International Applied Computational Electromagnetics Society Symposium (ACES 2019)

Miami, Florida, USA
14-18 April 2019

ISBN: 978-1-5108-8586-8

Printed from e-media with permission by:

Curran Associates, Inc.
57 Morehouse Lane
Red Hook, NY 12571

Some format issues inherent in the e-media version may also appear in this print version.

Printed by Curran Associates, Inc. (2019)

The Applied Computational Electromagnetics Society (ACES)
www.aces-society.org

Additional copies of this publication are available from:

Curran Associates, Inc.
57 Morehouse Lane
Red Hook, NY 12571 USA
Phone: 845-758-0400
Fax: 845-758-2633
Email: curran@proceedings.com
Web: www.proceedings.com

ACES 2019 Technical Review

Sunday, April 14

02:00PM-05:00PM	Conference Registration	Foyer
04:00PM-07:00PM	ACES Board of Directors Meeting	Metronome

Monday, April 15

07:30AM-05:00PM	Conference Registration	Foyer
08:00AM-12:00PM	Exhibitors Set-up	Ballroom Foyer
01:30PM-05:00PM	Exhibitors	Ballroom Foyer
06:00PM-09:00PM	Welcome Reception	Symphony Ballroom II
08:00AM-08:05AM	**Welcome Message** *John Volakis and Osama Mohammed*, Conference General Chairs	Symphony Ballroom I
08:05AM-08:10AM	**ACES Business Meeting** *Abd A. Arkadan*, ACES President	Symphony Ballroom I
Session 1 08:10AM-09:00AM	**Plenary Talk – 1** "Additively Manufactured Flexible, Wearable, Disposable Antennas and Sensors for Wireless Sensing Applications" *Atif Shamim*	Symphony Ballroom I
Session 2 09:10AM-10:00AM	**Plenary Talk – 2** "The Challenges of 5G Wireless Communication Systems" *Mark Newbury*	Symphony Ballroom I
10:00AM-10:20AM	Break	

		Page:
	Symphony Ballroom I	
Session 3 10:20AM-12:00PM	**Advances in Curved Patch Modeling** **Session Organizer: Andrew Peterson** **Session Chairs: Andrew Peterson and Branislav M. Notaroš**	
10:20AM-10:40AM	"Effect of Cell Curvature on the Convergence Rates of EFIE Numerical Solutions" Andrew F. Peterson	1
10:40AM-11:00AM	"Hybrid Integration Scheme for the Evaluation of Strongly Singular Integral over Curvilinear Triangle Surface" J. Rivero, F. Vipiana, D. R. Wilton, and W. A. Johnson	3
11:00AM-11:20AM	"On Higher-order Nyström Discretization of Scalar Potential Integral Equation for Penetrable Scatterers" Rui Chen and Hakan Bagci	5
11:20AM-11:40AM	"Evaluation of the Contour Integral on Curved Edges in Time Domain Equivalent Edge Currents" Aslihan Aktepe and H. Arda Ülkü	7
11:40AM-12:00PM	"Geometrically Conformal Quadrilateral Surface-Reconstruction for MoM-SIE Simulations" Jake Harmon, Cam Key, and Branislav M. Notaroš	9
12:00PM-01:30PM	Lunch	

	Lisseth Saavedra, Guilherme S. Rosa, and José R. Bergmann	
04:00PM-04:20PM	"Geometrically Conformal Quadrilateral Surface-Reconstruction for MoM-SIE Simulations" Jake Harmon, Cam Key, and Branislav M. Notaroš	81
04:20PM-04:40PM	"A Novel Mid-infrared Metalens using a Hyperbolic Metamaterial" Mohamed Kyamo, Navaneeth Premkumar, Abdelgader Alsalhin, and Brian A. Lail	83
04:40PM-05:00PM	"Determining the Dispersive Features of Nanophotonic Structures based on Hybrid FEM/TMM Technique" Abdelgader Alsalhin and Brian Lail	85
05:00PM-05:20PM	"Reconfigurable Metasurfaces for Index Modulation in 5G Wireless Communications" John A. Hodge, Kumar Vijay Mishra, and Amir I. Zaghloul	87

	Concerto Ballroom B	
Session 13 **03:20PM-05:20PM**	**Advanced Time Domain Solvers for Multiphysics Modeling in Photonics** **Session Organizers: Bill Henshaw and Alexander V. Kildishev** **Session Chairs: Ludmila Prokopeva and Derek Olson**	
03:20PM-03:40PM	"FDTD Modelling of Optical Polarisation Rotation in a Charged Quantum Dot - Micropillar System" G. Slavcheva, M. Koleva, and A. Rastelli	89
03:40PM-04:00PM	"Energy Stable Staggered High Order Finite Differences for Optical Media" Daniel Appelö, Vrushali Bokil, Yingda Cheng, and Fengyan Li	91
04:00PM-04:20PM	"On the Effect of Dissipation and Nonlocality on Unidirectional and Topological Surface Plasmon-Polaritons" S. Ali Hassani Gangaraj and Francesco Monticone	93
04:20PM-04:40PM	"Solving Maxwell's Equations with a Generalized Dispersive Material Model on Overset Grids" Jeffrey W. Banks, William D. Henshaw, Alexander V. Kildishev, Gregor Kovačič, Ludmila J. Prokopeva, and Donald W. Schwendeman	95
04:40PM-05:00PM	"Hermite Methods for Electromagnetic Waves in Dispersive Media" Thomas Hagstrom	97
05:00PM-05:20PM	"Material Models for Full Wave Nonlinear Optics" Michael Povolotskyi, Shaimaa Azzam, Ludmila J. Prokopeva, Samuel Peana, and Alexander V. Kildishev	99

	Concerto Ballroom C	
Session 14 **03:20PM-05:20PM**	**Advances in Multiscale and Multiphysics Computational Methods** **Session Organizers: Hakan Bagci, Ozgur Ergul, Huseyin Arda Ulku, and Abdulkadir C. Yucel** **Session Chairs: Hakan Bagci and Ozgur Ergul**	
03:20PM-03:40PM	"A Discontinuous Galerkin Framework for Multiphysics Simulation of Photoconductive Devices" Liang Chen and Hakan Bagci	101
03:40PM-04:00PM	"Computation of Fields from a Magnetic Dipole in a Conductive Medium using the QS-DGTD Method" M. Burak Özakın, Liang Chen, Shehab Ahmed, and Hakan Bagci	103
04:00PM-04:20PM	"Analysis of Composite Structures Involving Near-Zero-Index Materials" Yeşim Koyaz, Hande İbili, and Özgür Ergül	105
04:20PM-04:40PM	"Efficient Iterative Solution of Dense and Complex Linear Systems with Multiple Right-hand Sides in Electromagnetic Scattering" Bruno Carpentieri, Özgür Ergül, Barışcan Karaosmanoğlu, Sehar Naveed, and Donglin Sun	107

ACES 2019 Technical Review

Tuesday, April 16

07:30AM-05:00PM	**Conference Registration**	Foyer
08:30AM-05:00PM	**Exhibitors**	Ballroom Foyer
Session 15 **08:10AM-09:00AM**	**Plenary Talk – 3** "Electromagnetics Education: State of the Art, Assessment of Challenges, and Moving Forward" *Branislav M. Notaroš*	Symphony Ballroom I
Session 16 **09:10AM-10:00AM**	**Plenary Talk – 4** "Adjoint Sensitivity Analysis and its Low and High frequency Applications" *Mohamed H. Bakr*	Symphony Ballroom I
10:00AM-10:20AM	Break	

	Symphony Ballroom I	
Session 17 **10:20AM-12:00PM**	**Advances in Frequency-Domain CEM Techniques and Application - 1** **Session Organizer: Branislav M. Notaroš** **Session Chairs: Branislav M. Notaroš and Shubhendu Bhardwaj**	
10:20AM-10:40AM	"Platform-Aware In-Situ Antenna and Metamaterial Analysis and Design" Shu Wang, Brian MacKie-Mason, and Zhen Peng	113
10:40AM-11:00AM	"Acceleration of Volume-Volume (6-D) Integrals for Numerical Evaluation by Double Application of the Divergence Theorem" J. Rivero, F. Vipiana, D. R. Wilton, and W. A. Johnson	115
11:00AM-11:20AM	"Overview of the Iterative Solver in HFSS for Analyzing Frequency Domain Electromagnetic Problems" Ali Aghabarati, Kezhong Zhao, and L. E. Rickard Petersson	117
11:20AM-11:40AM	"Effective Electromagnetic Parameter Extractions for Porous Media Using a Potential-Based Formulation" Su Yan	119
11:40AM-12:00PM	"2D Integral Formulation with High Order Impedance Boundary Conditions for Transmission Lines" Luca Di Rienzo and Nathan Ida	121
12:00PM-01:30PM	Lunch	

Session 18 **10:20AM-12:00PM**	**Tutorial – 1** (Concerto Ballroom A) "Adjoint Sensitivity Analysis of High Frequency Structures and its Applications" *Mohamed H. Bakr*	N/A
12:00PM-01:30PM	Lunch	

	Concerto Ballroom B	
Session 19 **10:20AM-12:00PM**	**Finite Difference Methods and Other Techniques - 1** **Session Organizers: Yasushi Kanai and James Cole** **Session Chairs: Yasushi Kanai and James Cole**	
10:20AM-10:40AM	"Axial PML Performance Near the Axis of Rotation in Cylindrical FDTD" Mohammed F. Hadi and Atef Z. Elsherbeni	123
10:40AM-11:00AM	"Efficient RCS Evaluation for the Conventional TF/SF Separation Model in the FDTD Technique" Tadao Ohtani, Yasushi Kanai, and Nikolaos V. Kantartzis	125

	Sebastian Held, Adalbert Beyer, Rüdiger Follmann, Peter Waldow, and Dominique Schreurs	
02:00PM-02:20PM	"FDTD Modeling of Lightning Electromagnetic Field Propagation Over Mountainous Terrain" Dongshuai Li, Farhad Rachidi, and Marcos Rubinstein	151
02:20PM-02:40PM	"Time-Domain Magnetic Shielding of a Thin Conducting Screen Against a Small Loop" R. Araneo, G. Lovat, S. Celozzi, and P. Burghignoli	153
02:40PM-03:00PM	"Plasmonic Resonances and Light Generation in Nanoparticle Dimers" Viktoriia E. Babicheva, John M. Nehls, and Jerome V. Moloney	155
03:00PM-03:20PM	Break	

	Concerto Ballroom B	
Session 23 01:40PM-03:00PM	**Finite Difference Methods and Other Techniques - 2** **Session Organizers: Yasushi Kanai and James Cole** **Session Chairs: Yasushi Kanai and James Cole**	
01:40PM-02:00PM	"Point Source Transmitting Power Estimation of Wireless Avionics Intra-Communication Systems Using the Large-Scale FDTD Method" Shunichi Futatsumori, Kazuyuki Morioka, Takashi Hikage, Tetsuya Sekiguchi, Manabu Yamamoto, and Toshio Nojima	157
02:00PM-02:20PM	"FDTD Simulation of Multilayer-Coated and Rough Surface Metals Using Surface Impedance Method" Yong Wang and Scott Langdon	159
02:20PM-02:40PM	"Accelerating the FDTD Algorithm on CPUs with MATLAB's Parallel Computing Toolbox" Alec Weiss, Atef Elserbeni, Veysel Demir, and Mohammed Hadi	161
02:40PM-03:00PM	"Quantifying Subgridding Errors when Modeling Multiscale Structures with FDTD" Madison Le, Mohammed Hadi, and Atef Elsherbeni	163
03:00PM-03:20PM	Break	

	Concerto Ballroom C	
Session 24 01:40PM-03:00PM	**Applied EM for Biomedical and IoT Radar Technologies** **Session Organizers: Changzhi Li and Changzhan Gu** **Session Chairs: Changzhi Li**	
01:40PM-02:00PM	"In Vitro Dielectric Properties of Rat Skin Tissue for Microwave Skin Cancer Detection" Cemanur Aydinalp, Sulayman Joof, Tuba Yilmaz, Nural Pastacı Özsobacı, Fatma Ateş Alkan, and Ibrahim Akduman	165
02:00PM-02:20PM	"Monitoring of Food Contamination via Microwave Imaging" J. Tobon Vasquez, J. Rivero, R. Scapaticci, L. Farina, L. Crocco, and F. Vipiana	167
02:20PM-02:40PM	"Low-Profile Textile Antenna with Omni-Directional Radiation for Wearable Applications" Chunxu Mao, Pingjuan L. Werner, and Douglas H. Werner	169
02:40PM-03:00PM	"Analysis of Freshwater Curved and Flat Spiral Antennas" Ruben A. Llamas, Kumar Vijay Mishra, James J. Niemeier and Anton Kruger	171
03:00PM-03:20PM	Break	

ACES 2019 Technical Review

Wednesday, April 17

07:30AM-05:00PM	**Conference Registration**	**Foyer**
08:30AM-04:00PM	**Exhibitors**	**Ballroom Foyer**
07:00PM-10:00PM	**Awards Banquet**	**Symphony Ballroom II**
Session 28 **08:10AM-9:00AM**	**Plenary Talk – 5** "Arbitrary Manipulation of Electromagnetic Waves Through Engineered Materials" *Douglas H. Werner*	**Symphony Ballroom I**
Session 29 **09:10AM-10:00AM**	**Plenary Talk – 6** "Antenna Research at the Army Research Lab" *Steven Weiss*	**Symphony Ballroom I**
10:00AM-10:20AM	**Break**	

	Symphony Ballroom I	
Session 30 **10:20AM-12:00PM**	**Optimization and Inverse Problems in Low Frequency EM Applications - 1** **Session Organizer: Alessandro Formisano** **Session Chair: Alessandro Formisano**	
10:20AM-10:40AM	"Induction Heating of Thermoplastic Composites in the Presence of a Susceptor" Ankit Patel, Michel Van-Tooren, Frank D. Thomas, Robert Moore, and Mohammod Ali	201
10:40AM-11:00AM	"Two-Dimensional Electrical Properties Tomography Using a Simplified Contrast-Source Inversion Approach" Patrick Fuchs and Rob Remis	203
11:00AM-11:20AM	"A Comparison of Different Formulations for an Inverse Source Magnetostatic Problem" Alessandro Formisano	205
11:20AM-11:40AM	"An Accurate Technique for Modeling Realistic Well-Logging Sensors Inside Complex Media" Lisseth Saavedra, Guilherme S. Rosa, and José R. Bergmann	207
11:40AM-12:00PM	"Electromagnetic Induction Sensing for Buried Explosive Hazards Detection" Fridon Shubitidze, Benjamin E. Barrowes, Micheil Prishvin, and Irma Shamatava	209
12:00PM-01:30PM	**Lunch**	

	Concerto Ballroom A	
Session 31 **10:20AM-11:40AM**	**EM Modeling Using FEKO - 1** **Session Organizer: C.J. Reddy** **Session Chair: C.J. Reddy**	
10:20AM-10:40AM	"Recent Improvements in Feko" Johann van Tonder, Marianne Bingle, Elia Attardo, Ulrich Jakobus, Marlize Schoeman, and Kitty Longtin	212
10:40AM-11:00AM	"Co-Channel Simultaneous Transmit and Receive with 3-Element Array Antenna" Ehab A. Etellisi, Mohamed A. Elmansouri, and Dejan S. Filipovic	214
11:00AM-11:20AM	"Advanced Computational Methods for Transparency Control of Low Emissivity Windows"	216

	Gopinath Gampala and C. J. Reddy	
11:20AM-11:40AM	"A Simple Test for Quickly Measuring Shielding Effectiveness of Connectors Using Isotropic Broadband Electric Field Probe" Kenedy Marconi G. Santos, Marcela Silva Novo, Glauco Fontgalland, Marcelo Bender Perotoni, Décio Renno de Faria Mendonça, and Danilo Brito Almeida	218
12:00PM-01:30PM	**Lunch**	

	Concerto Ballroom B	
Session 32 **10:20AM-11:20AM**	**Modeling and Simulation of Electromagnetic Applications** **Session Chair: Abdullah Eroglu**	
10:20AM-10:40AM	"Hybrid-PIC Simulation of Nonlinear Wave-particle Interactions in the Earth's Radiation Belts" Hoyoung Kim and Vijay Harid	220
10:40AM-11:00AM	"Comparison of Methods for Dielectric Characterization of Additively Manufactured Materials" Gregory Mitchell, Quang Nguyen, and Theodore Anthony	222
11:00AM-11:20AM	"Impedance Matching of Layered Structures with Metamaterials" Brinta Chowdhury and Abdullah Eroglu	224
12:00PM-01:30PM	**Lunch**	

	Concerto Ballroom C	
Session 33 **10:20AM-12:00PM**	**Antenna Systems and Applications** **Session Organizer: Ahmed H. Abdelrahman** **Session Chair: Ahmed H. Abdelrahman**	
10:20AM-10:40AM	"EM-Driven Size Reduction of UWB MIMO Antennas with Feed Line Modifications" Muhammad Aziz ul Haq and Slawomir Koziel	226
10:40AM-11:00AM	"Polarization Transformations Based Metasurfaces for 5G Applications" Shraman Gupta and Abdel Razik Sebak	228
11:00AM-11:20AM	"An X-band Oblique Polarized Antenna Array" Jia Fang, Mouping Jin, and Feng Yu	230
11:20AM-11:40AM	"Proximity Effect of UWB U-Slot Patch Antenna on Human Body" Mahrukh Khan, Liaquat Ali, Abdul Hamid Yousuf, and Masud Chowdhury	232
11:40AM-12:00PM	"Design of a Novel Dual-Band, Electrically Small, Printed Octafilar Antenna" Joseph D. Majkowski	234
12:00PM-01:30PM	**Lunch**	

	Symphony Ballroom I	
Session 34 **01:40PM-02:40PM**	**Optimization and Inverse Problems in Low Frequency EM Applications - 2** **Session Organizer: Alessandro Formisano** **Session Chair: Alessandro Formisano**	
01:40PM-02:00PM	"A Fast 3D Imaging Method for Subsurface Metal Targets Using Time-Domain Electromagnetic System" Wupeng Xie, Xiaojuan Zhang, Yaoxin Zheng, Yaxin Mu, and Han Liu	236
02:00PM-02:20PM	"Deep Neural Networks Based Surrogate Model for Topology Optimization of Electromagnetic Devices" Mauro Tucci, Sami Barmada, Luca Sani, Dimitri Thomopulos, and Nunzia Fontana	238
02:20PM-02:40PM	"Driveability Optimization of HEV Powertrain" N. Al-Aawar and A.A. Arkadan	240
03:00PM-03:20PM	**Break**	

Thursday, April 18

07:30AM-11:00AM	**Conference Registration** Foyer	
	Symphony Ballroom I	
Session 41 **08:00AM-10:00AM**	**Recent Advancements in the Modeling, Design and Application of Metasurfaces - 1** **Session Organizers: Douglas Werner, Ping Werner, and Qiang Ren** **Session Chairs: Douglas Werner and Ping Werner**	
08:00AM-08:20AM	"Phonon-Polariton Resonances in Hexagonal Boron Nitride Transdimensional Lattices" Viktoriia E. Babicheva	284
08:20AM-08:40AM	"Plasmonic Colors and Memory with Al Metafilms" Maowen Song, Di Wang, Zhaxylyk Kudyshev, Yi Xuan, Honglin Yu, Alexandra Boltasseva, Vladimir M. Shalaev, and Alexander V. Kildishev	286
08:40AM-09:00AM	"Digital Metasurfaces Controlled by Light" Wei Xiang Jiang and Xin Ge Zhang	288
09:00AM-09:20AM	"Dual-Band Slot Dipole with AMC using Textiles" Fatin Nabilah Giman, Ping Jack Soh, Azremi Abdullah Al-Hadi, Herwansyah Lago, Sharul Kamal Abdul Rahim, Mohd Faizal Jamlos, Dominique Schreurs, and Adalbert Beyer	290
09:20AM-09:40AM	"Discontinuous Galerkin Time Domain Method for Periodic Dispersive Structure Analysis at Oblique Incidence" Huaguang Bao, Sawyer D. Campbell, Pingjuan L. Werner and Douglas H. Werner	292
09:40AM-10:00AM	"An Integrated, Broadband Circularly-polarized Millimeter-wave Metasurface-based Transmit-array" Zhi Hao Jiang and Xiao-Wei Zhu	294
10:00AM-10:20AM	Break	

	Concerto Ballroom A	
Session 42 **08:00AM-09:40AM**	**Physically Reconfigurable Antennas and Arrays: Design, Modeling and Materials - 1** **Session Organizer: Stavros Georgakopoulos** **Session Chair: Stavros Georgakopoulos**	
08:00AM-08:20AM	"Reconfigurable Origami Antennas" Stavros V. Georgakopoulos	296
08:20AM-08:40AM	"Coupled Structural-Electromagnetic Analysis of Origami-Inspired Adaptive Structures" Deanna Sessions, Gregory Huff, Joshua Ruff, Kazuko Fuchi, Alexander Cook, Andrew Gillman, Alexander Pankonien, and Philip Buskohl	298
08:40AM-09:00AM	"Automated CAD and Modeling of Origami Structures for Reconfigurable Antenna Applications" Md Rayhan Khan, Constantinos L. Zekios, Stavros V. Georgakopoulos, and Shubhendu Bhardwaj	300
09:00AM-09:20AM	"Origami-Tunable Frequency Selective Surfaces: A Design Optimization Approach"	302

2019 International Applied Computational Electromagnetics Society (ACES) Symposium
Miami, Florida, USA
April 14-18, 2019

ACES 2019 Conference Program

Organizing Committee

General Chair:
John L. Volakis
Florida International University, USA

General Chair/Finance Chair:
Osama A. Mohammed
Florida International University

Technical Program Chair:
Atef Elsherbeni
Colorado School of Mines, USA

Technical Program Co-Chair/
Student Paper Competition Chair:
Shubhendu Bhardwaj
Florida International University, USA

Technical Program Co-Chair/
Sponsorship/Exhibition Chair:
Stavros Georgakopoulos
Florida International University, USA

Student Paper Competition Chair:
Wuji Wang
Florida International University, USA

Awards Chair:
Sami Barmada
University of Pisa, Italy

Short Course/Tutorial Chair:
Andrew F. Peterson
Georgia Institute of Technology, USA

Sponsorship/Exhibition Chair:
C.J. Reddy
Altair, USA

Local Arrangements Chair::
Shubham Hemant Wagh
Florida International University, USA

Conference Secretary:
Shanell Lopez
Colorado School of Mines, USA

Website Administrator:
Matthew Inman
University of Mississippi, USA

Website Administrator:
Kyle Patel
Colorado School of Mines, USA

Welcome Message

Welcome to the 2019 International ACES Conference in Miami!

On behalf of the Steering Committee, we welcome you to the 2019 International Applied Computational Electromagnetics Society (ACES) Symposium at Miami, Florida, USA. This year ACES2019 is held from 14-18 April 2019 at the Hilton Miami Downtown.

We are grateful for your participation and we hope that you will enjoy the 4-day rich technical program, six plenary presentations, five tutorials, student competition and innovative talks during lunch by leaders. The technical program details can be found on the web at http://aces-society.org/conference/Miami_2019/, including details about the invited plenary talks and our generous sponsors and exhibitors.

Our many thanks to the steering committee and the special session organizers whose time and dedication were essential in making this conference a success. And we are indebted to our corporate sponsors whose support demonstrates their strong interest to the ACES conference and the organizing team from the Florida International University. We are also pleased to acknowledge our speakers who took the time from their busy schedule to discuss future innovations:

Following the traditional format of ACES, a single session format will be followed for the oral presentations, alongside with exhibitors to allow for technical interactions and networking.

To everyone attending the workshop, we are grateful for your participation and contributions to this workshop. Your presence and technical contributions are invaluable. The steering committee has made every effort to see that the oral presentations are of the highest quality. The plenary presentations and industry talks will certainly provide future directions in research and industry needs.

We promise you that the social programs (Monday reception, daily luncheons, and Wednesday banquet) will provide for a pleasant environment to network and enjoy one of the most attractive cities in the world. Please feel free to take the opportunity to visit many of the well-known attractions in Miami. Information for attractions like South Beach, Art Deco district, Little Havana and Brickell, Coral Gables Miracle Mile, Vizcaya Museum and Gardens, Key Biscayne, Key West, and much more can be found at the conference web site.

We look forward to seeing you at ACES2019 in Miami, Florida, USA from 14-18 April 2019.

John L. Volakis and Osama A. Mohammed
ACES2019 Miami General Chairs

Conference Sponsors

SILVER SPONSOR

Altair

ASSOCIATE SPONSORS

RFCOM Lab

RF Communications & Terahertz Lab

ENERGY SYSTEMS RESEARCH LABORATORY

FIU Engineering & Computing

Transforming Antennas Center

TECHNICAL CO-SPONSORS

FIU

IEEE

Miami Section

Conference Exhibitors

EXHIBITORS

Altair

IMST

RFCOM Lab

RF Communications & Terahertz Lab

Energy Systems Research Laboratory

Powering The Future

FIU

Electrical & Computer Engineering

ENERGY
SYSTEMS
RESEARCH
LABORATORY

FIU | Engineering & Computing

Transforming Antennas Center

Session Organizers

- Ahmed H. Abdelrahman
- Mohamed Abouzahra
- Rodolfo Araneo
- Hakan Bagci
- Mohamed H. Bakr
- Shubhendu Bhardwaj
- Hai-Tao Chen
- Pai-Yen Chen
- James Cole
- Khaled ElMahgoub
- Atef Elsherbeni
- Ozgur Ergul
- Abdullah Eroglu
- Nunzia Fontana
- Alessandro Formisano
- Stavros Georgakopoulos
- Changzhan Gu
- Mohammad Hadi
- Vijay Harid
- Bill Henshaw
- Haiyu Huang
- Lijun Jiang
- Thottam S. Kalkur
- Yasushi Kanai
- Alexander V. Kildishev
- Branko Kolundzija
- Slawomir Koziel
- Changzhi Li
- Osama Mohammed
- Branislav M. Notaros
- Abbas Omar
- Zhen Peng
- Andrew Peterson
- Shishir Punjala
- Mabel Ramirez
- C.J. Reddy
- Qiang Ren
- Sourajeet Roy
- Huseyin Arda Ulku
- Wujie Wen
- Douglas Werner
- Ping Werner
- Su Yan
- Cheng Yang
- Abdulkadir C. Yucel
- Ata Zadehgol
- Lei Zhao

Session Chairs

- Ahmed H. Abdelrahman
- Mohamed Abouzahra
- Elias A. Alwan
- Rodolfo Araneo
- Hakan Bagci
- Mohamed H. Bakr
- Sami Barmada
- Shubhendu Bhardwaj
- Sawyer Campbell
- Pai-Yen Chen
- James Cole
- Ozgur Ergul
- Abdullah Eroglu
- Nunzia Fontana
- Alessandro Formisano
- Stavros Georgakopoulos
- Matthew Inman
- Ulrich Jakobus
- Thottam S. Kalkur
- Yasushi Kanai
- Slawomir Koziel
- Zhaxylyk Kudyshev
- Changzhi Li
- Osama Mohammed
- Branislav M. Notaros
- Derek Olson
- Andrew Peterson
- Ludmila Prokopeva
- Mabel Ramirez
- C.J. Reddy
- Douglas Werner
- Ping Werner
- Yanli Zhang
- Haisen Zhao

Conference Reviewers

- Ahmed Abdelrahman
- Mohamed Abouzahra
- Mohamed Ahmed
- Rodolfo Araneo
- Abd A. Arkadan
- Ercument Arvas
- Nikolay Atanasov
- Mohamed H. Bakr
- Sami Barmada
- Adalbert Beyer
- Shubhendu Bhardwaj
- Subhradeep Chakraborty
- Hai-Tao Chen
- James Cole
- Veysel Demir
- Atef Elsherbeni
- Dejan Filipovic
- Nunzia Fontana
- Alessandro Formisano
- Mohammed Hadi
- Vijay Harid
- Mousa Hussein
- Jamie Infantolino
- Irum Jafri
- Lijun Jiang
- Omar Jibreel
- Yasushi Kanai
- Alexander V. Kildishev
- Slawomir Koziel
- Madison Le
- Changzhi Li
- Jau-Jr Lin
- Shanell Lopez
- Osama Mohammed
- Ranjit Momi
- Branislav M. Notaros
- Abbas Omar
- Zhengyu Peng
- Andrew Peterson
- Giuseppe Pelosi
- Shishir Punjala
- Hassan Ragheb
- Jalil Rashed-Mohassel
- C.J. Reddy
- Qiang Ren
- Sourajeet Roy
- Omar Saraereh
- Mustafa Secmen
- Chan See
- Fridon Shubitidze
- Ashok Kumar Srinivasan
- Prabhu Sundaramoorthy
- Yuvaraja T.
- Allison Tanner
- Huseyin Arda Ulku
- Irfan Ullah
- Erhiega Umayah
- Ana Vukovic
- Douglas Werner
- Su Yan
- Abdulkadir Yucel
- Amir Zaghloul
- Lei Zhao

Plenary Speaker

Dr. Atif Shamim

Computer, Electrical and Mathematical Sciences and Engineering Division
King Abdullah University Of Science & Technology (KAUST)

Additively Manufactured Flexible, Wearable, Disposable Antennas and Sensors for Wireless Sensing Applications

With the advent of wearable sensors and internet of things (IoT), there is a new focus on electronics which can be bent so that they can be worn or mounted on non-planar objects. Due to large volume (billions of devices), there is a requirement that the cost is extremely low, to the extent that they become disposable. The flexible and low-cost aspects can be addressed through additive manufacturing technologies such as inkjet, screen and 3D printing. This talk introduces additive manufacturing as an emerging technique to realize low cost, flexible, wearable antennas and sensors for wireless sensing applications. The ability to print electronics on unconventional mediums such as plastics, papers, and textiles has opened up a plethora of new applications. In this talk, various innovative antenna and sensor designs will be shown that have been realized through additive manufacturing. A multilayer process will be presented where dielectrics are also printed in addition to the metallic parts, thus demonstrating fully printed components. Many new functional inks and their use in tunable and reconfigurable components will be shown. In the end, many system level examples will be shown, primarily for wireless sensing applications. The promising results of these designs indicate that the day when electronics can be printed like newspapers and magazines through roll-to-roll and reel-to-reel printing is not far away.

Atif Shamim received his M.S. and Ph.D. degrees in Electrical Engineering from Carleton University, Canada in 2004 and 2009 respectively. He was an NSERC Alexander Graham Bell Graduate scholar at Carleton University from 2007 till 2009 and an NSERC postdoctoral Fellow in 2009-2010 at Royal Military College Canada and KAUST. In August 2010, he joined the Electrical Engineering Program at KAUST, where he is currently an Associate Professor and Principal Investigator of IMPACT Lab. He was an invited researcher at the VTT Micro-modules Research Center (Oulu, Finland) in 2006. His research work has won best paper awards in IEEE EuWiT 2008, IEEE IMS 2016, IEEE MECAP 2016 and honorable mention prizes in IEEE APS 2005, IEEE IWAT 2006, IEEE IMS 2014, IEEE IMS 2017 (3MT competition). He was given the Ottawa Centre of Research Innovation (OCRI) Researcher of the Year 2008 Award in Canada. His work on Wireless Dosimeter won the ITAC SMC Award at Canadian Microelectronics Corporation TEXPO in 2007. Prof. Shamim also won numerous business-related awards, including 1st prize in Canada's national business plan competition and was awarded OCRI Entrepreneur of the year award in 2010. He is an author/co-author of over 200 international publications, an inventor on 20 patents and has given over 40 invited talks at various international forums. His research interests are in innovative antenna designs and their integration strategies with circuits and sensors for flexible and wearable wireless sensing systems through a combination of CMOS and additive manufacturing technologies. Dr. Shamim is a Senior Member of IEEE and serves on the editorial board of IEEE Transactions on Antennas and Propagation.

Plenary Speaker

Mark Newbury

Futurewei Technologies
Bridgewater, NJ

The Challenges of 5G Wireless Communication Systems

We overview the challenges involved in realizing, or *productizing*, the 5G wireless system; with particular focus on the crucial role of simulation and modelling in pursuing innovation as well as in meeting industry 'gateways' for product. We begin by overviewing *context*; i.e., sharp market-driven requirements that range from 'do no harm' to cost-effectiveness, robustness, and speed to market. We then comment on the industry shift that has driven the need to pursue complex, non-convex optimization problems in order to achieve performance gains; and how this need in turn has driven a process of 'gateways' that takes innovation to deployment, with progressively more complex simulations at each step. We give examples of both the necessity and difficulty of achieving *realistic*, *market-reflective*, *discrete time* 5G simulations within this process. We offer radio channel modelling as a particular example of the value of modelling as well as the challenges of achieving accuracy at acceptable computational complexity. Finally, we comment on the lure and pitfalls of 'quick data'.

Mark Newbury is a Distinguished Engineer and Senior Director at Futurewei Technologies, where he leads a research and development team engaged in wireless network performance analysis, simulation, and innovation. Mr. Newbury holds degrees from Harvard University and Syracuse University, and has over 25 years of industry experience in the area of wireless network performance characterization and analysis. He is a past recipient of the Futurewei President's Award (2013), the Futurewei Black Swan Award (2014), and the Futurewei Most Valuable Innovation Award (2017); as well as a Futurewei Gold (2012) and "FutureStar" (2016) medalist. Mr. Newbury is also a Bell Labs Fellow; as well as a lifetime member of the Alcatel-Technical Academy and a past recipient of the Bell Labs President Gold Award. He holds several granted/pending patents in the areas of network load simulation, traffic spatial density estimation, wireless load management, network handover/reselection, and mobile video quality. He is the principal contributing author of "Handbook of CDMA Optimization" and has published within the Bell Labs Technical Journal in the areas of energy efficiency, performance measurement, trunking efficiency, and network planning.

Plenary Speaker

Dr. Branislav M. Notaroš

Department of Electrical and Computer Engineering

Colorado State University

Electromagnetics Education: State of the Art, Assessment of Challenges, and Moving Forward

Electromagnetics is rather difficult for students to grasp and for instructors to teach. On the other hand, its importance to technical education can hardly be overstated. This talk addresses the current state of the art in electromagnetics education and attempts to provide some answers and incite discussion around the following two general questions: 1. What are some of the major problems and challenges in the methodology and practice of electromagnetics teaching and learning globally? 2. What could be some proposed suggestions for advancing electromagnetics education in the near future, including existing strategies and new ideas? The talk will present some examples of general approaches to overcoming the difficulties in electromagnetics teaching and learning given the academic, societal, and economic contexts of today and outlooks for the future. It will also give some collaborative assessments of the state of electromagnetics education and suggestions for the near future based on discussions with colleagues worldwide. A goal of the talk is also to contribute to initiating and intensifying a broad discussion of the state and challenges of electromagnetics education globally and possible ways to move this essential topic forward.

Branislav M. Notaroš received the Dipl.Ing. (B.S.), M.S., and Ph.D. degrees in electrical engineering from the University of Belgrade, Belgrade, Yugoslavia, in 1988, 1992, and 1995, respectively. From 1996 to 1999, he was an Assistant Professor in the School of Electrical Engineering at the University of Belgrade. He spent the 1998-1999 academic year as a Visiting Scholar at the University of Colorado at Boulder. He was an Assistant Professor, from 1999 to 2004, and Associate Professor, from 2004 to 2006, in the Department of Electrical and Computer Engineering at the University of Massachusetts Dartmouth. From 2006 to 2012, he was an Associate Professor in the Department of Electrical and Computer Engineering at Colorado State University (CSU), where he is currently a Professor and University Distinguished Teaching Scholar, as well as Director of Electromagnetics Laboratory. His research interests and activities are in computational electromagnetics, higher order numerical methods, antennas, scattering, microwaves, metamaterials, characterization of snow and rain, surface and radar precipitation measurements, RF design for MRI at ultra-high magnetic fields, and electromagnetics education. He is the author of textbooks *Electromagnetics* (Prentice Hall, 2010), *MATLAB-Based Electromagnetics* (Prentice Hall, 2013), and *Conceptual Electromagnetics* (CRC Press, 2017).

Dr. Notaroš is Fellow of the IEEE and of the Applied Computational Electromagnetics Society. He served as General Chair of the 2018 International Applied Computational Electromagnetics Society Symposium – ACES2018, March 25-29, 2018, Denver, Colorado, USA, and of the 11th International Workshop on Finite Elements for Microwave Engineering – FEM2012, June 4-6, 2012, Estes Park, Colorado, USA. He served as General Chair of the 14th International Workshop on Finite Elements for Microwave Engineering – FEM2018, September 10-14, 2018, Cartagena de Indias, Colombia. He is Associate Editor for the IEEE Transactions on Antennas and Propagation, and served as Guest Editor of the Special Issue on Finite Elements for Microwave

Engineering, Electromagnetics, Vol. 34, Issue 3-4, 2014. He serves on the Board of Directors of ACES, as ACES Secretary, and as Vice-Chair of the US National Committee Commission B of the International Union of Radio Science (URSI), for which he previously served as Technical Activities Chair (2015–2018). He was the recipient of the 2005 IEEE MTT-S Microwave Prize (best-paper award for IEEE Transactions on MTT), 1999 IEE Marconi Premium (best-paper award for IEE Proceedings on Microwaves, Antennas and Propagation), 1999 URSI Young Scientist Award, 2005 UMass Dartmouth Scholar of the Year Award, 2004 UMass Dartmouth College of Engineering Dean's Recognition Award, 2010 CSU College of Engineering George T. Abell Outstanding Teaching and Service Faculty Award, 2012 CSU System Board of Governors Excellence in Undergraduate Teaching Award, 2014 CSU Provost's N. Preston Davis Award for Instructional Innovation, 2012 IEEE Region 5 Outstanding Engineering Educator Award, 2014 Carnegie Foundation for the Advancement of Teaching Colorado Professor of the Year Award, 2015 American Society for Engineering Education ECE Distinguished Educator Award, and 2015 IEEE Undergraduate Teaching Award.

Plenary Speaker

Dr. Mohamed H. Bakr

Electrical and Computer Engineering
McMaster University

Adjoint Sensitivity Analysis and its Low and High Frequency Applications

Adjoint sensitivity analysis (ASA) offers a powerful tool for accelerating the design optimization of low and high frequency structures. Using at most one extra simulation, the gradient of the desired time or frequency domain response can be estimated regardless of the number of parameters. This low computational cost can be easily contrasted with the $2n$ extra simulations required for the accurate central finite differences, where n is the number of parameters. The ASA was successfully demonstrated for electromagnetic problems with dispersive, anisotropic, and nonlinear materials at different frequency bands.

We give in this talk a global overview of the progress in adjoint sensitivity analysis and its applications in low and high frequency structures. We discuss how ASA can be used in high frequency applications such as the design of antennas and waveguide filters, microwave imaging, cloaking, and equalization of optical fiber impairments. We also cover some of its low frequency applications in the design of the emerging switched reluctance motors.

Mohamed H. Bakr is a Professor of Electrical and Computer Engineering, McMaster University, Hamilton, Ontario, Canada. Dr. Bakr received a B.Sc. degree in Electronics and Communications Engineering from Cairo University, Egypt in 1992 with distinction (honors). In June 1996, he received a Master's degree in Engineering Mathematics from Cairo University. He earned the Ph.D. degree in September 2000 from the Department of Electrical and Computer Engineering, McMaster University. In November 2000, he joined the Computational Electromagnetics Research Laboratory (CERL), University of Victoria, Victoria, Canada as an NSERC Post Doctoral Fellow. Dr. Bakr received a Premier's Research Excellence Award (PREA) from the province of Ontario, Canada, in 2003. He also received an NSERC Discovery Accelerator Supplement (DAS) award in 2011. In 2014, he was a Co-recipient of Chrysler's innovation award for project on novel designs of hybrid cars. Since 2015, he was listed on the Dean's Teaching Honour Roll several times in recognition of his success in utilizing flipped classrooms to teaching engineering courses. He was awarded in April 2018 a Leadership in Teaching and Learning (LTL) fellowship from the McPherson Institute, McMaster University. His research areas of interest include optimization methods, computational electromagnetics, computer-aided design and modeling of power circuits and motors, microwave circuits, THz, and photonic devices, nanotechnology, neural network applications, smart analysis of high frequency structures and efficient optimization using time/frequency domain methods. He is the author/coauthor of over 230 journal and conference papers, two books on the optimization and CAD of high frequency structures, two book chapters on optimization and electromagnetic modeling, and two patents.

Plenary Speaker

Dr. Douglas H. Werner

Department of Electrical Engineering and Materials Research Institute
The Pennsylvania State University

Arbitrary Manipulation of Electromagnetic Waves Through Engineered Materials

Recent advances in engineered materials (EnMats) have facilitated a plethora of RF/optical devices with an unprecedented ability to manipulate and control the behavior of electromagnetic waves. This has led to an ever increasing demand for more sophisticated design tools which can be utilized to customize the electromagnetic properties of engineered material systems. Examples of such tools include transformation electromagnetics as well as advanced multi-scale and multi-physics modeling techniques. In addition, practical EnMats-enabled system design requires powerful single- and multi-objective global optimization methods (e.g., genetic algorithms, particle swarm, covariance matrix adaptation evolutionary strategy, clonal section algorithms, wind driven optimization, lazy ant colony optimization, etc.), which transcend the current capabilities and limitations of commercially available software packages. These tools enable an unparalleled design flexibility for complex EnMats-based electromagnetic systems with increased functionality and/or significant size, weight and power (SWaP) reduction. The presentation will begin by providing a brief discussion of the most recent developments in the forward solvers and inverse design tools. Following this, several examples will be presented that showcase the successful application of these tools to the creation of transformative EnMat-enabled RF and optical devices.

Douglas H. Werner received the B.S., M.S., and Ph.D. degrees in Electrical Engineering and the M.A. degree in Mathematics from the Pennsylvania State University (Penn State), University Park, in 1983, 1985, 1989, and 1986, respectively. He holds the John L. and Genevieve H. McCain Chair Professorship in the Pennsylvania State University Department of Electrical Engineering. He is the Director of the Computational Electromagnetics and Antennas Research Lab (CEARL: http://cearl.ee.psu.edu/) as well as a Member of the Communications and Space Sciences Lab (CSSL). He is also a Faculty Member of the Materials Research Institute (MRI) at Penn State. Prof. Werner was presented with the 1993 Applied Computational Electromagnetics Society (ACES) Best Paper Award and was also the recipient of a 1993 International Union of Radio Science (URSI) Young Scientist Award. In 1994, Prof. Werner received the Pennsylvania State University Applied Research Laboratory Outstanding Publication Award. He was a co-author (with one of his graduate students) of a paper published in the IEEE Transactions on Antennas and Propagation which received the 2006 R. W. P. King Award. He received the inaugural IEEE Antennas and Propagation Society Edward E. Altshuler Prize Paper Award and the Harold A. Wheeler Applications Prize Paper Award in 2011 and 2014 respectively. In 2018, he received the DoD Ordnance Technology Consortium (DOTC) Outstanding Technical Achievement Award. He also received the 2015 ACES Technical Achievement Award. He was the recipient of a College of Engineering PSES Outstanding Research Award and Outstanding Teaching Award in March 2000 and March 2002, respectively. He was also presented with an IEEE Central Pennsylvania Section Millennium Medal. In March 2009, he received the PSES Premier Research Award. He is a Fellow of the IEEE, the IET, the OSA, and the ACES. He is also a Senior Member of the National Academy of Inventors (NAI). Prof. Werner is a former Associate Editor of Radio

Science, a former Editor of the IEEE Antennas and Propagation Magazine, an Editorial Board Member of Scientific Reports (a Nature subjournal), an Editorial Board Member for EPJ Applied Metamaterials, Editor for the IEEE Press Series on Electromagnetic Wave Theory & Applications, a Member of URSI Commissions B and G, Eta Kappa Nu, Tau Beta Pi and Sigma Xi. He holds 19 patents, has published over 800 technical papers and proceedings articles, and is the author of 29 book chapters with several additional chapters currently in preparation. He has published several books including Frontiers in Electromagnetics (Piscataway, NJ: IEEE Press, 2000), Genetic Algorithms in Electromagnetics (Hoboken, NJ: Wiley/IEEE, 2007), Transformation Electromagnetics and Metamaterials: Fundamental Principles and Applications (London, UK: Springer, 2014), Electromagnetics of Body Area Networks: Antennas, Propagation, and RF Systems (Hoboken, NJ: Wiley/IEEE, 2016), and Broadband Metamaterials in Electromagnetics: Technology and Applications (Pan Stanford Publishing, 2017). He has also contributed chapters for several books including Electromagnetic Optimization by Genetic Algorithms (New York: Wiley Interscience, 1999), Soft Computing in Communications (New York: Springer, 2004), Antenna Engineering Handbook (New York: McGraw-Hill, 2007), Frontiers in Antennas: Next Generation Design and Engineering (New York: McGraw-Hill, 2011), Numerical Methods for Metamaterial Design (New York: Springer, 2013), Computational Electromagnetics (New York: Springer, 2014), Graphene Science Handbook: Nanostructure and Atomic Arrangement (Abingdon, Oxfordshire, UK: CRC Press, 2016), Handbook of Antenna Technologies (New York: Springer, 2016), and Transformation Wave Physics: Electromagnetics, Elastodynamics and Thermodynamics (Boca Raton, FL: CRC Press, 2016). His research interests include computational electromagnetics (MoM, FEM, FEBI, FDTD, DGTD, CBFM, RCWA, GO, GTD/UTD, etc.) antenna theory and design, phased arrays (including ultra-wideband arrays), microwave devices, wireles and personal communication systems (including on-body networks), wearable and e-textile antennas, RFID tag antennas, conformal antennas, reconfigurable antennas, frequency selective surfaces, electromagnetic wave interactions with complex media, metamaterials, electromagnetic bandgap materials, zero and negative index materials, transformation optics, nanoscale electromagnetics (including nanoantennas), fractal and knot electrodynamics, and nature-inspired optimization techniques (genetic algorithms, clonal selection algorithms, particle swarm, wind driven optimization, and various other evolutionary programming schemes)

Plenary Speaker

Dr. Steven Weiss

US Army Research Lab
Adelphi, MD

Antenna Research at the Army Research Lab

Today's systems place ever more challenging requirements on antennas. Often, these requirements cannot be met by conventional technologies. Accordingly, this talk will give an overview of what ARL sees as the emerging technologies that will enable future antenna development for military and civilian applications. The talk will emphasize the need for new materials to enhance RF antenna performance as well as the exciting progress made in the field of additive manufacturing as it pertains to antennas.

Steven Weiss obtained his Bachelor's degree in Electrical Engineering from the Rochester Institute of Technology in 1985 (BSEE) and graduate degrees from The George Washington University in 1989 (MS) and 1995 (DSc) both with concentrations in Electrophysics.

Dr. Weiss is the team leader for the Antenna Team at the Army Research Lab and has worked with the Army since 1988. In this capacity, he has been instrumental in the development of numerous specialized antennas for military applications. The work has ranged from antennas for communications in the VHF band, radar antennas, antennas for Satellite on the Move (SOTM,) as well as antennas for collision avoidance. He has an active interest in beamformers and beamforming networks and has integrated a number of these into phased array architectures.

Dr. Weiss is a Fellow of the Washington Academy of Science and is on the board of directors of the Applied Computational Electromagnetics Society (ACES). He is a Senior Member of the IEEE and has served in all of the officer positions for the Washington Section of the IEEE. He is a Member of URSI Commissions A and B and served as the Vice-chair and Chair of Commission A. Additionally, he is an International Member of URSI.

Dr. Weiss has taught at The Johns Hopkins University since 2002, teaching courses in Antenna Systems, Advanced Antenna Systems, and Intermediate Electromagnetics. He has published numerous papers in the IEEE Antennas and Propagation societies' transactions, letters, and conferences. He is a registered Professional Engineer in the states of Maryland and Delaware and maintains an active status in both states.

ACES 2019 Plenary Speakers

Title and Presenter **Symphony Ballroom I**

Monday, April 15, 2019

Plenary - 1
08:10AM - 09:00AM
"Additively Manufactured Flexible, Wearable, Disposable Antennas and Sensors for Wireless Sensing Applications"
Atif Shamim

Plenary - 2
09:10AM - 10:00AM
"The Challenges of 5G Wireless Communication Systems"
Mark Newbury

Tuesday, April 16, 2019

Plenary - 3
08:10AM - 09:00AM
"Electromagnetics Education: State of the Art, Assessment of Challenges, and Moving Forward"
Branislav M. Notaroš

Plenary - 4
09:10AM - 10:00AM
"Adjoint Sensitivity Analysis and its Low and High frequency Applications"
Mohamed H. Bakr

Wednesday, April 17, 2019

Plenary - 5
08:10AM - 09:00AM
"Arbitrary Manipulation of Electromagnetic Waves Through Engineered Materials"
Douglas H. Werner

Plenary - 6
09:10AM - 10:00AM
"Antenna Research at the Army Research Lab"
Steven Weiss

ACES 2019 Tutorials

Title and Presenter **Room**

Tuesday, April 16, 2019

Tutorial – 1 **Concerto Ballroom A**
10:20AM - 12:00PM
"Adjoint Sensitivity Analysis of High Frequency Structures and its Applications"
Mohamed H Bakr

Wednesday, April 17, 2019

Tutorial – 2 **Concerto Ballroom A**
03:20PM - 05:20PM
"Effective Teaching of Engineering Courses Using Flipped Classrooms"
Mohamed H. Bakr

Tutorial – 3 **Concerto Ballroom B**
03:20PM - 05:20PM
"AI & FE Based Characterization and Design Optimization of Efficient and Renewable Energy Conversion Systems"
Abd A. Arkadan

Thursday, April 18, 2019

Tutorial – 4 **Concerto Ballroom B**
08:00AM - 10:00AM
"A Gentle Approach to Quantum Electrodynamics"
Alireza Baghai-Wadji

Tutorial – 5 **Concerto Ballroom C**
08:00AM - 10:00AM
"Domain Decomposition Methods for Differential and Integral Equations"
Zhen Peng

ACES 2019 Sessions Overview

Monday, April 15, 2019 (Sessions 1-14)

Session Title	Room
1- Plenary Talk – 1 "Additively Manufactured Flexible, Wearable, Disposable Antennas and Sensors for Wireless Sensing Applications"	Symphony Ballroom I
2- Plenary Talk – 2 "The Challenges of 5G Wireless Communication Systems"	Symphony Ballroom I
3- Advances in Curved Patch Modeling	Symphony Ballroom I
4- RF Filters and Resonators	Concerto Ballroom A
5- Efficient Optimization of High Frequency Structures – 1	Concerto Ballroom B
6- Advanced Radar Technologies and Techniques – 1	Concerto Ballroom C
7- Modeling of Novel Micro/Nano-Scale Electromagnetic Phenomena, and Applications	Symphony Ballroom I
8- Student Paper Competition – 1	Concerto Ballroom A
9- Efficient Optimization of High Frequency Structures – 2	Concerto Ballroom B
10- Advanced Radar Technologies and Techniques – 2	Concerto Ballroom C
11- Computational Electromagnetics, Advanced Algorithms and Emerging Applications	Symphony Ballroom I
12- Student Paper Competition – 2	Concerto Ballroom A
13- Advanced Time Domain Solvers for Multiphysics Modeling in Photonics	Concerto Ballroom B
14- Advances in Multiscale and Multiphysics Computational Methods	Concerto Ballroom C

ACES 2019 Sessions Overview

Tuesday, April 16, 2019 (Sessions 15-27)

Session Title	Room
15- Plenary Talk – 3 **"Electromagnetics Education: State of the Art, Assessment of Challenges, and Moving Forward"**	Symphony Ballroom I
16- Plenary Talk – 4 **"Adjoint Sensitivity Analysis and its Low and High frequency Applications"**	Symphony Ballroom I
17- Advances in Frequency-Domain CEM Techniques and Application – 1	Symphony Ballroom I
18- Tutorial – 1 **"Adjoint Sensitivity Analysis of High Frequency Structures and its Applications"**	Concerto Ballroom A
19- Finite Difference Methods and Other Techniques – 1	Concerto Ballroom B
20- Uncertainty Quantification Analysis in Networks, Devices, and Fields	Concerto Ballroom C
21- Advances in Frequency-Domain CEM Techniques and Application – 2	Symphony Ballroom I
22- Advances on Time Domain Modeling and Design – 1	Concerto Ballroom A
23- Finite Difference Methods and Other Techniques – 2	Concerto Ballroom B
24- Applied EM for Biomedical and IoT Radar Technologies	Concerto Ballroom C
25- Advances in Frequency-Domain CEM Techniques and Application – 3	Symphony Ballroom I
26- Advances on Time Domain Modeling and Design – 2	Concerto Ballroom A
27- Low Frequency Magnetics	Concerto Ballroom B

ACES 2019 Sessions Overview

Wednesday, April 17, 2019 (Sessions 28-40)

Session Title	Room
28- Plenary Talk – 5 **"Arbitrary Manipulation of Electromagnetic Waves Through Engineered Materials"**	Symphony Ballroom I
29- Plenary Talk – 6 **"Antenna Research at the Army Research Lab"**	Symphony Ballroom I
30- Optimization and Inverse Problems in Low Frequency EM Applications – 1	Symphony Ballroom I
31- EM Modeling Using FEKO – 1	Concerto Ballroom A
32- Modeling and Simulation of Electromagnetic Applications	Concerto Ballroom B
33- Antenna Systems and Applications	Concerto Ballroom C
34- Optimization and Inverse Problems in Low Frequency EM Applications – 2	Symphony Ballroom I
35- EM Modeling Using FEKO – 2	Concerto Ballroom A
36- Antennas and Arrays	Concerto Ballroom B
37- Wireless Power Transfer and Energy Harvesting: Advances in Modelling and Practice	Symphony Ballroom I
38- Tutorial – 2 **"Effective Teaching of Engineering Courses Using Flipped Classrooms"**	Concerto Ballroom A
39- Tutorial – 3 **"AI & FE Based Characterization and Design Optimization of Efficient and Renewable Energy Conversion Systems"**	Concerto Ballroom B
40- Design and Optimization for Nanophotonics: Multiscale Techniques	Concerto Ballroom C

ACES 2019 Sessions Overview

Thursday, April 18, 2019 (Sessions 41-46)

Session Title	Room
41- Recent Advancements in the Modeling, Design and Application of Metasurfaces – 1	Symphony Ballroom I
42- Physically Reconfigurable Antennas and Arrays: Design, Modeling and Materials – 1	Concerto Ballroom A
43- Tutorial – 4 "A Gentle Approach to Quantum Electrodynamics"	Concerto Ballroom B
44- Tutorial – 5 "Domain Decomposition Methods for Differential and Integral Equations"	Concerto Ballroom C
45- Recent Advancements in the Modeling, Design and Application of Metasurfaces – 2	Symphony Ballroom I
46- Physically Reconfigurable Antennas and Arrays: Design, Modeling and Materials – 2	Concerto Ballroom A

ACES 2019 Conference Program at a Glance - April 14-18, 2019

DATE	TIME	SYMPHONY BALLROOM I	CONCERTO BALLROOM A	CONCERTO BALLROOM B	CONCERTO BALLROOM C
			SUNDAY		
14-Apr	02:00PM - 05:00PM	Conference Registration			
	04:00PM - 07:00PM	ACES Board of Directors Meeting			
			MONDAY		
15-Apr	07:30AM - 05:00PM	Conference Registration			
	01:30PM - 05:00PM	Exhibitors			
	08:00AM - 08:10AM	Welcome Message/ACES Business Meeting			
	08:10AM - 09:00AM	(1) Plenary Talk 1: Atif Shamim			
	09:10AM - 10:00AM	(2) Plenary Talk 2: Mark Newbury			
	10:00AM - 10:20AM	BREAK			
	10:20AM - 12:00PM	(3) Advances in Curved Patch Modeling	(4) RF Filters and Resonators	(5) Efficient Optimization of High Frequency Structures - I	(6) Advanced Radar Technologies and Techniques - I
	12:00PM - 01:30PM	LUNCH			
	01:40PM - 03:00PM	(7) Modeling of Novel Micro/Nano-Scale Electromagnetic Phenomena, and Applications	(8) Student Paper Competition - I	(9) Efficient Optimization of High Frequency Structures - II	(10) Advanced Radar Technologies and Techniques - II
	03:00PM - 03:20PM	BREAK			
	03:20PM - 05:20PM	(11) Computational Electromagnetics, Advanced Algorithms and Emerging Applications	(12) Student Paper Competition - II	(13) Advanced Time Domain Solvers for Multiphysics Modeling in Photonics	(14) Advances in Multiscale and Multiphysics Computational Methods
	06:00PM - 09:00PM	WELCOME RECEPTION			
			TUESDAY		
16-Apr	07:30AM - 05:00PM	Conference Registration			
	08:30AM - 05:00PM	Exhibitors			
	08:10AM - 09:00AM	(15) Plenary Talk 3: Branislav M. Notaroš			
	09:10AM - 10:00AM	(16) Plenary Talk 4: Mohamed H. Bakr			
	10:00AM - 10:20AM	BREAK			
	10:20AM - 12:00PM	(17) Advances in Frequency-Domain CEM Techniques and Application - I	(18) Tutorial 1: Mohamed H. Bakr	(19) Finite Difference Methods and Other Techniques - I	(20) Uncertainty Quantification Analysis in Networks, Devices, and Fields
	12:00PM - 01:30PM	LUNCH			
	01:40PM - 03:00PM	(21) Advances in Frequency-Domain CEM Techniques and Application - II	(22) Advances on Time Domain Modeling and Design - I	(23) Finite Difference Methods and Other Techniques - II	(24) Applied EM for Biomedical and IoT Radar Technologies
	03:00PM - 03:20PM	BREAK			
	03:20PM - 05:20PM	(25) Advances in Frequency-Domain CEM Techniques and Application - III	(26) Advances on Time Domain Modeling and Design - II	(27) Low Frequency Magnetics	
			WEDNESDAY		
17-Apr	07:30AM - 05:00PM	Conference Registration			
	08:30AM - 04:00PM	Exhibitors			
	08:10AM - 09:00AM	(28) Plenary Talk 5: Douglas H. Werner			
	09:10AM - 10:00AM	(29) Plenary Talk 6: Steven Weiss			
	10:00AM - 10:20AM	BREAK			
	10:20AM - 12:00PM	(30) Optimization and Inverse Problems in Low Frequency EM Applications - I	(31) EM Modeling Using FEKO - I	(32) Modeling and Simulation of Electromagnetic Applications	(33) Antenna Systems and Applications
	12:00PM - 01:30PM	LUNCH			
	01:40PM - 03:00PM	(34) Optimization and Inverse Problems in Low Frequency EM Applications - II	(35) EM Modeling Using FEKO - II	(36) Antennas and Arrays	
	03:00PM - 03:20PM	BREAK			
	03:20PM - 05:40PM	(37) Wireless Power Transfer and Energy Harvesting: Advances in Modelling and Practice	(38) Tutorial 2: Mohamed H. Bakr	(39) Tutorial 3: Abd A. Arkadan	(40) Design and Optimization for Nanophotonics: Multiscale Techniques
	07:00PM - 10:00PM	AWARDS BANQUET			
			THURSDAY		
18-Apr	07:30AM - 11:00PM	Conference Registration			
	08:00AM - 10:00AM	(41) Recent Advancements in the Modeling, Design and Application of Metasurfaces - I	(42) Physically Reconfigurable Antennas and Arrays: Design, Modeling and Materials - I	(43) Tutorial 4: Alireza Baghai-Wadji	(44) Tutorial 5: Zhen Peng
	10:00AM - 10:20AM	BREAK			
	10:20AM - 12:00PM	(45) Recent Advancements in the Modeling, Design and Application of Metasurfaces - II	(46) Physically Reconfigurable Antennas and Arrays: Design, Modeling and Materials - II		

Effect of Cell Curvature on the Convergence Rates of EFIE Numerical Solutions

Andrew F. Peterson
School of Electrical and Computer Engineering
Georgia Institute of Technology
Atlanta, GA, USA
peterson@ece.gatech.edu

***Abstract*—The convergence rate of higher-order numerical solutions in electromagnetics depends on the fidelity of the target model, specifically on the order of curvature used in that model when analyzing curved targets. The effect of patch curvature is explored for canonical targets such as spheres and disks where exact reference solutions are available for comparison.**

Keywords—basis functions, curved patch models, electric field integral equation, numerical solutions.

I. Introduction

Numerical solutions of the electric field integral equation (EFIE) are widely employed in the analysis of electromagnetic antennas and scatterers. The majority of these computations involve low order expansions of the surface current density and flat-faceted patch models of the targets [1]. In recent years many higher-order polynomial and singular basis functions have been proposed to improve the accuracy and convergence of the numerical results [2-3]. Higher order representations are often used in conjunction with higher-order curved models of the targets, e.g., replacing the flat facets with curved patches based on polynomial mappings. In this presentation, the impact of patch curvature on the convergence rates of the EFIE numerical solution is studied using canonical examples such as spheres and disks for which exact reference solutions can be obtained. This work is the continuation of that presented in previous publications [4-7]. References [4-6] presented convergence data obtained using quadratic-curved patches, while [7] considered cubic-curved patch models but was limited to scattering cross section (SCS) results.

II. Formulation

We use divergence-conforming vector basis functions from the mixed-order Nedelec spaces [8] on curved triangular patches to discretize the EFIE. The Rao-Wilton-Glisson (RWG) basis functions [1] are the lowest order (p=0.5) members of this family. Hierarchical versions of these functions [2-3] were implemented in a Galerkin scheme. Functions of order p=0.5, p=1.5, and p=2.5 are considered, with occasional results for p=3.5. Inner integrals were evaluated using adaptive quadrature routines in conjunction with singularity cancellation procedures; these produce results accurate to 6 or more decimal places as desired. Testing integrals were evaluated with a 7-point Gauss rule (that can exactly integrate degree 5 functions) for p=0.5 and p=1.5, and a 12-point Gauss rule (that can exactly integrate degree 7 polynomials) for p=2.5 and p=3.5. These rules were selected after numerical experimentation showed that rules with more points do not improve the accuracy or convergence rates of the results. The error in the current density obtained from the EFIE under optimal conditions should converge at a rate of $O(h^{p+0.5})$, while the SCS should converge at a rate of $O(h^{2p+2})$ [4], where h denotes the nominal edge length in the model and half-integer indices are used for p to denote the mixed order functions. Optimal convergence rates are not expected if patch curvature is inadequate, since error in representing the target model may exceed the error in the representation of the numerical result.

To produce curved cells, each patch is mapped from a standard triangle to a curved triangle defined by the usual 6 Lagrange points (quadratic) or 10 Lagrange points (cubic), with all the points on the target surface. The divergence-conforming vector basis functions are defined on the curved cells using the procedures in [3] or [9].

III. Example

As an initial illustration, consider the surface current density induced on a perfectly conducting sphere of unit radius a ($ka = 2\pi$). A triangular-cell model is obtained by dividing the sphere uniformly in θ between its north pole and its south pole, and dividing it uniformly in ϕ so that the number of cell edges along the equator is twice the number of divisions in θ. Each triangle is defined by 10 points located on the actual sphere, and a cubic mapping. A sphere of unit radius has surface area equal to 12.6 square wavelengths, so reasonably accurate numerical results should be obtained with approximately 1000 unknowns. Figure 1 shows the 2-norm error in the current density obtained from various sphere models, and basis functions with order p=0.5 to p=3.5. The error is computed by sampling the normal-vector component of the numerical result at three points (two ends and center) along each edge in the sphere models and comparing to the exact solution. The two-norm error can be expressed as

$$E = \frac{\sqrt{\frac{1}{3N_{ed}} \sum_{n=1}^{3N_{ed}} \left| \hat{n}_n \bullet \bar{J}_{ex} - \hat{n}_n \bullet \bar{J}_{num} \right|^2}}{\left| \bar{J} \right|_{\max}}, \qquad (1)$$

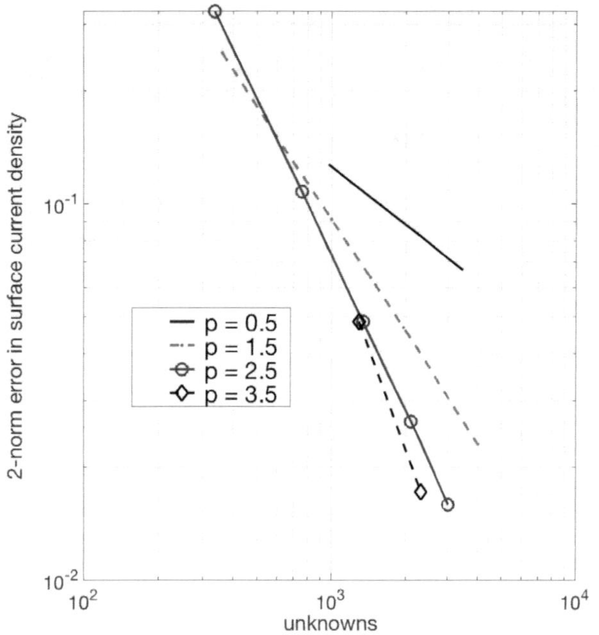

Fig. 1. Error in the surface current density for a sphere with $ka = 2\pi$, obtained with cubic-curved models and three sampling points per edge.

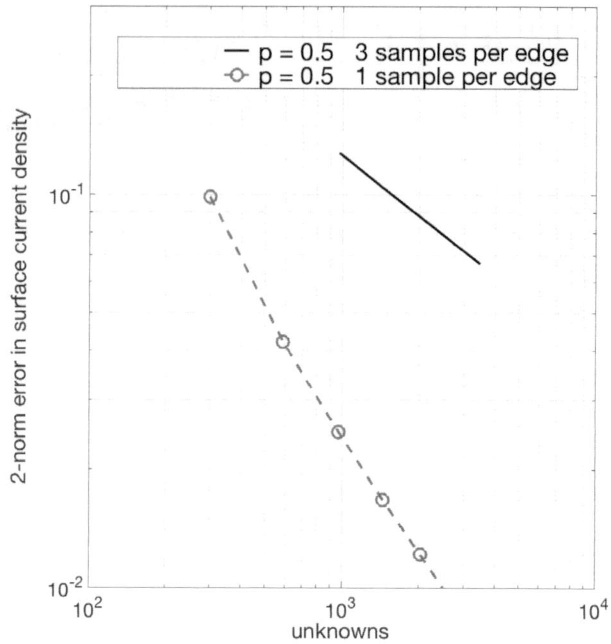

Fig. 2. Error in the surface current density produced by RWG basis functions when sampled at three points per edge and one point per edge, for a sphere with $ka = 2\pi$, and cubic-curved models.

where N_{ed} is the number of edges in the model and $\hat{n}_n$ is the normal vector at edge n. The maximum current density used to normalize (1) is approximated as 2.0 for this sphere.

The convergence rates illustrated by Fig. 1 are reasonably close to expected rates. The p=0.5 result appears to decrease as $O(N^{-0.5})$ or $O(h)$, while the p=1.5 result appears to decrease as $O(N^{-1})$ or $O(h^2)$, where N is the number of unknowns. The p=2.5 result appears to decrease as $O(N^{-1.5})$ or $O(h^3)$.

While the rates in Fig. 1 are close to ideal, there are effects that interfere with these rates, both favorably and unfavorably. An interesting observation, not directly related to the extent of cell curvature, is that it appears that the RWG basis functions exhibit superconvergence points at the center of cell edges. In other words, if the current density obtained with RWG functions (p=0.5) is sampled at the center of each edge, the result is much more accurate than shown in Fig. 1. Fig. 2 illustrates this effect for the preceding example of the sphere with $ka = 2\pi$. When sampled at the center of edges, the p=0.5 results converge at a rate of $O(h^2)$, and for this example are more accurate than the other higher-order representations depicted in Fig. 1.

IV. Additional Examples

Examples will be used in the presentation to illustrate other aspects of the impact of cell curvature by comparing results obtained with flat, quadratc-curved, and cubic-curved models. Other examples of superconvergence will be presented.

References

[1] S. M. Rao, D. R. Wilton, and A. W. Glisson, "Electromagnetic scattering by surfaces of arbitrary shape," IEEE Trans. Antennas Propagat., vol. AP-30, pp. 409-418, May 1982.

[2] A. F. Peterson and R. D. Graglia, "A review of hierarchical vector basis functions for triangular and quadrilateral domains," Forum for Electromagnetic Research Methods and Application Technologies (FERMAT), vol. 18, 24 pages, November-December 2016.

[3] R. D. Graglia and A. F. Peterson, Higher-order Techniques in Computational Electromagnetics. Edison NJ: SciTech Publishing, 2016.

[4] K. F. Warnick, Numerical Analysis for Electromagnetic Integral Equations. Boston: Artech House, 2008.

[5] A. F. Peterson, "Observed baseline convergence rates and superconvergence in the scattering cross section obtained from numerical solutions of the MFIE," IEEE Trans. Antennas Propagat., vol. 56, pp. 3510-3515, November 2008.

[6] A. F. Peterson, "Beyond RWG/Galerkin solutions of the EFIE: Investigations into point-matched, discontinuous, and higher order discretizations," Proceedings of the 27th Annual Review of Progress in Applied Computational Electromagnetics, Williamsburg, VA, pp. 117-120, March 2011.

[7] A. F. Peterson, "Cell curvature and far field superconvergence in numerical solutions of electromagnetic integral equations," International Journal of Antennas and Propagation, vol. 2016, Article ID 9808637, 7 pages, May 2016.

[8] J. C. Nedelec, "Mixed finite elements in R3," Num. Math., vol. 35, pp. 315-341, 1980.

[9] A. F. Peterson, Mapped Vector Basis Functions for Electromagnetic Integral Equations. San Rafael CA: Morgan & Claypool Synthesis Lectures, 2006.

Hybrid Integration Scheme for the Evaluation of Strongly Singular Integral over Curvilinear Triangle Surface

J. Rivero
Dept. of Electronics and Telecomunications
Politecnico di Torino
Torino, Italy
javier.rivero@polito.it

F. Vipiana
Dept. of Electronics and Telecomunications
Politecnico di Torino
Torino, Italy
francesca.vipiana@polito.it

D. R. Wilton
Dept. of Electrical and Computer Engineering
University of Houston
Houston, TX, USA
wilton@uh.edu

W. A. Johnson
Consultant
Albuquerque, NM, USA
w.johnson24@comcast.net

***Abstract*—This paper explores the possibility of combining two well-known schemes (singularity subtraction and singularity cancellation) to evaluate strongly near-singular integrals with the singularity present in the MoM discretization of the Magnetic Field Integral Equations, (MFIE). First, a subtraction of a singularity is applied. The resulting integrand presents a singular term, which is canceled with an appropriate variable transformation. The aim is to achieve good efficiency for a medium-low accuracy range and be able to reach machine precision increasing the quadrature order.**

***Index Terms*—Integral equations, moment methods, numerical analysis, singular integrals.**

I. Introduction

Typically, higher-order schemes are applied to refine the modeling of curved domains or boundaries or to provide more accurate representations of the fields or equivalent surface currents associated with them. However, the rigorous solution of either direct or inverse scattering problems using integral equation formulations for higher-order schemes, requires the development of numerical method of moments (MoM) codes able to accurately model and predict electromagnetic behavior. Accurate and efficient evaluation of singular and near-singular potential integrals is a key part of this requirement.

One of the most widely used and early methods to evaluate strongly near-singular integrals has been what is commonly called the "singularity subtraction" scheme [1], [2]. The idea is to subtract from the integrand one or more terms that have the same behavior as the integrand at its singularities. The remaining non-singular integrand is numerically evaluated by standard quadrature rules; the singular terms are then integrated analytically and added back into the final result.

A more recent approach is the "singularity cancellation" scheme, where the singularities are canceled via appropriate variable transformations [3]. Since the integral is calculated numerically, a singularity cancellation scheme is independent of bases, element shapes, and curvature. Moreover, it is possible to achieve machine precision by increasing the quadrature order [4]. This allows one to reach machine precision at the detriment of lower efficiency (greater number of integration points) in the low-medium accuracy range.

In this paper we propose to combined these two well-known schemes to evaluate strongly near-singular integrals, such as in the MoM discretization of the Magnetic Field Integral Equation (MFIE) for curved triangles. First, subtraction of the singularity of higher order is applied on the tangential triangle to the curved triangle. The remaining integrand shows an asymptotic behavior of $1/R$, which is canceled via an appropriate variable transformation. The goal of this work is to achieve good efficiency in the low-to-medium accuracy range and yet be able to reach machine precision by merely increasing the quadrature order. Preliminary results have demonstrated the possibility of achieving both goals. The method is relatively simple to implement, and applicable to flat triangles.

II. Formulation

Let's consider the vector integral present in the MFIE written in *area* coordinates $\boldsymbol{\xi} = (\xi_1, \xi_2, \xi_3)$, with $\xi_1 + \xi_2 + \xi_3 = 1$,

$$\mathbf{I}_n(\mathbf{r}) = \frac{1}{4\pi}\int_0^1 d\xi_2 \int_0^{1-\xi_2} d\xi_1 \boldsymbol{\Lambda}_n(\mathbf{r}'(\boldsymbol{\xi}))$$
$$(1 + jkR(\boldsymbol{\xi}))e^{-jkR(\boldsymbol{\xi})} \times \frac{\mathbf{R}(\boldsymbol{\xi})}{R(\boldsymbol{\xi})^3}\mathcal{J}(\boldsymbol{\xi}), \qquad (1)$$

where k is the wavenumber, $\mathbf{R}(\boldsymbol{\xi}) = \mathbf{r} - \mathbf{r}'(\boldsymbol{\xi})$, $R(\boldsymbol{\xi}) = |\mathbf{R}(\boldsymbol{\xi})|$, $\mathbf{r}$ is an observation point, and $\mathbf{r}'(\boldsymbol{\xi})$ is a point on the curvilinear triangle. Then, we consider a flat triangle, $\mathcal{T}_T'$, *tangent* to the curvilinear one at the projection of the observation point onto the curvilinear triangle, $\mathbf{r}_0 = \mathbf{r}'(\boldsymbol{\xi}_0)$, as shown in Fig. 1 and defined according to [5].

Now, we subtract, and sum back again a term with an asymptotic behavior $\mathbf{R}/R^3$ over the tangential triangle. This term is calculated analytically using the procedures described in [1]. The remaining integral shows an asymptotic behavior

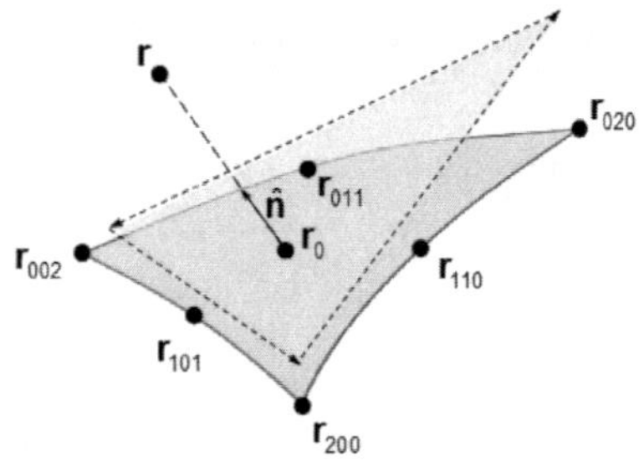

Fig. 1: Curvilinear triangle and corresponding flat tangent triangle at the projected observation point $\mathbf{r}_0$.

$1/R$ for $R \to 0$ that can be evaluated applying the radial angular transform for the curvilinear triangle shown in [5].

III. Preliminary Numerical Results

To show the accuracy of the proposed scheme, we analyze the convergence behavior of the vector integral (1). We consider a curved triangle/observation point pair where the projection of the observation point lies very close ($\lambda/100$) to the centroid of the curved triangle. We compared the behavior of three different schemes to deal with the strongly near-singular integral (1): the singularity subtraction scheme with two terms subtracted [1] and the standard Gauss-triangle (GT) quadrature scheme [6] for the remaining numerical integral, the singularity cancellation scheme with a Radial-Angular transform [3] numerically integrated using the GT quadrature scheme, and the hybrid scheme presented here, to a reference result obtained using the Radial-Angular transformation and GT quadrature scheme with the highest number of points we have available for this scheme (a total of around 60,000 points).

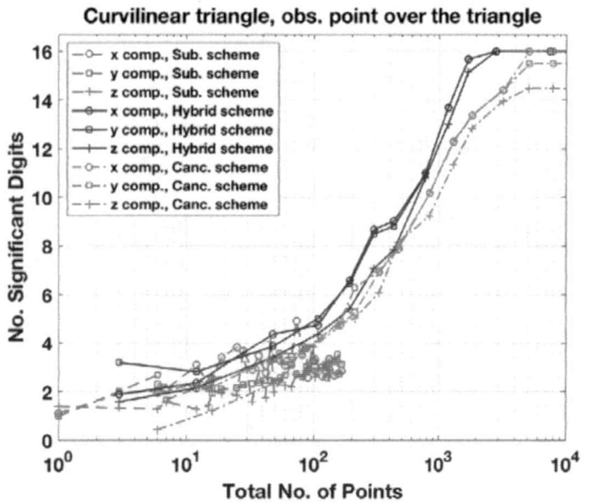

Fig. 2: Near-field convergence of the source integral.

In Fig. 2 the singularity subtraction scheme displays limited accuracy with a plateau at about 2-4 significant digits, while the singularity cancellation scheme can reach machine precision. The hybrid scheme displays better performance than the singularity subtraction scheme in the low-to-medium sample point range, and is able to reach machine precision using fewer integration points than the cancellation scheme.

IV. Conclusion

We propose an integration scheme based on a combination of two-existing well-known schemes to evaluate the strongly near-singular integrals present in MFIE for curve triangle.

In the proposed approach, a term with the appropriate asymptotic behavior over a tangent triangle and that is analytically integrable, is subtracted from the integrand. The remaining integrand is further smoothed using the Radial-Angular scheme. The method is relatively simple to implement, and its numerical behavior is as expected, replicating the good behavior of the two schemes on which is based.

References

[1] R. Graglia, "On the numerical integration of the linear shape functions times the 3-D Greens function or its gradient on a plane triangle," IEEE Transactions on Antennas and Propagation, vol. 41, no. 10, pp. 1448-1455, Oct. 1993.

[2] "Methods for the Evaluation of Regular, Weakly Singular and Strongly SingularSurface Reaction Integrals Arising in Method of Moments", A. Herschlein, J. v. Hagen, W. Wiesbeck, ACES Journal Paper, Year: 2002 vol. 17, no. 1, Mar 2002.

[3] F. Vipiana and D. R. Wilton, "Numerical evaluation via singularity cancellation schemes of near-singular integrals involving the gradient of Helmholtz-type potentials," IEEE Transactions on Antennas and Propagation, vol. 61, no. 3, pp. 12551265, Mar. 2013.

[4] P. W. Fink and M. A. Khayat, "A simple transformation for the numerical evaluation of near strongly singular integrals, IEEE Antennas and Wireless Propagation Letters, vol. 12, pp. 225228, 2013. [Online]. Available: http://ieeexplore.ieee.org/document/6420865.

[5] D. R. Wilton, F. Vipiana, and W. A. Johnson, "Evaluating singular, near-singular, and non-singular integrals on curvilinear elements," Electromagnetics, vol. 34, no. 3–4, pp. 307327, Apr. 2014.

[6] L. Zhang, T. Cui, and H. Liu, "A set of symmetric quadrature rules on triangles and tetrahedra," Journal of Computational Mathematics, vol. 27, no. 1, pp. 89-96, 2009.

On Higher-order Nyström Discretization of Scalar Potential Integral Equation for Penetrable Scatterers

Rui Chen, and Hakan Bagci
Division of Computer, Electrical, and Mathematical Science and Engineering
King Abdullah University of Science and Technology (KAUST), Thuwal, 23955-6900, Saudi Arabia
e-mails: {rui.chen, hakan.bagci}@kaust.edu.sa

Abstract—**A higher-order Nyström scheme is developed for discretizing the scalar potential integral equation (SPIE) for analyzing electromagnetic field/wave interactions on penetrable scatterers. The unknown scalar potential and its normal derivative are expanded using higher-order Lagrange interpolation functions. Inserting this expansion into the SPIE and point-testing the resulting equation yields a matrix system that is solved for the unknown expansion coefficients. Numerical results demonstrate that this matrix system is well-conditioned regardless of the discretization order and mesh density, and that its solution has higher-order convergence.**

I. Introduction

Electromagnetic scattering from homogeneous penetrable objects are often analyzed by solving different combinations of electric and magnetic field surface integral equations (EFIE and MFIE) [1]. However, it is well-known that the EFIE suffers from low-frequency and dense-mesh break downs [2], [3]. Even though the MFIE is always well-conditioned (thanks to its second-kind nature), its solution obtained using traditional methods at low-frequencies is inaccurate [4], [5]. Even though these problems can be alleviated using new discretization and preconditioning techniques, these often come at the expense of implementation simplicity.

In recent years, potential surface integral equations have been proposed as "break-down free" alternatives to field surface integral equations. These equations have first been formulated for perfect electrically conducting objects in [6], [7] and later extended for penetrable objects [8], [9]. In [9], a de-coupled formulation, which allows for solving for scalar and vector potential individually, has been proposed.

In this work, a higher-order Nyström method [10] is used to solve the scalar potential integral equation (SPIE) formulated in [9]. The proposed method uses higher-order basis functions defined at a set of discrete points to expand the unknown potential and its normal derivative on the surface of the scatterer, inserts this expansion in the SPIE, and point-tests the resulting equation to obtain a matrix system. This matrix system is solved for the unknown expansion coefficients. Numerical results demonstrate that this matrix system is well-conditioned regardless of the discretization order and mesh density, and that its solution has higher-order convergence.

II. Formulation

Let S denote the surface of a homogeneous penetrable scatterer residing in an unbounded background medium. The permittivity, permeability, and wavenumber of the background medium and scatterer are $\{\varepsilon_1, \mu_1, k_1\}$ and $\{\varepsilon_2, \mu_2, k_2\}$, respectively. The scatterer is excited by an incident scalar potential $\phi^{\mathrm{i}}(\mathbf{r})$. Using the scalar Green's theorem, the governing Helmholtz equation, and the equivalence principle, the scalar potentials outside S (exterior problem) and inside S (interior problem), $\phi_1(\mathbf{r})$ and $\phi_2(\mathbf{r})$, can be represented in terms of the integrals of $\{\phi_1(\mathbf{r}'), \partial_{n'}\phi_1(\mathbf{r}')\}$, $\mathbf{r}' \in S$ and $\{\phi_2(\mathbf{r}'), \partial_{n'}\phi_2(\mathbf{r}')\}$, $\mathbf{r}' \in S$, respectively. Here, $\partial_{n'} = \hat{\mathbf{n}}(\mathbf{r}') \cdot \nabla'$ and $\hat{\mathbf{n}}(\mathbf{r}')$ is the outward pointing unit normal vector on S at $\mathbf{r}'$ [9]. Linearly combining these representations and their normal derivatives on S, and enforcing the boundary conditions $\phi_1(\mathbf{r}') = \phi_2(\mathbf{r}')$, $\mathbf{r}' \in S$ and $\varepsilon_1 \partial_{n'}\phi_1(\mathbf{r}') = \varepsilon_2 \partial_{n'}\phi_2(\mathbf{r}')$, $\mathbf{r}' \in S$ yield the following SPIE [9]:

$$\begin{bmatrix} \frac{\alpha_1+\alpha_2}{2} I + C_{11} & C_{12} \\ C_{21} & \frac{\beta_1+\beta_2}{2} I + C_{22} \end{bmatrix} \begin{bmatrix} \phi \\ \frac{\varepsilon_1}{k_0\varepsilon_0}\partial_n \phi \end{bmatrix} = \begin{bmatrix} \alpha_1 \phi^{\mathrm{i}} \\ \frac{\beta_1\varepsilon_1}{k_0\varepsilon_0}\partial_n \phi^{\mathrm{i}} \end{bmatrix} \quad (1)$$

where $C_{11} = -\alpha_1 \tilde{D}_1 + \alpha_2 \tilde{D}_2$, $C_{12} = (\alpha_1 k_0 \varepsilon_0/\varepsilon_1) S_1 - (\alpha_2 k_0 \varepsilon_0/\varepsilon_2) S_2$, $C_{21} = -(\beta_1\varepsilon_1/k_0\varepsilon_0) N_1 + (\beta_2\varepsilon_2/k_0\varepsilon_0) N_2$, and $C_{22} = \beta_1 \tilde{D}_1' - \beta_2 \tilde{D}_2'$ with

$$S_i[x] = \int_S G_i(\mathbf{r}, \mathbf{r}') x(\mathbf{r}') d\mathbf{r}'$$
$$\tilde{D}_i[x] = \fint_S \partial_{n'} G_i(\mathbf{r}, \mathbf{r}') x(\mathbf{r}') d\mathbf{r}'$$
$$\tilde{D}_i'[x] = \fint_S \partial_{n} G_i(\mathbf{r}, \mathbf{r}') x(\mathbf{r}') d\mathbf{r}'$$
$$N_i[x] = \partial_n \int_S \partial_{n'} G_i(\mathbf{r}, \mathbf{r}') x(\mathbf{r}') d\mathbf{r}'$$

and $G_i(\mathbf{r}, \mathbf{r}') = e^{-jk_iR}/4\pi R$, $R = |\mathbf{r} - \mathbf{r}'|$. Here, ε_0, μ_0, and k_0 are the permittivity, permeability, and wavenumber in free-space, and α_1, α_2, β_1, and β_2 are constant coefficients. β_1 and β_2 are selected to satisfy $\beta_1\varepsilon_1 = \beta_2\varepsilon_2$ so that the hyper-singularity in C_{21} is cancelled out.

To numerically solve (1), S is discretized into N_{p} curvilinear triangular patches and $\phi(\mathbf{r}')$ and $(\varepsilon_1/k_0\varepsilon_0)\partial_{n'}\phi(\mathbf{r}')$ are expanded as:

$$\phi(\mathbf{r}') = \sum_{p=1}^{N_{\mathrm{p}}} \sum_{i=1}^{N_{\mathrm{i}}} \vartheta(\mathbf{r}') L_{ip}(\mathbf{r}') \{\mathbf{I}_1\}_{ip}$$
$$\frac{\varepsilon_1}{k_0\varepsilon_0}\partial_{n'}\phi(\mathbf{r}') = \sum_{p=1}^{N_{\mathrm{p}}} \sum_{i=1}^{N_{\mathrm{i}}} \vartheta(\mathbf{r}') L_{ip}(\mathbf{r}') \{\mathbf{I}_2\}_{ip} \quad (2)$$

where N_{i} is the number of interpolation points on each patch, $\vartheta(\mathbf{r})$ is the inverse of the Jacobian, $L_{ip}(\mathbf{r})$ is the Lagrange interpolator defined at $\mathbf{r}_{ip}$ (interpolation point i on patch p), and $\{\mathbf{I}_1\}_{ip}$ and $\{\mathbf{I}_2\}_{ip}$ are the unknown expansion coefficients. Inserting (2) into (1), and testing the resulting equation at $\mathbf{r}_{jq}$, $j = 1, .., N_\mathrm{i}$, $q = 1, .., N_\mathrm{p}$, yield a linear matrix system:

$$\begin{bmatrix} \mathbf{Z}_{11} & \mathbf{Z}_{12} \\ \mathbf{Z}_{21} & \mathbf{Z}_{22} \end{bmatrix} \begin{bmatrix} \mathbf{I}_1 \\ \mathbf{I}_2 \end{bmatrix} = \begin{bmatrix} \mathbf{V}_1 \\ \mathbf{V}_2 \end{bmatrix}. \tag{3}$$

Here, $\{\mathbf{V}_1\}_{jq} = \alpha_1 \phi^\mathrm{i}(\mathbf{r}_{jq})$, $\{\mathbf{V}_2\}_{jq} = (\beta_1\varepsilon_1/k_0\varepsilon_0)\partial_n \phi^\mathrm{i}(\mathbf{r}_{jq})$,

$\{\mathbf{Z}_{11}\}_{jq,ip} = (\alpha_1+\alpha_2)\vartheta(\mathbf{r}_{jq})\delta_{ij}\delta_{pq}/2 + C_{11}[\vartheta(\mathbf{r})L_{ip}(\mathbf{r})]$,
$\{\mathbf{Z}_{12}\}_{jq,ip} = C_{12}[\vartheta(\mathbf{r})L_{ip}(\mathbf{r})]$, $\{\mathbf{Z}_{21}\}_{jq,ip} = C_{21}[\vartheta(\mathbf{r})L_{ip}(\mathbf{r})]$,
$\{\mathbf{Z}_{22}\}_{jq,ip} = (\beta_1+\beta_2)\vartheta(\mathbf{r}_{jq})\delta_{ij}\delta_{pq}/2 + C_{22}[\vartheta(\mathbf{r})L_{ip}(\mathbf{r})]$.

III. Numerical Results

The proposed scheme is used for analyzing electromagnetic scattering from a unit dielectric sphere with $\varepsilon_2 = 2\varepsilon_0$ and $\mu_2 = \mu_0$ residing in a background medium with $\varepsilon_1 = \varepsilon_0$ and $\mu_1 = \mu_0$. The sphere is centered at the origin. The excitation is a plane wave: $\phi^\mathrm{i}(\mathbf{r}) = e^{-jk_1 z}/\sqrt{\mu_1\varepsilon_1}$ with frequency $f = 300$ MHz. The transpose-free quasi-minimal residual method [11] is used to solve the matrix system iteratively. The residual error threshold is set to 10^{-6}.

The sphere surface is discretized into seven different meshes using 2nd-order curvilinear patches with average edge lengths $h = \{0.4, 0.35, 0.3, 0.25, 0.2, 0.15, 0.1\}$ m. These meshes have $N_\mathrm{p} = \{136, 202, 280, 396, 622, 1126, 2560\}$ numbers of patches. The order of the interpolation functions (i.e., discretization order) is selected from $\{0, 1, 2, 3\}$, which corresponds to $N_\mathrm{i} = \{1, 3, 6, 12\}$ numbers of interpolation points on each curvilinear patch. The matrix system (3) is computed and solved for every combination of N_p and N_i, resulting in a total of 28 matrix solutions.

After each matrix solution, the scattered scalar potential $\phi^\mathrm{sca}(\mathbf{r}_0)$ is calculated on a circle described by $\mathbf{r}_0 = (4.0\sin\theta, 0.0, 4.0\cos\theta)$ m, for $\theta = [0^\circ, 180^\circ]$. The scattered scalar potential computed using 2nd-order discretization for $N_\mathrm{p} = 2560$ is used as the reference result (it has been reported in [10] 2nd-order interpolation gives the best accuracy). Then, relative norm errors in all other results are computed. Fig. 1 plots this error versus the product $2N_\mathrm{p}N_\mathrm{i}$ (total number of unknowns). The figure clearly shows that the Nyström scheme used here to solve (1) achieves higher-order convergence in the solution as expected. It is clear that for a given number of unknowns, higher-order discretizations reach higher accuracy levels. However, one can also see that the convergence rate of the solution of the 3rd-order discretization is smaller than that of the 2nd-order discretization. This is also observed in [10] and might be explained by the fact that only 2nd-order curvilinear patches are used to discretize the sphere surface.

Table I lists the condition number of the matrix in (3) for different combinations of the discretization order and h. It clearly shows that matrix system stays well-conditioned independent of the discretization order and mesh density. This is due to fact that diagonal and off-diagonal entries in (1) are second-kind and compact operators, respectively.

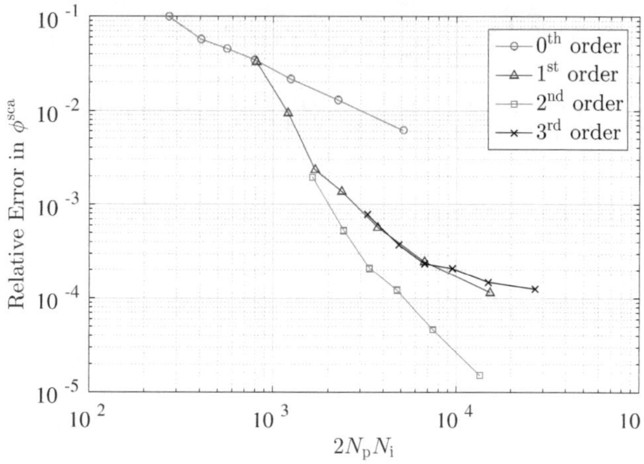

Fig. 1. Relative norm error in scattered scalar potential versus total number of unknowns for different discretization orders.

TABLE I
Condition Numbers for Different Discretization Orders and Different h

h	0.4 m	0.35 m	0.3 m	0.25 m	0.2 m
0th order	18.1	15.2	16.1	14.8	12.6
1st order	14.9	14.1	15.3	15.1	12.8
2nd order	14.3	15.0	16.6	16.2	13.8
3rd order	13.8	14.6	16.2	15.8	13.5

References

[1] P. Ylä-Oijala, S. P. Kiminki, K. Cools, F. Andriulli, and S. Järvenpää, "Mixed discretization schemes for electromagnetic surface integral equations," *Int. J. Numer. Model., Electron. Netw., Devices Fields*, vol. 25, no. 5–6, pp. 525–540, Jan. 2012.

[2] F. P. Andriulli, K. Cools, H. Bagci, F. Olyslager, A. Buffa, S. Christiansen, and E. Michielssen, "A multiplicative Calderon preconditioner for the electric field integral equation," *IEEE Trans. Antennas Propag.*, vol. 56, no. 8, pp. 2398–2412, Aug. 2008.

[3] G. Vecchi, "Loop-star decomposition of basis functions in the discretization of the EFIE," *IEEE Trans. Antennas Propag.*, vol. 47, no. 2, pp. 339–346, 1999.

[4] K. Cools, F. P. Andriulli, D. DeZutter, and E. Michielssen, "Accurate and conforming mixed discretization of the MFIE," *IEEE Antennas Wireless Propag. Lett.*, vol. 10, pp. 528–531, 2011.

[5] H. A. Ülkü, I. Bogaert, K. Cools, F. P. Andriulli, and H. Bagci, "Mixed discretization of the time-domain MFIE at low frequencies," *IEEE Antennas Wireless Propag. Lett.*, vol. 16, pp. 1565–1568, 2017.

[6] Q. S. Liu, S. Sun, and W. C. Chew, "A potential-based integral equation method for low-frequency electromagnetic problems," *IEEE Trans. Antennas Propag.*, vol. 66, no. 3, pp. 1413–1426, Mar. 2018.

[7] F. Vico, M. Ferrando, L. Greengard, and Z. Gimbutas, "The decoupled potential integral equation for time-harmonic electromagnetic scattering," *Commun. Pur. Appl. Math.*, vol. 69, no. 4, pp. 771–812, 2016.

[8] W. C. Chew, "Vector potential electromagnetics with generalized gauge for inhomogeneous media: Formulation," *Progr. Electromagn. Res.*, vol. 149, pp. 69–84, 2014.

[9] J. Li, B. Shanker, and X. Fu, "Potential integral equations in electromagnetics," *in IEEE Int. Symp. Antennas Propag.*, 2017.

[10] G. Kang, J. Song, W. C. Chew, K. C. Donepudi, and J. M. Jin, "A novel grid-robust higher order vector basis function for the method of moments," *IEEE Trans. Antennas Propag.*, vol. 49, no. 6, pp. 908–915, Jun. 2001.

[11] R. W. Freund, "A transpose-free quasi-minimal residual algorithm for non-Hermitian linear systems," *SIAM J. Sci. Comput.*, vol. 14, no. 2, pp. 470–482, 1993.

Evaluation of the Contour Integral on Curved Edges in Time Domain Equivalent Edge Currents

Aslihan Aktepe and H. Arda Ülkü
Department of Electronics Engineering
Gebze Technical University
41400 Kocaeli, Turkey
{aaktepe,haulku}@gtu.edu.tr

***Abstract*—The closed-form evaluation of the radiation integral in time domain physical theory of diffraction (PTD) equivalent edge currents (EECs) on quadratic edges of quadratic triangular surfaces, is presented. The radiation integral is interpreted as a Radon transform and the closed-form expressions are obtained by finding the intersection of the plane, which is formed by the propagation direction of the incident wave and the observation direction, and quadratic edge. A numerical example that shows the accuracy and validity of the scheme is presented.**

***Index Terms*—curved surfaces, Radon transform interpretation, quadratic triangles, time domain equivalent edge currents(TD-EEC).**

I. Introduction

The physical optics (PO) approximation is a well-known and useful high frequency technique to analyze electrically large structures. However PO approximation cannot model the diffracted fields, i.e. scattering from edges, sharp wedges, etc. Effects of the diffraction should be determined and added to the PO solution separately. There are several methods to determine the diffracted fields [1]–[3], e.g. physical theory of diffraction (PTD) – equivalent edge currents (EEC) [2], [3] can be used to determine the diffracted field contributions.

The PO approximation and EEC, require evaluation of a highly oscillatory radiation integral [4]–[9]. Efficient and accurate evaluation of this radiation integral has an important effect on the solution [4]–[9]. For the PO approximation, this integral is a surface integral and can be evaluated in closed-form using the Radon transform interpretation for linear triangles (LTs) in time and frequency domains [5], and for quadratic triangles (QTs) in time domain [6]. In addition approximate expressions for QTs [7] in frequency domain are available. For the EEC, the radiation integral is a contour integral and can be evaluated in closed-form in time domain for linear edges (LEs) of LTs using Radon transform interpretation [9].

In this work, closed-form evaluation of the contour integral on quadratic edges (QEs) of QTs in time domain EEC (TD-EEC) is presented. Using the Radon transform interpretation, the closed-form of the contour integral is obtained as the intersection of the QE and the plane formed by the incident plane wave's propagation and observation directions. Since the diffraction phenomena is local, diffraction coefficients for TD-EEC [2] with local parameters at the intersection point are used.

In the numerical example section, it is shown that PO and PTD-EEC contributions from curved scatterers can be determined accurately and efficiently using less number of QT and QE elements (compared to LT and LE) and the closed-form expressions.

II. Formulation

A. TD-EEC

Let S and l denote the illuminated surface and edge of a perfect electrically conducting (PEC) scatterer, respectively, and S is discretized with QTs as $S = \bigcup S_n$. Hence l can be represented by the QE segments l_n attached to S_n, as $l = \bigcup l_n$. The scattered electric field has contributions from PO and PTD-EEC, i.e., $\mathbf{E}^{\text{sca}}(\mathbf{r},t) = \mathbf{E}^{\text{sca}}_{\text{PO}}(\mathbf{r},t) + \mathbf{E}^{\text{sca}}_{\text{EEC}}(\mathbf{r},t)$. Here only the evaluation of TD-EEC contributions is considered, the evaluation of the closed-form expressions for time domain PO is given in [6]. For TD-EEC, at far field region, the scattered electric field due to an impulsively excited plane wave is:

$$\mathbf{E}^{\text{sca}}_{\text{EEC}}(\mathbf{r},t) = \frac{\delta(t - r/c)}{4\pi r} * \mathbf{E}^{\text{sca}}_{\text{rc}}(t) = \frac{\delta(t - r/c)}{4\pi r} * \sum_{n=1}^{N} \mathbf{h}_{\text{n}}(t). \tag{1}$$

Here, $\mathbf{E}^{\text{sca}}_{\text{rc}}(t)$ is the range-corrected scattered electric field, c is the speed of light, $\delta(\cdot)$ is the Dirac delta function, and "$*$" denotes temporal convolution. In (1), $\mathbf{h}_{\text{n}}(t)$ is defined as [2]:

$$\mathbf{h}_n(t) = \int_{l_n} \delta(t - \frac{2}{c}\mathbf{k}_{\text{r}} \cdot \mathbf{r}') \Big\{ \hat{\mathbf{k}}_{\text{s}} \times \hat{\mathbf{k}}_{\text{s}} \times \hat{\mathbf{t}}_n(\mathbf{r}') \Big[D^I_{\text{e},n} \hat{\mathbf{p}} \cdot \hat{\mathbf{t}}_n(\mathbf{r}') + D^I_{\text{h},n} (\hat{\mathbf{k}}_{\text{i}} \times \hat{\mathbf{p}}) \cdot \hat{\mathbf{t}}_n(\mathbf{r}') \Big] + \hat{\mathbf{k}}_{\text{s}} \times \hat{\mathbf{t}}_n(\mathbf{r}') \Big[D^M_{\text{h},n} (\hat{\mathbf{k}}_{\text{i}} \times \hat{\mathbf{p}}) \cdot \hat{\mathbf{t}}_n(\mathbf{r}') \Big] \Big\} \, dl', \tag{2}$$

where $\mathbf{k}_{\text{r}} = (\hat{\mathbf{k}}_{\text{i}} - \hat{\mathbf{k}}_{\text{s}})/2$, $\hat{\mathbf{k}}_{\text{s}}$ is the observation direction, $\hat{\mathbf{p}}$ and $\hat{\mathbf{k}}_{\text{i}}$ are the polarization and the propagation direction of the incident wave, and $\hat{\mathbf{t}}_n(\mathbf{r})$ is the unit tangent vector along the edge l_n. The diffraction coefficients $D^I_{\text{e},n}$, $D^I_{\text{h},n}$, $D^M_{\text{h},n}$ are defined in [2]. Note that even though it is not shown explicitly, $D^I_{\text{e},n}$, $D^I_{\text{h},n}$, $D^M_{\text{h},n}$ are functions of the surface normal at the edge, $\hat{\mathbf{t}}_n(\mathbf{r})$, and $\hat{\mathbf{k}}_\mathrm{i}$. For curved edges $\hat{\mathbf{t}}_n(\mathbf{r})$ and the diffraction coefficients are not constant through with the integration domain l_n, therefore they should be taken into account while evaluating $\mathbf{h}_n(t)$.

B. Evaluation of $\mathbf{h}_n(t)$

Assuming that $t = t_0$, $\mathbf{k}_\mathrm{r}$, and $\mathbf{r}_i$, $i = 1, 2, ..., 6$ nodes of the QE/QT are known, the steps of the scheme to evaluate $\mathbf{h}_\mathrm{n}(t)$ is as follows:

Step 1: The Dirac delta function in (2) defines a plane at the given time $t = t_0$, i.e., $ct_0 = 2\mathbf{k}_\mathrm{r} \cdot \mathbf{r}'$. Inserting the barycentric coordinates defined on QE/QT into the plane equation results in a quadratic equation. The solution of the quadratic equation yields the intersection point ($\mathbf{r}_\mathrm{int}$) on the QE. If there is no intersection, then $\mathbf{h}_n(t_0) = 0$.

Step 2: Using the Dirac delta function's properties, closed-form expression to $\mathbf{h}_n(t)$ can be determined at $(t, \mathbf{r}) = (t_0, \mathbf{r}_\mathrm{int})$. The values of the parameters for $\mathbf{h}_n(t)$ are determined using the intersection point $\mathbf{r}_\mathrm{int}$. It should be emphasized that $\hat{\mathbf{t}}_n(\mathbf{r})$, $D^I_{\mathrm{e},n}$, $D^I_{\mathrm{h},n}$, and $D^M_{\mathrm{h},n}$ are not constant through a QE and should be calculated for each time step and intersection point.

III. Numerical Example

A parabolic scatterer with radius of 0.5 m and focal depth of 0.9 m (shown in Fig. 1), is analyzed to show the accuracy and validity of the proposed scheme. The scatterer is illuminated with incident angles $\theta = 120°$ and $\varphi = 0°$, and backscattered fields are observed ($\hat{\mathbf{k}}_\mathrm{s} = -\hat{\mathbf{k}}_\mathrm{i}$), the time step size $\Delta t = 0.999$ ps is chosen.

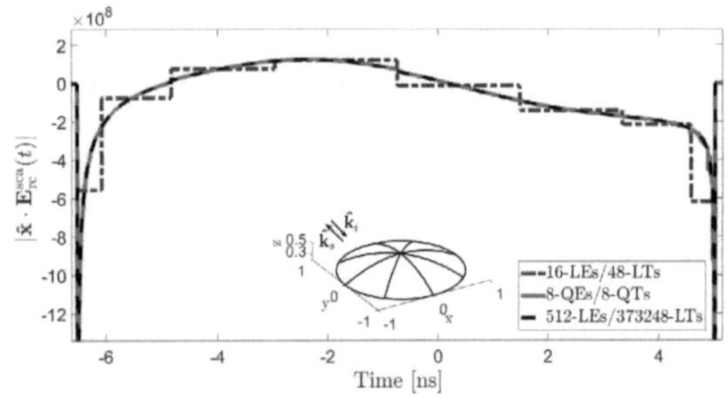

Fig. 1. Comparison of the $\hat{\mathbf{x}}$-component of the range corrected scattered electric fields.

Fig. 1 plots the $\hat{\mathbf{x}}$-component of the range corrected scattered electric fields due to the TD-EEC for 8-QEs/8-QTs, 16-LEs/48-LTs, and 512-LEs/373248-LTs. In this setup, $\hat{\mathbf{k}}_\mathrm{r} = \hat{\mathbf{k}}_\mathrm{i}$, and the plane starts to intersect with the scatterer at $t = -7.445$ ns and the intersection ends at $t = 5.036$ ns. Fig. 2 plots the radar cross section (RCS) (including the both PO and EEC contributions) obtained by Fourier transforming the time domain PO and EEC results for 8-QEs/8-QTs, 16-LEs/48-LTs and 512-LEs/373248-LTs. It can be seen from Figs. 1 and 2 that the results for LEs/LTs converges to the results for 8-QEs/8-QTs as the number of LTs increases. Fig. 3 plots the relative error between the RCS results for 8-QEs/8-QTs and the results obtained for (48-512)-LEs/(288-373248)-LTs. The convergence of the results can be seen clearly.

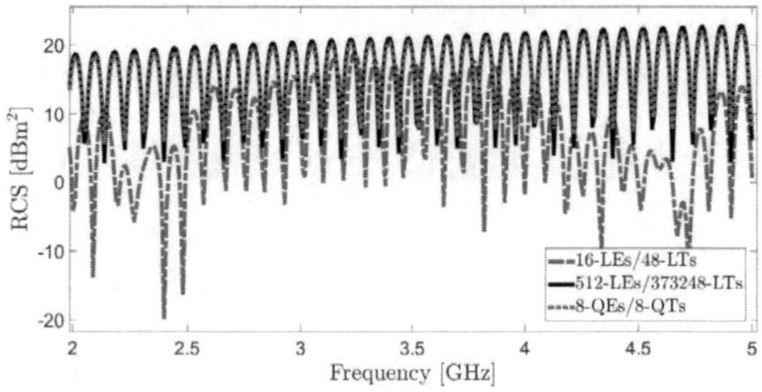

Fig. 2. Comparison of RCS results.

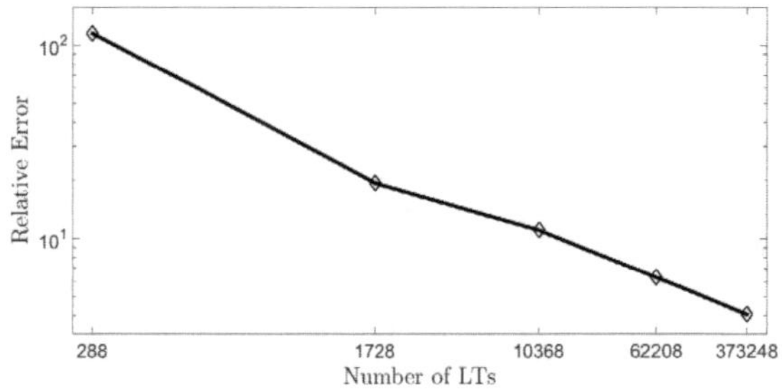

Fig. 3. Error in RCS results w.r.t. the RCS obtained for 8-QTs.

IV. Conclusion

In this work, the closed-form evaluation of the contour integral on QEs in TD-EEC is presented. The closed-form expressions are obtained by intersecting the plane, formed by the incidence and observation directions, and the QE segment. The numerical example demonstrates the accuracy and efficiency of the proposed method since accurate results can be obtained using fewer number of surface and edge elements.

References

[1] P. Y. Ufimtsev, "The 50-year anniversary of the PTD: Comments on the PTD's origin and development," IEEE Antennas Propag. Mag., vol. 55, no. 3, pp. 18–28, June 2013.

[2] A. Altintas and P. Russer, "Time-domain equivalent edge currents for transient scattering," IEEE Trans. Antennas Propag., vol. 49, no. 4, pp. 602–606, Apr. 2001.

[3] P. M. Johansen, "Time-domain version of the physical theory of diffraction," *IEEE Trans. Antennas Propag.*, vol. 47, no. 2, pp. 261–270, Feb. 1999.

[4] W. Gordon, "Far-field approximations to the Kirchoff-Helmholtz representations of scattered fields," IEEE Trans. Antennas Propag., vol. 23, no. 4, pp. 590–592, July 1975.

[5] D. Bölükbaş and A. A. Ergin, "A Radon transform interpretation of the physical optics integral," Microw. Opt. Technol. Lett., vol. 44, no. 3, pp. 284–288, 2005.

[6] A. Aktepe, H. A. Serim, and H. A. Ülkü, "Evaluation of time domain physical optics integral on curved surfaces," in 2018 2nd URSI Atlantic Radio Science Meeting (AT-RASC), May 2018, pp. 1–3.

[7] F. Vico-Bondia, *et al.*, "A new fast physical optics for smooth surfaces by means of a numerical theory of diffraction," IEEE Trans. Antennas Propag., vol. 58, no. 3, pp. 773–789, Mar. 2010.

[8] H. A. Ülkü and A. A. Ergin, "Radon transform interpretation of the physical optics integral and application to near and far field acoustic scattering problems," in 2010 IEEE Antennas and Propag. Society Int. Symp., July 2010, pp. 1–4.

[9] Y. Guan, S. Gong, S. Zhang, and Y. Xu, "A Radon transform interpretation of contour integral in time-domain equivalent edge currents," IEEE Antennas Wireless Propag. Lett., vol. 10, pp. 1247–1250, 2011.

Geometrically Conformal Quadrilateral Surface-Reconstruction for MoM-SIE Simulations

Jake Harmon, Cam Key, and Branislav M. Notaroš
Colorado State University, Electrical & Computer Engineering Department, Fort Collins, CO
j.harmon@colostate.edu, camkey@rams.colostate.edu, notaros@colostate.edu

***Abstract*—We present a higher order quadrilateral surface remeshing approach for application to the method of moments. We briefly introduce the motivation for high-quality quadrilateral meshes for accurate and efficient application of cutting edge integration and singularity extraction approaches. Results are demonstrated for simple surfaces and compared with a common quadrilateral remeshing algorithm.**

Keywords—computational electromagnetics, computational geometry, integral equations, method of moments, quadrilateral remeshing, surface reconstruction.

I. Introduction

One of the key challenges in numerical methods, geometric discretization, profoundly affects accuracy of a given simulation. An unnecessarily fine discretization (for a given frequency) produces an unnecessarily large number of unknowns, and therefore a correspondingly large linear system. Conversely, accurate geometric modeling of curved surfaces is essential for an overall optimal higher order solution [1]. In addition, even integration procedures strongly depend on the geometric discretization of a structure. Namely, improved singularity extraction and integration techniques have recently shown promise toward further improving the method of moments (MoM) in the surface integral equation (SIE) formulation based on higher order quadrilateral modeling; these novel approaches, however, are subject to increasing error as patch corner angles exceed ~120 degrees [2], [3]. Existing quadrilateral remeshing techniques, meanwhile, often neglect the corner angles of elements. A method, therefore, to efficiently remesh surfaces to quadrilaterals with concern for electrical size and corner angles provides benefits in terms of improving the applicability of these new integration schemes.

This paper focuses on the application of a geometrically conformal (angle preserving, explicitly biholomorphic) quadrilateral remeshing approach for computational electromagnetics problems to address these concerns. In particular, we provide examples in comparison to a non-conformal approach.

II. Conformal Remeshing

To produce a quadrilateral mesh with the desired properties, we begin, in general, with a point cloud describing the surface. The construction begins with a triangle meshing; Giesen, et al. provides a triangle meshing algorithm which offers several attractive guarantees, namely preservation of topology [4]. Following the reconstruction with an isotropic refinement assists in the parameterization.

Many methods exist to parameterize a surface, conformal or otherwise. However, for our application we require a conformal mapping. Conformal mappings such as discrete Ricci-flow [5], least squares conformal [6], and discrete conformal [7], each provide a means to map a surface to a parametric domain, ideally preserving the angles of the mapped surface. In this paper we show results using discrete-conformal mapping. Barycentric coordinates, unique on triangles, are then used to lift a sample pattern from a parametric domain to the original surface to produce vertices of the completed quadrilateral mesh. Crucially, as Barycentric coordinates depend on the corner angles of the triangles, conformality is preserved.

This method of remeshing provides several key advantages, especially for the higher order MoM-SIE. With a precomputed parameterization, additional remeshing is computed inexpensively; when coupled with adaptive sampling of the parametric domain, this permits a rapid means to adjust the electrical size of the patches for a given frequency. Additionally, curvilinear meshing arises naturally; given a separate sampling density for the patches and the interpolation points, quadrilateral-curvilinear patches can be generated identically to the linear case, with vertices used instead as geometric sample points for interpolation.

III. Results and Discussion

To demonstrate the viability of our implementation, we show results for two geometries: spherical and toroidal. For each case, we present several tiers of sampling density in the parametric domain to simulate a frequency-dependent remeshing.

As a comparison, we test against the 4 to 8 Subdivision method included in MeshLab [8].

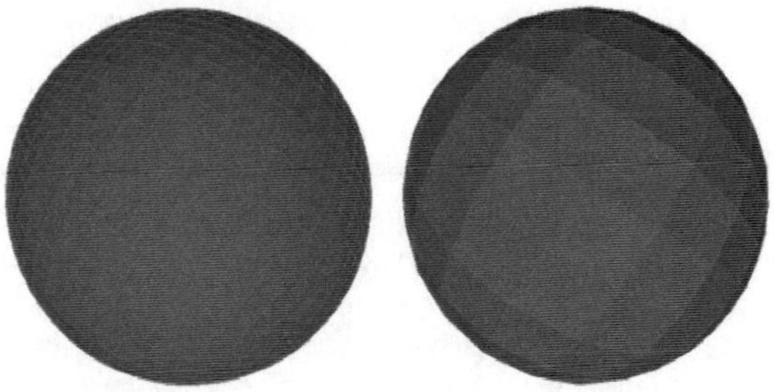

Fig. 1. Sphere quadrilateral remeshing for 2000 sample points (left) and 200 sample points (right).

We observe in Fig. 1 that a coarser sampling preserves the general constraints on the corner angles of the patches. Patch size decreases at the seams of the surface to maintain conformality. Note also that the quadrilateral remeshing does not exactly replicate the boundary of the original triangular surface mesh, with small distortions occurring; however, this effect is realized primarily for very coarse sampling or abrupt changes in curvature and is largely inconsequential.

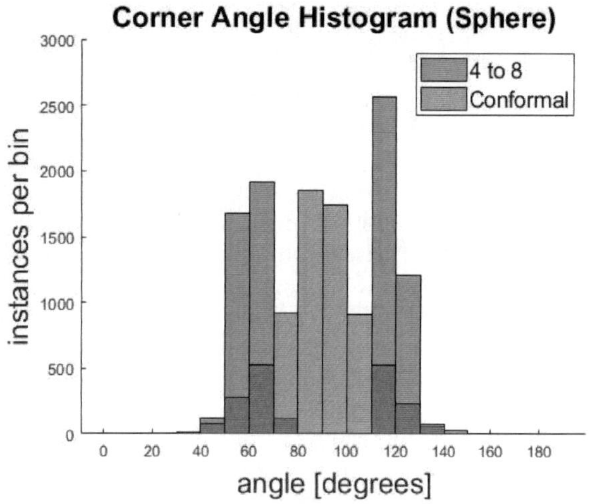

Fig. 2. Corner angle histogram for conformal remeshing and 4 to 8 subdivision for a sphere.

As seen in Fig. 2, the conformal remeshing distributes corner angles well within the desired range. In contrast, 4 to 8 subdivision—for the same number of patches—forces most angles outside this range. With further iterations of 4 to 8 subdivision, the distribution of corner angles improves, but at the expense of significantly greater element count compared to conformal remeshing.

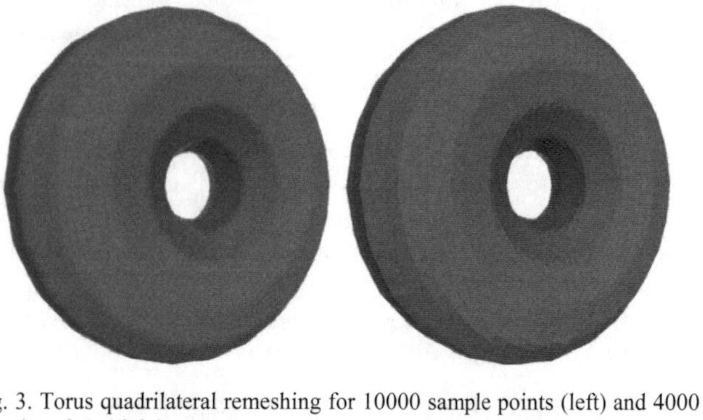

Fig. 3. Torus quadrilateral remeshing for 10000 sample points (left) and 4000 sample points (right).

As in Fig. 1, the torus of Fig. 3 exhibits similar behavior when varying sampling density. However, the change in quadrilateral size as a function of the curvature is much more apparent; note that in the center of the torus, the patch size shrinks rapidly to preserve conformality.

In terms of angle distribution, the histogram in Fig. 4 illustrates again the quality of the quadrilateral elements generated by a conformal remeshing. For the same number of elements, 4 to 8 subdivision produces many more nearly-degenerate quadrilateral elements, or elements with three collinear vertices.

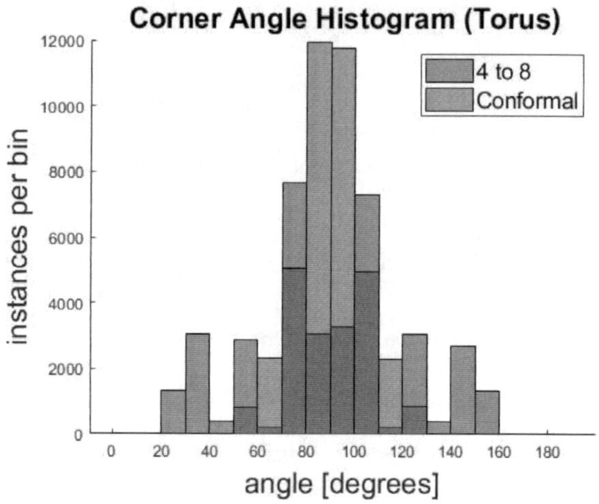

Fig. 4. Corner angle histogram for conformal remeshing and 4 to 8 subdivision for a torus.

By precomputing a conformal parameterization for a scatterer, new quadrilateral meshes with optimal corner angles can be constructed efficiently. The shape of the parent triangular mesh is also preserved well in the quadrilateral reconstruction. In principle, quadrilateral patches can be flat or curved, described by arbitrary geometric orders in parametric coordinates.

REFERENCES

[1] E. M. Klopf, N. J. Sekeljic, M. M. Ilic, and B. M. Notaros, "Optimal modeling parameters for higher order MoM-SIE and FEM-MoM electromagnetic simulations," IEEE Transactions on Antennas and Propogation, vol. 60, no.6, pp. 2790–2801, 2012.

[2] S. B. Manić and B. M. Notaroš, "Surface integral computation for the higher order surface integral equation method of moments," Proceedings of the 2018 International Applied Computational Electromagnetics Society (ACES) Symposium – ACES2018, March 25–29, 2018, Denver, Colorado, USA.

[3] A. A. Tambova, M. S. Litsarev, G. Guryev, and A. G. Polimeridis, "On the generalization of DIRECTFN for singular integrals over quadrilateral patches," IEEE Transactions on Antennas and Propogation, vol. 66, no.1, pp. 304-314, 2018.

[4] J. Giesen and M. John, "Surface reconstruction based on a dynamical system," In Proceedings of the 23rd Annual Conference of the European Association for Computer Graphics (Eurographics), Computer Graphics Forum 21, pp. 363-371, 2002.

[5] Y. Yang, R. Guo, F. Luo, S. Huo, and X. Gu, "Genearlized discrete Ricci flow," Computer Graphics Forum 28, pp. 2005-2014, 2009.

[6] B. Levy, S. Petitjean, N. Ray, and J. Maillot, "Least squares conformal maps for automatic texture atlas generation," ACM Transactions on Graphics, vol. 21, pp. 362-371, 2002.

[7] L. Kharevych, B. Springborn, and P. Schroder, "Discrete conformal mappings via circle patterns," ACM Transactions on Graphics, vol. 25, pp. 412-438, 2006.

[8] P. Cignoni, M. Callieri, M. Corsini, M. Dellepiane, F. Ganovelli, and G. Ranzuglia, "MeshLab: an open-source mesh processing tool," Sixth Eurographics Italian Chapter Conference, pp. 129-136, 2008.

Superformula-inspired Split-ring Resonators with Applications to Compact Bandpass Filters

Zephaniah Hill, Jack McShane, Roman Zapata, Khair Al Shamaileh
Electrical and Computer Engineering Department
Purdue University Northwest
Hammond, USA
kalshama@pnw.edu

Said Abushamleh
Physics Department–Engineering Program
University of Nebraska Kearney
Kearney, USA
abushamlehs2@unk.edu

***Abstract* — We introduce an effective technique for miniaturizing a split-ring resonator (SRR) structure by replacing its conventional circular rings with shapes obtained from the superformula. By maintaining the resonator's effective electrical lengths and the gaps between the rings, our experiments have found it possible to achieve a comparable electrical performance at a reduced physical size. To validate the design concept, cross-like SRR bandpass filter (BPF) layouts with a 1.2 GHz center frequency are simulated and measured. A 21.3% reduction in the physical area is achieved with acceptable ports matching and transmission parameters.**

Keywords—Bandpass filter (BPF), split-ring resonator (SRR), superformula.

I. Introduction

Split-ring resonators (SRRs) have recently found many applications in modern microwave front-end circuitry, including structural miniaturization and bandpass filtering [1, 2]. The resonance frequency (i.e., passband) of an SRR cell depends on the physical dimension, which is commonly in a circular form. However, at low frequencies, circular SRR structures are challenging to utilize due to the increased cell radius; and thus, the overall physical area.

The superformula concept allows the realization of complex and abstract shapes [3]. Such shapes could be of advantage in microwave circuits design. Superformula was recently applied in the design of a miniaturized circular patch antenna [4, 5]. The same technique can also be adopted in the design of compact SRRs as long as the effective rings radii, widths and separations are compared to the conventional circular SRR layout at a given frequency.

In this paper we utilize the superformula to design cross-like first- and second-order bandpass filters (BPFs). Structural tuning is carried out to achieve the optimum frequency response considering a 1.2 GHz passband.

II. Design Procedure

Fig. 1 shows examples of shapes created by the superformula. To begin the validation of these shapes as SRRs, dimensions of a 1.2 GHz circular SRR cell, shown in Fig. 2, are obtained considering a 0.813 mm-thick Rogers RO4003C substrate with a relative permittivity of 3.55.

Fig. 1. Sample geometries derived from the superformula.

Each individual ring has a width of $s_w = 1$ mm. The SRR cell and the aperture coupling ports are separated by 0.2 mm gap for optimum performance. The values of the other design parameters are listed in Table I.

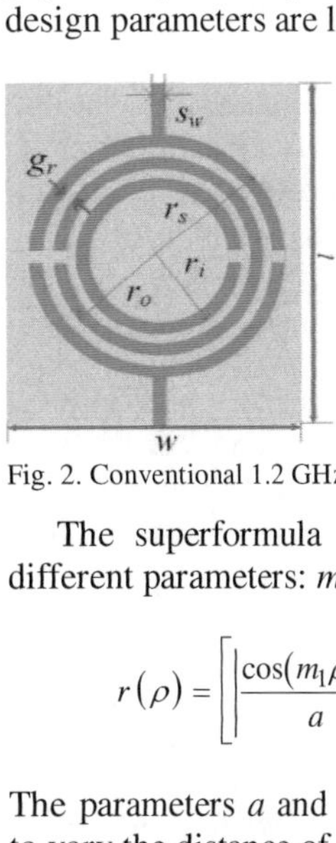

TABLE I. Parameters of the 1.2 GHz Circular SRR.

Parameter		Value (mm)
Substrate length	l	32.2
Substrate width	w	44.7
Strip ring radius	r_s	12.7
Outer ring radius	r_o	11.5
Inner ring radius	r_i	10.3
Strip width	s_w	01.0
Gap between rings	g_r	00.2

Fig. 2. Conventional 1.2 GHz circular SRR and corresponding parameters.

The superformula expression is governed with seven different parameters: $m_{1,2}$, $N_{1,2,3}$, a and b; and is given by:

$$r(\rho) = \left[\left| \frac{\cos(m_1 \rho/4)}{a} \right|^{N_2} + \left| \frac{\sin(m_2 \rho/4)}{b} \right|^{N_3} \right]^{-1/N_1} . \quad (1)$$

The parameters a and b are chosen with a different from b to vary the distance of inflection points from the origin. The parameters $m_{1,2}$ determine the number of points, corners, sectors, or hollows fixed on the shape and their spacing. The parameters N_2 and N_3 determine the concavity of the curves between points, corners, sectors or hollows. In our design, the superformula parameters are set to $a = 1.5$, $b = 1$, $m_1 = m_2 = 8$, $N_1 = 8$, $N_2 = N_3 = 1$. Such values result in a cross-like SRR profile as shown in Fig. 3.

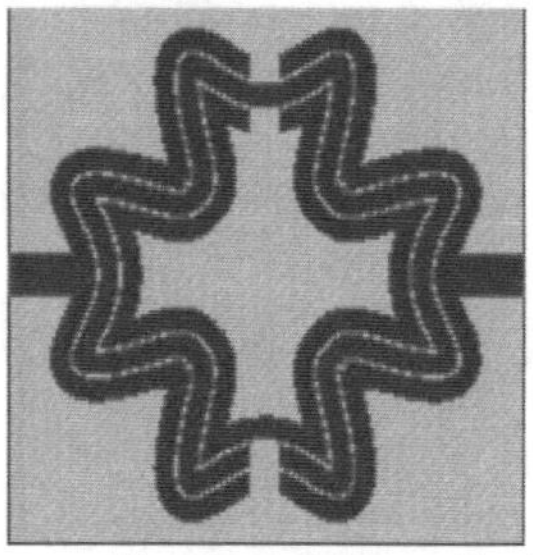

Fig. 3. The resulting cross-like shape SRR profile from setting a = 1.5, b = 1, $m_1 = m_2 = 8$, $N_1 = 8$, $N_2 = N_3 = 1$.

III. Simulations and Measurements

Fig. 4 shows photographs of the fabricated first- and second-order superformula-based cross-like shape BPFs using the substrate mentioned earlier. After performing a parametric analysis, the overall physical area of the cross-like SRR cell is found to be 507.7 mm^2 as compared to 645.2 mm^2 in the circular SRR. Thus a 21.3% reduction in the physical area is achieved.

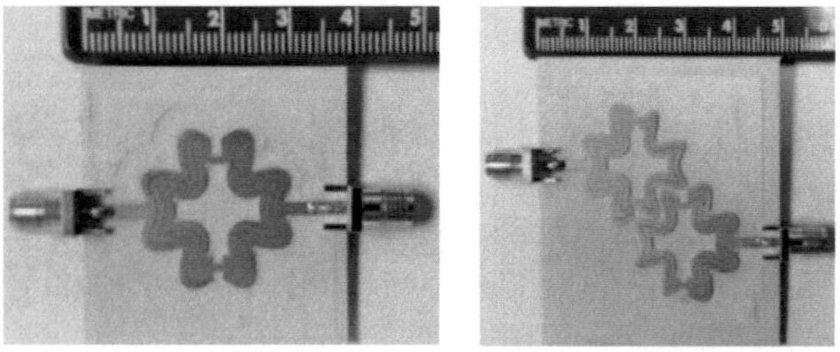

(a) (b)

Fig. 4. Photographs of the fabricated (a) first- and (b) second-order superformula-based cross-like shape BPFs.

Fig. 5 shows the simulated and measured response of the BPFs. As shown in Fig. 5(a), first-order bandpass filtering is obtained with input port matching parameter, S_{11}, better than –20 dB and transmission parameter, S_{21}, of –0.3 dB. The measured response shows a matching better than –12 dB and transmission loss of –1 dB. A second-order BPF circuit is designed by coupling two SRR-cell structures. As a result, an increased 10-dB passband fractional bandwidth of 2.42% (as compared to 1.17% in the first-order BPF) and an enhanced frequency response at the stopbands (i.e., roll-off) can be achieved. It is noteworthy to point out that higher order filters can be designed by integrating more cross-like SRR cells, allowing for more selective filtering with smaller circuitry area and added implementation convenience in higher order filtering arrays – demonstrating an advantage over circular cells. The two cross-like resonators in the second order filter are placed in close proximity with a configuration chosen to optimize coupling. At their respective closest points, the rings are separated by 0.5 mm gap. As shown in Fig. 5(b), the simulated and measured port matching are better than –10 dB; whereas the simulated and measured transmission loss are –0.8 dB and –3 dB, respectively, at the design band. The differences between the simulated and measured responses are thought to be due to the fabrication tolerances and measurement errors.

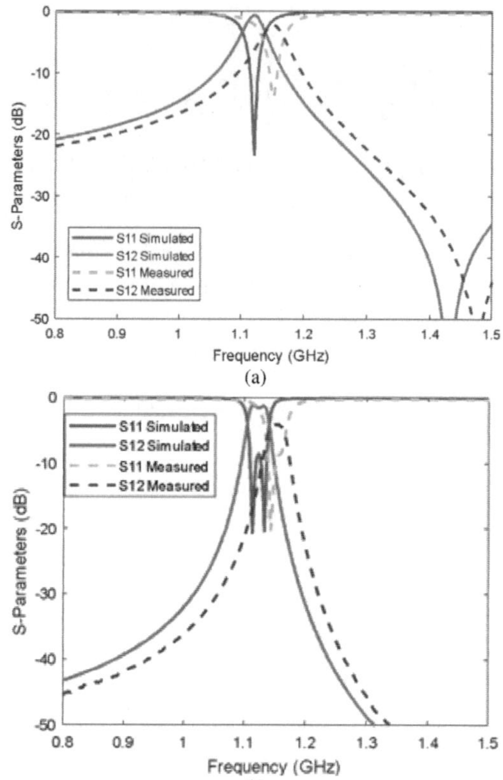

(a)

(b)

Fig. 5. Simulated and measured S-parameters of the superformula-shaped SRR-based BPFs: (a) 1st order and (b) 2nd order.

IV. Conclusion

In this paper, the physical area of the conventional circular SRR structure is reduced using shapes inspired and further optimized through the utilization of superformula-based geometries. The curvature of the resulting geometries allows for effective electrical lengths comparable to the conventional circular SRRs while allowing a reduction in circuitry area. The simulations and measurements of two BPF circuits are demonstrated, and the resulting electrical performance adjoined with the compact footprint validates the design methodology.

References

[1] M. Li, K.-M. Luk, L. Ge, and K. Zhang, "Miniaturization of magnetoelectric dipole antenna by using metamaterial loading," IEEE Trans. Anten. Propag., vol. 64, no. 11, pp. 4914 – 4918, 2016.

[2] A. Munir, "Development of dual-band microstrip bandpass filter based on split-ring resonator," Int. Conf. Electromag. Advanced Apps. (ICEAA), Cairns, Australia, pp. 712–715, 2016.

[3] J. Gielis, "A generic geometric transformation that unifies a wide range of natural and abstract shapes." American J. Botany, vol. 90, no. 3, pp. 333–338, 2003.

[4] A. Omar, M. Rashad, M. Al-Mulla, H. Attia, S. Naser, N. Dib, and R. Shubair, "Compact design of UWB CPW-fed-patch antenna using the superformula," Int. Conf. Electronic Devices, Syst. and Apps. (ICEDSA), UAE, pp. 1–4., 2016.

[5] A. Omar, S. Naser, M. Hussein, N. Dib, and M. Rashad, "Superformula-based compact UWB CPW-fed-patch antenna with and without dual frequency notches," Applied Comput. Electromag. Society (ACES), vol. 32, no. 11, pp. 979 – 986, 2017.

Compact tri-band pass filter using optimized Psi-shaped resonators

1st shahenda hatem
Communication and Electronics Engineering Departement. Institute of Engineering
Canadian International College *(CIC)*
Cairo, Egypt
shahenda_hatem@cic-cairo.com

2nd *Hesham A. Mohamed*
Electronics and Communication Department.
Electronics Research Institute (ERI)
Giza, Egypt
hesham_280@yahoo.com

3rd Roaa Mubarak
Electronics, Communication and Computer Department.Faculty of engineering
Helwan University
Cairo, Egypt
roaim79@yahoo.com

4th *Korany R. Mahmoud*
Electronics and Communication Department.
National Telecommunications Regulatory Authority, Ministry of Communication, and Information Technology
Cairo, Egypt
dr.aymanragab@yahoo.com

***Abstract*— In this paper, a compact tri-band pass filter (BPF) at 0.75 GHz, 2.1 GHz, and 3.5 GHz is introduced using a modified compact tri-mode Psi-shape resonator. The Psi-shape resonator is used to obtain three resonance frequencies and two transmission zeroes to improve the filter performance. The compact tri-band pass filter is proposed using fractal structure to reduce the size. The implemented design is simulated, fabricated, and measured. All measured results are consistent with the analysis and the simulations.**

***Keywords*— Band-pass filter (BPF), multi-mode resonator, compact filter**

I. Introduction

Recent advancement in mobile and satellite communication requires the miniaturization of tri-band pass filters (BPF) dimensions without affecting electrical performance. There are many ways to achieve this goal. One of them is to use high permittivity material as proposed in [1]. However, the compact (BPF) proposed in [2]–[5] used the fractural structure to reduce the size.

In this paper, a modified compact tri-mode Psi resonator with a compact size and low insertion loss is designed using high permittivity material and fractural structures to meet the requirements of wireless communication applications. Then, the proposed tri-band BPF is designed and implemented with high return loss and approximately zero insertion loss. The proposed design is fabricated to provide verified experimental measurements with respect to the simulated results.

II. Filter Design

A. Psi shape resonator

Fig. 1 represents the topology of the desired Psi-shape branch. It consists of a short and two open-circuited stubs with characteristic impedances of $\boldsymbol{Z_s}$ **and** $\boldsymbol{Z_o}$ respectively and an input transmission line with characteristic impedance $\boldsymbol{Z_1}$. For simplicity, all the transmission lines have the same electrical length $\boldsymbol{\theta}$. The input impedance of the Psi-shape resonator is expressed by [6]:

$$Z_{in} = Z_1 \frac{1 - 2\frac{Z_1}{Z_o}\tan^2\theta + \frac{Z_1}{Z_s}}{j[\left(2\frac{Z_1}{Z_o} + 1\right)\tan\theta - \frac{Z_1}{Z_s}\cot\theta]} \quad (1)$$

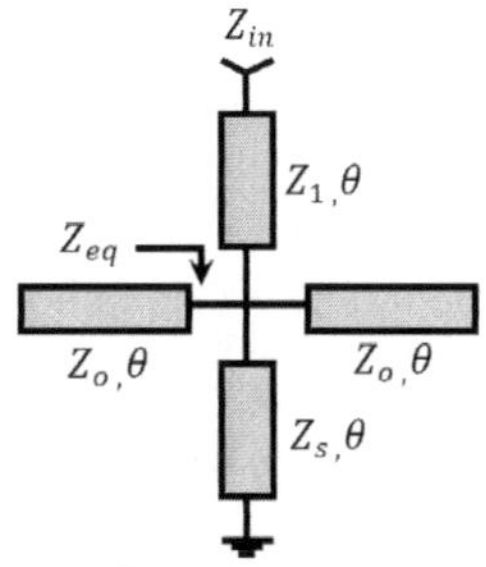

Fig. 2. The Psi-Shape resonator topology

The three resonant frequencies and the two zeros of the Psi -shape resonator can be obtained by zeroing the denominator and the numerator of (1) respectively. The third resonant frequency occurs at $\theta = \pi/2$, where the Z_{in} in (1) tends to infinity. Then the input impedance of the Psi-shape resonator can be written as

$$Z_{in} = j\frac{2Z_1{}^2\tan\theta}{2Z_1+Z_o}\Big|_{at\ \theta=\pi/2} \quad (2)$$

At this point, the Psi shape resonator can be considered as the short-circuited stub with the following characteristic impedance:

$$Z_{sc} = \frac{2Z_1{}^2}{2Z_1 + Z_o} \quad (3)$$

On the other hand, the first and the second resonance frequencies of the Psi-shape branch can be made equivalent to a shunt parallel resonator with an admittance slope related to passbands bandwidth . The admittance slope can be written as [7]:

$$b_{res_n} = \frac{dB_{in}}{d\omega} = \frac{dIm(Y_{in})}{d\omega}\Big|_{at\ \theta=\theta_{res_n}} \quad for\ n = \{1,2\}$$
$$= \frac{L\sqrt{\varepsilon_{eff}}}{Z_1 C}(1 + c_5)C_c \quad (4)$$

Where $C_c = \left[\frac{(c_1c_3-3c_2c_4)+c_1c_4c_5+\frac{c_2c_3}{c_5}}{(c_3-c_4c_5)^2}\right]$. Defining c_1, c_2, c_3, c_4, and c_5 for simplicity as: $c_1 = \frac{2Z_1}{Z_o}+1, c_2 = \frac{Z_1}{Z_s}, c_3 = \frac{Z_1}{Z_s}+1, c_4 = \frac{2Z_1}{Z_o}$, and $c_5 = \frac{Z_1Z_o}{Z_s(Zo+2Z_1)}$

L is the physical length of the transmission lines, ε_{eff} is the effective dielectric constant of the transmission lines, and c is the velocity of light. To make the design easier, it is assumed that, ε_{eff} does not change with the different impedance levels. Equations (3) and (4) summarize the necessary Ψ -shape resonator information for a bandpass filter design.

B. Design example

A 3-pole tri-band pass filter design is presented in Fig.2 to operate in the following bands with 300MHz ripple bandwidth:0.75GHz, 2.1GHz and 3.5GHz. A third order Chebyshev with in-band ripple of 0.01 dB is used in the filter design. Also, the input and output impedances are set to 50 Ω. The filter is fabricated on Rogers RT6010 substrate: a dielectric constant of 10.2, 0.635mm thickness, loss tangent of 0.0032, copper metallization thickness of 0.017mm, and a perfect electric conductor is used in the ground plane. The vias through the PCB board are implemented using 0.4mm copper wire expanding through substrate from the ground to the upper plan. The optimized filter dimensions are presented in TABLE I. The photograph of the fabricated proposed filter is illustrated in Fig. 3. Fig. 4 shows good agreement between the simulated and measured results.

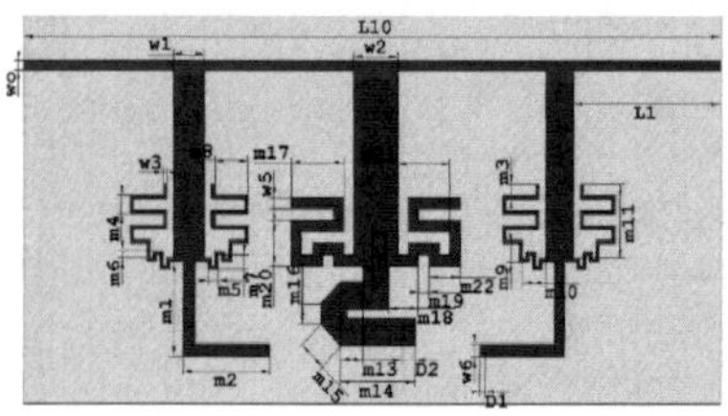

Fig. 2. Schematic of meandered tri-band pass filter

TABLE I. The optimized dimensions of the Compact tri-band pass filter (all dimensions in mm)

m1	m2	m3	m4	m5	m6	m7	m8	m9	m10
6.4	6.5	1	1.3	0.8	0.5	1	2.5	1.3	1.8
m12	**m13**	**m14**	**m15**	**m16**	**m17**	**m18**	**m19**	**m20**	**m21**
1	1.7	5.7	2.1	1.4	3.9	2.3	0.8	3.1	3.9
wo	***w1***	***w2***	***w3***	***w4***	***w5***	***w6***	***D1***	***D2***	***L1***
0.6	2.3	3.3	0.3	0.8	0.9	1.9	0.4	1	11.1

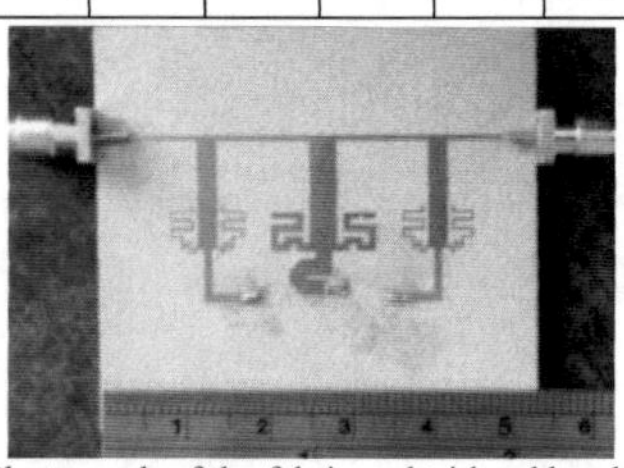

Fig. 3. Photograph of the fabricated tri-band bandpass filter.

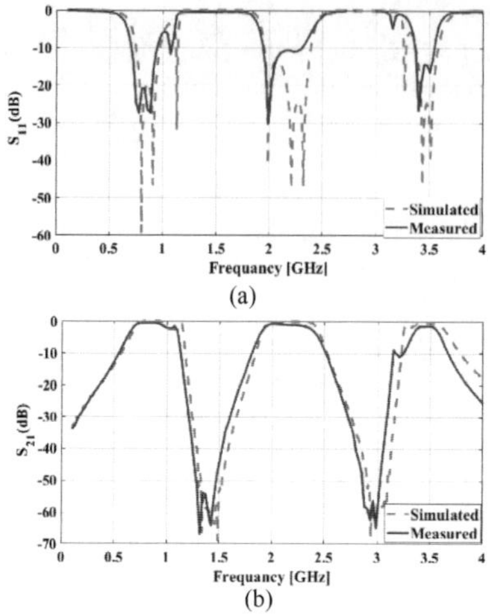

Fig. 4. Measured and Simulated S-parameter of the proposed compact filter. (a) S11, (b) S21

However, the three passbands center frequencies are shifted to higher frequencies to be 0.885GHz, 2.16GHz, and 3.44GHz with insertion losses of 0.038 dB, 0.13 dB, and 0.25dB respectively, and fractional 3dB bandwidths of 53.32%, 25%, and 12% respectively. This shift occurs because of the undesired magnetic coupling that is produced from the meander shape.

III. CONCLUSION

In this paper, a compact tri-band pass filter based on the Psi-shape resonator is analyzed, designed, and fabricated to be operate in the following applications LTE, WLAN, PDC, GSM, WCDMA, and WIMAX. The overall filter size is $0.26\lambda_g \times 0.16\lambda_g$ where λ_g is the guide wavelength at the center frequency of the first passband. Experimental results have been shown in excellent agreement with simulation results for the three required passbands (0.75, 2.1 and 3.5 GHz). The proposed filter provides two transmission zeros to improve the passband selectivity.

REFERENCES

[1] H. Lu, T. Xie, N. Yuan, and Q. Li, "Compact tri-band bandpass filter designed using stub-loaded stepped-impedance resonator," in *2017 7th IEEE International Conference on Electronics Information and Emergency Communication (ICEIEC)*, 2017, pp. 41–44.

[2] P. Wang, X. An, and Z.-Q. Lv, "A Compact Tri-Band Bandpass Filter with Independently Controllable Harmonic Bandwidth by Using Two Grounded Vias," *Progress In Electromagnetics Research*, vol. 74, pp. 1–8, 2018.

[3] G. Shen, W. Che, and Q. Xue, "Novel Tri-Band Bandpass Filter With Independently Controllable Frequencies, Bandwidths, and Return Losses," *IEEE Microwave and Wireless Components Letters*, vol. 27, no. 6, pp. 560–562, Jun. 2017.

[4] V. K. Killamsetty and B. Mukherjee, "Miniaturised highly selective bandpass filter with very wide stopband using meander coupled lines," *Electronics Letters*, vol. 53, pp. 889–890, 2017.

[5] A. Kumar, D. K. Choudhary, and R. K. Chaudhary, "Metamaterial Tri-Band Bandpass Filter Using Meander-Line with Rectangular-Stub," *Progress In Electromagnetics Research Letters*, vol. 66, pp. 121–126, 2017.

[6] S. Hatem, H. A. Mohamed, R. Mubarak, and K. R. Mahmoud, "Tri-band Pass Filter Using Optimized Psi-shaped Resonators," in *2019 International Conference on Innovative Trends in Computer Engineering (ITCE)*, 2019, pp. 275–280.

[7] Y. Liu, W.-B. Dou, and Y.-J. Zhao, "A tri-band bandpass filter realized using tri-mode T-shape branches," *Progress In Electromagnetics Research*, vol. 105, pp. 425–444, 2010.

A Simple Methodology to Eliminate Noise in the Antennas Dipoles Measurements

Décio Rennó de Faria Mendonça[1], Kenedy Marconi G. Santos[2],
Renan A. dos Santos[1], Danilo H. Spadoti[1]

UNIFEI[1] Federal University of Itajubá, Itajubá - MG, Brazil
IFBA[2]- Federal Institute of Bahia, Vitória da Conquista - BA, Brazil

Abstract— **The Measurements of dipole antenna outside the shielded room or semi anechoic chamber using an oscilloscope most often present problems due to the high input impedance of the dipole at low frequencies. The oscilloscope is susceptible to noise in low frequencies and 50 and 60 Hz is often the greatest signal received. Within this context, this paper presents a simple procedure with low costs to solve this problem.**

Index Terms— Antennas; Coaxial Cable; Oscilloscope Measurements.

I. INTRODUCTION

It is well known that measurements in time domain is very important in any application. The best way to make this measurement in order to see difference in phase of two signals or distortions is to use the oscilloscope. Beside this, some modern digital oscilloscopes can apply the FFT (Fast Fourier Transform) resulting in a frequency domain response. The FFT initial appeared when microprocessors entered commercial design in the 1970s. Today almost every oscilloscope from low to high prices offers the FFT analysis[1,2].

The Measurements of dipole antennas, outside the room shielded and semi anechoic chamber using the oscilloscope, most often present problems due to the high input impedance of the dipole at low frequencies, specially to 50 and 60 Hz, and the problem increases with the high sensibility of the oscilloscope port to all frequencies. This complication can have a diversity of effects on measurements and there are ways to mitigate them in practice. Real EMC mitigation methods may change by the type of setup and by the electromagnetic environment. For mitigation EMC problems, it is possible to act on the source, on the receiver or on the coupling environment [3,4]. This article presents a simple procedure with low costs to solve this problem.

II. METHODOLOGY

This paper proposes a methodology based on a setup, using dipole antennas in 900MHz as shown in Figure 1 connected directly in the input port of an oscilloscope. The transmitted signal in 900MHz was generated by the Signal Hound Vector Signal Generator model VSG25A and to receive the signals a High-Definition Oscilloscope Keysight model DSOS204A 2GHz 20GSa/s.

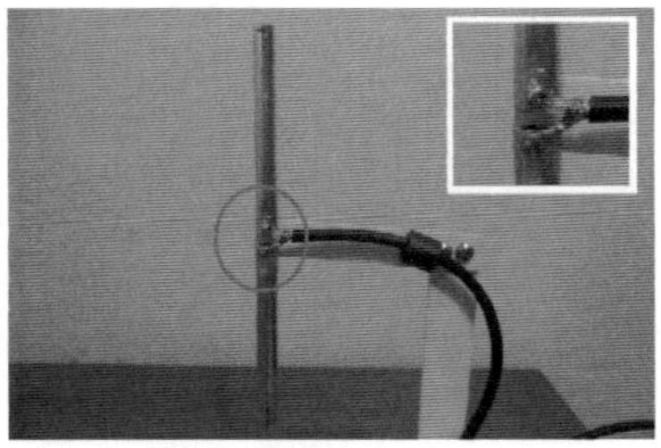

Fig. 1 – Dipole antenna used to receive the signal.

As any other conventional dipole, the coaxial cable was connected directly to the aluminum tubes. The result signal showed in 900MHz was completely distorted and the trigger circuit of the oscilloscope did not worked. The signal received was not only the expected 900MHz from the RF generator. There were a lot of unidentifiable signals. It is clear that, the greatest signal was an 60Hz from the electric power concessionaire. Figure 2 shows the got signal.

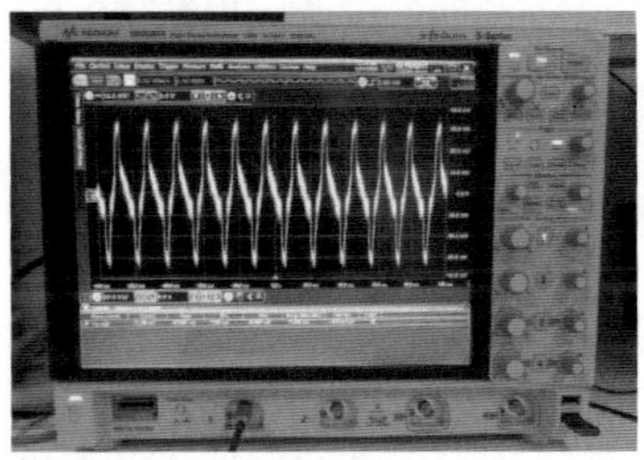

Fig. 2 – Received signal in a simple dipole.

III. PROPOSED SOLUTION

In order to reduce the sensibility of the oscilloscope at low frequencies, mainly at 50/60Hz, a resistance was introduced in parallel with the dipole as shown in Figure 3.

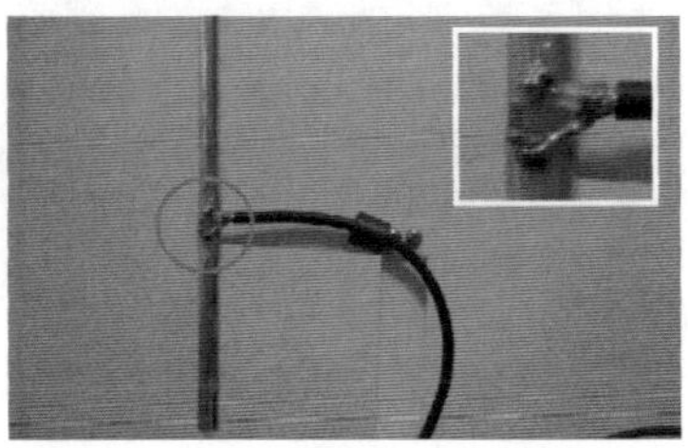

Fig. 3 – Dipole antenna with a 470Ω resistance in parallel.

This resistance reduced the impedance of the antenna in a different way for different frequencies. At 60Hz the impedance of this antenna is very high, because it is just an open pair of tubes without contact with each other. So, at low frequencies the impedance of the dipole is approximately infinite.

$$Zin \cong \infty$$

The signals at these frequencies will not be significantly transferred to the resistance as shown in Figure 4 since R is much smaller than Z_{dipole}.

$$V_{resistance} = \frac{V_{dipole} . R}{R + Z_{dipole}}$$

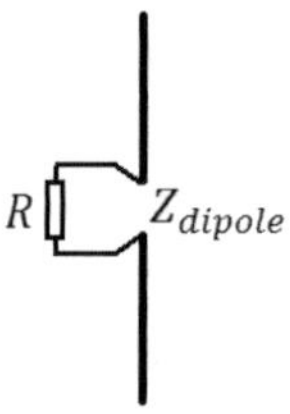

Fig. 4 – Voltage divider formed with the antenna and the resistance.

For the frequency of interest (900MHz) the dipole impedance is not infinite, it is near 50Ω [6], so the result of this parallel circuit is:

$$Z_{total} = \frac{50.470}{50+470}$$

$$Z_{total} = 45{,}19\Omega$$

The resistor do not affect significantly the impedance and neither the received signal. The total voltage reduction can be calculated by:

$$V_{out} = V_{signal} . \frac{470}{470 + 50}$$

$$V_{out} = V_{signal} . 0{,}904$$

The signal received after this modification is shown in Figure 5.

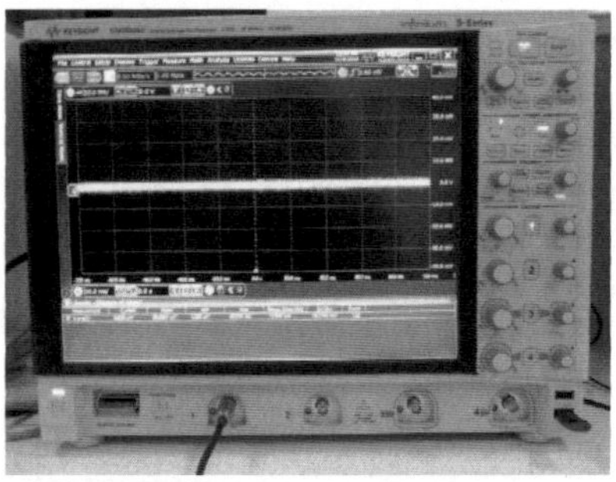

Fig. 5 – Received signal in the new arragment.

In order to confirm that the resistance did not reduce significantly the signal in 900MHz, an arrangement with two antennas using resistances was mounted in order to measure in the oscilloscope the difference in phase of the signals that arrives in these antennas. As it is possible to see in Figure 6 this measure was successfully done.

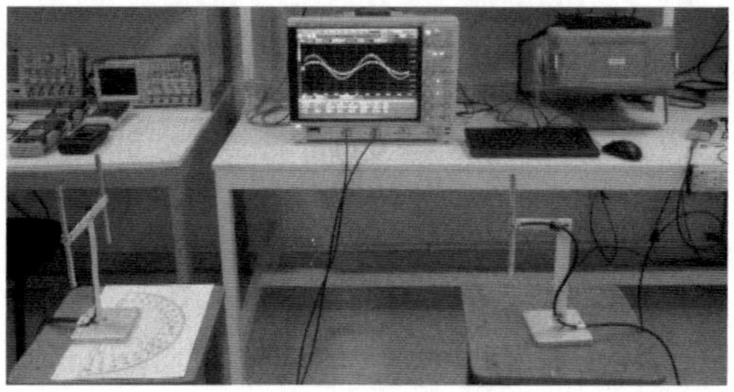

Fig. 6 – Two antennas receiving and in the oscilloscope the signals.

It is important to mention that, without the resistor the oscilloscope did not show any comprehensive information, trying all the time track the signal.

IV. CONCLUSION

It is possible to conclude that the use of a resistor in parallel with the dipole significantly reduces the signals at low frequencies in the antenna port and so makes it possible to analyses the higher frequencies with little noise. It is important to notice that, the resistor is not a band pass filter nor any type of high band pass filter. As demonstrated in this paper, what really happens is that near the resonance the dipole presents a low impedance and produces a measurable voltage in the resistance. In the opposite side, at low frequencies the dipole has a high impedance and no voltage appears over the resistance.

REFERENCES

[1] EDN, "FFTs and oscilloscopes: A practical guide", EDN Network, Sep. 2016. [Online]. Available: https://www.edn.com/ [Accessed Jan. 30, 2019].
[2] S. Gori and C. Narduzzi, "Application of a phase measurement algorithm to digitizing oscilloscope characterization", *IEEE Transactions on Instrumentation and Measurement*, vol. 49, no. 6, pp. 1211-1215, Dec. 2000.
[3] C. R. Paul, *Introduction to Electromagnetic Compatibility*, New York: John Wiley & Sons, 1992.
[4] H. W. Ott, *Electromagnetic Compatibility Engineering*, Livingston: John Wiley & Sons, 2009.
[5] D. Gerke and P. Cook, "60 Hz magnetic field susceptibility tests of CRT displays", IEEE International Symposium on Electromagnetic Compatibility, Washington, DC, 1990.
[6] J. D. Kraus and K. R. Carver, *Electromagnetics*, Tokio: McGraw-Hill, 1973.

Dualband Balanced Tunable Bandstop Filter

Dubari Borah
Dept. of Electrical and Computer Engineering
University of Colorado, Colorado Springs
Colorado Springs, USA
dborah@uccs.edu

Thottam S. Kalkur
Dept. of Electrical and Computer Engineering
University of Colorado, Colorado Springs
Colorado Springs, USA
tkalkur@uccs.edu

***Abstract*— This paper introduces a novel architecture of balanced (differential) dualband tunable bandstop filter (BSF) for the first time. In differential mode (DM), each symmetrical bisection of the filter incorporates in-series cascade of two reconfigurable dualband bandstop sections whereas common mode (CM) noise is highly eliminated by loading open stubs to the symmetry plane of the branch line structure. To validate the proposed topology, a microstrip prototype is designed and fabricated. Both simulation and measured results show a good agreement with each other.**

***Keywords*— Branch line structure, CM noise, CMRR, non-resonating node (NRN), tunability.**

I. Introduction

In modern wireless communication system, cognitive radios play an important role by addressing growing challenges of spectrum management [1]. The transceiver in such a radio uses wideband RF front end to sense and adapt over a wide frequency range. A wide-open RF front end usually operates under complex electromagnetic environment where the receiver signal is often affected by the jamming from high power signals. Therefore, bandstop filters are becoming useful blocks in such a system to protect the required signals from unwanted interference. Furthermore, modern wireless communication systems demand compact size and reduced system complexity, for which multiband reconfigurable filters are appealing to more attention for research and development.

Meanwhile, balanced topology is being widely employed in constructing microwave circuits and systems because they are more immune to signal noise as compared to single-ended systems. So far, people have investigated a variety of topologies to implement differential BPF whereas significantly less work has been done in the field of differential BSF. In [2], a balanced narrowband BSF is reported, which consists of four coupled line sections with open circuited stubs, two half wavelength transmission lines and two ground resistors. An octave tunable balanced BSF structure is introduced in [1], which is realized by coupling two high-Q tunable substrate integrated waveguide (SIW) resonators to two opposite polarity transmission lines. In [3], the CM noise of a wideband tunable differential BSF is eliminated by utilizing balanced properties of double-sided parallel-strip line (DSPSL). The directional filter in [4] uses a differential BSF which is a quarter wavelength branch line coupler with its coupled and isolated ports terminated in short and open, respectively. In [5], a K-th order N-band BSF topology has been realized by using in-series cascade of K N-band sections through K-1 static impedance inverters. However, to the best of the author's knowledge, no work has been published yet which applies differential topology to a dualband tunable BSF structure.

In this paper, a tunable balanced dualband BSF structure is proposed by integrating tunable dualband sections in a branch line structure. The flexible control of CM response is obtained by using the properties of stepped impedance resonator (SIR), which is necessary for noise elimination.

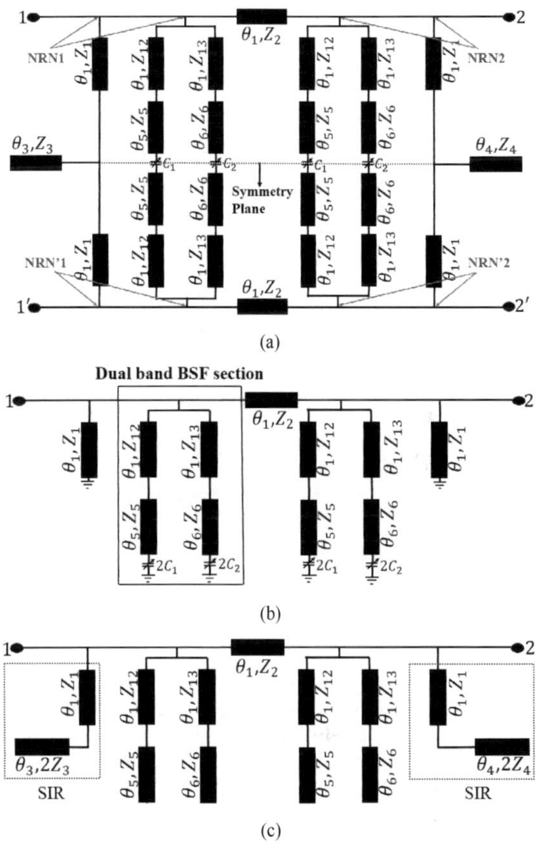

Fig. 1. (a) Schematic of the proposed topology (b) DM equivalent circuit (c) CM equivalent circuit.

II. Proposed Design

A. Filter Configuration

Fig. 1 (a) shows the schematic of the proposed balanced dualband tunable BSF structure. Fig. 1 (b) and (c) demonstrate that each symmetrical bisection of the structure (corresponding to horizontal central plane) consists of two dualband sections and each dualband section contains two quarter wavelength lines (θ_5, Z_5) and (θ_6, Z_6) at resonant frequencies f_1 and f_2 respectively. Varactors C_1 and C_2 in Fig. 1 (a) are used to obtain tunable response under DM operation. Each NRN and its image NRN' share an open stub in the horizontal symmetry plane for the flexible control of CM response. They are indicated as (θ_3, Z_3) and (θ_4, Z_4) at

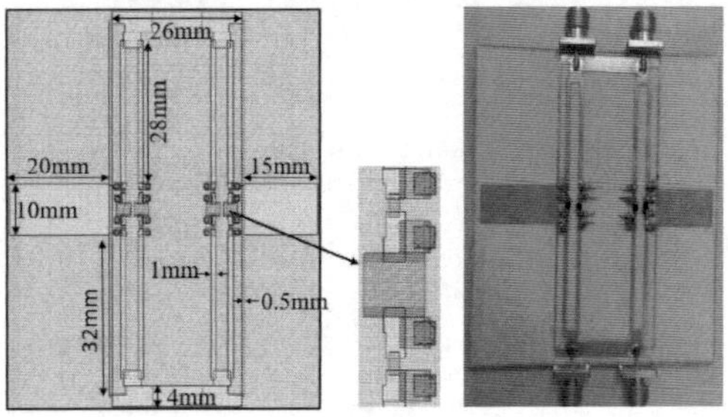

(a) (b)

Fig. 2. (a) Layout of the design with zoomed version of the lumped element section and (b) Fabricated prototype.

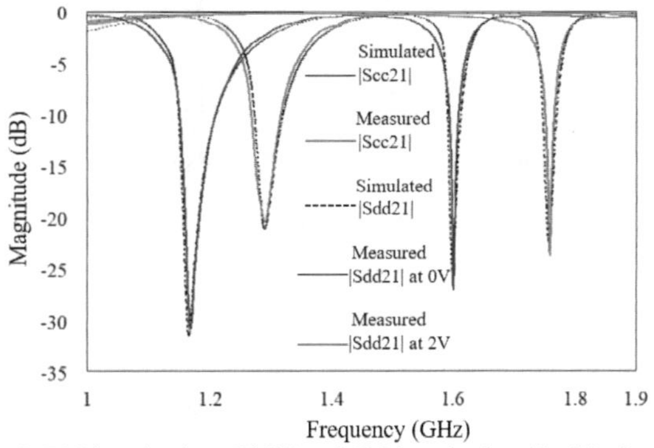

Fig. 3. DM insertion loss (Sdd21) and CM insertion loss (Scc21) plots of the proposed design.

center frequency $(f_1+f_2)/2$. The remaining line sections are quarter wavelength long at $(f_1+f_2)/2$, which are used as couplings between different nodes.

B. Differential mode (DM) operation

When the circuit in Fig. 1 (a) is excited by a differential signal, the horizontal symmetry plane acts as a perfect electric wall (PEW) i.e. electrical short circuit (Fig. 1 (b)). Therefore, the open stubs are short-circuited and have no effect on differential resonant frequencies. It should be noted that the capacitor values in this circuit become twice of their corresponding values in Fig. 1 (a).

C. Common mode (CM) operation

Under CM operation, the horizontal symmetry plane behaves as a perfect magnetic wall i.e. electrical open circuit (Fig. 1 (c)). Therefore, the open stubs loaded in the symmetry plane cause extension and reconstruction of their corresponding couplings from the NRNs. Now, each open stub and its coupling from the NRN form an SIR. At resonance, each SIR produces two transmission zeros (TZs) and their locations are determined by the impedance ratio and the length ratio of the SIR's constituent line sections [6]. This provides flexibility in achieving a flat CM bandpass response for each differential stopband.

III. Results and Discussion

To validate the proposed topology, a microstrip line prototype is fabricated on Rogers RO4003 substrate with relative dielectric constant 3.38, dielectric thickness 1.52mm and dielectric loss tangent 0.0027 (Fig. 2). The two line sections (θ_5, Z_5) and (θ_6, Z_6) are replaced by their equivalent low-pass π networks [7]. The π network for (θ_5, Z_5) consists of a series inductance of 3.6 nH (Coilcraft 0402CS series) and two shunt capacitances of 3 pF (ATC 100A series) each. Similarly, the π network for (θ_6, Z_6) consists of a series inductance of 1.4 nH (Coilcraft 0402CS series) and two shunt capacitances of 2 pF (ATC 100A series) each. Dimensions of the other line sections are presented in Fig. 2 (a). For both C_1 and C_2, Skyworks SMV1233 model is used.

Fig. 3 shows that the measured response is in good agreement with the simulated response. The design is simulated using NI/AWR microwave office and the fabricated model is characterized with the help of Keysight N5224A 4-port network. From the Sdd21 plot, the tuning ranges of the lower and upper stopbands are 1.16 GHz- 1.29 GHz and 1.6 GHz-1.76 GHz, respectively. The attenuation level of the lower stopband varies in the range of 20.5dB-30.7dB whereas for the upper stopband, it varies from 24dB to 26.7dB. The 3dB FBW of the lower band changes from 9% to 12% whereas the same for the upper band varies from 2.4% to 3.2%. Also, the Scc21 plot shows a flat 0 dB passband response to cover the entire spectral range of both reconfigurable stopbands. This results in the minimum CMRR values of 20.5 dB and 24 dB for the lower stopband and the upper stopband, respectively.

IV. Conclusion

A novel topology of tunable balanced dualband filter is proposed for the first time in this paper. Each DM bisection of this branch line structure consists of two dualband BSF sections separated by an impedance inverter. The CM noise is eliminated by loading the structure with open stubs in the horizontal symmetry plane. Finally, the simulated response and the measured response are compared to show a good match with each other.

References

[1] M. F. Hagag, M. Abdelfattah, and D. Peroulis, "Balanced octave-tunable absorptive bandstop filter," *2018 IEEE 19th Wireless and Microwave Technology Conference (WAMICON)*, Sand Key, FL, 2018, pp. 1-4.

[2] M. Kong, Y. Wu, Z. Zhuang, and Y. Liu, "Narrowband balanced absorptive bandstop filter integrated with wideband bandpass response," in *Electronics Letters*, vol. 54, no. 4, pp. 225-227, 2 22 2018.

[3] J. Cai, Y. J. Yang, W. Qin, and J. X. Chen, "Wideband Tunable Differential Bandstop Filter Based on Double-Sided Parallel-Strip Line," in *IEEE Transactions on Components, Packaging and Manufacturing Technology*.

[4] J. Sorocki, I. Piekarz, S. Gruszczynski, and K. Wincza, "Low-Loss Directional Filters Based on Differential Band-Reject Filters With Improved Isolation Using Phase Inverter," in *IEEE Microwave and Wireless Components Letters*, vol. 28, no. 4, pp. 314-316, April 2018.

[5] D. Psychogiou, R. Gomez-Garcia, and D. Peroulis, "A class of fully-reconfigurable planar multi-band bandstop filters," *2016 IEEE MTT-S International Microwave Symposium (IMS)*, 2016.

[6] Hui L., Weiping L., and Rong H. (2012) The Precise Design of Bandpass Filter Miniaturization Using Microstrip SIR. In: Lee G. (eds) Advances in Intelligent Systems. Advances in Intelligent and Soft Computing, vol 138. Springer, Berlin, Heidelberg.

[7] M. M. Elsbury, P. D. Dresselhaus, N. F. Bergren, C. J. Burroughs, S. P. Benz, and Z. Popovic, "Broadband Lumped-Element Integrated N-Way Power Dividers for Voltage Standards," in *IEEE Transactions on Microwave Theory and Techniques*, vol. 57, no. 8, pp. 2055-2063, Aug. 2009.

Design Trade-Offs for Spline-Parameterized Patch Coupler through Multi-Objective Optimization

Slawomir Koziel[1,2]
[1]School of Science and Engineering
Reykjavik University
Reykjavik, Iceland
koziel@ru.is

Adrian Bekasiewicz[1]
[2] Faculty of Electronics, Telecommunications and Informatics
Gdansk University of Technology
Gdansk, Poland
bekasiewicz@ru.is

***Abstract*—Investigations of design trade-offs for a miniaturized patch coupler are presented. Using surrogate-assisted multi-objective optimization, a set of designs representing available compromises between the coupler bandwidth and footprint area are obtained and analyzed. Sequential domain patching is utilized as the optimization engine to maintain acceptable computational cost despite a large number of design parameters. The presented approach is illustrated using a spline-parameterized coupler operating at 5.6 GHz.**

Keywords—Compact microwave circuits, patch couplers, design trade-offs, EM-driven optimization, multi-objective design.

I. Introduction

Identification of trade-offs between conflicting performance figures is an important part of the microwave and antenna design process. It is particularly important for miniaturized structures as size reduction normally leads to degradation of electrical performance. In practice, finding available compromises requires multi-objective optimization [1], [2].

In this work, design trade-offs for a 5.6 GHz spline-parameterized patch coupler are investigated. The set of alternative geometries are generated using sequential domain patching [3] supplemented by local surrogate-assisted tuning. The results indicate that when ensuring sufficient circuit flexibility (here, described by 17 parameters) the circuit bandwidth and footprint area can be changed in a wide range (from 940 MHz to 1843 MHz for bandwidth, and from 360 to 517 mm^2 for area, respectively).

II. Coupler Structure and Performance Figures

Consider a microstrip hybrid quadrature patch coupler shown in Fig. 1 [4]. The circuit consists of a spline-parameterized patch and four 50 ohm feed lines. The circuit (i.e., its two quarters; see Fig. 1) is represented using $K + 1$ variables $\boldsymbol{x} = [D\ r_1\ r_2\ \ldots\ r_K]^T$, where D defines maximum allowed distance from the model center (in a cylindrical coordinate system) and r_k, $k = 1, \ldots K$, are relative variables with respect to D. The angular distance between the control points is constant and equal to π/K radians. The absolute radial coordinate of the kth control point of the spline-based shape is $D{\cdot}r_k$. The EM model $\boldsymbol{R}(\boldsymbol{x})$ is implemented in CST Microwave Studio.

In this work, we set $K = 16$ to ensure sufficient flexibility of the circuit geometry. The coupler is to operate at $f_0 = 5.6$ GHz and we are interested in maximization of the coupler bandwidth B, defined as the symmetric (w.r.t. f_0) and continuous frequency range for which $|\,|S_{21}| - |S_{31}|\,| \leq 0.5$ dB, as well as minimization of the coupler footprint A (the area of the smallest rectangle containing the circuit). At the same time, we impose constraints $|S_{11}| \leq -20$ dB, and $|S_{41}| \leq -20$ dB (both at f_0). For the purpose of multi-objective optimization, we define objectives to be minimized as $F_1(\boldsymbol{R}(\boldsymbol{x})) = -B$, and $F_2(\boldsymbol{R}(\boldsymbol{x})) = A$.

III. Sequential Domain Patching

Design trade-offs for the coupler of Fig. 1 are identified using a sequential domain patching (SDP) algorithm [3]. SDP starts by identifying extreme Pareto-optimal designs (the best designs w.r.t. individual figures of interest) by solving

$$\boldsymbol{x}_k^* = \arg\min_{\boldsymbol{x}} F_k\left(\boldsymbol{R}(\boldsymbol{x})\right), \quad k = 1, 2 \tag{1}$$

The problem (1) is solved using trust-region gradient search with implicit constraint handling [4].

SDP works as follows (n is the number of parameters):

1. Set the patch size $\boldsymbol{d} = [d_1\ \ldots\ d_n]^T$ (here, sensitivity-based patch setup of [3] is utilized);
2. Set the current points $\boldsymbol{x}_1 = \boldsymbol{x}_1^*$ and $\boldsymbol{x}_2 = \boldsymbol{x}_2^*$;
3. Evaluate n perturbations of the size $\boldsymbol{d}$ around $\boldsymbol{x}_1^*$ (towards $\boldsymbol{x}_2^*$ only) and select the one that brings the largest improvement w.r.t. the second objective F_2.
4. Relocate the patch so that it is centered at the best perturbation selected in Step 2; update $\boldsymbol{x}_1$;
5. Evaluate n perturbations of the size $\boldsymbol{d}$ around $\boldsymbol{x}_2^*$ (towards $\boldsymbol{x}_1^*$ only) and select the one that brings the largest improvement w.r.t. the second objective F_1.
6. Relocate the patch so that it is centered at the best perturbation selected in Step 5; update $\boldsymbol{x}_2$;
7. If the path between $\boldsymbol{x}_1^*$ and $\boldsymbol{x}_2^*$ is not complete, go to 3;

The algorithm yields the initial approximation of the set of Pareto-optimal solutions, along with patches covering the part of the design space that contains these solutions. More details can be found in [3]. The cost of SDP is does not exceed $(M - 1){\cdot}(n - 1)$ EM coupler simulations, where $M = \sum_{k=1,\ldots,n} m_k$, and is m_k the number of intervals in the direction j.

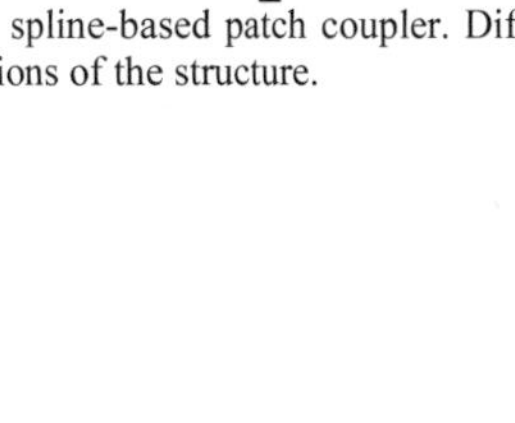

Fig. 1. Geometry of the spline-based patch coupler. Different shades of gray denote symmetrical sections of the structure.

The final set of design trade-offs is obtained by local tuning of selected designs $\boldsymbol{x}^{(k)}$, $k = 1, \ldots, K$, which is arranged as

$$\boldsymbol{x}^{(k)} \leftarrow \arg \min_{\boldsymbol{x},\, F_2(\boldsymbol{x}) \le F_2(\boldsymbol{x}^{(k)})} F_1\left(\boldsymbol{R}_s(\boldsymbol{x})\right) \qquad (2)$$

where $\boldsymbol{R}_s(\boldsymbol{x})$ is a second-order polynomial model without mixed terms established within the patch containing $\boldsymbol{x}^{(k)}$. Note that half of the data necessary to establish the model is already available from the patching procedure. The process (2) is embedded in the trust region framework [5] and iterated (typically, three to five iterations are necessary for convergence).

IV. NUMERICAL RESULTS

The coupler of Fig. 1 has been implemented on Arlon AD250 substrate (ε_r = 2.5, h = 0.762 mm). The extreme Pareto-optimal designs have been found as $\boldsymbol{x}_1^*$ = [12.4 0.6 0.84 0.62 0.39 0.63 0.78 0.92 0.57 0.92 0.90 0.79 0.64 0.77 0.91 0.89 0.65]^T, and $\boldsymbol{x}_2^*$ = [11.92 0.64 0.80 0.68 0.29 0.61 0.79 0.79 0.55 0.79 0.79 0.80 0.49 0.80 0.80 0.79 0.65]^T, respectively. The designs feature a bandwidth of 1843 MHz at size 517 mm^2 (design $\boldsymbol{x}_1^*$), and a bandwidth of 940 MHz at size 360 mm^2 (design $\boldsymbol{x}_2^*$). The initial set of design trade-offs obtained by SDP as well as the set of 10 re-tuned designs are shown in Fig. 2. Note that the initial set is very irregular which is due to the fact that even small design changes may lead to dramatic variations in the circuit bandwidth (defined through 0.5 dB power split error level). Also, SDP has no control over S_{11}/S_{41} constraints. These have been handled in the refinement process. The SDP has been run with the following interval setup $\boldsymbol{m}$ = [11 2 3 4 9 2 2 4 2 2 3 2 12 2 7 5 2], obtained using the method of [3]. The parameter values of the re-tuned trade-off designs have been gathered in Table I, whereas S-parameters for four selected designs are shown in Fig. 3.

The data obtained using the procedure described in this work can be utilized for quantifying available design trade-offs for the patch coupler at hand as well as to find particular design that satisfies prescribed specifications (here, pertinent to the bandwidth and/or footprint area).

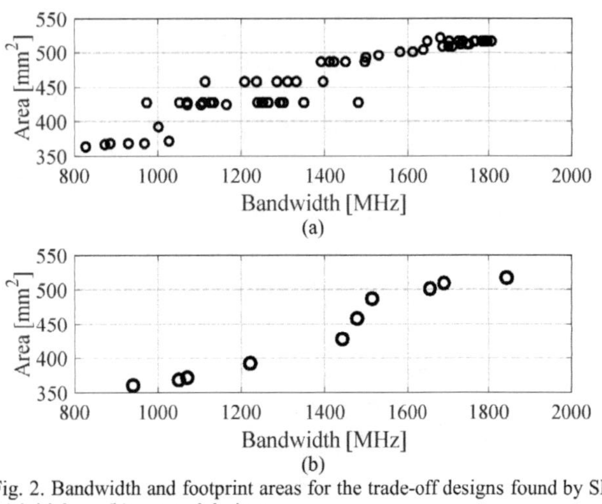

Fig. 2. Bandwidth and footprint areas for the trade-off designs found by SDP: (a) initial set, (b) re-tuned designs.

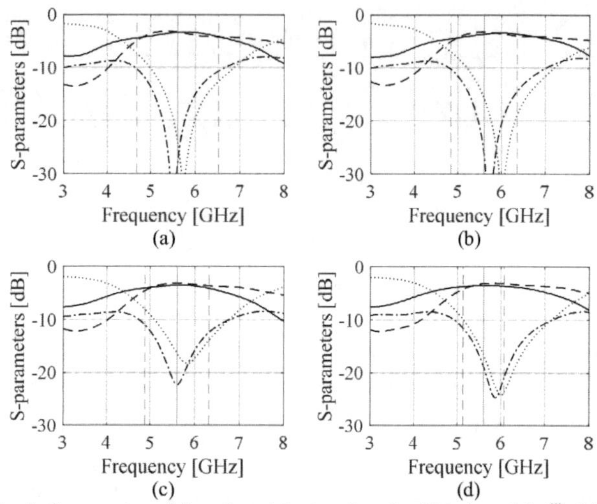

Fig. 3. S-parameters of the selected (re-tuned) trade-off designs: (a) $\boldsymbol{x}^{(1)}$, (b) $\boldsymbol{x}^{(4)}$, (c) $\boldsymbol{x}^{(6)}$, (d) $\boldsymbol{x}^{(10)}$; $|S_{11}|$ (····), $|S_{21}|$ (- - -), $|S_{31}|$ (—),$|S_{11}|$ (-·-·); vertical lines mark the center frequency (solid line) and ranges of symmetric bandwidth (dashed lines).

TABLE I PARAMETER VALUES OF TRADE-OFF COUPLER DESIGNS

Perform. /Variables	Trade-off design (re-tuned)									
	$\boldsymbol{x}^{(1)}$	$\boldsymbol{x}^{(2)}$	$\boldsymbol{x}^{(3)}$	$\boldsymbol{x}^{(4)}$	$\boldsymbol{x}^{(5)}$	$\boldsymbol{x}^{(6)}$	$\boldsymbol{x}^{(7)}$	$\boldsymbol{x}^{(8)}$	$\boldsymbol{x}^{(9)}$	$\boldsymbol{x}^{(10)}$
BW [GHz]	1.84	1.69	1.65	1.51	1.48	1.44	1.22	1.07	1.05	0.94
Area [mm^2]	517	509	501	486	457	427	392	372	369	360
D	12.4	13.3	12.2	12.1	12.1	12.1	12.1	12.1	12.0	11.9
r_1	0.63	0.64	0.65	0.64	0.64	0.64	0.64	0.64	0.64	0.64
r_2	0.84	0.84	0.86	0.84	0.84	0.82	0.82	0.80	0.80	0.80
r_3	0.62	0.62	0.63	0.66	0.63	0.63	0.62	0.63	0.62	0.68
r_4	0.39	0.38	0.38	0.37	0.35	0.30	0.29	0.30	0.29	0.29
r_5	0.63	0.63	0.63	0.63	0.63	0.63	0.63	0.63	0.63	0.61
r_6	0.78	0.76	0.78	0.77	0.77	0.78	0.81	0.78	0.80	0.80
r_7	0.92	0.92	0.92	0.91	0.87	0.85	0.81	0.80	0.80	0.80
r_8	0.57	0.58	0.57	0.57	0.56	0.57	0.57	0.56	0.57	0.55
r_9	0.92	0.92	0.92	0.80	0.87	0.85	0.80	0.80	0.79	0.79
r_{11}	0.90	0.89	0.89	0.88	0.88	0.85	0.79	0.79	0.79	0.80
r_{11}	0.80	0.80	0.80	0.80	0.80	0.80	0.80	0.80	0.80	0.80
r_{12}	0.64	0.63	0.64	0.64	0.59	0.50	0.50	0.50	0.50	0.50
r_{13}	0.77	0.77	0.77	0.79	0.77	0.77	0.78	0.78	0.77	0.80
r_{14}	0.91	0.89	0.88	0.86	0.84	0.82	0.80	0.80	0.80	0.80
r_{15}	0.89	0.86	0.86	0.85	0.85	0.84	0.80	0.80	0.80	0.80
r_{16}	0.65	0.65	0.73	0.71	0.70	0.65	0.65	0.65	0.65	0.65

ACKNOWLEDGMENT

This work has been partially supported by the Icelandic Centre for Research (RANNIS) Grant 163299051, and by National Science Centre of Poland Grant 2017/27/B/ST7/00563.

REFERENCES

[1] L. Wang, G. Wang, Y. He, R. Zhang, "Design of microstrip bandpass filters using fragment-type coupling structure based on multi-objective optimization," *IEEE MTT-S Int. Microwave Symp.*, pp. 1620-1623, 2017.

[2] P. Chen, J. Xia, B.M. Merrick, and T.J. Brazil, "Multiobjective Bayesian optimization for active load modulation in a broadband 20-W GaN Doherty power amplifier design," *IEEE Trans. Microwave Theory Techn.*, vol. 65, no. 3, pp. 860-871, 2017.

[3] S. Koziel and A. Bekasiewicz, "Multi-objective design optimization of antenna structures using sequential domain patching with automated patch size determination," *Eng. Opt.*, vol. 50, no. 2, pp. 218-234, 2018.

[4] A. Bekasiewicz and S. Koziel, "Novel structure and design of enhanced-bandwidth hybrid quadrature patch coupler," *Microwave and Optical Technology Letters*, 2018.

[5] S. Koziel and A. Bekasiewicz, "Conceptual design and automated optimization of a novel compact UWB MIMO slot antenna," *IET Microwaves Ant. Prop.*, vol. 11, no. 8, pp. 1162-1168, 2017.

Linear Adjoint Sensitivity Analysis of the Time-Dependent Schrödinger Equation

Mahmoud M.T. Maghrabi, Mohamed H. Bakr, and Shiva Kumar

Department of Electrical and Computer Engineering
McMaster University, Hamilton, Ontario, L8S 4K1, Canada
maghrabm@mcmaster.ca, mbakr@mcmaster.ca, kumars@mcmaster.ca

Abstract —We present a novel linear adjoint sensitivity analysis approach of the time-dependent Schrodinger equation. Regardless of the number of design parameters, the proposed approach estimates the sensitivities of a general objective function with respect to all the design parameters using only one extra system simulation. The efficiency of the approach is illustrated here through a numerical example.

I. INTRODUCTION

Recently, adjoint sensitivity analysis (ASA) has received wide interest as an efficient alternative to the computationally-expensive finite-difference approaches [1]. The ASA approach estimates the sensitivities of the desired objective function or response with respect to all design parameters using at most one extra system simulation. This can be contrasted with finite difference approximations whose computational cost scales linearly with the number of parameters. The gain of using ASA algorithms becomes more significant for structures with intensive computational time or with a large number of parameters.

Several ASA algorithms have been developed in literature for electromagnetic/photonic (high frequency) structures, based on Maxwell's equations or wave equation, using different numerical techniques such as the transmission line method, the method of moments, and the finite-difference time-domain method [1,2]. An efficient ASA approach is introduced for the time independent Schrödinger equation [3]. This approach estimates the sensitivities for static design problems, e.g., the semiconductor quantum structures in the static case. In this paper, we propose a simple and efficient ASA approach for the time-dependent Schrödinger equation (TDSE). The proposed ASA algorithm significantly accelerates the sensitivity analysis of all dynamic systems governed by the TDSE, e.g., short-reach fiber optic communication systems [4] and time-dependent quantum structures [5].

II. Adjoint Sensitivity Analysis Approach

The linear TDSE governing the light propagation within a short-reach optical fiber link is given by [4]:

$$-\frac{\beta_3}{6}\frac{\partial^3 q}{\partial t^3}+\frac{i\beta_2}{2}\frac{\partial^2 q}{\partial t^2}+\beta_1\frac{\partial q}{\partial t}+\frac{\partial q}{\partial z}+\frac{\alpha}{2}q=q_{Tx}\delta(z), \quad (1)$$

where $q = q(z,t)$ is the complex envelope of the propagated optical field, β_1 is the fiber propagation constant, β_2 and β_3 are the second- and third-order dispersion coefficients, and α is the fiber loss coefficient. The signal $q_{Tx} = q_{Tx}(t)$ is the optical field of the transmitter output and $i = \sqrt{-1}$. Expressing $q = q_{re} + iq_{im}$, substituting in equation (1), and separating the real and imaginary terms, we obtain:

$$\begin{bmatrix}-\tilde{\beta}_3 & 0\\ 0 & -\tilde{\beta}_3\end{bmatrix}\begin{bmatrix}\frac{\partial^3 q_{re}}{\partial t^3}\\ \frac{\partial^3 q_{im}}{\partial t^3}\end{bmatrix}+\begin{bmatrix}0 & -\tilde{\beta}_2\\ \tilde{\beta}_2 & 0\end{bmatrix}\begin{bmatrix}\frac{\partial^2 q_{re}}{\partial t^2}\\ \frac{\partial^2 q_{im}}{\partial t^2}\end{bmatrix}+\begin{bmatrix}\tilde{\beta}_1 & 0\\ 0 & \tilde{\beta}_1\end{bmatrix}\begin{bmatrix}\frac{\partial q_{re}}{\partial t}\\ \frac{\partial q_{im}}{\partial t}\end{bmatrix}+ \quad (2)$$

$$\begin{bmatrix}\partial/\partial z & 0\\ 0 & \partial/\partial z\end{bmatrix}\begin{bmatrix}q_{re}\\ q_{im}\end{bmatrix}+\begin{bmatrix}\tilde{\alpha} & 0\\ 0 & \tilde{\alpha}\end{bmatrix}\begin{bmatrix}q_{re}\\ q_{im}\end{bmatrix}=\begin{bmatrix}Re\{q_{Tx}\}\delta(z)\\ Im\{q_{Tx}\}\delta(z)\end{bmatrix},$$

where $\tilde{\beta}_1 = \beta_1$, $\tilde{\beta}_2 = \beta_2/2$, $\tilde{\beta}_3 = \beta_3/6$, and $\tilde{\alpha} = \alpha/2$. Writing equation (2) for the whole computational domain and approximating the derivatives using finite differences, we can rewrite (2) for the whole domain as:

$$\boldsymbol{B}_3\frac{\partial^3\boldsymbol{V}}{\partial t^3}+\boldsymbol{B}_2\frac{\partial^2\boldsymbol{V}}{\partial t^2}+\boldsymbol{B}_1\frac{\partial\boldsymbol{V}}{\partial t}+\boldsymbol{K}_c\boldsymbol{V}+\boldsymbol{A}\boldsymbol{V}=\boldsymbol{Q}_{in}, \quad (3)$$

where $\boldsymbol{V} = [\boldsymbol{q}_{re}^T\ \boldsymbol{q}_{im}^T]^T$ is the system state vector, $\boldsymbol{Q_{in}} = [Re\{q_{Tx}\}\boldsymbol{e}_1^T\ Im\{q_{Tx}\}\boldsymbol{e}_1^T]^T$ is the excitation vector, and $\boldsymbol{e}_1$ is an elementary column vector. The matrices are given by: $\boldsymbol{B}_3 = -\tilde{\beta}_3\boldsymbol{I}_{2m}$, $\boldsymbol{B}_2 = \tilde{\beta}_2\begin{bmatrix}\boldsymbol{0} & -\boldsymbol{I}_m\\ \boldsymbol{I}_m & \boldsymbol{0}\end{bmatrix}$, $\boldsymbol{B}_1 = \tilde{\beta}_1\boldsymbol{I}_{2m}$, and $\boldsymbol{A} = \tilde{\alpha}\boldsymbol{I}_{2m}$, where $\boldsymbol{I}$ is the identity matrix and m is the number of the spatial discretization cells. Equation (3) is typically solved numerically using the split-step Fourier-Scheme (SSFS) method [4].

After a lengthy derivation, it can be shown that the adjoint system corresponding to (3) is given by:

$$-\boldsymbol{B}_3\frac{\partial^3\boldsymbol{\lambda}}{\partial t^3}-\boldsymbol{B}_2\frac{\partial^2\boldsymbol{\lambda}}{\partial t^2}-\boldsymbol{B}_1\frac{\partial\boldsymbol{\lambda}}{\partial t}-\boldsymbol{K}_c\boldsymbol{\lambda}+\boldsymbol{A}\boldsymbol{\lambda}=\boldsymbol{Q}_{in}^{\lambda}, \quad (4)$$

where $\boldsymbol{\lambda} = [\boldsymbol{\lambda}_{re}^T \, \boldsymbol{\lambda}_{im}^T]^T$ is the adjoint state vector, $\boldsymbol{Q}_{in}^{\lambda} = [\partial\psi/\partial\boldsymbol{q}_{re}^T \, \partial\psi/\partial\boldsymbol{q}_{im}^T]^T$ is the adjoint excitation vector, and ψ is the kernel of the objective function integral [1]. As compared to the original simulation system (3), the adjoint system has a similar form but with different parameter values (opposite signs of the β_3, β_2, and β_1 parameters), and different excitation vector. It should also be clear that the adjoint problem is solved in a reversed spatial direction, $z' = L - z$, where L is the optical fiber length. Thus, the adjoint simulation can be solved using the same SSFS method used to solve the original problem.

Once the original and adjoint fields are determined using (3) and (4), the sensitivities of the desired objective function with respect to all parameters are estimated.

III. Results

To illustrate our algorithm, we consider a numerical example of a 10 Gbps short-reach optical fiber communication system. The optical channel is an anomalous single mode optical fiber whose design parameters' values are [4]: $\beta_3 = 0.1$ ps^3/km, $\beta_2 = -21$ ps^2/km, $\beta_1 = 0.016$ ps/km, and $\alpha = 0.2$ dB/km. The transmitted data are modulated with a return to zero on-off keying format with 50% duty cycle and the pulse shape is Gaussian. We aim at obtaining the sensitivities of an objective function of the form:

$$F = \int_{-T_m}^{T_m} \left| q_{Rx} - q_{ref} \right|^2 dt, \qquad (5)$$

where $q_{Rx} = q(L,t)$ is the complex envelope field of the received signal, $q_{ref} = q_{Tx}(z, t - \beta_1 L)$ is a time delayed version of the transmitted complex envelope field, and T_m is half of the computational time window size. This objective function is a measure of the bit error rate (BER). We estimate the sensitivities of (5) with respect to the design parameters $\boldsymbol{x} = [\beta_3 \, \beta_2 \, \beta_1 \, \alpha \, L]^T$. Fig. 1 shows the normalized sensitivities of the objective function with respect to the parameters: β_2 and L, for a sweep of the parameter L. Due to space limitation, we only show a subset of the obtained sensitivities. Good match is achieved with central finite differences (CFD) for all parameters. The ASA algorithm requires only one extra system simulation per gradient evaluation, while the CFD requires 10 extra simulations.

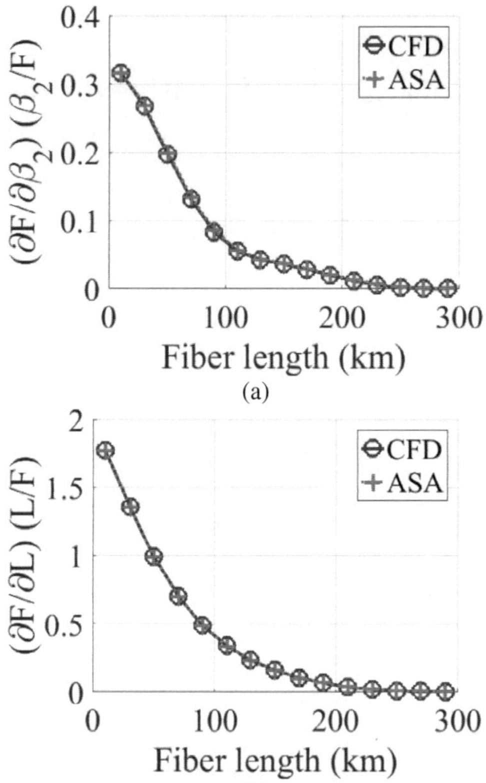

(b)

Fig. 1. The normalized ASA sensitivities of objective function (5) with respect to the second-order dispersion coefficient β_2, and the fiber length L, for a sweep of L, as compared to the more computationally expensive CFD approach.

IV. CONCLUSION

We presented a linear time-dependent Schrödinger equation based adjoint sensitivity analysis algorithm. As compared to the central finite-difference approach, the proposed algorithm is shown to estimate accurate sensitivities of the desired objective function with respect to all the design parameters but with a much lower computational cost.

REFERENCES

[1] M. Bakr, V. Demir, and A. Elsherbeni, *Adjoint Sensitivity Analysis of High Frequency Structures with MATLAB*, the Institution of Engineering and Technology (IET), 2017.

[2] M. H. Bakr, O.S. Ahmed, M. H. El Sherif, and T. Nomura, "Time domain adjoint sensitivity analysis of electromagnetic problems with nonlinear media," Optics Express, vol. 22, no. 9, pp. 10831-10843, 2014.

[3] M. A. Swillam, M. H. Bakr, X. Li, and M. J. Deen, "Efficient sensitivity analysis of the time independent Schrödinger equation with application to quantum lasers," *Optics Communications*, vol. 281, no. 17, pp. 4459-4463, 2008.

[4] S. Kumar and M. J. Deen, *Fiber Optic Communications: Fundamentals and Applications*, John Wiley & Sons, 2014.

[5] D. Bohm, *Quantum theory*, Courier Corporation, 2012.

On Reduced-Cost Design Optimization of Antennas Using Trust-Region Gradient Search

Anna Pietrenko-Dabrowska[1]
[1]*Faculty of Electronics, Telecommunications and Informatics*
Gdansk University of Technology
Gdansk, Poland
anndabr1@pg.edu.pl

Slawomir Koziel[1,2]
[2]*School of Science and Engineering*
Reykjavik University
Reykjavik, Iceland
koziel@ru.is

***Abstract*—A reduced-cost gradient search with numerical derivatives for design optimization of antenna structures is presented. Our approach involves management of the antenna response Jacobians based on relative relocation of the design during subsequent algorithm iterations, as well as the size of the trust region (i.e., optimization domain at current iteration). Consistent computational savings are demonstrated (40 percent on average as compared to the reference algorithm) for a set of benchmark antennas, along the algorithm robustness.**

Keywords—*Antenna design, EM-driven optimization, gradient search, Jacobian update, trust-region framework.*

I. Introduction

Electromagnetic (EM)-driven design closure is a necessary step in the design of modern antenna structures. Commonly used techniques are either expensive (e.g., conventional numerical procedures, both local [1] and global [2]) or laborious and unreliable (designer supervised parameter sweeping). Computational speedup can be achieved by means of surrogate-based optimization (SBO) algorithms, recently applied for antenna design (e.g., [3], [4]). Whether the task is direct optimization or solving particular sub-problems within the SBO procedures, limiting the number of EM simulations is essential to reduce the overall cost of the design process.

In this paper, a reduced-cost trust-region (TR) gradient search algorithm is proposed which allows for considerable reduction of the number of EM simulations by appropriate management of antenna response Jacobian updates throughout the algorithm run. Our method is validated using a set of benchmark UWB antennas and favorably compared to a reference TR algorithm.

II. Antenna Optimization with Sparse Jacobian Updates

The antenna design problem is formulated here as

$$x^* = \arg\min_{x} U(\boldsymbol{R}(x)) \tag{1}$$

where $\boldsymbol{R}(\boldsymbol{x})$ denotes a response of the EM-simulated antenna model with $\boldsymbol{x}$ being a vector of geometry parameters to be adjusted. The objective function U depends on a particular task to be addressed. In case of optimization for best matching as considered here, it is defined as

$$U(\boldsymbol{R}(\boldsymbol{x})) = \max\{f \in F : |S_{11}(\boldsymbol{x}, f)|\} \tag{2}$$

where $|S_{11}(\boldsymbol{x},f)|$ stands for the maximum in-band reflection, and F is the frequency range of interest.

The standard trust-region (TR)-based gradient-search algorithm [5] (the reference algorithm) solves (1) iteratively by generating approximations $\boldsymbol{x}^{(i)}$, $i = 0, 1, \ldots,$ to $\boldsymbol{x}^*$ as

$$\boldsymbol{x}^{(i+1)} = \arg\min_{\boldsymbol{x};\, -\boldsymbol{d}^{(i)} \le \boldsymbol{x}-\boldsymbol{x}^{(i)} \le \boldsymbol{d}^{(i)}} U(\boldsymbol{L}^{(i)}(\boldsymbol{x})) \tag{3}$$

where $\boldsymbol{L}^{(i)}(\boldsymbol{x}) = \boldsymbol{R}(\boldsymbol{x}^{(i)}) + \boldsymbol{J}_R(\boldsymbol{x}^{(i)})\cdot(\boldsymbol{x} - \boldsymbol{x}^{(i)})$ is a linear approximation of $\boldsymbol{R}$ at $\boldsymbol{x}^{(i)}$. If the Jacobian $\boldsymbol{J}_R$ is evaluated using finite differentiation (FD), n additional EM analyses (n being the number of antenna parameters) per algorithm iteration are necessary. The TR region size vector $\boldsymbol{d}^{(i)}$ is adjusted using the standard rules [5].

The algorithm proposed in this work allows us to reduce the number of Jacobian evaluations (as compared to full FD) by exploiting substantial differences of various components of $\boldsymbol{x}^{(i+1)} - \boldsymbol{x}^{(i)}$ in relation do $\boldsymbol{d}^{(i)}$. During the optimization process, the factors $\varphi_k^{\,i}$, defined as a relative design change of the kth parameter w.r.t. the TR size in the ith iteration, are used to decide which portion of the Jacobian $\boldsymbol{J}_R$ is not to be updated in the next iteration:

$$\varphi_k^i = \left|x_k^{(i+1)} - x_k^{(i)}\right| / d_k^{(i)}, \quad k = 1, \ldots, n, \tag{4}$$

The information about the update is stored in the binary Jacobian update matrix $\boldsymbol{A}^J$. Its nonzero elements $\boldsymbol{a}^J_{k,i}$ refer to the Jacobian component $\boldsymbol{J}_k(\boldsymbol{x}) = \partial\boldsymbol{R}/\partial x_k$, (being a vector of all antenna response sensitivities w.r.t. the kth parameter) that are to be updated in the $(i+1)$th iteration. If the update is omitted, the previous value of $\boldsymbol{J}_k$ is used.

In Step 1 of the proposed algorithm, the matrix is set to 1 for all $k = 1, \ldots, n$, meaning that the entire Jacobian $\boldsymbol{J}_R(\boldsymbol{x}^{(0)})$ is computed through FD. In the next iterations, $\boldsymbol{J}_R$ is updated on the basis of the $\boldsymbol{A}^J$ matrix (Step 2). Then, the candidate design $\boldsymbol{x}_{tmp}$ is found by solving (3) (Step 3), and the TR size is adjusted using the gain ratio $\rho = (U(\boldsymbol{R}(\boldsymbol{x}_{tmp}) - U(\boldsymbol{R}(\boldsymbol{x}^{(i)}))/(\boldsymbol{L}^{(i)}(\boldsymbol{x}_{tmp}) - \boldsymbol{L}^{(i)}(\boldsymbol{x}^{(i)}))$ (Step 4). In Step 5, the decision matrix $\boldsymbol{A}^J$ is updated using the procedure described in the next paragraph. If the termination criterion is satisfied, the optimization terminates, otherwise the algorithm returns to Step 3.

In the paper, two versions of the algorithm are presented and compared, different in terms of the update procedure of $\boldsymbol{A}^J$. In both versions, in the ith iteration, assuming that the candidate design $\boldsymbol{x}_{tmp}$ has been accepted ($\rho > 0$), the matrix is extended by adding an $(i+1)$th column that contains information about Jacobian calculation in the next iteration $i+1$. In the basic version of the algorithm, if the TR region size $\|\boldsymbol{d}^{(i+1)}\|$ is smaller than a user-specified threshold δ_{TR1}, the update is not performed for all parameters $k = 1, \ldots, n$. Moreover, if $\|\boldsymbol{d}^{(i+1)}\|$ • δ_{TR1}, the $\boldsymbol{J}_k$ part of the Jacobian is not computed for a given parameter k, if it was updated at least once in the last N_{iter} iterations (this is to ensure that $\boldsymbol{J}_k$ is computed at least every few iterations), and $\varphi_k^{\,i}$ is below the user-specified threshold φ_{high}. On the other hand, if the candidate design is rejected ($\rho < 0$), $\boldsymbol{A}^J$ is not extended. In the basic version of the algorithm, as a rule, the last column of the matrix is used for Jacobian update control. However, if $\|d^{(i+1)}\| < \delta_{TR1}$, the respective portion of the Jacobian J_k is not calculated if both $\varphi_k^i < \varphi_{low}$ and J_k was updated at least once in the last N_{iter} iterations.

The extended version of the algorithm includes two additional cases for the Jacobian update. Firstly, it is carried out if x_{tmp} has been accepted and both $\|d^{(i+1)}\| < \delta_{TR1}$ and J_k was not updated in the last N_{iter} iterations. Secondly, in the case of $\rho < 0$ (x_{tmp} rejected), additional updates are performed for all parameters, if $\|d^{(i+1)}\| > \delta_{TR1}$. The additional updates improve the quality of the solution obtained, however, at the expense of increasing the optimization cost. In this paper, the following values of the algorithm parameters are used: $\delta_{TR1} = 0.1$, and $\varphi_{low} = 0.33$, $\varphi_{high} = 0.66$ and $N_{iter} = 5$.

III. Numerical Results and Benchmarking

The performance of the proposed algorithm is demonstrated here using three UWB antennas shown in Fig. 1. Antenna I [6] is implemented on Taconic RF-35 substrate ($\varepsilon_r = 3.5$, $h = 0.762$ mm). The independent geometry parameters for this structure are $x = [L_0\ dR\ R\ r_{rel}\ dL\ dw\ L_g\ L_1\ R_1\ dr\ c_{rel}]^T$. Antenna II [7] is implemented on FR4 substrate ($\varepsilon_r = 4.3$, $h = 1.55$ mm). The design parameters are $x = [L_g\ L_0\ L_s\ W_s\ d\ dL\ d_s\ dW_s\ dW\ a\ b]^T$. Antenna III is based on the structure of [8] and implemented on RO4350 substrate ($\varepsilon_r = 3.48$, $h = 0.762$ mm); design variables are $x = [L_0\ L_1\ L_2\ L\ dL\ L_g\ w_1\ w_2\ w\ dw\ L_s\ w_s\ c]^T$. The computational models for all structures are implemented in CST Microwave Studio and evaluated using its transient solver. The EM models incorporate SMA connectors.

The antennas have been optimized for minimum reflection within the UWB band (3.1 GHz to 10.6 GHz). Statistical data on algorithm performance has been gathered by executing ten runs with random initial designs (Table I). Figure 2 shows the reflection responses at the initial and the optimized designs. It can be observed that the proposed algorithm (extended version) allows for considerable reduction of the computational cost as compared to the reference algorithm (over 40 percent on average) with slight degradation of the design quality (1.4 dB on average). The extended version of the algorithm can be considered as a cost-accuracy trade-off: the average computational savings are lower (33 percent on average) but design quality is improved (< 0.8 dB degradation on average).

The future work will include more extensive studies on algorithm control parameters and their effect on performance.

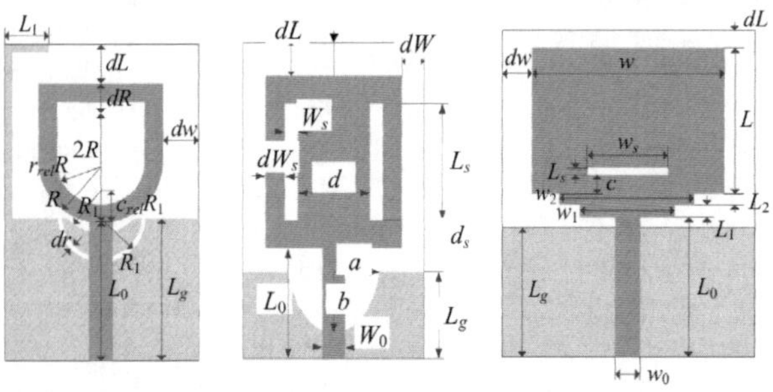

Fig. 1. Benchmark antenna structures: (a) Antenna I [6], (b) Antenna II [7], (c) Antenna III [8]. Ground plane marked using light gray shade.

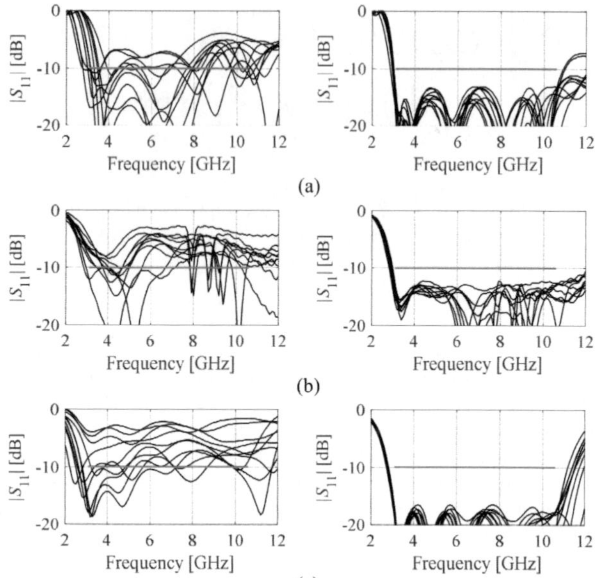

Fig. 2. Reflection responses at (left) initial designs and (right) optimized designs found using the proposed algorithm (extended version). Plots correspond to 10 random starting points. Horizontal line marks design specifications: (a) Antenna I, (b) Antenna II, (c) Antenna III.

TABLE I Optimization Results for Antennas I through III

Algorithm	Antenna					
	I		II		III	
	Cost*	max$\|S_{11}\|$#	Cost*	max$\|S_{11}\|$#	Cost*	max$\|S_{11}\|$#
Reference	111.2	–14.9	111.0	–13.9	139.7	–17.6
Basic	56.4 [49 %]	–13.6 [1.3 dB]	72.7 [35 %]	–12.8 [1.1 dB]	87.5 [37 %]	–15.8 [1.8 dB]
Extended	70.3 [37 %]	–14.2 [0.6 dB]	74.7 [33 %]	–12.9 [1.0 dB]	100.3 [28 %]	–16.9 [0.7 dB]

* Number of EM simulations averaged over 10 algorithm runs (random initial points). The values in brackets stand for relative computational savings in percent.

Objective function values (maximum in-band reflection in dB). The values in brackets represent degradation of the objective function value w.r.t. the reference algorithm (in dB).

Acknowledgment

This work is partially supported by the Icelandic Centre for Research (RANNIS) Grant 174114051, and by National Science Centre of Poland Grant 2015/17/B/ST6/01857.

References

[1] T.G. Kolda, R.M. Lewis, and V. Torczon, "Optimization by direct search: new perspectives on some classical and modern methods," SIAM Review, vol. 45, no. 3, pp. 385–482, 2003.

[2] S. K. Goudos, K. Siakavara, T. Samaras, E. E. Vafiadis, and J. N. Sahalos, "Self-adaptive differential evolution applied to real-valued antenna and microwave design problems," *IEEE Trans. Antennas Propag.*, vol. 59, no. 4, pp. 1286–1298, Apr. 2011.

[3] S. Koziel and S. Ogurtsov, *Antenna design by simulation-driven optimization. Surrogate-based approach*. Springer, New York, 2014.

[4] S. Koziel and A. Bekasiewicz. *Multi-objective design of antennas using surrogate models*. World Scientific, 2016.

[5] A.R. Conn, N.I.M. Gould, and P.L. Toint, *Trust Region Methods*, MPS-SIAM Series on Optimization, 2000.

[6] M.G.N. Alsath and M. Kanagasabai, "Compact UWB monopole antenna for automotive communications, *IEEE Trans. Ant. Prop.*, vol. 63, no. 9, pp. 4204-4208, 2015.

[7] M.A. Haq, S. Koziel, and Q.S. Cheng, "EM-driven size reduction of UWB antennas with ground plane modifications," *Int. Applied Comp. Electromagnetics Society (ACES China) Symposium*, 2017.

[8] D.R. Suryawanshi and B.A. Singh, "A compact UWB rectangular slotted monopole antenna," *IEEE Int. Conf. Control, Instrumentation, Comm. Comp. Tech. (ICCICCT)*, pp. 1130-1136, 2014.

A Compact Coplanar Waveguide Quad-band Wilkinson Power Divider Using Non-Uniform Transmission Lines

Heba H. Jaradat and Nihad I. Dib
Electrical Engineering Department
Jordan University of Science and Technology
Irbid, Jordan
hhjaradt16@eng.just.edu.jo, nihad@just.edu.jo

Khair A. Al Shamaileh
Electrical and Computer Engineering Department
Purdue University Northwest
Hammond, IN 46323,USA
kalshama@pnw.edu

***Abstract*— In this paper, varying-impedance coplanar waveguide (CPW) transmission lines are used to design a fully planar quad-band Wilkinson power divider (WPD). The design equations are presented, and an optimization process is carried out to obtain the quad-band operation with a small utilization area. The proposed divider is designed to operate at 0.5, 1.3, 2.2 and 3 GHz. The divider is simulated and fabricated. Simulated and the measured results are in a very good agreement. The input port matching parameter, S_{11}, is measured to be less than –19 dB at the design frequencies. Moreover, very good output ports matching and isolation between the output ports are achieved with a transmission parameter, S_{21}, of –3±2 dB at the design frequencies.**

Keywords*— *Coplanar waveguide (CPW), Non-uniform transmission lines (NTLs), Quad-band, Wilkinson power divider (WPD).

I. Introduction

Due to the importance of multi-band power dividers in designing different microwave components, many researches have been conducted to design multi-band Wilkinson power dividers (WPDs) using microstrip technology [1, 2]. Coplanar waveguide (CPW), which offers key advantages over microstrip, is still not widely used in this area. Furthermore, little attention is paid to design multi-band microwave components using CPW technology.

Replacing the uniform transmission line by a non-uniform transmission line (NTL) is considered one of the modern miniaturization techniques. The concept of NTLs in CPW was first introduced in [3] to design a single-band WPD. In this paper, the NTLs concept is extended, and a design based on continuously varying the signal trace and ground plane of a typical CPW through a truncated Fourier series expansion is introduced for quad-band operation. Fully-planar, low-cost and small-size quad-band WPD is designed, fabricated, simulated and measured considering an FR-4 substrate.

II. Design Procedure

Fig. 1 depicts the layout of the proposed quad-band WPD and its equivalent even/odd mode circuits. The WPD arms are composed of varying width CPW lines. The unwanted slot line mode in CPW is suppressed through incorporating the bond wires at the discontinuities and junctions as shown in the figure.

The optimum NTL transformer can be obtained by dividing the CPW-based NTL into K electrically short sections. Then, the varying center conductor width is written in terms of a Fourier series as follows:

$$\ln(W(z)/W_{ref}) = \sum_{n=0}^{N} a_n \cos\left(\frac{2\pi nz}{d}\right) + \sum_{n=1}^{N} b_n \sin\left(\frac{2\pi nz}{d}\right), \qquad (1)$$

where W_{ref} is the reference line width, N is the series coefficients number (N=5 is used here) and d is the optimum length of the non-uniform CPW.

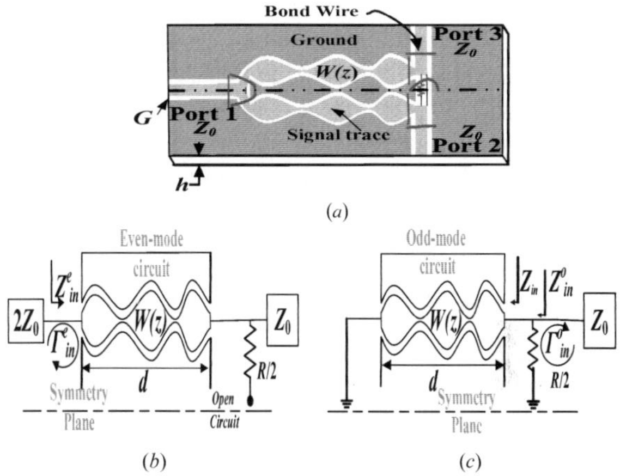

Fig. 1. (a) The layout of the proposed quad-band CPW-based WPD, (b) the equivalent even-mode circuit, and (c) the equivalent odd-mode circuit.

To determine the coefficients and the length d that attribute the quad-band operation and maximum compactness, respectively, an optimization process is carried out. The adopted Error function in the optimization process is intended to minimize the reflection coefficients of the input/output ports simultaneously at the target frequencies as follows:

$$\text{Error} = \sqrt{\sum_{j=1}^{M} \left|\Gamma^e_{in}(f_j)\right|^2} + \sqrt{\sum_{j=1}^{M} \left|\Gamma^o_{in}(f_j)\right|^2}, \qquad (2)$$

where $\Gamma^e_{in}(f_j)$ and $\Gamma^o_{in}(f_j)$ are the input reflection coefficients of the even and odd mode circuits, respectively, which can be written as follows :

$$\Gamma^e_{in}(f_j) = \frac{Z^e_{in}(f_j) - 2Z_o}{Z^e_{in}(f_j) + 2Z_o}, \qquad (3.a)$$

$$\Gamma^o_{in}(f_j) = \frac{Z^o_{in}(f_j) - Z_o}{Z^o_{in}(f_j) + Z_o}, \qquad (3.b)$$

where Z_o=50 Ω. The even and odd input impedances are defined as:

$$Z^e_{in} = \frac{A(f_j) + B(f_j)}{C(f_j)Z_o + D(f_j)}, \qquad (4.a)$$

$$Z_{in}^{o} = \frac{(R/2)Z_{in}(f_j)}{(R/2)+Z_{in}(f_j)}, \quad (4.b)$$

where $Z_{in} = B(f_j) / A(f_j)$. The total *ABCD* matrix of the non-uniform CPW is given by:

$$ABCD_{NTL} = ABCD_1 \times ABCD_2 ... \times ABCD_i ... \times ABCD_K, \quad (5)$$

where K is chosen here as 50. The *ABCD* parameters of the ith section are expressed as [4]:

$$A_i = D_i = \cos(\Delta\theta), \quad (6.a)$$

$$B_i = jZ((i-0.5)\Delta z)\sin(\Delta\theta), \quad (6.b)$$

$$C_i = j\sin(\Delta\theta)/(Z((i-0.5)\Delta z)), \quad (6.c)$$

where $\Delta\theta$ is the electrical length of each segment and $Z((i-0.5)\Delta z)$ is the characteristic impedance at the center of each segment.

III. Design Example and Results

The selected operating frequencies of a quad-band CPW-based WPD are 0.5, 1.3, 2.2 and 3 GHz. The obtained Fourier coefficients of the non-uniform CPW transformer are listed in Table 1. Then, each arm of the conventional WPD is replaced with non-uniform CPW transformer. The analytical results of the proposed WPD are depicted in Fig. 2. The divider is fabricated on an FR-4 substrate with 4.4 relative permittivity and 1.5 mm thickness. A photograph of the fabricated quad-band divider is shown in Fig. 3. Table 2 shows the physical dimensions of the proposed divider. In this approach, only one (100 Ω) resistor is used. The utilization area of the proposed design excluding the ports is 80.39 × 35.87 mm^2 which is around 0.21λ × 0.096λ where λ is the wavelength at the first design frequency for a 70.71 Ω CPW with center conductor of 1.5 mm.

Table 1: The Quad-Band NTL Fourier Coefficients

a_0	a_1	a_2	a_3	a_4	a_5
0.0767	–0.1468	–0.1237	–0.1839	–0.4648	0.8425
-	b_1	b_2	b_3	b_4	b_5
-	–0.2812	–0.0357	–0.0086	0.3311	–0.8393

Table 2: The Physical Dimensions of The Designed WPD (All dimensions are in mm)

Feed Lines		NTL			
Trace width	Gap width	W_{min}	W_{max}	d	Gap width
2	0.216	0.15	10.4062	90.4273	0.579

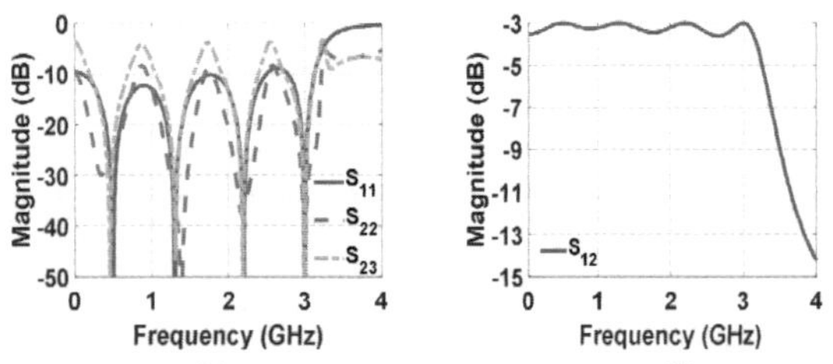

Fig. 2. The theoretical results of the proposed WPD.

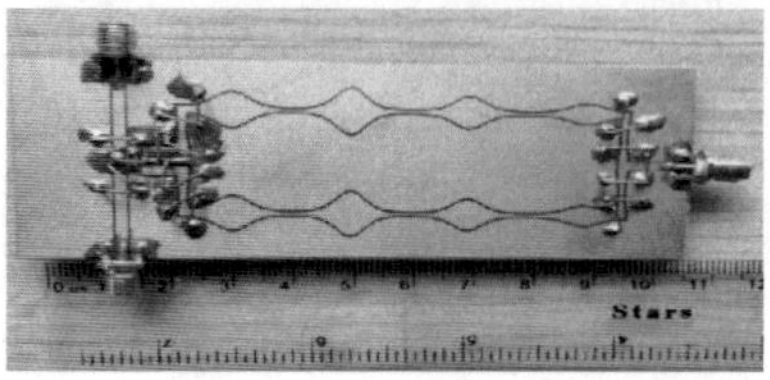

Fig. 3. Photograph of the fabricated WPD.

The designed divider is full-wave simulated using HFSS and CST. The simulated and the measured *S*-parameters are depicted in Fig. 4. The measured input matching and isolation between the output ports are better than –19 dB at the design frequencies. Output port matching is better than –15 dB. The measured transmission parameters are –3.4 dB, –3.7 dB, –4.3 dB and –5 dB at 0.5, 1.3, 2.2 and 3 GHz, respectively. The increase in the dielectric and conductor losses when the frequency increases is thought to be the reason behind the increase in the insertion loss at the fourth design frequency.

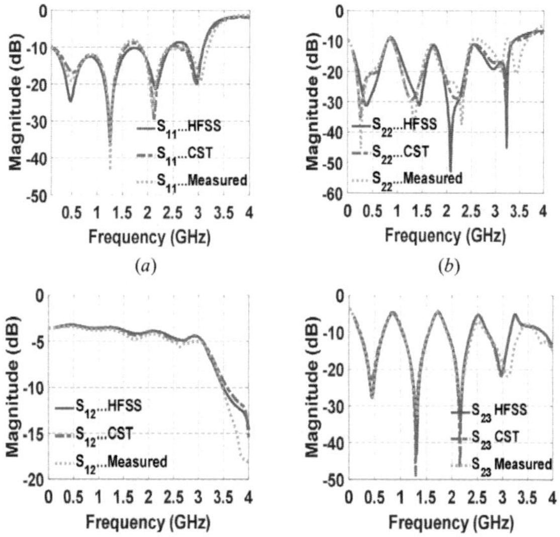

Fig. 4. The scattering parameters of the proposed WPD.

IV. Conclusion

In this paper, we introduced the concept of CPW-based NTLs in designing a quad-band WPD. The design approach was validated through simulating and fabricating the proposed divider. In terms of input/output return loss and transmission parameters, good performance was achieved and good agreement between simulated and measured results was realized.

References

[1] B. Xia, L. Sh. Wu, J. Mao, and L. Yang, "A new quad-band Wilkinson power divider," Journal of Electromagnetic Waves and Applications, vol. 28, no. 13, pp. 1622-1634, Aug. 2014.

[2] H. Younesiraad, M. Bemani, and M. Fozi, "A novel fully planar quad band Wilkinson power divider," AEU-International Journal of Electronics and Communications, vol. 74, pp. 75-82, 2017.

[3] K. Shamaileh, N. Dib, and S. Abu-Shamleh, "A compact coplanar waveguide Wilkinson power divider based on signal traces and adjacent grounds width modulation," Microwave and Optical Technology Letters, vol. 60, pp. 2224–2227, Aug. 2018.

[4] D. Pozar, Microwave engineering, 3rd ed., Wiley, 2005.

A Dual Band Plasmonic Metasurface Absorber for Energy Harvesting Applications

Ayman Negm
Department of Electrical and Computer Engineering
McMaster University
Hamilton, Canada
negma1@mcmaster.ca

Mohamed Bakr
Department of Electrical and Computer Engineering
McMaster University
Hamilton, Canada
mbakr@mcmaster.ca

Matiar Howlader
Department of Electrical and Computer Engineering
McMaster University
Hamilton, Canada
mrhowlader@ece.mcmaster.ca

Shirook Ali
School of Mechanical and Electrical Engineering Technology
Sheridan College
Brampton, Canada
shirook.ali@ieee.org

***Abstract*—A plasmonic dual-band polarization-insensitive metasurface absorber is proposed. The design provides sub-wavelength and confined collection of the absorbed energy in the gaps of the structure. In this paper, we study the absorption behavior of the metasurface operating in a dual-band mode targeting the mid-infrared range suitable for energy harvesting applications such as thermophotovoltaics. The design is optimized using a global optimization technique.**

***Index Terms*—dual-band, energy harvesting, metasurface, plasmonic, polarization-insensitive**

I. Introduction

The interest in perfect absorbers started from the first realization of a perfect absorber using metamaterials by Landy et al. [1] in 2008. Metasurfaces provide powerful absorption characteristics due to the impedance matching with air, especially in the terahertz range where materials with strong absorption characteristics cannot be found in nature [2]. Two main configurations are employed to achieve multiple bands structure namely the metal-dielectric-metal (MDM) structure in which a dielectric layer is sandwiched between a thick metal reflector and a patterned metal layer [3], and the stacked layers structure where each layer accounts for a different band [4]. Using symmetric shapes, polarization-independent absorption can be obtained [2].

Multiband MDM absorbers can be obtained by varying the number of elements in the unit cell of the metasurface [2], or by patterning a single element [3]. Many designs were proposed for the multiband perfect absorber such as circular rings [5], rectangular patches [6], and circular fishnets [7]. However, they do not provide confined absorption suitable for harvesting. This can be tackled by employing gap-based absorbers such as asymmetric double split ring [3] that can confine the absorbed energy in the gap. It was shown that hollow structures support higher surface current and consequently higher absorption, than filled structures [8].

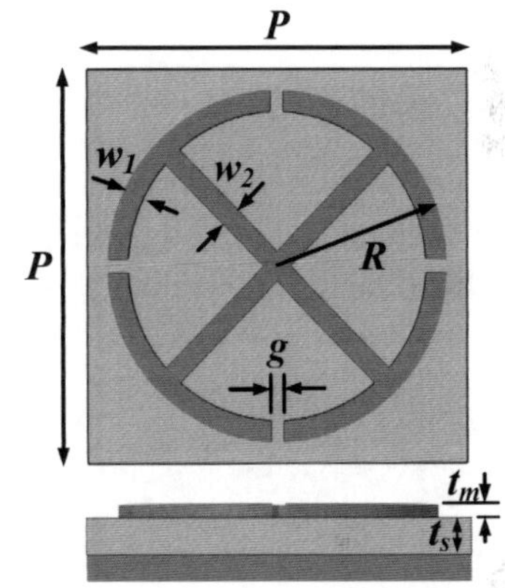

Fig. 1. Top and side views of the unit cell of the proposed absorber (P = 2860 nm, R = 1100 nm, w_1 = 140 nm, w_2 = 415 nm, g = 70 nm, t_m = 50 nm, t_s = 280 nm).

In this work, we introduce an MDM double-split ring with inner cross connection as a dual-band plasmonic nearly perfect absorber. The design provides enhanced field confinement within the gaps at the resonant frequencies by employing the plasmonic properties of gold. This facilitates energy harvesting using diodes placed within gaps. The proposed absorber operates in the mid-infrared range, which is suitable for energy harvesting applications such as thermophotovoltaics.

II. Proposed Structure

Fig. 1 shows the structure of the unit cell of the MDM metasurface absorber suggested in this work. The top gold layer of thickness tm is patterned in the form of a circular ring of radius R, width w_1, with four gaps each of width g cut in the ring, combined with an inner cross of width w_2. The gaps are intentionally included in the structure to act as regions for the confinement of electric field. The bottom layer is also a gold layer that is designed to be thick enough to prevent the

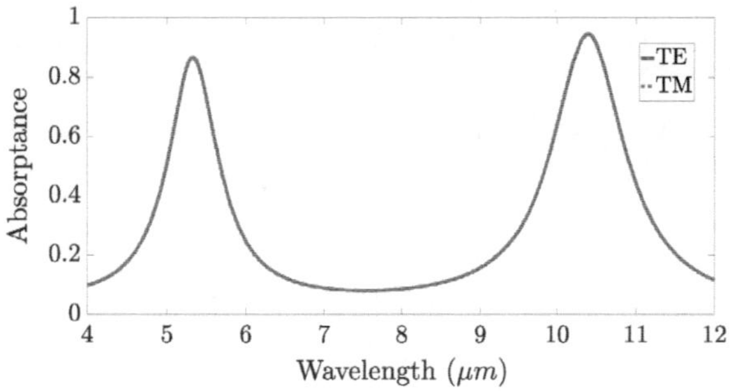

Fig. 2. Absorptance versus wavelength for TE and TM modes.

waves from propagating through it. A silicon dioxide layer of thickness ts separates the two gold layers.

To find the absorption characteristics of the structure, normally incident transverse electric (TE) and transverse magnetic (TM) plane waves are excited upon the metasurface. The absorption can be calculated as:

$$A = 1 - R - T, \tag{1}$$

where R and T are the reflectance and transmittance of the structure respectively. Since the bottom gold layer blocks the transmission, T can be ignored in the calculation of A. The values of the wavelength-dependent refractive index of gold was taken from [9], while the refractive index of silicon dioxide is taken as 1.5. Results were obtained using a finite-element method solver in COMSOL Multiphysics 5.3. Periodic boundary conditions are applied in x and y directions to model a metasurface response with periodicity P in both directions. To find the optimal values of the absorber parameters, genetic algorithm was employed as a global optimization technique [10]. Matlab optimization toolbox was used for the optimization process.

III. Results and Discussion

Fig. 2 shows the TM and TE responses of the absorber between 4 and 12 μm. Resonance peaks are located at 5.32 (86.6%) and 10.4 μm (94.4%). The peak locations are selected for infrared energy harvesting in the atmospheric windows where waves can be transmitted without being absorbed by the atmosphere [11]. The response for TM and TE waves is identical due to the symmetry of the structure.

Fig. 3 shows the field distribution over the structure corresponding to at the resonant wavelengths. It is observed that the electric field is highly confined in the gaps, which indicates that the gaps can act as energy collection spaces. The collected energy can then be harvested by connecting a diode in the gap space to provide conversion to DC current suitable for operating loads.

IV. Conclusion

A dual-band plasmonic metasurface absorber for energy harvesting in the mid-infrared range is proposed. The symmetry of the design provides a polarization-insensitive response, and the

Fig. 3. Electric field distribution at 5.32 μm (top) and 10.4 μm (bottom) for TE (left) and TM (right) polarizations.

gaps provide hot spots for energy collection. The dimensions of the structure are optimized using a global optimization technique.

References

[1] N. I. Landy, S. Sajuyigbe, J. J. Mock, D. R. Smith, and W. J. Padilla, "Perfect metamaterial absorber," *Physical review letters*, vol. 100, no. 20, p. 207402, 2008.

[2] S. Huang, Z. Xie, W. Chen, J. Lei, F. Wang, K. Liu, and L. Li, "Metasurface with multi-sized structure for multi-band coherent perfect absorption," *Optics express*, vol. 26, no. 6, pp. 7066–7078, 2018.

[3] T. Lu, D. Zhang, P. Qiu, J. Lian, M. Jing, B. Yu, and J. Wen, "Ultrathin terahertz dual-band perfect metamaterial absorber using asymmetric double-split rings resonator," *Symmetry*, vol. 10, no. 7, p. 293, 2018.

[4] Z. Zhang, Z. Yu, Y. Liang, and T. Xu, "Dual-band nearly perfect absorber at visible frequencies," *Optical Materials Express*, vol. 8, no. 2, pp. 463–468, 2018.

[5] P. Yu, J. Wu, E. Ashalley, A. Govorov, and Z. Wang, "Dual-band absorber for multispectral plasmon-enhanced infrared photodetection," *Journal of Physics D: Applied Physics*, vol. 49, no. 36, p. 365101, 2016.

[6] Y. Liu, Y. Q. Zhang, X. R. Jin, S. Zhang, and Y. P. Lee, "Dual-band infrared perfect absorber for plasmonic sensor based on the electromagnetically induced reflection-like effect," *Optics Communications*, vol. 371, pp. 173–177, 2016.

[7] Y. Ozturk and A. E. Yilmaz, "Multiband and perfect absorber with circular fishnet metamaterial and its variations," *Applied Computational Electromagnetics Society Journal*, vol. 31, no. 12, 2016.

[8] Y. J. Yoo, Y. J. Kim, P. Van Tuong, J. Y. Rhee, K. W. Kim, W. H. Jang, Y. Kim, H. Cheong, and Y. Lee, "Polarization-independent dual-band perfect absorber utilizing multiple magnetic resonances," *Optics Express*, vol. 21, no. 26, pp. 32 484–32 490, 2013.

[9] A. D. Rakić, A. B. Djurišić, J. M. Elazar, and M. L. Majewski, "Optical properties of metallic films for vertical-cavity optoelectronic devices," *Applied optics*, vol. 37, no. 22, pp. 5271–5283, 1998.

[10] M. Bakr, *Nonlinear optimization in electrical engineering with applications in matlab*. Institution of Engineering and Technology, 2013.

[11] R. Usamentiaga, P. Venegas, J. Guerediaga, L. Vega, J. Molleda, and F. Bulnes, "Infrared thermography for temperature measurement and non-destructive testing," *Sensors*, vol. 14, no. 7, pp. 12 305–12 348, 2014.

Space Fence Radar Overview

Gregory Fonder
Space Surveillance Programs
Lockheed Martin
Moorestown, NJ, USA
gregory.p.fonder@lmco.com

Matthew Hughes
Space Surveillance Programs
Lockheed Martin
Moorestown, NJ, USA
matthew.r.hughes@lmco.com

Dr. Mark Dickson
Advanced Sensors & Techniques
MIT Lincoln Laboratory
Lexington, MA, USA
mrd@ll.mit.edu

Melissa Schoenfeld
Advanced Sensors & Techniques
MIT Lincoln Laboratory
Lexington, MA, USA
schoenfeld@ll.mit.edu

Dr. Jennifer Gardner
Strategic Warning and
Surveillance Systems
AFLCMC/HBQB
Hanscom AFB, MA, USA

***Abstract*— The AN/FSY-3 Space Fence Radar, located on Kwajalein Atoll, is a ground-based S-band radar integrated with an Operations Center designed to greatly enhance the Air Force Space Surveillance Network. Space Fence will revolutionize Space Situational Awareness using advanced phased array radar technology. Space Fence will provide catalog completeness, accuracy and timeliness with vastly improved performance in Low Earth Orbit and capability to support missions in Geosynchronous Earth Orbit. Modeling & Simulation has played a key role in all phases of the Space Fence radar program. In addition, Modeling & Simulation will play an important role in the formal Government testing of requirements that depend on simulated environments or unique orbital events.**

Keywords—Space Situational Awareness (SSA), Phased Array, Digital Beamforming, Modeling & Simulation, Digital Array Radar

I. Space Fence Capabilities

The U.S. Air Force (USAF) is developing the AN/FSY-3 Space Fence (SF) System as part of its Space Surveillance Network (SSN) to provide unprecedented space object detection sensitivity, coverage and tracking accuracy. The SF design consists of two sensor sites; sensor site #1 in the Kwajalein Atoll and sensor site #2 in Western Australia as shown in Fig. 1. A SF Operations Control Center (SOC) is co-located with the Reagan Test Site (RTS) Operations Center in Huntsville, AL (ROC-H). The current Program of Record for site #1 is on track for Initial Operating Capability (IOC) in mid-2019. The preliminary design for site #2 is complete, but presently unfunded [1].

Lockheed Martin's SF System solution is a result of extensive cost-schedule-performance studies conducted during multiple concept and design phases. The design was shaped by the need for flexible sensor coverage and affordability through use of digital array technology that employs element-level Digital Beam Forming (DBF) and is capable of many independent beams to support simultaneous functions. Sensor site #1 is designed to provide assured coverage in Low Earth Orbit (LEO) down to 800 km altitude with the un-cued surveillance fence as well as provide cued tasking support of all altitudes including Geosynchronous Earth Orbit (GEO). The un-cued LEO surveillance fence is a fan-shaped search volume aligned in an east-west direction that detects objects as they pass through. When a detection occurs, SF tracks the object long enough to determine its observed locations. The observations are then combined to estimate its orbital element set. This is compared to the space catalog to determine if the object's element set correlates with one already cataloged or if it is an Un-Correlated Target (UCT) [2].

Use of element-level DBF permits SF to maintain persistent surveillance while tracking hundreds of simultaneous objects detected in the fence. The system automatically manages resources by performing long-arc tracks on UCTs to support accurate initial orbit determination (IOD) (See Fig. 1).

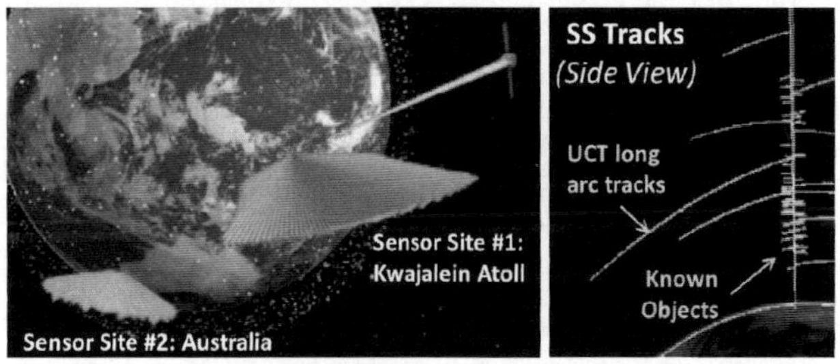

Fig. 1. Space Fence System Sensor Sites; Element-Level DBF Enables Long Arc Tracking Simultaneously With Un-cued Surveillance

The SF System is designed to run the un-cued surveillance mission with the majority of the radar's transmit power. A portion of the radar's remaining resources are available for precision tracking of high-interest objects. For such objects, a "mini-fence" can be electronically constructed to gather more track data, focusing radar resources specifically on that object, providing more timely and accurate information. Scheduling of the mini-fences is automated and based on orbital algorithms and system parameters. System resource control automatically adjusts the number of beams and range extents to cover the required volume. Use of element-level DBF allows SF to support cued tasks without interrupting un-cued surveillance.

Distribution Statement A – Cleared for public release by SMC PA. Case Number: 1128

The layout of a sensor site is depicted in Fig. 2. The radar site features closely-spaced, but separate, transmit and receive arrays that are mission-optimized for high availability and low lifetime support costs, including prime power. Arrays are built with scalable building block sections and Line Replaceable Units (LRUs). Array electronics can be serviced from beneath while arrays are operating, permitting high system availability. Liquid cooling enables high performance and reliability. Radar control, signal and data processing, and Mission Processing are hosted on Commercial off-the-Shelf (COTS) processing systems within the operations building. A portion of this processing is dedicated to automating many of the SF System functions, such as space object observation generation and system status monitoring.

Fig. 2. Space Fence Sensor Site Overview

II. Modeling and Simulation

Modeling & Simulation has played an important role in all phases of the SF radar program. MIT Lincoln Laboratory developed the Performance Assessment Simulator (PAS) for the SF Program Office to facilitate the development and testing of the SF radar software. The PAS provides a satellite simulation environment that interfaces with the radar model by providing space scenarios and collecting simulation performance results. The PAS has enabled the early validation of the SF radar design at the highest system level, which is often not possible in radar acquisition programs until the full radar system hardware comes online.

The PAS hardware as depicted in Fig. 3 was delivered by MIT Lincoln Laboratory as a fully installed rack. The PAS hardware architecture includes three multi-core servers: Computation Server, Logging Server, and Messaging Web Server. The Computation Server includes a NVIDIA Graphical Processing Unit (GPU) and is utilized for computationally intensive real-time propagation. All hardware, including the rack, servers, GPU, and other items depicted below are COTS products.

The PAS can flexibly support a wide range of space scenarios, allowing for thorough testing against many operational cases. Scenarios are derived from multiple sources, including the publicly available Space Track catalog and NASA orbital debris models. Synthetic, artificial scenarios designed to test specific requirements have also been developed including satellite collision and launch simulations. With these diverse scenarios, the flexibility of the PAS enables validation of many performance measures in simulation tied to the SF program requirements.

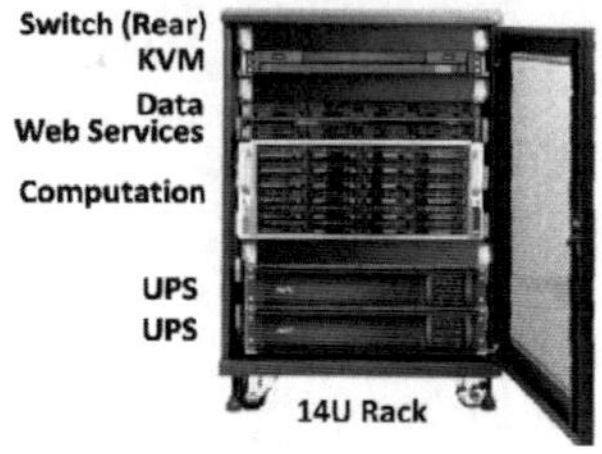

Fig. 3. Space Fence Performance Assessment Simulator (PAS)

Lockheed Martin's high fidelity model of the SF radar is used in conjunction with the PAS for capability analysis. The radar model runs using Mission and Radar control software used in the actual system, executing functions to point beams, analyze returns, determine orbits, and report observation data. Therefore, the model functions as a very accurate representation of the actual system. A modeling and simulation scenario is run by populating the simulated environment with orbiting objects, both cataloged and uncataloged, then executing the simulated SF System with both a surveillance fence and optional taskings reporting on detections, observations and tracks as the operational system would.

PAS scenarios are under development to support formal Government testing which will be conducted with the SF radar operating in a simulation mode. Simulation enables testing of space events that would not be otherwise available using live satellites. The simulation mode has the added fidelity of the real-world noise environment. The PAS will allow for testing of many stressing scenarios, such as breakups and docking or maneuvering events, as well as testing of a congested space environment, which would not be possible with live testing.

III. Summary

The AN/FSY-3 Space Fence Radar, located on Kwajalein Atoll, will revolutionize Space Situational Awareness (SSA) using advanced phased array radar technology. Throughout the acquisition of SF, the Performance Assessment Simulator has been key in the early evaluation of the SF radar design. As formal Government testing of requirements begins, PAS will play an important role in the testing of requirements which depend on simulated environments or unique orbital events.

References

[1] Gregory P. Fonder, Peter J. Hack, and Matthew R. Hughes "AN/FSY-3 Space Fence System – Sensor Site One / Operations Center Integration Status and Sensor Site Two Planned Capability", Advanced Maui Optical and Space Surveillance Technologies Conference Proceedings, September 2017.

[2] Michael G. Koltiska, 2^{d} Lt, Han Du, Dan Prochoda, and Kevin Kelly "AN/FSY-3 Space Fence System Support of Conjunction Assessment", Advanced Maui Optical and Space Surveillance Technologies Conference Proceedings, September 2016.

Radio Astronomy Techniques for Multistatic Radar Imaging and Localization of Space Objects

Robert L. Morrison, Jr.
MIT Lincoln Laboratory
Lexington, MA
rmorrison@ll.mit.edu

Eric B. Phelps
MIT Lincoln Laboratory
Lexington, MA
phelpse@ll.mit.edu

***Abstract*—This paper explores the application of aperture synthesis techniques for radio astronomy to multistatic radar with the goal of improving image quality and relative positioning precision for practical array geometries. In a step towards achieving this goal, a new multistatic radar approach is proposed that incorporates aperture synthesis processing. The feasibility of this approach is demonstrated via analytical results and simulation. The approach is then compared to conventional multistatic radar processing, where, for the same geometry, the conventional method is found to produce superior reconstructions in terms of signal-to-sidelobe level. However, the proposed approach is advantageous for two reasons. First, if a radio astronomy array and correlator already exist, the new method will generate acceptable images. Second, timing and synchronization requirements on the transmitters can be relaxed in the new method, allowing low-cost, low-complexity transmitters to be utilized.**

***Index Terms*—aperture synthesis, multistatic radar, space object characterization**

I. Introduction

Both resolved imaging and high-resolution relative localization of space objects are of continued interest to the space surveillance community. Radar imaging of space objects requires both bandwidth and aspect change to form a fully resolved 2D image. Likewise, localization of closely-spaced objects using radar requires fine angular resolution and high range precision. For both of these applications, an alternative for recovering cross-range information is to use a multistatic radar geometry with one or more transmitters and multiple receivers [1]. We define *conventional multistatic radar* to be a setup where the waveforms and timing of each transmitter are known at all of the receivers for use in pulse compression. Such an approach provides a limited, sparse set of 2D Fourier-domain samples for reconstructing an image or resolving targets, where the quantity of distinct measurements is equal to the product of the number of receivers and the number of transmitters.

A similar application is encountered in radio astronomy, where aperture synthesis techniques employ distributed arrays of receive sensors to generate maps of astronomical sources [2]. Here, celestial emissions in the radio-frequency range are observed by multiple receivers and correlated to recover the spatial distribution of sources. These techniques are effective in resolving closely-spaced sources.

The goal, then, is to apply radio astronomy aperture synthesis concepts to multistatic radar to improve both image quality and relative positioning precision. To that end, this paper considers the basic mechanism underlying aperture synthesis in radio astronomy and compares it to conventional radar data processing. A new approach is then proposed that modifies the traditional framework for collecting and processing multistatic radar data based on aperture synthesis. The approach uses multiple radars transmitting noise-like waveforms to generate spatially uncorrelated returns from the target. This enables measurements of the 2D Fourier Transform of the squared magnitude of the reflectivity to be generated by cross correlating signals from pairs of receivers. We will show that this approach is capable of spatially resolving the angular positions of multiple scattering centers on a target (or, through a similar mechanism, the relative angular positions of multiple separated objects in proximity).

II. Multistatic Radar Aperture Synthesis

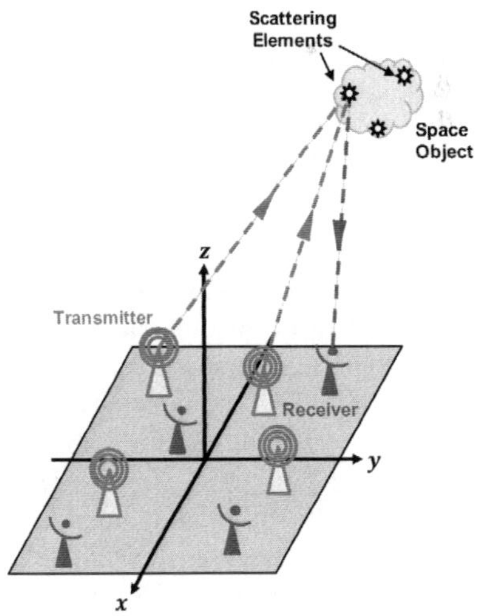

Fig. 1. Multistatic array for radar aperture synthesis imaging.

The primary distinction between radio astronomy and conventional multistatic radar is that, in radar, the returns from each part of the imaged scene are not spatially uncorrelated. The radar actively illuminates a target, and the aggregated return is a superposition of responses from each scattering element, or *scatterer*, on the object. If the signal collected at one receiver is correlated with that of another receiver, the correlation will contain cross-terms between scatterers. These cross-terms prevent a direct imaging relationship. Radio astronomy, in contrast, is a passive mode of imaging that relies on emissions from radio sources. The emissions may be modeled as uncorrelated at each point in the scene. Thus, the source cross-terms average out to generate a Fourier-transform relationship between the measurements and the image.

Now, the question is, how can radar be used to generate responses that are spatially uncorrelated from scatterer to scatterer? With one radar this is not possible, since the returns from different scatterers are simply delayed and scaled versions of each other. However, we will demonstrate that with multiple transmitters, it is possible to synthesize the spatially uncorrelated condition required for aperture synthesis, where the return from each scatterer can be approximated as an independent random process.

Figure 1 depicts a multistatic array with multiple transmitters and receivers. Suppose each transmitter transmits a passband noise process that is uncorrelated between transmitters. The signal incident on a particular scatterer is then the superposition of delayed and phase shifted noise signals from each transmitter. The phase shift affecting the signal contribution from a particular transmitter is essentially random, since it is proportional to the transmitter-to-scatterer range measured modulo one-half wavelength. Thus, the weighted sum of noise signals at a particular scatterer generates a new noise signal that is uncorrelated with other scatterer returns. In Figure 1, the signals from two transmitters converge at a particular scattering element. The return, which has been "randomized" by the multiple transmit sources with different path lengths, is collected at one of the receivers. Given such returns collected at multiple receivers with different geographic locations, aperture synthesis techniques can be applied to generate an image.

III. Simulation Example

Figure 2 presents a simulation result demonstrating the radar aperture synthesis technique. Figure 2(a) shows the sensor geometry with 10 transmitters and 50 receivers distributed over a 1000 km by 1000 km patch. The imaged target is a constellation of six point scatterers with magnitudes uniformly distributed between 0.8 and 1. The positions of the scatterers in the x-y plane are shown in Figure 2(b). The target is located in the far field of the array. Each transmitter transmits a noise signal with 50 kHz bandwidth centered at 10 GHz. Five seconds of simulated data are generated for each receiver. The signals from all unique baselines are cross correlated to produce a set of measurements for imaging.

Figure 2(c) presents the reconstruction result simulating the radar aperture synthesis process. The six scatterers are properly rendered in the image. The conventional multistatic reconstruction is displayed in Figure 2(d). There are significant sidelobes in the background of the aperture synthesis reconstruction that, while less intense than the desired features, are larger than the sidelobes in the conventional reconstruction. Image enhancement algorithms used in radio astronomy, such

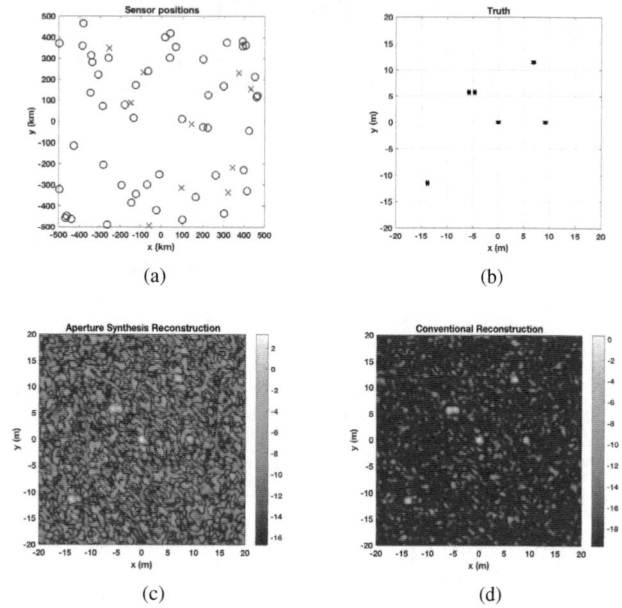

Fig. 2. Radar aperture synthesis simulation example: (a) sensor geometry, (b) truth scatterer positions, (c) aperture synthesis reconstruction, and (d) conventional multistatic reconstruction.

as CLEAN, could be used here to produce an improved restoration [2].

IV. Summary

In this paper, we explored the application of radio astronomy aperture synthesis techniques to multistatic radar, with the goal of determining whether the techniques could improve space object imaging and localization performance for practical arrays. We proposed a new technique for multistatic radar using aperture synthesis processing and compared this technique to conventional processing. Simulation results confirmed the validity of the approach in resolving the angular positions of targets. An advantage in the proposed approach is that it does not require the transmitters to have exquisite timing or to be synchronized with each other. The receive timing needs to be highly accurate, but the technology for accomplishing this has already been demonstrated [3]. Thus, the approach is beneficial when there is an existing receive array that can be leveraged, such as the VLBA or VLA. Work remains in more formally quantifying the information content available through the two approaches, examining link budgets, and investigating other imaging approaches.

References

[1] Y. Wu and D. C. Munson, Jr., "Multistatic Synthetic Aperture Imaging of Aircraft using Reflected Television Signals," *Proc. SPIE* vol. 4382, Algorithms for Synthetic Aperture Radar Imagery VIII, pp. 1-12, August 27, 2001.

[2] J. A. Högbom, "Aperture Synthesis with a Non-Regular Distribution of Interferometer Baselines," *Astronomy and Astrophysics Supplement*, vol. 15, pp. 417-426, 1974.

[3] K. Pazamickas, R. Hambly, and T. Clark, " High-Accuracy Time and Frequency in VLBI," 9th IVS Technical Operations Workshop, MIT Haystack Observatory, April 30-May 4 2017.

Validation of Wind Turbine Doppler Signatures in a Passive Bistatic Radar with a Point Scatterer Model

Martin Ummenhofer
Department of Passive Radar and Anti-Jamming Techniques (PSR)
Fraunhofer Institute for High Frequency Physics and Radar Techniques FHR
53343 Wachtberg, Germany
martin.ummenhofer@fhr.fraunhofer.de

***Abstract*—This paper presents a study on Doppler signatures of wind turbines in a passive bistatic radar system (PBR). Measurements of the turbine blades from a PBR operating in the UHF region are compared with a theoretical model derived from the assumption of point scatterers.**

***Index Terms*—Condition monitoring system, line model, passive radar, signatures, simulation, validation, wind turbine.**

I. Introduction

Passive Bistatic Radar (PBR) can be used to provide radar coverage in the vicinity of wind parks. This paper investigates the Doppler signatures of wind turbines (WT) observed using a PBR through the development of a point scatterer model [1]. In order to improve the understanding of WT returns in PBR systems and explore the possibility of using this technology for condition monitoring (CMS) [2], this study addresses phenomenology of the periodic flashing radar returns that are received by a PBR from nearby WT. A scattering model developed for the investigation of helicopter returns was adapted for the bistatic scenario and a closed form solution is derived in Section III to allow for a comparative analysis with measurements taken with a PBR in Section IV.

II. System Setup

PBR data was collected from an on-shore wind farm that consists of close to a hundred utility-scale WT with power generation ranging from 2 MW to 3.45 MW. The PBR sensor [3], is a two channel system capable of processing the signal received by a pair of vertically stacked antennas. Two broad band omni-directional antennas were used as receiving elements that had been tuned to the DVB-T (Digital Video Broadcasting Terrestrial) band specifications to operate in the Ultra High Frequency (UHF) range at 498 MHz. Measurements focused on a WT under test (TUT) of the type Vestas V112®at a distance of 4.9 km, which has a hub height of 94 m and a blade length of $l = 56$ m. In order to obtain truth information, this WT had been equipped with CMS sensors [2]. A DVB-T broadcasting transmitter at a distance of 5.6 km served as illuminator of opportunity.

III. Simulation Model

The modeling approach assumes that the predominant backscattering effects from the turbine blade originate from the lightning rod embedded into the the composite material of each blade. At UHF wavelengths of about 0.6 m, the cross section of this type of lightning protection can be considered negligible and the theory of point scatterers can be applied [4]. To obtain a closed form solution for the waveform being scattered back to the PBR, a theoretical model approach developed in [5] has been adapted for signal returns in the bistatic case.

This model assumes that a line structure can be described as a continuation of single point scatterers with a single point signal $s_s(t)$ given as:

$$s_s(t) = A \cdot e^{i(2\pi f_0 t - ck\tau + \Phi_0)}, \tag{1}$$

where the signal delay time is denoted $\tau = \frac{R_T + R_R}{c}$, amplitude A, sampling frequency f_0, wave number $k = \frac{2\pi}{\lambda}$, wave length λ and a constant phase Φ_0. The scatterer location $\boldsymbol{r}$ in spherical coordinates with the rotor hub at the origin, is determined by (r, ϕ_s, θ_s). With the instantaneous scatterer elevation angle given by the rotor's angular frequency ω, thus $\phi_s = \omega \cdot t$. Similarly the transmitter location $\boldsymbol{r_t}$ is determined by (r_t, ϕ_t, θ_t) and the receiver's $\boldsymbol{r_r}$ by (r_r, ϕ_r, θ_r) as shown in Fig. 1. Scattering effects of the receiver-to-scatterer path R_R

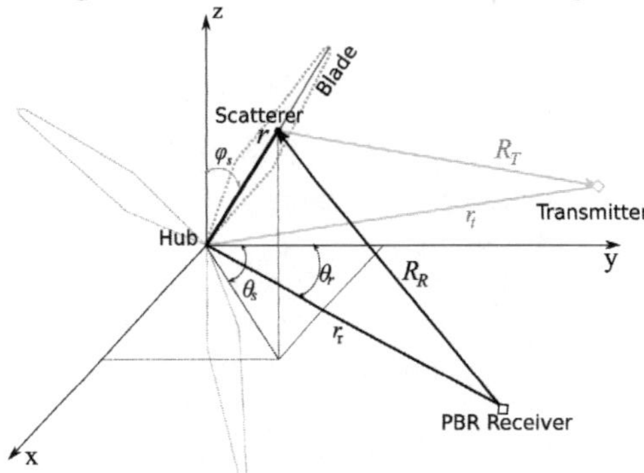

Fig. 1. Bistatic geometries for the rotor blades.

and transmitter-to-scatterer path R_T are in good approximation limited to the the horizontal plane which allows to neglect the elevation angles ϕ_r and ϕ_t. By taking into account that the blade length l is small compared to R_T, the approximation:

$$R_T = |\mathbf{r} - \mathbf{r_t}| = r_t - r \sin\phi_s \cos\theta_T \tag{2}$$

holds, where $\theta_T = \theta_s - \theta_t$. Similar consideration for the path length R_R with $\theta_R = \theta_s - \theta_r$ results in:

$$R_R = |\mathbf{r} - \mathbf{r_r}| = r_r - r \sin\phi_s \cos\theta_R. \quad (3)$$

Combining expressions (2) and (3) with (1) yield

$$s_s(t) = A \cdot e^{i(2\pi f_0 t + kr\sin(\omega t)(\cos\theta_R + \cos\theta_T) - k(r_r + r_t) + \Phi_0)}. \quad (4)$$

Integrating $s_s(t)$ over the length of the blade l and considering the returns of the entire rotor with N blades, results in the expression:

$$s_{Rotor}(t) = Al \cdot e^{i(2\pi f_0 t + \Phi_1)} \cdot \sum_{n=0}^{N-1} \exp\left(i\frac{kl}{2}(\cos\theta_R + \cos\theta_T)\sin\left(\omega t + \frac{2\pi n}{N}\right)\right) \cdot \mathrm{si}\left(\frac{kl}{2}(\cos\theta_R + \cos\theta_T)\sin\left(\omega t + \frac{2\pi n}{N}\right)\right), \quad (5)$$

with the constant phase term $\Phi_1 = -k(r_r + r_t) + \Phi_0$.

By taking the derivative of the time dependent phase term in (4), the blades Doppler frequency shift is obtained,

$$\dot{\Phi}(t) = 2\pi f_D = \omega kr(\cos\theta_R + \cos\theta_T)\cos(\omega t). \quad (6)$$

The maximum shift is expected at the blade tip with $r = l$ at time instances when $\cos(\omega t) = \pm 1$, thus:

$$f_{Dmax} = \left|\omega \frac{kl}{2\pi}(\cos\theta_R + \cos\theta_T)\right|. \quad (7)$$

IV. Experimental Validation

The PBR data from the TUT was obtained by extracting the appropriate bistatic range gate from the range profiles. The system is capable of sampling radar returns from a single gate at a rate of $f_0 = 892.9$ Hz. Time frequency analysis was performed by computing the signals discrete Gabor transform [6] using a Gauss distributed window function. The removal of the stationary clutter returns and the interference floor resulted in spectrogram shown in Fig. 2. Based on equation (5) a signal

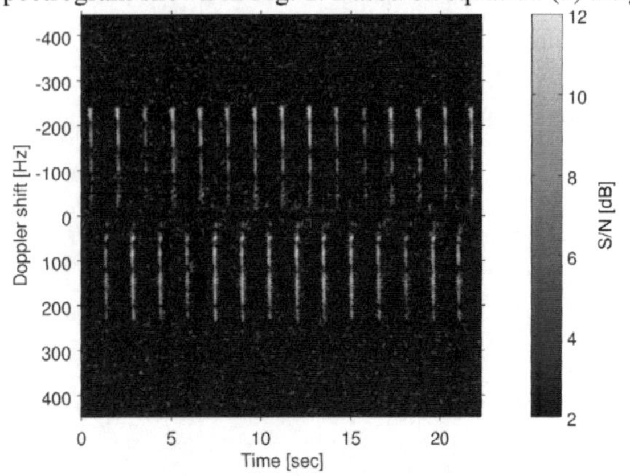

Fig. 2. WT spectrogram taken with the PBR system with f_{Dmax}=-240.4 Hz.

was generated using synchronized readings from the CMS sensors for ω, θ_T and θ_R with N=3 for a three bladed rotor. Based on the noise levels registered in the measured data, a Rayleigh distributed noise signal, 10.5 dB below $s(t)_{Rotor}$, was added. The resulting signal then underwent the same signal processing techniques as the PBR data which resulted in the spectrogram in Fig. 3.

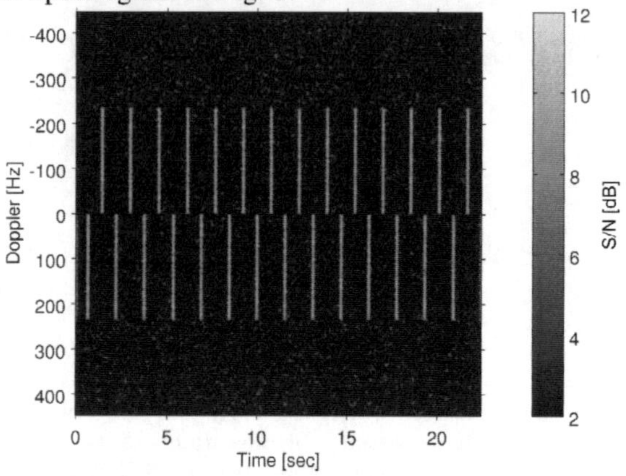

Fig. 3. Simulated WT spectrogram for ω=12.9 RPM, θ_R=160.1°, θ_R=202.4° with f_{Dmax} =-234.0 Hz.

Both spectrograms show the blade returns as distinct narrow flashes in the Doppler domain with matching levels, periodicity and maximum Doppler. It should be noted, that the flashes in the PBR data do not extend down to zero Doppler. A reason for this is that the model does not account for the solid metal rotor hub, which reflections are removed by clutter cancellation.

V. Conclusion

Results show the validity of the bistatic line model to describe the radar returns from the TUT. They indicate that the lightning rod in the turbine's blade is the predominant source of back scattering effect of an UHF based PBR.

Acknowledgment

The authors gratefully acknowledge the ongoing technical support of the team from Dirkshof EED GmbH & Co. KG in Reußenköge, Germany. This project is funded by the Federal Ministry of Economic Affairs and Energy on the basis of a decision of the German Bundestag.

Supported by: Federal Ministry for Economic Affairs and Energy on the basis of a decision by the German Bundestag

References

[1] H. Kuschel, J. Heckenbach and M. Ummenhofer, "Passive radar collision warning system parasol," IEEE Aerospace and Electronic Systems Magazine,vol. 32, no. 2, pp. 40–52, February 2017.

[2] C. Kress, S. Mechler, N. Denecke, A. Friedmann, R. S. C. Kühnert, M. Ummenhofer, C. Schwark, S. Leupold and R. Schelenz, "Iso.wind – A monitoring system for wind parks using passive radar," in Journal of Physics: Conference Series, 2018.

[3] M. Ummenhofer, C. Schwark, C. Kress, S. Mechlers, N. Denecke, A. Rohr, M. Fredebohm, M. Koch and A. Friedmann, "Practical investigation of using passive radar for structural health monitoring of wind farms," in 2018 IEEE International Conference on Environmental Engineering (EE), March 2018, pp. 1–5.

[4] V. C. Chen, The Micro-Doppler Effect in Radar, Artech House, 2011.

[5] G. Retzer, "Zur detektion von zielen im clutter unter ausnutzung von zielechomodulationen durch rotierende strukturen," Ph.D. dissertation, 2018.

[6] D. Gabor, "Theory of communication. Part 1: The analysis of information," Journal of the IET - Part III: Radio and Communication Engineering, pp. 429–441, 1946.

Overview of Electronic Attacks against Passive Radar

Daniel W. O'Hagan
Fraunhofer Institute for High Frequency Physics and Radar Techniques FHR
Wachtberg, Germany
Email: daniel.ohagan@fhr.fraunhofer.de

Stephen Paine
Radar Remote Sensing Group
University of Cape Town
Cape Town, South Africa
Email: PNXSTE002@myuct.ac.za

Christof Schüpbach
armasuisse Science + Technology
Thun, Switzerland
Email: christof.schuepbach@armasuisse.ch

***Abstract*—Passive radars (PR) are becoming more popular in both commercial and research environments. If, as they are expected to, become deployed in military surveillance applications, their vulnerability to electronic attacks (EA) needs to be thoroughly investigated. This paper presents aspects of countering FM, DAB and DVB-T based PR systems using various attack strategies. The effects of various jamming waveforms are investigated. It is shown that under certain conditions, successful EA can be achieved with relatively low power. We demonstrate the importance of a direct signal canceller which causes a FM based PR system to be more tolerant to jamming when the reference and surveillance antennas are co-located as opposed to being separated.**

***Index Terms*—Passive Radar, PCL, Jamming, Electronic Attack, FM, DVB-T, DAB**

I. Introduction

The performance of a passive radar (PR) can be intentionally degraded in a number of different ways. The required attack signal power strongly depends on the relative positions of the target, illuminator and all the relevant link budgets. We therefore assess the effectiveness of the attack on the level of the amplitude-range-Doppler (ARD) map. For systems employing digital signals that can be reconstructed using de- and re-modulation it is therefore unlikely that the quality of the reference signal can be corrupted enough to cause an issue. In this case, we assume that the attacking signal is only introduced into the surveillance channel.

II. FM Based Systems

FM based PR works by utilising two separate receive channels, one for the reference signal and one for target echos. As the target echo can be 90 dB lower than the direct signal, channel separation (typically 10 dB in a co-located configuration) poses a significant challenge. As a result, direct signal cancellation (DSC) is required whereby the direct signal appearing in the surveillance channel is typically suppressed by means of a least mean squares (LMS) filter. This section demonstrates that this has a significant impact on the performance of an FM based PR system in a hostile environment. A simple waveform analysis is performed using two different waveforms, Gaussian noise and a single tone applied to the carrier of the FM channel.

A. Waveform Analysis

Initial work on noise jamming of a FM based PR is shown in [1] and the complete simulation description and results can be found in [2]. Figure 1 illustrates measured results from [2] where a target which can clearly be seen within the red oval in Figure 1a. When noise jamming is applied, Figure 1b, the target becomes masked by the increased noise floor and is barely visible.

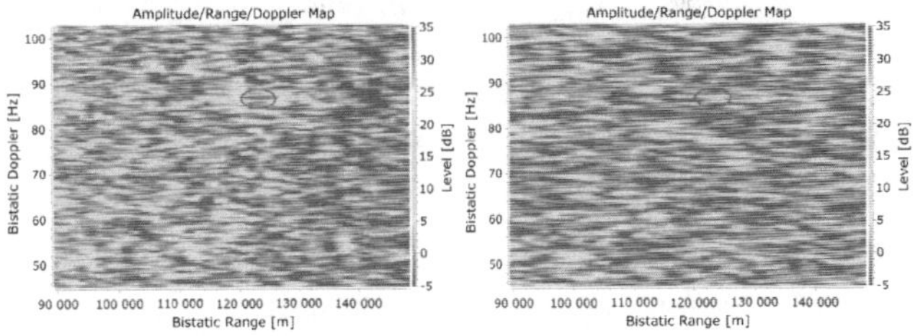

(a) No jamming (b) Noise jamming

Fig. 1: Measured system performance with Gaussian white noise.

Two measured targets shown Figure 2a. Figure 2b shows the same targets but with single tone jamming applied, leading to the targets being masked.

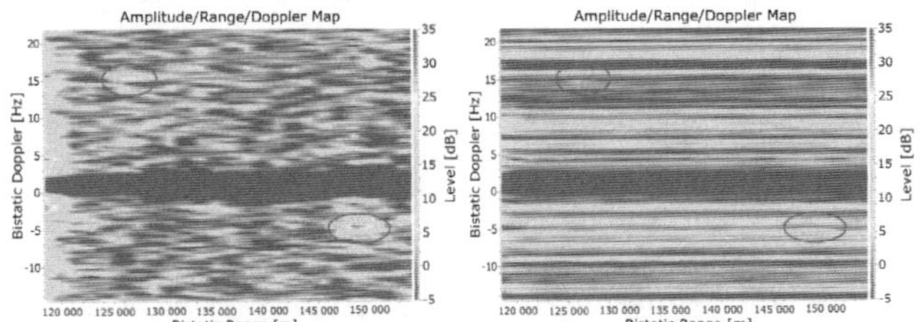

(a) No jamming (b) Tone jamming

Fig. 2: Measured system performance with tone jamming.

B. Direct Signal Cancellation Effects

To assess the effect of a DSC, 4 simulations were run using the FERS simulator [2]. The outputs of each simulation are shown in Figure 3. For each simulation run, a real recorded FM waveform transmitted at 10 kW ERP for 3 seconds with an aircraft approaching the receiver system at constant velocity.

A 5 W ERP Gaussian noise jammer is used and the resultant effects studied. For more details the reader is referred to [2].

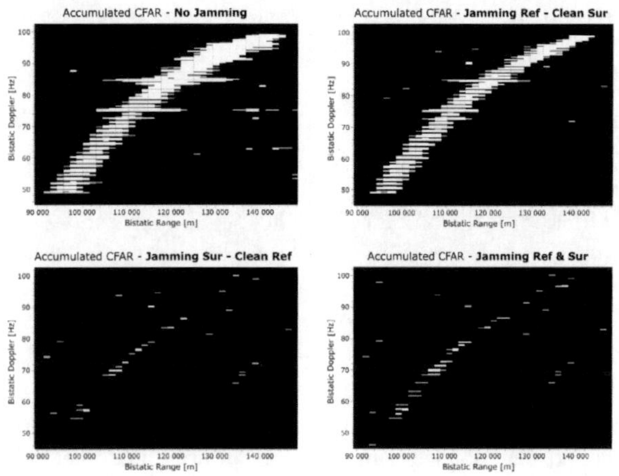

Fig. 3: Accumulated CFAR output for each simulation.

The top left plot of Figure 3 shows the accumulated CFAR output where no jamming is present to provide a reference benchmark for the simulation. Applying a jamming signal to the reference channel shows no visible reduction in the number of target detections (top right of Figure 3). Applying the jamming signal to only the surveillance channel (bottom left of Figure 3), results in a drastic reduction target detections (29%). Injecting the same jamming signal into both the reference and surveillance channels (bottom right of Figure 3) results in a relative improvement in detection performance (44% vs 29%). This is attributed to the DSC since if the jamming signal appears in both the channels, it will be partially suppressed.

III. Digital Waveform Based Systems

As the coding-standards of digital signals is known, they can be de-modulated and errors can be corrected. The disadvantage is that digital waveforms employ mechanisms for synchronization and channel equalization which can be used by an attacker to create unwanted effects in the ARD map. This section provides a brief overview of achievable effects using deterministic parts of DAB and DVB-T waveforms for jamming. More details can be found in [3], [4].

A. Digital Audio Broadcast (DAB)

In the case of DAB, every transmission frame starts with a known phase reference symbol (PRS). If it is used in an attack, the processing gain can reach up to 40 dB. Figure 4 shows the effects when the PRS attacked. The jammer operator can therefore selectively mask a target return along a particular range line regardless of which Doppler bin the target appears.

B. Digital Video Broadcast (DVB-T)

DVB-T, while similar to DAB, differs in that it uses absolute rather than relative carrier modulation where pilot tones are contained in every symbol. Once a receiver is synchronized to the signal, the pilot pattern is completely known from the

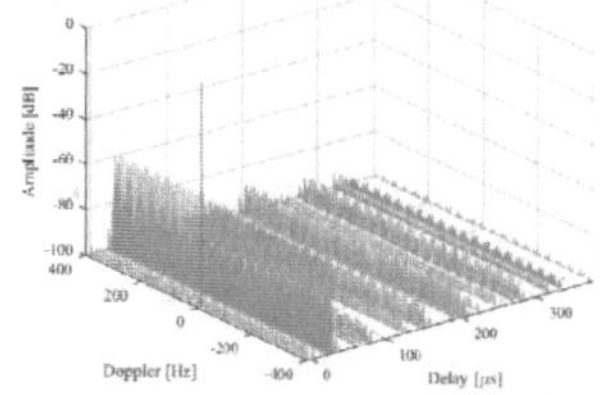

(a) DAB jamming PRS with a constant delay every frame.

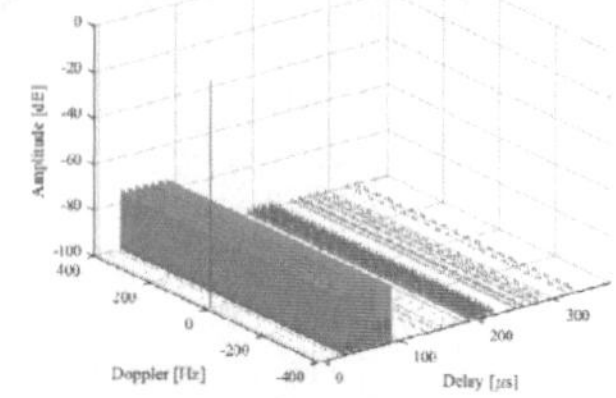

(b) DAB jamming PRS with a changing delay every frame.

Fig. 4: Output of DAB PR with PRS jamming applied

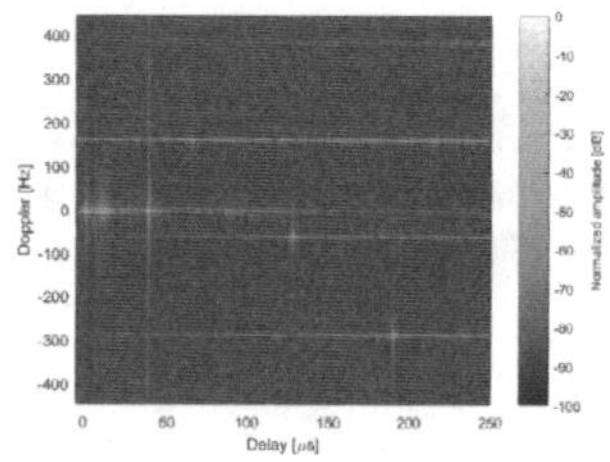

(a) DVB-T ARD with full pilot attack.

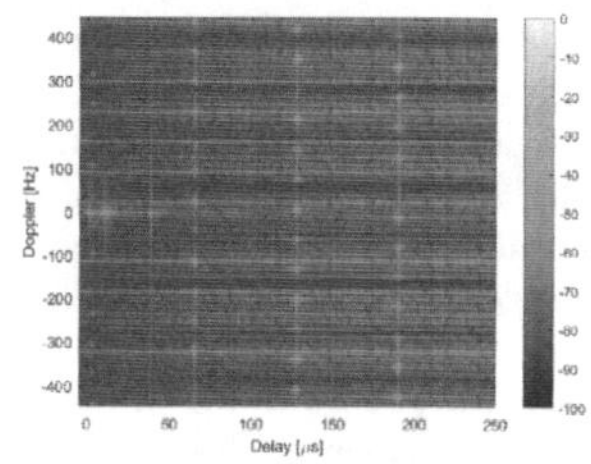

(b) DVB-T ARD with pulsed pilot attack every 13th symbol.

Fig. 5: Output of DVB-T PR with pilot jamming applied at $65\mu s$ delay and 160 Hz Doppler.

standard and can easily be used for an attack as shown in Figure 5.

In contrast to simple noise jamming, localised effects in the ARD map will not only increase the detection threshold but can also cause the system to report false targets.

IV. Conclusions

We have given a brief overview of investigations to counter FM, DAB and DVB-T based PR. In the case of FM based PR, we have shown that effective jamming can be achieved using relatively low power if the location of the receiver is known. The role of the DSC stage was investigated and it was shown that it has a significant impact on system performance in hostile environments. We also demonstrated that the deterministic parts of digital signals can be used to attack the PR.

References

[1] M. Inggs, C. Tong, D. W. O'Hagan, U. Böniger, U. Siegenthaler, C. Schüpbach, and H. Pratisto. *Noise Jamming of a FM Band Commensal Sensor.* IET Radar, Sonar Navigation, Volume 11, number 6, pages 946952, 2017.

[2] S. Paine and D. W. O'Hagan and M. Inggs and C. Schüpbach and U. Böniger *Evaluating the Performance of FM Based PCL Radar in the Presence of Jamming,*IEEE Transactions on Aerospace and Electronic Systems, pages 1-13, 2018

[3] C. Schüpbach, U. Böniger, 2016, *Jamming of DAB-based Passive Radar Systems*, 2016 European Radar conference (EuRAD)

[4] C. Schüpbach, D. W. OHagan, S. Paine, *Electronic Attacks on DVB-T-based Passive Radar Systems*, to be published in 2018 IEEE Radar Conference, 2018.

CW Radar Operation in the Focused Near-Field

Kristan A. Tuttle* and Herbert M. Aumann
Lincoln Laboratory, Massachusetts Institute of Technology
Lexington, MA 02420-6426
tuttle@ll.mit.edu

***Abstract*— In this paper we will show by computer simulation and by measurements that the horn antennas of a bi-static radar operating in the near-field have a distinct maximum at a non-zero range. By focusing the antennas on this hot spot a low-powered, continuous-wave Ku-band radar could detect flying mosquitoes at very short range.**

***Keywords*– Focused near-field antenna, CW radar, Mosquitoes**

I. INTRODUCTION

Most radars operate in the far-field of their antenna and the radar return, S, decreases as the fourth power of the range, R. This illustrated by the well known radar range equation [1]

$$S = \frac{P_t G^2 \lambda^2 \sigma}{(4\pi)^3 R^4} \tag{1}$$

where it is assumed that the transmit and receive antenna gains, G, are identical and the antennas and the target are in the far-field and can be treated as point sources. However, those assumptions are not valid in the near-field.

In this paper we consider the operation of a Ku-band continuous wave (CW) Doppler radar in the near-field. The radar uses separate transmit and receive horn antennas to minimize RF leakage. We will show by simulation and by measurements that the horn antennas have a region of increased field strength, or a "hot spot", in the near-field. Although this feature has been observed before [2], it has not been exploited by a radar. Focusing is a commonly employed technique for increasing the sensitivity of a radar in the near-field. We will show that the radar's sensitivity is further increased by operating in a bi-static mode which focuses the transmit and receive antennas on that hot spot. We will show that a low-powered radar can detect the vibrations of mosquitoes flying in the near-field of the antennas, a few wavelengths in front of the radar.

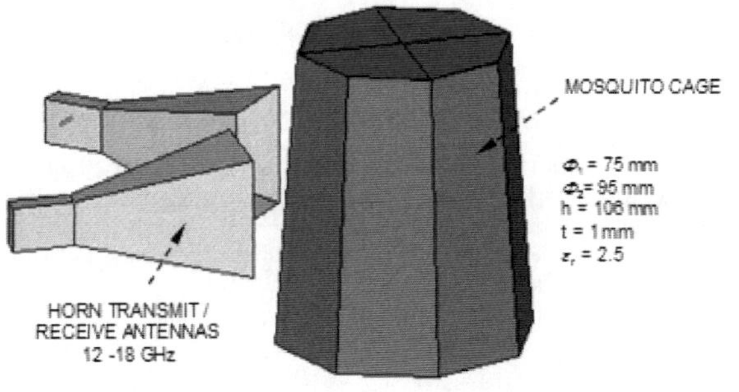

Fig. 1. Mosquito radar used in WIPL-D simulation

II. ANTENNA SIMULATION

The mosquito radar configuration shown in Fig. 1 was simulated in WIPL-D [3]. The transmit and receive antennas were $12-18$ GHz standard gain pyramidal horns. The horn feeds were 8 cm apart and angled 18 degrees to point to the center of a Styrofoam cup 12 cm away. The targets were mosquitoes flying inside the cup.

Near-field effects can be included in the radar range equation (1) by rewriting it as

$$S = \frac{P_t \lambda^2 \sigma}{(4\pi)^3} \cdot G^2(R) \tag{2}$$

where

$$G^2(R) = \left(\frac{G_T}{R_T^2}\right) \cdot \left(\frac{G_R}{R_R^2}\right) \tag{3}$$

and each term in (3) is proportional to the geometry dependent electric field strengths of the transmit and receive antennas calculated by an electromagnetic simulation.

EM simulations were carried out at 17.2 GHz with and without the Styrofoam cup. The results are show in Fig. 2 and Fig. 3.

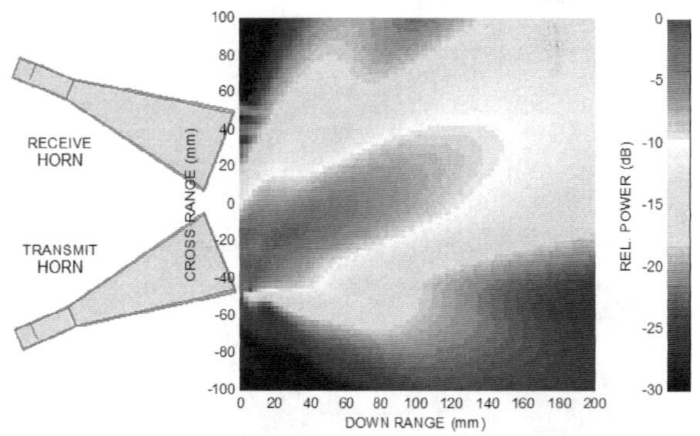

Fig. 2. Horn antenna near-field without mosquito cage

The field strength of the transmit horn antenna has a maximum about 30 mm in front of the horn face. The receive horn antenna field strength would be the vertical mirror image of Fig. 2. Fig. 3 is the product of the transmit and receive antenna fields and includes the effect of the Styrofoam cup. The maximum field strength now occurs about 40 mm in front to the antennas. Adding the Styrofoam cup to the simulation does not affect the location of this maximum. The simulation also shows a uniform illumination area inside the cup, enabling the radar to preferentially detect free-flying rather than resting mosquitoes.

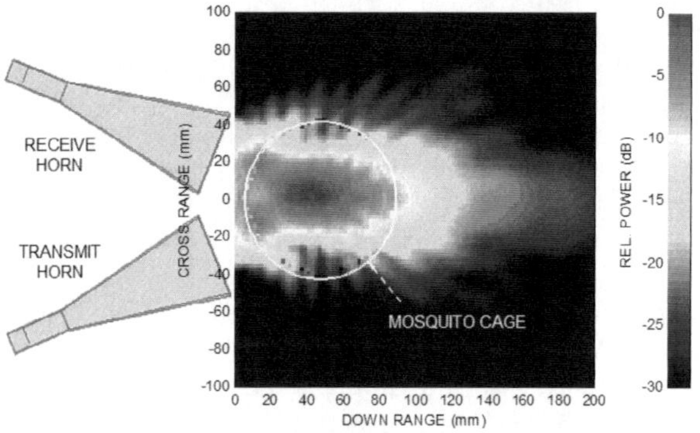

Fig. 3. Near-field of mosquito radar with cage

III. CW RADAR

The study of mosquito sounds is of interest in disease control [4]. An X-band Doppler radar microphone had been developed for detecting the vibrations of honeybees, which are perceived as sound by the human ear [5]. The block diagram of a similar Ku-band CW radar is shown in Fig. 4. Operating at a higher frequency had a significant sensitivity advantage in observing low radar cross section mosquitoes. The radar transmitted a maximum power of one watt. A picture of the antennas and mosquito cage is shown in Fig. 5.

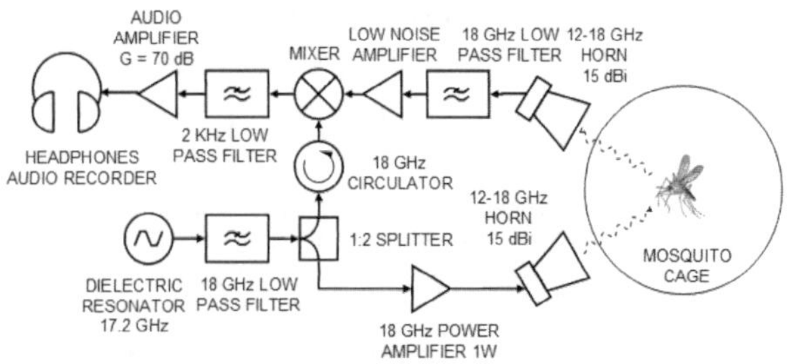

Fig. 4. Block diagram of CW Radar

Fig. 5. Transmit/receive horns and mosquito cage

IV. RESULTS

The radar sensitivity was determined as a function of range using as reference target a small earbud headphone broadcasting a 250 Hz tone. Fig. 6 illustrates that the EM simulations agreed with actual measurements, and the Styrofoam cup had negligible effects. Fig. 6 proves that there is a signal strength maximum in the near-field where the radar range equation (1) is no longer applicable.

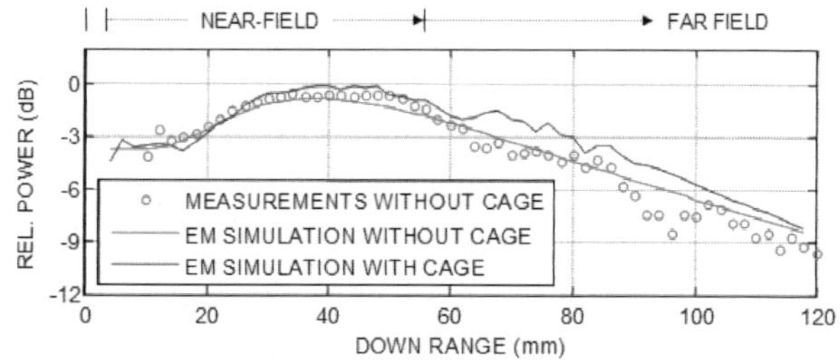

Fig. 6. Mosquito radar return with test target

Finally, the frequency spectrum in Fig. 7 illustrates that this radar is indeed capable of detecting the vibrations (sounds) of flying mosquitoes.

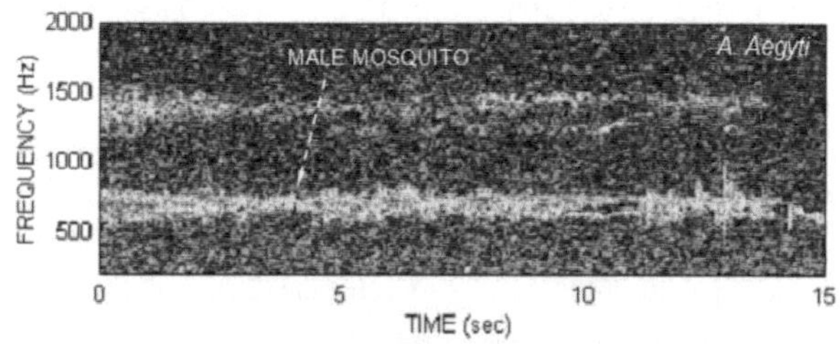

Fig. 7. Radar spectrum of flying mosquito

V. CONCLUSIONS

It has been shown through simulations and measurements that the mosquito radar has a near-field maximum at a non-zero range. The EM simulations provide the location in range of the near-field maximum.

DISTRIBUTION STATEMENT

Approved for public release: distribution unlimited.

This material is based upon work supported by the United States Air Force under Air Force Contract No. FA8702-15-D-0001. Any opinions, findings, conclusions or recommendations expressed in this material are those of the author(s) and do not necessarily reflect the views of the United States Air Force.

REFERENCES

[1] Merrill I. Skolnik, ed., *Introduction to Radar Systems,* McGraw-Hill, New York, 2001.

[2] A. Shishkova. N. Nikolay N and E. Ovsyannikova, "Near-field radiation from sectoral horns," Int. Conference on Antenna Theory and Techniques, 2007, pp 134 – 136.

[3] WIPL-D Microwave Pro CAD 2012, Software and User's Manual, WIPL-D d.o.o., Belgrade, 2012.

[4] L. Cator, B. Arthur, L. Harringtonand R. Hoy, "Harmonic Convergence in the Love Songs of the Dengue Vector Mosquito," Science, 2009, Vol. 323, pp. 1077 - 1079.

[5] H. Aumann and N. Emanetoglu, " The radar microphone: A new way of monitoring honey bee sounds,", 2016 IEEE Sensors, 2016, pp. 1 - 2.

A Boundary Element Method (BEM) for Modeling the Nonlocal Hydrodynamic Response in Deep-nm Plasmonic Wire Waveguides

Xuezhi Zheng
Department of Electrical Engineering (ESAT-TELEMIC)
KU Leuven
Leuven, Belgium
xuezhi.zheng@esat.kuleuven.be

Mario Kupresak
Department of Electrical Engineering (ESAT-TELEMIC)
KU Leuven
Leuven, Belgium
mario.kupresak@esat.kuleuven.be

Raj Mittra
Department of Electrical and Computer Engineering
University of Central Forida
Orlando, USA
rajmittr@gmail.com

Victor V. Moshchalkov
Laboratory of Solid State Physics and Magnetism
KU Leuven
Leuven, Belgium
victor.moshchalkov@fys.kuleuven.be

Guy A. E. Vandenbosch
Department of Electrical Engineering (ESAT-TELEMIC)
KU Leuven
Leuven, Belgiium
guy.vandenbosch@esat.kuleuven.be

***Abstract*—In this work, we present a Boundary Element Method (BEM) for modeling the optical response from a deep nanometric metallic wire waveguide with an arbitrary transverse cross section. Instead of using a *local* parameter, i.e. permittivity, to describe the electromagnetic (EM) property of the material constituting the guide, a *nonlocal* hydrodynamic model is considered to give a much finer description for the detailed dynamics of conduction electrons in the metal. Together with this nonlocal model, Maxwell's equations are solved within the framework of the Boundary Element Method (BEM). The numerical result is contrasted with the analytical one and a very good agreement is seen.**

***Keywords*—Boundary Element Method (BEM), Plasmonics, Deep-nanometer scale, Nonlocal Hydrodynamic Effects**

I. Introduction

Metallic nanowires that support surface plasmon waves (SPP) [1] have been considered as ideal sub-wavelength waveguiding structures at optical frequencies. Usually, the dynamics of free electrons inside the metal is described by *local* response material models, e.g. the Drude model [1]. However, when the critical size of the wire, e.g. the transverse dimension of the wire, approaches several nanometers, first order quantum effects, e.g. the quantum pressure, etc., start to appear and play a significant role in determining the optical response of the wire [2], which necessitates the introduction of the *nonlocal* hydrodynamic model. Computationally, the *nonlocal* model is described by a differential equation, and to obtain the full-wave solution from the wire, the differential equation must be solved together with Maxwell's equations. So far, both analytical and numerical approaches have been developed to solve the system of equations. On the one hand, for canonical structures [3], e.g. cylinders, solutions for both interior and exterior problems are derived, by matching the cylindrical wave functions on the boundary. On the other hand, as a general tool to tackle systems of differential equations, the differential-equation (DE) based algorithm, e.g. the Finite Difference Time Domain (FDTD) method, has been applied to study the *nonlocal* response of the wire guides. Alternatively, the integral-equation (IE) based methods have been pursued as a computationally more efficient replacement for the DE-based algorithms [4]. In this work, different than previous works based on EM fields, we describe the dynamics of the EM fields and electrons by using *vector and scalar* potentials. By further introducing the concepts of fictitious boundary charges and currents, we derive the boundary integral equations in terms of potentials. Then, the integral equations are solved by the MoM algorithm [5]. The dispersion relation of a gold nanowire guide is studied numerically. The numerical result agrees well with the analytical result.

II. Main Equations

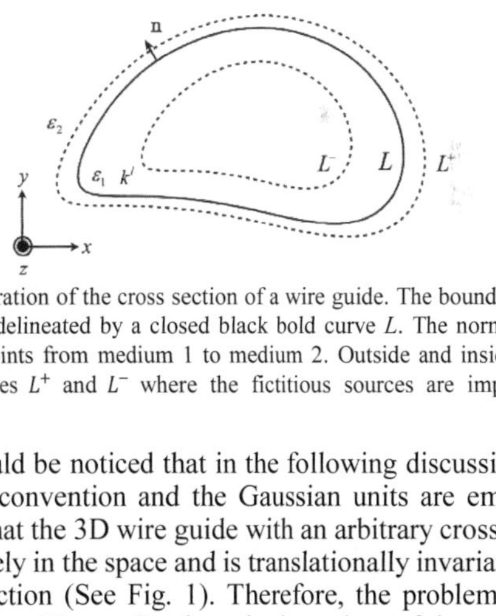

Fig. 1. Illustration of the cross section of a wire guide. The boundary of the structure is delineated by a closed black bold curve L. The normal of the boundary points from medium 1 to medium 2. Outside and inside L, two dashed curves L^+ and L^- where the fictitious sources are imposed are defined.

It should be noticed that in the following discussions, the $e^{-i\omega t}$ time convention and the Gaussian units are employed. Assume that the 3D wire guide with an arbitrary cross section stands freely in the space and is translationally invariant along the z direction (See Fig. 1). Therefore, the problem can be reduced to a 2D one. Further, the boundary of the transverse cross section (the L curve in Fig. 1) separates two regions, i.e., an external region (region 2), which is a *non-magnetic* homogeneous space characterized by a permittivity ε_2, and an interior region, which is a *nonlocal* metal characterized by a permittivity ε_1 for the transverse wave and a wave number k^l for the longitudinal wave. Lastly, a source is assumed to be in the external region. Given the above information, the main equations for the transverse waves in the external region are

$$\nabla^2 \mathbf{A}_2 + k_0^2 \varepsilon_2 \mathbf{A}_2 = -\frac{4\pi}{c}\mathbf{j},\ \nabla^2 \varphi_2 + k_0^2 \varepsilon_2 \varphi_2 = -4\pi \frac{\rho_2}{\varepsilon_2}. \quad (1)$$

The main equations for the internal region are

$$\nabla^2 \mathbf{A}_1 + k_0^2 \varepsilon_1 \mathbf{A}_1 = \mathbf{0},\ \nabla^2 \varphi_1 + k_0^2 \varepsilon_1 \varphi_1 = 0, \\ \nabla^2 \varphi_1^L + \left(k^l\right)^2 \varphi_1^L = 0. \tag{2}$$

In the above equations, $\mathbf{A}_i$ and φ_i are the vector and scalar potentials for the transverse waves, while φ^L represents the scalar potential for the longitudinal wave in the internal region. All the potentials are assumed to have a $e^{ik_z z}$ dependency. Across the boundary, the following physical quantities must be continuous

$$\mathbf{A}_i,\ \varphi_i,\ \frac{\partial \mathbf{A}_i}{\partial n} - ik_0 \varepsilon_i \varphi_i \mathbf{n},\ \varepsilon_i \mathbf{n} \cdot \left(ik_0 \mathbf{A}_i - \nabla \varphi_i\right). \tag{3}$$

In (3), **n** represents the normal of the boundary pointing from the internal region to the external region (See Fig. 1). Lastly, we assume that the normal component of the *free electron* polarization current is zero,

$$4\pi \chi_m \mathbf{n} \cdot \left(ik_0 \mathbf{A}_1 - \nabla \varphi_1\right) - \varepsilon_{bd} \mathbf{n} \cdot \left(-\nabla \varphi_1^L\right) = 0. \tag{4}$$

In the above equation, χ_m is the susceptibility of the metal and ε_{bd} is the permittivity for the bound electrons of the metal. For a detailed derivations for (1) - (4), we refer the readers to our previous work [6-7].

By introducing fictitious line charges and line currents on the boundary L (See Fig. 1) and matching the potentials on $L^{\pm}$ by the interface conditions in (3) and (4), the following boundary integral equations can be established,

$$\mathcal{G}_1 \sigma_1 - \mathcal{G}_2 \sigma_2 + \mathcal{G}_1^L \sigma_1^L = \phi^e, \tag{5}$$

$$\mathcal{G}_1 \mathbf{j}_1 - \mathcal{G}_2 \mathbf{j}_2 = \mathbf{A}^e, \tag{6}$$

$$\frac{\partial}{\partial n} \mathcal{G}_1 \mathbf{j}_1 - \frac{\partial}{\partial n} \mathcal{G}_2 \mathbf{j}_2 - ik\mathbf{n}\left(\varepsilon_1 \mathcal{G}_1 \sigma_1 - \varepsilon_2 \mathcal{G}_2 \sigma_2\right) = \boldsymbol{\alpha}, \tag{7}$$

$$\frac{\partial}{\partial n} \mathcal{G}_1 \varepsilon_1 \sigma_1 - \frac{\partial}{\partial n} \mathcal{G}_2 \varepsilon_2 \sigma_2 - ik\mathbf{n} \cdot \left(\mathcal{G}_1 \varepsilon_1 \mathbf{j}_1 - \mathcal{G}_2 \varepsilon_2 \mathbf{j}_2\right) = D^e, \tag{8}$$

$$4\pi \chi_{1,m} \left(\mathbf{n} \cdot ik \mathcal{G}_1 \mathbf{h}_1 - \frac{\partial}{\partial n} \mathcal{G}_1 \sigma_1\right) + \varepsilon_{1,bd} \frac{\partial}{\partial n} \mathcal{G}_1^L \sigma_1^L = 0. \tag{9}$$

ϕ^e, $\boldsymbol{A}^e$, $\boldsymbol{\alpha}$ and D^e are the quantities related with the external sources in region 2 and their definitions can be found in [6,7]. In (5) - (9), the $\mathcal{G}$ operator is defined as

$$\mathcal{G}\left(f\left(\boldsymbol{\rho}'\right)\right) = \int_L G\left(\boldsymbol{\rho}, \boldsymbol{\rho}'\right) f\left(\boldsymbol{\rho}'\right) d\boldsymbol{\rho}'. \tag{10}$$

The function $f(\boldsymbol{\rho}')$ in (10) can be *fictitious* surface charges and surface currents. Green's function in (10) is the Hankel function of the first kind,

$$G\left(\boldsymbol{\rho}, \boldsymbol{\rho}'\right) = 4\pi \cdot \frac{i}{4} H_0^{(1)}\left(k\left|\boldsymbol{\rho} - \boldsymbol{\rho}'\right|\right). \tag{11}$$

In (11), k can be the wave number of *transverse* or *longitudinal waves* in the external and internal regions.

III. Results

The system of equations in (5) - (9) can be solved by the MoM algorithm. We study the dispersion relation of an aluminum (Al) cylinder in vacuum. The radius of the cylinder is 1 nm. The boundary of the cylinder is discretized by N segments. In the calculations, we consider the cases where N are 30 and 40. The Al is characterized by three parameters: the plasma frequency $\omega_p = 14.2338$ ev; the damping frequency which is set to zero; and the Fermi velocity $v_f = 2.03 \times 10^8$ cm/s. The effects of bound electrons are neglected and hence the permittivity ε_{bd} is 1.

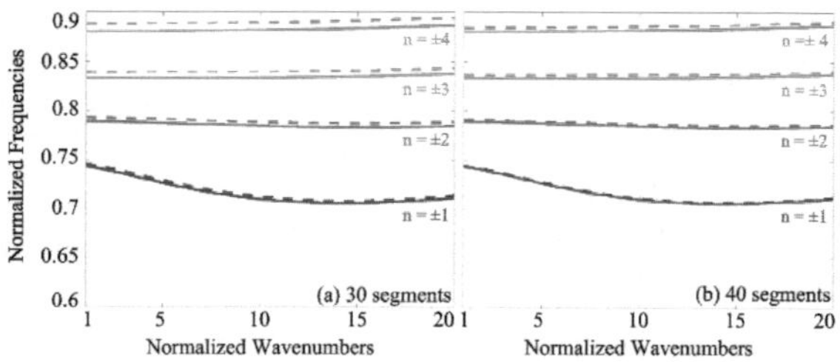

Fig. 2. Illustration of the dispersion diagram of an Al nanowire with a radius of 1 nm. In (a) and (b), the dispersion diagrams are presented for the cases N = 30 and N = 40. The solid and dashed lines represent the analytical and numerical results, respectively. The modes are marked by the blue, red, green and cyan colors to denote the cases $n = \pm 1, \pm 2, \pm 3$ and ± 4.

The dispersion diagram is generated by the generalized Mie theory [3] and the MoM codes, respectively. For both cases, we consider four guided wave modes that correspond to $n = \pm 1, \pm 2, \pm 3$ and ± 4 where n characterizes the order of the Bessel functions. It can be readily seen from Fig. 2 that the analytical and numerical results agree well with each other and the dispersion curves are almost identical for the case $N = 40$.

References

[1] S. A. Maier, "Plasmonics: fundamentals and applications," Springer (2007).

[2] F. Forstmann and R. R. Gerhardts, "Metal optics near the plasma frequency," Springer (2006).

[3] C. G. Aers, A. D. Boardman, and B. V. Paranjape, "Non-radiative surface plasmon-polariton modes of inhomogeneous metal circular cylinders," J. Phys. F: Metal Phys. 10, 53-65 (1980).

[4] W. Yan, N. A. Mortensen and M. Wubs, "Green's function surface-integral method for nonlocal response of plasmonic nanowires in arbitrary dielectric environments," Phys. Rev. B, 88, 155414 (2013).

[5] R. F. Harrington and J. L. Harrington, "Field computation by moment methods," Oxford University Press (1996).

[6] X. Zheng, M. Kupresak, R. Mittra, and G. A. E. Vandenbosch, "A boundary integral equation scheme for simulating the nonlocal hydrodynamic reponse of metallic antennas at deep-nanometer scales," IEEE Trans. Antennas Propag., vol. 66, no. 9, pp. 4759-4771 (2018).

[7] X. Zheng, M. Kupresak, V. V. Moshchalkov, R. Mittra and G. A. E. Vandenbosch, "A potential-based formalism for modeling local and hydrodynamic nonlocal responses from plasmonic waveguides," accepted by IEEE Trans. Antennas Propag. (2019).

Terahertz Modeling of 2D Electron Gas Systems using Multiphysics Time-Domain Solvers

Shubhendu Bhardwaj
Electrical and Computer Engineering
Florida International University
Miami, USA
sbhardwa@fiu.edu

***Abstract*—In this work, we present a rigorous numerical method for multiphysics and multiscale modeling of 2D electron gas (2DEG) systems at terahertz frequencies. Notably, we use finite difference time domain method for evaluation of Maxwell's equations, while hydrodynamic equations for electron transport modeling. The presented computation tools are useful for variety of terahertz modeling problems that use phenomenological understanding and optimization of the 2D electronics in transistors and graphene-like systems.**

Keywords—FDTD, 2D electron gas, HEMT, hydrodynamic, plasmonic modeling, terahertz.

I. Introduction

Modeling of 2D electron gas requires multiphysics approaches which should be accurate for electromagnetic wave propagation as well as for electron transport within semiconductor materials. This accurate modeling is useful for devices such as THz mixers, oscillators, waveguides, including those that are based on graphene. To achieve these, we present modeling methods that use finite difference time domain (FDTD) based solutions for electromagnetic wave propagation and hydrodynamic equations for electron transport modeling in the 2DEG systems. Contrary to prior approaches that either only use electron transport model (e.g. hydrodynamic modeling, Monte Carlo based modeling [1], among others) or only use full-wave type solutions and use Drude like modeling of the 2DEG [2], the current approach is rigorous in both- EM propagation as well as in transport of electrons.

In the following sections, we present the fundamental equations used in the modeling, solution-algorithms used and then pursue tests and validations using prior measurements and certain analytically solved canonical problems.

II. Governing Equations for Multiphysics Modeling

Solution requires modeling of electrodynamic fields via

$$\nabla \times \vec{H} = \frac{\partial \vec{D}}{\partial t} + \vec{J} + \sigma \vec{E}, \quad \text{and} \tag{1}$$

$$\nabla \times \vec{E} = -\frac{\partial \vec{B}}{\partial t} - \sigma^{*} \vec{H}. \tag{2}$$

For 2D TE_Z solution, electric field $\vec{E} = \hat{x}E_x + \hat{y}E_y$ is used (Fig. 1(a)). Electrical and magnetic conductivity parameters, i.e. σ and σ^*, are used for the modeling of anisotropic, perfectly matched layer surrounding the domain. Electron transport in the channel is modelled via hydrodynamic equations given by,

$$\frac{\partial n_{sh}}{\partial t} + \frac{\partial j}{\partial x} = 0, \quad \text{and} \tag{3}$$

$$\frac{\partial j}{\partial t} + v\frac{\partial j}{\partial x} + \frac{j\partial v}{\partial x} = -\frac{qnE_x}{m_e} - \frac{j}{\tau} - \frac{KT}{m_e}. \tag{4}$$

Here n_{sh} is the sheet carrier density, j (= $n_{sh}v$) is the sheet current and v is the electron velocity within the 2DEG channel. τ refers to the momentum relaxation time and m_e is the effective electron mass, q = 1.6×10−19 C is the charge-magnitude of a single electron, T is the electron temperature in the channel and K is the Boltzmann constant.

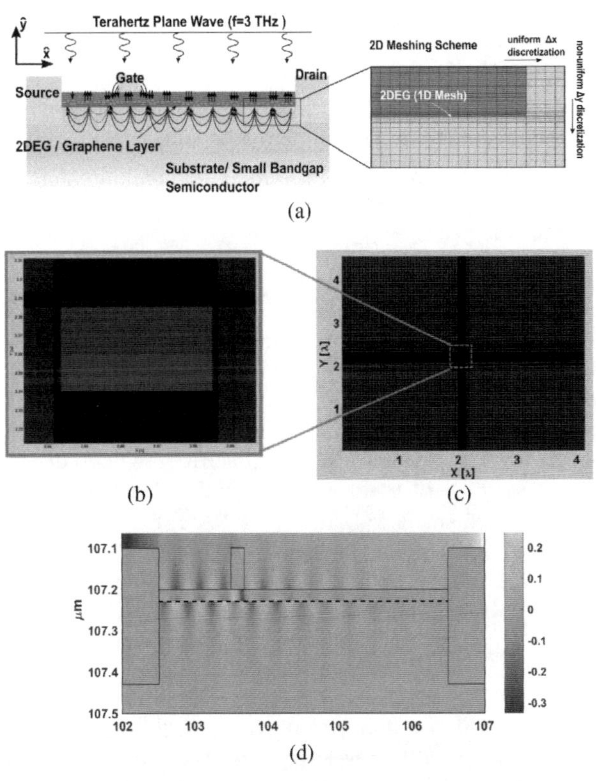

Fig. 1. (a) A typical HEMT with 2DEG (b) zoomed in view of the 2DEG region, showing dense meshing near the 2DEG (c) a typical to-scale model for the modeling of the 2DEG problems (d) plasmonic field distribution, illustrating propagation of the plasma-wave along the 2DEG.

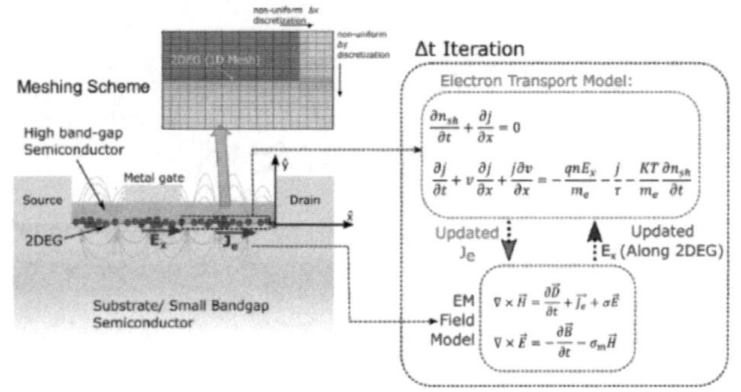

Fig. 2. Left: Coupled topology of hydrodynamic and Maxwell's equations as applied for plasmonic modeling of oscillations within High Electron Mobility Transistor (HEMT) device. Right: Typical mesh with minimum $\Delta x=\lambda/1000$, that limits the overall simulation time due to small step-size.

III. Modeling of HEMTs and Associated Challenges

Computational burden of global-full-wave models comes from its multiscale nature, i.e. the fact that computations for electron transport and electrodynamic fields must be carried out in the same numerical grid (Fig. 1(b), (c)). Since the cell-size of the grid, as required by the electron transport, is much finer (100 to 1000 times finer) than that needed for electromagnetic wave propagation, the electromagnetic solutions are unnecessarily over computed. This cannot be avoided in general due to coupled nature of solution. This is the core issue in all multiphysics, multiscale problems, including the ones targeted in this proposal. Mathematically, we state the above by considering the fundamental limitation on the Maxwell's equation solver Finite Difference Time Domain (FDTD)

$$\Delta t_{FDTD} \leq \frac{\frac{1}{c}}{\left(\sqrt{\frac{1}{\Delta x_{min}^2}+\frac{1}{\Delta y_{min}^2}}\right)}. \tag{5}$$

That is, the time step for one iteration of updating fields, Δt, is a limited by the smallest size-grid in the domain (Δx_{min} along x or Δy_{min}along y axis in Fig. 3). In physical terms, Δt cannot be larger than the time-taken by the wave to cross the smallest grid-size in the domain. In a multiscale problem due to subwavelength oscillations (as shown in Fig. 1(d)), Δx_{min} and Δy_{min} are much smaller ($\lambda/500$ to $\lambda/1000$) than in a single-physics electromagnetic simulation ($\lambda/10$). In other words, grids designed for electron transport modeling start to limit the efficiency of the Maxwell's equation solver. The solution algorithm is presented in Fig. 2 and is further outlined in the full-paper [3].

The fidelity of the developed model is demonstrated via its comparison with experimental data as well as with prior analytic models. Fig. 3 shows that plasmonic resonances observed in grating-gated 2DEG channel in large periodic HEMT structure. These experimental observations [4] have been verified by our multiphysics code as noted in the figure. Furthermore, Fig. 3 (right) shows results from model applications for two canonical problems- 1) wave-propagation in 2D electron gas (2DEG) placed in a dielectric media and 2) similar 2DEG with a metallic gate (gated-2DEG). The outcome of the simulation is compared against the analytical solutions for these problems, and comparisons are shown. The results clearly demonstrate that model-predicted values agree with the prior measurement data. Furthermore, analytical models also show close agreement with our simulations, where large 2DEG sheets are chosen for simulating canonical problems. Overall accuracy of the developed model is demonstrated for different cases.

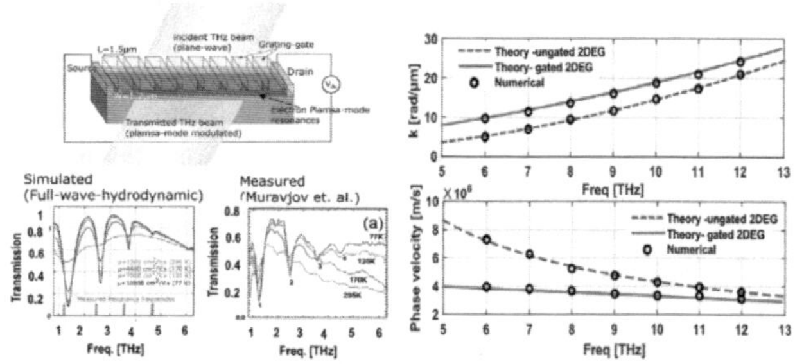

Fig. 3. Left: Experimental validation of previously developed codes. Transmission valleys due to resonant losses from [4] in 2DEG matched well with those predicted by the model. Right: Developed model used for identifying plasma-modes in two canonical problems, namely 2DEG layer in bulk dielectric media [5] and gated 2DEG in bulk dielectric media [6].

IV. Conclusions

In conclusion, a rigorous, multiphysics, multiscale model is developed, and its accuracy is demonstrated for 2DEG based devices. The model successfully incorporated the two-physical phenomenon, i.e. modeling of electron transport using hydrodynamic modeling as well as modeling of electrodynamic phenomenology using full-wave solution. The solution seems to show the required accuracy for terahertz problems and shows that such modeling can practical terahertz devices. We also note challenges associated with such modeling primarily point to need of unconditionally stable algorithms for such multiphysics problems, where the simulation times are not limited by the Courant condition.

References

[1] J. Mateos and T. Gonzalez, "Plasma Enhanced Terahertz Rectification and Noise in InGaAs HEMTs," IEEE Transactions on Terahertz Science and Technology, vol. 2, no. 5, pp. 562–569, Sept 2012.

[2] L. Vicarelli, M. S. Vitiello, D. Coquillat, A. Lombardo, A. C. Ferrari, W. Knap, M. Polini, V. Pellegrini, and A. Tredicucci, "Graphene field-effect transistors as room-temperature terahertz detectors," Nature Materials, vol. 11, pages 865–871 (2012).

[3] S. Bhardwaj, F. L. Teixeira, and J. L. Volakis, "Fast Modeling of Terahertz Plasma-Wave Devices Using Unconditionally Stable FDTD Methods," in IEEE Journal on Multiscale and Multiphysics Computational Techniques, vol. 3, pp. 29-36, 2018.

[4] A. V. Muravjov et. al., "Temperature dependence of plasmonic terahertz absorption in grating-gate gallium-nitride transistor structures," Applied Physics Letters, vol. 96, no. 4, p. 042105, 2010.

[5] W. Knap, Y. Deng, S. Rumyantsev, and M. S. Shur, "Resonant detection of subterahertz and terahertz radiation by plasma waves in submicron field-effect transistors," Appl. Phys. Lett., vol. 81, no. 24, p. 4637, 2002.

[6] El Fatimy et al., "Resonant and voltage-tunable terahertz detection in InGaAs/InP nanometer transistors," Appl. Phys. Lett., vol. 89, no. 13, pp. 131926-1–131926-3, Sep. 2006.

FPGA-Based FDTD Accelerators for 2DEG Plasma-Wave Device Modeling at THz

Hasantha Malavipathirana[1], Arjuna Madanayake[1], Fernando L. Teixeira[2], John L. Volakis[1], Shubhendu Bhardwaj[1]
[1]*Electrical and Computer Engineering, Florida International University (FIU), Miami, Florida, USA*
[2]*Electrical and Computer Engineering, The Ohio State University, Columbus, OH, USA*
hmala005@fiu.edu, amadanay@fiu.edu, teixeira.5@osu.edu, jvolakis@fiu.edu, sbhardwa@fiu.edu

***Abstract*—Plasmonic waves supported on 2DEG devices at terahertz (THz) frequencies are important for future high-bandwidth wireless communication and imaging systems. The design of such devices requires solution of computationally intensive Finite Difference Time Domain (FDTD) based multi-physics models which can be slow even with the use of GPUs. In this work, application-specific custom computing architectures based on reconfigurable deep nano-CMOS FPGA technologies, such as the 14nm Xilinx ZynQ RF SoC, are explored for solving the above problem using massively-parallel fine-grain pipelined multirate systolic-array processors.**

***Index Terms*—FDTD, PDE, plasmonic waves, THz, Xilinx.**

I. Introduction

High-frequency devices that use plasma-wave effects found in 2D electron gas (2DEG) are expected to find applications in high-speed communications, sensing, and imaging at frequencies in the 300 GHz - 10 THz range. The ability to conduct physics-based simulations using finite-difference time-domain (FDTD) models while also incorporating magnetohydrodynamics (MHD) for electron transport, is crucial for emerging device engineering/research, so that amplifiers, mixers, oscillators and detectors, can be reliably fabricated.

The time-limitation for the plasmonic FDTD simulations comes from slow-wave type plasma-wave oscillations, which exhibit wavelengths that are 10 to 1000 times smaller than free-space wavelength λ and require a mesh-size of around $\approx \lambda/5000$ [1], [2]. For such a simulation-domain, Courant-Friedrich-Levy (CFL) condition would require FDTD time-step to be $\approx 10^{-17}s$. Such a small time-step would result in long simulation time. Progress has been made recently in the unconditionally-stable simulation of 2DEG systems. These 2DEG systems can be implemented using a range of semiconductor heterojunctions (e.g., GaN/AlGaN GaAs/AlGaAs) or graphene [2], [3]. The FDTD models in [2], [3] enables the creation of multiphysics simulations that will be a platform for future generations of radio technologies in the THz regime.

We propose a fast implementation of 2DEG FDTD models using integrated circuits (ICs) [4] to enable real-time operation albeit at a suitably chosen slow-down factor. The proposed computing architecture using FPGA is shown in Fig. 1. FDTD algorithm allows such evaluation of wireless communication concepts, e.g, a slow-down factor of 1000 allows a 1 THz carrier frequency with bandwidth of 100 GHz to be scaled down to a 1 GHz carrier frequency and bandwidth of 100 MHz; now, the multi-physics modeling is still at 1 THz but the frequency and bandwidth scaling allows modulations and wireless waveforms to be applied in real-time to the digital simulator. This scheme is proposed to facilitate a better understanding of how the plasmonic THz devices would process information-rich symbols. Today's technologies such as an RF System on Chip (SoC) from Xilinx may allow THz device models to be excited by high-bandwidth modulated signals with FDTD models being evaluated at similar frame-rates. Keeping the FPGA accelerator fed with data at the required rates is a challenge that needs careful design.

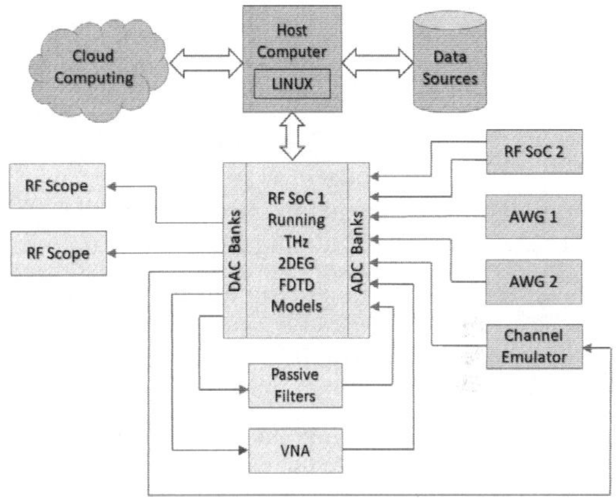

Fig. 1. Proposed FPGA computing architecture consisting of Xilinx RF SoC running fast 2DEG FDTD models, with interfaces to host-PC via ethernet, ADCs connecting to arbitrary waveform generators (AWG), RF scopes for visual monitoring via DACs, analog passives and RF instrumentation (hardware in the loop) capabilities.

II. Fast Multiphysics Modeling using FDTD

Unconditionally-stable fast FDTD models for terahertz plasmonic modeling of electron mobility transistors (HEMTs) can be referred from [2], [3]. This modeling requires electromagnetic field solver as well as electron transport solver in the 2DEG channel. The framework presented in [2] uses hydrodynamic equations for channel modeling and Maxwell's equation for the modeling of dielectric media. First two moments of Boltzmann transport equations (BTE), particle conservation and momentum conservation equations are used to model the channel. For 2-D confined electron gas, the hydrodynamic equations are; $\frac{\partial n_{sh}}{\partial t} + \frac{\partial j}{\partial x} = 0$ and $\frac{\partial j}{\partial t} + v\frac{\partial j}{\partial x} + j\frac{\partial v}{\partial x} = \frac{-qnE_x}{m_e} - \frac{j}{\tau} - \frac{KT}{m_e}\frac{\partial n_{sh}}{\partial x}$. Here n_{sh} is the sheet carrier density, $j(= n_{sh}v)$ is the sheet current and v is the electron velocity inside 2DEG channel. E_x is the x-directed electric field along the channel, τ is the momentum relaxation time and m_e refers to the effective electron mass. $q = 1.6 \times 10^{-19}C$ is the electron charge, T is the electron temperature in the channel and K is the Boltzmann constant. The field excitation term, $\frac{-qnE_x}{m_e}$, causes electromagnetic field variations and thus electron-density oscillations are created within the channel. This plasma-mode excitation results in propagation of AC power within the channel. The resulting electromagnetic field can be modeled using Maxwell's curl equations, namely, $\nabla \times \vec{H} = \frac{\partial \vec{D}}{\partial t} + \vec{J} + \sigma\vec{E}$ and $\nabla \times \vec{E} = -\frac{\partial \vec{B}}{\partial t} - \sigma^* \vec{H}$, that are solved self-consistently together with HD equations. 2D TE_z field polarization is considered and accordingly electric field $\vec{E} = \hat{x}E_x + \hat{y}E_y$ and magnetic field $\vec{H}$ are represented in the equation. Electric and magnetic flux densities are $\vec{D} = \epsilon\vec{E}$ and $\vec{B} = \mu\vec{H}$ where, permittivity ϵ and permeability μ are assumed to be scalar quantities. Electrical and magnetic conductivities are σ and σ^* respectively. Source term $\vec{J}$ is due to the current generated by plasmonic oscillations. This term is related to sheet current as $\vec{J} = \frac{-q(j-j_0)}{t_{2DEG}}\hat{x}$, where, t_{2DEG} is the thickness of 2DEG layer. Here, $j - j_0$ is the AC current responsible for radiation from the channel, with j_0 being the initial DC current which does not contribute to radiation.

A. *Time-Space Discretization of HD and ED Equations*

To obtain numerical solutions, partial differential equations (PDEs) are converted to corresponding time and space difference equations. An upwind difference scheme [2], [5], [6] is applied to maintain the stability of the algorithm. The obtained difference equations are [2],

$$n_{sh}\,|_{i+1/2}^{n+1} = n_{sh}\,|_{i+1/2}^{n} - \frac{\Delta t}{\Delta x}[j\,|_{i+1}^{n} - j\,|_{i-1}^{n}], \quad (1)$$

$$\begin{aligned} j\,|_i^{n+1} = j\,|_i^n - \Delta t\frac{qn_{sh}\,|_i^n\, E_{ch}\,|_i^n}{m_e} - \Delta t\frac{j\,|_i^n}{\tau_n} \\ -\Delta t\frac{KT}{m_e}\frac{[n_{sh}\,|_{i+1/2}^n - n_{sh}\,|_{i-1/2}^n]}{\Delta x} - Conv\,|_i^n, \end{aligned} \quad (2)$$

where, as per the upwind scheme, the convective term *Conv* is defined based on the direction of flow of electrons at that point. At any given spatial index *i* and time iteration *n*, if $v\,|_i^n > 0$, then

$$Conv\,|_i^n = \frac{\Delta t}{\Delta x} j\,|_i^n\,[v\,|_i^n - v\,|_{i-1}^n] + \frac{\Delta t}{\Delta x} v\,|_i^n\,[j\,|_i^n - j\,|_{i-1}^n], \quad (3)$$

and if $v\,|_i^n < 0$,

$$Conv\,|_i^n = \frac{\Delta t}{\Delta x} j\,|_i^n\,[v\,|_{i+1}^n - v\,|_i^n] + \frac{\Delta t}{\Delta x} v\,|_i^n\,[j\,|_{i+1}^n - j\,|_i^n]. \quad (4)$$

Here, *i* represents spatial grid-point index along $\hat{x}$ direction and *n* represents the time iteration index.

B. *Unconditionally Stable Fast FDTD Methods*

The two models in [2], [3] use alternating direction implicit (ADI) FDTD [7] coupled with hydrodynamic equations and an iterative-ADI based FDTD method [8], [9] coupled with hydrodynamic equations. More time reduction is allowed in the second method due to iterative corrections applied at large time steps. First, electrodynamic equations are solved using ADI based FDTD method and electric/magnetic field terms are updated in the domain. Then using the updated values of electric field (E_x), hydrodynamic equations are solved for the same time iteration. The resulting current values are used as source terms in electrodynamic solution for the next iteration.

III. Proposed Computing Architecture

The fast FDTD model is suited for massively-parallel systolic array implementation using digital CMOS. Software realizations on GPU are possible [10] but do not exploit digital computing capabilities because of instruction fetch-execute cycle that adds an overhead. A massively-parallel fine-grain pipelined hardware implementation, based on processor arrays that directly implement a parallel realization of FDTD makes maximum use of digital capabilities. Systolic arrays are locally interconnected and have low critical path delays, leading to maximum throughput. Information is moved along in pipelines and algorithms exploit local memory, making them fast and efficient. In presented work, we will present a method for designing computing cores that can map the outlined nonlinear problem to hardware architecture.

References

[1] M. A. Khorrami, S. El-Ghazaly, H. Naseem, and S. Yu, "Global modeling of active terahertz plasmonic devices," IEEE Transactions on Terahertz Science and Technology, vol. 4, no. 1, pp. 101–109, Jan. 2014.

[2] S. Bhardwaj, F. L. Teixeira, and J. L. Volakis, "Fast modeling of terahertz plasma-wave devices using unconditionally stable FDTD methods," IEEE Journal on Multiscale and Multiphysics Computational Techniques, vol. 3, pp. 29–36, 2018.

[3] S. Bhardwaj, "Hybrid Numerical Models for Fast Design of Terahertz Plasmonic Devices," Ph.D. dissertation, The Ohio State University, 2017.

[4] R. N. Schneider, M. M. Okoniewski, and L. E. Turner, "Finite-difference time-domain method in custom hardware," IEEE Microwave and Wireless Components Letters, vol. 12, no. 12, pp. 488–490, Dec. 2002.

[5] D. Vasileska, S. Goodnick, and G. Klimeck, Computational Electronics, Semiclassical and Quantum Device Modeling and Simulation. Boca Raton, FL, USA: CRC Press, 2010.

[6] A. Aste and R. Vahldieck, "Time-domain simulation of the full hydrodynamic model," Int. J. Numerical Model., Electron. Netw., Devices Fields, vol. 16, no. 2, pp. 161–174, 2003, [Online]. Available: http://dx.doi.org/10.1002/jnm.491.

[7] T. Namiki, "A new FDTD algorithm based on alternating-direction implicit method," IEEE Transactions on Microwave Theory and Techniques, vol. 47, no. 10, pp. 2003–2007, Oct. 1999.

[8] S. Wang, F. L. Teixeira, and J. Chen, "An iterative ADI-FDTD with reduced splitting error," IEEE Microwave and Wireless Components Letters, vol. 15, no. 2, pp. 92–94, Feb. 2005.

[9] F. Zheng, Z. Chen, and J. Zhang, "A finite-difference time-domain method without the courant stability conditions," IEEE Microwave and Guided Wave Letters, vol. 9, no. 11, pp. 441–443, Nov. 1999.

[10] C. Ong, M. Weldon, D. Cyca, and M. Okoniewski, "Acceleration of large-scale FDTD simulations on high performance GPU clusters," in 2009 IEEE Antennas and Propagation Society International Symposium, June 2009, pp. 1–4.

On Higher-order Nyström Discretization of Scalar Potential Integral Equation for Penetrable Scatterers

Rui Chen, and Hakan Bagci
Division of Computer, Electrical, and Mathematical Science and Engineering
King Abdullah University of Science and Technology (KAUST), Thuwal, 23955-6900, Saudi Arabia
e-mails: {rui.chen, hakan.bagci}@kaust.edu.sa

Abstract—**A higher-order Nyström scheme is developed for discretizing the scalar potential integral equation (SPIE) for analyzing electromagnetic field/wave interactions on penetrable scatterers. The unknown scalar potential and its normal derivative are expanded using higher-order Lagrange interpolation functions. Inserting this expansion into the SPIE and point-testing the resulting equation yields a matrix system that is solved for the unknown expansion coefficients. Numerical results demonstrate that this matrix system is well-conditioned regardless of the discretization order and mesh density, and that its solution has higher-order convergence.**

I. Introduction

Electromagnetic scattering from homogeneous penetrable objects are often analyzed by solving different combinations of electric and magnetic field surface integral equations (EFIE and MFIE) [1]. However, it is well-known that the EFIE suffers from low-frequency and dense-mesh break downs [2], [3]. Even though the MFIE is always well-conditioned (thanks to its second-kind nature), its solution obtained using traditional methods at low-frequencies is inaccurate [4], [5]. Even though these problems can be alleviated using new discretization and preconditioning techniques, these often come at the expense of implementation simplicity.

In recent years, potential surface integral equations have been proposed as "break-down free" alternatives to field surface integral equations. These equations have first been formulated for perfect electrically conducting objects in [6], [7] and later extended for penetrable objects [8], [9]. In [9], a de-coupled formulation, which allows for solving for scalar and vector potential individually, has been proposed.

In this work, a higher-order Nyström method [10] is used to solve the scalar potential integral equation (SPIE) formulated in [9]. The proposed method uses higher-order basis functions defined at a set of discrete points to expand the unknown potential and its normal derivative on the surface of the scatterer, inserts this expansion in the SPIE, and point-tests the resulting equation to obtain a matrix system. This matrix system is solved for the unknown expansion coefficients. Numerical results demonstrate that this matrix system is well-conditioned regardless of the discretization order and mesh density, and that its solution has higher-order convergence.

II. Formulation

Let S denote the surface of a homogeneous penetrable scatterer residing in an unbounded background medium. The permittivity, permeability, and wavenumber of the background medium and scatterer are $\{\varepsilon_1, \mu_1, k_1\}$ and $\{\varepsilon_2, \mu_2, k_2\}$, respectively. The scatterer is excited by an incident scalar potential $\phi^{\mathrm{i}}(\mathbf{r})$. Using the scalar Green's theorem, the governing Helmholtz equation, and the equivalence principle, the scalar potentials outside S (exterior problem) and inside S (interior problem), $\phi_1(\mathbf{r})$ and $\phi_2(\mathbf{r})$, can be represented in terms of the integrals of $\{\phi_1(\mathbf{r}'), \partial_{n'}\phi_1(\mathbf{r}')\}$, $\mathbf{r}' \in S$ and $\{\phi_2(\mathbf{r}'), \partial_{n'}\phi_2(\mathbf{r}')\}$, $\mathbf{r}' \in S$, respectively. Here, $\partial_{n'} = \hat{\mathbf{n}}(\mathbf{r}') \cdot \nabla'$ and $\hat{\mathbf{n}}(\mathbf{r}')$ is the outward pointing unit normal vector on S at $\mathbf{r}'$ [9]. Linearly combining these representations and their normal derivatives on S, and enforcing the boundary conditions $\phi_1(\mathbf{r}') = \phi_2(\mathbf{r}')$, $\mathbf{r}' \in S$ and $\varepsilon_1 \partial_{n'}\phi_1(\mathbf{r}') = \varepsilon_2 \partial_{n'}\phi_2(\mathbf{r}')$, $\mathbf{r}' \in S$ yield the following SPIE [9]:

$$\begin{bmatrix} \frac{\alpha_1+\alpha_2}{2} I + C_{11} & C_{12} \\ C_{21} & \frac{\beta_1+\beta_2}{2} I + C_{22} \end{bmatrix} \begin{bmatrix} \phi \\ \frac{\varepsilon_1}{k_0\varepsilon_0}\partial_n \phi \end{bmatrix} = \begin{bmatrix} \alpha_1 \phi^{\mathrm{i}} \\ \frac{\beta_1\varepsilon_1}{k_0\varepsilon_0}\partial_n \phi^{\mathrm{i}} \end{bmatrix} \quad (1)$$

where $C_{11} = -\alpha_1 \tilde{D}_1 + \alpha_2 \tilde{D}_2$, $C_{12} = (\alpha_1 k_0 \varepsilon_0/\varepsilon_1) S_1 - (\alpha_2 k_0 \varepsilon_0/\varepsilon_2) S_2$, $C_{21} = -(\beta_1\varepsilon_1/k_0\varepsilon_0) N_1 + (\beta_2\varepsilon_2/k_0\varepsilon_0) N_2$, and $C_{22} = \beta_1 \tilde{D}_1' - \beta_2 \tilde{D}_2'$ with

$$S_i[x] = \int_S G_i(\mathbf{r}, \mathbf{r}') x(\mathbf{r}') d\mathbf{r}'$$

$$\tilde{D}_i[x] = \fint_S \partial_{n'} G_i(\mathbf{r}, \mathbf{r}') x(\mathbf{r}') d\mathbf{r}'$$

$$\tilde{D}_i'[x] = \fint_S \partial_n G_i(\mathbf{r}, \mathbf{r}') x(\mathbf{r}') d\mathbf{r}'$$

$$N_i[x] = \partial_n \int_S \partial_{n'} G_i(\mathbf{r}, \mathbf{r}') x(\mathbf{r}') d\mathbf{r}'$$

and $G_i(\mathbf{r}, \mathbf{r}') = e^{-jk_i R}/4\pi R$, $R = |\mathbf{r} - \mathbf{r}'|$. Here, ε_0, μ_0, and k_0 are the permittivity, permeability, and wavenumber in free-space, and α_1, α_2, β_1, and β_2 are constant coefficients. β_1 and β_2 are selected to satisfy $\beta_1\varepsilon_1 = \beta_2\varepsilon_2$ so that the hyper-singularity in C_{21} is cancelled out.

To numerically solve (1), S is discretized into N_{p} curvilinear triangular patches and $\phi(\mathbf{r}')$ and $(\varepsilon_1/k_0\varepsilon_0)\partial_{n'}\phi(\mathbf{r}')$ are expanded as:

$$\phi(\mathbf{r}') = \sum_{p=1}^{N_{\mathrm{p}}} \sum_{i=1}^{N_{\mathrm{i}}} \vartheta(\mathbf{r}') L_{ip}(\mathbf{r}') \{\mathbf{I}_1\}_{ip}$$

$$\frac{\varepsilon_1}{k_0\varepsilon_0} \partial_{n'}\phi(\mathbf{r}') = \sum_{p=1}^{N_{\mathrm{p}}} \sum_{i=1}^{N_{\mathrm{i}}} \vartheta(\mathbf{r}') L_{ip}(\mathbf{r}') \{\mathbf{I}_2\}_{ip} \quad (2)$$

where N_{i} is the number of interpolation points on each patch, $\vartheta(\mathbf{r})$ is the inverse of the Jacobian, $L_{ip}(\mathbf{r})$ is the Lagrange interpolator defined at $\mathbf{r}_{ip}$ (interpolation point i on patch p), and $\{\mathbf{I}_1\}_{ip}$ and $\{\mathbf{I}_2\}_{ip}$ are the unknown expansion coefficients. Inserting (2) into (1), and testing the resulting equation at $\mathbf{r}_{jq}$, $j = 1,..,N_{\mathrm{i}}$, $q = 1,..,N_{\mathrm{p}}$, yield a linear matrix system:

$$\begin{bmatrix} \mathbf{Z}_{11} & \mathbf{Z}_{12} \\ \mathbf{Z}_{21} & \mathbf{Z}_{22} \end{bmatrix} \begin{bmatrix} \mathbf{I}_1 \\ \mathbf{I}_2 \end{bmatrix} = \begin{bmatrix} \mathbf{V}_1 \\ \mathbf{V}_2 \end{bmatrix}. \quad (3)$$

Here, $\{\mathbf{V}_1\}_{jq} = \alpha_1 \phi^{\mathrm{i}}(\mathbf{r}_{jq})$, $\{\mathbf{V}_2\}_{jq} = (\beta_1 \varepsilon_1 / k_0 \varepsilon_0)\partial_n \phi^{\mathrm{i}}(\mathbf{r}_{jq})$,

$\{\mathbf{Z}_{11}\}_{jq,ip} = (\alpha_1+\alpha_2)\vartheta(\mathbf{r}_{jq})\delta_{ij}\delta_{pq}/2 + C_{11}[\vartheta(\mathbf{r})L_{ip}(\mathbf{r})]$,
$\{\mathbf{Z}_{12}\}_{jq,ip} = C_{12}[\vartheta(\mathbf{r})L_{ip}(\mathbf{r})]$, $\{\mathbf{Z}_{21}\}_{jq,ip} = C_{21}[\vartheta(\mathbf{r})L_{ip}(\mathbf{r})]$,
$\{\mathbf{Z}_{22}\}_{jq,ip} = (\beta_1+\beta_2)\vartheta(\mathbf{r}_{jq})\delta_{ij}\delta_{pq}/2 + C_{22}[\vartheta(\mathbf{r})L_{ip}(\mathbf{r})]$.

III. Numerical Results

The proposed scheme is used for analyzing electromagnetic scattering from a unit dielectric sphere with $\varepsilon_2 = 2\varepsilon_0$ and $\mu_2 = \mu_0$ residing in a background medium with $\varepsilon_1 = \varepsilon_0$ and $\mu_1 = \mu_0$. The sphere is centered at the origin. The excitation is a plane wave: $\phi^{\mathrm{i}}(\mathbf{r}) = e^{-jk_1 z}/\sqrt{\mu_1 \varepsilon_1}$ with frequency $f = 300$ MHz. The transpose-free quasi-minimal residual method [11] is used to solve the matrix system iteratively. The residual error threshold is set to 10^{-6}.

The sphere surface is discretized into seven different meshes using 2nd-order curvilinear patches with average edge lengths $h = \{0.4, 0.35, 0.3, 0.25, 0.2, 0.15, 0.1\}$ m. These meshes have $N_{\mathrm{p}} = \{136, 202, 280, 396, 622, 1126, 2560\}$ numbers of patches. The order of the interpolation functions (i.e., discretization order) is selected from $\{0, 1, 2, 3\}$, which corresponds to $N_{\mathrm{i}} = \{1, 3, 6, 12\}$ numbers of interpolation points on each curvilinear patch. The matrix system (3) is computed and solved for every combination of N_{p} and N_{i}, resulting in a total of 28 matrix solutions.

After each matrix solution, the scattered scalar potential $\phi^{\mathrm{sca}}(\mathbf{r}_0)$ is calculated on a circle described by $\mathbf{r}_0 = (4.0\sin\theta, 0.0, 4.0\cos\theta)$ m, for $\theta = [0°, 180°]$. The scattered scalar potential computed using 2nd-order discretization for $N_{\mathrm{p}} = 2560$ is used as the reference result (it has been reported in [10] 2nd-order interpolation gives the best accuracy). Then, relative norm errors in all other results are computed. Fig. 1 plots this error versus the product $2N_{\mathrm{p}}N_{\mathrm{i}}$ (total number of unknowns). The figure clearly shows that the Nyström scheme used here to solve (1) achieves higher-order convergence in the solution as expected. It is clear that for a given number of unknowns, higher-order discretizations reach higher accuracy levels. However, one can also see that the convergence rate of the solution of the 3rd-order discretization is smaller than that of the 2nd-order discretization. This is also observed in [10] and might be explained by the fact that only 2nd-order curvilinear patches are used to discretize the sphere surface.

Table I lists the condition number of the matrix in (3) for different combinations of the discretization order and h. It clearly shows that matrix system stays well-conditioned independent of the discretization order and mesh density. This is due to fact that diagonal and off-diagonal entries in (1) are second-kind and compact operators, respectively.

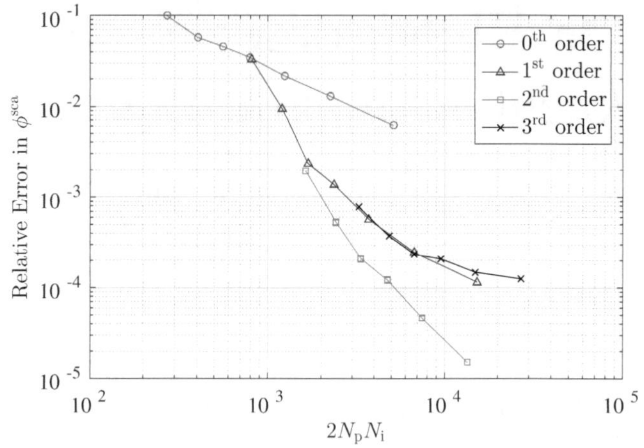

Fig. 1. Relative norm error in scattered scalar potential versus total number of unknowns for different discretization orders.

TABLE I
Condition Numbers for Different Discretization Orders and Different h

h	0.4 m	0.35 m	0.3 m	0.25 m	0.2 m
0th order	18.1	15.2	16.1	14.8	12.6
1st order	14.9	14.1	15.3	15.1	12.8
2nd order	14.3	15.0	16.6	16.2	13.8
3rd order	13.8	14.6	16.2	15.8	13.5

References

[1] P. Ylä-Oijala, S. P. Kiminki, K. Cools, F. Andriulli, and S. Järvenpää, "Mixed discretization schemes for electromagnetic surface integral equations," *Int. J. Numer. Model., Electron. Netw., Devices Fields*, vol. 25, no. 5–6, pp. 525–540, Jan. 2012.

[2] F. P. Andriulli, K. Cools, H. Bagci, F. Olyslager, A. Buffa, S. Christiansen, and E. Michielssen, "A multiplicative Calderon preconditioner for the electric field integral equation," *IEEE Trans. Antennas Propag.*, vol. 56, no. 8, pp. 2398–2412, Aug. 2008.

[3] G. Vecchi, "Loop-star decomposition of basis functions in the discretization of the EFIE," *IEEE Trans. Antennas Propag.*, vol. 47, no. 2, pp. 339–346, 1999.

[4] K. Cools, F. P. Andriulli, D. DeZutter, and E. Michielssen, "Accurate and conforming mixed discretization of the MFIE," *IEEE Antennas Wireless Propag. Lett.*, vol. 10, pp. 528–531, 2011.

[5] H. A. Ülkü, I. Bogaert, K. Cools, F. P. Andriulli, and H. Bagci, "Mixed discretization of the time-domain MFIE at low frequencies," *IEEE Antennas Wireless Propag. Lett.*, vol. 16, pp. 1565–1568, 2017.

[6] Q. S. Liu, S. Sun, and W. C. Chew, "A potential-based integral equation method for low-frequency electromagnetic problems," *IEEE Trans. Antennas Propag.*, vol. 66, no. 3, pp. 1413–1426, Mar. 2018.

[7] F. Vico, M. Ferrando, L. Greengard, and Z. Gimbutas, "The decoupled potential integral equation for time-harmonic electromagnetic scattering," *Commun. Pur. Appl. Math.*, vol. 69, no. 4, pp. 771–812, 2016.

[8] W. C. Chew, "Vector potential electromagnetics with generalized gauge for inhomogeneous media: Formulation," *Progr. Electromagn. Res.*, vol. 149, pp. 69–84, 2014.

[9] J. Li, B. Shanker, and X. Fu, "Potential integral equations in electromagnetics," *in IEEE Int. Symp. Antennas Propag.*, 2017.

[10] G. Kang, J. Song, W. C. Chew, K. C. Donepudi, and J. M. Jin, "A novel grid-robust higher order vector basis function for the method of moments," *IEEE Trans. Antennas Propag.*, vol. 49, no. 6, pp. 908–915, Jun. 2001.

[11] R. W. Freund, "A transpose-free quasi-minimal residual algorithm for non-Hermitian linear systems," *SIAM J. Sci. Comput.*, vol. 14, no. 2, pp. 470–482, 1993.

Two-Dimensional Electrical Properties Tomography Using a Simplified Contrast-Source Inversion Approach

1st Patrick Fuchs
Circuits and Systems, Microelectronics Department
Delft University of Technology
Delft, The Netherlands
p.s.fuchs@tudelft.nl

2nd Rob Remis
Circuits and Systems, Microelectronics Department
Delft University of Technology
Delft, The Netherlands
r.f.remis@tudelft.nl

***Abstract*—The contrast source inversion (CSI) method is a well-known inversion technique that has been utilized in a wide range of application areas. Here we show that in the specific situation of electrical properties tomography (EPT) in magnetic resonance imaging (MRI), which is a so-called hybrid inverse problem, since data is collected inside the reconstruction domain, the CSI method can be simplified to what is essentially a single forward simulation provided the electromagnetic field has an E-polarized field structure. As a consequence, the computational costs are significantly reduced and our experiments show that reconstructions obtained with the simplified CSI method have essentially the same accuracy as reconstructions obtained with the full CSI inversion method.**

***Index Terms*—Magnetic Resonance Imaging, Electrical Tissue Properties, Electromagnetic Inversion, Optimization**

I. Introduction

Magnetic resonance imaging (MRI) is a powerful imaging modality that can be used not only for imaging tissue contrasts but also to image the *in vivo* electrical properties of different tissue types. Specifically, in electrical properties tomography (EPT) the objective is to retrieve the conductivity and permittivity tissue profiles at the MR frequency of operation (Larmor frequency) and within an inversion domain of interest based on measured magnetic flux density data (the B_1^+-field) that has its support *inside* the inversion domain.

It has been shown in [1] that the contrast-source inversion (CSI) method applied to EPT (CSI-EPT) is able to retrieve the conductivity and permittivity maps within a domain of interest even for strongly inhomogeneous tissue profiles. However, convergence may be slow and it may take the CSI-EPT method many iterations to reach the desired error tolerance.

Fortunately, computation times and costs can be significantly reduced by taking advantage of the field structure that may be present inside the imaging domain of interest and the fact that data collection takes place inside this imaging domain. Specifically, we show that for two-dimensional field structures which can occur in the midplane of a birdcage coil [2], it is possible to image the induced currents in real-time and the electrical tissue maps in this plane can be obtained within at most a couple of seconds on a standard laptop or PC by solving a single forward problem. Since the simplified CSI-EPT method does rely on an E-polarized field structure, it is more limited in its applicability than standard CSI-EPT, but if it can be applied then significant speedups can be realized and accurate tissue profiles may be obtained at reduced computational costs.

II. Method

In the midplane of a birdcage coil, the electromagnetic field is essentially E-polarized meaning that the electric field strength has a longitudinal z-component only, while the magnetic field is purely transverse. With σ and ε denoting the conductivity and permittivity within the midplane of the coil, the induced electric-current density in this plane is given by

$$J_z^{\text{ind}} = (\sigma + \text{j}\omega\varepsilon)E_z. \tag{1}$$

The electric field strength E_z and the medium parameters σ and ε are all unknown, of course. Now in MRI, the so-called B_1^+ field

$$B_1^+ = \frac{B_x + \text{j}B_y}{2} \tag{2}$$

can be measured within the midplane of the birdcage coil. Introducing the differentiation operator $\partial^- = (\partial_x - \text{j}\partial_y)/2$, it follows from Maxwell's equations that

$$J_z^{\text{ind}} = \frac{4}{\text{j}\mu_0}\partial^- B_1^+. \tag{3}$$

In other words, the induced current follows from a first-order spatial differentiation of the B_1^+-data and the present method is therefore called foIC-EPT (first-order induced-current EPT). In practice, the data is typically filtered (explicitly or implicitly through the implementation of dedicated noise-suppressing finite-difference stencils) to avoid noise amplification. Clearly, computing the induced current density can be realized essentially in real-time.

Having the induced current available, the electric field strength within the midplane can be obtained by solving a particular integral equation for the electric field strength presented in [3]. Solving this equation is equivalent to solving

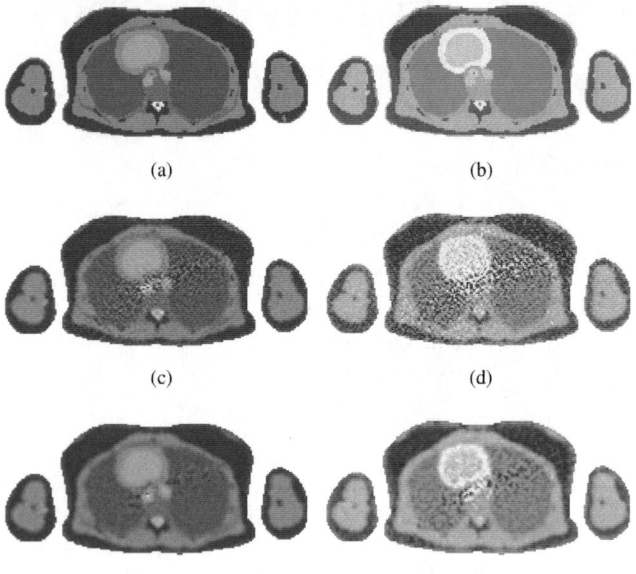

Fig. 1. (a),(c),(e), conductivity profiles of a thorax slice, (a) is the original conductivity, (c) the foIC-EPT reconstruction and (e) the 2D-CSI-EPT reconstruction. (b),(d),(f), permittivity profiles of a thorax slice, (b) is the original conductivity, (d) the foIC-EPT reconstruction and (f) the 2D-CSI-EPT reconstruction.

a forward problem and its solution can be obtained efficiently using iterative solvers such as CG-FFT or GMRES.

Finally, the conductivity and permittivity can be determined using the constitutive relation of equation (1), since the induced current density J_z^{ind} and the electric field strength E_z are now known. Note that at locations where the magnitude of the electric field strength is small it is difficult to retrieve the tissue parameters from the constitutive relation of equation (1).

III. Results

Simulations are performed to compare midplane tissue profile reconstructions obtained with CSI-EPT and the reconstruction method outlined above. Ideal B_1^+ data was obtained by simulating the wave field response due to 16 equally spaced line sources positioned on a circle with a radius of 34 cm that operate in quadrature mode at 128 MHz, which is the operating frequency that corresponds to a 3 tesla background field. For noiseless data, foIC-EPT and CSI-EPT produce essentially identical reconstructions. Therefore, to provide a more accurate representation of actual measured data, we corrupted the simulated B_1^+ data with noise at an SNR of 40dB. The current simplified reconstruction method and CSI-EPT were both implemented in Matlab 2018b on a desktop computer with an Intel i5 processor and 8Gb of RAM. Further implementation details can be found in [3].

Figures 1a and 1b show the exact conductivity and permittivity maps of a thorax model positioned at the midplane of the birdcage coil. Figures 1c and 1e show the conductivity reconstructions obtained with foIC-EPT and CSI-EPT, respectively. The corresponding permittivity reconstructions are shown in Figures 1d and 1f. The CSI-EPT reconstruction took 278 iterations (49.5 seconds) for the normalized residual to drop below the noise level, while five GMRES iterations were required to solve the E-field integral equation (normalized residual smaller than 10^{-6}) and it took 0.21 seconds for foIC-EPT to obtain the tissue reconstructions presented in Figures 1c and 1d.

IV. Discussion and Conclusion

In quadrature mode, the magnitude of the electric field strength is relatively small in an area around the center of the slice, and for both methods the effects of noise are clearly seen in this area. For foIC-EPT these noise effects are stronger due to the differentiation of the data (equation (3)). Such a step is absent in the CSI-EPT method. Noise effects can be suppressed, of course, by incorporating regularization techniques in both reconstruction methods. In addition, at 3T (128 MHz) both methods produce permittivity reconstructions that are of a lower quality than the conductivity reconstructions since the induced current density is dominated by the conduction current at 128 MHz.

In terms of computation time, the foIC-EPT method outperforms the CSI method and allows for real-time imaging. The main computational cost of foIC-EPT and CSI-EPT is the computation of FFT-based matrix-vector products at every iteration. For CSI-EPT, however, the total number of matrix-vector products that need to be computed is quite large and foIC-EPT is much more efficient in general. We conclude that if the radiofrequency transmit field has a two-dimensional E-polarized field structure in some imaging plane of interest, then foIC-EPT is able to reconstruct the dielectric tissue profiles within this plane essentially in real time.

Acknowledgment

The authors would like to thank Reijer Leijsen from the Gorter Center for High-Field MRI, Leiden University Medical Center in The Netherlands for fruitful discussions and feedback.

References

[1] Balidemaj, E., et al., "CSI-EPT: a contrast source inversion approach for improved MRI-based electrical properties tomography," IEEE Trans. Med. Imag., vol 34, pp. 1788 – 1796, 2015.

[2] van den Bergen, B., Stolk, C.C., van den Berg, J.B., Lagendijk, J.J.W., and Van den Berg, C.A.T., "Ultra fast electromagnetic field computations for RF multi-transmit techniques in high field MRI," Phys. Med. Biol. , vol. 54, pp. 1253 – 1264, 2009.

[3] Fuchs, P.S., et al., "First-order induced current density imaging and electrical properties tomography in MRI," IEEE Trans. Comp. Imag. , vol 4, pp. 624 – 631, 2018.

Platform-Aware In-Situ Antenna and Metamaterial Analysis and Design

Shu Wang, Brian MacKie-Mason, and Zhen Peng
Electrical and Computer Engineering Department, University of New Mexico, Albuquerque, U.S.A.
shuwang12@unm.edu, brimacki@unm.edu, pengz@unm.edu

***Abstract*—The objective of this paper is to build a reconfigurable, reusable, and parallel model reduction platform towards transformative in-situ antenna design. The key idea is to introduce a separable and compressible platform Green's function in an up-front offline computation. Once obtained, the online computational complexity does not depend on the size of the in-situ platform. As a result, in-situ design and optimization of multi-antenna systems can be performed at the same cost as the free-space radiation. The advancements make high-fidelity in-situ antenna design orders of magnitude faster.**

***Index Terms*—antenna, domain decomposition, Green's function, integral equation, model reduction.**

I. Overview

Modern military and commercial EM systems are routinely equipped with multiple antennas serving for radar and wireless communications. The computational electromagnetics (CEM) has emerged as a powerful and indispensable tool to evaluate the in-situ performance and co-site interference. These simulations are enabled by fast and rigorous numerical solutions of Maxwell's Equations as well as rapid advances in high-performance computing (HPC) systems. On present-day HPC clusters, the in-situ antenna performance on high-fidelity platforms of electrical length of the order of 1000 wavelengths can be analyzed within a couple of hours [1].

Nevertheless, the CEM based in-situ antenna design goes beyond just performing a single simulation. It often needs to perform a number of simulations in order to navigate highly complex design spaces. Each simulation should complete within at most a few minutes even a few seconds in an industrial design environment. Clearly, fundamental research into innovative mathematics and algorithms are required.

The aim of the paper is to address this pressing and challenging engineering need. For many in-situ antenna design and parameter studies, it is typical that those antennas are only allowed to be mounted on certain parts of the platform. Namely, the computational domain can be decomposed into large fixed parts and small portions involving the antenna design. The observation inspires us to investigate a highly efficient, reduced order in-situ antenna analysis framework.

Key ingredients are summarized as follows: **(1)** The discontinuous Galerkin (DG) boundary element (BE) method [2] and geometry-aware domain decomposition (DD) method [3] are employed to facilitate a modular design-oriented decomposition. **(2)** A novel platform Green's function (PGF) is introduced on the outer surface of those antennas. The PGF is calculated once in the offline phase to characterize the coupling with large, fixed platform. It can be reused for all future in-situ computation. **(3)** In the online phase, rapid solution for multi-query antenna design needs is achieved by a Schwarz DD solver of the reduced order system. The computational costs are the same as the free-space radiation.

II. Methodology

A. Problem decomposition

Consider the in-situ analysis of two antennas on the high-definition platform, as illustrated in Fig. 1. The problem can be decomposed into three sub-regions: sub-regions Ω_1 and Ω_2 contain two antennas, sub-region Ω_3 is electrically large PEC platform. We have used cubical surfaces, Γ_{31} and Γ_{32}, to facilitate the decomposition. The size of the surfaces is determined by the prescribed surface area where the antennas are allowed to be mounted.

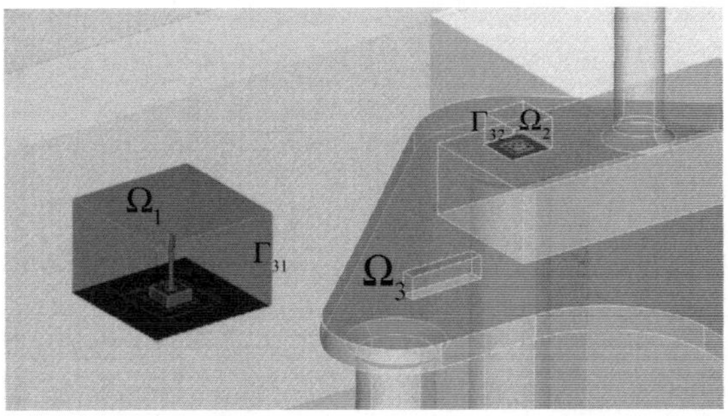

Fig. 1. DD based model reduction for in-situ antenna analysis.

The finite element (FE) method is used to discretized the volume domain of Ω_1 and Ω_2, and the DG boundary element method is applied to the exterior surface of Ω_1 and Ω_2 and platform Ω_3. The resulting system matrix can be written as:

$$\begin{bmatrix} \begin{bmatrix} \mathcal{A}_1^{\mathrm{FE}} & \mathcal{N}_1 \\ \mathcal{N}_1^T & \mathbf{A}_1^{\mathrm{BE}} \end{bmatrix} & \mathbf{C}_{12}^{\mathrm{BE}} & \mathbf{C}_{13}^{\mathrm{BE}} \\ \mathbf{C}_{21}^{\mathrm{BE}} & \begin{bmatrix} \mathcal{A}_2^{\mathrm{FE}} & \mathcal{N}_2 \\ \mathcal{N}_2^T & \mathbf{A}_2^{\mathrm{BE}} \end{bmatrix} & \mathbf{C}_{23}^{\mathrm{BE}} \\ \mathbf{C}_{31}^{\mathrm{BE}} & \mathbf{C}_{32}^{\mathrm{BE}} & \mathbf{A}_3^{\mathrm{BI}} \end{bmatrix}. \qquad (1)$$

The resulting sub-domain FE matrices, $\mathcal{A}_m^{\mathrm{FE}}$, m =1,2, have complex nonlinear dependency on a few design parameters (ϵ_m, μ_m, $\mathbf{r}_m$, etc.). The sub-domain BE matrices $\mathrm{A}_m^{\mathrm{BE}}$, m =1,2,3, and coupling matrices $\mathbf{C}_{mn}^{\mathrm{BE}}$ are resulting from free-space Green's function, and has no parametric dependency.

Evidently, the above non-overlapping and non-conforming DG and DD methods lead to a modular design-oriented decomposition. The modification of antenna types, parameters, locations in the design stage is reflected in local and sparse FE matrices, which are decoupled from exterior BE matrices. Nevertheless, every time antenna design is modified, we still need to solve the entire system matrix. That is where the platform Green's function comes into play.

B. Platform Green's function

The PGF is evaluated on the artificial surfaces, $\Gamma_3 = \Gamma_{31} \cup \Gamma_{32}$, in the offline computing phase. Once calculated, the large fixed platform is rigorously represented by the PGF. The direct calculation of the PGF matrix requires the solution of the large platform Ω_3 with respect to individual unit source currents on Γ_3. Recognizing the coupling between antennas and platform is considerably low-rank, we proposed a novel alternating and random interpolative decomposition (AR-ID) to select the skeleton source currents from the original ones on the exterior surface Γ_3. The AR-ID calculation can be achieved locally per antenna sub-system and embarrassingly in parallel. The reduced model of in-situ antenna system can be written as:

$$\begin{bmatrix} \begin{bmatrix} \mathcal{A}_1^{FE} & \mathcal{N}_1 \\ \mathcal{N}_1^T & \tilde{\mathbf{A}}_1^{BE} \end{bmatrix} & \begin{matrix} & \\ & \tilde{\mathbf{C}}_{12}^{BE} \end{matrix} \\ \begin{matrix} & \\ & \tilde{\mathbf{C}}_{21}^{BE} \end{matrix} & \begin{bmatrix} \mathcal{A}_2^{FE} & \mathcal{N}_2 \\ \mathcal{N}_2^T & \tilde{\mathbf{A}}_2^{BE} \end{bmatrix} \end{bmatrix} \begin{bmatrix} \mathbf{x}_1^{FE} \\ \mathbf{x}_1^{BE} \\ \mathbf{x}_2^{FE} \\ \mathbf{x}_2^{BE} \end{bmatrix} = \begin{bmatrix} \mathbf{b}_1^{FE} \\ 0 \\ \mathbf{b}_2^{FE} \\ 0 \end{bmatrix}. \quad (2)$$

The updated BE matrices consist of the free-space GF matrices and the AR-ID representation of PGF matrices:

$$\tilde{\mathbf{A}}_1^{BE} = \mathbf{A}_1^{BE} - \mathbf{R}_{13}^{n_1 \times k_1} \cdot \mathbf{S}_{11}^{k_1 \times k_1} \cdot \mathbf{R}_{31}^{k_1 \times n_1}, \quad (3)$$

$$\tilde{\mathbf{C}}_{12}^{BE} = \mathbf{C}_{12}^{BE} - \underbrace{\mathbf{R}_{13}^{n_1 \times k_1} \cdot \mathbf{S}_{12}^{k_1 \times k_2} \cdot \mathbf{R}_{32}^{k_2 \times n_2}}_{\text{Platform GF matrix}}, \quad (4)$$

where $\mathbf{S}_{mn}^{k_m \times k_n} = \mathbf{B}_{m3}^{k_m \times n_3} \cdot \left[\mathbf{A}_3^{BE}\right]^{-1} \cdot \mathbf{B}_{3n}^{n_3 \times k_n}$. The n_1, n_2, n_3 are the number of BE unknowns on antennas and platform. The k_1 and k_2 are skeleton BE unknowns.

During the design stage (online computing), (2) is solved by Krylov iterative methods with an additive Schwarz preconditioner [1]. We remark that the online computing complexity does not depend on the size of the in-situ platform. As a result, in-situ design and optimization of multi-antenna systems can be performed at the same cost as the free-space radiation.

III. ILLUSTRATION

We consider a metasurface antenna [4] mounted on the top surface of a PEC platform, as shown in Fig. 2. In the offline calculation, we first generate separate BE meshes on the exterior surface of antenna and the platform. The PGF matrix is then constructed and assembled in the AR-ID representation as in (3). We note that the PGF matrix is introduced to characterize the coupling with the platform only, and separately compressed with the free-space GF matrix. Thereby, the rank of the PGF matrix is extremely low, as the skeleton BE unknowns in Fig. 3(b), and the free-space GF matrix can still be compressed with the fast multipole method. In the online phase, we generate the volume meshes for different antennas independently. The FE matrices are combined with the same GF matrices in (3). The in-situ radiation patterns are shown in Fig. 4.

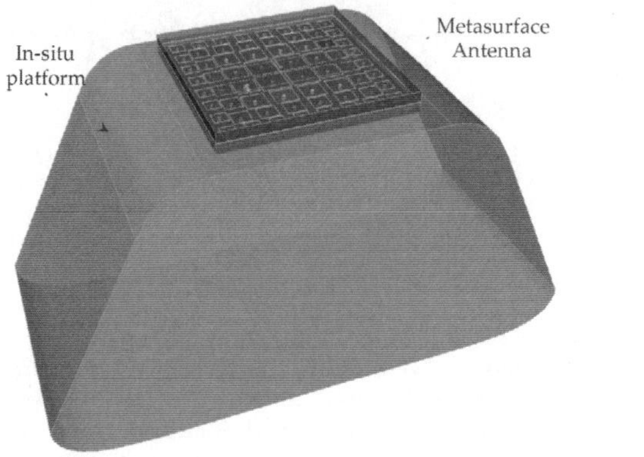

Fig. 2. Example of a metasurface antenna on PEC platform.

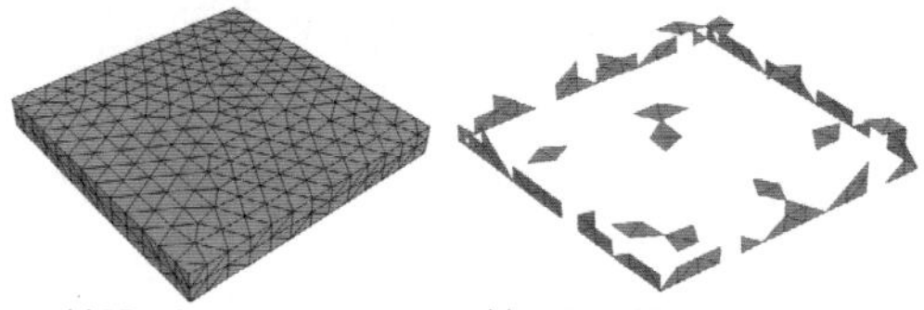

(a) BE unknowns: n = 859 (b) skeleton BE unknowns: k = 42

Fig. 3. Illustration of a data-sparse representation of PGF.

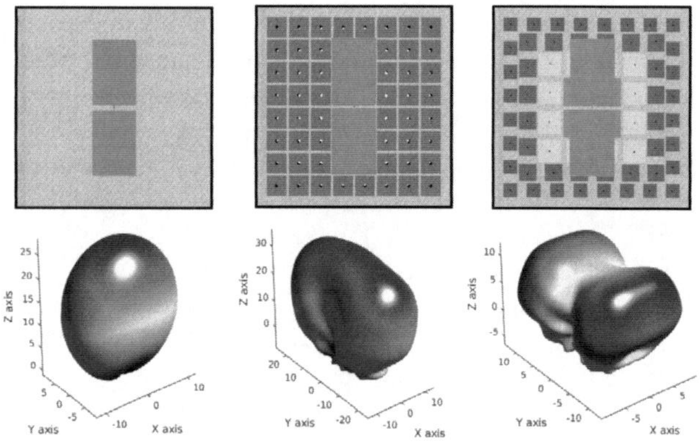

(a) Patch antenna (b) Patch antenna with uniform EBG (c) Patch antenna with NUA EBG

Fig. 4. Radiation pattern of in-situ antennas at 550MHz.

REFERENCES

[1] B. MacKie-Mason, Y. Shao, A. Greenwood, and Z. Peng, "Supercomputing-enabled first-principles analysis of radio wave propagation in urban environments," IEEE Trans. Antennas and Propagation, vol. 66, no. 12, pp. 6606-6617, Dec. 2018.

[2] Z. Peng, R. Hiptmair, Y. Shao, and B. MacKie-Mason, "Domain decomposition preconditioning for surface integral equations in solving challenging electromagnetic scattering problems," IEEE Trans. Antennas and Propagation, vol. 64, pp. 210-223, Jan. 2016.

[3] H. Gao, Z. Peng and X. Sheng, "A geometry-aware domain decomposition preconditioning for hybrid finite element-boundary integral method," IEEE Trans. Antennas and Propagation, vol. 65, no. 4, pp. 1875-1885, Apr. 2017.

[4] N. Chamok, M. Ali, T. Anthony, and S. J. Weiss, "Ultra-thin UHF broadband antenna on a non-uniform aperiodic (NUA) metaSurface," IEEE Antennas and Propagation Magazine, vol. 57, no. 2, pp. 167-180, Apr. 2015.

Quantifying Subgridding Errors when Modeling Multiscale Structures with FDTD

Madison Le
Electrical Engineering Department
Colorado School of Mines
Golden, USA
madisonle@mines.edu

Mohammed Hadi
Electrical Engineering Department
Colorado School of Mines
Golden, USA
mhadi@mines.edu

Atef Elsherbeni
Electrical Engineering Department
Colorado School of Mines
Golden, USA
aelsherb@mines.edu

***Abstract*—This paper discusses the growing subgridding errors in Finite-Difference Time-Domain (FDTD) analysis when applied on electrically large subgrids. FDTD simulations in 1D and 2D spaces are used with a 1:3 contrast ratio. Error levels are found to be linearly proportional to the subgrid's electrical dimension along the wave's propagation path. This linear growth suggests numerical phase error mismatch between coarse and fine grids as the subgridding error source.**

Keywords—Finite-difference time-domain method, numerical error analysis, subgridding, multi-scale problems.

I. Introduction

Finite-difference time-domain (FDTD) subgridding methods have become increasingly necessary as the operating frequency of modern electronic devices have risen and thus creating electrically large computational spaces. Using a traditional FDTD [1], the maximum Yee grid cell size is constrained by at least 10 cells per smallest wavelength [2]. Subgridding purportedly allows these electrically large domains to be analyzed accurately without the need for large allocations of memory and resources. The repercussions of subgridding in a FDTD calculation can lead to dispersion and stability errors, as seen in [3-5]. A larger subgrid enhances the maximum area an object of interest can be meshed to receive a more accurate analysis in a local grid. The deleterious effects of larger subgridding ratios have been discussed in the literature [6]. A topic that has not yet been investigated, is the relative error that arises with increased electrical sizes of subgridded regions, independent of the contrast ratio. This paper will discuss the effect the size of a subgridded region has on the resulting errors at a 1:3 contrast ratio within 1D and 2D FDTD simulations.

II. 1D and 2D FDTD Setups

The 1D FDTD setup (Fig. 1) involves a Gaussian pulse propagating through a leap-frogged 1D H_y and E_z grid of 500 cells. The discrete spatial step in the global coarse grid, $\Delta x = 4$ mm, is chosen such that the Gaussian pulse spans approximately 20 FDTD cells per wavelength. Within the global grid there is a localized region where a few coarse cells are replaced by a finer grid with one third the coarse grid's spatial step (Contrast Ratio = 1:3).

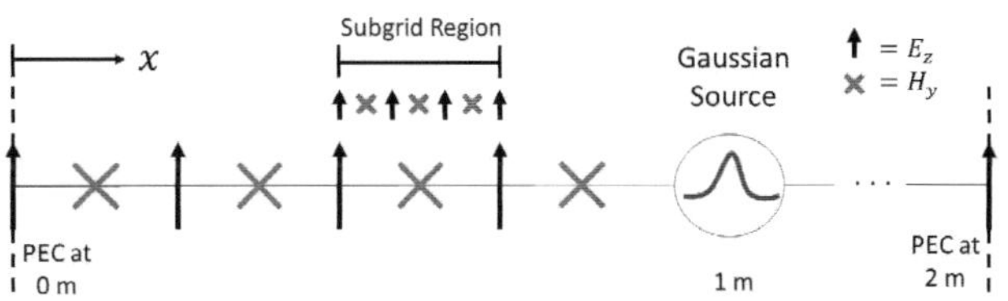

Fig. 1. The problem space of the 1D configuration. The coarse field components are indicated with the larger arrows and crosses while the fine grid components of the subgrid have smaller symbols.

The 2D problem space is depicted in Fig. 2 with 210 by 160 cells in the x and y directions, respectively. There is also a Gaussian pulse and a subgridded section replacing 60 by 10 coarse cells within the domain. In both setups, the time step is fixed for both coarse and fine update equations and of course is based on the smaller cell size to maintain stability throughout. Table I lists the discrete FDTD discrete steps used for both setups.

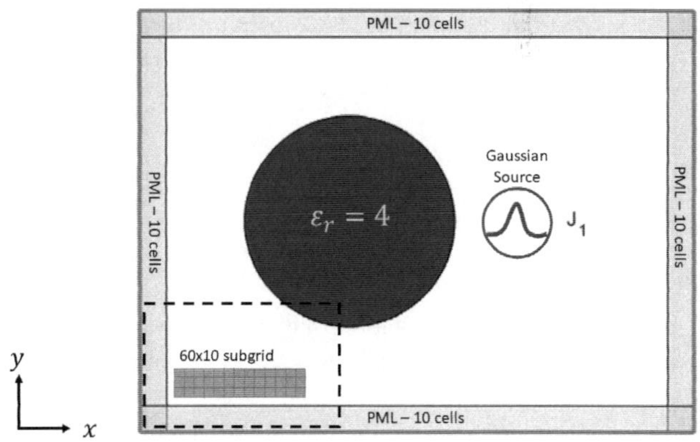

Fig. 2. Scattering example from [1, Section 7.5.2]: Line source parallel to a dielectric cylinder simulated with a 2D FDTD code. Dotted lines represent the lower left corner.

The 1D FDTD simulation is run long enough for the Gaussian pulse to fully traverse the subgrid region once and is ended before the pulse reaches the PEC boundary. The 2D FDTD simulation is run long enough for both the direct wave and the dielectric scattered wave fully interact with the subgrid region. Each FDTD code is run twice; once with the subgrid region included (subgrid run) and again with no subgridding (reference run). The normalized percentage error due to subgridding is quantified in (1):

$$Normalized\ Error = \frac{|E_{zSubgrid} - E_{zReference}|}{|E_{zReference}|_{Max}} \cdot 100\%\ . \quad (1)$$

The 1D code is tested for three subgrid sizes; the equivalent of 5, 10 and 100 coarse cells. The 2D code is tested for single size (60×10 coarse cells) subgrid.

TABLE I. SUBGRID PARAMETERS

	Δx	Δy	Δt	Number of Time Steps
1D	$4\ mm$	-	$4.4\ ps$	600
2D	$5\ mm$	$5\ mm$	$3.5\ ps$	3000

III. RESULTS & ANALYSIS

Figure 3 (a) demonstrates the normalized percentage error incurred when the Gaussian pulse traverses each of the three 1D subgrid configurations. As shown, the maximum error increases linearly with the subgrid size; 1.2%, 2.5% and 26% for subgrids replacing 5, 10 and 100 coarse cells, respectively. Equivalent electrical subgrid sizes are roughly a quarter wavelength, a half wavelength and 5 wavelengths, respectively, since the Gaussian pulse covers a total of 20 cells per wavelength. A 26% normalized error, as seen for 100 coarse cells, would be unacceptable for many applications. For example, antennas are designed for an electrical length of a half wavelength, however, and antenna array may consist of greater than 5 wavelengths. This large electrical size would produce significant errors.

Figure 3 (b) is a contour plot of the lower left corner of Fig. 2 after a Gaussian pulse is allowed to interact with both the cylindrical scatterer and the subgrid area there. Again, there is a normalized error which intensifies the longer (through space) the pulse interacts with the subgrid region. Maximum error value there is 2.6% which is also expected to increase linearly with increasing subgrid dimension along the pulse propagation path.

IV. CONCLUSION

1D and 2D FDTD simulations indicate a direct correlation between the subgrid electrical size and the cumulative errors caused due to the propagated waves. Linear increase of such errors suggests that the root cause is the disparate numerical phase velocities of waves propagating in the neighborhoods of subgridding interfaces. This in turn causes numerical impedance mismatches and subsequent reflections. Therefore, subgridding errors can be reduced by matching numerical phase velocities in fine and coarse grids. Further investigations will cover this phenomenon in hybrid FDTD schemes, utilizing higher-order calculations to reduce the coarse grid errors.

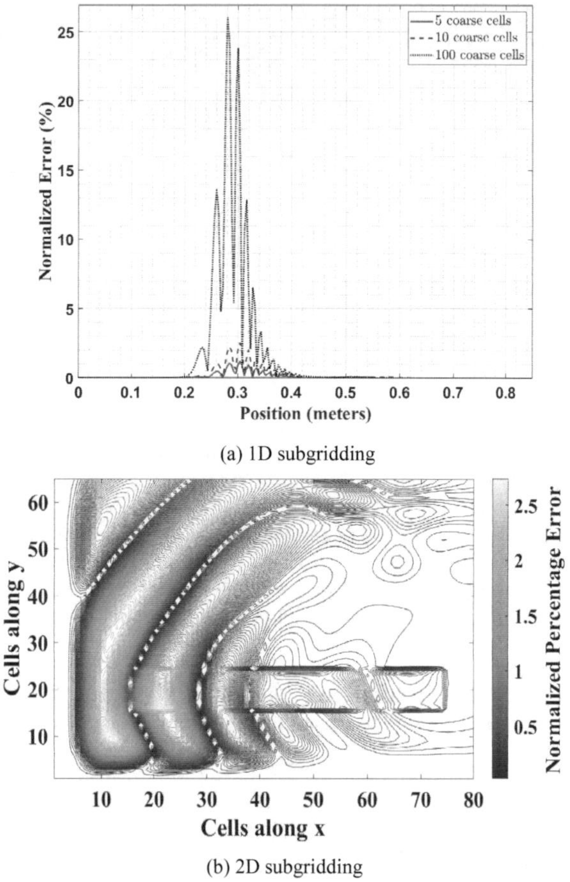

Fig. 3. The normalized errors calculated using (1). (a) Normalized percentage error in 1D subgridding. (b) Normalized percentage error in 2D subgridding.

ACKNOWLEDGMENTS

This project is supported by Futurewei Technology Inc., New Jersey Research Center, Bridgewater, NJ, USA.

REFERENCES

[1] A. Z. Elsherbeni and V. Demir, The Finite-Difference Time-Domain Method for Electromagnetics with MATLAB® Simulations, 2nd edition, Edison, New Jersey: SciTech Publishing, 2015.

[2] M. W. Chevalier, R. J. Luebbers, and V. P. Cable, "FDTD local grid with material traverse," IEEE Trans. Antennas Propagat., vol. 45, no. 3, Mar. 1997.

[3] S. Wang, "Numerical examinations of the stability of FDTD subgridding schemes," ACES Journal, vol. 22, no. 2, Jul. 2007.

[4] F. L. Teixeira, "A summary review on 25 years of progress and future challenges in FDTD and FETD techniques," ACES Journal, vol. 25, no. 1, Jan. 2010.

[5] M. F. Hadi and R. K. Dib, "Eliminating interface reflections in hybrid low-dispersion FDTD algorithms," ACES Journal, vol. 22, no. 3, Nov. 2007.

[6] J. Nehrbass and R. Lee, "Optimal finite-difference sub-gridding techniques applied to the Helmholtz equation," IEEE Transactions on Microwave Theory and Techniques, vol. 48, no. 6, pp. 976–984, Jun. 2000.

Compact Dual-Band Branch-Line Coupler With Enhanced Bandwidth for WLAN Applications

Adrian Bekasiewicz[1]
[1]*Faculty of Electronics, Telecommunications and Informatics*
Gdansk University of Technology
Gdansk, Poland
bekasiewicz@ru.is

Slawomir Koziel[1,2]
[2]*School of Science and Engineering*
Reykjavik University
Reykjavik, Iceland
koziel@ru.is

***Abstract*—Dual-band operation with enhanced bandwidth and small size are important performance figures of hybrid couplers for applications in modern communication systems. Unfortunately, maintaining broad frequency ranges of operation stays in conflict with circuit miniaturization. In this work, a compact dual-band branch-line coupler (BLC) with improved bandwidth has been proposed. Electrical performance of the structure has been improved by introducing an asymmetry into the cross-coupled branches of the reference dual-band circuit. The coupler has been optimized at a low computational cost using a surrogate-assisted method. It features 180 MHz and 450 MHz bandwidths at the center frequencies of 2.45 GHz and 5.4 GHz, respectively. The footprint of the optimized circuit is only 296 mm². The coupler has been benchmarked against competitive dual-band BLCs from the literature.**

Keywords—*Dual-band couplers, coupler miniaturization, surrogate-based optimization, bandwidth-enhanced operation.*

I. Introduction

Dual-band (DB) couplers are an interesting alternative for conventional BLCs in modern microwave systems. Enhanced functionality makes them useful for WLAN, as well as for other services operating within, e.g., industrial, scientific and medical (ISM) bands. Major disadvantages of dual-band BLCs include their relatively narrow operational bandwidths, as well as an increased size w.r.t. conventional single-band structures [1]-[4]. These limitations are rarely addressed in the literature. Nonetheless, in [1], a bandwidth-enhanced operation was obtained—at a cost of a large BLC footprint—using multi-section topology with stepped-impedance stubs. In [4], a miniaturized DB coupler was proposed where size reduction has been obtained by using meandered transmission lines. The structure, however, exhibits a degraded performance as compared to its non-miniaturized counterpart [2]. So far, explicit design of DB BLCs for bandwidth-enhanced operation and compact dimensions has not been reported in the literature.

In this work, a hybrid DB BLC with enhanced bandwidth for WLAN applications is proposed. Electrical performance of the structure is improved using asymmetrical cross-coupled branches which increase the number of degrees of freedom. At the same time, a small size of the BLC has been achieved by appropriate meandering of its transmission line sections. To achieve high-performance at a low design cost, the BLC has been optimized using surrogate-based optimization (SBO) techniques. The optimized circuit features 7.6% and 8.3% bandwidths (defined by $|S_{11}|$, $|S_{41}| \leq -20$ dB) for 2.45 GHz and 5.4 GHz center frequencies, respectively. A comparison of the circuit with state-of-the art DB BLCs is provided.

II. Coupler Structure and Performance Figures

Consider miniaturized hybrid dual-band BLC with enhanced bandwidth shown in Fig. 1. The structure is implemented in the microstrip technology on a Rogers RO4003C substrate (ε_r = 3.55, h = 0.813 mm, tanδ = 0.0021). The circuit is based on the structure of [2] where DB operation is achieved using cross-coupled branches. The proposed design is characterized by an increased number of degrees of freedom which is achieved by introducing asymmetry into the branches of [2]. The compact size is obtained by replacing the transmission line sections with their meandered counterparts. The vector of design parameters is $\boldsymbol{x} = [w_{11}\ w_{21}\ l_{11}\ s_{11}\ w_{12}\ w_{22}\ l_{12}\ s_{12}\ w_{13}\ w_{23}\ l_{13}\ l_{23}\ l_{33}\ l_{43}\ s_{13}]^T$. The dimensions w_0 = 1.7, c = 0.2, and g = 0.5 remain fixed, whereas parameters $l_1 = l_{11} + w_{11} - w_{21}$, $l_2 = 4s_{13} + 7w_{23} + 2g + w_{22} + \max(w_{22}, w_{21})$, and $l_3 = g + w_{21} + 2.5s_{11} + 2w_{11} + 0.5w_0 - 1.5w_{23} - 0.5c$. The unit for all parameters is mm.

To ensure a low design cost, two computational models of the coupler are utilized: the low-fidelity equivalent-circuit (Keysight ADS [5]) and the high-fidelity EM model (Keysight Momentum [5]; setup: 40 cells/wavelength, edge mesh, simulation time 5 min). The design objectives are to minimize the reflection $|S_{11}|$ and isolation $|S_{41}|$ within 2.4 GHz to 2.5 GHz and 5.2 GHz to 5.6 GHz bands, as well as to maintain the power-split imbalance for $f_{0.1}$ = 2.45 GHz and $f_{0.2}$ = 5.4 GHz below 0.3 dB.

III. Design Approach

Let $\boldsymbol{R}_f(\boldsymbol{x})$ and $\boldsymbol{R}_c(\boldsymbol{x})$ be responses of the high- and low-fidelity models at $\boldsymbol{x}$. The design problem can be formulated as a minimization task of the form

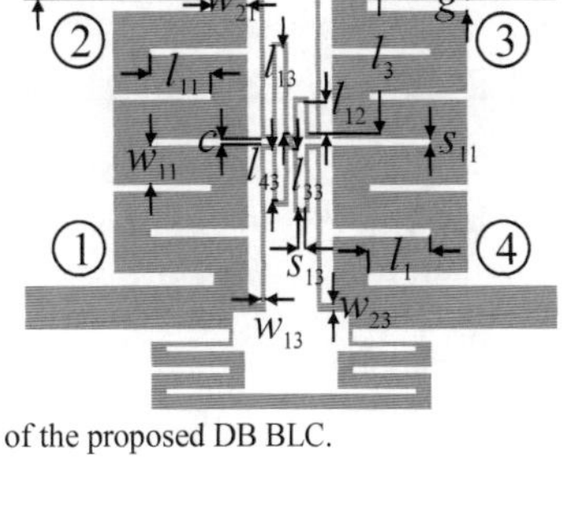

Fig. 1. Geometry of the proposed DB BLC.

$$x^* = \arg\min_x U\left(R_f(x)\right) \quad (1)$$

where U is a scalar objective function and x^* denotes the optimum design to be found. To ensure a low cost of the design process, direct solving of (1) is replaced by an SBO process which generates a series of approximations $x^{(i)}$, $i = 1, 2, \ldots$, to x^* through optimization of the surrogate model $R_s^{(i)}(x)$ which is iteratively updated based on occasional R_f evaluations [6]. The SBO process works as follows

$$x^{(i+1)} = \arg\min_x U\left(R_s^{(i)}(x)\right) \quad (2)$$

Here, the surrogate is constructed by correcting $R_c(x)$ through a combination of implicit and output space mapping, as well as frequency scaling [6].

The BLC is optimized in a two-step design framework involving minimization of the power-split imbalance for the center frequencies, followed by a constrained minimization of the in-band reflection and isolation. The objective function for the first step is given as $U = \max(d_1, d_2)$ where $d_k = ||S_{21}| - |S_{31}||$ at $f_{0.k}$, $k = 1, 2$. For the second step, the design objective is

$$U = \max\left(|S_{11}|, |S_{41}|\right)_{\substack{2.4\text{ GHz to }2.6\text{GHz}\\5.2\text{ GHz to }5.6\text{ GHz}}} + \beta\sum_{k=1}^{2} c_k \quad (3)$$

The penalty components of (3) are defined as $c_k = [\max(d_k - d, 0)/d]^2$. Note that they are only active if the respective power-split imbalance exceeds a user-defined threshold d (here, $d = 0.3$ dB). The penalty factor is set to $\beta = 5$.

IV. Numerical Results

The starting point for structure optimization has been obtained as follows. The electrical parameters of the coupler have been synthesized based on [2]. Subsequently, the structure topology has been modified using asymmetrical cross-coupled branches and optimized. The resulting electrical parameters have been utilized as a reference for determination of the equivalent-circuit model of the topology of Fig. 1. The initial design $x_0 = [1\ 1\ 3\ 0.3\ 0.4\ 0.2\ 3\ 0.2\ 0.8\ 0.2\ 0.2\ 3\ 3\ 3\ 3\ 0.3]^T$ has been optimized using the SBO approach outlined in Section II. The final design $x^* = [1.49\ 1.4\ 2.38\ 0.27\ 0.61\ 0.16\ 2.5\ 0.2\ 0.79\ 0.2\ 0.32\ 2\ 0.1\ 2.26\ 1.98\ 0.29]^T$ has been found after 5 and 8 iterations of optimization for minimum power-split imbalance and for constrained reflection improvement (cf. (3)), respectively. Figure 2 shows a comparison of the structure responses at the initial and the final designs. The optimized BLC features 180 MHz and 450 MHz bandwidths (defined for $|S_{11}|$ and $|S_{41}|$ being both below –20 dB) with power split errors of 0.05 dB and 0.5 dB for the lower and upper center frequencies, respectively. Note that a slight violation of the power-split imbalance condition for the upper band results from the implicit constraint handling of (3).

The computational cost of coupler optimization (excluding the structure development) corresponds to 29.5 EM model simulations (~2.5 hours of CPU-time) and it includes a total of 1087 R_c model simulations and 16 R_f model evaluations. The cost of direct TR-based BLC optimization in the outlined bi-step setup is 213 R_f simulations (over seven times higher than for the SBO approach considered in this work).

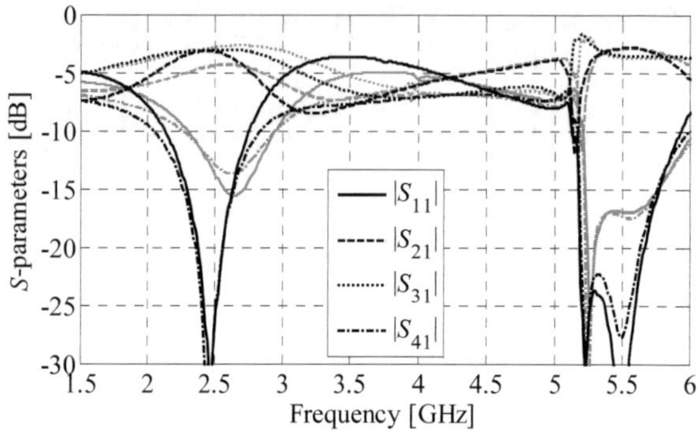

Fig. 2. Responses of the proposed BLC at the initial (gray) and the optimized (black) designs.

Table I Comparison with State-of-the-Art Couplers

Design	$f_{0.1}/f_{0.2}$ [GHz]	BW1/BW2 [%]*	Dimensions [mm × mm]	Size [mm²]	Size [λ_g^2]	SRF [%]$
[1]	2.2/5.5	28.2/11.3	100 × 65.8	6575	0.944	1388
[2]	1.0/2.0	12.4/6.2	64.3 × 64.3	4134	0.126	185
[3]	1.0/2.0	13.5/6.5	99.2 × 48.0	4762	0.095	140
[4]	1.0/2.0	12.0/4.0	32.3 × 32.3	1041	0.032	47
This work	2.45/5.4	14.0/10.7	20.7 × 14.3	296	0.055	81

* Calculated for $|S_{11}|$ and $|S_{41}|$ both below –15 dB (w.r.t. $f_{0.1}$ and $f_{0.2}$)
$ Calculated w.r.t. the size of conventional single-band BLC designed for $f_{0.1}$

The proposed circuit has been compared with state-of-the-art dual-band couplers from the literature [1]-[4] with respect to the operational bandwidths (defined for $|S_{11}|$ and $|S_{41}|$ being both below–15 dB) and the size defined in terms of the guided wavelength calculated for the lower center frequency and given substrate parameters. The circuit footprints have been compared in terms of size with a conventional single-band BLC designed for their respective $f_{0.1}$ frequencies. The results gathered in Table I indicate that the proposed structure is the only one within the considered set, which offers both size reduction w.r.t. conventional design and over 10% lower- and upper-bandwidth, respectively.

Acknowledgment

This work has been partially supported by the Icelandic Centre for Research (RANNIS) Grant 163299051, and by National Science Centre of Poland Grant 2017/27/B/ST7/00563.

References

[1] K. Chin, K. Lin, Y. Wei, T. Tseng, and Y. Yang, "Compact dual-band branch-line and rat-race couplers with stepped-impedance-stub lines," *IEEE Trans. Microwave Theory Tech.*, vol. 58, no. 5, pp. 1213–1221, 2010.

[2] M.-J. Park and B. Lee, "Dual-band, cross coupled branch line coupler," *IEEE Microwave Wireless Comp. Lett.*, vol. 15, no. 10, pp. 655–657, 2005.

[3] H. Kim, B. Lee, and M. Park, "Dual-band branch-line coupler with port extensions," *IEEE Trans. Microwave Theory Tech.*, vol. 58, no. 3, pp. 651–655, 2010.

[4] A. Bekasiewicz and S. Koziel, "Miniaturised dual-band branch-line coupler," *Electronics Lett.*, vol. 51, no. 10, pp. 769–771, 2015.

[5] Agilent (Keysight) ADS, ver. 2011.10, Agilent Technologies, 1400 Fountaingrove Parkway, Santa Rosa, CA 95403-1799, 2011.

[6] S. Koziel, Q.S. Cheng, and J.W. Bandler, "Space mapping," *IEEE Microwave Mag.*, vol. 9, no. 6, pp. 105–122, 2008.

The Impact of Surface Roughness on Avalanche Frequency

Talal Al-Attar
Computer, Electrical and Mathematical Science & Engineering Division
King Abdullah University of Science and Technology, Thuwal, Saudi Arabia
Talal.Attar@kaust.edu.sa

Abstract— **IMPATT diodes were designed and fabricated in standard CMOS technology to study the impact of the RMS value of surface roughness on the avalanche frequency. By comparing the on-chip measurements of an IMPATT diode integrated in a CPW to an integrated one with a microstrip patch antenna at the same biasing conditions, the results demonstrated a reduction in the avalanche frequency in the antenna integrated structure by 34% compared to the CPW one. Such variation is strongly associated with the increase in the conduction losses by 40%~80% based on the biasing conditions and hence the avalanche frequency.**

Keywords— ***avalanche frequency, coplanar waveguide, high frequency, IMPATT diode, microstrip patch antenna, skin depth, surface roughness, transmission line.***

I. Introduction

The need for accurate on-chip measurements of (Impact Avalanche Transit Time) IMPATT diodes is increasing due to the recent developments in IMPATT-Antenna integration for monolithic millimeter-wave applications in standard CMOS technology [1]. This accuracy affects the design and the optimization of the oscillation and the radiation frequency.

IMPATT diode is a solid state device that converts the DC power into RF one by generating negative resistance beyond avalanche frequency [2-3]. CMOS IMPATT diodes revealed the capabilities of generating avalanche frequency beyond 30 GHz and negative resistance up to 80GHz [1-4]. Gilden and Hines (G&H) model was used to extract the avalanche frequency and the desired matching impedance [5]. The creation of the negative resistance and the capacitive reactive part at frequencies beyond the avalanche frequency is affected by the selection of the breakdown voltage and the operating current [1-4].

Although de-embedding techniques would be applied to arrive directly to the device under test (DUT) [6], the surface roughness factor would still kick in and impact the operation of the IMPATT diode because of its direct influence on the operating current and hence the inaccuracy in extracting the avalanche frequency.

The advances reported in modeling Coplanar Waveguide transmission lines (CPW) fabricated in standard CMOS technology at high frequencies was extended up to 110GHz [7] which revealed the importance of including the surface roughness to accurately extract the avalanche frequency in the neighborhood of 30GHz and beyond.

In this paper, we demonstrate the impact of surface roughness on avalanche frequency by comparing the on-chip measurement of a monolithic integrated IMPATT diode with CPW to an integrated one with a microstrip patch antenna at the same biasing conditions.

II. The Impact of Surface Roughness

IMPATT diodes have been have been monolithically integrated in coplanar waveguides (Fig. 1) and successfully de-embedded and characterized by S-parameter measurements from 40 MHz to 110 GHz [1]. This will be considered the first test structure.

In addition, we designed, measured and modeled the Ground-Signal-Ground (GSG) RF pads (Fig. 2) utilizing the conduction losses used in [7] and shown in Equation (1) including the surface roughness (Δ) as a frequency dependent factor [7] and the skin depth δ, proposed by Hammerstad and Jensen [8];

$$\alpha_{condution\ total} = \alpha_c \left[1 + \frac{2}{\pi} tan^{-1}\left(1.4\left(\frac{\Delta}{\delta}\right)^2\right)\right]. \qquad (1)$$

Fig. 3 shows a plot of the correction factor used in Equation (2) up to 110GHz proposed by [7];

$$\alpha_{condution\ total} = \alpha_c\ [Correction\ Factor\ ]. \qquad (2)$$

The extracted avalanche frequency range between ~30GHz to ~50GHz for different biasing conditions is shown in Table 1. In addition, a special case for a DC bias of 11V with measured current of 55mA is demonstrated in Fig. 4.

Fig. 5 shows the second test structure where the IMPATT diodes integrated with mircostrip patch antenna as a mean to measure the oscillation and the radiation frequency and hence extract the avalanche frequency compared to the same bias conditions of the first structure.

III. Results and Discussion

Multiple IMPATT diodes integrated in a CPW and microstrip patch antenna were designed and fabricated in five metal layers standard CMOS technology. The CPW test structures demonstrated avalanche frequency range between 30GHz and 50GHz (Table 1). At the same range and in Fig. 3 we observed an increase in the conduction losses by 40% ~80% due to the presence of the surface roughness in Equation (1). We thoroughly investigated a case of DC bias of 11V and 55mA in both structures in order to study the impact of surface roughness on avalanche frequency. The case revealed a reduction in the second structure's avalanche frequency by 34% where the correction factor of the conductor losses was increased by 40% as shown in Fig. 3.

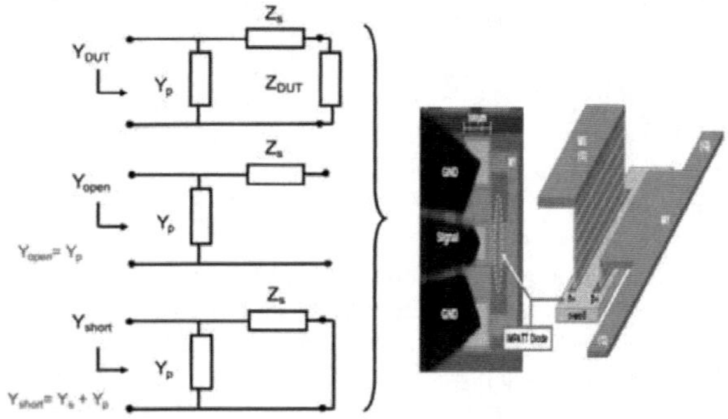

Fig. 1. Die photo of integrated IMPATT diode and GSG RF probe with the de-embedding steps [6].

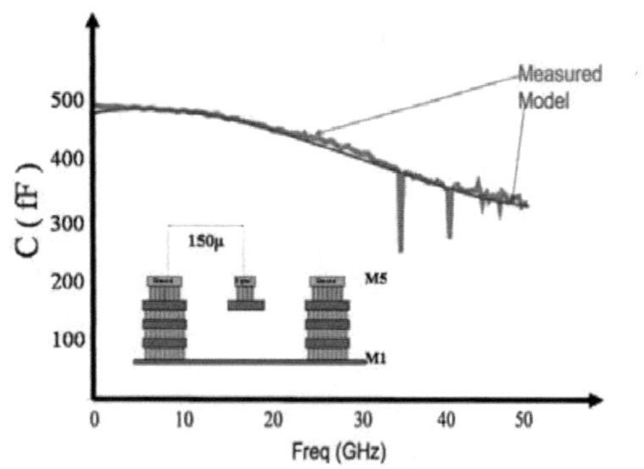

Fig. 2. The measured and modeled capacitance of the GSG RF pad.

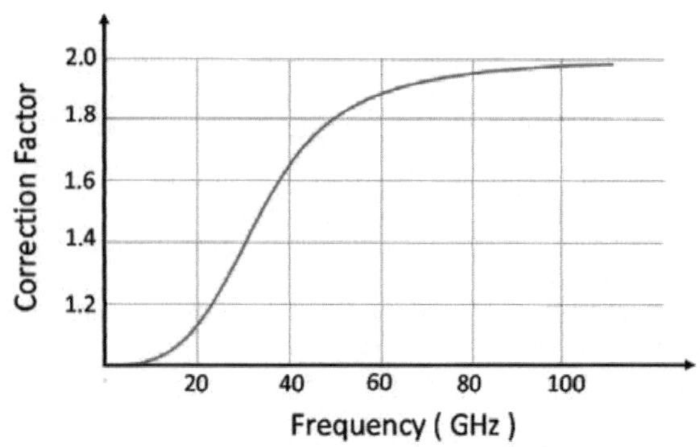

Fig. 3. Correction factor given in Equation (2) adding 40% ~ 80% losses in the avalanche frequency range of 30GHz ~50GHz shown in Table 1.

Table 1: Measured avalanche frequency based on different bias conditions

Bias Voltage [V]	Bias Current [mA]	Avalanche Frequency f_a [GHz]
9.8	23	28.3
10.0	28	31.1
10.5	40	37.0
11.0	55	43.0
11.5	67	47.0

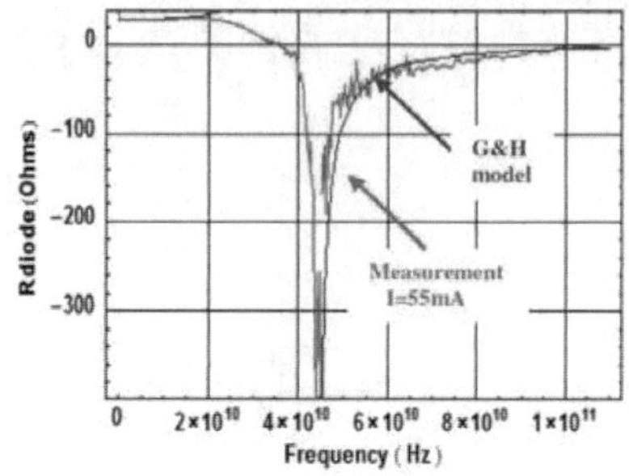

Fig. 4. Measured real part of the IMPATT impedance at I=55mA [4] and G&H model [5].

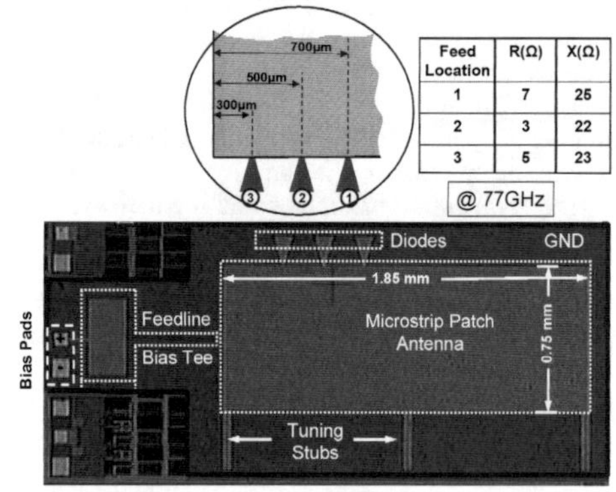

Fig. 5. Die photo of integrated IMPATT diode with microstrip patch antenna on-chip.

IV. Conclusion

The realized IMPATT diodes demonstrated considerable changes in the extracted avalanche frequency based on different integration environments. This paper revealed the impact of the surface roughness on the avalanche frequency and a strong correlation of the correction factor to the changes noticed. A thoroughly investigated case; with two different structures, was presented with the same biasing conditions and demonstrated a reduction in the avalanche frequency by 34%.

References

[1] T. Al-Attar and T. H. Lee, "Monolithic integrated millimeter-wave IMPATT transmitter in standard CMOS technology," IEEE Transactions on Microwave Theory and Techniques, vol. 53, pp. 3557-3561, 2005.

[2] W. T. Read Jr. "A proposed high-frequency negativeresistance diode," Bell Syst. Tech. J., vol. 37, pp. 401- 446, Mar. 1958.

[3] T. Al-Attar, M. D. Mulligan, and T. H. Lee, "Lateral IMPATT Diodes in Standard CMOS Technology," IEEE International Electron Devices Meeting, IEDM, December, 2004.

[4] T. Al-Attar, "CMOS diodes operating beyond avalanche frequency," 12th International Symposium on Quality Electronic Design, pp. 1-6, 2011.

[5] M. Gilden and M. E. Hines, "Electronic tuning effects in the Read microwave avalanche diode," IEEE Trans. Electron Devices (Special Issue on Semiconductor Bulk-Effect and Transit Time Devices), vol. ED-13, pp. 169-175, Jan. 1966.

[6] M. C. A. M. Koolen, J. A. M. Geelen, and M. P. J. G. Versleijen, "An Improved De-embedding Technique for On-wafer High Frequency Characterization," Proceedings of the Bipolar Circuits and Technology Meeting, pp. 188-191, 1991.

[7] T. Al-Attar, A. Alshehri, A. Almansouri, and A. Alturki, "Critical parameters affecting the design of high frequency transmission lines in standard CMOS technology," Applied Computational Electromagnetics Society Symposium-Italy (ACES), pp. 1-2, Mar. 2017.

[8] E. Hammerstad and O. Jensen, "Accurate Models for Microstrip Computer-Aided Design," in 1980 IEEE MTT-S International Microwave Symposium Digest, 1980, pp. 407-

Dual-Band High Split Ratio Bagley Power Divider Based on Multi-T-Section Characterizaion of High Impedance Transmission Lines

Omar Jibreel and Nihad Dib
Electrical Engineering Department
Jordan University of Science and Technology
Irbid, Jordan
omar.j.jibreel@hotmail.com, nihad@just.edu.jo

Khair Al Shamaileh
Electrical and Computer Engineering Department
Purdue University Northwest
IN, USA
kalshama@pnw.edu

***Abstract*— We propose a dual-band 10:1:10 3-way Bagley power divider (BPD). The high characteristic impedance transmission lines in the conventional divider are replaced by dual-band T-shaped structures. To validate the design methodology, a prototype is designed to operate at 1 and 2 GHz. Simulation results show input port matching better than −20 dB, and transmission parameters, S_{21} (equals S_{41}) and S_{31}, around −4 dB and −14 dB, at the design frequencies, respectively.**

Keywords—Bagley power divider (BPD), dual-band, high characteristic impedance, high split ratio, T-sections.

I. Introduction

Unequal-split dual-band power dividers are main components in the modern RF/microwave subsystems, such as antenna arrays beam-forming, where unequal energy is required at each antenna element. The Bagley power divider (BPD) attracted some attention as a multi-way equal split divider that can be extended to any number of output ports [1]. In [2], the BPD was modified to split the power unequally using new analytically derived design equations. However, high-split ratio power dividers require transmission lines (TLs) with impractical, very narrow widths. In [3], a dual-band 1:10 Wilkinson power divider (WPD) was proposed, where the high-impedance impractical TLs were replaced by cascaded dual-band T-shaped sections. Herein, a 3-way dual-band 10:1:10 BPD is proposed. The rest of this paper is organized as follows: Section II presents the theory and design equations for designing the unequal-split BPD and characterizing the resulting high impedance TLs using T-sections; Section III presents simulation and measurements of the designed divider; and finally, conclusions are given in Section VI.

II. Theory and Design Equations

A. The Unequal-Split BPD

Fig. 1 presents the schematic of the 3-way unequal-split BPD proposed in [2]. The interconnecting TLs between ports have the length of quarter-wavelength at the design frequency. Considering a unit incident power at port 1, the characteristic impedances of the TLs, Z_1 and Z_2, are set to obtain the desired splitting ratio using the following design equations:

$$P_2 = P_4 = \left(Z_1/2Z_o\right)^2, \quad (1.a)$$

$$P_2/P_3 = \left(Z_2/2Z_o\right)^2, \quad (1.b)$$

The authors acknowledge the financial support of the Deanship of Scientific Research at the Jordan University of Science and Technology under research grant number 2017/331.

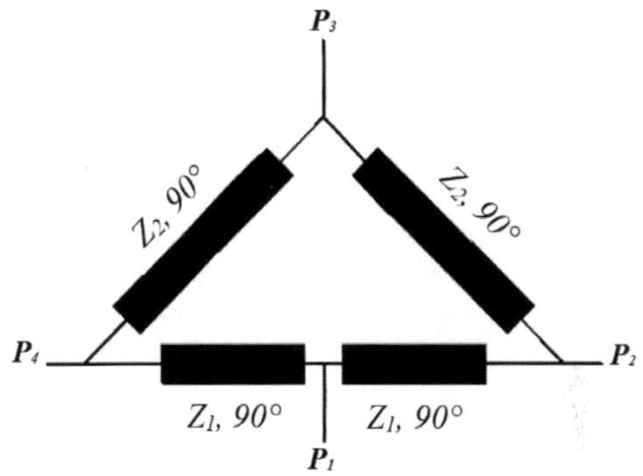

Fig. 1. Schematic of the 3-way unequal split BPD.

TABLE I. Characteristic Impedance Values of 3-Way BPD TLs with Different Split Ratios

P_2: P_3: P_4	Z_1 (Ω)	Z_2 (Ω)
2:1:2	63	141
5:1:5	67	223
10:1:10	69	316

where Z_0 is the impedance of ports termination. Table I shows the characteristic impedance values of the TLs for different splitting ratios, considering (Z_0 = 50 Ω). As the desired split ratio becomes higher, TLs with a higher impedance are required. Such lines are impractical and cannot be fabricated due to their narrow width. In this case, it is mandated to replace these impractical lines with realizable structures as will be presented in the next subsection.

B. High-Impedance Characterization Using T-Sections

Fig. 2 shows a conventional TL and its equivalent T-shaped structure. θ_i is the electrical length of the ith TL, at the design frequency. The T-section parameters are set to keep the same transmission properties of the replaced conventional line as follows [3]:

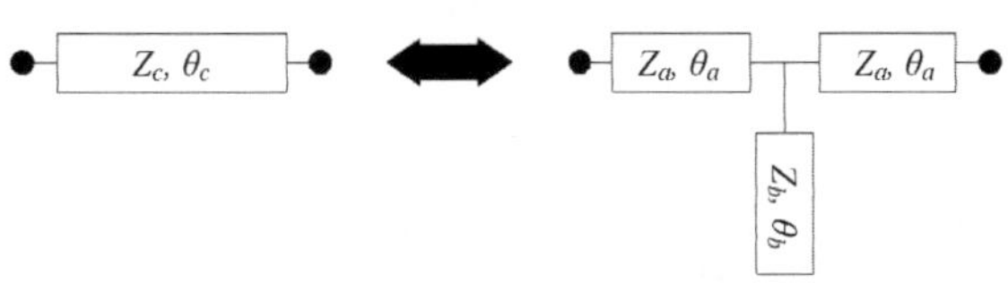

Fig. 2. Conventional TL characterization using a T-section.

$$Z_a = Z_c \cot(\theta_a)\left[\frac{\sin(\theta_c)}{1+\cos(\theta_c)}\right], \quad (2.a)$$

$$Z_b = \frac{1}{2} Z_a \left[\frac{\sin(2\theta_a)}{\cos(2\theta_a)-\cos(\theta_c)}\right]\tan(\theta_b). \quad (2.b)$$

By choosing the appropriate values for $\theta_{a,b}$, the impractical thin lines can be replaced by a realizable structure. To attain dual-band operation for the T-section at $f_{1,2}$ ($f_2 > f_1$), the following constraints should be satisfied:

$$\frac{Z_a\left[1+\cos(\theta_c)\right]\tan(\theta_a)}{\sin(\theta_c)} = \pm Z_c, \quad (3.a)$$

$$\theta_{a(f_2)} = l\pi \pm \theta_{a(f_1)}, \quad (3.b)$$

$$\theta_{b(f_2)} = m\pi \pm \theta_{b(f_1)}, \quad (3.c)$$

where l and m are positive integers. Let's define the frequency ratio as $K = f_2/f_1$ and subsequently, $K = \theta_{a(f_2)}/\theta_{a(f_1)}$. Hence, to obtain a dual-band T-section, the electrical lengths should be chosen as follows:

$$\theta_{a(f_1)} = l\pi/(K \pm 1), \quad (4.a)$$

$$\theta_{b(f_1)} = m\pi/(K \pm 1). \quad (4.b)$$

To maintain compactness, l is set to 1, and the positive sign is considered in the above equations. To obtain a realizable characteristic impedance value (i.e., positive value is obtained from equation (2.b)), m is set to 2 (i.e. $\theta_{b(f_1)} = 2\theta_{a(f_1)}$).

Let's consider the 10:1:10 BPD TLs with the characteristic impedance values shown in Table I. For the (90°, 69 Ω) TL, a realizable dual-band T-section can be obtained using the above equations considering the frequency ratio (K = 2). However, applying the equations to the (90°, 316 Ω) TL will lead to a dual-band T-section with impractical lines too. For such lines with very high characteristic impedance, it is efficient to divide it into smaller lines and replace each segment with its equivalent dual-band T-section. Table II represents the parameters of the equivalent dual -band T-sections of the 10:1:10 BPD.

III. Simulation and Measurments

Fig. 3 illustrates a photograph of the dual-band 10:1:10 BPD that operates at 1 and 2 GHz using the FR-4 substrate ($\varepsilon_r = 4.4$ and thickness = 1.5 mm). The low impedance line is substituted by one dual-band T-section, while the high impedance line is replaced by two cascaded sections with the parameters listed in Table II. Fig. 4 shows the simulated and the measured S-parameters of the proposed divider.

TABLE II. Dual-Band T-Sections Characterization of The 10:1:10 BPD Transmission Lines (K=2)

Z_i	*Impedance* (Ω)	θ_c (°)	Z_a (Ω), θ_a (°)	Z_b (Ω), θ_b (°)
Z_1	69	90	40, 60	60, 120
Z_2	316	45	75.4, 60	47.2, 120

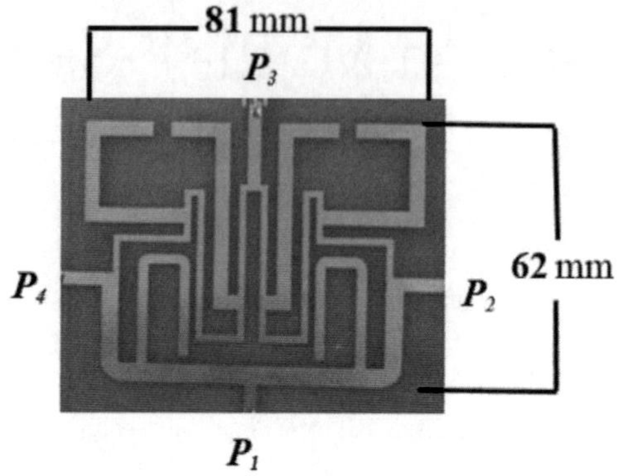

Fig. 3. A photograph of the dual-band 10:1:10 BPD.

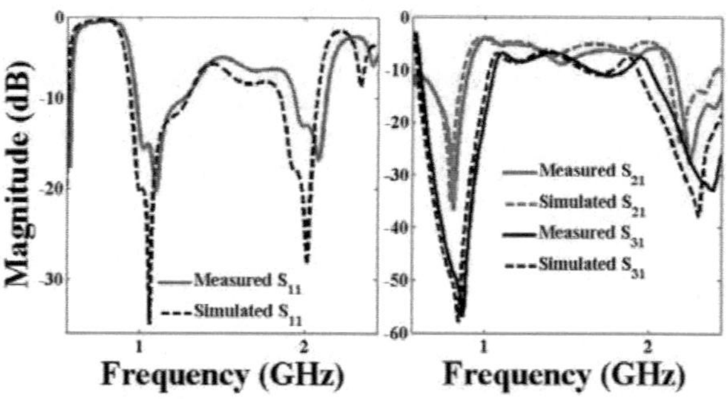

Fig. 4. Simulated and measured S-parameters of the proposed BPD.

Full-wave simulation results show an input port matching better than −20 dB at the design frequencies. The transmission parameter S_{21} ($S_{21} = S_{41}$) has the values of −3.9 dB and −4.7 dB at 1 GHz and 2 GHz, respectively. While the simulated S_{31} is −14 dB at 1 GHz, and −14.8 dB at 2 GHz. Such values are considered close to the theoretical ones (S_{21} = S_{41} = −3.22 dB, S_{31} = −13.22 dB). The small difference between simulated and measured results is due to conductor losses, and the soldering of the connectors to the lines.

IV. Conclusions

A dual-band BPD with high split ratio was designed by employing dual-band T-sections to characterize the divider lines. For extremely high characteristic impedance lines, the line is divided into several segments, then, each segment is replaced by its equivalent dual-band T-section. To validate the proposed procedure, a 10:1:10 BPD was designed to operate at 1 and 2 GHz. The designed divider was fabricated and measured. Simulated and measured results are in a good agreement and close to the theoretical results at the design frequencies.

References

[1] I. Skagami, T. Wuren, M. Fujii, and Y. Tomoda, "A new type of multi-way microwave power divider based on Bagley polygon power divider," Asia-Pacific Microwave Conference Proc., vol. 2, pp. 1353–1356, Dec. 2006.

[2] O. Abu-Alnadi, N. Dib, K. Al-Shamaileh, and A. Sheta, "Design and analysis of unequal split Bagley power dividers," *International Journal of Electronics*, vol. 102, pp. 500–513, 2015.

[3] K. Al-Shamaileh, N. Dib, and S. Abushamleh, "A dual-band 1:10 Wilkinson power divider based on multi-T-section characterization of high-impedance transmission lines," *IEEE Microwave and Wireless Components Letters*, vol. 27, pp. 897–899, Oct. 2017.

Design Optimization of Dual-Band and Double-Polarization IR Perfect Absorbers Using Adjoint Sensitivities

Ahmed Y. Elsharabasy
Electrical and Computer Engineering
McMaster University
Hamilton, ON, Canada
elsharay@mcmaster.ca

Mohamed H. Bakr
Electrical and Computer Engineering
McMaster University
Hamilton, ON, Canada
mbakr@mcmaster.ca

M.Jamal Deen
Electrical and Computer Engineering
McMaster University
Hamilton, ON, Canada
jamal@mcmaster.ca

***Abstract*—In this work, we utilize adjoint sensitivity approach within a constrained optimization algorithm to design a dual band infrared perfect absorber (IR-PA). The structure is composed of a silver circular ring and an elliptic cross centered on top of a two layer substrate. Dimensions of the ring and crossed ellipses in addition to the thicknesses are considered the design parameters. Careful parameters' optimization leads to a dual-band and near unity absorber at 2.7 µm and 6.0 µm, respectively. The symmetry of the design allows the operation at a polarization free electromagnetic excitation. The absorption peak wavelengths and their bandwidths can be tailored to match with a wide range of applications such as detection, energy harvesting, imaging, and stealth technologies.**

Keywords—adjoint sensitivity, double polarization, dual-band, metal-insulator-metal, optimization, perfect absorber.

I. Introduction

Infrared absorbers that are able to reach near-unity absorption of incident IR energy offer the opportunity as important building blocks in many emerging applications such as energy harvesting [1], IR detection [2], and thermal imaging [2]. Additionally, perfect absorbers in IR and visible regime provide a suitable solution for stealth technology [3]. One of the ways to design a perfect absorber is through using the exotic properties of metal-insulator-metal (MIM) structures. The occurrence of plasmonic resonances enables MIM structures to reach near-unity absorption. These perfect absorbers are considered one of the highly attractive metamaterial applications to researchers.

Infrared perfect absorber (IR-PA) has the ability to harvest the untapped energy coming from sun in the IR range and to efficiently absorb the IR laser light in military applications. By introducing more design parameters, the absorption peaks at center wavelengths can be tuned. The bandwidths around these peaks can be tailored as well. Optimization algorithms are required to take care of these multi-objectives with large number of parameters. Adjoint sensitivity allows exploiting constrained optimization algorithms in order to obtain the optimal parameters' values quickly [4].

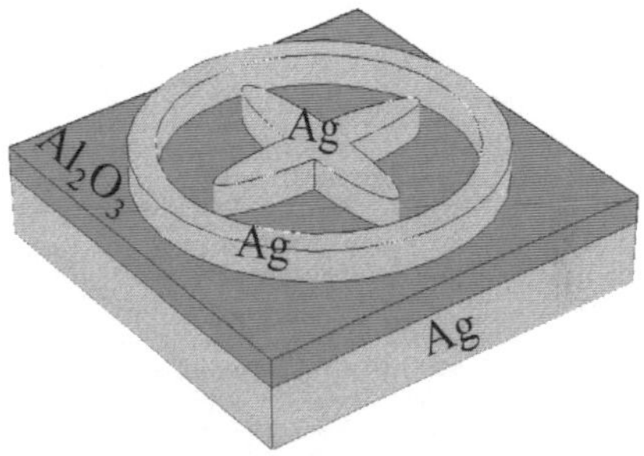

Fig. 1. A schematic 3D view of a unit cell of the proposed IR-PA.

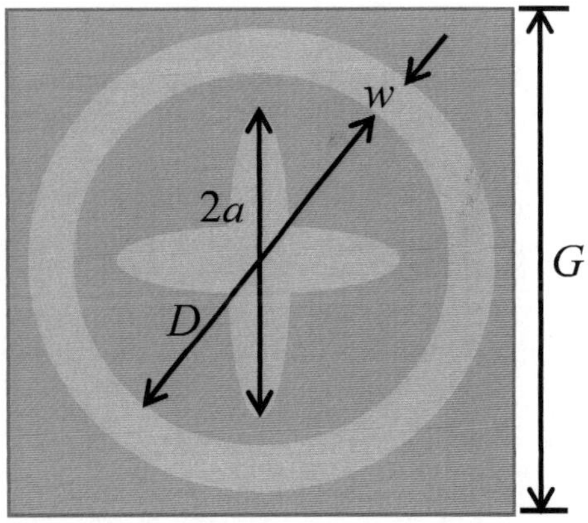

Fig. 2. A top view of an IR-PA unit cell with defined dimensions.

II. Proposed Design

Fig. 1 shows the unit cell of the proposed design. The MIM structure used in this work is composed of a silver structure built over another silver ground plane and separated by a thin Al_2O_3 dielectric layer. An elliptic cross centered inside a circular ring form the top metallic layer. The structure has 7 design parameters. These parameters include the ring inner radius D, its width w, the semi radii of the ellipses a, and b, the periodicity of the unit cell G, and the thicknesses of the top layer and dielectric t_m, and t_d, respectively. The design parameters are presented in Fig. 2.

The objective function describes the absorption at specific wavelengths is defined using *S*-parameters. Owing to the ground plane, the transmission vanishes. Therefore, the optimization problem can be formulated as in (1):

$$\max_{x}\left\{1-\left|S_{11}(\lambda_i,\boldsymbol{x})\right|^2-\left|S_{21}(\lambda_i,\boldsymbol{x})\right|^2\right\}, \quad (1)$$

$$\text{subject to} \quad \boldsymbol{x}_l \le \boldsymbol{x} \le \boldsymbol{x}_u,$$

$$\lambda_i = 2.7\ \mu\text{m},\ 6.0\ \mu\text{m}.$$

The vectors $\boldsymbol{x}_l$ and $\boldsymbol{x}_u$ are the predefined upper and lower bounds to avoid undesirable overlaps. The *S*-parameters are calculated from simulations carried out using COMSOL Multiphysics [5]. The simulator supplies the gradients with respect to all design parameters. This technique is known as self-adjoint sensitivity analysis (SASA) [6, 7].

III. Results

In our proposed design, the optimization algorithm reveals an optimal performance as plotted in Fig. 3 according to the set of optimal parameters listed in Table I.

TABLE I. THE OPTIMAL PARAMAETERS

Parameter	Optimal Value
G	1400 nm
D	500 nm
w	100 nm
a	400 nm
b	75 nm
t_m	100 nm
t_d	90 nm

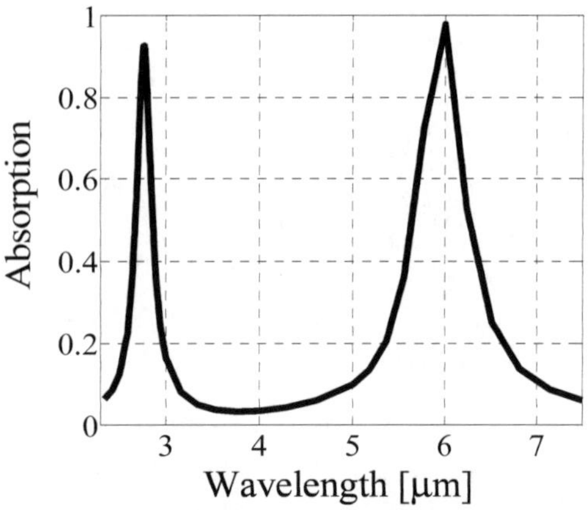

Fig. 3. Absorption spectra of the proposed MPA; 98% at 2.7µm, and 93% at 2.7µm.

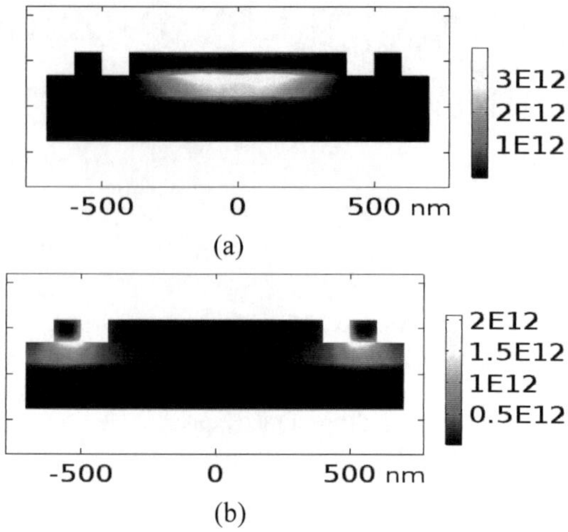

Fig. 4. Magnetic field intensity $|H|^2$ distribution in the xz-plane at the absorption peaks: (a) 2.7µm and (b) 6 µm.

The IR-PA possesses dual absorption peaks of 93% at 2.7 µm and 98% at 6 µm, respectively. The magnetic field intensity is shown at each peak wavelength in Fig. 4. As expected, the resonance at the shorter wavelength is according to elliptic cross, while the outer ring is responsible of the longer resonance wavelength. The proposed approach can be used to design perfect absorbers at predefined resonance wavelengths. In addition, a wideband response is expected when moving the two resonance wavelengths closer to each other.

References

[1] H. Wang and L. Wang, "Perfect selective metamaterial solar absorbers," Opt. Exp., vol. 21, pp. A1078–A1093, 2013.
[2] N. I. Zheludev and Y. S. Kivshar, "From metamaterials to metadevices," Nature Mater., vol. 11, p. 917, 2012.
[3] K. Iwaszczuk, et al., "Flexible metamaterial absorbers for stealth applications at terahertz frequencies," Opt. Exp., vol. 20, pp. 635–643, 2012.
[4] M. H. Bakr, Nonlinear Optimization in Electrical Engineering with Applications in Matlab, IET, 2013.
[5] 'COMSOL Multiphysics' ver. 5.3, COMSOL AB, Stockholm, Sweden, 2018.
[6] H. Akel and J. P. Webb, "Design sensitivities for scattering-matrix calculation with tetrahedral edge elements," IEEE Trans. Magn., vol. 36, no. 4, pp. 1043–1046, July 2000.
[7] M. H. Bakr, A. Elsherbeni, and V. Demir, Adjoint Sensitivity Analysis of High Frequency Structures With MATLAB, IET, 2017.

RF Compressed Sensing Radar Based on Digital Beamforming for Localization and IoT Applications

Prateek Nallabolu and Changzhi Li
Department of Electrical Engineering
Texas Tech University
Lubbock, USA
prateek-reddy.nallabolu@ttu.edu, changzhi.li@ttu.edu

Abstract—**This paper presents the concept of a radio frequency (RF) compressed sensing radar for indoor localization. A digital beamforming architecture for RF physical layer compressed sensing is discussed. Compressed sensing can reconstruct an under-sampled signal provided it is sparse in nature. A pseudo random multi-beam radiation pattern will be used to scan the target frame. The spatial sparsity in the target frame helps in recovering the entire frame using less number of scans compared to the conventional indoor localization system.**

Keywords—compressed sensing, pseudo random multi-beam radiation pattern, sparsity.

I. INTRODUCTION

As the internet of things (IoT) becomes the infrastructure of the information society, many solutions have been developed to meet the increasing demand for short-range localization. Examples include systems based on wireless communication networks (WCN), wireless sensor networks (WSN) [1], radio frequency identification (RFID) [2], as well as frequency modulated continuous-wave (FMCW) and ultra-wideband (UWB) cooperative localization systems [3]. Using a variety of estimated metrics obtained by data fusion of information represented by the received signal strength (RSS) [4], time of arrival (TOA) and direction of arrival (DOA), such wireless localization systems have achieved significant success. However, most of the solutions rely on established networks or interrogators, and the targets to be localized are mainly active sources, such as cellular/Wi-Fi devices and RFID tags. Some FMCW/UWB systems can localize objects without requiring the targets to carry any device. However, deploying in practical short-range mobile applications could be challenging because a high resolution requires a large signal bandwidth, and the beam scanning mechanism requires complex front-end circuits.

Recently, compressed sensing (CS) has aroused significant interests [5]. CS can recover a signal from far fewer samples by exploiting the sparsity of a signal through optimization. This means reduced system complexity and less resources consumed by the sampling front-end, leading to potential of reduced cost and spectrum- and energy-efficiency for mobile devices. Randomness is the key for the success of CS. Among many applications of compressed sensing, compressed sensing radars are directly related to wireless localization [6,7]. Most existing researches introduce randomness by using different methods such as random filtering and convolution based on digital signal processing [8]. Since the RF front-end is one of the most expensive and power-hungry building blocks, a system that takes full advantages of compressed sensing should execute physical-layer compressed sensing by introducing randomness directly into the RF front-end.

Ideally, randomness can be introduced using an RF phased array system by randomly switching radiation beams in time sequence, so that the target is illuminated by spatially randomized radiation. However, an RF phased array system suffers from high complexity and cost. To reduce complexity, digital beamforming can be used which provides more flexibility to achieve a high level of randomness.

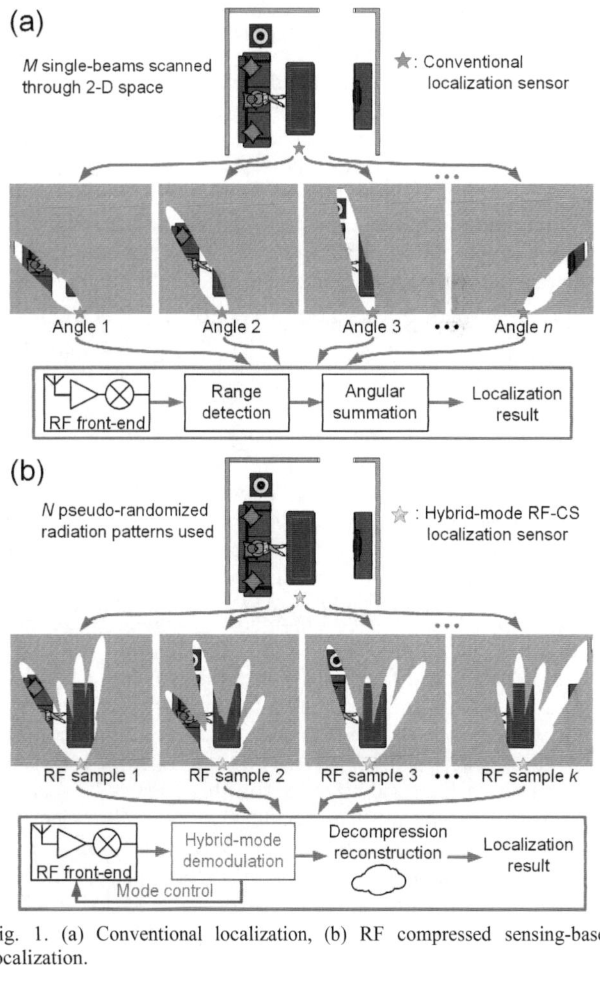

Fig. 1. (a) Conventional localization, (b) RF compressed sensing-based localization.

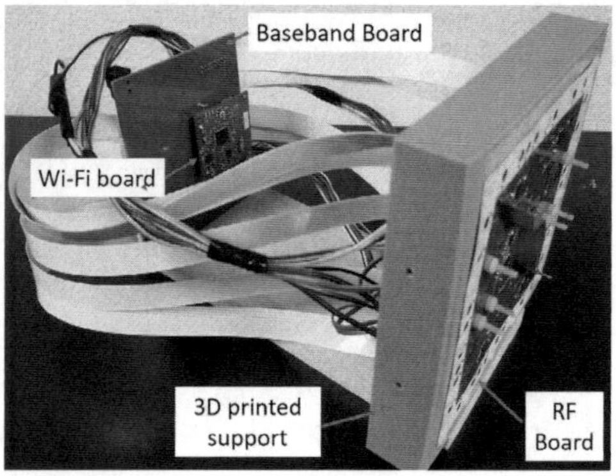

Fig. 2. Prototype of a digital beamforming radar.

In this paper, a short-range wireless localization system for modern IoT applications, which employs a physical layer RF compressed sensing based on a novel digital beamforming architecture is discussed. The digital beamforming architecture probes the space of interest with pseudo-random radiation patterns instead of a focused scanning beam. Compared with RF beamforming, the proposed solution reduces the hardware complexity of the system.

II. THEORY

Compressed sensing states that a signal x of length n and k-sparse, i.e., the signal contains not more than k non-zero elements, can be reconstructed using m measurements, where $m << n$. The sparsity of the signal x determines the sampling rate in CS. To achieve a high probability of reconstruction, the measurements must be random in nature. A mathematical measure of the randomness of the measurements is the mutual coherence of the $m \times n$ measurement matrix ϕ. The measurement matrix takes the form $y = \phi x$, where y is the measurement vector of length m. To reconstruct the signal x with high probability, the mutual coherence μ of the measurement matrix must be low.

In indoor localization application, the target of interest is usually sparse in spatial domain in most realistic situations. This sparsity in the spatial domain enables the use of compressed sensing. The spatial frame to be scanned can be divided into M equivalent blocks. In the conventional indoor localization system, the radar scans through each of the M blocks sequentially. Due to the spatial sparsity of the target frame, compressed sensing can be used to scan the blocks randomly and reconstruct the entire frame using CS reconstruction algorithms. Furthermore, an antenna array which can generate multiple random beams at a time can be used to scan multiple blocks at a time.

Fig. 1 shows the difference between the conventional indoor localization system and the proposed compressed sensing radar based indoor localization system. In conventional indoor localization system shown in Fig. 1 (a), the RF front-end steers its beam with a fixed step size to scan the space of interest. M beams will be used, and it is desirable to have a very narrow scanning beam to achieve a high cross-range resolution. For the proposed solution, the RF front-end generates a pseudo random radiation pattern with multiple beams radiated to different directions at the same time as shown in Fig. 1 (b). The number of scans N will be less than M, corresponding to RF compressed sensing and thus significantly reducing the power consumption and complexity of the RF front-end.

The digital beamforming front-end will provide a randomized illumination with multiple beams transmitted simultaneously. The receiver will detect a mixed-up range spectrum in response to targets covered by the multi-beam. This measurement data can be represented by a matrix g similar to the matrix y. Using f to represent the sparse locations to be solved and H to represent the measurement matrix, the localization problem can be implemented by solving a matrix equation $g = Hf$ using reconstruction algorithms such as basis pursuit (BP) or orthogonal matching pursuit (OMP).

Fig. 2 shows a multiple-input multiple-output FMCW radar capable of digital beamforming [9], which can provide the maximum flexibility for forming various radiation patterns. The radar consists of 8×8 non-uniform antenna array designed to achieve 2-D beam scanning. The radar operates at a center frequency of 24.125 GHz and a bandwidth of 240 MHz. It achieves an angular resolution of 7.2° with a 90° field of view. The radar is capable of short-range localization with an estimated accuracy of 5 cm.

III. CONCLUSION

In this paper, a novel solution for short-range localization was proposed. An RF compressed sensing radar with a digital beamforming architecture was discussed, which aims to significantly improve the efficiency by generating pseudo random multi-beams to scan through a target frame. The spatial sparsity of the target frame ensures that the target frame can be completely reconstructed using less number of scans as compared to conventional indoor localization systems.

REFERENCES

[1] A. Boukerche, H. A. Oliveira, E. F. Nakamura, and A. A. Loureiro, "Localization systems for wireless sensor networks," IEEE Wireless Communications, vol. 14, no. 6, pp. 6-12, 2007.

[2] L. M. Ni, D. Zhang, and M. R. Souryal, "RFID-based localization and tracking technologies," IEEE Wireless Communications, vol. 18, no. 2, pp. 45-51, 2011.

[3] R. Feger, C. Pfeffer, W. Scheiblhofer, C. M. Schmid, M. J. Lang, and A. Stelzer, "A 77-GHz cooperative radar system based on multi-channel FMCW stations for local positioning applications," IEEE Transactions on Microwave Theory and Techniques, vol. 61, no. 1, pp. 676-684, 2013.

[4] H. A. Obeidat, Y. A. Dama, R. A. Abd-Alhameed, Y.-F. Hu, R. S. Qahwaji, J. M. Noras, et al., "A comparison between vector algorithm and CRSS algorithms for indoor localization using received signal strength," The Applied Computational Electromagnetics Society (ACES), vol. 31, pp. 868-876, August 2016.

[5] D. L. Donoho, "Compressed sensing," IEEE Transactions on Information Theory, vol. 52, no. 4, pp. 1289-1306, 2006.

[6] M. Herman and T. Strohmer, "Compressed sensing radar," in 2008 IEEE Radar Conference, 2008, pp. 1-6: IEEE.

[7] D. Yang, H. Li, G. D. Peterson and A. Fathy, "Compressive sensing TDOA for UWB positioning systems," 2011 IEEE Radio and Wireless Symposium, Phoenix, AZ, 2011, pp. 194-197.

[8] J. Romberg, "Compressive sensing by random convolution," SIAM Journal on Imaging Sciences, vol. 2, no. 4, pp. 1098-1128, 2009.

[9] Z. Peng and C. Li, "A portable K-band 3-D MIMO radar with nonuniformly spaced array for short-range localization," in IEEE Transactions on Microwave Theory and Techniques, vol. 66, no. 11, pp. 5075-5086, Nov. 2018.

The Optimization of Arbitrary-Shape Conformal Array Antenna's Performance Based on CSHPSO

Zhu Qingchao
Anhui Province Engineering Laboratory for Antenna and Microwave
East China Research Institute of Electronic Engineeing
Hefei, China
zhu_qingchao@sina.com

Zhang Xiaolin
Anhui Province Engineering Laboratory for Antenna and Microwave
East China Research Institute of Electronic Engineeing
Hefei, China

Fang Jia
Anhui Province Engineering Laboratory for Antenna and Microwave
East China Research Institute of Electronic Engineeing
Hefei, China

***Abstract*—In order to optimize the arbitrary-shape conformal array antenna's performance, the Cloud Self-adaptive Hybrid Particle Swarm Optimization (CSHPSO) is introduced in this paper. The inertia weight coefficient is introduced into Hybrid Particle Swarm Optimization (HPSO), which is built upon PSO, to avoid the premature convergence. The introduction of cloud self-adaptive model makes particles in HPSO more intelligent. An arbitrary-shape conformal array is optimized by CSHPSO and results show that the gain is improved compared with the situation that all elements are excited. It is obvious that the algorithm is effective to optimize arbitrary-shape conformal array antenna's performance such as gain, beam-width and side-lobe.**

***Keywords*—arbitrary-shape, conformal array antenna, CSHPSO, cloud self-adaptive model, intelligent**

I. Introduction

Particle swarm optimization (PSO) is widely used because it can effectively solve complex problems such as antenna array optimization for better radiation characteristics. D. Mandal used improved swarm intelligence to design concentric circular antenna array[1]. Pradhan used PSO to design and optimize a mutually coupled planar array antenna[2]. It was derived in the migration model of birds and abstracted from the bird migration to deals with problems in which variables are defined in continuous domain. Yu combines PSO and GA to design low side-lobe level conformal antenna array[3]. In paper[4], the cloud self-adaptive model and rule of variation are introduced into PSO to build CVCPSO to avoid premature convergence.

The sparse of array is necessary in conformal array antenna design and the optimization can improve performance of the pattern by eliminating the elements that have negative contribution to the directivity at the same time. The platform we often use is not regular in shape. Teng realizes stationary targets imaging and moving targets detection based on airship conformal sparse array[5]. In paper[6], Oliveri optimized sparse conformal array through a versatile BCS-based method. For arbitrary-shape conformal array antenna, the contribution of element to array's gain is determined by the angle between the maximum radiation direction of element and the maximum radiation direction of array, which can be calculated according to elements' positions while elements' ground are placed on the plane perpendicular to the normal direction of the placed point. However, it is impossible to determine whether the element needs to be excited according to the position for arbitrary-shape conformal array antenna while elements are not arranged in obvious rules and the normal direction of each element cannot be directly obtained. In this paper, the cloud self-adaptive model, which optimizes the weight, is used to form CSHPSO built on the HPSO.

II. Principle of CSHPSO

PSO is applied for optimizing problems with variables defined in continuous domain. It needs to be discretized when it is used to optimize the excitation coefficients of array. It is assumed that the system consists of p groups and each group consists of q particles which carries n-dimensional information. What is different from PSO is that particles update information through cross-substitution in the iterative process of HPSO. The specific approach is that part of information of the optimal solution will be given to the particle and used for next iteration when the particle update its information after its t-th iteration. The cross-substitution process actually replaces the partial information with the information at the corresponding position of the better solution according to weight coefficient.

The particles are not filtered in HPSO since the weight coefficient keeps unchanged and all particles are approaching to the group and system optimal solution at the same speed. In order to avoid premature convergence, the inertia weight coefficient is introduced. The specific approach is that different weight coefficients are chosen according to the value η which is obtained by calculating the ratio of result in the t-th iteration and the optimal solution of the iteration. The weighting progress is based on cloud self-adaptive model which is derived from the cloud model in which the ambiguity and randomness are quantified by expectation Ex, entropy En, and hyper-entropy He. The positive generation process of cloud drop is that any x is assumed to satisfy x-N(E_x-$E_n{}'^2$) under the qualitative concept in the universe U, then the membership degree of x to the qualitative concept is:

$$u(x) = e^{-\frac{(x-Ex)^2}{2En'^2}}.$$

Where En' is a normally distributed random number with En as the expected value and He as the standard deviation.

The birds which are closer to the temporary migration site will slow down while the far-side birds increase the speed after the t-th iteration so that the whole bird flock will be closer to the known optimal migration and the model provides better starting points for next birds addressing. The weight coefficients of cross-substitution are obtained from cloud self-adaptive model.

The model makes the optimization more intelligent because weight coefficients are assigned to particles according to the group and system optimal solution at the every iteration. The proportion of particles which find better positions at the next iteration is larger after carrying the optimal solution information of the group and system at the same time and it is more likely to find the best solution after many iterations.

III. Optimization of Conformal Array Antenna

In order to optimize conformal array antenna, an arbitrary-shape surface is selected for antenna modeling. The antenna element is optimized by two-dimensional periodic boundary and the spacing is approximately half wavelength of the high frequency. The shape of surface which is obtained from body of airplane is shown in Fig. 1. The elements' positions keep unchanged after acquiring their positions through commercial software such as Hypermesh and some of elements are chosen excited to obtain better directivity. The scanning angle is fixed at the normal direction which is based on the coordinate system of the central element.

The element factor is considered in the optimization and the beam width is consistent with the simulation result. The normal and referenced vector of element at the point can be obtained through commercial software and the element factor can be rotated until the element's maximum direction is consistent with the normal vector.

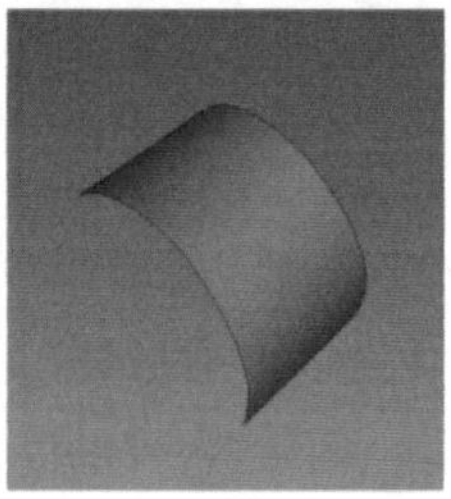

Fig. 1. Surface of airplane's body.

The antenna is optimized by CSHPSO to obtain higher gain at the normal direction and the results are shown in Fig. 2 and Fig. 3. The patterns of array are shown in Fig. 2 and the excitation coefficient is shown in Fig. 3.

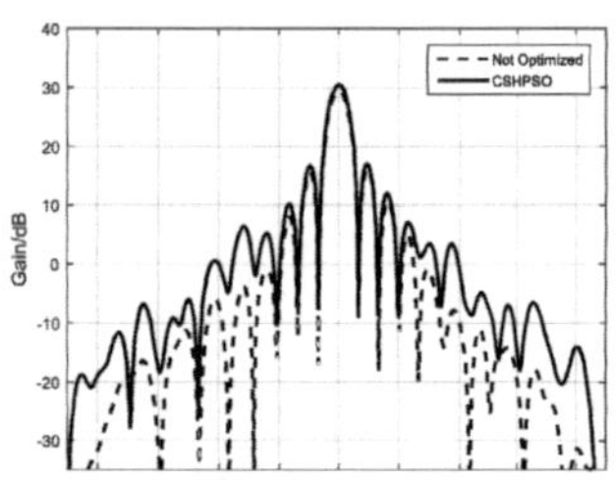

Fig. 2. The patterns of array.

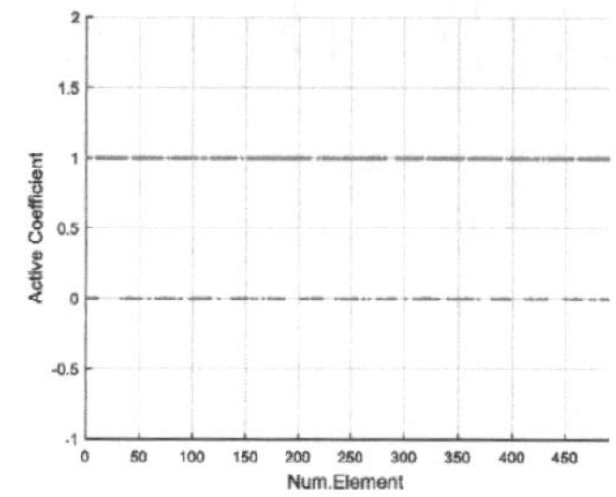

Fig. 3. The excitation coefficients.

It is obvious that the normal gain is improved by partly exciting elements compared with all elements excited and the gain is increased from 29.44 dBi to 30.48 dBi. The excitation coefficients are shown in Fig.3. The number of array elements is 490 while the excited is only 317 when the optimal gain is obtained. The optimization process greatly reduces the number of excitation elements. Considering the order number of antenna elements, the elements which are placed in central part of the surface are almost fully excited when the optimizing direction is set at normal of the coordinate system because the maximum directions of elements away from the central part deviate far from the normal direction and they contribute little or show negative influence to the antenna's normal gain. The optimization results show that CSHPSO can effectively optimize the performance of arbitrary-shape conformal array antenna. Besides, the algorithm not only is available with the antenna's gain but also can be applied to the beam width and side-lobe level optimization of pattern.

IV. Conclusion

This paper presents the principle of CSHPSO and the algorithm is modified to optimize arbitrary-shape conformal array antenna's performance based on the BPSO. Results show that CSHPSO exhibits better ability to find the global optimal position and is effective to optimize antenna's pattern.

References

[1] D. Mandal, S. P. Ghoshal and A. K. Bhattacharjee. "Improved Swarm Intelligence Based Optimal Design of Concentric Circular Antenna Array," 2009. IEEE 978-1-4244-4819-7/09

[2] Hrudananda Pradhan, Biswa Binayak Mangaraj and Iti Saha Misra. "Designing and optimizing a mutually coupled planar array antenna using PSO for UHF application," AEMC, Dec. 2013

[3] Xiao-meng Yu, Yan Zhang, Tao Dong and Li-wei Wang. "Design of low side-lobe level conformal antenna array by PSO-GA," ICUWB, Oct. 2016I.

[4] Qingchao Zhu and Qinghua Lai. "The optimization of conformal array based on CVCPSO[J]," ICEICT, Aug. 2016K.

[5] Xiu-min Teng and Dao-jing Li. "Stationary targets imaging and moving targets detection based on airship conformal sparse array," APSAR, 2011, pp 1-4

[6] Giacomo Oliveri, Ephrem T. Bekele, Fabrizio Robol and Andrea Massa. "Sparsening Conformal Arrays Through a Versatile BCS-based Method," pp: 1681-1689, 2014

Fast Algorithm of Arbitrary Beam Propagation Based on Adaptive Elliptical Gaussian Beam Decomposition

Dong Xia
School of Electronics and Information Engineering
Beihang University
Beijing, China
buaaxd@buaa.edu.cn

Liao Ma
School of Electronics and Information Engineering
Beihang University
Beijing, China
ma_liao@buaa.edu.cn

Xiya Shao
School of Electronics and Information Engineering
Beihang University
Beijing, China
865458215@qq.com

Ming Bai*
School of Electronics and Information Engineering
Beihang University
Beijing, China
mbai@buaa.edu.cn

***Abstract*—An algorithm for arbitrary electromagnetic (EM) beam propagation is proposed and well demonstrated in this paper. The essential idea of this algorithm is to decompose arbitrary beam into a small number of elliptical Gaussian beams, which is similar but different from existing diffracted Gaussian beam analysis (DGBA) based on Gabor expansion. The proposed algorithm utilizing adaptive Gaussian beam matching method is much more efficient than regular decomposition strategy by Gabor expansion. Beam propagation is then calculated by these elliptical Gaussian beams' superposed analytical results, with accuracy comparable with physical optics (PO) theory. This fast algorithm can be suitable for analyzing beam propagation in electrically-large systems, such as reflector antennas and quasi-optical (QO) transforming systems.**

***Keywords*—adaptive matching, beam propagation, Gaussian beam.**

I. Introduction

The beam propagation in systems with large electrical sizes has always been a popular issue, which involves beam modification, beam transformation and beam prediction, such as in reflector antennas, high frequency quasi-optical (QO) beam transforming systems, etc. [1,2]. There have been considerable algorithms for solving such propagation problems. To improve the computational efficiency, fast algorithms based on the concept of mode decomposition and synthesis have been developed. The plane wave spectrum (PWS) [1,3,4] is based on the idea that arbitrary electromagnetic (EM) beam can be decomposed into a set of plane waves with different propagating directions. Gabor expansion based diffracted Gaussian beam analysis (DGBA) [5,6], alternatively, decomposes the EM beam into a set of elementary circular Gaussian beams. Both plane wave expansion and Gabor expansion conform with orthogonal completeness principle, therefore have broad applicability. However, both algorithms follow routine decomposition procedures, during which distribution characteristics of the beam are barely involved. Gabor expansion divides arbitrary beam distribution into small square grids and results in thousands of circular Gaussian beam elements, which limits the calculating efficiency. In addition, efficiency of Gabor expansion relies on several manually chosen parameters, such as radius of elementary circular Gaussian beam and dual frame function [6].

In this paper, a novel algorithm which takes advantage of beam's distribution characteristics is proposed based on a different mode decomposition strategy and EM field equivalence principle. The local undulating distribution of the beam with different scales is matched with Gaussian beam of elliptical type. An adaptive matching method is developed to efficiently decompose the beam's complex distribution into a few hundred elliptical Gaussian beams with different sizes and orientations, much less than those by Gabor expansion. After decomposition, vectorial propagation of the beam can be simply reconstructed by the superposition of these elliptical Gaussian beams' propagating results.

This work was supported by the National Natural Science Foundation of China under Grant 61671032.

II. Fast Calculation of Propagation and Numerical Results

For better illustration of this fast algorithm, calculating procedure of an arbitrary sample aperture field's propagation ($\boldsymbol{E_0}$(x, y, 0) in Fig. 1), which is the output field of a certain QO beam transformation design, is given in this section.

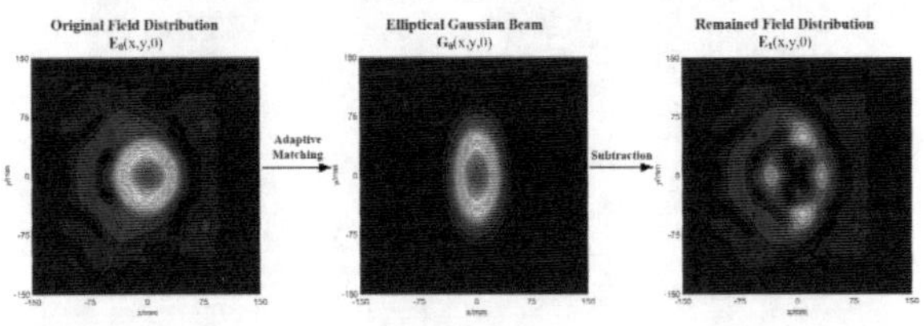

Fig. 1. First round of beam decomposition for aperture field $\boldsymbol{E_0}$(x, y, 0).

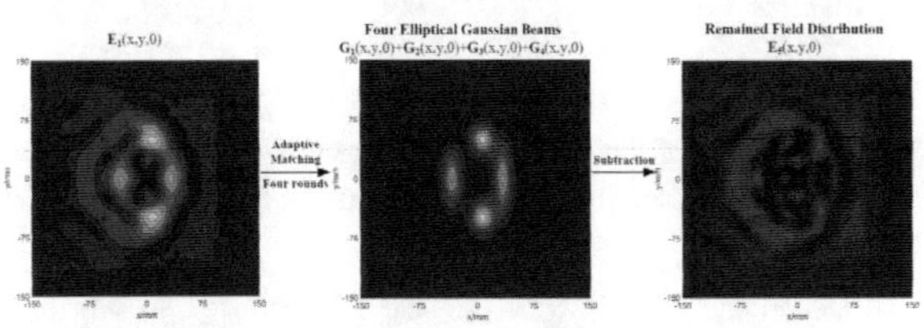

Fig. 2. Next four rounds of beam decomposition.

For the aperture field $\boldsymbol{E_0}$(x, y, 0) with two-dimensional distribution, the number of its sampling points is $N\times N$. Steps of single-round decomposition based on adaptive elliptical Gaussian beam matching are given as follows.

1. Find point $\boldsymbol{P_0}$=(x_0, y_0, 0) of maximum field value in the field distribution $\boldsymbol{E_0}$(x, y, 0).
2. Based on the wave-front principle of EM wave, $\boldsymbol{P_0}$'s wave propagating direction $\overrightarrow{\boldsymbol{D_0}}$ is calculated by the phases at its adjacent points.
3. According to the undulating distribution of $\boldsymbol{E_0}$(x, y, 0) in vicinity of $\boldsymbol{P_0}$, calculate the beam-waist radiuses $\boldsymbol{\omega u_0}$ and $\boldsymbol{\omega v_0}$ of matching elliptical Gaussian beam with maximum matching degree. It should be noted that the matched elliptical Gaussian beam is vectorial and fully reflects the characteristics of local propagating direction and polarization around $\boldsymbol{P_0}$.
4. Express this matched elliptical Gaussian beam [2] by $\boldsymbol{G_{00}}$(u, v, n) in its local coordinate, then further by $\boldsymbol{G_0}$(x, y, z) in universal coordinate.
5. Subtract matched elliptical Gaussian beam distribution $\boldsymbol{G_0}$(x, y, 0) from $\boldsymbol{E_0}$(x, y, 0) to obtain a remained field distribution $\boldsymbol{E_1}$(x, y, 0), as shown in Fig. 1. $\boldsymbol{E_1}$(x, y, 0) is later set as the original field distribution for the next round of decomposition and subtraction.

The results of next four rounds of decomposition are together shown in Fig. 2. In such decomposition and subtraction cycles, the energy of the remained field will continuously decrease, until the remaining energy is considered negligible, which can be controlled by a preset threshold value, for example -30dB (0.1%). In this case of the example EM beam presented in Fig. 1, after only 260 rounds, that is to say, by 260 elliptical Gaussian beams, the original field $\boldsymbol{E_0}$(x, y, 0) can be represented with error less than -30dB, and is expressed by:

$$\boldsymbol{E}(x, y, z) = \sum_i \boldsymbol{G}_i(x, y, z). \tag{1}$$

Amplitude and phase distributions of $\boldsymbol{E_0}$(x, y, z=0.2m) after beam propagation by implemented algorithm and typical physical optics (PO) integration are given in Fig. 3.

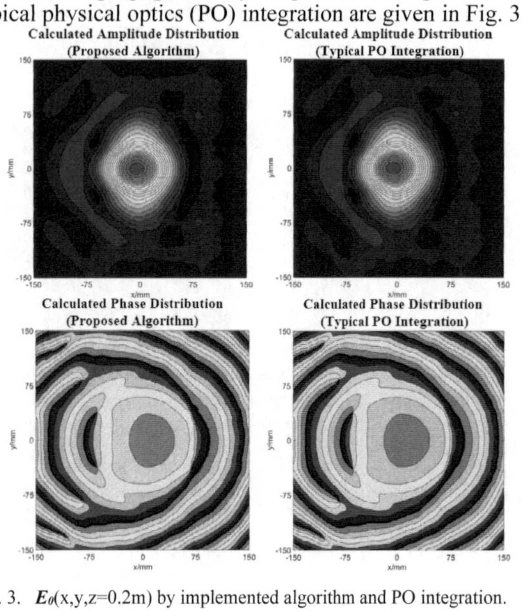

Fig. 3. $\boldsymbol{E_0}$(x,y,z=0.2m) by implemented algorithm and PO integration.

Comparison of the distributions along beam propagating direction, briefly as $\boldsymbol{E_0}$(x=0, y, z), is also given in Fig. 4.

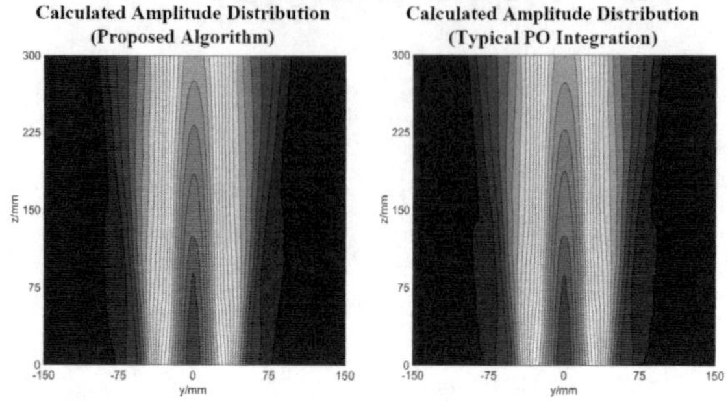

Fig. 4. $\boldsymbol{E_0}$(x=0,y,z) along propagating direction by implemented algorithm and and PO integration.

In this example, with 200×200 sampling points (45λ×45λ), beam propagating calculation from source plane to another plane only takes tens of seconds by proposed algorithm, while typical PO integration takes tens of minutes with same computational configuration. Also, corresponding consuming time by commercial software FEKO is over ten minutes with method of moment (MoM) solver, which is still much longer than this proposed algorithm.

III. Conclusion

A novel algorithm for analyzing beam propagation with high efficiency is demonstrated and verified in this paper. Based on the developed adaptive elliptical Gaussian beam matching method, this algorithm operates fast beam decomposition and accurate propagation calculation. Numerical results indicate that proposed algorithm has comparable accuracy with PO while much higher computational efficiency. It is very promising in applications of EM analysis of electrically large reflector antennas and high frequency QO beam transforming systems.

References

[1] P. J. Wood, Reflector antenna analysis and design. Stevenage Herts, England: Peter Peregrinus Ltd IEE Electromagnetic Waves Series, 1980.

[2] P. F. Goldsmith, Quasioptical Systems-Gaussian Beam, Quasioptical Propagation, and Applications. Piscataway, NJ: IEEE Press, 1998.

[3] A. Muñoz-Acevedo and M. Sierra-Castañer, "An efficient hybrid GO-PWS algorithm to analyze conformal serrated-edge reflectors for millimeter-wave compact range," IEEE Trans. Antennas Propag., vol. 60, pp. 1192–1197, Feburary 2012.

[4] M. Bai, N. Ou, and M. Jin, "Reflector antenna analysis method using Poynting vector tracing between virtual apertures," IET Microw. Antennas Propag., vol. 9, pp. 1279-1286, 2015.

[5] H. T. Chou, P. H. Pathak, and R. J. Burkholder, "Novel Gaussian beam method for the rapid analysis of large reflector antennas," IEEE Trans. Antennas Propag., vol. 49, pp. 880–893, June 2001.

[6] C. Rieckmann, M. R. Rayner, C. G. Parini, D. H. Martin, and R. S. Donnan, "Novel modular approach based on Gaussian beam diffraction for analysing quasi-optical multi-reflector antennas," IEE Proc. Microw, Antennas Propag., vol. 149, pp. 160-167, 2002.

Modeling and Experiments of High-Quality Factor Cavity Shielding Effectiveness

Salvatore Campione, Larry K. Warne, Isak C. Reines, Jeffery T. Williams, Roy K. Gutierrez, Rebecca S. Coats, and Lorena I. Basilio
Sandia National Laboratories
Albuquerque, NM, USA
sncampi@sandia.gov, lkwarne@sandia.gov, icreine@sandia.gov, jtwill@sandia.gov, rkgutie@sandia.gov, rscoats@sandia.gov, libasil@sandia.gov

Abstract—**In this paper, we investigate the coupling from external electromagnetic (EM) fields to the interior EM fields of a high-quality factor cylindrical cavity through a small perturbing slot. We illustrate the shielding effectiveness versus frequency, highlighting bounds on the penetrant power through the slot. Because internal fields may become larger than external ones, we then introduce a small amount of microwave absorbing materials decorating the slot to improve shielding effectiveness considerably, as shown by both simulations and experiments. Although the cylindrical cavity is used for demonstration purposes in this paper, the conclusions presented here can be leveraged for use with more complex cavity structures.**

Keywords—cavity, electromagnetic dampener, microwave absorbing materials, power balance bounds, quality factor, shielding effectiveness.

I. INTRODUCTION

Harsh external electromagnetic (EM) environments may adversely affect the electrical performance and reliability of many electrical circuits and systems. These are often enclosed by a metallic cavity that acts as a shield against unwanted interactions with external EM fields. This cavity may become resonant at certain frequencies. Unfortunately, since shields are not perfect, external fields can couple to the interior of the cavity, for example, through mechanical joints, seams, and rivets of the cavity, or other ports of entry. For high-quality factor resonant cavities, internal field levels can be much higher than the incoming field [1-6].

Using modeling and experiments, we first illustrate the quantity shielding effectiveness (SE) versus frequency for empty slotted cylindrical cavities. SE measures the ratio of the EM field at a given point in space with and without the cavity shield, respectively, and is defined as $\mathrm{SE} = \left|\mathbf{E}_{\text{cavity}}(\mathbf{r})\right| / E_0$, with $\mathbf{E}_{\text{cavity}}(\mathbf{r})$ the field inside the cavity at a probe position $\mathbf{r}$ and E_0 the external incident field. We define an upper bound, wide band SE result for a slot aperture by treating the backing cavity as a uniformly distributed matched load [5].

Finally, we decorate the slot with microwave absorbing materials to improve significantly system shielding effectiveness [6].

II. EMPTY SLOTTED CYLINDRICAL CAVITY

We investigate the 0.25 inch thick aluminum alloy cylinder (modeled with a conductivity $\sigma = 2.6\times10^{7}$ S/m) in Fig. 1 (a) with a 24 inch interior height and a 4 inch interior radius. The cavity comprises a 0.02 inch x 2 inch slot on one side (representative, for example, of a slot in the array created by a bolted flange), located midway along the cylinder length as shown in Fig. 1 (a). The cavity is excited with a plane wave incident towards the slot (-*x* direction) with the electric field oriented in the *z*-direction with $E_0 = 1$ V/m. The slot resonates at $f_{\text{slot}} = c/(2l_{\text{slot}}) = 3\times10^{8}/0.1016 \approx 2.96$ GHz.

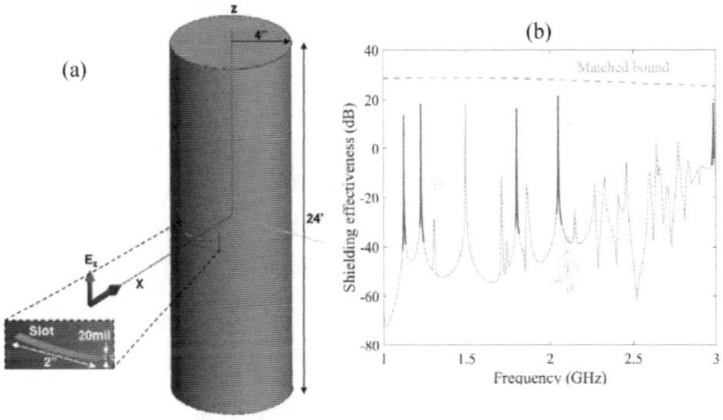

Fig. 1. (a) Schematic of a cylindrical cavity with a small slot being excited by a plane-wave incident field with electric field along the *z*-direction. (b) Full-wave simulation SE of an empty cavity versus frequency. The dotted gray line reports a broad frequency sweep in the band 1 to 3 GHz computed with FEKO, while the blue lines have been simulated with fine frequency sampling in CST Microwave Studio to capture their high-quality factors. The dashed orange line represents an upper bound, wide band SE result.

In Fig. 1 (b), we show in dotted gray the SE from full-wave simulations 4.3 mm away from one plate of the cylinder and 1 inch off center in the frequency band 1 to 3 GHz. Five resonances in solid blue have been simulated with fine frequency sampling to capture their high-quality factors. One can clearly see that, at some frequencies, SE reaches values larger than 0 dB, indicating that internal EM fields are larger than external ones. Figure 1 (b) also shows the dashed orange line as an upper bound, wide band SE result. This bound has been computed using conservation of power arguments [5, 7], by assuming that the matched received power P_{rec} of the aperture is delivered to be absorbed by the interior cavity walls P_{wall}. In other words, we impose $P_{rec} = P_{wall}$, with $P_{wall} = \sigma_{wall} S$ and $P_{rec} = \sigma_{rec} S_0$, where S_0 is the incident power flux density and S is the interior power density, and σ_{wall} and σ_{rec} are the wall loss cross section and the matched slot cross section, respectively [5]. The extreme level (or bound) is then defined as $SE_{\max} = 10\log_{10}(8S/S_0)$. One can see that the cavity SE is always below this bound, providing guidelines for maximum achievable levels of interior fields.

III. Slotted Cylindrical Cavity Loaded with Microwave Absorbing Materials

As observed in Fig. 1 (b), internal field levels can be much higher than the incoming field. Therefore, we decorate the aperture with a 2 mm thick patch of ECCOSORB MCS microwave absorbing material [8] as detailed in Fig. 2 (a), with the objective of improving shielding effectiveness; the absorber permittivity and permeability were modeled as $\varepsilon_m = \varepsilon_0(38 + i1)$ and $\mu_m = \mu_0(4.5 + i3)$ in the analyzed frequency band, respectively (see [6] for more details).

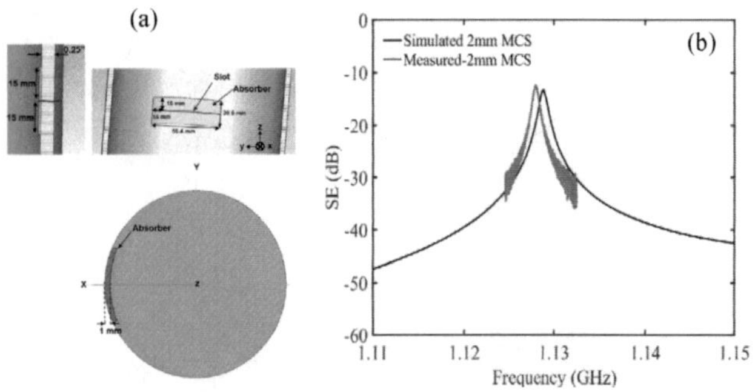

Fig. 2. (a) Schematic of the placement of the absorber around the slot. (b) Comparison of full-wave simulation and experimental results of a cavity with a microwave absorbing material for the TM_{010} mode around $f = 1.13$ GHz.

In Fig. 2 (b) we show the SE from full-wave simulations (black) as well as measurements performed in an anechoic chamber (blue) for the TM_{010} mode, in good agreement. In particular, we note that decorating the aperture with a small magnetic absorber (0.026% cavity volume) leads to improvements in peak SE values, with respect to the empty cavity (Fig. 1), of about 20 dB. Future investigations will provide insight into optimum absorber properties and placement for maximum wide-band internal field reduction.

IV. Conclusion

In this paper, we have addressed the coupling to a high-quality factor cylindrical cavity through a small perturbing slot. We have first shown plots of shielding effectiveness versus frequency, as well as formulated an upper bound on the penetrant power through the slot, which provides initial guidelines for maximum achievable levels of interior EM fields. Since for high-quality factor resonant cavities, internal field levels can be much higher than the incoming field, we decorated the slot with a small amount of microwave absorbing materials to improve shielding effectiveness considerably, as attested by both simulations and experiments. Although we focused on the treatment of a canonical slotted cylindrical cavity, the conclusions presented here can be extended to more complex cavity structures.

Acknowledgment

This work was supported by the Laboratory Directed Research and Development program at Sandia National Laboratories. Sandia National Laboratories is a multimission laboratory managed and operated by National Technology and Engineering Solutions of Sandia, LLC, a wholly owned subsidiary of Honeywell International, Inc., for the U.S. Department of Energy's National Nuclear Security Administration under contract DE-NA-0003525. This paper describes objective technical results and analysis. Any subjective views or opinions that might be expressed in the paper do not necessarily represent the views of the U.S. Department of Energy or the United States Government.

References

[1] M. P. Robinson, T. M. Benson, C. Christopoulos, J. F. Dawson, M. D. Ganley, A. C. Marvin, et al., "Analytical formulation for the shielding effectiveness of enclosures with apertures," IEEE Transactions on Electromagnetic Compatibility, vol. 40, pp. 240-248, 1998.

[2] X.-C. Nie and N. Yuan, "Accurate modeling of monopole antennas in shielded enclosures with apertures," Progress in Electromagnetics Research, vol. 79, pp. 251-262, 2008.

[3] S. Eng Swee, K. Sertel, J. L. Volakis, V. V. Liepa, and R. Wiese, "Coupling studies and shielding techniques for electromagnetic penetration through apertures on complex cavities and vehicular platforms," IEEE Transactions on Electromagnetic Compatibility, vol. 45, pp. 245-257, 2003.

[4] G. B. Tait, C. Hager, M. B. Slocum, and M. O. Hatfield, "On measuring shielding effectiveness of sparsely moded enclosures in a reverberation chamber," IEEE Transactions on Electromagnetic Compatibility, vol. 55, pp. 231-240, 2013.

[5] L. K. Warne, R. E. Jorgenson, J. T. Williams, L. I. Basilio, W. L. Langston, R. S. Coats, et al., "A Bound on Electromagnetic Penetration through a Slot Aperture with Backing Cavity," Sandia National Laboratories report SAND2016-9029, Albuquerque, NM, 2016.

[6] S. Campione, I. C. Reines, L. K. Warne, J. T. Williams, R. K. Gutierrez, R. S. Coats, et al., "Preliminary Survey on the Effectiveness of an Electromagnetic Dampener to Improve System Shielding Effectiveness," Sandia National Laboratories report, SAND2018-10548, Albuquerque, NM, 2018.

[7] K. S. H. Lee and F.-C. Yang, "Trends and bounds in RF coupling to a wire inside a slotted cavity," IEEE Transactions on Electromagnetic Compatibility, vol. 34, pp. 154-160, 1992.

[8] ECCOSORB MCS, Emerson & Cuming Microwave Products, http://www.eccosorb.com/products-eccosorb-mcs.htm

Electromagnetic Analysis of Multilayer Structures with Arbitrarily Shaped Interfaces.

Gérard Granet
Institut Pascal
Université Clermont Auvergne,
CNRS,Sigma Clermont,Institut Pascal,F-63000
Clermont-Ferrand, France
gerard.granet@uca.fr

Denis Prémel
CEA LIST
Laboratoire Simulation et Modlisation
91191 Gif-sur-Yvette,France
denis.premel@cea.fr

***Abstract*—A general formulation for electromagnetic analysis of multilayer structures with arbitrarily shaped interfaces is presented. The formulation belongs to modal methods. Its originality lies in the use of coordinates systems attached to the profile shape of the interfaces that separate the layers and to Maxwell's equations written under the covariant form. Each interface coincides with a coordinate surface which makes it elementary to enforce boundary conditions.**

***Index Terms*—Modal Methods, Curvilinear Coordinate Method, Computational Electromagnetics.**

I. Introduction

Many applications rely on the interaction of an electromagnetic field with multilayer structures. For instance, radar remote sensing of soils content requires an accurate model of soils which often involves multilayer rough surfaces and dielectric profiles. In an other frequency range, the performance of solar cells highly depend on light trapping which may be optimized by front and back gratings. At low frequencies, non-destructive testing of stratified conductors characterized by a set of arbitrary interfaces of complex shape may rely on the computation of the response of a 3D Eddy Current probe [1]. From the electromagnetic point of view, all three cited examples are similar. They represent problems of diffraction by layers with non-parallel faces, the case of parallel faces being a particular case. This paper is aimed at presenting a general method based on curvilinear coordinates for solving such problems.

II. Formulation

A. New Coordinates

Let us consider a stratified media characterized by a set of interfaces as is shown in Fig.1. Each interface separating two consecutive media with optical indexes ν_{p-1} and ν_p is described by an analytic function $a_p(x, y)$ depending on two directions x and y. The air domain, denoted by 0, contains the source. The last media is assumed to be infinite.

Each interface is associated with a non-orthogonal coordinate system such as:

$$x = x^1, \quad y = x^2, \quad z = x_p^3 + a_p(x^1, x^2). \tag{1}$$

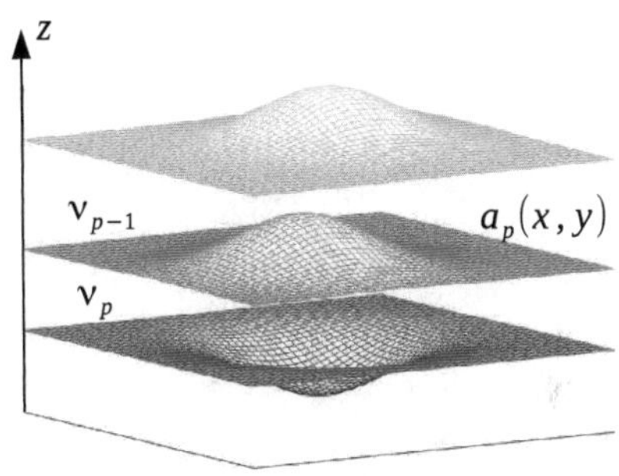

Fig. 1. Illustration of a multilayer structure. The pth layer is between a_{p-1} and a_p.

Therefore, boundary conditions at the interface of two adjacent layers becomes elementary since the latter is now a coordinate surface characterized by $x_p^3 =$ constante.. Due to the change of coordinates, a new metric tensor must be introduced [2]. Denoting (x, y, z) by $(x^{1'}, x^{2'}, x^{3'})$, the components of the metric tensor g_{ij} are given by $\sum_{i'j'}(\partial x^{i'}\partial x^{j'}/(\partial x^i \partial x^j)\delta_{i'j'}$ where $\delta_{i'j'}$is the Kronecker symbol. The inverse of the matrix formed by the g_{ij} gives the components of the conjugate metric tensor g^{ij}:

$$[g^{ij}] = [g_{ij}]^{-1} = \begin{bmatrix} 1 & 0 & -\dot{a}_1 \\ 0 & 1 & -\dot{a}_2 \\ -\dot{a}_1 & -\dot{a}_2 & 1 + \dot{a}_1^2 + \dot{a}_2^2 \end{bmatrix}, \tag{2}$$

where $\dot{a}_i$, $i = 1, 2$ are the partial derivative of $a_p(x^i)$ with respect to x^i. Here, the determinant g of $[g_{ij}]$ is equal to one. Since the coordinate system is non-orthogonal, it is convenient to write Maxwell's equations under the covariant form. Assuming a time dependence of the form $\exp(i\omega t)$, we have:

$$\begin{aligned} \xi^{lmn}\partial_m E_n &= -ik\sqrt{g}g^{lm} Z_0 H_m, \\ \xi^{lmn}\partial_m Z_0 H_n &= ik\nu^2\sqrt{g}g^{lm} E_m, \end{aligned} \tag{3}$$

where $l, m, n \in \{1, 2, 3\}$, k is the wave number, Z_0 is the vacuum wave impedance, ∂_j, $j \in \{1, 2, 3\}$ stands for $\partial/\partial x^j$, ξ^{lmn} is the Levi-Civita indicator.

B. Method of Solution

Since the components of the metric tensor do not depend on the x^3 variable, it is possible to express the four tangential components E_1, E_2, H_1 and H_2 in terms of the two longitudinal components E_3 and H_3 which satisfy the same scalar propagation equation [3]:

$$\left(\partial_m g^{mn} \partial_n + k^2 \nu^2\right) \psi = 0 \quad \psi = E_3 \text{ or } \psi = H_3. \quad (4)$$

Moreover any of the six components takes the form :

$$\Psi(x^1, x^2, x^3) = \psi(x^1, x^2) \exp(-i\gamma x^3). \quad (5)$$

Taking into account (5), (4) can be recast as a first order differential system of the form:

$$[\mathcal{L}_p^q] \begin{bmatrix} \psi_p^q \\ \psi_p'^q \end{bmatrix} = \gamma_p^q \begin{bmatrix} \psi_p^q \\ \psi_p'^q \end{bmatrix} \quad \psi_p'^q = -i\gamma_p^q \psi_p^q. \quad (6)$$

In equation (6), the subscript p refers to the interface whereas the superscript q refers to the media. According to the notations illustrated on Fig.1, we see that $q = p$ or $q = p - 1$. Equation (6) is transformed into an algebraic eigenvalue system by using the method of moments after a suitable basis is chosen. The numerical solution is then obtained thanks to standard linear algebra libraries. It can be shown that there are two sets of modes which correspond to forward waves and backward waves respectively. Finally the solution is a linear combination of eigen-modes depending on both the media and the coordinate system. Hence, inside a layer whose faces are not identical, the field is represented by two different sets of eigenvectors:

$$\psi_p^{\pm q} = \sum_{l=1}^{L} \left(A_{el,p}^{\pm q} \psi_{elp}^{\pm q} + A_{hlp}^{\pm q} \psi_{hlp}^{\pm q} \right) \exp(-i\gamma^{\pm q}{}_p(x_p^3)), \quad (7)$$

with $q = p-1$ or $q = p$. Vector ψ is the concatenation of the four tangential components. The subscript e, (respectively h) designates a vector generated by E_3, (respectively H_3). L is the number of numerically computed eigen-modes.

C. Boundary Conditions

The unknown constant coefficients depend on two physical phenomena of different nature. On the one hand, crossing an interface, the total tangential field components are continuous which implies that forward and backward waves are coupled. On the other hand, the propagation from one interface to the next one in the same media, creates only a phase shift or an attenuation without coupling the two kind of waves. Boundary conditions are enforced thanks to the the S-matrix formalism. At the pth interface which separates media $p-1$ and media p, that is at $x_p^3 = 0$, we have an interface $S_p^{p-1,p}$ matrix such that:

$$\begin{bmatrix} A_{elp}^{+(p-1)} \\ A_{hlp}^{+(p-1)} \\ A_{el,p}^{-p} \\ A_{hlp}^{-p} \end{bmatrix} = S_p^{p-1,p} \begin{bmatrix} [A_{elp}^{-(p-1)} \\ A_{hlp}^{-(p-1)} \\ A_{elp}^{+p} \\ A_{hlp}^{+p} \end{bmatrix}. \quad (8)$$

Between interface $p-1$ and interface p, we have derived two modal expansions for the field: one is attached to a_{p-1} and the other one to a_p. The corresponding coordinate systems are linked by

$$x_{p-1}^3 = x_p^3 + a_{p-1}(x^1, x^2) - a_p(x^1, x^2) = x_p^3 + t_p(x^1, x^2). \quad (9)$$

In the case of layers with parallel faces, function $t_p(x^1, x^2)$ reduces to a constant. We consider the pth layer as a generalized transmission line which connects input field ψ_{p-1}^{-p-1} and ψ_p^{+p-1} to output fields ψ_{p-1}^{+p-1} and ψ_p^{-p-1}. As already mentioned, no coupling occurs between forward waves and backward waves. Hence the definition of the bloc anti-diagonal layer $S_{p-1\,p}^{p-1}$ matrix:

$$\begin{bmatrix} A_{el(p-1)}^{+(p-1)} \\ A_{hl(p-1)}^{+(p-1)} \\ [A_{el,p}^{-,p} \\ A_{hlp}^{-,p} \end{bmatrix} = S_{p-1\,p}^{p-1} \begin{bmatrix} [A_{elp-1}^{-(p-1)} \\ A_{hlp-1}^{-(p-1)} \\ [A_{elp}^{+p} \\ A_{hlp}^{+p} \end{bmatrix}. \quad (10)$$

At the input of the pth layer that is at $z_{p-1}^3 = 0$, the outgoing waves correspond to the incoming waves of the output plane. Similarly, at the output of the same layer, that is at $z_p^3 = 0$, the outgoing waves correspond to the incoming waves of the input. Hence the two relations from which the coefficients of the layer S matrix are computed:

$$\begin{aligned} \psi_{p-1}^{+(p-1)}(x_{p-1}^3 = 0) &= \psi_p^{+(p-1)}(x_p^3 = t_p), \\ \psi_p^{-(p-1)}(x_p^3 = 0) &= \psi_{p-1}^{-(p-1)}(x_p^3 = -t_p). \end{aligned} \quad (11)$$

D. Excitation

The structure is exited from air with a known field which is expanded onto the eigenvectors associated to the first interface which determine input amplitude coefficients $A_{el,1}^{-0}, A_{hl,1}^{-0}$. All other coefficients are obtained from the usual recursion formulas of the S matrix algorithm.

III. Conclusion

We have described an efficient and versatile algorithm for modeling arbitrarily shaped faces multilayer structures. Its advantage over pure numerical methods like Finite Elements Methods is that no mesh is needed in the z direction which makes it competitive in terms of computational speed especially for layers with rather large thickness. In the presentation, we will focus on the numerical implementation and give some examples of applications.

References

[1] F.Caire, D. Prémel and G. Granet,"Fast Computation of the Fields Diffracted by a Multi-Layered Conductor With Non-Parallel Rough Interfaces. Application to Eddy-Current Non-Destructive Testing Simulation", IEEE transaction on magnetics, Vol. 51,No.3, March 2015, pp.6200604

[2] G. Granet, "Analysis of diffraction by surface-relief crossed gratings with use of the Chandezon method: application to multilayer crossed gratings", J. Opt. Soc. Am. A, vol. 15, N. 5, pp. 1121-1131, 1998.

[3] R. Dusséaux, K. Edee, G. Granet, S. Afifi "Electromagnetic scattering from rough layered interfaces: Analysis with the curvilinear coordinate method", The 26th Annual Review of Progress in Applied Computational Electromagnetics, Tampere, Finland. pp.508-513, 2010.

A Novel Mid-infrared Metalens using a Hyperbolic Metamaterial

Mohamed Kyamo, Navaneeth Premkumar, Abdelgader Alsalhin, and Brian A. Lail
Dept. of Computer Engineering and Sciences Florida Institute of Technology
Melbourne, Florida
mkyamo2016@my.fit.edu, npremkumar2013@my.fit.edu, aalshiekh2014@my.fit.edu blail@fit.ed

Abstract— **A novel metalens in the mid infrared range from 6.4um to 10um is designed. It consists of a plasmonic waveguide coupler (PWC), on a slab of type I hyperbolic metamaterial (HMM) on the top of a substrate of undoped InAs with a Au nanoantenna at the other end. The metalens serves to focus both propagating and evanescent waves into a focal point at which the field confinement and enhancement are improved using the plasmonic nanoantenna. This paper shows the design and performance of the metalens, which has applications in sub-wavelength imaging and sensing.**

Keywords- Enhancement, Hyperbolic metamaterial, Metalens, Mid-infrared, Plasmonic, Resolution.

I. Introduction

In [1] it was shown that electromagnetic plane waves in a medium having negative permittivity and permeability would propagate toward a path against to that of the flow of energy. Lately in [2], they designed a flat lens using a slab of material with a negative index of refraction while a metalens at visible light was designed in [3]. The motivation behind the design in this paper is to make a three-dimensional super-resolution metalens with high electric-field enhancement in the mid-infrared range of 6.4-10μm. Here we use a plasmonic waveguide coupler (PWC), which is made out of rings of doped InAs working as a Fresnel zone plate (FZP) to focus waves like a conventional lens. The PWC is placed on hyperbolic metamaterial (HMM) which is constructed using a periodic stack of doped and undoped InAs layers where the bulk material properties are calculated using effective medium theory (EMT). The HMM allows us to break the diffraction limit and convert evanescent waves to propagating waves. Together the PWC and the HMM slab serve to focus incoming radiation onto a focal point located in the gap between a plasmonic nanodisk made using two gold (Au) disks.

II. Design and Optmization

The metalens was designed and simulated using ANSYS HFSS software and the structure is excited by an incident plane wave. Fig. 1 shows the structure of the metalens which consists of a PWC with annular rings of doped InAs , a slab of HMM in [4] and a nanoantenna situated on a dielectric substrate. The PWC has a thickness of 70nm and ring width of 20 and it is illuminated by normally incident TM plane waves. The PWC is placed on the cylindrical slab of HMM which consists of undoped InAs and doped InAs. The Drude model is used to generate the data of the constituent material properties for InAs. Complex permittivity for undoped InAs is found by using $\omega_p = 3x10^{13}\ \text{rads}^{-1}, \gamma = 10^{12}$ rad, and $\epsilon_r = 12.3$, while the doped InAs parameters are $\omega_p = 2.95x10^{14}\ \text{rads}^{-1}, \gamma = 10^{12}$ rad, and $\epsilon_r = 10.4$; where ω_p is the plasmonic resonance frequency, γ is electron relaxation in radians and ϵ_r is the relative permittivity. The metamaterial is a uniaxial material with permittivities $\boldsymbol{\epsilon}_{\parallel}$ and $\boldsymbol{\epsilon}_{\perp}$. The dispersion relation of a uniaxial material is given by:

$$\frac{k_{\parallel}^2}{\epsilon_{\perp}} + \frac{k_{\perp}^2}{\epsilon_{\parallel}} = \frac{\omega^2}{c^2}. \quad (1)$$

The effective permittivity is calculated by effective medium theory (EMT) [5]:

$$\epsilon_{\parallel} = \epsilon_{xx} = \epsilon_{yy} = p\epsilon_m + (1-p)\epsilon_d\,.$$
$$\epsilon_{\perp} = \epsilon_z = \frac{\epsilon_m.\epsilon_d}{p\epsilon_d + (1-p)\epsilon_m}, \quad p = \frac{t_m}{t_m + t_d}. \quad (2)$$

Here t_m is the thickness of metallic layer (doped InAs) and t_d is the thickness of the dielectric layer (undoped InAs). ϵ_m is permitivity of doped InAs and ϵ_d is permitivity of undoped InAs ,t_m is 290nm and t_d is 370nm .

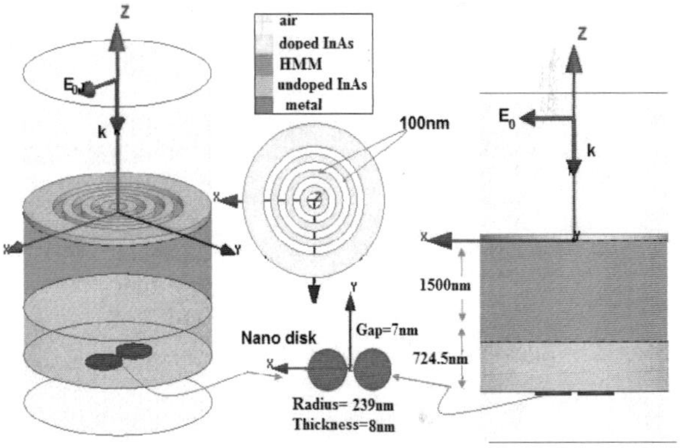

Fig. 1. Metalens structure.

The perpendicular and parallel permittivities are shown in Fig. 2. The resulting material is a type I HMM with a diagonal dielectric tensor described as $\epsilon_{xx} = \epsilon_{yy} > 0, \epsilon_z < 0$ in the wavelength range of 6.366μm to 8.837μm, and a type II HMM with $\epsilon_{xx} = \epsilon_{yy} < 0$, $\epsilon_z > 0$ in the wavelength range 10.4μm to 12μm. It also acts as an anisotropic metal in the range 8.838μm to 10.03μm. Here we use the type I HMM.

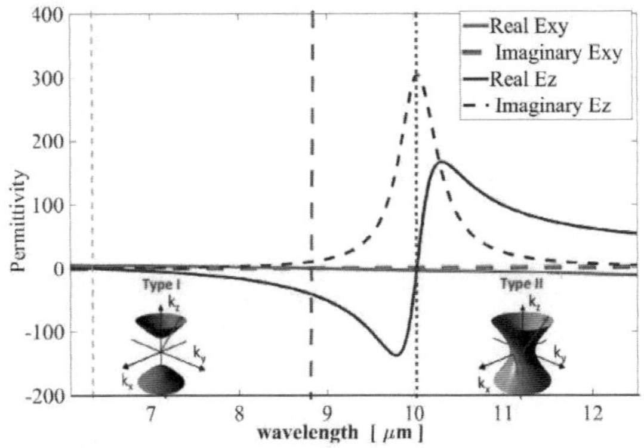

Fig. 2. Effective permittivity as a function of wavelength.

III. Results and Discussion

Fig. 3 is shows the magnitude of electric field distribution for metalens with and without nano disks at the focal point of the metalens in the XZ plane with a X-polarized normal plane wave at 7.739um. The focal length is 2.248um. The FWHM values along the x-axis and the y-axis without the nano disks are 800nm and its electric field enhancement on the order of 10^2. The electric field distribution is enhanced in the gap of two gold nano disks. This enhancement is controlled by varying the height and radii of the disks.

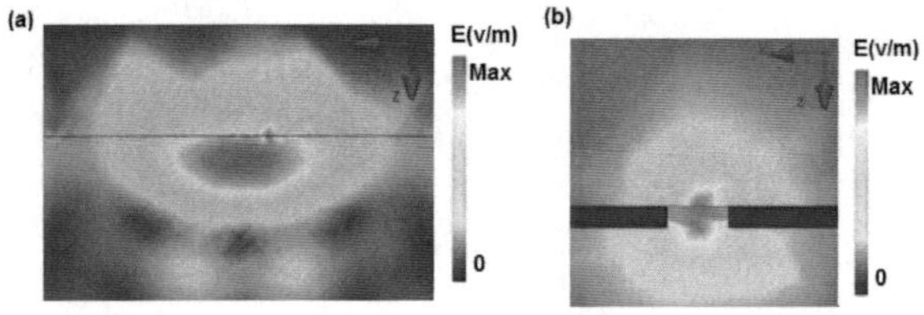

Fig. 3. The magnitude of electric field distribution at the focal point: (a) without nano disk and (b) with nano disk.

Fig. 4 shows the variation of electric-field enhancement at the focal point with variation in the gap between the two disks. The electric field enhancement on the order of 10^6.

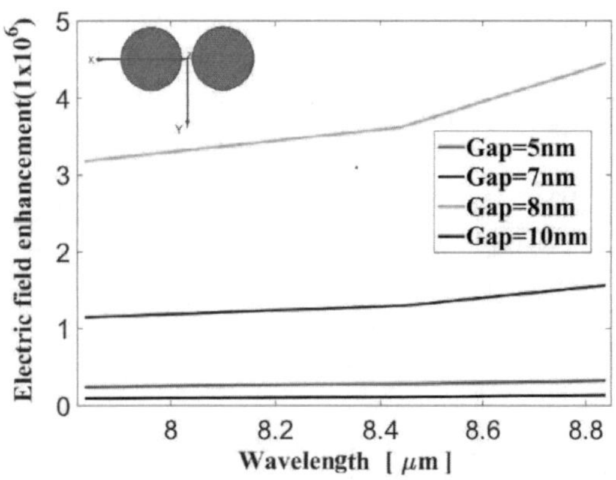

Fig. 4. The electric field distribution of the focal point with different values for separation between the disks.

In Fig. 5, electric field at the focal point is plotted on the x-axis (blue) and y-axis (red). The full-width half maximum (FWHM) is 8.18nm and 13.64nm on the x-axis and y-axis, respectively. The FWHM values along the x-axis and the y-axis are smaller than the diffraction limit of the 0.5λ, thus allowing us to image particles that are 1/1000 times the wavelength.

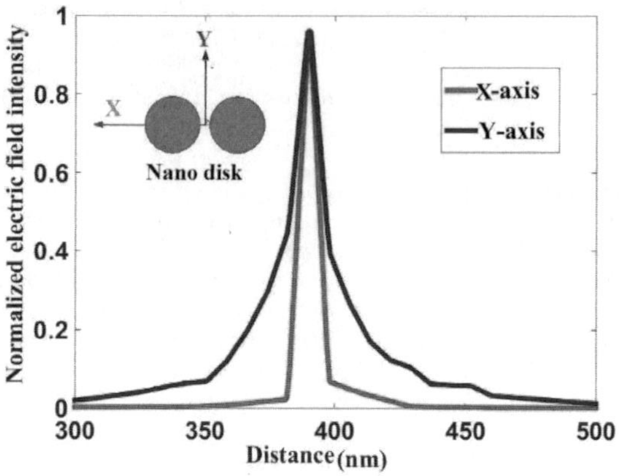

Fig. 5. Field intensity profile the x-axis and y-axis.

IV. Conclusion

As shown by using a PWC made using doped InAs, a hyperbolic metamaterial made using layers of doped InAs and undoped InAs and an Au plasmonic nan disk, a new metalens was designed in the mid infrared capable of super-resolution focusing with high electric-field enhancement. Using InAs as an alternative to metals reduces losses. The hyperbolic metamaterial allows the lens to support the propagation of waves with high wave vectors. The electric field at the focal point is enhanced when using the Au nanoadisk. The full-width half maximum (FWHM) of the field at the focal point is 8.18nm x 13.64nm on the x-axis and y-axis, respectively. This allows us to image particles that are 1/1000 times the wavelength. Such a metalens may be used for sub-wavelength imaging and sensing with super resolution and high electric field enhancement.

References

[1] G. Veselago, "The electrodynamics of substances with simultaneously negative values of permittivity and permeability," Sov. Phys. Usp. 10, 509-514, 1968.

[2] J. B. Pendry, "Negative refraction makes a perfect lens," Phys. Rev. Lett., vol. 85, no. 18, pp. 3966–3969, Oct. 2000.

[3] C. B. Ma and Z. W Liu," A super resolution metalens with phase compensation mechanism," Appl. Phys. Lett. 96, 183103, 2010.

[4] F. Peragut, L. Cerutti, A. Baranovj, P. Hugonin, T. Taliercio, Y. De Wilde, and J. J. Greffet, "Hyperbolic metamaterials and surface plasmon polaritons," Optica. vol. 4, no. 11, pp. 1409-1415, Nov. 2017.

[5] P Shekhar, J Atkinson, Z. Jacob, "Hyperbolic metamaterials: Fundamentals and applications," Nano Convergence, 2014.

Determining the Dispersive Features of Nanophotonic Structures based on Hybrid FEM/TMM Technique

Abdelgader Alsalhin and Brian Lail
Computer Engineering and Sciences
Florida Institute of Technology
Melbourne, Florida
aalshiekh2014@my.fit.edu

***Abstract*—Determining the dispersion relation of nanophotonic structures is one of the biggest challenges especially for nano-scale inhomogeneous structures where several efforts have been directed. Here, we present a technique that leverages the accuracy and simplicity of the combination of transfer matrix method (TMM) and finite element method (FEM). This hybrid technique allows us to find the spatial dispersion, coupling strength and nature of the generated modes.**

Keywords—dispersion, finite element method, HFSS, nanophotonics, transfer matrix method,

I. Introduction

In the field of nanophononics (or nano-optics), determining the dispersion relation of inhomogeneous structures is one of the biggest challenges. There are numerous efforts in this direction with techniques of varying levels of complexity [1]. Each technique has its advantages and limitations where the outcomes, in general, are affected by the trade-off with the accuracy and the time. Therefore, looking for accurate techniques to determine the dispersion relations for nano-scale grating structures has been gaining momentum recently. The transfer matrix method (TMM) is a one-dimensional method (1D) that is used to calculate the dispersion in the incident direction (longitudinal) while the other directions (transversal) are assumed to be infinite. As detailed in the next section, TMM is a valid technique used to approximate the dispersion behavior inside a structure. In contrast, a three-dimensional (3D) technique like the finite element method (FEM) could deal with a structure having discontinuous content (grating) in 3D. Practically, modeling the geometry of interest using a full wave simulator (FEM-based) and modifying the outputs to match a simpler technique of extracting the dispersion based on TMM is the new hybrid technique that is suggested here.

II. Principles and Methodology

A. TMM

The TMM is a rigorous semi-analytical method where an approximated solution is adopted for transversal directions while the analytical solution is in longitudinal direction. It is usually applied for infinite slabs and it neither accounts for diffraction effects nor handles inhomogeneous transversal gratings. On the other hand, it is very fast, simple, robust and unconditionally stable [2]. Also, much like scattering techniques, it is well explained in the available literature [2], [3]. Starting with Maxwell's equations, the physical boundary conditions are applied, where the tangential fields are equal at both sides of an interface, and finally the wave equations of these tangential fields are extracted in matrix form. Typically, the overall solution of the second order differential wave equation is represented in matrix form as:

$$[\Psi_t(L)]_{m\times 1} = [W]_{m\times m}\,[E_d]_{m\times m}\,([W]_{m\times m})^{-1}\,[a^{\pm}]_{m\times 1} \quad (1),$$

where the relevant terms of this equation are defined as the following:
$[\Psi_t(L)]_{m\times 1}$ are the tangential field vectors at distance L, $[W]_{m\times m}$ contains the eigen vectors and is called the Dynamical Matrix, $[Ed]_{m\times m}$ is termed the Propagation Matrix and is a diagonal matrix that contains the eigen values, $([W]_{m\times m})^{-1}\,[a^{\pm}]_{m\times 1} = (C^{\pm})$ = proportionality coefficients and $[W]_{m\times m}\,[Ed]_{m\times m}\,([W]_{m\times m})^{-1}$ is the Transfer Matrix (Tr).

In case of multilayers, as shown in Fig. 1, the overall tangential fields equation in terms of TMM is:

$$\left[\Psi_{t(\text{trnsmitted Side})}\right] = \mathrm{Tr}_{(\text{total})}\left[\Psi_{t(\text{reflected Side})}\right] \quad (2),$$

where $\mathrm{Tr}_{(\text{total})}$ is the total transfer matrix and equals to $(\mathrm{Tr}_{\text{Layer}\#1})(\mathrm{Tr}_{\text{Layer}\#2})\ldots(\mathrm{Tr}_{\text{Layer}\#N})$. TMM represents the relation between the modes at one side of a layer to the modes at the other side while S-matrix describes the relationship between inputs to the outputs of that layer. For instance, medium #2 as seen in Fig. 1 has;

$$\begin{bmatrix} C_1^- \\ C_3^+ \end{bmatrix} = \begin{bmatrix} \mathbb{S}_{11}^{M\#2} & \mathbb{S}_{12}^{M\#2} \\ \mathbb{S}_{21}^{M\#2} & \mathbb{S}_{22}^{M\#2} \end{bmatrix} \begin{bmatrix} C_1^+ \\ C_3^- \end{bmatrix} \ldots\ldots\ldots\ldots\ \text{S-matrix for medium \#2,}$$

$$\begin{bmatrix} \mathbb{O} & -\mathbb{S}_{12}^{M\#2} \\ \mathbb{I} & -\mathbb{S}_{22}^{M\#2} \end{bmatrix} \begin{bmatrix} C_3^+ \\ C_3^- \end{bmatrix} = \begin{bmatrix} \mathbb{S}_{11}^{M\#2} & -\mathbb{I} \\ \mathbb{S}_{21}^{M\#2} & \mathbb{O} \end{bmatrix} \begin{bmatrix} C_1^+ \\ C_1^- \end{bmatrix} \text{TMM for medium \#2,}$$

where $[C^{\pm}]$ are the vectors of mode proportionality (amplitudes), $[\mathbb{S}]$ is the S-matrix components, $[\mathbb{I}]$ is the identity matrix, and $[\mathbb{O}]$ is a zero matrix [2].

B. FEM

FEM is very mature and versatile method, and allows for solving inside of complex shapes, but its implementation is tedious, and often a numerical implementation using a full-wave commercially-available simulator overcomes this issue. Here the FEM software used is ANSYS HFSS. When modeling the geometry in HFSS, we apply Floquet ports as a source, with master-slave periodic boundaries to simulate infinite slabs, and a fine mesh. The Floquet port provides a built-in tool (mode calculator) to control the type and the order of the modes (TE or TM) whilst periodic boundaries can handle the incident angles based on Floquet theory [4]. Finally, the meshing operator controls the solution accuracy and convergence. As a result, the S-matrix of the selected modes can be extracted as a function of either the wavelength or the dimensions of the structure.

C. Hybrid Techniuqe

The proposed method starts by extracting TMM from the S-matrix (output of FEM-based software) as a following;

$$\begin{bmatrix} \mathbb{O} & -\mathbb{S}_{12}^{\text{total}} \\ \mathbb{I} & -\mathbb{S}_{22}^{\text{total}} \end{bmatrix} \begin{bmatrix} C_{\text{Output}}^+ \\ C_{\text{Output}}^- \end{bmatrix} = \begin{bmatrix} \mathbb{S}_{11}^{\text{total}} & -\mathbb{I} \\ \mathbb{S}_{21}^{\text{total}} & \mathbb{O} \end{bmatrix} \begin{bmatrix} C_{\text{input}}^+ \\ C_{\text{input}}^- \end{bmatrix} \quad (3),$$

and using the following periodic boundary conditions [2],

$$\begin{bmatrix} C_{\text{Output}}^+ & C_{\text{Output}}^- \end{bmatrix}^T = \left[\exp^{j(K_z)d}\right]_{\text{diagonal}} \begin{bmatrix} C_{\text{input}}^+ & C_{\text{input}}^- \end{bmatrix}^T$$

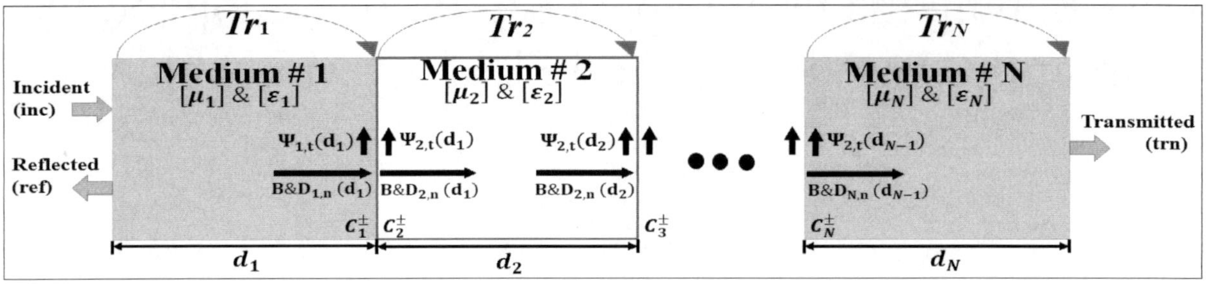

Fig. 1. A physical description of applying TMM for 1D stack of layers where [μ] and [ε] are permeability and permittivity of each medium, while (Bn) and (Dn) are the normal components of magnetic and electric flux densities, respectively.

$$\begin{bmatrix} \mathbb{S}_{11}^{total} & -\mathbb{I} \\ \mathbb{S}_{21}^{total} & \mathbb{O}\end{bmatrix}\begin{bmatrix} C_{input}^{+} \\ C_{input}^{-}\end{bmatrix} = \left[\exp^{j(K_z)d}\right]_{diag}\begin{bmatrix}\mathbb{O} & -\mathbb{S}_{12}^{total} \\ \mathbb{I} & -\mathbb{S}_{22}^{total}\end{bmatrix}\begin{bmatrix} C_{input}^{+} \\ C_{input}^{-}\end{bmatrix} \quad (4),$$

where (K_Z) and (d), respectively, are the complex wave vector and the total thickness in longitudinal direction (assumed to be Z-axis). Hence, (4) should be solved as a generalized eigen-value problem, (Ax = λBx), using the MATLAB function [W, Ed] = eig (A, B). The output will be eigen vector matrix ($[W]_{m\times m}$) represents the amplitudes of the modes, and diagonal eigen value matrix ($[Ed]_{m\times m} \equiv \lambda$) describes the mode propagation (Bloch modes) [2]. Eventually, in MATLAB also:

$$\lambda k = j(K_Z)d = \text{diag}\,(\text{diag}\,(\log\,(\text{diag}\,(Ed)))) \quad (5),$$

$$K_z = (\beta) \pm j(\alpha) = \left(\frac{\text{imag}(\lambda K)+(M\pi)}{d}\right) \pm j\left(\frac{\text{real}(\lambda K)-(M\pi)}{d}\right) \quad (6),$$

where (M) is the order of the modes, will be assumed 0 here.

III. Investigation

The hybrid technique was implemented to the geometry shown in Fig. 2, consisting of hexagonal boron nitride (hBN, type II) where his material supports phonon polaritons [5].

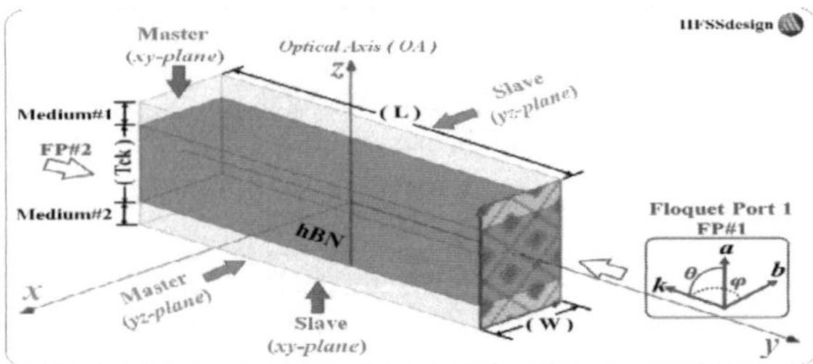

Fig. 2. Modeling [Medium1/hBN/Medium2] in HFSS.

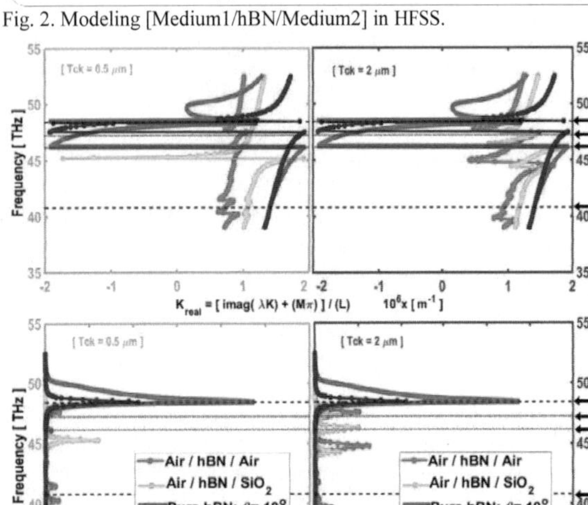

Fig. 3. Dispersion relations for the model in Fig. 2.

After modeling the structure seen in Fig. 2, the thickness of hBN (Tck), medium 2, and the angle θ are varied as [0.5μm, 2μm], [air, SiO2], and [0° to 90°], respectively. Here L=W=1.618μm, φ=90°, and medium 1 is air. Under these conditions, the best momentum matching is obtained with θ=60°, i.e., $(\text{absorbance})_{max} = 1 - |S_{11}|^2 - |S_{21}|^2$. Accordingly, all results in Fig. 3 are plotted for θ=60° except the red curves at θ=10° to show the effect of θ variation. Figs. 3(a-1) and (b-1) illustrate the real wave vector, and (a-2) and (b-2) show the imaginary part (losses), for Tck = 0.5 and 2 μm. The four horizontal black lines in Fig. 3 define the localized modes (see [5]) where UI, for example, represents surface modes at the upper interface. The red (θ=10°) and blue (θ=60°) curves represent the dispersion inside a pure hBN where medium 1 and 2 are nonexistent, and these results are compatible with the dispersion presented in [6]. The anticrossing (or repulsion) behavior is a distinctive signature known for coupling [5]. Therefore, each anti-crossing signature describes coupled mode where wider repulsion means stronger coupling. Based on that, only one coupled mode is noticed for a pure hBN cases at LO, and the stronger is when (θ=60°). Moreover, the effect of substrate (medium2) is illustrated by comparing the green (silica) and the purple curves (air) where the number and the strength of the modes are different. In fact, it should be mention that there are two floquet modes excited, and these results reflect TM_{00} input mode only while results for TE_{00} were ignored because they didn't give the highest absorbance. As mention in Section II (B), input modes are handling at ports where largest energy at TM_{00}, so, fewer modes means best accuracy [4].

IV. Conclusion

This technique is suitable for few-input modes in order to determining the number of coupled modes, and the nature of these modes, regardless of the ingredients or the geometry.

References

[1] W. Stutzman and G. Thiele, Antenna Theory and Design, 3rd ed., John Wiley & Sons, Inc., 2013.

[2] R. C. Rumpf, "Improved formulation of scattering matrices for semianalytical methods that is consistent with convention," Progr. Electromagn. Res. B, vol. 35, pp. 241–261, Oct. 2011.

[3] H. Kitahara, M. W. Takeda, M. Iida, M. Tani, M. Watanabe, and K. Sakai, "Reflection losses of finite periodic photonic crystals," Laser Optics 14(5), pp. 654-659, 2004.

[4] HFSS™, "Getting started with HFSS: Floquet Ports," Report 2010.

[5] A. A. Alsalhin, M. F. Finch, and B. A. Lail, "Coupling between metallic structure and phonon polaritons for sensing applications," Proc. SPIE 10719, Metamaterials, Metadevices, and Metasystems, Sep. 2018.

[6] S. Dai, Q. Ma, et al., "Subdiffractional focusing and guiding of polaritonic rays in a natural hyperbolic material," Nature Communications, vol. 6, p. 6963, 2015.

Numerical Simulation and Analyses of SAR Images from Ship Wakes

Min Zhang and Jinxing Li
School of Physics and Optoelectronic Engineering
Xidian University
Xi'an, Chia
mzhang@mail.xidian.edu.cn

***Abstract*—The study of SAR images from ship wakes is of great value to the detection and information inversion of ship targets in a marine environment. In this paper, a facet-based simplified small-slope approximation (FBS-SSA) is used to investigate the electromagnetic (EM) scattering from a sea surface with Kelvin wakes, based on which the SAR echoes can be simulated. Then, SAR images are readily obtained with the range-Doppler algorithm (RDA). SAR images under different incident angles, ship directions are analyzed, it is concluded that for a low incident angle, wakes show more clearly due to an obvious comparison of strong scatters and weak scatters. In addition, both the transverse and divergent waves can be seen when SAR flies across ship heading while only divergent waves can be seen when SAR flies along ship heading. Only one arm can be seen when the angle between SAR's flight direction and ship's heading is 45°.**

Keywords—EM scattering, SAR image, Ship wake.

I. Introduction

As an active microwave remote sensor, synthetic aperture radar (SAR) has been an important tool for the detection, tracking and recognition of ship targets in a marine environment [1-3]. In addition, ship wakes contain the geometrical, motion information of ships, etc. Therefore, the study on the characteristics of ship wakes in SAR images is of great value to the detection of ships.

To investigate the characteristics of ship wakes in SAR images, a reliable scattering model for rough surfaces is necessary for the generation of SAR echoes. At present, the small slope approximation (SSA) [4] has been widely applied to the calculation of rough surface scattering problems because of its good accuracy. However, it needs a mesh size less than one-eighth of the wavelength, which leads to large computer consumption and higher computational complexity for electrically large surfaces, especially for higher microwave bands. Thus, this paper employed a simplified facet-based SSA (FBS-SSA) [5] to generate SAR echoes in different cases, based on which SAR images are simulated with the help of range-Doppler algorithm (RDA) [6]. From the numerical results, one can see the different characteristics of Kelvin wakes in SAR images, which will benefit the information inversion of ships.

II. Theoretical Foundation

A. Generation of Sea Surface with Kelvin Wakes

The composite scene of interest can be regarded as the superposition of sea surface and Kelvin wakes. Geometry structure of sea surface can be simulated by the Monte Carlo method, in which Elfouhaily's wave spectrum [7] is adopted.

This work was supported by the National Natural Science Foundation of China under Grant No. 61771355, the Fundamental Research Funds for the Central Universities, the Innovation Fund of Xidian University.

With regard to the ship wake, the model for Kelvin wake proposed in [8] is utilized. For a ship moving in the x direction at a speed of V, the wave elevations are

$$h_{wake}(x,y) = \mathrm{Re}\int_{-\pi/2}^{\pi/2} A(\theta)\exp\left[k_0\sec^2\theta(i\cos\theta x + i\sin\theta x)\right], \quad (1)$$

where $A(\theta)=\frac{4k_0}{V}\sec^3\theta\cdot\mathcal{H}\left(k_0\sec^2\theta,\theta\right)$, $k_0 = g/V^2$, $\mathcal{H}$ is the Kochin function, and θ is the direction of wave propagation with respect to the x direction.

Fig.1 shows geometry structure of a sea surface with a Kelvin wake. In the simulations, the wind speed at 10m height above the sea level is 5m/s with up-wind direction. The velocity of the ship is 6m/s.

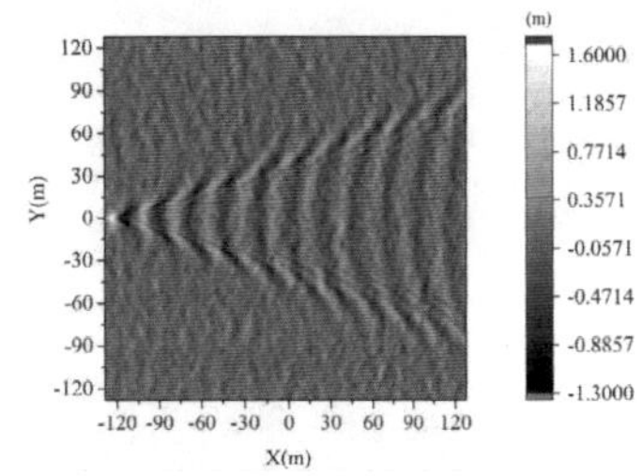

Fig.1 Geometry structure of a sea surface with a Kelvin wake.

B. EM Scattering Model

A reliable scattering model is the foundation to simulate the SAR echoes from a scene of interest. In this paper, the facet-based simplified scattering model proposed in our earlier work [5] is utilized. Based on FBS-SSA, the scattering amplitude (SA) from a facet on the sea surface is

$$\mathbf{S}^{facet}_{\alpha\alpha_0} = \frac{2\sqrt{qq_0}}{(2\pi)^2(q+q_0)\sqrt{P_{inc}}}B_{pq}(\boldsymbol{k},\boldsymbol{k}_0)\cdot\Lambda(\boldsymbol{r}) \cdot\exp\left[-i(\boldsymbol{k}-\boldsymbol{k}_0)\cdot\boldsymbol{r}_0 - i(q+q_0)h(\boldsymbol{r}_0)\right], \quad (2)$$

where $\alpha\alpha_0$ indicates the polarization mode, $\boldsymbol{k}_0$ and $-q_0$ are the horizontal and vertical projections of the incident wave vector, respectively. $\boldsymbol{k}$ and q are the horizontal and vertical projections of the scattered wave vector, respectively. $\boldsymbol{B}$ is available in [4] and $\Lambda(\boldsymbol{r})$ is available in [5].

C. Simulation of SAR Image

SAR echo of a sea surface is

$$s(\tau,\eta) = \sigma w_r(\tau)w_a(\eta)\exp\left[j2\pi f_c\left(\tau - 2R(\eta)/c\right)\right] \cdot\exp\left[j\pi K_r\left(\tau-2R(\eta)/c\right)^2\right], \quad (3)$$

where σ is the scattering coefficient of a facet, τ,η are respectively the fast time and the slow time, w_r, w_a are respectively the window functions in range and azimuthal directions. f_c is the central frequency of the incident wave and K_r is the chirp rate. R is the range between the SAR platform and a facet. It should be note that σ changes with time because of the variation of sea surface.

III. NUMERICAL RESULTS

A. *SAR Images for Different Incident Angles*

First, the effect of incident angles on the SAR images of Kelvin wakes are simulated and compared in Fig.2. In the simulations, the incident frequency is 5GHz, the resolution cell of the HH polarized SAR is $2\text{m}\times 2\text{m}$. The ship moves at a speed of 10 m/s, the SAR flies across the ship's heading direction. The wind speed of sea surface is 3m/s. The incident angles for the three figures are $20°, 45°, 70°$ respectively. As is shown in Fig.2, we can see that ship wakes can be seen in all of the three images. However, for a low incident angle, it shows much clearer due to an obvious comparison of strong and weak scatters. Thus, Kelvin wakes are easier to be detected with a low incident angle.

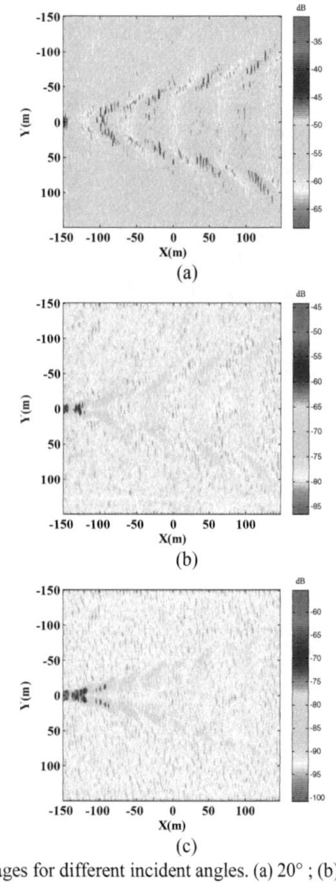

Fig.2 SAR images for different incident angles. (a) 20° ; (b) 45° ; (c) 70° .

B. *SAR Images for Different Heading Directions*

In this part, SAR images with different ship directions are simulated and compared. The angles between the SAR's flight direction and the ship's heading direction are 0° for Fig.3 (a), 45° for Fig.3 (b), and 90° for Fig.3 (c). The ship moves at a speed of 6m/s. The incident angle of the SAR is 45° . We can see that both the transverse and divergent waves can be seen when SAR flies across ship's heading, however only transverse waves can be seen when SAR flies along ship's heading. Moreover, it is interesting that only one arm can be seen when the angle between the SAR's flight direction and the ship's heading is 45°. The reason is that only the waves moving along the direction of radar line-of-sight can be detected by the radar.

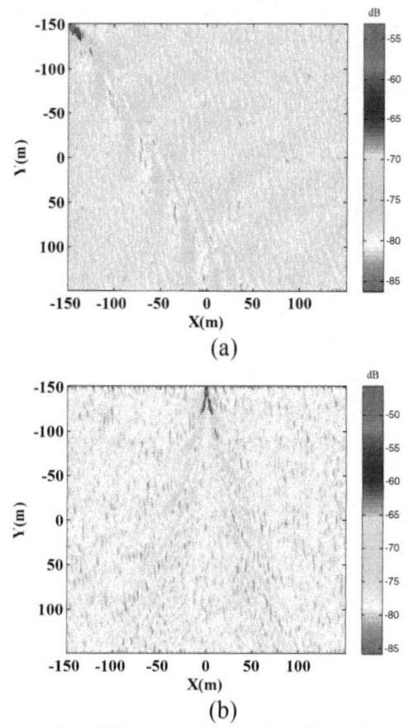

Fig.3 SAR images for different ship moving directions. (a) 45° ; (b) 90° .

IV. CONCLUSIONS

In this paper, SAR images of sea surfaces with Kelvin wakes are simulated based on a facet-based scattering model and the RDA. Characteristics of Kelvin wakes in SAR images under different incident angles and ship directions are compared. It is seen that Kelvin wakes are easier to be detected with a low incident angle. In addition, the angle between the SAR's flight direction and the ship's heading direction has effect on the image as well. These studies will absolutely benefit the detection of ships and inversion of the moving information of ships based on wakes.

REFERENCES

[1] D. L. Schuler, J. S. Lee, and D. D. Grandi, "Measurement of topography using polarimetric SAR images," *IEEE Transactions on Geoscience and Remote Sensing,* vol. 34, pp. 1266–1277, 1996.

[2] H. Mo, W. Xu, and Z. Zeng, "Moving targets imaging in spaceborne TOPS SAR," ACES Journal, vol. 31, no. 11, pp. 1286-1292, 2016.

[3] Y. Li, et al. "Squint SAR imaging of complex targets on the sea," in ACES 2018, China, 2018.

[4] A. Voronovich, "Small slope approximation for electromagnetic wave scattering at a rough interface of two dielectric half-spaces," *Waves in Random Media*, vol. 4, no.3, pp.337-367, 2006.

[5] J. X. Li, M. Zhang, P. B. Wei, and W. Q. Jiang, "An improvement on SSA method for EM scattering from electrically large rough sea surface," *IEEE Geoscience and Remote Sensing Letters*, vol.13, no.8, pp. 1144-1148, 2016.

[6] I. Cumming, F. Wong, *Digital processing of synthetic aperture radar data algorithms and implementation.* Boston, MA, USA: Artech House, 2005.

[7] T. Elfouhaily, B. Chapron, and K. Katarsos, "A unified directional spectrum for long and short wind-driven waves," *J. Geophys. Res.*, vol. 102, no. C7, pp. 15 781–15 796, 1997.

[8] K. Oumansour, Y. Wang, and J. Saillard, "Multifrequency SAR obaservation of a ship wake," *IEE Proceeding- Radar, Sonar and Navigation*, vol. 143, no. 4, pp. 275-280, 1996.

Radiated EM Flux based Diagnostic Approach for Stator Insulation Failures in Inverter fed Motors

Hassan H. Eldeeb[1], Alberto Berzoy[2], *Student Members, ACES & IEEE,* and Osama Mohammed[1], *ACES, Fellow, IEEE*

1. Energy System Research Laboratory, ECE Department, Florida International University, Miami, FL33174, USA
2. R&D Department, Sonnen Batterie Inc, Tucker, GA 30084, USA

helde002@fiu.edu; a.berzoyllerena@sonnen-batterie.com; mohammed@fiu.edu

***Abstract*— Analysis of harmonics and inter-harmonics components in the spectrum of the radiated electromagnetic (EM) field is proposed for the detection of induction motor (IM) windings' insulation failure. The IM is fed through a voltage source inverter (VSI) operating under the classical direct torque controller (DTC). To investigate the EM spectrum, the radiated magnetic field intensity ($\vec{H}$) was calculated at an observer point in a physics-based finite element analysis (FEA) platform.**

***Index Terms*— DTC, Fault detection, Induction machine, Inter-turn short-circuit, FEA co-simulation, Emitted magnetic flux.**

I. INTRODUCTION

The early detection of turn-to-turn faults (TTF) in the stator's winding of induction motors (IM), to improve the reliability and secure operation of the IM drive system, has been a hot research topic for decades. With the massive increase in the transportation electrification industry, TTF detection in closed-loop driven IMs became more momentous. Owing to the fact that closed-loop controllers hides the signatures available in faulty IM connected directly on-line (DOL) or fed from an open loop controlled voltage source inverter (VSI) [1]. Due to its simplicity and independency on machine's parameters, the direct torque control (DTC) algorithm is widely used in industry. Turn fault detection (FD) in DTC driven IMs is more challenging due to the switching activities of the VSI, which injects significant harmonics not directly related to the fault. Few studies addressed the detection of TTFs in DTC driven IMs.

Among the non-invasive diagnostic methods used to detect TTFs in DTC driven IMs: motor current signature analysis (MCSA) and positive sequence component of the stator's current [2], harmonic spectrum of the developed power [3], and impedance sequence component in [4]. The FD of TTFs using the radiated magnetic flux intensity ($\vec{H}$) is also non-invasive, and it doesn't rely on the current or voltage sensors [5], which are subjected to saturation due to the high (dv/dt) rate applied by the VSI to the IM. This article investigates the online FD of TTFs in a DTC driven IM using the magnetic signature.

II. IM DRIVE SYSTEM MODELLING

A short dipole conductor whose length (l) is significantly shorter than the wave length (λ). The magnetic potential ($\vec{A}$) at an observer point (op), placed at a distance (d) in the spherical coordinates from the dipole with current (I) is as in (1):

$$\vec{A} = \frac{\mu I l}{4\pi d} e^{-j\xi d}(\cos\theta\, a_R - \sin\theta\, a_\Phi) \quad (1)$$

where ξ is the phase, μ is the permeability. The field $\vec{H}$ is evaluated is as in(3):

$$\vec{H} = \frac{\mu I l}{4\pi}\xi^2 \sin(\theta)\left[\frac{1}{j\xi d} - \frac{1}{(\xi d)^2}\right] e^{-j\xi d}\, a_\Phi \quad (2)$$

From (2) it is obvious that the radiated $\vec{H}$ will carries the same signatures in the current. The IM has thousands of short dipole, the entire $\vec{H}$ is the summation of the radiated $\vec{H}$ of each dipole.

DTC is a predictive controller that aims to control $|\boldsymbol{\lambda}_s|$and T_e. Whereas for faulty IM driven by DTC other harmonics are presented, per instance: the 3rd order harmonic in $\boldsymbol{i}_s$ inserted by DTC to counter-balance the 2nd order harmonics inT_e, and the inter-harmonics due to ITSC as in (3)

$$f_{TTF} = f\left[\frac{m}{p}(1-s) \pm l\right] \quad (3)$$

and the inter-harmonics due to the interaction between ITSC and saturation effect as in (4)

$$f_{3h} = f\left[\frac{R}{p}(1-s) \pm 3\right] \quad (4)$$

where, $m = 0,1,2\ldots$, $l = 0,1,3,5\ldots$,, p is the number of pole pairs, s is the slip, and R is the number of rotor's slots. Details about DTC and its reaction to TTF is available in [6].

III. FEA MODEL

Physics-based model of the faulty IM was done. Fig.2 shows the magnetic flux density distribution for the IM in the FEA software. The ratings of the IM under study are shown in Table I. Each phase has number of turns $N_{as} = 510$. The fault severity factor (μ_f) is a ratio between the number of faulty turns and N_{sa}. The faulty case is for $\mu_f = 1.08\%$. The fault resistance is $R_f = 0.67\ \Omega$. The two cases studied at reference torque of 2 Nm. The op was placed at 30 cm from the stator's frame in FEA environment.

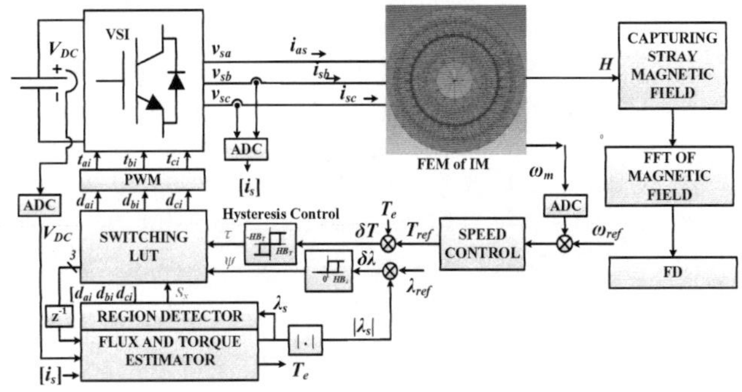

Fig. 1. The FEA co-simulation platform of the DTC driven IM under study.

This work was partially supported by grants from the Office of Naval Research and Department of Energy. Corresponding author: Prof. Mohammed, email: mohammed@fiu.edu

TABLE I. NAMEPLATE RATINGS OF THE 1 HP WEG IM UNDER STUDY.

Rating	Value	Param.	Value
Pr (W)	750	Stator outer diameter	160
U (V)	460	Stator inner diameter	100
I (A)	1.47	Rotor inner diameter	22
f (HZ)	60	Air-gap length	0.31
n (rpm)	1730	Parallel branch	1
J (kgm^2)	0.053	Slot numbers (Z1/Z2)	36/44

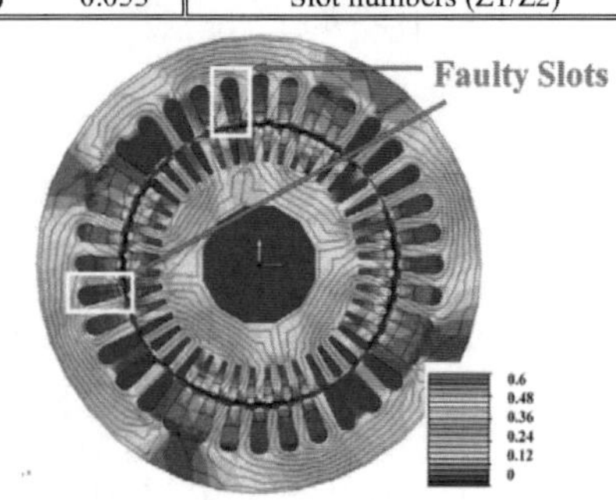

Fig. 2. 2D distribution of $|B|$

The spectrum in Fig.3 indicates the existence of several harmonics and inter-harmonics in both cases. However, the amplitude in the faulty case is not always higher than the healthy case. Moreover, the integral harmonic components are not always indicators to the fault. Consequently, statistical analysis was done to evaluate the density of existence of inter-harmonics around each integral harmonic. The histograms in Fig.4 depicts that the inter-harmonics around the fundamental components has higher value for the healthy than the faulty, while the faulty inter-harmonics have higher amplitude elsewhere. The fault could be detected easily via monitoring the inter-harmonics around $h = 3$ and 7, as shown in Fig.4 (d) and (h), respectively.

IV. CONCLUSION

Investigation of the inter-harmonics components in the radiated magnetic field was presented for the purpose of TTF detection in DTC driven IM. The FEA co-simulation showed that monitoring the inter-harmonics is more trustworthy to detect the fault from monitoring the harmonic components. Furthermore,

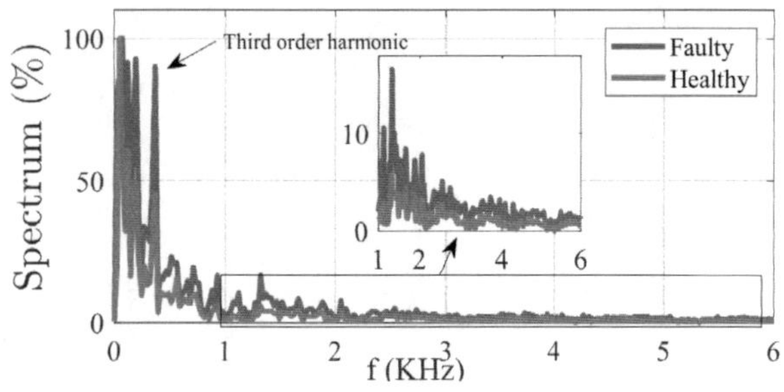

Fig. 3. The spectrum of the radiated $\vec{H}$ at the observer point

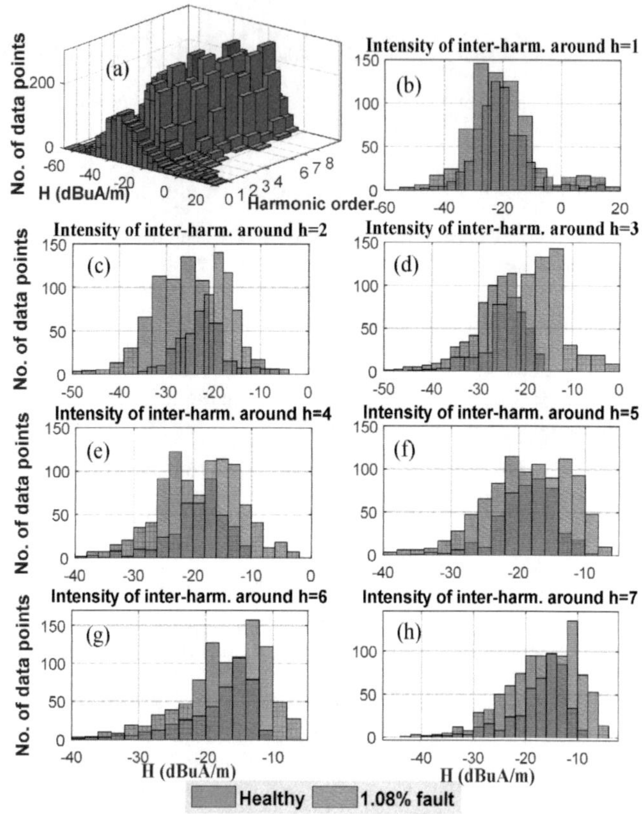

Fig. 4. Histogram of the radiated $\vec{H}$ around each integral harmonic component

results showed that the inter-harmonic components around the 3rd and 5th order harmonics are more sensitive to the fault from other inter-harmonics.

REFERENCES

[1] H. H. Eldeeb, A. Berzoy and O. Mohammed, "Stator Fault Detection on DTC-Driven IM via Magnetic Signatures Aided by 2-D FEA Co-Simulation," in *IEEE Transactions on Magnetics* [in press].

[2] S. M. A. Cruz and A. J. M. Cardoso, "Diagnosis of stator inter-turn short circuits in DTC induction motor drives," *IEEE Trans. Ind. Appl.*, vol. 40, no. 5, pp. 1349–1360, Sep. 2004.

[3] M. Drif and A. J. M. Cardoso, "Stator Fault Diagnostics in Squirrel Cage Three-Phase Induction Motor Drives Using the Instantaneous Active and Reactive Power Signature Analyses," in *IEEE Transactions on Industrial Informatics*, vol. 10, no. 2, pp. 1348-1360, May 2014.

[4] A. Berzoy, H. H. Eldeeb and O. Mohammed, "Online fault detection of stator winding faults in IM driven by DTC using the off-diagonal term of the symmetrical component impedance matrix," *2018 IEEE Applied Power Electronics Conference and Exposition (APEC)*, San Antonio, TX, USA, 2018, pp. 2482-2487.

[5] M. Irhoumah, R. Pusca, E. Lefevre, D. Mercier, R. Romary and C. Demian, "Information Fusion With Belief Functions for Detection of Interturn Short-Circuit Faults in Electrical Machines Using External Flux Sensors," in *IEEE Transactions on Industrial Electronics*, vol. 65, no. 3, pp. 2642-2652, March 2018.

[6] H. H. Eldeeb, A. Berzoy and O. Mohammed, "Comprehensive Investigation of Harmonic Signatures Resulting from Inter- Tum Short-Circuit Faults in DTC Driven IM Operating in Harsh Environments," 2018 *XIII International Conference on Electrical Machines (ICEM)*, Alexandroupoli, Greece, 2018, pp. 2579-2585

An Accurate Technique for Modeling Realistic Well-Logging Sensors Inside Complex Media

Lisseth Saavedra, Guilherme S. Rosa, and José R. Bergmann
Center for Telecommunications Studies, CETUC
Pontifical Catholic University of Rio de Janeiro
Rio de Janeiro, Brazil
lissethsaavedra@cetuc.puc-rio.br

***Abstract*—In this paper, a pseudoanalytical mode-matching formulation is introduced for the analysis of electromagnetic well-logging tools. We present numerical results for several representative scenarios to validate and explore the input (self) impedance of typical logging-while-drilling (LWD) sensors comprised by an array of coil antennas. Preliminary conclusions are presented and the potential of this approach for modeling realistic LWD sensors is then summarized.**

***Index Terms*—Antenna impedance, inhomogeneous media, logging-while-drilling (LWD) tools.**

I. Introduction

Logging-while-drilling (LWD) tools have enabled the real-time characterization of lithological variations in the soil surrounding a prospecting oil well and the consequent identification of potential pay zones. Typical LWD sensors employed by the oil and gas industry [1], [2] are comprised by an array of coil antennas wrapped around a metallic mandrel, as illustrated in Fig. 1. The geophysical environment in this type of problem is complex, and the prevalence of large contrasts of resistivity requires accurate and robust computational electromagnetics (CEM) techniques for addressing the propagation sensor response. This topic has been receiving much attention for several subsurface applications. To the best of our knowledge, the modeling of the mutual- and self-impedance of antenna sensors, however, is a topic that was not properly addressed in the literature because it demands high-cost brute-force CEM based on finite-differences (FD) and finite-elements (FE). In this paper, we overcome these difficulties by using a combination of the Bessel-Fourier expansion with an analytic version of the mode-matching technique for representing self-impedance of real dimensions LWD sensors in a borehole environment described by cylindrical-stratified media [3], [4]. Numerical simulations are presented to validate our formulation versus finite-difference-time-domain (FDTD) results. In addition, present a sensitivity analysis of the sensor impedance in terms of its physical dimension, operating frequency, and constitutive parameters of the medium where it is immersed.

II. Electromagnetic Modeling

Fig. 1 shows the geometry used to model the geophysical formation around a typical well-logging tool. Field solutions for Maxwell's equations in uniaxially anisotropic multilayered cylindrical structures (with radial and longitudinal stratifications) are well known from a prior study, and to avoid repetition, we adopt here a notation similar to that in [4] by assuming a time-harmonic dependence in the form $\exp(-i\omega t)$. The electromagnetic fields radiated by the transmitter (TX) antenna are computed by considering first it as an electric-coil with an infinitesimal cross-section. Such fields are then used as a basis for computing the input impedance of a finite-cross-section TX by using [5]:

$$Z_{\text{in}} = -\frac{1}{I_{\text{TX}}^2} \oiint \mathbf{E} \cdot \mathbf{J}_s \, ds, \tag{1}$$

where I_{TX} and $\mathbf{J}_s$ are the electrical current of the TX and its associated current density distribution over the antenna surface. The electric field $\mathbf{E}$ is computed considering all the radial and longitudinal stratifications of the problem. The mode-matching method used for computing $\mathbf{E}$ (due to an infinitesimal coil) in (1) has been extensively validated against FD and FE methods as shown in the results in [4]. In what follows, we are only concerned with the calculation of the antenna impedances of the well-logging tool.

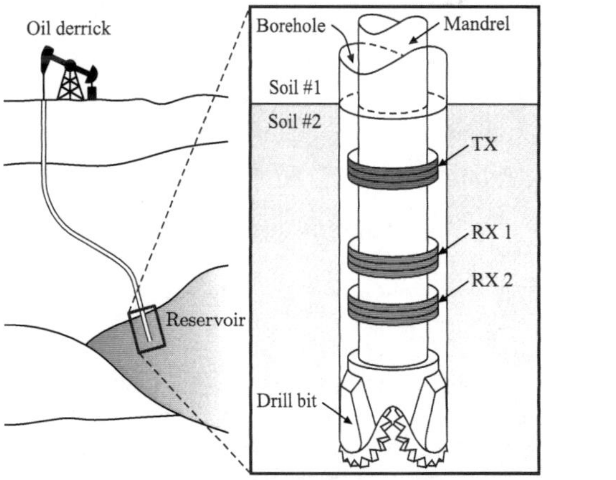

Fig. 1. Geometry of a triaxial LWD sensor within a geophysical formation.

As a first example, we first consider a 4-in-radius metallic mandrel inside a 7-in-radius borehole, where 1 in $= 2.54 \times 10^{-2}$ m. The borehole is filled with oil-based mud with 5×10^{-4} S/m and the soil formation has 1 S/m. Fig. 2 shows the impedance of two rectangular cross-section antennas as the frequency evolves from 0.5 MHz–2 MHz. Good agreement is observed versus FDTD results. To avoid very long simulation times in the FDTD, the radial domain was truncated at 10 in.

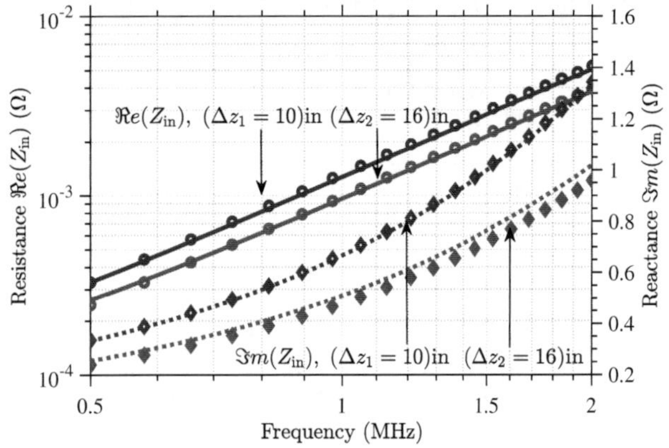

Fig. 2. Impedance of the antenna with cross-section width $\Delta\rho = 0.2$ in and heights $\Delta z = 10$ in and 16 in. The results from the present algorithm are indicated by small symbols. The solid and dashed lines are FDTD results.

As a second example, we consider a formation similar to that presented above, but now we investigate the influence of the conductivity of the soil formation. Fig. 3 shows the impedance of an antenna with cross-section $\Delta\rho = 0.2$ in by $\Delta z = 10$ in operating at 500 kHz and 2 MHz as the conductivity of the soil formation evolves.

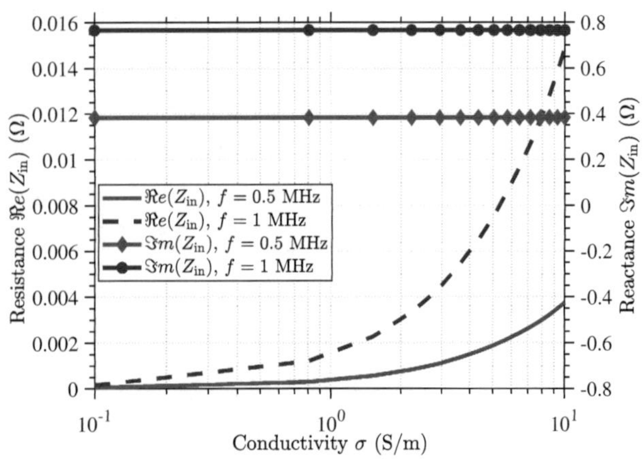

Fig. 3. Impedance of the antenna as a function of the soil conductivity.

We next evaluate a scenario similar to the first example, but now we investigate the influence of the antenna dimensions. Fig. 4 and Fig. 5 show impedance results as a function of the antenna width $\Delta\rho$ and height Δz, when the operating frequency is fixed at 0.5 MHz.

III. Conclusions

In this paper, we present a novel semi-analytical technique for modeling realistic LWD sensors immersed in complex media. Numerical results show that the technique can accurately describe the sensor impedance using low computational resources. A sensitivity analysis shows that the antenna impedance changes dramatically in terms of its dimensions, operating frequency, and media parameters of the medium where it is immersed.

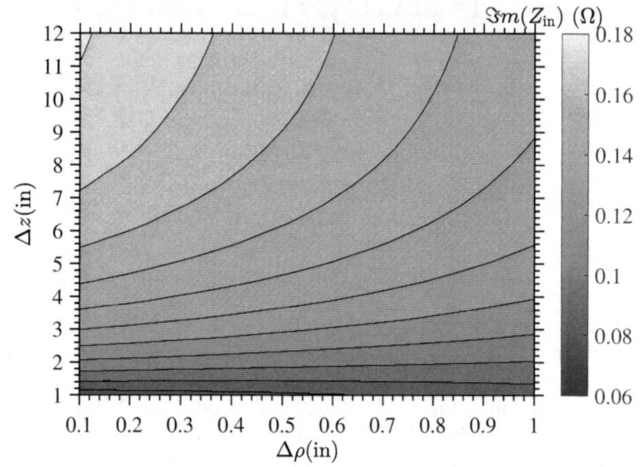

Fig. 4. Input reactance of the antenna as a function of the cross-section width $\Delta\rho$ and height Δz.

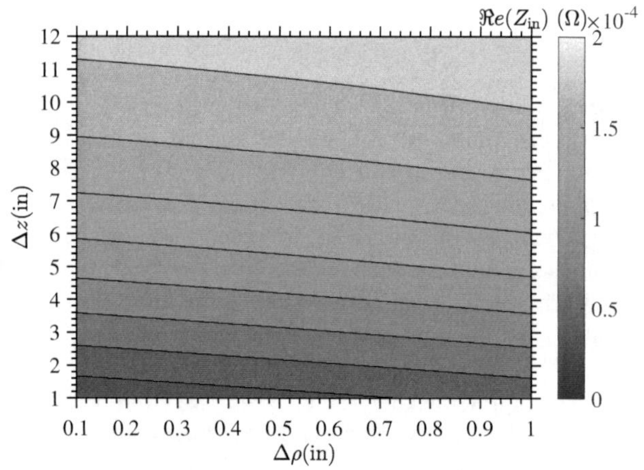

Fig. 5. Input resistance of the antenna as a function of the cross-section width $\Delta\rho$ and height Δz.

Acknowledgment

The first author thanks support from the Brazilian Agency CNPq. This study was financed in part by the Coordenação de Aperfeiçoamento de Pessoal de Nível Superior - Brasil (CAPES) - Finance Code PROCAD 068419/2014-01.

References

[1] "ADR azimuthal deep resistivity sensor datasheet," Halliburton Sperry-Drilling, Houston, TX, USA, 2016.
[2] "EarthStar^{TM} Ultra-Deep Resistivity Service datasheet," Halliburton-Sperry Drilling, Houston, TX, USA, 2018.
[3] W. C. Chew, Waves and Fields in Inhomogeneous Media. New York,NY, USA: John Wiley & Sons, 1995.
[4] G. S. Rosa, J. R. Bergmann, and F. L. Teixeira, "A robust mode-matching algorithm for the analysis of triaxial well-logging tools in anisotropic geophysical formations,"IEEE Trans. Geosci. Remote Sens., vol. 55,no. 5, pp. 2534–2545, May 2017.
[5] R. F. Harrington,Time-harmonic electromagnetic fields. New York, NY,USA: McGraw-Hill, 1961.

Geometrically Conformal Quadrilateral Surface-Reconstruction for MoM-SIE Simulations

Jake Harmon, Cam Key, and Branislav M. Notaroš
Colorado State University, Electrical & Computer Engineering Department, Fort Collins, CO
j.harmon@colostate.edu, camkey@rams.colostate.edu, notaros@colostate.edu

***Abstract*—We present a higher order quadrilateral surface remeshing approach for application to the method of moments. We briefly introduce the motivation for high-quality quadrilateral meshes for accurate and efficient application of cutting edge integration and singularity extraction approaches. Results are demonstrated for simple surfaces and compared with a common quadrilateral remeshing algorithm.**

Keywords—computational electromagnetics, computational geometry, integral equations, method of moments, quadrilateral remeshing, surface reconstruction.

I. INTRODUCTION

One of the key challenges in numerical methods, geometric discretization, profoundly affects accuracy of a given simulation. An unnecessarily fine discretization (for a given frequency) produces an unnecessarily large number of unknowns, and therefore a correspondingly large linear system. Conversely, accurate geometric modeling of curved surfaces is essential for an overall optimal higher order solution [1]. In addition, even integration procedures strongly depend on the geometric discretization of a structure. Namely, improved singularity extraction and integration techniques have recently shown promise toward further improving the method of moments (MoM) in the surface integral equation (SIE) formulation based on higher order quadrilateral modeling; these novel approaches, however, are subject to increasing error as patch corner angles exceed ~120 degrees [2], [3]. Existing quadrilateral remeshing techniques, meanwhile, often neglect the corner angles of elements. A method, therefore, to efficiently remesh surfaces to quadrilaterals with concern for electrical size and corner angles provides benefits in terms of improving the applicability of these new integration schemes.

This paper focuses on the application of a geometrically conformal (angle preserving, explicitly biholomorphic) quadrilateral remeshing approach for computational electromagnetics problems to address these concerns. In particular, we provide examples in comparison to a non-conformal approach.

II. CONFORMAL REMESHING

To produce a quadrilateral mesh with the desired properties, we begin, in general, with a point cloud describing the surface. The construction begins with a triangle meshing; Giesen, et al. provides a triangle meshing algorithm which offers several attractive guarantees, namely preservation of topology [4]. Following the reconstruction with an isotropic refinement assists in the parameterization.

Many methods exist to parameterize a surface, conformal or otherwise. However, for our application we require a conformal mapping. Conformal mappings such as discrete Ricci-flow [5], least squares conformal [6], and discrete conformal [7], each provide a means to map a surface to a parametric domain, ideally preserving the angles of the mapped surface. In this paper we show results using discrete-conformal mapping. Barycentric coordinates, unique on triangles, are then used to lift a sample pattern from a parametric domain to the original surface to produce vertices of the completed quadrilateral mesh. Crucially, as Barycentric coordinates depend on the corner angles of the triangles, conformality is preserved.

This method of remeshing provides several key advantages, especially for the higher order MoM-SIE. With a precomputed parameterization, additional remeshing is computed inexpensively; when coupled with adaptive sampling of the parametric domain, this permits a rapid means to adjust the electrical size of the patches for a given frequency. Additionally, curvilinear meshing arises naturally; given a separate sampling density for the patches and the interpolation points, quadrilateral-curvilinear patches can be generated identically to the linear case, with vertices used instead as geometric sample points for interpolation.

III. RESULTS AND DISCUSSION

To demonstrate the viability of our implementation, we show results for two geometries: spherical and toroidal. For each case, we present several tiers of sampling density in the parametric domain to simulate a frequency-dependent remeshing.

As a comparison, we test against the 4 to 8 Subdivision method included in MeshLab [8].

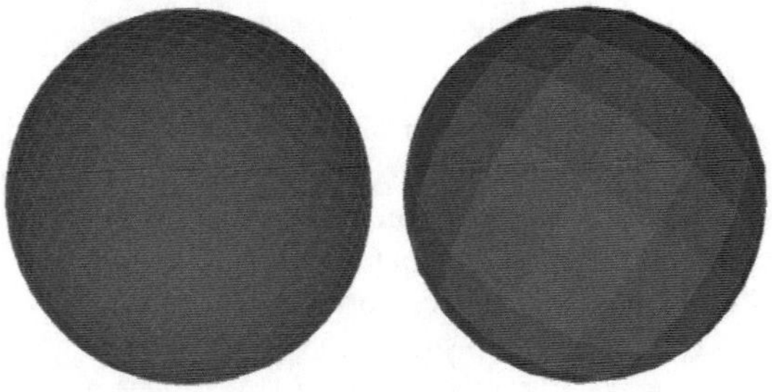

Fig. 1. Sphere quadrilateral remeshing for 2000 sample points (left) and 200 sample points (right).

We observe in Fig. 1 that a coarser sampling preserves the general constraints on the corner angles of the patches. Patch size decreases at the seams of the surface to maintain conformality. Note also that the quadrilateral remeshing does not exactly replicate the boundary of the original triangular surface mesh, with small distortions occurring; however, this effect is realized primarily for very coarse sampling or abrupt changes in curvature and is largely inconsequential.

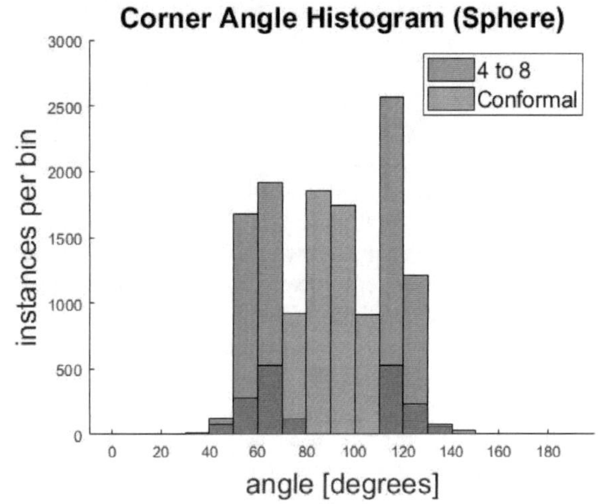

Fig. 2. Corner angle histogram for conformal remeshing and 4 to 8 subdivision for a sphere.

As seen in Fig. 2, the conformal remeshing distributes corner angles well within the desired range. In contrast, 4 to 8 subdivision—for the same number of patches—forces most angles outside this range. With further iterations of 4 to 8 subdivision, the distribution of corner angles improves, but at the expense of significantly greater element count compared to conformal remeshing.

Fig. 3. Torus quadrilateral remeshing for 10000 sample points (left) and 4000 sample points (right).

As in Fig. 1, the torus of Fig. 3 exhibits similar behavior when varying sampling density. However, the change in quadrilateral size as a function of the curvature is much more apparent; note that in the center of the torus, the patch size shrinks rapidly to preserve conformality.

In terms of angle distribution, the histogram in Fig. 4 illustrates again the quality of the quadrilateral elements generated by a conformal remeshing. For the same number of elements, 4 to 8 subdivision produces many more nearly-degenerate quadrilateral elements, or elements with three collinear vertices.

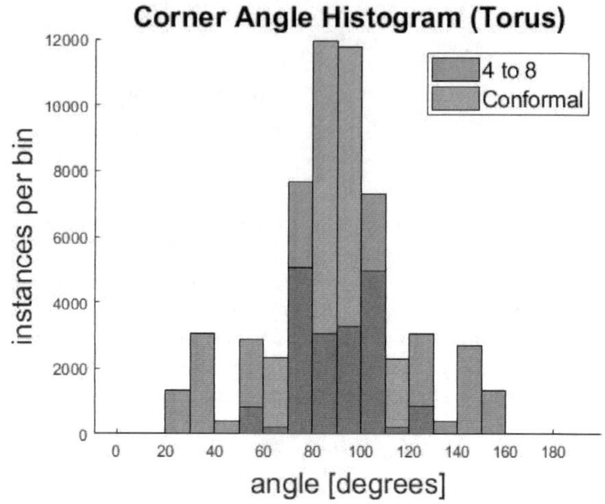

Fig. 4. Corner angle histogram for conformal remeshing and 4 to 8 subdivision for a torus.

By precomputing a conformal parameterization for a scatterer, new quadrilateral meshes with optimal corner angles can be constructed efficiently. The shape of the parent triangular mesh is also preserved well in the quadrilateral reconstruction. In principle, quadrilateral patches can be flat or curved, described by arbitrary geometric orders in parametric coordinates.

REFERENCES

[1] E. M. Klopf, N. J. Sekeljic, M. M. Ilic, and B. M. Notaros, "Optimal modeling parameters for higher order MoM-SIE and FEM-MoM electromagnetic simulations," IEEE Transactions on Antennas and Propogation, vol. 60, no.6, pp. 2790–2801, 2012.

[2] S. B. Manić and B. M. Notaroš, "Surface integral computation for the higher order surface integral equation method of moments," Proceedings of the 2018 International Applied Computational Electromagnetics Society (ACES) Symposium – ACES2018, March 25–29, 2018, Denver, Colorado, USA.

[3] A. A. Tambova, M. S. Litsarev, G. Guryev, and A. G. Polimeridis, "On the generalization of DIRECTFN for singular integrals over quadrilateral patches," IEEE Transactions on Antennas and Propogation, vol. 66, no.1, pp. 304-314, 2018.

[4] J. Giesen and M. John, "Surface reconstruction based on a dynamical system," In Proceedings of the 23rd Annual Conference of the European Association for Computer Graphics (Eurographics), Computer Graphics Forum 21, pp. 363-371, 2002.

[5] Y. Yang, R. Guo, F. Luo, S. Huo, and X. Gu, "Genearlized discrete Ricci flow," Computer Graphics Forum 28, pp. 2005-2014, 2009.

[6] B. Levy, S. Petitjean, N. Ray, and J. Maillot, "Least squares conformal maps for automatic texture atlas generation," ACM Transactions on Graphics, vol. 21, pp. 362-371, 2002.

[7] L. Kharevych, B. Springborn, and P. Schroder, "Discrete conformal mappings via circle patterns," ACM Transactions on Graphics, vol. 25, pp. 412-438, 2006.

[8] P. Cignoni, M. Callieri, M. Corsini, M. Dellepiane, F. Ganovelli, and G. Ranzuglia, "MeshLab: an open-source mesh processing tool," Sixth Eurographics Italian Chapter Conference, pp. 129-136, 2008.

A Novel Mid-infrared Metalens using a Hyperbolic Metamaterial

Mohamed Kyamo, Navaneeth Premkumar, Abdelgader Alsalhin, and Brian A. Lail
Dept. of Computer Engineering and Sciences Florida Institute of Technology
Melbourne, Florida
mkyamo2016@my.fit.edu, npremkumar2013@my.fit.edu, aalshiekh2014@my.fit.edu blail@fit.ed

***Abstract*— A novel metalens in the mid infrared range from 6.4um to 10um is designed. It consists of a plasmonic waveguide coupler (PWC), on a slab of type I hyperbolic metamaterial (HMM) on the top of a substrate of undoped InAs with a Au nanoantenna at the other end. The metalens serves to focus both propagating and evanescent waves into a focal point at which the field confinement and enhancement are improved using the plasmonic nanoantenna. This paper shows the design and performance of the metalens, which has applications in sub-wavelength imaging and sensing.**

Keywords- Enhancement, Hyperbolic metamaterial, Metalens, Mid-infrared, Plasmonic, Resolution.

I. Introduction

In [1] it was shown that electromagnetic plane waves in a medium having negative permittivity and permeability would propagate toward a path against to that of the flow of energy. Lately in [2], they designed a flat lens using a slab of material with a negative index of refraction while a metalens at visible light was designed in [3]. The motivation behind the design in this paper is to make a three-dimensional super-resolution metalens with high electric-field enhancement in the mid-infrared range of 6.4-10μm. Here we use a plasmonic waveguide coupler (PWC), which is made out of rings of doped InAs working as a Fresnel zone plate (FZP) to focus waves like a conventional lens. The PWC is placed on hyperbolic metamaterial (HMM) which is constructed using a periodic stack of doped and undoped InAs layers where the bulk material properties are calculated using effective medium theory (EMT). The HMM allows us to break the diffraction limit and convert evanescent waves to propagating waves. Together the PWC and the HMM slab serve to focus incoming radiation onto a focal point located in the gap between a plasmonic nanodisk made using two gold (Au) disks.

II. Design and Optmization

The metalens was designed and simulated using ANSYS HFSS software and the structure is excited by an incident plane wave. Fig. 1 shows the structure of the metalens which consists of a PWC with annular rings of doped InAs , a slab of HMM in [4] and a nanoantenna situated on a dielectric substrate. The PWC has a thickness of 70nm and ring width of 20 and it is illuminated by normally incident TM plane waves. The PWC is placed on the cylindrical slab of HMM which consists of undoped InAs and doped InAs. The Drude model is used to generate the data of the constituent material properties for InAs. Complex permittivity for undoped InAs is found by using $\omega_p = 3x10^{13}\ rads^{-1}, \gamma = 10^{12}$ rad, and $\epsilon_r = 12.3$, while the doped InAs parameters are $\omega_p = 2.95x10^{14}\ rads^{-1}, \gamma = 10^{12}$ rad, and $\epsilon_r = 10.4$; where ω_p is the plasmonic resonance frequency, γ is electron relaxation in radians and ϵ_r is the relative permittivity. The metamaterial is a uniaxial material with permittivities $\epsilon_\parallel$ and $\epsilon_\perp$. The dispersion relation of a uniaxial material is given by:

$$\frac{k_\parallel^2}{\epsilon_\perp} + \frac{k_\perp^2}{\epsilon_\parallel} = \frac{\omega^2}{c^2}. \qquad (1)$$

The effective permittivity is calculated by effective medium theory (EMT) [5]:

$$\epsilon_\parallel = \epsilon_{xx} = \epsilon_{yy} = p\epsilon_m + (1-p)\epsilon_d .$$
$$\epsilon_\perp = \epsilon_z = \frac{\epsilon_m \cdot \epsilon_d}{p\epsilon_d + (1-p)\epsilon_m}, \quad p = \frac{t_m}{t_m + t_d}. \qquad (2)$$

Here t_m is the thickness of metallic layer (doped InAs) and t_d is the thickness of the dielectric layer (undoped InAs). ϵ_m is permitivity of doped InAs and ϵ_d is permitivity of undoped InAs ,t_m is 290nm and t_d is 370nm .

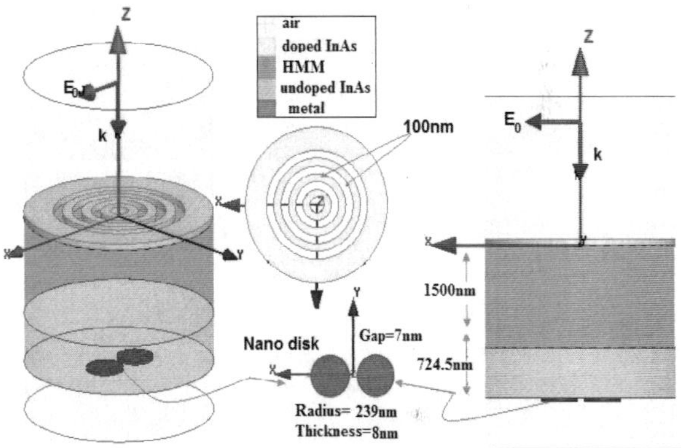

Fig. 1. Metalens structure.

The perpendicular and parallel permittivities are shown in Fig. 2. The resulting material is a type I HMM with a diagonal dielectric tensor described as $\epsilon_{xx} = \epsilon_{yy} > 0, \epsilon_z < 0$ in the wavelength range of 6.366μm to 8.837μm, and a type II HMM with $\epsilon_{xx} = \epsilon_{yy} < 0$, $\epsilon_z > 0$ in the wavelength range 10.4μm to 12μm. It also acts as an anisotropic metal in the range 8.838μm to 10.03μm. Here we use the type I HMM.

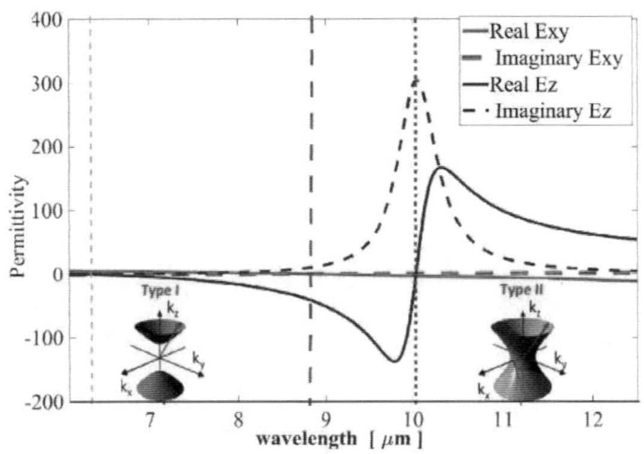

Fig. 2. Effective permittivity as a function of wavelength.

III. Results and Discussion

Fig. 3 is shows the magnitude of electric field distribution for metalens with and without nano disks at the focal point of the metalens in the XZ plane with a X-polarized normal plane wave at 7.739um. The focal length is 2.248um. The FWHM values along the x-axis and the y-axis without the nano disks are 800nm and its electric field enhancement on the order of 10^2. The electric field distribution is enhanced in the gap of two gold nano disks. This enhancement is controlled by varying the height and radii of the disks.

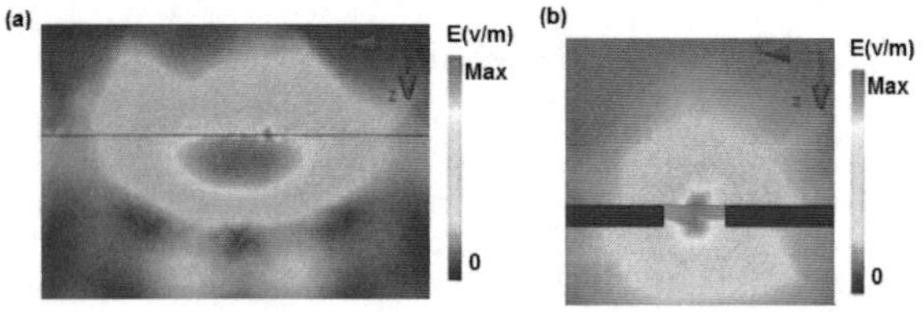

Fig. 3. The magnitude of electric field distribution at the focal point: (a) without nano disk and (b) with nano disk.

Fig. 4 shows the variation of electric-field enhancement at the focal point with variation in the gap between the two disks. The electric field enhancement on the order of 10^6.

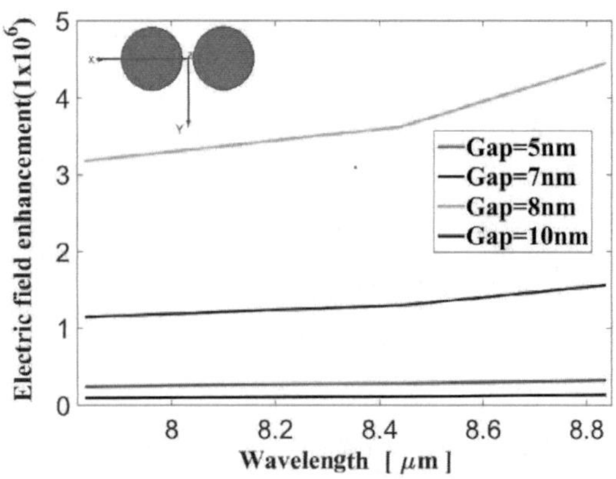

Fig. 4. The electric field distribution of the focal point with different values for separation between the disks.

In Fig. 5, electric field at the focal point is plotted on the x-axis (blue) and y-axis (red). The full-width half maximum (FWHM) is 8.18nm and 13.64nm on the x-axis and y-axis, respectively. The FWHM values along the x-axis and the y-axis are smaller than the diffraction limit of the 0.5λ, thus allowing us to image particles that are 1/1000 times the wavelength.

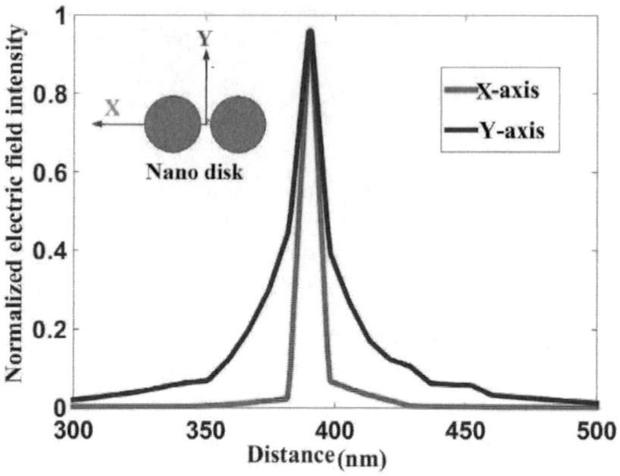

Fig. 5. Field intensity profile the x-axis and y-axis.

IV. Conclusion

As shown by using a PWC made using doped InAs, a hyperbolic metamaterial made using layers of doped InAs and undoped InAs and an Au plasmonic nan disk, a new metalens was designed in the mid infrared capable of super-resolution focusing with high electric-field enhancement. Using InAs as an alternative to metals reduces losses. The hyperbolic metamaterial allows the lens to support the propagation of waves with high wave vectors. The electric field at the focal point is enhanced when using the Au nanoadisk. The full-width half maximum (FWHM) of the field at the focal point is 8.18nm x 13.64nm on the x-axis and y-axis, respectively. This allows us to image particles that are 1/1000 times the wavelength. Such a metalens may be used for sub-wavelength imaging and sensing with super resolution and high electric field enhancement.

References

[1] G. Veselago, "The electrodynamics of substances with simultaneously negative values of permittivity and permeability," Sov. Phys. Usp. 10, 509-514, 1968.

[2] J. B. Pendry, "Negative refraction makes a perfect lens," Phys. Rev. Lett., vol. 85, no. 18, pp. 3966–3969, Oct. 2000.

[3] C. B. Ma and Z. W Liu," A super resolution metalens with phase compensation mechanism," Appl. Phys. Lett. 96, 183103, 2010.

[4] F. Peragut, L. Cerutti, A. Baranovj, P. Hugonin, T. Taliercio, Y. De Wilde, and J. J. Greffet, "Hyperbolic metamaterials and surface plasmon polaritons," Optica. vol. 4, no. 11, pp. 1409-1415, Nov. 2017.

[5] P Shekhar, J Atkinson, Z. Jacob, "Hyperbolic metamaterials: Fundamentals and applications," Nano Convergence, 2014.

Determining the Dispersive Features of Nanophotonic Structures based on Hybrid FEM/TMM Technique

Abdelgader Alsalhin and Brian Lail
Computer Engineering and Sciences
Florida Institute of Technology
Melbourne, Florida
aalshiekh2014@my.fit.edu

***Abstract*—Determining the dispersion relation of nanophotonic structures is one of the biggest challenges especially for nano-scale inhomogeneous structures where several efforts have been directed. Here, we present a technique that leverages the accuracy and simplicity of the combination of transfer matrix method (TMM) and finite element method (FEM). This hybrid technique allows us to find the spatial dispersion, coupling strength and nature of the generated modes.**

Keywords—dispersion, finite element method, HFSS, nanophotonics, transfer matrix method.

I. INTRODUCTION

In the field of nanophononics (or nano-optics), determining the dispersion relation of inhomogeneous structures is one of the biggest challenges. There are numerous efforts in this direction with techniques of varying levels of complexity [1]. Each technique has its advantages and limitations where the outcomes, in general, are affected by the trade-off with the accuracy and the time. Therefore, looking for accurate techniques to determine the dispersion relations for nano-scale grating structures has been gaining momentum recently. The transfer matrix method (TMM) is a one-dimensional method (1D) that is used to calculate the dispersion in the incident direction (longitudinal) while the other directions (transversal) are assumed to be infinite. As detailed in the next section, TMM is a valid technique used to approximate the dispersion behavior inside a structure. In contrast, a three-dimensional (3D) technique like the finite element method (FEM) could deal with a structure having discontinuous content (grating) in 3D. Practically, modeling the geometry of interest using a full wave simulator (FEM-based) and modifying the outputs to match a simpler technique of extracting the dispersion based on TMM is the new hybrid technique that is suggested here.

II. PRINCIPLES AND METHODOLOGY

A. TMM

The TMM is a rigorous semi-analytical method where an approximated solution is adopted for transversal directions while the analytical solution is in longitudinal direction. It is usually applied for infinite slabs and it neither accounts for diffraction effects nor handles inhomogeneous transversal gratings. On the other hand, it is very fast, simple, robust and unconditionally stable [2]. Also, much like scattering techniques, it is well explained in the available literature [2], [3]. Starting with Maxwell's equations, the physical boundary conditions are applied, where the tangential fields are equal at both sides of an interface, and finally the wave equations of these tangential fields are extracted in matrix form. Typically, the overall solution of the second order differential wave equation is represented in matrix form as:

$$[\Psi_t(L)]_{m\times1} = [W]_{m\times m}\,[E_d]_{m\times m}\,([W]_{m\times m})^{-1}\,[a^{\pm}]_{m\times1}, \quad (1)$$

where the relevant terms of this equation are defined as the following:
$[\Psi_t(L)]_{m\times1}$ are the tangential field vectors at distance L, $[W]_{m\times m}$ contains the eigen vectors and is called the Dynamical Matrix, $[Ed]_{m\times m}$ is termed the Propagation Matrix and is a diagonal matrix that contains the eigen values, $([W]_{m\times m})^{-1}\,[a^{\pm}]_{m\times1} = (C^{\pm})$ = proportionality coefficients and $[W]_{m\times m}\,[Ed]_{m\times m}\,([W]_{m\times m})^{-1}$ is the Transfer Matrix (*Tr*).

In case of multilayers, as shown in Fig. 1, the overall tangential fields equation in terms of TMM is:

$$\left[\Psi_{t(\text{trnsmitted Side})}\right] = \text{Tr}_{(\text{total})}\left[\Psi_{t(\text{reflected Side})}\right], \quad (2)$$

where $\text{Tr}_{(\text{total})}$ is the total transfer matrix and equals to $(\text{Tr}_{\text{Layer\#1}})(\text{Tr}_{\text{Layer\#2}})\ldots(\text{Tr}_{\text{Layer\#N}})$. TMM represents the relation between the modes at one side of a layer to the modes at the other side while S-matrix describes the relationship between inputs to the outputs of that layer. For instance, medium #2 as seen in Fig. 1 has;

$$\begin{bmatrix} C_1^- \\ C_3^+ \end{bmatrix} = \begin{bmatrix} \mathbb{S}_{11}^{M\#2} & \mathbb{S}_{12}^{M\#2} \\ \mathbb{S}_{21}^{M\#2} & \mathbb{S}_{22}^{M\#2} \end{bmatrix}\begin{bmatrix} C_1^+ \\ C_3^- \end{bmatrix} \text{............... S-matrix for medium \#2,}$$

$$\begin{bmatrix} \mathbb{O} & -\mathbb{S}_{12}^{M\#2} \\ \mathbb{I} & -\mathbb{S}_{22}^{M\#2} \end{bmatrix}\begin{bmatrix} C_3^+ \\ C_3^- \end{bmatrix} = \begin{bmatrix} \mathbb{S}_{11}^{M\#2} & -\mathbb{I} \\ \mathbb{S}_{21}^{M\#2} & \mathbb{O} \end{bmatrix}\begin{bmatrix} C_1^+ \\ C_1^- \end{bmatrix} \text{TMM for medium \#2,}$$

where $[C^{\pm}]$ are the vectors of mode proportionality (amplitudes), $[\mathbb{S}]$ is the S-matrix components, $[\mathbb{I}]$ is the identity matrix, and $[\mathbb{O}]$ is a zero matrix [2].

B. FEM

FEM is very mature and versatile method, and allows for solving inside of complex shapes, but its implementation is tedious, and often a numerical implementation using a full-wave commercially-available simulator overcomes this issue. Here the FEM software used is ANSYS HFSS. When modeling the geometry in HFSS, we apply Floquet ports as a source, with master-slave periodic boundaries to simulate infinite slabs, and a fine mesh. The Floquet port provides a built-in tool (mode calculator) to control the type and the order of the modes (TE or TM) whilst periodic boundaries can handle the incident angles based on Floquet theory [4]. Finally, the meshing operator controls the solution accuracy and convergence. As a result, the S-matrix of the selected modes can be extracted as a function of either the wavelength or the dimensions of the structure.

C. Hybrid Techniuqe

The proposed method starts by extracting TMM from the S-matrix (output of FEM-based software) as a following;

$$\begin{bmatrix} \mathbb{O} & -\mathbb{S}_{12}^{\text{total}} \\ \mathbb{I} & -\mathbb{S}_{22}^{\text{total}} \end{bmatrix}\begin{bmatrix} C_{\text{Output}}^+ \\ C_{\text{Output}}^- \end{bmatrix} = \begin{bmatrix} \mathbb{S}_{11}^{\text{total}} & -\mathbb{I} \\ \mathbb{S}_{21}^{\text{total}} & \mathbb{O} \end{bmatrix}\begin{bmatrix} C_{\text{input}}^+ \\ C_{\text{input}}^- \end{bmatrix}, \quad (3)$$

and using the following periodic boundary conditions [2],

$$\begin{bmatrix} C_{\text{Output}}^+ & C_{\text{Output}}^- \end{bmatrix}^T = \left[\exp^{j(K_z)d}\right]_{\text{diagonal}}\begin{bmatrix} C_{\text{input}}^+ & C_{\text{input}}^- \end{bmatrix}^T$$

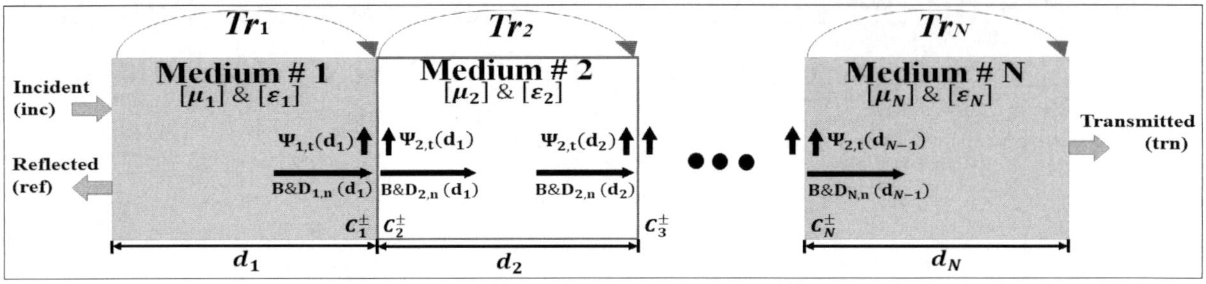

Fig. 1. A physical description of applying TMM for 1D stack of layers where [μ] and [ε] are permeability and permittivity of each medium, while (Bn) and (Dn) are the normal components of magnetic and electric flux densities, respectively.

$$\begin{bmatrix} \mathbb{S}_{11}^{total} & -\mathbb{I} \\ \mathbb{S}_{21}^{total} & \mathbb{O} \end{bmatrix} \begin{bmatrix} C_{input}^{+} \\ C_{input}^{-} \end{bmatrix} = \left[\exp^{j(K_z)d}\right]_{diag} \begin{bmatrix} \mathbb{O} & -\mathbb{S}_{12}^{total} \\ \mathbb{I} & -\mathbb{S}_{22}^{total} \end{bmatrix} \begin{bmatrix} C_{input}^{+} \\ C_{input}^{-} \end{bmatrix}, \quad (4)$$

where (K_Z) and (d), respectively, are the complex wave vector and the total thickness in longitudinal direction (assumed to be Z-axis). Hence, (4) should be solved as a generalized eigen-value problem, (Ax = λBx), using the MATLAB function [W, Ed] = eig (A, B). The output will be eigen vector matrix ($[W]_{m\times m}$) represents the amplitudes of the modes, and diagonal eigen value matrix ($[Ed]_{m\times m} \equiv \lambda$) describes the mode propagation (Bloch modes) [2]. Eventually, in MATLAB also:

$$\lambda k = j(K_Z)d = \text{diag}\,(\text{diag}\,(\log\,(\text{diag}\,(Ed)))), \quad (5)$$

$$K_z = (\beta) \pm j(\alpha) = \left(\frac{\text{imag}(\lambda K)+(M\pi)}{d}\right) \pm j\left(\frac{\text{real}(\lambda K)-(M\pi)}{d}\right), \quad (6)$$

where (M) is the order of the modes, will be assumed 0 here.

III. Investigation

The hybrid technique was implemented to the geometry shown in Fig. 2, consisting of hexagonal boron nitride (hBN, type II) where his material supports phonon polaritons [5].

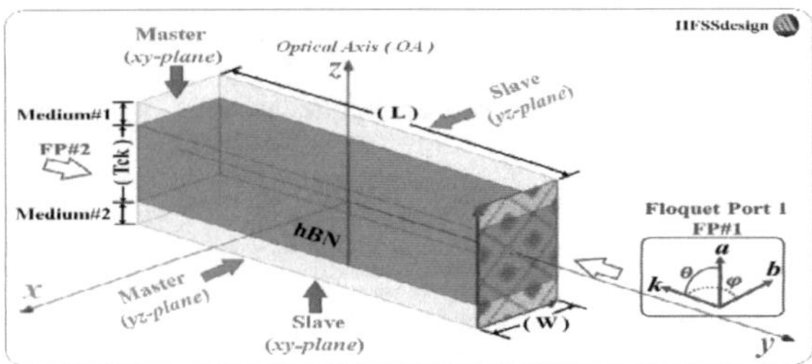

Fig. 2. Modeling [Medium1/hBN/Medium2] in HFSS.

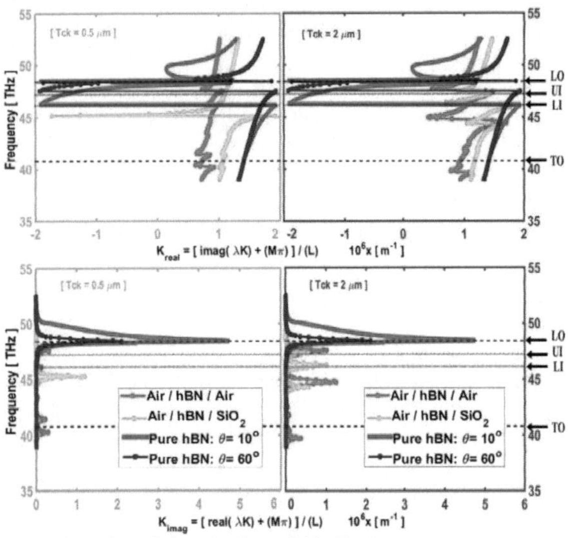

Fig. 3. Dispersion relations for the model in Fig. 2.

After modeling the structure seen in Fig. 2, the thickness of hBN (Tck), medium 2, and the angle θ are varied as [0.5μm, 2μm], [air, SiO2], and [0° to 90°], respectively. Here L=W=1.618μm, φ=90°, and medium 1 is air. Under these conditions, the best momentum matching is obtained with θ=60°, i.e., $(\text{absorbance})_{max} = 1 - |S_{11}|^2 - |S_{21}|^2$. Accordingly, all results in Fig. 3 are plotted for θ=60° except the red curves at θ=10° to show the effect of θ variation. Figs. 3 (a-1) and (b-1) illustrate the real wave vector, and (a-2) and (b-2) show the imaginary part (losses), for Tck = 0.5 and 2 μm. The four horizontal black lines in Fig. 3 define the localized modes (see [5]) where UI, for example, represents surface modes at the upper interface. The red (θ=10°) and blue (θ=60°) curves represent the dispersion inside a pure hBN where medium 1 and 2 are nonexistent, and these results are compatible with the dispersion presented in [6]. The anticrossing (or repulsion) behavior is a distinctive signature known for coupling [5]. Therefore, each anti-crossing signature describes coupled mode where wider repulsion means stronger coupling. Based on that, only one coupled mode is noticed for a pure hBN cases at LO, and the stronger is when (θ=60°). Moreover, the effect of substrate (medium2) is illustrated by comparing the green (silica) and the purple curves (air) where the number and the strength of the modes are different. In fact, it should be mention that there are two floquet modes excited, and these results reflect TM_{00} input mode only while results for TE_{00} were ignored because they didn't give the highest absorbance. As mention in Section II (B), input modes are handling at ports where largest energy at TM_{00}, so, fewer modes means best accuracy [4].

IV. Conclusion

This technique is suitable for few-input modes in order to determining the number of coupled modes, and the nature of these modes, regardless of the ingredients or the geometry.

References

[1] W. Stutzman and G. Thiele, Antenna Theory and Design, 3rd ed., John Wiley & Sons, Inc., 2013.

[2] R. C. Rumpf, "Improved formulation of scattering matrices for semianalytical methods that is consistent with convention," Progr. Electromagn. Res. B, vol. 35, pp. 241–261, Oct. 2011.

[3] H. Kitahara, M. W. Takeda, M. Iida, M. Tani, M. Watanabe, and K. Sakai, "Reflection losses of finite periodic photonic crystals," Laser Optics 14(5), pp. 654-659, 2004.

[4] HFSS™, "Getting started with HFSS: Floquet Ports," Report 2010.

[5] A. A. Alsalhin, M. F. Finch, and B. A. Lail, "Coupling between metallic structure and phonon polaritons for sensing applications," Proc. SPIE 10719, Metamaterials, Metadevices, and Metasystems, Sep. 2018.

[6] S. Dai, Q. Ma, et al., "Subdiffractional focusing and guiding of polaritonic rays in a natural hyperbolic material," Nature Communications, vol. 6, p. 6963, 2015.

Reconfigurable Metasurfaces for Index Modulation in 5G Wireless Communications

John A. Hodge[1], Kumar Vijay Mishra[2] and Amir I. Zaghloul[1,2]
[1]Virginia Tech, Falls Church, VA 22043 USA
[2]United States Army Research Laboratory, Adelphi, MD 20783 USA
jah70@vt.edu

***Abstract*—Recent research on index modulation (IM) techniques shows great promise in improving the energy and spectral efficiencies of high data-rate 5G wireless communications. In this work, we introduce a reconfigurable software-defined metasurface to implement IM techniques in 5G transceivers. In particular, we define implementation of spatial and subcarrier index modulations using a reconfigurable metasurface antenna, including beam steering and phase modulation capabilities. We present a metasurface aperture that can modulate and multiplex communications signals over the spectral, spatial, and temporal domains using space-time coding of unit elements.**

***Index Terms*—5G, index modulation, OFDM, reconfigurable metasurfaces, spatial modulation.**

I. Introduction

Demands for higher data rates within the limited electromagnetic spectrum have increased multi-fold with the onset of fifth-generation (5G) wireless communications systems. Further, growing global usage of smart phones and internet-of-things (IoT) devices requires 5G networks to support higher spectral and energy efficiencies (SE and EE) [1, 2]. In this context, index modulation (IM) has emerged as a potential 5G waveform because it offers high EE and SE by relying on the indices or permutation of some variable of carrier signals to convey additional bits of information [2]. In this paper, we focus on two particular forms of IM. The first is spatial modulation (SM) which encodes part of the transmit data onto the spatial position of each transmit antenna in the antenna array [3]. The other is the subcarrier index modulation (SIM), also known as orthogonal frequency division multiplexing (OFDM)-IM, wherein the frequency subcarrier-index of the transmitted symbol carries information bits [1–4].

Typically, 5G links employ several multiple-input-multiple-output (MIMO) antenna arrays with many radio-frequency (RF) chains [1], resulting in complex RF systems with prohibitive cost, size, weight, and power (SWaP). These limitations can be offset by employing a variety of techniques. At the modulation level, SM conveys bits of information without additional power through antenna indices and only requires a single RF chain thereby reducing the complexity at both transmitter and receiver, without decreasing the SE or EE of conventional systems [2]. At the RF and antenna stage, recently RF reconfigurable metasurfaces (R-MTSs) have been developed to provide antennas with active beamforming capabilities with significantly lower cost and complexity than the traditional phased arrays [5–9]. In this work, we combine these two ideas to propose MTS-enabled IM to meet the spectral and hardware requirements of next-generation communications systems.

II. Metasurface Control

An MTS antenna is an electrically-large aperture antenna comprising of subwavelength resonant metamaterial elements. By changing the phase coding across the MTS over time, functions such as phase modulation, amplitude attenuation, and frequency-domain multiplexing, are performed all over the MTS surface without RF components such as mixers and phase shifters. Each MTS unit cell is characterized by its transmission or reflection coefficient. This coefficient is tuned to the desired frequency-dependent phase and amplitude by sending a voltage control signal to an active element, e.g. a diode, embedded in the unit cell [10].

In this paper, we assume the active MTS is in a reflectarray configuration [7] and is controlled by a MTS control module, which is an FPGA controller that calculates the necessary phase of each unit cell to perform MTS beam scanning and phase modulation. The MTS control module also sends voltage signals to each unit cell to realize the desired phase states. Let θ_r and θ_i be the reflected and incident wave directions, respectively. If $\frac{d\Phi}{dx}$ is the gradient of phase discontinuity along the MTS, then the MTS beam scanning is modeled using the generalized law of reflection as [11]

$$\sin(\theta_r) - \sin(\theta_i) = \frac{\lambda_0}{2\pi}\frac{d\Phi}{dx}. \tag{1}$$

Assuming $\theta_i = 0$ and taking MTS unit cell parameters into account, the beam scanning equation becomes

$$\theta_r = \sin^{-1}\left(\frac{\lambda_0}{2\pi}\frac{\Delta\phi_e}{Qd}\right), \tag{2}$$

where $\Delta\phi_e$ is the phase tuning range of the unit cell element, Q is the selected period of unit cells, and d is the element spacing of each unit cell. From this relation, we calculate the phase difference between each unit cell necessary to scan the beam in the desired direction. Figure 1 demonstrates a progressive phase shift calculated using (2) that scans the beam to $\theta_r = 30\,\text{deg}$ with a desired phase. The FPGA-based MTS control module computes the values of $\Delta\phi_e$ and Q accordingly for beam scanning and calculates the phase of each unit cell column ($\phi_{steer}(m)$) using

$$\phi_{steer}(m) = \text{mod}(m/Q)(\Delta\phi_e/Q), \tag{3}$$

where $\text{mod}(\cdot)$ denotes the modulo operation. The unit cell grid spacing in each dimension is denoted by d_x and d_y and the wavenumber is $k_c = \frac{2\pi}{\lambda_c}$. The far-field phase of each element due to the array factor of the MTS is

$$\phi_{ff}(m,n) = k_c \sin\theta((m-1)d_x\cos\phi + (n-1)d_y\sin\phi). \tag{4}$$

Let $\phi_{mod}(m,n,t)$ be the time-varying phase modulation term that accounts for the desired phase shift keying (PSK) or quadrature amplitude modulation (QAM) modulation symbols. We denote the reflection amplitude and phase of each MTS unit cell as $a_e(m,n)$ and $\phi_e(m,n)$, respectively [6]. For simplicity, assume $a_e = 1$; in practice, a scan-dependent element pattern may be used. The desired reflection phase of each unit cell is

$$\phi_e(m,n,t) = \phi_{mod}(m,n,t) + \phi_{steer}(m,n) + \phi_{ff}(m,n). \tag{5}$$

From (3)-(5), the far-field radiation pattern of the signal-modulating-MTS is

$$f(\phi,\theta) = \sum_{m=1}^{M}\sum_{n=1}^{N} a_e(m,n)\exp\{j\phi_e(m,n,t)\}. \tag{6}$$

III. MTS-enabled Index Modulation

We now explain MTS implementation for two 5G IM techniques, i.e., SM and OFDM-IM.

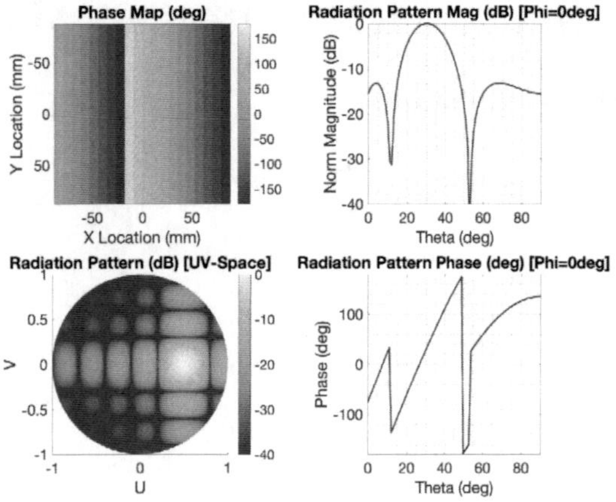

Fig. 1. Phase map of MTS scanning beam to 30° at 6 GHz with far-field radiated phase tuned to +45°. The MTS consisted of 20 × 20 unit cells with element spacing of 8.3 mm ($\lambda/6$). The radiation pattern is normalized.

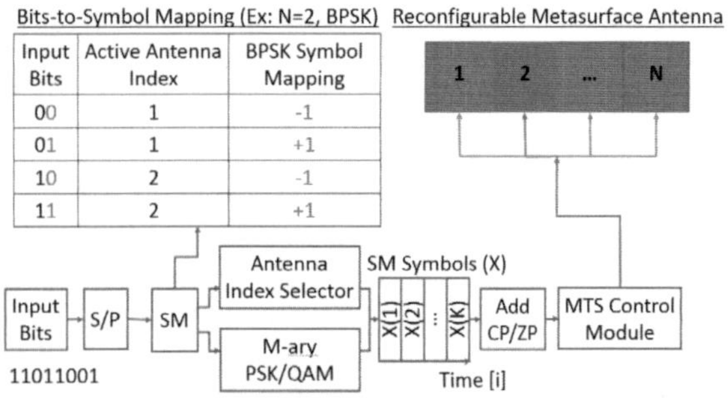

Fig. 2. Simplified system block diagram of an active MTS-based SM transmit chain. The communications signal bit stream input is converted from serial-to-parallel (S/P). The SM splits input into antenna index and M-ary modulation bits; the outputs of the two form SM symbols. Next, zero padding (ZP) or cyclical prefix (CP) add a guard interval. The SM symbols are fed to the MTS Control Module which computes the reflection phase of each unit cell for modulation and outputs voltage signals to control the unit cell at each time step to modulate and transmit the reflected signal from the feed.

In SM, bits are split into index bits and M-ary (PSK/QAM) constellation bits [2]. The R-MTS implements SM by dividing the MTS into sub-apertures with sufficient phase center separation to create a spatial antenna constellation (Figure 2). The SM is particularly well suited for MTS implementation because it employs a single-RF feed. The single-carrier SM MIMO provides the benefits of a low-complexity, low-cost single-RF transmitter while attaining high MIMO multiplexing gain [12]. At the cost of added complexity, generalized spatial modulation (GSM) [2] can be performed using MTSs by illuminating more than one subaperture simultaneously. Additionally, more sophisticated SM modulation schemes, such as space-time block codes (STBCs) (as in, e.g. Vertical-Bell Laboratories Layered Space-Time or VBLAST) [12], can also be implemented using MTSs with most of the added complexity handled digitally inside of the FPGA that controls the MTS.

Many modern wireless communication systems utilize OFDM to multiplex PSK or QAM signals on orthogonal frequency subcarriers to increase data rates. The IM has been extended to OFDM to create SIM (or OFDM-IM) for greater SE and EE. Through space-time coding of an R-MTS, frequency harmonics [13] or subcarriers are generated for SIM. For MTS implementation of OFDM and OFDM-IM, signal amplitude and phase control can each be controlled

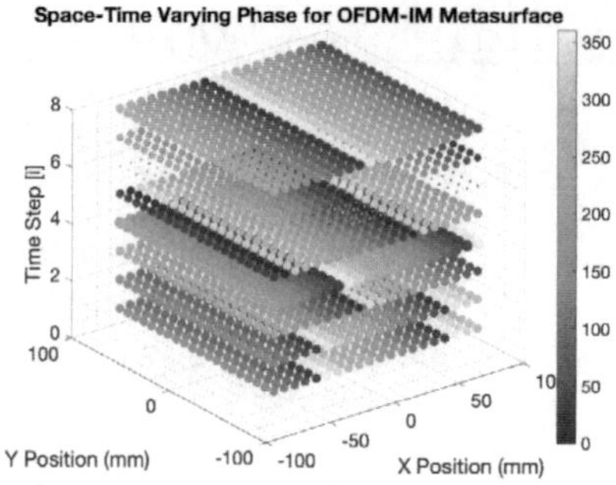

Fig. 3. Illustration of space-time varying phases of an MTS-based OFDM-IM for a random bit signal sequence. The colored dots represent phase in degrees.

either in the RF feed circuitry or directly through switching in the active MTS. Figure 3 shows space-time MTS varying phases that implement OFDM-IM for random bit signal sequence.

ACKNOWLEDGEMENTS

K. V. M. acknowledges support from the National Academies of Sciences, Engineering, and Medicine via Army Research Laboratory Harry Diamond Distinguished Postdoctoral Fellowship.

REFERENCES

[1] X. Cheng, M. Zhang, M. Wen, and L. Yang, "Index modulation for 5G: Striving to do more with less," IEEE Wireless Communications, vol. 25, no. 2, pp. 126–132, 2018.

[2] E. Basar, M. Wen, R. Mesleh, M. Di Renzo, Y. Xiao, and H. Haas, "Index modulation techniques for next-generation wireless networks," IEEE Access, vol. 5, pp. 16 693–16 746, 2017.

[3] R. Mesleh, H. Haas, S. Sinanovic, C. W. Ahn, and S. Yun, "Spatial modulation," IEEE Transactions on Vehicular Techology, vol. 57, no. 4, pp. 2228–2241, 2008.

[4] R. Abu-Alhiga and H. Haas, "Subcarrier-index modulation OFDM," in IEEE International Symposium on Personal, Indoor and Mobile Radio Communications, 2009, pp. 177–181.

[5] D. R. Smith, O. Yurduseven, L. P. Mancera, P. Bowen, and N. B. Kundtz, "Analysis of a waveguide-fed metasurface antenna," Physical Review Applied, vol. 8, no. 5, p. 054048, 2017.

[6] X. Wan, M. Q. Qi, T. Y. Chen, and T. J. Cui, "Field-programmable beam reconfiguring based on digitally-controlled coding metasurface," Scientific Reports, vol. 6, p. 20663, 2016.

[7] K. V. Mishra, J. A. Hodge, and A. I. Zaghloul, "Reconfigurable metasurfaces for radar and communications systems," in URSI Asia-Pacific Radio Science Conference, 2019, in press.

[8] K. Chen, Y. Feng, F. Monticone, J. Zhao, B. Zhu, T. Jiang, L. Zhang, Y. Kim, X. Ding, S. Zhang et al., "A reconfigurable active huygens' metalens," Advanced Materials, vol. 29, no. 17, 2017.

[9] D. Cabric, D. Markovic, and R. W. Brodersen, "On MIMO signal processing for adaptive W-CDMA and OFDM wireless transceivers," in IEEE/ACES International Conference on Wireless Communications and Applied Computational Electromagnetics, 2005, pp. 58–61.

[10] J. A. Hodge, T. K. Anthony, and A. I. Zaghloul, "Utilizing active circuit elements for dynamic tuning and electronic scanning of CLL-loaded dipole antenna structure," in URSI Radio Science Meeting, 2015, p. 16.

[11] N. Yu, P. Genevet, M. A. Kats, F. Aieta, J.-P. Tetienne, F. Capasso, and Z. Gaburro, "Light propagation with phase discontinuities: Generalized laws of reflection and refraction," Science, p. 1210713, 2011.

[12] P. Yang, Y. Xiao, Y. L. Guan, K. V. S. Hari, A. Chockalingam, S. Sugiura, H. Haas, M. D. Renzo, C. Masouros, Z. Liu, L. Xiao, S. Li, and L. Hanzo, "Single-carrier SM-MIMO: A promising design for broadband large-scale antenna systems," IEEE Communications Surveys & Tutorials, vol. 18, no. 3, pp. 1687–1716, 2016.

[13] L. Zhang, X. Q. Chen, S. Liu, Q. Zhang, J. Zhao, J. Y. Dai, G. D. Bai, X. Wan, Q. Cheng, G. Castaldi, V. Galdi, and T. J. Cui, "Space-time-coding digital metasurfaces," Nature Communications, vol. 9, no. 1, p. 4334, 2018.

FDTD Modelling of Optical Polarisation Rotation in a Charged Quantum Dot - Micropillar System

G. Slavcheva
Inst. of Semicond. and Sol. State Physics
Johannes Kepler University Linz, A-4040
Linz, Austria
g.slavcheva@jku.at

M. Koleva
Faculty of Life Sciences
King's College London, SE1 1UL
London, United Kingdom
mirella.koleva@kcl.ac.uk

A. Rastelli
Inst. of Semicond. and Sol. State Physics
Johannes Kepler University Linz, A-4040
Linz, Austria
armando.rastelli@jku.at

***Abstract*—We employ a quantum master equations approach based on a full-wave Maxwell-pseudospin model to describe the polarisation dynamics of a negatively charged quantum dot embedded in a micropillar cavity upon an ultrashort optical excitation. The set of equations is solved self-consistently in the time domain by the Finite-Difference Time-Domain method (FDTD). We demonstrate numerically a giant optical polarisation rotation ($\sim \pm\pi/2$) of a resonant circularly polarised pulse in realistic dot-cavity geometries. The model allows for optimisation of the polarisation rotation angle for realisation of spin-photon entanglement and ultrafast polarisation switching on a chip.**

***Index Terms*—cavity-dot system, polarisation rotation, trion.**

I. Introduction

Realisation of a deterministic spin-photon entanglement in semiconductor quantum dots (QDs) is one of the major goals of integrated quantum photonics. In general, there are two possible ways of realising a quantum superposition of states: through controlled rotations of either 1) the material spin qubit or 2) the photon polarisation state representing the qubit. Coupling a stationary spin qubit to an optical cavity enhances the efficiency of spin-photon interaction. Recently, a macroscopic Kerr rotation of photon polarisation ($\sim 6°$) has been observed in both the strong- [1] and weak-coupling [2] regimes in a charged QD-micropillar.

In this work, we develop a dynamical model and investigate numerically realistic micropillar cavity-dot geometries. We show that a resonant coherent interaction of an ultrashort circularly polarised pulse with the trion transition results in a giant rotation angle of π in the weak-coupling regime. Large rotation angles are highly desirable for fabrication of phase gates for optical quantum computing and enable using charged QD-cavities as ultrafast polarisation switches on a chip.

II. Theoretical Model

We consider a negatively charged InGaAs QD embedded in a AlAs/AGaAs micropillar cavity Fig. 1 (a). An equivalent four-level scheme of the ground trion singlet transition and the relevant spin relaxation processes is shown in Fig. 1 (b). The dynamical evolution of an open 4-level quantum system under a time-dependent perturbation is described by a master pseudospin equation for the real state vector, S_j [3], [4]:

$$\frac{\partial S_j}{\partial t} = \begin{cases} f_{jkl}\Gamma_k S_l + \frac{1}{2}Tr\left(\hat{\sigma}.\hat{\lambda}_j\right) - \frac{1}{T_j}\left(S_j - S_{je}\right), & j = 1,2,..,12 \\ f_{jkl}\Gamma_k S_l + \frac{1}{2}Tr\left(\hat{\sigma}.\hat{\lambda}_j\right), & j = 13,14,15, \end{cases} \tag{1}$$

where Γ_k – torque vector, $\widehat{\lambda}_j$ –generators of $SU(4)$ Lie group algebra, f – fully-antisymmetric tensor of the structure constants; $\hat{\sigma}$ – population relaxation; S_{je} – equilibrium coherence vector, and T_j – phenomenological decay times towards S_{je}.

We solve self-consistently the quantum evolution equations Eqs. (1) and the vector Maxwell equations for a resonant circularly polarised optical pulse interacting with an ensemble of four-level systems (charged QDs) with density N_d:

$$\begin{aligned} \frac{\partial H_x(z,t)}{\partial t} &= \frac{1}{\mu}\frac{\partial E_y(z,t)}{\partial z} \\ \frac{\partial H_y(z,t)}{\partial t} &= -\frac{1}{\mu}\frac{\partial E_x(z,t)}{\partial z} \\ \frac{\partial E_x(z,t)}{\partial t} &= -\frac{1}{\varepsilon}\frac{\partial H_y(z,t)}{\partial z} - \frac{1}{\varepsilon}\frac{\partial P_x(z,t)}{\partial t} \\ \frac{\partial E_y(z,t)}{\partial t} &= \frac{1}{\varepsilon}\frac{\partial H_x(z,t)}{\partial z} - \frac{1}{\varepsilon}\frac{\partial P_y(z,t)}{\partial t}, \end{aligned} \tag{2}$$

where the polarisation components are given by: $P_x = -\wp N_d S_1$;$P_y = -\wp N_d S_7$. $\wp = \langle 1\,|e\mathbf{r}|\,2\rangle = \langle 3\,|e\mathbf{r}|\,4\rangle$ is the dipole matrix element. The optical rotation angle of a transmitted through the cavity pulse is calculated from the phase shift induced by the resonant absorption of the QD layer with thickness $l = z_2 - z_1$. The resonant phase shift is given by $\Delta\varphi_{x,y} = \beta_{x,y}l$, where $\beta_{x,y} = \frac{1}{l}\arctan\left(\frac{\mathrm{Im}(z_{x,y})}{\mathrm{Re}(z_{x,y})}\right)$ and $z_{x,y} = \frac{E_{x,y}(z_2,\omega)}{E_{x,y}(z_1,\omega)} = e^{ik_{cx,y}l}$ is the complex propagation factor, given by Fourier transform of the time traces of the E_x and E_y sampled at the end points of the QD layer (Fig. 2 (a)).

TABLE I
Model Parameters

E_{trion} [eV]	λ_0 [nm]	T_p [fs]	E_0 $[Vm^{-1}]$	$\wp$ [e.nm]	N_d $[m^{-3}]$	Relaxation Times [ps]				
						Γ	γ_1	γ_2	γ_3	Γ_τ
1.388	894	100	1.44×10^8	0.57	3.18×10^{24}	820 [2]	500 [5]	450 [7]	170 [6]	340

III. Numerical Method and Results

Eqs. (1-2) are solved directly in the time domain by the Finite-Difference Time-Domain (FDTD) method. The resonant Gaussian circularly polarised pulse, is given by:

$$\sigma^{\pm} \begin{cases} E_x(z=L,t) = E_0 exp\left[-(t-t_0)^2/t_d^2\right]\cos(\omega_o t) \\ E_y(z=L,t) = \pm E_0 exp\left[-(t-t_0)^2/t_d^2\right]\sin(\omega_o t), \end{cases} \tag{3}$$

G.S. gratefully acknowledges funding through the Austrian LIT 213221001 project. G.S. and M.K. are with Quantopticon Ltd., Guildford GU2 8LQ, United Kingdom; info@quantopticon.co.uk.

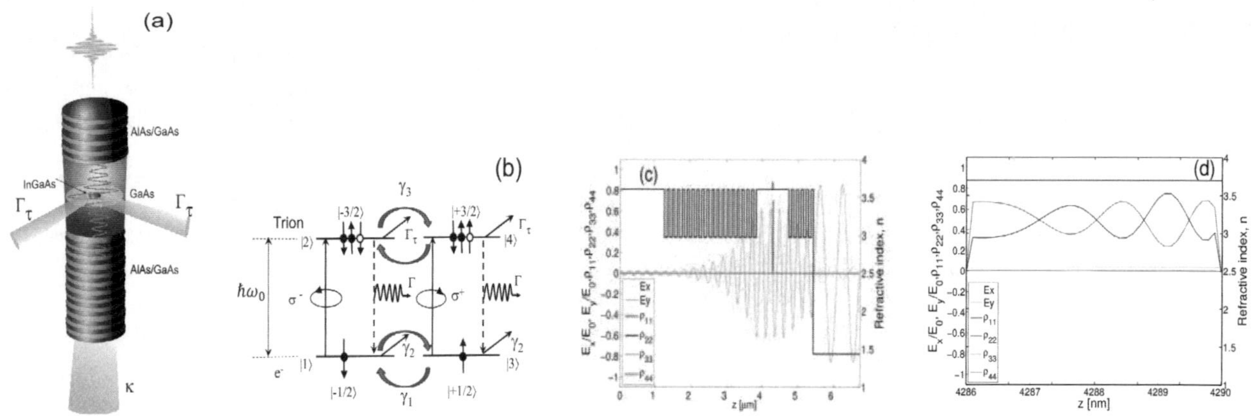

(a) (b) (c) (d)

Fig. 1. (a) Sketch of a charged QD-micropillar structure; κ - cavity loss, Γ_τ - trion decay rate to non-cavity modes. The micropillar cavity is pumped from the top (through an optical fibre) by an ultrashort circularly polarised pulse; (b) Energy-level diagram of the negative trion ground singlet transition driven resonantly by either left- (σ^-) or right-(σ^+) circularly polarised light. Electron (γ_1) / hole (γ_3): spin flip relaxation rates; Γ: spontaneous emission rate; γ_2, Γ_τ: spin decoherence rates. (c) Refractive-index profile (black line) of the micropillar with embedded QD [2], and a snapshot of the E-field components (yellow and cyan curves) and level populations (red, blue, green and magenta) at t=3.33 ps. (d) Zoom-in on (c) of the QD layer.

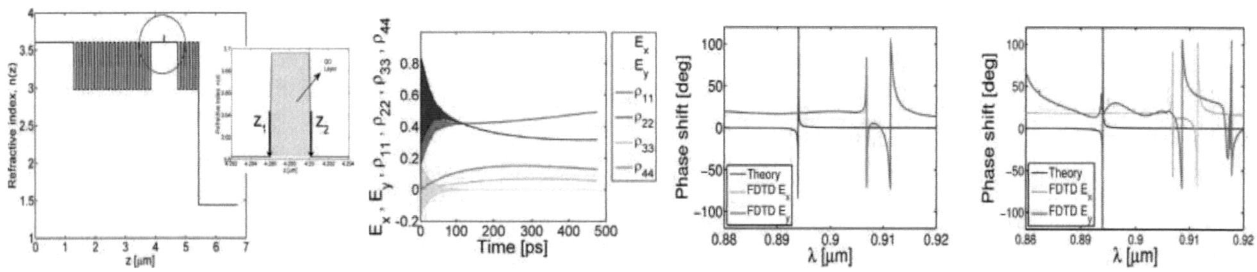

(a) (b) (c) (d)

Fig. 2. (a) Refractive index profile of the micropillar from [2]; inset: zoom-in of the region around the QD layer; z_1 and z_2 denote the left and right end points of the QD layer; (b) Time evolution of the E-field components of a σ^- pulse and level populations at z_2 for a spin-down initial state; ρ_{22} (blue curve) proportional to experimentally detected TRPL; (c) Phase shift (in degrees) of the E_x and E_y pulse components of a σ^- - pulse. Blue curve: stationary solution of the density-matrix equations for a two-level system (no cavity), (d) Phase shift of the E-field components of a linearly x-polarised pulse.

where $\pm$ corresponds to right(left) circularly polarised pulse with amplitude E_0, or $E_y = 0$ for $x-$ linearly polarised pulse. The model parameters are summarised in Table I.

Consider initial spin-down population prepared entirely in ground level $|1\rangle$ e.g. by e.g. optical pumping [8]. The temporal dynamics of the E-field components of a σ^- pulse and populations of all levels is calculated at the end points, z_1 and z_2, of the QD layer (see Fig. 2 (a, b)). We numerically demonstrate a giant phase shift of $\pm\pi/2$, induced by the single spin confined in the QD in a range of realistic micropillar cavities (Fig. 2 (c)). We calculate the cavity transmission spectrum and the cavity loss, $\kappa = 1.25 \text{ ps}^{-1} \gg \Omega_R \sim 125 \text{ ps}^{-1}$ – weak coupling regime. By contrast, when the trion transition is driven by a resonant x-linearly polarised pulse, we show that the orthogonal (y) E-field pulse component (initially set to zero) is building up in time, thereby leading to a polarisation rotation. The time delay in the E_y amplitude build-up results in a red shift in the phase shift spectrum with respect to the one for the E_x (Fig. 2 (d)). This displacement effectively leads to destructive interference and significant reduction of the optical rotation angle. In summary, we demonstrate numerically a giant $\sim \pm\pi/2$ optical rotation for a circularly polarised ultrashort pulse, which exceeds by an order of magnitude the Kerr polarisation rotation angles obtained by cw linearly polarised excitations. Our method allows to design and test cavity-dot structures with maximised photon polarisation rotation angles and thus prepare high-fidelity photon qubit states.

REFERENCES

[1] C. Arnold, et al., "Macroscopic rotation of photon polarization induced by a single spin," Nature Comm., vol. 6, p. 6236, 2015.
[2] P. Androvitsaneas, et al., "Charged quantum dot micropillar system for deterministic light-matter interactions," PRB, vol. 93, p. 241409(R), 2016.
[3] G. Slavcheva, Phys. Rev. B, vol. 77, pp. 115347-1–115347-10, 2008.
[4] G. Slavcheva and M. Koleva, Chapter in Handbook of Optoelectronic Device Modeling and Simulation, J. Piprek, Taylor Francis, 2017.
[5] I. A. Merkulov, et al., "Electron spin relaxation by nuclei in semiconductor quantum dots, " PRB, vol. 65, pp. 205309-1–205309-8, 2002.
[6] A. Greilich, et al., "Optical Control of Spin Coherence in Singly Charged (In,Ga)As/GaAS QDs," PRL, vol. 96, pp. 227401, 2006.
[7] S. E. Economou, et al., "Unified theory of consequences of spontaneous emission in a Λ system," PRB, vol. 71, pp. 195327-1–195327-11, 2005.
[8] M. Atatüre, J. Dreiser, A. Badolato, A. Högele, K. Karrai, and A. Imamoglu, Science, vol. 312, pp. 551-553, 2006.

Energy Stable Staggered High Order Finite Differences for Optical Media*

Daniel Appelö
Department of Applied Mathematics
University of Colorado, Boulder
daniel.appelo@colorado.edu

Vrushali Bokil
Department of Mathematics
Oregon State University
bokilv@math.oregonstate.edu

Yingda Cheng
Department of Mathematics
Michigan State University
ycheng@msu.edu

Fengyan Li
Department of Mathematical Sciences
Rensselaer Polytechnic Institute
lif@rpi.edu

***Abstract*—We present high order energy stable staggered summation by parts discretizations for Maxwell's equations in a non-magnetic dispersive optical medium.**

***Index Terms*—Finite Differences, High Order, Optical Media.**

I. Introduction

Accurate, stable and efficient simulation of wave propagation in optical media is becoming increasingly important as high power lasers become more common both in the laboratory and industrial setting. It is well known, [3], that high order accurate methods are more efficient for hyperbolic problems than low (second and below) order accurate methods but despite this fact it is still very common to use the Yee scheme (FDTD for short). A reason for the persisting popularity is the staggered nature of FDTD which results in attractive mimetic properties, another reason might be that most of the legacy software has been built to fit with staggered grids so that modern element based methods are difficult to retro-fit.

Here we consider staggered discretizations of Maxwell's equations in a non-magnetic dispersive optical medium by summation by parts operators, [4]. We show that these are high order and that they are energy stable and conserve a discrete version of the continuous energy of the physical system. The analysis of the discretization is done in a discrete version of the L_2-norm indicating that future coupling with the discontinuous Galerkin methods of [1], [2] should be possible.

II. Governing Equations

The constitutive laws for the model we consider here are, $D = \varepsilon_0(\varepsilon_\infty E + P)$, $B = \mu_0 H$. This results in a one dimensional version of Maxwell's equations governing the electric and magnetic fields, E and H, in a non-magnetic dispersive optical medium:

$$\begin{aligned} \varepsilon_0\varepsilon_\infty E_t &= H_x - \varepsilon_0 J, && (1)\\ \mu_0 H_t &= E_x, && (2)\\ P_t &= J, && (3)\\ J_t &= -J/\tau - \omega_0^2 P + \omega_p^2 E. && (4) \end{aligned}$$

Here we assume that all the material parameters to be constant. The equation governing the polarization P modeling the linear response of the dispersive material takes the form of a single (damped) harmonic oscillator, see [1] for details which we write as a first order system. by introducing the auxiliary variable J.

III. Discretization

We define the staggered grids $x_+ = [x_0, x_1, \ldots, x_{n-1}, x_n]$ and $x_- = [x_0, x_{1/2}, \ldots, x_{n-1/2}, x_n]$ and use the summation by parts operators, $D_+ \equiv P_+^{-1}Q_+$ and $D_- \equiv P_-^{-1}Q_-$ derived in [4]. Here P_+ and P_- are diagonal norms and D_+ and D_- approximate the derivatives on the grid x_+ using values from x_- and vice versa. A crucial property of the operators is that they satisfy:

$$Q_+ + Q_- = B = (e_n e_n^T - e_0 e_0^T). \qquad (5)$$

Here $e_0 = (1, 0, \ldots, 0)^T$ and $e_n = (0, \ldots, 0, 1)^T$.

Let E^h and H^h be grid functions approximating E and H (etc.), we then approximate the derivatives according to

$$\begin{aligned} E_x &\approx D_- E^h + \sigma_n P_+^{-1} e_n E_n^h + \sigma_0 P_+^{-1} e_0 E_0^h,\\ H_x &\approx D_+ H^h. \end{aligned}$$

Resulting in the semi-discretization:

$$\begin{aligned} E_t^h &= \frac{1}{\varepsilon_0\varepsilon_\infty}\left(D_+ H^h - \varepsilon_0 J^h\right), && (6)\\ H_t &= \frac{1}{\mu_0}\left(D_- E^h + \sigma_n P_+^{-1} e_n E_n^h + \sigma_0 P_+^{-1} e_0 E_0^h\right), && (7)\\ P_t^h &= J^h, && (8)\\ J_t^h &= -J^h/\tau - \omega_0^2 P^h + \omega_p^2 E^h. && (9) \end{aligned}$$

IV. Energy Estimates

Let (u, v) denote the standard L_2 inner product and let $\|u\| = \sqrt{(u,u)}$ be the norm induced by the inner product.

Multiplying the above equations by suitable quantities and integrating we find:

$$
\begin{aligned}
(\varepsilon_0\varepsilon_\infty E, E_t) &= (E, H_x) - \varepsilon_0(E, J),\\
(\mu_0 H, H_t) &= (H, E_x),\\
\frac{\varepsilon_0\omega_0^2}{\omega_p^2}(P, P_t) &= \frac{\varepsilon_0\omega_0^2}{\omega_p^2}(P, J),\\
\frac{\varepsilon_0}{\omega_p^2}(J, J_t) &= -\frac{\varepsilon_0}{\omega_p^2\tau}(J, J) - \frac{\varepsilon_0\omega_0^2}{\omega_p^2}(J, P) + \omega_p^2(J, E).
\end{aligned}
$$

Summing up these equations we arrive at the energy identity:

$$
\begin{aligned}
\frac{1}{2}\frac{d}{dt}\left(\varepsilon_0\varepsilon_\infty\|E\|^2 + \mu_0\|H\|^2 + \frac{\varepsilon_0\omega_0^2}{\omega_p^2}\|P\|^2 + \frac{\varepsilon_0}{\omega_p^2}\|J\|^2\right)&\\
= (E, H_x) + (E_x, H) - \frac{\varepsilon_0}{\omega_p^2\tau}\|J\|^2. \quad (10)&
\end{aligned}
$$

It is also straightforward to derive a discrete estimate simply multiply (6)-(9) by $(E^h)^T P_+$, $(H^h)^T P_-$, $(P^h)^T P_+$ and $(J^h)^T P_+$, respectively. After adding these equations we find that the right hand side is:

$$
\begin{aligned}
&(E^h)^T P_+ P_+^{-1} Q_+ H^h + (H^h)^T P_-(P_-^{-1} Q_- E^h\\
&\quad + \sigma_n P_+^{-1} e_n E_n^h + \sigma_0 P_+^{-1} e_0 E_0^h)\\
&= (E^h)^T Q_+ H^h + (H^h)^T Q_- + \sigma_n H_n^h e_n E_n^h + \sigma_0 H_0^h E_0^h.
\end{aligned}
$$

Using (5) the discrete energy identity becomes

$$
\begin{aligned}
&\frac{1}{2}\frac{d}{dt}\Big(\varepsilon_0\varepsilon_\infty (E^h)^T P_+ E^h + \mu_0 (H^h)^T P_- H^h\\
&\quad + \frac{\varepsilon_0\omega_0^2}{\omega_p^2}(P^h)^T P_+ P^h + \frac{\varepsilon_0}{\omega_p^2}(J^h)^T P_+ J^h\Big) =\\
&- \frac{\varepsilon_0}{\omega_p^2\tau}(J^h)^T P_+ J^h + (\sigma_n + 1) H_n^h E_n^h + (\sigma_0 - 1) H_0^h E_0^h.
\end{aligned}
$$

An obvious choice for the penalty parameters is $\sigma_n = -1$ and $\sigma_0 = 1$. This yields an energy conserving discretization when the relaxation time is $\tau = \infty$.

V. Numerical Examples

To check the energy conservation properties of the method we use a grid with $n = 50$ and $\Delta t = h/2$ and evolve the equations with a 24th order Taylor series method. The initial data are drawn from a uniform random variable between -1/2 and 1/2 for all the fields ($E_n = E_0 = 0$ to be consistent with the boundary conditions). The various parameters in the model are taken from a lottery hat. They are $\tau = \infty, \mu_0 = 1.2, \varepsilon_0 = 1.12, \varepsilon_\infty = 2.15, \omega_0 = 1.1$ and $\omega_p = 10.1$. The results, displayed in Figure 1 , indicate that the spatial discretization is conservative for interior orders of accuracy 2, 4, and 6. The small decay of energy relative to the initial energy is most likely due to the dissipative nature of the Taylor series methods.

Finally we perform a self-convergence study with the initial data $E = \exp(-72x^2)$, $H = \exp(-72(x-0.5)^2)$, $x \in [-1, 1]$, and $P = J = 0$. We take the parameters as above with the exceptions $\tau = 185$ and $\omega_p = 1.1$. The results are displayed in Figure 2 and clearly show the rates of convergence that are expected for a diagonal norm summation by parts operator. That is, no less than half the interior order plus one.

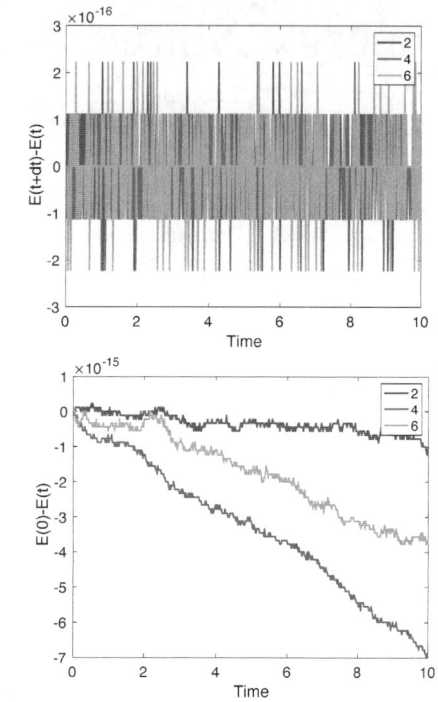

Fig. 1. Difference in energy between subsequent timesteps (top) and between initial energy and current energy.

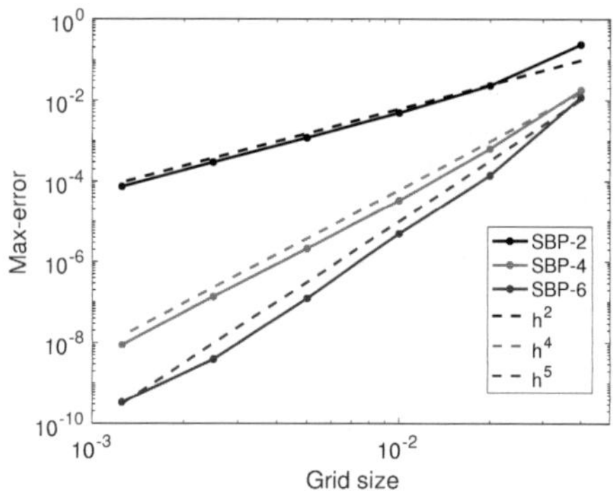

Fig. 2. Self convergence study for the operators with interior order of accuracy $2s = 2, 4$ and 6 an interior order 2, 3 and 4. The rates of convergence are expected to be at least $s + 1$. This is confirmed by the experiments.

References

[1] V. A. Bokil, Y. Cheng, Y. Jiang, and F. Li, "Energy stable discontinuous Galerkin methods for Maxwell's equations in nonlinear optical media," Journal of Computational Physics, vol. 350, pp. 420–452, 2017.

[2] Y. Jiang, P. Sakkaplangkul, V. A. Bokil, Y. Cheng and F. Li, "Dispersion Analysis of Finite Difference and Discontinuous Galerkin Schemes for Maxwell's Equations in Linear Lorentz Media," arXiv preprint arXiv:1810.01723.

[3] H.-O. Kreiss and J. Oliger, "Comparison of accurate methods for the integration of hyperbolic equations," Tellus, 24:199-215, 1972.

[4] O. O'Reilly, T. Lundquist, E. M. Dunham, J. Nordström, "Energy stable and high-order-accurate finite difference methods on staggered grids," Journal of Computational Physics, vol. 346, pp. 572–589, 2017.

On the Effect of Dissipation and Nonlocality on Unidirectional and Topological Surface Plasmon-Polaritons

S. Ali Hassani Gangaraj
School of Electrical and Computer Engineering
Cornell University
Ithaca, New York, USA
ali.gangaraj@gmail.com

Francesco Monticone
School of Electrical and Computer Engineering
Cornell University
Ithaca, New York, USA
francesco.monticone@cornell.edu

***Abstract*—Unidirectional surface plasmon polaritons (SPPs) on nonreciprocal material platforms are currently the subject of significant interest. In this abstract, we revisit this exciting topic, discussing the role of the nonlocal response of a magnetized plasmonic material. Our analytical calculations and frequency-domain finite-element simulations confirm that a nonlocal correction in the material model implies the absence of purely unidirectional SPP modes below the plasma frequency. However, we also show that, depending on the considered configuration, the presence of even moderate levels of loss (absorption or radiation) can practically restore the unidirectionality of this mode. Our findings have important implications in the context of nonreciprocal and topological electromagnetic systems.**

***Index Terms*—Finite Element Method, Nonlocality, Nonreciprocity, Spatial Dispersion, Surface Plasmon Polaritons.**

I. Introduction

It has been known for several decades that, at the interface between a magnetized plasma (a gyrotropic medium) and an isotropic material, unidirectional surface plasmon-polaritons (SPPs) can emerge under certain conditions and in certain frequency ranges [1]. This topic has seen a resurgence of interest recently in the context of nonreciprocal and topological electromagnetics [2], [3]. Interestingly, however, it has been recently shown that some of these SPP modes lose their strict unidirectionality if more realistic material models that include nonlocal effects are employed [4]. Indeed, in the large-wavenumber (small-wavelength) regime the inherent granularity of any medium becomes apparent, and the effect of carrier convection and diffusion becomes important, leading to a non-negligible nonlocal response. Here, we consider a hydrodynamic nonlocal Drude model following [4]–[6], which we implement in a frequency-domain finite-element commercial software [7]. Based on this approach, we systematically study how nonlocality and dissipation affect the excitation and propagation properties of unidirectional and topological SPPs.

The authors acknowledge partial support from the National Science Foundation (NSF) with Grant No. 1741694.

II. Theoretical Model

Following [4]–[6], the problem of wave propagation in a nonlocal magnetized plasma or plasmonic material can be solved by simultaneously solving two coupled equations: (i) The electromagnetic wave equation, written in the following form (under a $e^{-i\omega t}$ time-harmonic convention):

$$\nabla \times \nabla \times \mathbf{E} = \frac{\omega^2}{c^2}\epsilon_\infty \mathbf{E} - i\omega\mu_0 \mathbf{J}, \quad (1)$$

where ϵ_∞ models the dielectric response due to bound charges, and the total current density in the system $\mathbf{J} = \mathbf{J}_{ext} + \mathbf{J}_i$ is the sum of the external impressed currents (sources) $\mathbf{J}_{ext}$ and the induced current $\mathbf{J}_i$. (ii) From a microscopic analysis of the equation of motion of the free carriers under Thomas-Fermi approximation, Ref. [4] shows that the polarization current satisfies the following frequency-domain equation:

$$\beta^2\nabla(\nabla \cdot \mathbf{J}_i) + \omega(\omega + i\gamma)\mathbf{J}_i = -i\omega(\omega_p^2\epsilon_\infty\epsilon_0\mathbf{E} - \frac{e}{m^*}\mathbf{J}_i \times \mathbf{B}_0), \quad (2)$$

where β is the nonlocal parameter, γ is the collision frequency representing the level of loss, e is the electric charge, m^* is the effective mass of the electrons in the plasmonic material, ω_p is the plasma frequency, and $\mathbf{B}_0$ is an externally applied DC magnetic field. For a given excitation current (or no current, i.e., an eigenvalue problem), these two coupled equations should then be solved simultaneously, considering conventional electromagnetic boundary conditions, together with the additional boundary condition of zero normal induced current at a dielectric-metal interface. We solved this problem numerically using COMSOL Multiphysics [7], implementing Eq. (2) as a weak form equation.

III. Numerical Results and Discussion

As an example, we considered a linear dipole source at the interface between a gyrotropic magnetized plasma and vacuum, as seen in Fig. 1. First, we set the nonlocal parameter $\beta = 0$, such that our model becomes equal to a conventional local Drude model. Fig. 1, top panel, shows a unidirectional SPP propagating along the interface. No backward surface wave is launched on the interface since backward propagation is prohibited [3]. The bottom panel shows the profile of the SPP electric field (y-component) along the interface.

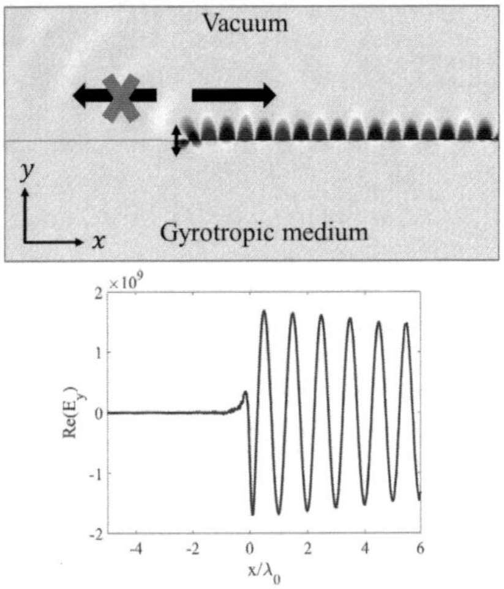

Fig. 1. Top panel: An interface between a magnetized plasmonic material (nonreciprocal gyrotropic medium) and vacuum. A y-polarized dipolar source radiating at frequency ω_0 is placed at the interface. Considering a local material model (Drude plasma), a unidirectional SPP is launched toward right while backward propagation is prohibited. The plasmonic material is biased along the $-z$-axis , with $\omega_c = 0.4\omega_p$, $\epsilon_\infty = 1$ and $\omega_0 = 0.76\omega_p$. Bottom panel: electric-field profile (y-component) of the SPP at the interface. The source is located at $x/\lambda_0 = 0$ where λ_0 is the free-space wavelength at the source frequency. The material is assumed to be local with $\beta = 0$, and with low loss rate $\gamma = 0.005\omega_p$.

Next, we considered the effect of non-zero nonlocality ($\beta^2 = 0.1[\mathrm{m}^2/\mathrm{rad}\cdot\mathrm{s}] \times \omega_p$) for the same geometry. Fig. 2 shows the electric-field profile near the interface, as in Fig. 1. As clearly seen, in addition to the forward-propagating surface wave, now there exists a weak backward-propagating wave launched by the source toward the negative x-axis. Furthermore, it can be seen that the wavelength (wavenumber) of the backward wave is smaller (larger) than that of the forward wave, consistent with the findings in [4]. This suggests that the backward mode may be much more sensitive to loss compared to the forward mode. To verify this fact, we then considered a lossy material model with higher loss rate and investigated its effect on both forward and backward modes.

Fig. 3 corresponds to the case of a nonlocal and dissipative magnetized plasmonic material, with $\gamma = 0.02\omega_p$. Our numerical calculations show that, in the considered configuration, this moderate level of loss is sufficient to completely suppress the backward-propagating SPP, while the forward-propagating SPP is only moderately attenuated. Hence, the unidirectionality of the SPP mode is restored by the presence of loss (the presence of non-zero dissipation also avoids apparent thermodynamic paradoxes associated with the problem of a lossless cavity fed by a unidirectional channel; this is also consistent with the fact that perfect lossless isolators cannot exist). Mathematically, the relative effect of loss and nonlocality can be understood by inspecting the left-hand-side of Eq. (2), where, depending on the configuration under study, a moderate level of loss in the material model may make the second term (dissipation/dispersion effects) dominant with respect to the first term (nonlocal effects). In this way, practically unidirectional SPPs can exist in a nonlocal dissipative scenario, almost indistinguishable from a local dissipative scenario. We should, however, stress that the level of loss necessary to recover this unidirectional response depends on the specific materials/configuration under study. At the conference, we will elaborate further on the effect of loss and nonlocality on the unidirectional and topological nature of SPP modes of different types supported by nonreciprocal plasmonic platforms.

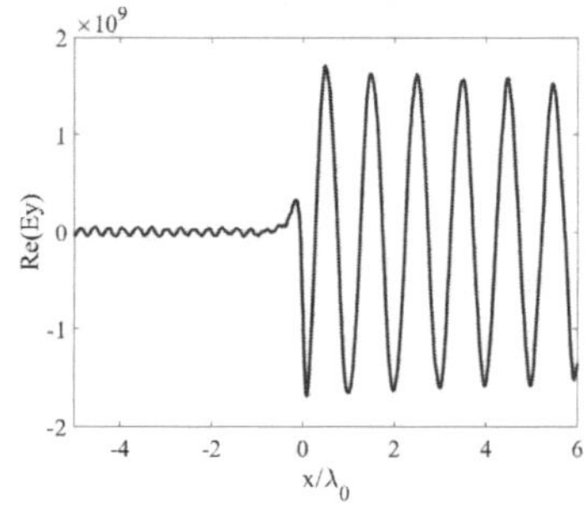

Fig. 2. Electric-field profile (y-component) of the SPP at the interface, for the same structure as in Fig. 1. In this figure, the magnetized plasmonic material is nonlocal with $\beta^2 = 0.1[\mathrm{m}^2/\mathrm{rad}\cdot\mathrm{s}] \times \omega_p$, and with low loss rate $\gamma = 0.005\omega_p$.

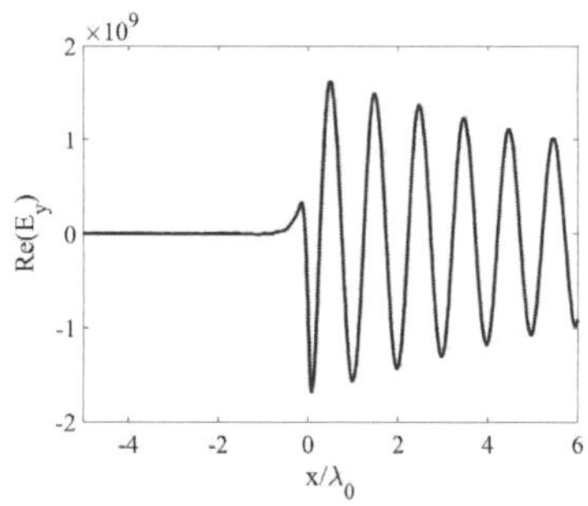

Fig. 3. Similar to Fig. 2, but for a moderately lossy magnetized plasmonic material, with loss rate $\gamma = 0.02\omega_p$.

References

[1] S. R. Seshadri, "Excitation of surface waves on a perfectly conducting screen covered with anisotropic plasma," IRE Trans. Microwave Theory Tech. 10, 573, 1962.

[2] M. G. Silveirinha, et al., "Fluctuation-induced forces on an atom near a photonic topological material," Phys. Rev. A 97, 022509, Feb. 2018.

[3] S. Ali Hassani Gangaraj, et al., "Truly unidirectional excitation and propagation of diffractionless surface plasmon-polaritons," arXiv:1811.00463v2, 2018.

[4] S. Buddhiraju, et al., "Absence of unidirectionally propagating surface plasmon-polaritons in nonreciprocal plasmonics," arXiv:1809.05100v1, 2018.

[5] A. J. Bennett, "Influence of the electron charge distribution on surface-plasmon dispersion," Phys. Rev. B 1, Jan. 1970.

[6] S. Raza, et al., "Nonlocal optical response in metallic nanostructures," Journal of Physics: Condensed Matter 27, 183204, 2015.

[7] COMSOL MULTIPHYSICS ver. 5.4, COMSOL AB, Stockholm. http://comsol.com

Solving Maxwell's Equations with a Generalized Dispersive Material Model on Overset Grids

Jeffrey W. Banks
Depart. of Mathematical Sciences
Rensselaer Polytechnic Institute
Troy, New York USA
banksj3@rpi.edu

William D. Henshaw
Mathematical Sciences
Rensselaer Polytechnic Institute
Troy, New York USA
henshw@rpi.edu

Alexander V. Kildishev
Electrical and Computer Engineering
Purdue University
West Lafayette, IN 47907, USA
kildishev@purdue.edu

Gregor Kovačič
Mathematical Sciences
Rensselaer Polytechnic Institute
Troy, New York USA
kovacg@rpi.edu

Ludmila J. Prokopeva
Electrical and Computer Engineering
Purdue University
West Lafayette, IN 47907, USA
lprokop@purdue.edu

Donald W. Schwendeman
Mathematical Sciences
Rensselaer Polytechnic Institute
Troy, New York USA
schwed@rpi.edu

***Abstract*—An efficient and high-order accurate time-domain (FDTD) scheme for solving Maxwell's equations in second-order form with a generalized dispersive material (GDM) model is described. The equations are discretized using finite-differences, and advanced in time with a single-stage, three-level, space-time scheme which remains stable up to the usual explicit CFL-one restriction, as proven using mode analysis. Composite overlapping grids are used to treat complex geometries with boundary-conforming grids, and a high-order upwind dissipation is added to ensure robust and stable approximations on overlapping grids. Properties of the GDM model, which can represent arbitrary dispersive bahaviours, are analysed. Numerical results for some newly developed exact solutions confirm the accuracy and stability of the new scheme.**

***Keywords*—FDTD, dispersive Maxwell's equations, overset grids, upwind schemes.**

I. Introduction

We consider the solution of the dispersive Maxwell equations in second-order form using high-order finite difference approximations and an auxiliary differential equation (ADE) approach to model dispersive effects. A generalized dispersive material (GDM) model is used to represent arbitrary dispersive effects [1]. Overset grids are used to represent complex geometry using structured body-fitted curvilinear-grids to represent boundaries and interfaces and Cartesian background grids to cover the majority of the domain. The use of structured and Cartesian grids along with high-order accurate finite difference approximations leads to very efficient schemes. To provide stable and robust schemes on overset and non-orthogonal grids we use a novel upwind scheme for the second-order wave equation as described in [2]. The new ADE-GDM scheme is described in more detail in [3].

This work was partially performed under DOE contracts from the ASCR Applied Math Program, and by the DARPA Defense Sciences Office.

II. The ADE-GDM Scheme

The second-order formulation of the governing equations using an ADE approach is

$$\partial_t^2 \mathbf{E} = c^2 \Delta \mathbf{E} - \epsilon_0^{-1}\, \partial_t^2 \mathbf{P} \tag{1}$$

$$\big(\partial_t^2 + b_{1,m}\partial_t + b_{0,m}\big)\mathbf{P}_m = \epsilon_0\big(a_{0,m} + a_{1,m}\partial_t\big)\mathbf{E}, \tag{2}$$

$$\mathbf{P} = \sum_{m=1}^{N_p} \mathbf{P}_m. \tag{3}$$

where $c^2 = 1/(\epsilon_0\mu_0)$ is the nominal wave speed, and the total polarization vector, $\mathbf{P}$, is the sum of N_p component polarization vectors $\mathbf{P}_m$. Each $\mathbf{P}_m$ satisfies an ordinary differential equation whose coefficients $a_{0,m}$, $a_{1,m}$, $b_{0,m}$, and $b_{1,m}$ are chosen to fit a given dispersion model or spectroscopic data.

The GDM model for the electric permittivity in the frequency domain, $\hat{\epsilon}$, takes the form

$$\hat{\epsilon}(\omega) = \epsilon_0\big(1 + \hat{\chi}(-i\omega)\big), \tag{4}$$

where the electric susceptibility $\hat{\chi}$ is given by

$$\hat{\chi}(s) \stackrel{\text{def}}{=} \sum_{m=1}^{N_p} \hat{\chi}_m(s), \quad \hat{\chi}_m(s) \stackrel{\text{def}}{=} \frac{a_{0,m} + s\, a_{1,m}}{b_{0,m} + s\, b_{1,m} + s^2}. \tag{5}$$

Given a representation for the susceptibility $\hat{\chi}(-i\omega)$ (from theory or experiment), the real-valued GDM coefficients $a_{0,m}$, $a_{1,m}$, $b_{0,m}$ and $b_{1,m}$ can be determined to fit the representation as a sum of Padé approximants of the above form with N_p terms. Note that the Debye, Drude, Lorentz, Sellmeier, and critical point (CP) models (or combinations thereof) are all special cases of the GDM model. A plane-wave analysis of solutions to the ADE-GDM equations shows the existence of non-resonant modes that are modified versions of the typical non-dispersive plane waves as well as N_p different resonant-modes that have much slower phase speeds. An analysis using Routh-Hurwitz theory provides constraints on the GDM

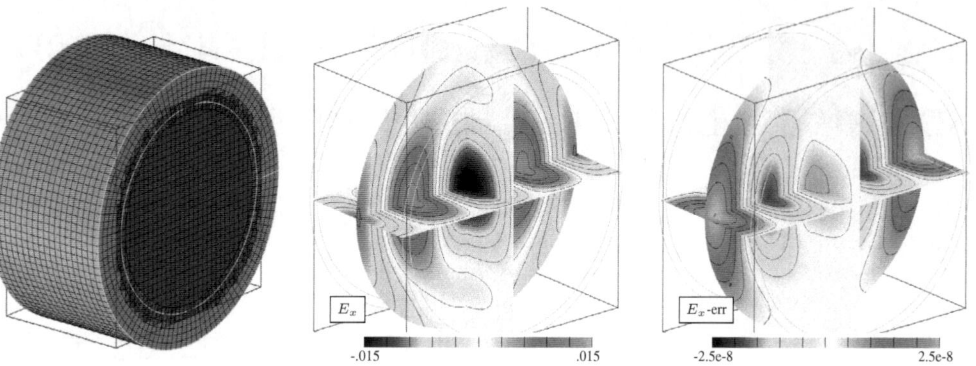

Fig. 1. At left a coarse grid representation of the cylinder $\mathcal{G}^{(1)}$. At center is the E_x field for a GDM eigenmode of a cylinder with PEC BCs on grid $\mathcal{G}^{(4)}$ at $t = 1$ computed using the fourth-order accurate ADE-GDM scheme and $C_{\rm cfl} = 0.9$, and at right is the error in the computed E_x field.

parameters to ensure that solutions do not grow in time. For $N_p = 1$, for example, a sufficient condition is that all coefficients be positive and $a_0 b_1 > a_1 b_0$.

High-order accurate space-time schemes for the ADE-GDM equations are derived using a Lax-Wendroff type expansion that only require three-time levels of $\mathbf{E}^n$ and $\mathbf{P}_m^n$ and these take the form

$$\begin{bmatrix} \mathbf{E} \\ \mathbf{P}_m \end{bmatrix}_{\mathbf{j}}^{n+1} = \mathbf{L}_h \left(\begin{bmatrix} \mathbf{E} \\ \mathbf{P}_m \end{bmatrix}_{\mathbf{j}}^{n}, \begin{bmatrix} \mathbf{E} \\ \mathbf{P}_m \end{bmatrix}_{\mathbf{j}}^{n-1} \right). \qquad (6)$$

For a fourth-order accurate scheme in space and time this would involve a 5^d-point stencil in d-dimensions. This means that the storage requirements are very small, even as the order of accuracy increases, or as the number of polarization vectors increases. Note that the entire fourth-order (or high-order) update occurs in one stage (in contrast to Runge-Kutta time-stepping) and is thus very efficient. High-order upwind dissipation is added as a separate stage in the algorithm and does not change the order of accuracy. This upwinding ensures that the scheme remains stable on overset grids, even for the difficult case when there are narrow boundary fitted grids. Accurate boundary conditions are implemented using compatibility conditions [4]. A mode analysis of the ADE-GDM scheme shows that the stable time-step is essentially the same as for the non-dispersive algorithm so that a large CFL-one time-step can be chosen, independent of the order of accuracy. This is to be contrasted with many other high-order schemes where the time-step decreases as the order increases.

III. Numerical Results

For verification of the new scheme, several new exact solutions to the ADE-GDM equations have been derived including the eigenmodes of a cylindrical domain that contains a GDM material as illustrated in Fig. 1. This figure shows a coarse version of the overset grid used in the computations, as well as the computed solution for E_x and the error in E_x. Note that the error is smooth even across the overset grid interpolation boundaries which suggests an accurate treatment. A grid convergence study is shown in Fig. 2. Results are shown for a resonant and non-resonant solution computed

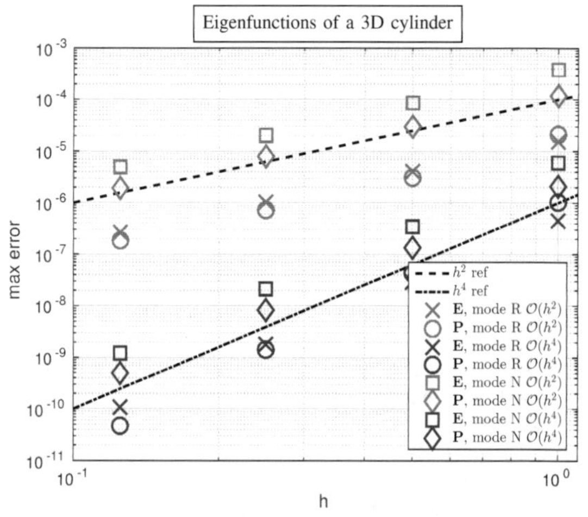

Fig. 2. Grid convergence of the max-norm errors in $\|\mathbf{E}\|_\infty$ and $\|\mathbf{P}\|_\infty$ for resonant (R) and non-resonant (N) eigenmodes of a PEC cylinder using the second- and fourth-order accurate ADE-GDM schemes.

using the second-order and fourth-order accurate versions of the scheme. The convergence results confirm the expected order of accuracy.

In current work, the ADE-GDM scheme is being extended to treat material interfaces. When the interface is represented with conforming grids, the resulting scheme is designed to retain the full accuracy of the base scheme, with no loss of accuracy near the interface.

References

[1] L. J. Prokopeva, J. D. Borneman, and A. V. Kildishev, "Optical dispersion models for time-domain modeling of metal-dielectric nanostructures," IEEE Transactions on Magnetics, vol. 47, pp. 1150–1153, 2011.

[2] J. W. Banks and W. D. Henshaw, "Upwind schemes for the wave equation in second-order form," J. Comput. Phys., vol. 231, no. 17, pp. 5854–5889, 2012.

[3] J. Angel, J. W. Banks, W. D. Henshaw, M. J. Jenkinson, A. V. Kildishev, G. Kovačič, L. J. Prokopeva, and D. W. Schwendeman, "A high-order accurate scheme for Maxwell's equations with a generalized dispersion model," J. Comput. Phys., vol. 378, pp. 441–444, 2018.

[4] W. D. Henshaw, "A high-order accurate parallel solver for Maxwell's equations on overlapping grids," SIAM J. Sci. Comput., vol. 28, no. 5, pp. 1730–1765, 2006.

Hermite Methods for Electromagnetic Waves in Dispersive Media

Thomas Hagstrom
Department of Mathematics
Southern Methodist University
Dallas TX, USA
thagstrom@smu.edu

***Abstract*—We describe arbitrary-order discretization methods based on Hermite-Birkhoff interpolation for Maxwell's equations in dispersive media. We consider generalized Lorentz models, not only for the permittivity, but also for the permeability to account for approximations to negative index metamaterials. Both conservative and dissipative methods are considered.**

***Index Terms*—dispersive media, high-order methods.**

I. Introduction

Hermite methods are general-purpose methods for solving time dependent PDEs [1] which are particularly well-suited for hyperbolic equations. Examples of their application in the hyperbolic case include the original dissipative formulation [2] as well as more recent energy-conserving forms [3], [4]. In contrast with typical polynomial-based element methods, Hermite methods for hyperbolic problems can march in time with a time step, Δt, limited only by domain-of-dependence constraints, $c\Delta t \lesssim \Delta x$, independent of order. Moreover, the cell updates require no communication with neighboring cells, and thus high-order Hermite methods essentially maximize the computation-to-communication ratio, which, as seen in [3]–[5], enables efficient implementations on GPUs.

Here we consider the general dispersive Maxwell system:

$$\epsilon\left(1+\mathcal{K}_e *\right)\frac{\partial E}{\partial t}=\nabla\times H,\quad \mu\left(1+\mathcal{K}_m *\right)\frac{\partial H}{\partial t}=-\nabla\times E.$$

We assume Lorentz models for the temporal convolutions; precisely, with s the Laplace transform variable dual to time,

$$\hat{\mathcal{K}}_e=\sum_{j=1}^{N_e}\frac{\omega_{e,j}^2}{s^2+\gamma_{e,j}s+\Omega_{e,j}^2},\quad \hat{\mathcal{K}}_m=\sum_{j=1}^{N_m}\frac{\omega_{m,j}^2}{s^2+\gamma_{m,j}s+\Omega_{m,j}^2}.$$

Here we include frequency dependence not only of the permittivity but also of the permeability to account for simple homogenized models of metamaterials and note that more general models, as discussed in [6], could be treated. We eliminate the convolutions by introducing additional fields P_j, Q_j, R_j and S_j to obtain:

$$\frac{\partial E}{\partial t} = \frac{1}{\epsilon}\nabla\times H-\sum_{j=1}^{N_e}\omega_{e,j}^2 P_j, \tag{1}$$

$$\frac{\partial P_j}{\partial t} = -\gamma_{e,j}P_j-\Omega_{e,j}^2 Q_j+E, \tag{2}$$

$$\frac{\partial H}{\partial t} = -\frac{1}{\mu}\nabla\times E-\sum_{j=1}^{N_m}\omega_{m,j}^2 R_j, \tag{3}$$

$$\frac{\partial R_j}{\partial t} = -\gamma_{m,j}R_j-\Omega_{m,j}^2 S_j+H, \tag{4}$$

$$\frac{\partial Q_j}{\partial t}=P_j,\qquad \frac{\partial S_j}{\partial t}=R_j. \tag{5}$$

After rescaling the variables we can rewrite (1)-(5) in the form:

$$\frac{\partial V}{\partial t} = \sum_k A_k\frac{\partial W}{\partial x_k}+MW-\Gamma_V V, \tag{6}$$

$$\frac{\partial W}{\partial t} = \sum_k A_k^T\frac{\partial V}{\partial x_k}-M^TV-\Gamma_W W, \tag{7}$$

where V contains rescalings of E, Q_j and R_j, W contains rescalings of H, S_j, and P_j, and the nonnegative diagonal matrices $\Gamma_{V,W}$ vanish if dissipation is absent. Spatial derivatives are only applied to E and H and the characteristic speeds are $c=(\epsilon\mu)^{-1/2}$, 0. We thus conclude that the domain-of-dependence is unaffected by the dispersive corrections, an energy given by $\|V\|_{L^2}^2+\|W\|_{L^2}^2$ is conserved or dissipated (modulo boundary contributions), and that the number and type of admissible boundary conditions is the same as for Maxwell's equations in a simple dielectric.

II. Hermite Discretization of (6)-(7)

The essential ingredients of both the dissipative and conservative Hermite methods are:
(i.) A cuboidal primal and dual grid,
(ii.) Degrees of freedom defined by tensor-product Taylor polynomials at the cell vertices - for multi-indices α, $0\leq\alpha_j\leq m$, and U representing either V or W, $U_{j_1,j_2,j_3}^{\alpha}(t_n)\approx\frac{\Delta x^{|\alpha|}}{\alpha!}D^{\alpha}U(x_{1,j_1},x_{2,j_2},x_{3,j_3},t_n)$.
(iii.) The cell polynomial, $P_U(x)$, is the tensor-product Hermite-Birkhoff interpolant of the vertex data:

$$\frac{\Delta x^{|\alpha|}}{\alpha!}D^{\alpha}P_U(x_{1,j},x_{2,k},x_{3,\ell})=U_{j,k,\ell}^{\alpha},$$

for all α and for $j = j_1, j_1+1$, $k = j_2, j_2+1$, $\ell = j_3, j_3+1$. (iv.) The evolution problem, (6) and/or (7), is solved locally with data P to time $t_{n+1/2}$, producing updated data at the dual node $(x_{1,j_1+1/2}, x_{2,j_2+1/2}, x_{3,j_3+1/2})$.

The stability of the process generally follows if we satisfy the CFL condition, $\Delta t < c\Delta x$, due to the smoothing property of the Hermite interpolation process. Precisely, if we define,

$$|f|_m^2 = \|\frac{\partial^{3m+3} f}{\partial x_1^{m+1} \partial x_2^{m+1} \partial x_3^{m+1}}\|_{L^2}^2,$$

and denote by $\mathcal{I}_m f$ the interpolant defined above, then the Pythagorean Theorem holds:

$$|f|_m^2 = |\mathcal{I}_m f|_m^2 + |f - \mathcal{I}_m f|_m^2.$$

See [2]–[4] for details of proofs when the lower order terms, M, $\Gamma_{V,W}$ are 0. Note that these proofs assume that the local evolution problem is solved exactly (which is possible in piecewise contant dielectric media), but as we see in numerical experiments high-order local time stepping suffices.

Specific methods now differ depending on whether one or two time levels are used and whether or not the approximations to V and W are defined on every time level or whether they are staggered, as in the well-known Yee scheme [7].

A. Dissipative Method

For the dissipative method both V and W are defined at every time level and, assuming piecewise constant, we time step here using a simple Taylor method (from now on we drop the cell indices for ease of writing):

$$V^0 = P_V, \quad W^0 = P_U,$$

and for $\ell = 1, \ldots, q$

$$\begin{aligned}
V^\ell &= \sum_k A_k \frac{\partial W^{\ell-1}}{\partial x_k} + M W^{\ell-1} - \Gamma_V V^{\ell-1}, \\
W^\ell &= \sum_k A_k^T \frac{\partial V^{\ell-1}}{\partial x_k} - M^T V^{\ell-1} - \Gamma_W W^{\ell-1}, \\
V(\mathbf{x}, t_{n+1/2}) &= \sum_{\ell=0}^{q} \frac{(\Delta t/2)^\ell}{\ell!} V^\ell, \\
W(\mathbf{x}, t_{n+1/2}) &= \sum_{\ell=0}^{q} \frac{(\Delta t/2)^\ell}{\ell!} W^\ell.
\end{aligned}$$

For $q > 2m+1$ large enough we expect convergence at order $2m+1$ in space and time.

B. Conservative Method

Now we define V and W at different time levels and thus on different grids. Also, to pursue a conservative method, we take $\gamma_{e,j} = \gamma_{m,j} = 0$ - including dissipation is possible but it leads to a more complicated method. Now we have:

$$V^1 = \sum_k A_k \frac{\partial P_W}{\partial x_k} + M P_W,$$

$$V^\ell = \left(\sum_k A_k \frac{\partial}{\partial x_k} + M\right)\left(\sum_k A_k^T \frac{\partial V^{\ell-1}}{\partial x_k} - M^T V^{\ell-1}\right),$$

$$V(\mathbf{x}, t_{n+1/2}) = V(\mathbf{x}, t_{n+1/2}) + 2\sum_{\ell=1}^{q} \frac{(\Delta t/2)^{2\ell-1}}{(2\ell-1)!} V^\ell,$$

$$W^1 = \sum_k A_k^T \frac{\partial P_V}{\partial x_k} - M^T P_V,$$

$$W^\ell = \left(\sum_k A_k^T \frac{\partial}{\partial x_k} - M^T\right)\left(\sum_k A_k \frac{\partial W^{\ell-1}}{\partial x_k} + M W^{\ell-1}\right),$$

$$W(\mathbf{x}, t_{n+1}) = W(\mathbf{x}, t_n) + 2\sum_{\ell=1}^{q} \frac{(\Delta t/2)^{2\ell-1}}{(2\ell-1)!} W^\ell.$$

Here setting $q > m+2$ large enough we expect convergence at order $2m$ or $2m+2$ (see [4]). Obviously the conservative method uses less work and storage per time step.

III. Numerical Experiment

We solve (1)-(5) in the TE case with both methods, $m = 6$, $\Delta t/\Delta x = 0.9$, on the domain $(-8, 8)^2$ up to $T = 100$. The parameters in the Lorentz models with $N_e = N_m = 1$ are:

$$\epsilon = 1.25, \quad \mu = 0.8, \quad \omega_m^2 = 3, \quad \Omega_m^2 = 6, \quad \omega_e^2 = 2, \quad \Omega_e^2 = 5,$$

and we force the equation for H_z by $e^{-10(x^2+y^2)} \sin(7t)$, a frequency in the negative index regime. Using as reference the dissipative solution on a mesh of 96^2 cells, we obtain the results displayed in Table I. We observe that the dissipative scheme converges roughly at the expected order of 13. The convergence of the conservative scheme is far choppier, but overall consistent with the design accuracy. A comparison of costs suggests that the conservative scheme, though needing a finer grid, is more efficient. The codes for this experiment will be made available in the CHIDES repository [8].

TABLE I
Relative Errors in H_z at $T = 100$.

Dissipative			Conservative		
Mesh	Error	Rate	Mesh	Error	Rate
24 × 24	7.3(−4)		32 × 32	8.8(−3)	
32 × 32	1.5(−5)	13.6	48 × 48	1.1(−6)	22.2
48 × 48	4.7(−8)	14.2	64 × 64	1.1(−7)	8.0
64 × 64	1.3(−9)	12.4	96 × 96	2.2(−10)	15.3

References

[1] D. Appelö and T. Hagstrom, "Solving PDEs with Hermite interpolation", Lecture Notes in Computational Science, Springer, 2015, pp. 31–49.

[2] J. Goodrich, T. Hagstrom, and J. Lorenz, "Hermite methods for hyperbolic initial-boundary value problems," Math. Comp., vol. 75, pp. 595–630, 2006.

[3] D. Appelö, T. Hagstrom, and A. Vargas, "Hermite methods for the scalar wave equation," SIAM J. Sci. Comput., vol. 40, pp. A3902–A3927, 2018.

[4] A. Vargas, T. Hagstrom, J. Chan, and T. Warburton, "Leapfrog time-stepping for Hermite methods," J. Sci. Comput., 2018, in revision.

[5] A. Vargas, J. Chan, T. Hagstrom, and T. Warburton, "GPU acceleration of Hermite methods for simulation of wave propagation", Lecture Notes in Computational Science, Springer, 2017, pp. 357–368.

[6] L. Prokopeva, J. Borneman, and A. Kildishev, "Optical dispersion models for time-domain modeling of metal-dielectric nanostructures," IEEE Trans. on Magnetics, vol. 47, pp. 1150–1153, 2011.

[7] K. Yee, "Numerical solution of initial boundary value problems involving maxwell's equations in isotropic media," IEEE Trans. on Antennas and Prop., vol. 14, p. 302307, 1966.

[8] D. Appelö and T. Hagstrom, "CHIDES," http://www.chides.org.

Material Models in Full-Wave Nonlinear Optics (invited)

Michael Povolotskyi
Birck Nanotechnology Center
Purdue University
West Lafayette IN, USA
mpovolot@purdue.edu

Shaimaa Azzam
School of ECE and Birck Nanotechnology Center
Purdue University
West Lafayette IN, USA
sazzam@purdue.edu

Ludmila J. Prokopeva
School of ECE and Birck Nanotechnology Center
Purdue University
West Lafayette IN, USA
lprokop@purdue.edu

Samuel Peana
School of ECE and Birck Nanotechnology Center
Purdue University
West Lafayette IN, USA
speana@purdue.edu

Alexander V. Kildishev
School of ECE and Birck Nanotechnology Center
Purdue University
West Lafayette IN, USA
kildisha@purdue.edu

***Abstract* — We present advanced material models describing light-matter interaction for numerical simulation of nonlinear optical responses. We build the models on electron transport equations, carrier kinetics equations, and the effective dipole oscillator equation. Coupled to the Maxwell equations, they enable the study of nonlinear photonic elements such as nonlinear absorbers, optical modulators, and switches.**

Keywords* — *absorption saturation, electron hydrodynamic models, light-matter coupling, Maxwell's equations.

I. Introduction

A new generation of nonlinear optical devices is imperative for on-a-chip integration of photonics with electronics, nanolasing, and reconfigurable ultrafast optical switching. To design and optimize these next generation devices sophisticated material models are critically needed. In particular, new models are required to simulate nonlinear optical effects such as stimulated emission and saturable absorption of light, and the heating of electrons. In this work we report our newly developed numerically efficient models which can describe the discussed nonlinear effects on femtosecond time scales with up to 10-nm resolution. We couple the developed models to the full-wave time-domain Maxwell equations.

II. Material Models

A. Systems with Reverse Saturable Absorption

Accurate numerical simulation of nonlinear materials that exhibit reverse saturation of absorption, known as reverse saturable absorbers (RSAs), requires explicit modeling of electron level populations. Here, the atomic rate equations are employed to model the dynamics of reverse saturable absorption. A schematic of a four-level atom system used to model RSA, is shown in Fig. 1, indicating the allowed transitions with the corresponding lifetimes. We model the nonlinear material response as a sum of two polarizations: P_G, the singlet states transition polarization and P_T, as the triplet states transition polarization.

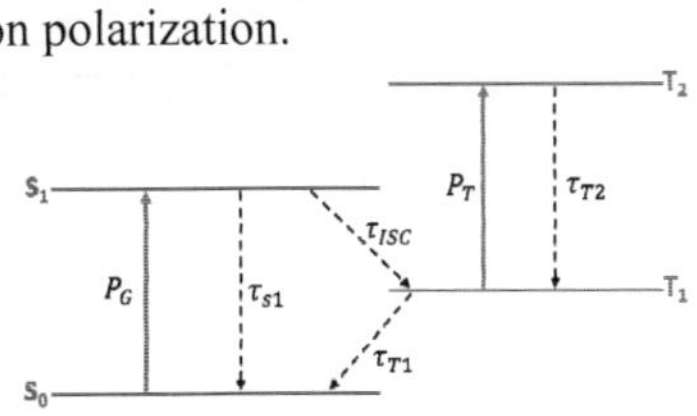

Fig. 1. Schematic of a four-level system representing the RSA.

Supported by DARPA/DSO Extreme Optics and Imaging (EXTREME) Program, Award HR00111720032.

Figure 2 (a) depicts the transmittance of 1-μm film, as a function of the input fluence, exhibiting reverse saturable absorption. Figs. 2 (b-d) describe the simulated dynamics of carrier populations and transition polarizations. Refs. [1,2] include more details on the time-domain modeling and simulation results. The proposed time-domain model based on rate equations enables full-wave 3D multiphysics analysis of RSA effects. In particular, this versatile technique makes possible modeling and optimization of micro- and nano-structured devices and opens up new opportunities to explore high-sensitivity, low-threshold optical limiters beyond homogeneous RSA materials.

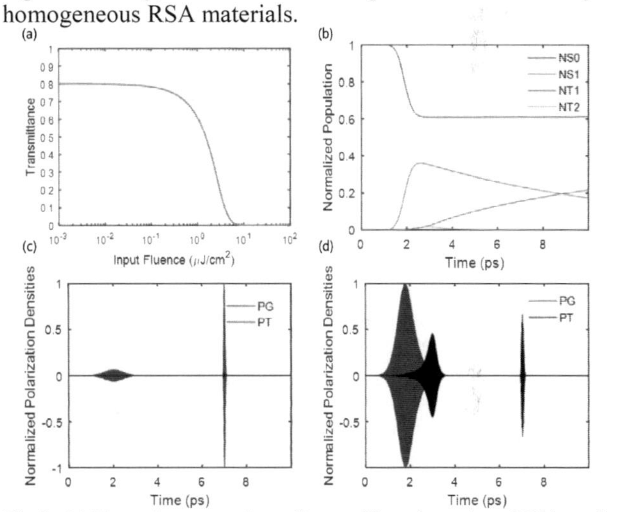

Fig. 2. (a) Transmittance vs. input fluence. Time dynamics of RSA medium including (b) population densities, (c) polarization densities at 0.01 μJ/cm² (linear regime), and (d) polarization densities at 50 μJ/cm² (nonlinear regime).

B. Transparent Conducting Oxides

Our material model of transparent conduction oxides (TCOs) describes interaction of light with a high density ($n \sim 1021$ cm^{-3}) electron gas. In this study, we assume that the frequency of light is small enough to neglect interband transitions. Hence, we limit the electron kinetics model to transport in the lowest conduction band and use the effective mass approximation. In the hydrodynamic approximation, the model considers conservation of electrons, momentum, and energy of the electron gas under light excitation [3,4]:

$$\partial_t n + \nabla(n\mathbf{v}) = 0, \quad m_e \partial_t \mathbf{v} + m_e \mathbf{v}\nabla\mathbf{v} - q\mathbf{F} + \frac{\nabla p}{n_e} = -\frac{m_e \mathbf{v}}{\tau_v}, \qquad (1)$$

$$\partial_t w + \mathbf{v}\nabla w - \mathbf{F}\mathbf{v} + \frac{1}{n}\nabla(\mathbf{v}p) = -\frac{w_e - w_e^0}{\tau_w},$$

where $n, \mathbf{v}, w$ are density, average velocity, and energy of electrons, respectively. Electron motion is caused by the Lorentz force $\mathbf{F}$ and gradient of electron pressure ∇p.

Figure 3 shows simulation results of normal light incidence on a 50-nm TCO film. The incident electric field only has the lateral component. As the electron gas is heated, it creates an electron pressure gradient in the normal direction. That gradient consequently, generates an oscillating normal component of current density and electric field. Hence, one can compute a nonlinear anisotropic response of a TCO film.

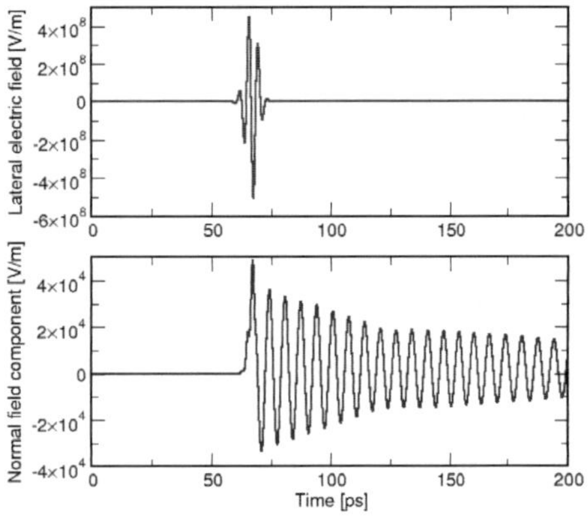

Fig. 3. Lateral and normal E-field in TCO film upon high-intensity excitation.

C. Coupling with Linear Dispersion

The nonlinear effects discussed can be enhanced with device designs that provide high field localization, e.g., [5]. For accurate and computationally efficient implementation of linear dispersion in time domain, we additionally couple our nonlinear solver with the Generalized Dispersive Material (GDM) model [6], where generality comes from the Pade approximation of the dielectric function. Previously we reported that this approach could be used to model the dispersion of noble metals, graphene, and phase change materials with just the Drude term and two critical points oscillators [6,7]. We have demonstrated the implementation of the GDM model in various time-domain methods, including FDTD, FVTD, and FETD, and confirmed its superiority over more computationally expensive Drude-Lorentz models.

III. Online Availability

To share our nonlinear numerical models and design examples we have developed a compact, versatile 2D FDTD multiphysics simulator that is available online on nanoHUB [8]. There, we provide a constellation of well documented interactive Jupyter notebooks with simulation examples. The examples can be run "as is" or with modified parameters. Additionally, these notebooks are full Python development environments allowing end users to write custom pre-/post-processing, parametric sweeps, or optimization scripts entirely on the cloud. This platform allows full and interactive online cloud access to the developed computational core, which supports modeling with any multi-level atomic system and arbitrary dispersion. Figure 4 presents the look and feel of the interface; it shows a partial snapshot of a notebook, where the geometry and the parameters of the incident pulse are defined.

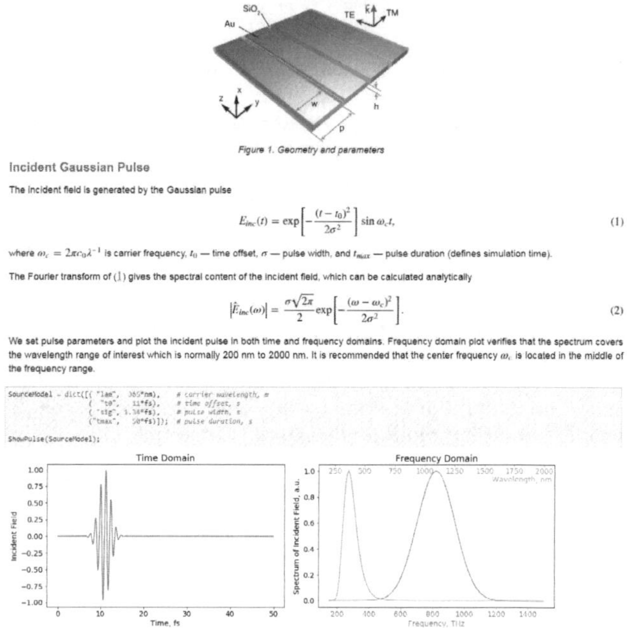

Fig. 4. "Look and feel" screenshot of the developed Jupyter notebook.

IV. Summary

The reported models cover a broad range of light-matter interaction phenomena. Choice of a model and its parameters requires validation and fitting to the experiment. For this reason, the models and simulation examples are made accessible online using Jupyter notebooks.

References

[1] S. I. Azzam and A. V. Kildishev, "Full-wave analysis of reverse saturable absorption in time-domain," Nanophotonics, Published Online: Nov 23, 2018. DOI: https://doi.org/10.1515/nanoph-2018-0139

[2] L. J. Prokopeva, et al., "Numerical modeling of active plasmonic metamaterials," Optical Complex Systems: OCS11, vol. 8172, International Society for Optics and Photonics, 2011.

[3] D. L. Woolard, et al., "Hydrodynamic electron-transport model: Nonparabolic corrections to the streaming terms," Phys. Rev. B, 44(11119), 2009.

[4] S. Bhardwaj, F. L. Teixeira and J. L. Volakis, "Fast Modeling of Terahertz Plasma-Wave Devices Using Unconditionally Stable FDTD Methods," in IEEE Journal on Multiscale and Multiphysics Computational Techniques, vol. 3, pp. 29-36, 2018.

[5] X. Meng, A. V. Kildishev, K. Fujita, K. Tanaka, and V. M. Shalaev, "Wavelength-tunable spasing in the visible," Nano Lett., 13(9), pp. 4106-4112, 2013.

[6] L. J. Prokopeva, J. D. Borneman, and A. V. Kildishev, "Optical dispersion models for time-domain modeling of metal-dielectric nanostructures," IEEE Trans. on Magnetics, 47(5), pp. 1150-1153, 2011.

[7] L. J. Prokopeva and A. V. Kildishev, "Efficient time-domain model of the graphene dielectric function," Metamaterials: Fundamentals and Applications VI, vol. 8806, International Society for Optics and Photonics, 2013.

[8] L. J. Prokopeva, S. Peana, A. V. Kildishev, "Sandbox2D FDTD Multiphysics Simulator," 2018, https://nanohub.org/resources/sandbox2d (DOI: 10.4231/D36W96C0S)

A Discontinuous Galerkin Framework for Multiphysics Simulation of Photoconductive Devices

Liang Chen and Hakan Bagci
Division of Computer, Electrical, and Mathematical Science and Engineering
King Abdullah University of Science and Technology (KAUST), Thuwal, Saudi Arabia
{liang.chen, hakan.bagci}@kaust.edu.sa

***Abstract*—A discontinuous Galerkin (DG) framework is developed for multiphysics simulation of plasmonic photoconductive devices. The nonequilibrium steady state is modeled by the coupled system of Poisson and drift-diffusion (DD) equations and this system is solved using a nonlinear DG scheme. The optical-to-terahertz (THz) conversion process is modeled by the coupled system of Maxwell and time dependent DD equations and this system is solved using a time domain DG scheme. Numerical experiments show that the proposed scheme provides accurate results.**

***Keywords*—Discontinuous Galerkin method, drift-diffusion equations, Maxwell equations, plasmonic photoconductive antennas, Poisson equation, semiconductor device modeling, Terahertz sources.**

I. Introduction

Recently, plasmonic photoconductive devices (PCDs) have emerged as the most promising candidates for Terahertz (THz) source generation because they can be designed to achieve high optical-to-THz conversion efficiency [1-3]. While the inclusion of plasmonic nanostructures dramatically enhances the efficiency of PCDs, they also introduce new challenges to numerical simulations because of their geometrically more intricate design resulting in more complex electromagnetic (EM) scattering behaviour. Previous numerical approaches making use of finite difference method (FDM) [4-6] are targeted for more conventional PCDs with simpler geometries, where the photocarrier generation is modeled using analytical expressions. This approach is not applicable to plasmonic PCDs, where the pumping EM wave scattering is more complex. Additionally, the uniform/structured mesh used by the FDM is inefficient for the complex plasmonic nanostructures and fields. Recent approaches to numerical modeling of plasmonic PCDs [7,8] make use of the finite element method (FEM), which provides the mesh flexibility to better approximate the plasmonic nanostructures. However, these approaches ignore the nonlinear coupling in the optical-to-THz conversion process. In practice, EM wave scattering, carrier generation, and carrier movements all happen simultaneously and are strongly coupled. For example, the scattering of the pumping EM wave results in a space-time dependent carrier generation rate. The nonuniform carrier distribution, in turn, results in EM wave scattering, which again changes the carrier generation. Accurate modeling of this strongly nonlinear process calls for time domain methods.

In this work, a two-stage discontinuous Galerkin (DG) framework is developed for multiphysics simulation of plasmonic PCDs. The nonequilibrium steady state is modeled by the coupled system of Poisson and drift-diffusion (DD) equations; and this system is solved using a (nonlinear) DG scheme. The optical-to-THz conversion process is modeled by the coupled system of Maxwell and time dependent DD equations. This system is solved using a time domain DG scheme. Unlike the previous approaches, the proposed DG-based framework can account for complex geometries and EM scattering as well as the nonlinear coupling between different physical processes. It should be noted here that the proposed framework is used only for simulation of the PCDs but it is general enough to take into account the antennas that can be attached to the device for transmitting the generated THz energy.

II. Formulation

The physical process behind the operation of the PCDs can be analyzed in two stages. Before the optical pumping starts, the device is under a nonequilibrium steady state, where carrier dynamics are described under only an external bias voltage. During optical pumping, the device is in a transient stage involving EM wave scattering, carrier generation, and carrier dynamics.

A. The Steady State

The steady state is described by the coupled system of Poisson and DD equations:

$$\nabla\cdot(\varepsilon\nabla\varphi) = -q(C + n_h^s - n_e^s), \tag{1}$$

$$\nabla\cdot(-\mu_e n_e^s \nabla\varphi + D_e \nabla n_e^s) = R^s, \tag{2}$$

$$\nabla\cdot(-\mu_h n_h^s \nabla\varphi - D_h \nabla n_h^s) = -R^s, \tag{3}$$

where the electric potential φ and the carrier densities $n_{e(h)}^s$ are unknowns to be solved for, C is the doping concentration, R^s is the recombination rate, and $\mu_{e(h)}$ and $D_{e(h)}$ are the mobility and the diffusion coefficient, respectively. This nonlinear coupled equation set is discretized using the local DG (LDG) scheme [10]. The LDG alternate flux is used for the Laplace operator and the local Lax-Friedrichs flux is used for the drift term. The resulting (coupled) matrix systems are solved using the iterative Gummel method [9].

B. The Transient Stage

The transient stage is described by the coupled system of Maxwell and DD equations:

$$\mu\partial_t \vec{H}^t = -\nabla\times\vec{E}^t, \tag{4}$$

$$\varepsilon\partial_t \vec{E}^t = \nabla\times\vec{H}^t - (\vec{J}_e^t + \vec{J}_h^t), \tag{5}$$

$$q\partial_t n_e^t = \nabla\cdot\vec{J}_e^t - q(R^t - G), \tag{6}$$

$$q\partial_t n_h^t = -\nabla\cdot\vec{J}_h^t - q(R^t - G), \tag{7}$$

$$\vec{J}_e^t = q\mu_e[(-\nabla\varphi + \vec{E}^t)n_e^t + \vec{E}^t n_e^s] + qD_e\nabla n_e^t, \tag{8}$$

$$\vec{J}_h^t = q\mu_h[(-\nabla\varphi + \vec{E}^t)n_h^t + \vec{E}^t n_h^s] - qD_h\nabla n_h^t, \tag{9}$$

where the time-dependent EM fields $\vec{E}^t$ and $\vec{H}^t$, and carrier densities $n_{e(h)}^t$ are unknowns to be solved for, G is the carrier generation rate (a function of optical wave energy).

Equations (4)-(9) are discretized using the time domain DG scheme [11]. For Maxwell equations, the upwind flux is used. For DD equations, the LDG alternate flux is used for the Laplace operator and the local Lax-Friedrichs flux is used for the drift term. The resulting systems of Maxwell and DD equations are updated separately using the explicit fourth-order five-stage low-storage Runge-Kutta scheme, while the solutions of these systems are alternately fed into each other through the coupling terms.

III. Numerical Experiments

The proposed framework is used to analyze photocurrent generation on a PCD [5-7]. The simulation domain is shown in Fig.1. DD equations are solved in the LT-GaAs layer. The domains for Poisson and Maxwell equations are respectively truncated by the outer air boundary and perfectly matched layers (PMLs). Second order Legendre-Gauss-Lobatto nodal basis functions [11] are used in the DG methods. The (average) mesh sizes are 10 nm near the boundaries of the LT-GaAs layer, 80 nm in the SI-GaAs layer, and 150 nm in air and PML, resulting in a total of 20,000 mesh elements. In the transient simulation, a Gaussian beam of 3μm width is injected from top. The center frequency is 375 THz and the pulse length is 8×10^{-14} s. The time step size is 2×10^{-19} s and the simulation time is 4×10^{-12} s. The semiconductor parameters, mobility and recombination models are the same as those in [5].

Fig. 2 shows the electron density at $y=0.5\mu$m and $y=0$ lines, obtained using the proposed (steady state) DG solver and the COMSOL semiconductor module. The results match well with each other. The differences between the two results are two orders smaller than the solutions. Transient response is also computed using the proposed (time domain) DG scheme. Fig. 3 shows the normalized photocurrent and the power spectrum obtained using the proposed DG framework [Fig. 3 (a)] and the FDM [5] [Fig. 3 (b)]. The results agree well with each other.

Acknowledgment

This publication is based upon work supported by the King Abdullah University of Science and Technology (KAUST) Office of Sponsored Research (OSR) under Award No 2016-CRG5-2953. The authors would like to thank the King Abdullah University of Science and Technology Supercomputing Laboratory (KSL) for providing the required computational resources.

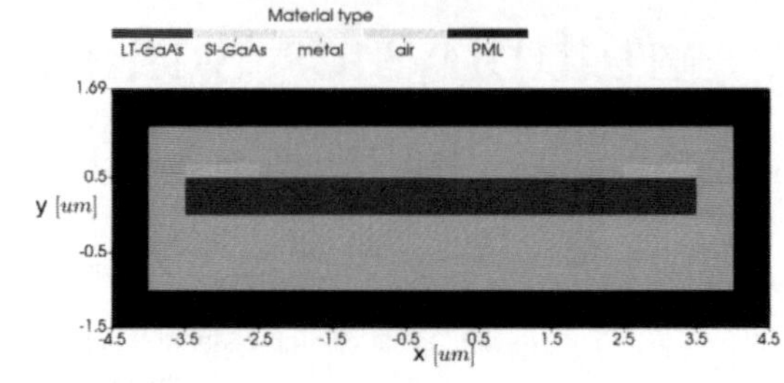

Fig. 1. Simulation domain of the conventional PCD.

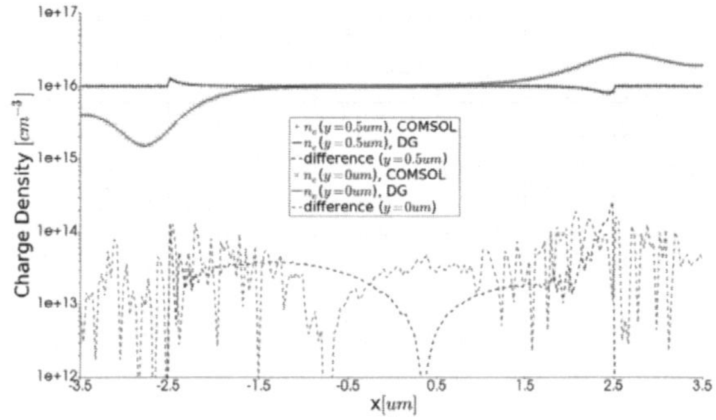

Fig. 2. Steady state electron density distribution computed by the proposed DG scheme in comparison with COMSOL.

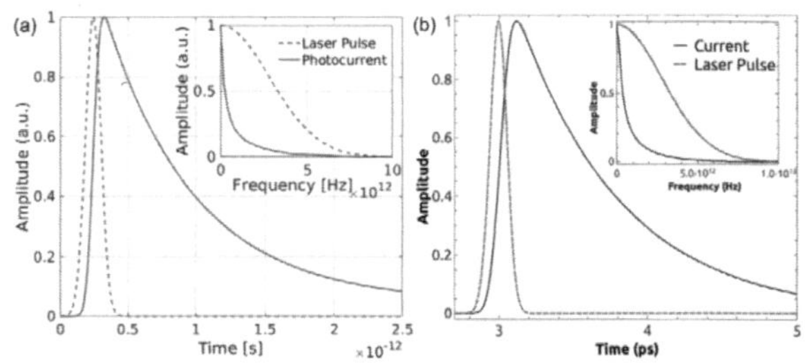

Fig. 3. Photocurrent and power spectrum computed using (a) the proposed DG framework and (b) the FDM [5].

References

[1] C. W. Berry, N. Wang, M. R. Hashemi, M. Unlu, and M. Jarrahi, "Significant performance enhancement in photoconductive terahertz optoelectronics incorporating plasmonic contact electrodes," Nat. Commun., vol. 4, no. 1622, 2013.

[2] S.-H. Yang, M. R. Hashemi, C. W. Berry, and M. Jarrahi, "7.5% optical-to-terahertz conversion efficiency offered by photoconductive emitters with three-dimensional plasmonic contact electrodes," IEEE Trans. Terahertz Sci. Tech., vol. 4, no. 5, pp. 575-581, 2014.

[3] S. Lepeshov, A. Gorodetsky, A. Krasnok, E. Rafailov, and P. Belov, "Enhancement of terahertz photoconductive antenna operation by optical nanoantennas," Laser Photon. Rev., vol. 11, no. 1, pp. 1600199, 2017.

[4] B. Tissafi, F. Aniel, L. Pichon, B. Essakhi, C. Guiffaut, S. Lepaul, "Comparative study of three wave propagation software programs for the modeling of coupled Maxwell and Boltzmann equations at THz frequency,"Applied Computational Electromagnetics Society Journal, vol. 24, no. 4, pp. 382-389, 2009.

[5] E. Moreno, M. F. Pantoja, S. G. Garcia, A. R. Bretones, and R. G. Martin, "Time-domain numerical modeling of THz photoconductive antennas," IEEE Trans. Terahertz Sci. Tech., vol. 4, no. 4, pp. 490-500, 2014.

[6] E. Moreno, M. F. Pantoja, F. G. Ruiz, J. B. Roldan, and S. G. Garcia, "On the numerical modeling of terahertz photoconductive antennas," J. Infrared Millim. Terahertz Waves, vol. 35, pp. 432-444, 2014.

[7] N. Burford and M. El-Shenawee, "Computational modeling of plasmonic thin-film terahertz photoconductive antennas," J. Opt. Soc. Am. B, vol. 33, no. 4, pp. 748-759, 2016.

[8] M. Bashirpour, S. Ghorbani, M. Kolahdouz, M. Neshat, M. Masnadi-Shirazi, and H. Aghababa, "Significant performance improvement of a terahertz photoconductive antenna using a hybrid structure," RSC Adv., vol. 7, pp. 53010-53017, 2017.

[9] H. K. Gummel, "A self-consistent iterative scheme for one-dimensional steady state transistor calculations," IEEE Trans. Electron Devices, vol. 11, pp. 455–65, 1964.

[10] B. Cockburn and C. W. Shu, "The local discontinuous Galerkin method for time-dependent convection-diffusion systems," SIAM J. Numer. Anal., vol. 35, no. 6, pp. 2440-2463, 1998.

[11] J. Hesthaven and T. Warburton, Nodal Discontinuous Galerkin Methods: Algorithms, Analysis, and Applications, NY, USA: Springer, 2008.

Computation of Fields from a Magnetic Dipole in a Conductive Medium using the QS-DGTD Method

M. Burak Özakın
Division of Computer, Electrical and Mathematical Science and Engineering, King Abdullah University of Science and Technology (KAUST), Thuwal 23955-6900, Saudi Arabia
mehmet.ozakin@kaust.edu.sa
Department of Electronics Engineering
Gebze Technical University, Kocaeli 41400, Turkey
bozakin@gtu.edu.tr

Liang Chen, Shehab Ahmed, and Hakan Bagci
Division of Computer, Electrical and Mathematical Science and Engineering, King Abdullah University of Science and Technology (KAUST), Thuwal 23955-6900, Saudi Arabia
{liang.cheng, shehab.ahmed, hakan.bagci}@kaust.edu.sa

***Abstract*—Loop antennas are often used for field generation in low-frequency electromagnetic applications. Since the antenna dimensions are much smaller than the wavelength, the antenna can accurately be replaced by its equivalent magnetic dipole model in simulations. In this paper, low-frequency magnetic dipole radiation fields in a conductive medium are computed using a three-dimensional discontinuous Galerkin Time-Domain (DGTD) scheme. It is shown that this computation can be accelerated using a material scaling scheme under Quasi-Static (QS) approximation, i.e., time step size can be scaled up without sacrificing from the accuracy and the stability of the time marching scheme. Radiated fields from a magnetic dipole in a conductive medium computed by this accelerated scheme are compared to those obtained using analytical expressions. Results are in good agreement.**

Keywords—Discontinuous Galerkin time-domain method, magnetic dipole, Quasi-static approximation.

I. INTRODUCTION

Electromagnetic induction (EMI) sensors consisting of loop antennas are often used in electromagnetic systems operating at very low frequencies. Many of these systems, such as those used for underwater remote sensing and wellbore integrity monitoring are designed to operate in conductive media. For these low-frequency applications, since the dimensions of the loop antenna are much smaller than the wavelength, the antenna can be replaced by its equivalent magnetic dipole model in simulations. For numerical investigation of these low-frequency systems, Maxwell equations are often solved using time-domain methods, such as discontinuous Galerkin time-domain (DGTD) [1-2] and finite-difference time-domain (FDTD) [3] schemes. However, these methods require very long execution times since they sample low-frequency (slowly varying) fields with a very small time step size. To overcome this problem, quasi-static FDTD (QS-FDTD) method [4] has been developed. This method scales the dielectric permittivity (ε) by a constant of α, i.e., $\varepsilon^{QS} = \alpha\varepsilon$, to effectively "slow down" the wave propagation velocity. This means that, for the same spatial discretization, time step size can also be scaled-up as $\Delta t^{QS} = \sqrt{\alpha}\Delta t$. Consequently, the simulation can carried out $\sqrt{\alpha}$ times faster for the same duration. It should be noted here that this "material scaling" concept is valid only under QS approximation limits and the selection of α should maintain the low-frequency nature of the problem and the stability and the accuracy of the time marching scheme. A method for the choosing α within the framework of the QS-FDTD method was described in [4].

In this work, a DGTD scheme is used as an alternative to the FDTD method to simulate low-frequency electromagnetic field/wave interactions. This choice is motivated by the advantages offered by the DGTD, namely the ability to model using unstructured meshes and the flexibility to easily increase the solution accuracy [2]. More specifically, fields radiated from a magnetic dipole in a conductive medium are computed using a three-dimensional (3D) DGTD method (termed as QS-DGTD here), which is accelerated using the same material scaling technique used by the QS-FDTD [4-5].

II. METHODOLOGY

In this section, first, the analytical expressions of fields generated by a magnetic dipole in a conductive medium are provided. Then, the equations underlying the DGTD scheme used for solving the Maxwell curl equations in a conductive medium are very briefly described.

A. Magnetic Dipole Fields in a Conductive Medium

The expressions of the fields generated by a magnetic dipole (or a small loop with area S and carrying a constant current I_0) are given in spherical coordinate system [6]:

$$H_r = \frac{I_m l \cos\theta}{2\pi\eta r^2}\left(1+\frac{1}{jkr}\right)e^{-jkr}, \tag{1.a}$$

$$H_\theta = j\frac{kI_m l \sin\theta}{4\pi\eta r}\left(1+\frac{1}{jkr}-\frac{1}{(kr)^2}\right)e^{-jkr}, \tag{1.b}$$

$$E_\phi = -j\frac{kI_m l \sin\theta}{4\pi r}\left(1+\frac{1}{jkr}\right)e^{-jkr}, \tag{1.c}$$

$$E_r = E_\theta = H_\phi = 0\ . \tag{1.d}$$

Here, $I_m l = jS\omega\mu I_0$ is the magnetic moment of the dipole, $j=\sqrt{-1}$, ω is the frequency, μ is the permeability, η is the wave impedance, and k is the wave number. Conductivity of the background medium is defined within k and η.

B. DGTD Scheme for Maxwell-curl Equations in a Conductive Medium

The nodal DG discretization of the unit-free normalized Maxwell-curl equations yields a semi-discrete coupled system of equations, each of which is enforced on discretization element k [2], [7]:

$$\mu^k \partial_t \vec{H}^k(t) = -\overline{D}^k \times \vec{E}^k(t) - \overline{N}^k \vec{F}_H^k(t) \, , \qquad (2.a)$$

$$\varepsilon^k \partial_t \vec{E}^k(t) = \overline{D}^k \times \vec{H}^k(t) + \overline{N}^k \vec{F}_E^k(t) - \sigma^k \eta_0 \vec{E}^k(t) \, . \qquad (2.b)$$

Here, $\vec{H}^k(t)$ and $\vec{E}^k(t)$ store the unknown time dependent coefficients of the electric and magnetic field components at the nodes of element k, ε^k, μ^k, and σ^k are the relative permittivity, permeability, and conductivity values in element k, and η_0 is the wave impedance in free space. The (elemental) differentiation matrix $\overline{D}^k$ implements the curl operation, $\overline{N}^k$ is a block diagonal matrix constructed using face and mass matrices, and $\vec{F}_H^k(t)$ and $\vec{F}_E^k(t)$ represent the upwind numerical flux [2]. Semi-discretized equations (2.a) and (2.b) are integrated in time to yield the samples of $\vec{H}^k(t)$ and $\vec{E}^k(t)$ using the explicit fourth- order five-stage low-storage Runge-Kutta scheme. The time step size of this time marching is scaled-up as described in [4] under QS approximation limits for low-frequency simulations in a conductive medium.

III. Numerical Results

In this section, electromagnetic fields generated by magnetic dipole in a conductive medium is computed using the 3D QS-DGTD scheme described in Section II-B (in time domain) and using the analytical expression provided in Section II-A (in frequency domain).

The z-directed magnetic dipole is located placed at the center of the investigation domain. The dipole generates a single-frequency (100 kHz) continuous wave. The conductive of the medium is 10^{-2} S/m. The up-scaling parameter α is selected as 100 using following the guidelines described in [4]. This consequently means that the QS-DGTD method is 10 times faster than classical DGTD method since $\Delta t^{QS-DGTD} = \sqrt{\alpha}.\Delta t^{DGTD}$. Also, the outer boundaries of the numerical problem space truncated by UPML. The fields are computed at 120 observation points, which are equally spaced on circle around the dipole. Assuming the dipole is located at the center of the observer coordinate system, $r = 4$ m, $\theta = \pi/4$, and $0 < \phi < 2\pi$ for these observation points. Time domain fields computed by the QS-DGTD scheme at the observation points are transformed to the frequency-domain using Fast Fourier Transform. Transformed results are compared to those computed directly in frequency domain using the analytical expression given in Section II-A in Fig. 1. Very good agreement is observed between the two sets of results.

IV. Conclusion

Very-low frequency electromagnetic fields generated by a magnetic dipole in conductive medium are computed using the 3D QS-DGTD scheme. Material scaling idea is applied to accelerate this computation by ten times. Comparison to analytical results show that the accuracy of the QS-DGTD is maintained even after the up-scaling of the permittivity and the time step size.

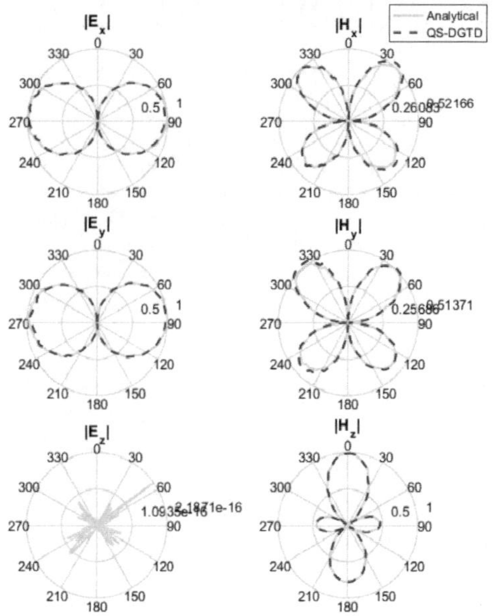

Fig. 1. Magnetic dipole fields at ($r = 4$ m, $\theta = \pi/4$, $\phi = 0:2\pi$), its compared with the analytical and the QS-DGTD method.

Acknowledgment

This publication is based upon work partially supported by the King Abdullah University of Science and Technology (KAUST) Office of Sponsored Research (OSR) under Award No: 2016-CRG5-2953.

References

[1] J. S. Hesthaven and T. Warburton, Nodal Discontinuous Galerkin Methods: Algorithms, Analysis, and Applications, Springer Science & Business Media, 2008.

[2] M. Liu, K. Sirenko, and H. Bagci, "An efficient discontinuous Galerkin finite element method for highly accurate solution of Maxwell equations," IEEE Transactions on Antennas and Propagation, 60(8), 3992-3998, 2012.

[3] A. Taflove and S. C. Hagness, Computational Electrodynamics: The Finite-Difference Time-Domain Method, Artech House, 2005.

[4] M. B. Özakın, and S. Aksoy, "On the application of magneto quasi-static approximation in the finite difference time domain method", IEEE Transactions on Magnetics, 52.8, 2016: 7209809.

[5] M. B. Özakın and S. Aksoy, "Numerical calculation of magnetic dipole fields by three-dimensional QS-FDTD method," In Progress In Electromagnetics Research Symposium-Spring (PIERS), May 2017, pp. 3293-3296.

[6] C. A. Balanis, Antenna Theory: Analysis and Design, 3rd Edition, John Wiley & Sons, 2005.

[7] J. Yang, W. Cai, and X. Wu, "A high-order time domain discontinuous galerkin method with orthogonal tetrahedral basis for electromagnetic simulations in 3-D heterogeneous conductive media," Communications in Computational Physics, 21(4), 1065-1089, 2017.

Analysis of Composite Structures Involving Near-Zero-Index Materials

Yeşim Koyaz, Hande İbili, and Özgür Ergül
Department of Electrical and Electronics Engineering
Middle East Technical University
Ankara, Turkey
ozergul@metu.edu.tr

Abstract—**We consider numerical solutions of electromagnetic problems involving near-zero-index materials with permittivity and/or permeability values close to zero. These types of problems are inherently multiscale due to the large variety of wavelength from very large values to ordinary values in the same problem. In addition to developing a stable formulation for extreme values of the intrinsic impedance, we employ a broadband multilevel fast multipole algorithm based on approximate diagonalization for efficient solutions. Examples involving near-zone-index materials inside ordinary waveguides are presented to demonstrate interesting electromagnetic responses of these exotic materials, as well as the effectiveness of the developed solver.**

I. INTRODUCTION

Zero-index and near-zero-index (NZI) materials have attracted the interest of researchers [1]–[6], since they demonstrate interesting electromagnetic behaviors that can be useful in diverse applications, such as normal refraction, light bending, energy squeezing, and tunneling. While, NZI materials are obtained via alternative approaches, e.g., by regular arrangements of unit cells (metamaterials), in practice, computational studies often focus on their homogeneous representations, where zero-valued electromagnetic parameters (permittivity, permeability, or both) are directly used. Volume-type formulations are commonly used to analyze such models; but, surface formulations are attractive due to their lower computational costs. In fact, frequency-domain surface formulations are readily available to formulate zero-index media, while not all of them are stable when parameter values go to zero [7]. Besides, in electromagnetic applications, zero-index materials often coexist with ordinary materials, which require surface formulations that can handle multi-region problems.

In this study, we present computational solutions of composite problems involving zero-index and NZI materials. These problems can be considered to be multiscale, since the wavelength goes to infinity inside zero-index bodies or become very large in NZI bodies, while it takes ordinary values in other regions. We use a combined-type integral equation, where operators are scaled properly such that extreme impedance values are handled. In addition, a broadband multilevel fast multipole algorithm (MLFMA) is used for efficient simulations. We present various examples, in which zero-index materials are used to improve the performances of electromagnetic devices.

II. IMPLEMENTATION OF THE SOLVER

In the frequency domain, surface formulations can be obtained by properly combining integral equations derived at boundaries. It is well known that the selection of integral equations and their combinations with appropriate scaling factors are crucial to obtain well-conditioned systems and accurate solutions [8]. For problems involving zero-index parts, scaling should be done by considering extreme cases of the intrinsic impedance, i.e., $\eta \ll \eta_o$ (mu-near-zero cases) and $\eta \gg \eta_o$ (epsilon-near-zero cases), as well as for perfect impedance matching ($\eta \approx \eta_o$), where $\eta_o \approx 377$ Ω. The derived integral-equation formulation is discretized by using the Rao-Wilton-Glisson functions so that the implementation is obtained by combining integral/interaction routines that are already available.

For fast analysis of composite structures, a broadband MLFMA based on approximate diagonalization is used [9]. This way, without any restriction on the size of interaction boxes, the same tree structure is used for electromagnetic interactions in the host media and inside zero-index bodies, as well as in ordinary materials. Depending on its dimensions, a portion of the master tree structure can be used effectively for computing far-zone interactions related to a zero-index object, while this does not lead to any inefficiency. Once the expansion coefficients for electric/magnetic currents are obtained, they are used to generate near-zone electromagnetic fields, as usual. Accuracy of solutions is tested by null radiations of equivalent sources.

III. NUMERICAL EXAMPLES

As two sets of examples, we consider WR90-sized waveguides with sharp corners. The walls are modeled as perfectly conducting, while epsilon-near-zero (ENZ), mu-near-zero (MNZ), and epsilon-mu-near-zone (EMNZ) blocks are used to enhance power transmission. As the excitation, Hertzian dipoles are used near the closed sides of the waveguides, while the other ends are considered to be open. The whole structures are located in vacuum. Fig. 1 presents the results when an $51 + 51$ mm waveguide with a corner is investigated at 12 GHz. The electric field intensity (in dBV/m), the magnetic field intensity (in dBA/m), and the power density (in dBW/sm) are plotted in the cross-sectional plane. Without using any material in the corner region, reflections deteriorate the transmission. Using a cubic ENZ (with 0.1 permittivity), the transmission is slightly improved, while MNZ (0.1 permeability) leads to better transmission. Using EMNZ of the same size, the transmission is clearly enhanced with large field and density values inside the waveguide, as well as at its output.

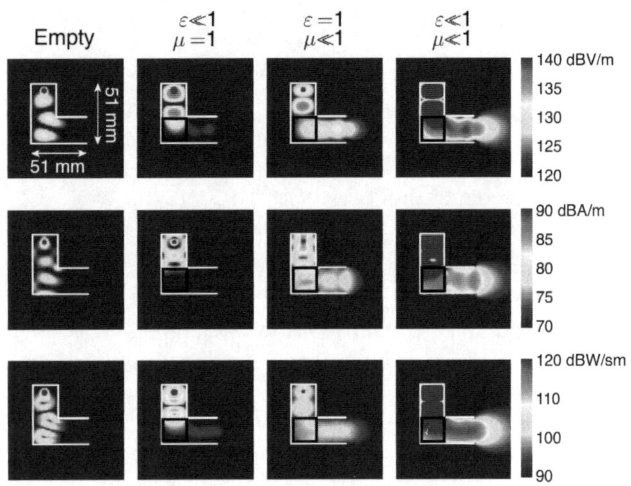

Fig. 1. Simulations involving a WR90-sized waveguide with a sharp corner. The overall cross-sectional size of the structure is 51×51 mm. One end of the waveguide is closed, while the other end is open. Excitation is a Hertzian dipole near the closed side. NZI cubes are used to improve the transmission.

Fig. 2 presents the results for a waveguide with three sharp corners. The overall cross section of the waveguide is 79×79 mm. We consider the electric field intensity and the magnetic field intensity at 11.5 GHz, 12.0 GHz, 12.5 GHz, and 13.0 GHz without any inner material and with an MNZ (0.1 permeability) that fills $3/5$ of the waveguide. Without any material, the transmission is weak at 11.5 GHz and 12.0 GHz, while relatively better levels of transmission with irregular magnetic-field distributions are observed at 12.5 GHz and 13.0 GHz. On the other hand, using MNZ, the transmission is improved at all frequencies. It is remarkable that a cavity is formed on the excitation side due to the wall of MNZ; but, the electromagnetic energy is still pumped into the MNZ due to its nonzero relative permeability of 0.1.

In conclusion, this study is devoted to computational simulations of three-dimensional composite structures involving NZI materials together with ordinary bodies, such as waveguides. Using a broadband implementation based on surface integral equations and MLFMA, accurate and efficient solutions can be obtained, without resorting to volume-based solvers.

ACKNOWLEDGEMENT

This work was supported by the Scientific and Technical Research Council of Turkey (TUBITAK) under the Research Grant 118E243 and by the Turkish Academy of Sciences (TUBA) in the framework of the Young Scientist Award Program.

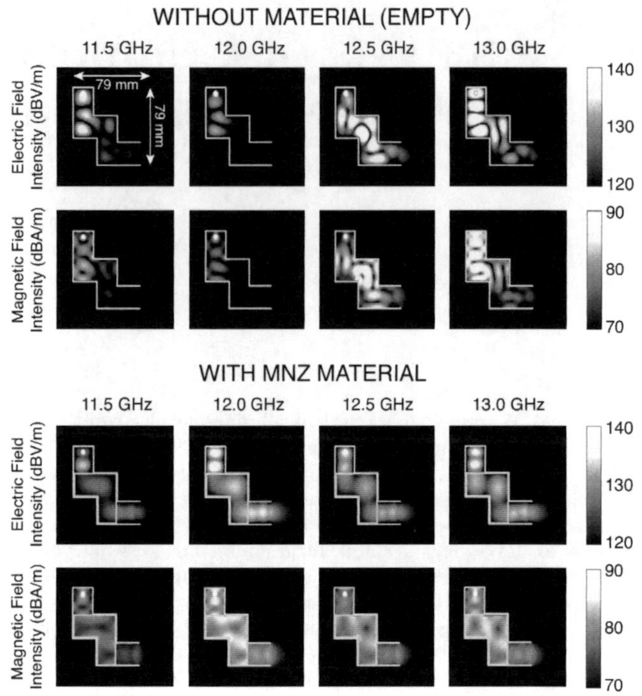

Fig. 2. Simulations involving a WR90-sized waveguide with three sharp corners. The overall cross-sectional size of the structure is 79×79 mm. One end of the waveguide is closed, while the other end is open. Excitation is a Hertzian dipole near the closed side. MNZ filling material is used to improve the transmission.

REFERENCES

[1] R. W. Ziolkowski, "Propagation in and scattering from a matched metamaterial having a zero index of refraction," Phys. Rev. E, vol. 70, no. 046608, Oct. 2004.

[2] M. Silveirinha and N. Engheta, "Tunneling of electromagnetic energy through subwavelength channels and bends using ϵ-near-zero materials," Phys. Rev. B, vol. 97, no. 157403, Oct. 2006.

[3] B. Edwards, et al., "Experimental verification of epsilon-near-zero metamaterial coupling and energy squeezing using a microwave waveguide," Phys. Rev. Lett., vol. 100, no. 033903, Jan. 2008.

[4] J. Luo and Y. Lai, "Anisotropic zero-index waveguide with arbitrary shapes," Sci. Rep., vol. 4, no. 5875, Jul. 2014.

[5] I. Liberal and N. Engheta, "Near-zero refractive index photonics," Nat. Photonics, vol. 11, pp. 149–158, Mar. 2017.

[6] I. V. Lindell, et al., "Realization of spherical D'B' boundary by a layer of wave-guiding medium," Metamaterials, vol. 5, no. 4, pp. 149–154, Dec. 2011.

[7] P. Ylä-Oijala, et al., "Surface and volume integral equation methods for time-harmonic solutions of Maxwells equations," Prog. Electromagn. Res., vol. 149, pp. 15–44, 2010.

[8] B. Karaosmanoğlu, A. Yılmaz, and Ö. Ergül, "A comparative study of surface integral equations for accurate and efficient analysis of plasmonic structures," IEEE Trans. Antennas Propag., vol. 65, no. 6, pp. 3049–3057, Jun. 2017.

[9] Ö. Ergül and B. Karaosmanoğlu, "Broadband multilevel fast multipole algorithm based on an approximate diagonalization of the Green's function," IEEE Trans. Antennas Propag., vol. 63, no. 7, pp. 3035–3041, Jul. 2015.

Efficient Iterative Solution of Dense and Complex Linear Systems with Multiple Right-hand Sides in Electromagnetic Scattering

Bruno Carpentieri[1], Özgür Ergül[2], Barışcan Karaosmanoğlu[2], Sehar Naveed[1], and Donglin Sun[3]

[1]*Free University of Bozen-Bolzano, Bolzano, 39100, Italy*

[2]*Middle East Technical University, Ankara, TR-06800, Turkey*

[3]*University of Electronic Science and Technology of China, Chengdu, Sichuan 611731, PR China*

Corresponding author: bruno.carpentieri@unibz.it

***Abstract*—The solution of large linear systems with multiple right-hand sides given simultaneously is required in many large-scale scientific and engineering applications modelled by either partial differential or boundary integral equations. In this paper we introduce variants of the block GMRES method that combine initial deflation and eigenvalue recycling strategies to remedy some typical convergence problems of block Krylov methods.**

I. Introduction

The Method of Moments discretization of boundary integral equations in electromagnetic scattering require the simultaneous solution of multiple right-hand sides linear systems of the form:

$$AX = B, \tag{1}$$

where $A \in \mathbb{C}^{n\times n}$ is a large dense nonsingular matrix of dimension n, $B = [b_1, b_2, \ldots, b_p] \in \mathbb{C}^{n\times p}$ is the right-hand side matrix, and $X \in \mathbb{C}^{n\times p}$ is the unknown solution matrix. This core computation often represents the most time-consuming task of the simulation, due to the large values of n and p in practical engineering applications. Block Krylov subspace methods can solve the whole sequence (1) at once by using only one Krylov subspace and performing cache-effective block operations. Although they lack the typical robustness of direct solution methods, their convergence performance can be significantly improved by transforming systems (1) into the equivalent linear system:

$$MAX = MB, \tag{2}$$

(or $AMY = B$, for $X = MY$). In (2), M is a nonsingular matrix close to A^{-1} in some sense, cheap to compute and to apply, called the preconditioner matrix.

Many of the preconditioners proposed in the literature succeed in clustering most of the eigenvalues of the preconditioned matrix MA far from the origin. However, they often tend to leave a few eigenvalues close to zero in the spectrum of MA, potentially slowing down the convergence of the iterative solver. Another practical difficulty in the robust implementation of block Krylov methods for solving multiple right-hand sides linear systems is to handle the approximate linear dependence of the block of right-hand sides that may slow down or even prevent the convergence. In this study, we propose a variant of the popular block Generalized Minimum Residual (BGMRES) method [1] that attempts to remedy these two computational problems by combining in the same Krylov subspace formulation for the first time eigenspace recycling and eigenvalue deflation.

II. The SPID-BGMRES Method

The BGMRES algorithm finds the minimal residual norm over block Krylov subspaces:

$$\mathbb{K}_m(A, R_0) = \text{blockspan}\left\{R_0, AR_0, \ldots, A^{m-1}R_0\right\}, \tag{3}$$

of increasing dimension m. To limit the memory costs due to the construction and representation of the Krylov basis, the method is typically restarted periodically after a given number of steps, as m increases, using the last computed approximation, at the price of slowing down the convergence to some extent. We propose a new spectrally preconditioned and initially deflated variant of the BGMRES method (shortly, SPID-BGMRES) that aims at accelerating the convergence of the standard restarted BGMRES method by gathering spectral information during the block Arnoldi process, and using this information to adapt an existing preconditioner M.

We denote by M the first-level preconditioner and let $\{\lambda_1, \ldots, \lambda_n\}$ be the set of eigenvalues of MA in any order. Let the columns of V_k be the basis of a right invariant subspace of MA of dimension k associated to the eigenvalues $\{\lambda_1, \ldots, \lambda_k\}$, that is $MAV_k = V_k J_k$ where the eigenvalues of J_k are $\{\lambda_1, \ldots, \lambda_k\}$. Finally, let $V_k^{\perp}$ be an orthogonal complement of V_k. Then we can write:

$$MAV = V\begin{pmatrix} J_k & E \\ 0 & F \end{pmatrix},$$

where $V = [V_k, V_k^{\perp}]$, the eigenvalues of J_k are $\{\lambda_1, \ldots, \lambda_k\}$ and those of F are $\{\lambda_{k+1}, \ldots, \lambda_n\}$.

In the same spirit of standard multigrid cycles, the first-level preconditioner M is used to define a smoother for a weighted stationary iterative method. After, say μ_1, pre-smoothing steps using the restriction operator $R = V_k^H$, we project the residual onto the coarse subspace and we solve the coarse space error equation defined by the projected matrix $A_c = V_k^H A V_k$. Finally, we project back the error to the original space using V_k and we smooth again the new approximation. The preconditioning operator M_{mul} has the following expression:

$$M_{mul} = A^{-1} - (I - \omega A)^{\mu_2}(I - M_c A)(I - \omega A)^{\mu_1} A^{-1}, \quad (4)$$

where $M_c = V_k(V_k^H A V_k)^{-1} V_k^H$ is the coarse grid correction. The following result can be established [2].

Proposition. *The preconditioner M_{mul} is such that the preconditioned matrix M_{mul} has eigenvalues:*

$$\begin{cases} \eta_i = 1 & \text{if} \quad i < k, \\ \eta_i = 1 - (1 - \omega\lambda_i)^{\mu_1+\mu_2} & \text{if} \quad i \geq k. \end{cases}$$

The result shows that, if M has the ability to cluster most of the eigenvalues close to one, possibly leaving relatively few outliers near zero, due to the choice of V_k the eigenvalues closest to the origin are shifted exactly to one and those that were grouped close to one get more clustered closer to this point after applying M_{mul}. Therefore, we can expect a significant reduction of the number of BGMRES iterations.

In SPID-BGMRES, the eigenvectors V_k's are approximated from the block Arnoldi process at low computational cost [2]. The spectrally preconditioned BGMRES method with eigenspace recycling presented earlier is combined with an initial deflation strategy to handle the case of the approximate linear dependence of the p right-hand sides [3].

III. Numerical Results

We illustrate the numerical behavior of the SPID-BGMRES method for solving multiple right-hand sides linear systems (1) arising from the boundary integral discretization of scattering problems in computational electromagnetics. The iterative solution was started from the initial guess $0 \in \mathbb{C}^{n\times p}$ and was terminated when;

$$\frac{\|B_m(:,s) - AX(:,s)\|_2}{\|B(:,s)\|_2} \leq tol, \quad s = 1,\dots,p,$$

or the number of iterations exceeded the value $maxiter$. The experiments were run under Ubuntu 18.04 and MATLAB version 2018a Intel(R) Xeon(R) CPU E5-26800 @2.70GHz. We set the maximum number of iterations $maxiter$ equal to 5000, the convergence tolerance tol equal to 10^{-6} and the maximum dimension m of the Krylov search space equal to 50. The coefficient matrix A was dense complex symmetric. The right-hand side has excitation at multiple frequencies and different illuminating directions. The first-level preconditioner M was a sparse approximation of A^{-1}.

Figs. 1-2 plots the convergence histories of the conventional BGMRES method versus the initially deflated variant (DBGMRES) and the SPID-BGMRES method on two selected boundary element problems. The benefits of the initial deflation strategy are evident. Eigenvector recycling can further help to reduce the number of iterations. Combination of the SPID-BGMRES method with acceleration techniques such as Multilevel Fast Multipole Method (MLFMA) for the (block) matrix-vector products is currently being investigated.

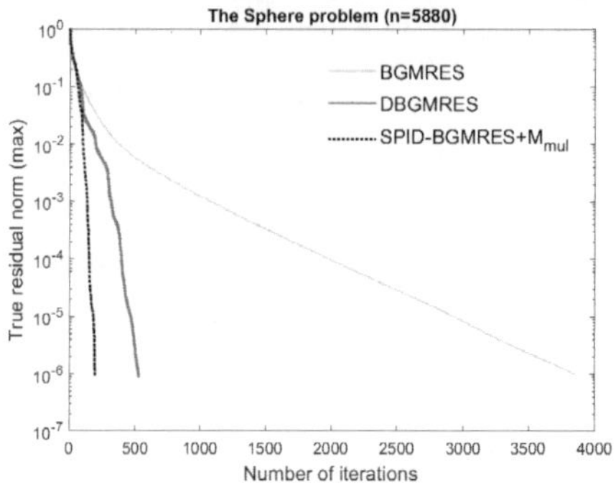

Fig. 1. Convergence histories of iterative solutions on the sphere problem ($n = 5880$). We used $p = 11$, $k = 10$, $\mu_1 = 2, \mu_2 = 1$, and restart=50. The integral equation model is EFIE (Electric Field Integral Equation).

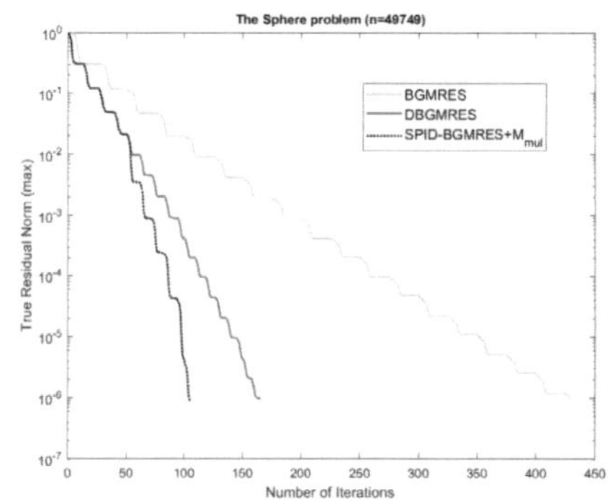

Fig. 2. Convergence histories of iterative solutions on the sphere problem ($n = 49749$). We used $p = 26$, $k = 10$, $\mu_1 = 2$, $\mu_2 = 1$ in M_{mul} and restart $= 50$. The integral equation model is CFIE (Combined Field Integral Equation). Block matrix-vector products are carried out using MLFMA.

IV. Conclusions

In this paper, novel variants of the BGMRES method were presented for the simultaneous solution of sequences of linear systems with multiple right-hand sides. The proposed spectrally preconditioned and initially deflated BGMRES algorithm can outperform the conventional BGMRES method. To the best of our knowledge, our method is the first block Krylov solver that can combine initial deflation with eigenspace recycling.

References

[1] Y. Saad, Iterative Methods for Sparse Linear Systems. vol. 82, SIAM, 2003.

[2] D.-L. Sun, B. Carpentieri, T.-Z. Huang, and Y.-F. Jing, "A spectrally preconditioned and initially deflated variant of the restarted block GMRES method for solving multiple right-hand sides linear systems," International Journal of Mechanical Sciences 144, 775-787, 2018.

[3] H. Calandra, S. Gratton, R. Lago, X. Pinel, and X. Vasseur, "Two-level preconditioned Krylov subspace methods for the solution of three-dimensional heterogeneous Helmholtz problems in seismics," Numerical Analysis and Applications 5, no. 2, 175-181, 2012.

Tensor Decompositions for Reducing the Memory Requirement of Translation Operator Tensors in FMM-FFT Accelerated IE Solvers

Cheng Qian, Zhuotong Chen, and Abdulkadir C. Yucel
School of Electrical and Electronic Engineering
Nanyang Technological University
Singapore, 639798
cqian@ntu.edu.sg, chenz313@myumanitoba.ca, acyucel@ntu.edu.sg

***Abstract*—Tensor decompositions are applied to lessen the memory requirements of translation operator tensors in fast multipole method-fast Fourier transform (FMM-FFT) accelerated integral equation (IE) solvers. In particular, methodologies leveraging Tucker and tensor train (TT) decompositions are developed to compress the three-dimensional (3D) arrays and four-dimensional (4D) array storing the *FFT'ed* translation operator values. Preliminary results show the achieved memory reduction as well as imposed computational overhead via the developed methodologies.**

Keywords—Fast Fourier transform, fast multipole method, memory reduction, translation operator, tensor decompositions, tensor train, Tucker decomposition.

I. INTRODUCTION

The FMM-FFT accelerated IE solvers permit efficient and accurate characterization of electromagnetic (EM) phenomena on electrically large and complex platforms [1-4]. For many practical scenarios, these solvers' applicability is limited by their memory requirement. One of the primary data structures limiting their applicability is the tensors holding the *FFT'ed* translation operator values on a structured grid. Recently, Tucker decompositions (a.k.a. high-order singular value decompositions) were proposed to lessen the memory requirement of *FFT'ed* translation operator tensors [5, 6]. These decompositions achieved more than 90% memory reduction in the memory requirement of these tensors and required negligible computational overhead. Such decompositions were recently used to reduce the memory requirement of *FFT'ed* system tensors arising in volume IE simulators as well [7, 8].

In [5], the memory reduction, computational overhead, and accuracy (i.e., performance metrics) of Tucker decompositions are investigated for compressing the *FFT'ed* translation operator tensors computed at each plane-wave direction and generated for different structure and FMM box sizes. That said, a detailed performance analysis is missing for the *FFT'ed* translation operator tensors generated for different wavenumbers and FMM accuracies. Furthermore, the performance of other decompositions for reducing the memory requirement of *FFT'ed* translation operator tensors is not analyzed so far. Moreover, the performance of neither Tucker nor other decompositions is demonstrated for compressing the 4D array holding the *FFT'ed* translation operator values on a structured grid for all plane-wave directions.

This study aims to fill the abovementioned gaps in the application of tensor decompositions to the compression of *FFT'ed* translation operator tensors. To this end, methodologies leveraging the Tucker and TT decompositions are developed for compressing 3D arrays storing the *FFT'ed* translation operator tensors for each plane-wave direction as well as 4D array storing the *FFT'ed* translation operator values for all plane-wave directions. During the setup stage of solvers, the Tucker and TT-based methodologies for compressing 3D arrays and 4D array, called Tucker-3D, TT-3D, Tucker-4D and TT-4D, respectively, are used to obtain compressed tensors efficiently via cross-based approximations [8, 9] for given tolerance. During the iterative solution stage of the solvers, the compressed tensors are *fully* or *partially* restored to obtain the *FFT'ed* translation operator tensor for each plane-wave direction. Then the restored tensor is used to perform the convolution for each plane-wave direction via 3D FFTs. Due to limited space, here we provide the general idea of methodologies and preliminary results. Details of the developed methodologies as well as their performances with respect to different parameters will be provided in the talk.

II. FORMULATION

In FMM-FFT acceleration scheme, a hypothetical box enclosing the structure is divided into N_x, N_y, and N_z small boxes along principle axes. The boxes are centered on a uniform 3D grid points and labeled by $B_{\mathbf{u}}$ with $\mathbf{u}=(u_x,u_y,u_z)$, $u_x=1,\ldots,N_x, u_y=1,\ldots,N_y, u_z=1,\ldots,N_z$. In this scheme, while the interactions between basis functions in adjacent boxes are computed classically, those in the remaining boxes are accounted for as follows. First, the basis functions' far-field patterns along a plane-wave direction $\hat{\mathbf{k}}_i$, $i=1,\ldots,N_{\text{dir}}$, are summed for each box and stored in aggregation tensor $\mathcal{F}_{\mathbf{u}}(\hat{\mathbf{k}}_i)$. Next, $\mathcal{F}_{\mathbf{u}}(\hat{\mathbf{k}}_i)$ is convolved with *FFT'ed* translation operator tensor $\mathcal{T}_{\mathbf{u}'-\mathbf{u}}(\hat{\mathbf{k}}_i)$ via 3D FFT operations. Finally, the plane-wave spectra for $\hat{\mathbf{k}}_i$ obtained as the result of convolution is projected onto the basis functions. The same procedure is applied for all N_{dir} directions and the far-field contribution to the matrix-vector multiplication is computed; here N_{dir} is a function of FMM accuracy, box size, and wavenumber [6].

$\mathcal{T}_{\mathbf{u}'-\mathbf{u}}(\hat{\mathbf{k}}_i)$ with dimensions $2N_x \times 2N_y \times 2N_z$ is computed and stored during setup stage of the solvers. The memory requirement of $\mathcal{T}_{\mathbf{u}'-\mathbf{u}}(\hat{\mathbf{k}}_i)$ for each $\hat{\mathbf{k}}_i$ can be significantly lowered by applying Tucker or TT decompositions as

$$\mathcal{T}_{\mathbf{u}'-\mathbf{u}} \approx \mathcal{C}_{\text{Tucker}} \times_1 \bar{\mathbf{U}}^1_{\text{Tucker}} \times_2 \bar{\mathbf{U}}^2_{\text{Tucker}} \times_3 \bar{\mathbf{U}}^3_{\text{Tucker}}, \quad (1)$$

$$\mathcal{T}_{\mathbf{u}'-\mathbf{u}} \approx \mathcal{C}_{\text{TT}} \times_1 \bar{\mathbf{U}}^1_{\text{TT}} \times_3 \bar{\mathbf{U}}^3_{\text{TT}}. \quad (2)$$

Here $\times_j$, $j=1,\ldots,3$, denotes the mode$-j$ matrix product of a tensor. The 3D array $\mathcal{C}$ and matrix $\bar{\mathbf{U}}^j$ along mode $-j$, pertinent to Tucker or TT decompositions (as indicated at the subscripts), can be efficiently obtained for a given tolerance by utilizing the cross approximation [8] and AMEN-cross approximation [9], respectively. Likewise, $\mathcal{T}_{\mathbf{u}'-\mathbf{u}}(\hat{\mathbf{k}}_i)$ for all $\hat{\mathbf{k}}_i$, $i=1,\ldots,N_{\text{dir}}$, constitutes a 4D array, $\mathcal{T}_{\text{4D}}$, with dimensions $2N_x \times 2N_y \times 2N_z \times N_{\text{dir}}$, which can be compressed via Tucker or TT decompositions as

$$\mathcal{T}_{\text{4D}} \approx \mathcal{C}_{\text{Tucker}} \times_1 \bar{\mathbf{U}}^1_{\text{Tucker}} \times_2 \bar{\mathbf{U}}^2_{\text{Tucker}} \times_3 \bar{\mathbf{U}}^3_{\text{Tucker}} \times_4 \bar{\mathbf{U}}^4_{\text{Tucker}}, \quad (3)$$

$$\mathcal{T}_{\text{4D}} \approx (\mathcal{C}_{\text{TT1}} \times_1 \bar{\mathbf{U}}^1_{\text{TT}}) \times^1_3 (\mathcal{C}_{\text{TT2}} \times_3 \bar{\mathbf{U}}^3_{\text{TT}}). \quad (4)$$

Here ($\mathbf{A} \times^k_j \mathbf{B}$) represents the tensor contraction along mode $-j$ in $\mathbf{A}$ and mode $-k$ in $\mathbf{B}$. By effectively performing matrix-tensor products, the compressed tensor can be *fully* or *partially* restored to obtain the *FFT'ed* translation operator tensor for each plane-wave direction, during the iterative solution stage.

III. Numerical Result

In this section, EM scattering analysis of a perfect electric conductor sphere with unit radius is considered for comparing the performances of developed methodologies. The analysis is performed at 2.39 GHz and 4.79 GHz, at which the diameter of sphere becomes 16λ and 32 λ, respectively, where λ denotes the wavelength. For the analysis at these frequencies, once the FMM box size and accuracy are set to 0.5λ and 5 digits, there exist 435 *FFT'ed* translation operator tensors with dimensions 64×64×64 and 128×128×128, respectively ($N_{\text{dir}} = 435$). While Tucker-3D and TT-3D methodologies compress each $\mathcal{T}_{\mathbf{u}'-\mathbf{u}}(\hat{\mathbf{k}}_i)$ for each $\hat{\mathbf{k}}_i$ separately, Tucker-4D and TT-4D methodologies compress $\mathcal{T}_{\text{4D}}$. In Fig.1, we plot the memory reductions achieved by these methodologies versus the relative error in the tensors restored after applying the decompositions. Clearly, TT-4D performs the best when very high accuracy (more than 10^{-6}) is needed. Both Tucker-4D and TT-4D methodologies yield higher memory savings compared to the Tucker-3D and TT-3D methodologies.

For the analysis at 4.79 GHz and relative error 10^{-6}, the TT-4D and Tucker-4D methodologies reduced the memory of original *FFT'ed* translation operator tensors from 13,920 MB to 473 MB and 541 MB, achieving 96.60% and 96.12% memory reduction, respectively. On the other hand, Tucker-3D reduced it to 1,007 MB, which is twice the total memory of compressed tensors obtained in TT-4D methodology. Moreover, TT-3D reduced it to 1,794 MB, corresponding to 87.11% memory reduction. For the same analysis, the computational overhead introduced by methodologies is computed by taking the ratio of the time required to restore one *FFT'ed* translation operator to the convolution time. While this ratio is 0.34 and 0.40 for TT-3D and Tucker-3D, that is 2.26 and 1.5 for TT-4D and Tucker-4D, respectively.

IV. Conclusion

The Tucker and TT-based methodologies are developed to reduce the memory requirement of *FFT'ed* translation operator tensors in FMM-FFT accelerated IE solvers. Preliminary results demonstrate the achieved memory saving and required computational overhead of the developed methodologies.

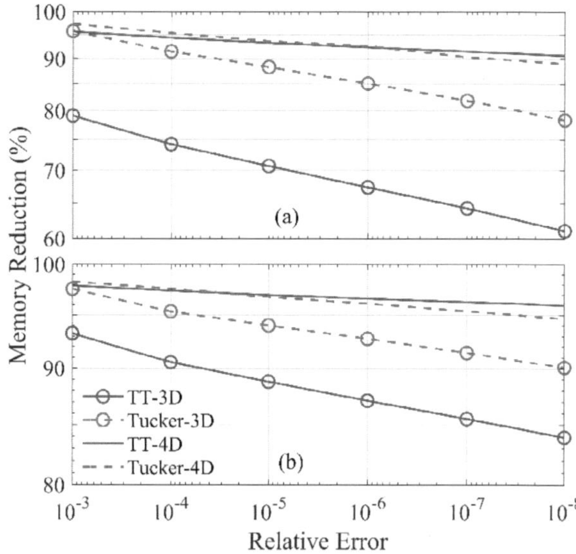

Fig. 1. The memory reduction w.r.t. the relative error when the dimensions of translation operator tensors are (a) 64×64×64 and (b) 128×128×128.

References

[1] R. L. Wagner, S. Jiming, and W. C. Chew, "Monte Carlo simulation of electromagnetic scattering from two-dimensional random rough surfaces," *IEEE Trans. Antennas Propag.*, vol. 45, no. 2, pp. 235–245, 1997.

[2] J. M. Taboada et al., "High scalability FMM-FFT electromagnetic solver for supercomputer systems," *IEEE Antennas Propag. Mag.*, vol. 51, no. 6, pp. 20–28, 2009.

[3] M. Vikram and B. Shanker, "An incomplete review of fast multipole methods-from static to wideband-as applied to problems in computational electromagnetics," *Appl. Computat. Electromagn. Society J.*, vol. 24, no. 2, pp. 79-108, 2009.

[4] A.C. Yucel et al., "An FFT-accelerated inductance extractor for voxelized structures," *2018 International ACES*, Denver, CO, pp. 1-2, 2018.

[5] A. C. Yucel, L. J. Gomez, and E. Michielssen, "Compression of translation operator tensors in FMM-FFT-accelerated SIE solvers via Tucker decomposition," *IEEE Antennas Wireless Propag. Lett.*, vol. 16, pp. 2667-2670, 2017.

[6] A. C. Yucel et al., "An FMM-FFT accelerated SIE simulator for analyzing EM wave propagation in mine enviroments loaded with conductors," *IEEE J. Multiscale and Multiphys. Comput. Techn.*, vol. 3, pp. 3-15, 2018.

[7] A. G. Polimeridis and J. K. White, "On the compression of system tensors arising in FFT-VIE solvers," in *Proc. IEEE Antennas Propag. Soc. Int. Symp.*, pp. 2144–2145, 2014.

[8] I. I. Giannakopoulos, M. S. Litsarev, and A. G. Polimeridis, "Memory footprint reduction for the FFT-based volume integral equation method via tensor decompositions," arXiv:1811.00484, 2018.

[9] M. V. Rakhuba and I. V. Oseledets, "Fast multidimensional convolution in low-rank tensor formats via cross approximation," *SIAM J. Sci. Comput.*, vol. 37, no. 2, pp. A565-A582, 2015.

Computational Analysis of Nanoantenna Arrays for Nanoparticle Detection

Göktuğ Işıklar and Özgür Ergül
Department of Electrical and Electronics Engineering
Middle East Technical University
Ankara, Turkey
ozergul@metu.edu.tr

***Abstract*—We present computational analysis of nanoantenna arrays when they are used to detect and identify nearby nanoparticles. Solutions of frequency-domain scattering problems are performed by using a surface-integral-equation formulation that is suitable for composite structures involving metallic, dielectric, magnetic, and/or plasmonic objects. Acceleration is further achieved via the multilevel fast multipole algorithm that is developed for composite structures. Numerical results demonstrate the feasibility of particle detection and identification, even with sparse arrays with relatively large periodicities.**

I. Introduction

Strong electromagnetic responses of nanoantennas at optical frequencies make them suitable for a plethora of applications, such as bio-sensing [1], nano-optical imaging [2], nano-optical power links [3], and optical energy harvesting [4], [5]. Array arrangements of nanoparticles, such as nano-cubes, can provide further ability to control radiation [6]. As shown in this contribution, such nanoantenna arrays can also be excellent tools for nanoparticle detection. For this purpose, however, nanoantenna geometries and array parameters must be designed carefully. This becomes possible by using a fast and efficient computational solver that enables rigorous simulations of three-dimensional structures involving nanoarrays and nanoparticles. In this study, we present a computational study of nanoantenna arrays for the detection of nearby nanoparticles. An implementation based on surface integral equations and the multilevel fast multipole algorithm (MLFMA) is used for numerical solutions. Initial results demonstrate the capabilities of nanoarrays for both particle detection and identification.

II. Implementation of the Solver

Simulations are carried out in the frequency domain assuming time-harmonic sources. The considered problems involve nanoarrays and nanoparticles that typically have different electrical parameters. Surfaces are discretized by using triangles, while equivalent electric and magnetic currents are expanded with the Rao-Wilton-Glisson functions. Scattering problems are formulated by using a modified combined tangential formulation [7], which has been extended to composite (multi-region) scenarios in this study. Electrical parameters of silver (Ag), which is the main material for nanoantennas, are extracted from tabulated data available in the literature. Specifically, at optical frequencies, Ag has complex permittivity values with negative real parts, as well as imaginary parts to account for ohmic losses. The considered nanoparticles are also modelled as penetrable, and typically as dielectrics that are generally difficult to detect in comparison to metallic particles. MLFMA is used with different tree structures in different regions, i.e., the host medium (vacuum), inside particles (dielectric), and inside nanoantennas (plasmonic). In plasmonic regions, MLFMA interactions are truncated whenever possible without sacrificing the accuracy [8].

III. Numerical Examples

As an example, we consider an arrangement of 3×3 Ag bowtie nanoantennas, which can be a part of a larger array, as depicted in Fig. 1. The size of a single nanoantenna is $214 \times 100 \times 20$ nm, while the gap width is 14 nm. With these dimensions and the material (Ag), nanoantennas are active with high enhancement factors in the 400–500 THz range. In the following results, the frequency is fixed to 450 THz. The center-to-center distance is set to 475 nm, which is larger than $\lambda/2$, where λ is the wavelength. As also illustrated in Fig. 1, we consider dielectric particles with different shapes, i.e., sphere, cube, cylinder, as well as cones with two different orientations, which are symmetrically located above the array. All particles fit into $300 \times 300 \times 300$ nm volumes, while they are 50 nm away from nanoantenna surfaces. In the results presented below, the relative permittivity of the particles is selected as 8.0, while they are assumed to be non-magnetic. The overall structures (array and particles) are illuminated by a 1 V/m linearly polarized plane wave from the top.

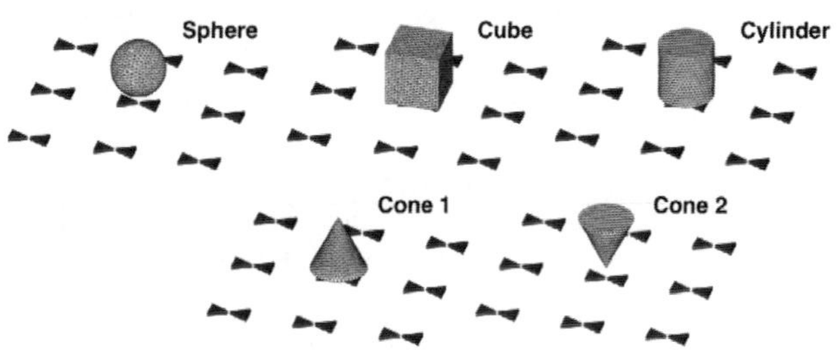

Fig. 1. Dielectric particles with different shapes located above an array of 3×3 nanoantennas.

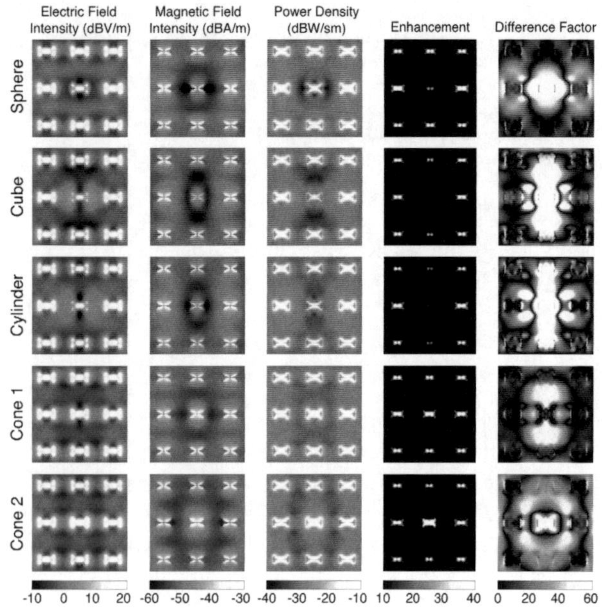

Fig. 2. Intensity, density, enhancement, and difference factor distributions on the $z = -20$ nm plane.

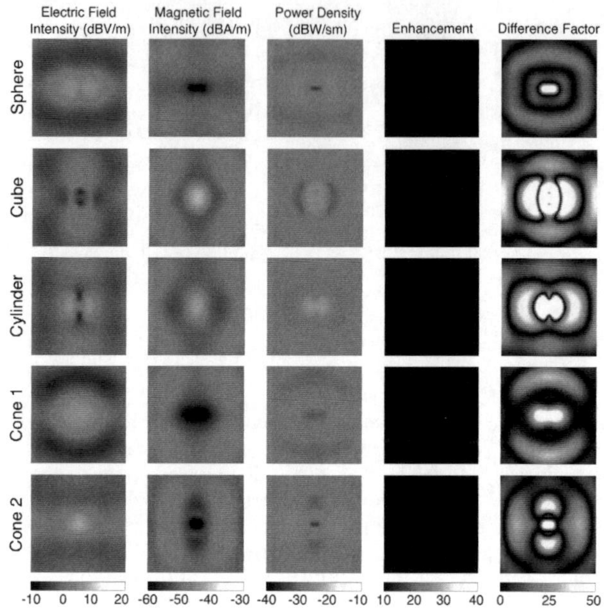

Fig. 3. Intensity, density, enhancement, and difference factor distributions on the $z = 400$ nm plane.

Figs. 2 and 3 present the electric field intensity ($[-10, 20]$ dBV/m), the magnetic field intensity ($[-60, -30]$ dBA/m), the power density ($[-40, -10]$ dBW/sm), as well as the power enhancement (unitless) and the difference factor (unitless), at two different planes, i.e., at $z = -20$ nm (below the array) and $z = 400$ nm (above the array), respectively, assuming that the array is located on the x-y plane symmetrically from $z = -10$ nm (bottom surfaces) to $z = 10$ nm (top surfaces). The enhancement factor is computed as usual, by normalizing the power density with the incident power density of approximately -25.8 dBW/sm. As shown in Fig. 2, particles introduce perturbations in field and density distributions, while their effects are mainly visible as shadowing in the enhancement factor distributions. Nevertheless, even for relatively large sizes of the particles, it can be difficult to detect and identify them via field, density, and enhancement characteristics. Therefore, we further compute the difference factor as $\mathrm{DF}(\boldsymbol{r}) = 100 \times |e_{\text{array}}(\boldsymbol{r}) - e_{\text{array+particle}}(\boldsymbol{r})|/e_{\text{array}}(\boldsymbol{r})$ as a function of position $\boldsymbol{r}$, where $e_{\text{array}}(\boldsymbol{r})$ represents enhancement factor values obtained with only the excited nanoantenna array and $e_{\text{array+particle}}(\boldsymbol{r})$ represents the corresponding values when particles exist. It can be observed in the fifth column of Fig. 2 that particles lead diverse difference factors, making them distinguishable from each other. The results are more remarkable in Fig. 3, where the sample plane is at 400 nm such that field, density, and enhancement plots are quite uniform, while the position-dependent difference factor makes it possible to identify the shape of the particles. We note that, depending on the application, sampling far away above the array (e.g., at 400 nm) may be more practical and feasible than sampling close to the array (e.g., at -20 nm).

To sum up, as shown in the numerical examples, nanoantenna arrays can be very suitable to detect and identify nearby particles. This can be useful in many applications, particularly for bio-sensing and imaging. In order to distinguish particles, we define a difference factor, considering that positions of nanoparticles can be controlled in measurement setups. Estimation of particle shapes from difference factor distributions is under investigation.

ACKNOWLEDGEMENT

This work was supported by the Scientific and Technical Research Council of Turkey (TUBITAK) under the Research Grant 118E243 and by the Turkish Academy of Sciences (TUBA) in the framework of the Young Scientist Award Program.

REFERENCES

[1] M. Alavirad, L. Roy, and P. Berini, "Optimization of plasmonic nanodipole antenna arrays for sensing applications," IEEE J. Sel. Top. Quantum Electron., vol. 20, no. 3, May/June 2014.

[2] E. G. Mironov, et al., "Enhancing weak optical signals using a plasmonic Yagi-Uda nanoantenna array," IEEE Photon. Technol. Lett., vol. 26, no. 22, pp. 2236–2239, Aug. 2014.

[3] D. M. Solis, et al., "Optimization of an optical wireless nanolink using directive nanoantennas," Opt. Exp., vol. 21, no. 2, pp. 2369–2377, Jan. 2013.

[4] Y. M. El-Toukhy, et al., "Optimized tapered dipole nanoantenna as efficient energy harvester," Opt. Exp., vol. 24, no. 14, pp. 1107–1122, Jul. 2016.

[5] U. M. Gür, et al., "Computational demonstration of multiband nanoantennas for power enhancement," in Proc. IEEE Antennas and Propagation Soc. Int. Symp., 2017, pp. 135–136.

[6] A. Altınoklu and Ö. Ergül, "Computational analysis and full-wave optimizations of nanoantenna arrays for desired scattering and radiation characteristics," in Proc. URSI General Assembly and Scientific Symp. (URSI-GASS), 2017.

[7] B. Karaosmanoğlu, A. Yılmaz, and Ö. Ergül, "A comparative study of surface integral equations for accurate and efficient analysis of plasmonic structures," IEEE Trans. Antennas Propag., vol. 65, no. 6, pp. 3049–3057, Jun. 2017.

[8] B. Karaosmanoğlu, et al., "Solutions of plasmonic structures using the multilevel fast multipole algorithm," Int. J. RF Microwave Comput.-Aided. Eng., vol. 26, no. 4, pp. 335–341, May 2016.

Platform-Aware In-Situ Antenna and Metamaterial Analysis and Design

Shu Wang, Brian MacKie-Mason, and Zhen Peng
Electrical and Computer Engineering Department, University of New Mexico, Albuquerque, U.S.A.
shuwang12@unm.edu, brimacki@unm.edu, pengz@unm.edu

Abstract—**The objective of this paper is to build a reconfigurable, reusable, and parallel model reduction platform towards transformative in-situ antenna design. The key idea is to introduce a separable and compressible platform Green's function in an up-front offline computation. Once obtained, the online computational complexity does not depend on the size of the in-situ platform. As a result, in-situ design and optimization of multi-antenna systems can be performed at the same cost as the free-space radiation. The advancements make high-fidelity in-situ antenna design orders of magnitude faster.**

Index Terms—**antenna, domain decomposition, Green's function, integral equation, model reduction.**

I. Overview

Modern military and commercial EM systems are routinely equipped with multiple antennas serving for radar and wireless communications. The computational electromagnetics (CEM) has emerged as a powerful and indispensable tool to evaluate the in-situ performance and co-site interference. These simulations are enabled by fast and rigorous numerical solutions of Maxwell's Equations as well as rapid advances in high-performance computing (HPC) systems. On present-day HPC clusters, the in-situ antenna performance on high-fidelity platforms of electrical length of the order of 1000 wavelengths can be analyzed within a couple of hours [1].

Nevertheless, the CEM based in-situ antenna design goes beyond just performing a single simulation. It often needs to perform a number of simulations in order to navigate highly complex design spaces. Each simulation should complete within at most a few minutes even a few seconds in an industrial design environment. Clearly, fundamental research into innovative mathematics and algorithms are required.

The aim of the paper is to address this pressing and challenging engineering need. For many in-situ antenna design and parameter studies, it is typical that those antennas are only allowed to be mounted on certain parts of the platform. Namely, the computational domain can be decomposed into large fixed parts and small portions involving the antenna design. The observation inspires us to investigate a highly efficient, reduced order in-situ antenna analysis framework.

Key ingredients are summarized as follows: **(1)** The discontinuous Galerkin (DG) boundary element (BE) method [2] and geometry-aware domain decomposition (DD) method [3] are employed to facilitate a modular design-oriented decomposition. **(2)** A novel platform Green's function (PGF) is introduced on the outer surface of those antennas. The PGF is calculated once in the offline phase to characterize the coupling with large, fixed platform. It can be reused for all future in-situ computation. **(3)** In the online phase, rapid solution for multi-query antenna design needs is achieved by a Schwarz DD solver of the reduced order system. The computational costs are the same as the free-space radiation.

II. Methodology

A. Problem decomposition

Consider the in-situ analysis of two antennas on the high-definition platform, as illustrated in Fig. 1. The problem can be decomposed into three sub-regions: sub-regions Ω_1 and Ω_2 contain two antennas, sub-region Ω_3 is electrically large PEC platform. We have used cubical surfaces, Γ_{31} and Γ_{32}, to facilitate the decomposition. The size of the surfaces is determined by the prescribed surface area where the antennas are allowed to be mounted.

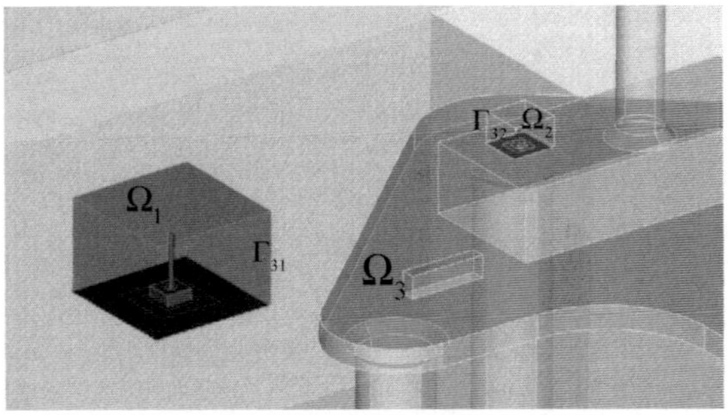

Fig. 1. DD based model reduction for in-situ antenna analysis.

The finite element (FE) method is used to discretized the volume domain of Ω_1 and Ω_2, and the DG boundary element method is applied to the exterior surface of Ω_1 and Ω_2 and platform Ω_3. The resulting system matrix can be written as:

$$\begin{bmatrix} \begin{bmatrix} \mathcal{A}_1^{\rm FE} & \mathcal{N}_1 \\ \mathcal{N}_1^T & \mathbf{A}_1^{\rm BE} \end{bmatrix} & \mathbf{C}_{12}^{\rm BE} & \mathbf{C}_{13}^{\rm BE} \\ \mathbf{C}_{21}^{\rm BE} & \begin{bmatrix} \mathcal{A}_2^{\rm FE} & \mathcal{N}_2 \\ \mathcal{N}_2^T & \mathbf{A}_2^{\rm BE} \end{bmatrix} & \mathbf{C}_{23}^{\rm BE} \\ \mathbf{C}_{31}^{\rm BE} & \mathbf{C}_{32}^{\rm BE} & \mathbf{A}_3^{\rm BI} \end{bmatrix}. \qquad (1)$$

The resulting sub-domain FE matrices, $\mathcal{A}_m^{\rm FE}$, m =1,2, have complex nonlinear dependency on a few design parameters (ϵ_m, μ_m, $\mathbf{r}_m$, etc.). The sub-domain BE matrices $\mathrm{A}_m^{\rm BE}$, m =1,2,3, and coupling matrices $\mathbf{C}_{mn}^{\rm BE}$ are resulting from free-space Green's function, and has no parametric dependency.

Evidently, the above non-overlapping and non-conforming DG and DD methods lead to a modular design-oriented decomposition. The modification of antenna types, parameters, locations in the design stage is reflected in local and sparse FE matrices, which are decoupled from exterior BE matrices. Nevertheless, every time antenna design is modified, we still need to solve the entire system matrix. That is where the platform Green's function comes into play.

B. Platform Green's function

The PGF is evaluated on the artificial surfaces, $\Gamma_3 = \Gamma_{31} \cup \Gamma_{32}$, in the offline computing phase. Once calculated, the large fixed platform is rigorously represented by the PGF. The direct calculation of the PGF matrix requires the solution of the large platform Ω_3 with respect to individual unit source currents on Γ_3. Recognizing the coupling between antennas and platform is considerably low-rank, we proposed a novel alternating and random interpolative decomposition (AR-ID) to select the skeleton source currents from the original ones on the exterior surface Γ_3. The AR-ID calculation can be achieved locally per antenna sub-system and embarrassingly in parallel. The reduced model of in-situ antenna system can be written as:

$$\begin{bmatrix} \begin{bmatrix} \mathcal{A}_1^{\mathrm{FE}} & \mathcal{N}_1 \\ \mathcal{N}_1^T & \tilde{\mathbf{A}}_1^{\mathrm{BE}} \end{bmatrix} & \begin{matrix} & \\ & \tilde{\mathbf{C}}_{12}^{\mathrm{BE}} \end{matrix} \\ \begin{matrix} & \\ & \tilde{\mathbf{C}}_{21}^{\mathrm{BE}} \end{matrix} & \begin{bmatrix} \mathcal{A}_2^{\mathrm{FE}} & \mathcal{N}_2 \\ \mathcal{N}_2^T & \tilde{\mathbf{A}}_2^{\mathrm{BE}} \end{bmatrix} \end{bmatrix} \begin{bmatrix} \mathbf{x}_1^{\mathrm{FE}} \\ \mathbf{x}_1^{\mathrm{BE}} \\ \mathbf{x}_2^{\mathrm{FE}} \\ \mathbf{x}_2^{\mathrm{BE}} \end{bmatrix} = \begin{bmatrix} \mathbf{b}_1^{\mathrm{FE}} \\ 0 \\ \mathbf{b}_2^{\mathrm{FE}} \\ 0 \end{bmatrix}. \quad (2)$$

The updated BE matrices consist of the free-space GF matrices and the AR-ID representation of PGF matrices:

$$\tilde{\mathbf{A}}_1^{\mathrm{BE}} = \mathbf{A}_1^{\mathrm{BE}} - \mathbf{R}_{13}^{\mathrm{n}_1\times\mathrm{k}_1} \cdot \mathbf{S}_{11}^{\mathrm{k}_1\times\mathrm{k}_1} \cdot \mathbf{R}_{31}^{\mathrm{k}_1\times\mathrm{n}_1}, \quad (3)$$

$$\tilde{\mathbf{C}}_{12}^{\mathrm{BE}} = \mathbf{C}_{12}^{\mathrm{BE}} - \underbrace{\mathbf{R}_{13}^{\mathrm{n}_1\times\mathrm{k}_1} \cdot \mathbf{S}_{12}^{\mathrm{k}_1\times\mathrm{k}_2} \cdot \mathbf{R}_{32}^{\mathrm{k}_2\times\mathrm{n}_2}}_{\text{Platform GF matrix}}, \quad (4)$$

where $\mathbf{S}_{\mathrm{mn}}^{\mathrm{k_m}\times\mathrm{k_n}} = \mathbf{B}_{\mathrm{m3}}^{\mathrm{k_m}\times\mathrm{n}_3} \cdot \left[\mathbf{A}_3^{\mathrm{BE}}\right]^{-1} \cdot \mathbf{B}_{\mathrm{3n}}^{\mathrm{n}_3\times\mathrm{k_n}}$. The n_1, n_2, n_3 are the number of BE unknowns on antennas and platform. The k_1 and k_2 are skeleton BE unknowns.

During the design stage (online computing), (2) is solved by Krylov iterative methods with an additive Schwarz preconditioner [1]. We remark that the online computing complexity does not depend on the size of the in-situ platform. As a result, in-situ design and optimization of multi-antenna systems can be performed at the same cost as the free-space radiation.

III. Illustration

We consider a metasurface antenna [4] mounted on the top surface of a PEC platform, as shown in Fig. 2. In the offline calculation, we first generate separate BE meshes on the exterior surface of antenna and the platform. The PGF matrix is then constructed and assembled in the AR-ID representation as in (3). We note that the PGF matrix is introduced to characterize the coupling with the platform only, and separately compressed with the free-space GF matrix. Thereby, the rank of the PGF matrix is extremely low, as the skeleton BE unknowns in Fig. 3(b), and the free-space GF matrix can still be compressed with the fast multipole method. In the online phase, we generate the volume meshes for different antennas independently. The FE matrices are combined with the same GF matrices in (3). The in-situ radiation patterns are shown in Fig. 4.

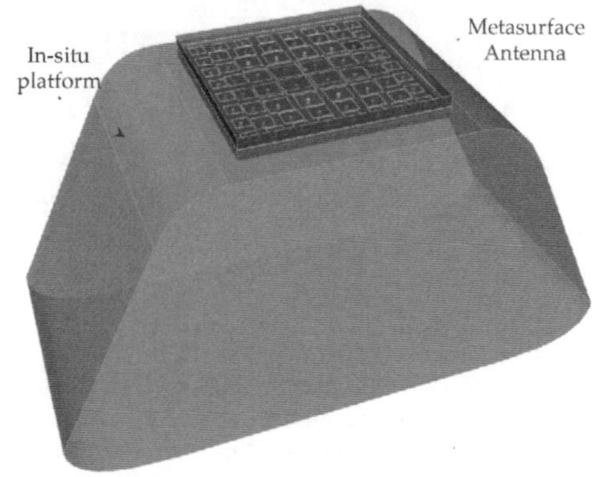

Fig. 2. Example of a metasurface antenna on PEC platform.

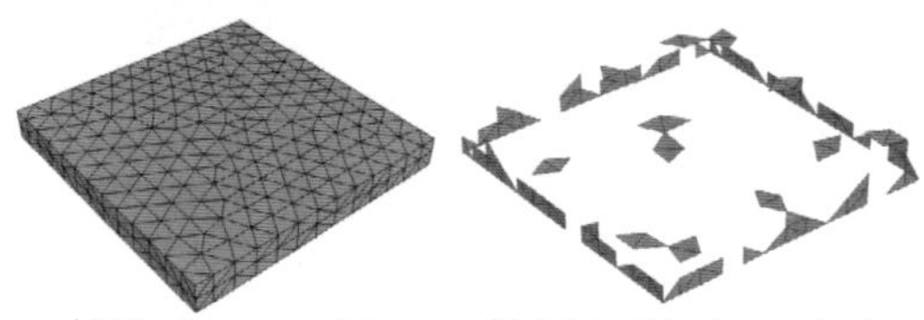

(a) BE unknowns: n = 859 (b) skeleton BE unknowns: k = 42

Fig. 3. Illustration of a data-sparse representation of PGF.

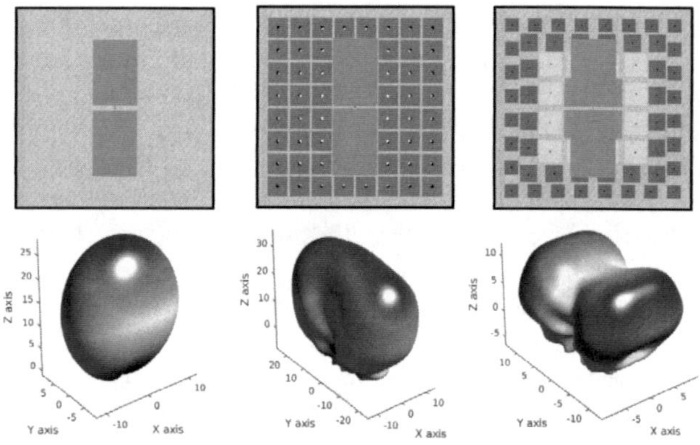

(a) Patch antenna (b) Patch antenna with uniform EBG (c) Patch antenna with NUA EBG

Fig. 4. Radiation pattern of in-situ antennas at 550MHz.

References

[1] B. MacKie-Mason, Y. Shao, A. Greenwood, and Z. Peng, "Supercomputing-enabled first-principles analysis of radio wave propagation in urban environments," IEEE Trans. Antennas and Propagation, vol. 66, no. 12, pp. 6606-6617, Dec. 2018.

[2] Z. Peng, R. Hiptmair, Y. Shao, and B. MacKie-Mason, "Domain decomposition preconditioning for surface integral equations in solving challenging electromagnetic scattering problems," IEEE Trans. Antennas and Propagation, vol. 64, pp. 210-223, Jan. 2016.

[3] H. Gao, Z. Peng and X. Sheng, "A geometry-aware domain decomposition preconditioning for hybrid finite element-boundary integral method," IEEE Trans. Antennas and Propagation, vol. 65, no. 4, pp. 1875-1885, Apr. 2017.

[4] N. Chamok, M. Ali, T. Anthony, and S. J. Weiss, "Ultra-thin UHF broadband antenna on a non-uniform aperiodic (NUA) metaSurface," IEEE Antennas and Propagation Magazine, vol. 57, no. 2, pp. 167-180, Apr. 2015.

Acceleration of Volume-Volume (6-D) Integrals for Numerical Evaluation by Double Application of the Divergence Theorem

J. Rivero
Dept. of Electronics and Telecomunications
Politecnico di Torino
Torino, Italy
javier.rivero@polito.it

F. Vipiana
Dept. of Electronics and Telecomunications
Politecnico di Torino
Torino, Italy
francesca.vipiana@polito.it

D. R. Wilton
Dept. of Electrical and Computer Engineering
University of Houston
Houston, TX, USA
wilton@uh.edu

W. A. Johnson
Consultant
Albuquerque, NM, USA
w.johnson24@comcast.net

***Abstract*—In the present paper, we propose the application of the surface divergence theorem for the integration of double volumetric integrals for both source and test domain of the 6-D reaction integrals. The resulting 6-D volume integrals are expressed as two radial integrals plus two surface integrals over the source and observation domain boundaries. The radial integrations in the physical domain should be well-behaved and easily performed for arbitrary polyhedral domains. The method is numerically validated for static and dynamic kernels arising in the Electric Field Integral Equation (EFIE), i.e., for kernels with 1/R singularities, and linear basis functions.**

***Index Terms*—integral equations, moment methods, numerical analysis, singular integrals.**

I. Introduction

Volume integral equation (VIE) techniques based on the method of moments (MoM) are especially useful in cases involving inhomogeneous materials [1] either in the direct scattering problem or in the inverse scattering problem, as in microwave imaging techniques. The rigorous solution of radiation and scattering problems using VIEs requires the accurate and efficient numerical evaluation of double volume reaction integrals. Lately, powerful numerical methods for handling the entire integration of surface integrals on test and observation element pairs in moment method solutions have been demonstrated in several papers, e.g. see [2]–[4]. Their approach is based on an interchange of integration orders to first perform radial integrations for both source and observation point integrals. However, the approach was limited to surface elements.

Recently Bleszynski et al. presented a method allowing an analytical conversion of expressions for matrix elements of the tensor and vector Green functions from 6-D volumetric to 4-D surface integrals with nonsingular integrands [5].

In this paper we extend the applicability of the method of [3], [4] to the evaluation of double volumetric integrals on source and test domains of the 6-D reaction integrals, which also produces radial source and test integrals. The divergence theorem is applied directly in the physical domains for both the source and observation point integrals, and the resulting radial integrals are well-behaved for polygonal domains. In this sense, the scheme is quite general, i.e., is not limited to well-shaped elements nor to ad-hoc treatments of self-, edge-, or vertex-adjacent geometries. Unlike the surface element case, in the volumetric case, neither source nor test points need to be imaged on a plane associated with the other element. Preliminary results have shown good accuracy for the proposed method.

This work was supported by Compagnia di San Paolo, under the research project MIT-Food, Microwave Imaging Technology for Food Contamination Monitoring

II. Formulation

First let us consider the inner volume integral

$$\int_{V'} F(\mathbf{r},\mathbf{r}')dV'. \tag{1}$$

If we can find a vector function $\mathbf{H}(\mathbf{r},\mathbf{r}')$ such that $\nabla'\cdot\mathbf{H} = F(\mathbf{r},\mathbf{r}')$, then by the divergence theorem (1) can be written as

$$\int_{V'} F(\mathbf{r},\mathbf{r}')dV' = \oint_{S'} \mathbf{H}(\mathbf{r},\mathbf{r}'_{S'})\cdot\hat{\mathbf{n}}'dS', \tag{2}$$

where the volume integral over a tetrahedral element, such as shown in Fig. 1, is reduced to a surface integral over its faces. $\mathbf{r}'_{S'}$ is a point on the boundary S' of V', $\hat{\mathbf{n}}'$ is the external normal to the boundary surface of the tetrahedral volume, and

$$\mathbf{H}(\mathbf{r},\mathbf{r}'_{S'}) = \frac{\hat{\mathbf{R}}'}{R^2}\int_0^R F(\mathbf{r},\mathbf{r}')\,R'^2dR', \tag{3}$$

where $\mathbf{r}' = \mathbf{r} + R'\hat{\mathbf{R}}'$, $\hat{\mathbf{R}}' = (\mathbf{r}'-\mathbf{r})/R'$, $0 \le R' \le R \equiv |\mathbf{r}-\mathbf{r}'_{S'}|$, $R' = |\mathbf{r}'-\mathbf{r}|$ as seen in Fig. 1. Using (3) we can write (2) as

$$\int_{V'} F(\mathbf{r},\mathbf{r}')dV' = \oint_{S'}\left(\frac{\hat{\mathbf{n}}'\cdot\hat{\mathbf{R}}'}{R^2}\int_0^R F(\mathbf{r},\mathbf{r}')\,R'^2dR'\right)dS'. \tag{4}$$

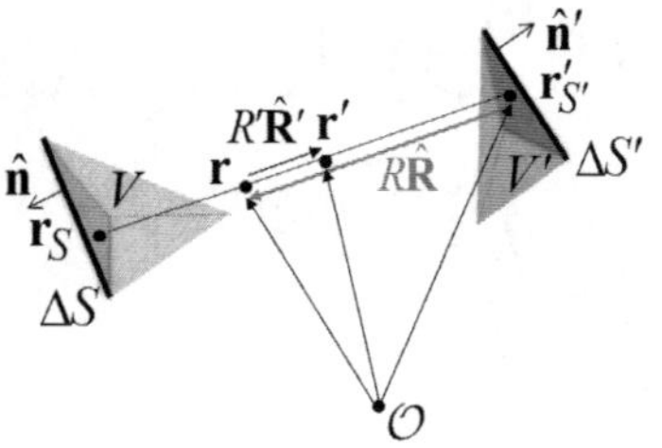

Fig. 1. The orientation of a pair of tetrahedral elements in space and the definition of quantities for the computation of radial integrals associated with a pair of interacting surface $\Delta S'$ and ΔS for source V' and test V tetrahedral, respectively.

Next, we consider an additional testing integration over the planar observer domain S in order to evaluate the following double surface integral:

$$\int_V \int_{V'} F(\mathbf{r}, \mathbf{r}') dV' dV = \oint_{S'} \hat{\mathbf{n}}' \cdot \left[\int_V \left(\frac{\hat{\mathbf{R}}'}{R^2} \int_0^R F(\mathbf{r}, \mathbf{r}') \, R'^2 dR' \right) dV \right] dS', \quad (5)$$

where the interchange of integration order is permitted by the independence of the source and observation coordinates and their associated domains. Again applying the divergence theorem to the volumetric integral in (5) and rearranging the order of the resulting integrals, we obtain

$$\oint_{S'} \oint_S \frac{(\hat{\mathbf{n}} \cdot \hat{\mathbf{R}})(\hat{\mathbf{n}}' \cdot \hat{\mathbf{R}}')}{R_{SS'}{}^2} \int_0^{R_{SS'}} \int_0^R F(\mathbf{r}, \mathbf{r}') R'^2 dR' dR \, dS \, dS', \quad (6)$$

where S is the boundary of V, $\hat{\mathbf{n}}$ is the outward pointing normal to S, $\mathbf{r} = \mathbf{r}'_{S'} + R\hat{\mathbf{R}}$, $\hat{\mathbf{R}} = -\hat{\mathbf{R}}' = (\mathbf{r}_S - \mathbf{r}_{S'})/R_{SS'}$, $0 \leq R \leq R_{SS'}$, $R_{SS'} = |\mathbf{r}_S - \mathbf{r}'_{S'}|$, and $\mathbf{r}_S$ is a point on S. The radial integrals can be performed in closed form for both the dynamic and static forms of the free space Greens function $G\left(|\mathbf{r} - \mathbf{r}'|^{-1}\right)$ and $\nabla G\left(|\mathbf{r} - \mathbf{r}'|^{-1}\right)$, with or without polynomial vector bases. The two outer surface integrals can be analyzed using any appropriate scheme implemented for surface integration.

III. Preliminary Numerical Results

To analyze the accuracy of the 6-D reaction integral reported in (6), we examine the contribution of the three different sets of faces iterations occurring when analyzing a pair of tetrahedra in the Method of Moment discretization of the Electric Field Integral Equation (EFIE). We consider a pair of source and test tetrahedra with a common edge, as shown in Fig. 2 (inset). The surface integrals are evaluated numerically using the standard Gauss quadrature scheme for triangles (GT) to a reference result obtained using the GT scheme with the highest number of points we have available for this schema (166 points).

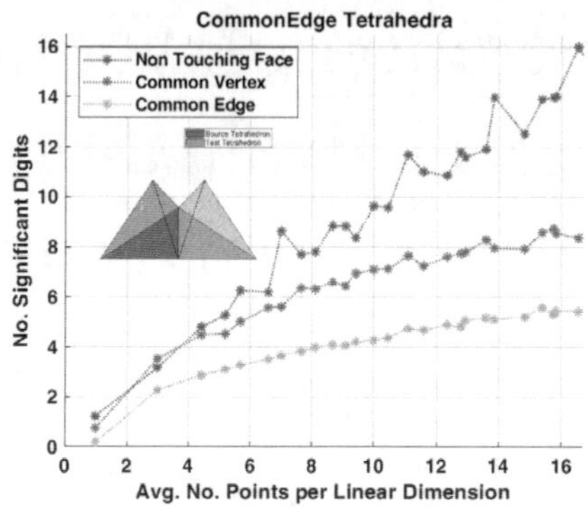

Fig. 2. Near-field convergence of surface integrals. Inset: Orientation of a pair of tetrahedral elements in space.The orientation of a pair of tetrahedral elements in space.

In Fig. 2, the convergence of the different sets of interaction faces is separately investigated. Fig. 2 shows the number of correct significant digits obtained increasing the number of surface sample points for the boundary integrals, using exact results for the radial integrals. The sets of non-touching faces show the best convergence, as expected, approaching machine precision accuracy with about 16 points per linear dimension. However, the behavior of the set of faces with a common vertex or a common edge is not as good. In order to improve the convergence for this set of faces it is possible to use some variable transform or another surface integration scheme.

IV. Conclusion

The proposed scheme is based on two applications of the divergence theorem with an appropriate integration reordering. The 6-D integrals are expressed as two radial integrals plus two surface integrals over source and observation domain boundaries. The method is numerically validated for static and dynamic kernels arising in the EFIE and similar formulations. Numerical results highlighted the need of accelerated convergence of the method with appropriate transformations for the surface contour integrals when the faces of the tetrahedral are touching.

References

[1] M. Hasanovic, C. Mei, J. R. Mautz, E. Arvas, "MoM Solution to Scattering from Three-Dimensional Inhomogeneous Magnetic and Dielectric Bodies," ACES Journal Paper, Vol. 22, no. 1, Mar. 2017.
[2] A. G. Polimeridis, F. Vipiana, J. R. Mosig, and D. R. Wilton, "DIRECTFN: fully numerical algorithms for high precision computation of singular integrals in Galerkin SIE methods," IEEE Transactions on Antennas and Propagation, vol. 61, no. 6, pp. 3112-3122, Jun. 2013.
[3] D. Wilton, F. Vipiana, and W. Johnson, "Evaluation of 4-D reaction integrals in the method of moments: co-planar element case," IEEE Transactions on Antennas and Propagation, vol. 65, no. 5, pp. 2479-2493, May 2017.
[4] J. Rivero, F. Vipiana, D. R. Wilton, and W. A. Johnson, "Evaluation of 4-D reaction integrals via double application of the divergence theorem," IEEE Transactions on Antennas and Propagation, to be published.
[5] E. H. Bleszynski, M. K. Bleszynski, and T. Jaroszewicz, "Reduction of volume integrals to nonsingular surface integrals for matrix elements of tensor and vector green functions of Maxwell equations," IEEE Transactions on Antennas and Propagation, vol. 61, no. 7, pp. 3642-3647, Jul. 2013.

Overview of the Iterative Solver in HFSS for Analyzing Frequency Domain Electromagnetic Problems

Ali Aghabarati, Kezhong Zhao, and L. E. Rickard Petersson
ANSYS, Inc.
Pittsburgh, PA, USA
Ali.Aghabarati@ansys.com, Kezhong.Zhao@ansys.com, Rickard.Petersson@ansys.com

***Abstract*—This paper presents an overview of the iterative solver in ANSYS HFSS for solving large-scale problems obtained from the finite element analysis of time-harmonic Maxwell's Equations. To this end, Krylov subspace methods with effective preconditioning and parallelizable routines are presented to extend the applicability and efficiency of frequency domain solver. Several real-life examples are presented to demonstrate the accuracy as well as efficiency of the iterative approach.**

Index Terms —Frequency Domain Solver, Krylov Subspace Methods, Large Scale Electromagnetic Simulations.

I. INTRODUCTION

The finite element method (FEM) has been one of the most popular methods in the engineering community due to its ability to handle complex heterogeneous and anisotropic materials and its capability to accurately represent complicated geometries via tetrahedral elements. It is well known that the linear system resulting from a finite element discretization of time-harmonic Maxwell's equations is indefinite. Because of this indefiniteness, direct sparse solvers such as multifrontal solver [1]-[2] are quite popular. However, for electrically large 3-dimensional problems, direct solvers potentially require prohibitive amounts of memory and suffer poor parallel scalability. Therefore, iterative solvers remain an attractive option and thus a robust and effective preconditioner is highly desirable.

HFSS (High Frequency Structure Simulator) [3] is a commercial solver for analyzing arbitrary 3-dimensional electromagnetic structures. It is one of the most popular and powerful tools used for antenna design as well as the design of complex RF electronic circuits including filters, transmission lines, and electronic packaging. In this paper, we present an overview of the iterative solver employed in HFSS for analyzing electrically large EM problems with complex geometries along with initial findings from a new enhanced iterative solver.

In HFSS, we have successfully incorporated an efficient multilevel Schwarz preconditioner to accelerate the convergence of iterative algorithms [4]-[6]. By using a hierarchical multilevel technique over $\mathcal{H}^p(\text{curl})$, an inexpensive but effective approximate inverse is obtained by starting from the highest level and proceeding to the lowest level for computing a series of improving corrections. It has been shown that for simulations involving a large number of higher order unknowns, which is necessary for more accurate representation of the vector fields, a carefully designed multilevel preconditioning cycle significantly reduces the memory requirements at the solve step.

Krylov sub-space solvers employed in HFSS support both Lanczos and Arnoldi algorithms for handling indefinite symmetric and unsymmetrical linear systems [7]-[8]. For the new enhanced solver, all algorithms now use multithreaded routines from the latest Intel MKL sparse library for BLAS level 1 vector operations and BLAS level 2 matrix operations [9]. The solver first inspects the linear system in terms of sparsity structure and sparse matrix format. Next, it chooses the best computational kernel for multicore platforms and selects an optimum balancing strategy for efficient parallel execution. Significant speedup factors are observed by executing preconditioned Krylov solvers in parallel mode using optimized BLAS routines.

For problems with multiple right-hand sides (RHS), such as monostatic RCS and S-parameter calculations, the iterative solver in HFSS supports acceleration by both shared memory parallel as well as MPI distributed RHS solve. The large set of right-hand side vectors is divided into blocks among the available processes, and each process is responsible for the update of solution vectors in its block. Furthermore, for a wideband problem we employ a multi-level parallelization scheme where frequencies as well as RHS vectors are solved in parallel to achieve the optimum parallel efficiency.

This paper is organized as follows. Section II presents the results obtained from a simulation study of large electromagnetic problems. Section III discusses conclusions on the strength of iterative methods in HFSS.

II. NUMERICAL RESULTS

In this section, we demonstrate the efficiency of the new enhanced iterative solver by analyzing some challenging problems.

For the first study, a dish antenna is considered as shown in Fig. 1. The perfect electric conductor (PEC) structure is excited by a wave port in HFSS. Simulations were performed at 10 GHz, at which the diameter of the dish is about 25λ and the dish is about 13λ away from the feed. The FEM region is enclosed by an absorbing boundary condition (ABC) surface, and the volume is discretized using 287,446 tetrahedral elements. Using tangential vector elements up to 3rd order results in 5,317,558 unknows for approximating the electric field. For this experiment, the performances of two solvers in HFSS are compared: 1) Multifrontal direct solver; 2) Preconditioned Krylov iterative solver with tolerance accuracy of 10^{-6}. As summarized in Fig. 1, the iterative solution reduces memory requirements significantly. It converges in 56 iterations and performs 2.7x faster than the direct solver.

For the second example, we demonstrate the capability of the iterative solver through adaptive mesh analysis of a filter structure at the operating frequency of 1.95 GHz. The dimensions of the filter, shown in Fig. 2 (a), are $5in \times 2.2in \times 0.8in$. For this experiment, we used the iterative solver with and without optimized BLAS routines in the Krylov algorithm to demonstrate the efficiency of our multithreaded parallel algorithm with 20 cores. Fig. 2 (a) illustrates the memory requirements at the solve step for the multifrontal direct solver and iterative solvers as system size increases to 15.6 million unknows. Fig. 2 (b) also shows cumulative solver time for all solvers after 11 adaptive passes. We can observe from the final adaptive pass that Krylov solvers require about 4 times less memory than the direct approach, reducing the peak RAM usage from 235 GB. The new iterative solver in HFSS also achieves about 2 times reduction in total CPU time by incorporating routines that are highly optimized for speed on multicore machines.

III. Conclusions

In this paper, we presented the capabilities of a preconditioned Krylov method in ANSYS HFSS for analysing time-harmonic Maxwell's equations problems. The results show that a Krylov algorithm with effective multilevel preconditiong methods and optimized BLAS routines can significantly accelerate the finite element solution and reduce its memory requirements.

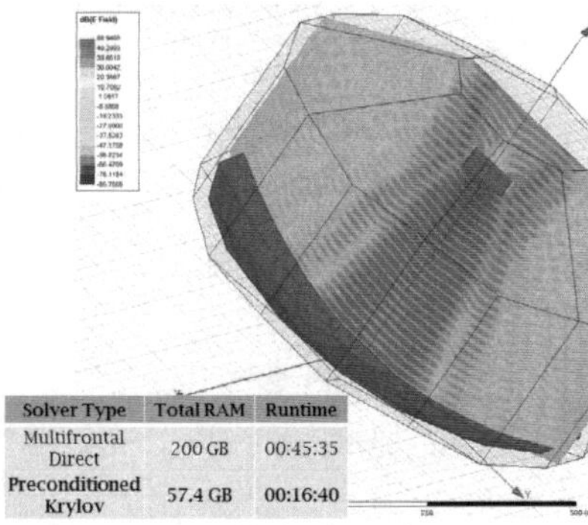

Fig. 1. Dish antenna with feeding port.

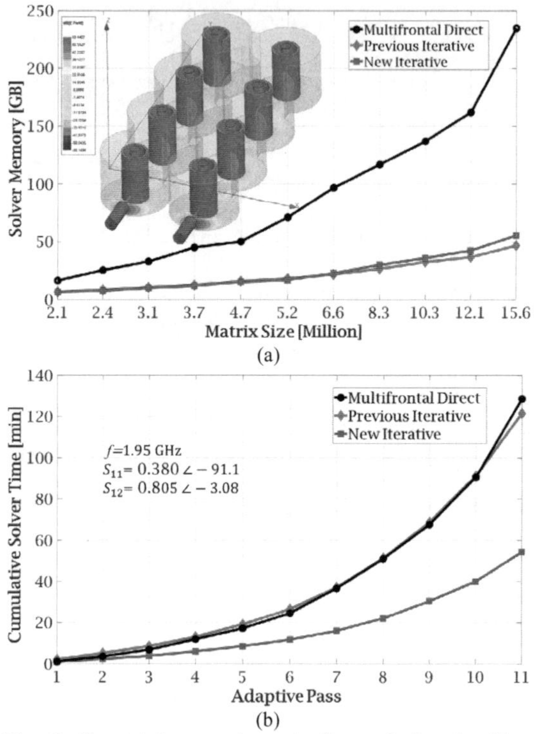

Fig. 2. Computation requirements for analyzing the filter structure in HFSS up to 11 adaptive passes (a) Solver memory usage (GB); (b) Solver cumulative CPU time (min).

References

[1] J. W. H. Liu, "The multifrontal method for sparse matrix solution: theory and practice," SIAM Rev, vol. 34, no. 1, pp. 82-109, Mar. 1992.

[2] J. A. Scott, "A frontal solver for the 21st century," Commun. Numer. Meth. Engng., vol. 22, pp. 1015-1029, 2006.

[3] "ANSYS HFSS," ANSYS, Inc., 2018, [Online]. Available: www.ansys.com/products/electronics/ansys-hfss.

[4] D. K. Sun, J. F. Lee, and Z. J. Cendes, "Construction of nearly orthogonal nedelec bases for rapid convergence with multilevel preconditioned solvers," SIAM Journal on Scientific Computing, vol. 23, no. 4, pp. 1053-1076, 2002.

[5] J. F. Lee and D. K. Sun, "p-Type multiplicative schwarz (pMUS) method with vector finite elements for modeling three-dimensional waveguide discontinuities," IEEE Trans. Microw. Theory Techn., vol. 52, no 3, pp. 864-870, 2004.

[6] A. Aghabarati and J. P. Webb, "Multilevel methods for p-adaptive finite element analysis of electromagnetic scattering," IEEE Trans. Antennas Propagat., vol. 61, no. 11, pp. 5597-5606, 2013.

[7] R. W. Freund, "Conjugate gradient-type methods for linear systems with complex symmetric coefficient matrices," SIAM J. Sci. Statist. Comput., vol. 13, no. 1, pp. 425–448, Jan. 1992.

[8] Y. Saad, Iterative Methods for Sparse Linear Systems, 2nd ed. Philadelphia, PA, USA: SIAM, 2003.

[9] "Intel Math Kernel Library (Intel MKL)," Intel Corporation, 2018, [Online] Available: https://software.intel.com/en-us/mkl.

Effective Electromagnetic Parameter Extractions for Porous Media Using a Potential-Based Formulation

Su Yan
Department of Electrical Engineering and Computer Science
Howard University, Washington, DC 20059-1015, USA
E-mail: su.yan@howard.edu

***Abstract*—In this paper, a potential-based partial differential formulation is utilized to extract the effective electromagnetic parameters of multiphase porous media. To overcome the low-frequency catastrophe, the magnetic vector and electric scalar potentials are employed to formulate the vector wave equation that governs the electromagnetic problems. The magnetic vector potential is then gauged by the generalized Lorentz gauge, which is supplemented to the vector wave equation to form a complete system of equations. It is shown that, after a proper discretization of the resulting potential-based formulation, the low-frequency breakdown issue is successfully removed without the need to perform a tree-cotree splitting and the effective parameters of the porous media can be extracted in a wide frequency range with an excellent accuracy.**

I. Introduction

Multiphase porous media have many important applications in geophysics and remote sensing. In such media, different phases refer to microscopic constituents with different physical properties. To better understand the macroscopic behaviors of porous media, homogenization of material properties is required. Among various homogenization methods developed in recent decades, the ones based on full-wave solutions of Maxwell's equations usually have a better accuracy over those based on simple mixing formulas [1]. Unfortunately, due to the extremely small geometrical sizes of the constituents, numerical solutions of the field-based full-wave formulations break down in a wide range of frequencies. This low-frequency, or equivalently, dense-mesh, breakdown issue can be resolved by applying the loop-tree decomposition and tree-cotree splitting (TCS) techniques to the integral- and partial-differential-equation-based formulations, respectively. However, the construction of the loop and tree structures can be difficult when dealing with geometries with multiply-connected regions.

In this work, the vector wave equation is rewritten by expressing the electric field into the magnetic vector and electric scalar potentials. The generalized Lorentz gauge [2] is then supplemented as the second equation to obtain an unique solution for the vector potential. The resulting potential-based formulation is used in the effective electromagnetic parameter extraction of porous media. It is shown that with the potential-based formulation, the low-frequency breakdown problem is removed and the effective parameters can be obtained accurately without the application of the TCS technique.

II. Potential-Based Finite Element Formulation

An electrodynamic problem can be formulated in terms of the electric field into a vector wave equation [3]

$$\nabla\times\frac{1}{\mu_{\rm r}}\nabla\times\boldsymbol{E}-k_0^2\tilde{\epsilon}_{\rm r}\boldsymbol{E}=-{\rm j}k_0\eta_0\boldsymbol{J} \tag{1}$$

where $\mu_{\rm r}$ stands for the relative permeability of the material, $\tilde{\epsilon}_{\rm r}=\epsilon_{\rm r}-{\rm j}\sigma/\omega\epsilon_0$ stands for the complex relative permittivity that takes into account the relative permittivity $\epsilon_{\rm r}$ and conductivity σ of the material with ω being the angular frequency, k_0 and η_0 stand for the wavenumber and intrinsic impedance in vacuum, respectively. This wave equation suffers from the low-frequency breakdown problem when the operating frequency approaches zero. To remove such a problem, the TCS technique can be applied based on the Helmholtz decomposition of the electric field to describe the contributions from the purely gradient and the rotational-like components separately. Alternatively, a potential-based formulation can be obtained by expressing the electric field into the magnetic vector potential $\boldsymbol{A}$ and the electric scalar potential ϕ as $\boldsymbol{E}=-{\rm j}\omega\boldsymbol{A}-\nabla\phi$, which, when substituted into (1), yields

$$\nabla\times\frac{1}{\mu_{\rm r}}\nabla\times\boldsymbol{A}-k_0^2\tilde{\epsilon}_{\rm r}\boldsymbol{A}+{\rm j}\omega\mu_0\epsilon_0\tilde{\epsilon}_{\rm r}\nabla\phi=\mu_0\boldsymbol{J}. \tag{2}$$

In order to determine the vector potential $\boldsymbol{A}$ uniquely, the generalized Lorentz gauge [2]

$$\nabla\cdot\epsilon_{\rm r}\boldsymbol{A}=-{\rm j}\omega\mu_0\epsilon_0\,\phi \tag{3}$$

is applied as a constraint relating $\boldsymbol{A}$ to ϕ. By defining an intermediate variable $\varphi=-{\rm j}\omega\mu_0\epsilon_0\,\phi$, the frequency dependence in the gauge condition is removed such that (2) and (3) are rewritten as

$$\nabla\times\frac{1}{\mu_{\rm r}}\nabla\times\boldsymbol{A}-k_0^2\tilde{\epsilon}_{\rm r}\boldsymbol{A}-\tilde{\epsilon}_{\rm r}\nabla\varphi=\mu_0\boldsymbol{J} \tag{4}$$

$$\nabla\cdot\epsilon_{\rm r}\boldsymbol{A}-\varphi=0. \tag{5}$$

To solve the potential-based equations (4) and (5) with the finite element method, $\boldsymbol{A}$ and φ are expanded using the vector and scalar basis functions, respectively, as

$$\boldsymbol{A}=\sum_{j=1}^{N_v}\boldsymbol{N}_j a_j,\qquad \varphi=\sum_{j=1}^{N_s}N_j\varphi_j \tag{6}$$

where N_v and N_s denote the numbers of vector basis functions $\boldsymbol{N}_j$ and scalar basis functions N_j, respectively. Applying the Galerkin test of (4) and (5), the following matrix equation can be obtained

$$\begin{bmatrix} K_{aa}+A_{aa} & -M_{a\varphi}+A_{a\varphi} \\ -M_{\varphi a}+A_{\varphi a} & -M_{\varphi\varphi} \end{bmatrix} \begin{Bmatrix} a \\ \varphi \end{Bmatrix} = \begin{Bmatrix} b \\ 0 \end{Bmatrix} \tag{7}$$

where

$$[K_{aa}]_{ij} = \int_{\Omega} \frac{1}{\mu_{\mathrm{r}}} \nabla\times\boldsymbol{N}_i \cdot \nabla\times\boldsymbol{N}_j - k_0^2 \tilde{\epsilon}_{\mathrm{r}} \boldsymbol{N}_i \cdot \boldsymbol{N}_j \,\mathrm{d}\Omega \tag{8}$$

$$[M_{a\varphi}]_{ij} = \int_{\Omega} \tilde{\epsilon}_{\mathrm{r}} \boldsymbol{N}_i \cdot \nabla N_j \,\mathrm{d}\Omega \tag{9}$$

$$[M_{\varphi a}]_{ij} = \int_{\Omega} \epsilon_{\mathrm{r}} \nabla N_i \cdot \boldsymbol{N}_j \,\mathrm{d}\Omega \tag{10}$$

$$[M_{\varphi\varphi}]_{ij} = \int_{\Omega} N_i \, N_j \,\mathrm{d}\Omega \tag{11}$$

$$[A_{aa}]_{ij} = \int_{\Gamma_{\mathrm{ABC}}} \frac{\mathrm{j}k_0}{\eta_{\mathrm{r}}} \hat{\boldsymbol{n}}\times\boldsymbol{N}_i \cdot \hat{\boldsymbol{n}}\times\boldsymbol{N}_j \,\mathrm{d}\Gamma \tag{12}$$

$$[A_{a\varphi}]_{ij} = \int_{\Gamma_{\mathrm{ABC}}} \frac{\mathrm{j}}{k_0\eta_{\mathrm{r}}} \hat{\boldsymbol{n}}\times\boldsymbol{N}_i \cdot \hat{\boldsymbol{n}}\times\nabla N_j \,\mathrm{d}\Gamma \tag{13}$$

$$[A_{\varphi a}]_{ij} = \int_{\Gamma_{\mathrm{ABC}}} \epsilon_{\mathrm{r}} N_i \, \hat{\boldsymbol{n}} \cdot \boldsymbol{N}_j \,\mathrm{d}\Gamma \tag{14}$$

$$b_i = \mu_0 \int_{\Omega} \boldsymbol{N}_i \cdot \boldsymbol{J} \,\mathrm{d}\Omega + \frac{1}{c_0} \int_{\Gamma_{\mathrm{ABC}}} \boldsymbol{N}_i \cdot \boldsymbol{F}^{\mathrm{inc}} \,\mathrm{d}\Gamma. \tag{15}$$

Inn these expressions, $\eta_{\mathrm{r}} = \sqrt{\mu_{\mathrm{r}}/\epsilon_{\mathrm{r}}}$ is the relative wave impedance and $\boldsymbol{F}^{\mathrm{inc}} = \hat{\boldsymbol{n}} \times \hat{\boldsymbol{n}} \times \boldsymbol{E}^{\mathrm{inc}}/\eta_{\mathrm{r}} - \eta_0 \hat{\boldsymbol{n}} \times \boldsymbol{H}^{\mathrm{inc}}$ describes the incident plane wave. Note that the $[A]$ matrices are obtained on the absorbing boundary Γ_{ABC} where the incident wave $\boldsymbol{F}^{\mathrm{inc}}$ is introduced. Once (7) is solved, the electric field can be recovered by

$$\boldsymbol{E} = -\mathrm{j}\omega \left(\sum_{j=1}^{N_v} \boldsymbol{N}_j a_j + \frac{1}{k_0^2} \sum_{j=1}^{N_s} \nabla N_j \varphi_j \right) \tag{16}$$

and other quantities of interest can be calculated accordingly.

III. Numerical Example

Shown in Fig. 1, the two-phase non-magnetic porous material under consideration consists of a background matrix with a relative permittivity $\epsilon_{\mathrm{r}} = 7$ and conductivity $\sigma = 5 \times 10^{-4}$ S/m and 48 spherical inclusions of various sizes with a relative permittivity $\epsilon_{\mathrm{r}} = 65$ and conductivity $\sigma = 5$ S/m. The geometric size of the sample is 1 mm by 1 mm by 0.4 mm, and the frequency range under consideration is from 10 KHz to 10 GHz. In the numerical experiment, an incident plane wave is launched from one side of the sample and propagates across the porous material. After the governing equation is solved for the electric field, the reflection and transmission coefficients are calculated, based on which the effective material parameters are calculated using the formulas given in [4]. Shown in Fig. 2 is the numerically extracted effective permittivity and conductivity as functions of frequency using the field-based formulation (1) and the potential-based formulation (4) and (5). Clearly, the field-based formulation produces erroneous solutions when frequency is below 100 MHz. But the effective parameters extracted by solving the potential-based formulation agree very well with the reference solution in the entire frequency range.

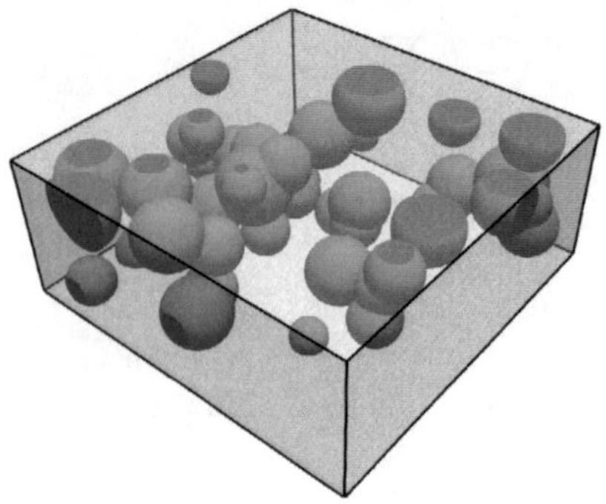

Fig. 1: Geometry of the porous material sample.

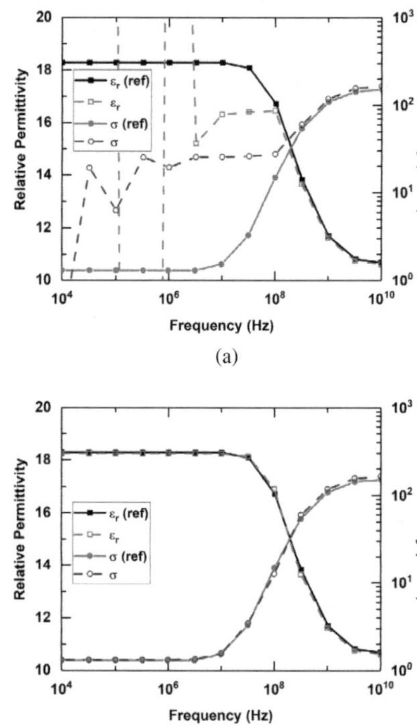

(a)

(b)

Fig. 2: Numerically extracted effective permittivity and conductivity versus frequency using (a) the field-based formulation (1) and (b) the potential-based formulation (4) and (5).

References

[1] A. H. Sihvola, *Electromagnetic Mixing Formulas and Applications*. London: IET Press, 1999.

[2] W. C. Chew, "Vector potential electromagnetics with generalized gauge for inhomogeneous media: Formulation," *Progress In Electromagnetics Research*, vol. 149, pp. 69–84, Sep. 2014.

[3] J.-M. Jin, *The Finite Element Method in Electromagnetics*, 3rd ed. Hoboken, NJ: Wiley, 2014.

[4] D. R. Smith, S. Schultz, P. Markoš, and C. M. Soukoulis, "Determination of effective permittivity and permeability of metamaterials from reflection and transmission coefficients," *Phys. Rev. B*, vol. 65, p. 195104, Apr. 2002.

2D Integral Formulation with High Order Impedance Boundary Conditions for Transmission Lines

1st Luca Di Rienzo
Dipartimento di Elettronica, Informazione e Bioingegneria
Politecnico di Milano
Milan, Italy
luca.dirienzo@polimi.it

2nd Nathan Ida
Department of Electrical and Computer Engineering
The University of Akron
Akron, Ohio. USA
ida@uakron.edu

***Abstract*—High order impedance boundary conditions take into account the curvature of the conductive surface and the diffusion of the electromagnetic field in all directions into the conductor. A previously published two dimensional boundary integral formulation based on magnetic vector potential and perturbation theory is compared here with the corresponding non-perturbative version. Some of the limitations of the perturbative approach are shown and overcome by the present formulation.**

***Index Terms*—BEM, high order impedance boundary condition, integral formulation, transmission lines.**

I. Introduction

An integral formulation for coupling high order Surface Impedance Boundary Conditions (SIBCs) [1], [2] with the Boundary Element Method (BEM) for the computation of series per-unit-length parameters of uniform multiconductor transmission lines of arbitrary cross-sections is proposed in [3], [4]. Despite the strong advantage of this approach, that is to require the numerical discretization of the integral equations only once so that the solution is then easily obtained in the whole frequency range of interest, the formulation suffers from some limitations. First, it becomes inaccurate when the conductors are very near to each others, independent of the discretization method. Second, it cannot take into account the case of conductors with relative permeability different from that of the dielectric space. The formulation presented here is the direct coupling of Neumann-to-Dirichlet SIBCs ([4], [5]) with the boundary integral equation.

II. Integral Formulation

Let us consider C infinitely long parallel conductors (in the z-direction), with cross sections Ω_c, $c = 1, \ldots, C$. Each conductor is assumed to have electrical conductivity σ_c and magnetic permeability μ_c. Under the hypothesis of time-harmonic regime with angular frequency ω, the vector fields are represented using phasors, and from now on all field quantities are assumed to be complex. We assume that for each conductor the condition $\sigma_c \gg \omega\varepsilon_c$ is satisfied, and that the size of the computational domain is much smaller than the wavelength, so that displacement currents are neglected in Ampére's law.

The 2D formulation in terms of the Magnetic Vector Potential (MVP) reported in [4] is applied here. The unknown is the z-component of the MVP, that is separated into "source" and "eddy" components, $A = A^s + A^e$, with A^s constant in each conductor. The eddy component A^e satisfies the diffusion equation in each conductor

$$\nabla^2 A^e_{\text{int}} = j\omega\mu_c\sigma_c A^e_{\text{int}} \qquad \text{in } \Omega_c, \tag{1}$$

and Laplace's equation in the nonconducting domains

$$\nabla^2 A^e_{\text{ext}} = 0 \qquad \text{in } \Omega_0. \tag{2}$$

Denoting by Γ_c the boundary of the cross section of each conductor and by $\mathbf{n}$ the unit normal vector exterior to Ω_0, the equations for A^e are completed with interface conditions on Γ_c

$$A^e_{\text{int}} - A^e_{\text{ext}} = -A^s, \tag{3}$$

$$\frac{1}{\mu_c}\frac{\partial A^e_{\text{int}}}{\partial \mathbf{n}} = \frac{1}{\mu_0}\frac{\partial A^e_{\text{ext}}}{\partial \mathbf{n}}. \tag{4}$$

Let us indicate the normal derivative at each interface by

$$K^c = \left.\frac{\partial A^e_{\text{ext}}}{\partial \mathbf{n}}\right|_{\Gamma_c}, \quad c = 1, \ldots, C. \tag{5}$$

From equations (2)-(3), applying the Boundary Integral Equation Method we obtain

$$A^s(s) - \sum_{c=1}^{C} S_c K^c(s) = \left(-\frac{I}{2} - \sum_{c=1}^{C} D_c\right) A^e_{\text{int}}(s), \tag{6}$$

where I is the identity operator, and S_c and D_c are the operators for the single and the double layer potential on the interface Γ_c, as follows:

$$S_c u = \oint_{\Gamma_c} g u \, \mathrm{d}s, \qquad D_c u = \oint_{\Gamma_c} \frac{\partial g}{\partial \mathbf{n}} u \, \mathrm{d}s,$$

with $g = -\frac{1}{2\pi}\ln r$. Since the source component A^s is unknown, the condition on current intensity flowing in each conductor is also imposed

$$\oint_{\Gamma_c} K^c(s)\,\mathrm{d}s = \mu_0 I_c, \quad c = 1, \ldots, C. \tag{7}$$

III. Non-Perturbative Formulation

Defining $\alpha = \sqrt{2j}$, the first order (Leontovich), second order (Mitzner) and third order (Rytov) SIBCs on Γ_c are respectively given by ([5], [6])

$$A^e_{\text{int}} = -\frac{\delta_c}{\alpha}\frac{\partial A^e_{\text{int}}}{\partial \mathbf{n}}, \tag{8}$$

$$A^e_{\text{int}} = -\frac{\delta_c^2\kappa + 2\alpha\delta_c}{2\alpha^2}\frac{\partial A^e_{\text{int}}}{\partial \mathbf{n}}, \tag{9}$$

$$A^e_{\text{int}} = -\left(\frac{\delta_c}{\alpha} + \frac{\kappa\delta_c^2}{2\alpha^2} + \frac{3\kappa^2\delta_c^3}{8\alpha^3}\right)\frac{\partial A^e_{\text{int}}}{\partial \mathbf{n}} - \frac{\delta_c^3}{2\alpha^3}\frac{\partial^2}{\partial s^2}\left(\frac{\partial A^e_{\text{int}}}{\partial \mathbf{n}}\right), \tag{10}$$

where $\kappa = \kappa(s)$ is the (signed) curvature of the contour's cross section.

The implementation of Rytov's SIBC (10) requires the computation of the second order derivative of K with respect to the curvilinear coordinate s. Exploiting (4) and (10) in the integral equation (6), results in

$$A^s_c - \sum_{c=1}^{C}\int_{\Gamma_c} gK^c\mathrm{d}s - \frac{I}{2}G_cK^c - \sum_{c=1}^{C}\int_{\Gamma_c} G_c\frac{\partial g}{\partial \mathbf{n}}K^c\mathrm{d}s$$
$$-\frac{I}{2}F_c\frac{\partial^2 K^c}{\partial s^2} - \sum_{c=1}^{C}F_c\int_{\Gamma_c}\frac{\partial g}{\partial \mathbf{n}}\frac{\partial^2 K^c}{\partial s^2}\mathrm{d}s = 0, \tag{11}$$

where

$$G_c = \frac{\mu_c}{\mu_0}\left(\frac{\delta_c}{\alpha} + \frac{\kappa\delta_c^2}{2\alpha^2} + \frac{3\kappa^2\delta_c^3}{8\alpha^3}\right), \qquad F_c = \frac{\mu_c}{\mu_0}\frac{\delta_c^3}{2\alpha^3}.$$

IV. Numerical Results

The canonical problem of two identical parallel circular copper conductors is solved (conductivity is $\sigma = 5.8 \times 10^7$ S/m, relative permeability is $\mu_r = 1$ and radius is $R = 2$ mm), for which the analytical solution is available. Each conductor is discretized by means of second order BEM elements.

The perturbative (P) and non-perturbative (NP) formulations are compared for different distances between the conductors. If conductors are far enough the two formulations give similar results, while in the case of conductors very near to each other the P-formulation [3], [4] suffers of a kind of instability and cannot provide accurate results (Fig. 1, 2). On the other hand the NP-formulation still guarantees accurate results.

V. Conclusion

Some limitations of a previously proposed perturbative boundary integral formulation are overcome by the corresponding non-perturbative approach. Both formulations are implemented using second order isoparametric boundary elements. Comparison with the anaytical solution show that

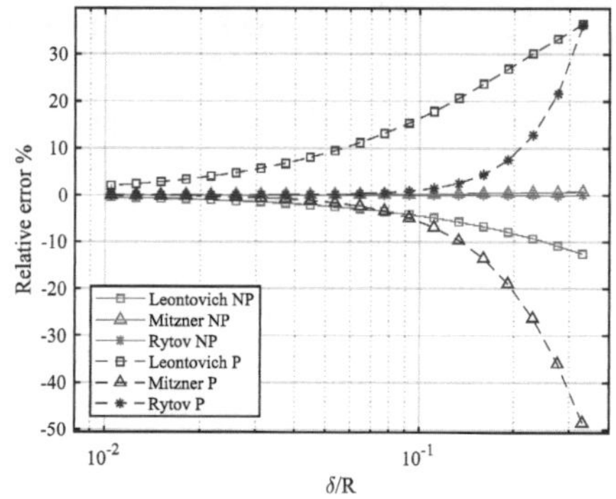

Figure 1. Relative error in the computation of p.u.l. resistance. Distance between the centers of the conductors is $d = 2.2R$.

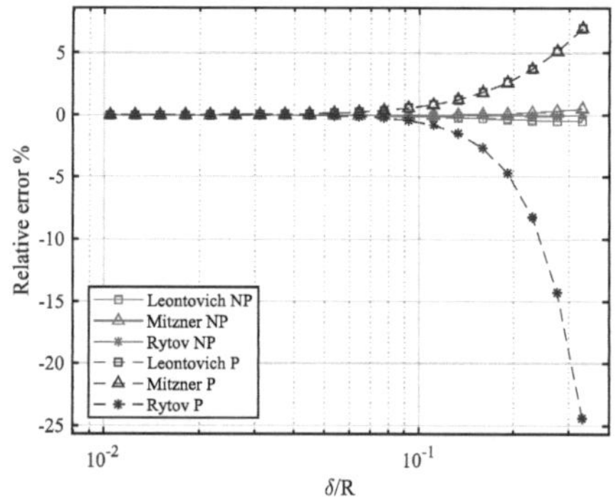

Figure 2. Relative error in the computation of p.u.l. inductance. Distance between the centers of the conductors is $d = 2.2R$.

the non-perturbative approach is more accurate in the case of strong skin-effect. In the full paper also the case of magnetic conductors will be analysed.

References

[1] Yuferev, S. and Di Rienzo, L., "Surface impedance boundary conditions in terms of various formalisms," IEEE Trans. Magn., Vol. 46, No. 9, 3617 –3628, 2010.

[2] Barmada, S. and Di Rienzo, L. and Ida, N. and Yuferev, S., "Time domain surface impedance concept for low frequency electromagnetic problems - Part II: Application to transient skin and proximity effect problems in cylindrical conductors," IEE Proceedings: Science, Measurement and Technology, Vol. 152, No. 5, 207-216, 2005.

[3] Vazquez, R. and Buffa, A. and Di Rienzo, L., "NURBS-Based BEM implementation of high-order surface impedance boundary conditions," IEEE Trans.Magn., Vol. 48, No. 12, 4757–4766, 2012.

[4] Di Rienzo, L. and Yuferev, S. and Ida, N., "Computation of the impedance matrix of multiconductor transmission lines using high-order surface impedance boundary conditions," IEEE Trans.Electromagn. Compat., Vol. 50, No. 4, 974–984, 2008.

[5] Haddar, H. and Joly, P. and Nguyen, H.-M., "Generalized impedance boundary conditions for scattering by strongly absorbing obstacles: the scalar case," Math. Models Methods Appl. Sci., Vol. 15, No. 8, 1273–1300, 2005.

[6] Vazquez, R. and Buffa, A. and Di Rienzo, L., "Isogeometric FEM implementation of high-order surface impedance boundary conditions," IEEE Trans. Magn., Vol. 50, No. 50,2014.

Axial PML Performance Near the Axis of Rotation in Cylindrical FDTD

Mohammed F. Hadi
Electrical Engineering, Colorado School of Mines
Golden, USA
mhadi@mines.edu

Atef Z. Elsherbeni
Electrical Engineering, Colorado School of Mines
Golden, USA
aelsherb@mines.edu

***Abstract*—This work investigates the effect of proximity to the axis of rotation on the perfectly-matched-layer (PML) absorbing boundary condition when used to truncate cylindrical finite-difference time-domain (FDTD) simulations along the axial dimension. The investigation is based on deriving predictive equations for the overall reflection coefficient off the innermost PML interface which rely heavily on a recently derived numerical dispersion relation for cylindrical FDTD. Accounting for cylindrical waves behavior near the axis of rotation is critical in realizing appropriate cylindrical FDTD and PML performance near the axis of rotation.**

***Index Terms*—Absorbing boundary conditions, cylindrical coordinates, cylindrical FDTD, numerical dispersion, perfectly-matched-layer (PML), .**

I. FDTD Theory-Based Reflection Coefficient Matrix

The governing reflection matrix for the Perfectly-Matched-Layer (PML) absorbing boundary condition derived for Cartesian FDTD [1], [2] applies for the most part to the PML region terminating the axial (z) dimension in cylindrical FDTD. There are two restrictions that need to be observed, though. First, the requisite numerical wavenumber should be obtained from the numerical dispersion relation for cylindrical FDTD [3] rather than from that for Cartesian FDTD [4]. This implies that excessive numerical errors near the axis of rotation need to be accounted for. Second, PML analysis in cylindrical FDTD need to be restricted to cases where TE and TM modes are decoupled [5] in order for the Cartesian FDTD reflection matrix to apply. Therefore, analysis need to be restricted to rotationally invariant modes ($\partial/\partial\phi = 0$) [5].

Under these circumstances, the PML reflection matrix for axial cylindrical regions can be written as [1] $\mathbf{UT} = \mathbf{V}$, where $\mathbf{U}$ is the tri-diagonal matrix:

$$\mathbf{U} = \begin{bmatrix} U_0 & G_0 & & & & \\ -G_{\frac{1}{2}} & 1 & G_{\frac{1}{2}} & & & \\ & -G_1 & 1 & G_1 & & \\ & & & \ddots & & \\ & & & -G_{N-1} & 1 & G_{N-1} \\ & & & & -G_{N-\frac{1}{2}} & 1 \end{bmatrix} \tag{1}$$

and

$$\mathbf{T} = \left[\Gamma \;\; T_{\frac{1}{2}} \;\; T_1 \;\; \cdots \;\; T_{N-1} \;\; T_{N-\frac{1}{2}}\right]^T \tag{2}$$

$$\mathbf{V} = \left[V_0 \;\; G_{\frac{1}{2}} \;\; 0 \;\; \cdots \;\; 0 \;\; 0\right]^T. \tag{3}$$

Element subscripts in the above refer to PML layers' indices starting with the innermost PML interface, whereas N represents the number of PML layers used. Γ represents the overall reflection coefficient off the innermost PML interface, and the interior layers' T_i parameters are place holders for inter-layer wave interaction mechanisms as explained in [1]. The remaining matrix parameters are given by,

$$G_i = \left[\frac{\cos\theta_0^P \Delta z\sqrt{\mu\epsilon}}{B_i\Delta t}\left(e^{j\omega\Delta t/2} - A_i e^{-j\omega\Delta t/2}\right)\right]^{-1} \tag{4}$$

$$U_0 = +1 + G_0 e^{-j\tilde{\beta}_{z0}\Delta z/2} \tag{5}$$

$$V_0 = -1 + G_0 e^{+j\tilde{\beta}_{z0}\Delta z/2}, \tag{6}$$

where $i = 0$ references the innermost PML interface (see Fig. 1).

The numerical wavenumber $\tilde{\beta}_{z0}$ corresponds to the innermost PML interface position and is obtained from the rotationally-invariant cylindrical FDTD numerical dispersion relation [3],

$$\mu\epsilon D_t^2 = D_\rho^\phi D_\rho^z + D_z^2 \tag{7}$$

where

$$D_t = j\,\frac{\sin(\omega\Delta t/2)}{\Delta t/2} \tag{8}$$

$$D_\rho^\phi = \frac{\rho^+ H_0^{'(2)}(\tilde{\beta}_\rho\rho^+) - \rho^- H_0^{'(2)}(\tilde{\beta}_\rho\rho^-)}{\rho\Delta\rho H_0^{(2)}(\tilde{\beta}_\rho\rho)} \tag{9}$$

$$D_\rho^z = \frac{H_0^{(2)}(\tilde{\beta}_\rho\rho^+) - H_0^{(2)}(\tilde{\beta}_\rho\rho^-)}{\Delta\rho H_0^{'(2)}(\tilde{\beta}_\rho\rho)} \tag{10}$$

$$D_z = -j\,\frac{\sin(\tilde{\beta}_z\Delta z/2)}{\Delta z/2}. \tag{11}$$

The incidence angle (θ) is defined such that $\theta = 0$ corresponds to wave propagation parallel to and along the positive z-axis. Therefore, $\tilde{\beta}_z = \tilde{\beta}\cos\theta$ and $\tilde{\beta}_\rho = \tilde{\beta}\sin\theta$. The H functions are the cylindrical Hankel functions with $\rho^\pm = \rho \pm \Delta\rho/2$.

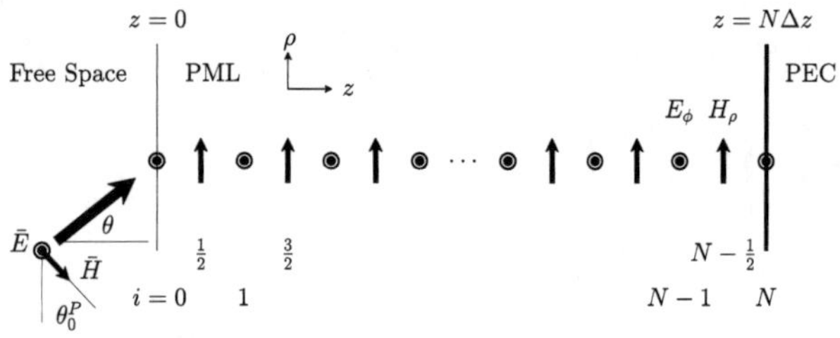

Fig. 1. A cylindrical wave impinging obliquely on a PML region terminating the z-axis. θ is incidence angle and θ^P is field polarization angle as manifested in FDTD's discrete space. Axis of rotation is horizontally oriented, below the shown field components.

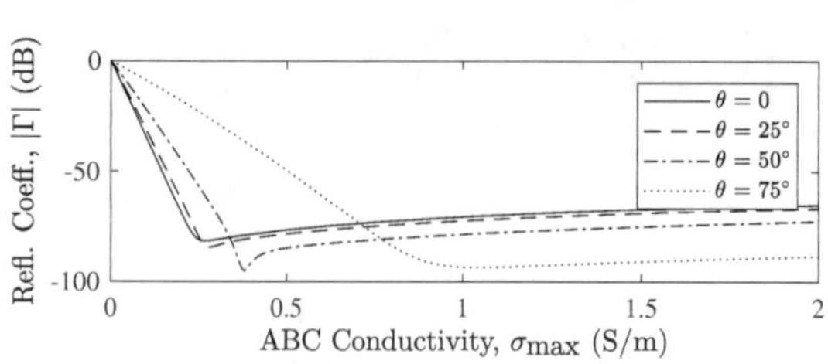

Fig. 2. Axial PML performance, compared at different wave incidence angles.

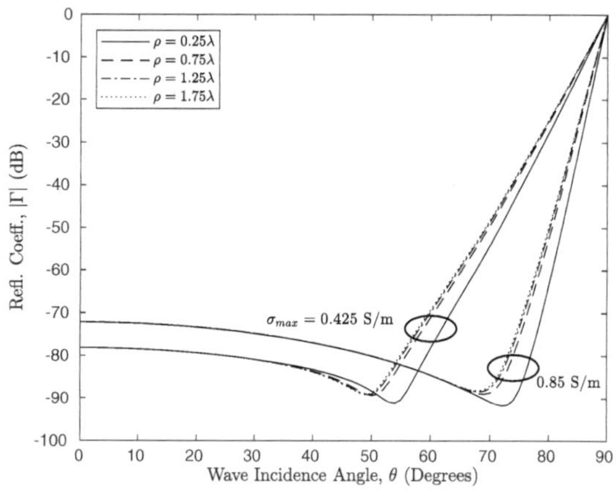

Fig. 3. Axial PML performance, compared at different radial positions.

The angle θ_0^P corresponds to the wave polarization angle at the innermost PML interface and is likewise obtained from the above numerical dispersion relation [1],

$$\cos\theta_0^P = \left|\frac{D_z}{\sqrt{\mu\epsilon}D_t}\right|. \tag{12}$$

Rounding up these definitions, the parameters A_i and B_i host the details of the particular PML flavor used. Since a complex-valued numerical wavenumber is anticipated near the axis of rotation, it is prudent to use the convolutional PML variant [6], based on the stretched coordinate variable,

$$s(z,\omega) = \kappa(z) + \frac{\sigma(z)}{\alpha(z) + j\omega\epsilon}, \tag{13}$$

which translates into [2] $A_i = 1$ and

$$\begin{aligned}
B_i &= \frac{1}{\kappa_i} + \frac{q_i}{1 - p_i e^{-j\omega\Delta t}} && (14)\\
p_i &= e^{-(\sigma_i/\kappa_i + \alpha_i)\Delta t/\epsilon} && (15)\\
q_i &= \frac{\sigma_i(p_i - 1)}{\kappa_i(\sigma_i + \alpha_i\kappa_i)} && (16)\\
\sigma_i &= \sigma_{\max}\,(i/N)^{n_\sigma} && (17)\\
\kappa_i &= 1 + (\kappa_{\max} - 1)\,(i/N)^{n_\kappa} && (18)\\
\alpha_i &= \alpha_{\max}\,(1 - i/N)^{n_\alpha}, && (19)
\end{aligned}$$

with all variables above as defined in [6].

II. Reflection Sensitivity Analysis

The following analysis discuss the cases where $\kappa_{\max} = 1$ and $\alpha_{\max} = 0$. Other frequency shifting cases will be discussed during the conference presentation. A 3-D cylindrical FDTD code is used at 1 GHz where $\Delta\rho = \Delta z = \lambda/20$, $\Delta\phi \simeq \Delta\rho/\rho$ with $\rho = \lambda/4$ and

$$\Delta t = \sqrt{\mu\epsilon}\left[\left(\frac{1}{\Delta\rho}\right)^2 + \left(\frac{1}{\Delta z}\right)^2 + \left(\frac{1}{\Delta\rho\Delta\phi}\right)^2\right]^{-\frac{1}{2}}.$$

PML setup is $N = 10$ and $n_\sigma = 2$. Fig. 2 compares the predicted overall reflection coefficient (Γ) at different incidence angles while $\sigma_{\max}$ is swept from zero to 2 S/m. The figure suggests the possibility of using smaller losses (and gentler PML loss profile) if wave incidence is expected to be near normal. Otherwise, $\sigma_{\max}$ choice should be based on the largest anticipated incidence angle.

Fig. 3 uses the optimum $\sigma_{\max}$ values for $\theta = 55°$, $75°$ and compares PML performance at several radial positions while θ is swept from normal incidence to near grazing. Even though cylindrical FDTD suffers excessive numerical dispersion errors near the axis of rotation [7], axial PML performance remains relatively unperturbed, as demonstrated in the above analysis, and maintains its high performance everywhere, at least for the rotationally invariant mode.

References

[1] M. F. Hadi, "Near-field PML optimization for low and high order FDTD algorithms using closed-form predictive equations," *IEEE Trans. Antennas Propagat.*, vol. 59, no. 8, pp. 2933–2942, Aug. 2011.

[2] J.-P. Bérenger, "Numerical reflection from FDTD-PMLs: A comparison of the split PML with the unsplit and CFS PML," *IEEE Trans. Antennas Propagat.*, vol. 50, no. 3, pp. 258–265, Mar. 2002.

[3] M. F. Hadi and A. Z. Elsherbeni, "Numerical dispersion and stability for three-dimensional cylindrical FDTD near the axis of rotation," in *11th European Conference on Antennas and Propagation*, Paris, France, Mar. 2017, pp. 936–938.

[4] A. Z. Elsherbeni and V. Demir, *The Finite-Difference Time-Domain Method for Electromagnetics with MATLAB Simulations, 2nd Edition* (ACES Series on Computational Electromagnetics and Engineering). Edison, NJ: SciTech Publishing, an Imprint of the IET, 2015.

[5] W. C. Chew, *Waves and Fields in Inhomogeneous Media.* New York: Van Nostrand Reinhold, 1990.

[6] J. A. Roden and S. D. Gedney, "Convolution PML (CPML): An efficient FDTD implementation of the CFS-PML for arbitrary media," *Microwave Opt. Technol. Lett.*, vol. 27, no. 5, pp. 334–339, Dec. 2000.

[7] M. F. Hadi, A. Z. Elsherbeni, M. J. Piket-May, and S. F. Mahmoud, "Radial waves based dispersion analysis of the body-of-revolution FDTD method," *IEEE Trans. Antennas Propagat.*, vol. 65, no. 2, pp. 721–729, Feb. 2017.

Efficient RCS Evaluation for the Conventional TF/SF Separation Model in the FDTD Technique

Tadao Ohtani
Asahikawa 070-0841, Japan
bytcg100@ybb.ne.jp

Yasushi Kanai
Engineering Department,
Niigata Institute of Technology
Kashiwazaki, 945-1195, Japan
kanai@iee.niit.ac.jp

Nikolaos V. Kantartzis
ECE Department,
Aristotle University of Thessaloniki
GR-54124 Thessaloniki, Greece
kant@auth.gr

***Abstract*—A systematic radar cross-section (RCS) evaluation scheme to enhance the total-field/scattered-field (TF/SF) separation scheme is developed in this paper for the nonstandard finite-difference time-domain (NS-FDTD) and FDTD method. Usually, the direct launch of an electromagnetic wave on the TF/SF separation surface generates undesired scattered artifacts. To avoid the influence of these forms in RCS, we introduce an error prediction model via pre-calculated data from vector parasites. It is numerically shown that our technique can improve the reliability of the RCS analysis for aircrafts with electrically large size.**

Keywords*—*FDTD methods, nonstandard (NS)-FDTD techniques, numerical analysis, radar cross section.

I. INTRODUCTION

The total-field/scattered-field (TF/SF) separation model is a very instructive tool for the radar cross-section (RCS) analysis via the finite-difference time-domain (FDTD) [1] and the nonstandard (NS)-FDTD method [2]. Basically, the traditional TF/SF scheme is straightforward to implement, yet it creates significant non-physical scattered waves, especially around reflection directions at the TF/SF separation surface. The intensity of these artifacts augments depending on the size of the separation surface, thus degrading the reliability of the RCS analysis by means of the FDTD approach. To alleviate this defect, a modified TF/SF model has been previously presented, considering the potential of NS-FDTD operators to reduce the influence of such undesired vector forms [3]. However, the specific model uses a very complex algorithm to attain its goals. Considering the study of realistic structures, such as modern aircrafts, the RCS prediction tool must remain simple, while exhibiting high levels of algorithmic reliability.

In this paper, a robust RCS evaluation technique employing the regular TF/SF separation model [1] is introduced. Although the new model requires a pre-calculation step for the undesired scattered waves, it can fully estimate their effect on the RCS analysis. Moreover, the featured approach is suitable for combination with the FDTD method, since it utilizes the original TF/SF formulation. Initially, we describe the TF/SF characteristics in the FDTD and NS-FDTD technique. Next, the RCS calculation process via the normal TF/SF separation model is explained. Finally, the featured algorithm is numerically verified in terms of real-world aircraft applications.

II. ENHANCED RCS PREDICTION SCHEME CONSIDERING UNDESIRED SCATTERING WAVES

A. Conventional TF/SF Separation Model

To verify, the separation competence of the conventional TF/SF scheme, lets us consider Fig. 1, which shows the RCS

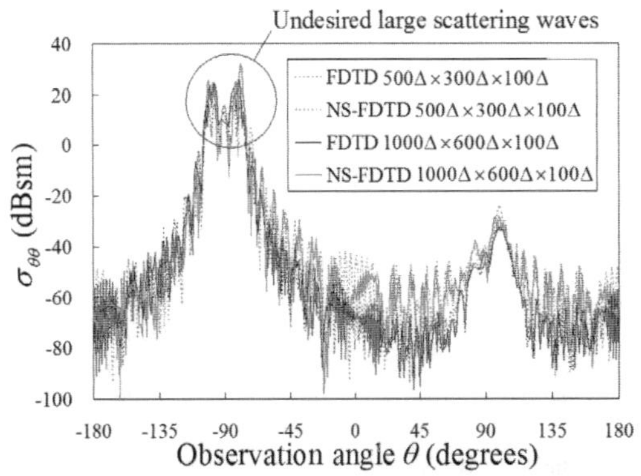

Fig. 1. A typical RCS caused by undesired scattering waves and calculated via the FDTD and the NS-FDTD method. The $\sigma_{\theta\theta}$ parameter refers to the RCS values for an E_θ incident (E_θ^{inc}) plane wave, while the evaluation angle is $\theta^{inc} = 80°$ and $\phi^{inc,\,\mathrm{observation}} = 30°$. Note that the undesired scattering waves are found to be rather intense along the reflection direction.

caused by undesired scattering waves. Here, the TF/SF separation area is either 500Δ×300Δ×100Δ or 1000Δ×600Δ ×100Δ, with Δ= λ /10 and λ =1 m, while the time-step is $\Delta t = 1/(20f)$ for f the frequency. Therefore, even without the scatterer, the usual TF/SF model causes non-negligible RCS errors, both for the FDTD and the NS-FDTD techniques. Essentially, the intensity of these undesired scattering waves depends on the TF/SF separation area size, as in Fig. 1, an issue which hinders the correct RCS design of low observation aircrafts.

B. The Proposed RCS Evaluation Scheme

To avoid the prior non-nonphysical effect of the scattering waves, generated due to the TF/SF separation area, we introduce a new "error prediction model", defined as

$$\overline{\varphi}^{s}(N) = \varphi^{s,\mathrm{raw}} - \varphi^{s,\mathrm{undesired}} e^{j\omega N\Delta t}, \qquad (1)$$

where, $\varphi^{s,\mathrm{raw}}$ and $\varphi^{s,\mathrm{undesired}}$ are the scattering waves in the presence and absence of scatterer, respectively, $j^2 = -1$, ω the angular frequency, and $N = 1, 2, \ldots 1/(f\Delta t)$. It should be stressed that $\varphi^{s,\mathrm{raw}}$ and $\varphi^{s,\mathrm{undesired}}$ are, actually, raw data extracted via the conventional TF/SF separation scheme. Furthermore, the well-known near-to-far-field transformation approach [1] is conducted for all $\overline{\varphi}^{s}(N)$. Our key concept is based on the formulation that since, in (1), $\varphi^{s,\mathrm{raw}}$ is the converged value, we may utilize $\varphi^{s,\mathrm{undesired}}$ when the TF/SF separation region contains the incident wave, however for a smaller time-step number than the one required for the $\varphi^{s,\mathrm{raw}}$ counterpart. This significant reduction of the total amount of time steps for the $\varphi^{s,\mathrm{undesired}}$ quantity leads to substantial CPU time savings, particularly in the FDTD analysis.

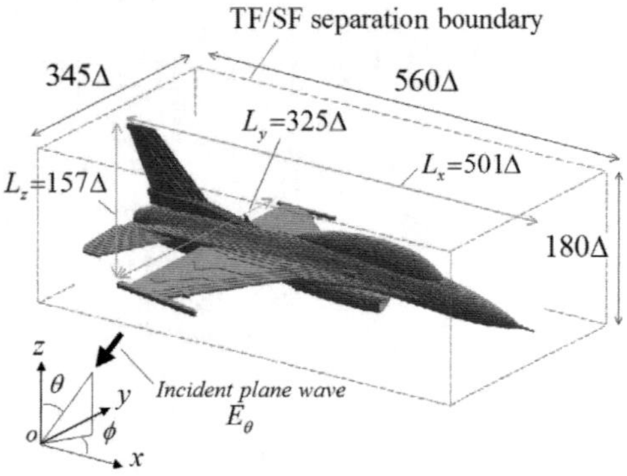

Fig. 2. The RCS evaluation model of an F-16 aircraft model with a total length of L_x = 501Δ, a width of L_y = 325Δ, a height of L_z = 157Δ, and a total number of 194560 cells for the F-16 body. The structure is excited by an E_θ plane wave, while the computational domain is truncated by a 15Δ-layer perfectly matched layer (PML) [1] [Note: the F-16 FDTD model has been created with the assistance of Dr. Shunichi Futatsumori, Electronic Navigation Research Institute (ENIR, Japan)].

By means of (1), the influence of the undesired scattering waves is represented as fluctuations of the RCS value in the proposed procedure. Consequently, in all the results obtained through the conventional TF/SF separation model, we consider the RCS values as valid in the observation angle range, without any fluctuations. Only when, one must, particularly, pay attention to the RCS in the fluctuation angle range, the $\varphi^{s,\mathrm{raw}}$ and $\varphi^{s,\mathrm{undesired}}$ quantities are implemented for the same time-step number, with $N = 0$ set in (1).

III. Application to a Practical Aircraft-Results

To verify our RCS evaluation method, we apply it to the scattering analysis of a real-world aircraft model, depicted in Fig. 2 along with its overall lattice configuration. The model consists of a perfect electric conductor (PEC) medium and is discretized via cubic cells with a spatial increment of $\Delta = \lambda/10$, for $\lambda = 1$ m, and $\Delta t = 1/(20f)$. Moreover, the total simulation time for our calculations is $7000\Delta t$ for the $\varphi^{s,\mathrm{raw}}$ and $2000\Delta t$ for the $\varphi^{s,\mathrm{undesired}}$, respectively. In this context, a set of indicative RCS results, i.e., the variation of the $\sigma_{\theta\theta,\theta\phi}$ parameters as a function of the observation angle θ, is illustrated in Figs. 3 and 4, for an the incident angle $\theta^{inc} = 80°$ and $\phi^{inc} = 30°$ in the FDTD and NS-FDTD realizations. Observe that the "Reference" plot is the RCS outcome acquired via $N = 0$ and an $\varphi^{s,\mathrm{undesired}}$ at $t = 7000\Delta t$ in (1), whereas the "Conventional" plot is the result of $\varphi^{s,\mathrm{raw}}$. As detected from Figs. 3 and 4, the angle range with error of the "Conventional" and "Reference" plots is in agreement with the fluctuation angle range of their "Proposed" counterpart. So, our technique can clarify the angle range, influenced by the undesired scattering waves in terms of the fluctuated RCS values. As an upshot, it is found that the novel method is indeed useful for the validation of RCS data extracted by means of the conventional TF/SF separation model in electrically-large scale analyses.

References

[1] A. Taflove and S. Hagness, *Computational Electrodynamics:* The Finite-Difference Time-Domain Method. Norwood, MA: Artech House, 2005. Chapter 5.

[2] J. B. Cole, "High-accuracy Yee algorithm based on nonstandard finite differences: New developments and verifications," IEEE Trans. Antennas Propag., vol. 50, no. 9, pp. 1185–1191, 2002.

[3] T. Ohtani, Y. Kanai, and N. V. Kantartzis, "Total-field/Scattered-field separation based on H-field correction for the nonstandard finite-difference time-domain," IEEE Trans. Magn., vol. 54, no. 3, art. no. 7000204, 2018.

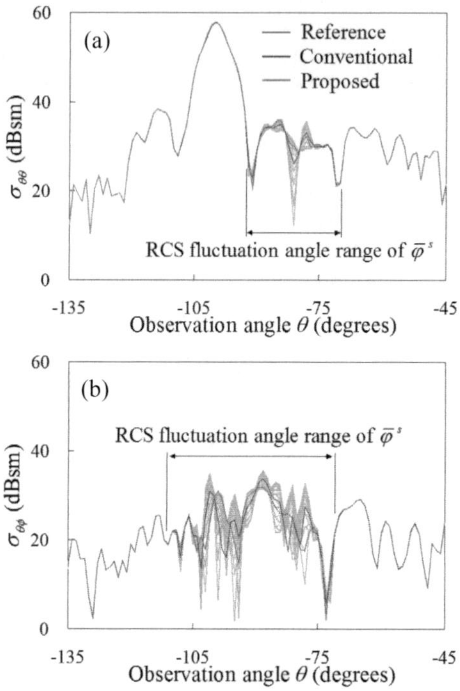

Fig. 3. The NS-FDTD case. The observation is (a) E_θ^s and (b) E_ϕ^s at ϕ = 30°, with $\sigma_{\theta\phi}$ referring to the RCS for an E_θ^{inc} and an $E_\phi^{\mathrm{observation}}$ component.

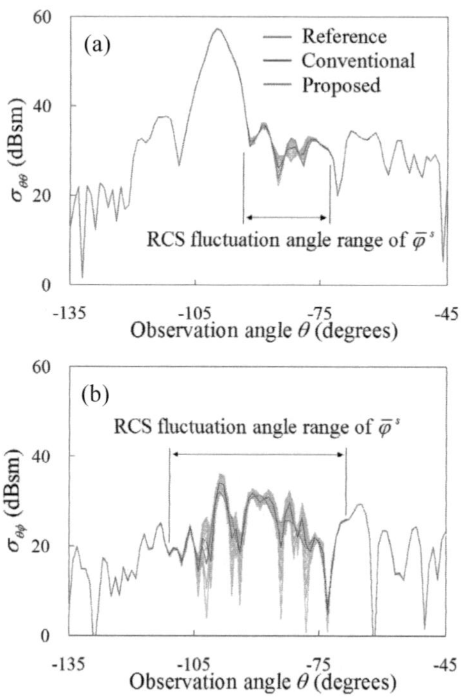

Fig. 4. The FDTD case. The observation is (a) E_θ^s and (b) E_ϕ^s at ϕ = 30°, with $\sigma_{\theta\phi}$ referring to the RCS for an E_θ^{inc} and an $E_\phi^{\mathrm{observation}}$ component.

Heating Characteristics of a Newly Developed RF Cavity Resonator for Hyperthermia that targets Deep-Seated Tumor

Yutaka Tange
Dept. of Electrical and Computer Engineering
National Institute of Technology, Maizuru College
Maizuru, Japan
tange@maizuru-ct.ac.jp

Yasushi Kanai
Dept.of Engineering
Niigata Institute of Technology
Kashiwazaki, Japan
kanai@iee.niit.ac.jp

***Abstract*—We have numerically and experimentally investigated the heating characteristics of a newly developed RF cavity resonator for hyperthermia that targets deep-seated tumor. The new cavity resonator allows only the affected part to be inserted. From calculated and measured results, while the surface region in the phantom inside the cavity is heated to a high temperature, the deep region is heated to a slightly higher temperature. Although it is necessary to cool down the surface of the phantom by the water bolus, it is found that this applicator can heat the deep-seated tumor.**

Keywords—FD-TD method, cavity resonator, hyperthermia, deep-seated tumor

I. INTRODUCTION

Cancer is the uncontrolled growth and spread of cells. It can affect almost any part of the body. The growths often invade the surrounding tissues and even metastasize to distant sites [1]. Therefore, it is desirable to remove the cancer from the human body as soon as possible. Hyperthermia is a cancer therapy that focuses on the difference in heating sensitivity between a tumor and non-tumor cells. In comparison to non-tumor cells that live up to 44°C, the tumor dies from 42.5°C upward. By using electromagnetic energy, the tumor cells are heated up to a temperature at which they die.

We had already developed an RF resonant cavity applicator for a large model with deep-seated tumor [2]. In order to realize local heating, conductive caps were attached to the dielectric phantom [3]. As a result, while we could heat the selective region, the conductive caps obtained large effect on the electromagnetic field in the cavity. Therefore, it can be said that the function as a resonator could not be fully demonstrated because temperature was directly affected by the antenna.

In this study, we have numerically and experimentally investigated the heating characteristics of a newly developed RF cavity resonator for hyperthermia that targets deep-seated tumor. Since the new cavity resonator does not have the conductor cap attached to it, better deep heating can be obtained by this applicator.

II. NEWLY DEVELOPED RF RESONANT CAVITY APPLICATOR

The experimental setup used in our study is illustrated in Fig. 1. The applicator consists of copper plates with the following dimensions: 1.3 m in length x 1.5 m in width x 0.4 m in thickness.

In the cavity applicator, the heated object is placed on a wooden table. Loop antenna is placed beside the object at the center of the applicator in the x-direction. The electric power is applied to the antenna set inside the applicator. Then, the electric and magnetic fields occur in the cavity. In order to realize deep heating, the lowest resonant frequency (TE011 mode) is used. In this study, the electric field strength along x direction of the cavity does not change.

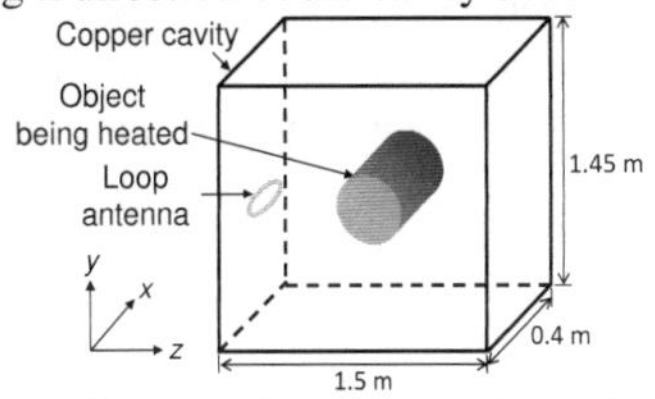

Fig. 1 Arrangement of a rectangular resonant cavity applicator.

III. ELECTROMAGNETIC ANALYSIS

We have solved Maxwell's equations by using three dimensional Finite Difference Time Domain (3D FD-TD) methods:

$$\nabla \times \mathbf{E} = -\mu \frac{\partial \mathbf{H}}{\partial t},\ \nabla \times \mathbf{H} = \sigma \mathbf{E} + \varepsilon \frac{\partial \mathbf{E}}{\partial t} \qquad (1)$$

where μ, σ, and ε represent the permeability, electrical conductivity, and permittivity, respectively. First, we derive resonant frequency of the cavity, and the lowest resonant frequency is applied. After analyzing the electromagnetic field distributions, the electromagnetic energy applied to the heating object is evaluated as

$$Q = \frac{1}{\mathrm{T}} \sigma \int |\mathbf{E}|^2 \mathrm{dt}, \qquad (2)$$

where heat generation is expressed by Q, and periodic time by T.

IV. ANALYSIS MODEL

We modeled the cavity containing the dielectric phantom for electromagnetic calculations as shown in Fig. 2. The whole volume has been divided by our automatic mesh generator into regular cells with a side length of 25 mm. Loop antennas were modeled by using magnetic field. Note that the cavity walls are assumed to be perfect electrical conductors. The electric properties of the phantom are shown in Table I.

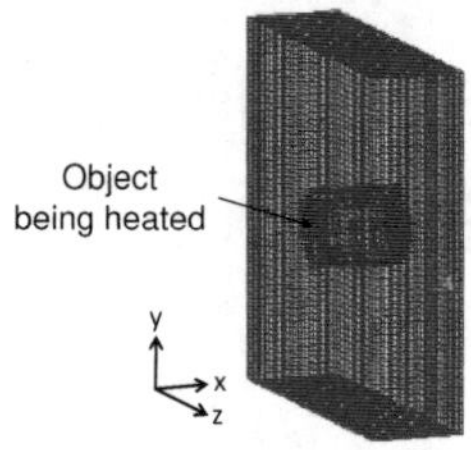

Fig. 2 A model for an RF resonant cavity applicator taking a dielectric phantom into account.

Table I The electric properties and thermal properties of the phantom

Electrical conductivity	σ=0.7 (S/m)
Relative permittivity	ε_r=70
Relative permeability	μ_r= 1

V. Experimental Procedure

Before the experiments, we kept the phantom and room temperature at approximately 20 degrees centigrade by using an air conditioner.

Electromagnetic energy of 400 watts in the frequency range of 90 – 100 MHz at the amplifiers' terminal was generated from the amplifiers. While the phantom is heating, the reflected power increases because of the temperature dependencies of material properties of the phantom. Adjusting the impedance matching box during heating minimizes the amount of reflected power. So the resonant state is maintained by changing the capacitance of the impedance matching box. After heating for 30 minutes, the phantom was cut. Then the temperature distribution was observed using a thermograph (Infra-Eye210; Fujitsu Co. Ltd.).

VI. Results and Discussion

Fig. 3 shows the normalized electromagnetic energy distribution in phantom. In Figs. 3, it is observed that energy is focused on the central region of the phantom and also strongly distributed to the surface region. These results signify that the lowest resonant frequency (TE011 mode) was used.

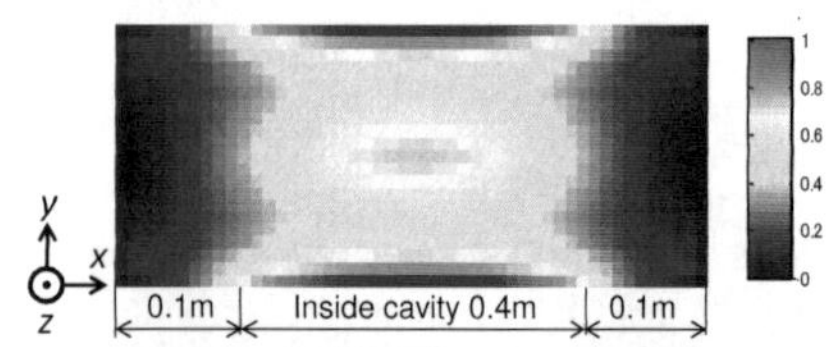

(a) X-Y plane

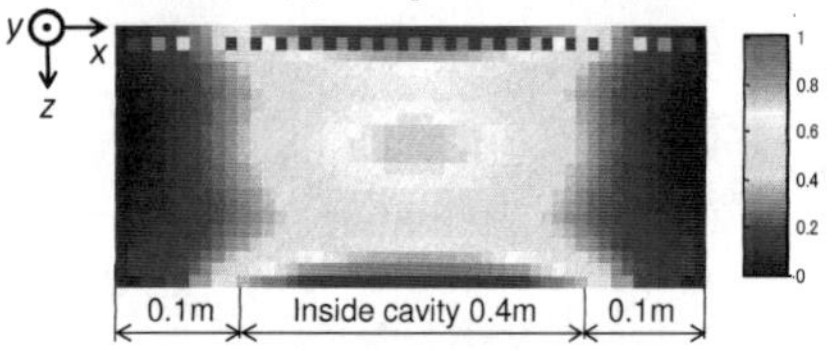

(b) Z-X plane

(c) Y-Z plane (center)

Fig. 3 Normalized electromagnetic energy of the phantom

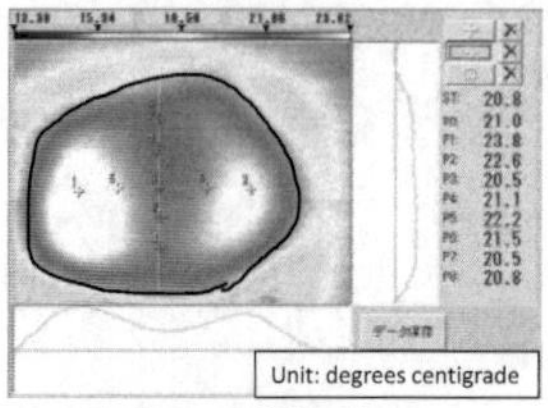

(a) Center of the phantom

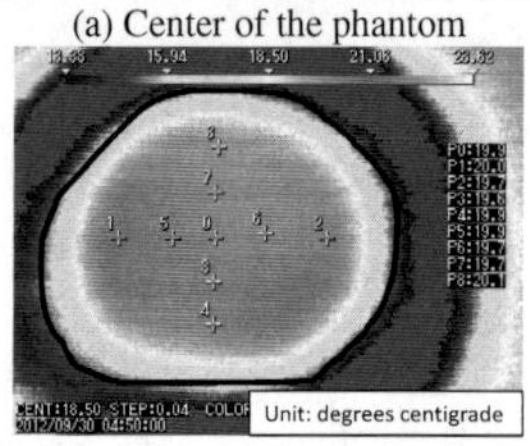

(b) Directly under the conductive wall

Fig. 4 Temperature distributions for a dielectric phantom. Here, T_0, T_c, and f_r are 18.6 degrees centigrade, 19.0 degrees centigrade, and 97.93 MHz, respectively.

Fig. 4 show the measured temperature distribution of the phantom at the center (x = 0.3 m) and directly under the wall (x = 0.1 m). The starting temperature T_0, room temperature T_c, and resonance frequency f_r for each condition are listed in the figure captions. Note that the dielectric phantom is made of gel. For that reason, it does not maintain its original shape, as shown in these figures. The shape distortion is a major reason for the difference in heating patterns between the measured and calculated results.

As observed in Fig. 4 (a), the measured result is in good agreement with the trend of the energy pattern in Fig. 3 (c). While the surface region in the phantom is heated to a high temperature, the deep region is heated to a slightly higher temperature than the initial temperature. In Fig. 4 (b), the temperature distribution directly under the wall is heated about 1.0 degree centigrade higher than the initial temperature. Compared with our previous results [3], it is found that this applicator can heat a tumor located in the deep region within 9 cm in diameter, except for normal cells with a conductive cap. However, it is necessary to reduce the surface temperature by using a cooling system such as a water bolus at clinical stage.

VII. Conclusion

We have developed a new type of RF resonant cavity applicator for hyperthermia that eliminates the need for a conductor cap. By using this applicator, we obtained better heating patterns for a deep-seated tumor as compared to the previous works. Therefore, this applicator is suitable for heating deep-seated tumors during hyperthermia treatment.

References

[1] World Health Organization web site [Online]. Available: http://www.who.int/cancer/en/.

[2] Y. Tange, Y. Kanai, and Y. Saitoh, "Analysis and development of a radio frequency rectangular resonant cavity applicator with multiple antennas for a hyperthermic treatment," IEEE Trans. on Magn., vol. 41, no. 5, pp. 1880–1883, May 2005.

[3] Y. Tange, Y. Kanai, and Y. Saitoh, "Discussion Based on Numerical and Experimental Studies on Heating Characteristics of an RF Rectangular Resonant Cavity Applicator for Hyperthermia Targeting Deep-seated Tumors," The 29th Annual International Conference of the IEEE Engineering in Medicine and Biology Society, pp. 3536–3539, Sep 2007.

Microwave Non-Destructive Testing Technique for Defect Detection of Composite Piles via Electromagnetic Waves with FDTD

Ummu Sahin Sener
Department of Mathematical Engineering
Yıldız Technical University
Istanbul, Turkey
ummusahin@klu.edu.tr

Sebahattin Eker
Informatics Institute
Istanbul Technical University
Istanbul, Turkey
ekerseb@itu.edu.tr

***Abstract*—** Radar and microwave non-destructive testing (NDT) technique is used to simulate a concrete-filled Fiber Reinforced Polymer (FRP) tubes and a concrete pile containing defects (delamination, crack, void). The delamination that occurs as a result of external factors is modeled as closest to the reality. Interaction of electromagnetic wave and the concrete pile is utilized for numerical simulation. A Finite-Difference Time-Domain (FDTD) method with Perfectly Matched Layer (PML) Absorbing Boundary Condition (ABC) is proposed to simulate electromagnetic wave propagation in FRP tube and composite pile. 2D simulation of a wave generated from a point source at microwave frequencies is obtained by using MATLAB®.

Keywords*— *fiber reinforced polymer pile, crack, rebar, finite-difference time-domain simulation, perfectly matched layer

I. INTRODUCTION

FRP composites are widely used for the improvement and strengthening of structures due to their lightness and robustness [1,2]. Structural reinforcement using FRP composites is investigated for two different conditions. Structural reinforcement can be done by covering FRP composites outside of the concrete pile containing defects (delamination, void, crack) and FRP tubes. Although these composite structures are more robust to corrosion and biological threats than conventional piles, delamination or other defects in the concrete may occur. There are many NDT techniques used to detect defects in the structures, such as acoustic, thermal, radiographic, microwave and radar methods. Radar and microwave NDT techniques consist of waveguides, microwave radiometry, coaxial probes and radar horn antenna [3]. Radar NDT includes the generation and transmission of electromagnetic waves using antennas, imaging algorithms, interpretation of the data. Materials that have different dielectric properties can be specified via radar NDT. The response of the concrete-filled FRP tube including rebar and FRP wrapped concrete structure containing void and delamination is investigated by numerical simulation. In the following section, Maxwell curl equations and FDTD methods with PML boundary conditions are ensured. The geometrical configuration of the 2D piles is described and reflection responses of concrete cylinders are revealed.

II. THEORY AND NUMERICAL SIMULATION EXPERIMENTS

The propagation of the electromagnetic wave is expressed by Maxwell's equations. Maxwell curl equations in cartesian coordinates for the linear, isotropic, nondispersive and lossy medium is presented below:

$$\frac{\partial \vec{H}}{\partial t} = -\frac{1}{\mu}\left(\nabla \times \vec{E} + \sigma^* \vec{H}\right) \quad (1)$$

$$\frac{\partial \vec{E}}{\partial t} = \frac{1}{\varepsilon}\left(\nabla \times \vec{H} - \sigma \vec{E}\right) \quad (2)$$

When components of (1) and (2) are reformulated two decoupled groups of equations are obtained, and the decoupled equations are evaluated separately. These two groups are TE or HH-polarized waves, which contain E_x, E_y and H_z components and TM or VV-polarized waves, which contains H_x, H_y and E_z components. In our simulation, HH-polarized or TE waves will be used. In Cartesian coordinate system TE waves has three components as follows:

$$\frac{\partial E_x}{\partial t} = \frac{1}{\varepsilon}\left(\frac{\partial H_z}{\partial y} + \sigma E_x\right) \quad (3)$$

$$\frac{\partial E_y}{\partial t} = \frac{1}{\varepsilon}\left(-\frac{\partial H_z}{\partial x} + \sigma E_y\right) \quad (4)$$

$$\frac{\partial H_z}{\partial t} = -\frac{1}{\mu}\left(\frac{\partial E_y}{\partial x} - \frac{\partial E_x}{\partial y}\right) \quad (5)$$

Thanks to FDTD the Maxwell's curl equations are discretized both space and time domains based on the Yee's algorithm [4, 5]. Central differences are applied for time and space derivatives in (3-5). Thus, the equations that will be used in the algorithm are attained and then the algorithm is implemented for 2D simulations in MATLAB®.

In numerical wave propagation computations, an artificial boundary must be defined to restrict the computation domain and absorb the outgoing waves. In numerical simulation absorber medium has a few mesh cell thickness. In PML boundary condition the waves, which have arbitrary incidence angle, frequency and polarization, are matched at the boundary [6].

The two-dimensional geometry is divided into cells of a much smaller size than the wavelength. The computational domain is a quadratic region of 0.5 m × 0.5 m. The numerical domain is obtained by dividing into 200 grids both the x-axis and the z-axis, $\Delta x = \Delta z = 0.0025$ m and $\Delta x = \Delta z \cong \lambda / 120$. In the first numerical experiment, a three-layered cylinder with eight embedded rebar is used to test the method. The thickness of the Layer 1 (FRP epoxy) and Layer 2 (epoxy) is 0.025 m and the diameter of the inner concrete cylinder is 0.35 m. In the second experiment two-layered concrete cylinder is investigated. The thickness of the FRP epoxy layer that used to strengthen the concrete is 0.0025 m and diameter of the concrete column is 0.4 m.

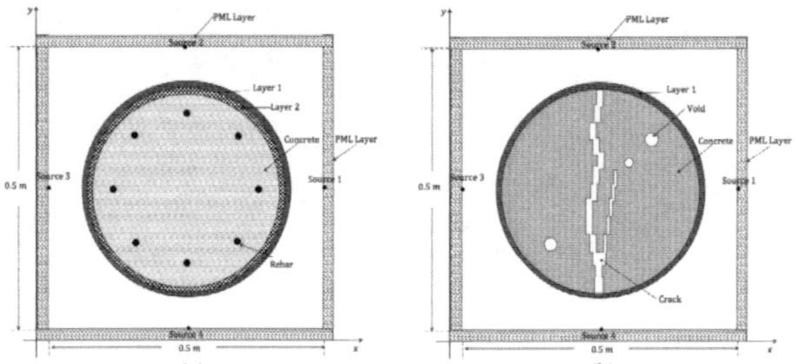

(a) (b)

Fig. 1. (a) FRP tube and (b) Composite Pile

III. Simulation Results

Since the structures are excited by TE plane wave only E_x, E_y and H_z components are calculated. 1 GHz, 2 GHz and 4 GHz pointwise H hard sources in one dimension is used for simulation. The dielectric constants of Layer 1, Layer 2 and concrete are $\varepsilon_1 = 2.6$, $\varepsilon_2 = 4.2$ and $\varepsilon_3 = 5.0$ respectively in Fig. 1 (a). The dielectric constant of Layer 1 is $\varepsilon_1 = 2.6$ in Fig.1 (b). The conductivity of Layer 1, Layer 2, concrete and rebar is $\sigma_1 = \sigma_2 = 0.0\ (S/m)$, $\sigma_3 = 2.6\ (S/m)$ and $\sigma_4 = 10^7\ (S/m)$ respectively.

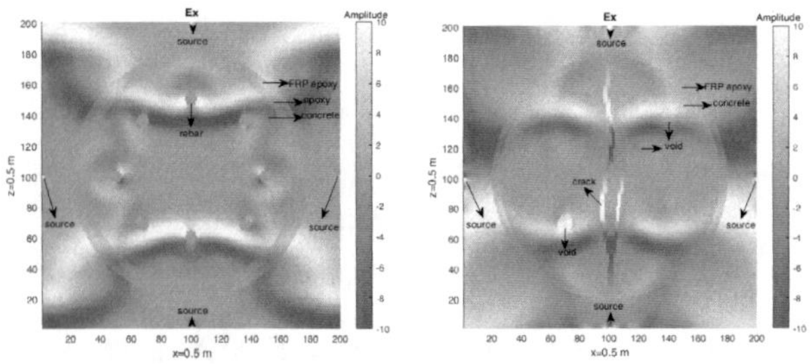

(a) (b)

Fig. 2. E_x for FRP tube and Composite pile at 1 GHz

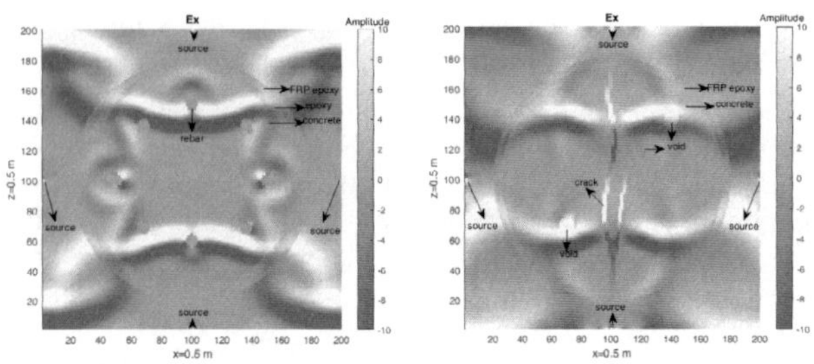

(a) (b)

Fig. 3. E_x for FRP tube and Composite pile at 2 GHz

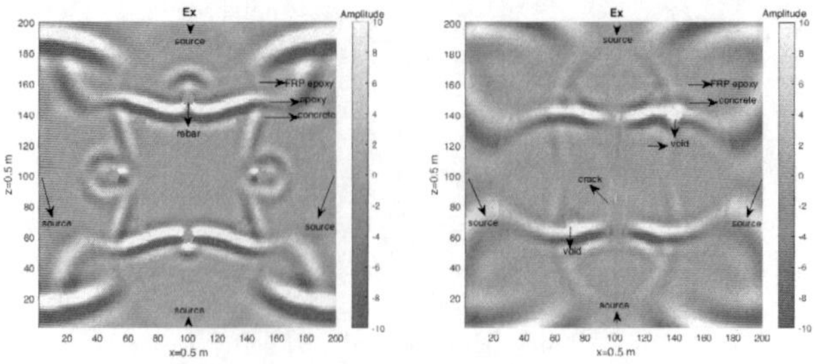

(a) (b)

Fig. 4. E_x for FRP tube and Composite pile at 4 GHz

In Fig. 2 (a) E_x field distributions and amplitudes are obtained, the layers of the FRP tube and rebar can be seen clearly. In Fig. 3 (a) rebars can be seen, but the layers are less clear. In Fig. 4 (a) even though the rebars are visible, the layers are almost indistinguishable. In Fig. 2 (b) the crack inside composite pile is like delamination and the right part of it thinner than the left part and it contains three voids. One of the voids is smaller than the others. A similar situation can be seen in Fig. 3 (b). In Fig. 4 (b) the void which is at the left side is seen, but the crack is noticed vaguely.

IV. Conclusions

The composite pile used in the construction technology and the reinforcement of concrete piles, which are one of the most commonly used strengthening methods, are designed as a numerical simulation experiment. The capability of the FDTD method for simulation of the concrete-filled FRP tubes and a concrete pile containing defects (delamination, crack, void) is investigated. The layers of the composite structure filled inside the concrete and the rebar inside it are successfully viewed. Also, the delamination in the reinforced concrete is observed in such a way that the thickness of the crack is noticeable and the best simulation result is obtained at 1 GHz frequency for microwave radar NDT technique.

References

[1] W. Naguib and A. Mirmiran, "Flexural creep tests and modeling of concrete-filled fiber reinforced polymer tubes", *Journal of Composites for Construction*, vol. *6*(4), pp. 272-279, 2002.

[2] A. Mirmiran, "Stay-in-place FRP form for concrete columns", *Advances in Structural Engineering*, vol. *6*(3), pp. 231-241, 2003.

[3] T. Yu, T. K. Cheng, A. Zhou and D. Lau, "Remote defect detection of FRP-bonded concrete system using acoustic-laser and imaging radar techniques", *Construction and Building Materials*, vol. *109*, pp. 146-155, 2016.

[4] K. Yee, "Numerical solution of initial boundary value problems involving Maxwell's equations in isotropic media", *IEEE Transactions on Antennas and Propagation*, vol. *14*(3), pp. 302-307, 1966.

[5] A. Taflove and S. C. Hagness, Computational electrodynamics: the finite-difference time-domain method, Artech house, 2005.

[6] J. P. Berenger, "A perfectly matched layer for the absorption of electromagnetic waves", *Journal of computational physics*, vol. *114*(2), pp. 185-200, 1994.

A Numerical Approach of Graphene Non-Linear Electromagnetic Response

Stamatios Amanatiadis
ECE Department
Aristotle Univ. of Thessaloniki
Thessaloniki, Greece
samanati@auth.gr

Tadao Ohtani
Asahikawa 070-0841, Japan
bytcg100@ybb.ne.jp

Yasushi Kanai
Engineering Department
Niigata Inst. of Technology
Kashiwazaki, Japan
kanai@iee.niit.ac.jp

Nikolaos Kantartzis
ECE Department
Aristotle Univ. of Thessaloniki
Thessaloniki, Greece
kant@ece.auth.gr

***Abstract*—In the present work, graphene non-linear phenomena are introduced in the finite-difference time-domain algorithm through the dynamic evaluation of its surface conductivity at each time-step. The latter is influenced via the action of the carrier density on graphene that is significantly altered when strong excitation is applied. The developed algorithm is validated by the quantification of the normal propagation distortion.**

***Index Terms*—Carrier density, chemical potential, graphene, non-linearity.**

I. Introduction

During the past decade, the two-dimensional carbon allotrope, namely the graphene, drew the attention of the research community due to its outstanding properties. This one-atom thick material, presents a finite conductivity, despite its negligible thickness, leading to various interesting properties. Regarding its electromagnetic response, graphene is capable of supporting the propagation of strongly confined surface plasmon polariton (SPP) waves at the terahertz regime. The latter feature enables the design of several devices for advanced applications at these frequencies.

However, graphene's properties are based on the effective Dirac equation that describes the behaviour of electrons holded in it. This fact results in a strong non-linear electromagnetic response that has to be taken into account during the design process of any apparatus [1]. Consequently, such traits for complicated devices can not be investigated theoretically and modified algorithms of popular numerical schemes must be utilized. In our work, a flexible method is proposed in order to introduce non-linear features in the popular finite-difference time-domain (FDTD) algorithm.

First of all, the surface conductivity of graphene is presented, focusing on the chemical potential. This potential is influenced from the carrier density on the two-dimensional sheet, that is evaluated via the discontinuity of the electric displacement on graphene. The prior aspects are imported in the conventional FDTD algorithm and the surface conductivity is updated both spatially and temporally. Numerical results prove the consistent incorporation of non-linear effects owing to the response of graphene at strong excitation fields.

II. Theoretical Aspects

Our concept to introduce the non-linear properties of graphene is based on the alteration of carrier density n_s because of the strongly confined SPP waves. This is computed through the boundary conditions on graphene and specifically in terms of the discontinuity of electric displacement $D_n^+ - D_n^- = q_e n_s$, with q_e the electron charge. Therefore, the properties, related to the carrier density, are influenced locally, especially the chemical potential μ_c via [2]:

$$n_s = \frac{2}{\pi(\hbar v_F)^2} \int_0^\infty E\left[f_d(E) - f_d(E + 2\mu_c)\right] \mathrm{d}E, \quad (1)$$

where v_F is the Fermi velocity, $\hbar$ the reduced Planck constant, and $f_d(E)$ the Fermi-Dirac distribution.

Essentially, the chemical potential has an effect on the surface conductivity of graphene that is considered throughout this work as an infinitesimally thin layer $\sigma(\omega, \mu_c, \Gamma, T)$, with ω the radian frequency, Γ a phenomenological scattering rate assumed to be independent of energy, and T the temperature. Then, graphene's conductivity can be reliably calculated by the compact expression of:

$$\sigma_{\text{intra}}(\omega, \mu_c, \Gamma, T) = \frac{A}{j\omega + 2\Gamma}, \quad (2)$$

obtained from the Kubo formula [3] that involves only the dominant, at the far-infrared spectrum, intraband term, where A is a parameter (independent of frequency), defined as:

$$A = \frac{q_e^2 k_B T}{\pi \hbar^2}\left[\frac{\mu_c}{k_B T} + 2\ln(e^{-\mu_c/k_B T} + 1)\right], \quad (3)$$

and k_B the Boltzmann constant.

In summary, the SPP waves on graphene, due to an external electromagnetic field, are leading in the local variation of the surface conductivity, enabling non-linear phenomena. The conventional FDTD algorithm is upgraded to support the two-dimensional material, while proper modifications are applied according to the discussed procedure. Graphene is introduced in the FDTD method as the surface current $\mathbf{J}_{gr} = \sigma_{\text{intra}}\mathbf{E}$, estimated through the auxiliary differential equation (ADE) approach, and is placed exactly at the corresponding tangential electric field components. The update equation of the electic field is firstly calculated through the conventional algorithm and then the surface current density contribution is added [4]:

$$E_x\big|_{i+1/2,j}^{n+1} = E_x\big|_{i+1/2,j}^{n+1} - \frac{\Delta t}{\varepsilon_0 \Delta z} J_x\big|_{i+1/2,j}^{n+1/2}, \quad (4)$$

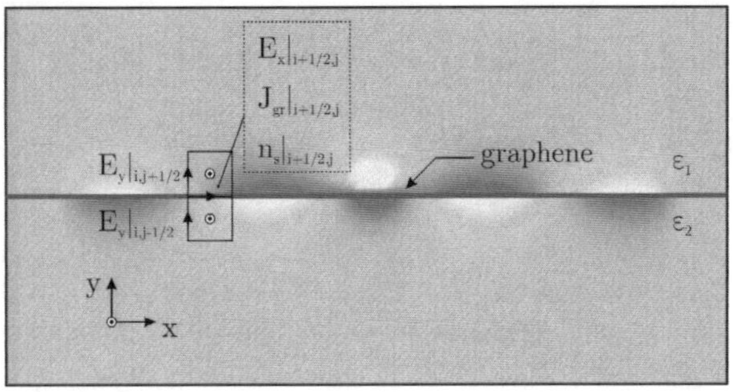

Fig. 1. Field components and auxiliary parameters of graphene for a real propagation scenario.

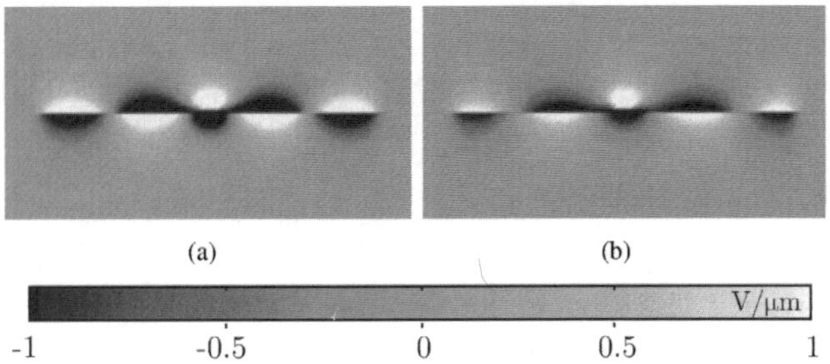

Fig. 2. Electric field distribution for an excitation of $1\,\mathrm{V}/\mu\mathrm{m}$ for (a) the conventional FDTD algorithm, (b) the proposed modification.

$$J_x|^{n+1/2}_{i+1/2,j} = \frac{1-\Gamma\Delta t}{1+\Gamma\Delta t} J_x|^{n-1/2}_{i+1/2,j} + \frac{A|^n_{i+1/2,j}\Delta t}{1+\Gamma\Delta t} E_x|^n_{i+1/2,j}. \quad (5)$$

Parameter $A|^n_{i+1/2,j}$ is not constant, as in the linear case, yet it is computed at each time-step and cell via (3). Here, the chemical potential is evaluated through (1) for carrier density:

$$n_s|^n_{i+1/2,j} = \frac{\varepsilon_1 E_y|^n_{i,j+1/2} - \varepsilon_2 E_y|^n_{i,j-1/2}}{q_e}, \quad (6)$$

where ε_1 and ε_2 are the dielectric permittivity of the superstrate and substrate, respectively. The described configuration is depicted in Fig. 1, while the rest of the components, not related to graphene, are updated through the conventional FDTD algorithm.

III. Numerical Results

For the numerical validation, graphene starting parameters are selected as $\Gamma = 0.11\,\mathrm{meV}$ and $\mu_c = 0\,\mathrm{eV}$ at room's temperature $T = 300\,\mathrm{K}$ and the far-infrared spectrum. The scattering rate is near its lower limit in order to sufficiently observe the phenomenon. Moreover, the dimensions of our computation domain are $200\,\mu\mathrm{m}\times 100\,\mu\mathrm{m}$ and those of the cubic cells are $\Delta x = \Delta y = 1.45\,\mu\mathrm{m}$, while the time-step is set to $\Delta t = 2.4\,\mathrm{fs}$. All open boundaries are terminated via an 8-cell thick perfectly matched layer (PML), extending graphene in its interior to attenuate efficiently SPP waves.

The conducted simulations are of identical characteristics except for the strength of the excitation field, since it enables the non-linear response. The initial observation of the phenomenon is performed via the distribution of the field

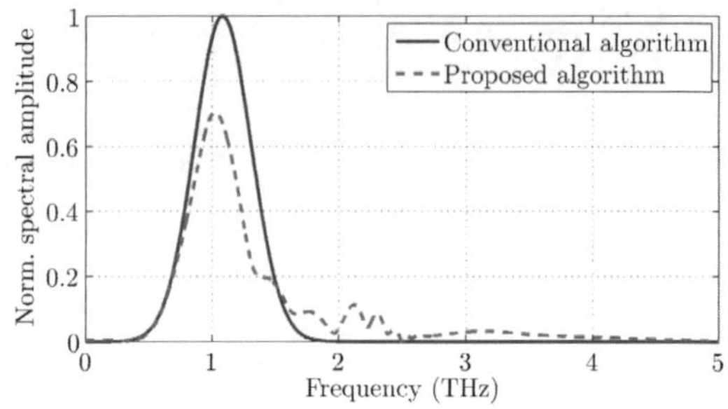

Fig. 3. Spectral amplitude of the surface current for an excitation of $1\,\mathrm{V}/\mu\mathrm{m}$.

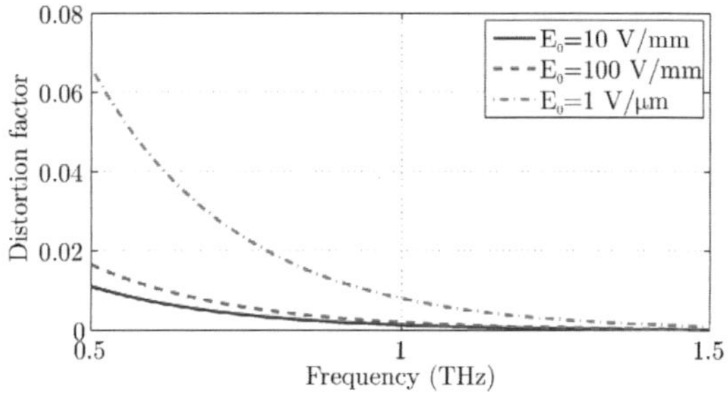

Fig. 4. Distortion factor versus frequency for different excitation fields, calculated by means of the proposed algorithm.

components in the computational domain. Specifically, the normal, to graphene, electric field component, namely E_y, is illustrated in Fig. 2 for a strong excitation field of $1\,\mathrm{V}/\mu\mathrm{m}$. Observe that the proposed modification of the FDTD algorithm has, indeed, an effect on the propagation of the SPP wave, as the harmonic pulse is broadened. Moreover, the surface current spectral amplitude, normalized to the maximum obtained value of the conventional algorithm, is compared in Fig. 3 where the higher harmonics are clearly indicated in our approach.

Also, a quantitative result is demonstrated in Fig. 4, where the distortion factor depends on the surface current density:

$$\frac{|J_{x,\mathrm{conventional}} - J_{x,\mathrm{proposed}}|}{\max\{J_{x,\mathrm{conventional}}\}}. \quad (7)$$

It is observed that the non-linear phenomena are more prominently revealed at lower frequencies and for stronger excitation fields, as expected. It should be stressed that an electromagnetic field over $1\,\mathrm{V}/\mu\mathrm{m}$ has to be applied in order to adequately distort the normal propagation of the SPP waves.

References

[1] S. Mikhailov and K. Ziegler, "Nonlinear electromagnetic response of graphene: Frequency multiplication and the self-consistent-field effects," *J. Phys.: Condensed Matter*, vol. 20, no. 38, pp. 384 204 (1–10), 2008.

[2] G. W. Hanson, "Dyadic Green's functions and guided surface waves for a surface conductivity model of graphene," *J. Appl. Phys.*, vol. 103, no. 6, pp. 064 302(1–8), 2008.

[3] V. Gusynin, S. Sharapov, and J. Carbotte, "Magneto-optical conductivity in graphene," *J. Phys.: Condensed Matter*, vol. 19, no. 2, pp. 026 222(1–12), 2006.

[4] S. A. Amanatiadis and N. V. Kantartzis, "Rigorous time-domain graphene representation as a surface boundary condition," in *Proc. 8th Int. Congr. Advanced Electromagn. Materials in Microwaves and Optics (METAMATERIALS)*. Lyngby, Denmark, 2014, pp. 13–15.

On the Validity of Time Domain Methods for Complex Cavities

Michael R. Johnson
205 West D Ave Suite 348
Eglin AFB, FL 32542 USA
michael.johnson.10@us.af.mil

***Abstract*—This work evaluates the applicability of computational electromagnetic methods for simulating the response of a typical aircraft weapon bay. The goal is to develop a prediction of maximum expected electric field levels in the bay for evaluating EMC, including hazards of electromagnetic radiation to ordnance. A generalized geometry is created with traits similar to an aircraft bay. The Transmission Line Matrix method is used to simulate the response of the bay at 1830 MHz using a near field source in CST Microwave Studio. Results are evaluated for Chi-squared distribution with six degrees of freedom and the predicted number of modes.**

***Keywords*—CEM, E3, EMC, Complex Cavity, Weapon bay.**

I. Background

Aircraft weapon bays present a difficult challenge when evaluating Electromagnetic Environmental Effects (E3) of stores within those bays. The bay Radio Frequency (RF) environment is quite chaotic and sensitive to minute changes in a host of independent variables, leading to the conclusion that a stochastic approach might be a practical analysis alternative. Stochastic characteristics of Reverberation Chambers (RC) are understood and have been expanded over the years to describe many types of complex enclosures [1], [2], and [3].

This paper explores the use of a time-domain Computational Electromagnetics (CEM) method as a substitute for traditional test data. While the goal is to provide broadband data—data at frequencies just above the first cutoff of the bay to as high as practical in simulation—this work focuses in a band around 1830 MHz, since it coincides with other projects.

II. Critical Assumptions

A complex cavity is such that the irregularity of the walls insures that only the incoherent part of the fields contributes to the distribution of the fields in a cavity. In order to stochastically represent a complex cavity two assumptions must be made [1]: one, the number of modes M at a given frequency is high ([4] suggests $M > 100$), i.e., overmoded; and two, that the energy of every excited mode is the same. This paper asserts that these assumptions can be justified with simulated data as a viable substitute for test data.

Mean normalized e-fields in an overmoded cavity can be represented as a chi-square random variable with six degrees of freedom (X_6^2) [1]. Further, the standard deviation of the *per probe maximum* simulated e-fields relative to the mean and standard deviation of those maximums as a set ($\overline{E}_{max}$, σ_{max}) is given by (1) as shown in [5]. Energy can be considered uniform if $\sigma_{max/mean}(dB) \leq 3$ dB for frequencies above 400 MHz [5]:

$$\sigma_{max/mean}(dB) = 20log_{10}\frac{\sigma_{max} + \overline{E}_{max}}{\overline{E}_{max}}. \qquad (1)$$

The number of modes M for a wavelength λ in a complex cavity with volume V and quality factor Q [4], [5] is:

$$M(\lambda) = \frac{8\pi V}{\lambda^3 Q}. \qquad (2)$$

For this work Q is defined at a frequency f_p as:

$$Q(f) = \frac{f_p}{\Delta f}, \qquad (3)$$

where Δf is the bandwidth determined by two frequencies coincidental with field values at half a significant peak value within a band centered at frequency f_p within a total band $0.95f_p < f < 1.05f_p$.

For example, in Fig. 1 e-field data is plotted for seven field probes within the bay simulation centered at f_p = 1830 MHz. Frequency stirring techniques [6] are used to set conditions to adhere to the modal energy assumption in the post-processing of the simulation data. Several strong modes exist (implying an overmoded condition), although the modes at 1830 MHz are fairly weak. The peak at 1806 MHz from one of the probes (probe 5 as described below) was selected to define Q since it is the nearest dominant mode.

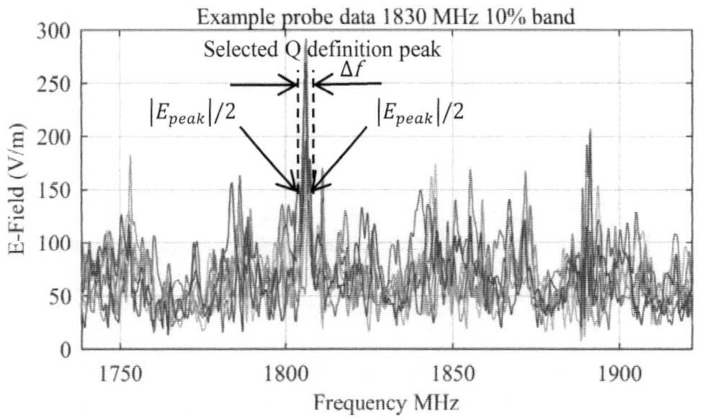

Fig. 1. Example probe data centered around 1830 MHz. Magnitudes for seven probes are plotted. The peak at 1806 MHz is chosen to define Q.

III. Simulation Setup

The modeling and simulations were performed using the TLM method [7] in CST Microwave Studio. A chamber meant to be a reasonable representation of an aircraft weapon bay with simplified shape and content was constructed from geometric primitives within CST (Fig. 2).

The x axis is longitudinal to the bay along its center, y across the bay, and z is vertical. Several structural ribs were included to add a level of complexity. Both ends of the main chamber open into smaller chambers through various openings in bulkheads. The left end has a large square aperture while the right has two smaller circular and one small rectangular aperture. The lower portion of the chamber is a flat sheet modeled as multilayer 1.5 mm carbon Fiber Composite (CFC) thin panel material with a conductivity of 4.09×10^4 S/m. The sheet has three 3 mm slits; one on either end of the bay running from side to side, connected by a center slit running along the center axis, intended to represent closed bay doors. The surrounding walls are simulated as sheet lossy metal aluminum (Al) with a conductivity of 3.56×10^7 S/m. The volume critical to M and Q is that of the main bay; 2.828 m^3. All surrounding simulation boundaries are absorbing. The top, sides and both ends of the bay are flush with the absorbing boundary. The bottom boundary is offset by 0.2 m. A Near Field Source (NFS) replicating a horn antenna was used.

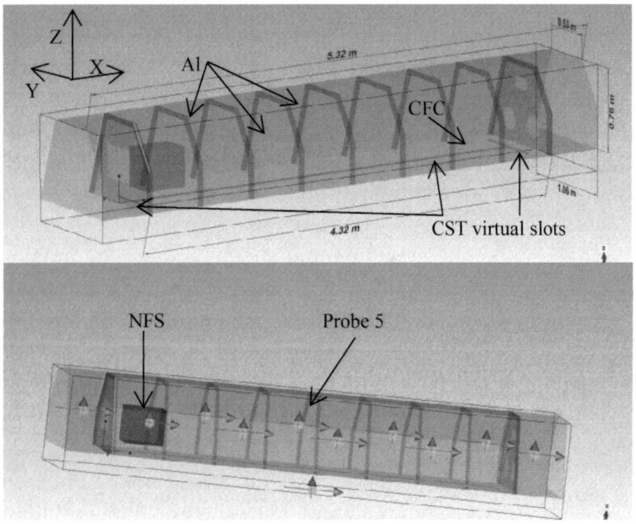

Fig. 2. Simulated bay with dimensions (top), and probe locations in the bay (bottom). Probes are numbered 1–11 from left to right. Probes 1 and 11 are in the end chambers, and probe 6 is below the bay outside the door. The dark blue box near the left end is the location of the NFS.

IV. Simulation Results

Fig. 1 typifies the simulation output for all probes. There are very high peaks spread out between minor peaks and valleys in the data, generally indicating a highly moded result all across the spectrum. Probe responses were then mean-normalized in order to compare with an ideal X_6^2 distribution for the range of the mean-normalized probe data. Using probe 5 as an example, a typical stochastic comparison is shown in Fig. 3. The agreement to theory is obvious, implying that the use of simulation could be successful.

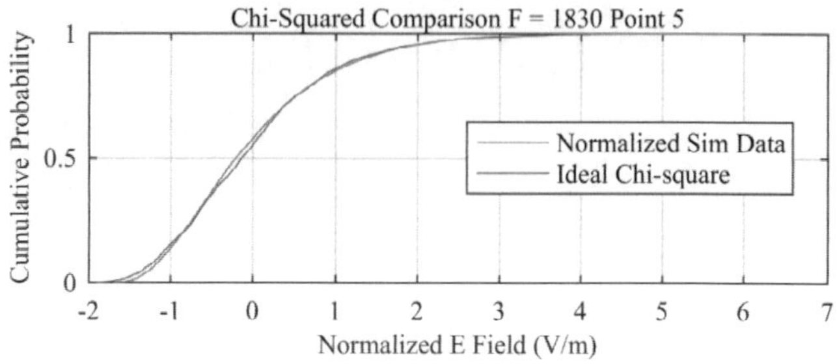

Fig. 3. Chi-squared comparison of 1830 MHz data for probe 5.

Data from four probes was excluded from the statistics: the probes in either end; outside the door; and the probe coincidental with the NFS. Table 1 summarizes results, using the average maximum simulated e-field, $\overline{E}_{max}$.

TABLE I. Vital Metrics

Frequency (MHz)	*Q*	*Modes*	$\sigma_{max/mean}$*(dB)*	$\overline{E}_{max}$ *(V/m)*
1830	44	336	1.03	219

V. Conclusions

It can be concluded that this bay model displays the characteristics of a complex cavity. Anecdotally it is reasonable to conclude that simulation data conforms to the X_6^2 distribution requirement. Qualitative analysis is sufficient considering the near perfect agreement as exemplified in Fig. 3. The number of modes is quite high and $\sigma_{max/mean}$ is well below the required 3 dB.

Although this bay is not particularly resonant at 1830 MHz, it is at nearby frequencies. It may be advantageous to evaluate several frequencies once a broadband simulation is completed. Quality factors of complex, highly resonant structures are difficult to quantify. Since the values for Q and therefore M in this work are based on an approximation it is risky to draw presise conclusions from them. Considering the high magnitude of the maximum e-fields, the values for Q seem somewhat low and (3) may need to be readdressed.

References

[1] T. H. Lehman, "A Statistical Theory of Electromagnetic Fields in Complex Cavities," EMP Int. Note 494, 1993.

[2] R. H. Price, et al., "Determination of the Statistical Distribution of Electromagnetic Field Amplitudes in Complex Cavities, JAYCOR Rep. 88-JAL129, June 1988.

[3] D. Hill, *Electromagnetic Fields in Cavities, Deterministic and Statistical Theories*, John Wiley & Sons, Inc., Hoboken, HJ, USA, 2009, pp. 81–148.

[4] MIL-STD-461F: Requirement of the Control of Electromagnetic Interference Characteristics of Subsystems and Equipment. US DoD Interface Standard, 10 December 2007.

[5] IEC 61000-4-21, Electromagnetic Compatibility (EMC) – Part 4-21: Testing and measurements techniques – Reverberation chamber test methods, International Electrotechnical Commission, 2008.

[6] D. A. Hill, "Electronic mode stirring for reverberation chambers," IEEE Trans. On Electromagnetic Compatibility, vol. 36, no. 4, pp 294–299, November 1994.

[7] P. B. Johns and M. O'Brien. "Use of the transmission line modelling (T.L.M) method to solve nonlinear lumped networks," The Radio Electron and Engineer, 1980.

Stochastic LIM for Transient Solution of Electromagnetic and Circuit Problems with Uncertainties

Xu Chen, José E. Schutt-Ainé, and Andreas C. Cangellaris
Department of Electrical and Computer Engineering
University of Illinois at Urbana-Champaign
Urbana, IL 61801
Email: {xuchen1, jesa, cangella}@illinois.edu

***Abstract*—Stochastic LIM was introduced for fast and accurate simulation of circuits with random elements. The method combines Latency Insertion Method with Stochastic Galerkin Method to formulate a finite difference-based transient circuit solver for simulation of circuits with uncertainties. The random nodal voltages and branch currents, along with the random circuit element values, are expanded using generalized Polynomial Chaos basis functions to form an augmented system which is solved using LIM. A sampling-based method proposed to calculate expansion coefficients as inputs to Stochastic LIM.**

I. Introduction

Stochastic LIM was introduced for the solution of transient circuit problems [1], [2] containing random variables. It has been demonstrated to be effective for resistor networks and ideal transmission line models. In this paper, we review the formulation of Stochastic LIM and propose a sampling-based electromagnetic (EM) extraction routine to obtain inputs for Stochastic LIM using existing EM solvers.

II. Stochastic LIM

Latency Insertion Method (LIM) [3] is a finite-difference time-domain circuit solver that utilizes a leapfrogging algorithm, similar to FDTD, to solve for transient voltages and currents in circuits. Stochastic LIM is an extension of LIM that takes into account Polynomial Chaos (PC) expansion of random variables in a circuit. The PC expansion coefficients of random variables are similar to Fourier Series coefficients of the random process, and thus they encapsulate the randomness in the voltages, currents, and circuit element values:

$$F(\omega) = \sum_{k=0}^{\infty} F_k \phi_k(\xi(\omega)), \tag{1}$$

where the basis functions ψ_k are orthogonal polynomials whose weighting function $W(\xi)$ takes on the same form as the probability density function of the random variables. For instance, Hermite polynomials are used if the random variables exhibit Gaussian distribution.

When Stochastic LIM is formulated to include the PC expansion, the scalar update equations for voltages and currents at each time step becomes an augmented state-space system. The size of the state space is only proportional to the number of truncated PC expansion terms used to represent the random variables. Each node voltage and branch current is still updated independently, thus the numerical complexity of the method still scales favorably with respect to the number of nodes and branches in the circuit. Once one simulation is needed to propagate the uncertainties in the system. Using Galerkin project, the vector update equations are:

$$\mathbf{V}_i^{n+\frac{1}{2}} = \left(\frac{\mathbf{C}_i}{\Delta t} + \frac{\mathbf{G}_i}{2}\right)^{-1} \times \left[\left(\frac{\mathbf{C}_i}{\Delta t} - \frac{\mathbf{G}_i}{2}\right)\mathbf{V}_i^{n-\frac{1}{2}} + \mathbf{H}_i^n - \sum_{j=1}^{M_i} \mathbf{I}_{ij}^n\right], \tag{2}$$

$$\mathbf{I}_{ij}^{n+1} = \left(\frac{\mathbf{L}_{ij}}{\Delta t} + \frac{\mathbf{R}_{ij}}{2}\right)^{-1} \times \left[\left(\frac{\mathbf{L}_{ij}}{\Delta t} - \frac{\mathbf{R}_{ij}}{2}\right)\mathbf{I}_{ij}^n + \mathbf{E}_{ij}^{n+\frac{1}{2}} + \mathbf{V}_i^{n+\frac{1}{2}} - \mathbf{V}_j^{n+\frac{1}{2}}\right], \tag{3}$$

$$\mathbf{V}_i^n = \left[V_{i,0}^n, V_{i,1}^n, \cdots, V_{i,P}^n\right]^T, \quad \mathbf{I}_{ij}^n = \left[I_{ij,0}^n, I_{ij,1}^n, \cdots, I_{ij,P}^n\right]^T, \tag{4}$$

$$\mathbf{S}_k = \begin{bmatrix} \frac{\langle\psi_k,\psi_0,\psi_0\rangle}{\langle\psi_0^2\rangle} & \frac{\langle\psi_k,\psi_0,\psi_1\rangle}{\langle\psi_0^2\rangle} & \cdots & \frac{\langle\psi_k,\psi_0,\psi_P\rangle}{\langle\psi_0^2\rangle} \\ \frac{\langle\psi_k,\psi_1,\psi_0\rangle}{\langle\psi_1^2\rangle} & \ddots & & \vdots \\ \vdots & & \ddots & \vdots \\ \frac{\langle\psi_k,\psi_P,\psi_0\rangle}{\langle\psi_P^2\rangle} & \frac{\langle\psi_k,\psi_P,\psi_1\rangle}{\langle\psi_P^2\rangle} & \cdots & \frac{\langle\psi_k,\psi_P,\psi_P\rangle}{\langle\psi_P^2\rangle} \end{bmatrix}, \tag{5}$$

$$\mathbf{C}_i = \sum_{k=0}^{P} C_{i,k}\mathbf{S}_k, \quad \mathbf{G}_i = \sum_{k=0}^{P} G_{i,k}\mathbf{S}_k, \tag{6}$$

$$\mathbf{R}_{ij} = \sum_{k=0}^{P} R_{ij,k}\mathbf{S}_k, \quad \mathbf{L}_{ij} = \sum_{k=0}^{P} L_{ij,k}\mathbf{S}_k. \tag{7}$$

Once the PC coefficients of unknown voltages and currents are solved, their statistics can be obtained from post-processing:

$$\mathbb{E}[V_i^n] = V_{i,0}^n, \quad \sigma(V_i^n) = \sqrt{\sum_{k=1}^{P} V_{i,k}^n \langle \psi_k^2 \rangle}. \qquad (8)$$

III. Sampling-based EM Extraction

Electromagnetic problems such as transmission lines (TL) can be solved using LIM and an equivalent circuit. To extract an EM model containing uncertainties, we use sparse grid quadrature in the multi-dimensional random space. A deterministic EM extraction is performed at each quadrature node, then the PC expansion coefficients in (6) and (7) can be approximated as:

$$C_k \approx \frac{1}{\langle \psi_k^2(\boldsymbol{\xi}) \rangle} \sum_{i=1}^{M_{d,l}} C(\boldsymbol{\xi}_i)\psi(\boldsymbol{\xi}_i)W(\boldsymbol{\xi}_i)w(\boldsymbol{\xi}_i), \qquad (9)$$

where the number of EM extractions requires is

$$M_{d,l} \approx \frac{2^l d^l}{l!}, \quad \text{for } d \gg 1. \qquad (10)$$

Notice this number scales more favorably with respect to the dimensionality of the random space when compared to tensor product grid.

IV. Numerical Example

We consider a microstrip line of length $L = 50$ cm excited by a trapezoidal pulse voltage source with source impedance $50\,\Omega$, switching from $V_{low} = 0\,\text{V}$ to $V_{high} = 1\,\text{V}$, with rise and fall time $t_{rf} = 500\,\text{ps}$, pulse width $pw = 20\,\text{ns}$, and is terminated with a load impedance of $50\,\Omega$. The random parameters are the width $W \sim \mathcal{N}(0.1, 0.01)$ mm, the substrate thickness $h \sim \mathcal{N}(0.2, 0.02)$ mm, and dielectric constant $\epsilon_r \sim \mathcal{N}(4.4, 0.44)$.

Using the sampling-based modeling, 177 deterministic EM extractions are needed to obtain the PC expansion coefficients for RLGC. Then an equivalent $\pi-$topology model is used to solve the problem in Stochastic LIM with a single transient simulation. The results are compared to Monte Carlo, where 2000 EM extractions and 2000 LIM runs are needed. The standard deviation of the near- and far-end voltages calculated by both methods are shown in Figure 1.

The total run-time using Stochastic LIM and proposed EM modeling strategy is 1195 seconds, whereas the Monte Carlo simulation required 9420 seconds. Additionally, the post-process of results to obtain the statistics in Stochastic LIM is much quicker and required less data storage. Only 2.5 MB of data needed to be processed in under 10 seconds, whereas Monte Carlo resulted in 632 MB of data that took 6935 seconds to post-process for statistics.

V. Conclusions

We demonstrated some preliminary results for quantifying uncertainties in circuit voltages and currents resulting from random variables in the underlying EM problem. The proposed approach utilizes existing EM code to perform the extraction and modeling part of the process, and uses Stochastic LIM to obtain the uncertainties with a single simulation. Notable improvements over Monte Carlo technique [4] is observed.

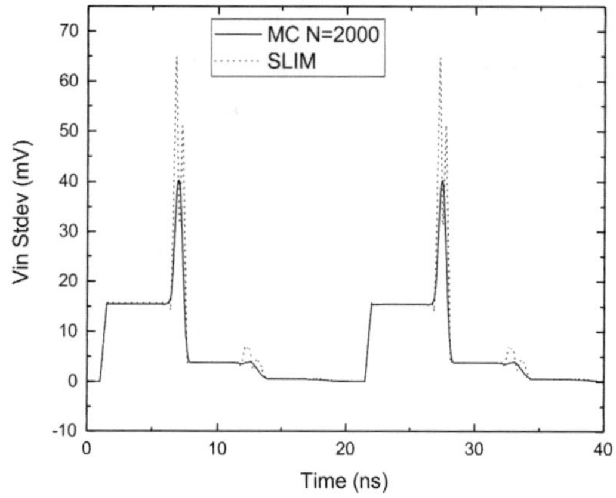

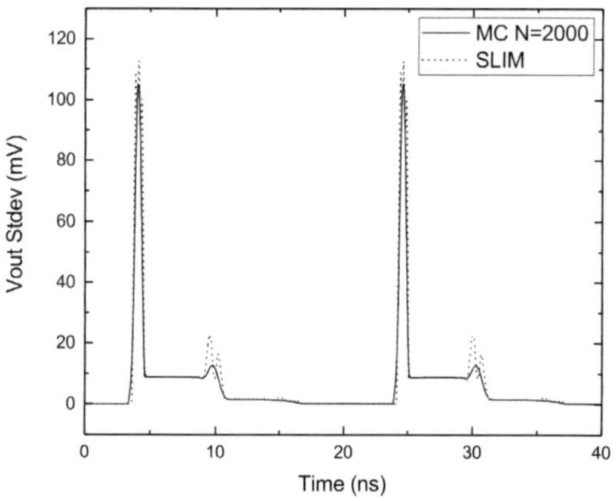

Fig. 1. Standard deviation σ of near- (a) and far-end (b) voltages on single-line microstrip with geometric uncertainties as calculated by Monte Carlo $N = 2000$ and Stochastic LIM.

References

[1] X. Chen, M. Qiu, J. E. Schutt-Ainé, and A. C. Cangellaris, "Stochastic LIM for transient simulation of circuits with uncertainties," in *Proc. IEEE 23rd Conf. Electrical Performance of Electronic Packaging and Systems*, pp. 29–32, Oct. 2014.

[2] X. Chen, J. E. Schutt-Ainé, and A. C. Cangellaris, "Stochastic LIM for transient simulations of printed circuit board transmission lines with uncertainties," in *Proc. IEEE 66th Electronic Components and Technology Conf. (ECTC)*, pp. 2297–2304, May 2016.

[3] J. E. Schutt-Aine, "Latency insertion method (LIM) for the fast transient simulation of large networks," *Circuits and Systems I: Fundamental Theory and Applications, IEEE Transactions on*, vol. 48, pp. 81–89, Jan. 2001.

[4] M. Mishra and N. Gupta, "Quasi monte carlo integration technique for method of moments solution of efie in radiation problems," *Applied Computational Electromagnetics Society Journal*, vol. 24, no. 3, pp. 300–305, 2009. cited By 6.

A Modified Polynomial Chaos Modeling Approach for Uncertainty Quantification

Majid Ahadi Dolatsara[1], Ambrish Varma[2], Kumar Keshavan[2], and Madhavan Swaminathan[1]
[1] School of Electrical and Computer Engineering, Center for Co-Design of Chip, Package, System (C3PS), Georgia Institute of Technology, Atlanta, Ga, email: mad6@gatech.edu, madhavan.swaminathan@ece.gatech.edu.
[2] Cadence Design Systems, Inc., Chelmsford, MA, email: ambrishv@cadence.com, ckumar@cadence.com.

Abstract—**Uncertainty quantification is a key element for modeling high speed circuits, which is often done with Monte Carlo analysis. However, because this method is computationally expensive, new approaches with higher efficiency have been developed. Many popular methods are based on the surrogate models developed with Polynomial Chaos theory. However, size of these models can be prohibitively large for realistic examples. Hence, this paper provides a novel methodology to use an ensemble of weaker models to improve efficiency. Finally, a numerical example with a DDR4 topology is provided.**

Keywords—DDR4, Design space exploration, Polynomial Chaos theory, Uncertainty quantification.

I. Introduction

As the complexity of high speed circuits increases, and their size miniaturizes, uncertainty of parameters needs to be carefully considered. Uncertainty can happen in fabrication; nevertheless, it is also seen in the design stage, where designers are not sure about the best value for a parameter. Therefore, they need to find it with tuning, also called design space exploration. This type of uncertainty quantification is the focus of this paper. In the past decade, various uncertainty quantification methods have been developed to estimate the distribution of random variables. In other words, they find how the randomness propagates from input random variables to the output. The most popular and straightforward approach is Monte Carlo (MC) analysis, which works by simulating the system at numerous samples to find the distribution of the output. However, MC can be extremely time consuming, especially for complex systems where running one instance of a deterministic simulation is computationally expensive. Therefore, more efficient uncertainty quantification methods have been developed [1]. Many of these methods, apply the concept of generalized Polynomial Chaos (PC) theory, using an expansion of orthogonal polynomials to estimate the random variables [2]. This method is popular because of fast convergence, and provides statistical results at no extra cost. However, its computational cost increases polynomially with number of random variables, also called curse of dimensionality. Moreover, its complexity increases exponentially with order of the expansion. Therefore, PC techniques are limited to relatively low number of variables, where the output is a smooth function, and random variables have a small range of variation. However, in design space exploration we often need to examine several parameters over a wide range. To partially alleviate this problem, in this paper a novel approach is suggested that expands the PC approach to a wider range of variation with nominal increase in the computational cost. In the next section, basics of the PC theory are discussed.

II. Polynomial Chaos Theory

To model a function of random variables, PC theory suggests estimation with sum of a series of orthogonal polynomials [3]. If $\boldsymbol{\lambda} = [\lambda_1, \lambda_2, \dots, \lambda_n]$ shows a vector of n random variables, a smooth function of them is estimated as:

$$f(\boldsymbol{\lambda}) \approx \sum_{i=0}^{P} c_i \phi_i(\boldsymbol{\lambda}), \quad (1)$$

where, c_i shows unknown coefficients, and $\phi_i(\boldsymbol{\lambda})$ are multidimensional orthogonal polynomials. Moreover, $P+1$ is the length of expansion, and it is set as $P+1 = (m+n)!/m!\,n!$, with m being the maximum order used in the polynomials. For smooth functions with a limited range, $m = 2$ or 3 often provides acceptable accuracy. Furthermore, ϕ_i are chosen based on the distribution of random variables. Additionally, statistics of $f(\boldsymbol{\lambda})$ are found directly from the coefficients of PC expansion. Using the orthogonality condition it is proven that:

$$E\big(f(\boldsymbol{\lambda})\big) = c_0, \quad V\big(f(\boldsymbol{\lambda})\big) = \sum_{i=1}^{P} c_i^2, \quad (2)$$

where, E and V show expectation and variance of $f(\boldsymbol{\lambda})$, respectively. Various approaches have been suggested to find the coefficients of PC expansion. However, for now we use a simple regression technique [4], and leave more advanced methods for future work. First, the system is sampled and simulated at N points $\boldsymbol{\lambda}^1$ to $\boldsymbol{\lambda}^N$, where $N \geq 2(P+1)$. Then, the samples and outputs are plugged in (1), and the results are written in the matrix form as:

$$\boldsymbol{A\Gamma} = \boldsymbol{E}, \quad (3)$$

$$\boldsymbol{A} = \begin{bmatrix} \phi_0(\boldsymbol{\lambda}^1) & \dots & \phi_P(\boldsymbol{\lambda}^1) \\ \vdots & \ddots & \vdots \\ \phi_0(\boldsymbol{\lambda}^N) & \dots & \phi_P(\boldsymbol{\lambda}^N) \end{bmatrix}, \boldsymbol{\Gamma} = \begin{bmatrix} c_0 \\ \vdots \\ c_P \end{bmatrix}, \mathbf{E} = \begin{bmatrix} f(\boldsymbol{\lambda}^1) \\ \vdots \\ f(\boldsymbol{\lambda}^N) \end{bmatrix}. \quad (4)$$

This system is over sampled, and the minimum error can be achieved by using least squares approximation. Hence, coefficients are found as:

$$\boldsymbol{\Gamma} = (\boldsymbol{A}^T\boldsymbol{A})^{-1}\boldsymbol{A}^T\boldsymbol{E}, \quad (5)$$

with T being the transpose sign. Note that after finding the coefficients, (1) can be used as a surrogate model to evaluate the system at arbitrary sample points. We used this model for design space exploration.

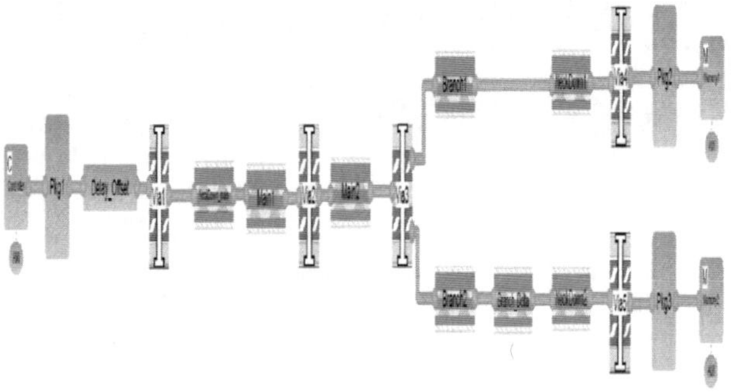

Fig. 1. Numerical example: A DDR4 topology with uncertain paramete

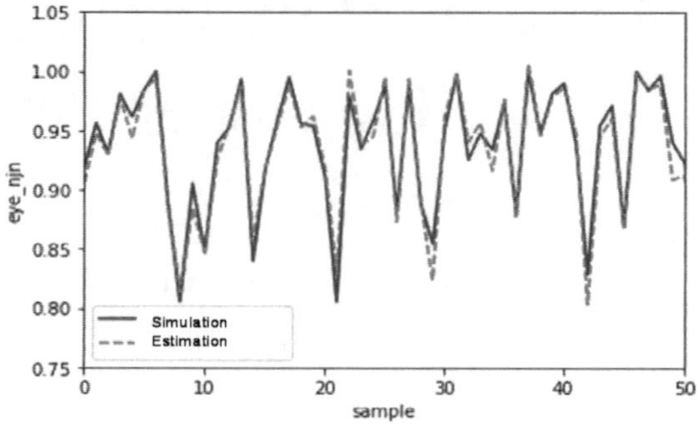

Fig. 2. Estimation results using the proposed PC model.

III. Proposed PC Approach

PC surrogate models provide a good approximation of a smooth function, when random variables have a small variance. However, when the surrogate models are needed for tuning parameters and design space exploration, the variation might be much larger (e.g. more than 50%). Higher order polynomials can be used to increase the accuracy for a wide range. In other words, we can increase *m*; however, size of the model increases exponentially with *m*. Combined with curse of dimensionality, this would be problematic when *n* is large. Therefore, we suggest breaking down the range of each variable to multiple intervals, and develop lower order PC models for each range. This work is inspired by ensemble methods such as AdaBoost in the machine learning field, where a combination of a group of weak learners is used to create a strong learner [5]. Similarly, we suggest developing several small PC models, where each model is different based on the range of training data. For instance, consider the case of two random variables, λ_1 and λ_2. First, λ_1 is divided to two equal ranges, and it is described with two new random variables, called λ_{1_1} and λ_{1_2}. Meanwhile, λ_2 is kept unbroken. With sampling λ_{1_1} and λ_2 the following model is developed:

$$f(\lambda_{1\_1}, \lambda_2) \approx \sum_{i=0}^{P} c_{1\_i} \phi_i(\lambda_{1\_1}, \lambda_2). \quad (6)$$

Similarly, with sampling λ_{1_2} and λ_2 a new model is developed:

$$f(\lambda_{1\_2}, \lambda_2) \approx \sum_{i=0}^{P} c_{1\_i} \phi_i(\lambda_{1\_2}, \lambda_2). \quad (7)$$

This process is repeated for λ_2, while λ_1 is kept unbroken; hence, four models are trained in total. Note that samples are reused, which means half of the samples used for training (6) and (7) are used again for $f(\lambda_1, \lambda_{2\_1})$ or $f(\lambda_1, \lambda_{2\_2})$, depending on their range. For evaluating the system at a new sample point, two of the four models are selected, based on the ranges where the new sample is located. Finally, the estimation of output is provided as the average of reported values by selected models. This approach is generalized for *n* variables, where *nq* models are developed, with *q* being number of intervals in range of each variable. Then, *n* models are selected, and used for finding the output at new samples.

IV. Numerical Example

To evaluate performance of the proposed approach, the DDR4 topology in Fig. 1 is considered, and simulated with Cadence SystemSI.

In this circuit, package 1 capacitance, package 1 inductance, package 2 capacitance, package 2 inductance, length of neck down 1, and length of neck down 2 need tuning. Their mean values are 2 pF, 2 nH, 2 pF, 2nH, 6 mm, and 6 mm, respectively. Moreover, each parameter needs to be inspected for +/- 90% variation of its average value with uniform distribution. The output is a measure of openness of the eye-diagram, which is called eye_njn, and equal to ratio of noise area to total area in the eye-diagram. Manually sweeping parameters or MC analysis are excessively time consuming; therefore, developing surrogate models is necessary. A single PC model needs a high order to cover this wide range; hence, the proposed approach is used, where $m = 3$. The range of each parameter is divided to two; thus, 12 smaller models are developed, and in total 420 samples were used for training. For validation, the final surrogate model is evaluated at 50 new samples and compared with actual simulation. Results are presented in Fig. 2. The accuracy is relatively good; however, it is not a perfect match. The reason can be that even 45% variation is high for PC surrogate models. Finally, the system is evaluated at 1000 new samples, and compared with simulation, where the L2-norm of error is observed to be 0.360. For comparison, this system was also modeled with a traditional PC model with $m = 3$. The L2-norm of error for 1000 estimated samples was 0.385, showing the decrease in accuracy compared to the proposed approach.

Acknowledgment

This material is partially supported by the National Science Foundation under Grant NO CNS 16-24810 – Center for Advanced Electronics through Machine Learning (CAEML).

References

[1] MA Dolatsara, "Efficient multidimensional uncertainty quantification of high speed circuits using advanced polynomial chaos approaches," Master's Thesis, Colorado State University, Fort Collins, CO, 2016.

[2] D. Xiu and G. E. Karniadakis, "The Wiener-Askey Polynomial chaos for stochastic differential equations", SIAM Journal on Scientific Computing, vol. 24, no. 2, pp. 619-644, 2002.

[3] P. Manfredi, "High-speed interconnect models with stochastic parameter variability," Ph.D. dissertation, Informat. Comm. Tech., Politecnico di Torino, Turin, Italy, 2013.

[4] D. Spina, F. Ferranti, G. Antonini, T. Dhaene and L. Knockaert, "Non-intrusive polynomial chaos-based stochastic macromodeling of multiport systems", in Proc. IEEE 18th Workshop on SPI, pp. 1-4, May 2014.

[5] M. Mohri, A. Rostamizadeh, and A. Talwalkar, Foundations of Machine Learning, MIT Press, Cambridge, MA, Chapter 6, 2012.

Hierarchical Polynomial Chaos for Variation Analysis of Silicon Photonics Microresonators

Xinzhe Cao, Sakshi Bhatnagar, Mahdi Nikdast, Sourajeet Roy
Department of Electrical and Computer Engineering, Colorado State University, Fort Collins, USA
Email: Sourajeet.Roy@colostate.edu

Abstract— **This paper presents a polynomial chaos (PC) based numerical approach for the variation analysis of silicon photonics microresonators (MRs) in the presence of inevitable fabrication process variations. In particular, we develop low-dimensional component-level PC metamodels of standard quantities of interest which are then used to model the impact of fabrication process variations on the higher dimensional device-level quantities of interest. We demonstrate that the proposed indirect approach is much more computationally efficient when compared with the conventional approach of directly generating PC metamodels for device-level quantities of interest.**

Keywords— Fabrication process variations, microresonators, polynomial chaos, silicon photonics, variation analysis.

I. Introduction

Microresonators (MRs) are often considered as the primary building block in silicon photonics integrated circuits. They are compact (*e.g.,* 5 μm in radius) and have various functionalities for signal modulation, switching, and filtering [1]. Nevertheless, MRs are highly susceptible to fabrication process variations [2]-[3]. For example, small variations in the critical dimensions of MRs (*e.g.,* waveguide width and thickness) as well as those in the doped materials (*i.e.,* silicon (Si) in the waveguide core and silicon dioxide (SiO_2) in the cladding and substrate) lead to large uncertainty in the operating frequency (*i.e.,* the resonant wavelength) of MRs (see Fig. 1) [4].

Recently, polynomial chaos (PC) has emerged as a reliable and powerful numerical tool to quantify the impact of fabrication process variations on the response of silicon photonics devices [5]-[6]. In particular, PC models the fabrication process variations as random variables (or random dimensions) with well-known probability density functions (PDFs). Next, it represents the resultant variability in the device response using a linear combination of orthonormal polynomial basis functions of the input random variables [5]-[6]. The coefficients of the basis functions form the new unknowns of the system. These coefficients are determined using repeated deterministic simulations of the original device model at prescribed nodes in the multidimensional random space. Once known, the combination of the coefficients and orthonormal bases form a closed-form surrogate model or metamodel of the response that can be easily probed to capture the statistical variability of the response quantity of interest (*e.g.,* the resonant wavelength in MRs). The key advantage of PC lies in its fast convergence to the correct results even in the presence of large number of random dimensions. However, this advantage is balanced by the fact that the number of deterministic model simulations required to determine all the coefficients scale in a near-exponential manner with respect to the number of random dimensions. This poor scalability makes it infeasible to consider the full set of random dimensions.

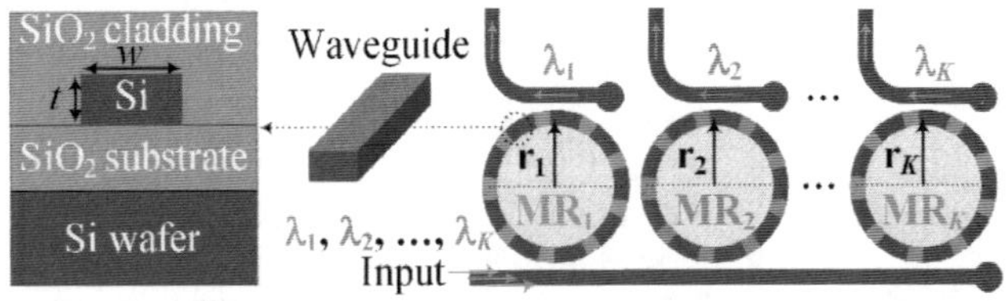

Fig. 1. Geometrical structure of an MR-based filter (right-hand side) with K MRs, and a cross-section of a strip waveguide (left-hand side).

In this paper, a new hierarchical PC approach is developed to study the resonant wavelength shift in MRs under fabrication process variations. We consider passive MRs based on strip waveguides (see Fig. 1). The proposed approach first constructs PC metamodels for the component-level quantities of interest (*i.e.,* the refractive effective index for the strip waveguides in the MR). In doing so, only the random dimensions that arise at the component-level need to be considered while the dimensions that arise at the device-level can be ignored. This means that a reduced set of dimension need to be considered for the component-level PC metamodels. This significantly reduces the number of deterministic model simulations required to determine the coefficients. Finally, the impact of the component-level PC metamodels and the impact of the device-level random dimensions on the device-level quantity (*i.e.,* the resonant wavelength in an MR) is modeled analytically. Thus, hierarchical but analytic statistical models are derived at the device-level far more efficiently than the conventional approach of generating device-level PC metamodels directly.

II. Hierarchical PC Metamodels

A general MR-based filter consisting of K MRs is shown in Fig. 1. The impact of fabrication process variation on the device-level quantity (*i.e.,* the resonant wavelength ($\lambda_{res}^{(i)}$) of the ith MR) is usually described using a PC metamodel as

$$\lambda_{res}^{(i)}(\boldsymbol{\alpha}) = \sum_{j=0}^{P} \lambda_j^{(i)} \phi_j(\boldsymbol{\alpha}); \quad 1 \le i \le K \ , \tag{1}$$

where $\phi(\alpha)$ is the jth multivariate polynomial, $\lambda_j^{(i)}$ is the corresponding PC coefficient, $\boldsymbol{\alpha} = [\alpha_1, \alpha_2, \ldots, \alpha_n]$ is the set of n random dimensions used to describe the fabrication process variations and the number of terms in the expansion of (1) is truncated to $P+1 = (n+m)!/(n!m!)$, m being the maximum degree of the expansion. Evaluating the coefficients of (1) requires $O(2(P+1)K)$ or $O(n^m K)$ number of deterministic

This work is partially supported by the National Science Foundation (NSF) through the NSF award CCF-1813370.

solutions of the model in (1) – a computationally expensive task for even modest values of n, m, and K. This challenge is addressed using the proposed hierarchical PC approach.

TABLE I
UNCERTAIN PARAMETERS OF MR-BASED FILTER EXAMPLE (FIG. 1)

Random Parameter (Normal PDFs)	Mean	Relative Standard Deviation
Waveguide thickness (t)	220 nm	0.758%
Waveguide width (w)	500 nm	0.667%
Refractive index of core	3.47	1.5%
Refractive index of substrate	1.44	
Refractive index of cladding	1.44	
Radius of MR1	10.022 μm	0.05%
Radius of MR2	10.044 μm	
Radius of MR3	10.066 μm	
Radius of MR4	10.088 μm	

A. Proposed Hierarchical PC Approach

In this paper, instead of directly constructing the PC metamodel of (1), the variability in the resonant wavelengths ($\lambda_{res}^{(i)}$) caused by fabrication process variations is analytically modeled as a function of the variation in the effective index ($\Delta n_{eff}^{(i)}$) and the variation in the radius of the MR (ΔR_i) as

$$\lambda_{res}^{(i)}(\boldsymbol{\alpha}) = \lambda_{res,0}^{(i)} + \frac{\left(\Delta n_{eff}^{(i)} + \dfrac{n_{eff,0}^{(i)}}{R_{i,0}}\Delta R_i\right)\lambda_{res,0}^{(i)}}{n_{g,0}^{(i)}}; \quad 1 \le i \le K , \quad (2)$$

where $n_{g,0}^{(i)}$ and $n_{eff,0}^{(i)}$ are, respectively, the nominal values of the group index and effective index calculated at the nominal value of the resonant wavelength $\lambda_{res,0}^{(i)}$, and $R_{i,0}$ is the nominal radius of the ith MR. Thus, equation (2) propagates the variability of the component-level effective index ($\Delta n_{eff}^{(i)}$) to the device-level resonant wavelength quantity ($\lambda_{res}^{(i)}$). The key advantage of using (2) is that the variability of the component-level effective index ($\Delta n_{eff}^{(i)}$) can now be represented using a PC metamodel as

$$\Delta n_{eff}^{(i)} = \sum_{j=1}^{Q} \Delta n_j^{(i)} \psi_j(\boldsymbol{\beta}); \quad 1 \le i \le K , \quad (3)$$

where $\psi_j(\boldsymbol{\beta})$ is the jth multivariate polynomial and $\Delta n_j^{(i)}$ is the corresponding PC coefficient. Note that the variability in the MR radii (ΔR_i) does not affect the variability of the effective index ($\Delta n_{eff}^{(i)}$). Hence, the vector $\boldsymbol{\beta}$ includes all component-level random dimensions directly impacting $\Delta n_{eff}^{(i)}$ but does not include the device-level random dimensions associated with the MR radius. Due to this reduction in dimensions, the number of PC coefficients of (3) is much smaller than that of (1) and needs smaller number of deterministic simulations to determine (*i.e.*, $Q << P+1$). Once the coefficients of (3) are determined, they can be used in the analytic model of (2). The model in (2) can be probed repeatedly using Monte Carlo samples to determine any statistical moment of the resonant wavelengths. The standard deviation of the resonant wavelengths is expressed as

$$SD\left(\lambda_{res}^{(i)}(\boldsymbol{\alpha})\right) = \frac{\lambda_{res,0}^{(i)}}{n_{g,0}} \sqrt{\left(\sum_{j=1}^{Q}\left(\Delta n_j^{(i)}\right)^2\right) + \left(n_{eff,0} s_i\right)^2}; \quad 1 \le i \le K , \quad (4)$$

where s_i is the relative standard deviation of the MR with a radius R_i.

TABLE II
RESULTS FOR RESONANT WAVELENGTHS OF NUMERICAL EXAMPLE

Resonant wavelength	Hierarchical PC Mean (nm)	Hierarchical PC SD (nm)	Monte Carlo Mean (nm)	Monte Carlo SD (nm)
MR1 ($\lambda_{res}^{(1)}$)	1550	21.60	1550	21.60
MR2 ($\lambda_{res}^{(2)}$)	1551.70		1552	
MR3 ($\lambda_{res}^{(3)}$)	1554.30		1554	
MR4 ($\lambda_{res}^{(4)}$)	1555.90		1556	

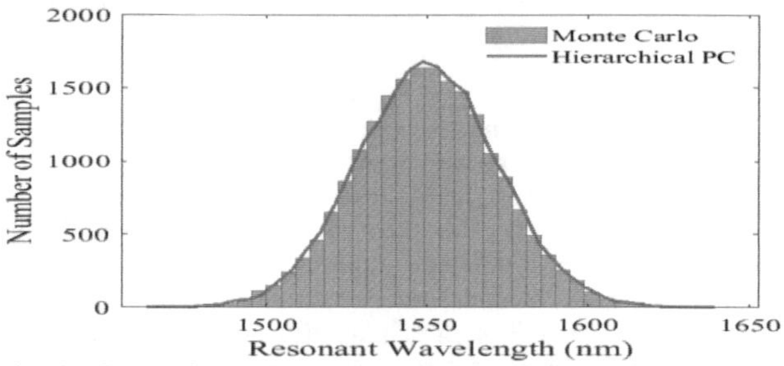

Fig. 2. Comparison of the PDF obtained from the hierarchical PC approach and the Monte Carlo approach for $\lambda_{res}^{(1)}$ (20,000 samples).

III. NUMERICAL EXAMPLE FOR VALIDATION

In order to validate the proposed approach, a MR-based filter consisting of $K = 4$ MRs is considered (see Fig. 1). The nominal values and the relative standard deviation of the different parameters of this device is listed in Table I. We used the analytic models in [4] to calculate the effective and group indices values required in (2), (3), and (4). The device-level quantities of interest for this example are the resonant wavelength for each MR: $\lambda_{res}^{(1)}$- $\lambda_{res}^{(4)}$. For accuracy analysis, the mean and standard deviation of each resonant wavelength is calculated using the proposed hierarchical PC approach and the results are compared against a brute-force Monte Carlo approach where 20,000 deterministic simulations of the model of Fig. 1 is used. The results are provided in Table II. As can be seen, the proposed approach exhibits excellent agreement with Monte Carlo results. Fig. 2 further illustrates this excellent accuracy for the PDF of the resonant wavelength of the first MR. To create the PC metamodels of (3) only $2KQ = 1000$ deterministic model simulations are required which is in contrast to the conventional $2K(P+1) = 1680$ deterministic simulations required for (1) (a reduction of 680 deterministic simulations).

REFERENCES

[1] M. Bahadori, M. Nikdast, et al., "Design space exploration of microring resonators in silicon photonic interconnects: impact of the ring curvature," IEEE JLT, vol. 36, no. 13, pp. 2767-2782, 2018.

[2] L. Chrostowski, X. Wang, et al., "Impact of fabrication non-uniformity on chip-scale silicon photonic integrated circuits," OSA/IEEE OFC, CA, USA, 2014, paper Th2A.37.

[3] M. Nikdast, G. Nicolescu, et al., "Photonic integrated circuits: A study on process variations," OSA/IEEE OFC, Anaheim, USA, 2016, paper W2A.22.

[4] M. Nikdast, G. Nicolescu, et al., "Chip-scale silicon photonic interconnects: a formal study on fabrication non-uniformity," IEEE JLT, vol. 34, no. 16, pp. 3682-3695, 2016

[5] T. Weng, D. Melati, A. Melloni, and L. Daniel, "Stochastic simulation and robust design optimization of integrated photonic filters," Nanophotonics, vol. 6, no. 1, pp. 299-308, 2016.

[6] A. Waqas, D. Melati, et al., "Stochastic process design kits for photonic circuits based on polynomial chaos augmented macro-modelling," Optics Express, vol. 26, pp. 5894-5907, 2018.

Comparison of Extruded and Capstone Meshes for Finite Element Analysis

Leo Kempel
Dept. of Electrical and Computer Engineering
Michigan State University
East Lansing, MI, USA
kempel@egr.msu.edu

B. Shanker
Dept. of Electrical and Computer Engineering
Michigan State University
East Lansing, MI, USA
bshanker@egr.msu.ed

Abstract—**Meshes generation is often one of the most time-consuming and challenging aspects of performing an analysis of a radio-frequency (RF) design. New powerful tools are becoming available that simplify the mesh generation task. This paper introduces a new meshing tool – Capstone – to the community with comparison to an extruded mesh. The example presented is a coaxial line since it is readily meshed both by extrusion and using Capstone.**

Keywords—mesh generation, RF, electromagnetic, tetrahedra

I. INTRODUCTION

Traditionally, mesh generation has been a significant challenge due to the need to generate meshes for a variety of applications (e.g., electromagnetic, fluid dynamics, thermodynamics, etc.) and still be realtively easy-to-use so as to garner a large user community. In the early days of development of the finite element method for electromagnetics, all meshes were hand generated. That is, the mesh was generated for a specific geometry and those geometries tended to be rather simple for that reason. One significant advantage of meshes generated by hand or "hand meshes" is that the creator can enforce symetries that are intuitive based on the expected field distributions. Nevertheless, while these meshes are acceptable for research purposes, it is not sufficient for even the most simplistic design requirements. The finite element-boundary intergral (FE-BI) methods has been implemented for many types of elements; most often bricks, prisms, and tetrahedra [1]. In a practical sense, the type of elements used for a hand mesh are limited to hexahedra and prisms.

Extruded meshes offer a compromise between a hand mesh and a full unconstrained mesh generator. For extruded meshes, the cross-sectional mesh is generated first using either an hand mesh or a planar mesh generator. There are a number of elements that can be used as the basis for extrusion; triangular and quadratic elements are the most common. As an example, figure 1 illustrates the surface mesh for a coaxial section. In this, the region in the center ($0 \le \rho \le 0.3$ cm) is assumed to be metal while the exterior region ($0.3 < \rho \le 1.0$ cm) is assumed to be a dielectric such as Teflon ($\varepsilon_r = 2$). The outer boundary is assumed to be metal in this case. The transverse electromagnetic (TEM) mode for this design yields a predicted guided wave impedance of 51Ω and a cut-off frequency of 5.2 GHz. Above the cut-off frequency, higher-order modes can exist and hence the impedance of the device is no longer constant.

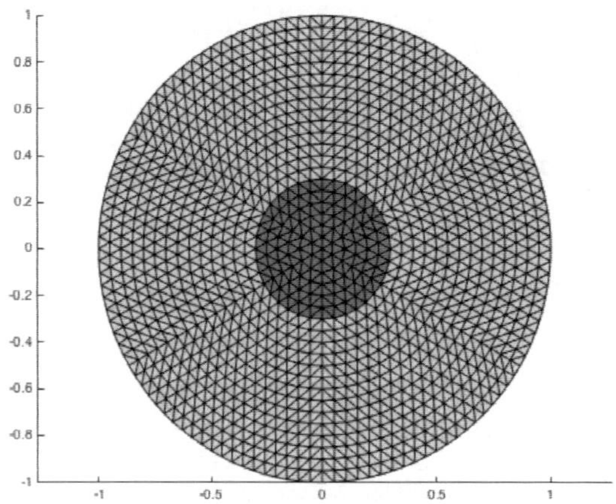

Figure 1. 2-D Mesh of Coaxial Structure.

Tetrahedra are some of the most useful elements in the computational electromagnetics toolbox. One way to form Tetrahedra elements from an extruded mesh is to first build prisms and then splitting the prisms into tetrahedral [2]. Such a mesh has considerable structure since the mesh looks the same no matter what cross-section is examined; this is of course also a limitation of such meshes for modeling complex geometries.

II. CAPSTONE

The US Department of Defense initiated a major computational model development effort in 2006 under the Computational Research and Engineering Acquisition Tools and Environments (CREATE) program [3]. The HPCMP CREATE™ program has developed a suite of software tools in areas of high need within the Department of Defense – both Government and Contractors. These are:

1. RF antenna design and integration with platforms
2. Military ship design
3. Military ground vehicle design
4. Military aircraft design
5. Meshing and geometry generation

The latter two are part of the Genesis software distribution [4] that is available to the academic and research communities free-of-charge. Genesis includes a powerful computational fluid dynamics tool, examples of various aircraft components geared towards the aerospace engineering community, and a meshing tool – Capstone. This is a powerful tool for 3-D geometry generation and meshing. The example used in this paper in no way demonstrates the power of Capstone as a tool – it was chosen because the S-parameter results are predicatable. Capstone comes with a number of examples that demonstrate the ability of it to model complex geometries such as filters, aircraft, etc. Figure 2 illustrates the coaxial line geometry.

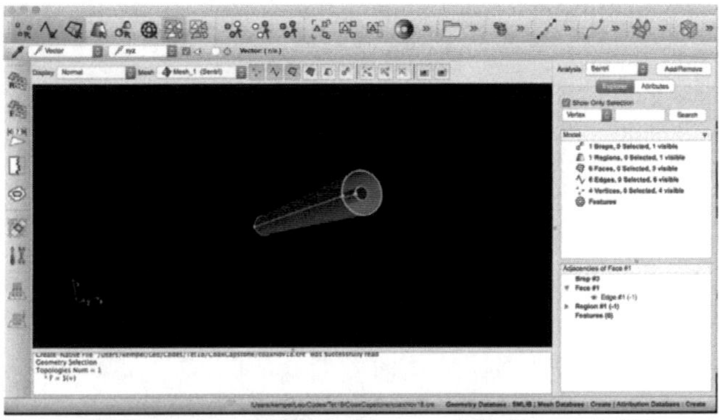

Figure 2. Screenshot of Capstone model of a coaxial line.

III. Comparison of Data

A first-pass comparison of results for a mesh generated by extrusion (from Figure 1) and one created with Capstone is to compare the S-parameters for a coaxial line. This was chosen since the TEM mode has a constant impedance up to a cut-off frequency (approaximately 5.2 GHz for the inner and outer radii chosen for this test). As a practical matter, the length of the device also matters in the analysis since at lower frequencies it is "short" and at higher frequencies it is "long". For the example, a port impedance of 50Ω is assumed. The same tetrahedra finite element computer program was used for both cases. Figure 3 illustrates the comparison of S_{11} and S_{12} calculated using the method described in [5]. As shown, there are slight deviations in the calculated S_{11} between the two meshes. This is due to the fact that the feed structures are not exactly the same. For the extruded case, the feed is concentric with the center conductor and axially directed. For the Capstone mesh, this could not be guaranteed although care was take for the feed to bridge the gap between each end face of the coax and the center conductor end face. Accordingly, the electric fields at those feeds can be slightly different (although of course more dense sampling will eventually minimize the difference). The fact that the nulls and peaks align well indicates that the boundary conditions (metallic walls and reference impedance) are consistent between the two meshes.

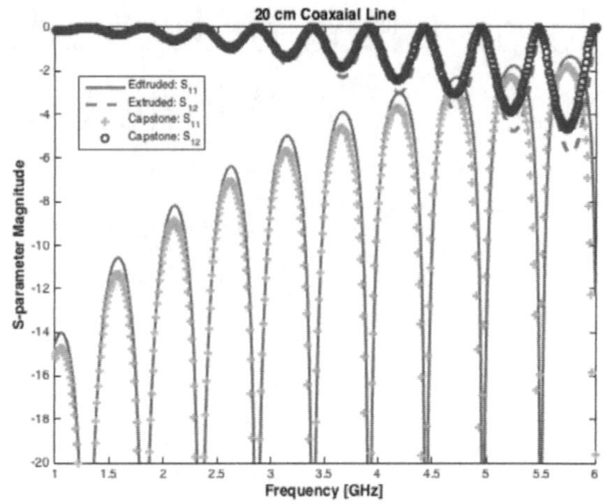

Figure 3. Comparison of S-parameters for extruded and Capstone meshes.

The comparison between the simulations using both meshes is good.

IV. Summary

In this paper, a new meshing capability is introduces to the computational electromagnetics communtiy – Capstone. This tool was developed by the Department of Defense through the High Performance Computing Modernization Office Program and is available to the education and research community. A mesh was generated for a coaxial line and compared with the results when an extruded mesh was used. Additional examples will be presented at the conference.

Acknowledgment

This work was supported in part by high performance computer time and resources from the DOD High Performance Computing Modernization Program.

References

[1] L.C. Kempel, "Implementation of Various Hybrid Finite Element-Boundary Integral Methods: Bricks, Prisms, and Tets," *1999 ACES Meeting*, Monterey, CA, 1999, pp. 242-249.

[2] J.Meese, L. Kempel, and S. Schneider, "Subdividing distorted prisms into tetrahedra," *19th Review of Progress in Applied Computational Electromagnetics*, Monterey, CA, 2003, pp. 224-227.

[3] D. Post, C. Atwood, K. Newmeyer, S. Landsberg, and F. Shull, "The Computational Research and Engineering Acquisition Tools and Environments (CREATE) Program," *Comp. in Sci & Egr*, Jan/Feb 2016, 10-13.

[4] Genesis software distribution, https://www.hpcmpcreategenesis.org

[5] L. Kempel, "Calculation of dual leaky-wave antenna performance using quad-core processors and OpenMP," *ACES Conf.*, Niagara Falls, CANADA, March 2008.

Adjoint-Based Uncertainty Quantification in Frequency-Domain Double Higher-Order FEM

Jake Harmon, Cam Key, and Branislav M. Notaroš
Colorado State University, Electrical & Computer Engineering Department, Fort Collins, CO
j.harmon@colostate.edu, camkey@rams.colostate.edu, notaros@colostate.edu

Donald Estep
Department of Statistics
Colorado State University, Fort Collins, CO
donald.estep@colostate.edu

Troy Butler
Department of Mathematical and Statistical Sciences
University of Colorado Denver, Denver, CO
troy.butler@ucdenver.edu

***Abstract*—We summarize an adjoint-based uncertainty quantification technique for a double higher-order finite element method solution in frequency-domain computational electromagnetics. We introduce the motivation and structure of the adjoint for the double-curl wave equation. We demonstrate scattering results for a lossy dielectric sphere.**

Keywords—adjoint methods, computational electromagnetics, finite element method, frequency domain, scattering, sensitivity analysis, uncertainty quantification.

I. Introduction

Error contribution estimates, sensitivity analysis, and adaptive mesh refinement provide powerful tools to optimize a solution in terms of accuracy and computation time. As a practical numerical problem lacks an analytical solution, separating computational error from measurement error when comparing to real-world data proves difficult. Additionally, the computation times inherent to techniques like Monte-Carlo simulation preclude practical usability for sensitivity analysis and optimization.

Recently, explorations in computational electromagnetics (CEM) have shown promising results in terms of adjoint based adaptive refinement for the one-dimensional finite element method (FEM) [1].

This paper focuses on an application of adjoint methods to uncertainty quantification in CEM. We present estimates of error in a quantity of interest (QoI) for the double higher-order (DHO) three-dimensional FEM solution [2]. We describe possibilities of applying such error contribution estimates to adjust the resolution of an element's geometric structure and basis function order.

II. Motivation and Construction of the Adjoint Solution

For many CEM problems, rather than the field solution as a whole, we are interested in a particular QoI, such as radar cross-section (RCS), S-parameters, or input-impedance. Practical applications also mandate successive solves when frequency sweep, parameter sweep, or optimization is desired. These methods, then, benefit from information regarding the efficiency and/or sufficiency of the discretization. Adjoint-based *a posteriori* error estimation permits such analysis, fostering an efficient method to categorize the elements of a mesh for refinement or coarsening both in element density and field expansion order

To frame the construction of the adjoint solution, we analyze scattering from a dielectric body. We consider a lossy dielectric sphere surrounded first by an air layer, followed by a perfectly matched layer (PML).

We then apply the double-curl wave equation:

$$\nabla\times\mu_r^{-1}\nabla\times\mathbf{E}^{sc} - k_0^2\varepsilon_r\mathbf{E}^{sc} = -\nabla\times\mu_r^{-1}\nabla\times\mathbf{E}^{inc} + k_0^2\varepsilon_r\mathbf{E}^{inc}, \qquad (1)$$

where ε_r and μ_r are, respectively, complex relative permittivity and permeability of the inhomogeneous medium (tensors for anisotropic materials), $\mathbf{E}^{inc}$ and $\mathbf{E}^{sc}$ are the incident and scattered electric field complex intensity vectors, and k_0 is the free-space wave number. Then, by expressing (1) in linear operator form:

$$L\mathbf{u} = \mathbf{f}, \qquad (2)$$

we can isolate the forward operator L such that the adjoint operator L^* can be constructed to satisfy the Lagrange identity,

$$\langle L\mathbf{u}, \mathbf{v}\rangle = \langle \mathbf{u}, L^*\mathbf{v}\rangle, \qquad (3)$$

where $\langle\cdot,\cdot\rangle$ denotes the L^2 inner product as in [3]. The adjoint problem is then stated:

$$L^*\mathbf{v} = \mathbf{p}, \qquad (4)$$

where the vector quantity $\mathbf{p}$ denotes a linear functional defining a given quantity of interest from the forward solution. Finally, with the approximation of the quantity of interest, we can form the error in the functional of interest by an inner product involving the solutions to the forward and adjoint problems – the dual-weighted residual [3].

The building block for DHO FEM modeling is a Lagrange-type interpolation generalized hexahedron shown in Fig. 1,

This work was supported by the US Air Force Research Laboratory, CREATE SENTRi, Riverside Research Institute, under contract FA8650-14-D-1725(6F1957).

with arbitrary geometrical orders, and the electric field vector inside FEM hexahedra is approximated by curl-conforming hierarchical polynomial vector bases of arbitrary field-expansion orders [2]. The FEM elements can be large and filled with inhomogeneous (and anisotropic) materials.

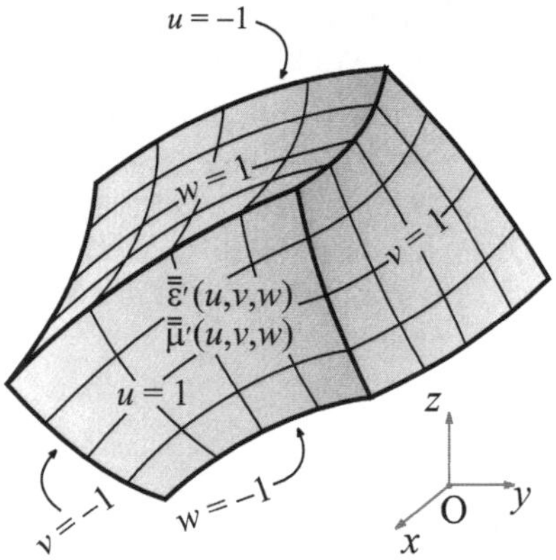

Fig. 1. Curved hexahedral volume finite element for DHO FEM.

III. Results and Discussion

To demonstrate the practical value of adjoint-based uncertainty quantification, we consider the dielectric sphere suspended in air (and modeled with a truncating PML) with an incident plane wave directed towards the center of the sphere.

The process to estimate the uncertainty for our particular QoI, the scattered field (in the far-field limit), begins by computing both the adjoint and forward solutions. While just the Nth order approximation for the forward solution must be computed, the error estimates necessitate the $(N+1)^{th}$ order approximation for the adjoint solution as well. However, to minimize the computational impact, the lower order integrals are stored for reuse in computing the error estimate, and only the integrals of the adjoint solution with the higher order basis functions are computed.

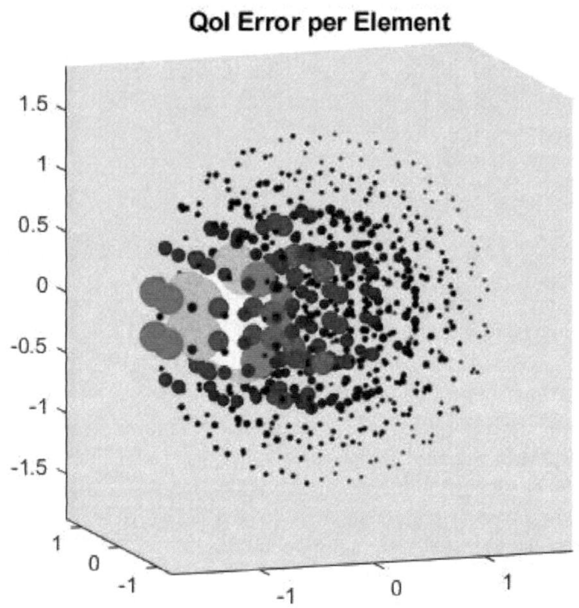

Fig. 2. QoI error contribution estimate per element for dielectric sphere.

Based on this formulation, computing the error estimate on a per-element develops naturally. As seen in Fig. 2, the QoI error is distributed primarily in a symmetric region where the incident plane wave initially strikes the dielectric. Opposite this region of the incidence, the QoI error is significantly lower.

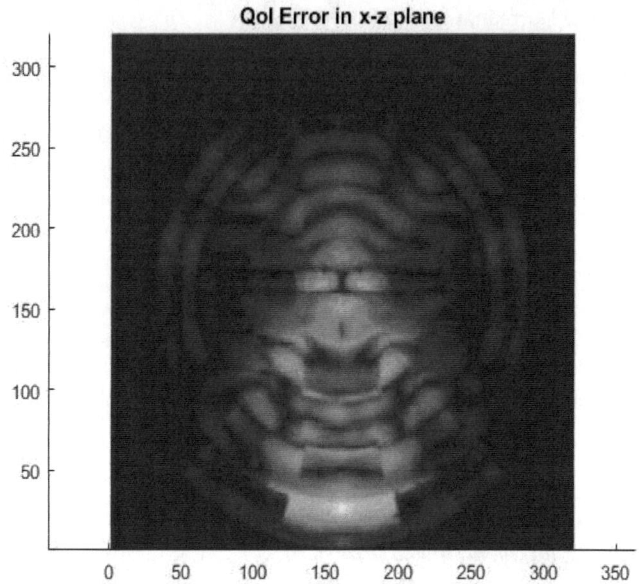

Fig. 3. Central planar cross section of QoI error contribution field.

Analogously to the per-element distribution of the QoI error, the QoI per-basis function can be computed. This generates a QoI error "field" which provides a less discrete visualization of the distribution of the error. Note, of course, that the per-element QoI error is implicit in this QoI error field approximation.

In Fig. 3 we see a similar representation to that of Fig. 2; the QoI error behaves symmetrically and is maximal at the region of incidence (as expected for this test case).

With estimates of the error contribution, adaptive refinement can be performed. Field expansion order refinement, geometric refinement, and the simultaneous execution of the two refinement strategies together can leverage element-wise QoI error contribution estimates to increase or decrease discretization resolution to optimize accuracy and computation time of the solution.

References

[1] C. Key, A. Smull, B. M. Notaroš, D. Estep and T. Butler, "Adjoint methods for uncertainty quantification in applied computational electromagnetics: FEM scattering examples," 2018 International Applied Computational Electromagnetics Society Symposium (ACES), Denver, CO, 2018, pp. 1-2.

[2] M. M. Ilic and B. M. Notaros, "Higher order hierarchical curved hexahedral vector finite elements for electromagnetic modeling," IEEE Transactions on Microwave Theory and Techniques, 51(3), 1026-1033.

[3] D. Estep and D. Neckels, "Fast and reliable methods for determining the evolution of uncertain parameters in differential equations," Journal of Computational Physics, 2006, 213(2), 530-556.

Numerical Mesh Truncation Boundary Conditions Optimized via Machine Learning

Tayfun Özdemir*(1), Daniel N. Aloi(1), Kevin Bi(2), and Robert J. Burkholder(3)
(1) Oakland University, Rochester, Michigan, USA, www.oakland.edu
(2) Virtual EM, Inc., Ann Arbor, Michigan, USA, www.virtualem.com
(3) The Ohio State University, Columbus, Ohio, USA, www.osu.edu

Abstract— **Mesh truncation in Finite Element Method (FEM) is critical and presents conflicting options. Boundary Integral (BI) option yields very accurate results but results in non-sparse solution matrix while Artificial Absorbers (AAs) or Absorbing Boundary Conditions (ABCs) preserves sparsity of the matrix, they need to be placed sufficiently far away from the structure to yield accurate data, resulting in large number of unknowns. Paper presents a method to optimize the placement of the truncation boundary close to the object being modeled to minimize the size of the problem and the run time Optimization is object-dependent as it should be and is achieved using Machine Learning (ML). The proposed scheme is promising but needs further study to fully explore its potential to be of practical use.**

I. Introduction

FEM is a differential equation formulation and hence requires boundary conditions (BCs) applied at the outer-boundary or some distance from the surface of the object being modeled in order to arrive at a unique solution. The type of BC used determines the properties of the resulting linear system of equations and hence the accuracy of the solution and the time it takes to arrive at it. Boundary Integral (BI) option yields very accurate results but results in non-sparse solution matrix while Artificial Absorbers (AAs) or Absorbing Boundary Conditions (ABCs) preserves sparsity of the matrix but they need to be placed sufficiently far away from the structure to yield accurate solution, resulting in large number of unknowns. Placing AAs and ABCs too close to the structure produces unreliable accuracy and hence the sparse truncation methods were virtually abandoned in favor of the BI two decades ago [1]. As a result, much of the scientific literature on the subject concentrated on improving the computational efficiency of the BI approach trough techniques such as Fast Multi-pole Method (FMM) and domain decomposition. During the same period, hardware acceleration received a lot of attention and is still going strong. While multi-core Central Processing Units (CPUs) demonstrated the best across-the-board performance, careful implementations based on Graphical Processing Units (GPUs) for some applications proved beneficial. Latest additions to the mix are the Many Integrated Core (MIC) platforms such as Intel's Knights Landing offering that bridges that gap between GPUs and CPUs. Despite the unprecedented advance in raw computational power offered by such hardware, memory access speed and inter-nodal communication overhead remain a fundamental bottleneck in achieving scalable implementations. BI is a suspect for this bottleneck due to the fact that it produces a full-matrix albeit moderated by FMM.

Therefore, it may be time to revisit the sparse mesh truncation methods such as AAs and ABCs to see if there is a way to reduce the storage penalty associated with them without compromising the accuracy of the solution. AA is a simple Perfect Electric Conductor (PEC) surface with a thin lining of lossy dielectric on the side of the structure and absorbs the incoming energy to mimic free-space [2]. ABC is a mathematical expression to relate local tangential electric and magnetic fields to each other and is typically derived through the expansion of the near-field in terms of spherical expansion functions. The most accurate ABC is the Sommerfeld BC imposed at the far-field as shown in Figure 1(a) and such terminations have been shown to produce accurate results [3]. However, far-field termination results in a large FEM matrix and so the researchers looked at developing higher order sparse BCs called ABCs or optimized AAs imposed conformal to the structure at sub-wavelength distances to minimize the size of the FEM matrix as illustrated in Figure 1(b). Such close placements produced mixed results in terms of accuracy and the authors believe that the reason was that these boundary conditions were applied uniformly making general assumptions about the behavior of the near field, i.e., in a sense, it was a one-size-fits-all approach.

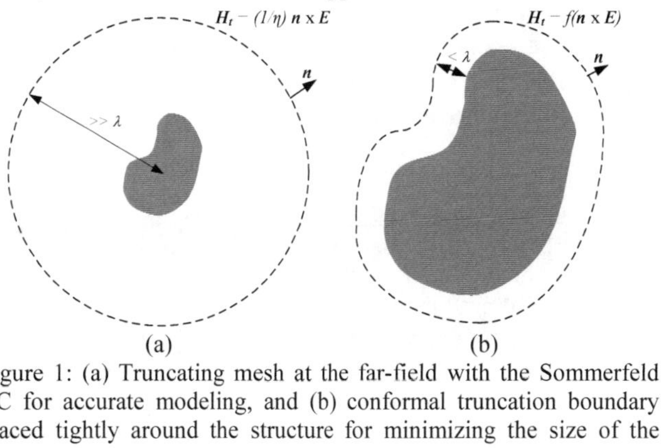

Figure 1: (a) Truncating mesh at the far-field with the Sommerfeld BC for accurate modeling, and (b) conformal truncation boundary placed tightly around the structure for minimizing the size of the FEM matrix.

The Sommerfeld BC is the only one that can be applied uniformly since every structure eventually produces a spherical phase-front at a sufficiently large distance. The near-field is very structure-dependent (i.e., is a function of its material make up, shape and excitation) and the BC must be constructed by considering this fact. For example, the termination boundary in Figure 1(b) makes a concave intrusion into the dent located on the upper-left quadrant of the structure effectively cutting off the direct propagation path between two peaks at the beginning and the end of the dent. Regardless of the BC imposed at that location, it is unlikely to make up for that interference and hence will produce inaccurate results. BC must possess some elements of the near field of the particular structure being modeled. This is a "chicken-and-egg" conundrum because, if we knew the new field, we would not need to solve for it. Authors, however, postulate that, perhaps, there is a way out of this impasse by recognizing that structures sharing similar features (such as excitation, shape, size and material content) would yield similar near-fields and so are the forms of the BCs that can be applied close to the structure. Further, the variation in the BCs could be even smaller than the near-fields themselves, which is not an unreasonable expectation. The question then to ask is how to arrive at such BCs and the answer may lie in Machine Learning (ML), which works well when the two spaces that are being mapped are uniquely deduced from each other, and that is the case here [4]. Paper presents a case study of generating numerical BCs using ML algorithms, which demonstrates its potential but further studies are needed to fully explore the merits of the proposed method.

II. Case Study

A resonant patch antenna was used a case study where the FEM mesh was terminated using an AA optimized via ML as depicted in Figure 2. Complex permittivity, complex permeability, and the thickness of the material lining of the AA layer vary with space as well as the contour of the PEC backing. Multiple realizations of the patch antenna (with varying permittivity of the substrate, ground plane size and the patch size) were modeled via Method of Moment (MoM) and observation parameters (input impedance and maximum gain including its direction) were recorded and considered the "accurate solution." Same antenna was modeled next using FEM and the AA truncation was optimized to minimize the deviation of the observation parameters from the reference MoM solution. Optimization was performed over various realizations of the truncation layer by varying thickness, material properties and the PEC contour. During the optimization, the maximum distance of the PEC contour from the geometric center of the antenna structure was forced to be 0.5 free-space wavelength or smaller. Pairs of antenna realization and the optimum truncation layer were used to train the ML algorithm to map the two. Then few realizations of the antenna, that were not part of the training set, were used to test the algorithms. In these testing cases, antenna was modeled using FEM and the AA truncation layer that the ML algorithm predicts. Results are very encouraging and details will be shared during the event.

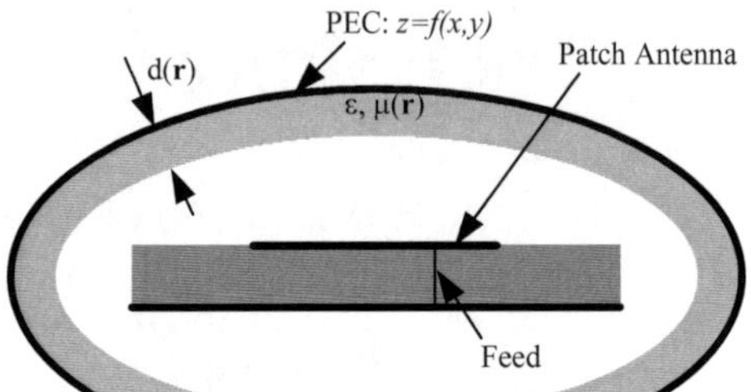

Figure 2: Case study of a resonant patch antenna modeled by FEM with AA mesh truncation.

III. Machine Learning (ML) Algorithms

ML algorithms operate as neural networks (mimicking how human brain learns) and are excellent in establishing very accurate relationships between the input and the output data sets when the training data set is a good representation of the sampling space. Therefore, care must be taken to ensure the structure models used in training are balanced representation of the types to be encountered in practice. The type of ML algorithms used in this study are called Dense Neural Network (DNN), which is composed of layers with weights and biases, where *output* = *weight* * *input* + *bias*, where *output, input* and *bias* are vectors and *weight* is a matrix (see Figure 3). *Biases* and w*eights* are updated at every training iteration by gradient descent.

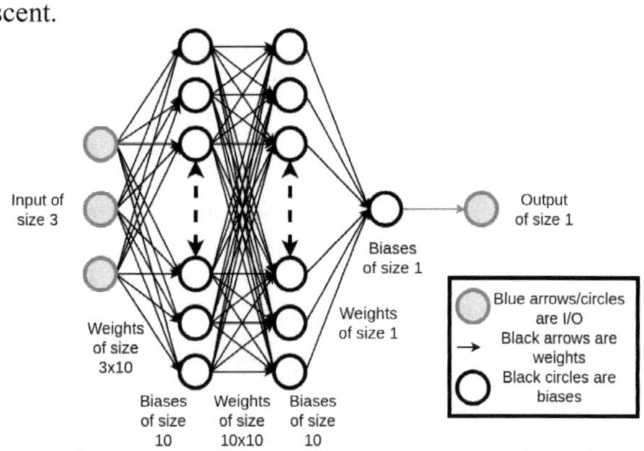

Figure 3: Dense Neural Network (DNN) used for training and testing.

References

[1] J. L. Volakis, A. Chatterjee, and L. C. Kempel, *Finite Element Method for Electromagnetics: Antennas, Microwave Circuits, and Scattering*, Ch.6, IEEE Press, New York, New York, 1998.

[2] T. Özdemir and J. L. Volakis, "A comparative study of an absorbing boundary condition and an artificial absorber for truncating finite element meshes," *Radio Science*, Vol. 29, No. 5, pp. 1255-1263, Sept.-Oct. 1994.

[3] A. Sommerfeld, *Partial Differential Equations in Physics*, Academic Press, New York, New York, 1949

[4] T. Özdemir, K. Bi, S. Campos and R. J. Burkholder, "Sparse Recovery Method for Order-of-Magnitude Reduction in RCS Measurments," *Int'l ACES Symp.*, March 2018.

A New Perspective on an Old Problem: Scattering by a Perfect Electric Conductor

Alex J. Yuffa*, Johannes Markkanen†, Qiang Sun‡, Evert Klaseboe§, and Derek Y. C. Chan‡¶
* National Institute of Standards and Technology, 325 Broadway, Boulder, Colorado 80305, USA
alex.yuffa@nist.gov
† Max Planck Institute for Solar System Research, Justus-von-Liebi-Weg 3, 37077 Göttingen, Germany
‡ University of Melbourne, Parkville 3010 VIC, Australia
§ Institute of High Performance Computing, 1 Fusionopolis Way, Singapore 138632, Singapore
¶ Swinburne University of Technology, Hawthorn 3122 VIC, Australia

***Abstract*—We explore several different singular surface integral equation formulations. These formulations are specifically designed for time-harmonic scattering by a perfect electric conductor and are obtained by choosing non-conventional boundary unknowns.**

***Index Terms*—Boundary element method, electromagnetic scattering, surface integral equations.**

I. Introduction

Electromagnetic scattering by a perfect electric conductor (PEC) is a century old problem. This scattering problem is illustrated in Fig. 1, where $\boldsymbol{N}$ denotes the outward unit normal to the surface of scatterer denoted by Σ. It is well-known that the total electric field satisfies

$$\boldsymbol{N} \times \boldsymbol{E} = 0 \quad \text{on} \quad \Sigma \tag{1}$$

and the total magnetic field satisfies $\boldsymbol{N} \cdot \boldsymbol{H} = 0$ on Σ. In a typical Stratton–Chu integral equation formalism of the above scattering problem [1] the induced surface current density $\boldsymbol{N} \times \boldsymbol{H}$ is related to the induced surface charge density $\boldsymbol{N} \cdot \boldsymbol{E}$ via the continuity equation. This approach yields an integral equation where the surface current density is chosen as the boundary unknown. In this contribution, we explore integral equation formulations with other boundary unknown(s).

Throughout the paper, we assume that all fields are harmonic in time with a suppressed $\exp(-\mathrm{i}\omega t)$ time factor. Furthermore, we use tensor notation with the Einstein summation convention and assume that the incident E-field $\overset{\text{inc}}{\boldsymbol{E}}$ satisfies the vector Helmholtz equation.

II. Integral Equation Formalism

Let the coordinates of a point in the three-dimensional Euclidean space be denoted by Z^i or simply by Z. The covariant ambient basis are then derived from the position vector $\boldsymbol{R}$ via

$$\boldsymbol{Z}_i = \frac{\partial}{\partial Z^i}\boldsymbol{R}(Z) \tag{2}$$

and the covariant metric tensor is given by $Z_{ij} = \boldsymbol{Z}_i \cdot \boldsymbol{Z}_j$.

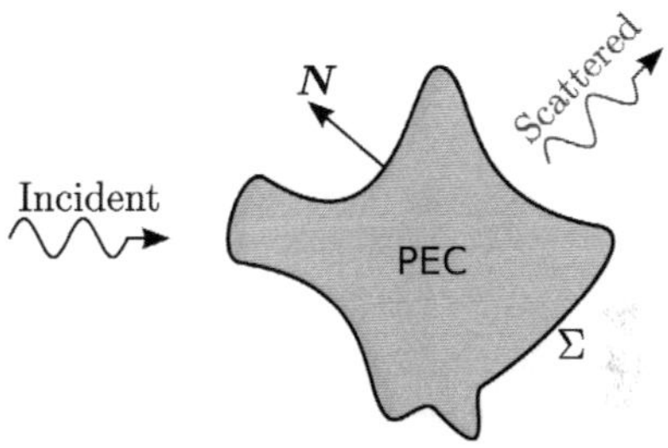

Fig. 1. (Color online) A typical scattering geometry is shown. The scatterer is bounded by the surface Σ with the unit normal vector $\boldsymbol{N}$.

It is well-known that the E-field in a source-free region is divergenceless and satisfies the vector Helmholtz equation. In the tensor notation, the Laplacian may be written as $\nabla^j \nabla_j$ and thus, the vector Helmholtz equation is written as

$$\left(\nabla^j \nabla_j + k^2\right) \boldsymbol{E} = \boldsymbol{0}, \tag{3}$$

where $\nabla^j = Z^{jk}\nabla_k$ and ∇_k denotes the covariant derivative. In order to derive an integral representation of the E-field, we introduce a free-space Green's function G. The Green's function satisfies

$$(\nabla^i \nabla_i + k^2)G = -\delta(\widetilde{\boldsymbol{P}} - \boldsymbol{P}), \tag{4}$$

where $\delta(\widetilde{\boldsymbol{P}} - \boldsymbol{P})$ denotes the Dirac delta function and the position vectors of a source point and a field point are given by $\boldsymbol{P} = \boldsymbol{R}(Z)$ and $\widetilde{\boldsymbol{P}} = \boldsymbol{R}(\widetilde{Z})$, respectively. To obtain an integral representation of the E-field, we multiply (3) by $G(\widetilde{\boldsymbol{P}}, \boldsymbol{P})$ and (4) by $\boldsymbol{E}(Z)$, then take the difference between the two equations. After integrating the resultant equation via Gauss's theorem, we obtain

$$\overset{\text{inc}}{\boldsymbol{E}}(\widetilde{Z}) - \int_\Sigma \left[G\frac{\partial \boldsymbol{E}}{\partial N} - \boldsymbol{E}\frac{\partial G}{\partial N}\right] \mathrm{d}S = \boldsymbol{E}(\widetilde{Z}), \quad \widetilde{Z} \notin \text{PEC}, \tag{5}$$

where $\partial/\partial N = N^i \nabla_i$ denotes the normal derivative with respect to the source coordinates. Finally, taking the limit as $\widetilde{Z}$ approaches the surface and accounting for the Green's function singular nature [2], we obtain

$$\overset{\text{inc}}{\boldsymbol{E}} - \fint_{\Sigma} \left[G \frac{\partial \boldsymbol{E}}{\partial N} - (\boldsymbol{N} \cdot \boldsymbol{E}) \boldsymbol{N} \frac{\partial G}{\partial N} \right] \mathrm{d}S = \frac{1}{2} (\boldsymbol{N} \cdot \boldsymbol{E}) \boldsymbol{N}, \quad (6)$$

where $\fint$ denotes the Cauchy principal value integral and the tangential components of the E-field vanish because of the boundary condition (1). Notice that (6) contains *three* scalar equations. Thus, if we choose $\boldsymbol{N} \cdot \boldsymbol{E}$ (surface charge) and $\partial \boldsymbol{E}/\partial N$ as the boundary unknowns, then we will have *more* unknowns than equations. To remedy this situation, either the number of equations must be increased by one or the number of unknowns must be decreased by one. We discuss both of these approaches below.

A. Increasing the Number of Equations

We can increase the number of equations by noticing that if the E-field is divergenceless, then $\boldsymbol{R} \cdot \boldsymbol{E}$ satisfies the *scalar* Helmholtz equation [3], [4]. Thus, after applying Green's second identity and taking the limit as $\tilde{Z}$ approaches the surface, we obtain

$$\boldsymbol{R} \cdot \overset{\text{inc}}{\boldsymbol{E}} - \fint_{\Sigma} \left[G \frac{\partial (\boldsymbol{R} \cdot \boldsymbol{E})}{\partial N} - (\boldsymbol{R} \cdot \boldsymbol{E}) \frac{\partial G}{\partial N} \right] \mathrm{d}S = \frac{1}{2} (\boldsymbol{R} \cdot \boldsymbol{E}) . \quad (7)$$

The normal derivative of $\boldsymbol{R} \cdot \boldsymbol{E}$ can be related to the surface charge and the normal derivative of the E-field; namely,

$$\begin{aligned} N^i \nabla_i (\boldsymbol{R} \cdot \boldsymbol{E}) &= N^i (\nabla_i \boldsymbol{R}) \cdot \boldsymbol{E} + \boldsymbol{R} \cdot (N^i \nabla_i \boldsymbol{E}) \\ &= \boldsymbol{N} \cdot \boldsymbol{E} + \boldsymbol{R} \cdot \frac{\partial \boldsymbol{E}}{\partial N}. \end{aligned} \quad (8)$$

Substituting (8) into (7) and using (1) yields the desired additional equation; namely,

$$\begin{aligned} \fint_{\Sigma} \left[G \left(\boldsymbol{N} \cdot \boldsymbol{E} + \boldsymbol{R} \cdot \frac{\partial \boldsymbol{E}}{\partial N} \right) - (\boldsymbol{R} \cdot \boldsymbol{N}) (\boldsymbol{N} \cdot \boldsymbol{E}) \frac{\partial G}{\partial N} \right] \mathrm{d}S \\ = \boldsymbol{R} \cdot \overset{\text{inc}}{\boldsymbol{E}} - \frac{1}{2} (\boldsymbol{R} \cdot \boldsymbol{N}) (\boldsymbol{N} \cdot \boldsymbol{E}) . \end{aligned} \quad (9)$$

Notice that (II-A) contains *one* scalar equation and thus, together with (6), we have *four* scalar equations that we can solve for the *four* scalar unknowns; namely, $\boldsymbol{N} \cdot \boldsymbol{E}$ and $\partial \boldsymbol{E}/\partial N$.

The above coordinate invariant singular integral equation formulation is analogous to the formulation presented in [3], [4]. However, in [3], [4] the singular behavior of the Green's function was removed via a clever subtraction of an auxiliary function.

B. Decreasing the Number of Unknowns

We can decrease the number of unknowns by relating the normal component of the normal derivative of the E-field to the surface charge on Σ. The desired relationship is

$$\boldsymbol{N} \cdot \frac{\partial \boldsymbol{E}}{\partial N} = (\boldsymbol{N} \cdot \boldsymbol{E}) W, \quad (10)$$

where W is the mean curvature. The derivation of (10) is built upon the work presented in [5], [6] and is outside of the scope of this paper. To apply (10) to (6), we decompose the normal derivative of the E-field into normal and tangential parts, i.e.,

$$\frac{\partial \boldsymbol{E}}{\partial N} = \left(\boldsymbol{N} \cdot \frac{\partial \boldsymbol{E}}{\partial N} \right) \boldsymbol{N} + \left(\boldsymbol{S}^{\alpha} \cdot \frac{\partial \boldsymbol{E}}{\partial N} \right) \boldsymbol{S}_{\alpha}, \quad (11)$$

where $\boldsymbol{S}_{\alpha=1,2}$ are the surface covariant basis, i.e., two vectors tangential to Σ. Putting (10) into (11) and the resultant into (6) yields

$$\begin{aligned} \fint_{\Sigma} \left\{ \left[W G - \frac{\partial G}{\partial N} \right] (\boldsymbol{N} \cdot \boldsymbol{E}) \boldsymbol{N} + G \left(\boldsymbol{S}^{\alpha} \cdot \frac{\partial \boldsymbol{E}}{\partial N} \right) \boldsymbol{S}_{\alpha} \right\} \mathrm{d}S \\ = \overset{\text{inc}}{\boldsymbol{E}} - \frac{1}{2} (\boldsymbol{N} \cdot \boldsymbol{E}) \boldsymbol{N}. \end{aligned} \quad (12)$$

Notice that (II-B) contains *three* scalar equations and *three* scalar unknowns; namely, the surface charge $\boldsymbol{N} \cdot \boldsymbol{E}$ and the tangential components of the normal derivative of the E-field, $(\boldsymbol{S}^{\alpha} \cdot \frac{\partial \boldsymbol{E}}{\partial N})_{\alpha=1,2}$. Thus, we can obtain the boundary unknowns directly from (II-B).

If the mean curvature is different from zero, i.e., $W \neq 0$, then another formulation is possible. Putting (10) directly into (6) yields

$$\begin{aligned} \fint_{\Sigma} \left\{ \left[G - \frac{1}{W} \frac{\partial G}{\partial N} \right] \left(\boldsymbol{N} \cdot \frac{\partial \boldsymbol{E}}{\partial N} \right) \boldsymbol{N} + G \left(\boldsymbol{S}^{\alpha} \cdot \frac{\partial \boldsymbol{E}}{\partial N} \right) \boldsymbol{S}_{\alpha} \right\} \mathrm{d}S \\ = \overset{\text{inc}}{\boldsymbol{E}} - \frac{1}{2W} \left(\boldsymbol{N} \cdot \frac{\partial \boldsymbol{E}}{\partial N} \right) \boldsymbol{N}. \end{aligned} \quad (13)$$

In (II-B), we can choose the normal and tangential components of the normal derivative of the E-field as the boundary unknowns. In other words, after discretization we can numerically solve (II-B) for $\boldsymbol{N} \cdot \partial \boldsymbol{E}/\partial N$ and $(\boldsymbol{S}^{\alpha} \cdot \partial \boldsymbol{E}/\partial N)_{\alpha=1,2}$ via well-known methods such as the Galerkin's method [7] or the Nyström method [8].

III. Conclusions

We derived three alternative singular surface integral equation formulations for electromagnetic scattering by a perfect electric conductor. These formulations were obtained by choosing non-conventional boundary unknowns. We showed that the number of the scalar integral equations needed in each formulation depends on the choice of the boundary unknowns. These formulations show an interesting interplay between the normal component of the E-field and its the normal derivative.

References

[1] J. A. Stratton and L. J. Chu, "Diffraction theory of electromagnetic waves," Phys. Rev., vol. 56, no. 1, pp. 99–107, Jul. 1939.

[2] J. DeSanto and A. Yuffa, "A new integral equation method for direct electromagnetic scattering in homogeneous media and its numerical confirmation," Waves in Random and Complex Media, vol. 16, no. 4, pp. 397–408, Nov. 2006.

[3] E. Klaseboer, Q. Sun, and D. Y. C. Chan, "Nonsingular field-only surface integral equations for electromagnetic scattering," IEEE Trans. Antennas Propag., vol. 65, no. 2, pp. 972–977, 2017.

[4] Q. Sun, E. Klaseboer, and D. Y. C. Chan, "Robust multiscale field-only formulation of electromagnetic scattering," Phys. Rev. B, vol. 95, no. 4, p. 045137, 2017.

[5] A. J. Yuffa and J. Markkanen, "A 3-D tensorial integral formulation of scattering containing intriguing relations," IEEE Transactions on Antennas and Propagation, vol. 66, no. 10, pp. 5274–5281, Oct. 2018.

[6] J. Markkanen, A. J. Yuffa, and J. A. Gordon, "Numerical validation of a boundary element method with electric field and its normal derivative as the boundary unknowns," Appl. Comput. Electromagn. Soc. J., 2019, (to be published).

[7] K. E. Atkinson, The Numerical Solution of Integral Equations of the Second Kind. Cambridge University Press, 1997.

[8] A. F. Peterson and M. M. Bibby, An Introduction to the Locally-Corrected Nyström Method, ser. Synthesis Lectures on Computational Electromagnetics. Morgan and Claypool Publishers, 2010.

Powerful TLM Technique for Analyzing Antennas

Sebastian Held and Adalbert Beyer
Department of Electrical Engineering and Informatics
Duisburg-Essen University
Campus Duisburg, Germany
a.beyer@ieee.org

Rüdiger Follmann and Peter Waldow
System and Circuit Integration
IMST GmbH
Kamp-Lintfort, Germany
waldow@imst.de

Dominique Schreurs
Department of Electrical Engineering (ESAT)
KU Leuven,
Leuven, Belgium
dominique.schreurs@kuleuven.be

***Abstract*—In this paper, a time-domain technique for analyzing antennas efficiently with the help of Transmission Line Matrix (TLM) Method is presented. This procedure requires the simulation of free space, and, the near-to- far-field transformation. Numerical, as well as experimental results are introduced and discussed, underlining the applicability of this technique for broad-band antenna design.**

***Keywords*— near-to-far-field transformation, perfectly matched layer (PML), transient behavior, Transmission Line Matrix (TLM) Method, Ultra-Wide Band (UWB) antenna.**

I. Introduction

The analysis and design of antennas in micro-strip technology are often carried out by means of CAD (Computer Aided Design) programs. These packages are valid only up to a certain frequency, and, describe a particular type of an antenna, only [1].

For realistic description of an antenna, it is necessary to use full-wave simulators like the method of moments that is applied in the simulator ADS (Advanced Design System), and FEM (Finite Element Method) method that is applied in HFSS (High Frequency Structure Simulator). These operate in the frequency domain performing exclusively the analysis of the steady state.

In order to avoid this drawback, a time domain method is used in this work. The most applied techniques are FDTD- (Finite Difference Time Domain) [2] and TLM (Transmission Line Matrix) methods [3]. In this paper, the TLM method is applied, which is based on the Huygens' Principle. TLM is theoretically very simple providing all field components are at the same time and space, which is an advantage compared to FDTD. In addition, handling the boundary conditions in TLM requires considerably lower mathematical efforts compared to FDTD and other time domain methods. In this work, it is shown by means of numerical experiments that by the help of modified equations for a PML-SCN (perfect matched layer) node - originally suggested by Le Maguer and Ney in [4] -, the highest degree of stability can be reached for simulating a given antenna arrangement. This technique renders also possible applying a very efficient near zone to far zone transformation.

II. Theoretical Background

A disadvantage of time-domain method compared to frequency domain techniques is that the simulation space must be limited by appropriate boundary conditions. This is especially the case when determining antenna properties. A finite simulation field always contains limitations on which reflections occur. The 3D FDTD PML and its implementation in TLM have been originally proposed in [4].

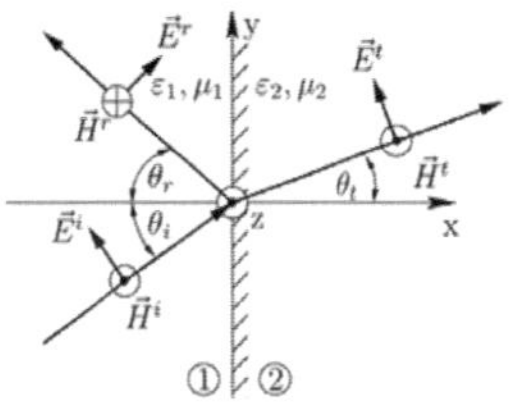

Fig. 1. Boundary conditions of a TE_z wave.

Fig. 1 shows the reflection-transmission behavior of a TE_z wave at a boundary between two half-spaces. The aim of using PML is that no reflections occur. In this case (and for θ_i=0), the following conditions are to be fulfilled:

$$\varepsilon_1 = \varepsilon_2 = \varepsilon,\ \mu_1 = \mu_2 = \mu, \text{and}\ \sigma_e/\varepsilon = \sigma_m/\mu, \quad (1)$$

where ε is the dielectric constant, and μ is the magnetic permeability. Furthermore, the values σ_e and σ_m are the electric and magnetic losses, respectively.

For the simulation of an antenna discrete space is used, which may represent only an approximation of the continuous space. Therefore, the governing relationships are no longer differential equations, but difference equations. This fact has the consequence that abrupt changes in the conductivity of the media (e.g., vacuum-PML boundary layer) lead to unphysical reflections. For that reason, it is not possible to reduce to a width of only one cell, which might have a very high conductivity. Rather, one must construct a PML so that the jumps between the different conductivities remain low. Such a PML can be constructed by using several layers.

This work builds on the principle of PML-SCN node as suggested in [4]. The governing equations obtained in [4] are modified and used in the numerical experiments in this work.

III. Results and Discussion

Using the particular EPML (Extended Perfectly Matched Layer) suggested in [4], the spatial distance between the AUT (antenna under test) and the surrounding absorber can be kept very small. In addition to that, attenuation of evanescent energy is considered. This approach has proven superior stability in antenna analysis. All simulations were done using the SCN (Symmetrical Condensed Node) [5] with the condition of discretization: $\Delta\ell = \Delta x = \Delta y = \Delta z$. Also, a near-to-far-field transformation [6], applied for the TLM method, was performed in order to get the antenna properties. The perfectly matched layer surrounds the computation domain. Its properties beside the geometric profile are: Thickness = 5 $\Delta\ell$, Reflection factor R (0) = 0.1%, Evanescent damping F = 3. The latter is defined in [4].

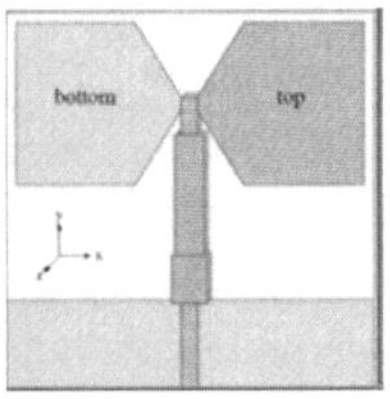

Fig. 2. Geometry of the bow-tie antenna.

In order to demonstrate the effectiveness of this technique, the bow-tie antenna is investigated. This type of antenna is often used for different Ultra-Wide Band (UWB) purposes. In particular, it is a double-sided printed bow-tie antenna, which is fabricated on Duroid Substrate with a relative permittivity ε_r = 6.15 and a thickness of 1.27 mm (see Fig. 2).

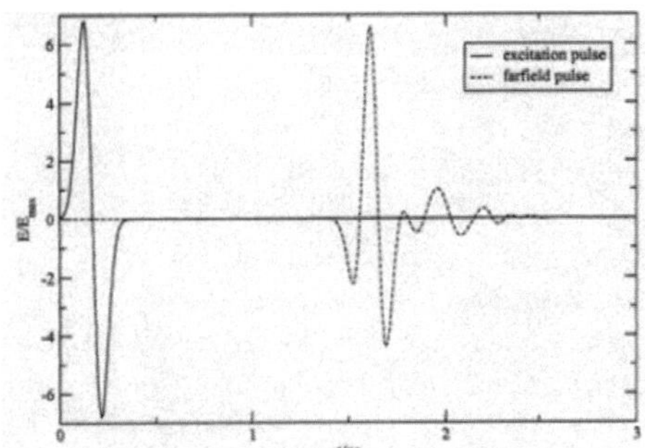

Fig. 3. Normalized radiated E-field pulse from the bow-tie antenna.

Fig. 3 shows a Gauss monocycle pulse as excitation signal and the transmitted pulse (Θ-polarized e-field) in the farfield (Φ= 90°, Θ = 90°). Time and amplitude are normalized for better displaying. The far-field signal exhibits only small disturbances, so called ringing. It can be recognized that his antenna is well suited for pulse transmission.

The magnitude of the reflection coefficient S_{11} is plotted in Fig. 4. It can be recognized that the values of simulated reflection coefficient reasonably agree with the measured ones.

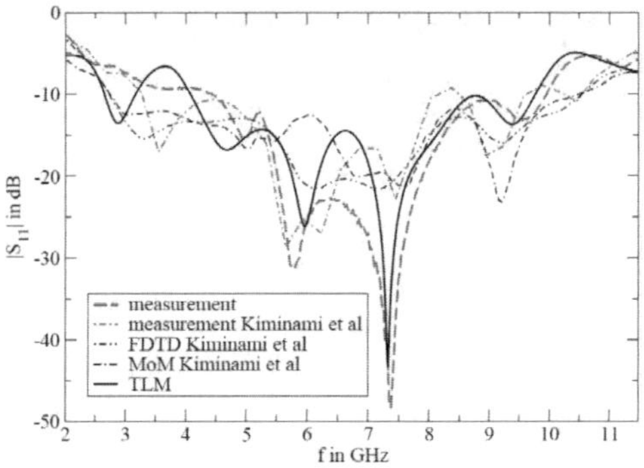

Fig. 4. Reflection coefficient $|S_{11}|$ for the bow-tie antenna.

Compared to the results given by [7], the resonance at 7.4 GHz is well predicted in the simulation. It is a common practice to consider an antenna matched, if the reflection coefficient is smaller than -10 dB. Hence, this antenna is usable between 4.5 GHz - 10 GHz, where the reflection coefficient is below -10 dB.

With the help of this very powerful tool further simulation results such as antenna-radiation diagrams could be obtained. and, will be presented and discussed in the planned presentation.

IV. Conclusion

For analyzing antennas in micro-strip technology, the Transmission Line Matrix (TLM) method - in conjunction with the Extended Perfectly Matched Layer (EPML) - is used in this work. The feasibility of the technique proposed has been demonstrated by analyzing a double-sided printed bow-tie antenna. Transient behavior as well as scattering parameters are introduced and discussed.

References

[1] H. J. Visser, Approximate Antenna Analysis for CAD , 2009 John Wiley & Sons, Ltd, March 2009.

[2] EMPIRE XPU 7.62 Released July 2018, IMST, Kamp-Lintfort, Germany.

[3] T. Itoh (Editor), Planar Transmission Line Structures, IEEE Press, The Institute of Electrical and Electronics Engineers, Inc., New York, 1987.

[4] S. Le Maguer and M. M. Ney, "Extended PML-TLM node: An efficient approach for full-wave analysis of open structures," International Journal of Numerical Modeling: Electronic Networks, Devices and Fields, no. 14, pp. 129144, 2001.

[5] P. B. Johns, "A symmetrical condensed node for the TLM method," IEEE Transaction of Microwave Theory and Techniques, vol. MTT-35, no. 4, pp. 370-377, April 1987.

[6] R. J. Luebbers, et al., "A finite-difference time domain near zone to far zone transformation," IEEE Transactions on Antennas and , Propagation, vol. 39, no. 4, pp. 428-433, April 1991.

[7] K. Kiminami, A. Hirata, and T. Shiozawa, "Double-sided printed bow-tie antenna for UWB communications," IEEE Antennas and Wireless Propagation Letters, vol. 3, pp. 152-153, 2004.

FDTD Modeling of Lightning Electromagnetic Field Propagation Over Mountainous Terrain

1st Dongshuai Li
Instituto de Astrofísica de Andalucía (IAA)-CSIC
Granada, Spain
dsl@iaa.es

2nd Farhad Rachidi
Electromagnetic Compatibility Laboratory
Swiss Federal Institute of Technology (EPFL)
Lausanne, Switzerland
farhad.rachidi@epfl.ch

3rd Marcos Rubinstein
University of Applied Sciences
Western Switzerland
Yverdon-les-Bains, Switzerland
marcos.rubinstein@heig-vd.ch

***Abstract*—The Full-Wave Finite-Difference-Time-Domain (FDTD) electromagnetic (EM) simulation method can simulate large domains and produce time-marching solutions for arbitrary time-domain sources, making it ideal for many lightning applications. In this paper, a two-dimensional (2D) axial-symmetric and a three-dimensional (3D) FDTD model are developed that include irregular terrain based on real topographic data. The models open the door to a wide variety of advanced modeling applications in the analysis of the lightning EM field propagation over mountainous terrain and the location error of lightning location systems (LLSs) in the presence of in mountainous regions.**

***Index Terms*—FDTD, Mountainous terrain, Säntis Tower**

I. INTRODUCTION

Full-Wave FDTD numerical simulations have a number of advantages with respect to other methods, including the ability to simulate large domains without having to solve matrix equations, the time-marching nature of the solutions and the possibility of using arbitrary time-domain sources. These advantages make FDTD especially well-suited for lightning EM field simulations with engineering Return Stroke (RS) models.

In this study, we present two full-wave FDTD models based on available topographic data that can be used to analyze propagation effects of the lightning EM field over mountainous terrain and to evaluate the location error associated with the Time of Arrival (ToA)-based LLSs.

II. ADOPTED MODELS AND METHODS

In this study, as shown in Fig.1, we focus on the region around the Säntis Tower located in the Swiss Alps. The 124-m Säntis Tower has been instrumented since 2010 and it serves as an experimental station for the direct measurement of lightning currents [1]. We consider the topography between the Säntis Tower and nearby LLS sensors (see Fig.1) based on the global digital elevation model version 2 (GDEM V2) data. The current distribution along the lightning channel is specified according to the modified transmission line model with exponential decay (MTLE) with the channel-base current directly measured at the Säntis Tower. More details of the FDTD simulation of the return stroke can be found in [2], [3] and the references quoted there.

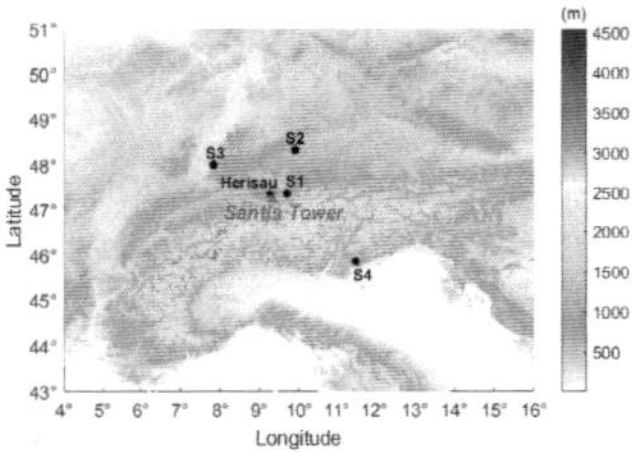

Fig. 1. The topographic map of the selected region around the Säntis Tower (red triangle) including the locations of four sensors (S1, S2, S3 and S4, black dots) and the Herisau station (black star).

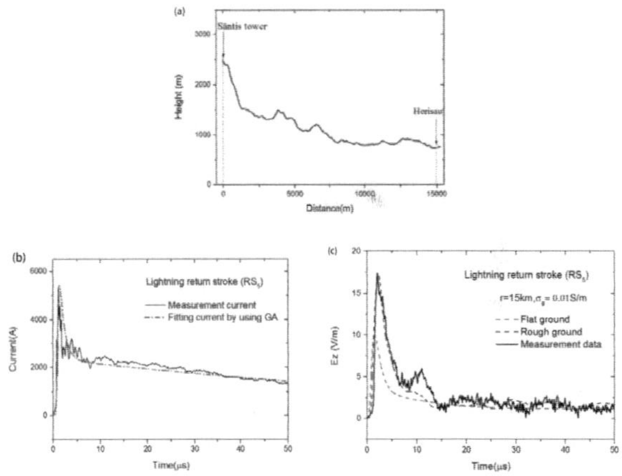

Fig. 2. (a) The 2D cross-section of the topographic map along the direct path between the Säntis Tower and the Herisau E-field measurement station. (b) Measured and simulated lightning RS current. (c) Associated electric field (adapted from [2]).

III. SIMULATION RESULTS AND DISCUSSION

A. 2D axial-symmetric FDTD model

In this section, to save computational cost with sufficient accuracy, we use a 2D axial symmetric FDTD model that assumes that the 2D cross-section of the topographic map along the direct path between the Säntis Tower and the Herisau station in Switzerland is the same in all azimuthal directions (see Fig. 2(a)).

For comparison purposes, two terrain profiles are considered in our 2D axial-symmetric FDTD modeling, namely the irregular ground model based on the topographic map shown in Fig.2(a), and a flat ground. Experimental observations consist of simultaneous records of lightning RS currents measured at the Säntis Tower and the associated electric fields measured at the Herisau station, about 15 km away from the Tower. The measured channel-base current and a fitted version using genetic algorithms are presented in Fig.2(b). As shown in Fig.2(c), after considering the real irregular terrain between the Säntis Tower and the field measurement station, both the waveshape and amplitude of the simulated electric fields are in excellent agreement with the measured waveforms. On the other hand, the assumption of a flat ground results in a significant underestimation of the peak electric field.

B. 3D FDTD model

As discussed in [3], a 3D FDTD simulation of the full domain would require prohibitively high computational resources. In this section, we consider a reduced 3D FDTD model and we compare it with the 2D axial-symmetric model presented in the previous section A. The 3D model utilizes a reduced version of the full 3D space consisting of a 20-km wide rectangular area between the lightning at the Säntis Tower and the field point (See Fig.3(a), (c), (e), (g)).

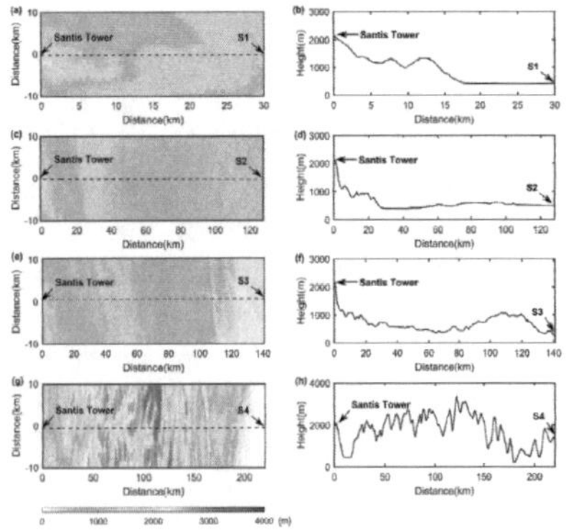

Fig. 3. The rectangular region (left) and the 2D cross section (right) of the topographic profiles along the direct path between the Säntis Tower and the observation sensor site S1 (a,b), S2 (c,d), S3 (e,f) and S4 (g,h) (adopted from [3]).

We use four field points corresponding to lightning location system sensors S1, S2, S3, and S4 belonging to the European Cooperation for Lightning Detection (EUCLID) network. For comparison, as shown in Fig.4, we consider four different conditions for the ground: (i) Perfectly-conducting flat ground, (ii) Finitely-conducting flat ground, (iii) Finitely-conducting ground taking into account the 3D terrain profile, and (iv) finitely-conducting ground, taking into account the 2D terrain profile. From Fig.4, it is found that the peak and the rise times of vertical electric fields can be strongly affected by the presence of mountainous terrain and the finite ground conductivity. It is interesting to note that the results obtained using the approximate 2D approach [2] are very similar to those obtained using the 3D FDTD model for the cases corresponding to sensors S1, S2 and S3. However, for Sensor S4, the results obtained using the 2D FDTD approach are significantly different from those obtained using the 3D approach. This is due, on the one hand, to the fact that the propagation distance to Sensor 4 is much longer than for the other sensors and, on the other hand, to the complex terrain profile along the path between the Säntis Tower and S4 sensor site (see Fig.3(g, h)).

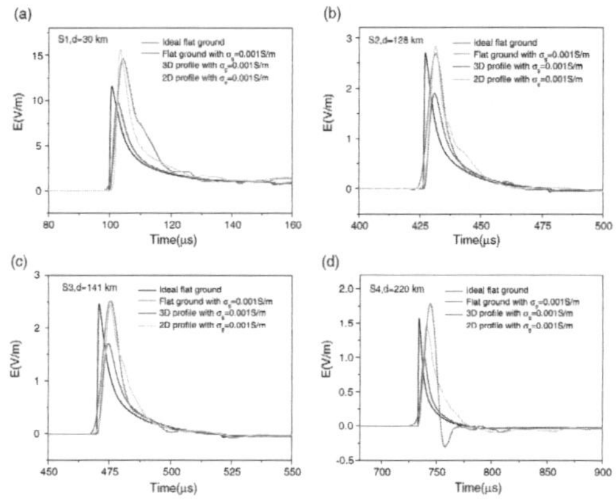

Fig. 4. Vertical electric fields at sensor S1(a) , S2(b), S3(c) and S4(d) considering four different conditions for the ground corresponding to the cases from (i) to (iv). Note that cases (i), (ii) and (iii) are calculated using the 3D FDTD method, while the results corresponding to case (iv) are computed by way of the 2D FDTD approach presented by in Section A. (adopted from [3]).

IV. CONCLUSION

In this paper, based on two proposed full-wave FDTD models, we presented an analysis of the propagation effects of lightning EM fields over mountainous terrain, to illustrate the use of FDTD in complex models for lightning EM field calculations. It is noted that the lightning EM fields can be significantly affected by the presence of mountainous terrain. After considering the real irregular terrain over which propagation occurs, the simulated electric fields are in excellent agreement with the measured waveforms, validating the accuracy of the FDTD technique and of the implemented models. On the other hand, the results obtained using our 2D axial-symmetric FDTD model can save considerable computation time and agree well in most cases (e.g., sensors S1, S2 and S3) with those obtained by using a more complex 3D FDTD approach. However, the 2D axial-symmetric assumption analysis might lead to inaccuracies in the cases when the terrain is characterized by a particularly complex profile (e.g. sensor S4).

REFERENCES

[1] C. Romero, M. Paolone, M. Rubinstein et al., "A system for the measurements of lightning currents at the Säntis Tower," Electric Power Systems Research, vol. 82, no. 1, pp. 34–43, 2012.

[2] D. Li, M. Azadifar, F. Rachidi et al., "On lightning electromagnetic field propagation along an irregular terrain," IEEE Transactions on Electromagnetic Compatibility, vol. 58, no. 1, pp. 161–171, 2016.

[3] D. Li, M. Rubinstein, F. Rachidi et al., "Location accuracy evaluation of ToA-based lightning location systems over mountainous terrain," Journal of Geophysical Research: Atmospheres, vol. 122, no. 21, 2017.

Time-Domain Magnetic Shielding of a Thin Conducting Screen Against a Small Loop

R. Araneo, G. Lovat, and S. Celozzi
DIAEE - EE Division
Sapienza University of Rome
Rome, Italy
rodolfo.araneo, giampiero.lovat, salvatore.celozzi@uniroma1.it

P. Burghignoli
D.I.E.T.
Sapienza University of Rome
Rome, Italy
burghignoli@diet.uniroma1.it

***Abstract*—The classical electromagnetic problem represented by a small loop axially parallel to a thin conductive planar shield of infinite extent is addressed in the time domain. The problem is solved analytically through a modified Cagniard-de Hoop approach and numerically through the double inverse Hankel/Fourier transform. Although some approximations are made, the analytical method is the most useful in predicting the main time-domain shielding characteristics.**

I. Introduction

Recently, time-domain (TD) electromagnetic analysis of classical shielding configurations has received a renewed attention [1]–[6] aimed at assessing the relevant theoretical electromagnetic (EM) phenomena. When the screen is thin and the sources are pulsed dipoles, the solution can be obtained in semi-analytical form through modified Cagniard-de Hoop (CdH) approaches [7]–[9], while, in the more general case of thick and/or multilayered screens, the numerical approach remains the only possible way. Using the CdH approach originally proposed in [10], the TD potential Green's function in planar multilayered structures has been derived in [11] through a generalized ray theory; yet the proposed formulation is valid only for non-dispersive and lossless media. Other approaches have been proposed in [12], but their applicability, and hence their practical interest, remains limited.

In this paper we present some preliminary results concerning the TD shielding properties of a thin conductive sheet against transient fields excited by a pulsed small loop axially parallel to a thin conductive planar shield of infinite extent. The small loop is represented by an equivalent horizontal magnetic dipole (HMD) and the solution of the problem is obtained in a semi-analytical form by means of a modified CdH approach extending the formulation developed by the authors in [6], [13]. As a numerical benchmark, a conventional pure numerical two-step procedure is considered: first, the frequency-domain (FD) solution is obtained via a spatial-wavenumber synthesis through the inverse Fourier-Hankel transform; then, the TD solution via the inverse Fourier transform (IFT) is computed. By using efficient techniques based on the double-exponential (DE) formulas, the numerical burden related to the evaluation of oscillatory infinite integrals is drastically reduced, thus allowing for a rapid solution of the problem.

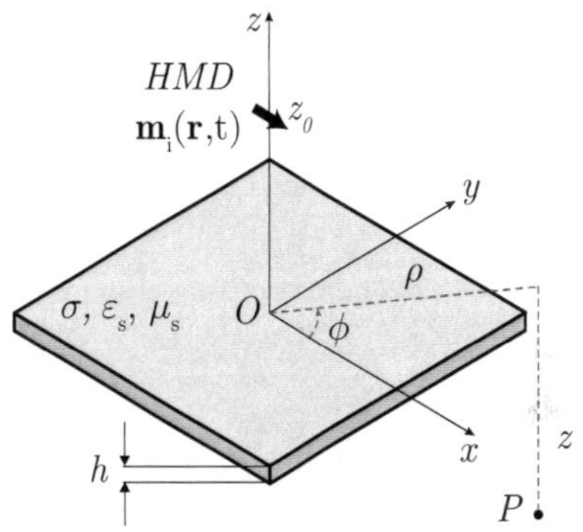

Fig. 1. The configuration under analysis with the relevant reference system and physical parameters.

II. The Problem and its Numerical Solution

The configuration under analysis is shown in Figure 1. It consists of an infinite planar conductive sheet with thickness h, electric permittivity $\varepsilon_s = \varepsilon_0\varepsilon_{sr}$, magnetic permeability $\mu_s = \mu_0\mu_{sr}$, and (bulk) conductivity σ; the sheet is orthogonal to the vertical z axis and is excited by a horizontal magnetic dipole source of length ℓ, located along the x axis at $z = z_0 > 0$ in air and carrying a voltage $v(t)$. The source is thus modeled as an impressed magnetic current

$$\mathbf{j}_{mi}(\mathbf{r}, t) = v(t)\ell\delta(x)\delta(y)\delta(z - z_0)\mathbf{u}_x \quad (1)$$

The considered source excites both TM^z and TE^z fields, which can be derived in the spectral domain through a standard formulation. Once the general component of the dyadic field Green's function $\tilde{G}(k_x, k_y; \omega; z, z_0)$ is computed in the spectral domain, in order to obtain the spatial-domain counterparts, a double inverse Fourier transform has to be performed, that is

$$G(\mathbf{r}, z_0; \omega) = \frac{1}{(2\pi)^2} \cdot \int_{-\infty}^{+\infty}\int_{-\infty}^{+\infty} \tilde{G}(k_x, k_y; \omega; z, z_0)\, e^{-j(k_x x + k_y y)}\, \mathrm{d}k_x\, \mathrm{d}k_y \,. \quad (2)$$

Subsequently, the TD electromagnetic field can be recovered by inverse-Fourier transforming the product of the relevant component of the dyadic spatial-domain Green's function times the Fourier trasform of the voltage profile $V(\omega)\,\ell$, i.e.,

$$f(\mathbf{r},t)=\frac{1}{2\pi}\int_{-\infty}^{+\infty}G(\mathbf{r},z_0;\omega)\,V(\omega)\,\ell e^{j\omega t}\,\mathrm{d}\omega\,. \quad (3)$$

Starting from the field expressions in the spectral domain, using a modified CdH approach we derive efficient expressions for the calculation of the relevant time-domain electromagnetic field in the halfspace beyond the screen. After some cumbersome manipulations of the integral (2), it is possible to derive the following expression

$$G(\mathbf{r},z_0;s)=-j\frac{s^2}{(4\pi)^2}\int_{-\infty}^{+\infty}\int_{-\infty}^{+\infty}\bar{G}(-jss_x,-sq;-js)\,e^{-s(s_x\rho+s_z\Delta_z)}\,\mathrm{d}s_x\,\mathrm{d}q\,, \quad (4)$$

where $s_z=\sqrt{s_0^2+q^2-s_x^2}$, $s_y=-jq$ and $s=j\omega$. Evaluating the inner integral in (4) with the CdH technique we obtain the final expression

$$f(\boldsymbol{r},t)=\int_{s_0 r}^{t}\frac{\ell\,\mathrm{d}\tau}{2\pi^2 r}\int_{-\sqrt{\frac{\tau^2}{r^2}-s_0^2}}^{+\sqrt{\frac{\tau^2}{r^2}-s_0^2}}\frac{\mathrm{Re}\left\{\left[s_z\bar{G}\right]_{P_U}\right\}}{\sqrt{\frac{\tau^2}{r^2}-s_0^2-q^2}}\left.\frac{\mathrm{d}^2 v}{\mathrm{d}t^2}\right|_{t-\tau}\mathrm{d}q\,. \quad (5)$$

Figures 2 shows the results for the transmitted magnetic field $h_\phi(t)$ components produced at $z=-30$ cm, $\rho=30$ cm and $\phi=\pi/3$, by a transient HMD located at $z_0=30$ cm above an ideally thin sheet represented by a surface conductance $G_s=37.7$ S. For the time waveforms of the magnetic current sources, we consider the first Derivative of the Power Exponential Pulse (DPEP) [13], expressed in the TD by

$$v(t)=nV_0\left(1-\frac{t}{T_c}\right)\left(\frac{t}{T_c}\right)^{n-1}\exp\left[-n\left(\frac{t}{T_c}-1\right)\right]H(t)\,, \quad (6)$$

where V_0 is the PEP pulse amplitude, T_c its rise time, and n is the exponent of its initial algebraic increase (in the following, $n=16$ and $T_c=5$ μs). Figure 3 show the peak-reduction (PR) efficiency of an aluminum shield ($\sigma=37.7$ MS/m) as a function of the thickness h.

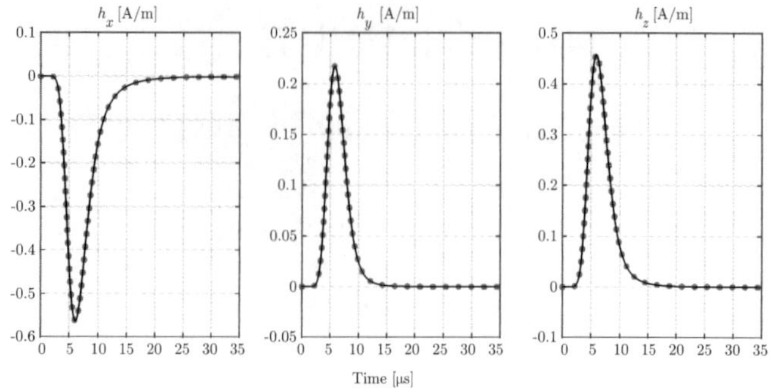

Fig. 2. Transmitted magnetic field $h(t)$ components produced at $z=-30$ cm, $\rho=30$ cm, and $\phi=\pi/3$, by a transient HMD placed at $z_0=30$ cm above an ideally thin conducting sheet with $G_s=37.7$ S. *Solid line*: analytical solution obtained with the proposed CDH approach. *Dots*: numerical solution obtained by inverse-Bessel-Fourier transforms of the spectral-domain solutions.

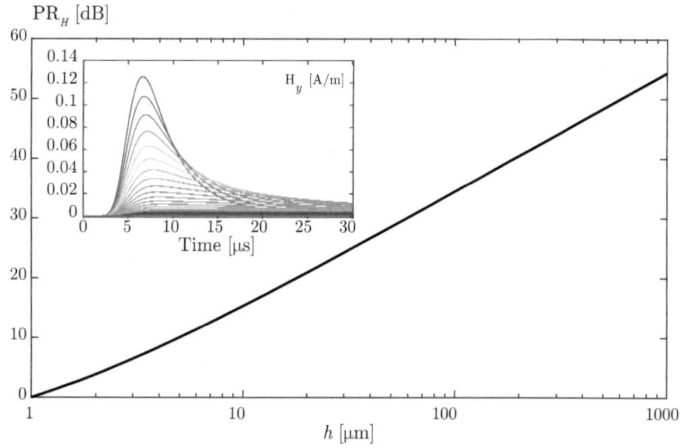

Fig. 3. Peak reduction efficiency SE_{PR} as a function of the screen thickness h. *Parameters*: $\sigma=37.7$ MS/m, $z_0=30$ cm, $z=-30$ cm, $\rho=30$ cm and $\phi=\pi/3$.

REFERENCES

[1] H. Karami, R. Moini, S. H. H. Sadeghi, H. Maftooli, M. Mattes, and J. R. Mosig, "Efficient analysis of shielding effectiveness of metallic rectangular enclosures using unconditionally stable time-domain integral equations," *IEEE Trans. Electromagn. Compat.*, vol. 56, no. 6, pp. 1412–1419, Dec. 2014.

[2] S. Celozzi and R. Araneo, "Alternative definitions for the time-domain shielding effectiveness of enclosures," *IEEE Trans. Electromagn. Compat.*, vol. 56, no. 2, pp. 482–485, Apr. 2014.

[3] R. Araneo, S. Celozzi, A. Tatematsu, and F. Rachidi, "Time-domain analysis of building shielding against lightning electromagnetic fields," *IEEE Trans. Electromagn. Compat.*, vol. 57, no. 3, pp. 397–404, Jun. 2015.

[4] R. Araneo, G. Attolini, S. Celozzi, and G. Lovat, "Time-domain shielding performance of enclosures: A comparison of different global approaches," *IEEE Trans. Electromagn. Compat.*, vol. 58, no. 2, pp. 434–441, Apr. 2016.

[5] M. R. Cabello, L. D. Angulo, J. Alvarez, I. D. Flintoft, S. Bourke, J. F. Dawson, R. G. Martín, and S. G. Garcia, "A hybrid Crank-Nicolson FDTD subgridding boundary condition for lossy thin-layer modeling," *IEEE Trans. Microw. Theory Techn.*, vol. 65, no. 5, pp. 1397–1406, May 2017.

[6] P. Burghignoli, G. Lovat, R. Araneo, and S. Celozzi, "Time-domain shielding of a thin conductive sheet in the presence of pulsed vertical dipoles," *IEEE Trans. Electromagn. Compat.*, vol. 60, no. 1, pp. 157–165, Feb. 2018.

[7] A. T. D. Hoop, M. Stumpf, and I. E. Lager, "Pulsed electromagnetic field radiation from a wide slot antenna with a dielectric layer," *IEEE Trans. Antennas Propag.*, vol. 59, no. 8, pp. 2789–2798, Aug. 2011.

[8] G. Lovat, R. Araneo, and S. Celozzi, "Near-field time-domain shielding effectiveness of thin conductive screens," *Progr. Electromag. Res.*, vol. 146, pp. 47–56, 2014.

[9] G. Lovat and R. Araneo, "Semi-analytical representation of the two-dimensional time-domain Green's function of a graphene sheet in the intraband regime," *IEEE Trans. Nanotechnol.*, vol. 14, no. 4, pp. 681–688, Jul. 2015.

[10] R. Dai and C. T. Young, "Transient fields of a horizontal electric dipole on a multilayered dielectric medium," *IEEE Trans. Antennas Propag.*, vol. 45, no. 6, pp. 1023–1031, Jun. 1997.

[11] M. Štumpf, A. T. D. Hoop, and G. A. E. Vandenbosch, "Generalized ray theory for time-domain electromagnetic fields in horizontally layered media," *IEEE Trans. Antennas Propag.*, vol. 61, no. 5, pp. 2676–2687, May 2013.

[12] G. W. Hanson, A. B. Yakovlev, and J. Hao, "Leaky-wave analysis of transient fields due to sources in planarly layered media," *IEEE Trans. Antennas Propag.*, vol. 51, no. 2, pp. 146–159, Feb. 2003.

[13] P. Burghignoli, G. Lovat, R. Araneo, and S. Celozzi, "Pulsed vertical dipole response of a thin sheet with high-contrast dielectric and conductive properties," *IEEE Trans. Antennas Propag.*, vol. 66, no. 1, pp. 217–225, Jan. 2018.

Plasmonic Resonances and Light Generation in Nanoparticle Dimers *(Invited)*

Viktoriia E. Babicheva
College of Optical Sciences
University of Arizona
Tucson, US
vbab.dtu@gmail.com

John M. Nehls
College of Optical Sciences
University of Arizona
Tucson, US
nehls@email.arizona.edu

Jerome V. Moloney
College of Optical Sciences
University of Arizona
Tucson, US
jml@acms.arizona.edu

***Abstract*—We numerically study nanoparticle dimer (two closely-spaced nanoparticles) with the aim to resolve gap plasmon mode using finite-difference time-domain (FDTD) method. Our semi-conformal meshing based on transformation optics principles allows for accurate accounting of nanoparticle gaps and other curved shapes. We calculate surface plasmon amplification by stimulated emission of radiation (SPASER) in the dimer modes using Bloch equations.**

Keywords—field enhancement, finite-difference time-domain, plasmons, spaser, surface plasmon amplification by stimulated emission of radiation.

I. Introduction

Plasmonic nanostructures can significantly enhance electric and magnetic fields at nanoscale dimensions. Fields localized in the narrow gaps of plasmonic nanostructures can be several orders of magnitude higher than the incident light field [1], and this field enhancement strongly affects light-matter interaction processes in plasmonic nanostructures.

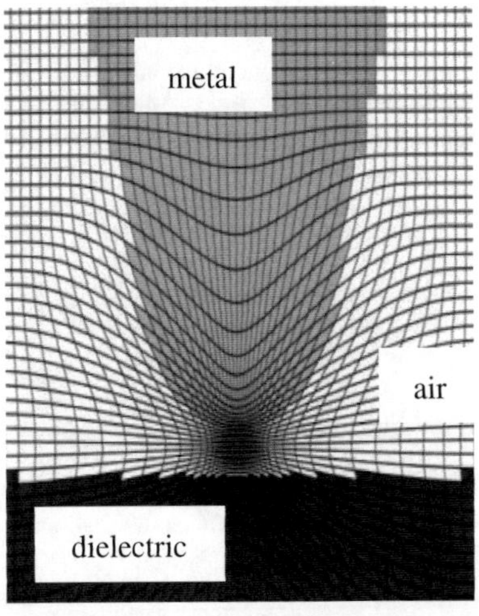

Fig. 1. Example of our FDTD modeling with semi-conformal mesh based on transformation optics. The simulation domain shows a microscope tip on top of the sample, and the intermediate region is highly resolved.

Our in-house FDTD method includes non-uniform, geometry-specific, semi-conformal meshing of the nanostructures (Fig. 1) and enables accurate resolution of electromagnetic 'hot spots' in the nanoparticle gap without parasitic staircasing. Our technique allows for FDTD simulations of fully-anisotropic permittivity and permeability material tensors [2]. Semi-conformal meshing is enabled by placing grid boundaries in critical areas along the surfaces and interfaces of the simulated nanostructure and Maxwell's equations encapsulating a coordinate transformation into the material tensors [3].

II. Dimer Plasmonic Resonances

Here, we study field enhancement in nanoparticle dimers (two nanospheres with a small gap in between, Fig. 2) and analyze surface plasmon amplification by stimulated emission (spaser) in the dimer gap. Using our FDTD approach, we numerically study gap modes with even and odd field distributions within the 10-nm dimer gap and identify spatial regions with nodes and anti-nodes of the field enhancement (Fig. 3). We consider both sphere and disk silver nanoparticles and FDTD simulations for modeling field enhancement in the dimer.

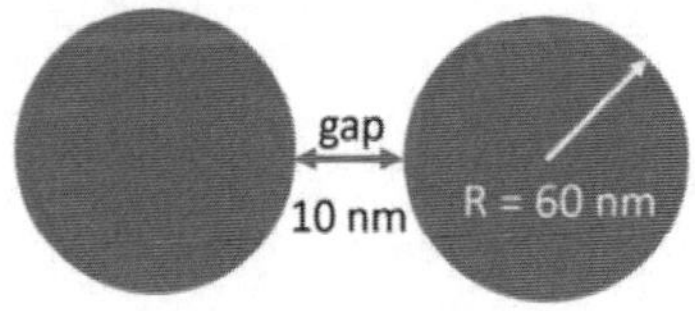

Fig. 2. Schematic of nanosphere dimer.

III. Spasing

We use quantum density matrix (optical Bloch) equations for the spaser, calculate the plasmon amplification in the gap, and show its correspondence to the mode characteristics [4]. Fig. 4 shows preliminary results obtained by finite-element calculations using partial differential equations toolkit in MATLAB. Because of the strong field enhancement in the gap, amplification of plasmons in a nanoparticle dimer is more efficient than ones in the proximity to a single nanoparticle and can be used as an ultra-compact light source in optical devices and medical applications. The effective mode increase (Fig. 4, top) and number of plasmons in the mode (Fig. 4, bottom) agree well.

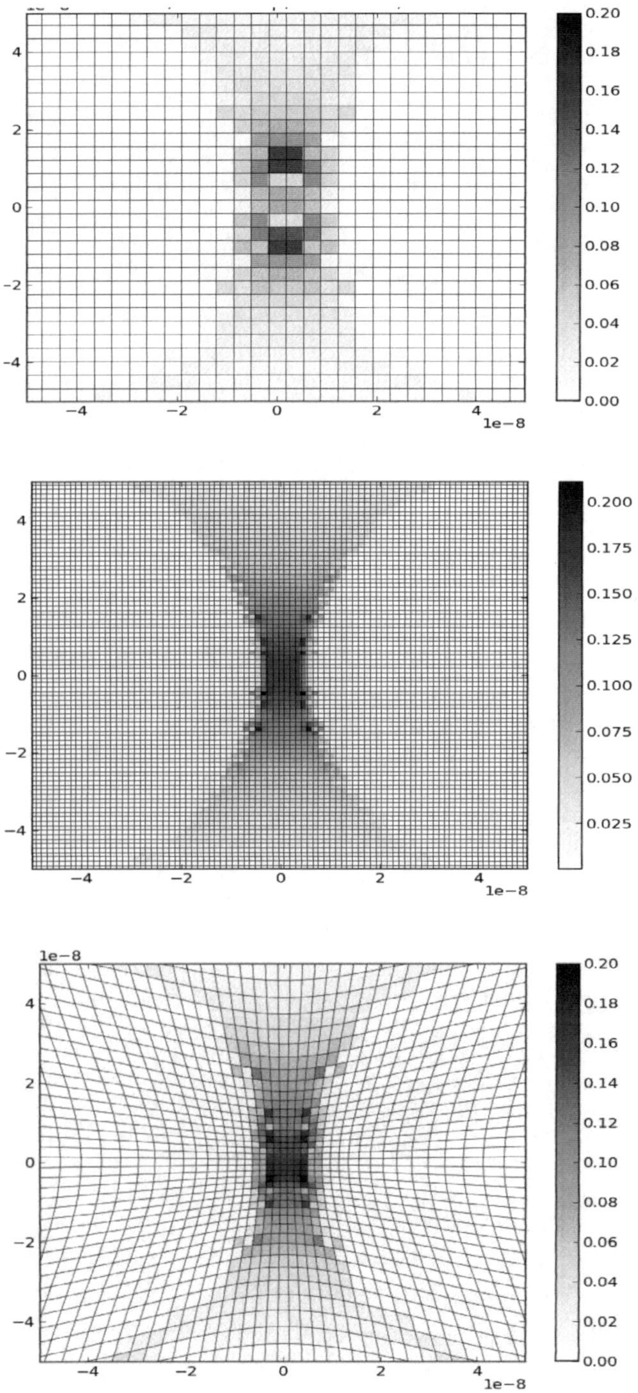

Fig. 3. FDTD modeling of nanosphere dimer. All panels show the Fourier transform of the electric field at the center frequency of the pulse (λ = 500 nm), on the plane symmetrically intersecting the dimer structure, with the propagation direction in the *y*-direction and the dimer axis and polarization direction in the *x*-direction. Top: low, 3.5 nm resolution in the uniform mesh; Middle: high, 1.2 nm resolution in the uniform mesh (takes ~80x longer to run); Bottom: semi-conformal, refined mesh (takes ~4x longer to run). Both runs are compared to the low-resolution simulations.

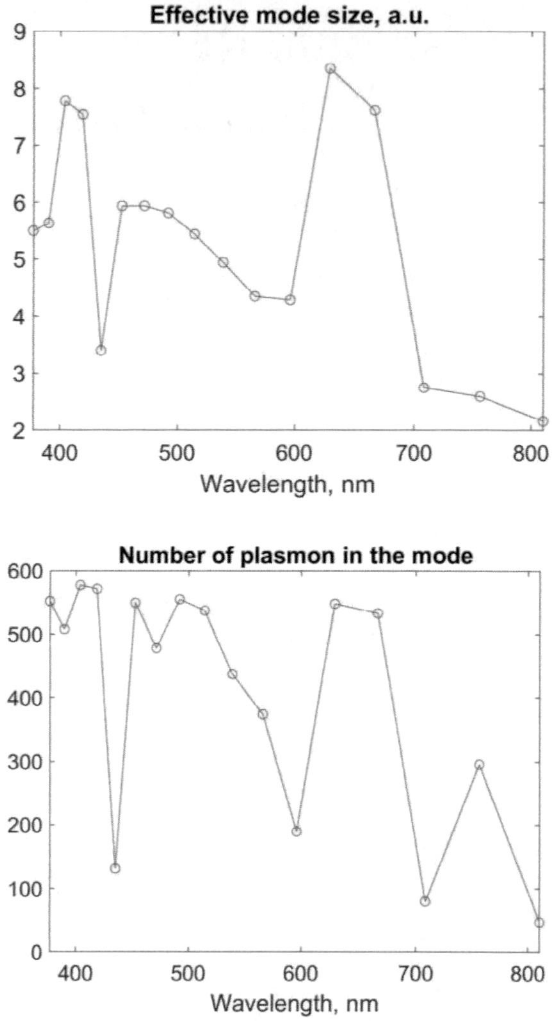

Fig. 4. Calculations of mode size (top) and number of plasmons (bottom) in quasi-static approximation obtained with finite-element modeling. Wavelength is defined based on the dispersion of nanoparticle permittivity.

ACKNOWLEDGMENT

The work is supported by the Air Force Office of Scientific Research under Grant No. FA9550-19-1-0032.

REFERENCES

[1] V. E. Babicheva, S. S. Vergeles, P. E. Vorobev, and S. Burger, “Localized surface plasmon modes in a system of two interacting metallic cylinders,” JOSA B 29, 1263-1269, 2012.

[2] J. Nehls, C. Dineen, J. Liu, C. Poole, M. Bio, and J. V. Moloney, “Stable 3D FDTD method for arbitrary fully electric and magnetic anisotropic Maxwell equations,” International Journal of Numerical Modelling: Electronic Networks, Devices and Fields, 2018. https://doi.org/10.1002/jnm.2521

[3] J. Liu, M. Brio, and J. V. Moloney, “Transformation optics based local mesh refinement for solving Maxwell's equations,” Journal of Computational Physics 258, 359–370, 2014.

[4] M. I. Stockman, "The spaser as a nanoscale quantum generator and ultrafast amplifier," Journal of Optics 12, 024004, 2010.

Point Source Transmitting Power Estimation of Wireless Avionics Intra-Communication Systems Using the Large-Scale FDTD Method

Shunichi Futatsumori
Surveillance and Communications Department, Electronic Navigation Research Institute
National Institute of Maritime, Port and Aviation Technology
Chofu, Japan
futatsumori@mpat.go.jp

Kazuyuki Morioka
Surveillance and Communications Department, Electronic Navigation Research Institute
National Institute of Maritime, Port and Aviation Technology
Chofu, Japan
morioka@mpat.go.jp

Takashi Hikage
Graduate School of Information Science and Technology
Hokkaido University
Sapporo, Japan
hikage@wtemc.ist.hokudai.ac.jp

Tetsuya Sekiguchi
Graduate School of Information Science and Technology
Hokkaido University
Sapporo, Japan
t-sekiguchi@wtemc.ist.hokudai.ac.jp

Manabu Yamamoto
Graduate School of Information Science and Technology
Hokkaido University
Sapporo, Japan
yamamoto@wtemc.ist.hokudai.ac.jp

Toshio Nojima
Graduate School of Information Science and Technology
Hokkaido University
Sapporo, Japan
nojima@wtemc.ist.hokudai.ac.jp

***Abstract*—Wireless avionics intra-communication (WAIC) systems are operated at the same frequency bands as aircraft radio altimeters, i.e., 4,200–4,400 MHz. The coexistence conditions of WAIC systems and radio altimeters are investigated in detail with respect to electromagnetic compatibility. Firstly, the 4-GHz electromagnetic field around a three-dimensional Airbus A320 aircraft model is obtained through large-scale finite-difference time-domain analysis. Then, a transmitting antenna is modeled at the center of the aircraft at window height. Finally, the point source transmitting power at the geometrical center of the aircraft is estimated for the coexistence investigation.**

Keywords—aircraft, large-scale finite-difference time-domain method, point source transmitting power, radio altimeter interference, wireless avionics intra-communication.

I. INTRODUCTION

Wireless avionics intra-communication (WAIC) systems enable wireless communication among aircraft components such as monitoring sensors and controllers. The frequency band assigned for the WAIC systems is 4,200–4,400 MHz at WRC-15 [1]. However, an aircraft radio altimeter is operated at the same frequency band [2]. Therefore, potential electromagnetic compatibility (EMC) issues must be investigated to ensure the safety and security of aircraft operation. The coexistence conditions of WAIC systems and radio altimeters have been discussed in relation to the standardization of WAIC devices. We have developed an electromagnetic field (EMF) estimation method based on large-scale finite-difference time-domain (FDTD) analysis to investigate the EMC issues of WAIC systems [3].

In this paper, the point source transmitting power of a WAIC system is estimated to investigate its coexistence conditions with the radio altimeters of other aircraft. Firstly, FDTD analysis using a three-dimensional aircraft model based on the Airbus A320-200 is discussed. The detailed electric field (E-field) strength around the aircraft is obtained to estimate the point source transmitting power at the geometrical center of the aircraft. Then, the maximum point source equivalent isotopically radiated power (EIRP) is calculated from the obtained E-field strength. The maximum point source EIRP values at different evaluation heights are obtained to confirm the fundamental EMF characteristics.

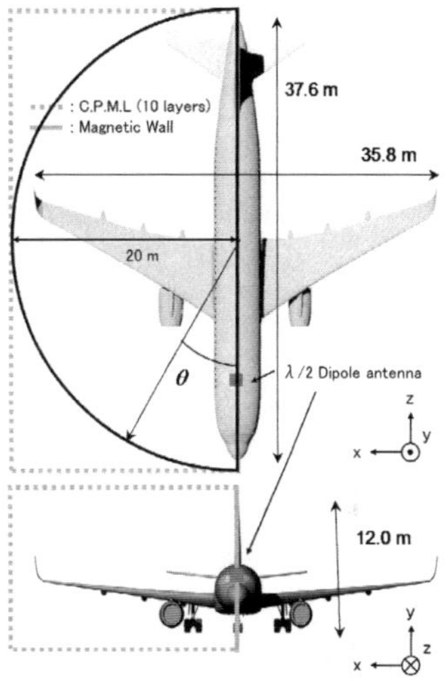

Fig. 1. Three-dimensional aircraft model based on Airbus A320-200, including the evaluation circle.

II. FDTD ANAYSIS MODEL BASED ON A320-200

The point source transmitting power at the geometrical center of the aircraft is estimated through large-scale FDTD analysis. WAIC devices are installed at various locations on the aircraft; however, the point source EIRP power at the geometrical center of the aircraft is required for WAIC/radio altimeter coexistence evaluation. Fig. 1 shows a three-dimensional aircraft model based on the Airbus A320-200 the evaluation circle. The E-field strength obtained for the evaluation circle is converted to the point source transmitting power. The aircraft model include the detailed internal structures as well as the electrical parameters [3]. The evaluation points are shown on the circle, the center of which is the same as the geometrical center of the aircraft. The radius of the circle is 20 m. In addition, perfect magnetic walls are located at the center of the aircraft to reduce the analysis memory. The vertical polarized transmitting dipole antenna

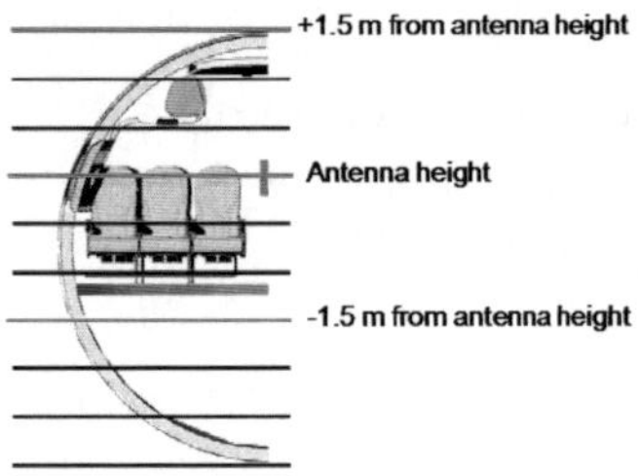

Fig. 2. Evaluation height of the point source power estimation. Three heights, antenna height +1.5 m, antenna height, and antenna height −1.5 m, were evaluated.

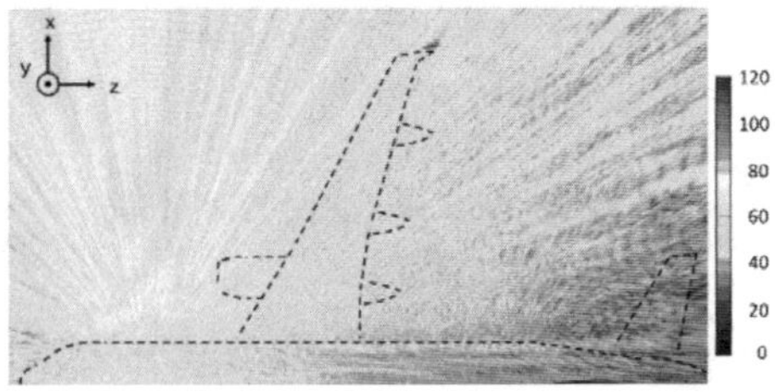

(a) Antenna height +1.5 m (6.6 m from the ground)

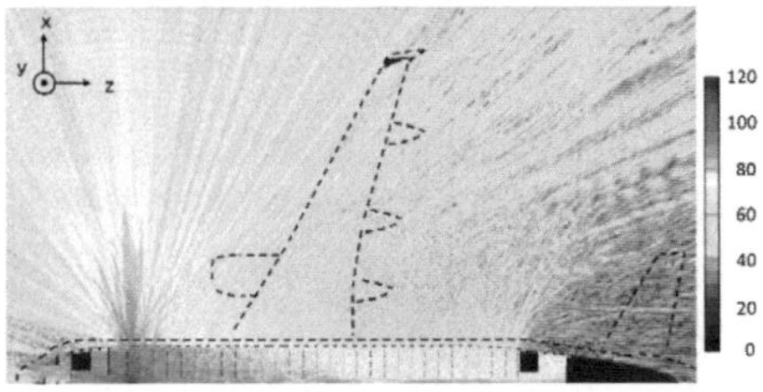

(b) Antenna height (5.1 m from the ground)

(c) Antenna height −1.5 m (3.6 m from the ground)

Fig. 3. Typical analyzed two-dimensional E-field strength distributions at the xz-plane for (a) antenna height +1.5 m, (b) antenna height, and (c) antenna height −1.5 m.

is modeled at the center of the aisle at window height. The transmitting frequency and transmitting power are 4.4 GHz and 0.1 W, respectively. In addition, dry ground of 10-cm thickness (relative dielectric constant: 15, conductivity: 0.001 S/m) is modeled. Fig. 2 shows the evaluation height of the point source power estimation. Three heights, i.e., antenna height +1.5 m (6.6 m from the ground), antenna height (5.5 m from the ground), and antenna height −1.5 m (3.6 m from the ground), are evaluated. Uniform 5-mm cubic cells are employed for the analysis. The number of grid points per wavelength is around 14 in free space. In addition, the numbers of cells are 3,625 × 2,449 × 7,525. The detailed FDTD analysis parameters are given in a previous paper [3]. Fig. 3 shows the typical analyzed two-dimensional E-field strength distributions at each evaluation height. The obtained E-field strength at the evaluation circle is shown in Fig. 4. Angles smaller than 40° have high E-field strengths because of the short distance between the transmitting antenna and

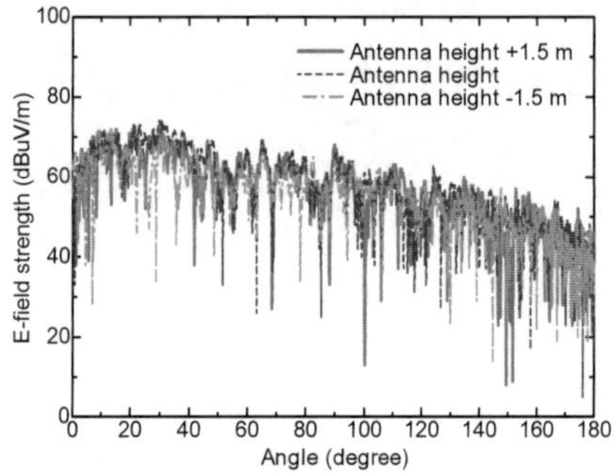

Fig. 4. Analyzed E-field strength at the circle around the aircraft for different evaluation planes.

the analyzed point at the evaluation circle.

III. Point Source Power Estimation

As an example, point source EIRP estimation is performed on the basis of the results of the analysis described pervious section. The point source EIRP P_T is calculated from the following equation:

$$P_T = \frac{P_R}{G_T G_R} \times \frac{(4\pi r)^2}{\lambda^2}, \quad (1)$$

where G_T and G_R are the transmitting and receiving antenna gains, respectively. In addition, P_R is the received power at each point on the measurement circle. The terms r and λ denote the radius of the measurement circle and the wavelength, respectively. Assuming point source radiation, G_T and G_R are both 0 dBi, and r and λ are 20 m and 0.068 m, respectively. From the analysis results shown in Fig. 4, the maximum point source EIRP at the antenna height is −4.7 dBm (angle: 29.8 degrees). The maximum point source EIRP at the antenna heights +1.5 m and −1.5 m are −6.8 dBm (angle: 15.1 degrees) and −6.8 dBm (angle: 8.6 degrees), respectively.

IV. Conclusions

A point source transmitting power estimation method for 4-GHz band WAIC systems, based on large-scale FDTD analysis, is demonstrated. An aircraft model based on the Airbus A320-200, which contains a WAIC system inside the cabin, is used to estimate the EMF characteristics. Then, the point source EIRPs are estimated using the obtained E-field strength around the aircraft. The maximum point source EIRP at the geometrical center of the aircraft is obtained. The present method is useful to investigate the coexistence issues of WAIC systems and radio altimeters.

References

[1] International Telecommunication Union, Resolution 424 of World Radiocommunication Conference 2015, "Use of wireless avionics intra-communications in the frequency band 4200-4400 MHz," Nov. 2015.

[2] International Telecommunication Union, "Operational and technical characteristics and protection criteria of radio altimeters utilizing the band 4 200-4 400 MHz," Report M.2059-0, Feb. 2014.

[3] S. Futatsumori, K. Morioka, A. Kohmura, N. Yonemoto, T. Hikage, T. Sekiguchi, M. Yamamoto, and T. Nojima, "Analysis of radar altimeter interference due to wireless avionics intra-communication systems by using large-scale FDTD method—Investigation on Airbus A320 class passenger aircraft," Proceedings of the 34th International Review of Progress in Applied Computational Electromagnetics, pp. 1-2, Mar. 2018.

FDTD Simulation of Multilayer-Coated and Rough Surface Metals Using Surface Impedance Method

Yong Wang and Scott Langdon
Remcom Inc., 315 S. Allen St., Suite 416, State College, PA 16801, USA
yong.wang@remcom.com, scott.langdon@remcom.com

Abstract — **A surface impedance method with synchronization in time and its application to the FDTD simulation of multilayer-coated metals and rough surface metals are presented. The numerical results showed that the presented method is accurate and efficient.**

I. Introduction

There are two major surface impedance methods in FDTD simulation of conductors [1]. One is the convolution based and the other is the equivalent-circuit based. The convolution-based surface impedance method is more general and can be applied to the multilayer-coated metals and rough surface metals.

In this paper, a surface impedance method with synchronization in time is presented. The method is based on the piecewise linear recursive convolution method [2] and is slightly more accurate than the original surface impedance method without synchronization.

The synchronized surface impedance method is applied to the FDTD simulation of multilayer-coated metals and rough surface metals. The surface impedance of multilayer-coated metals and rough surface metals can be found in [3]-[5]. The surface impedance can be approximated by the national models [6] before the surface impedance method is applied in the FDTD simulation. The numerical experiments showed that the FDTD simulation agrees well with the analytical solution.

II. The Formulations

Using the piecewise linear recursive convolution technique, the update equation for the tangential electric field on a conductor surface can be written as:

$$E_t^{n+1} = k_0 \hat{n} \times H_t^{n+1/2} + \textstyle\sum_{i=1}^{N} \psi_i^{n+1/2}, \quad (1)$$

where $\hat{n}$ is the surface normal, $\psi_i^{n+1/2} = (\chi_i - \xi_i)\hat{n} \times H_t^{n+1/2} + \xi_i \hat{n} \times H_t^{n-1/2} + \rho_i \psi_i^{n-1/2}$, $\chi_i = -\frac{r_i}{p_i}(1 - e^{p_i \Delta t})$, $\xi_i = -\frac{r_i}{p_i^2 \Delta t}[(1 - p_i \Delta t)e^{p_i \Delta t} - 1]$, and $\rho_i = e^{p_i \Delta t}$.

Here r_i and p_i are the residues and poles extracted from the surface impedance, Δt is the timestep and N is the number of the order. Note that the electric and magnetic fields are not collocated in space and also have half a time step offset.

To synchronize the time, the interpolation of time for the magnetic fields is applied to (1). The following update equation can be obtained:

$$H_x^{n+3/2} = \frac{1}{1+\Delta t/\mu \Delta z} \frac{k_0 + \sum_{i=1}^{N}(\chi_i - \xi_i)}{2} \Big\{ H_x^{n+1/2} + \frac{\Delta t}{\mu}\Big(-\frac{E_{z\,j+1}^{n+1} - E_{z\,j}^{n+1}}{\Delta y} + \frac{E_{y\,k+1}^{n+1} - E_{t-}^{n+1}}{\Delta z} \Big) \Big\}, \quad (2)$$

where $E_{t-}^{n+1} = k_0 \hat{n} \times \frac{H_t^{n+\frac{1}{2}}}{2} + \sum_{i=1}^{N} \psi_{i-}^{n+1}$, $\psi_{i-}^{n+1} = \chi_i \hat{n} \times \frac{H_t^{n+\frac{1}{2}}}{2} + \xi_i \hat{n} \times \frac{H_t^{n-\frac{1}{2}}}{2} + \rho_i \psi_i^n$ and $\psi_i^n = (\chi_i - \xi_i)\hat{n} \times \frac{H_t^{n+\frac{1}{2}}}{2} + \psi_{i-}^n$.

The synchronization is applied to every timestep and is stable without any change to the stability condition. The surface impedance method can be applied to multilayer-coated metals and rough surface metals once their surface impedances are available. The surface impedance of multilayer-coated metals can be calculated analytically as follows. It is assumed that there are n layers of coatings. The layer number from the air to the lossy metal is 0 to n+1. The surface impedance can be expressed by [3]:

$$Z = \frac{\omega \mu_0}{k_1} \tanh\Bigg\{ jk_1 d_1 + tanh^{-1}\Bigg[\frac{k_1}{k_2}\tanh\Bigg[jk_2 d_2 + tanh^{-1}\Bigg[\frac{k_2}{k_3}\tanh\Bigg[jk_3 d_3 + \cdots tanh^{-1}\Big[\frac{k_{n-1}}{k_n}\tanh\Big(jk_n d_n + tanh^{-1}\frac{k_n}{k_{n+1}}\Big)\cdots\Big]\Bigg]\Bigg]\Bigg]\Bigg]\Bigg\}, \quad (3)$$

where $k_i = \omega\sqrt{\varepsilon_i \mu_i}$ is the wavenumber of layer i, ω is the angular frequency, ε_i is the permittivity, μ_i is the permeability and d_i is the thickness of layer i. Note that this equation is a little different from that in the original book. The coating can be various kinds of materials, normal or dispersive, dielectric or magnetic.

The rough surfaces can be represented by using the popular Hammerstad and Jensen model and causal Huray model [4], [5]. The surface impedance can be calculated using these models and the rational representations of these surface impedance can be obtained by the vector fitting technique [6].

III. Numerical Results

A number of examples have been tested and a few of them are given here to demonstrate the efficacy of the approach.

A. Smooth Metals

The reflection from a smooth metal surface is first analyzed. The conductivity is 1000 S/m. Six real poles are extracted for the frequency range of 0 – 30 GHz and are used in the presented approach. Fig. 1 shows the validation of the approach against the analytical method and the regular FDTD update with surface conductivity correction (SCC) [7]. It is seen that the results from surface conductivity correction at the particular frequencies agree quite well with those calculated from the analytical solution, but the results calculated from the the presented approach agree well with the analytical solution in a broad frequency band. The approach is very accurate at low frequencies although the error increases slightly at high frequencies. This demonstrated that the surface impedance method is significantly more accurate in broadband than the regular update for a good conductor using a constant conductivity.

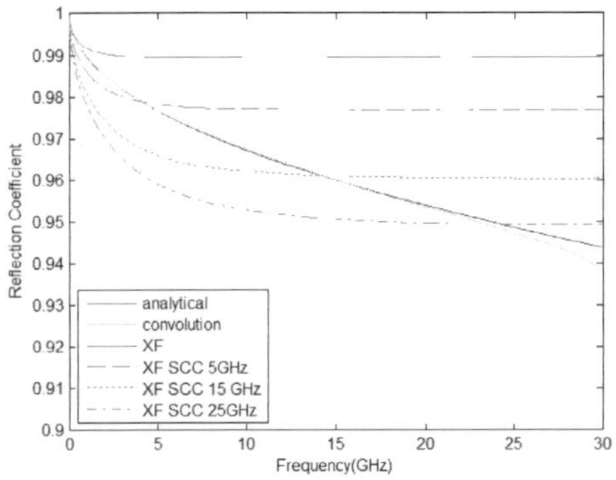

Fig. 1. Validation of convolution-based method against analytical method and regular FDTD update with SCC method where XF means XFdtd®

B. Coated Metals

A metal with one-layer coating is analyzed using the convolution-based methods. The surface impedance of the coated metal is fitted using six poles in the frequency range of 0 – 30 GHz. Fig. 2 shows the reflection coefficients from the coated metal. It is seen that the FDTD simulation results agree well with the analytical solution. The synchronization in time slightly improved the accuracy at high frequencies.

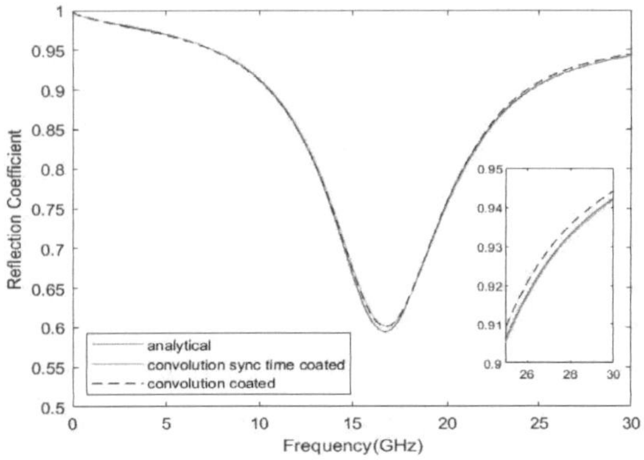

Fig. 2. The reflection coefficients from the coated metal (σ=1000) with one layer of normal material (thickness d=0.25 mm, conductivity σ=0.1, dielectric constant ε_r=200) using the convolution-based methods with and without synchronization in time and analytical method.

C. Rough Surface Metals

Rough surface metals are also analyzed using the convolution-based methods. Fig. 3 shows the reflection coefficients from rough surface copper using the Hammerstad and Jensen model simulated by the convolution-based methods without/with the synchronization in time. The results from the FDTD simulation actually follows the analytical solution reasonably well, noting that the range of the y-axis is between 0.999 and 1. Fig. 4 shows the reflection coefficients from rough surface copper using the causal Huray model. The results of the two rough surface models look similar.

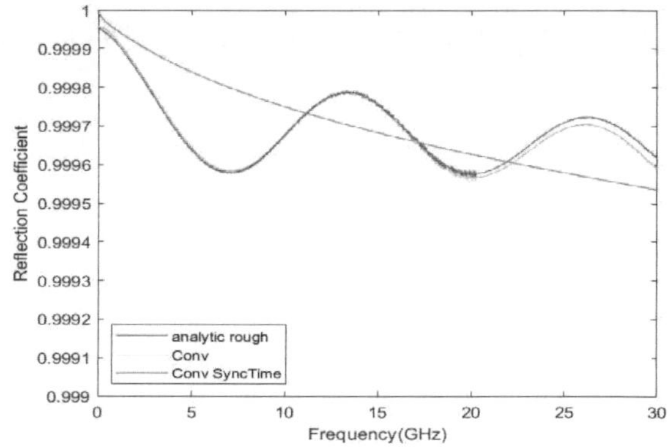

Fig. 3. Reflection coefficients from rough surface copper using Hammerstad and Jensen model (conductivity σ=5.8e7, roughness Δ=1 µm): analytical solution vs. convolution-based methods.

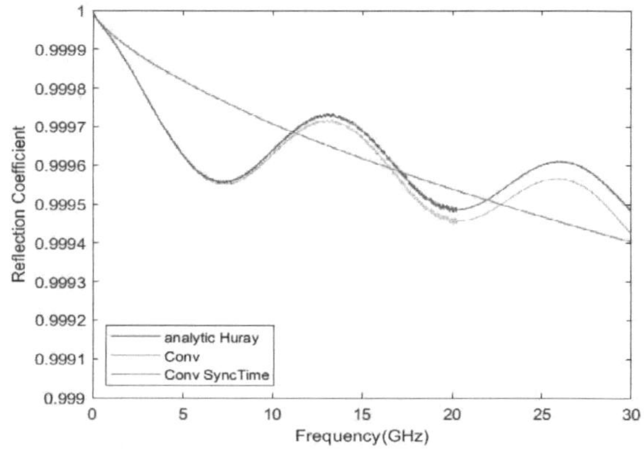

Fig. 4. The reflection coefficients from rough surface copper using causal Huray model (radius a=0.85 µm, area A=65 µm^2 and number of spheres N=11): analytical solution vs. convolution-based methods.

IV. CONCLUSION

The surface impedance method with synchronization in time is demonstrated to be well suited for FDTD simulation of multilayer-coated metals and rough surface metals.

REFERENCES

[1] A. Taflove and S. Hagness, Computational Electrodynamics: The Finite-Difference Time-Domain Method, 3rd ed., Norwood: Artech House, Inc., 2005.

[2] D. Kelley and R. Luebbers, "Piecewise linear recursive convolution for dispersive media using FDTD," IEEE Trans. on Antennas and Propagation, vol. 44, no. 6, pp. 792-797, June 1996.

[3] R. W. P. King, et al., Lateral Electromagnetic Waves: Theory and Applications to Communications, Geophysical Exploration, Remote Sensing, Springer-Verlag New York, 1992.

[4] E. Hammerstad and O. Jensen, "Accurate models of computer aided microstrip design," in IEEE MTT-S Int. Microw. Symp. Dig., pp. 407-409, May 1980.

[5] Eric Bracken, "A causal Huray model for surface roughness," DesignCon, vol.4, pp. 2880-2914, Santa Clara, USA, Jan.-Feb., 2012.

[6] B. Gustavsen and A. Semlyen, "Rational approximation of frequency domain responses by vector fitting, " IEEE Trans. Power Del., vol. 14, no. 3, pp. 1052–1061, July 1999.

[7] K. Chamberlin and L. Gordon, "Modeling of good conductors using the finite difference time domain technique," IEEE Trans. on Electromagnetic Compatibility, vol. 37, no. 2, pp. 210-216, May 1995.

Accelerating the FDTD Algorithm on CPUs with MATLAB's Parallel Computing Toolbox

Alec Weiss
Dept. of Electrical Engineering
Colorado School of Mines
Golden, Colorado
aweiss@mines.edu

Atef Elserbeni
Dept. of Electrical Engineering
Colorado School of Mines
Golden, Colorado
aelsherb@mines.edu

Veysel Demir
Dept. of Electrical Engineering
Northern Illinois University
Dekalb, Illinois
vdemir@niu.edu

Mohammed Hadi
Dept. of Electrical Engineering
Colorado School of Mines
Golden, Colorado
mhadi@mines.edu

***Abstract*— Investigating the improvement of MATLAB based finite difference time domain (FDTD) simulations using central processing units (CPUs) is the goal of this paper. The MATLAB parallel toolbox along with modern multi-core CPUs are used with no external dependencies or libraries and no expensive or complicated hardware acceleration units.**

Keywords*— *FDTD, MATLAB, Parallel Computing.

I. Introduction

The finite difference time domain (FDTD) method provides high bandwidth simulations using time domain techniques to provide accurate, full wave electromagnetic simulations. This method is inherently parallel due to each cell within the simulation grid relying on values all of which have been calculated locally at a previous time. MATLAB is a good testbed for prototyping new FDTD techniques as it provides quick programming and debugging compared to languages like C or FORTRAN. While most previous work focuses on parallelization of FDTD in lower level programming languages using various software and hardware acceleration techniques such as in [1]–[3], only a small number have researched parallelization using simpler languages such as MATLAB in [4], [5]. This paper explores the use of MATLAB's parallel computing toolbox to extend the FDTD computation onto multiple central processing unit (CPU) cores.

II. Parallel CPU Computing in MATLAB

The MATLAB environment has two types of parallelization that can be performed. These two types are built-in parallelization also known as implicit parallelization and parallelism using MATLAB workers also known as explicit parallelization. This is further described in [6], [7].

A. Implicit Parallelization with MATLAB

Implicit parallelization in MATLAB takes place without any extra work from the user. When performing operations such as elementwise multiplication as done in many FDTD codes, MATLAB automatically will parallelize this to use multiple cores on a CPU. This provides speed increases for large and computationally dense problems. Unfortunately, this method gives the user no control over the parallelization of the code.

B. Explicit Parallelization with MATLAB

Contrary to MATLAB's implicit parallelization, explicit parallelization in MATLAB does require extra work from the programmer to instruct the system on how to parallelize the code. This is done by first launching worker threads using the parpool() command. Once a parallel pool has been started in MATLAB, the single program multiple data (SPMD) keyword can be used to directly address each of the workers in the parallel pool. Once this keyword has been used, each of the workers can be individually addressed and communicate with one another using constructs similar to the message passing interface (MPI).

III. Explicit Parallelization of FDTD with MATLAB

The developed multi-processor code is an edited version of the code generated from [8] based on the second order accurate FDTD method. Because of this, the FDTD solver is completely in MATLAB and has many capabilities such as convolutional perfectly matched layer (CPML) boundary conditions, the ability to change material properties, and the capability to add lumped elements, sources, and test ports for full S parameter simulations.

A. Distribution of Domain

For the parallelization of the FDTD algorithm, the FDTD domain was split up amongst cores. To minimize communication time and programming difficulty, the domain is only split along the z-axis. To ensure the smallest amount of data possible is transferred, the simulation space is rotated such that the largest dimension of the domain is along the z-axis. This rotation ensures that the boundaries along which the domain is split where data are communicated across are the smallest possible.

B. Distribution of Sources, Samples, and Lumped Elements

With the domain split across cores, the sources, sampling locations, and lumped elements in the simulation must also be distributed. The lumped elements are simply contained as coefficients in the FDTD as formulated in [8]. This means that they are precalculated before the simulation time marching begins and are distributed with the rest of the domain. Because of this no further work is required to distribute them.

The sources and sampling locations are distributed in similar ways to the lumped elements, again as formulated in [8]. Before the simulation begins, the core that contains the piece of the simulation grid containing each of the sources and samples is found. Its global domain coordinates are then mapped to local coordinates for the core on which it is contained. This mapping allows these sources and samples to be updated in the same way they are in a non-multicore implementation during the time marching loop. Once the end of the loop is reached, one final step must be taken to gather the sampled domain parameters back to the host CPU from which post-processing steps can be performed in the same way as a non-multicore implementation.

C. Transfer of Domain Boundaries

As previously mentioned, the domain is split evenly among cores along the z-axis where field values must be transferred across the boundaries. We used an approach similar to that implemented in [9] where a single xy-plane slice of the H-fields would be transferred up to the core containing the next section of the domain, and a single xy-plane of the E-fields would be transferred down providing full continuity across the boundary. Each of these transfers in MATLAB can be performed using the labSend() and labReceive() commands.

IV. RESULTS

With the multicore code completed, correct operation was ensured by directly comparing results of a microstrip band pass filter problem (pages 171-177 in [8]) from the multicore code to a verified non-multicore code. This problem proved the simulation capability and correct operation of the new multicore code.

Once the new multicore code had been verified, the throughput was timed on various computers with a varying number of cores using MATLAB R2018. This timing was also performed using the non-multicore code and compared. Sample of the results from two computers can be seen in Figs. 1 and 2.

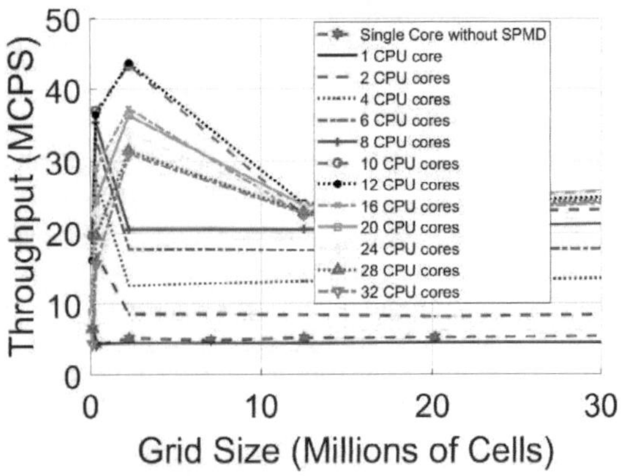

Fig. 2. Throughput vs grid size with various core counts on two Intel Xeon E5-2680 with 20MB of cache. Each processor has 8 physical cores for a total of 16 physical cores and 32 total threads

When comparing the throughput in million cells per second (MCPS) of a single core without using SPMD (i.e., the original non-multicore code), it can be noticed that on every machine the non-multicore code outperformed the multicore code when using a single core. Again, this is due to the implicit parallelization MATLAB performs. Once the multicore code begins utilizing more than a single core, the benefits of explicit parallelization in MATLAB quickly surpass the throughput of implicit parallelization.

It should also be noticed that on each system there exists a region of higher throughputs when the grid size is sufficiently small. The size of the grid that this bump exists at is relative to the size of the CPU system cache. This is shown clearly on the systems with multiple processors. The length of the bump can clearly be seen to extend when moving from utilizing a single processor to multiple processors (e.g., Fig. 1 when moving from 8 cores to greater than 8 cores).

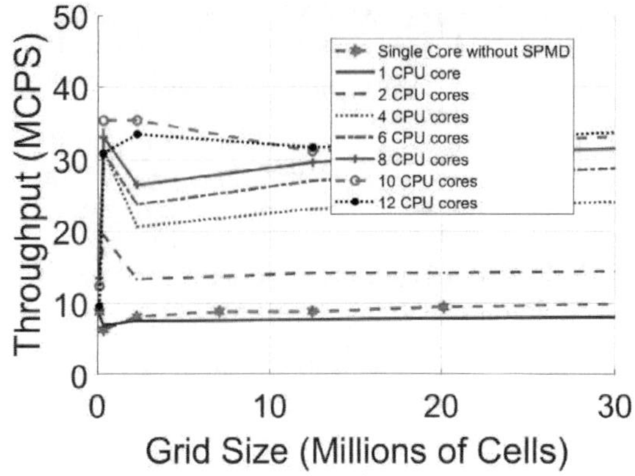

Fig. 1. Throughput vs grid size with various core counts on a Intel Core i7-5820K with 15MB of cache. This system has 6 physical cores on a single CPU with 12 total threads.

The final important trend to be observed is the effect on throughput by extending past a systems physical core count. Once the requested core count extends past the number of physical cores the system begins using hyperthreading. As this requires a lot of resource sharing within a core, in most cases we see little or no speedup by using hyperthreading. The only case where this does not hold true is for the single CPU system used in Fig. 2 where substantial gains can be seen by utilizing both physical cores and hyperthreading.

ACKNOWLEDGMENT

This project is partially supported by Futurewei Technology Inc., New Jersey Research Center, Bridgewater, NJ, USA.

REFERENCES

[1] M. J. Inman, A. Z. Elsherbeni, J. G. Maloney, and B. N. Baker, "GPU based FDTD solver with CPML boundaries," in 2007 IEEE Antennas and Propagation Society International Symposium, pp. 5255–5258, 2007.

[2] K. hayakawa and R. Yamano, "Multi-core FPGA Execution for Electromagnetic Simulation by FDTD," in 2015 2nd International Conference on Information Science and Control Engineering, pp. 829–833, 2015.

[3] X.-M. Guo, Q.-X. Guo, W. Zhao, and W. Yu, "Parallel FDTD Simulation Using NUMA Acceleration Technique," Prog. Electromagn. Res. Lett., vol. 28, pp. 1–8, 2012.

[4] J. E. Diener and A. Z. Elsherbeni, "FDTD Acceleration using MATLAB Parallel Computing Toolbox and GPU," vol. 32, p. 6, 2017.

[5] W. Shao and W. McCollough, "Multiple-GPU-Based Frequency-Dependent Finite-Difference Time Domain Formulation Using MATLAB Parallel Computing Toolbox," Prog. Electromagn. Res. M, vol. 60, pp. 93–100, 2017.

[6] "Parallel MATLAB: Multiple Processors and Multiple Cores." [Online]. Available: https://www.mathworks.com/company/newsletters/articles/parallel-matlab-multiple-processors-and-multiple-cores.html. [Accessed: 10-Jan-2019].

[7] "MATLAB Multicore." [Online]. Available: https://www.mathworks.com/discovery/matlab-multicore.html. [Accessed: 10-Jan-2019].

[8] A. Z. Elsherbeni and V. Demir, The Finite-Difference Time-Domain Method for Electromagnetics with MATLAB® Simulations, 2 edition. Edison, NJ: Scitech Publishing, 2015.

[9] P. F. Baumeister, T. Hater, J. Kraus, D. Pleiter, and P. Wahl, "A Performance Model for GPU-Accelerated FDTD Applications," in 2015 IEEE 22nd International Conference on High Performance Computing (HiPC), pp. 185–193, 2015.

Quantifying Subgridding Errors when Modeling Multiscale Structures with FDTD

Madison Le
Electrical Engineering Department
Colorado School of Mines
Golden, USA
madisonle@mines.edu

Mohammed Hadi
Electrical Engineering Department
Colorado School of Mines
Golden, USA
mhadi@mines.edu

Atef Elsherbeni
Electrical Engineering Department
Colorado School of Mines
Golden, USA
aelsherb@mines.edu

***Abstract*—This paper discusses the growing subgridding errors in Finite-Difference Time-Domain (FDTD) analysis when applied on electrically large subgrids. FDTD simulations in 1D and 2D spaces are used with a 1:3 contrast ratio. Error levels are found to be linearly proportional to the subgrid's electrical dimension along the wave's propagation path. This linear growth suggests numerical phase error mismatch between coarse and fine grids as the subgridding error source.**

Keywords—Finite-difference time-domain method, numerical error analysis, subgridding, multi-scale problems.

I. Introduction

Finite-difference time-domain (FDTD) subgridding methods have become increasingly necessary as the operating frequency of modern electronic devices have risen and thus creating electrically large computational spaces. Using a traditional FDTD [1], the maximum Yee grid cell size is constrained by at least 10 cells per smallest wavelength [2]. Subgridding purportedly allows these electrically large domains to be analyzed accurately without the need for large allocations of memory and resources. The repercussions of subgridding in a FDTD calculation can lead to dispersion and stability errors, as seen in [3-5]. A larger subgrid enhances the maximum area an object of interest can be meshed to receive a more accurate analysis in a local grid. The deleterious effects of larger subgridding ratios have been discussed in the literature [6]. A topic that has not yet been investigated, is the relative error that arises with increased electrical sizes of subgridded regions, independent of the contrast ratio. This paper will discuss the effect the size of a subgridded region has on the resulting errors at a 1:3 contrast ratio within 1D and 2D FDTD simulations.

II. 1D and 2D FDTD Setups

The 1D FDTD setup (Fig. 1) involves a Gaussian pulse propagating through a leap-frogged 1D H_y and E_z grid of 500 cells. The discrete spatial step in the global coarse grid, $\Delta x = 4$ mm, is chosen such that the Gaussian pulse spans approximately 20 FDTD cells per wavelength. Within the global grid there is a localized region where a few coarse cells are replaced by a finer grid with one third the coarse grid's spatial step (Contrast Ratio = 1:3).

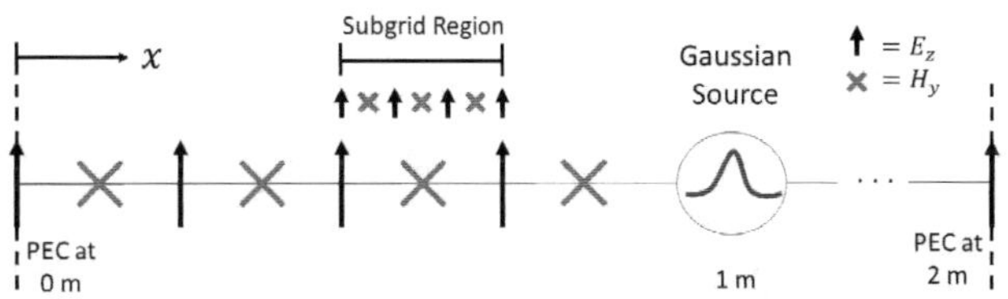

Fig. 1. The problem space of the 1D configuration. The coarse field components are indicated with the larger arrows and crosses while the fine grid components of the subgrid have smaller symbols.

The 2D problem space is depicted in Fig. 2 with 210 by 160 cells in the x and y directions, respectively. There is also a Gaussian pulse and a subgridded section replacing 60 by 10 coarse cells within the domain. In both setups, the time step is fixed for both coarse and fine update equations and of course is based on the smaller cell size to maintain stability throughout. Table I lists the discrete FDTD discrete steps used for both setups.

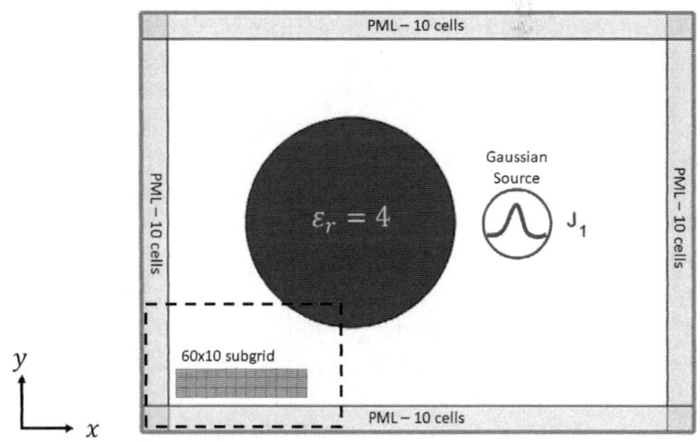

Fig. 2. Scattering example from [1, Section 7.5.2]: Line source parallel to a dielectric cylinder simulated with a 2D FDTD code. Dotted lines represent the lower left corner.

The 1D FDTD simulation is run long enough for the Gaussian pulse to fully traverse the subgrid region once and is ended before the pulse reaches the PEC boundary. The 2D FDTD simulation is run long enough for both the direct wave and the dielectric scattered wave fully interact with the subgrid region. Each FDTD code is run twice; once with the subgrid region included (subgrid run) and again with no subgridding (reference run). The normalized percentage error due to subgridding is quantified in (1):

$$Normalized\ Error = \frac{|E_{zSubgrid} - E_{zReference}|}{|E_{zReference}|_{Max}} \cdot 100\% \ . \quad (1)$$

The 1D code is tested for three subgrid sizes; the equivalent of 5, 10 and 100 coarse cells. The 2D code is tested for single size (60×10 coarse cells) subgrid.

TABLE I. SUBGRID PARAMETERS

	Δx	Δy	Δt	Number of Time Steps
1D	$4\,mm$	-	$4.4\,ps$	600
2D	$5\,mm$	$5\,mm$	$3.5\,ps$	3000

III. RESULTS & ANALYSIS

Figure 3 (a) demonstrates the normalized percentage error incurred when the Gaussian pulse traverses each of the three 1D subgrid configurations. As shown, the maximum error increases linearly with the subgrid size; 1.2%, 2.5% and 26% for subgrids replacing 5, 10 and 100 coarse cells, respectively. Equivalent electrical subgrid sizes are roughly a quarter wavelength, a half wavelength and 5 wavelengths, respectively, since the Gaussian pulse covers a total of 20 cells per wavelength. A 26% normalized error, as seen for 100 coarse cells, would be unacceptable for many applications. For example, antennas are designed for an electrical length of a half wavelength, however, and antenna array may consist of greater than 5 wavelengths. This large electrical size would produce significant errors.

Figure 3 (b) is a contour plot of the lower left corner of Fig. 2 after a Gaussian pulse is allowed to interact with both the cylindrical scatterer and the subgrid area there. Again, there is a normalized error which intensifies the longer (through space) the pulse interacts with the subgrid region. Maximum error value there is 2.6% which is also expected to increase linearly with increasing subgrid dimension along the pulse propagation path.

IV. CONCLUSION

1D and 2D FDTD simulations indicate a direct correlation between the subgrid electrical size and the cumulative errors caused due to the propagated waves. Linear increase of such errors suggests that the root cause is the disparate numerical phase velocities of waves propagating in the neighborhoods of subgridding interfaces. This in turn causes numerical impedance mismatches and subsequent reflections. Therefore, subgridding errors can be reduced by matching numerical phase velocities in fine and coarse grids. Further investigations will cover this phenomenon in hybrid FDTD schemes, utilizing higher-order calculations to reduce the coarse grid errors.

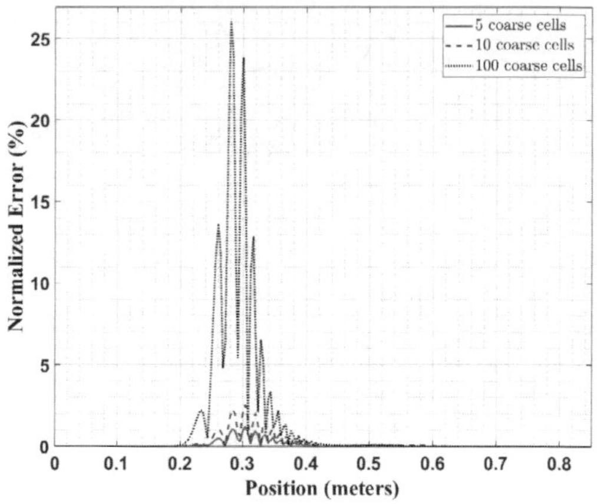

(a) 1D subgridding

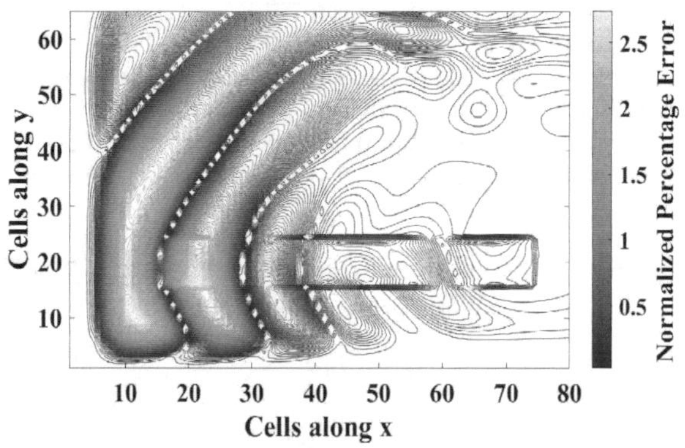

(b) 2D subgridding

Fig. 3. The normalized errors calculated using (1). (a) Normalized percentage error in 1D subgridding. (b) Normalized percentage error in 2D subgridding.

ACKNOWLEDGMENTS

This project is supported by Futurewei Technology Inc., New Jersey Research Center, Bridgewater, NJ, USA.

REFERENCES

[1] A. Z. Elsherbeni and V. Demir, The Finite-Difference Time-Domain Method for Electromagnetics with MATLAB® Simulations, 2nd edition, Edison, New Jersey: SciTech Publishing, 2015.

[2] M. W. Chevalier, R. J. Luebbers, and V. P. Cable, "FDTD local grid with material traverse," IEEE Trans. Antennas Propagat., vol. 45, no. 3, Mar. 1997.

[3] S. Wang, "Numerical examinations of the stability of FDTD subgridding schemes," ACES Journal, vol. 22, no. 2, Jul. 2007.

[4] F. L. Teixeira, "A summary review on 25 years of progress and future challenges in FDTD and FETD techniques," ACES Journal, vol. 25, no. 1, Jan. 2010.

[5] M. F. Hadi and R. K. Dib, "Eliminating interface reflections in hybrid low-dispersion FDTD algorithms," ACES Journal, vol. 22, no. 3, Nov. 2007.

[6] J. Nehrbass and R. Lee, "Optimal finite-difference sub-gridding techniques applied to the Helmholtz equation," IEEE Transactions on Microwave Theory and Techniques, vol. 48, no. 6, pp. 976–984, Jun. 2000.

In Vitro Dielectric Properties of Rat Skin Tissue for Microwave Skin Cancer Detection

Cemanur Aydinalp, Sulayman Joof, Tuba Yilmaz
Department of Electronics and Communication Engineering
Istanbul Technical University
Istanbul, Turkey
{aydinalp16,joof,yilmazabdolsahe } @itu.edu.tr

Nural Pastacı Özsobacı
Department of Biophysics, Cerrahpasa Medical Faculty, Istanbul University - Cerrahpasa
Istanbul, Turkey
nuralp@istanbul.edu.tr

Fatma Ateş Alkan
Department of Biophysics, Medical School, Beykent University,
Istanbul, Turkey
fatmaalkan@beykent.edu.tr

Ibrahim Akduman
Department of Electronics and Communication Engineering
Istanbul Technical University
Istanbul, Turkey
akduman@itu.edu.tr

***Abstract*—Dermal tissue characterization based on dielectric properties can be utilized as a non-invasive method for diagnosis of skin cancers. To enable such technology, there is a need to develop techniques that can rapidly and accurately collect the dielectric properties of the skin tissues. Therefore, the current measurement techniques and tools has to be optimized for skin cancer detection. To this end, this study presents dielectric property measurements with open-ended coaxial probes having small apertures customized for detection of skin cancer. Relative permittivity and conductivity of rat skin tissue is characterized with open-ended coaxial probes with outer diameters of 0.9mm and 0.5mm between 0.5GHz-6GHz and the measurement results are compared with the traditional probes having diameter of 2.2mm. The results agree well with the reported literature data.**

Keywords—Dielectric properties, in vitro measurement, open-ended coaxial probe, rat skin tissue, skin cancer.

I. Introduction

Skin cancer, comprising 40% of cancer cases globally, is one of the most common form of cancers in the world [1]. Basal cell carcinoma (BCC), squamous cell carcinoma (SCC), melanoma are main types of skin cancer. BCC and SCC are also called as non-melanoma skin cancer (NMSC) [2]. The number of diagnosed melanoma cases annually has increased by 53% since 2008 [3]. The diagnosis methods for melanoma are dermoscopy, digital dermoscopy, and pathological analysis of skin biopsy [2]. Dermoscope has several drawbacks such as low accuracy and risk of false positive detections that can stem from alteration of melanoma over time and human observation error. Digital dermoscope provides the map of moles in body by photographing and recording dermoscopic images in order to detect the point localization. Thus, it becomes possible to follow-up of high-risk skin cancer patients [2]. Even though pathological analysis of skin biopsy provides highly accurate results, it is not suitable for patients with multiple moles since biopsy process results in undesirable scars.

Recently, it was concluded that the tumors lead to changes in the physiological composition of tissues via changes in water, sodium and protein content of the tissue and such changes can be detected with electromagnetic technology operating at microwave region [3]. One such technology is reported in [4], where the dielectric property discrepancy at microwave frequencies between hepatic malignancies and healthy liver tissues has been identified with open-ended coaxial probes. Open-ended coaxial probes can also be employed to identify the skin cancer. However, there is a need to characterize the dielectric properties of different moles and customize the technique for skin cancer diagnosis. The possibility of using microwave diagnostic technologies for melanoma detection attracted the interest of researchers and dielectric property measurements have been reported in the literature. In [5], dielectric properties of freshly excised normal and malignant human skin is measured via slim-form open-ended coaxial probe in the range of 0.5-50GHz. In another recent study [6], a formula has been derived to calculate the dielectric properties of skin cancer tissues and healthy tissues based on a function of water content in the frequency range of 1GHz to 50GHz. In order to estimate the dielectric properties of malignant and healthy skin tissues, [7] has utilized the effective medium theory in the range of 20-100GHz. Moreover, [7] introduced mm-wave reflectometry as a potential non-invasive tool for skin cancer diagnosis. The dielectric properties of porcine skin tissue have been measured in the frequency range of 300MHz-3GHz because of the possibility that porcine skin tissue may be used as a substitute for human skin in medical research [8]. Knowledge of dielectric characteristics of skin tissue is fundamental to develop new diagnostic methods.

In this paper, the dielectric properties of rat skin tissues have been measured between 500MHz–6GHz frequency range with slim-form open-ended coaxial probes having three different aperture diameters in an attempt to customize the open-ended coaxial probes for skin cancer characterization. The rest of the paper is organized as follows, measurement methods and sample details are given in Section II, dielectric property measurement results are given in Section III, and conclusion is drawn in Section IV.

II. Materials And Methods

Measurement samples included skin sample from 3 months old, 180g Sprague-Dawley rat was obtained from Center for Life Sciences and Technologies Department, Bogazici University (BU), Istanbul, Turkey. The experimental protocol was in accordance with the regulations on animal experiments approved by the Animal Experiments Local Ethics Committee of Bogazici University.

The measurement set-up included Agilent N9923A FieldFox Handheld RF Vector Network Analyzer 6GHz, Agilent 85070E software, slim form open-ended coaxial probes with outer diameters 2.2mm, 0.9mm, and 0.5mm all manufactured by Mitos Medical Technologies.

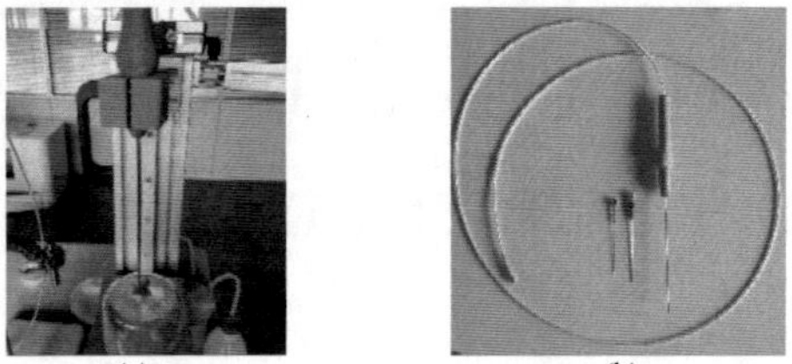

(a) (b)

Fig. 1. Measurement set-up: (a) probe with the in vitro rat skin sample, and (b) three probes with 0.5mm, 0.9mm and 2.2mm diameters from left to right.

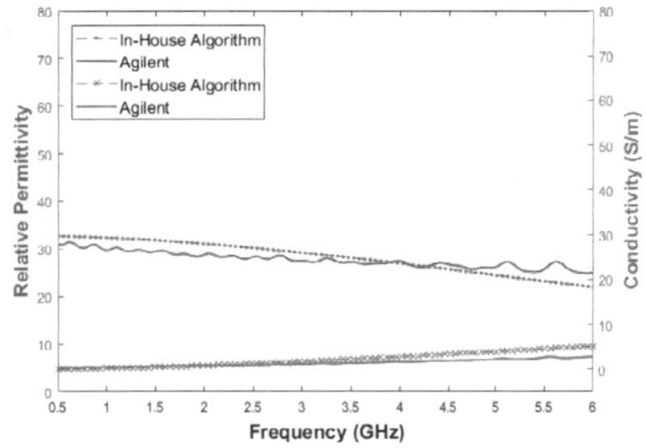

(a)

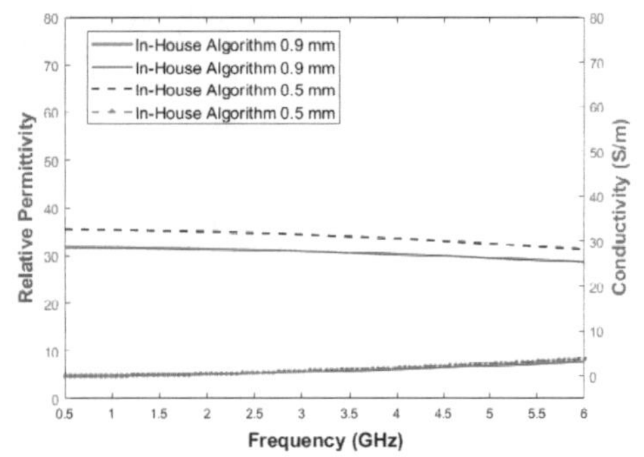

(b)

Fig. 2. Dielectric property measurements: (a) comparison of Agilent's and in-house algorithm's relative permittivity and conductivity of rat skin tissue samples using 2.2mm probe, and (b) the relative permittivity and conductivity of rat skin tissue samples using 0.9mm and 0.5mm probes with in-house algorithm.

Also, a laptop computer to run the commercial software for dielectric property verification.The measurement set up and the probes are shown in Fig. 1 (a) and Fig. 1 (b), respectively. The dielectric material sandwiched between the inner and outer conductor of the probes is Teflon (ε_r=2.1).

III. Results

The calibration process has been performed with measurement sequence of air, a conductive textile and distilled water. The relative dielectric constant (ε_r) and conductivity (σ) measurements were performed in the range of 0.5GHz–6GHz with 55MHz intervals. The measurements were taken within 1 hour following the excision. To obtain reliable results for each position, five measurements were performed and their medians were used for computation of the relative dielectric constant (ε_r) and the conductivity (σ) of the sample. In order to calculate the relative permittivity and conductivity with the in-house algorithm, S-parameter response of the probes is also collected. The results from in-house software have been validated with Agilent 85070E software by using slim form probe with diameter 2.2mm.

The relative permittivity and conductivity measurements are shown in Fig. 2. The relative permittivity and conductivity computed by in-house software and verified with Agilent 85070E software via 2.2mm aperture probe are shown in Fig. 2 (a). The relative permittivity and conductivity calculated through in-house software from the data collected by the probes with diameters 0.9mm and 0.5mm are shown in Fig. 2 (b). In this study, the relative permittivity conductivity values agree well with the data reported in the literature [9].

IV. Conclusion

Classification of anomalies based on dielectric properties emerges as a new diagnostic and therapeutic method. In this study, dielectric properties of rat skin tissues have been measured via open-ended coaxial probes with outer diameters 2.2mm, 0.9mm and 0.5mm in the frequency range 0.5GHz and 6GHz. Obtained results are in agreement with the literature.

Acknowledgment

This project has received funding from the European Union's Horizon 2020 research and innovation program under the Marie Sklodowska-Curie grant agreement No. 750346 and COST Action CA17115.

References

[1] B. Ö. Cakir, P. Adamson, and C. Cingi. "Epidemiology and economic burden of nonmelanoma skin cancer," Facial Plastic Surgery Clinics of North America, 20, pp. 419-22, 2012.

[2] L. Thomas and S. Puig, "Dermoscopy, Digital Dermoscopy and Other Diagnostic Tools in the Early Detection of Melanoma and Follow-up of High-risk Skin Cancer Patients," vol. 97, 2018.

[3] M. Gniadecka, O. F. Nielsen, and H. C. Wulf, "Water content and structure in malignant and benign skin tumours," Journal of Molecular Structure, vol. 661-662, pp. 405-410, 2003.

[4] T. Yilmaz, et al., "Machine learning aided diagnosis of hepatic malignancies through in vivo dielectric measurements with microwaves," Physics in Medicine & Biology, 61.13 (2016): 5089.

[5] A. Mirbeik-Sabzevari, R. Ashinoff, and N. Tavassolian, "Ultra-wideband millimeter-wave dielectric characteristics of freshly excised normal and malignant human skin tissues," in IEEE Transactions on Biomedical Engineering, vol. 65, no. 6, pp. 1320-1329, June 2018.

[6] B. J. Mohammed, S. A. R. Naqvi, M. Manoufali, K. Bialkowski, and A. M. Abbosh, "Changes in epidermal dielectric properties due to skin cancer across the band 1 to 50 GHz," 2018 Australian Microwave Symposium (AMS), Brisbane, QLD, 2018, pp. 77-78.

[7] R. Aminzadeh, M. Saviz, and A. A. Shishegar, "Dielectric properties estimation of normal and malignant skin tissues at millimeter-wave frequencies using effective medium theory," 2014 22nd Iranian Conference on Electrical Engineering (ICEE), Tehran, 2014, pp. 1657-1661.

[8] T. Karacolak, R. Cooper, E. S. Unlu, and E. Topsakal, "Dielectric properties of porcine skin tissue and in vivo testing of implantable antennas using pigs as model animals," IEEE Antennas and Wireless Propagation Lett., vol. 11, pp. 1686-1689, Jan. 2013.

[9] A. Peyman, A. A. Rezazadeh, and C. Gabriel, "Changes in the dielectric properties of rat tissue as a function of age at microwave frequencies," Phys. Med. Biol., vol. 46, no. 6, pp. 1617-1629, June 2001.

Monitoring of Food Contamination via Microwave Imaging

J. Tobon Vasquez
Dept. of Electronics and Telecomunications
Politecnico di Torino
Torino, Italy
jorge.tobon@polito.it

J. Rivero
Dept. of Electronics and Telecomunications
Politecnico di Torino
Torino, Italy
javier.rivero@polito.it

R. Scapaticci
CNR-IREA
Consiglio Nazionale delle Ricerche
Napoli, Italy
scapaticci.r@irea.cnr.it

L. Farina
Translational Medical Device Lab
National University of Ireland Galway
Galway, Ireland
laura.farina@nuigalway.ie

L. Crocco
CNR-IREA
Consiglio Nazionale delle Ricerche
Napoli, Italy
crocco.l@irea.cnr.it

F. Vipiana
Dept. of Electronics and Telecomunications
Politecnico di Torino
Torino, Italy
francesca.vipiana@polito.it

***Abstract*—Detecting food contamination in products moving along the production chain is a priority for every established food producer. Although detection technologies have been widely used in last years, low-density foreign bodies such as plastic, thin glass or wood are still undetectable to all established detection systems. Hence, the use of microwave imaging system to be used along the production chain is proposed in this work. This scenario implies a reduced time for data gathering and hence a limited amount of available data. To face this issue, an imaging system taking advantage of the targets movement and of the expected small size of the sought contamination is developed. The rationale of the approach is described and assessed in a simple, yet meaningful case.**

***Index Terms*—food inspection, food security, food safety, microwave imaging, non-invasive diagnostics.**

I. INTRODUCTION

Food industry is particularly aware to foreign body contamination in the packaging of processed food. This kind of contamination is among the main causes of costumers complaint against manufacturers, resulting in loss of brand loyalty and large recall expenses for food industries [1].

There are very capable metal detectors (MD), X-ray (XRI) or near infrared (NIR) imaging sensors available today. However these systems do not offer a complete solution and the occurrence of accidents remains significant. In fact, these technologies suffer several limitations. For instance, MD can only detect metallic objects, whereas XRI cannot easily recognize low-density foreign objects such as most plastics, thin glass and wood (the most common type of contaminants) and can be harmful for operators. Finally, NIR techniques are rapid and safe but limited by the short penetrating length and the strong absorption in water. For these reasons, novel technologies must be developed to address all the requirements of food-industry.

This work was supported by Compagnia di San Paolo, under the research project MIT-Food, Microwave Imaging Technology for Food Contamination Monitoring

To overcome this limitations, microwave imaging devices represent an attractive, cost-effective candidate [2]. Actually, water content in food affect its EM properties at microwaves, which suggests to use EM devices to detect foreign contaminants. In this paper, the use of microwave imaging for food safety inspection is investigated considering a challenging case study. In particular, the validation concerns the assessment of a plastic or glass jar system designed for emulsions and pumpable products such as baby food, yogurt with fruit berries, chocolate-based spreads, honey, moving along the packaging line. The system is particularly suited to detect foreign bodies such as plastic or glass fragments few millimeters in size that, up until now, have gone undetected and straight to the consumer.

II. FOOD MONITORING SYSTEM

A. Rationale of the Monitoring System

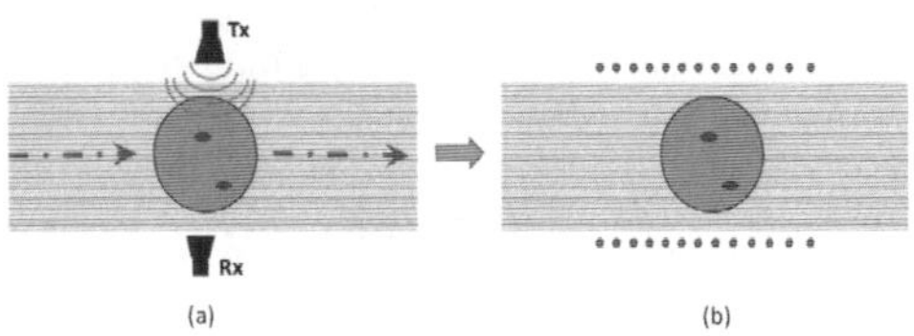

Fig. 1. Conceptual scheme of the microwave device for food monitoring. (a) The target moving along the production chain probed by the two-antennas system; (b) the scenario modeled in the imaging problem.

Considering the paradigm work previously mention, the main pitfall is the speed of the object under test over the production line that constrains on the speed of acquisition (and therefore amount of available data) and elaboration. As such, developing an MWI device capable to assess products without interrupting or delaying the production process requires suitable strategies to cope with these aspects.

To this end, we have explored the feasibility of a synthetic aperture approach, by considering only a pair of antennas placed at the sides of the chain, see Fig.1(a). The relative movement of the object under test with respect to the measurement device is exploited to introduce the diversity in observation needed to implement a tomographic imaging algorithm, see Fig.1(b). It is important to observe that, in this arrangement, no cross-position information is available.

In addition, to enable real-time monitoring, a model-based differential imaging approach based on the distorted Born approximation [3] has been developed. In particular, the tomographic images are obtained by processing the data obtained from the difference of the signals measured for the object under test and those measured for a standard i.e., uncontaminated - object. Such an approach is reasonable in this kind of applications, wherein objects are indeed expected to be identical. Moreover, given the small size of the sought contaminations, it is also reasonable to assume a linearized model of the electromagnetic scattering, as the one underlying the adopted approximation.

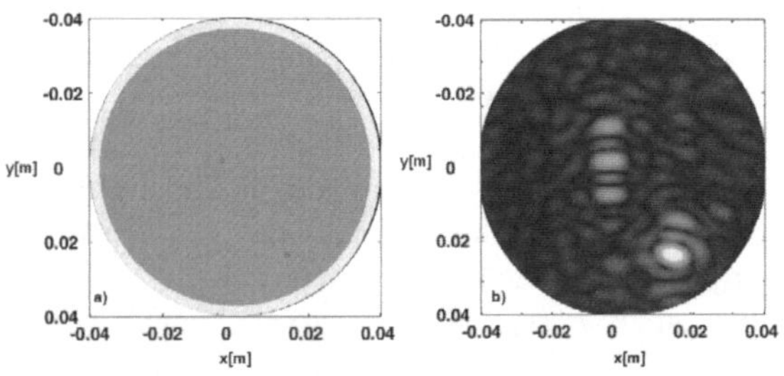

Fig. 2. Numerical imaging example. (a) Reference profile; (b) Normalized TSVD reconstruction.

B. *Implementation and Numerical Assessment*

Considering this scenario, we assume we are able to collect data from one test jar. Likewise, we have gathered data *a priori* for a reference jar which certainly is not contaminated. Taking into account the distorted Born approximation (DBA) with a fix working frequency f, the differential data from the current jar with respect to the reference one is given by

$$\begin{aligned} \Delta S(\mathbf{r}_p, \mathbf{r}_q) &= \frac{-j\omega\varepsilon_b}{4} \int_D \mathbf{E}_b(\mathbf{r}_p, \mathbf{r}) \cdot \mathbf{E}_b(\mathbf{r}, \mathbf{r}_q) \Delta\chi(\mathbf{r}) d\mathbf{r} \\ &= L(\Delta\chi), \qquad (1) \end{aligned}$$

where D is the domain of interest, p and q are the transmitter and the receiver probes indexes and $\Delta\chi$ is the variation of the contrast with respect to the reference scenario due to the food contamination. $\mathbf{E}_b$ is the total field radiated by the pth antenna in absence of $\Delta\chi$ (and in presence of the uncontaminated jar). L is the linear scattering operator, which relates the differential data ΔS to the unknown $\Delta\chi$ of the problem.

The tomographic image is formed by using the truncated singular value decomposition (TSVD) scheme [**?**]:

$$\Delta\chi = \sum_{n=1}^{T} \frac{1}{\sigma_n} \langle \Delta S, u_n \rangle v_n, \qquad (2)$$

where $[u_n, \sigma_n, v_n]$ is the singular value decomposition of L in eq. (1), while T is the truncation index representing the regularization parameter of the linear and ill-posed inverse problem in (1) and it is chosen as a trade-off between accuracy and stability of the reconstruction.

The considered test-bed is the monitoring of a 3 mm thick glass jar filled with hazelnut-cocoa cream. The validation has been carried out with respect to 2D geometry, modelling the jar as an infinite cylinder and the antennas as line currents aligned with the cylinder axis.

First, as a result of a broad numerical analysis, the setting of the frequency range was chosen around 10 GHz, which represents the best trade-off between penetration depth and achievable spatial resolution. Hence, nine evenly spaced frequencies with a step of 250 MHz in the range [9 - 11] GHz have been selected and used in the numerical validation.

As far as the number of data points is concerned, assuming that the spacing between the jars moving along the chain is the same as their size (8.5 cm in diameter), a measurement line 12 cm long, centered with respect to the jar, has been considered. This choice minimizes the sensing of the previous or next jar with respect to the one under test. Given the typical size of the belt, the measurement line is positioned at 3 cm from the side of the jar and 13 sampling positions have been considered.

At the working frequency range, the electric properties of glass and cocoa cream are $\varepsilon_{glass} = 4.7$, $\sigma_{glass} = 0$ S/m and $\varepsilon_{cream} = 3$, $\sigma_{cream} = 0.25$ S/m, respectively. The contaminant has been modeled as two plastic inclusions of 2 mm in size, whose electric properties in the frequency range of interest are $\varepsilon_{plastic} = 2.3$, $\sigma_{plastic} = 0$ S/m. The testbed scenario is depicted in Fig. 2a. Synthetic data have been corrupted with a Gaussian noise with SNR = 60 dB on the total field.

In Fig.2(b), the reconstruction obtained via TSVD is shown. As can be seen, some replicas in the direction orthogonal to the measurement line are present. This is due to the lack of measurements on the left and right sides of the jar and is consistent with the spatial spectral content of the operator L (not reported for the sake of brevity).

III. Conclusion

We have presented a feasibility study on the use of microwave technology for food contamination monitoring, possibly exploitable on the production chain. The results from the presented analysis are promising, motivating further investigation concerned with an experimental proof-of-concept.

References

[1] B. S. Editor, Plant Operations, "Innovations Keep Food Processing Conveyors Flexible," [Online]. Available: https://www.foodprocessing.com/articles/2011/conveyor-innovation/.

[2] K. Wang, D.-W. Sun, and H. Pu, "Emerging non-destructive terahertz spectroscopic imaging technique: Principle and applications in the agrifood industry," Trends in Food Science & Technology, vol. 67, pp. 93105, Sep. 2017.

[3] M. Pastorino, Microwave Imaging. Wiley, 2010.

[4] M. Bertero and P. Boccacci, Introduction to inverse problems in imaging. Bristol, U.K.: Institute of Physics Pub, 1998.

Low-Profile Textile Antenna with Omni-Directional Radiation for Wearable Applications

Chunxu Mao, Pingjuan L. Werner and Douglas H. Werner
Department of Electrical Engineering
The Pennsylvania State University, University Park, PA, 16802 USA
cxm2088@psu.edu, dhw@psu.edu

***Abstract*— A novel planar textile antenna with an omni-directional radiation pattern is presented for wearable applications. The omnidirectional radiation is achieved by exciting four rotated open-ended slots with uniform amplitude and phase. The operating principles are explained with the help of equivalent circuit models and current distribution. The antenna is verified experimentally, showing good performance in terms of impedance bandwidth, omni-directional pattern, radiation efficiency and robustness to deformation and phantom loading.**

***Keywords*— Antenna, omni-directional, textile antenna, wearable applications.**

I. Introduction

Antennas with a low profile and omni-directional radiation patterns are very attractive for a wide range of applications, such as wireless terminals [1], wearable devices [2], and Internet-of-Things (IoT) [3]. For wearable applications, omni-directional radiation from an antenna can support the exchange of information with sensors located at a variety of positions on the body. Another important issue to be concerned with in the design of the antenna is its thickness, which should be minimized in order to achieve compactness. Traditional dipole and monopole antennas suffer from a high profile, and thus are not suitable for the wearable applications. A number of omni-directional antennas have been proposed for wearable applications in the past decades [4]-[9]. However, these antennas are all 3-D structures with high profiles in order to realize the desired omni-directional radiation pattern, which makes them unsuitable for integration into garments.

In this paper, a novel single-layer, low-profile antenna with an omni-directional radiation pattern is proposed for the 2.45 GHz wireless body area network (WBAN) band. The antenna design is developed from a group of rotated microstrip fed slot antennas, which have uniform power amplitude and phase. This results in a circular current distribution allowing omni-directional radiation to be achieved. The operating mechanism of the antenna is discussed with the help of an equivalent circuit and current distribution analysis. The experimental results verify the proposed antenna has a very good performance.

This work was supported by the National Science Foundation ASSIST Nanosystems ERC under Award EEC-1160483.

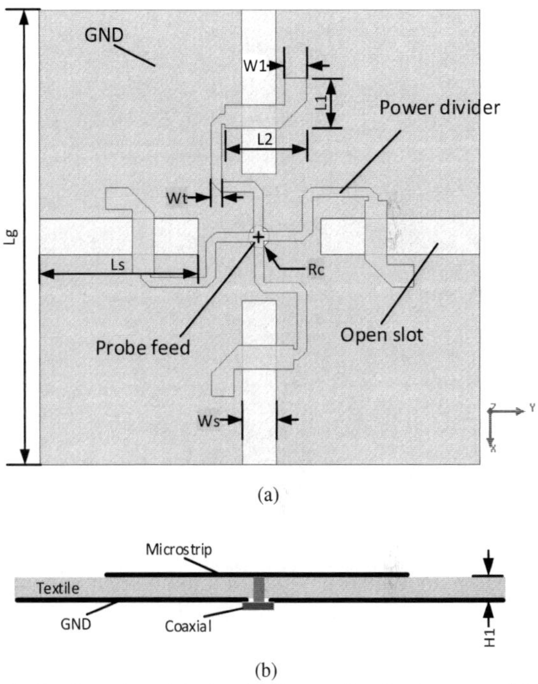

Fig. 1. Configuration of the low-band omni-directional antenna: (a) top view, (b) side view. Lg = 56 mm, Ls = 18 mm, Ws = 4 mm, $L1$ = 4.5 mm, $L2$ = 9.5 mm, $W1$ = 2.5 mm, Wt = 0.8 mm, Rc = 1.2 mm, $H1$ = 1.5 mm.

II. Antenna Design

A. Geometry

Fig. 1 shows the configuration of the proposed planar omni-directional textile antenna, which is composed of four rotated and symmetrical microstrip-fed open slots in the ground, which serve as the radiating elements. The slots are fed by a four-way microstrip power divider on the top layer. The four slots are designed to have uniform amplitude and phase, which generates an omnidirectional radiation pattern in the horizontal plane (xy-plane). A textile substrate with a relative permittivity of 1.65 is used in the design. The thickness of the textile is around 1.5 mm. An optimization was performed using the High Frequency Structural Simulator (HFSS), where the optimized parameters are listed in the figure caption.

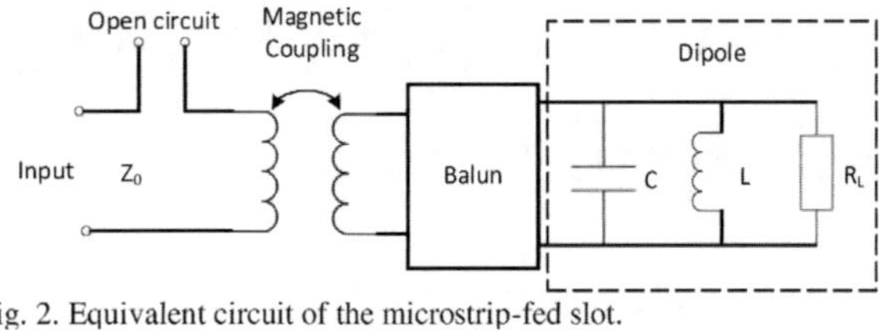

Fig. 2. Equivalent circuit of the microstrip-fed slot.

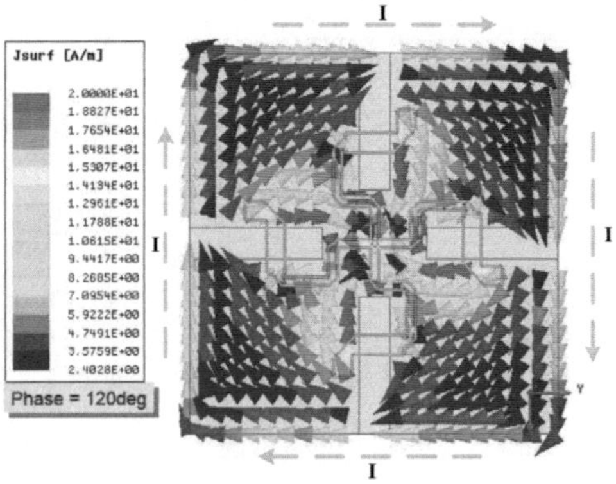

(a)

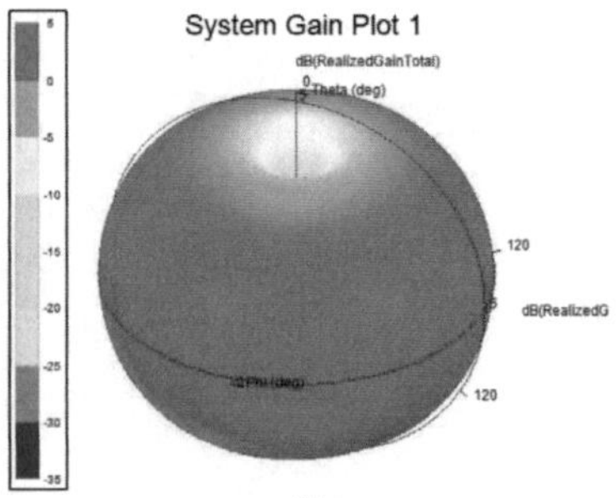

(b)

Fig. 3. (a) Simulated current distribution of the rotation-fed antenna at 2.45 GHz and (b) simulated 3-D radiation pattern at 2.45 GHz.

B. Operating Principle

Fig. 2 shows an equivalent circuit for each of the microstrip-fed radiating elements. The radiating edge is equivalent to a shunt RLC resonator. The open-ended slot serves as a balun, which is enables the input power to be evenly distributed over the conductive plane. The power from the microstrip is coupled to the slot via magnetic coupling. The center frequency of the antenna is mainly determined by the radiation section.

Fig. 3(a) shows the simulated current distribution at 2.45 GHz. The four open slots are excited simultaneously, generating four current paths along the contour of the antenna, which combine to form a magnetic-dipole-like current distribution. As a result, an omni-directional radiation pattern can be achieved. Fig. 3(b) shows the simulated radiation pattern at 2.45 GHz, which exhibits omni-directional radiation in the horizontal plane (xy-plane).

III. Experimental Results

The experimental results are summarized in Fig. 4. The antenna has a bandwidth that ranges from 2.35 to 2.5 GHz. In the band of interest, the antenna has a gain of over 2 dBi and an efficiency of over 90%.

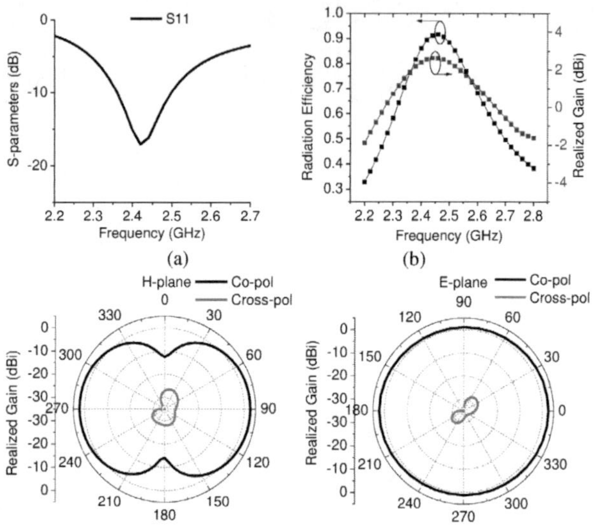

Fig. 4. Experimental results: (a) S_{11}, (b) radiation efficiency and realized gain, (c) radiation pattern in xz plane, (d) radiation pattern in xy plane.

The antenna exhibits a dipole-like radiation pattern that is omni-directional in the E-plane (xy-plane). The cross-polarization discrimination (XPD) is over 30 dB.

IV. Conclusion

In this paper, a novel planar textile antenna with a low profile and omni-directional radiation characteristics is proposed for wearable applications. The operating principles are detailed using equivalent circuit models and analysis of the current distribution. The performance of the antenna is verified experimentally and found to exhibit excellent bandwidth, gain, and radiation efficiency, which makes it ideally suited for wearable applications.

References

[1] Q. Chu, and C. Mao, "A compact notched band UWB slot antenna with sharp selectivity and controllable bandwidth," *IEEE Trans. Antennas Propag.*, vol. 61, no. 8, pp. 3961–3966, Aug. 2013.

[2] Z. H. Jiang, D. E. Brocker, P. E. Sieber, and D. H. Werner, "A compact, low-profile metasurface-enabled antenna for wearable medical bodyarea network devices," *IEEE Trans. Antennas Propag.*, vol. 62, no. 8, pp. 4021–4030, Aug. 2014.

[3] K. Venugopal, M. Valenti, and R. Heath, "Device-to-device millimeter wave communications: Interference, coverage, rate, and finite topologies," *IEEE Trans. Commu.*, vol. 15, no. 9, pp. 6175-6188, 2016.

[4] B. Sanz-Izquierdo, F. Huang, and J. Batchelor, "Small size wearable button antenna," *European Conference on Antennas and Propagation* (EuCAP), pp. 1-4, 2006.

[5] B. Sanz-Izquierdo, J. Batchelor, and M. Sobhy, "UWB wearable button antenna," *European Conference on Antennas and Propagation* (EuCAP), pp. 1-4, 2006.

[6] S. Chang, G. Liu, D. Wang, C. Du, "A Compact monopole antenna for wearable computer system," *International Conference on Transportation, Mechanical, and Electrical Engineering (TMEE)*, pp. 332-335, 2011.

[7] L. H. Salman, and L. Talbi, "G-shaped wearable cuff button antenna for 2.45 GHZ ISM band applications," *14th International Symposium on Antenna Technology and Applied Electromagnetics (ANTEM) and the American Electromagnetics Conference (AMEREM)*, pp. 1-4, 2010.

[8] S. T. Yu, Y. Liu, W. Jiang, and S. Gong, "A novel textile UWB antenna," *2012 International Symposium on Antennas and Propagation (ISAP)*, pp. 1051-1054, 2012.

Analysis of Freshwater Curved and Flat Spiral Antennas

Ruben A. Llamas, Kumar Vijay Mishra, James J. Niemeier and Anton Kruger
IIHR - Hydroscience and Engineering, The University of Iowa, Iowa City, IA 52242 USA
{ruben-llamas, kumarvijay-mishra, james-niemeier, anton-kruger}@uiowa.edu

***Abstract*—Recent research shows that freshwater mussels are very effective as biological sensors for measuring pollutant levels in rivers. Electronic assembly mounted on top of mussel shells, or backpacks, measures the periodic opening and closing of the valves that is directly related to the nitrogen content of the water. These sensors communicate with a surface station through a radio operating at 300 MHz. Mussel backpacks require light-weight, small, broadband antennas with high efficiency in freshwater environment. Conventional spiral antennas satisfy these requirements but are ill-fitted to the curved shell surface. In this work, we design low-cost curved spiral antennas for mussel backpacks. Our numerical experiments with FEKO indicate relatively constant reflection coefficient of curved spiral antenna in freshwater at 300 MHz with values comparable with the flat spiral geometry.**

***Index Terms*—Broadband antennas, biosensors, curved spiral antennas, FEKO, underwater communications**

I. Introduction

Freshwater mussels (*lampsilis cardium* or Pocketbook) are sentinel species whose health is correlated to the overall pollutant level of their river environment. By monitoring the *gape* - the rhythmic opening and closing of mussel valves - an estimate of the nitrogen content of the river can be obtained. In our previous research, we developed electronic sensors that can be deployed on the mussels in their natural underwater habitat for environmental monitoring [1–3]. These *mussel backpacks* (Fig. 1a) consist of sensors to measure gape [2] and heart rate [4], a micro-controller [5], and a small radio to transmit data from the sensors to an on-shore receiver [6]. The underwater propagation environment is a complex radio channel in which a reliable data transmission requires a specialized antenna. In this paper, we focus on the antenna design for this application.

The backpack radio operates at ~300 MHz, which corresponds to a freshwater wavelength of about 0.1 m. Backpack antennas must be small and lightweight. Further, the mussel orientation is unpredictable thereby requiring the antennas to have broad radiation patterns. In this context, the spiral antennas are a natural fit; they are broadband, compact and allow for small antennas at 0.1 m wavelength. Conventional spiral antennas are flat [7–9] while the mussel shell is curved. Mounting flat antennas on such a surface will impede mussel motion. Therefore, we developed a procedure to design curved spiral antennas (Fig. 1b). We start with the well-known flat spiral antenna and project it onto the mussel shell. Although the projection disturbs the intrinsic properties of the flat spiral antenna, our technique compensates for this perturbation.

II. Curved Spiral Antennas

A typical spiral antenna is flat but possibilities of curved spirals with square and Archimedean configurations have been explored before [10]. Simulation studies [7] of curved spiral antennas printed on a dielectric and conducting cylinders show that the frequency dependence of input impedance and gain fluctuates greatly in case of dielectric substrate while the same is relatively constant in case of conducting cylinder above a certain threshold cylinder height. Further, in case of conducting substrate, the antenna input impedance was largely independent of the cylinder radius while the gain exhibited a slight increase with the cylinder radius. The radiation patterns showed marked dependence on both the cylinder height and radius. The

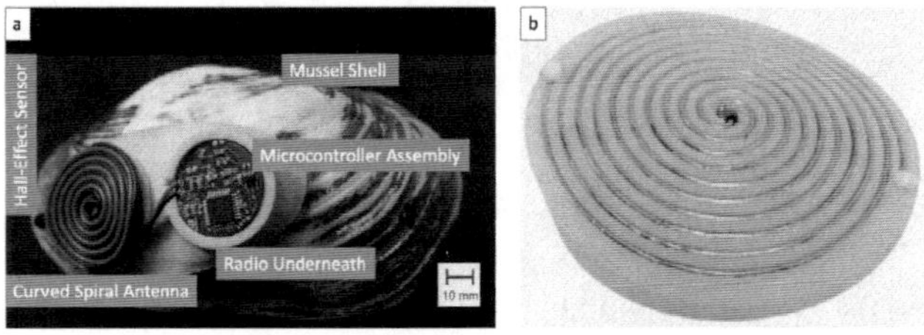

Fig. 1. (a) Illustration of the freshwater mussel and its backpack (b) Our lab-fabricated spiral antenna

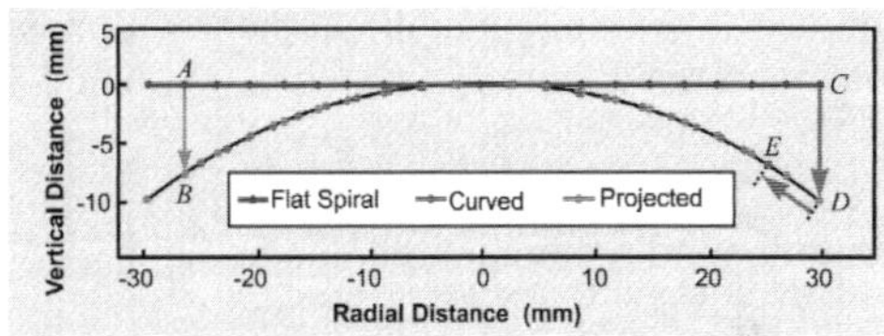

Fig. 2. Cross-section showing element locations of flat spiral, projected spiral, and corrected (curved) spiral antenna

overall gain of the curved spiral antenna was lower than that of the reference flat spiral by ~2.7 dB. In the cross-sectional view, similar to the flat design, the ideal curved spiral antenna has equispaced turns (Fig. 2). However, it is very difficult to maintain identical spacing while inlaying the antenna wire on a curved geometry (Fig. 1b). We, therefore, adopted following approach to design an effective low-cost antenna: design a flat spiral antenna and then vertically project its coordinates onto the spherical surface (which approximates a mussel shell). The result is a *projected spiral* antenna. However, such a design produces non-uniform spacing between the turns. Consequently, the phase relationships of waves emanating from differential radiating elements observed at a certain range are not the same as an ideal curved spiral antenna. This effect is observed in the radiation pattern and S_{11} parameter measurements.

In this work, we develop a correction procedure to account for this perturbation. For a given aperture, the location of equispaced curved spiral turns is known. Hence, after projecting the flat spiral turn points (points A and C in Fig. 2) on the curved surface (points B and D, respectively), the turn points are moved to new locations (e.g. point E) to mimic an ideal curved design. This procedure is then applied to all the wire elements and the distances moved along the shell surface are such that the spacing (between green dots) are as close as possible to the spacing between the flat spiral elements (blue dots).

Let r be the radius of the sphere on which the projection is intended (Fig. 3). Assuming plane-wave approximation, a given point O in far-range subtends an angle of $(\theta_1 + \theta_2)$ (rad) over the arc that connects the flat spiral turn (point C) to its ideal curved spiral turn (point E) on the mussel shell. The chord length for this arc is [10]

$$d_3 = 2d \sin\left(\frac{\theta_1 + \theta_2}{2}\right). \qquad (1)$$

The observation point subtends angles θ_1 (θ_2) between the points C (E) and the projected curved spiral point D from which the range is d_1. The vertical distance between C and D is d_2. The goal is to

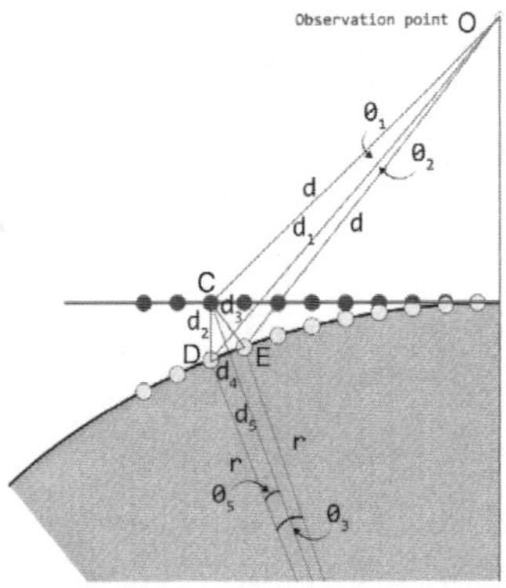

Fig. 3. Geometry of flat and curved spiral antenna cross-sections

find the arc distance Δd between points D and E. The corresponding chord length with respect to the centre of the circle (at the cross-section of the spherical surface) is

$$d_4 = 2r \sin\left(\frac{\theta_3}{2}\right), \tag{2}$$

where θ_3 is angle subtended by the centre of the sphere on this chord. Further, from the triangle DEO, we have

$$d_4 = \sqrt{d_1^2 + d^2 - 2dd_1 \cos\theta_2}, \tag{3}$$

where θ_2 is to be determined. Substituting (3) in (2) yields

$$\theta_3 = 2\sin^{-1}\left(\frac{\sqrt{d_1^2 + d^2 - 2d_1 d \cos\theta_2}}{2r}\right). \tag{4}$$

In order to find unknown angle θ_2, we exploit the relation between d_3 of (1) and the known length d_5 from the center of the sphere to point C, i.e.,

$$d_3^2 = d_5^2 + r^2 - 2d_5 r \cos(\theta_3 - \theta_5), \tag{5}$$

where d_5, r,

$$\theta_5 = \cos^{-1}\left(\frac{d_5^2 + r^2 - d_2^2}{2d_5 r}\right), \tag{6}$$

are known quantities and θ_3 can be computed from (4). Substituting (1) in (5) gives θ_2:

$$\theta_2 = 2\sin^{-1}\left(\frac{\sqrt{d_5^2 + r^2 - 2d_5 r \cos(\theta_3 - \theta_5)}}{2d}\right) - \theta_1 \tag{7}$$

where θ_1 is known. Thus, the correction Δd is

$$\Delta d = r\theta_3 = 2r \sin^{-1}\left(\frac{\sqrt{d_1^2 + d^2 - 2d_1 d \cos\theta_2}}{2r}\right). \tag{8}$$

After this correction, the next step is a rotational procedure to mark new locations of the 3D elements over the curved surface, using cross-section elements as a departure point. We generate trajectories on the surfaces of successive hemispheres with increasing radii. This new design effectively provides us with a curved spiral antenna.

III. Numerical and Field Experiments

We used FEKO electromagnetic simulation software tool to verify the performance of our design. Figure 4 depicts the 3-D simulation geometry. In our experiments, the voltage source magnitude was 1 V, zero phase, with port impedance of 50 Ω. The simulations were performed at 315 MHz - the operating frequency of the transmitter module mounted on the mussel backpack. We examined the S_{11} parameter over a range of frequencies. The frequency bounds for the simulation were such that their geometric mean was 315 MHz. We used human muscle tissue from FEKO's built-in materials library

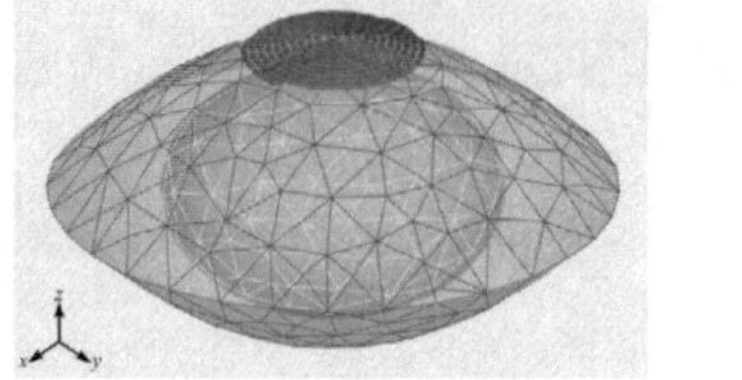

Fig. 4. Three-dimensional (3-D) model and mesh for FEKO simulation. The radiation patterns were calculated in spherical coordinates in increments of radius, azimuth and polar angle by 10 cm, 5°, and 5°, respectively.

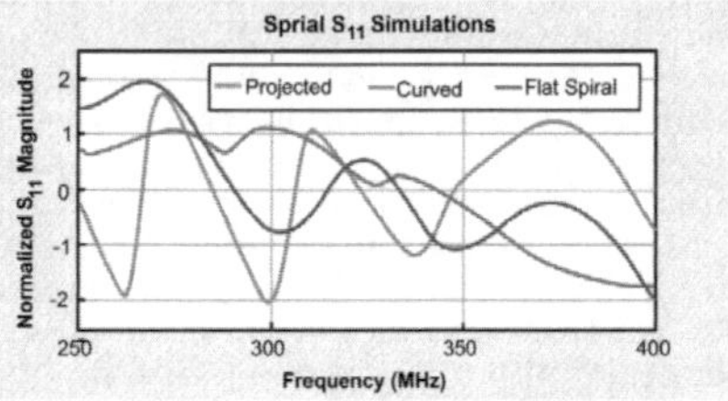

Fig. 5. Simulated normalized magnitude of S_{11} for various geometries

to simulate the mussel flesh. A spheroid of radii $x = 4$ cm, $y = 3$ cm, and $z = 2$ cm was used to mimic the bulk mussel tissue. The mussel shells were approximated using a paraboloid with radius of 5 cm and focal depth of 2.5 cm. These are representative of an adult Pocketbook mussel dimensions, e.g. the mussel shells have an average thickness of ~3 mm.

Figure 5 depicts FEKO results for flat, projected, and curved spiral antennas. It shows that the curved spiral antenna has lesser variation in S_{11} over the range of frequencies than both flat and projected spiral cases. These results show that it is feasible to fabricate a curved spiral antenna to fit on the contour of the mussel shell, obtain relatively constant reflection coefficient in freshwater and, thus, providing a consistent match to the radio-antenna system.

References

[1] H. Hodson, "Mussels with backpacks monitor Mississippi's health," New Scientist, 16 January 2013.

[2] K. P. Hunt, J. J. Niemeier, and A. Kruger, "Antennas for mussel-based underwater biological sensor networks in rivers," in ACM International Workshop on Underwater Networks. ACM, 2010, p. 13.

[3] H. F. Rezaei, A. Kruger, and C. Just, "An energy harvesting scheme for underwater sensor applications," in IEEE International Conference on Electro/Information Technology, 2012, pp. 1–4.

[4] C. Just, D. Vial, A. Kruger, J. Niemeier, H. Lee, and H. Schroer, "Heart rate sensor for freshwater mussels," in AGU Fall Meeting Abstracts, 2014.

[5] H. Taylor, A. Kruger, and J. Niemeier, "Embedded electronics for a mussel-based biological sensor," in IEEE Sensors Applications Symposium, 2013, pp. 148–151.

[6] K. P. Hunt, J. J. Niemeier, and A. Kruger, "RF communications in underwater wireless sensor networks," in IEEE International Conference on Electro/Information Technology, 2010, pp. 1–6.

[7] H. Nakano, "Helical and spiral antennas," in Wiley Encyclopedia of Telecommunications Vol II, J. G. Proakis, Ed. Wiley Online Library, 2003.

[8] C. Fumeaux, D. Baumann, and R. Vahldieck, "FVTD characterization of substrate effects for Archimedean spiral antennas in planar and conformal configurations," Applied Computational Electromagnetics Society Journal, vol. 20, no. 3, pp. 186–197, 2005.

[9] B. Xiao, L. Zhong, J.-S. Hong, and S.-L. Li, "A novel compact planar spiral-shaped antenna," Applied Computational Electromagnetics Society Journal, vol. 28, no. 1, pp. 57–63, 2013.

[10] R. A. Llamas, J. J. Niemeier, and A. Kruger, "Curved spiral antennas for freshwater applications," in IEEE Radio and Wireless Symposium, 2015, pp. 53–55.

3D Diagonalization and Supplementation of Maxwell's Magneto-static Field Equations in Fully Anisotropic and Inhomogeneous Media - Part I: Proof of Existence by Construction

A. R. Baghai-Wadji

Electrical Engineering Department
University of Cape Town, Cape Town, 7701, South Africa
alireza.baghai-wadji@uct.ac.za

College of Science
Xi'an University of Science and Technology, Xi'an, Shaanxi, 710054, China

Abstract – Consider the Maxwell's magneto-static equations $\nabla \times \mathbf{H} = \mathbf{J}$ and $\nabla \cdot \mathbf{B} = 0$ in fully anisotropic and inhomogeneous media characterized by the 3×3 positive-definite permeability matrix $\boldsymbol{\mu}^{3\times3}(x, y, z)$. This paper establishes - for the first time - that the aforementioned system of the governing and constitutive equations can be diagonalized with respect to the arbitrarily chosen $z-$axis leading to the $\mathcal{D}_c-$ and the associated supplementary $\mathcal{S}_c-$forms. The existence of the $(\mathcal{D}_c, \mathcal{S}_c)-$forms is demonstrated by construction. The accompanying paper (Part II) proves the internal consistency of the $(\mathcal{D}_c, \mathcal{S}_c)-$forms rigorously by showing the sharp equivalence of the $(\mathcal{D}_c, \mathcal{S}_c)-$forms with the originating Maxwell's and constitutive equations.

Index Terms – Maxwell's magneto-static equations, diagonalization, supplementation.

I. INTRODUCTION

Consider the Maxwell's magneto-static equations for the magnetic field $\mathbf{H}$ and the magnetic induction $\mathbf{B}$ in fully anisotropic and inhomogeneous magnetic media,

$$\nabla \times \mathbf{H} = \mathbf{J}, \quad \nabla \cdot \mathbf{B} = 0, \quad \mathbf{B} = \boldsymbol{\mu}^{3\times3}(x, y, z)\mathbf{H}, \tag{1}$$

with $\boldsymbol{\mu}^{3\times3}(x, y, z)$ being a 3×3 positive-definite position-dependent matrix. The main objective in this paper is two-fold: (i) to prove that the set of equations in (1) are diagonalizable with respect to the arbitrarily-chosen $z-$coordinate, leading to the $\mathcal{D}_c-$form. (ii) There exists an associated set of supplementary equations the $\mathcal{S}_c-$form. For the general properties of the $(\mathcal{D}_c, \mathcal{S}_c)-$forms and the nomenclature refer to [1]. Writing $\nabla \times \mathbf{H} = \mathbf{J}$ in component form and rearranging to distinguish the (arbitrarily chosen) $z-$coordinate,

$$\begin{bmatrix} \partial_x \\ \partial_y \end{bmatrix} H_3 + \begin{bmatrix} J_2 \\ -J_1 \end{bmatrix} = \partial_z \begin{bmatrix} H_1 \\ H_2 \end{bmatrix} \tag{2a}$$

$$\begin{bmatrix} -\partial_y & \partial_x \end{bmatrix} \begin{bmatrix} H_1 \\ H_2 \end{bmatrix} = J_3. \tag{2b}$$

Comment: Applying the operator $[-\partial_y \ \ \partial_x]$ to (2a) from the left

$$\underbrace{\begin{bmatrix} -\partial_y & \partial_x \end{bmatrix} \begin{bmatrix} \partial_x \\ \partial_y \end{bmatrix}}_{=0} H_3 + \begin{bmatrix} -\partial_y & \partial_x \end{bmatrix} \begin{bmatrix} J_2 \\ -J_1 \end{bmatrix}$$

$$= \underbrace{\begin{bmatrix} -\partial_y & \partial_x \end{bmatrix} \partial_z}_{=\partial_z[-\partial_y \ \ \partial_x]} \begin{bmatrix} H_1 \\ H_2 \end{bmatrix}. \tag{3}$$

Taking into account the indicated relationships in (3) and employing (2b) imply the charge conservation law $\nabla \cdot \mathbf{J} = 0$ for the current density $\mathbf{J}$.

II. On the construction of the $\mathcal{S}_c-$ and $\mathcal{D}_c-$ forms

A. The $\mathcal{S}_c-$form

It is easily seen that $\mathbf{B} = \boldsymbol{\mu}^{3\times3}(x, y, z)\mathbf{H}$ in (1) can be judiciously split and partitioned into

$$\begin{bmatrix} B_1 \\ B_2 \end{bmatrix} = \underbrace{\begin{bmatrix} \mu_{11} & \mu_{12} \\ \mu_{21} & \mu_{22} \end{bmatrix}}_{\boldsymbol{\mu}_{aa}^{2\times2}} \begin{bmatrix} H_1 \\ H_2 \end{bmatrix} + \underbrace{\begin{bmatrix} \mu_{13} \\ \mu_{23} \end{bmatrix}}_{\boldsymbol{\mu}_{ab}^{2\times1}} H_3 \tag{4a}$$

$$B_3 = \underbrace{\begin{bmatrix} \mu_{31} & \mu_{32} \end{bmatrix}}_{\boldsymbol{\mu}_{ba}^{1\times2}} \begin{bmatrix} H_1 \\ H_2 \end{bmatrix} + \underbrace{\begin{bmatrix} \mu_{33} \end{bmatrix}}_{\boldsymbol{\mu}_{bb}^{1\times1}} H_3. \tag{4b}$$

Multiplying (4b) by the inverse $\boldsymbol{\mu}_{bb}^{-1}$ from the left permits expressing H_3 in terms of the "essential" field variables H_1, H_2, and B_3, which are - as we shall see - the only field components accompanied by the differential operator ∂_z. Substituting the resulting equation for H_3 into (4a), $[B_1, B_2]^T$ can be expressed in terms of H_1, H_2, and B_3 as well. In summary,

$$\begin{bmatrix} B_1 \\ B_2 \end{bmatrix} = \overbrace{[\boldsymbol{\mu}_{aa} - \boldsymbol{\mu}_{ab}\boldsymbol{\mu}_{bb}^{-1}\boldsymbol{\mu}_{ba}]}^{\mathcal{A}_{11}^{2\times 2}} \begin{bmatrix} H_1 \\ H_2 \end{bmatrix} + \underbrace{[\boldsymbol{\mu}_{ab}\boldsymbol{\mu}_{bb}^{-1}]}_{\mathcal{A}_{12}^{2\times 1}} B_3 \tag{5a}$$

$$H_3 = \underbrace{[-\boldsymbol{\mu}_{bb}^{-1}\boldsymbol{\mu}_{ba}]}_{\mathcal{A}_{21}^{1\times 2}} \begin{bmatrix} H_1 \\ H_2 \end{bmatrix} + \underbrace{[\boldsymbol{\mu}_{bb}^{-1}]}_{\mathcal{A}_{22}^{1\times 1}} B_3 \tag{5b}$$

$$\begin{bmatrix} B_1 \\ B_2 \\ H_3 \end{bmatrix} = \begin{bmatrix} \mathcal{A}_{11}^{2\times 2} & \mathcal{A}_{12}^{2\times 1} \\ \mathcal{A}_{21}^{1\times 2} & \mathcal{A}_{22}^{1\times 1} \end{bmatrix} \begin{bmatrix} H_1 \\ H_2 \\ B_3 \end{bmatrix}. \tag{6}$$

Defining $\mathcal{A}_{31}^{1\times 2} = [-\partial_y \ \partial_x]$, and the null matrix $\mathbf{0}^{1\times 1}$, J_3 in (2b), is also expressible in terms of the "essential" field components H_1, H_2, and B_3,

$$J_3 = \begin{bmatrix} \mathcal{A}_{31}^{1\times 2} & \mathbf{0}^{1\times 1} \end{bmatrix} \begin{bmatrix} H_1 \\ H_2 \\ B_3 \end{bmatrix}. \tag{7}$$

Equations (6) and (7), taken together, completes the construction of the set of supplementary equations,

$$\begin{bmatrix} B_1 \\ B_2 \\ H_3 \\ J_3 \end{bmatrix} = \begin{bmatrix} \mathcal{A}_{11}^{2\times 2} & \mathcal{A}_{12}^{2\times 1} \\ \mathcal{A}_{21}^{1\times 2} & \mathcal{A}_{22}^{1\times 1} \\ \mathcal{A}_{31}^{1\times 2} & \mathbf{0}^{1\times 1} \end{bmatrix} \begin{bmatrix} H_1 \\ H_2 \\ B_3 \end{bmatrix}. \quad \square \tag{8}$$

B. The $\mathcal{D}_c$−form

Substituting (5b) into (2a) and defining

$$\mathcal{L}_{11}^{2\times 2} = \begin{bmatrix} \partial_x \\ \partial_y \end{bmatrix} \mathcal{A}_{21}^{1\times 2}, \quad \mathcal{L}_{12}^{2\times 1} = \begin{bmatrix} \partial_x \\ \partial_y \end{bmatrix} \mathcal{A}_{22}^{1\times 1} \tag{9}$$

lead to:

$$\begin{bmatrix} \mathcal{L}_{11}^{2\times 2} & \mathcal{L}_{12}^{2\times 1} \end{bmatrix} \begin{bmatrix} H_1 \\ H_2 \\ B_3 \end{bmatrix} + \begin{bmatrix} J_2 \\ -J_1 \end{bmatrix} = \partial_z \begin{bmatrix} H_1 \\ H_2 \end{bmatrix} \tag{10}$$

Consider $\nabla \cdot \mathbf{B} = 0$ in (1). Emphasizing the role of "z" it is straightforward to cast $\nabla \cdot \mathbf{B} = 0$ in the form

$$\begin{bmatrix} -\partial_x & -\partial_y \end{bmatrix} \begin{bmatrix} B_1 \\ B_2 \end{bmatrix} = \partial_z B_3. \tag{11}$$

Substituting (5a) into (11) and defining

$$\mathcal{L}_{21}^{1\times 2} = \begin{bmatrix} -\partial_x & -\partial_y \end{bmatrix} \mathcal{A}_{11}^{2\times 2} \tag{12a}$$

$$\mathcal{L}_{22}^{1\times 1} = \begin{bmatrix} -\partial_x & -\partial_y \end{bmatrix} \mathcal{A}_{12}^{2\times 1} \tag{12b}$$

result in

$$\begin{bmatrix} \mathcal{L}_{21}^{1\times 2} & \mathcal{L}_{22}^{1\times 1} \end{bmatrix} \begin{bmatrix} H_1 \\ H_2 \\ B_3 \end{bmatrix} = \partial_z B_3. \tag{13}$$

Equations (10) and (13), taken together, build the set of diagonalized equations:

$$\begin{bmatrix} \mathcal{L}_{11}^{2\times 2} & \mathcal{L}_{12}^{2\times 1} \\ \mathcal{L}_{21}^{1\times 2} & \mathcal{L}_{22}^{1\times 1} \end{bmatrix} \begin{bmatrix} H_1 \\ H_2 \\ B_3 \end{bmatrix} + \begin{bmatrix} J_2 \\ -J_1 \\ 0 \end{bmatrix} = \partial_z \begin{bmatrix} H_1 \\ H_2 \\ B_3 \end{bmatrix}. \tag{14}$$

This completes the construction of the $\mathcal{D}_c$−form. $\square$

C. Interface conditions

Using Heaviside's unit step function $H(\cdot)$:

$$\begin{bmatrix} H_1 \\ H_2 \\ B_3 \end{bmatrix} = \begin{bmatrix} H_1 \\ H_2 \\ B_3 \end{bmatrix}^{<} H(z' - z) + \begin{bmatrix} H_1 \\ H_2 \\ B_3 \end{bmatrix}^{>} H(z - z') \tag{15}$$

Substituting (15) into (14) leads to the "interface" conditions, as byproducts of the diagonalization,

$$H_2^{>}(x, y, z'_+) - H_2^{<}(x, y, z'_-) = -J_1(x, y, z') \tag{16a}$$

$$H_1^{>}(x, y, z'_+) - H_1^{<}(x, y, z'_-) = J_2(x, y, z') \tag{16b}$$

$$B_3^{>}(x, y, z'_+) - B_3^{<}(x, y, z'_-) = 0. \tag{16c}$$

III. CONCLUSION

It was demonstrated constructively that Maxwell's magneto-static equations are diagonalizable. Furthermore, it was shown that there exists an associated supplementary form. The internal consistency of the derived diagonalized and supplementary forms will be established in the accompanying paper (Part II), [2].

REFERENCES

[1] A. R. Baghai-Wadji, "3-D Electrostatic Charge Distribution on Finitely Thick Busbars in Micro Acoustic Devices: Combined Regularization in the Near- and far-Field," IEEE Transactions on Ultrasonics, Ferroelectrics, and Frequency Control (UFFC), Vol. 62, No. 6, June 2015, pp. 1132-1144.

[2] A. R. Baghai-Wadji, "3D Diagonalization and Supplementation of Maxwell's Magneto-static Field Equations in Fully Anisotropic and Inhomogeneous Media - Part II: Relative Proof of Consistency," this proceedings.

3D Diagonalization and Supplementation of Maxwell's Magneto-static Field Equations in Fully Anisotropic and Inhomogeneous Media - Part II: Relative Proof of Consistency

A. R. Baghai-Wadji

Electrical Engineering Department
University of Cape Town, Cape Town, 7701, South Africa
alireza.baghai-wadji@uct.ac.za

College of Science
Xi'an University of Science and Technology, Xi'an, Shaanxi, 710054, China

Abstract – Consider the Maxwell's magneto-static equations $\nabla \times \mathbf{H} = \mathbf{J}$ and $\nabla \cdot \mathbf{B} = 0$ in fully anisotropic and inhomogeneous media characterized by the 3×3 positive-definite position-dependent permeability matrix $\boldsymbol{\mu}^{3\times3}(x, y, z)$. In the accompanying paper (Part I) the existence of the diagonalized $\mathcal{D}_c-$ and the associated supplementary $\mathcal{S}_c-$forms was demonstrated constructively. In this paper the internal consistency of the $(\mathcal{D}_c, \mathcal{S}_c)-$forms is established rigorously by proving the sharp equivalence of the $(\mathcal{D}_c, \mathcal{S}_c)-$forms with the originating Maxwell's and constitutive equations.

Index Terms – Maxwell's magneto-static equations, diagonalization, supplementaion.

I. INTRODUCTION

General virtues of the concept of the diagonalized $(\mathcal{D}_c-)$ and the associated supplementary $(\mathcal{S}_c-)$forms were discussed in [1] in greater length. Furthermore, considering magneto-static fields, the existence of the $(\mathcal{D}_c, \mathcal{S}_c)-$forms was established in the accompanying paper [2]. In this paper the internal consistency of the $(\mathcal{D}_c, \mathcal{S}_c)-$forms is shown rigorously by proving the sharp equivalence of the $(\mathcal{D}_c, \mathcal{S}_c)-$forms with the originating governing and constitutive equations.

A. Implications from the $\mathcal{S}_c-$form

Consider the $\mathcal{S}_c-$form constructed in [2],

$$\begin{bmatrix} B_1 \\ B_2 \\ H_3 \\ J_3 \end{bmatrix} = \begin{bmatrix} \mathcal{A}_{11}^{2\times2} & \mathcal{A}_{12}^{2\times1} \\ \mathcal{A}_{21}^{1\times2} & \mathcal{A}_{22}^{1\times1} \\ \mathcal{A}_{31}^{1\times2} & \mathbf{0}^{1\times1} \end{bmatrix} \begin{bmatrix} H_1 \\ H_2 \\ B_3 \end{bmatrix}. \quad (1)$$

It is instructive to rewrite (1) by splitting the field components judiciously and separating equations,

$$\begin{bmatrix} B_1 \\ B_2 \end{bmatrix} = \mathcal{A}_{11}^{2\times2} \begin{bmatrix} H_1 \\ H_2 \end{bmatrix} + \mathcal{A}_{12}^{2\times1} B_3 \quad (2a)$$

$$H_3 = \mathcal{A}_{21}^{1\times2} \begin{bmatrix} H_1 \\ H_2 \end{bmatrix} + \mathcal{A}_{22}^{1\times1} B_3 \quad (2b)$$

$$J_3 = \mathcal{A}_{31}^{1\times2} \begin{bmatrix} H_1 \\ H_2 \end{bmatrix}. \quad (2c)$$

The various $\mathcal{A}-$operators are defined by

$$\begin{aligned} \mathcal{A}_{11}^{2\times2} &= \boldsymbol{\mu}_{aa}^{2\times2} + \boldsymbol{\mu}_{ab}^{2\times1} \mathcal{A}_{21}^{1\times2} && (3a) \\ \mathcal{A}_{12}^{2\times1} &= \boldsymbol{\mu}_{ab}^{2\times1} \mathcal{A}_{22}^{1\times1} && (3b) \\ \mathcal{A}_{21}^{1\times2} &= -\boldsymbol{\mu}_{bb}^{-1} \boldsymbol{\mu}_{ba}^{1\times2} && (3c) \\ \mathcal{A}_{22}^{1\times1} &= \boldsymbol{\mu}_{bb}^{-1} && (3d) \\ \mathcal{A}_{31}^{1\times2} &= \begin{bmatrix} -\partial_y & \partial_x \end{bmatrix}. && (3e) \end{aligned}$$

The involved material characteristic matrices are

$$\boldsymbol{\mu}_{aa}^{2\times2} = \begin{bmatrix} \mu_{11} & \mu_{12} \\ \mu_{21} & \mu_{22} \end{bmatrix}, \quad \boldsymbol{\mu}_{ab}^{2\times1} = \begin{bmatrix} \mu_{13} \\ \mu_{23} \end{bmatrix} \quad (4a)$$

$$\boldsymbol{\mu}_{ba}^{1\times2} = \begin{bmatrix} \mu_{31} & \mu_{32} \end{bmatrix}, \quad \boldsymbol{\mu}_{bb}^{1\times1} = \mu_{33}. \quad (4b)$$

Substituting (3a) and (3b) into (2a) and rearranging

$$\begin{aligned} \begin{bmatrix} B_1 \\ B_2 \end{bmatrix} &= \boldsymbol{\mu}_{aa}^{2\times2} \begin{bmatrix} H_1 \\ H_2 \end{bmatrix} \\ &+ \boldsymbol{\mu}_{ab}^{2\times1} \underbrace{\left(\mathcal{A}_{21}^{1\times2} \begin{bmatrix} H_1 \\ H_2 \end{bmatrix} + \mathcal{A}_{22}^{1\times1} B_3 \right)}_{=H_3 \text{ according to (2b)}} && (5a) \\ &= \boldsymbol{\mu}_{aa}^{2\times2} \begin{bmatrix} H_1 \\ H_2 \end{bmatrix} + \boldsymbol{\mu}_{ab}^{2\times1} H_3. && (5b) \end{aligned}$$

Considering (3c) and (3d), (2b) becomes

$$H_3 = -\boldsymbol{\mu}_{bb}^{-1}\boldsymbol{\mu}_{ba}^{1\times 2}\begin{bmatrix} H_1 \\ H_2 \end{bmatrix} + \boldsymbol{\mu}_{bb}^{-1}B_3. \tag{6}$$

Multiplying by $\boldsymbol{\mu}_{bb}^{1\times 1}$ from the left and rearranging

$$B_3 = \boldsymbol{\mu}_{ba}^{1\times 2}\begin{bmatrix} H_1 \\ H_2 \end{bmatrix} + \boldsymbol{\mu}_{bb}^{1\times 1}H_3. \tag{7}$$

Equations (5) and (7) taken together permit the reconstruction of the constitutive equation

$$\mathbf{B} = \boldsymbol{\mu}^{3\times 3}\mathbf{H}. \tag{8}$$

Furthermore, in virtue of (3e), (2c) becomes

$$J_3 = \begin{bmatrix} -\partial_y & \partial_x \end{bmatrix}\begin{bmatrix} H_1 \\ H_2 \end{bmatrix}. \tag{9}$$

B. Implications from the $\mathcal{D}_c$−form

In [2] we also constructed the $\mathcal{D}_c$−form consisting of

$$\mathcal{L}_{11}^{2\times 2}\begin{bmatrix} H_1 \\ H_2 \end{bmatrix} + \mathcal{L}_{12}^{2\times 1}B_3 + \begin{bmatrix} J_2 \\ -J_1 \end{bmatrix} = \partial_z\begin{bmatrix} H_1 \\ H_2 \end{bmatrix} \tag{10a}$$

$$\mathcal{L}_{21}^{1\times 2}\begin{bmatrix} H_1 \\ H_2 \end{bmatrix} + \mathcal{L}_{22}^{1\times 1}B_3 = \partial_z B_3, \tag{10b}$$

with the $\mathcal{L}$−operators being defined by

$$\mathcal{L}_{11}^{2\times 2} = \begin{bmatrix} \partial_x \\ \partial_y \end{bmatrix}\mathcal{A}_{21}^{1\times 2} \tag{11a}$$

$$\mathcal{L}_{12}^{2\times 1} = \begin{bmatrix} \partial_x \\ \partial_y \end{bmatrix}\mathcal{A}_{22}^{1\times 1} \tag{11b}$$

$$\mathcal{L}_{21}^{1\times 2} = \begin{bmatrix} -\partial_x & -\partial_y \end{bmatrix}\mathcal{A}_{11}^{2\times 2} \tag{11c}$$

$$\mathcal{L}_{22}^{1\times 1} = \begin{bmatrix} -\partial_x & -\partial_y \end{bmatrix}\mathcal{A}_{12}^{2\times 1}. \tag{11d}$$

Substituting (11) into (10),

$$\begin{bmatrix} \partial_x \\ \partial_y \end{bmatrix}\overbrace{\left(\mathcal{A}_{21}^{1\times 2}\begin{bmatrix} H_1 \\ H_2 \end{bmatrix} + \mathcal{A}_{22}^{1\times 1}B_3\right)}^{=H_3,\ \text{according to } (2b)} + \begin{bmatrix} J_2 \\ -J_1 \end{bmatrix} = \partial_z\begin{bmatrix} H_1 \\ H_2 \end{bmatrix} \tag{12a}$$

$$\begin{bmatrix} -\partial_x & -\partial_y \end{bmatrix}\underbrace{\left(\mathcal{A}_{11}^{2\times 2}\begin{bmatrix} H_1 \\ H_2 \end{bmatrix} + \mathcal{A}_{12}^{2\times 1}B_3\right)}_{=[B_1\ B_2]^T,\ \text{according to } (2a)} = \partial_z B_3. \tag{12b}$$

Or, equivalently,

$$\begin{bmatrix} \partial_x \\ \partial_y \end{bmatrix}H_3 + \begin{bmatrix} J_2 \\ -J_1 \end{bmatrix} = \partial_z\begin{bmatrix} H_1 \\ H_2 \end{bmatrix} \tag{13a}$$

$$\begin{bmatrix} -\partial_x & -\partial_y \end{bmatrix}\begin{bmatrix} B_1 \\ B_2 \end{bmatrix} = \partial_z B_3. \tag{13b}$$

Equation (13b) implies

$$\nabla\cdot\mathbf{B} = 0. \tag{14}$$

Furthermore, Eqs. (13a) and (9) are equivalent with

$$\nabla\times\mathbf{H} = \mathbf{J}. \tag{15}$$

Finally, applying $\begin{bmatrix} -\partial_y & \partial_x \end{bmatrix}$ to (13a) from the left, considering $\begin{bmatrix} -\partial_y & \partial_x \end{bmatrix}\begin{bmatrix} \partial_x \\ \partial_y \end{bmatrix} = \mathbf{0}$, and $\begin{bmatrix} -\partial_y & \partial_x \end{bmatrix}\partial_z = \partial_z\begin{bmatrix} -\partial_y & \partial_x \end{bmatrix}$, in virtue of (9),

$$\begin{bmatrix} -\partial_y & \partial_x \end{bmatrix}\begin{bmatrix} J_2 \\ -J_1 \end{bmatrix} = \partial_z J_3. \tag{16}$$

This equation is equivalent with the charge conservation law,

$$\nabla\cdot\mathbf{J} = 0. \tag{17}$$

II. CONCLUSION

In the accompanying paper (Part I), [2], it was established that the Maxwell's magneto-static equations together with the constitutive equations can be diagonalized with respect to the arbitrarily chosen z−direction leading to the $\mathcal{D}_c$−form. An associated supplementary equation (the $\mathcal{S}_c$−form) was also derived. In this paper it was rigorously shown that the $(\mathcal{D}_c, \mathcal{S}_c)$−forms are sharply equivalent with the originating governing and constitutive equations, and thus internally consistent.

REFERENCES

[1] A. R. Baghai-Wadji, "3-D Electrostatic Charge Distribution on Finitely Thick Busbars in Micro Acoustic Devices: Combined Regularization in the Near- and far-Field," IEEE Transactions on Ultrasonics, Ferroelectrics, and Frequency Control (UFFC), Vol. 62, No. 6, June 2015, pp. 1132-1144.

[2] A. R. Baghai-Wadji, "3D Diagonalization and Supplementation of Maxwell's Magneto-static Field Equations in Fully Anisotropic and Inhomogeneous Media - Part I: Proof of Existence by Construction," this proceedings.

Data-Enabled Poisson Equation Solver using Multiple Input Artificial Neural Networks (ANNs)

Shubhendu Bhardwaj
Electrical and Computer Engineering
Florida International University
10555, W. Flagler Street, Miami, USA
sbhardwa@fiu.edu

***Abstract*—We explore the possibility of using multiple input artificial neural networks for the solution of Poisson Equation. Results are shown for 1D case considering a boundary value problem with Dirichlet boundary conditions. As opposed to previous work, we consider the cases where input to the ANN is provided at multiple input nodes. A typical variation is considered containing sinc and cosine type functions and output validation is shown for different discretization steps. Time and error performances of the algorithm are presented.**

Keywords—Artificial neural network, Boundary Value Problem, Poisson Equation, Numerical.

I. INTRODUCTION

A unique feature in machine learning (ML) and artificial intelligent (AI) techniques is their ability to predict new information using learning of past data. This ability has specifically allowed the techniques to reduce computation for generating new information, which has found practical applications in healthcare, marketing, stock market, engineering and power systems. These are interesting new areas, where exact physical model of the phenomenon is not needed to be known, as long sufficiently large data is available for learning a trend. Within electromagnetic optimization and design, there has been some interest in using such techniques [1], [2].

In computational electromagnetics, artificial neural networks may be used to obtain the same effect. However, whether the data-learning and prediction is to be applied on physics level, i.e. model the data from other simulators, or at mathematics level, i.e. solve the partial differential equations using ANNs, is an important question which requires considerations of data reliability. Recent works has been shown in the physics-modeling to solve 3D Poison equation [3], while a body of work exists in solving the partial differential equations using ANNs [4], [5]. In this work, we pursue the latter, to maintain the physical integrity of the modeler in question.

In this paper, we show preliminary results on the use of multiple input ANNs for the solution of second order boundary value problem (BVP) enforced with Dirichlet boundary conditions. In distinction with previous work on this topic, we show the use of multiple inputs to the ANNs, which have better convergence for modeling typical electromagnetic functions such as sin, sinc, exponential, among others.

II. 1D POISSON EQUATION UNDER CONSIDERATION

The solution is pursued for a 1D Poisson equation (for a homogenous media) where second derivative of the function and the function values at the two boundaries are known. We define the BVP as

$$\frac{\partial^2 f(x)}{\partial x^2} = g(x), \tag{1}$$

with Dirichlet boundary conditions, given by

$$\begin{aligned} f(x = x_o) = C_1, \quad \text{and} \\ f(x = x_{end}) = C_2 \end{aligned} \tag{2}$$

To illustrate the model, we choose the function g(x) as

$$g(x) = \mathrm{sinc}\left(x + \frac{\pi}{2}\right) + \cos^2\left(\frac{3}{2}x\right)\,\mathrm{sinc}\left(\frac{3}{2}x\right) \tag{3}$$

for domain $x \in (-\pi, \pi)$. For this problem, the boundary values $C_1 = 2$ and C_2=3 have been used in this paper. Use of sinc and cosine functions is to model typical functions used to express electromagnetic fields. The shape of curve g(x) is shown in Fig. 1 for reference.

III. NEURAL NETWORK ARCHITECTURE

For the problem under consideration, neural network was developed consisting of 5 fully connected hidden layers consisting of 10, 10, 15, 20 and 30 nodes respectively. The input was varied with the level of discretization of domains. For example, if the domain was discretized with 30 steps, the number of input nodes was 30. Detailed information on the neural network, and parameters that were optimized, will be discussed at the conference and here we focus on summarizing the results.

IV. RESULTS, VALIDATION AND ERROR PERFORMANCE

The developed neural network was used for calculation of the function f(x). The NN was optimized using the algorithm of steepest decent and back propagation of error to calculate new weights. The calculated function f(x) is obtained by the optimization of the NN, such that error calculated using

$$\text{Error} = \frac{\sqrt{\sum_n \left(g(x_n) - g_c(x_n)\right)^2}}{\sqrt{\sum_n \left(g(x_n)\right)^2}} \tag{4}$$

was minimized. Here $g(x_n)$ is the ground truth value provided by the function in (3), whereas $g_c(x_n)$ is the optimized value using the ANN. x_n represents the nth step within the discretized domain $x \in (-\pi, \pi)$ at which the ANNs is being optimized.

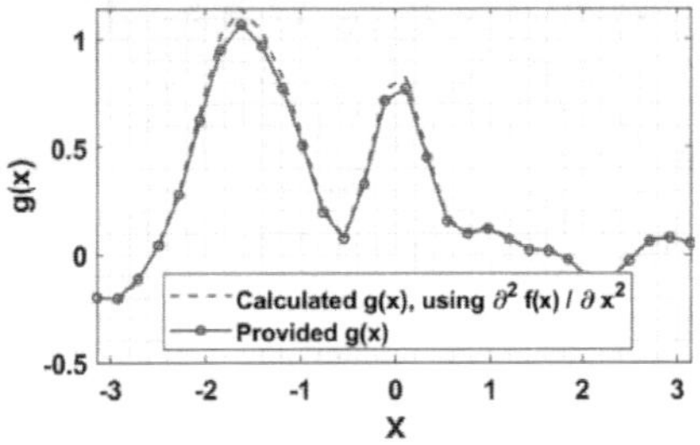

Fig. 1. Validation check the case N=30. The comparison is performed between calculated g(x) using NN-optimized f(x) from equation (1) and g(x) from equation (3).

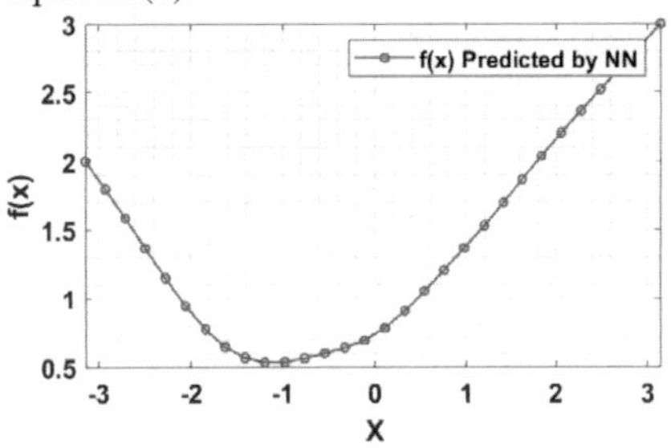

Fig. 2. Neural network optimized function f(x), using N=30 step discretized domain.

We consider two cases in this study, where the discretization steps in the domain were chosen to be N=30 and N=50. The results corresponding to these cases are shown in Fig. 1 to 4. Fig. 1 and Fig. 3 represent the validation of the output from the NN for discretization steps N=30 and 50 respectively, while Fig. 2 and 4 represent the output function for these cases, i.e. the result of the solution of the BVP or function f(x).

To conduct validation, second order derivative of the f(x) is calculated as per equation (1) and compared with g(x). There is close agreement between the two showing that the basic optimization algorithm of the NN is implemented accurately (Fig. 1 and 3). Function f(x) calculated in the two cases is shown in Fig. 2 and 4. In each case boundary value of $C_1 = 2$ and $C_2 = 3$ is achieved which further confirms the solution.

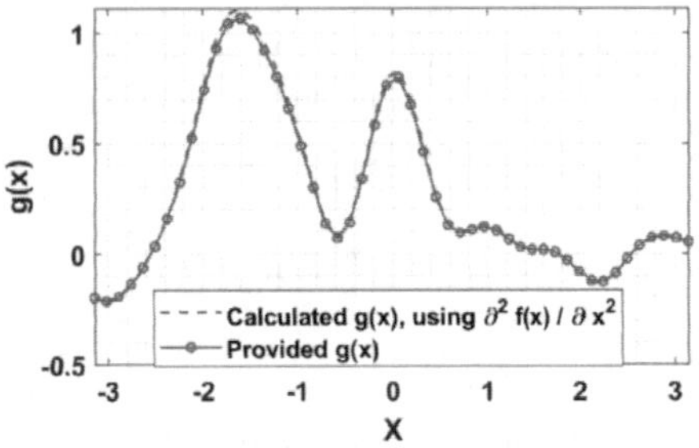

Fig. 3. Validation check the case N=50. The comparison is performed between calculated g(x) using NN-optimized f(x) from equation (1) and g(x) from equation (3).

To compare the error-performance of the algorithm over the generations, the error versus epoch plots for the two cases are shown in Fig. 5. The rate of error reduction is approximately exponential and becomes saturated after 1000 epochs for N=30 and after 5000 epochs for N=50. Further error reduction is possible by optimization of the NN parameters, such as number of nodes and number of hidden layers.

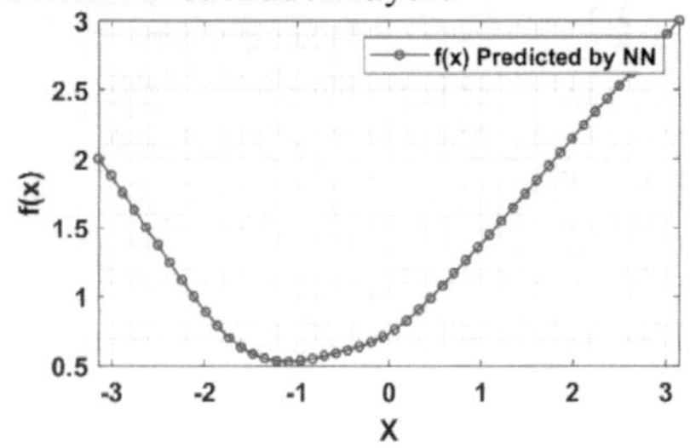

Fig. 4. Neural network optimized function f(x), using N=50 step discretized domain.

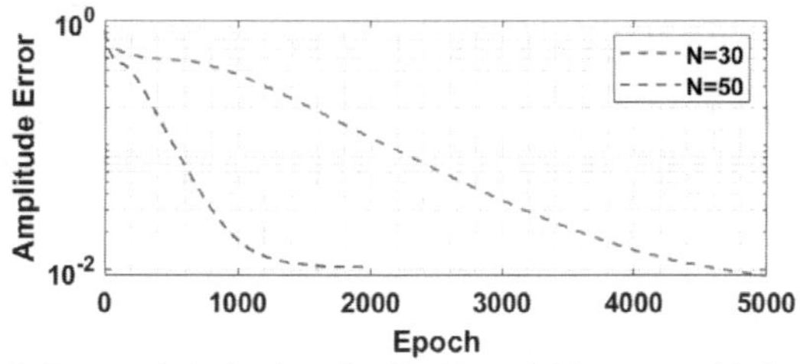

Fig. 5. Error minimization for N=30 and 50 cases with increasing number of generations.

The total simulation time for the N=30 case was 1.92 seconds and for N=50 case was 8.3 seconds. The code was developed on MATLAB, running on a Core I7, 6600 CPU with typical clock frequency of 2.6 GHz.

V. Conclusion

In this paper, we show the solution of a boundary value problem for a 1D Poisson equation using multiple input neural network architecture. The solution shows an error minimization of -40 dB (0.01 in amplitude) for an equation containing sinc and cosine type functions that model typical cases in electromagnetic functions. Two cases with different discretization levels were considered to understand the time-efficiency performance of the algorithms. In conclusion, the presented results show promise of numerical solution of electromagnetic problems using the artificial neural networks.

References

[1] H. M. Yao and L. Jiang, "Machine-Learning-Based PML for the FDTD Method," IEEE Antennas Wirel. Propag. Lett., vol. 18, no. 1, pp. 192–196, 2019.

[2] C. Erredir, M. L. Riabi, H. Ammari, and E. Bouarroudj, "Design of waveguide structures using improved neural networks," J. Microwaves, Optoelectron. Electromagn. Appl., vol. 16, no. 4, pp. 900–907, 2017.

[3] W. Tang et al., "Study on a Poisson's equation solver based on deep learning technique," 2017 IEEE Electr. Des. Adv. Packag. Syst. Symp. EDAPS 2017, vol. 2018–Janua, pp. 1–3, 2018.

[4] J. Sirignano and K. Spiliopoulos, "DGM: A deep learning algorithm for solving partial differential equations," J. Comput. Phys., vol. 375, no. Dms 1550918, pp. 1339–1364, 2018.

[5] I. E. Lagaris, A. Likas, and D. I. Fotiadis, "Artificial neural networks for solving ordinary and partial differential equations," IEEE Trans. Neural Networks, vol. 9, no. 5, pp. 987–1000, 1998.

Fast Structure Preserving HSS Matrix Inversion Algorithm in Exact Arithmetic and Its Application to Electromagnetic Analysis

Miaomiao Ma and Dan Jiao
School of Electrical and Computer Engineering, Purdue University, West Lafayette, IN 47907, USA

***Abstract*—A new matrix inversion algorithm in exact arithmetic is developed for general HSS (*H*ierarchically *S*emiseparable) matrices, which also preserves the HSS structure in inverse by updating the cluster basis based on actual computations performed. No theoretical nor numerical approximation is involved in the proposed inverse. The resulting computational complexity is strictly $O(N)$ (linear) for constant-rank HSS matrices. For variable-rank HSS matrices like those encountered in electrodynamic analysis, the complexity is minimized as well because each computation is performed on a small matrix of rank size. For solving electrically large volume integral equations (VIE), taking into account the rank's growth with electrical size, the proposed inverse has an $O(N)$ complexity in memory and solution, and $O(NlogN)$ complexity in inversion. Numerical experiments on electrically large VIE analysis have demonstrated the machine-precision accuracy and low complexity of the proposed new inverse algorithm.**

I. INTRODUCTION

HSS (Hierarchically Semiseparable) matrices [1] have been used to develop fast direct or iterative solvers for both dense and sparse linear systems of equations due to its simple structure and nested low-rank property. In literature, fast HSS factorization algorithms have been developed for symmetric positive definite (SPD) matrices [1]. For general complex-valued HSS matrices, factorization and inversion algorithms are also developed [2]. These algorithms perform HSS ULV/URV factorizations and factorize the HSS matrix into a series of factors. There also exist other HSS inversion-based solution schemes. However, all these algorithms do not preserve the original HSS structure in the inverse. Preserving the HSS structure in inverse facilitates fast computation of matrix-matrix products when multiple right hand sides are involved. In this work, we develop a new HSS inverse algorithm in exact arithmetic. Furthermore, the structure of the original HSS is preserved in its inverse without making any approximation, as we update cluster bases to rigorously account for the change to the original matrix during the inversion. Moreover, we keep the inverse complexity to be linear for constant-rank HSS matrices, and also achieve low complexity for variable-rank HSS. For example, the resultant direct VIE solver for electrically large analysis has an $O(NlogN)$ complexity in inversion, $O(N)$ complexity in solution and memory, whose accuracy is also achieved at machine precision since no approximations are utilized in the inversion.

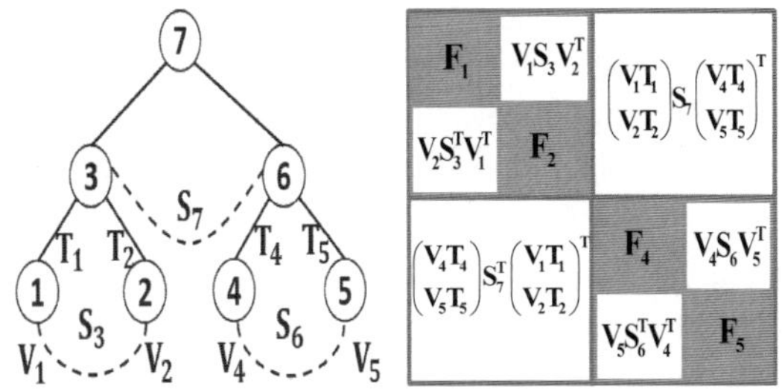

(a) (b)

Fig. 1. An HSS matrix. (a) Tree. (b) A two-level matrix.

II. PROPOSED HSS INVERSION ALGORITHM

In an HSS-matrix, the entire matrix is partitioned into leaf level inadmissible blocks, noted as **F**, and off-diagonal admissible blocks at multiple levels, noted as **R**. The **R** block has a nested low-rank form of $\mathbf{Z}_{t,s} = (\mathbf{V}_t)_{\#t\times k}(\mathbf{S}_{t,s})_{k\times k}(\mathbf{V}_s)^T_{\#s\times k}$, where $\mathbf{V}_t$ ($\mathbf{V}_s$) is called cluster basis associated with cluster t (s), $\mathbf{S}_{t,s}$ is called a coupling matrix. In Fig. 1 (b), we give an HSS matrix **G** of two levels, shown in blue and red color respectively. Using

$$\mathbf{G}^{-1} = \begin{bmatrix} \mathbf{G}_{11}^{-1} + \mathbf{G}_{11}^{-1} \times \mathbf{G}_{12} \times \mathbf{S}^{-1} \times \mathbf{G}_{21} \times \mathbf{G}_{11}^{-1} & -\mathbf{G}_{11}^{-1} \times \mathbf{G}_{12} \times \mathbf{S}^{-1} \\ -\mathbf{S}^{-1} \times \mathbf{G}_{21} \times \mathbf{G}_{11}^{-1} & \mathbf{S}^{-1} \end{bmatrix}, \quad (1)$$

where $\mathbf{S} = \mathbf{G}_{22} - \mathbf{G}_{21}\mathbf{G}_{11}^{-1}\mathbf{G}_{12}$, we can compute the inverse recursively. At each level, we compute the inverse of **G** as an HSS-inverse ($\underline{\mathbf{G}}$, $\mathbf{G}$), which is carried out as the following:

1) HSS-inverse ($\underline{\mathbf{G}}_{11}$, $\mathbf{G}_{11}$);
2) $\mathbf{G}_{21} \times \underline{\mathbf{G}}_{11} \rightarrow \mathbf{X}_{21}$, $\underline{\mathbf{G}}_{11} \times \mathbf{G}_{12} \rightarrow \mathbf{X}_{12}$;
3) $\mathbf{G}_{22} - \mathbf{X}_{21} \times \mathbf{G}_{12} \rightarrow \mathbf{G}_{22}$;
4) HSS-inverse ($\underline{\mathbf{G}}_{22}$, $\mathbf{G}_{22}$);
5) $-\underline{\mathbf{G}}_{22} \times \mathbf{X}_{21} \rightarrow \mathbf{G}_{21}, -\mathbf{X}_{12} \times \underline{\mathbf{G}}_{22} \rightarrow \mathbf{G}_{12}$;
6) $\underline{\mathbf{G}}_{11} - \underline{\mathbf{G}}_{12} \times \mathbf{X}_{21} \rightarrow \mathbf{G}_{11}$.

At the end of the computation, the **G** is overwritten by $\mathbf{G}^{-1}$.

We use the matrix in Fig. 1 (b) as an example to illustrate the overall procedure, however the proposed algorithm is applicable to general HSS-matrices. At leaf level L, for Step 1, we compute the dense matrix inverse of $\mathbf{G}_{11}^L$, which is $\mathbf{F}_1$ matrix in Fig. 1 (b). Here, the superscript of $\mathbf{G}_{11}^L$ denotes tree level. At level L, since the matrix is of $leafsize$, its inverse is computed as a full-matrix inverse, and stored in $\underline{\mathbf{G}}_{11}^L$.

Then we compute two matrix-matrix multiplications shown in Step 2. Since $\mathbf{G}_{12}^L$ is low-rank,

$$\mathbf{X}_{12}^L = \underline{\mathbf{G}}_{11}^L \times \mathbf{G}_{12}^L = (\underline{\mathbf{G}}_{11}^L \times \mathbf{V}_1) \times \mathbf{S}_3 \times \mathbf{V}_2^T, \qquad (2)$$

must also be low rank. Furthermore, this admissible block clearly has a new row cluster basis of $\underline{\mathbf{G}}_{11}^L \mathbf{V}_1$ instead of the original $\mathbf{V}_1$. Hence, we need to update the cluster basis of cluster 1 from $\mathbf{V}_1$ to $\tilde{\mathbf{V}}_1 = \underline{\mathbf{G}}_{11}\mathbf{V}_1$. We further orthogonalize $\tilde{\mathbf{V}}_1$ so that it satisfies $\tilde{\mathbf{V}}_1^H \tilde{\mathbf{V}}_1 = \mathbf{I}$. With the row cluster basis updated, the product $\mathbf{X}_{12}^L$ now can be rewritten as $\mathbf{X}_{12}^L = \tilde{\mathbf{V}}_1 \tilde{\mathbf{S}}_3 \mathbf{V}_2^T$, where the new coupling matrix $\tilde{\mathbf{S}}_3 = (\tilde{\mathbf{V}}_1^H \underline{\mathbf{G}}_{11}^L \mathbf{V}_1)\mathbf{S}_3 = \underline{\mathbf{G}}_{11,collect}^L \mathbf{S}_3$, the computational cost of which is $O(k'^3)$, where $k' = max(k_L, leafsize)$ and k_L is the rank at level L. For symmetric matrix, $\mathbf{X}_{21}^L$ is nothing but $\left(\mathbf{X}_{12}^L\right)^T$. For non-symmetric ones, a similar procedure can be performed to obtain $\mathbf{X}_{21}^L$.

Then we proceed to Step 3, we first compute $\mathbf{X}_{21}^L \mathbf{G}_{12}^L = \left(\mathbf{V}_2 \tilde{\mathbf{S}}_3^T \tilde{\mathbf{V}}_1^T\right)\left(\mathbf{V}_1 \mathbf{S}_3 \mathbf{V}_2^T\right)$, which can be written in short as $\mathbf{X}_{21}^L \mathbf{G}_{12}^L = \mathbf{V}_2 \mathbf{S} \mathbf{V}_2^T$, where the coupling matrix is $\mathbf{S} = \tilde{\mathbf{S}}_3^T \tilde{\mathbf{V}}_1^T \mathbf{V}_1 \mathbf{S}_3$. Hence, the computation of $\mathbf{X}_{21}^L \mathbf{G}_{12}^L$ results in an admissible block, whose computation is simply the coupling matrix computation, as the cluster bases remain to be the original ones. The cost of this step is $O(k'^3)$. We then convert the admissible block of $\mathbf{X}_{21}^L \mathbf{G}_{12}^L$ to a full matrix and perform the subtraction in Step 3, the cost of which is $O(leafsize^3)$. Next, in Step 4, we compute the inverse of the updated $\mathbf{G}_{22}^L$ by a normal full matrix inverse. Step 5 and Step 6 are calculated in the same way as Step 2 and Step 3. In Step 5, we need to update the row cluster bases of $\mathbf{V}_2$ to $\tilde{\mathbf{V}}_2 = \underline{\mathbf{G}}_{22}^L \mathbf{V}_2$, which is then orthogonalized. After performing the above 6 steps, we obtain the inverse of $\mathbf{G}_{11}^{L-1}$ and continue to the non-leaf level.

At a nonleaf level l, we perform the 6 steps similar to the leaf level. Take Step 2 as an example, $\underline{\mathbf{G}}_{11}$ at level l is now a non-leaf block. This block needs to be multiplied by $\mathbf{G}_{12}$ at level l, which is admissible. The product clearly remains to be admissible. However, the matrix size involved in the computation doubles at every level. To efficiently carry out this computation, we can use two children's updated cluster bases (transfer matrices for non-leaf levels) as the row bases, and the two children's original cluster bases (transfer matrices) as the column bases to first collect $\underline{\mathbf{G}}_{11}^l$ obtained at previous level to be a small matrix of rank size, and then multiply the resultant with the coupling matrix of $\mathbf{G}_{12}$. Such an operation is exact without making any approximation since we have updated cluster bases level by level. To explain, take $L-1$ level as an example, since

$$\mathbf{X}_{12}^{L-1} = \underline{\mathbf{G}}_{11}^{L-1}\mathbf{G}_{12}^{L-1} = \underline{\mathbf{G}}_{11}^{L-1}\begin{bmatrix}\mathbf{V}_1 & \mathbf{0}\\ \mathbf{0} & \mathbf{V}_2\end{bmatrix}\mathbf{T}_3\mathbf{S}_7\mathbf{T}_6^T\begin{bmatrix}\mathbf{V}_1^T & \mathbf{0}\\ \mathbf{0} & \mathbf{V}_2^T\end{bmatrix}, \qquad (3)$$

and $\underline{\mathbf{G}}_{11}^{L-1}$ is nothing but the inverse of $\mathbf{G}_{11}^{L-1}$, which has a form shown in (1), the product of (3) clearly has a row cluster basis being $\begin{bmatrix}\tilde{\mathbf{V}}_1 & \mathbf{0}\\ \mathbf{0} & \tilde{\mathbf{V}}_2\end{bmatrix}$, and a column cluster basis of the original two children's cluster bases. Thus, the above product can be represented as:

$$\mathbf{X}_{12}^{L-1} = \begin{bmatrix}\tilde{\mathbf{V}}_1 & \mathbf{0}\\ \mathbf{0} & \tilde{\mathbf{V}}_2\end{bmatrix}\underline{\mathbf{G}}_{11,collect}^{L-1}\mathbf{T}_3\mathbf{S}_7\mathbf{T}_6^T\begin{bmatrix}\mathbf{V}_1^T & \mathbf{0}\\ \mathbf{0} & \mathbf{V}_2^T\end{bmatrix}, \qquad (4)$$

where

$$\underline{\mathbf{G}}_{11,collect}^{L-1} = \begin{bmatrix}\tilde{\mathbf{V}}_1^H & \mathbf{0}\\ \mathbf{0} & \tilde{\mathbf{V}}_2^H\end{bmatrix}\underline{\mathbf{G}}_{11}^{L-1}\begin{bmatrix}\mathbf{V}_1 & \mathbf{0}\\ \mathbf{0} & \mathbf{V}_2\end{bmatrix}, \qquad (5)$$

is the collected $\underline{\mathbf{G}}_{11}^{L-1}$ which is of rank size. Here, $\tilde{\mathbf{T}}_3 = \underline{\mathbf{G}}_{11,collect}^{L-1}\mathbf{T}_3$ can be viewed as an updated transfer matrix of cluster 3. As a result, $\underline{\mathbf{G}}_{11}^{L-1}\mathbf{G}_{12}^{L-1}$ is an admissible block whose row and column cluster bases are as shown in (4), and the only computation associated with this block is the updated transfer matrix of $\tilde{\mathbf{T}}_3$, the cost of which is of $O(k_l)^3$. If $\tilde{\mathbf{T}}_3$ is further orthogonalized just like leaf-level updated cluster basis, then we update the coupling matrix to be $\tilde{\mathbf{T}}_3^H \underline{\mathbf{G}}_{11,collect}^{L-1}\mathbf{T}_3\mathbf{S}_7$, the cost of which is also $O(k_l)^3$. Notice that at any non-leaf level higher than $L-1$, in (5), the row cluster basis becomes the updated transfer matrices of two children; and the column cluster bases are the original transfer matrices of two children, while the center block is the collected $\underline{\mathbf{G}}_{11,collect}$ at previous level. Hence, at each level, the computation is performed on matrices of rank size, thus efficient.

III. Numerical Results

We use HSS matrices resulting from electrically large VIE as an example, whose kernels are highly oscillatory. A large-scale dielectric cube array is simulated via VIE from $2\times2\times2$ to $8\times16\times16$ elements at 300 MHz, whose unknown size N is from 3,024 to 774,144. Each cube is of size $0.3\times0.3\times0.3m^3$. The dielectric constant is 2.54 and the $leafsize$ used is 378. The center-to-center distance between cube elements is set to keep the admissibility parameter $\eta = 1$. In Fig. 2, we plot the time and memory of the proposed inverse with respect to N, which shows clear linear scaling. Meanwhile, it is shown to take less time and memory as compared to the state-of-the-art HSS factorization solver in [2], while achieving the same machine-precision accuracy, as can be seen from Table I.

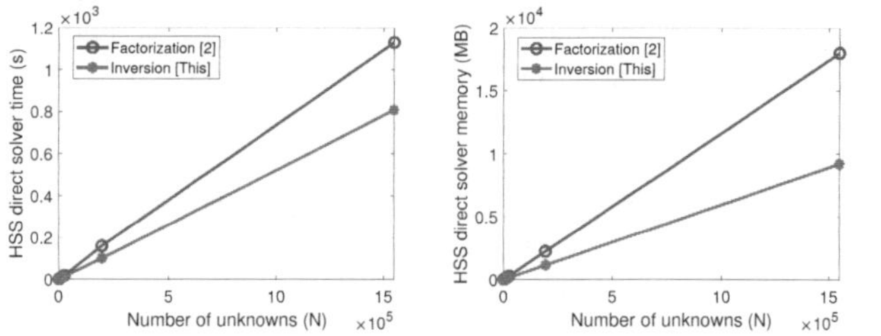

(a) (b)

Fig. 2. Performance comparison with [2].

TABLE I: Relative residual of the proposed HSS inversion

N	3,024	24,192	193,536	774,144
Relative residual	1.73E-15	2.37E-15	3.84E-15	4.17E-15

References

[1] J. Xia, S. Chandrasekaran, M. Gu, and X. S. Li, "Fast algorithm for hierarchically semiseparable matrices," Number. Linear Algebra Appl., 17 (2010), pp. 953-976.

[2] M. Ma and D. Jiao, "New HSS-factorization and inversion algorithms with exact arithmetic for efficient direct solution of large-scale volume integral equations," IEEE International Symposium on Antennas and Propagation (APSURSI), Jul. 2016.

FEM-MTLN Hybridization Technique to Evaluate Electrical Current on Multiconductor Cables inside Enclosures Illuminated by a Plane Wave

Pierre Schickele
pierre.schickele@onera.fr

Xavier Ferrieres
xavier.ferrieres@onera.fr

Jean-Philippe Parmantier
jean-philippe.parmantier@onera.fr

ONERA / DEMR
University of Toulouse, F-31055 Toulouse, France

***Abstract*—In this paper, we introduce a strategy to evaluate current on multiconductor electrical cables installed inside enclosures. This strategy consists of the hybridization of a FEM and a MTLN approach. The motivation of this strategy relies on the fact that the high order FEM scheme has less numerical dispersive effect than a usual first order scheme such as an FDTD scheme. More accuracy is thereby obtained in the MTLN response. This property is demonstrated on a generic test case configuration.**

***Index Terms*—EM modeling, Maxwell's equations, multiconductor cables, hybridization, multiconductor transmission lines, FEM, field-to-transmission-line, EMC**

I. Introduction

Marketing industrial vehicles requires compliance with Electromagnetic Compatibility (EMC) standards. In this context, we are interested in the problem of currents induced on electrical cables installed in a vehicle illuminated by a electromagnetic (EM) plane wave. A commonly adopted approach to solve this problem consists in solving Maxwell's equations coupled with Multiconductor Transmission Line Network (MTLN) equations to model respectively the EM fields in the 3D structure and the electrical currents on complex multiconductor cables. When reaction on the induced currents on the incident fields (taken as sources to drive those currents) are neglected, this approach is known under the name "Field-to-Transmission-Line" (FTL) and allows modeling of large wiring systems of industrial complexity because of its capacity to decouple 3D and MTLN problems as well as to account for MTLN models (whereas cable models embedded in 3D models are usually limited to thin single-wire models, which is a significant simplification). In EMC studies, the Yee scheme applied on a Cartesian mesh to evaluate Maxwell's equations is a widely used approach because of its numerous advantages. However, this technique is known to introduce a numerical dispersion error on the EM fields driving themselves an error on the induced currents on the cable models. To avoid this problem, one solution is to reduce the size of the mesh cells, but this strongly increases the computational costs. Therefore an other idea consists in applying a higher order scheme such as the Finite Element Method (FEM) to solve both Maxwell's equations, still on a Cartesian grid and MTLN equations. This approach gives more accuracy with fewer cells in the mesh and maintains reasonable computational costs. Moreover, by taking into account a higher order of approximation for the solution, calculations can be done at higher frequencies using the same cell size in the mesh. In the first and second sections of this paper, we describe the FEM method for Maxwell's equations and the MTLN equations. In the third section, we describe the hybridization principle between the two methods. Finally, in the last section, we present some results obtained for a wire in a generic enclosure.

II. High spatial order FEM method to solve Maxwell's equations

To evaluate EM fields (E, H) on $\Omega \times [0, T]$, we solve Maxwell's equations, on a computational domain Ω approximated by a Cartesian mesh with a high order (r) Finite Element Method (FEM) [1].

As an illustration, (1) shows the approximation used for fields. In the FEM scheme, for E_x and H_z components :

$$\begin{aligned} E_x(t,x,y,z) &= \textstyle\sum_{i,j,k=1}^{r} E^x_{ijk}(t) L^G_i(x) L^{GL}_j(y) L^{GL}_k(z) \\ H_z(t,x,y,z) &= \textstyle\sum_{i,j,k=1}^{r} H^z_{ijk}(t) L^G_i(x) L^G_j(y) L^{GL}_k(z) \end{aligned} \tag{1}$$

where L^G_i and L^{GL}_i are Lagrange polynomials defined on $[0, 1]$ respectively by using r Gauss $((\xi^g_k)_{k=1\ldots r})$ and $r+1$ Gauss-Lobatto $((\xi^{gl}_k)_{k=1\ldots r+1})$ points. These points are also the quadrature points used to evaluate the integrals in the FEM scheme. By considering this approximation, we obtain a numerical scheme which provides an efficient and accurate solution for Maxwell's equations on EM fields.

III. MTLN formalism for complex harness

The organization of cables inside vehicles define networks of Multiconductor Transmission Lines (MTL) connected to nodes (also called "junctions") as presented in Fig. 1. On each MTL, we define unknown currents I_i and voltages V_i distributed along the conductors of the MTL that verify (2).

$$\begin{cases} C_i \partial_t V_i + G_i V_i = -\partial_l I_i \\ L_i \partial_t I_i + R I_i = -\partial_l V_i + E_i \\ V_i(t=0) = I_i(t=0) = 0 \end{cases} \tag{2}$$

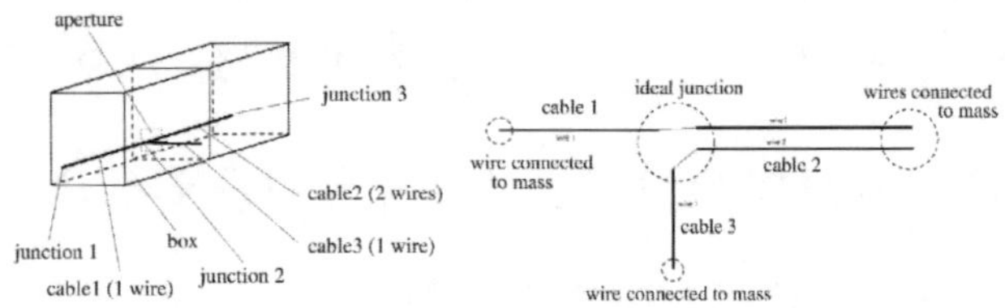

Fig. 1. Example of a multiconductor cable network modeling.

C_i, L_i, R_i and G_i are the capacitance, inductance, resistance and conductance matrices of the MTL and E_i the incident field. To close (2), we introduce on each conductor some limit conditions at the ends of the MTLs using several models of junctions that represent electrical circuits as illustrated in Fig. 2.

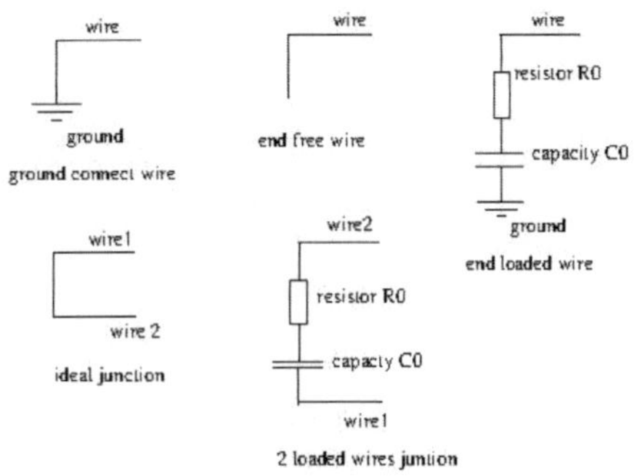

Fig. 2. Examples of electrical circuits in junctions.

To approximate (2), we decompose each MTL into several segments where the unknowns I and V are located respectively at Gauss and Gauss-Lobatto quadrature points. By using the Lagrange polynoms previously defined for the EM fields, we have :

$$I(t,x) = \sum_{i=1}^{r} I_i(t) L_i^G(x) \text{ and } V(t,x) = \sum_{i=1}^{r+1} V_i(t) L^{GL}(x) \tag{3}$$

As for Maxwell's equations on EM fields, this high order FEM to solve MTLN equations gives an efficient and accurate solution with low dispersion.

IV. Hybridization Process

The coupling terms between Maxwell's equations and the MTLN equations are given by the electric fields along the MTLs for the MTLN equations and the currents on the wires for Maxwell's equations [2]. In this coupling process, the electric fields evaluated along the direction of the MTLs are taken as distributed generators of the MTLs and the J source term in Maxwell's equations is approximated by the sum of currents on the conductors of the MTLs, for the unknown fields located in the cell where the MTLs are located.

V. Test Case

In this preliminary version of the paper, we consider a perfectly metallic enclosure with an aperture. An electric wire connected to 50 Ω loads to the ground is routed inside the enclosure. The enclosure is illuminated by a Gaussian plane wave (of mean 3e-10 s and standard deviation 1e-10 s) at the level of the aperture, as shown in Fig. 3.

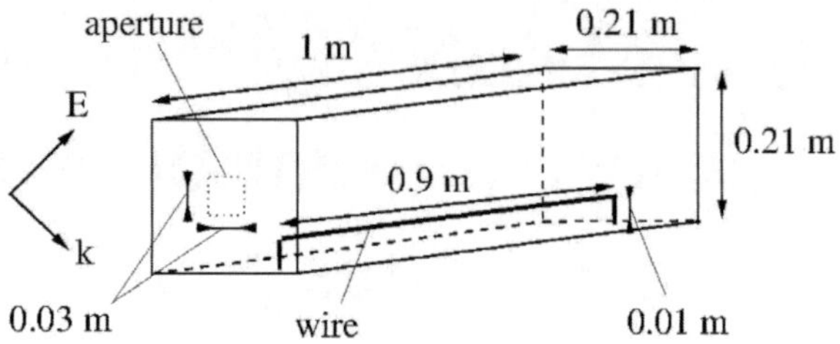

Fig. 3. Wire in an enclosure illuminated by an EM plane wave.

The electrical current has been calculated in the middle of the wire using "full" FDTD and 3-order FEM models (for which the wire model is imbedded in the solver) on the one side (Fig. 4) and the full FEM model and a FEM/MTLN hybridized model on the other side (Fig. 5). FDTD and FEM models have a 0.5 cm cell-size and a 1.5 cm cell-size meshes respectively. Fig. 4 clearly shows a shift in time on the FDTD solution due to FDTD numerical dispersion. Fig. 5 shows that the hybridization technique using FEM provides almost the same results as the FEM full reference results. The slight amplitude difference is due to the fact that the hybridization used here did not account for the reaction of the wire current on the field (the FTL approximation which does not reproduce EM radiation phenomenon).

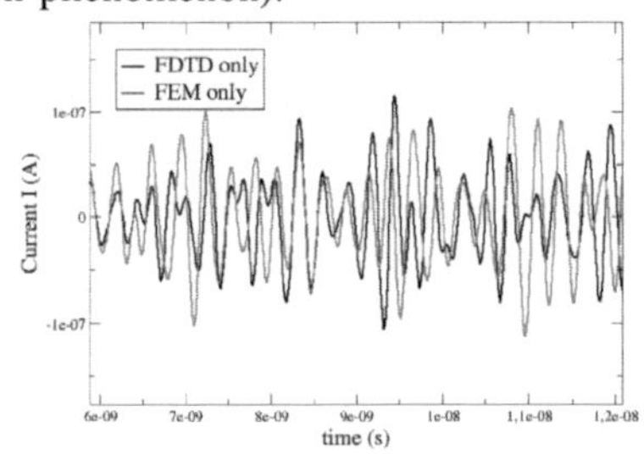

Fig. 4. Current obtained in the middle of the wire by full FDTD and FEM methods.

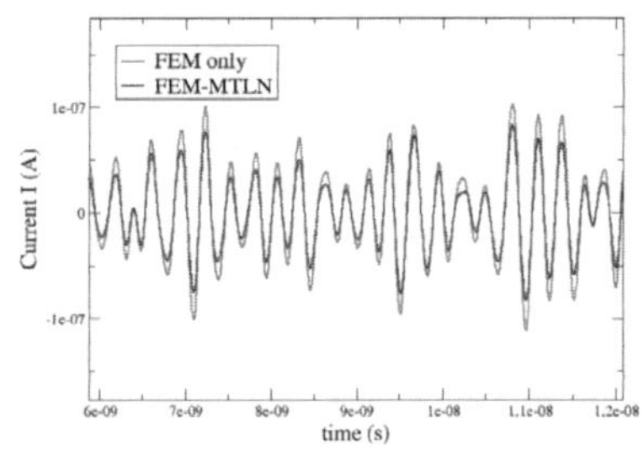

Fig. 5. Current obtained in the middle of the wire by full FEM method and the hybridization of MTLN with FEM method.

References

[1] N. Deymier, T. Volpert, X. Ferrieres, V. Mouysset, B. Pecqueux, "New High order FDTD method to solve EMC problem", Advanced Electromagnetics, vol.4, No.2, october 2015.

[2] N. Muot, C. Girard, X. Ferrieres and E. Bachelier, "A combined FDTD/TLM time domain method to solve efficiently electromagnetic problems", PIERS B, vol.56, 409-427, 2013.

[3] D. Thiel, J. Lu, "EMC Computer Modeling and Simulation Techniques", ACES Conference Paper, 2006 – Applied CEM for EMC Applications.

Lightning Performance of Overhead Distribution Lines with Underbuilt Ground Wires

R. Araneo, S. Celozzi
DIAEE - Electrical Engineering Division
University of Rome "La Sapienza"
Via Eudossiana 18, 00184 Rome, Italy
rodolfo.araneo@uniroma1.it

J. Brandão Faria
Instituto de Telecomunicações
Instituto Superior Técnico
Universidade de Lisboa, Lisboa, Portugal
brandao.faria@tecnico.ulisboa.pt

A. Andreotti, L. Verolino
Electrical Engineering Department
University Federico II of Napoli
Napoli 80125, Italy
andreot@unina.it

***Abstract*—We investigate the improvement of the lightning performance of overhead distribution lines by additional ground wires placed beneath phase conductors. We adopt a time-domain method based on the matrix formalism of multiconductor (MTL) transmission lines that allows for the computation of overvoltages across insulator strings, when direct lightning hits a tower or a ground wire.**

I. Introduction

Ground wires are generally used to protect power lines against lightning [1], [2]. Their function is to intercept lightning strokes with currents that can produce overvoltages larger than the so-called critical flashover overvoltage (CFO). HV lines have ground wires that are usually grounded at every tower. Meanwhile, there are many possible reasons for sectionalizing the ground wires at certain points [3]–[5]. Indeed, in case of direct stroke, the lightning currents should not be allowed to travel too much along the line, because they may increase the chances of back-flashover for the conductors insulators. It has been shown in the literature [6] that additional underbuilt ground wires can improve the lightning performance of HV lines. In medium voltage (MV) lines, the beneficial role played by the ground wires in reducing voltages due to indirect lightning is widely recognized [7]. Oppositely, when dealing with direct lightning, their usefulness is still under debate.

It was thought that the lightning performance of MV lines against direct strokes could not be improved by the use of ground wires as the ground potential rise (GPR) generally causes overvoltages on the insulator strings larger than the CFO. However, in the recent years it is progressively consolidating the idea that by using continuously grounded ground wires (e.g., grounded at every tower) it is possible to improve the performance of MV overhead lines also against direct hits [8].

In this paper we propose a time-domain (TD) approach [9] to assess the role of additional underbuilt ground wires. A particular attention is focused on overvoltages that appear when a ground wire is hit.

II. The Problem and its Numerical Solution

The overhead power line is constituted of N_p phase conductors and N_g ground wires, that can be placed above and/or below the phase conductors (see Fig. 1). The line is assumed of length L and the tower-to-tower span distance is assumed to be ℓ. The ground wires are assumed to be grounded at each tower by a constant ground admittance G.

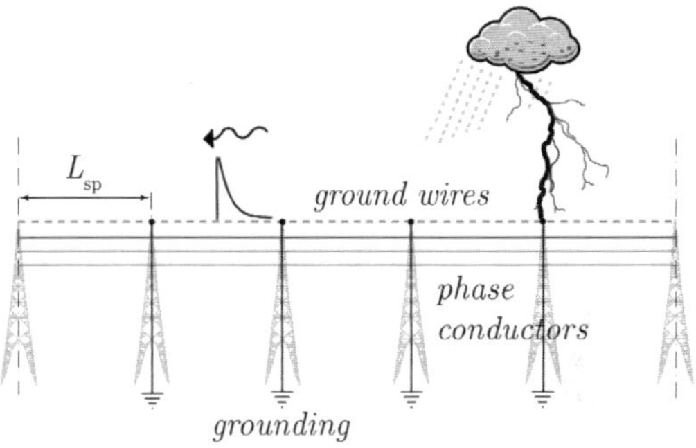

Fig. 1. Longitudinal view of the reference line.

We assume that lightning hits directly the ground wire at the tower position, and we compute the overvoltages across the insulators strings under the hypothesis that there is no back-flashover of the insulation.

In this paper we mainly follow the numerical approach developed in [9] for high-voltage (HV) lines, with some main novelties: (*i*) here we study how to improve the lightning performance of MV distribution lines with additional underbuilt ground wires; (*ii*) usually the classical configurations of MV distribution lines require two ground wires, one above and one below the phase conductors; (*iii*) parametric analyses are conducted on the position of the ground wires to search for the existence of optimum configurations.

The numerical approach consists in segmenting the overhead line into uniform sections of length equal to the tower-to-tower span distance ℓ and applying the MTL approach under the quasi-TEM approximation [9, eq.1] in the frequency domain to compute the chain matrix $\mathbf{T}$ and the characteristic impedance $\mathbf{Z}_\mathrm{c}$ of the single uniform section, from which the transmission propagation along the line can be successively computed. The time domain waveforms are finally obtained through the Inverse Fourier Transform (IFT).

Using the classical chain matrix notation and distinguishing between the N_p phase conductors and N_g ground wires, it is possibile to define a chain matrix of the uniform MTL

$$\mathbf{T} = \begin{bmatrix} \mathbf{A}_{\mathrm{pp}} & \mathbf{A}_{\mathrm{pg}} & \mathbf{B}_{\mathrm{pp}} & \mathbf{B}_{\mathrm{pg}} \\ \mathbf{A}_{\mathrm{gp}} & \mathbf{A}_{\mathrm{gg}} & \mathbf{B}_{\mathrm{gp}} & \mathbf{B}_{\mathrm{gg}} \\ \mathbf{C}_{\mathrm{pp}} & \mathbf{C}_{\mathrm{pg}} & \mathbf{D}_{\mathrm{pp}} & \mathbf{D}_{\mathrm{pg}} \\ \mathbf{C}_{\mathrm{gp}} & \mathbf{C}_{\mathrm{gg}} & \mathbf{D}_{\mathrm{gp}} & \mathbf{D}_{\mathrm{gg}} \end{bmatrix}, \tag{1}$$

and a chain matrix $\mathbf{T}_{\mathrm{G}}$ of the grounding connection [10]

$$\mathbf{T}_{\mathrm{G}} = \begin{bmatrix} \mathbf{1}_{\mathrm{pp}} & 0 & 0 & 0 \\ 0 & \mathbf{1}_{\mathrm{gg}} & 0 & 0 \\ 0 & 0 & \mathbf{1}_{\mathrm{pp}} & 0 \\ 0 & \mathbf{G}_{\mathrm{gg}} & 0 & \mathbf{1}_{\mathrm{gg}} \end{bmatrix}. \tag{2}$$

Cascading the two chain matrices, we can obtain the final chain matrix $\mathbf{T}_{\mathrm{FIN}}$ of the single uniform section as

$$\begin{bmatrix} \mathbf{V}_1^{\mathrm{p}} \\ \mathbf{V}_1^{\mathrm{g}} \\ \mathbf{I}_1^{\mathrm{p}} \\ \mathbf{I}_1^{\mathrm{g}} \end{bmatrix} = \underbrace{\mathbf{T}\mathbf{T}_{\mathrm{G}}}_{\mathbf{T}_{\mathrm{FIN}}} \begin{bmatrix} \mathbf{V}_2^{\mathrm{p}} \\ \mathbf{V}_2^{\mathrm{g}} \\ \mathbf{I}_2^{\mathrm{p}} \\ \mathbf{I}_2^{\mathrm{g}} \end{bmatrix}, \tag{3}$$

from which it is possible to study the propagation properties along the phase conductors and the ground wires.

In order to assess the performance of the line without any reflection effect, we assume that it is closed on the characteristic impedance $\mathbf{Z}_{\mathrm{c}}$ at both ends. For nonsymmetrical MTLs, it has been shown that it is necessary to solve the complete eigenvalue problem of order $2N_{\mathrm{w}}$:

$$\begin{bmatrix} \mathbf{M}_{11} & \mathbf{M}_{12} \\ \mathbf{M}_{21} & \mathbf{M}_{22} \end{bmatrix}^{-1} \begin{bmatrix} \mathbf{A} & \mathbf{B} \\ \mathbf{C} & \mathbf{D} \end{bmatrix} \begin{bmatrix} \mathbf{M}_{11} & \mathbf{M}_{12} \\ \mathbf{M}_{21} & \mathbf{M}_{22} \end{bmatrix} = \begin{bmatrix} e^{+\gamma l} & \\ & e^{-\gamma l} \end{bmatrix} \tag{4}$$

obtaining the backward $\mathbf{Z}_B$ and the forward $\mathbf{Y}_F$ through

$$\mathbf{Z}_B = -\mathbf{M}_{12}\mathbf{M}_{22}^{-1}, \ \mathbf{Y}_F = +\mathbf{M}_{21}\mathbf{M}_{11}^{-1}. \tag{5}$$

The proposed approach is applied to evaluate the lightning performance of the classical MV Italian distribution line reported in Fig. 2: the three-phase conductors (number #1, #2 and #3) can be shielded by introducing two ground wires (number #g1 and #g2, respectively) placed with an x offset with respect to the vertical axis and y with respect to the outer phase conductors. The distance ℓ between adjacent towers is assumed to be equal to 100 m. Fig. 3(a) and 3(b) show the trend of the peak value of overvoltages across insulator strings on conductor $\#1$ and $\#2$, respectively, at the tower subject to the direct strike (red line) and at a distance equal to 5ℓ (blue line) with respect to the distance y (with $x = 0.45$ m), with ground line $\#g1$ (dotted line) and both ground lines $\#g1$ and $\#g2$ (solid line). It is interesting to note that overvoltages produced on the phase conductors are deeply reduced by adding the underbuilt ground wire.

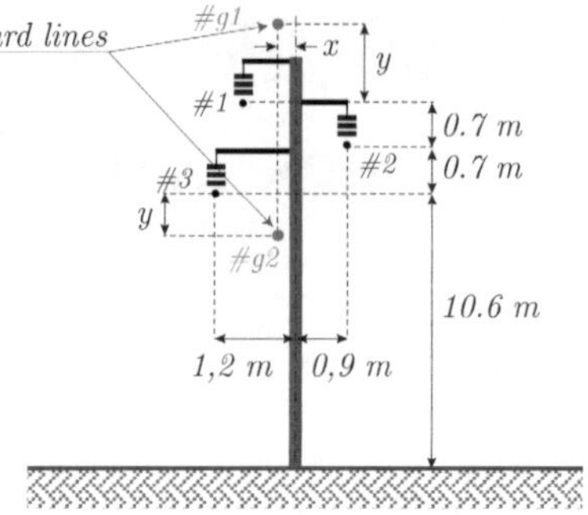

Fig. 2. MV Italian power configuration considered for the analysis.

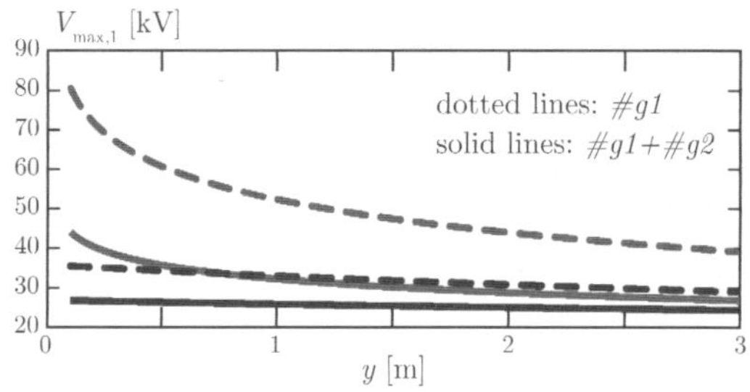

(a) Conductor #1

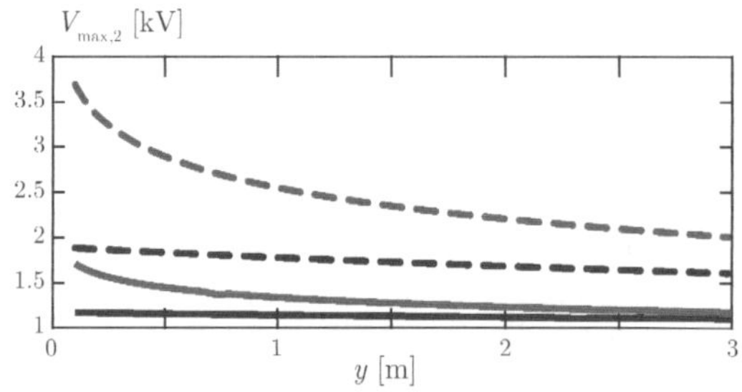

(b) Conductor #2

Fig. 3. Peak-value of overvoltages across insulator strings at the tower subject to the direct strike (red line) and at a distance equal to 5ℓ (blu line).

REFERENCES

[1] A. Andreotti, A. Pierno, and V. A. Rakov, "An analytical approach to calculation of lightning induced voltages on overhead lines in case of lossy ground - Part I: Model development," *IEEE Trans. Power Del.*, vol. 28, no. 2, pp. 1213–1223, Apr. 2013.

[2] ——, "An analytical approach to calculation of lightning induced voltages on overhead lines in case of lossy ground - Part II: Comparison with other models," *IEEE Trans. Power Del.*, vol. 28, no. 2, pp. 1224–1230, Apr. 2013.

[3] R. Araneo, J. A. Brandão Faria, and S. Celozzi, "Frequency-domain analysis of sectionalized shield wires on PLC transmission over high-voltage lines," *IEEE Trans. Electromagn. Compat.*, no. 99, pp. 1–9, 2016.

[4] J. A. Brandão Faria and R. Araneo, "Computation, properties and realizability of the characteristic immittance matrices of nonuniform multiconductor transmission lines," *IEEE Trans. Power Del.*, pp. 1–10, 2018.

[5] R. Araneo, S. Celozzi, and J. A. Brandão Faria, "Direct TD analysis of PLC channels in HV transmission lines with sectionalized shield wires," in *16th Int. Conf. Environ. and Electr. Eng.*, Jun. 2016, pp. 1–4.

[6] S. Visacro, F. H. Silveira, and A. D. Conti, "The use of underbuilt wires to improve the lightning performance of transmission lines," *IEEE Trans. Power Del.*, vol. 27, no. 1, pp. 205–213, Jan. 2012.

[7] A. Piantini, "Lightning-induced voltages on distribution lines with shield wires," in *2016 33rd International Conference on Lightning Protection (ICLP)*, Sep. 2016, pp. 1–5.

[8] M. Brignone, D. Mestriner, R. Procopio, A. Piantini, and F. Rachidi, "Evaluation of the mitigation effect of the shield wires on lightning induced overvoltages in mv distribution systems using statistical analysis," *IEEE Trans. Electromagn. Compat.*, vol. 60, no. 5, pp. 1400–1408, Oct. 2018.

[9] R. Araneo, G. Lovat, S. Celozzi, J. B. Faria, A. Andreotti, and L. Verolino, "Improvement of lightning performance of overhead power lines by addition of underbuilt ground wires," in *18th Int. Conf. Environ. and Electr. Eng. and 2nd Ind. and Com. Power Systems Europe*, June 2018, pp. 1–5.

[10] A. Andreotti, D. Assante, and L. Verolino, "Characteristic impedance of periodically grounded lossless multiconductor transmission lines and time-domain equivalent representation," *IEEE Trans. Electromagn. Compat.*, vol. 56, no. 1, pp. 221–230, Feb. 2014.

Improved Heating Uniformity of a 3-kWatt 2.45GHz Microwave Dryer Using Multiple Multi-Slotted Waveguides

S.-H. Ahn, C.-H. Jeong, D.-G. Seo, and W.-S. Lee*
Dept.of Elect. Eng./Eng. Res. Inst. (ERI)
Gyeongsang National University
52828 Jinju-si, Gyeongnam, Republic of Korea
*wsang@gnu.ac.kr

***Abstract*—For improving heating uniformity we propose a 3-kWatt 2.45GHz microwave dryer using multiple multi-slotted waveguides with the horizontal and vertical array slots. Microwave source of each 2.45GHz magnetron is controlled to improve heating uniformity. The proposed dryer consists of two waveguide with the horizontal slots and one waveguide with the vertical slots. The input power was optimized for improved uniformity of temperature. The optimized power applied to each waveguide. Compared with the conventional microwave dryer, the proposed microwave dryer has improved the heating uniformity up to approximately 55%.**

Keywords—Array slots, controlling the power, heating uniformity, microwave dryer, slotted waveguide.

I. Introduction

Microwave dryer is becoming increasingly popular for cooking and reheating foods in homes as well as hospitals, restaurants, etc. Before microwave drying, natural drying and hot air drying were mainly used. But these are characteristic of natural drying has little damage to the product, but takes a long time and is susceptible to contamination [1]. Microwave drying has the advantages over the natural drying and hot air drying. Microwave drying can apply thermal energy to the outside of the material to minimize damage to the product and reduce bacteria and air pollution with fast drying time. However, the microwave dryers still require further improvement in their performance [2], [3]. Microwave heating has non-uniformity temperatures in the drying chamber. To reduce these non-uniformity, various studies are underway to improve the combination of various drying methods [4], [5]. To solve this non-uniform microwave heating, we use a turntable or a microwave source and a hybrid dryer of various frequencies. However, these require additional components. Recently, the studies using slotted waveguide without additional components are underway. There are proposed methods for improving the internal heating uniformity by using a waveguide in which slots are arranged in the microwave dryer [6], [7].

This work was supported by the National Research Foundation of Korea (NRF) grant funded by the Korea government (MSIT) (NO.2019R1C1C1008102) and by the Human Resources Program and the Industrial Technology Innovation Program in Energy Technology of the Korea Institute of Energy Technology of the Korea Institute of Energy Technology Evaluation and Planning funded by the Ministry of Trade, Industry and Energy, under Grant 20174030201440 and 20192010106020 respectively.

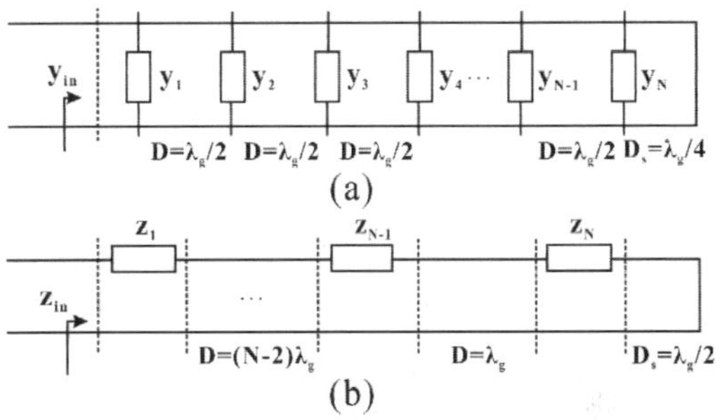

Fig. 1. Equivalent transmission line circuit of: (a) horizontally polarized, and (b) vertically polarized resonant slotted waveguide.

In this paper, we propose the microwave dryer with multiple slotted waveguides consisting of horizontal and vertical array slots and the power-controlling method that improve the heating uniformity of the material.

II. Proposed Dryer with Slotted Waveguides

When a microwave source is applied to a waveguide through a magnetron, the slots interrupt the currents flow, which causes the electric field from the slots. The radiation of electric field is determined by the resonance of the slot and the interference of the current. When the length of slot is half-wavelength (l = 61mm in 2.45 GHz), the resonance of a slot occurs. When resonance occurs, the linearly polarized electric field is radiated from the slots.

In general, the slotted waveguide consists of the horizontal or vertical slots. The slotted waveguide is divided in resonant and non-resonant type. The array slots have a constant spacing according to the current flow. Fig. 1 is equivalent transmission line circuit of the resonant type slotted waveguide consisting of the horizontal and vertical array slots. In the resonant slot arrays, the susceptance component of the admittance of the elements is zero and the phases of the elements are same. For resonated admittance at the used frequency and phase equalization, the horizontal slots are arranged at intervals of $\lambda_g/2$, and the vertical slots are arranged at the intervals of λ_g so that the phases become the same. In order to improve the heating uniformity of the heating material in the microwave chamber using such slotted waveguide, the microwave dryer using multiple slotted waveguide consisting of the array slots are proposed.

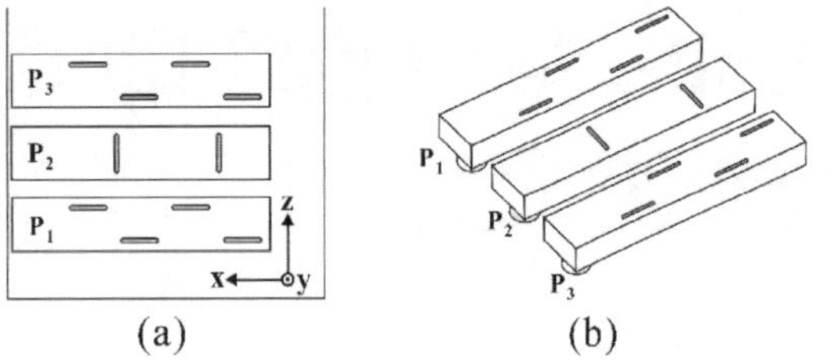

Fig. 2. Configuration of the proposed dryer consisting of array slots: (a) distribution of slots in chamber, and (b) distribution of slots in the waveguide.

The proposed microwave dryer using multiple slotted waveguide and the power-control method. Fig. 2 shows the configuration of array slots in the dryer. The slots in the odd waveguides be arranged horizontally and the slots in even waveguide be arranged vertically. When the slot resonates, the horizontal and vertical slot arrays radiate the electric field in the same direction slots. In the waveguide, the phase difference exists between the horizontal and vertical slots. From the relative phase difference of the slots, the electric fields in the horizontal and vertical directions are sequentially radiated to the microwave chamber. However, when the input power is simultaneously applied to the waveguide, the temperature have different peak magnitudes in each case. Therefore, to equalize the peak magnitudes, we adjust the input power. When the input power of 250W is applied to the odd waveguide and the power of 1kW is applied to the even waveguide, the peak magnitude of the temperature becomes equal. Accordingly, the heating uniformity can be improved.

III. Result and Discussion

To verify the heating uniformity of the proposed microwave dryer, we designed the proposed microwave dryer consisting of the multi-slotted waveguides having horizontal and vertical slot arrays. Fig. 3 shows the geometry of the conventional and proposed microwave dryer. The waveguide was designed as WR-340, and the water was used as a general material. The size of WR-340 is w_{wg} = 86.36mm, l_{wg} = 43.18mm, and h_{wg} = 141mm. The total microwave signal power is 1.5kW on each dryer.

We use a high frequency time solver analysis method of CST Microwave Studio 2018 for performing thermal analysis of the each dryer. Figs. 4 (a)-(c) show the theoretical analysis results of conventional dryer, the proposed dryer with same power, and the proposed dryer using power control respectively. Table I shows the number of waveguides, the input power, maximum, minimum and

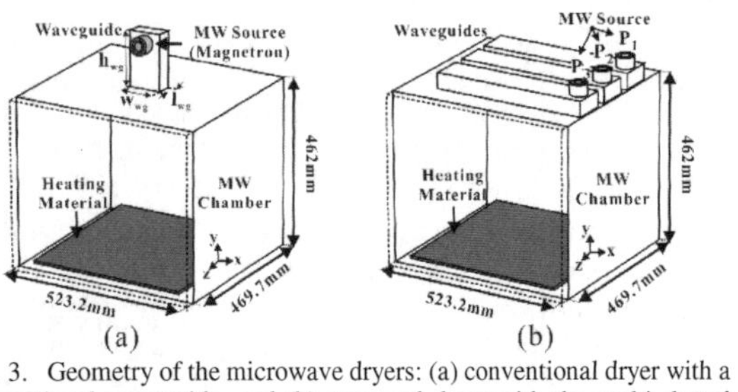

Fig. 3. Geometry of the microwave dryers: (a) conventional dryer with a conventional waveguide, and (b) proposed dryer with the multi-slotted waveguides.

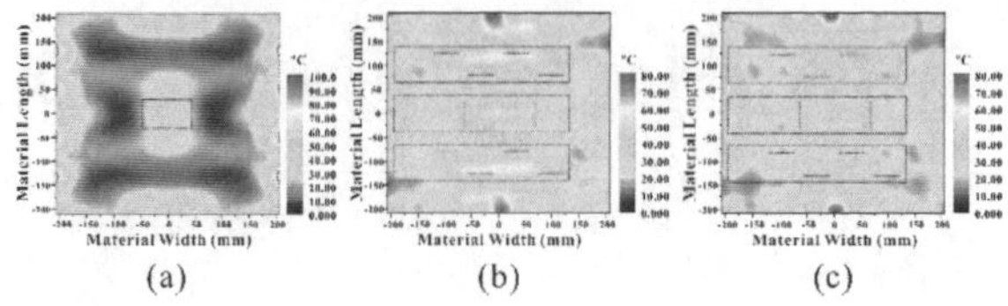

Fig. 4. Result of the analysis of the temperature on the material according to the structure and power difference: (a) conventional dryer, (b) proposed dryer applying same power, and (c) proposed dryer using the power control.

average temperature, and ratio on the material. The ratio of temperature in three cases are gradually improved.

TABLE I. Comparison of Temperature of Each Dryer

Characteristics	Conv'l Dryer	Prop. Dryer	
		Same Power	*Power Control*
Num. of Wg.(EA)	1	3	3
Power (kWatt)	1.5	All Port : 0.5	P_1 & P_3 :0.25, P_2 : 1
Min. Temp. (°C)	7.02	9.3	11.1
Max. Temp. (°C)	112	79.8	80.26
Avg. Temp. (°C)	26.29	33.85	30.08
Ratio Max./Min.	15.95	8.58	7.23

IV. Conclusion

In this paper, we proposed the microwave dryer that can improve the heating uniformity using the slotted waveguides and the power-controlling method. The intersecting direction electric fields are sequentially applied to the chamber according to the phase difference of the slots, thereby increasing the overall internal heating uniformity. Compared with the conventional dryer, the proposed dryer is improved maximum approximately 55% by the power control. By using a power control method and the slotted waveguides, the temperature uniformity in the microwave dryer can be improved without additional components.

References

[1] J. M. Osepchuk, "A history of microwave heating applications," IEEE Trans. Microw. Theory Techn., vol. 32, no. 9, pp. 1200-1224, Sep. 1984.

[2] S. Mishin, M. Gutkin, A. Bizyukov, and V. Sleptsov, "Improving frequency control of temperature compensated surface acoustic wave devices," European Frequency and Time Forum & International Frequency Control Symposium (EFTF/IFC) 2013 Joint, pp. 111-113, 2013.

[3] Z. Y. Li, R. E. Wang, and T. Kudra, "Uniformity issue in microwave drying," Drying Tech., vol. 29, no. 6, pp. 652-660, Apr. 2011.

[4] W. S. Che and J. Ma, "The study on the uniform drying of microwave heating system with multiple waveguides," Applied Mechanics and Materials, vol. 329, pp. 219-223, 2013.

[5] S. Bae, M. Jeong, J. Kim, and W. Lee, "A continuous power-controlled microwave belt drier improving heating uniformity," IEEE Microwave and Wireless Components Letters, vol. 27, no. 5, pp. 527-529, May 2017.

[6] E. D. Tortajada, P.-P. Gonzalez, A. B.-D. Morcile, and J. V. Ballbastre, "Optimisation of electric field uniformity in microwave heating systems by means of multi-feeding and genetic algorithms," International Journal of Materials and Product Technologhy, Jan. 2007.

[7] M. Razmhosseini and R. G. Vaughan, "Impedance bandwidth of a slotted waveguide array: Impact of waveguide length and element shape," 2017 IEEE International Symposium on Antennas and Propagation & USNC/URSI National Radio Science Meeting, pp. 1587-1588, 2017.

Time-domain development of negative refraction

Timothy J. Garner
Radio Frequency Communications Division
US Army CERDEC
Aberdeen Proving Ground, MD, USA

Distribution A: Approved for Public Release

***Abstract*—Negative refraction in prisms built of periodic unit cells is a steady-state phenomenon that requires a finite amount time to develop. A signal transmitted through such a prism will initially be refracted positively. As time increases, the direction of refraction shifts toward the steady state angle of refraction. Signals that are shorter than the time required to reach steady state are not negatively refracted.**

***Index Terms*—negative refraction, finite-difference time-domain method, periodic structures, metamaterials**

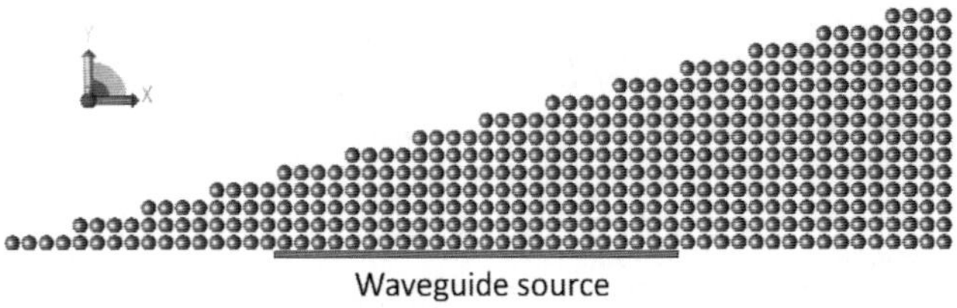

Fig. 1. Prism and waveguide source.

I. Introduction

Negative refraction has been observed in prisms made of periodic structures both experimentally and in numerical computations [1], [2]. In such circumstances, negative refraction may be predicted from a consideration of the array factor of the aperture radiators sitting upon the stairs of the hypotenuse [3]. Each such stair-step upon the hypotenuse is preceded in the y-direction by a column of unit cells that increase in number as we proceed up the staircase. A progressive phase is thus prescribed, and the prism constitutes a scanning array, which will occasionally achieve scan angles consistent with negative refraction. However, because of the relative delays through the unit cells, several cycles of the carrier wave must be transmitted through the prism before negative refraction develops. In this presentation, we use the finite-difference time-domain (FDTD) method [4] to explore the development of negative refraction by examining the electric field transmitted through a metamaterial prism at several instants of time.

II. Methods

We computed the electromagnetic fields transmitted through a prism constructed of cubic unit cells based on that shown by Liu and Alu [2]. Each unit cell contained a magneto-dielectric sphere of radius $r = 0.45d$, where d is the edge length of the unit cell. The prism was illuminated by a transverse-electromagnetic waveguide source, as shown in Fig. 1. The electric field was polarized in the z direction.

We used XFdtd, a commercial implementation of the FDTD method, to compute the time-domain electromagnetic fields transmitted through a metamaterial prism. We used a mesh grid with 15 cells per carrier wavelength. In all simulations, the carrier frequency f_c was chosen such that $k_0d = 0.7$. The time-step length in the simulations was $t_s = 1/(351.2f_c)$. At the carrier frequency, the excess time delay through each unit cell was $t_d = 248.1t_s$. The excess phase delay through each unit cell at the carrier frequency was $254.4°$

III. Results

Figure 2 shows the electric fields transmitted through the metamaterial prism. The incident signal is a ramped sinusoid with frequency chosen such that $k_0d = 0.7$, where k_0 is the free-space wave number. At this frequency, the prism refracts negatively, but only after the fields have reached a steady state. When $t = 2 \times 10^3 t_s$, the transmitted electric fields propagate in a direction consistent with positive refraction, as shown in Fig. 2a. Figures 2b–d show the electric fields at $t = 4 \times 10^3 t_s$, $t = 6 \times 10^3 t_s$, and $t = 8 \times 10^3 t_s$. As the time increases, the transmitted beam shifts toward a direction consistent with negative refraction. By $t = 8 \times 10^3 t_s$, the transmitted beam propagates in its final direction, as shown in Fig. 2d. It therefore takes approximately twenty cycles of the sinusoid before the transmitted signal is negatively refracted. Figures 2e and f show the electric field at $t = 10^4 t_s$ and $t = 2 \times 10^4 t_s$, respectively. These final two panels show the electric field as it reaches a steady state.

Figures 3 and 4 show the time-domain electric fields of a modulated Gaussian signal transmitted through the prism at various instants of time. The carrier frequency in both Figs. 3 and 4 is such that $k0d = 0.7$. The width w of the modulated Gaussian signal is the length of time that the Gaussian function is greater than 2% of its maximum. In Fig. 3, $w = 5/f_c$, and in Fig. 4, $w = 2/f_c$. As with the ramped sinusoid, the modulated Gaussian signal in Fig. 3 initially propagates in a direction consistent with positive refraction. As time increases, the direction of transmission shifts toward a negatively refracted direction before dying out. Because of the shorter duration of the incident signal in Fig. 4, the transmitted signal largely dies out before it can shift to the negative refraction direction.

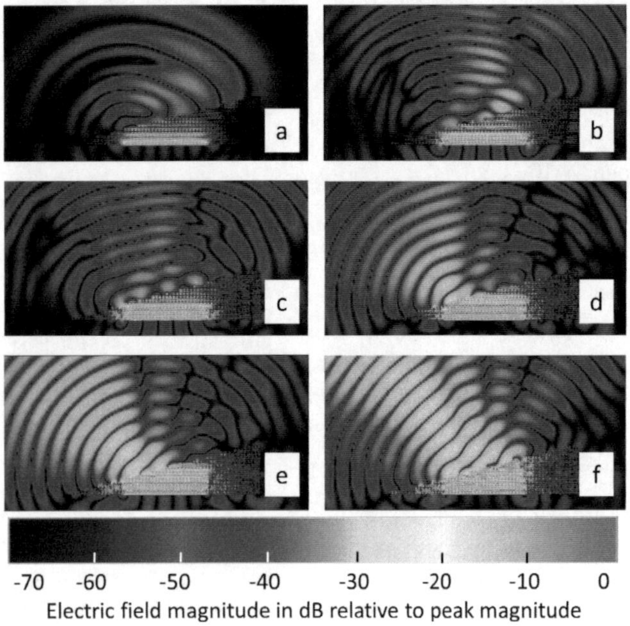

Fig. 2. Normalized, time-domain electric fields transmitted through prism. The input signal is a ramped sinusoid with frequency such that $k_0 d = 0.7$. Each panel shows the electric fields at a different times. a) $t = 2 \times 10^3 t_s$, b) $t = 4 \times 10^3 t_s$, c) $t = 6 \times 10^3 t_s$, d) $t = 8 \times 10^3 t_s$, e) $t = 10^4 t_s$, f) $t = 2 \times 10^4 t_s$.

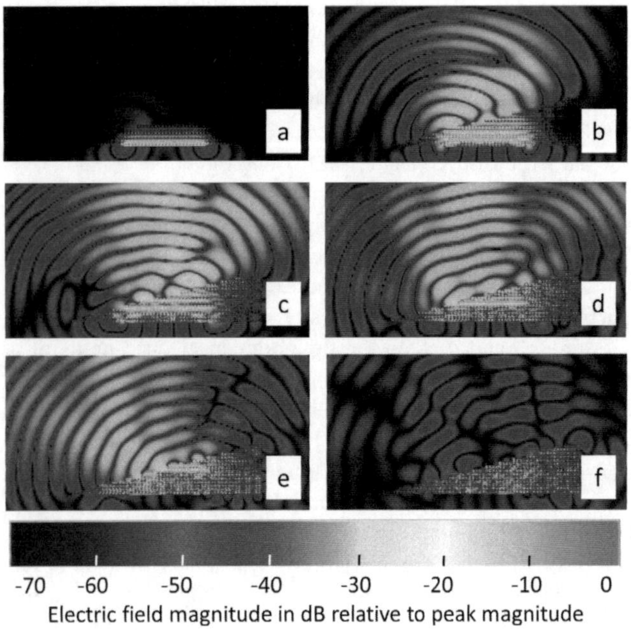

Fig. 3. Same as Fig. 2 but with a modulated-Gaussian input signal with carrier frequency f_c such that $k_0 d = 0.7$ and width $w = 5/f_c$.

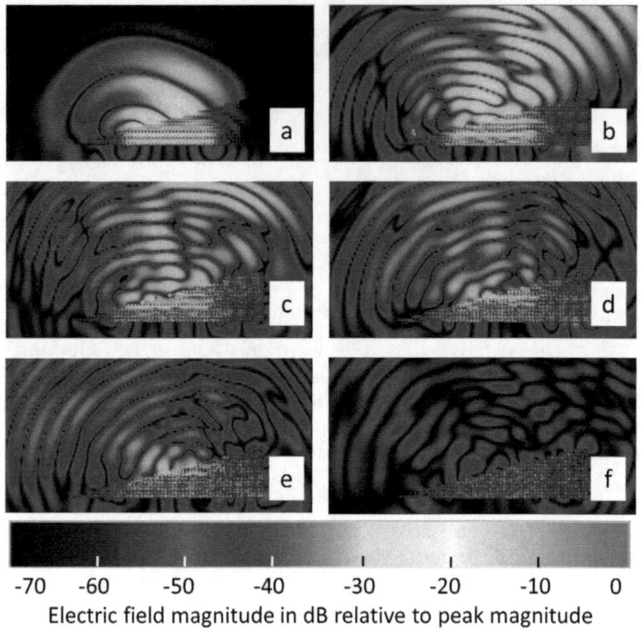

Fig. 4. Same as Fig. 2 but with a modulated-Gaussian input signal with carrier frequency f_c such that $k_0 d = 0.7$ and width $w = 2/f_c$.

IV. Concluding Remarks

Negative refraction through a prism comprised of a periodic structure is a steady-state phenomenon that takes several cycles of the carrier wave to develop. A signal that is too short will not negatively refract, even if a time-harmonic signal at its carrier frequency would be negatively refracted. This has been demonstrated for a modulated Gaussian signal with a width equal to two periods of its carrier wave. The time required for negative refraction to develop is large relative to the time it takes for the signal to initially emerge from the prism. It is apparent that during the start-up time that radiation will occur in unintended directions.

Further research may determine the implications for digitally modulated signals transmitted through materials that refract negatively. If the symbol duration is too short, the transmitted signal may be distorted enough that information cannot be recovered from the signal.

References

[1] R. A. Shelby, D. R. Smith, and S. Schultz, "Experimental verification of a negative index of refraction," *Science*, vol. 292, pp. 77–79, Apr. 2001.

[2] X. X. Lui and A. Alu, "Homogenization of quasi-isotropic metamaterials composed by dense arrays of magnetodielectric spheres," *Metamaterials*, vol. 5, pp. 56–63, June 2011.

[3] G. A. Talalai, T. J. Garner, and S. J. Weiss, "Explaining negative refraction without negative indices," *JOSA A*, vol. 35, pp. 437–441, Feb. 2018.

[4] A. Taflove and S. C. Hagness, *Computational Electrodynamics: The Finite-Difference Time-Domain Method*, Artech House: Boston, 2005.

Improved Efficiency and Accuracy Using Duality in Hybrid SIBC-BEM Formulation

Aldo Canova
Department of Energy
Politecnico di Torino
Torino, Italy
aldo.canova@polito.it

Fabio Freschi
Department of Energy
Politecnico di Torino
Torino, Italy
fabio.freschi@polito.it

Luca Giaccone
Department of Energy
Politecnico di Torino
Torino, Italy
luca.giaccone@polito.it

Maurizio Repetto
Department of Energy
Politecnico di Torino
Torino, Italy
maurizio.repetto@polito.it

***Abstract*—The paper presents a hybrid formulation coupling the surface impedance boundary condition, to deal with conductive and magnetic materials, and the boundary element method to account rigorously for the regularity conditions of the magnetic field at infinity. Based on duality relations, the field variables are associated to spatial elements starting from the dual mesh, overcoming some of the performance issues of the previously published results. The new formulation is suitable to be used to study wireless power transfer devices for automotive applications.**

***Index Terms*—Boundary element method, duality, hybrid formulation, surface impedance boundary condition, wireless power transfer.**

I. Introduction

In the last decade, the development of wireless power transmission devices increased the challenges of electromagnetic simulations. In particular, when high power is required, for example for automotive applications [1], the electromagnetic structure present many peculiar characteristics that do not fit with standard simulation tools:

- the frequency range involves low-medium frequencies, up to 100 kHz, due to the availability of suitable power electronics;
- the domain under study is characterised by open boundaries, whereas the active structures have limited extension;
- the thickness of active structures like car bodies is much smaller than other dimensions (order of millimetres compared with meters);
- the penetration depth is much smaller than the thickness.

For these reasons, ad-hoc formulations are required to efficiently and effectively solve such problems. In papers [2], [3] the possibility of coupling nonlinear surface impedance boundary conditions (SIBC) [4] with the boundary element method (BEM) was presented. The BEM-SIBC hybrid formulation was based on the definition of integral variables over two intertwined surface meshes, namely primal and dual meshes, linked by duality relations. This particular choice gave rise to a lumped circuit network of admittances in the conductive domain which was coupled with the boundary element formulated in terms of reduced scalar potential and its normal derivative. The method showed the benefits of the two formulations: the SIBC allowed the use of analytical or semi-analytical solution of the electromagnetic field in thin conductive layers [5], also in case of nonlinear material, while the BEM rigorously accounted for the regularity conditions of the magnetic field at infinity. The original method had two main drawbacks: unknowns were associated to the faces of the surface mesh, giving rise to very large simulations also for limited structures. In addition SIBC equations were defined in terms of the admittance matrix $\mathbf{Y}$, that required a direct LU factorisation in order to obtain the impedance matrix $\mathbf{Z}$ necessary for the solution of the final system. The aim of this paper is to overcome these limitations by swapping the variable association between the primal and dual mesh, using nodal unknowns and building the matrix $\mathbf{Z}$ directly on the dual mesh.

II. Dual SIBC-BEM

The domain under study is constituted by conductive regions, where eddy currents occur, external sources and external open space. It is assumed that the combination of the material properties and the source frequency is such that the penetration depth δ can be considered small with respect to the conductive region dimension. Under this hypothesis, it is possible to discretise only the surface of the domain by an unstructured mesh, referred to as simplicial mesh. Starting from this mesh, a second based on barycentric subdivision is derived. This second discretisation is referred to as barycentric mesh.

The magnetic scalar potential ψ and its normal derivative $\partial_n\psi$, the magneto-motive force and the electric current are defined on the nodes, edges and faces of the simplicial mesh. The electric voltages e and the magnetic fluxes b are associated to the edges and the faces of the barycentric mesh, Fig. 1. In terms of matrix operators, Faraday's law reads $\tilde{\mathbf{C}}\mathbf{e} = \mathrm{j}\omega\mathbf{b}$ where, in 2-dimensional discretisation, the discrete curl operator $\tilde{\mathbf{C}}$ is the incidence matrix linking the barycentric faces (in blue in Fig. 1) to their bounding edges. The Ampère's equation reads $\mathbf{h} = \mathbf{i}$. The constitutive equation links the voltages to the currents. The electric voltage can be calculated by integration of the electric field along dual edges:

$$e'_j = \int_{\tilde{L}_j} \vec{E}_0 \cdot \vec{t}\mathrm{d}L = \int_{\tilde{L}_j} \frac{1}{\sigma}\vec{J}_0 \cdot \vec{t}\mathrm{d}L, \qquad (1)$$

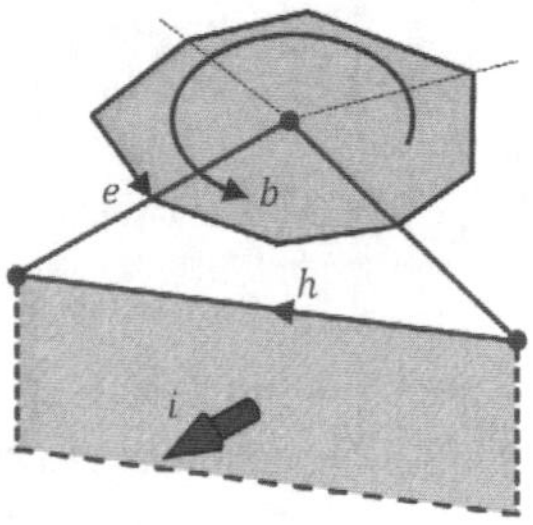

Fig. 1. Definition of variables with dual association.

where $\vec{t}$ is the unit vector tangent to the dual edge. The current density $\vec{J}(z)$ is a function of the depth coordinate z and is expressed as:

$$\vec{J}(z) = \vec{J}_0 f(z) = \vec{J}_0 \exp^{-(1+\mathrm{j})\frac{z}{\delta}}. \quad (2)$$

Expanding the current density using facet elements $\vec{w}_m$, the surface current density becomes:

$$\vec{J}_0 = \frac{\sum_{m=1}^{3} \vec{w}_m i_m}{\int_0^{\infty} f(z)\mathrm{d}z} = \frac{1+\mathrm{j}}{\delta} \sum_{m=1}^{3} \vec{w}_m i_m. \quad (3)$$

Thus, (1) becomes

$$e'_j = \sum_{m=1}^{3} i_m \frac{1+\mathrm{j}}{\sigma\delta} \int_{\tilde{L}_j} \vec{w}_m \cdot \vec{t}\mathrm{d}L = \sum_{m=1}^{3} Z'_{jm} i_m. \quad (4)$$

Assembling element-by-element the impedance matrix $\mathbf{Z}$, the voltage-current relation becomes $\mathbf{e} = \mathbf{Zi}$.

A. Interface Conditions and BEM Formulation

The interface conditions are used to imposed the continuity of the tangential component of the magnetic filed and the normal component of the magnetic flux density. Similarly to the conventional SIBC-BEM formulation, these equations are:

$$\mathbf{h} = -\mathbf{G}\boldsymbol{\psi} + \mathbf{h}_{\mathrm{S}} \quad (5)$$

$$\mathbf{b} = \mu_0 \mathbf{S}(-\partial_n \boldsymbol{\psi} + \mathbf{H}_{\mathrm{S}n}), \quad (6)$$

where $\mathbf{G}$ is the edge-to-node incidence matrix, $\mathbf{S}$ is the area matrix of each barycentric faces. Note that $\tilde{\mathbf{C}} = \mathbf{G}^{\mathrm{T}}$ $\mathbf{H}_{\mathrm{S}n}$ and $\mathbf{h}_{\mathrm{S}}$ are the normal component of the magnetic field on barycentric faces and the magneto-motive force along simplicial edges due to the source currents. Because the scalar potentials and their normal derivative are defined on the nodes of the simplicial mesh, linear elements are used. This requires the use of nodal functions N and the calculation of the integrals of the Green's function $G(\vec{r}_i, \vec{r}_j)$:

$$\{\mathbf{H}\}_{ij} = \delta_{ij}\alpha - \int_{S_j} N_i \frac{\partial G(\vec{r}_i, \vec{r}_j)}{\partial n} \mathrm{d}S \quad (7)$$

$$\{\mathbf{W}\}_{ij} = \int_{S_j} N_i G(\vec{r}_i, \vec{r}_j) \mathrm{d}S. \quad (8)$$

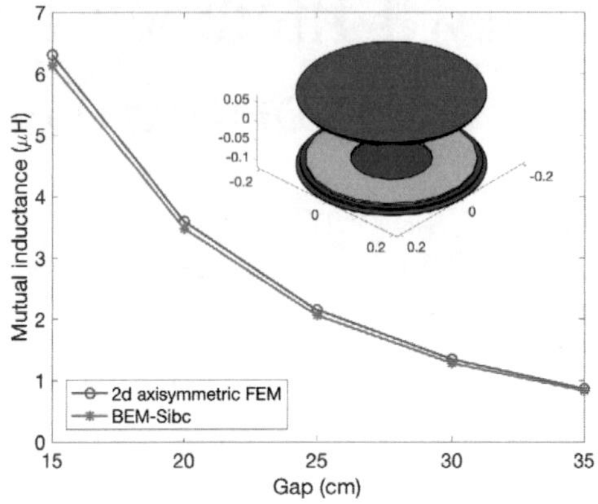

Fig. 2. Mutual inductance at different gaps evaluated with axially symmetric FEM and SIBC-BEM formulation (dimensions of the structure in meters).

The additional burden with respect to the BEM formulation with constant elements is usually negligible when using analytical formulas [6]. The final system, having $\boldsymbol{\psi}$ and $\partial_n\boldsymbol{\psi}$ as unknowns, is:

$$\begin{bmatrix} -\mathbf{H} & \mathbf{W} \\ \mathbf{G}^{\mathrm{T}}\mathbf{Z}\mathbf{G} & \mathrm{j}\omega\mu_0\mathbf{S} \end{bmatrix} \begin{bmatrix} \boldsymbol{\psi} \\ \partial_n\boldsymbol{\psi} \end{bmatrix} = \begin{bmatrix} \mathbf{0} \\ \mathbf{f} \end{bmatrix}, \quad (9)$$

where $\mathbf{f} = \mathbf{G}^{\mathrm{T}}\mathbf{Z}\mathbf{h}_{\mathrm{S}} + \mathrm{j}\omega\mu_0\mathbf{S}\mathbf{H}_{\mathrm{S}n}$.

III. Preliminary Results

The effectiveness of the formulation is compared using the transmission system proposed by IEC [7]. The structure is modified such that an axially symmetric device is obtained, making it possible to compare results with a solution obtained with good accuracy. Fig. 2 shows the comparison of the mutual inductance at different gaps for this structure. Details about the formulation, the convergence issues and the applicability with the presence of the car body will be presented at the conference.

References

[1] V. Cirimele, M. Diana, F. Freschi, and M. Mitolo, "Inductive power transfer for automotive applications: State-of-the-art and future trends," *IEEE Transactions on Industry Applications*, vol. 54, no. 5, pp. 4069–4079, 2018.

[2] V. Cirimele, F. Freschi, L. Giaccone, and M. Repetto, "Finite formulation of surface impedance boundary conditions," *IEEE Transactions on Magnetics*, vol. 52, no. 3, pp. 7 206 504/1–7 206 504/4, 2016.

[3] F. Freschi, L. Giaccone, and M. Repetto, "Algebraic formulation of nonlinear surface impedance boundary condition coupled with bem for unstructured meshes," *Engineering Analysis with Boundary Elements*, vol. 88, pp. 104–114, 2018.

[4] L. Di Rienzo, N. Ida, and S. Yuferev, "Surface impedance boundary conditions of high order of approximation for the finite integration technique," *ACES Journal*, vol. 22, no. 1, pp. 53–59, 2007.

[5] B. Ancelle, A. Nicolas, and J. Sabonnadiere, "A boundary integral equation method for high frequency eddy currents," *IEEE Transactions on Magnetics*, vol. 17, no. 6, pp. 2568–2570, 1981.

[6] R. Graglia, "On the numerical integration of the linear shape functions times the 3-D Green's function or its gradient on a plane triangle," *IEEE Transactions on Antennas and Propagation*, vol. 41, pp. 1448–1455, 1993.

[7] IEC 61980-1, *Electric vehicle wireless power transfer systems (WPT) - Part 1: General requirements*, 1st ed., 2015.

Finite Element Analysis of Starting Performance of Induction Motors with Non-Skewed Asymmetric Rotor Bars

Haisen Zhao, *Senior Member, IEEE*, Chengyang Chu, Yang Zhan, *Member, IEEE,* Guorui Xu, *Member, IEEE*, and Xiaofang Liu

State Key Laboratory of Alternate Electrical Power System with Renewable Energy Sources, North China Electric Power University, Beijing 102206, China

zhaohisen@163.com

Abstract— Non-skewed asymmetric rotor bars can be used to replace the skewed rotors for eliminating the slot harmonic field and weaken the noise and vibration of effectively in cage induction motors. However, due to the complex spatial distribution of rotor bars, the starting performance may be affected by the modulated air-gap flux density. This paper studies the starting performances of a 5.5-kW, 4-pole induction motor, such as the starting current, the starting torque and the maximum torque, by using Finite Element Method (FEM). Prototpes of 5.5 kW induction motor with asymmetric rotor bars are manufactured and experiment validations are also performed.

Key Words—Cage induction motor, non-skewed rotor, starting perforamnce, Finite Element Method (FEM).

I. Introduction

In small and medium cage induction motors, skewed or double-skewed rotor bars are used to weaken the additional torque and noise caused by slot harmonics field. However, the skew may cause higher iron losses and additional loss resulting from inter-bar currents [1]. Asymmetric non-skewed rotor bars based on phase shift effect was proposed to lower the noise and vibration levels of cage induction motor, and the influence of slot combination and spatial position of the rotor bars on the operation performance was studied [2-3]. However, due to the complex special distribution of rotor bars, the starting performance may be affected by the modulated air-gap flux density, therefore, it is necessary to analyze the influence of different asymmetric parameters on the starting performance of induction motors.

This paper studies the starting performance of cage induction motors with non-skewed asymmetric rotor bars by using FEM. The variation of starting current, starting torque and maximum torque with the modulation coefficient and the sine wave coefficient are analyzed. Three prototypes of 5.5-kW induction motor are designed and manufactured, and the starting performances are validated by experiments.

II. Design Method for Induction Motors with Asymmetric Rotor Bars

A. Design Method of Asymmetric Rotor Bars

Sinusoidal modulation of the spatial positions of rotor bar is adopted in this paper as it can make symmetric air-gap field. The sinusoidal modulated positions of rotor slot are given by [3].

$$\theta_n = \theta_{n0} + K\zeta \tag{1}$$

where θ_n is the spatial position of the *n*th rotor slot, θ_{n0} is the spatial position of evenly distributed rotor slots that is given by $\theta_{n0}=2\pi n/Z_2$ (Z_2 is the number of rotor slots), K is the modulation coefficient of spatial position whose value is 0 to 0.03, ζ is the angle obtained by the sinusoidal modulation method. ζ is given by $\zeta=\sin(2\pi n\varepsilon/Z_2)$, where ε is the sine wave coefficient that can be set to 0 to 4. Z is a crucial parameter in the sinusoidal modulation method.

B. Calculation Method of Starting Performance

The transient electromagnetic torque in the process of starting is calculated by the improved Maxwell stress method as follows

$$T_{\mathrm{e}} = \frac{L_{\mathrm{ef}}}{g\mu_0}\sum_{e=1}^{N}\gamma B_{\mathrm{r}} B_{\mathrm{t}} \Delta_{\mathrm{e}} \tag{2}$$

where Δ_{e} is the area of element; g is the air gap length; γ represents the radius of the center of gravity; B_{r} and B_{t} are the radial and tangential flux densities, respectively; L_{eff} is the effective length of core; μ_0 is permeability.

III. Influence of Different Asymmetric Parameters on Starting Performance

A. Starting Performance with Different Asymmetric Parameters

Considering the various extent of asymmetry to be compared, tremendous calculations should be carried out. The slot combinations of 36/32, 36/33 and 36/42 were compared in previous work, and 36/42 has relatively low risk of vibration [1-2]. In this paper, with the slot combination of 36/42, 25 cases of K and ε combination that have relatively small loss and low vibration are obtained. These cases are given in Table I. The calculated torque-speed curves of the 25 cases are given in Fig. 1. The torque performance is summarized as follows.

1) The starting performance can be affected obviously if the parameters of K and ε are greater than 0.02 and 2, respectively. For example, the torque-speed curves of cases 1, 4, 5, 17 and 19 fluctuate severely at the initial stage of starting, and the torque-speed curves of the other 20 cases are relatively smooth. This indicates that the starting ability of cases 1, 4, 5, 17 and 19 is lower than the others. Those 20 cases are not considered in the following sections.

2) The maximum per-unit torques $T_{\text{m-pu}}$ of the 25 cases are between 3.2 and 3.5. $T_{\text{m-pu}}$ of case 1 is the smallest, and $T_{\text{m-pu}}$ of case 19 is the largest, roughly 3.42.

3) The starting per-unit torques $T_{\text{st-pu}}$ of the 25 cases are between 2.2 and 3. The value of $T_{\text{st-pu}}$ may vary with the initial position of rotor. The simulations of the starting for all the 25 cases are implemented with same initial position of rotor. $T_{\text{st-pu}}$ of case 7 is 2.27 that is the smallest, and $T_{\text{st-pu}}$ of case 19 is 2.88 that is the largest. This indicates that the extent of rotor

asymmetry significantly influences the starting torque. Cases 3, 15 and 23 have the best starting performances. The following sections focus on these cases only.

TABLE I
DIFFERENT CASES OF K AND ε

K, ε (cases 1-5)	K, ε (cases 6-10)	K, ε (cases 11-15)	K, ε (cases 16-20)	K, ε (cases 21-25)
0.023, 2.54	0.015, 3.82	0.028, 3.64	0.035, 3.93	0.004, 1.22
0.026, 0.717	0.038, 2.37	0.036, 0.052	0.029, 1.6	0.013, 2.95
0.020, 1.4	0.0067, 2.14	0.021, 3.22	0.012, 1.73	0.031, 2.77
0.019, 1.97	0.017, 0.453	0.0056, 3.19	0.025, 1.9	0.001, 2.65
0.039, 3.41	0.0021, 0.616	0.011, 0.173	0.0095, 0.807	0.033, 1.06

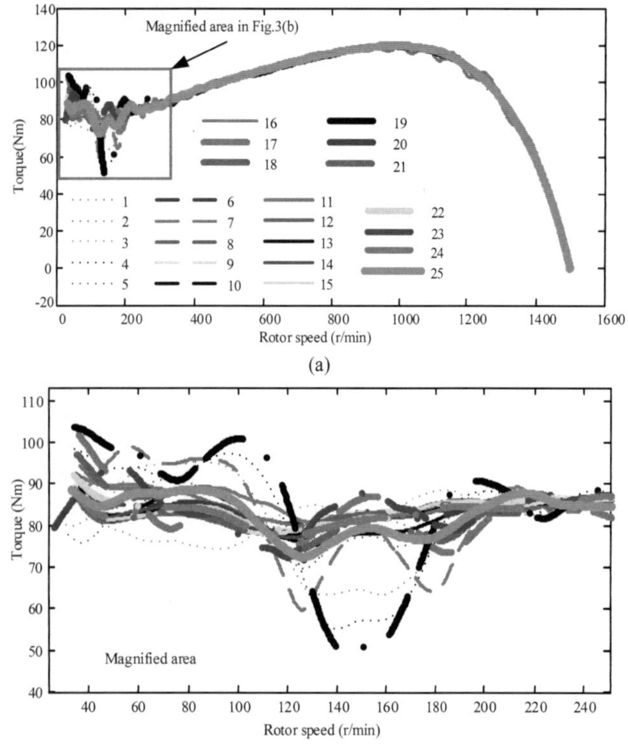

Fig. 1. Torque-speed curves with different asymmetric parameters. (a) Torque-speed curves. (b) Magnified area.

B. Torque-Speed Curves with Skewed Rotor Bars and 3 Typical Asymmetric Rotor Bars

The torque-speed curves with skewed rotor bars and 3 typical asymmetric rotor bars (cases 3, 15 and 23) are calculated and compared. The comparison of the calculated results shown in Fig. 2 indicate that

1) Compared with the skewed case, the torque-speed curves of the 3 typical asymmetric cases, particularly case 23, show apparently larger fluctuation at the initial stage of starting.

2) $T_{m\text{-}pu}$ of the 3 cases are between 3.4 and 4, which is larger than that of skewed rotor. $T_{st\text{-}pu}$ of cases 3 and 15 are greater than 2.6, larger than that of skewed rotor. $T_{st\text{-}pu}$ of case 23 is only 2.08, a lot smaller than those of cases 3 and 15.

it can be concluded that the appropriate asymmetrical parameters can be achieve the better starting ability similar during the starting initial stage. As for the 5.5kW motor, the recommended values for K and ε are 0.02 and 1.4, respectively, for avoiding the better starting ability.

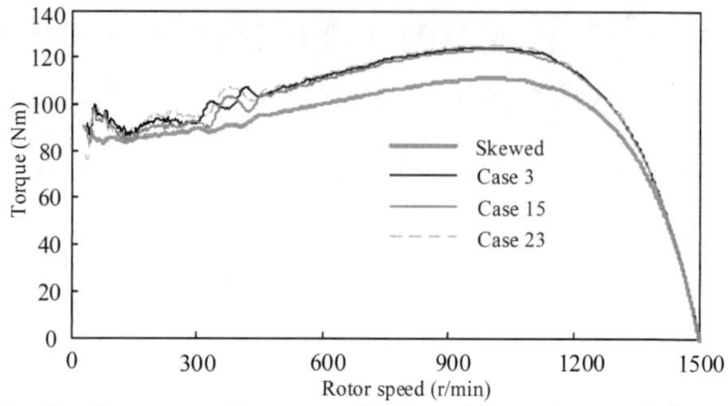

Fig. 2. Torque-speed curves with skewed rotor bars and 3 types of asymmetric rotor bars.

IV. EXPERIMENTAL VALIDATIONS

A 5.5-kW prototype is designed and manufactured, as given in Fig. 3. The test results are given in Table II, in which the per-unit values are used for comparing easily. The non-skewed asymmetric rotor bars have better starting performance than skewed rotor bars, and the loss and vibration also meet the requirement.

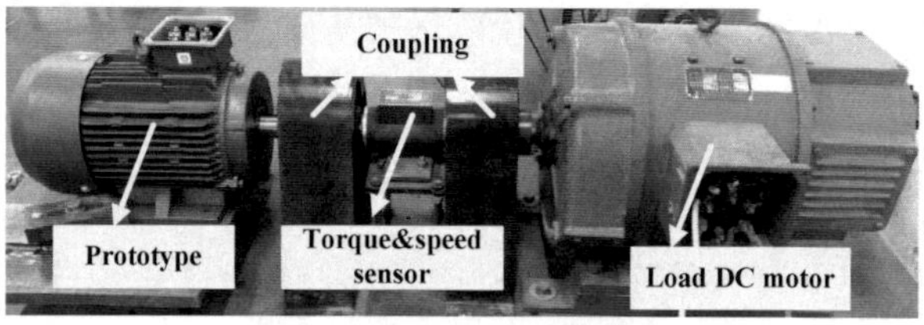

Fig. 3. Prototypes and test rig.

TABLE II
PROTOTYPES AND TESTED STARTING PERFORMANCE

	Skewed	Prototype
Slot combination	36/32	36/42
K, ε	0, 0	0.02, 1.4
$T_{m\text{-}pu}$	2.69	3.62
$T_{st\text{-}pu}$	2.43	2.65
$I_{st\text{-}pu}$	6.90	7.04

V. CONCLUSIONS

This paper studies the starting performance of induction motors with non-skewed asymmetric rotor bars by FEM and experiments. Those induction motors outperform conventional skewed induction motors in producing larger maximum torque and starting torque. The slot harmonics in the rotor flux density and current density can be significantly reduced by appropriate selection of the asymmetric parameters.

REFERENCES

[1] H. S. Zhao, X. F. Liu, Y. L. Luo, W. H. Chen, and B. Peter, "Time-stepping finite element analysis on the influence of skewed rotors and different skew angles on the losses of squirrel cage asynchronous motors," *Sci China Tech Sci*, vol. 54, no. 9, pp. 2511-2519, Sep. 2011.

[2] H. S. Zhao, J. Zhang, X. Y. Wang, Q. Wang, X. F. Liu, and Y. L. Luo, "A design method for cage induction motors with non-skewed rotor bars," *IEEE Trans. Magn.*, vol. 50, no. 2, pp. 769-772, Feb., 2014

[3] H. S. Zhao, Y. L. Wang, Y. H. Wang, Y. Zhan, and G. R. Xu, "Loss and air-gap force analysis of cage induction motors with non-skewed asymmetrical rotor bars based on FEM," *IEEE Trans. Magn.*, vol. 53, no.6, 8103004, Jun. 2017

Loss and Starting Performance of Inverter-fed Induction Motors Considering Semi-Closed Effect of Closed slot

Haisen Zhao, *Senior Member, IEEE*, Cong Liu, Yang Zhan, *Member, IEEE*, Guorui Xu, *Member, IEEE*
State Key Laboratory of Alternate Electrical Power System with Renewable Energy Sources, North China Electric Power University, Changping District, Beijing, 102206
zhaohisen@163.com

Abstract— Due to the interaction of fundamental and harmonic fields, semi-closed slot effect in iron bridge area may not only increase the leakage reactance, but also reduce the stray losses caused by harmonic flux density and high frequency current density in rotor bars, which is useful to design the inverter-fed cage induction motors. This paper analyzes the starting performance, such as slot leakage reactance, starting current and maximum torque, considering semi-closed slot effect of closed rotor bars with different parameters by FEM, meanwhile, a prototype is manufactured and the experimental validation is also carried out.

***Index Terms*— Cage induction motors, closed slot, inverted-fed, semi-closed slot effect, Finite Element Method (FEM)**

I. Introduction

In industrial induction motors, semi-closed rotor slots are preferred because it can reduce the rotor leakage inductance for better operating performance under inverter-fed conditions. Meanwhile, closed rotor slots can reduce the stator copper loss and stray losses of cage induction motors, but they also result in the drop of starting current, starting torque and maximum torque, due to the increase of leakage reactance in iron bridge areas [1].

Previous studies have focused on analyzing its relationship to the structure of the slot from the perspective of leakage impedance. It was revealed that open rotor slots contribute to a substantial reduction of the rotor leakage inductance and closed rotor slots produce higher rotor leakage inductance for better current filtering in the presence of an inverter-fed supply [2-3]. However, closed rotor slots of induction motors for high-speed applications are not mandatory [4].

This paper intends to study the semi-closed slot effect in inverted-fed induction motors with closed slot. The identification of semi-closed slot caused by local saturation and abnormal operating condition caused by closed slot is firstly emphasized. A 37-kW cage induction motor with closed-slot rotor and 300 Hz supply is manufactured and experimental validation is also performed.

II. Semi-closed Slot Effect in Cage Induction Motors with Closed Rotor Slots

A. Semi-Closed Effect in Induction Motors with Closed Slot

Fig.1 (a) shows the typical structure of semi-closed and closed slot, in which the main parameters are given, such as width of slot br1 and br2, as well as, height and width of semi-closed slot opening hr0 and br0. As for the closed slot, the height of iron bridge hr0 is the key parameter. With FE simulation analysis, magnetic flux line of semi-closed slot and closed slot with full-load condition are given in Fig.1 (b) and (c). It can be seen that the main flux in both open rotor slot area and iron bridge area are basically the same, which suggests that the semi-closed slot effect caused by local saturation in iron bridge area is noticeable, and this effect would be more significant in inverter-fed motors due to the variety of harmonic fields.

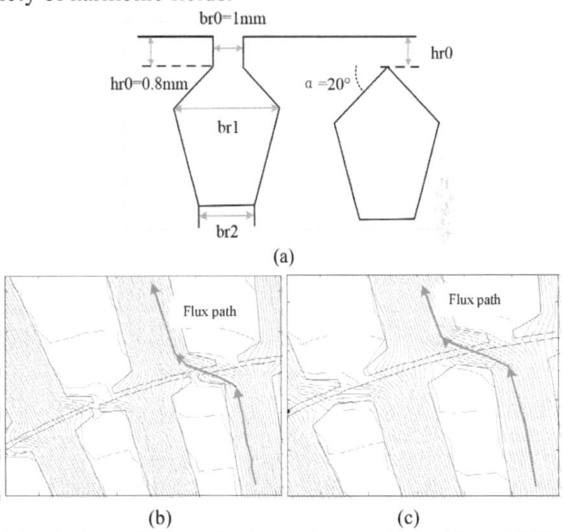

Fig.1 Typical closed slot and calculated magnetic flux lines. (a) Typical structure of closed slot. (b). Magnetic flux line of semi-closed slot. (c). Magnetic flux line of closed slot.

B. Abnormal Operation of Induction Motors with Closed Slot and High Frequency Supply

Fig.2 (a) and Fig.2 (b) show the abnormal operating conditions of a 300-Hz, 37-kW motor with closed slot, with increasing load, from no-load to 50% rated load ($0.5P_N$), and from no-load to rated load (P_N). It can be seen that, with 0.5 P_N condition, stator phase current is larger than the rated 75 A. In addition, the motor cannot operate normally under rated load condition, due to the increasing stator current, as shown in Fig.2(b), which result in activation of the over-load protect device when the motor is loaded in field. Therefore, the reasonable design of the parameters of the closed slot should be further studied with leakage reactance considered under high frequency condition, for avoiding the abnormal operation.

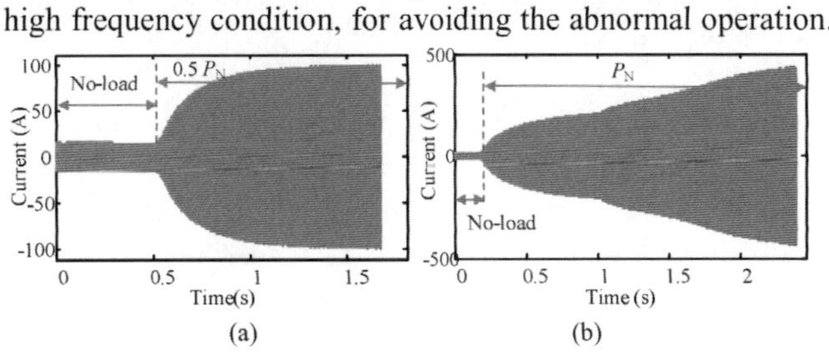

Fig.2 Abnormal operation of a 37-kW motor with closed rotor slot and 300Hz supply. (a) 50% rated load. (b) Rated load.

III. FE ANALYSIS

To avoid the abnormal operation stated in section II, a normally operated 30-kW induction motor with semi-closed slot is used to study the influence of closed slot on motor performance. The loss and starting performances of the motor with the different parameters of closed rotors are analyzed, under full-load condition. The calculated results are given in Table II. The gray area shows the results with the semi-closed motor with h_{r0}=0.8mm and b_{r0}=1mm, while the others are the results of the motor with closed slot. It can be concluded that,

1) Under full-load condition, the trend of rotor copper loss P_{cu2}, iron loss P_{fe}, and stray loss P_s decrease, it is the reason that the harmonic field at rotor iron surface and harmonic current density in rotor bars can be effectively weakened by closed slot. However, the stator copper loss P_{cu1} increases, it is the reason that the loading ability of motor with closed slot is lower than that with semi-closed rotor slots, that is, more active power should be consumed from the power source to meet the demand of constant loads. Furthermore, increase of leakage reactance of the motor with higher iron bridge may cause the increase of corresponding reactive power absorbed from the power source, which also results in an increase of the stator copper losses.

3) With the increasing of iron bridge h_{r0}, starting current I_{st}, starting torque T_{st} and maximum torque T_{max} decreases, since the leakage reactance of closed rotor increased. The calculated torque-speed curves of different closed slots are given in Fig.3.

TABLE II

COMPARISON OF LOSSES UNDER FULL-LOAD CONDITIONS WITH 50HZ SUPPLY

Type	P_{cu1}(w)	P_{cu2}(w)	$P_{fe}+P_s$(w)	η (%)	n(rpm)
hr0=0.8	736.70	743.33	510.27	92.938	1477.2
hr0=0.2	745.15	750.09	507.56	92.902	1477.1
hr0=0.3	751.13	742.54	502.74	92.919	1477.0
hr0=0.4	758.48	737.03	495.89	92.933	1476.9
hr0=0.5	766.01	731.50	493.49	92.936	1476.8
hr0=0.6	772.68	727.26	492.81	92.928	1476.7
hr0=0.7	779.93	724.02	489.14	92.927	1476.6
hr0=0.8	788.04	720.26	484.12	92.926	1476.5
hr0=0.9	795.30	717.17	484.40	92.921	1476.3
hr0=1.0	803.03	714.52	481.65	92.908	1476.2
hr0=1.1	811.22	713.25	480.85	92.889	1476.1
hr0=1.2	819.50	712.58	479.13	92.872	1475.9
hr0=1.3	827.42	711.51	477.28	92.857	1475.7
hr0=1.4	836.50	712.15	478.68	92.824	1475.6
hr0=1.5	843.54	711.91	480.68	92.798	1475.5

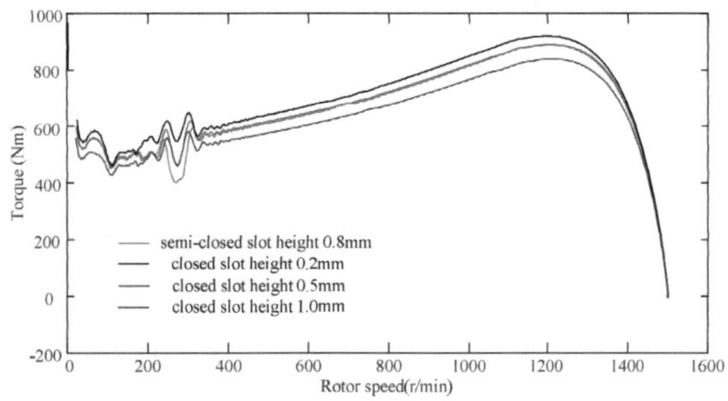

Fig.3 Comparison of the starting torque

IV. EXPERIMENTAL VALIDATION

Based on the above analysis, a new 300-Hz, 37-kW inverted-fed induction motor is designed and manufactured, as shown in Fig.4. Fig.4 (a) shows the rotor and Fig.4 (b) shows the prototype of 37-kW motor with closed slots of hr0=0.3. Experimental validation is also performed, and the tested results are given in Table III. Through field application, the problem of abnormal operation stated in section II can be avoided effectively, and the motor performance can meet the requirement of the consumer. It can be further concluded that, with the closed rotor, the inverter-fed motor can achieve the same performance as that with semi-closed rotors.

(a) (b)

Fig.4 Manufactured prototype with closed slot rotor. (a) Closed slot rotor. (b) Prototype

TABLE III

TESTED RESULTS WITH DIFFERENT CONDITIONS

Load ratio	$0.25P_N$	$0.5P_N$	$0.75P_N$	$1.0P_N$
I(A)	75.02	91.78	114.4	141.1
P_{fe}(W)	1190.0	1184.4	1178.5	1172.2
P_{cu1} (W)	124.8	190.0	301.6	470.2
P_{cu2} (W)	10.4	39.7	90.8	165.2
P_s(W)	188.9	351.3	516.3	684.2
s (%)	0.11	0.21	0.32	0.43
η (%)	82.95	89.58	91.82	92.78

V. CONCLUSIONS

This paper mainly studies the influence of semi-closed slot effect caused by local magnetic saturation on loss and starting performance of induction motors, for high-frequency application. The main contribution is as follows.

1) Closed slot may increase the rotor leakage reactance, which is helpful to improve the slot harmonic field and reducing the stray loss caused by the harmonic field, but stator copper loss may be increased and starting performance can also be weakened due to the higher leakage reactance.

2) Unreasonable closed slot may weaken the loading ability, but a suitable height and width design can also achieve the same performance of semi-closed slot. A prototype is designed and manufactured and experimental validation is performed.

REFERENCES

[1] A. Boglietti, A. Cavagnino, and M. Lazzari., "Computational algorithms for induction-motor equivalent circuit parameter determination-part I: resistances and leakage resistances," *IEEE Trans. Ind. Electron.*, vol. 58, no. 9, pp. 3723-3733, Sept., 2011.

[2] A. Boglietti, R. I. Bojoi, A. Cavagnino, and P. Guglielmi, "Analysis and modeling of rotor slot enclosure effects in high-speed induction motors," *IEEE Trans. Ind. Appl.*, vol. 48, no. 4, pp. 1279-1281, July./Aug., 2012.

[3] R. Zhou, G. L. Li, Q. J. Wang, G. H. Fang, and X. W. Guo, "Leakage field computational analysis of closed slot motor based on Ansoft," in *Proc. IEEE ICEMS*, 2014.

[4] M. Bortolozzi, L. Branz, A. Tessarolo, and C. Bruzzese, "An improved analytical expression for computing the leakage inductance of a circular bar in a semi-closed slot," in *Proc. IEEE SMART. Meeting,* Kuwait City, Kuwait, 2015.

Measurement and Modeling of Magnetostriction in Transformer Core Based on a BPNN Method Assisted with Levenberg-Marquardt Algorithm

Zhen Wang
School of Electrical Engineering,
Shenyang University of Technology
Shenyang, China
597814237@qq.com

Yanli Zhang, ACES *Member*
[1]*Shenyang University of Technology*
[1]Shenyang, China
[2]*Energy Systems Research Laboratory*
[2]*College of Electrical and Computer Engineering*
[2]*Florida International University*
[2]Miami, USA
yanzhang@fiu.edu

Osama A. Mohammed, ACES *Fellow*
Energy Systems Research Laboratory
College of Electrical and Computer Engineering
Florida International University
Miami, USA
mohammed@fiu.edu

***Abstract*— The reasons causing the vabriations and noises of tranformer cores include the magnetostrictiove force in the core material and electromagnetic forces acting on lapped seams of cores and among silicon steel sheets. This paper carried out the measurement of magnetostrictive strains in a grain-oriented steel sheet under alternating magnetizations and dicussed the effect of a dc bias present in the exciting current on the magnetostriction. Based on the experimental data, the magnetostrictive characteristics are modeled by a back propagation neural network (BPNN) method. In order to achive an acceptable convergence condition, the Levenberg-Marquardt (LM) algorithm instead of the traditional gradient descent algorithm was employed to assist the BPNN.**

Keywords—BPNN model, dc bias, Epstein frame, magnetostriction.

I. INTRODUCTION

Direct current (dc) bias is a kind of abnormal working state of power transformer [1]. For the transformer operating under a dc bias condition, the vibration and noise of cores are obviously greater than the one without dc bias. Until now, there are some methods that have been implemented to reduce the dc bias' effects [2]-[4]. However, in order to make more accurate performance predictions, these procedures require an accurate estimation for the material characteristics. The influence of presence of a dc bias on the magnetostrictive characteristics has not been well explained and modeled yet.

In this paper, an experimental setup, aimed to measure the in-plane magnetostriction, was built by means of an Epstein frame when a dc biased magnetic field was present in the alternating magnetization. The magnetostrictive behaviors of electrical steel sheet under both the alternating magnetizations and a dc bias were investigated. Based on the experimental test, a description of the magnetostrictive behavior in the presence of dc bias was proposed by using a back propagation neural network (BPNN) model assisted with the Levenberg-Marquardt (LM) algorithm. The validity of the BPNN model was verified.

II. MEASUREMENT AND ANALYSIS OF MAGNETOSTRICTION

A measured system of the magnetostrictive property in an electrical steel sheet is shown in Fig. 1, in which the Epstein frame is employed to magnetize the double-overlapped samples. During the measurement, the magnetic field intensity $\boldsymbol{H}$ created by the main winding in the Epstein frame can be superposed with a dc biased field with 0 A/m, 15 A/m, 30 A/m, or 50 A/m and the magnetic flux density $\boldsymbol{B}$ measured by the second winding can be controlled as a purely alternating $\boldsymbol{B}$ with amplitudes of 0.1 T to 1.8 T and 50 Hz. A rosette foil resistance strain gauge is mounted on the surface of electrical steel sheet to obtain an in-plane magnetostriction in an arbitrary direction. The strain gauge is connected to the strain bridge box and strain amplifier, then the strain signals are transferred to a NI PXIe-6368 data acquisition card and processed by LabView program.

A. *Anisotropic Magnetostriction Characterizations under Alternating Magnetizations*

Fig. 2 depicts the measured magnetostrictive loop when the sample is magnetized with a purely alternating magnetic flux density $\boldsymbol{B}$ at 50 Hz along the rolling direction (RD) and the transverse direction (TD), respectively. It can be seen that the peak to peak value increases with the increase of magnetic induction $\boldsymbol{B}$. In Fig. 2 (a), the peak to peak value of magnetostrictive strain measured at $B_{\max}$ = 1.6 T is around 3 times greater than that at a peak magnetic induction $B_{\max}$ = 1.0 T. It can also be seen that when the sample is magnetized along the RD, the strain value is

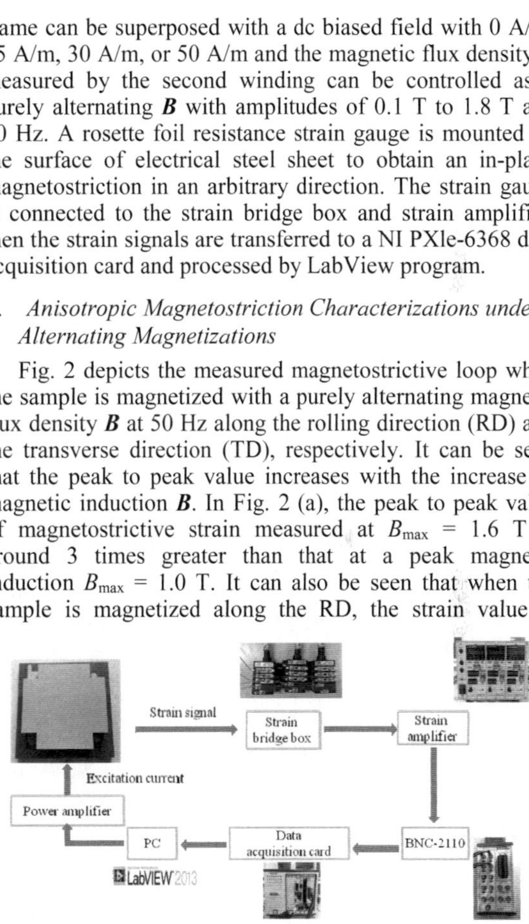

Fig.1. Measurement system of in-plane magnetostriction in an Epstein frame.

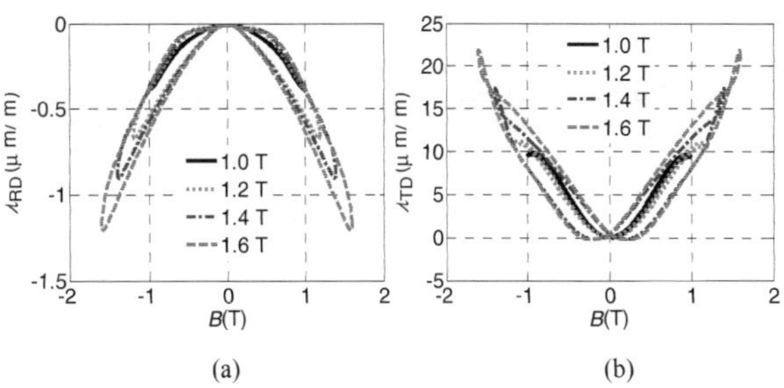

Fig.2. Magnetostrictive loop under alternating magnetization at 50 Hz. (a) magnetized along the RD, (b) magnetized along the TD.

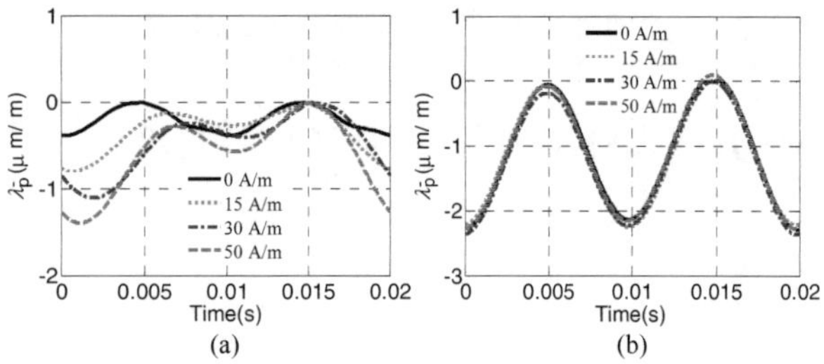

Fig. 3. Principal strain waveform λ_p^- under several imposed dc biased fields H_{dc} when the samples magnetized along the RD. (a) λ_p^- vs. t at B_{max} = 1.0 T, (b) λ_p^- vs. t at B_{max} = 1.8 T.

TABLE I. COMPARISON OF MEASURED AND CALCULATED RESULTS OF λ_{pp}^- UNDER AN IMPOSED 30 A/M BIASED FIELD.

	B_{max} = 0.82 T	B_{max} = 1.43 T	B_{max} = 1.81 T
Measured λ_{pp}^- (μm/m)	0.815	1.625	2.362
Calculated λ_{pp}^- (μm/m)	0.762	1.584	2.303

negative, which represents that the contractive strain occurs. However, in Fig. 2 (b), when the sample is magnetized along the TD, the strain is of elongation with the positive value. Moreover, the strain in the TD is obviously greater than that in the RD.

B. *Variations of Magnetostrictive Characterizations at the Presence of DC Biased Magnetic Field*

Fig. 3 represents the principal strain waveform λ_p^- in one time period with several imposed dc biased fields H_{dc} when the samples are magnetized along the RD and magnetic flux density $\boldsymbol{B}$ are controlled as 1.0 T and 1.8 T, respectively. In the case of H_{dc} = 0 A/m in Fig. 3 (a), the waveform of magnetostriction varies at a frequency of 100 Hz that is twice that of $\boldsymbol{B}$ signal (50 Hz). In the presence of a dc bias magnetic field, such as 15 A/m, 30 A/m, and 50 A/m, however, the waveform does not change periodically two times and lose its symmetry at time 0.01 s. We can see that the asymmetry trend increases with the increase of the dc biased magnetic field, and the peak to peak value also increases. However, the symmetry of the magnetostrictive waveform in Fig. 3 (b) is restored at high induction $\boldsymbol{B}$ of 1.8 T, and the peak to peak value is basically the same. It can be concluded that the influence of the dc biased field on the magnetostrictive strain is little when the samples are magnetized gradually into the saturation stage.

III. ESTIMATIONS OF MAGNETOSTRICTIVE PROPERTIES

The BPNN model has been employed to predict the dynamic magnetostriction along the unidirectional magnetization with different magnetic inductions under purely sinusoidal induction and can offer fast evaluation time [5, 6]. However, when studying the anisotropic principal strain of magnetostriction along various excitation directions different from the RD, the BPNN based on the gradient descent (GD) algorithm is hard to reach the acceptable convergence condition due to the increase of the numbers of weights and thresholds of the neural network [7]. In this paper, a BPNN model assisted with the LM algorithm is presented to describe anisotropic magnetostriction characteristics in the presence of dc bias mentioned above.

The general training scheme of the BPNN is as follows: The input of the model is two waveforms data in one time period for the two components of the magnetic flux density $B_x(t)$ and $B_y(t)$ in the time domain. After that, a fast Fourier transform (FFT) is applied on these two waves, and the frequency components including the amplitude and phase are obtained. The FNN returns the frequency components of the magnetostriction on three different directions, on which an inverse fast Fourier transform (IFFT) is applied. Also, the magnetostriction waves on three different directions $\lambda_a(t)$, $\lambda_b(t)$, $\lambda_c(t)$ corresponding to the input waves in the time domain are obtained. Finally, based on the knowledge of plane strain in material mechanics, the principal strain and its direction are calculated.

Table I compares measured results of magnetostriction and computed ones using the BPNN model in the Fig. 1 under an imposed 30 A/m dc bias field. From Table I, it can be seen that the peak to peak value of calculated contractive strains (λ_{pp}^-) are closed to the measured ones, which verifies that it is feasible to use the BPNN model assisted with LM algorithm to describe the magnetostriction in the presence of dc bias.

IV. CONCLUSION

The transformer core is laminated from the silicon steel sheets and its magnetostriction brings out the core vibrations. The study in this paper shows that the magnetostiction along the RD is of contraction and its value increases with the increase of the magnetic flux density. The dc biased magnetic field induces more frequency harmonics into the magnetostrictive waveforms which will aggrevate the vibration of core. It is also concluded that a BPNN model assisted with LM algorithm can be effectively proposed to describe magnetostriction behavior under a dc bias.

REFERENCES

[1] X. M. Liu, Y. M. Yang, and Y. C. Huang, "**Vibration analysis of transformer DC bias caused by HVDC based on EMD reconstruction**," J. Electr. Eng. Technol., vol. 13, no. 2, pp. 781-789, Jan. 2018.

[2] S. Liu, S. Ganu, N. Abed, O. Mohammed, "Acoustic noise signal evaluation due to magnetostrictive effects in electrical equipment," ACES Conference Paper, Year: 2005 - Hybrid CEM Techniques.

[3] A. J. Moses, P. I. Anderson, and T. Phophongviwat, "Localized surface vibration and acoustic noise emitted from laboratory-scale transformer cores assembled from grain-oriented electrical steel," IEEE Trans. Magn., vol. 52, no. 10, pp. 1-15, Oct. 2016.

[4] L. Zhu, H. S. Yoon, and D. J. Um, "Finite-element analysis of magnetostriction force in power transformer based on the measurement of anisotropic magnetostriction of highly grain-oriented electrical steel sheet," *IEEE Trans. Magn.*, vol. 52, no. 3, pp. 1-4, Mar. 2015.

[5] T. Hilgert, "Comparison of magnetostriction models for use in calculations of vibrations in magnetic cores," IEEE Trans. Magn., vol. 44, no. 6, pp. 874-877, Jun. 2008.

[6] J. Dong, W. W. Qin, Y. J. Li, et al., "Fast multi-objective antenna design based on BPNN surrogate Model," ACES Conference Paper, Year: 2018 - 9-P-2 Poster.

[7] Hang Zhou, Yanli Zhang, Dianhai Zhang, Ziyan Ren and Dexin Xie, "An anisotropic magnetostriction model based on BP neural network combining levenberg-marquardt algorithm and particle swarm optimization," International Journal of Applied Electromagnetics and Mechanics, vol. 55, no. s1, pp. s193-s201, Sep. 2017.

Calculation on Magnetostrictive Deformation of Motor Core Under the Non-Sinusoidal Excitation

Litao Jiang
School of Electrical Engineering,
Shenyang University of Technology
Shenyang, China
847766822@qq.com

Yanli Zhang, ACES *Member*
[1]*Shenyang University of Technology*
[1]Shenyang, China
[2]*Energy Systems Research Laboratory*
[2]*College of Electrical and Computer Engineering*
[2]*Florida International University*
[2]Miami, USA
yanzhang@fiu.edu

Osama A. Mohammed, ACES *Fellow*
Energy Systems Research Laboratory
College of Electrical and Computer Engineering
Florida International University
Miami, USA
mohammed@fiu.edu

***Abstract*—The magnetostrictions in a non-oriented electrical steel sheets are an important cause of motor vibrations and noises. The presence of non-sinusoidal magnetic flux density brings about larger vibrations and noises. In this paper, a standard monolithic measurement system is employed to measure the magnetostriction in a non-oriented electrical steel sheet when a third harmonic is overlapped on a pure sinusoidal magnetic flux density. Based on the analysis of measured magnetostrictive property, a dynamic estimation model of magnetostrictive strain is proposed and verified. The results are helpful for further investigation of motor vibrations and noises.**

Keywords—Higher harmonics, magnetostriction, motor stator core, non-oriented silicon steel.

I. Introduction

The motor noise originated from mechanical sources, pneumatic sources, and magnetic sources has been studied [1]. Magnetostriction defined as the deformation of ferromagnetic material under an external magnetic field is one of the main factors that result in magnetic noise. Motor stator cores are laminated by electrical steel sheets and have a deformation with an amount of several micrometers per meter. However, most studies have focused on the magnetostrictive behavior under a pure sinusoidal excitation. In an engineering application, there are always some higher harmonics of the voltage present in the grid due to non-linear load, which can induce harmonics to the flux density. Recently, the effect of the harmonic magnetic field on the magnetostrictive behavior of the electrical steel sheet has been discussed in [2]-[4].

In this paper, the magnetostrictive strain of non-oriented electrical steel was measured by using a triaxial strain gauge under a sinusoidal magnetic field overlapped with a third harmonic, and the effect of presence of harmonic on magnetostriction was discussed. A magnetostrictive estimation model for non-sinusoidal excitation was proposed, and its validity was verified with the experimental results.

II. Magnetostrictive Property under Non-Sinusoidal Magnetic Flux Density

The magnetostrictive measurement setup is shown in Fig. 1, in which the excitation device adopts a single yoke structure, and the sample is a long plate having a length of 600 mm and a width of 100 mm. The excitation voltage in the winding can be controlled in a closed loop way to generate non-sinusoidal magnetic flux density ***B*** waveforms in the sample as required. The magnetostrictive strain was measured by triaxial strain gauge. In order to study the anisotropy of magnetostriction, the samples were cut at 15° intervals from the rolling direction (RD) to the transverse direction (TD). During the measurement, the magnetic flux density is controlled to change from 0.5 T to 1.6 T in the interval of 0.1 T, and the amplitude of the third harmonic is set as 10% of the fundamental component of magnetic flux density and without phase delay.

Fig. 2 (a) shows a series of magnetostrictive loops corresponding to different magnitudes of ***B*** values when the magnetization direction θ_B is 30°, and Fig. 2 (b) depicts the variation of magnetostrictive loop due to the presence of harmonic field. From Fig. 2 (b), it can be seen that the amplitude of principal strain of magnetostriction is increased by almost 39% and the shape of loop is also changed. Further, Fig. 3 shows the Fourier series expansion results for measured magnetostrictive waveform

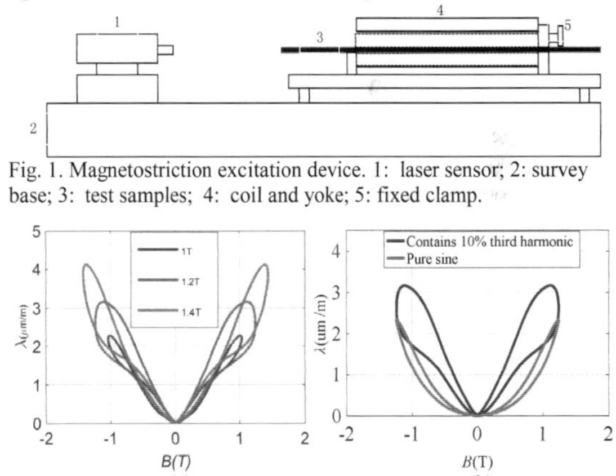

Fig. 1. Magnetostriction excitation device. 1: laser sensor; 2: survey base; 3: test samples; 4: coil and yoke; 5: fixed clamp.

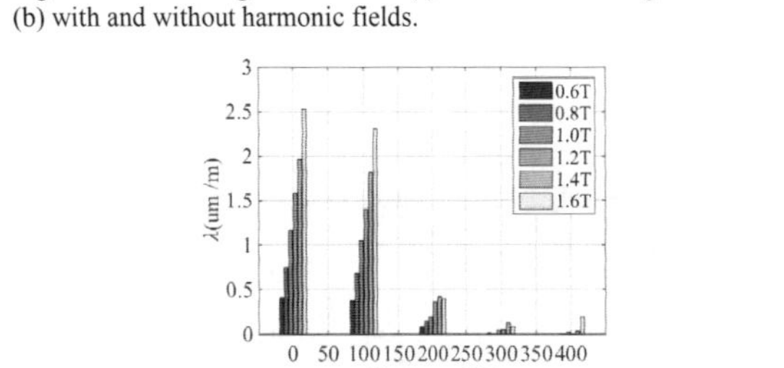

Fig. 2. Measured magnetostrictions. (a) under different magnitudes of ***B***, (b) with and without harmonic fields.

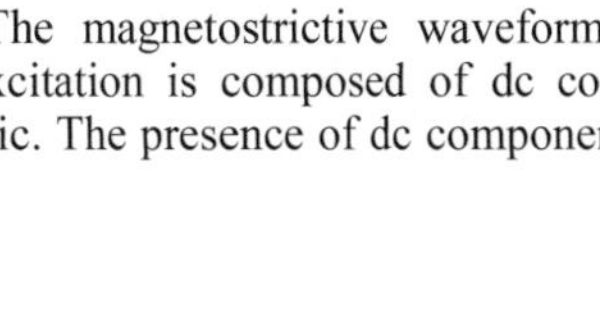

Fig. 3. Fourier analysis of magnetostrictive waveforms in Fig. 2.

in Fig. 2. The magnetostrictive waveform under non-sinusoidal excitation is composed of dc component and even harmonic. The presence of dc components are due to

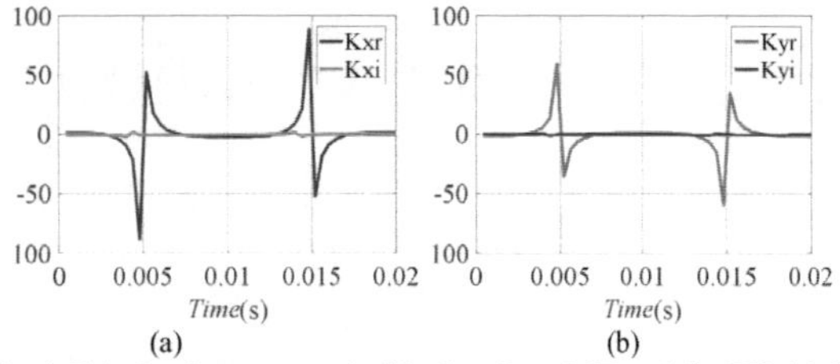

Fig. 4. Calculated parameters in (1) when B_{max}=1.2T, and θ_B=30°. (a) K_{xr} and K_{xi}, (b) K_{yr} and K_{ui}.

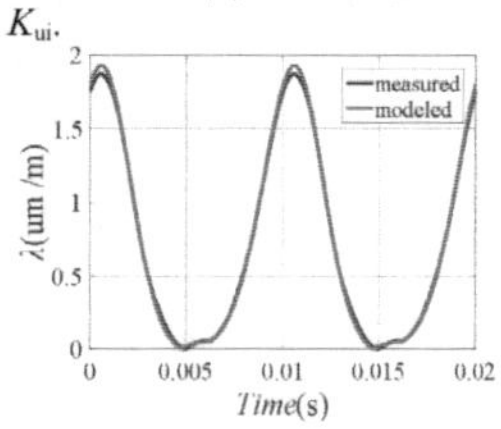

Fig. 5. Comparison of the value of measured and modeled magnetostriction when a=10%, B_{max}=1.055T, and θ_B=30°

the nonsymmetry of magnetostrictive waveforms about the horizontal axis in Fig.2.

III. Magnetostrictive Estimation Model and its Verification

A. Derivation of Dynamic Magnetostrictive Model

There is a complex vector relationship between the magnetostrictive strain and the magnetic flux density under non-sinusoidal excitation, as shown in Fig. 2, and in order to estimate their relation, a dynamic vector model is proposed in this paper as follows

$$\begin{cases} \lambda_x(\tau) = C_x + K_{xr}B_x(\tau) + K_{xi}\dfrac{\partial B_x(\tau)}{\partial \tau} \\ \lambda_y(\tau) = C_y + K_{yr}B_y(\tau) + K_{yi}\dfrac{\partial B_y(\tau)}{\partial \tau} \end{cases}, \quad (1)$$

where λ_x and λ_y are x- and y- component of principal strain of magnetostriction, respectively; C_x, C_y K_{xr}, K_{xi}, K_{yr}, and K_{yi} are the magnetostrictive coefficients to be determined. During the measurement, the B-waveforms are controlled as follows

$$\begin{cases} B_x = B_{max}\cos\theta_B\cos\tau + \sum_{n=2}^{N}\alpha B_{max}\cos\theta_B\left[\cos(2n-1)\tau+\varphi\right] \\ B_y = B_{max}\sin\theta_B\cos\tau + \sum_{n=2}^{N}\alpha B_{max}\sin\theta_B\left[\cos(2n-1)\tau+\varphi\right] \end{cases}, \quad (2)$$

where B_{max} is fundamental amplitude of flux density, θ_B is the magnetization angle, α is the percentage of higher harmonic accounting for B_{max}, and φ is the phase delay.

Rewriting magnetic density $\boldsymbol{B}$ to Fourier expansion, we have

$$B_k = \sum_{n=1}^{N}\left\{R_{(2n-1)B_k}\cos[(2n-1)\tau] + I_{(2n-1)B_k}\sin[(2n-1)\tau]\right\}. \quad (3)$$

Further, by substitute (3) into (1), we can obtain

$$\lambda_k = C_k + K_{kr}\left\{\sum_{n=1}^{N}\left[R_{(2n-1)B_k}\cos(2n-1)\tau + I_{(2n-1)_{B_k}}\sin(2n-1)\tau\right]\right\} + K_{ki}\left\{\sum_{n=1}^{N}(2n-1)I_{(2n-1)B_k}\cos[(2n-1)\tau] - (2n-1)R_{(2n-1)B_k}\sin[(2n-1)\tau]\right\}, \quad (4)$$

where k represents x or y, N is harmonic number, and $R_{(2n-1)Bk}$ and $I_{(2n-1)Bk}$ correspond to the real and imaginary parts of magnetic density $\boldsymbol{B}$ Fourier decomposition result, respectively. On the other hand, the measured magnetostrictive strain waveforms can be expanded by the Fourier analysis as

$$\lambda_k = C_k + \sum_{m=1}^{M}R_{2m\lambda_k}\cos(2m\tau) + \sum_{m=1}^{M}I_{2m\lambda_k}\sin(2m\tau), \quad (5)$$

where $R_{2m\lambda k}$ and $I_{2m\lambda k}$ correspond to the real and imaginary parts in the magnetostrictive strain $\boldsymbol{\lambda}$ decomposition result, C_k is the dc component, and M=4.

By comparing (4) and (5) and considering that the corresponding terms of λ_k are equal, thus we can obtain the parameters as

$$\begin{cases} K_{kr} = \dfrac{\sum_{m=1}^{M}[R_{2m\lambda_k}\cos(2m\tau)]}{\sum_{n=1}^{N}\left[R_{(2n-1)B_k}\cos(2n-1)\tau + I_{2n-1}\sin(2n-1)\tau\right]} \\ K_{ki} = \dfrac{\sum_{m=1}^{M}[I_{2m\lambda_k}\sin(2m\tau)]}{\sum_{n=1}^{N}\left[(2n-1)I_{(2n-1)B_k}\cos(2n-1)\tau - (2n-1)R_{(2n-1)B_k}\sin(2n-1)\tau\right]} \end{cases}. \quad (6)$$

B. Identification of Model Parameters and Verification

The results of some parameters in (1) are illustrated in Fig. 4 based on the measurement data. Fig. 5 shows the comparison of measured and modeled magnetostriction under non-sinusoidal magnetization which is not part of the grid data. This is done for a=10%, B_{max}=1.055T, and θ_B=30°. There is a good agreement between the measured and modeled results.

IV. Conclusion

In this paper, the magnetostrictive property of a non-oriented steel sheet containing 10% of the third harmonic in a sinusoidal magnetic density is measured and analyzed. From the measurement results, the presence of higher harmonics in the magnetic field increases the magnetostrictive strain of the electrical steel sheet, which may cause larger noise and vibration of the motor. The mathematical model of magnetostriction proposed here has been verified that it can be effectively used to estimate the deformation of electrical steel caused by the non-sinusoidal excitation, which will be significant to optimal design of the motor in order to reduce core vibration and noise.

References

[1] L. Vandevelde , J. A. A. Melkebeek, "Magnetic forces and magnetostriction in electrical machines and transformer cores," IEEE Trans. Magn., vol. 39, no. 3, pp. 1618–1621, May 2003.

[2] S. G. Ghalamestani, L. Vandevelde, J. J. J. Dirckx, et al., "Magnetostriction and the influence of higher harmonics in the magnetic field," IEEE Trans. Magn., vol. 48, no. 11, pp. 3981-3984, Nov. 2012.

[3] W. J. Gong, Z. G. Zhang, R. F. Hou, et al., "Magnetostriction and the influence of harmonics in flux density in electrical steel," IEEE Trans. Magn., vol. 51 no. 11, pp. 1-4, Nov. 2015.

[4] S. G. Ghalamestani, A Darba, L Vandevelde, et al., "Macroscopic description of the magnetostrictive behavior of electrical steel in the presence of high-order harmonics in the magnetization," IEEE Trans. Magn., vol. 52, no. 5 pp. 1-4, May 2016.

Radiated EM Flux based Diagnostic Approach for Stator Insulation Failures in Inverter fed Motors

Hassan H. Eldeeb[1], Alberto Berzoy[2], *Student Members, ACES & IEEE,* and Osama Mohammed[1], *ACES, Fellow, IEEE*

1. Energy System Research Laboratory, ECE Department, Florida International University, Miami, FL33174, USA

2. R&D Department, Sonnen Batterie Inc, Tucker, GA 30084, USA

helde002@fiu.edu; a.berzoyllerena@sonnen-batterie.com; mohammed@fiu.edu

***Abstract*— Analysis of harmonics and inter-harmonics components in the spectrum of the radiated electromagnetic (EM) field is proposed for the detection of induction motor (IM) windings' insulation failure. The IM is fed through a voltage source inverter (VSI) operating under the classical direct torque controller (DTC). To investigate the EM spectrum, the radiated magnetic field intensity ($\vec{H}$) was calculated at an observer point in a physics-based finite element analysis (FEA) platform.**

***Index Terms*— DTC, Fault detection, Induction machine, Inter-turn short-circuit, FEA co-simulation, Emitted magnetic flux.**

I. INTRODUCTION

The early detection of turn-to-turn faults (TTF) in the stator's winding of induction motors (IM), to improve the reliability and secure operation of the IM drive system, has been a hot research topic for decades. With the massive increase in the transportation electrification industry, TTF detection in closed-loop driven IMs became more momentous. Owing to the fact that closed-loop controllers hides the signatures available in faulty IM connected directly on-line (DOL) or fed from an open loop controlled voltage source inverter (VSI) [1]. Due to its simplicity and independency on machine's parameters, the direct torque control (DTC) algorithm is widely used in industry. Turn fault detection (FD) in DTC driven IMs is more challenging due to the switching activities of the VSI, which injects significant harmonics not directly related to the fault. Few studies addressed the detection of TTFs in DTC driven IMs.

Among the non-invasive diagnostic methods used to detect TTFs in DTC driven IMs: motor current signature analysis (MCSA) and positive sequence component of the stator's current [2], harmonic spectrum of the developed power [3], and impedance sequence component in [4]. The FD of TTFs using the radiated magnetic flux intensity ($\vec{H}$) is also non-invasive, and it doesn't rely on the current or voltage sensors [5], which are subjected to saturation due to the high (dv/dt) rate applied by the VSI to the IM. This article investigates the online FD of TTFs in a DTC driven IM using the magnetic signature.

II. IM DRIVE SYSTEM MODELLING

A short dipole conductor whose length (l) is significantly shorter than the wave length (λ). The magnetic potential $(\vec{A})$ at an observer point (op), placed at a distance (d) in the spherical coordinates from the dipole with current (I) is as in (1):

$$\vec{A} = \frac{\mu I l}{4\pi d} e^{-j\xi d}(\cos\theta \, a_R - \sin\theta \, a_\Phi) \quad (1)$$

where ξ is the phase, μ is the permeability. The field $\vec{H}$ is evaluated is as in(3):

$$\vec{H} = \frac{\mu I l}{4\pi} \xi^2 \sin(\theta) \left[\frac{1}{j\xi d} - \frac{1}{(\xi d)^2}\right] e^{-j\xi d} \, a_\Phi \quad (2)$$

From (2) it is obvious that the radiated $\vec{H}$ will carries the same signatures in the current. The IM has thousands of short dipole, the entire $\vec{H}$ is the summation of the radiated $\vec{H}$ of each dipole.

DTC is a predictive controller that aims to control $|\boldsymbol{\lambda}_s|$and T_e. Whereas for faulty IM driven by DTC other harmonics are presented, per instance: the 3rd order harmonic in $\boldsymbol{i}_s$ inserted by DTC to counter-balance the 2nd order harmonics inT_e, and the inter-harmonics due to ITSC as in (3)

$$f_{TTF} = f\left[\frac{m}{p}(1-s) \pm l\right] \quad (3)$$

and the inter-harmonics due to the interaction between ITSC and saturation effect as in (4)

$$f_{3h} = f\left[\frac{R}{p}(1-s) \pm 3\right] \quad (4)$$

where, $m = 0,1,2 \ldots$, $l = 0,1,3,5 \ldots$,, p is the number of pole pairs, s is the slip, and R is the number of rotor's slots. Details about DTC and its reaction to TTF is available in [6].

III. FEA MODEL

Physics-based model of the faulty IM was done. Fig.2 shows the magnetic flux density distribution for the IM in the FEA software. The ratings of the IM under study are shown in Table I. Each phase has number of turns $N_{as} = 510$. The fault severity factor (μ_f) is a ratio between the number of faulty turns and N_{sa}. The faulty case is for $\mu_f = 1.08\%$. The fault resistance is $R_f = 0.67\ \Omega$. The two cases studied at reference torque of 2 Nm. The op was placed at $30\,cm$ from the stator's frame in FEA environment.

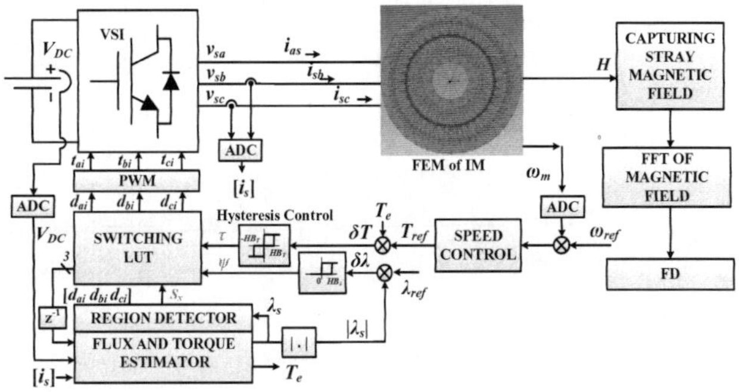

Fig. 1. The FEA co-simulation platform of the DTC driven IM under study.

This work was partially supported by grants from the Office of Naval Research and Department of Energy. Corresponding author: Prof. Mohammed, email: mohammed@fiu.edu

TABLE I. NAMEPLATE RATINGS OF THE 1 HP WEG IM UNDER STUDY.

Rating	Value	Param.	Value
Pr (W)	750	Stator outer diameter	160
U (V)	460	Stator inner diameter	100
I (A)	1.47	Rotor inner diameter	22
f (HZ)	60	Air-gap length	0.31
n (rpm)	1730	Parallel branch	1
J (kgm^2)	0.053	Slot numbers (Z1/Z2)	36/44

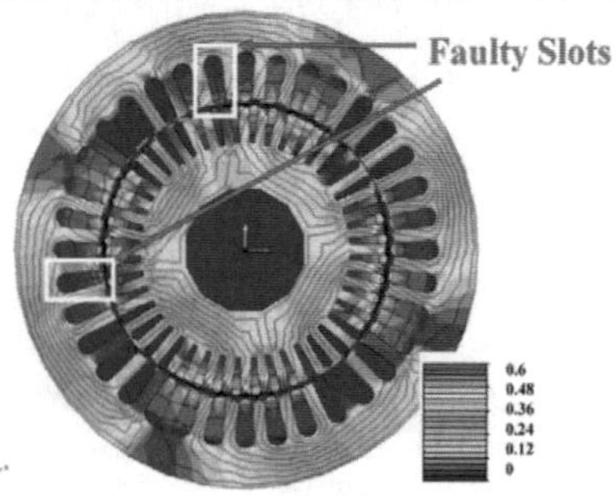

Fig. 2. 2D distribution of $|B|$

The spectrum in Fig.3 indicates the existence of several harmonics and inter-harmonics in both cases. However, the amplitude in the faulty case is not always higher than the healthy case. Moreover, the integral harmonic components are not always indicators to the fault. Consequently, statistical analysis was done to evaluate the density of existence of inter-harmonics around each integral harmonic. The histograms in Fig.4 depicts that the inter-harmonics around the fundamental components has higher value for the healthy than the faulty, while the faulty inter-harmonics have higher amplitude elsewhere. The fault could be detected easily via monitoring the inter-harmonics around $h = 3$ and 7, as shown in Fig.4 (d) and (h), respectively.

IV. CONCLUSION

Investigation of the inter-harmonics components in the radiated magnetic field was presented for the purpose of TTF detection in DTC driven IM. The FEA co-simulation showed that monitoring the inter-harmonics is more trustworthy to detect the fault from monitoring the harmonic components. Furthermore,

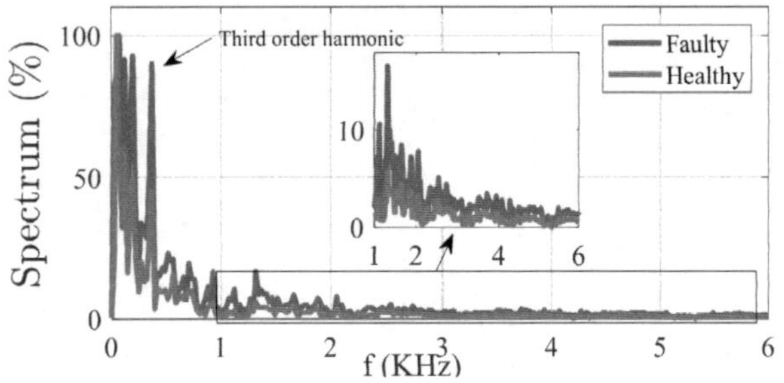

Fig. 3. The spectrum of the radiated $\vec{H}$ at the observer point

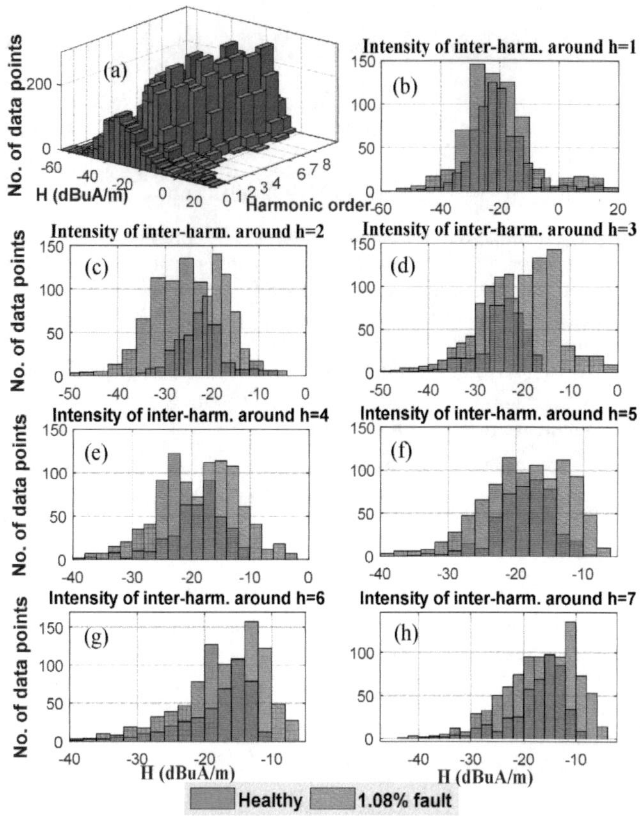

Fig. 4. Histogram of the radiated $\vec{H}$ around each integral harmonic component

results showed that the inter-harmonic components around the 3rd and 5th order harmonics are more sensitive to the fault from other inter-harmonics.

REFERENCES

[1] H. H. Eldeeb, A. Berzoy and O. Mohammed, "Stator Fault Detection on DTC-Driven IM via Magnetic Signatures Aided by 2-D FEA Co-Simulation," in *IEEE Transactions on Magnetics* [in press].

[2] S. M. A. Cruz and A. J. M. Cardoso, "Diagnosis of stator inter-turn short circuits in DTC induction motor drives," *IEEE Trans. Ind. Appl.*, vol. 40, no. 5, pp. 1349–1360, Sep. 2004.

[3] M. Drif and A. J. M. Cardoso, "Stator Fault Diagnostics in Squirrel Cage Three-Phase Induction Motor Drives Using the Instantaneous Active and Reactive Power Signature Analyses," in *IEEE Transactions on Industrial Informatics*, vol. 10, no. 2, pp. 1348-1360, May 2014.

[4] A. Berzoy, H. H. Eldeeb and O. Mohammed, "Online fault detection of stator winding faults in IM driven by DTC using the off-diagonal term of the symmetrical component impedance matrix," *2018 IEEE Applied Power Electronics Conference and Exposition (APEC)*, San Antonio, TX, USA, 2018, pp. 2482-2487.

[5] M. Irhoumah, R. Pusca, E. Lefevre, D. Mercier, R. Romary and C. Demian, "Information Fusion With Belief Functions for Detection of Interturn Short-Circuit Faults in Electrical Machines Using External Flux Sensors," in *IEEE Transactions on Industrial Electronics*, vol. 65, no. 3, pp. 2642-2652, March 2018.

[6] H. H. Eldeeb, A. Berzoy and O. Mohammed, "Comprehensive Investigation of Harmonic Signatures Resulting from Inter- Turn Short-Circuit Faults in DTC Driven IM Operating in Harsh Environments," 2018 *XIII International Conference on Electrical Machines (ICEM)*, Alexandroupoli, Greece, 2018, pp. 2579-2585

Induction Heating of Thermoplastic Composites in the Presence of a Susceptor

Ankit Patel
Department of Electrical Engineering
University of South Carolina
Columbia, SC USA
akpatel@email.sc.edu

Michel Van-Tooren
Department of Mechanical Engineering
University of South Carolina
Columbia, SC USA
vantooren@cec.sc.edu

Frank D. Thomas and Robert Moore
Department of Mechanical Engineering
University of South Carolina
Columbia, SC USA
fthomas@email.sc.edu, rm3@email.sc.edu

Mohammod Ali
Department of Electrical Engineering
University of South Carolina
Columbia, SC USA
alimo@cec.sc.edu

***Abstract*—The issue of inductive heating and welding of two pieces of thermoplastic composites in the presence of a susceptor alloy consisting of 67% nickel and 27% copper is studied using Maxwell. Simulation results clearly show solid losses in the material which can be used to heat and weld the composite panels. Location based temperature increase due to I^2R losses are calculated which show significant heating and welding potentials.**

***Keywords*— Composites, electromagnetic, inductive heating, thermoplastic, welding.**

I. Introduction

Induction welding [1-5] of thermoplastic composite laminates is an exciting topic. The non-contact method of heating and welding is being adopted in aircraft parts, engine parts, and turbine parts manufacturing among many other things. While in most circumstances carbon fiber composite parts are welded together there are examples of other non-carbon composites such as fiberglass composites welding as well. Typically for non-carbon welding a susceptor material is placed in between the composite parts to be welded together. The combined ensemble is then exposed to intense electromagnetic (EM) fields created by a low frequency high current source. The source of the fields can travel on a gantry and expose large section of the composite to weld it fully. Understanding the heating behavior of the objects under consideration is important to ensure proper and homogenous heating and welding so that there are no premature burning or damage in certain areas while other areas remain unexposed completely. The focus of this paper is to conduct a numerical simulation study of the induction heating of thermoplastic composites in the presence of a susceptor called Monel. All simulations were performed using Ansys Maxwell. An experiment was conducted to validate the simulated findings.

II. Simulation Models and Results

A. Initial Simulation Model

First, a simulation model of the Monel mesh was created using cylindrical conductor segments as shown in Fig. 1. The electrical property used for the Monel were conductivity, $\sigma = 3\times10^7$ S/m and relative permeability, $\mu_r = 350$. Since Monel is an alloy consisting of 67% nickel and 27% copper average conductivity and relative permeability values were estimated using their individual conductivity and relative permeability and their percentage contributions in forming the alloy. These values were used in Ansys Maxwell simulation. A current carrying loop with 500A of current excited at 292 kHz was placed 3 mm above the mesh. Simulated total solid loss in the Monel was 0.47W. This apparent low loss is concerning yet explainable because the mesh although looking inter-woven the orthogonal segments do not touch each other.

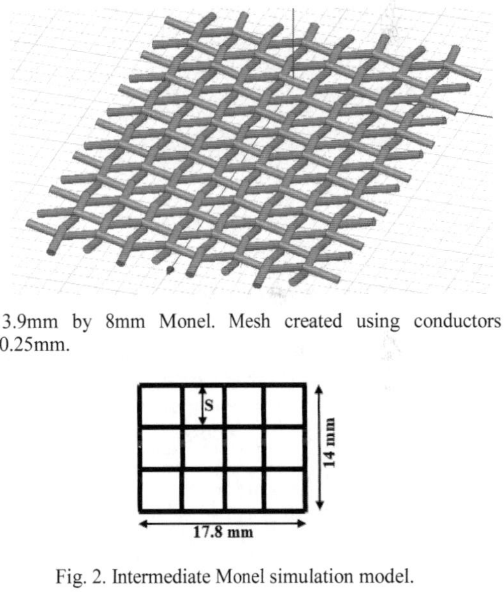

Fig. 1. 13.9mm by 8mm Monel. Mesh created using conductors with diameter=0.25mm.

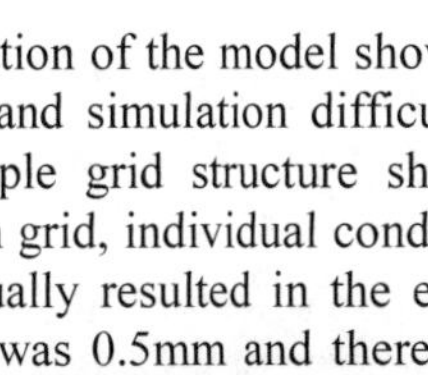

Fig. 2. Intermediate Monel simulation model.

B. Intermedicate Simulation Model

Due to the limitation of the model shown in Fig. 1 and due to the construction and simulation difficulty of a truly inter-woven mesh a simple grid structure shown in Fig. 2 was considered. For each grid, individual conductor segments were modeled that eventually resulted in the entire geometry. The conductor diameter was 0.5mm and there were 127 segments used in the model with the parameter s=2 mm. This Monel mesh which was also excited using a 292 kHz 500A current resulted in 1.35W of total solid loss in the material.

Subsequently denser meshes were created by considering 40X40 and 50X50 mesh within a square inch. For example, for a 50X50 mesh the conductor radius is 0.1143mm and the grid size is 0.28mm (conductor edge to edge). First, simulations with Monel under a coil with 500A current excited by a 292 kHz source alone was conducted. Subsequently the Monel susceptor was placed in between two 3 mm thick Plexiglass ($\varepsilon_r = 3.7$ and $\tan\delta = 0.001$) sheets and then simulated. The results with and without Plexiglass are compared in Table I. There are a few things to observe. As expected, the larger the structure size, the higher is the solid loss in the material. For a specific size structure, the presence of the two Plexiglass sheets reduces the amount of solid loss in the Monel material.

TABLE I. SIMULATED RESULTS FOR 50X50 MESH

Structure Size	Segments	Solid Loss (W) No Plexiglass	Solid Loss (W) With Plexiglass
5mm by 5mm	200	0.1626	0.02118
10mm by 10mm	800	1.1342	0.21627
15 mm by 15mm	1800	2.0693	0.52950

TABLE II. SIMULATED RESULTS COMPARISON

Structure Size	Solid Loss (mW) With Plexi-glass 50X50 mesh	Solid Loss (mW) With Plexi-glass 40X40 mesh
5mm by 5mm	21.184	18.2
10mm by 10mm	216.27	196.1
15 mm by 15mm	529.50	497.5
20 mm by 20 mm	-	785.21

Table II shows a comparison between the solid loss in the material in the presence of the Plexiglass sheets but with two different mesh densities. As apparent, the denser mesh yields more loss.

C. Final Simulation Model

The final simulation model can be seen in Fig. 3. The geometry of the model and is construction mechanism are illustrated in Fig. 3. Simulated total solid loss was 2.39W.

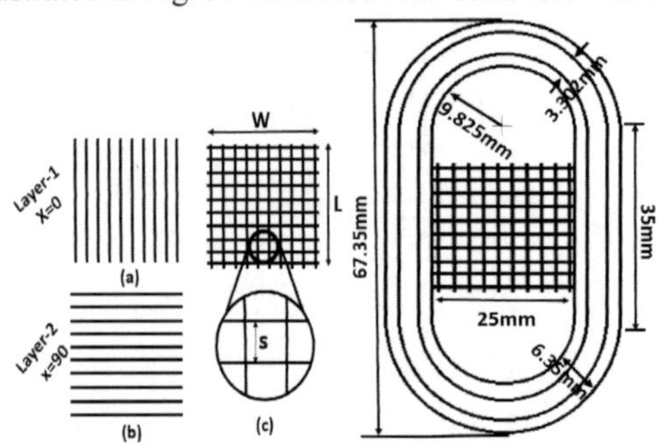

Fig. 3. Final Monel simulation model 40X40 mesh. Parameters: L=W=25mm, S=0.381mm, and conductor radius=0.127mm.

However, to estimate the temperature rise in specific areas of the mesh a current density plot as shown in Fig. 4 was generated where markers were used to determine the current density values. The current density values were then used to calculate the currents in the specific locations marked using the small circles in Fig. 4. Losses in those locations were calculated as I^2R loss where the resistance, R is given by $R = R_s/(2\pi r)$ (Ω) where $R_s = \sqrt{\omega\mu/(2\sigma)}$ where $\mu = \mu_0\mu_r$ and $\mu_0 = 4\pi\times10^{-7}$ (H/m). If exposure time in seconds is known, then the temperature increase in those specific locations can be calculated as $\Delta T = E/(mC)$ (degree C) where E = energy in joules, m = mass of Monel in g, and C = heat capacity of Monel in J/g-$^{\circ}C$. Considering C=0.44 J/g-$^{\circ}C$ and density of 8.9 g/m^3 calculated ΔT is 38.97 degree C at the marker location for 1 second of exposure time.

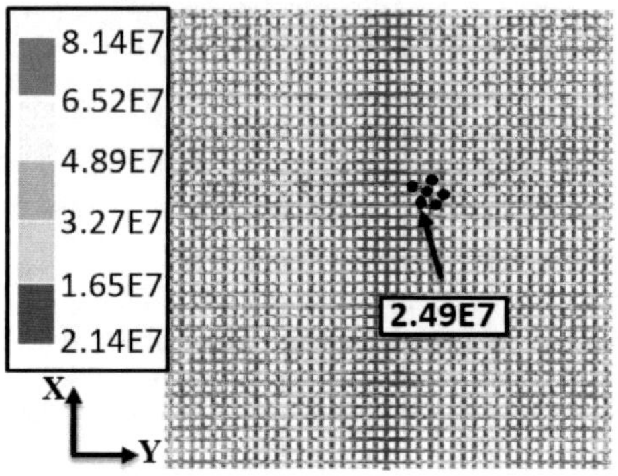

Fig. 4. Simulated current density for the Monel mesh sandwiched between two 3 mm thick sheets of Plexiglass.

An experiment was performed to verify the simulation results. A small thermocouple was placed on top of the Monel mesh approximately at the same location as one of the markers in Fig. 4. Temperature increase was also measured using an infrared camera. Two pieces of Plexiglass sheets were placed on the top and bottom of the Monel mesh as done in the simulation. A coil was placed at the same distance from the test material as in the simulation. Although the coil had multiple turns, at one instance only two turns were located on the specimen as it would be for the case illustrated in Fig. 3. The coil was excited using 500A current from a 292 kHz source. Measured temperature increase showed readings of 40 and 43.9 degrees respectively (thermocouple and IR camera). These numbers compare favorably with the simulated temperature increase of 38.97 degrees C.

ACKNOWLEDGEMENT

Authors would like to acknowledge the help from Burton Rhodes who supported the development of the equipment.

REFERENCES

[1] C. Ageorges and L. Ye, "Simulation of impulse resistance welding for thermoplastic matrix composites," Applied Composite Materials, vol. 8, no. 2, pp. 133-147, March 2001.

[2] C. Ageorges, L. Ye, and M. Hou, "Experimental investigation of the resistance welding for thermoplastic-matrix composites. Part I: Heating element and heat transfer," Composites Science and Technology, vol. 60, no.7, pp. 1027-1039, May 2000.

[3] A. Yousefpour, M. Hojjati, and J.-P. Immarigeon, "Fusion bonding/welding of thermoplastics composites," J. Thermoplastic Composite Materials, vol. 17, no. 4, pp. 303-341, July 2004.

[4] L. Moser and A. K. Schlarb, "Induction welding of thermoplastic polymer composites using robotics techniques," Sample Journal, vol. 44, no.5, pp. 43-48, 2008.

[5] V. K. Stokes, "Experiments on the induction welding of thermoplastics," Polymer Engineering and Science, vol. 43, no. 9, pp. 1523-1541, 2004.

Two-Dimensional Electrical Properties Tomography Using a Simplified Contrast-Source Inversion Approach

Patrick Fuchs
Circuits and Systems, Microelectronics Department
Delft University of Technology
Delft, The Netherlands
p.s.fuchs@tudelft.nl

Rob Remis
Circuits and Systems, Microelectronics Department
Delft University of Technology
Delft, The Netherlands
r.f.remis@tudelft.nl

***Abstract*—The contrast source inversion (CSI) method is a well-known inversion technique that has been utilized in a wide range of application areas. Here we show that in the specific situation of electrical properties tomography (EPT) in magnetic resonance imaging (MRI), which is a so-called hybrid inverse problem, since data is collected inside the reconstruction domain, the CSI method can be simplified to what is essentially a single forward simulation provided the electromagnetic field has an E-polarized field structure. As a consequence, the computational costs are significantly reduced and our experiments show that reconstructions obtained with the simplified CSI method have essentially the same accuracy as reconstructions obtained with the full CSI inversion method.**

***Index Terms*—Electrical Tissue Properties, Electromagnetic Inversion, Magnetic Resonance Imaging, Optimization.**

I. Introduction

Magnetic resonance imaging (MRI) is a powerful imaging modality that can be used not only for imaging tissue contrasts but also to image the *in vivo* electrical properties of different tissue types. Specifically, in electrical properties tomography (EPT) the objective is to retrieve the conductivity and permittivity tissue profiles at the MR frequency of operation (Larmor frequency) and within an inversion domain of interest based on measured magnetic flux density data (the B_1^+-field) that has its support *inside* the inversion domain.

It has been shown in [1] that the contrast-source inversion (CSI) method applied to EPT (CSI-EPT) is able to retrieve the conductivity and permittivity maps within a domain of interest even for strongly inhomogeneous tissue profiles. However, convergence may be slow and it may take the CSI-EPT method many iterations to reach the desired error tolerance.

Fortunately, computation times and costs can be significantly reduced by taking advantage of the field structure that may be present inside the imaging domain of interest and the fact that data collection takes place inside this imaging domain. Specifically, we show that for two-dimensional field structures which can occur in the midplane of a birdcage coil [2], it is possible to image the induced currents in real-time and the electrical tissue maps in this plane can be obtained within at most a couple of seconds on a standard laptop or PC by solving a single forward problem. Since the simplified CSI-EPT method does rely on an E-polarized field structure, it is more limited in its applicability than standard CSI-EPT, but if it can be applied then significant speedups can be realized and accurate tissue profiles may be obtained at reduced computational costs.

In previous work this has been shown for a head model, but to show that the method can handle larger domains where the speedup is even more significant here we focus on the computationally more challenging abdomen.

II. Method

In the midplane of a birdcage coil, the electromagnetic field is essentially E-polarized meaning that the electric field strength has a longitudinal z-component only, while the magnetic field is purely transverse (see [2] for a detailed discussion). With σ and ε denoting the conductivity and permittivity within the midplane of the coil, the induced electric-current density in this plane is given by:

$$J_z^{\text{ind}} = (\sigma + \mathrm{j}\omega\varepsilon)E_z. \tag{1}$$

The electric field strength E_z and the medium parameters σ and ε are all unknown, of course. Now in MRI, the so-called B_1^+ field:

$$B_1^+ = \frac{B_x + \mathrm{j}B_y}{2}, \tag{2}$$

can be measured inside the object in the midplane of a birdcage coil. Given a B_1^+ measurement, and introducing the differentiation operator $\partial^- = (\partial_x - \mathrm{j}\partial_y)/2$, it follows from Ampere's law and the fact that the magnetic flux density is divergence free that:

$$J_z^{\text{ind}} = \frac{4}{\mathrm{j}\mu_0}\partial^- B_1^+. \tag{3}$$

In other words, the induced current follows from a first-order spatial differentiation of the B_1^+-data and the present method is therefore called foIC-EPT (first-order induced-current EPT). In practice, the data is typically filtered to avoid noise amplification. Clearly, computing the induced current density can be realized essentially in real-time.

Having the induced current available, the electric field strength within the midplane can be obtained by solving a particular integral equation for the electric field strength presented in [3]. Solving this equation is equivalent to solving a forward problem and its solution can be obtained efficiently using iterative solvers such as CG-FFT or GMRES.

Finally, the conductivity and permittivity can be determined using the constitutive relation of equation (1), since the induced current density J_z^{ind} and the electric field strength E_z are now known. Note that at locations where the magnitude of the electric field strength is small it is difficult to retrieve the tissue parameters from the constitutive relation of equation (1).

III. Results

Simulations are performed to compare midplane tissue profile reconstructions obtained with CSI-EPT and the reconstruction method outlined above. Ideal B_1^+ data was obtained by simulating the wave field response due to 16 equally spaced line sources positioned on a circle with a radius of 34 cm that operate in quadrature mode at 128 MHz, which is the operating frequency that corresponds to a 3 tesla background field. For noiseless data, foIC-EPT and CSI-EPT produce essentially identical reconstructions. Therefore, to provide a more accurate representation of actual measured data, we corrupted the simulated B_1^+ data with noise at an SNR of 40dB. The current simplified reconstruction method and CSI-EPT were both implemented in Matlab 2018b on a desktop computer with an Intel i5 processor and 8Gb of RAM. Further implementation details can be found in [3].

Figures 1 (a) and 1 (d) show the exact conductivity and permittivity maps of a thorax model positioned at the midplane of the birdcage coil. Figures 1 (b) and 1 (c) show the conductivity reconstructions obtained with foIC-EPT and CSI-EPT, respectively. The corresponding permittivity reconstructions are shown in Figs 1 (e) and 1 (f). The normalised global error for the conductivity and permittivity are 0.118 and 0.1399 for foIC-EPT and 0.1157 and 0.1342 for CSI-EPT methods respectively. The CSI-EPT reconstruction took 278 iterations (49.5 seconds) for the normalized residual to drop below the noise level, while five GMRES iterations were required to solve the E-field integral equation (normalized residual smaller than 10^{-6}) and it took 0.21 seconds for foIC-EPT to obtain the tissue reconstructions presented in Figs 1 (b) and 1 (e).

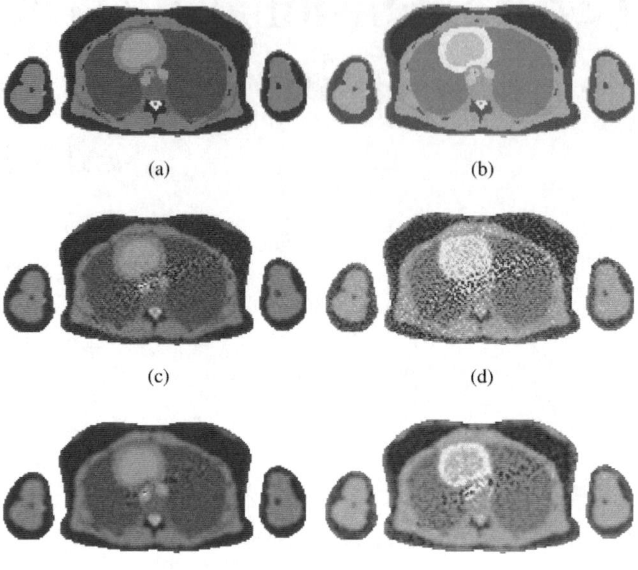

Fig. 1. (a), (c), (e), Conductivity profiles of a thorax slice; (a) is the original conductivity, (c) the foIC-EPT reconstruction, and (e) the 2D-CSI-EPT reconstruction. (b), (d), (f), permittivity profiles of a thorax slice; (b) is the original conductivity, (d) the foIC-EPT reconstruction, and (f) the 2D-CSI-EPT reconstruction.

IV. Discussion and Conclusion

In quadrature mode, the magnitude of the electric field strength is relatively small in an area around the center of the slice, and for both methods the effects of noise are clearly seen in this area. For foIC-EPT these noise effects are stronger due to the differentiation of the data (equation (3)). Such a step is absent in the CSI-EPT method. Noise effects can be suppressed, of course, by incorporating regularization techniques in both reconstruction methods. In addition, at 3T (128 MHz) both methods produce lower quality permittivity than the conductivity reconstructions since the conduction current dominates the induced current density at 128 MHz.

In terms of computation time, the foIC-EPT method is 100 times faster for the region considered here, which allows for real-time imaging. The main computational cost of foIC-EPT and CSI-EPT is the computation of FFT-based matrix-vector products at every iteration, therefore, both have an equal complexity of $\mathcal{O}(n\log(n))$. For CSI-EPT, however, the total number of matrix-vector products that need to be computed is typically for thousands of iterations and foIC-EPT takes less than ten. We conclude that if the radiofrequency transmit field has a two-dimensional E-polarized field structure in some imaging plane of interest, then foIC-EPT is able to reconstruct these dielectric tissue profiles essentially in real time.

Acknowledgment

The authors would like to thank Reijer Leijsen from the Gorter Center for High-Field MRI, Leiden University Medical Center in The Netherlands for fruitful discussions.

References

[1] E. Balidemaj, et al., "CSI-EPT: A contrast source inversion approach for improved MRI-based electrical properties tomography," IEEE Trans. Med. Imag., vol. 34, pp. 1788–1796, 2015.

[2] B. van den Bergen, C. C. Stolk, J. B. van den Berg, J. J. W. Lagendijk, and C. A. T. van den Berg, "Ultra fast electromagnetic field computations for RF multi-transmit techniques in high field MRI," Phys. Med. Biol., vol. 54, pp. 1253–1264, 2009.

[3] P.S. Fuchs, et al., "First-order induced current density imaging and electrical properties tomography in MRI," IEEE Trans. Comp. Imag., vol. 4, pp. 624–631, 2018.

A Comparison of Different Formulations for an Inverse Source Magnetostatic Problem

Alessandro Formisano
Department of Engineering
Univ.della Campania "Luigi Vanvitelli"
Aversa (CE), Italy
Alessandro.Formisano@unicampania.it

***Abstract*—The resolution of inverse problems is a quite common task in the diagnostic processes based on electromagnetic field measurements, in particular when internal characteristics of the object under test are to be estimated from external measurements. This class of problems are well known to be ill posed, and a number of different techniques have been proposed to make the estimation process reliable. In this paper, with reference to an application in the framework of low frequency magnetic fields measurements, the effects of different choices for the degrees of freedom are discussed, with the aim of improving the solution reliability.**

Keywords—Inverse Problems, Magnetostatics, Numerical Analysis, Superconducting Coils.

I. Introduction

Current measurement and current distribution reconstruction from external magnetic field is gathering increasing interest in a number of applications where a direct current measurement is not feasible, but system or device correct operation depends on the availability of such information. Examples are power distribution lines, electric arcs, but also, in a broader sense, high field magnets, such as those for magnetically confined thermonuclear fusion [1-4]. In these cases, indirect measurement of source characteristics can also help determining discrepancies from nominal design due to manufacturing and assembly tolerances [5]. The resulting inverse problem is ill posed, and the solution is highly influenced by measurement uncertainty. A number of different approaches have been proposed to regularize this problem, based on classical general-purpose schemes (e.g. Tikhonov or Truncated Singular Values Decomposition - TSVD [6]), or taking advantage of the problem physics [7, 8]. Other possibilities, not yet fully explored in the area of low frequency electromagnetism, are based on the ideas behind Model Order Reduction [9, 10]. All of these possibilities present advantages and drawbacks, which makes it quite hard to find a real general winner, and trade-offs among accuracy, promptness and availability of measurements and *a-priori* information drive towards the best choice for the problem at hand. The aim of this contribution is to assess the impact of different choices of Degrees of Freedom (DOF). The key aspect here is on the matrix projecting standard DOF onto alternative ones: actually, by suitably choosing such a matrix, it is possible to redefine the singular vectors, mapping reconstruction error onto components associated with less significant current configurations, much like as in the analysis of dynamical systems. A very simple test example of current reconstruction is used here for illustration purposes, and a brief description of the example is first given. Then, in this digest, just an alternative for the DOF choice is considered. The reliability of these DOF is compared to a more straightforward choice, to show the impact on the inverse problem resolution. Both TSVD and an iterative scheme are used to solve for both sets of DOF. In the full paper, a larger number of projection bases are introduced, with the related mapping matrices, and their advantages and drawbacks discussed.

II. The Illustrative Example

In the remaining, for the sake of exposition, we will refer to a conceptually simple situation, yet showing all the relevant aspects required to gain insight in the considered problem. We will consider the (inverse) problem of estimating the current in each turn of a multi-turn circular coil from the magnetic field map measured on a circumference encircling the Winding Pack (WP). Although usually turns are series connected, in this illustrative example we will remove this hypothesis to let currents differ each from the others. A schematic view of the measurement layout, with reference to a WP of N_c=25 conductors, arranged in five layers, is sketched in Fig. 1.

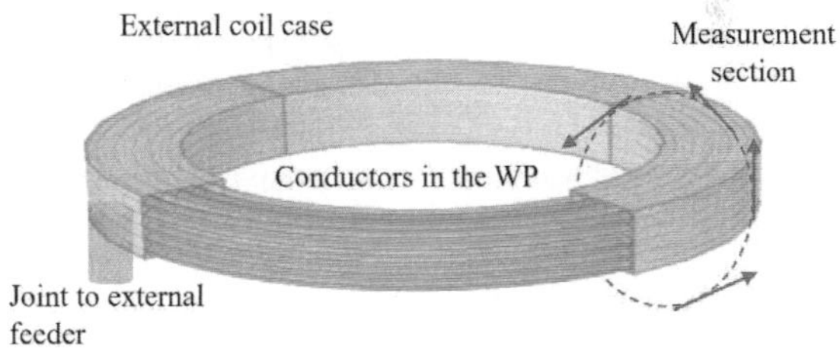

Fig. 1. Sketch of the measurement layout for a circular coil.

Taking into account: (i) the limitations on the frequency, that must be very low to avoid inducing eddy currents in the coil metallic case and support structures, (ii) the expected amplitude of the field, assumed in the order of some mT in the considered case, and (iii) the need of measuring the field with high spatial resolution to catch small local field map variations, in this study the underlying measurement system is assumed to be based on a set of three-dimensional Hall probes, fixed to a plastic holder encircling the magnet. This "system" measures simultaneously the tangential and normal components of flux density in N_p=30 points. If no magnetic material is present, and assuming a DC power supply, the linear magneto-static model applies, and the currents estimation process can be easily formulated as a matrix inversion. Real world systems are by far more complex, but this quite simple model allows a straightforward performance comparison of different choices for the DOF. Thanks to the linearity assumption, the contribution of each conductor, fed by a unit current, in each measurement point can be computed in advance, providing a matrix **G**, which is known as "lead matrix". In this paper, matrix elements are computed using the classical expression for a thin circular coil [11]. The resulting "direct" problem, that is the measurement of the flux density from known sources, can be stated as:

$$\underline{m} = \boldsymbol{G}(\underline{\boldsymbol{x}}_{\mathrm{m}}, \underline{\boldsymbol{s}}_{\mathrm{m}}; \underline{\boldsymbol{x}}_{\mathrm{c}}) * \underline{I} + \underline{\varepsilon}, \quad (1)$$

where $\underline{m}$ is the measurement values array, $\underline{\boldsymbol{x}}_m$ and $\underline{\boldsymbol{s}}_{\mathrm{m}}$ are the arrays of probes position and alignment respectively, $\underline{\boldsymbol{x}}_c$ the array of coils positions, $\underline{I}$ is the array of currents in each of the k coil turns and $\underline{\varepsilon}$ is the measurement uncertainty, due to noise, probes incorrect positioning and alignment, and "model" errors, introduced by an approximate modeling of the actual coil and by poor knowledge of possible background field and material characteristics. The inverse problem can now be formulated as:

$$\underline{\tilde{I}} = pinv(\boldsymbol{G}) * \underline{m}, \qquad (2)$$

or as an alternative suited for iterative estimation process:

$$\min_{\underline{\tilde{I}}} \left\| \boldsymbol{G} * \underline{\tilde{I}} - \underline{m} \right\|, \qquad (3)$$

where $\underline{\tilde{I}}$ is the array of estimated currents.

III. Different Reconstruction Approaches

Since the seminal proposal of Tikhonov [12], many regularization algorithms have been proposed to counteract the ill conditioning of linear inverse problems, as discussed above. As anticipated, the attention here will be focused on the effect on reconstruction reliability of different choices for DOF. In this digest, just a single alternative is considered, namely DOF represented by the total fluxes linked by each coil. This amounts to pre- and post-multiplying the matrix **G** times the square, invertible inductances matrix **M**. Two possible methods based on this transformation are considered, namely a TSVD approach, and an iterative approach (ν-method, [6]), which uses the lead matrix to create a "succession" of solutions. A comparison of different regularization techniques for a very similar problem has been proposed in [13]. Note that for the particular problem at hand a more regular approach, based on a direct estimation of current distribution moments, is provided in [7]. Since this approach can be applied only to current reconstruction, for the sake of generality it is not considered here.

IV. Results and discussion

In order to show the impact of a re-definition of DOF from current to fluxes linked by each of the coils, we show the singular values distribution of **G** and **G*M**$^{-1}$ in fig. 2. To appreciate the different decrease rates, singular values are normalized to the first one for both matrices. The conditioning number of **G** is $C_G=1.3\times10^5$, while for **M** is $C_M=2717$, and finally for **G*M**$^{-1}$ is $C_{GM}=12850$. Average reconstruction errors on 1000 randomly generated current distributions, adding white Gaussian noise with a std. dev. of 0.01% of full scale, are reported in Table I for two different truncation index in the case of TSVD and iterations number for ν-method. As the aim of the reconstruction is to detect current variations from small variations of the measured field, taking into account the ill conditioned nature of the problem, also using apparently accurate measurements, the estimation error is still not acceptable for practical applications. On the other hand, the purpose in this work is just to reveal the effects of DOF redefinitions, so we did not apply any measure to improve the quality of reconstructions.

TABLE I. AVERAGE RECONTRUCTION ERRORS

DOF basis	Average error on 1000 random current distributions			
	TSVD		*ν-method*	
	7 modes	21 modes	3 iterations	5 iterations
Currents	86%	143%	88%	753%
Fluxes	97%	72%	78%	90%

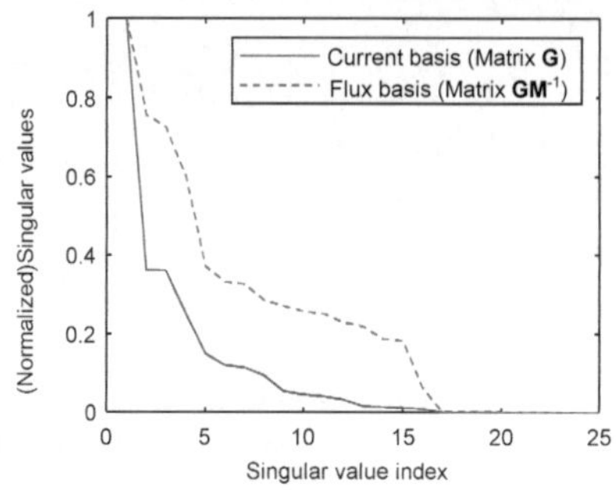

Fig. 2. Comparison of (normalized) singular values distribution for **G** and **GM**$^{-1}$.

In all cases, when using very severe truncation (or limited number of iterations), the details of current distribution are lost. When augmenting the singular modes, or increasing the number of iterations, it is possible to recognize the effect of the slower singular values decrease of **GM**$^{-1}$, which leads to a reduction of the average reconstruction error both for TSVD and for iterative method. When using optimized transformation, the impact on the singular values can be "tailored" to enhance or depress specific modes, thus filtering out uncertainty.

Acknowledgements

This work was partly founded by Engineering Dept., Univ. of Campania, and partly by ENEA/EURATOM/CREATE.

References

[1] S. Ziegler, R. C. Woodward, H. Ho-Ching Iu, and L. J. Borle, "Current Sensing Techniques: A Review, IEEE Sensors Journal," Vol. 9, n° 4, 2009, pp. 354-376.

[2] L. Di Rienzo, R. Bazzocchi, and A. Manara, "Circular arrays of magnetic sensors for current measurement," IEEE Trans. Instrum. Meas., Vol. 50, n° 2, 2001, pp. 1093-1096.

[3] M. Norgren and S. He, "Exact and explicit solution to a class of degaussing problems," IEEE Trans. On Magnetics., Vol. 36, n° 1, 2000, pp. 308-312.

[4] A. Formisano et al., "DC and transient current distribution analysis from self-field measurements on ITER PFIS conductor," Fusion Engineering and Design, Vol. 75-79, 2005, pp. 11-15.

[5] A. Bonito Oliva et al, "Characterization of deformed magnets from external magnetic measurements," IEEE Trans. on Magnetics, Vol. 50 n° 2, 2014, pp. 1001-1004.

[6] P.C. Hansen, *Rank-Deficient and Discrete Ill-Posed Problems. Numerical Aspects of Linear Inversion*, SIAM. Philadelphia, 1997.

[7] B. Braams, "The interpretation of tokamak magnetic diagnostics," Plasma Phys. Control. Fusion, Vol. 33, pp. 715-748.

[8] M. Vikram, B. Shanker, "An Incomplete Review of Fast Multipole Methods-from Static to Wideband-as Applied to Problems in Computational Electromagnetics," ACES Journal, Vol. 24, n°2, pp. 79-108.

[9] J. R. Shenefelt, R. Luck, R. P. Taylor, and J. T. Berry, "Solution to inverse heat conduction problems employing singular values decomposition and model-reduction," Int. J. of Heat and Mass Transfer, Vol. 45, 2002, pp. 67-74.

[10] S. Gazzola, P..C. Hanse, and J. G. Nagy, "IR Tools: a MATLAB package of iterative regularization methods and large scale test problems," Numer. Algor., 2018, DOI: 10.1007/s11075-018-0570-7.

[11] É. Durand, *Magnétostatique*, Masson er Cie, 1968, Paris (FR).

[12] A. N. Tikhonov and V. Y. Arsenin, *Solutions of Ill-Posed Problems*, Winston&Sons, Washington D.C., 1977.

[13] A. Formisano and R. Martone, "Different regularization methods for an inverse magnetostatic problem," in press on Int. Journ. of Applied Electromagnetics and Mechanics.

An Accurate Technique for Modeling Realistic Well-Logging Sensors Inside Complex Media

Lisseth Saavedra, Guilherme S. Rosa, and José R. Bergmann
Center for Telecommunications Studies, CETUC
Pontifical Catholic University of Rio de Janeiro
Rio de Janeiro, Brazil
lissethsaavedra@cetuc.puc-rio.br

***Abstract*—In this paper, a pseudoanalytical mode-matching formulation is introduced for the analysis of electromagnetic well-logging tools. We present numerical results for several representative scenarios to validate and explore the input (self) impedance of typical logging-while-drilling (LWD) sensors comprised by an array of coil antennas. Preliminary conclusions are presented and the potential of this approach for modeling realistic LWD sensors is then summarized.**

***Index Terms*—Antenna impedance, inhomogeneous media, logging-while-drilling (LWD) tools.**

I. Introduction

Logging-while-drilling (LWD) tools have enabled the real-time characterization of lithological variations in the soil surrounding a prospecting oil well and the consequent identification of potential pay zones. Typical LWD sensors employed by the oil and gas industry [1], [2] are comprised by an array of coil antennas wrapped around a metallic mandrel, as illustrated in Fig. 1. The geophysical environment in this type of problem is complex, and the prevalence of large contrasts of resistivity requires accurate and robust computational electromagnetics (CEM) techniques for addressing the propagation sensor response. This topic has been receiving much attention for several subsurface applications. To the best of our knowledge, the modeling of the mutual- and self-impedance of antenna sensors, however, is a topic that was not properly addressed in the literature because it demands high-cost brute-force CEM based on finite-differences (FD) and finite-elements (FE). In this paper, we overcome these difficulties by using a combination of the Bessel-Fourier expansion with an analytic version of the mode-matching technique for representing self-impedance of real dimensions LWD sensors in a borehole environment described by cylindrical-stratified media [3], [4]. Numerical simulations are presented to validate our formulation versus finite-difference-time-domain (FDTD) results. In addition, present a sensitivity analysis of the sensor impedance in terms of its physical dimension, operating frequency, and constitutive parameters of the medium where it is immersed.

II. Electromagnetic Modeling

Fig. 1 shows the geometry used to model the geophysical formation around a typical well-logging tool. Field solutions for Maxwell's equations in uniaxially anisotropic multilayered cylindrical structures (with radial and longitudinal stratifications) are well known from a prior study, and to avoid repetition, we adopt here a notation similar to that in [4] by assuming a time-harmonic dependence in the form $\exp(-i\omega t)$. The electromagnetic fields radiated by the transmitter (TX) antenna are computed by considering first it as an electric-coil with an infinitesimal cross-section. Such fields are then used as a basis for computing the input impedance of a finite-cross-section TX by using [5]:

$$Z_{\text{in}} = -\frac{1}{I_{\text{TX}}^2} \oiint \mathbf{E} \cdot \mathbf{J}_s \, ds, \tag{1}$$

where I_{TX} and $\mathbf{J}_s$ are the electrical current of the TX and its associated current density distribution over the antenna surface. The electric field $\mathbf{E}$ is computed considering all the radial and longitudinal stratifications of the problem. The mode-matching method used for computing $\mathbf{E}$ (due to an infinitesimal coil) in (1) has been extensively validated against FD and FE methods as shown in the results in [4]. In what follows, we are only concerned with the calculation of the antenna impedances of the well-logging tool.

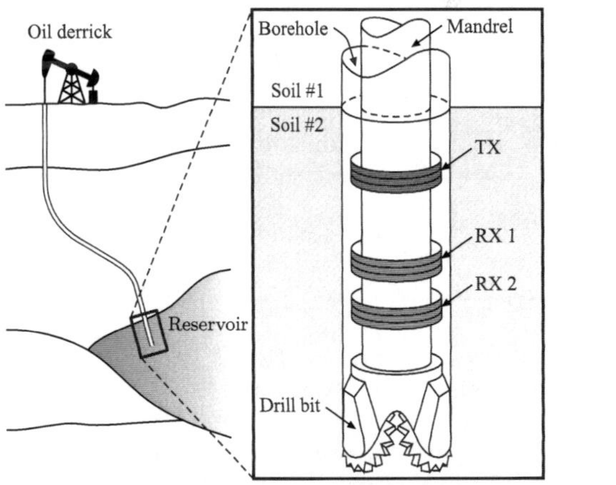

Fig. 1. Geometry of a triaxial LWD sensor within a geophysical formation.

As a first example, we first consider a 4-in-radius metallic mandrel inside a 7-in-radius borehole, where 1 in $= 2.54 \times 10^{-2}$ m. The borehole is filled with oil-based mud with 5×10^{-4} S/m and the soil formation has 1 S/m. Fig. 2 shows the impedance of two rectangular cross-section antennas as the frequency evolves from 0.5 MHz–2 MHz. Good agreement is observed versus FDTD results. To avoid very long simulation times in the FDTD, the radial domain was truncated at 10 in.

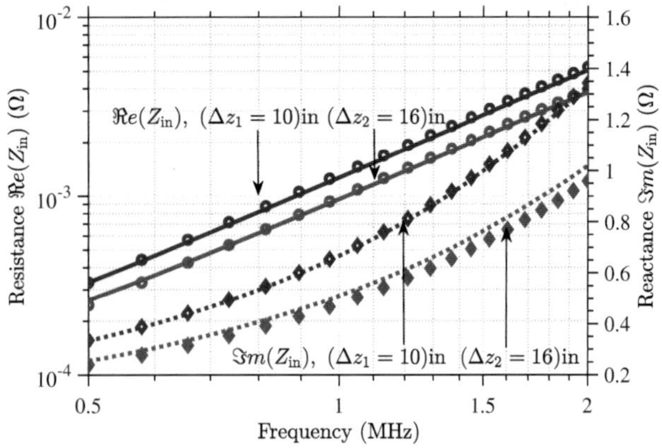

Fig. 2. Impedance of the antenna with cross-section width $\Delta\rho = 0.2$ in and heights $\Delta z = 10$ in and 16 in. The results from the present algorithm are indicated by small symbols. The solid and dashed lines are FDTD results.

As a second example, we consider a formation similar to that presented above, but now we investigate the influence of the conductivity of the soil formation. Fig. 3 shows the impedance of an antenna with cross-section $\Delta\rho = 0.2$ in by $\Delta z = 10$ in operating at 500 kHz and 2 MHz as the conductivity of the soil formation evolves.

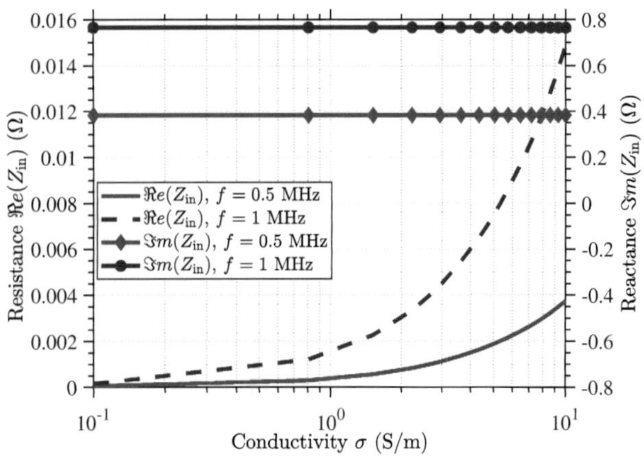

Fig. 3. Impedance of the antenna as a function of the soil conductivity.

We next evaluate a scenario similar to the first example, but now we investigate the influence of the antenna dimensions. Fig. 4 and Fig. 5 show impedance results as a function of the antenna width $\Delta\rho$ and height Δz, when the operating frequency is fixed at 0.5 MHz.

III. Conclusions

In this paper, we present a novel semi-analytical technique for modeling realistic LWD sensors immersed in complex media. Numerical results show that the technique can accurately describe the sensor impedance using low computational resources. A sensitivity analysis shows that the antenna impedance changes dramatically in terms of its dimensions, operating frequency, and media parameters of the medium where it is immersed.

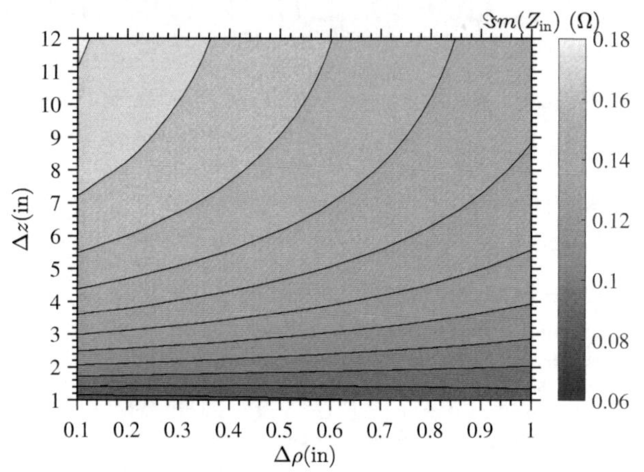

Fig. 4. Input reactance of the antenna as a function of the cross-section width $\Delta\rho$ and height Δz.

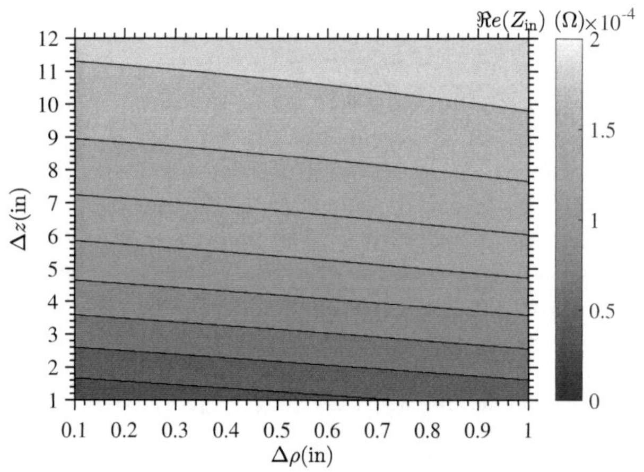

Fig. 5. Input resistance of the antenna as a function of the cross-section width $\Delta\rho$ and height Δz.

Acknowledgment

The first author thanks support from the Brazilian Agency CNPq. This study was financed in part by the Coordenação de Aperfeiçoamento de Pessoal de Nível Superior - Brasil (CAPES) - Finance Code PROCAD 068419/2014-01.

References

[1] "ADR azimuthal deep resistivity sensor datasheet," Halliburton Sperry-Drilling, Houston, TX, USA, 2016.

[2] "EarthStar™ Ultra-Deep Resistivity Service datasheet," Halliburton-Sperry Drilling, Houston, TX, USA, 2018.

[3] W. C. Chew, Waves and Fields in Inhomogeneous Media. New York,NY, USA: John Wiley & Sons, 1995.

[4] G. S. Rosa, J. R. Bergmann, and F. L. Teixeira, "A robust mode-matching algorithm for the analysis of triaxial well-logging tools in anisotropic geophysical formations,"IEEE Trans. Geosci. Remote Sens., vol. 55,no. 5, pp. 2534–2545, May 2017.

[5] R. F. Harrington,Time-harmonic electromagnetic fields. New York, NY,USA: McGraw-Hill, 1961.

Electromagnetic Induction Sensing for Buried Explosive Hazards Detection

Fridon Shubitidze[1,3], Benjamin E. Barrowes[2], Micheil Prishvin[1], Irma Shamatava[3,1]

[1]Thayer School of Engineering
Dartmouth College, Hanover, NH, 03755, USA
Fridon.Shubitidze@Dartmouth.edu; Mikheil.Prishvin@Dartmouth.edu

[2]Cold Regions Research and Engineering Laboratory
USA Army ERDC, Hanover, NH, 03755, USA
Benjamin.E.Barrowes@erdc.dren.mil

[3]White River Technologies, Inc,
Lebanon, NH, 03766, USA
Shamatava@Whiterivertech.com

Abstract — Detection and identification of subsurface improvised explosive devices (IED) remains one of the most pressing military and civilian problems worldwide. Usually, IED-s are made only with low conducting and/or no metallic parts and therefore are undetectable with conventional metal detectors and electromagnetic induction (EMI) sensors. To overcome this limitation and to fill the gap between the conventional EMI induction and radar sensing frequency bands, our group has developed a next generation High Frequency EMI (HFEMI) sensor, operating between 50 kHz and 15 MHz. Both numerical and in-lab experimental studies have showed that the new EMI sensor is able to detect high conducting (metals) as well as low conducting (carbon rods), low metal content (short wires) and non-conducting (voids in conducting soil) targets. For validating the system's detection capabilities under real world conditions, the system was deployed at an IED test site and EMI data were collected for a set of targets. In this paper, measured and numerical data are presented and analyzed for subsurface IEDs.

Index Terms—Carbon-Rods, Detection, EMI, Explosive-Hazards, IED, Sensing, Voids.

I. INTRODUCTION

Detection and identification of subsurface IEDs remains the number one problem for military and public safety worldwide. Recent IED constituents are either non-metallic, use intermediate electrical conductivity (IEC) materials ($1<\sigma<10^5$ S/m such as a Carbon Rod (CR)), or use low metal content objects (such as wires) for detonator elements and triggering mechanisms. Since the conductivity of these IEC materials are orders of magnitude less than the conductivity of metallic targets, IECs as well as low metal content wires are undetectable using traditional metal detectors (DC) and EMI instruments (30 Hz to 100kHz) [1]-[3].Therefore, detection and identification of CR and wires have become a high priority for the US military during recent conflicts. To address this need, a new EMI sensor was developed. The HFEMI sensor, which operates between 50 kHz and 15 MHz (Fig. 1), can detect buried IEC and low metal content targets including wires.

During EMI sensing a time-varying magnetic field illuminates a target. This primary electromagnetic field penetrates a conducting and potentially permeable metallic object and induces currents within it. The induced currents produce a secondary field that is sensed outside the object. Once signals are detected, the measured data are processed and a target's intrinsic and extrinsic parameters are extracted for identification [2].

Fig. 1. A new EMI system has co-located circular Tx and Figure 8 Rx coils;

The HFEMI system consists of collocated Tx/Rx coils with high gain amplifiers for improved signals [4]. The Tx coil is 25cm in diameter while the figure-8 receiver coil lobes are each 7.5-cm diameter circles. The figure-8 windings are in opposite directions to cancel the voltage produced by the primary magnetic fields. The National Instruments VirtualBench all-in-one function generator/oscilloscope is used for generating and measuring the primary and secondary electromagnetic fields, respectively.

Numerical results presented here were obtained using the Method of Auxiliary Sources (MAS), which was adapted for solving the EMI diffusion problems. The MAS solves boundary value problems numerically by representing the electromagnetic fields in each domain of the structure under investigation by finite linear combinations of analytical solutions of the relevant field equations, corresponding to sources situated some distance away from the boundaries of each domain [5].

II. RESULTS

To demonstrate the applicability of the MAS for solving high frequency EMI induction problems first the comparisons between modeled and actual data are presented for a carbon rod (CR) the 2-1/4 "length and 5/16 "diameter, Fig.2 The CR, that is used as a triggering mechanism in IEDS, has been identified as a target of interest by the US army. The comparisons between the modeled and actual responses are shown in Fig. 3 for the CR. The data were taken in a lab and CR was placed at 1" and 2" depths from the HFEMI sensor.

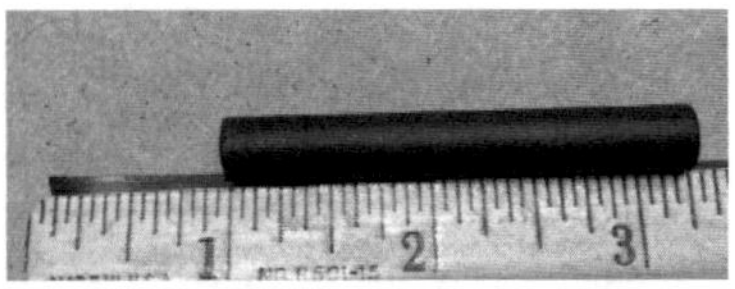

Fig. 2. Carbon rod: Length 2 ¼ "; diameter 5/16 ".

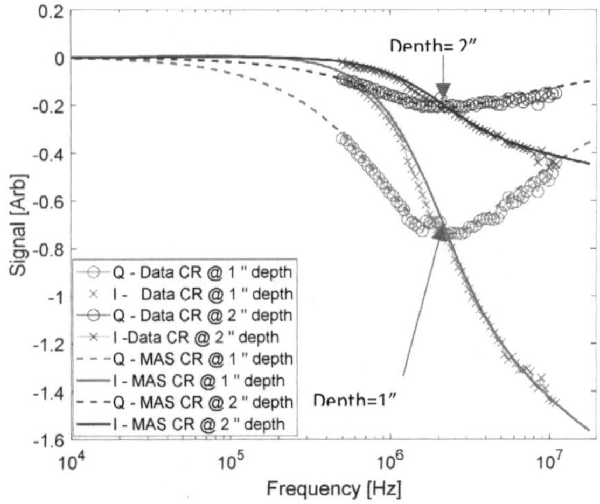

Fig. 3. Comparisons between modeled and measured EMI data for an IED carbon rod.

The comparisons show good agreements between the modeled and measured data, for both depths. As the separation (depth) between the HFEMI sensor and CR rod increases the signal decays but the CR is still detectable in the middle frequency range.

To validate the MAS method and applicability of the new EMI sensing system for subsurface IED detection in realistic field conditions, the system was deployed at the Fort AP-Hill IED test site on April 3, 2018. Using a data collection protocol as: 1) background, 2) ferrite and 3) anomaly shots, we collected data over a set of anomalies. The EMI system's detection results for carbon rod and tire rubber pressure plates and low-metal-content wire AP-HILL IED targets are illustrated below. Namely, Fig. 4 shows the measured data for the flush CR pressure plate. The measured data are correlated with modeled data up to 1 MHz and divergences between the measured and modeled data at high (> 1MHz) frequencies are due to the EMI response of the IED wires, which are not included in the model.

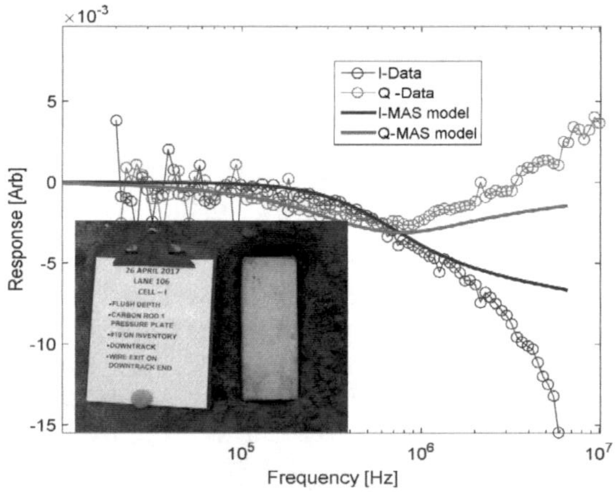

Fig. 4. Lines with circles: EMI signals (in-phase and quadrature parts) for a carbon rod pressure plate buried in AP-Hill soil. Solid lines: modeled HFEMI responses using the MAS.

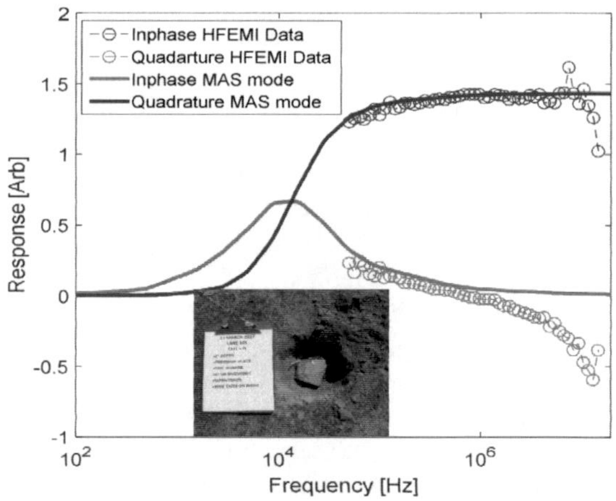

Fig. 5. Modeled and actual data for a Fort AP-Hill IED-Tire Rubber pressure plate buried at 2'' depth.

Fig. 5 shows comparisons between modeled and actual data for a tire rubber pressure plate buried at 2" depth. The comparisons show the model matched the data up to 1 MHz. In the model, data was calculated for the plate placed in free space using the MAS techniques. The mismatches between the modeled and actual data are due to the soil's responses at high frequencies. Fig. 6 illustrates measured EMI responses for 1 m long dual 24 AWG lamp wire buried at 4". For comparison, the EMI response for background soil is shown. The system detects buried wire. Note that the responses are caused to linear and not induction (eddy) currents.

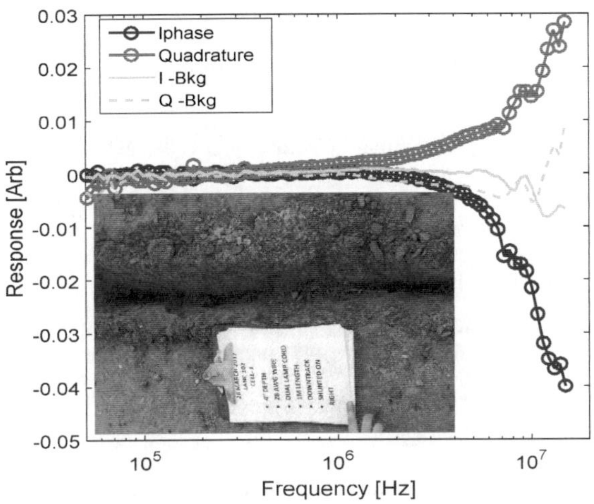

Fig. 6. Measured EMI responses for buried 1 m length cord 24 AWG wire (blue and red lines with circles) and for background soil (green lines). The wire was buried at 4".

III. CONCLUSIONS

The MAS is applied to HHEMI problems. The comparisons between modeled and actual HFEMI data are demonstrated for IED targets. The studies show good agreements between numerical and actual data were illustrated. In addition, the applicability of the HFEMI system to detect IED constituents such as carbon rods and tire rubber pressure plates and low-metal-content wire targets was demonstrated. The results show that HFEMI sensing is a promising approach for detecting, locating and identifying subsurface IEDs.

ACKNOWLEDGMENT

This work was sponsored by the Office of Naval Research under the project: N00014-16-1-2332.

References

[1] J. Won and *et al.,* "Electromagnetic Induction Spectroscopy for Clearing Landmines," *IEEE Rem. Sensing,* vol. 39, no. 4, April, 2001.

[2] E. Gasperikova and *et al.*, "UXO detection and identification based on intrinsic target polarizabilities—A case history," *Geophysics*, vol. 74, no. 1,pp. B1–B8, 2009.

[3] H. H. Nelson and J. R. McDonald, "Multi-sensor towed array detection system for UXO detection," *IEEE Trans. Geosci. Remote Sens.*, vol. 39, pp. 1139–1145, 2001.

[4] John B. and et al., "High-frequency electromagnetic induction sensing of non-metallic materials", *IEEE Trans. Geosci. Remote Sens.*, 2017.

[5] F. Shubitidze and *et al.* "Application of the method of auxiliary sources to the wide-band electromagnetic induction problem," *IEEE Transactions on Geoscience and Remote Sensing,* vol. 40, pp. 928-942, Apr 2002.

Recent Improvements in Feko

Johann van Tonder
Altair Development S.A. (Pty) Ltd
Stellenbosch, South Africa
jvtonder@altair.co.za

Marianne Bingle
Altair Development S.A. (Pty) Ltd
Stellenbosch, South Africa
mbingle@altair.co.za

Elia Attardo
Altair Engineering GmbH
Böblingen, Germany
attardo@altair.de

Ulrich Jakobus
Altair Engineering GmbH
Böblingen, Germany
jakobus@altair.de

Marlize Schoeman
Altair Development S.A. (Pty) Ltd
Stellenbosch, South Africa
schoeman@altair.co.za

Kitty Longtin
Altair Engineering, Inc.
Hampton, VA, USA
klongtin@altair.com

***Abstract*—This paper describes the latest improvements to the commercial electromagnetic software Feko. These include the hybridization of the MLFMM based on the surface equivalence principle, the finite element method and windscreen antenna analysis; periodic boundary conditions are accelerated and extended to support the finite element method; and the number of options to model a cable shield has been extended to include direct modeling of a double shield and single-layered braided shield formulas described by Tyni and Demoulin.**

Keywords—cable shield models, fast techniques, Feko, MLFMM, periodic boundaries, windscreen antennas.

I. Introduction

For many years, Altair Feko [1] has been a popular computational electromagnetics code widely used for academic research and commercial applications. To remain an industry leader in this field, continuous improvements and extensions are required. This paper highlights some of the recent extensions made.

II. Windscreen Antenna Analysis

Feko has a wide range of techniques to model complex dielectrics, including the method of moments (MoM) based on either the surface equivalence principle (SEP) or the volume equivalence principle (VEP), the finite element method (FEM), the finite difference time domain method (FDTD), and special formulations for planar multilayer structures, windscreen antennas, skin effect, thin sheets, coatings, etc. For large structures the MoM is accelerated by using the multilevel fast multiple method (MLFMM). Since each formulation has its own advantages and limitations, it is often required to use a combination of these techniques for optimal performance.

The SEP represents homogeneous dielectric regions by modeling their surfaces as mesh triangles applying there equivalent electric and magnetic currents. It is the preferred solution for low contrast homogeneous dielectrics. However, antenna modules with multiple dielectrics and fine geometry details will require a fine mesh leading to a dense near field matrix in the MLFMM for this block. For parallel runs, this highly inhomogeneous mesh will degrade the runtime and memory efficiency due to the "load imbalance". The FEM, on the other hand, represents dielectric regions as tetrahedral volume elements where each element could have its own dielectric properties. For a hybrid FEM/MLFMM method, the MLFMM is only applied to the boundary elements of the FEM, significantly improving the efficiency of the MLFMM for cases with high levels of geometrical detail and for highly lossy dielectrics. To combine their advantages, the MLFMM (for metallic parts and dielectrics with SEP) and FEM are now allowed in the same model during windscreen antenna analysis. Feko automatically takes the multiple windscreen layers and curvature into account, requiring only the metallic elements on the windscreen to be meshed.

The runtime and memory requirements for the model in Fig. 1 are given in Table I, where we compare resources when the SEP versus the FEM are used to model the complex antenna module. The FEM model reduces both the total runtime and memory footprint by a factor of 2. Calculation of the matrix elements is 4.4 times faster, and the iterative solution of the linear equations is 5.6 times faster. For this relatively small problem, the time to initialise the Green's function for the windscreen antenna is significant. For larger problems this time will be less dominant in the total runtime, resulting in final speed-ups greater than the factor of 2 reported here.

Fig. 1. Windscreen antenna analysis including complex antenna module.

TABLE I
COMPUTATIONAL RESOURCES

	MLFMM-SEP + WINDSCREEN	MLFMM + FEM + WINDSCREEN
Initialisation of the Green's function	1088 sec	1088 sec
Calculation of matrix elements	589 sec	134 sec
Solution of the system of linear eqns.	1723 sec	307 sec
Other	372 sec	343 sec
Total times	3772 sec	1872 sec
Sum of peak memory of all processes	8.668 GByte	4.374 GByte

160k unknowns; 4 parallel processes on Intel(R) Xeon(R) CPU E7-4820 v3 @ 1.90GHz

III. PERIODIC BOUNDARY CONDITIONS

Periodic boundary conditions (PBC) was already implemented a decade ago in Suite 5.4 for metallic triangles, wires, connections and dielectrics using the SEP. Recently the PBC was extended to include the FEM to enable Feko to treat complex dielectrics with fine details more efficiently. The general PBC formulation was also improved and a tremendous acceleration was obtained by extracting singularities before filling the PBC interpolation tables. The second order compact frequency selective surface (FSS) example in Fig. 2 was solved from 5-15 GHz requiring only 10 adaptive frequency samples. Results in Fig. 3 are in excellent agreement to [2] and took less than 5 minutes using 6 parallel processes on Intel(R) Core(TM) i7-8700 CPU @ 3.20GHz.

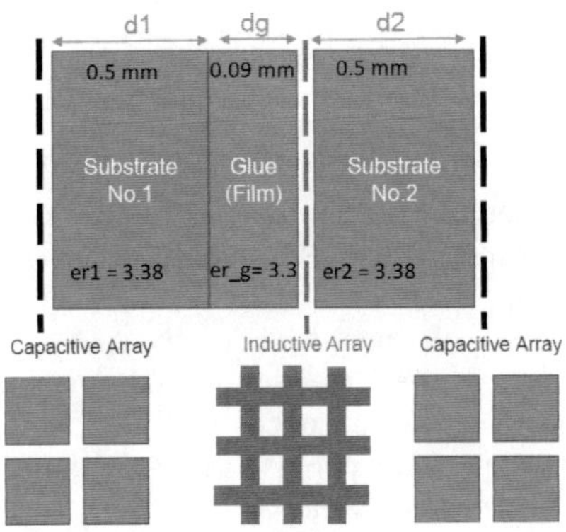

Fig. 2. Second order compact FSS layout [2].

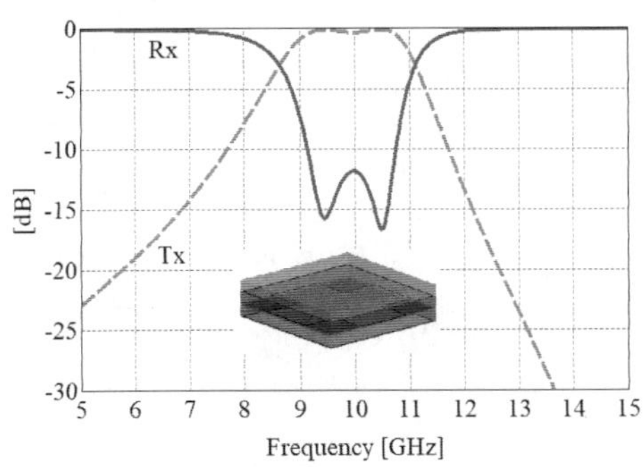

Fig. 3. FSS reflection (Rx) and transmission (Tx) coefficients [2].

IV. CABLE SHIELD MODELS

Shielded cables are commonly used in multiconductor cable analysis for electronic systems to transmit/receive information between equipment contained within protective systems. The transfer impedance and admittance of a cable shield serves as a measure to describe the effectiveness of coupling through a shield to ultimately limit unwanted field penetration through imperfections in a shield and possible damage to sub-systems.

The complexity in the way the electromagnetic field penetrates a shield has presented difficulties in the attempts of modeling the transfer impedance/admittance of cables and as such the most reliable method for determining these transfer quantities is still by measurement. Over the years Feko added support for several cable shield models (measured data, Schelkunoff formula, Kley and Vance expressions) in connection with its built-in cable harness solver based on Multiconductor Transmission Line (MTL) theory. This offering was now extended by adding the Tyni and Demoulin [3] expressions that may be applied to practical single-layered braided shields. Furthermore, flexibility was added to specify the transfer admittance independently through a transfer capacitance value and finally support for an equivalent transfer impedance applied to a double braid which is periodically shorted together was also added [4].

In Fig. 4 subtle differences between the transfer impedance as predicted by empirical models for a single-layered braided shield are compared. The braid is characterized by the following parameters: diameter under the braid $D_0 = 6.8$ mm; the number of carriers $m = 24$ in the braid; the number of wires $n = 7$ in each carrier; the wire diameter $d = 0.15$ mm; the electrical conductivity $\sigma = 57.3$ MS/m of the shield material; and the weave angle $\psi = 32.78°$.

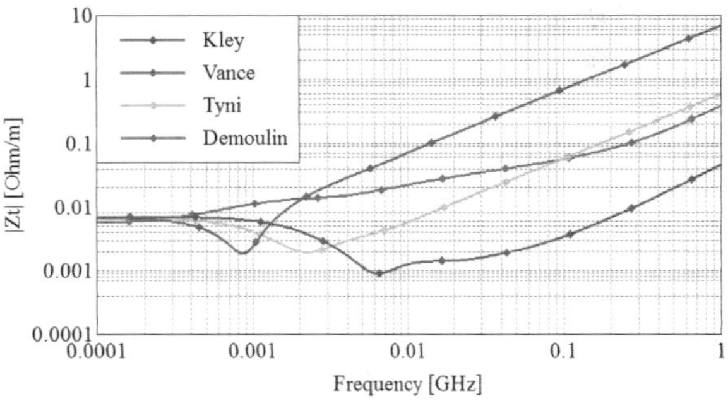

Fig. 4. The transfer impedance of Coroplast 9-2610 FLR2GCB2G 16mm2 when compared using different single-layered braided shield models.

REFERENCES

[1] Altair Feko, Altair Engineering, Inc., www.altairhyperworks.com/feko

[2] M. Al-Joumayly and N. Behdad, "A new technique for design of low-profile, second-order, bandpass frequency selective surfaces," IEEE Trans. AP, vol. 57, no. 2, pp. 452-459, February 2009.

[3] F. M. Tesche, M. V. Ianoz, and T. Karlsson, "EMC analysis methods and computational models," Wiley Interscience, Chapter 9, 1997.

[4] D. W. P. Thomas, "Simulation of cable coupling," Final report, January 2009, pp. 6-7.

Co-Channel Simultaneous Transmit and Receive with 3-Element Array Antenna

Ehab A. Etellisi, Mohamed A. Elmansouri, and Dejan S. Filipovic
Department of Electrical, Computer, and Energy Engineering
University of Colorado, Boulder, CO 80309-0425, USA
{Ehab.Etellisi, Mohamed.Elmansouri, Dejan.Filipovic}@Colorado.EDU

***Abstract*—A novel co-polarized wideband array antenna is proposed for co-channel simultaneous transmit and receive (C-STAR) applications. The proposed C-STAR configuration is composed of three (spiral) antennas sequentially rotated by 120°. Two antennas are used for transmitting (TX) and one for receiving (RX) or vice versa. The high isolation is achieved in this approach by utilizing antennas' orientation, symmetry, and phase cancellation to ideally eliminate the coupled TX signals at the RX port. To demonstrate the performance of the proposed C-STAR configuration, numerical modelling is conducted using method of moments (MoM) solver.**

Keywords— C-STAR, isolation, self-interference, spiral antenna.

I. Introduction

One of the most difficult challenges for wireless RF systems is to simultaneously transmit and receive from an aperture without any time/frequency/polarization multiplexing while achieving broadband co-channel high-isolation. To obtain the necessary isolation over wide bandwidth, the demand-driven front-end topologies typically combine multiple isolation layers and digital back-end processing. Depending on the TX power and bandwidth, this isolation is in the order of 110-140 dB [1]. Our recent studies have demonstrated that >30% of the total isolation at the aperture layer can be achieved by re-routing the coupled TX signals away from the RX port in beam-former networks (BFN), near-field cancellation, and modes multiplexing to mention a few [2]. Clearly, some of these C-STAR approaches can mitigate self-interferences (SI), but at least four antennas/ports are needed. In this paper, antenna orientation and phase cancellation are utilized to improve the TX/RX isolation by using only three antenna elements and a simple BFN (1 power divider). The achieved isolation is theoretically infinite over multi-octave bandwidth as long as the symmetry is maintained. However, the operational bandwidth of the proposed approach is limited by the far-field quality of the two-element TX array due to increased side lobe level (SLL) at higher frequencies. Therefore, about an octave of bandwidth can be achieved with reasonable SLL. To prove the concept, spiral antenna is used due to its inherent consistent far-field performance [3]-[4]. The C-STAR array is computationally studied using the commercial MoM (Altair FEKO) solver.

This research is supported by the Office of Naval Research (ONR) award # N00014-15-1-2125.

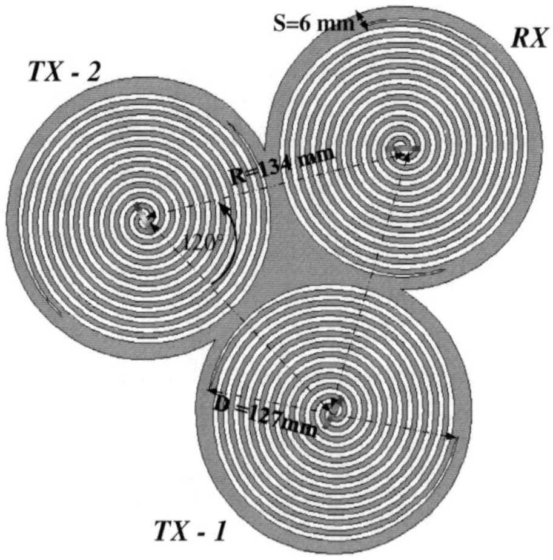

Fig. 1. Proposed C-STAR 3-element spiral array antenna system. The 3-element sequentially rotated by 120°.

II. C-STAR Array Antenna

The proposed co-polarized C-STAR configuration is composed of three antennas sequentially rotated by 120°; two for TX and one for RX as illustrated in Fig. 1. To demonstrate the principle of operation, free-standing right-handed circularly-polarized (CP) two-arm spiral antenna is considered. The full geometrical parameters of the designed C-STAR antenna array are shown in Fig. 1. Each self-complementary slot spiral antenna element has an outer diameter of D=127 mm and an inner dimeter of 0.4 mm. A differential port (i.e. edge port in FEKO) is used to excite each spiral element in the desired mode of CP operation. The feed polarity of TX-1 antenna is reversed to use a power divider instead of 180° hybrid to combine TX spirals coherently. Note, antenna orientation, symmetry, and feeds' polarity are essential to ensure full SI cancellation of the two out-of-phase coupled TX signals at the RX antenna port while maintaining good TX and RX far-field performances.

III. Performance

The C-STAR spiral array antenna system is modeled in FEKO. As seen from Fig. 2, TX and RX antennas have good VSWR<1.5 over most of the bandwidth with respect to their nominal impedance (180 Ω). The match of TX side is at the power divider input port.

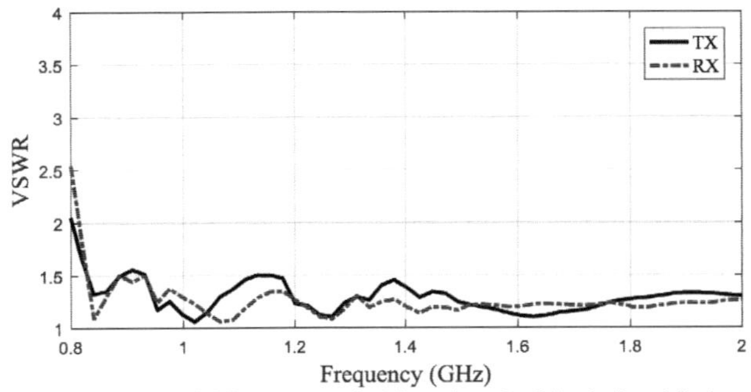

Fig. 2. Simulated VSWR (w.r.t nominal impedance) of the designed 3-element spiral array antenna.

The gain and radiation patterns of the TX and RX spirals are shown in Fig. 3. As seen, the gain increases with the frequency and reaching 6 dBic for the TX side at 2GHz. As expected, higher gain is achieved with the TX array since two elements are used. TX SLL increases at higher frequencies due to the increased electrical separation between the two TX spiral antennas. Better quality radiation patterns are obtained for the single RX spiral antenna.

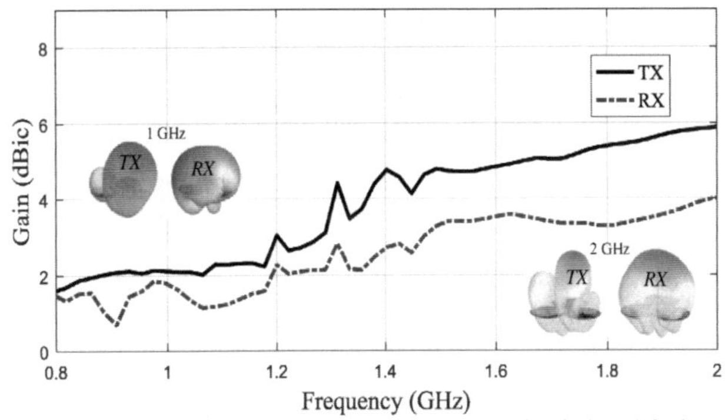

Fig. 3. Simulated gain and 3D-radiation patterns of the designed 3-element spiral array antenna.

To determine the overall system isolation, the non-radiating network is added to CADFEKO model, as illustrated in Fig. 4 (a). One ideal power divider is used at the TX side to combine the two antenna ports. As seen in Fig. 4 (b), the two mutual coupled TX signals have similar magnitudes and 180° phase difference (not shown), so once they reach the RX port, they are cancelled leading to very high isolation. As shown in Fig. 4 (b), the TX/RX isolation is improved by >30 dB compared to the mutual coupling between the TX and RX antenna elements without physically increasing the separation. The obtained isolation level is limited by the simulation noise floor and the symmetry/size of the mesh and it can be enhanced by improving those. Once the amplitude and phase imbalances are introduced, the two TX mutual coupled signals becomes asymmetric leading to degradation in isolation as shown by the shaded area in Fig. 4 (c). However, the average isolation remains high (>50 dB) over most of the band. Amplitude and phase imbalances up to 0.4 dB and 4° are considered, and this imbalances study is done in AWR after exporting the S-parameters touchstone file from FEKO. The power loss is very low over the entire band because of the low mutual coupling "$|S_{RX-TX_i}|$" between the TX and RX antennas (>15 dB), as seen in Fig. 4 (b) (right y-axis). This model is solved using MoM in FEKO using custom mesh with triangle edge length of ($\lambda/75$ at 2GHz) and basis function of 24,498 unknown. Total of 4.54 GByte memory is required. The practical realization of the array over a ground plane with resistive terminations is part of the future work.

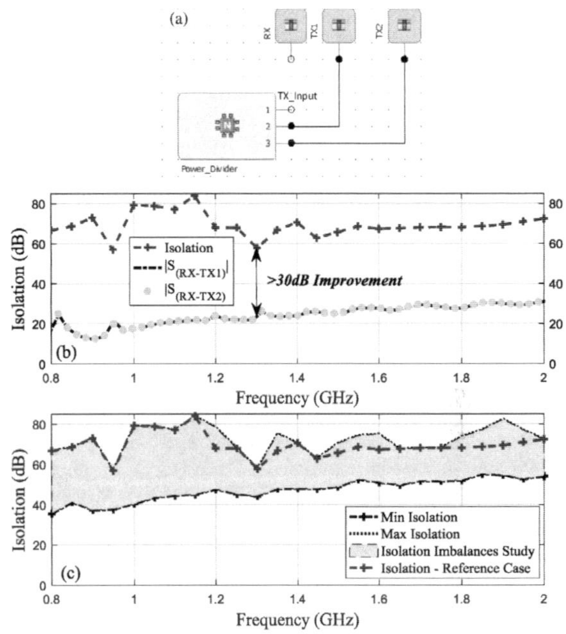

Fig. 4. (a) Non-radiating feed network, (b) simulated mutual coupling and isolation of the designed 3-element spiral array antenna, and (c) simulated isolation once the amplitude and phase imbalances are introduced.

IV. Conclusion

A novel wideband co-polarized co-channel C-STAR 3-element array antenna with a power divider feed is presented. The approach utilizes antenna element orientation and phase cancellation to obtain very high-isolation (>56 dB) between the TX and RX antennas without increasing the physical separation between the elements. Good simulated TX-RX isolation and far-field performance over an octave of bandwidth are achieved.

References

[1] J. Choi, M. Jain, K. Srinivasan, P. Levis, and S. Katti, "Achieving single channel, full duplex wireless communication," The 16th Annual Int. Conf. on Mobile Comp. Net., Chicago, IL, July 2010, pp. 1-12.

[2] E. A. Etellisi, M. A. Elmansouri and D. Filipovic, "Wideband monostatic co-polarized co-channel simultaneous transmit and receive (C-STAR) broadside circular array antenna," in IEEE Trans. Antennas and Propag., vol. 67, no. 2, Nov. 2018.

[3] D. S. Filipovic and T. P. Cencich Sr., Frequency Independent Antennas, in Antenna Engineering Handbook, 4th ed., New York: Mc-Graw Hill, 2007, ch. 13.

[4] C. Fumeaux, D. Baumann and R. Vahldieck, "FVTD simulations of Archimedean spiral antennas on thin substrates in planar and conformal configurations," IEEE/ACES International Conference on Wireless Communications and Applied Computational Electromagnetics, 2005., Honolulu, HI, 2005, pp. 277-28.

Advanced Computational Methods for Transparency Control of Low Emissivity Windows

Gopinath Gampala
Altair Engineering, Inc.
Phoenix, USA
gopi@altair.com

C. J. Reddy
Altair Engineering, Inc.
Hampton, USA
cjreddy@altair.com

***Abstract*—Low emissivity (low-E) windows have thin layers of metallic oxides for extra thermal insulation. These metallic layers not only block infrared and ultraviolet waves but also attenuate cellular signals. Cellular coverage can be improved by using Frequency Selective Surface (FSS) layers that will act as bandpass filters, instead of solid layers. This paper discusses the type of FSS structures that can be integrated into the window glass. A workflow process is demonstrated for efficient design and analysis of such structures using Periodic Boundary Conditions (PBC), Characterised Surfaces in conjunction with Ray-Launching Geometrical Optics (RL-GO) method.**

Keywords—Characterised surfaces, FSS, low-E windows, PBC, RL-GO.

I. Introduction

Power saving or energy consumption is one of the prominent factors in a majority of the fields, ranging from cellular communications to building homes. Modern day designers and architects are opting for low-E windows to reduce the energy consumption of buildings. Low-E windows are made by applying an extremely thin metallic layers on one side of the glass pane. The metallic layer blocks most of the infrared and ultraviolet rays and maintain cooler temperatures inside the building. However, this layer is not transparent to the incoming cellular signals, resulting in poor reception inside the buildings [1]. When attenuation of cellular signals is too strong inside the buildings, repeaters are used to amplify the signal. The repeater systems are in general expensive and energy consuming.

The aim of this work is to provide a solution for the low cellular reception, with FSS integrated low-E windows. This paper will also provide an overview of the advanced computational methods used to design the FSS and analyze the entire building with FSS integrated low-E windows. All the results presented in this paper are using the commercial 3D computational electromagnetics simulation software Altair Feko [2].

II. Computational Methods

The operating frequencies for present day cellular technologies range from 800 MHz to 2.4 GHz. However, designing an FSS for a required bandwidth involves several design iterations and opting for measurements to evaluate the performance in each iteration will be very expensive, whereas a numerical analysis will be extremely cost effective. This section discusses the PBC formulation for the design and analysis of FSS and RL-GO with characterised surfaces for a full-size building.

A. Periodic Boundary Conditions

The PBC technique enables the analysis of both 1-dimensional (1-D) and 2-dimensional (2-D) infinite periodic structures by analyzing only a single unit cell. High accuracy can be achieved by using the Ewald transformation in order to get fast convergence for the infinite sums [2]. The PBC formulation in combination with MoM defines the periodic Green's function as the sum of modified spatial portion and a modified spectral portion, where the number of terms in the infinite sum are automatically determined. The advantage of using PBC with MoM, specifically in the case of dielectric structures is that the vertical side walls coinciding with the vertical walls of the unit cell can be ignored through the use of Surface Equivalence Principle (SEP). If one has to use the Finite Element Boundary Integral (FEBI) method, the boundary conditions must also be imposed on the Finite Element mesh on the vertical side walls.

PBC minimizes the total number of unknowns as well as the computational resources when analyzing large but finite size arrays. More information on this can be found in [3].

B. Ray-Launching Geometrical Optics (RL-GO)

RL-GO is particularly useful when modeling the transmission of rays through objects, like windows and walls. With RL-GO, rays are launched at a fixed angular increment, independent of the number of observation points. Equivalent Huygens sources are established on the surface of the dielectric body at every instance of a ray hitting the surface. The RL-GO is hybridized with MoM where the equivalent Huygens sources are used to evaluate the impact of the GO region, both with respect to coupling back to the MoM region and the scattering/radiation of the GO region itself. More information on RL-GO can be found in [4, 5].

C. Characterised Surfaces

The special formulation of characterised surfaces allows for the analysis of multiple layers of thin dielectrics, as well as dielectric layers with FSSs integrated in between, using a single equivalent layer. The main difference between characterised surface and the traditional Thin Dielectric Sheet (TDS) approximation is, this formulation takes every angle of incidence into account, unlike TDS which is valid only for normal incidence. As such, this formulation will be extremely useful in analyzing multi-layer thin wall dielectric radomes, FSS radomes and FSS integrated low-E windows.

RL-GO technique described above is well suited for use with characterised surfaces, where the surface characteristics are assigned based on the incident angle.

III. Low-E FSS Windows

Typical residential glass panes have a thickness ranging from 3.175 mm to 6.35 mm, with dielectric constant of 7.0 and loss tangent of 0.001. A glass pane with a thickness of 5 mm is chosen for this study. The thickness of the metallic coatings on the low-E windows is in the order of micro meters, and their conductivity is maintained confidential. However, manufacturers give the equivalent surface impedance, which is normally 4 Ω/sq.

A. FSS Design

Two-dimensional arrays of periodic resonant elements (printed/bandstop or slot/bandpass) interact with electromagnetic waves within certain frequency band(s) and can be characterized as frequency selective surfaces. An FSS can be designed by using the PBC formulation in Altair Feko.

The metallic coating on the low-E windows blocks all the incoming signals, whereas a cross-slot FSS improves the transmission over the entire bandwidth of the typical cellular frequencies, as shown in Fig. 1. The slot width of the FSS design shown in this paper is 40 µm in a 5 mm unit cell. The comparison of the transparency of the low-E windows for varied slot and unit cell sizes will be presented at the conference.

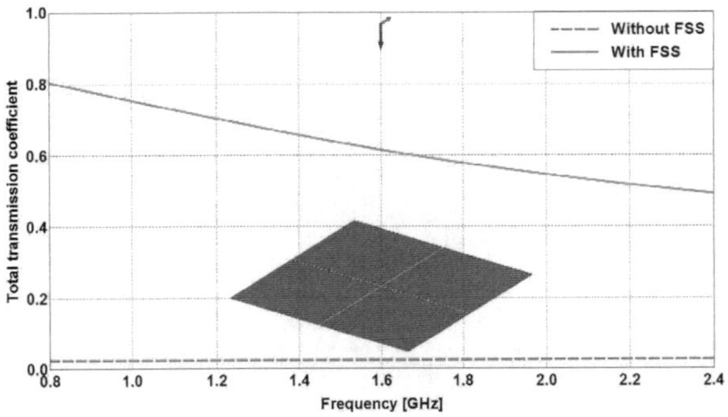

Fig. 1. Transmission coefficient of the low-E window with and without FSS.

B. Analysis of Entire Building

It is important to analyze the effect of FSS integrated low-E windows in a real building environment to evaluate their benefits, before opting for mass production. A typical residential building itself will be electrically large at the cellular frequencies and a commercial multi-story building will be manifold larger. Analyzing these electrically large buildings with any rigorous computational electromagnetic method will be impractical, whereas RL-GO technique described above can handle these with reasonable computational resources.

It is also impractical to model the low-E window as a thick glass with thin metallic coating and the periodic FSS slots in the coating layer. Instead, the low-E windows are modelled as characterised surfaces. With this formulation, the transmission/reflection coefficients of the low-E glass configuration are computed for every incident angle in orthogonal polarizations and the matrix of these coefficients is then applied to a single surface. Analyzing a single equivalent surface in place of the layered glass configuration will be computationally less expensive.

To demonstrate the effect of FSS, buildings with low-E windows are analyzed at the 1900 MHz LTE frequency band. The field strength inside a building room with FSS integrated low-E windows is much stronger than the building with regular windows, as shown in Fig. 2 and Fig. 3.

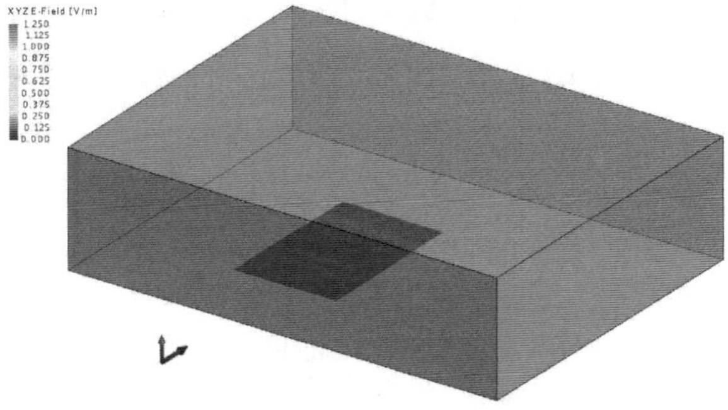

Fig. 2. Field strength inside the room with regular low-E windows.

Fig. 3. Field strength inside room with FSS integrated low-E windows.

IV. Conclusions

The benefits of FSS integrated low-E windows in solving the poor cellular reception inside the buildings is discussed along with the advanced computational methods that can be used in designing the FSS and analyzing the entire building.

References

[1] Mobile network reception problems in low energy buildings. Working group report. Ministry of Transport and Communications Working Group, chaired by Mr Olli-Pekka Rantala, 2013.

[2] Altair Feko, https://altairhyperworks.com/product/FEKO, 2018.

[3] I. Stevanovic, P. Crespo-Valero, K. Blagovic, F. Bongard, and J. R. Mosig, "Integral-equation analysis of 3-D metallic objects arranged in 2-D lattices using Ewald transformation," IEEE Transactions on Microwave theory and Techniqmes, vol. 54, no. 10, pp. 3688-3697, October 2006.

[4] J. van Tonder and U. Jakobus, "Infinite periodic boundaries in FEKO," 25th Annual Review of Progress in Applied Computational Electromagnetics, pp. 237-242, ACES 2009.

[5] H. Ling, Ri-C. Chou, and S-Wu Lee, "Shooting and bouncing rays: calculating the RCS of an arbitrarily shaped cavity," IEEE Trans. Antennas Propagat., vol. 37, no. 2, pp. 194-205, 1989.

[6] U. Jakobus, M. Bingle, M. Schoeman, J. J. van Tonder, and F. Illenseer, "New FEKO modeling capabilities: waveguide ports with dielectrics, fast MLFMM based near-field calculations, integrated network modeling, and dielectric GO," 24th International Review of Progress in Applied Computational Electromagnetics, ACES 2008.

A Simple Test for Quickly Measuring Shielding Effectiveness of Connectors Using Isotropic Broadband Electric Field Probe

Kenedy Marconi G. Santos[1], Marcela Silva Novo [2], Glauco Fontgalland [3]
Marcelo Bender Perotoni[4], Décio Renno de Faria Mendonça[5] and Danilo Brito Almeida[1]

IFBA[1]- Federal Institute of Bahia / UFBA[2]- Federal University of Bahia, Salvador-BA, Brazil
UFCG[3]- Federal University of Campina Grande, Campina Grande - PB, Brazil
UFABC[4] Federal University of ABC, Santo André -SP, Brazil
UNIFEI[5] Federal University of Itajubá, Itajubá - MG, Brazil

Abstract—**The shielding of coaxial cables and connectors is an important parameter for the electromagnetic compatibility of electro-electronic systems. It is of paramount importance the detection of failures as soon as possible in order to consider improved systems and avoid unexpected costs. Within this context, this paper presents a simple procedure to measure the electric field radiated by connectors, with and without solder. A virtual simulation was performed using the commercial package FEKO with a good correlation between simulation and measurement.**

Index Terms—Connectors; Computational analysis; VSWR; Shielding effectiveness.

I. Introduction

Electromagnetic Compatibility (EMC) is the electro-electronic ability for an apparatus to operate correctly in a determined electromagnetic environment, without disturbing the nearby systems and without being disturbed by other devices or by itself [1,2]. EMC problems can have a variety of effects on equipment and there are many ways to mitigate them in practice. Real EMC mitigation techniques may differ by the type of apparatus and by the electromagnetic environment. For mitigating EMC problems, it is possible to act on the source, on the receiver or on the coupling environment. The connector is the element that is hereby investigated in order to diminish the radiated electromagnetic signal.

II. Methodology

In order to determine the electric field radiated by the connectors, this paper proposes a methodology based on a setup, using the R&S ® EMC32 Measurement Software. Fig.1 and Fig.2 show the connector under test and the setup, respectively. The distance between the Isotropic Broadband Electric Field Probe (IBEFP) and the cable center was defined as 100 mm.

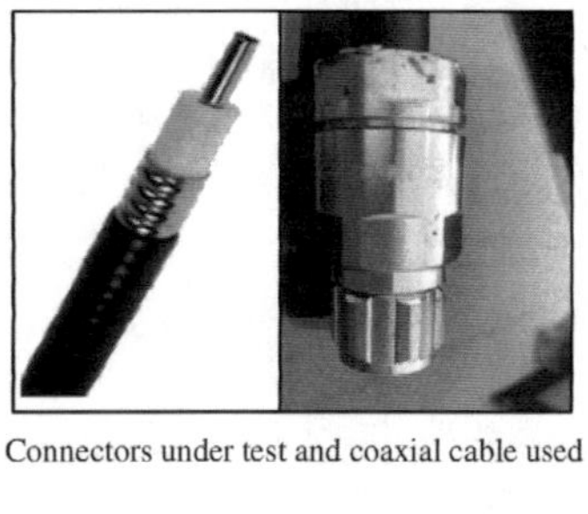

Fig. 1 – Connectors under test and coaxial cable used

The measurement setup contains an electric field probe, a ground plane, a 50 ohms load and a low loss foam coaxial cable (The solid outer conductor of coaxial cable creates a continuous RFI/EMI shield that minimizes system interference by the coaxial cable). The connectors under test is the NM LCF 12-C02.

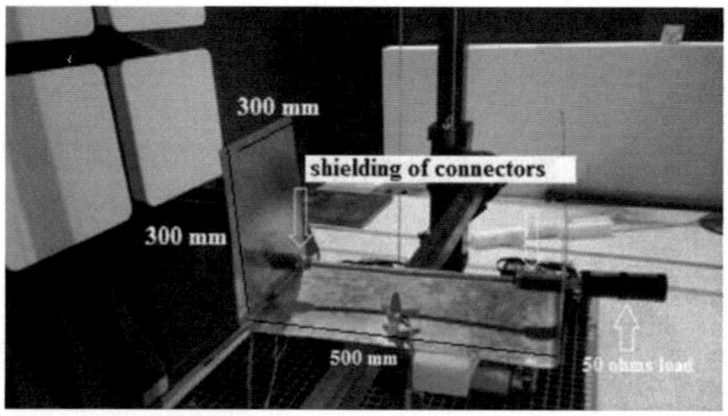

Fig.2 - Measurement setup

The electric field is measured using the EMC32 integration software that controls the injected power and the electric field measured. A continuous power of 10 W(sweeping the range of 1 GHz to 3 GHz) is injected into the cable and the electric field is measured inside a semi-anechoic chamber. A ground plane has been used to simulate the automobile metal body and the cable under test has been positioned at 50 mm height from the ground plane, as prerequisite in CISPR25 [3,4,5].

Fig. 3 shows the measured electric field radiated by the connectors NM LCF 12-C02 with and without solder.

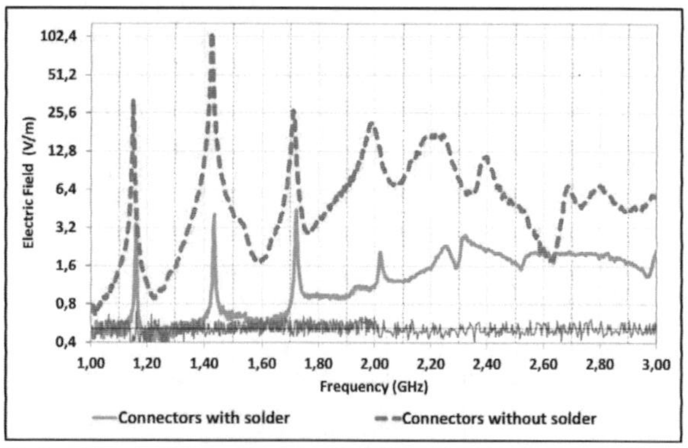

Fig.3 - Electric field radiated by NM LCF 12-C02 connectors with and without solder

The blue trace shows the environment noise floor. A measurement with the shielding of the connectors was performed to make sure the coaxial cable was not radiating.

Fig.4 shows the Shielding Effectiveness (SE) [1,2] calculated with the measured data and shown in the Fig.4. The Shielding Effectiveness (SE) can be defined by equation (1):

$$SE = 20\,Log\left|\frac{E1}{E2}\right| \quad (1)$$

Were *E1* is the electric field radiated by the connectors without solder and *E2* is the electric field radiate by the connectors with solder.

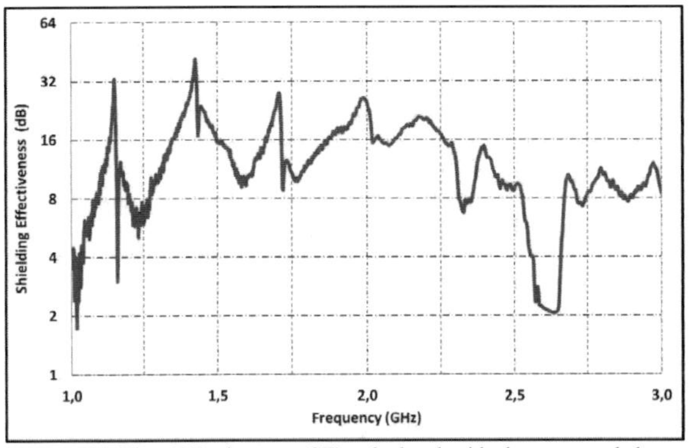

Fig. 4- Shielding Effectiveness (SE) calculated with the measured data and shown in the Fig.4

Fig.3 and Fig.4 show that there are main differences between the electric field radiated by connector with and without solder. For example, at 1.4 GHz there is variation in the electric field from 3.4 V/m to 112.4 V/m. It can be also noticed that there are not an amplitude big difference in the electric field between 2.5 GHz to 3 GHz. The data shows the importance of proper soldering of the connector in a system.

III. Virtual Simulation

In order to determine the Voltage Standing Wave Ratio (VSWR) of the device under test (DUT), this work proposes the computer simulation of the NM LCF 12-C02 connectors using the Feko software[6]. Fig. 5 shows the NM LCF 12-C02 connector design for simulation via FEKO.

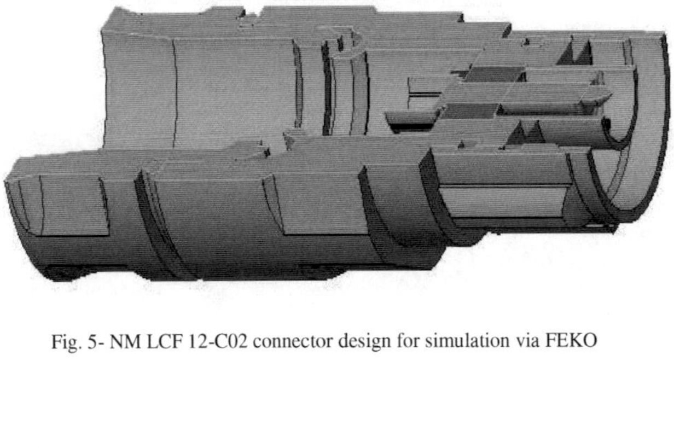

Fig. 5- NM LCF 12-C02 connector design for simulation via FEKO

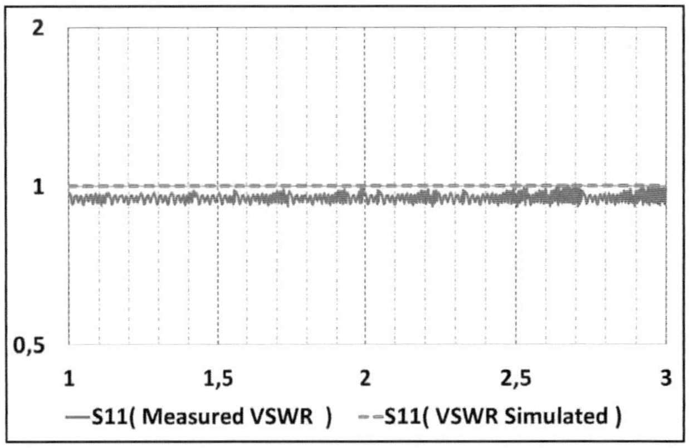

Fig. 6- VSWR measured and simulated via FEKO

Fig. 6 shows the simulated and measured voltage standing wave ration (VSWR) with 50 Ω load connected in the connector. Fig 6 show the VSWR simulation also presented an excellent correlation with measurement.

IV. Conclusion

It can be concluded that the methodology presented here is efficient for the measurement of the radiated electric field leaking from the connectors [3]. The proposed methodology is a simple and quick way to perform qualitative and quantitative tests for shielded connectors in high frequencies. The Voltage Standing Wave Ratio simulation also presented an excellent correlation with measurement. All these results showed that excellent quality coaxial cables can be inefficient if connectors are not well installed and shielded.

V. Acknowledgments

The authors would like to thank SENAI-CIMATEC plant in Salvador-BA, for the use of semi-anechoic chamber and devices, as well as CAPES/CNPq for the financial support and FAPESB doctoral scholarship.

References

[1] PAUL, C.R, Introduction to Electromagnetic Compatibility, John Wiley & Sons, *Inc., New York, New York,* 1992.

[2] OTT, Henry W., Electromagnetic Compatibility Engineering, John Wiley & Sons, 2011.

[3] FE Analysis on Temperature, Electromagnetic Force and Load Capacities of Imperfect Assembled GIB Plug-in Connectors," X. Guan, X. Wei, X. Song, N. Shu, H. Peng, ACES Journal Paper, Year: 2018 Volume: 33 Number: 6

[4] Santos, K. M. G. et al., A Simple Test for Measuring the Shielding Effectiveness of Coaxial Cables and Connectors, International Journal of Applied Electromagnetics and Mechanics,Vol.55, no1, pp.151-166, July 7, 2017.

[5] CISPR 25: Edition 3.0 2008-03: Vehicles, boats and internal combustion engines - Radio Disturbance Characteristics - Limits and methods for the protection on board receiver.

[6] Altair Feko, Altair Engineering, Inc, USA, https://altairhyperworks.com/product/FEKO.

Hybrid-PIC Simulation of Nonlinear Wave-Particle Interactions in the Earth's Radiation Belts

Hoyoung Kim
Electrical Engineering
University of Colorado Denver
Denver, CO, USA
hoyoung.kim@ucdenver.edu

Vijay Harid
Electrical Engineering
University of Colorado Denver
Denver, CO, USA
vijay.harid@ucdenver.edu

***Abstract*—The Earth's magnetosphere is a complex plasma environment that is heavily influenced by the geomagnetic field. The particles in the near-Earth space environment can be classified into two major "cold" and "hot" plasma populations. The cold plasma is dense and can be modeled as a fluid with linear physics. However, the hot plasma drives nonlinear interactions and resonances with the waves. To model the physics of the system, we have developed a hybrid simulation which combines a fluid and Particle In Cell (PIC) simulation using the finite-difference time-domain method (FDTD) for broadband whistler wave interactions in the magnetosphere. In this work, we consider the nonlinear amplification of whistler mode waves injected into the radiation belts as well as the precipitation of hot plasma electrons interacting with the waves.**

Keywords—hybrid-PIC simulation, Computational Electromagnetics, whistler mode wave, Earth's radiation belts,

I. Introduction

In the Earth's magnetosphere, the geomagnetic field heavily influences physical processes, particularly that of near-Earth space plasmas [1]. The plasma populations in the magnetosphere can be divided into a cold, dense component (~0.5 eV, 10~1000 el/cm^3) and a hot but rarified plasma referred to as the radiation belts (100 keV~10 MeV, 1 el/cm^3). The cold plasma supports the propagation of whistler mode waves. These whistler waves can trap and accelerate or precipitate (i.e. be collide with the neutral atmosphere) radiation belt electrons depending on their initial energies and momenta. Moreover, the collective effect of the radiation belt particles can in turn nonlinearly feed back to the whistler mode waves. In order to investigate complex nonlinear wave-particle interactions, we have developed a hybrid simulation in which the cold plasma current is modeled by a fluid equation while the radiation belt particles are simulated with a Particle in Cell (PIC) code. Additionally, the finite-difference time-domain method (FDTD) is utilized to self-consistently determine the evolution of the wave electric and magnetic fields. This method provides a broadband, time-domain numerical solution to the wave-particle interactions problem. The hybrid simulation method is an effective means to investigate self-consistent nonlinear wave phenomena such as the generation of magnetospheric chorus, nonlinear whistler wave amplification, and the triggering of free-running emissions. The acceleration and precipitation of radiation belt particles induced by wave-particle interactions can also be self-consistently determined. Using this hybrid simulation technique, several unanswered questions in magnetospheric physics can be quantitatively approached via numerical experiments.

II. Method

A. Single Particle Motion with the Whistler Mode Wave

Single electron motion with the whistler mode wave is shown in Fig. 1. B_0, B_w, and E_w correspond to the geomagnetic field, wave magnetic and electric field respectively. V represents the particle velocity and consists of parallel ($V_\parallel$) and perpendicular ($V_\perp$) velocity components. The direction of parallel velocity is the same as the wave number (k). The quantity Φ is the angle between perpendicular velocity and wave magnetic field. It is the angle of wave (Φ_w) subtracted from the angle of particle (Φ_p). These parameters are converted to Cartesian coordinates for simulations.

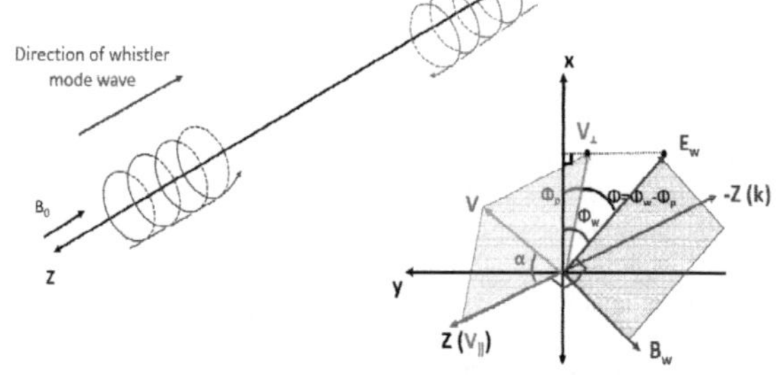

Fig. 1. Single radiation belt electron motion with the whistler mode wave [1].

B. Particle Movement

The Lorentz force governs motion of a single particle in presence of electromagnetic forces. In the presence of whistler mode waves and an inhomogenous geomagnetic field the particle equations of motion in cylindrical coordinates are given by:

$$\frac{dv_\parallel}{dt} = -\frac{v_\perp^2}{2w_c}\frac{\partial w_c}{\partial z} + \frac{q}{m}B_w v_\perp sin\phi \quad (1),$$

$$\frac{dv_\perp}{dt} = \frac{v_\perp v_\parallel}{2w_c}\frac{\partial w_c}{\partial z} - \frac{q}{m}(B_w v_\parallel + E_w)sin\phi \quad (2),$$

$$\frac{d\phi}{dt} = \frac{d\phi_w}{dt} - \left(w_c + \frac{q}{mv_\perp}(B_w v_\parallel + E_w)cos\phi\right) \quad (3),$$

where V_{res}, m, q, and w_c are the resonance velocity, mass and electric charge of an electron, and cyclotron frequency [2]. In equations (1)-(3), the first terms on the right sides are related to geomagnetic field and the second terms are related to injected whistler mode wave. These equations are utilized by the particle pusher within the PIC simulation framework.

C. Wave Propagation

The wave magnetic and electric fields are calculated using the FDTD algorithm [3]. The fields as well as the current density are updated via the equations,

$$B_x^{n+\frac{1}{2}}(k) = B_x^{n-\frac{1}{2}}(k) - \frac{dt}{dz}\left[E_y^n\left(k+\frac{1}{2}\right) - E_y^n\left(k-\frac{1}{2}\right)\right] \quad (4),$$

$$B_y^{n+\frac{1}{2}}(k) = B_y^{n-\frac{1}{2}}(k) + \frac{dt}{dz}\left[E_x^n\left(k+\frac{1}{2}\right) - E_x^n\left(k-\frac{1}{2}\right)\right] \quad (5),$$

$$E_x^{n+1}\left(k+\frac{1}{2}\right) = E_x^n\left(k+\frac{1}{2}\right) + \frac{C^2 dt}{dz}\left(B_y^{n+\frac{1}{2}}(k+1) - B_y^{n+\frac{1}{2}}(k)\right)$$
$$-\frac{C^2\mu\, dt}{2}\left(J_x^{n+\frac{1}{2}}\left(k+\frac{1}{2}\right) + J_x^{n-\frac{1}{2}}\left(k+\frac{1}{2}\right)\right) \quad (6),$$

$$E_y^{n+1}\left(k+\frac{1}{2}\right) = E_y^n\left(k+\frac{1}{2}\right) - \frac{C^2 dt}{dz}\left(B_x^{n+\frac{1}{2}}(k+1) - B_x^{n+\frac{1}{2}}(k)\right)$$
$$-\frac{C^2\mu\, dt}{2}\left(J_y^{n+\frac{1}{2}}\left(k+\frac{1}{2}\right) + J_y^{n-\frac{1}{2}}\left(k+\frac{1}{2}\right)\right) \quad (7),$$

where dt, dz, C, μ and J are time step, a cell size, the speed of light, permeability and current density. The direction of wave is the opposite against the direction of particle movement as shown in Fig. 1.

III. HYBRID-PIC SIMULATION

A 1-dimensional Hybrid-PIC simulation with FDTD method has been developed to investigate nonlinear wave-particles interactions. The calculation of the electric current is a summation of the cold and hot plasma current densities. Figure 2 shows preliminary results for the case of a negligibly small hot plasma density and is in agreement with the theoretical cold plasma dispersion relation. More complex simulations with a larger hot plasma density are not included in this paper in the interest of space.

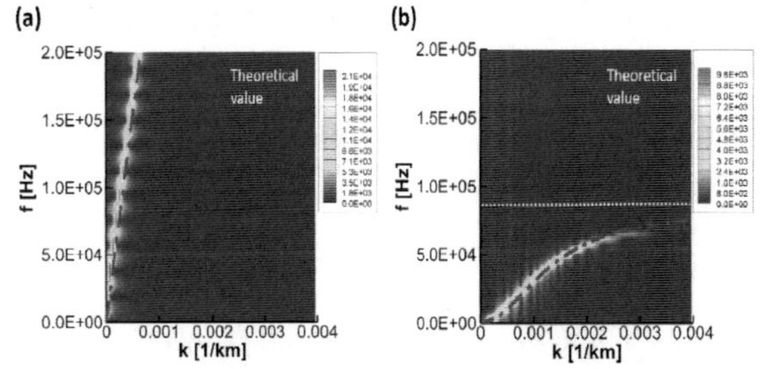

Fig. 2. Theoredical and computational cold plasma dispersion relations. (a) No cold plasma and (b) the density of cold plasma is 5e7 [m^{-3}].

The number of cells are 128 and time step is 5e-8 s. The size of simulation domain is 100 km and The initial velocity in z direction is 0.07*C. The frequency of injected whistler mode wave is 2e3 Hz and the maximum of cyclotron frequency is 8.73e4 Hz which is a white dotted line in Fig. 2 (b).

REFERENCES

[1] M. Gołkowski and A. R. Gibby, "On the conditions for nonlinear growth in magnetospheric chorus and triggered emissions," Physics of Plasmas, 24(092904), 1-11, 2017.

[2] V. Harid, M. Gołkowski, T. Bell, and U. S. Inan, "Theoretical and numerical analysis of radiation belt electron precipitation by coherent whistler mode wave," Journal of Geophysical Research: Space Physics, 119(6), 4370-4388, 2014.

[3] J. H. Lee and D. K. Kalluri, "Three-dimensional FDTD simulation of electromagnetic wave transformation in a dynamic inhomogeneous magnetized plasma," IEEE Transactions on Antennas and Propagation, 47(7), 1146-1151, 1999.

Comparison of Methods for Dielectric Characterization of Additively Manufactured Materials

Gregory Mitchell, Quang Nguyen, Theodore Anthony
US Army Research Laboratory, Adelphi, MD, 20783, USA
gregory.a.mitchell1.civ@mail.mil, 93nguyen@cua.edu

***Abstract* — As additive manufacturing (AM) gains traction in the field of antennas, characterizing the electromagnetic properties of AM materials becomes paramount for comparison to simulation and modeling. The Nicholson-Ross-Weir (NRW) and reference-plane invariant (RPI) methods are two well-known algorithms used for the extraction of complex permittivity from *S*-parameters of material samples measured in a waveguide. This paper gives a brief overview of the two methods and then compares the measured complex permittivity of various AM samples.**

***Index Terms*—Additive manufacturing, complex permittivity Nicholson-Ross-Weir, Reference-plane invariant.**

I. Introduction

As additive manufacturing (AM) receives more attention from electromagnetic (EM) community, the measurement of EM properties of AM substrates has become a topic of emphasis. The EM properties of AM materials can vary from print to print due to bounding interfaces between printed layers, surface roughness and porosity [1-3]. Moreover, utilizing techniques such space filling curves to vary complex permittivity (ε) or permeability (μ) across the volume of AM structures necessitates post-print EM measurements to compare to expected values. Accurate wideband retrieval methods to obtain the EM properties of AM materials is crucial.

Several techniques exist including waveguide retrieval methods and free space retrieval methods. Typical retrieval methods utilize measured *S*-parameters to characterize the complex ε and μ of materials. The free space retrieval method requires a focused EM beam utilizing lenses, arrays, or horn antennas which become cumbersome as they scale in electrical size at UHF frequencies and below. An ideal candidate to measure material properties at wide bandwidths as well as low frequencies is a coaxial waveguide because there is no lower bound on the propagation of the TEM mode. The size of the measurement setup would not have to scale with frequency.

An established technique for retrieval of EM parameters is based on the Nicolson-Ross-Weir (NRW) method. The NRW method inverts Fresnel equations of an equivalent slab to extract the constitutive parameters. The *S*-parameters are transformed from the calibration reference plane to the surface of the material under test (MUT) [4, 5]. In other words, the precise location of the MUT in the sample holder must be known. This adds unnecessarily complicated steps in calibrating the measurement setup up to the reference plane of the sample holder itself. Both improper calibration and/or imprecise knowledge of the exact position of the MUT within the waveguide can add significant errors in the calculation of ε and μ using NRW methods.

The reference-plane invariant (RPI) method attempts to overcome this challenge. In this work, we compare the measured ε of AM materials using both the NRW and RPI methods. For all measurements in this paper we utilize an air-filled coaxial waveguide of fixed dimensions. In all instances we are careful to stay below the frequency that would introduce additional propagating modes into the waveguide which could skew the measurement.

II. NRW Versus RPI Methodology

In this section, we briefly discuss the key concepts involved in the NRW and RPI methods. Since the main focus of the paper is comparison of measured data, we direct the reader to the suggested references for more detailed information on the parameter retrieval processes.

The fundamentals of NRW are as follows. We obtain the effective refractive index (n) and impedance (Z) using *S*-parameters measured or simulated from a wave incident normally on the surface of a MUT. We determine ε and μ by $\mu=nZ$ and $\varepsilon=n/Z$ respectively. The equation details can be found in references [4, 5]. The reader should note that the known location of the MUT in the sample holder is essential in this version of the NRW method.

By introducing a specific set of RPI equations and combining these with the original set of NWR equations, we no longer need the position of the MUT in the sample holder to calculate ε. We construct the RPI equations from measured *S*-parameters of the waveguide when there is no MUT in the sample holder. First the total reflection and total transmission is written in terms of the measured *S*-parameters [6]. We should note that, the only information required is the waveguide. Once we know the RPI equations, we follow the traditional NRW procedure as described in references [4, 5].

III. Comparison of Methods Through Measured Data

We now compare the results of calculated ε_r and loss tangent ($\tan\delta$). In order to verify our measurements we initially measure a standard dielectric substrate of Rogers 5870 which has expected values for ε_r of 2.43 and for $\tan\delta$ from 0.0009 to 0.0024 [7]. Figures 1a and 1b shows that these measured values for the NRW method fall within the expected values.

Figures 2a and 2b show the measured ε_r and $\tan\delta$ of ABS with green dye mixed into the thermoplastic filaments while Figures 3a and 3b show measurements for the same ABS from the same company with blue dye mixed into the thermoplastic filaments. This material was printed from filaments using fused deposition modeling (FDM) on an nScrypt printer.

The two methods give excellent agreement in the calculation of ε_r. However, in calculating $\tan\delta$ there are differences as high as 16% between the two methods, especially as we increase in frequency. We are unsure of the underlying reasons for this discrepancy at this time; however we consider the traditional NRW measurements to be more accurate based on the results shown in Figures 1a and 1b. These results encourage further investigation. Another takeaway is that materials purported to have similar properties (blue and green ABS) in fact vary quite a bit in $\tan\delta$ which shows why post-print characterization is important. These differences could result from properties of the two dyes used or simply by differences from print to print as discussed in previous sections.

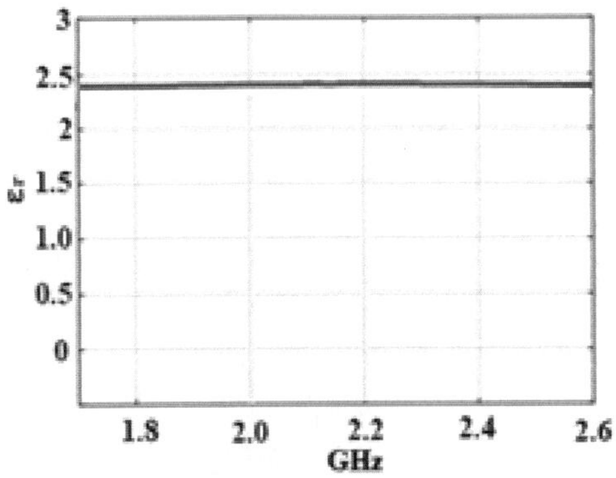

(a)

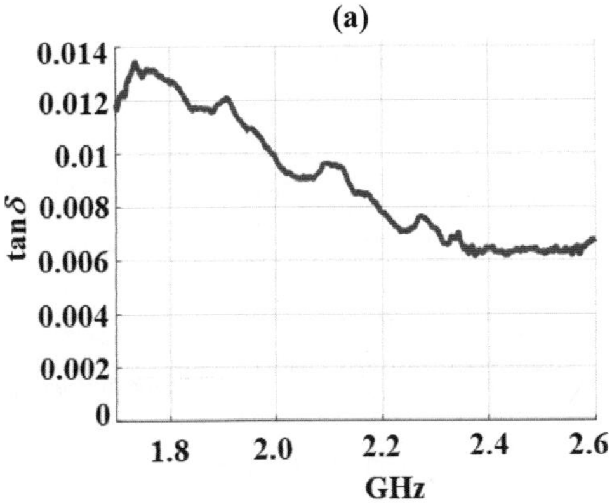

(b)

Figure 1: Measured permittivity of Rogers 5870 using NRW method: a) relative permittivity b) loss tangent.

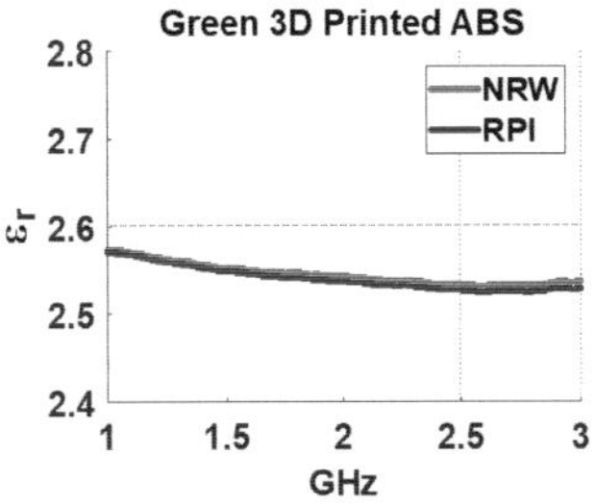

(a)

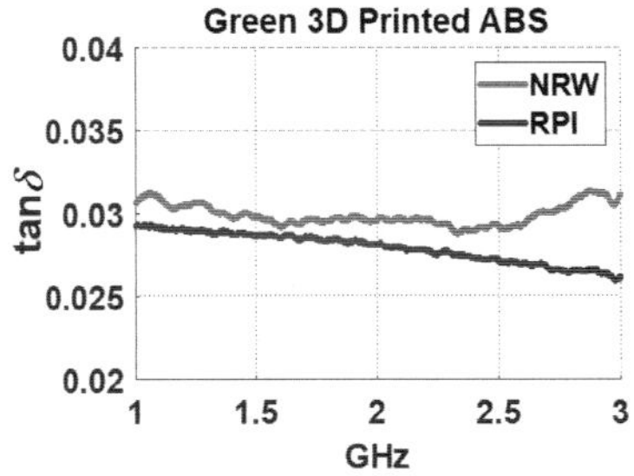

(b)

Figure 2: Measured permittivity of ABS using NRW and RPI method: a) relative permittivity b) loss tangent.

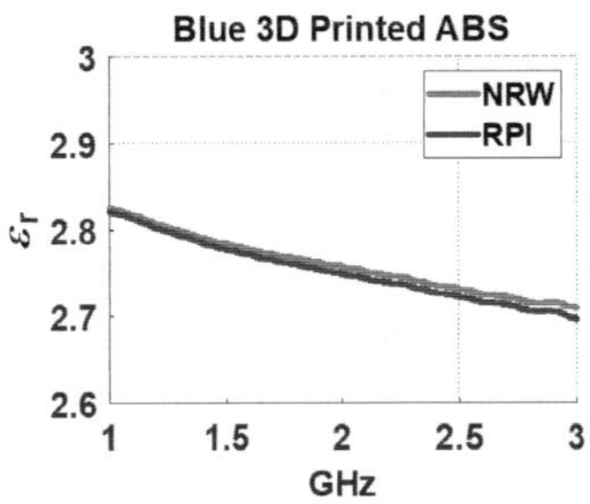

(a)

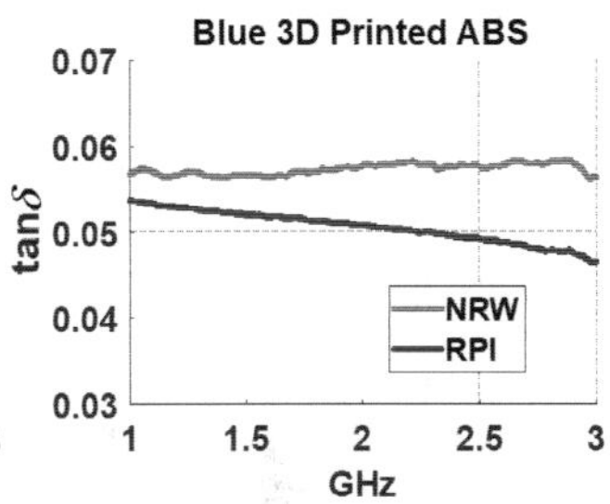

(b)

Figure 3: Measured permittivity of ABS using NRW and RPI method: a) relative permittivity b) loss tangent.

IV. Conculsion

This paper presents measured results for the NRW and RPI measurement methods of ε_r and $\tan\delta$ for two AM substrates. We show that both methods agree on ε_r, but the differences in $\tan\delta$ would result in unexpected device performance if one method is relied upon over the other. In conclusion, we suggest further investigation into the mechanisms producing the variations in $\tan\delta$ between the two methods.

References

[1] C. Bellehumeur, et al., "Modeling of bond formation between polymer filaments in the fused deposition modeling process", Journal of Manufacturing Processes, vol. 6, iss. 2, pgs. 170-178, 2004.

[2] D. Ahn, *et al*., "Representation of surface roughness in fused deposition modeling", Journal of Materials Processing Technology, vol. 209, iss. 15-16, pgs. 5593-5600, 2009.

[3] K. Ang, et al., "Investigation of the mechanical properties and porosity relationships in fused deposition modeling-fabricated porous structures", Rapid Prototyping Journal, vol. 12, iss. 2, pgs. 100-105, 2006.

[4] A. M. Nicolson, G. F. Ross, "Measurement of the intrinsic properties of materials by time domain techniques." *IEEE Trans. Instrum. Meas*., vol. IM-17, pp. 395-402, Dec. 1968.

[5] W. B. Weir, "Automatic measurement of complex dielectric constant and permeability at microwave frequencies.", *Proc. IEEE*., vol. 62, pp. 33-36, Jan. 1974.

[6] K. Chalapat, K. Sarvala, J. Li, and G. S. Paraoanu, "Wideband reference-plane invariant method for measuring electromagnetic parameters of materials", *IEEE Tran. Microw. Theory Tech*., vol. 57, no. 9, pp. 2257–22267, Sep. 2009.

[7] "The Advantage of Nearly Isotropic Dielectric Constant for RT/duroid 5870-5880 Glass Microfiber-PTFE Composite", Rogers Corporation, Printed in USA, 2015. www.rogerscorp.com.

Impedance Matching of Layered Structures with Metamaterials

Brinta Chowdhury and Abdullah Eroglu

Department of Electrical and Computer Engineering
North Carolina A&T State University
Greensboro, NC 27411
bchowdhury@aggies.ncat.edu, aeroglu@ncat.edu

***Abstract*— Impedance matching of layered structures involving metamaterial is investigated. The base isotropic material is selected from commonly used microwave materials with dielectric permittivity ranging from 2.1 to 10.2, such as Teflon and Alumina. The method adapted is immune to polarization of the incident wave regardless if it is TE or TM wave. The metamaterial permittivity and permeability parameters are obtained for the minimum reflectivity by varying the thickness of the metamaterial for each isotropic material for broad range of incident angles and operational frequency. The results presented in this paper can be used for applications where antireflection (AR) is a requirement.**

Keywords—Anisotropic, Metamaterial, Antireflection (AR), Radome, Matching.

I. Introduction

Impinging of propagating electromagnetic waves on an interface of two different materials cause reflections. In several applications, reflections are required to be minimized due to associated insertion loss. Antireflection becomes even more critical for low power in many far infrared or terahertz (THz) systems. As a result, there have been several studies reported in the literature for development of antireflective (AR) coatings for the last two decades [1-3].

AR can be done using single or multilayer configurations. The simplest antireflection can be done using refractive index matching with a quarter wave length (λ/4) matching layer with refractive index, n_f, that is equal to the square root of the refractive indexes of the substrate materials, $n_f = \sqrt{n_1 n_3}$ [4]. While this configuration is simple and practical, the matching requirements make it difficult with available natural material properties. It also provides solution for only a single frequency operation when wave has normal incidence. One of the methods to overcome the limitation in frequency range and incidence angle is using the multilayer configuration with alternating high and low index materials. However, this approach suffers for large incident angles [5].

In this paper, we adapt the method proposed in [6] to have AR with minimum reflectance for both TM and TE polarized waves and apply it for several commonly used microwave materials. The proposed method in [6] is based on the transfer matrix method discussed in [7]. The method is then used to identify the permittivity and permeability constants of the metamaterial versus incident angle when the thickness of the matching layer is varied from 0.1 λ to 0.7 λ as shown in Fig. 2. The metamaterial is selected to be a magneto electric uniaxial metamaterial (MEUM) where its material properties are represented with the equation given in (1). The detailed analysis of the formulation is also provided in this paper;

$$\bar{\bar{\varepsilon}}_2 = \begin{bmatrix} \varepsilon_{2t} & 0 & 0 \\ 0 & \varepsilon_{2t} & 0 \\ 0 & 0 & \varepsilon_{2n} \end{bmatrix}, \bar{\bar{\mu}}_2 = \begin{bmatrix} \mu_{2t} & & 0 \\ 0 & \mu_{2t} & 0 \\ 0 & 0 & \mu_{2n} \end{bmatrix}. \quad (1)$$

In (1), t represents the tangential and n represents longitudinal components of the constitutive parameters.

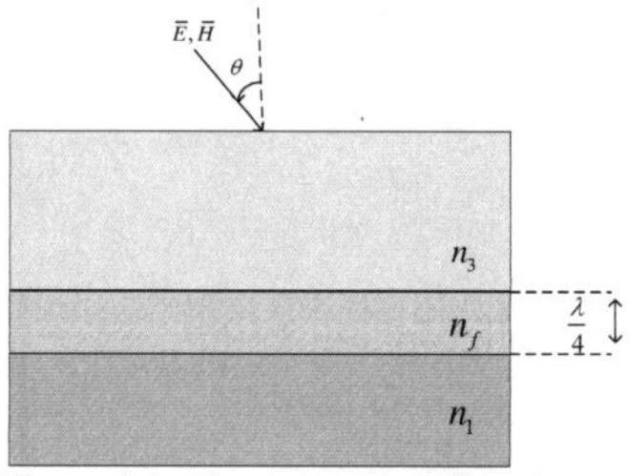

Fig. 1. Illustration of a quarter-wavelength AR coating.

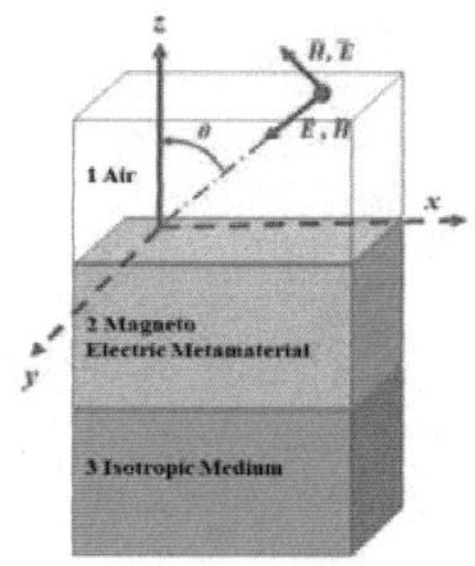

Fig. 2. Configuration of the proposed AR layered structure with MEUM [6].

II. Formulation

The reflection coefficient in medium 1 shown in Fig. 1 is calculated from:

$$r^{TM/TE} = \frac{r_{12}^{TM/TE} + r_{23}^{TM/TE} e^{-i2\varphi^{TM/TE}}}{1 + r_{12}^{TM/TE} r_{23}^{TM/TE} e^{-i2\varphi^{TM/TE}}}. \quad (2)$$

The reflection coefficent given in (2) is equal to zero when

$$r_{12}^{TM/TE} + r_{23}^{TM/TE} e^{-i2\varphi^{TM/TE}} = 0 . \qquad (3)$$

From (3). we can write

$$r_{12}^{TM/TE} - r_{23}^{TM/TE} = 0 . \qquad (4)$$

It is assumed that all permittivity and permeability parameters are real and $e^{-i2\varphi^{TM/TE}}$ = -1. Equation (4) then can be expressed as:

$$e^{-i2\varphi^{TM/TE}} = -1 = e^{-i2\pi} . \qquad (5)$$

This leads to:

$$(Z_2^{TM/TE})^2 = Z_1^{TM/TE} Z_3^{TM/TE} , \qquad (6)$$

and

$$k_{2z}^{TM/TE} = \frac{\pi}{2d} . \qquad (7)$$

Simultaneous solutions of the equations for TM and TE waves for the layered structure shown in Fig. 2 lead to the solution of constitutive relations for permittivity and permeability parameters in equation (1) as:

$$\mu_{2t} = \frac{\lambda_o}{4d}\frac{1}{\sqrt{\cos\theta_1\sqrt{\varepsilon_3-\sin^2\theta_1}}} , \qquad (8a)$$

$$\varepsilon_{2t} = \mu_{2t}\cos\theta_1\sqrt{\varepsilon_3-\sin^2\theta_1} + \sin^2\theta_1\frac{1}{\mu_{2n}} , \qquad (8b)$$

and

$$\varepsilon_{2n} = \frac{4d}{\lambda_o}\frac{\sin^2\theta_1\sqrt{\varepsilon_3}\sqrt{\cos\theta_1\sqrt{\varepsilon_3-\sin^2\theta_1}}}{\sqrt{\varepsilon_3}-\cos\theta_1\sqrt{\varepsilon_3-\sin^2\theta_1}} , \qquad (9a)$$

$$\mu_{2n} = \frac{4d}{\lambda_o}\frac{\sin^2\theta_1\sqrt{\varepsilon_3}\sqrt{\varepsilon_3}\sqrt{\cos\theta_1\sqrt{\varepsilon_3-\sin^2\theta_1}}}{\sqrt{\varepsilon_3}-\cos\theta_1\sqrt{\varepsilon_3-\sin^2\theta_1}} . \qquad (9b)$$

The permittivity and permeability parameters obtained in (8)-(9) align with the results given in [6].

III. Simulation Results

In this section simulation results are obtained for the constitutive parameters given in (8)-(9) when the isotropic substrate material in Fig. 2 (medium 3) is selected to be commonly used microwave materials such as Teflon, Polyamide, Quartz, Porcelain and Alumina with permittivity constants ranging from 2.1 to 10.2. The simulation results depicting the constitutive parameters of the metamaterial when the substrate material is Teflon and Alumina is illustrated in Fig. 3.

Simulation results show that the proposed method can be applied using available microwave materials to obtain constitutive parameters of MEUM to give minimum reflectivity for broad range of incidennt angles and operational frequency.

IV. Conclusion

In this paper, the method proposed in [6] is extended to implement commonly used microwave materials as isotropic substrate for the layered structures when magneto electric uniaxial metamaterial (MEUM) is utilized as matching layer.

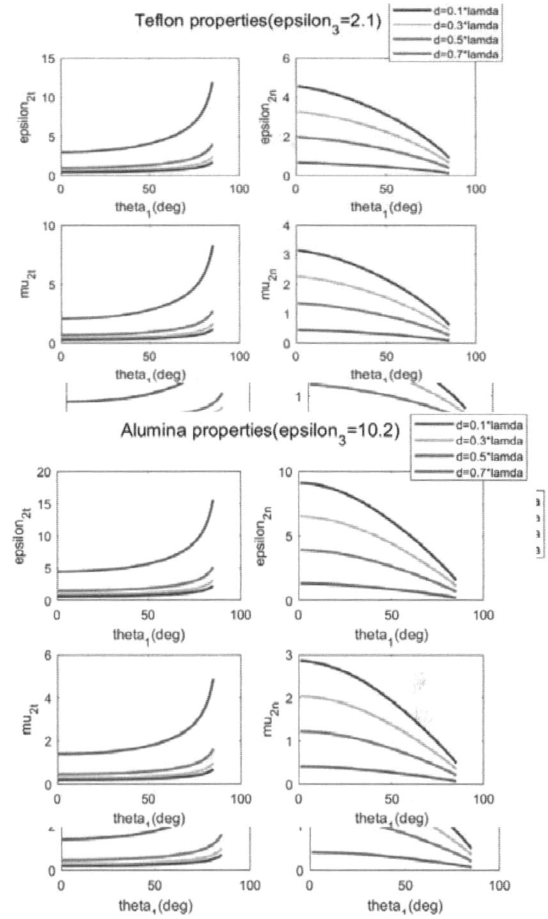

Fig. 3. Constitutive parameters of MEUM when the substrate is Teflon and Alumina.

The constitutive parameters of MEUM is obtained for several cases with different layer thickness and incident angles. It is shown that the efficient impedance matching with minimum reflectivity is obtained for various practical microwave materials. The method proposed in this paper can be easily adapted for AR applications including radome design.

References

[1] H. K. Raut, V. A. Ganesh, A. S. Nair, and S. Ramakrishna, “Antireflectivecoatings: A critical, in-depth review,” Energy Environ. Sci., vol. 4, no. 10, pp. 3779–3804, 2011.

[2] A. J. Gatesman, J. Waldman, M. Ji, C. Musante, and S. Yngvesson, "An nti-reflection coating for ailicon optics at terahertz frequencies," IEEE Microwave and Guided Wave Letters, vol. 10, no. 7, July 2000.

[3] J. Lau, J. Fowler, T. Marriage, L. Page, J. Leong, E. Wishnow, R. Henry, E. Wollack, M. Halpern, D. Marsden, et al., "Millimeter-wave antireflection coating for cryogenic silicon lenses," Appl. Opt., vol. 45, no. 3746, 2006.

[4] M. Born and E. Wolf, Principles of optics, Pergamon Press, New York, 6th ed, 1980.

[5] J. A. Dobrowolski, D. Poitras, P. Ma, H. Vakil, and M. Acree,“Toward perfect antireflection coatings: Numerical investigation,” Appl. Opt., vol. 41, no. 16, pp. 3075–3083, June, 2002.

[6] Y. He and G. V. Eleftheriades, "Magneto-electric uniaxial metamaterials as wide-angle, polarization-insensitive matching Layers," Phys. Rev. B 98, 205404, 2018.

[7] R. Collin, Field Theory of Guided Waves, Wiley-IEEE Press, 1960.

EM-Driven Size Reduction of UWB MIMO Antennas with Feed Line Modifications

Muhammad Aziz ul Haq and Slawomir Koziel
School of Science and Engineering
Reykjavik University
Reykjavik, Iceland
muhammadu16@ru.is, koziel@ru.is

***Abstract*— In this paper, we discuss an efficient size reduction technique for wideband MIMO antennas in a parallel configuration. Our approach exploits tapered feed lines of various complexities (from two to five sections), applied in order to improve antenna matching, thus creating a room for footprint reduction. Obtaining the minimum possible size while ensuring acceptable performance (especially, isolation $|S_{21}| \le -20$ dB within the operating band) is secured by rigorous constrained EM-driven design optimization involving all geometry parameters of the antenna. Numerical results indicate that increasing the feed line complexity has a positive impact on antenna miniaturization.**

Keywords—*EM-driven design; MIMO antennas; antenna miniaturization; feed line modifications; isolation characteristic.*

I. Introduction

In recent years, Multiple-Input-Multiple-Output (MIMO) antenna systems have gained considerable attention because of their ability to improve the channel capacity in complex and scattering environments, as compared to a Single-Input-Single-Output (SISO) systems [1]. At the same time, utilization of wideband antennas is an effective way of covering multiple communication channels, for which the MIMO technology has been implemented. Consequently, wideband MIMO antennas are essential parts of modern communication systems (e.g., 4G or 5G technology) [2]. One of the challenges in the design of such structures is a limited space available to install the radiator [3], [4]. Therefore, development of techniques that permit compact size while ensuring sufficient performance, in particular, high element isolation, has become an important research direction for this class of antennas.

In this paper, a systematic approach to miniaturization of MIMO antennas is developed and implemented. Our technique exploits modified (tapered) feedline structures which allow for considerable improvement of the antenna matching, thus creating a room for size reduction. The latter is achieved by constrained EM-driven optimization of antenna geometry parameters, with the constraints securing both the sufficient impedance bandwidth and element isolation ($|S_{21}| \le -20$). A similar technique has been successfully used in the context of size reduction of SISO antenna systems [5]. However, its suitability for MIMO systems has not yet been reported in the literature. The results obtained for an exemplary MIMO structure indicate that considerable reduction of the antenna footprint (by over 30.2 percent) can be obtained without compromising electrical performance.

II. MIMO Antenna Structure and Numerical Results

The proposed miniaturization concepts are illustrated using the MIMO antenna shown in Fig. 1. The structure is implemented on a 1.55-mm-thick FR-4 substrate with $\varepsilon_r = 4.4$. The computational model of the structure is simulated using CST Microwave Studio [6]. Initially, the antenna is designed and optimized using the same specifications as described in [7]. The design parameters are $\boldsymbol{x} = [l_g\ l_0\ r\ d\ d_l\ d_w\ l_{p1}\ w_{p1}\ w_{g1}\ l_{g2}\ w_{g2}]^T$. The numerical values of the optimized antenna are: $\boldsymbol{x}^{\mathbf{1}} = [4.9\ 6.6\ 3.7\ 13.5\ 4.7\ 2.4\ 2.5\ 6.2\ 6.6\ 1.7\ 18.2]^T$ (all dimensions in mm). The antenna is supposed to operate for the same frequency range as in [7], i.e., 2.8 GHz to 20 GHz). The design parameter vector is extended due to introducing additional feed line sections. It is then optimized for each case (different by the number of sections). The numerical values are given in Table I. Table II contains the antenna footprint area corresponding to each case. It is clear that increasing the feedline complexity has a significant impact on the miniaturization capability.

Figure 2 shows the $|S_{11}|$ and $|S_{21}|$ characteristics of the size-optimized MIMO antennas. It can be observed that $|S_{11}| \le -10$ dB for the entire frequency range of interest. Meanwhile, the isolation $|S_{21}|$ has been improved from –20 dB to –25 dB level, owing to a rigorous optimization process. This shows that simultaneous adjustment of all antenna parameters is mandatory in order to yield the truly optimum design. Figure 3 shows the realized gain of the size-optimized MIMO antenna. The effect of additional size reduction on gain characteristics is minor. The MIMO antenna efficiency (Fig. 4) is over 75% despite using a high loss substrate (FR-4). Figures 5 and 6 illustrate the E- and H-plane pattern of the size-optimized MIMO antennas at 3 GHz, 9GHz, and 11 GHz and 20 GHz. The patterns are almost omnidirectional for the entire frequency range. At the same time, the Envelop Coefficient Correlation (ECC) is lower than 0.005. These confirm the suitability of the antenna for mobile communication applications.

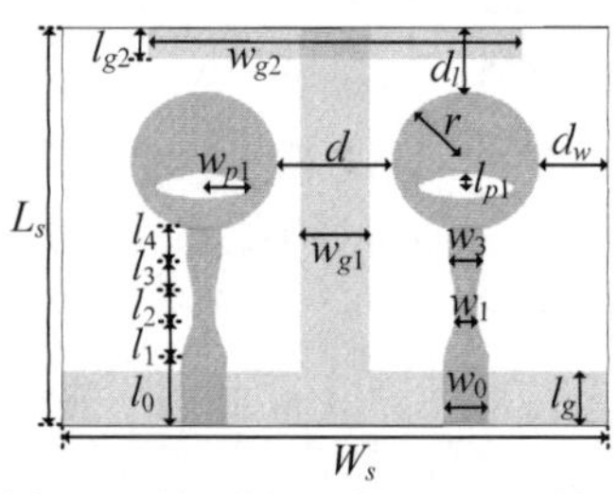

Fig. 1. Geometry of the considered MIMO antenna with optional feed line modifications. Ground plane is highlighted using a light gray shade.

TABLE I OPTIMIZED PARAMETRIC VALUES

	l_g	l_0	r	d	d_l	d_w	l_{p1}	w_{p1}	w_{g1}	l_{g2}	w_{g2}	l_1	w_1	l_2	l_3	w_3	l_4
$\boldsymbol{x}^{I}$	4.9	6.6	3.7	13.5	4.7	2.4	2.5	6.2	6.6	1.7	18.2	-	-	-	-	-	-
$\boldsymbol{x}^{II}$	4.4	2.9	3.2	13.4	5.4	2.6	1.7	6.1	5.9	2.8	17.5	3.2	0.4	-	-	-	-
$\boldsymbol{x}^{III}$	2.5	1.5	3.9	12.1	5.8	1.1	1.7	7.4	7.3	3.5	19.1	1.6	1.0	0.3	-	-	-
$\boldsymbol{x}^{IV}$	2.5	1.4	3.5	13.1	6.3	0.4	1.8	6.3	7.3	4.6	18.4	1.0	0.9	0.2	1.1	0.4	-
$\boldsymbol{x}^{V}$	2.0	0.9	3.2	12.8	6.9	0.7	1.7	5.5	6.0	3.3	16.2	1.0	0.3	0.7	0.2	0.3	0.4

*All values are in mm.

TABLE II OPTIMIZED MIMO ANTENNA SIZE

MIMO Antenna Footprint Area [mm^2]				
$\boldsymbol{x}^{I}$	$\boldsymbol{x}^{II}$	$\boldsymbol{x}^{III}$	$\boldsymbol{x}^{IV}$	$\boldsymbol{x}^{V}$
648	576	522	488	452

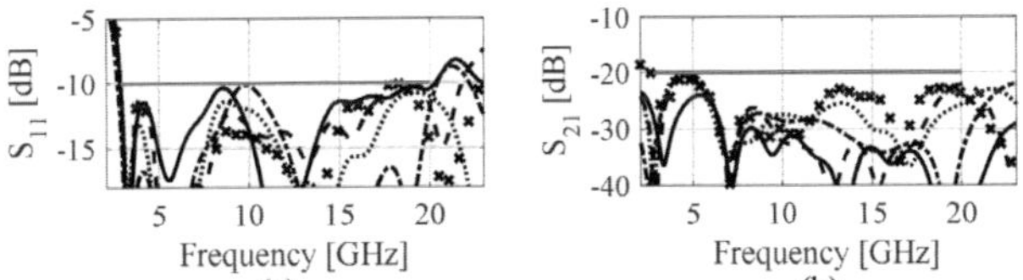

Fig. 2. Reflection responses of the size-optimized MIMO antennas with design vector $\boldsymbol{x}^{I}$ (xxx), $\boldsymbol{x}^{II}$ (---), $\boldsymbol{x}^{III}$ (...), $\boldsymbol{x}^{IV}$ (— — —), and $\boldsymbol{x}^{V}$ (—): (a) $|S_{11}|$ and (b) $|S_{21}|$.

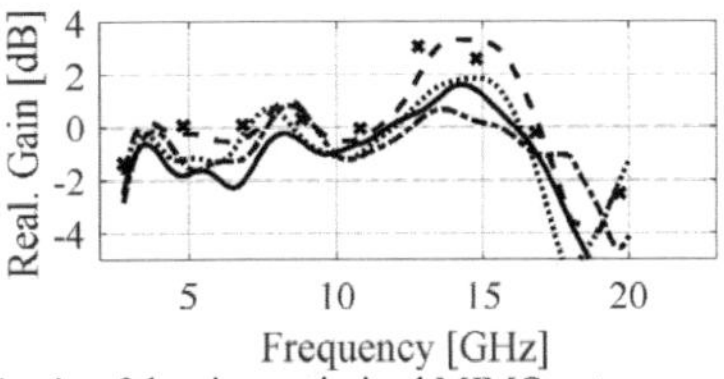

Fig. 3. Realized gain of the size-optimized MIMO antennas with design vector $\boldsymbol{x}^{I}$ (xxx), $\boldsymbol{x}^{II}$ (---), $\boldsymbol{x}^{III}$ (...), $\boldsymbol{x}^{IV}$ (— — —), and $\boldsymbol{x}^{V}$ (—).

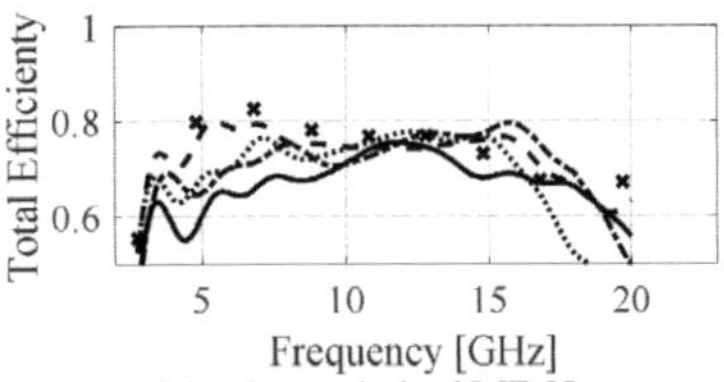

Fig. 4. Total efficiency of the size-optimized MIMO antennas with design vector $\boldsymbol{x}^{I}$ (xxx), $\boldsymbol{x}^{II}$ (---), $\boldsymbol{x}^{III}$ (...), $\boldsymbol{x}^{IV}$ (— — —), and $\boldsymbol{x}^{V}$ (—).

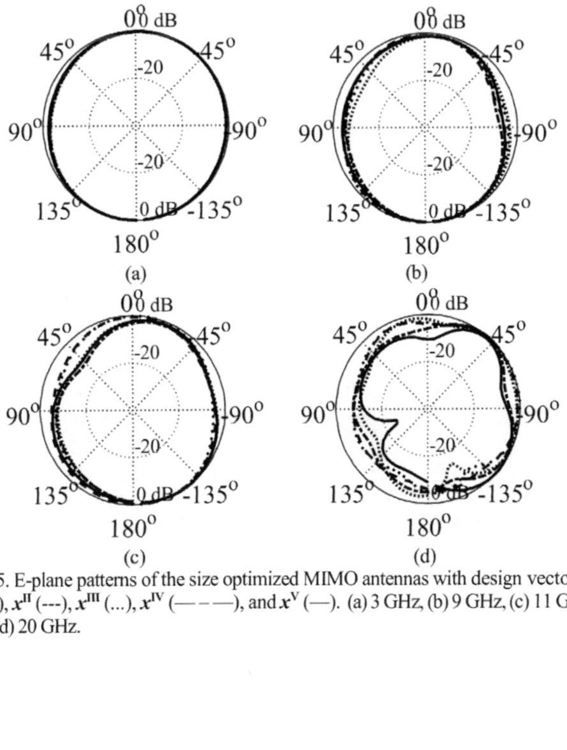

Fig. 5. E-plane patterns of the size optimized MIMO antennas with design vector $\boldsymbol{x}^{I}$ (xxx), $\boldsymbol{x}^{II}$ (---), $\boldsymbol{x}^{III}$ (...), $\boldsymbol{x}^{IV}$ (— — —), and $\boldsymbol{x}^{V}$ (—). (a) 3 GHz, (b) 9 GHz, (c) 11 GHz, and (d) 20 GHz.

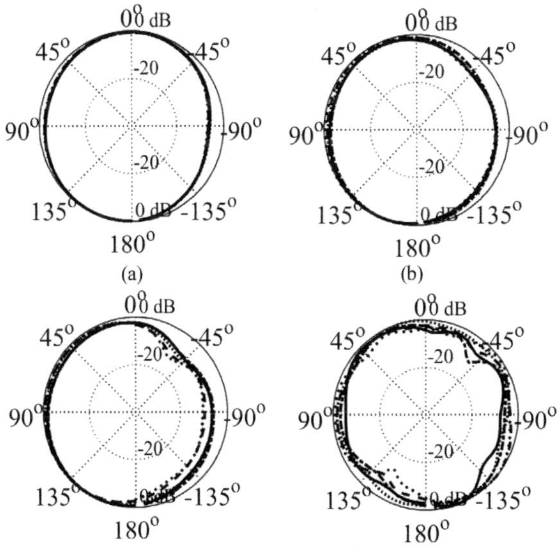

Fig. 6. H-plane patterns of the size-optimized MIMO antennas with design vector $\boldsymbol{x}^{I}$ (xxx), $\boldsymbol{x}^{II}$ (---), $\boldsymbol{x}^{III}$ (...), $\boldsymbol{x}^{IV}$ (— — —), and $\boldsymbol{x}^{V}$ (—). (a) 3 GHz, (b) 9 GHz, (c) 11 GHz, and (d) 20 GHz.

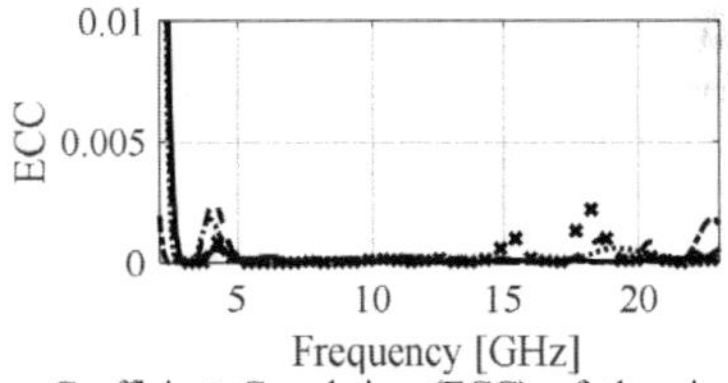

Fig. 7. Envelop Coefficient Correlation (ECC) of the size-optimized MIMO antennas with design vector $\boldsymbol{x}^{I}$ (xxx), $\boldsymbol{x}^{II}$ (—), $\boldsymbol{x}^{III}$ (...), $\boldsymbol{x}^{IV}$ (— — —), and $\boldsymbol{x}^{V}$ (—).

ACKNOWLEDGMENT

The authors thank Dassault Systemes, France, for making CST Microwave Studio available. This work is partially supported by the Icelandic Centre for Research (RANNIS) Grant 163299051.

REFERENCES

[1] S. Tripathi, A. Mohan, and S. Yadav, "A compact koch fractal UWB MIMO antenna with WLAN band-rejection," *IEEE Ant. Wireless Prop. Lett.*, vol. 14, pp. 1565-1568, 2015.

[2] X. Liu, Y. Liu, X. Wang, and H. Lin, "Highly efficient 3D resource allocation techniques in 5G for NOMA-enabled massive MIMO and relaying systems," *IEEE Jouornal of Selected Areas on Commun.*, vol. 35, no. 12, pp. 2785–2797, 2017.

[3] M. A. Haq and S. Koziel, "Ground plane alterations for design of high isolation compact wideband MIMO antenna," *IEEE Access*, vol. 6, pp. 48978-48983, 2018.

[4] U. Ullah and S. Koziel, "A broadband circularly polarized wide-slot antenna with a miniaturized footprint," *IEEE Ant. Wireless Prop. Lett.*, 2018.

[5] M. A. Haq, S. Koziel, and Q. S. Cheng, "Miniaturization of wideband antennas by means of feed line topology alterations," *IET Microwaves, Antennas & Propagation*, vol. 12, Iss. 13, pp. 2128-2134, 2018.

[6] CST Microwave Studio, ver. 2016. CST AG, Bad Nauheimer Str. 19, D64289 Darmstadt, Germany, 2016.

[7] R. Chandel, A. K. Gautam and K. Rambabu, "Design and packaging of an eye-shaped multiplc-input–multiple-output antenna with high isolation for wireless UWB applications," *IEEE Trans. on Comp, Pack. and Manu. Tech.*, vol. 8, no. 4, pp. 635-642, 2018.

Polarization Transformations Based Metasurfaces for 5G Applications

Shraman Gupta*, Abdel Razik Sebak
Department of Electrical and Computer Engineering
Concordia University
Montréal, QC, Canada
*shraman.gupta@concordia.ca

***Abstract*—This paper presents two different configurations of metasurfaces for 5G applications. The field transformations (polarization transformations) can be achieved using metasurfaces modelled through Generalized Sheet Transition Conditions (GSTCs). The configurations used in this paper are dielectric resonator and metallic metasurfaces that can be used to obtain quarter-wave transformations for an operating frequency range 28-33 GHz and 26-40 GHz respectively. The unit cell analysis for both types of metasurfaces using *TE* and *TM* polarization and phase difference between transmitted fields for both polarizations is maintained within 90° ± 20°.**

***Index Terms*—5G applications, Circular polarization, Metasurfaces, Linear polarization.**

I. Introduction

Metasurface is considered as a two dimensional subwavelength electromagnetic discontinuity ($t \ll \lambda$) in the free space. In today's world, frequency selective surface (*FSS*), reflectarray, transmitarray and phase-shifting arrays can be concluded as metasurfaces. Such surfaces are also known as controllable surfaces and are basically desired for field transformations. The metasurfaces can provide controllable reflection and transmission coefficients [1], holograms [2], orbital angular momentum (OAM) production [3] and as a solar sail for radiation pressure control [4].

In this paper, two types of metasurfaces are discussed. Firstly, the dielectric resonator metasurface is presented to achieve quarter-wave transformations at 28-33 GHz. Secondly, the four layer metasurface is used to convert the linear polarization to a circular polarization covering 2π transmission phase range over 26-40 GHz.

II. Mathematical Formulation Using GSTCs

The rigorous boundary conditions for zero-thickness sheet is developed by Idemen [5, Chap. 4] where the Maxwell equations are re-written in the form of distributions and later applied to metasurfaces by Kuester & Holloway in [6]. The GSTCs in the absence of impressed sources is given as

$$\hat{z} \times \Delta\mathbf{H} = \jmath\omega\mathbf{P}_{||} - \hat{z} \times \nabla_{||} M_z \tag{1a}$$

$$\Delta\mathbf{E} \times \hat{z} = \jmath\omega\mu_0\mathbf{M}_{||} - \nabla_{||}\left(\frac{P_z}{\epsilon_0}\right) \times \hat{z} \tag{1b}$$

$$\hat{z} \cdot \Delta\mathbf{D} = -\nabla \cdot \mathbf{P}_{||} \tag{1c}$$

$$\hat{z} \cdot \Delta\mathbf{B} = -\mu_0\nabla \cdot \mathbf{M}_{||} \tag{1d}$$

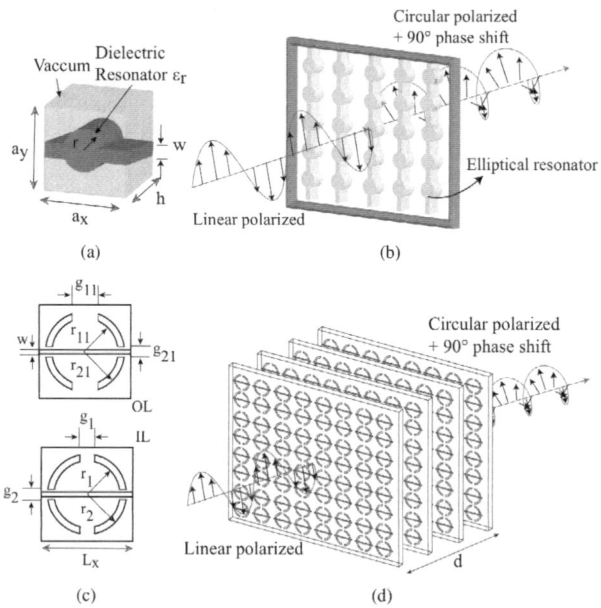

Fig. 1. (a) DR Unit cell. (b) DR metasurface linear to circular polarization. (c) Outer layer and inner layer unit cell for four layer metasurface polarizer. (d) Four Layer metasurface linear to circular polarization.

where the discontinuity on the two sides of the metasurfaces is presented by $\Delta\mathbf{E}$ and $\Delta\mathbf{H}$. The polarization densities can be defined using the concept of average fields and susceptibility tensors as stated in [4, Eq.(2.7)].

$$\mathbf{P} = \epsilon_0\bar{\bar{\chi}}_{ee} \cdot \mathbf{E}_{av} + \frac{1}{c_0}\bar{\bar{\chi}}_{em} \cdot \mathbf{H}_{av} \tag{2a}$$

$$\mathbf{M} = \bar{\bar{\chi}}_{mm} \cdot \mathbf{H}_{av} + \frac{1}{\eta_0}\bar{\bar{\chi}}_{me} \cdot \mathbf{E}_{av} \tag{2b}$$

III. Polarization Transformations Using Metasurfaces

The objective of these polarization transformation based metasurfaces is to achieve linear (*LP*) to circular (*CP*) polarization at millimeter wave frequency band. In general, the aim to work at millimeter wave is to achieve broadband response and we have tried to work on surfaces that can achieve broadband response and *CP* within $90^\circ \pm 20^\circ$. In this paper, broadband response of dielectric resonator and metallic metasurfaces is determined with transmission coefficient as $T(\omega) \geq 0.8$ and phase difference between TE and TM polarization as $\Delta\varphi = \varphi_{TE} - \varphi_{TM} \approx 90^\circ$.

A. Dielectric Resonator Metasurface

The dielectric resonator (DR) unit cell and its metasurface are illustrated in Fig. 1(a) and 1(b). The material used for DR is Rogers RO3210 having a permittivity of $\epsilon_r = 10.2$ with $\tan\delta = 0.0027$, thickness $h = 2.54$ mm ($\approx \lambda_0/4.2$), axis dimensions of $a = 2.7$ mm ($\approx \lambda_0/3.9$) and $b = 1.85$ mm ($\approx \lambda_0/5.78$), and unit period cell $ax = ay = 7.45$ mm ($\approx \lambda_0/1.4$). The simulated results for DR metasurface are illustrated in Fig. 2(a) and 2(b). It is seen that the satisfied response of this metasurface is achieved between $28 - 33$ GHz and electric and magnetic susceptibility are retrieved using reflection and transmission parameters using GSTCs, mentioned in Section II, for both TE and TM polarization. The simulated response is of limited bandwidth due to resonating properties of dielectric resonator.

B. Four Layer Metallic Metasurface

The four layer metallic unit cell along with its metasurface are illustrated in Fig. 1(c) and 1(d). The material used for dielectric substrate is Rogers RO5880 having a permittivity of $\epsilon_r = 2.2$ with $\tan\delta = 0.0009$, thickness $h = 0.127$ mm and periodicity of $L_x = 2.5$ mm of each layer consisting of different unit cell for inner and outer layers. The radius of the inner and outer rings for both types of unit cell are $r_1 = 1.2$ mm, $r_2 = 1.9$ mm, $r_{11} = 1.5$ mm, and $r_{21} = 2.2$ mm. The gaps along *y-axis* and *x-axis* are given as $g_1 = 1$ mm, $g_{11} = 2$ mm, $g_2 = 0.5$ mm, and $g_{21} = 0.5$ mm. The four layers are created to cover 2π phase range coverage over for transmitted fields. The total thickness of the metasurface is considered subwavelength ($d \ll \lambda_0$) and is $d = 0.508$ mm. The simulated results for four layer unit cell are illustrated in Fig. 2(c) and 2(d). The bandwidth achieved to obtain linear and circular polarization is within $90^\circ \pm 10^\circ$ over 26-40 GHz. In addition, the transmission coefficients are greater than 0.9 over the whole frequency band.

IV. Conclusion

In this paper, the demonstration of polarization transformation using metasurfaces is presented. The metasurfaces shown here can be of two types: dielectric resonator and metallic and linear to circular polarization is aimed using such surfaces. It is seen the dielectric resonator, due to its limited bandwidth, cover only 28-33 GHz for such polarization conversion. On the other hand, due to increase in the number of the layers for metallic metasurfaces, we are able to increase the 2π phase range transmission coverage resulting in better performance than dielectric resonator based metasurfaces.

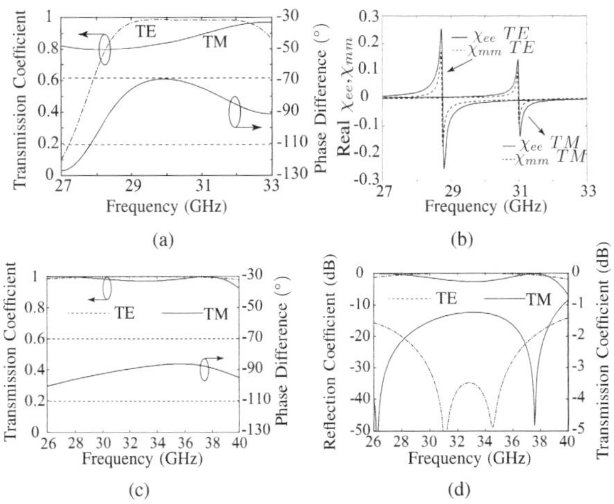

Fig. 2. (a) Transmission Coefficients and phase difference between TE and TM polarization for DR unit cell. (b)Real Electric and magnetic susceptibilities for TE and TM polarization. (c) Transmission coefficients and phase difference between TE and TM polarization for four layer unit cell. (d) Reflection and Transmission coefficient in dB for four layer metasurface.

Acknowledgment

We acknowledge the support of the Natural Sciences and Engineering Research Council of Canada (NSERC), PGSD3-519470-2018. Cette recherche a été financée par le Conseil de recherches en sciences naturelles et en génie du Canada (CRSNG), PGSD3-519470-2018.

References

[1] C. L. Holloway, M. A. Mohamed, E. F. Kuester, and A. Dienstfrey, "Reflection and transmission properties of a metafilm: with an application to a controllable surface composed of resonant particles," in IEEE Transactions on Electromagnetic Compatibility, vol. 47, no. 4, pp. 853-865, Nov. 2005.

[2] G. Zheng, H. Mühlenbernd, M. Kenney, G. Li, T. Zentgraf, and S. Zhang, "Metasurface holograms reaching 80% efficiency," Nature Nanotechnol. vol. 10, no. 4, pp. 308–312, 2015.

[3] E. Karimi, S. A. Schulz, I. D. Leon, H. Qassim, J. Upham, and R. W. Boyd, "Generating optical orbital angular momentum at visible wavelengths using a plasmonic metasurface," Light, Sci. Appl., vol. 3,no.5, p. e167, 2014.

[4] K. Achouri, "Synthesis and applications of electromagnetic metasurfaces," Ph.D. dissertation, Ecole Polytechnique de Montreal, 2017.

[5] M. M. Idemen, Discontinuities in the electromagnetic field. John Wiley & Sons, 2011, vol. 40.

[6] E. F. Kuester, M. A. Mohamed, M. Piket-May, and C. L. Holloway, "Averaged transition conditions for electromagnetic fields at a metafilm," IEEE Transactions on Antennas and Propagation, vol. 51, no. 10, pp. 2641–2651, 2003.

An X-band Oblique Polarized Antenna Array

Jia Fang, Mouping Jin, and Feng Yu
ECRIEE, East China Research Institute of Electronic Engineering
APELAM, Anhui Province Engineering Laboratory for Antennas and Microwave
Hefei, China
fjftt@mail.ustc.edu.cn

***Abstract*—An X-band oblique polarized array is designed and manufactured, the scan range is positive negative 45deg. The antenna choose the printed dipole antenna. By using a short-circuited probe balun and adding a parasitic patch on the top of the dipole, the bandwidth of it is extended to be whole X-band. The antenna is improved to be double plates with two face radiation dipoles and a lot of metallization holes to close the balun radiation, which could reduce the difference between the horizontal polarization patterns and the vertical polarization patterns when wide-angle scan. The array is measured and the results show it can achieve X-band 45deg scan work.**

***Keywords*—45deg oblique polarized, balun, printed dipole antenna, wide-angle scan, wideband.**

I. INTRODUCTION

Because the wideband work can reduce a lot of equipments and costs, the wide-angle scan work can cover more airspace, the 45° oblique polarized work can receive and send both the horizontal polarization and vertical polarization radar signal, the wideband wide-angle scan 45° oblique polarized antenna array is used for the electronic warfare domain [1-2].

II. STRUCTURE

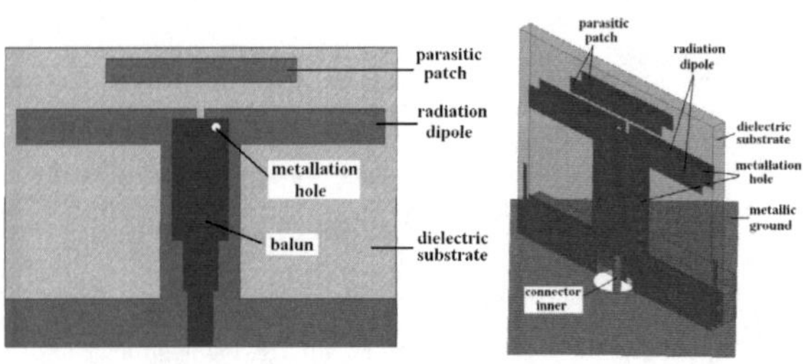

Fig. 1. Structure of the printed dipole antenna.

The printed dipole antenna is choose to be the antenna element of the array, which has a lot of advantages such as low cost, little weight, easy manufacture and integration, high accuracy and consistency [3-4]. The bandwith of the traditional printed dipole antenna is not enough for the whole X-band [5], so the antenna is feed by a new balun and add a parasitic patch, as shown in the left picture of Fig. 1. By using a short-circuited probe balun which introduced a parallel capacitor to compensated the series reactance, and adding a parasitic patch on the top of the antenna, the work bandwidth of it is extended to be 50%.

To reduce the effect of the balun radiation, the printed dipole antenna is change to be double plates. There are two radiation dipoles at both sides of the dielectric substrates. The balun is in the middle, and there are a lot of metallization holes connect both two face radiation dipoles to close the radiation of the balun, as shown in the right picture of Fig. 1 . The strip-line at the bottom of the antenna is changed to micro-strip line to connect the RF connector.

III. SIMULATION

The couple between antennas of the wideband wide-angle scan array is powerful, so the performance of the single antenna and the antenna in the array is not the same [6]. The antenna is simulated and optimized by HFSS with two-dimensional periodic boundary to simulation the antenna in the array, as shown in Fig. 2. The antenna element is positioned 45° from the X axis and the Y axis to achieve 45° oblique polarized work. The active-VSWR simulated results of the antenna in the array are shown in Fig. 3. The red real line and the blue dot line are the results with no scan and scan ±45° , and they are under 1.75 between 8.5GHz to 11.9GHz ,and under 2.5 at whole X-band.

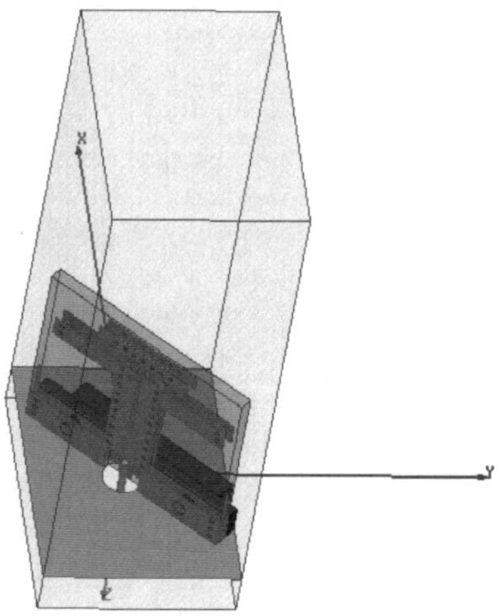

Fig. 2. Simulation model of the antenna.

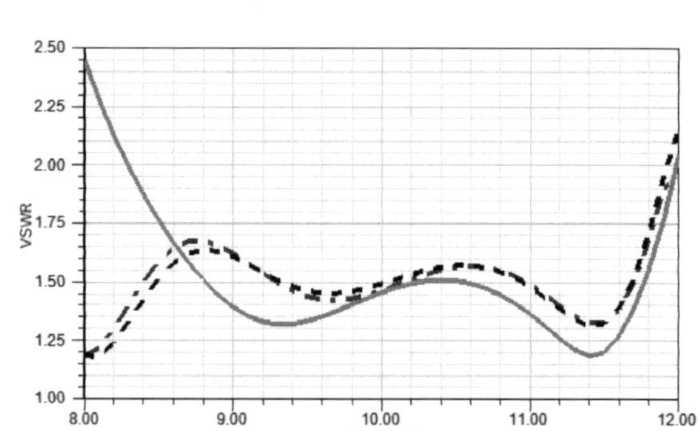

Fig. 3. Active-VSWR simulated results.

IV. Results

The array size is 16×12. Because there's no need scan in the pitching direction, each 12 elements in one row are combined by an integrated Wilkinson power divider, as shown in Fig. 4.

The antenna is manufactured and tested. Figure 5 is the VSWR measured results of one row antenna elements, the maximum number is under 2.5 at whole X-band. The array antenna is measured in the microwave darkroom, as shown in Fig. 6. The measured E-plane radiation patterns of the array at 10GHz with no scan and scan ±45° are shown in Fig. 7. The red line is the horizontal polarization result and the black line is the vertical polarization result, and they are almost same at the main-lobe, the maximum difference is under 1dB.

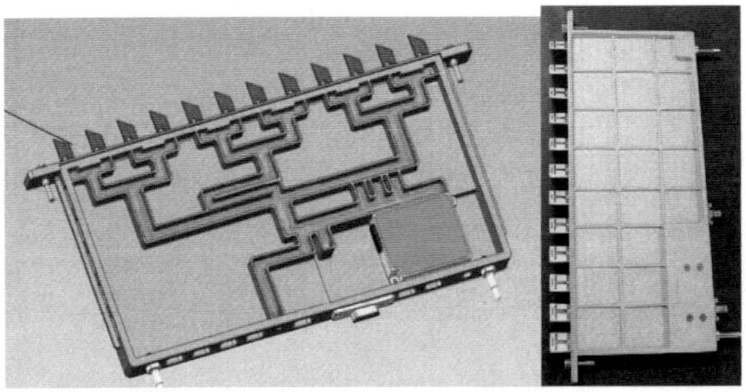

Fig. 4. A low antenna elements.

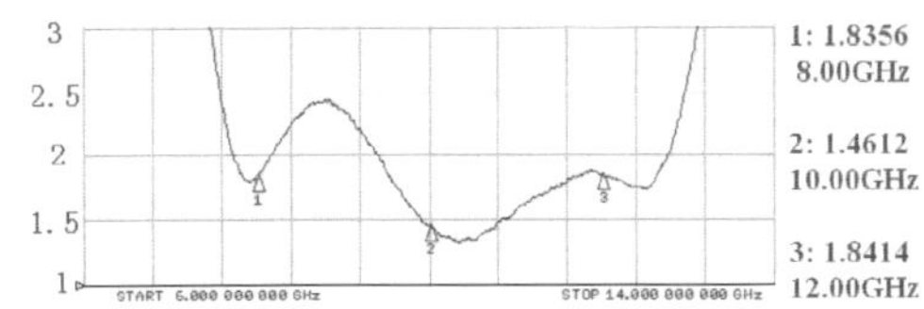

Fig. 5. VSWR measured results.

V. Conclusion

A new printed dipole antenna is designed for wideband wide-angle scan 45° oblique polarized antenna array. By using a short-circuited probe balun and adding a parasitic patch on the top of the dipole, the bandwidth of it is extended to be whole X-band. The antenna is improved to be double plates with two face radiation dipoles and a lot of metallization holes to close the balun radiation, which could reduce the difference between the horizontal polarization patterns and the vertical polarization patterns when wide-angle scan. The measured results show its VSWR at whole X-band are under 2.5, the scan range can reach ±45°, and the difference between two polarizations are less than 1dB, which could meet the needs of the system work.

Fig. 6. The antenna array.

References

[1] J. Mouping and F. Jia, "Technology of ultra-wideband antenna array," The Journal of Advanced Radar Detection Technology, vol. 20, pp. 1-6, Oct. 2016.

[2] F. Jia and J. Mouping, "An UWB printed log-periodic array antenna," [C]. 2018 IEEE International Workshop on Antenna Technology, Nanjing, China, pp. 125- 127, Mar. 2018.

[3] F. Tefiku, "A broad-band antenna of double-sided printed strip dipoles," [C]. Int. Symp. Antennas Propagation (ISAP 96), Tokyo, Japan, pp. 361-364, Sept. 1996.

[4] Z. Zhou, S. Yang, and Z. Nie, "A novel broad-band printed dipole antenna with low cross-polarization," [J]. IEEE Trans. Antennas Propagation, vol. 55, pp. 3091-3093, 2007.

[5] L. Xiaopeng and L. Yan, "A novel BALUN for printed dipole," Radar Science and Technology, vol. 4, no. 4, Aug. 2006.

[6] F. Jia and J. Mouping, "Design and Research of An UWB 45deg Oblique Polarized Antenna Array"[C] . CIE RADAR2016 , Guangzhou, Chian, pp. 238－240, Oct. 2016.

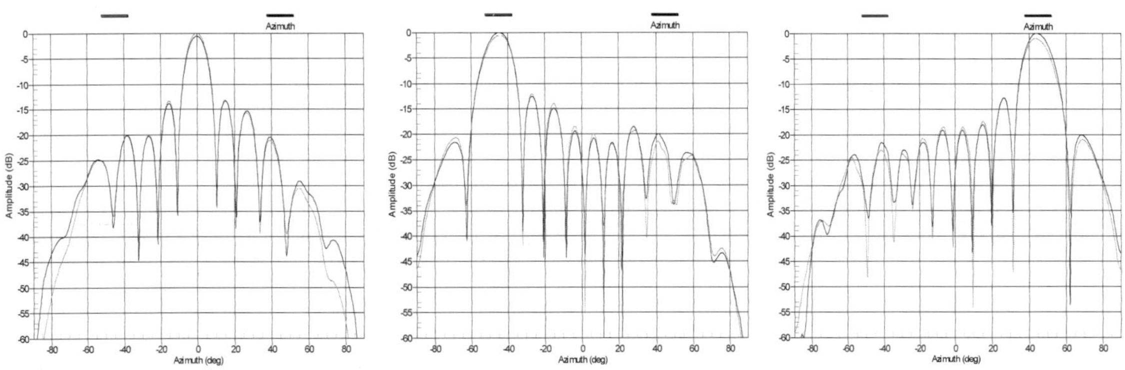

Fig. 7. E-plane patterns of the antenna array with no scan and scan ±45° at 10GHz.

Proximity Effect of UWB U-Slot Patch Antenna on Human Body

Mahrukh Khan, Liaquat Ali, Abdul Hamid Yousuf and Masud Chowdhury

Computer Science and Electrical Engineering Department, University of Missouri Kansas City, Missouri, 64131, USA

***Abstract*-In this paper, the proximity effect of Ultra-wideband (UWB) antenna on human body is considered and demonstrated. A U-Slot loaded planar UWB antenna is designed on TMM3 (ε_r=3.27) using single layer circuit board technology. The antenna has shown 75% impedance bandwidth in free space. A human body model having three layers (skin, fat and muscle) is developed. The effect of the human body on the antenna performance is analyzed and characterized in terms of the reflection-coefficient and specific absorption rate (SAR). The effect of the antenna-body is analyzed for off body applications. The UWB U-Slot antenna exhibits low SAR while maintaining reasonable impedance bandwidth.**

***Index Terms* — antennas, bandwidth biomedical, microwaves.**

I. Introduction

Ultra-wideband (UWB) technology is a highly promising solution for Wireless Body area Networks (WBANs), particularly for healthcare applications [1]. The 3.1–10.6 GHz frequency band was selected by the FCC for the unlicensed usage of this technology. The main advantages of UWB are potentially high data rates, low power consumption, and increased resilience to multipath interference. The antenna is an essential element of such systems, and its design becomes more demanding in health care applications due to the proximity effects of complex human body electromagnetic characteristics [3]. From an electromagnetic field point of view, the human body can be considered as an irregular, inhomogeneous, and lossy dielectric object positioned near the antennas. The effect of the human body on the performance of the antenna must be considered in the antenna design, because it severely affects the antenna's characteristics [2].

General studies have been conducted on the evaluation of the power absorbed by the human body and the Specific Absorption Rate (SAR). Kuster [4] has evaluated the absorption mechanism for homogenous body model while Kivekas [5] has considered homogenous and layered body model. Specific Absorption Rate (SAR) is defined as the amount of radio frequency energy absorbed by human tissue. Higher SAR level means more electromagnetic signals absorbed by the body and more harm to the health [7].

In this paper, we examine U-Slot antenna performance in free space and in presence of layered human body phantom. The main objective is to analyze the potential capability of U-Slot antenna for health care applications. We have presented here that how the antenna parameters are changed by introducing the human body in proximity of UWB U-Slot microstrip antenna.

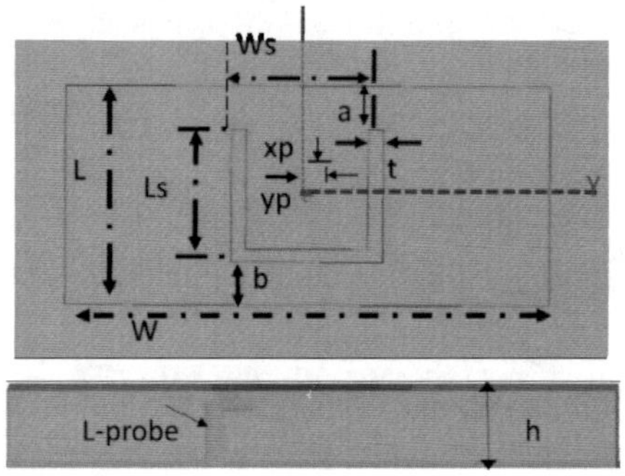

Fig. 1. UWB slot loaded microstrip patch antenna. All patch design values are given in [6].

II. UWB U-Slot Design and Effect ON Human Body

The structure of the UWB slot loaded micro-strip antenna is shown in Fig. 1. The UWB antenna on Rogers TMM3 (ε_r=3.27) operates for a wide range from the frequency of 4.4 GHz to 9.5 GHz as shown in Fig. 3. The design values of antenna are given in [6]. Addition of L-probe feed increased its bandwidth from 29.74% to 75%. Fig. 2 shows a setup of the antenna with a layered human body model for off body application. The distance between antenna and human body phantom is 50mm. For a tissue, to have a greater impact on microwave signals, permittivity and water content play a major role [5]. The layered human body model comprises of three different tissues namely skin (dry), fat and muscle. This layered model can represent most of the body regions, since the fat has similar properties to the bone tissue, and the electrical parameters of the muscle and many inner organs are alike. Since the human body tissues are frequency dispersive materials, that's why their effect on antenna parameters varies with frequency. Table I shows the relative permittivity(ε_r), conductivity (σ) (taken from FEKO library) and thickness of human model at center frequency. Commercial electromagnetic simulation package FEKO was used for design & simulation purposes.

The antenna's impedance bandwidth behavior is analyzed in the presence of human body. It can be seen from Fig. 3 that reflection coefficient is not affected much when antenna is placed at 50 mm from the body except the lower resonant frequency which is shifted to 4.6 GHZ from 4.4 GHz

TABLE I. HUMAN TISSUE MODEL @ 7.3 GHz

Tissue	ε_r	σ(S/m)	Thickness(mm)
Skin	32.31	5.06	4
Fat	4.13	0.38	4
Muscle	47.56	8.3	8

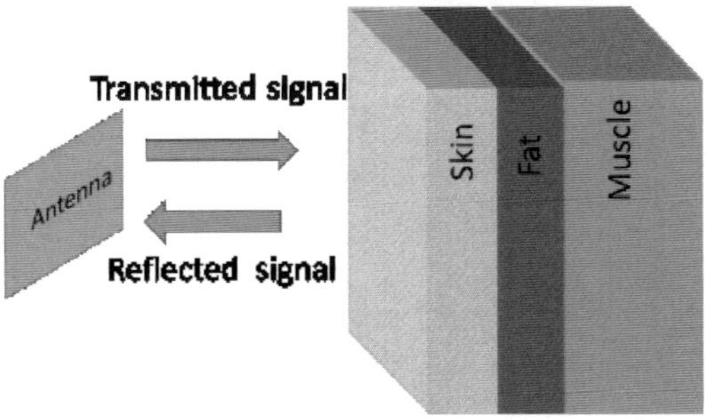

Fig. 2. UWB antenna setup for noninvasive detection.

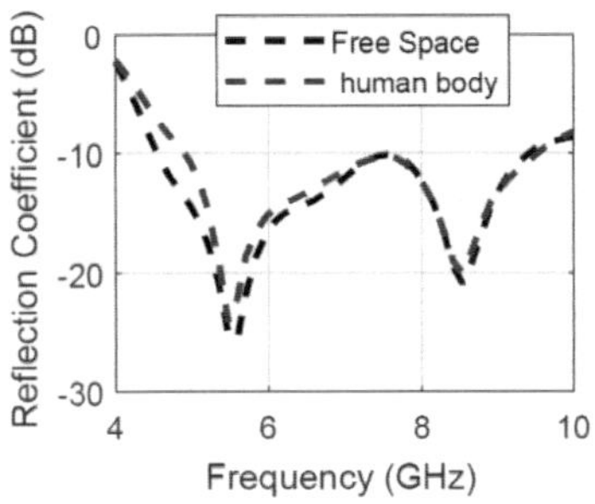

Fig. 3. Return loss in free space vs. in presence of human body.

In Fig. 4, A 2D rectangular cross section is drawn in the middle to show SAR in all the layers as shown in Fig.4. SAR's value is shown at center frequency, i.e.,7.3 GHz. It can be observed that thermal absorption is more for the muscle layer and skin layer but less for the fat layer. The maximum SAR value observed at this frequency is 50mW/kg. Among the three tissue layers, skin tissue has absorbed more energy than the other tissues due to its high permittivity. Peak SAR values vs frequency are given in Fig 5. averaged on 1g of tissue which are within defined limits of FCC for 1g of tissue content i.e. 1.6 (W/Kg).

III. SUMMARY

Recently, Health issues due to EM radiation are becoming an important concern for many countries that's why accurate modeling of the UWB antenna requires the inclusion of the human tissue frequency dispersion in the UWB frequency range. In this paper, the proximity effect of U-Slot antenna on human body is analysed. It is shown that antenna maintains its impedance bandwidth if human body is present at 50 mm. SAR values show that there is thermal absorption in human body phantom which is significant at skin layer than other layers. Peak SAR values are within FCC defined limits which make this antenna safer for off body application.

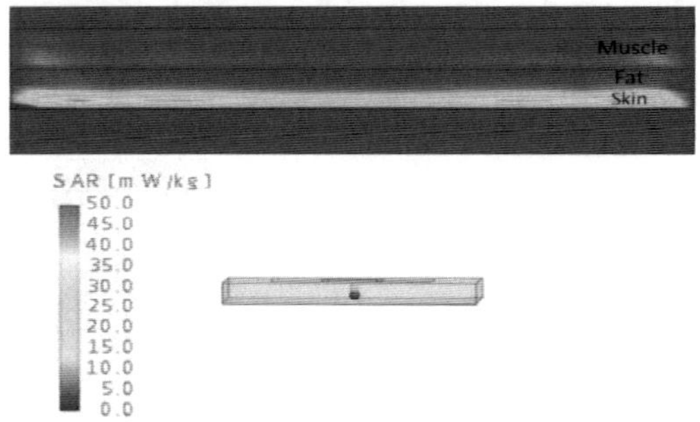

Fig. 4. Simulated SAR (Specific absorption rate) for off-body applications at 7.3GHz.

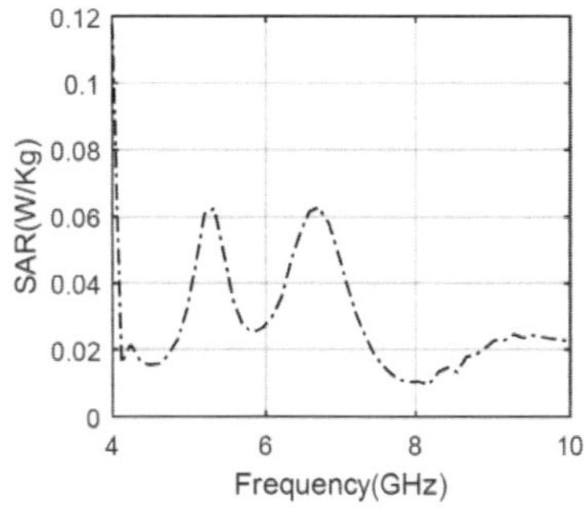

Fig. 5. Peak SAR averaged over 1g of tissue.

REFERENCES

[1] E. M. Staderini, "UWB radars in medicine," *IEEE Aerosp. Electron.Syst. Mag.*, vol. 17, no. 1, pp. 13–18, Jan. 2002.

[2] Z. N. Chen, A. Cai, T. S. P. See, X. Qing, and M. Y. W. Chia "Small Planar UWB Antennas in Proximity of the Human Head." *IEEE Transactions on Microwave Theory and Techniques*, vol .54, no. 4 pp., April 2006.

[3] P. A. Floor, et al., "In-Body to On-Body Ultra wideband Propagation Model Derived From Measurements in Living Animals," in *IEEE Journal of Biomedical and Health Informatics,* vol. 19, no. 3, May 2015.

[4] K. Meier, V. Hombach, R. Kastle, R. Y.-S. Tay, and N. Kuster, "The dependence of electromagnetic energy absorption upon human-head modeling at 1800 MHz," IEEE Transactions on Microwave Theory and Techniques, vol. 45, no. 11, pp. 2058–2062, 199

[5] O. Kivekäs, T. Lehtiniemi, and P. Vainikainen, "On the general energy-absorption mechanism in the human tissue," Microwave and Optical Technology Letters, vol. 43, no. 3, pp. 195–201, 2004.

[6] M. Khan and D. Chatterjee, "Characteristic mode analysis of a class of empirical design techniques for probe-fed U-Slot microstrip patch antennas," *IEEE Trans. Antennas Propag.*, vol. 64, no. 7, pp. 2758-2770, Jul. 2016.

[7] Florence, Esther S., et al. "An Investigation of a Wearable Antenna Using Human Body Modelling." *Applied Computational Electromagnetics Society Journal*, vol. 29, no. 10, pp. 777–783, Oct. 2014.

Design of a Novel Dual-Band, Electrically Small, Printed Octafilar Antenna

Joseph D. Majkowski

Harris Communication Systems
Rochester NY, 14610, United States

Abstract — This paper presents several innovative techniques for the design and optimization of a dual band octafilar helix antenna. The antenna was designed to fit inside a radome with .07λ diameter. This was achieved through a novel technique of applying differing pitches and terminations to the upper and lower frequency antenna filars and then feeding them from the same point at the base. The final design produced gain greater than 0dBic at zenith across both .07*F1 bands of operation. The differing pitch approach to the elements was seen to improve impedance and hence overall gain performance at the low frequency band by about 2 dBic.

Index Terms — Dualband, Octafilar, QHA.

I. INTRODUCTION

In this paper, a novel, dual quadrifilar, or octafilar, is designed, fabricated, and measured. The two filar structures have differing loop connection heights which allows for proper resonant length to be set individually for each loop. The high and low frequency filar structures are also set at differing pitch angles to maximize isolation of the two elements while maintaining a small coupling factor to improve low frequency impedance. This improvement came at marginal cost of the impedance of the high frequency structure. The high frequency band structure's orthogonal elements also needed to be electrically isolated from one another to prevent improper current distribution from being induced due to the proximity and frequency of the low frequency element. Finally, a G-10 radome utilized to house the antenna, while the antenna structure itself was choked off with Baluns to isolate it from the transmitter and fed through a 90 degree hybrid. Details of the proposed antenna are shown in Fig. 1. and described along with both experimental and numerical results.

II. SEPARATED LOOP TERMINATIONS

The optimal design for a dualband, multi-filar helix antenna would be to have two separate radiating structures set to their proper electrical lengths for operation in their respective frequency ranges [3]. Thus, the two quadrifilar antennas were fed from a single point at the base of the antenna with this being the only point of DC connection between the two different frequency structures. The two differing quadrifilar structures have their own unique height corresponding to the frequency of operation. This was accomplished with two rigid PWBs being soldered into place at the end of the two differing quadrifilar structures. The proposed antenna can be seen below in Fig. 1.

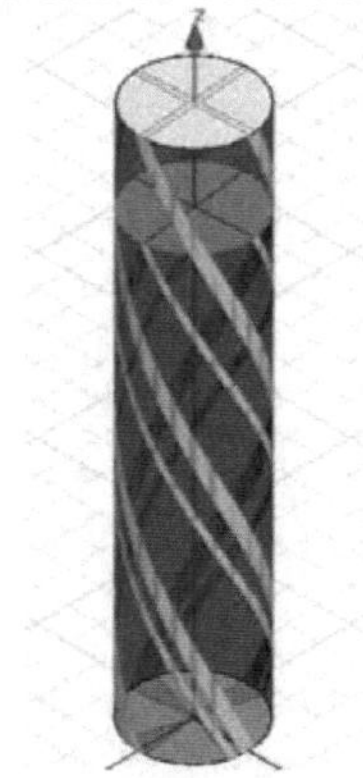

Fig. 1. HFSS model of octafilar antenna design.

III. DIVERGING ELEMENTS

As the radius of the structure decreases relative to the wavelength of operation the radiation resistance of the structure starts to decrease [1]. Ideally the elements should be located at 45 degrees of separation to maximize isolation between the high frequency and low frequency elements. However, it was observed that the closer the elements are at the feed side of the antenna the better the impedance and radiation resistance gets. This comes at a marginal cost of performance of the upper frequency element. Optimal performance was found when the higher frequency element was placed at an angle of 4 degrees more than the lower frequency elements.

IV. UNEVEN CURRENT DISTRIBUTIONS

It is standard practice to allow all branches of the loops to meet at a singular point at the top of the antenna structure [2]. This technique allows for the currents to balance out and the overall structure to be balanced. Due to proximity, as well as frequency, of the nested quadrifilars, connecting the orthogonal components of the high frequency structure to a singular point induced a resonance and subsequently loss in the upper frequency band. The orthogonal components of the high frequency quadrifilar needed to be DC isolated at their crossing points. This was achieved by completing the first loop on the top of the circuit board and the perpendicular component on the bottom of the circuit board.

V. ANTENNA RADOME

The antenna structure was printed on a 4 mil thick strip of pyralux material. This material was rolled and housed within a 1/32" wall thickness G-10 cylinder. This material was chosen due to its high electrical transparency, light weight, and good structural integrity which allows for the antenna to pass all MIL-STD 810G testing. Expanding foam was utilized inside the rolled up pyralux material to create consistent contact and hence dielectric loading unit to unit. This dielectric loading shifted performance .05λ which was compensated for by reducing overall antenna length.

VI. CONCLUSION

An electrically small diameter, light weight, dual-band, octafilar antenna was designed and fabricated for operation over two .07λ bands of operation. The return loss of the antenna structure matched very closely numerically to measurement, with a roughly 1 dB delta in magnitude as seen in Fig. 2. The pattern and gain performance of the prototype also matched very closely to simulation results as seen in Fig. 3.

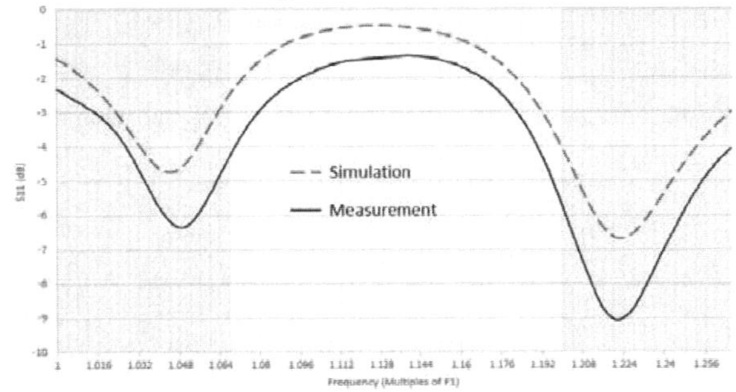

Figure 2. Return Loss Comparisons

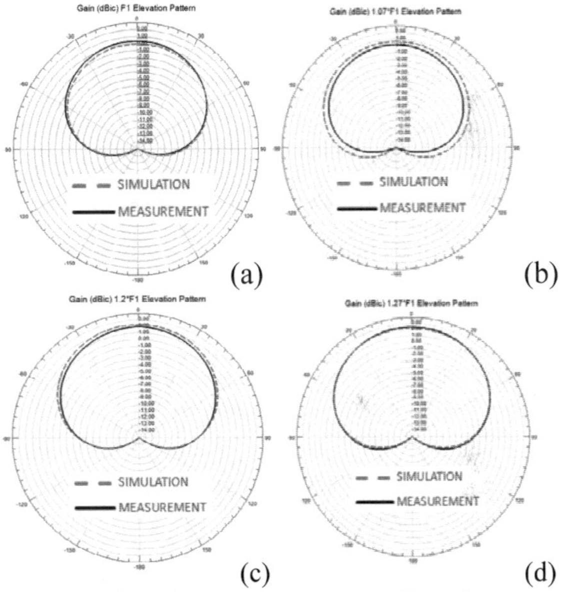

Fig. 3. Elevation Pattern Comparison for:
(a) F1, (b) 1.07*F1, (c) 1.2*F1, (d) 1.27*F1.

VII. ACKNOWLEDGEMENTS

The author would like to acknowledge Harris Communication Systems of Rochester, NY for their support.

REFERENCES

[1] C. Gerst and R. A. Worden, "Helix antenna take turn for the better," *Electronics*, vol. 39, no. 17, pp.100-110, Aug. 1966.

[2] C. Kilgus, "Multielement fractional turn helices," IEEE Trans. Antennas Propag., vol. 16, pp. 499–500, Jul. 1968.

[3] C. Kilgus, "Resonant quadrafilar helix," IEEE Trans. Antennas Propag., vol. AP-17, no. 3, pp. 349–351, May 1969.

A Fast 3D Imaging Method for Subsurface Metal Targets Using Time-Domain Electromagnetic System

Wupeng Xie
Key Laboratory of Electromagnetic Radiation and Sensing Technology,
Chinese Academy of Sciences
Beijing, China
xwpucas@163.com

Xiaojuan Zhang*
Key Laboratory of Electromagnetic Radiation and Sensing Technology,
Chinese Academy of Sciences
Beijing, China
xjzhang@mail.ie.ac.cn

Yaoxin Zheng
Key Laboratory of Electromagnetic Radiation and Sensing Technology,
Chinese Academy of Sciences
Beijing, China
yxzheng1996@126.com

Yaxin Mu
Key Laboratory of Electromagnetic Radiation and Sensing Technology,
Chinese Academy of Sciences
Beijing, China
muyaxin15@mails.ucas.ac.cn

Han Liu
Key Laboratory of Electromagnetic Radiation and Sensing Technology,
Chinese Academy of Sciences
Beijing, China
635264270@qq.com

***Abstract*—We propose a fast 3D imaging method to image subsurface metal targets using time-domain electromagnetic system. The method is based on the discretization of the underground into several grids which represent the independent magnetic dipoles contribute to the measured responses collectively. The strength of every dipole is obtained by minimizing the mismatch between the computed and observed secondary response from the targets using the iterative optimization method. The method proposed herein has a small amount of computation and strong robustness, which help visualize the underground target in three dimensions accurately and rapidly.**

***Keywords*—Magnetic dipole, Optimization method, Three-dimensional imaging, Time-domain electromagnetic (TEM) method.**

I. Introduction

The detection of subsurface targets such as unexploded ordnance, pipes, communication cables and archaeological artifacts has been drawing more and more attention. In recent years, due to its good performance of detection, the time-domain electromagnetic (TEM) method is widely used in the field, including shallow surface mapping [1], detection of unexploded ordnance [2] and archeology [3].

The TEM method is an artificial source detection approach based on electromagnetic induction, which uses an un-grounded loop source (magnetic source) or grounded line source (electric source) to launch a primary field to the ground, and under its excitation, eddy currents induced in subsurface conductor targets will produce an induced secondary field. The ANSYS finite-element programming has been used to compute the electromagnetic induction (EMI) response of arbitrary, ordnance-like objects, which usually take several hours, even a day, and it is not suitable for real-time recognition of the subsurface targets [4]. The EMI responses of the metal targets can be represented by the single point magnetic dipole fields when the subsurface detection where the target-sensor distance is 3-5 times the dimension of a target [5], [6]. The TEM method satisfies the electromagnetic wave diffusion equation rather than the wave equation as EMI frequencies range from tens of Hz to hundreds of kHz, and it results in the impossibility of forming high-resolution images of the subsurface targets.

II. 3D Imaging Method

Our method is based on the discretization of the underground into several grids which represent the independent magnetic dipoles contribute to the measured responses collectively. To be noticed, the direction of every dipole is fixedly z-axis, which means the position and orientation of each dipole are already known but not their dipole moment strength (The tri-axial magnetic dipole is unnecessary. For our detection system, both the transmitting and the receiving coil are z-axis, and the x-axis and y-axis magnetic dipole contributes negligibly to the received signal).

The magnetic field generated by each dipole is:

$$H^S(\vec{r},t) = \frac{1}{4\pi|\vec{r}|^3}\left(\frac{3\vec{r}\vec{r}}{|\vec{r}|^2} - \bar{\bar{I}}\right) \cdot \vec{m}(t). \tag{1}$$

Where $\vec{r}$ represents the distance vector, which is from the dipole to the observation point and the dipole moment is:

$$\vec{m}(t) = \hat{z}\beta_z(t) \cdot H_z^{pr}, \tag{2}$$

where $\beta_z(t)$ is the polarizability and H_z^{pr} is the primary field generated by the transmitting coil.

We use the optimization method to calculate:

$$\min_{\left\{\frac{\partial\beta_z(t)}{\partial t}\right\}} \left\| \oint \sum_j^{N_m} \frac{1}{4\pi|\vec{r_j}|^3}\left(\frac{3\vec{r_j}\vec{r_j}}{|\vec{r_j}|^2} - \bar{\bar{I}}\right) \cdot \frac{\overrightarrow{\partial m_j}}{\partial \mathrm{t}} dS - V^{obs} \right\|_2, \quad s.t. \left\{\frac{\partial\beta_z(t)}{\partial t}\right\} > 0 \tag{3}$$

where observation measurement is:

$$V^{obs} = \begin{bmatrix} V_1^{obs} \\ \vdots \\ V_N^{obs} \end{bmatrix}, \tag{4}$$

where N_m and N are the number of observed data and the number of magnetic dipoles, respectively. Then, we use the first time gate of the observation response near the anomaly region to image. Taking a profile as an example, the x-z plane along the y-coordinate of the anomaly is divided into several dipoles. In the same way, we discretize the y-z plane and the x-y plane, and finally the three-dimensional imaging results of the subsurface target can be obtained.

III. NUMERICAL EXAMPLES

This section shows the results using the 3D imaging method proposed herein with synthetic data. The schematic of target detection is shown in Fig. 1, the steel and barrel target (20*5*5)(cm) is buried at (1,0.5,-0.6)(m), and the z-axis transmitter (1m*1m) and receiving coil (0.5m*0.5m) are placed concentrically with a measured point spacing of 25cm.

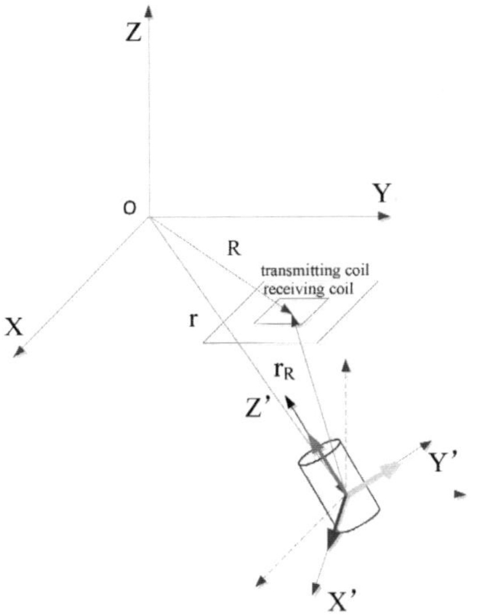

Fig. 1. The schematic of target detection.

Then we use the method proposed herein with first time gate measured response to image the subsurface target. The Fig. 2 shows that it converges quickly within 10 steps. The final 3D imaging result is shown in Fig. 3, and we can see that the imaging result agree well with the true position of target.

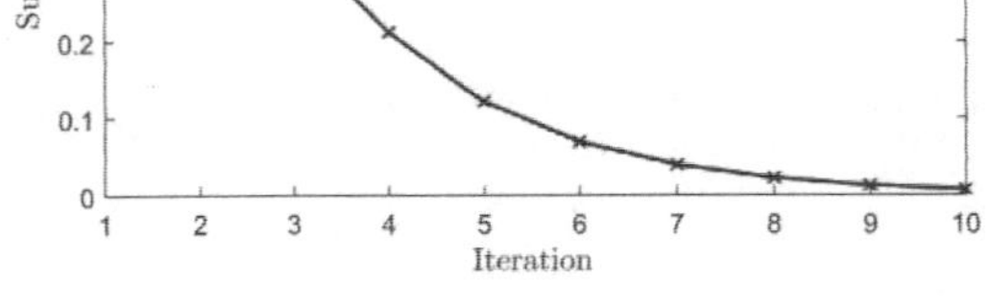

Fig. 2. The convergence curve.

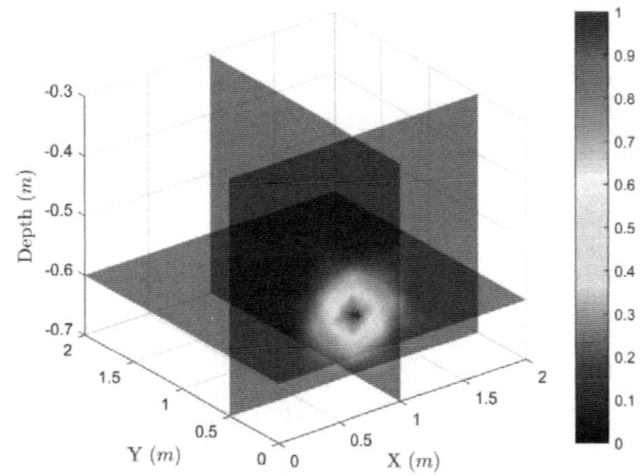

Fig. 3. The 3D imaging result. (the symbol "+" in this figure indicates the actual position of the target).

IV. CONCLUSION

In this work, a fast 3D imaging method for subsurface metal targets using time-domain electromagnetic system has been proposed. The synthetic example demonstrates the effectiveness of our method. Compared with the finite element method, it requires smaller amount of computation, and can locate the subsurface targets in three dimensions accurately and quickly to visualize the detection results. Future work will be to image the details of the subsurface targets, such as the shape and inclination of the targets.

ACKNOWLEDGMENT

This research work is supported by the Innovation Project of Chinese Academy of Sciences. Also, the authors would like to thank Ms. Boxuan Dong from Beijing Forestry University for many fruitful discussions and the guidance on manuscript editing.

REFERENCES

[1] S. P. Sharma, K. Anbarasu, S. Gupta, et al., "Integrated very low-frequency EM, electrical resistivity, and geological studies on the LantaKhola landslide, North Sikkim, India," Landslides, vol. 7, no. 7, pp. 43–53, Feb. 2010.

[2] H. H. Nelson and D. A. Steinhurst, "Enhanced UXO discrimination using frequency-domain electromagnetic induction," ResearchGate, Jul. 2007.

[3] Y. Manstein and A. Manstein, "EMI sensor NEMFIS: Method, equipment and case stories of archaeological prospection," Arch´eosciences, vol. 33, no. 1, pp. 321-324, Oct. 2009.

[4] R. E. Grimm, "Time Domain Measurements and Modeling of UXO," Uxo Forum, 2001.

[5] L. P. Song, D. W. Oldenburg, L. R. Pasion, and S. D. Billings, "Transient electromagnetic inversion of multiple targets," Proc. SPIE, vol. 7303, pp. 73030R–73030R12, 2009.

[6] J. T. Smith and H. F. Morrison, "Estimating equivalent dipole polarizabilities for the inductive response of isolated conductive bodies," IEEE Trans. Geosci. Remote Sens., vol. 42, no. 6, pp. 1208–1214, Jun. 2004.

Deep Neural Networks Based Surrogate Model for Topology Optimization of Electromagnetic Devices

Mauro Tucci
DESTEC
University of Pisa
Pisa, Italy
mauro.tucci@unipi.it

Sami Barmada
DESTEC
University of Pisa
Pisa, Italy
sami.barmada@unipi.it

Luca Sani
DESTEC
University of Pisa
Pisa, Italy
luca.sani@unipi.it

Dimitri Thomopulos
DESTEC
University of Pisa
Pisa, Italy
thomopulos@lix.polytechnique.fr

Nunzia Fontana
DESTEC
University of Pisa
Pisa, Italy
nunzia.fontana@gmail.com

***Abstract*—In this work a novel approach is presented for topology optimization of low frequency electromagnetic devices. In particular a surrogate model based on deep neural networks with encoder-decoder architecture is introduced. A first autoencoder deep neural network learns to represent the input images that describe the topology, i.e. geometry and materials. The novel idea is to use the low dimensional output space of the encoder as the search space of the optimization algorithm, instead of using the higher dimensional space represented by the input images. A second deep neural network learns the relationship between the encoder outputs and the objective function (i.e., torque), which is calculated by means of a finite element analysis. The calculation time for the optimization is greatly improved by reducing the dimensionality of the search space, and by introducing the surrogate model, whereas the quality of the result is slightly affected.**

***Index Terms*—deep nerual networks, surrogate model, topology optimization.**

I. Introduction

Design optimization of rotating machines and electromagnetic (EM) devices based on field computation is nowadays of interest both for research and industries. The conventional approach usually faces the following main challenges:

- it is often difficult to set an adequate design space that includes a solution with satisfactory performance, as the design variables introduced by the user restrict the ability of the optimization models to deal with any arbitrary change in the design of a machine;
- employing Finite Element Analysis (FEA) for modeling and simulation purposes remains a computationally expensive process.

The first problem is overcome by topology optimization [1], which does not require the definition of the design variables. In fact, geometries and materials are flexibly represented using a bitmap approach, which describes a device as a set of pixels. This allows free modification of material boundaries and appearance of holes in the design region, resulting in new machine shapes which may outperform conventional machines. The remarkable drawback is the increased dimensionality of the optimization search space, related to the bitmap resolution and color space.

The second problem has led to the development of several surrogate models to aid the optimization process [2], [3]. Extensive research has been carried out in the field of magnetic equivalent circuits and neural networks, based on curve fitting, to partially or completely bypass computing the field solution using FEA. Most of these methods are usually suitable for specific types of problems and describe systems with very few parameters, i.e., they suffer of the first problem. Some preliminary studies used deep learning convolutional neural networks (CNNs) as surrogate models for the computation of EM quantities such as torque and fields [4]. In fact, CNNs have excellent capability in extracting relevant features from the input image and relating them to EM quantities. However, evolutionary optimization algorithms are not as well suited as deep neural networks to deal with high dimensional bitmaps as search space.

The motivation of this work is the need to reduce the dimensionality of the search space for topology optimization. In particular, we exploit the feature extraction capabilities of a CNN based autoencoder that learns the space of input bitmaps, and we use the encoded space as the search space for the optimization.

The main contributions are the following:

- the evolutionary optimization algorithm works in a coded reduced space that represents the original high dimensional bitmap space almost perfectly;
- a new surrogate model approach is proposed and applied during optimization, reducing the time cost for calculating the FEA solutions;
- the constraints are defined both in the encoded space and in the decoded (original) space.

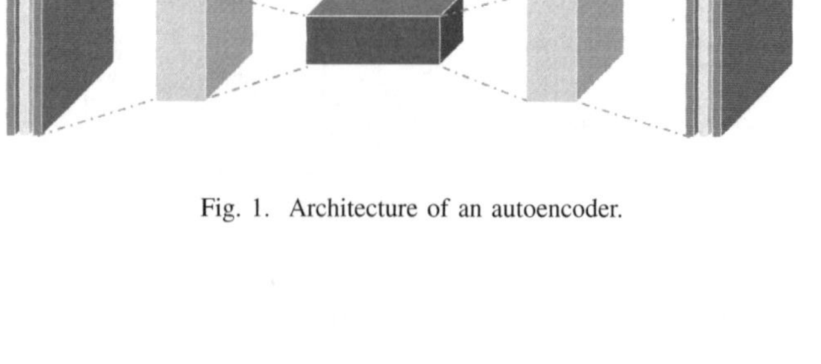

Fig. 1. Architecture of an autoencoder.

Results show that the search process is accelerated with a minimal impact on the quality of the solutions.

II. Autoencoder for Dimensionality Reduction

An autoencoder [5], depicted in Fig. 1 is an unsupervised neural network composed by an encoder, that maps the input space to a reduced number of features, denoted as code or latent space, and a decoder that maps the latent variables back to the original data. The compression made by the encoder is learned in order to minimize the error between the decoder output and original input, i.e. the reconstruction error. Then, the latent representation can be considered as a reduced feature space that fully describes the original high dimensional input space. A data-set of images, in the order of thousands, depicting different machine shapes and materials boundaries is used to train the autoencoder and define the latent space. The resolution of the original images was 250X250 pixels, while the size of the layers of the autoencoder CNN was optimized using a 5-fold cross validation, leading to a latent space representation using hundreds of variables. In order to well represent the input space the autoencoder needed to be trained with a large variety of geometries, including shapes that correspond to low performance designs. The latent space corresponding to the training data was then analyzed by means of determining the upper and lower bounds of each latent variable. These bounds are used in the following as constraints for the optimization, which will be performed in the space of the latent variables. It is important to note that decoder and encoder networks are tightly interconnected, and cannot be adopted separately, and that a properly trained autoencoder ensures univocity of mapping of training data.

III. Surrogate CNN Model

For each image (design solution) of the training set we pre-calculated the corresponding EM quantity to be optimized, i.e., the torque, by means of a FEA. A second CNN based surrogate model is then also trained using the latent representation of the image as input, and the torque as output. This approach allows the surrogate model to benefit from the dimensionality reduction provided by the autoencoder. The role of the surrogate model is to provide a fast prediction of the objective function, bypassing the FEA. The surrogate model is trained offline before optimization, and it is also updated online using the new input-output pairs generated during the optimization process. In particular, all the calculated FEA solutions are included in a set that we call FEA_{data}. For each solution in this set we calculate the Euclidean distance to the nearest neighbor, and we set the $dist_{max}$ thershold as the maximum among these distances.

IV. Optimization

An evolutionary optimization algorithm, previously proposed by the authors is used [6], which is based on self-organizing maps SOM, and denoted as self-organizing centroids optimization, SOC-opt. It was shown that SOC-opt outperforms many standard evolutionary optimization algorithms in a number of benchmarks. The algorithm uses a population of fixed size, and implements selection and mutation operators. The optimization is carried out as follows:

1) initialize the population in the latent space randomly within the bounds of the latent variables;
2) provide each solution to the surrogate model in order to calculate the corresponding torque;
3) calculate the new population of feasible solutions;
4) divide the population in two subsets: subset 1 (eventually empty) contains solutions to be simulated with FEA, subset 2 the rest of the population;
5) decompress each solution of subset 1 to the corresponding bitmap using the decoder section of the autoencoder, provide the bitmap to the FEA software to calculate the torque, update the surrogate model with such solutions, add the solutions to FEA_{data};
6) provide each solution of subset 2 to the surrogate model in order to calculate the corresponding torque;
7) iterate steps 3 to 6 until a stop criterion is verified.

The selection of the solutions in subset 1 is carried out by means of the following heuristic strategy: a point is included in subset 1 if its distance to the nearest point in FEA_{data} is greater than $dist_{max}$.

V. Conclusion

Optimizing rotating machines in the latent representation space of an autoencoder was shown to be a promising approach, allowing the flexibility of topology optimization and reducing the dimensionality of both the search space and the surrogate model. Through the decoder it is possible to observe the solutions and include constraints in the original space, and the introduction of a surrogate model approach, which also works in the latent space, reduces the number of required FEA simulations. Further work will be devoted to study the potential application in the case of multiobjective optimization.

References

[1] T. Sato, K. Watanabe, and H. Igarashi, "Multimaterial topology optimization of electric machines based on normalized Gaussian network," IEEE Transactions on Magnetics, vol. 51, no. 3, pp. 1-4, Mar. 2015.

[2] B. Xia, Z. Ren, and C. Koh, "Utilizing Kriging surrogate models for multi-objective robust optimization of electromagnetic devices," in IEEE Transactions on Magnetics, vol. 50, no. 2, pp. 693-696, Feb. 2014.

[3] A. Khan, V. Ghorbanian, and D. A. Lowther, "Deep Learning for magnetic field estimation," 2018 IEEE Conference on Electromagnetic Field Computation (CEFC), Hangzhou, China, 2018.

[4] H. Igarashi and H. Sasaki, "Topology optimization accelerated by Deep Learning," 2018 IEEE Conference on Electromagnetic Field Computation (CEFC), Hangzhou, China, 2018.

[5] I. Goodfellow, Y. Bengio, and A. Courville, Deep Learning, vol. 1, Cambridge: MIT Press, 2016.

[6] S. Barmada, M. Raugi, and M. Tucci, "An evolutionary algorithm for global optimization based on self-organizing maps," Engineering Optimization, vol. 48, no. 10, pp. 1740-1758, Jan. 2016.

Driveability Optimization of HEV Powertrain

N. Al-Aawar[1] and A.A. Arkadan[2]
[1]Marquette University, ECE Department, Milwaukee WI, 53203, USA
[2]Colorado School of Mines, Electrical Engineering Department, Golden CO 80401, USA
aaarkadan@mines.edu

***Abstract*— The work investigates the optimization of a Hybrid Electric Vehicle, HEV, powertrain to achieve good driveability (comfort). This involves the development of a robust identifier utilizing state space, SS, models and electromagnetic, EM, field computations to predict accurately the performance of the powertrain and a Fuzzy Logic, FL, based algorithm to ensure good driveability. The developed model is applied in a case study of a HEV and the predicted simulation results are validated by comparison to readily available benchmark data.**

Keywords*— *Computational Electromagnetics, Driveability, Hybrid Electric Vehicles, Optimization.

I. Introduction

The need for energy efficient and environmentally friendly transportation systems increased the demand for Hybrid Electric Vehicles, HEV. Typically, a HEV makes use of a hybrid powertrain that consists of an internal combustion engine, ICE, and one or more Electrical Motor Generator, EMG, units, Fig. 1. The performance of a HEV depends on the design of the powertrain system and the integration of the power sources. Accordingly, accurate performance characterization, including the interaction of mechanical and electrical components, is essential to optimize the design of the powertrain and thus the performance of the HEV [1,2].

This work, utilizes two modules to optimize the powertrain design. The first is a robust identifier utilizing state space, SS, models and electromagnetic, EM, field computations to accurately predict the performance characteristics of a powertrain. The second employs a Fuzzy Logic based algorithm to ensure good driveability (comfort) by minimizing the torque hole during shifting and limiting the Root Mean Square, RMS, of the acceleration of the HEV in the comfort zone [3,4].

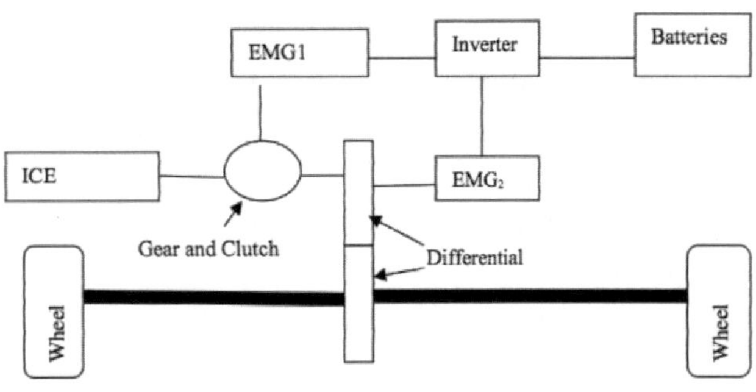

Fig. 1. Powertrain Split–Power Configuration.

II. The Modeling Approach

In the EM-SS module developed, the following state space, SS, model is used to represent the EMG:

$$\dot{I} = L^{-1}\left(R + \omega\frac{\partial L}{\partial \theta}\right)I + L^{-1}V, \tag{1}$$

$$\dot{\omega} = \frac{T_{EMG} - T_{load}}{J}, \tag{2}$$

$$P_{EMG} = I^{T}\omega^{2}\frac{\partial L}{\partial \theta}I, \tag{3}$$

where, I is the current vector, R is the resistance matrix, L is the inductance matrix, ω is the electric angular speed, θ is the rotor position, V is the voltage vector, J is the moment of inertia of the rotor, T_{load} is the load torque, T_{EMG} is developed torque and P_{EMG} is the output power of the EMG. The SS model is used with a Finite Element, FE, analysis model to develop the robust identifier module for the EMG and associated converters. This module accounts for the non-linearity of the EMG magnetic material, space harmonics due to its geometry, as well as time harmonics resulting from the switching electronics in the powertrain converters. It utilizes an indirectly coupled an FE-SS approach to compute sets of winding inductances as function of load and rotor positions [5]. The powertrain of Fig. 1 utilizes two Motor/generator, EMG, sets. The EMG_2 machine shown here is of the synchronous type with Internal PM rotor, rated at a 500 V, 67 hp (50 kW), and 1200-1540 rpm [3, 6]. The geometry and field distribution of a sample FE solution for EMG2 is shown in Fig. 2. In addition, the family of curves for the armature mutual inductance, L_{ab}, function of rotor position and load conditions, spanning No-load to Full-Load, is shown in Fig. 3.

Fig. 2. EMG Sample Finite Element Field Solution.

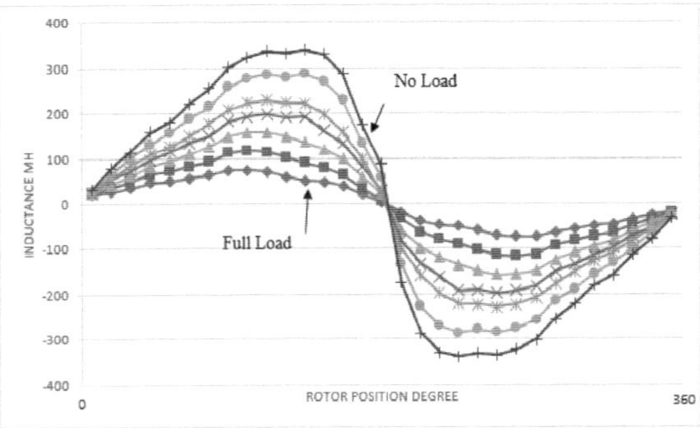

Fig. 3. Computed Family of Curves Set of Mutual Inductance L_{ab}.

In this work, we develop and implement a strategy to optimize the performance of a HEV power train and its drivability. This strategy manages the interaction between the ICE and the EMG [5, 6]. Essential to this strategy is the prediction of the required speed for the next time step, which is implemented by using an Adaptive Neural Fuzzy Inference System, ANFIS, where the pedal position and velocity in previous time steps are used as inputs, Fig. 4. The rules of the ANFIS are constructed based on knowledge of the driving cycle, such as the City and Highway driving cycles used in this work [2]. The ICE/EMG model of Fig. 4 uses the battery bank voltage and pedal position as inputs to compute the values of EMG power, P_{EMG}, and the ICE power, P_{ICE}. In addition, the calculus of variation is utilized to compute the optimum power $P_{ICE\text{-}opt}$ and the optimum power $P_{EMG\text{-}opt}$ [5]. Next, $P_{ICE\text{-}opt}$ and $P_{EMG\text{-}opt}$ values are added to determine the total output power of the powertrain, P_{req} which is used to calculate the speed of the HEV. As a result, the pedal position and the batteries bank voltage are updated and used iteratively to update the speed. The process is terminated when the error between calculated and predicted speeds is less than 5%. Finally, a Driveability Fuzzy Logic algorithm is implemented to ensure good driveability (comfort) by minimizing the torque hole during shifting and limit the RMS of the acceleration of the HEV in the comfort zone [4,7]. This algorithm employs an ANFIS to accurately characterize the ICE. It is trained by data generated from the ICE state space equations over defined search space. The input to this algorithm is the Driveability Index, DI, [6] and the output is P_{ICE} which is adjusted to achieve a speed error of less than 5% and corresponding DI greater than 7.

III. EM-FL Model Results

The algorithm of Fig. 4 was developed for use with a split–power configuration of a Toyota Prius prototype powertrain, Fig. 1. This configuration consists of two EMGs of the Internal Permanent Magnet, IPM, type, rated at 28 kW and 50 kW, respectively. The bank of batteries consists of 168 cells of the Nickel Metal Hydride (NiMH) type, rated at 21 kW. The ICE is a 4-cylinder aluminum double overhead cam with 16-valves and displacement of 1.5L. In addition, the prototype powertrain was tested for the Urban Driving Cycle, UDC [2]. The application of the developed control algorithm resulted in the performance characteristics for the benchmarked and optimized controllers. The values of the drivability index, DI, are shown in Table 1.

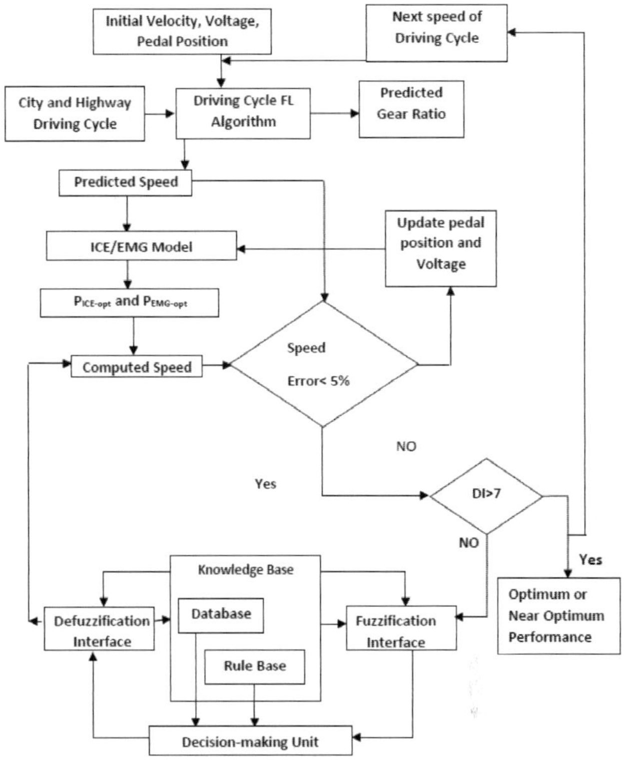

Fig. 4. Control Strategy of HEV.

Table 1. Comparison of Performance Indicators

Description	Benchmark	Optimal Controller	% Change
DI	6.5	8.4	29%

Conclusion

A control algorithm was developed and applied to optimize the HEV powertrain drivability. The FL based algorithm utilized a FE-SS robust identifier. As can be appreciated, the application of the developed strategy improved the performance characteristics of the HEV, including the driveability (comfort) index DI that was improved by 29%.

References

[1] S. G. Wirasingha and A. Emadi, "Classification and Review of Control Strategies for Plug-In Hybrid Electric Vehicles," IEEE Transaction on Vehicular Technology, vol. 6, iss. 1, pp. 111-122, January 2011.

[2] U.S. DOE Plug-in Hybrid Electric Vehicle R&D Plan, 2007.

[3] J. Liu and H. Peng, "Modeling and Control of a Power-Split Hybrid Vehicle," IEEE Transactions on Control Systems Technology, vol. 16, no. 6, pp. 1242-1251, 2008.

[4] A. Sciarretta, M. Black, and L. Guzzella, "Optimal Control of Parallel HEV," IEEE Transactions on Control System Technology, vol. 12, no. 3, pp. 352-363, May 2004.

[5] Al-Aawar, N., and Arkadan, A.A., "Hybrid Electric Vehicle Characterization Using Generalized Notion of Power," Applied Computational Electromagnetics Society Journal, ACES, Vol. 28, No. 11, pp. 1080-1087, November, 2013

[6] N. Al-Aawar, and A.A. Arkadan, "Optimal Control Strategy for Hybrid Electric Vehicle Powertrain," IEEE Journal of Emerging and Selected Topics in Power Electronics, vol. 03, no. 2, pp. 362-370, June 2015.

[7] T. Megli, M. Haghooie, and D. Colvin, "Shift characteristics of a 4 speedautomatic transmission," in Proc. SAE, 1999, paper 1999-01-1060.

FEKO™ Analysis of Surface Treatments for Mitigating the EM Coupling between Conformal Antennas

Robert J. Burkholder
The Ohio State University ElectroScience Lab
Dept. of Electrical and Computer Engineering
Columbus, U. S. A.
burkholder.1@osu.edu

***Abstract*—Conformal antenna arrays that are embedded in the same planar or convex curved surface can interfere with each other via the electromagnetic waves propagating along the surface. Various surface treatments on a metallic ground plane for suppressing the surface waves are investigated using FEKO™ with numerical and layered media Green's functions solutions. These include metallic fences, corrugations, radar absorbing structures (RAS), and thin magnetic radar absorbing materials (magRAM). It is found that magRAM offers the best trade-off between wideband surface wave suppression and low profile.**

Keywords — conformal antennas, coupling, electromagnetic compatibility, electromagnetic interference, materials, surface treatment, surface waves.

I. Introduction

Electromagnetic interference (EMI) between antennas mounted on the same platform can be a serious issue, especially when one antenna is transmitting a high power signal while another antenna is receiving weak signals. The in-band coupling between antennas may be reduced using shielding methods, wide separation, orthogonal polarizations, and material treatment, to name a few common approaches. Conformal antennas that are embedded in the same planar structure or in a convex curved platform surface such as on an aerodynamic structure, couple via the surface wave [1]-[3]. It is therefore of interest to develop practical techniques for suppressing the surface wave.

In this paper we investigate the coupling between two conformal antennas embedded in a ground plane, as illustrated in Fig. 1. FEKO™ is used for numerical solutions and for studying surface wave suppression with multi-layered materials on a ground plane. Two classes of approach are considered: 1) physical structures and 2) material treatments. Section II discusses physical structures and Section III presents a surface wave analysis of a material coated ground plane. Conclusions are presented in Section IV.

II. Physical Structures for Mitigating Antenna Coupling

Physical structures can be used to reduce the coupling between conformal antennas, but have the disadvantage of significantly modifying the geometry of the surface. Examples

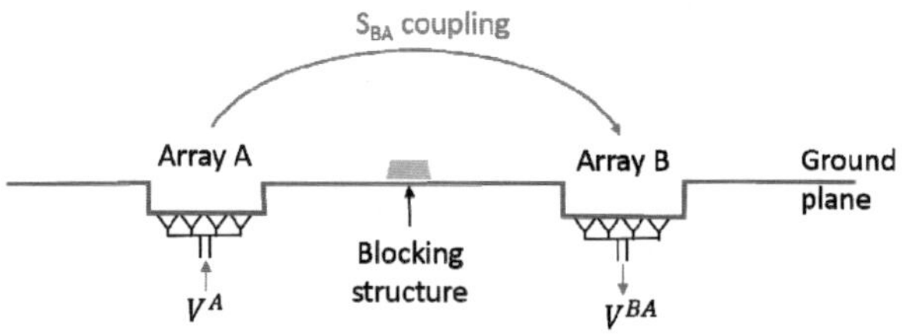

Fig. 1: Coupling between two antenna arrays embedded in a ground plane. The surface wave is suppressed using a blocking or absorbing structure.

that are considered here include metal fences, corrugations, and radar absorbing structures (RAS). A fence is designed to isolate the two arrays by blocking or deflecting EM waves from Array A so that they do not reach Array B (see Fig. 1). Of course, edge diffraction always causes some energy to propagate over the fence. A well-designed fence should therefore also consider deflection of the diffracted rays [4]. Another type of blocking structure is made from RAS. This could be a block of foam microwave absorber, for example. It can work extremely well for suppressing the surface wave, but it too will allow some energy to diffract over the top.

Fences and RAS must protrude from the surface to provide blockage of the surface wave. This may not be acceptable because conformal antennas are usually embedded in smooth surfaces or aerodynamic platforms. Corrugations offer a more conformal solution. Quarter-wavelength deep notches in a perfect electrical conductor (PEC) surface can be used to cancel the tangential magnetic field, thereby producing an artificial perfect magnetic conductor (PMC) [5]. Since the surface wave coupling along a PEC surface is due primarily to the tangential magnetic field, canceling it can greatly reduce the coupling. However, this solution has very narrow bandwidth because the notch depth depends on the wavelength. Wider bandwidth is achieved by using a large number of notches with depth that is tapered with distance. A smooth conformal surface can be preserved by filling the notches with a dielectric material. However, cutting notches in a PEC surface may compromise the structural integrity of the platform.

Physical structures are modeled in FEKO using the finite element/boundary integral solution option.

III. Material Treatment for Suppressing Surface Waves

Material treatments of the surface reduce coupling by attenuating the surface wave. They take the form of a thin material coating with a single layer or multiple layers. It is possible for the coating to have properties that vary with position (such as thickness, permittivity, permeability and conductivity), but here we will consider only uniform coatings. Coatings are analyzed using the spectral Green's function solution for multi-layered media [6]. A computer code is being developed for evaluating and optimizing these types of coatings for suppressing surface waves. FEKO has a multi-layered media Green's function implemented for integral equation solutions and is used for validation.

Fig. 2 shows a validation plot comparing FEKO and the layered media spectral Green's function (LMGF) for a ground plane coated with magRAM as a function of frequency. The electric field component normal to the ground plane is computed 30.5 cm from a magnetic dipole source. The magRAM is DD-10007 available from ARC Technologies, Inc., [7]. According to the spec sheet it is 2.413 mm thick. The relative dielectric permittivity is approximately 8.3 with loss tangent 0.002, and the relative magnetic permeability is approximately 1.8 with loss tangent 0.5. As Fig. 2 shows, the agreement between FEKO and the LMGF solution is very good.

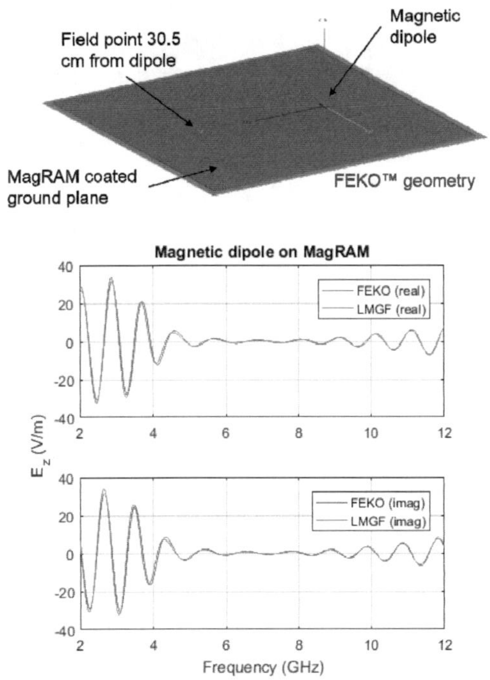

Fig. 2. Normal electric field of a magnetic dipole source on a ground plane coated with magRAM material. The field is computed 30.5 cm from the source.

Fig. 3 plots the attenuation performance vs. frequency of the magRAM for the same case as Fig. 2, relative to the same magnetic source on a ground plane. It is observed that the magRAM provides 25-45 dB attenuation for frequencies above 5 GHz. Below 5 GHz, a thicker coating would be needed.

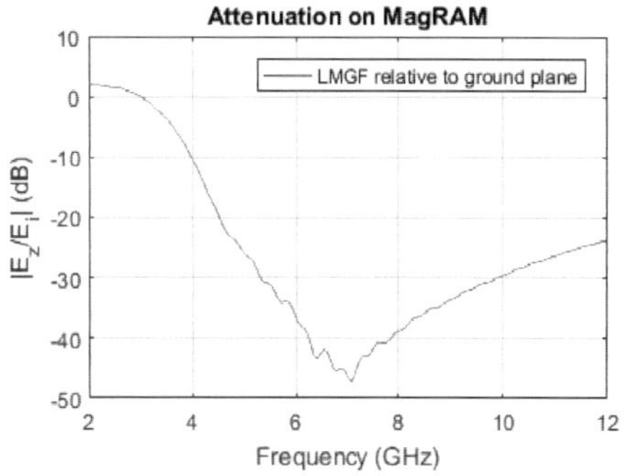

Fig. 3. Attenuation performance of the magRAM coating for a magnetic dipole source. The attenuation relative to an uncoated ground plane is plotted on a decibel scale.

IV. Conclusions

Surface treatments for reducing the coupling between conformal antennas embedded in the same platform have been investigated using FEKO and the layered media Green's function. Physical structures can achieve good performance for isolating a transmitting and receiving antenna through blockage, deflection, absorption, and field cancellation. However, they are more intrusive than a thin material coating, and may spoil an otherwise smooth aerodynamic surface. It has been shown that a thin layer of magRAM can provide excellent attenuation of the EM field radiated by a magnetic dipole source on a ground plane. A 2.413 mm thick layer has been shown to achieve 25-45 dB attenuation relative to an uncoated ground plane at a distance of 30 cm from the source.

V. Acknowledgement

The author wishes to thank Dr. C. J. Reddy and Altair for providing HyperWorks with FEKO™ to The Ohio State University ElectroScience Lab with an academic discount for education and research purposes.

References

[1] V. B. Erturk and R. G. Rojas, "Efficient analysis of input impedance and mutual coupling of microstrip antennas mounted on large coated cylinders," IEEE Trans. on Antennas and Propagation, vol. 51, no. 4, pp: 739-749, April 2003.

[2] P. Persson, "Modeling conformal array antennas of various shapes using uniform theory of diffraction (UTD)," J. of the Applied Computational Electromagnetics Society (ACES), vol. 21, no. 3, pp. 305-317, Nov. 2006.

[3] A. G. Aguilar, Z. Sipus and M. Sierra-Pérez, "An asymptotic solution for surface fields on a dielectric-coated circular cylinder with an effective impedance boundary condition," IEEE Trans. on Antennas and Propagation, vol. 61, no. 10, pp. 5175-5183, Oct. 2013.

[4] R. G. Kouijiam and P. H. Pathak, "A uniform geometrical theory of diffraction for an edge in a perfectly conducting surface," Proc. IEEE, vol. 62, pp. 1448-1461, Nov. 1974.

[5] C. A. Balanis, Artificial Impedance Surfaces for Antennas, in Modern Antenna Handbook, Wilely Telecom, 2008.

[6] N. K. Das and D. M. Pozar, "A generalized spectral-domain Green's function for multilayer dielectric substrates with application to multilayer transmission lines," IEEE Trans. Microw. Theory Techn., vol. MTT-35, no. 3, pp. 326–335, Mar. 1987.

[7] Technical Data Sheet, DD-10007, Arc Technologies, Inc., Amesbury, MA, April 2016.

Radiated Fields of Patch Antennas – a Comparison of Simulated and Analytic Results

Steven Weiss
US Army Research Lab
Adelphi, MD
steven.j.weiss14.civ@mail.mil

***Abstract*—This paper compares the beamwidth of the fields radiated by a rectangular patch antenna using FEKO simulations and analytic formulations. Typical analytic estimates use over-simplified models that fail to account for the air-dielectric boundary. The analytic estimates in this work realize the radiated fields using Green's functions that presume filaments of magnetic current about the perimeter of the patch antenna. Accordingly, the formulation accounts for the air dielectric boundary as well as surface waves. The filaments of magnetic current are based on the cavity model operating at resonance. Comparisons are made to the approximations found in [1] as well as to simulations by the commercial software FEKO.**

Keywords—Green's functions, Patch antenna, Radiated field.

I. Formulas for the Radiated Fields of Patch Antennas

The radiated fields of patch antennas can be approximated by formulas given in [1]. These formulas are approximations that assume the relative dielectric constant of the substrate material is close to unity and the thickness of the substrate is small. The geometry of the antenna is shown in Fig. 1. Based on the cavity model, the equivalent magnetic surface currents are placed on the radiating apertures. The model ignores the dielectric external to the patch and radiates into free space. A ground plane is presumed and is located at the bottom of the cavity in the y-z plane. The height of the cavity is designated as *h*.

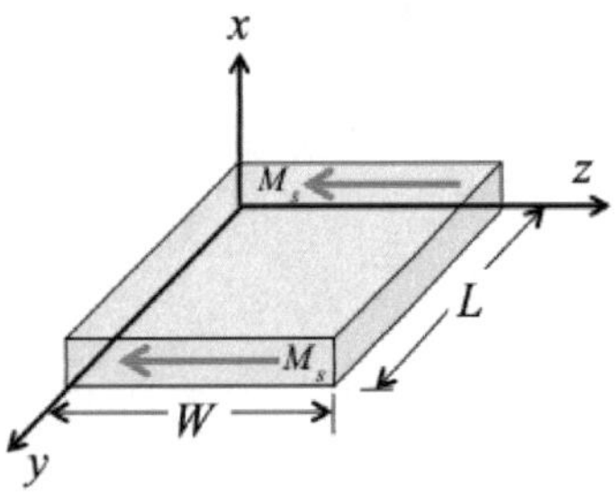

Fig. 1. Approximate model for determining the field radiated by a patch antenna.

The equations for the E-plane and H-plane are found in [1, eq. 14-45 and 14-46]. For the E-plane:

$$E_{\emptyset}^{t} \approx j\frac{k_0 W V_0}{\pi r} e^{-jk_0 r} Sinc\left(\frac{k_0 h}{2} cos\emptyset\right) cos\left(\frac{k_0 L_e}{2} sin\emptyset\right) \quad (1)$$

$$\theta = 90^{\circ}, 0^{\circ} \le \emptyset \le 90^{\circ} \; and \; 270^{\circ} \le \emptyset \le 360^{\circ}.$$

For the H-plane:

$$E_{\emptyset}^{t} \approx j\frac{k_0 W V_0}{\pi r} e^{-jk_0 r} Sinc\left(\frac{k_0 h}{2} sin\theta\right) Sinc\left(\frac{k_0 W}{2} cos\theta\right) sin\theta \quad (2)$$

$$\emptyset = 0^{\circ}, 180^{\circ}, 0^{\circ} \le \theta \le 90^{\circ}.$$

The definition of the equivalent length, L_e, is found in [1, pp. 790.]

A more detailed model takes the air-dielectric boundary into account and predicts the radiated fields using filaments of magnetic current about the perimeter of the patch. The equivalent filaments are based on the lowest resonant mode of the cavity model. The details are lengthy [2] and omitted for brevity. The geometry of the structure is shown on Fig. 2. Note that the z-axis is now normal to the surface of the patch.

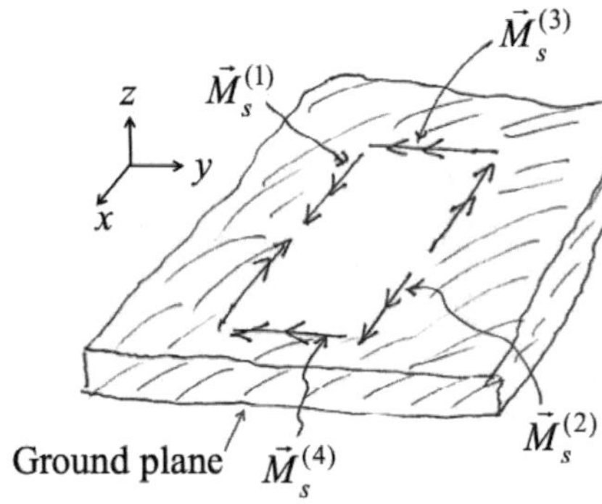

Fig. 2. Model for determining the field radiated by a patch antenna.

The analytic expressions for the fields radiated by the patch antenna model, using filaments of magnetic current about the perimeter of the patch are given by (3.) Note that the region denoted by the subscript "2" is above the air dielectric boundary while a subscript of "1" is in the dielectric region:

$$\begin{bmatrix} E_\theta(r,\theta,\phi) \\ E_\phi(r,\theta,\phi) \end{bmatrix} = jk_0 \cos\theta \frac{e^{-jkr}}{2\pi r} \cos(k_{z_{1s}} d) e^{+jk_{z_{2s}} d} \cdot \begin{bmatrix} \dfrac{+\varepsilon_r k_0 \sin\phi}{T_m(k_{x_S},k_{y_S})} & \dfrac{-\varepsilon_r k_0 \cos\phi}{T_m(k_{x_S},k_{y_S})} \\ \dfrac{k_{z_{1s}} \cos\phi}{T_e(k_{x_S},k_{y_S})} & \dfrac{k_{z_{1s}} \sin\phi}{T_e(k_{x_S},k_{y_S})} \end{bmatrix} \begin{bmatrix} \tilde{M}_{s_x}(k_{x_S},k_{y_S}) \\ \tilde{M}_{s_y}(k_{x_S},k_{y_S}) \end{bmatrix} \quad (3)$$

The transformed filaments of current and various stationary wavenumbers are given by:

$$\tilde{M}_{s_x}(k_{x_s},k_{y_s}) = -dE_{0_{1,0}} 2L^2 k_{x_s} \sin(k_{y_s} W/2) \frac{\cos\left(k_{x_s} L/2\right)}{\left(\pi^2 - \left(k_{x_s} L\right)^2\right)}$$

$$\tilde{M}_{s_y}(k_{x_s},k_{y_s}) = -dE_{0_{1,0}} 2\cos(k_{x_s} L/2) W \frac{\sin\left(k_{y_s} W/2\right)}{\left(k_{y_s} W/2\right)} \qquad (4)$$

$$T_m(k_{x_s},k_{y_s}) = \left(\varepsilon_r k_{z_{2s}} cos(k_{z_{1s}} d) + jk_{z_1} sin(k_{z_{1s}} d)\right)$$

$$T_m(k_{x_s},k_{y_s}) = \left(k_{z_{1s}} cos(k_{z_1} d) + jk_{z_{2s}} \mu_r sin(k_{z_{1s}} d)\right)$$

$$k_{x_s} = k_0 \sin\theta \cos\phi \quad k_{y_s} = k_0 \sin\theta \cos\phi \quad k_{z_{2s}} = k_0 \cos\theta$$

$$k_{z_{1s}} = k_0 \sqrt{\varepsilon_r \mu_r - \sin^2(\theta)}$$

$\phi = 0^\circ, 180^\circ, 0 \le \theta \le 90^\circ$ E-plane

$\phi = 90^\circ, 270^\circ, 0 \le \theta \le 90^\circ$ H-plane.

Equations 1, 2, 3, and 4 are plotted for the E- and H-plane patterns and compared to computer-simulated fields. The simulations are done using FEKO.

II. Plots of the Fields

The case studies use the patch antenna dimensions found on page 587 of [1]: $L = 0.906$ *cm*, $W = 1.186$ *cm*, $d = h = 0.1588$, $\varepsilon_r = 2.2$. Plots are given in Figs. 3, 4, and 5.

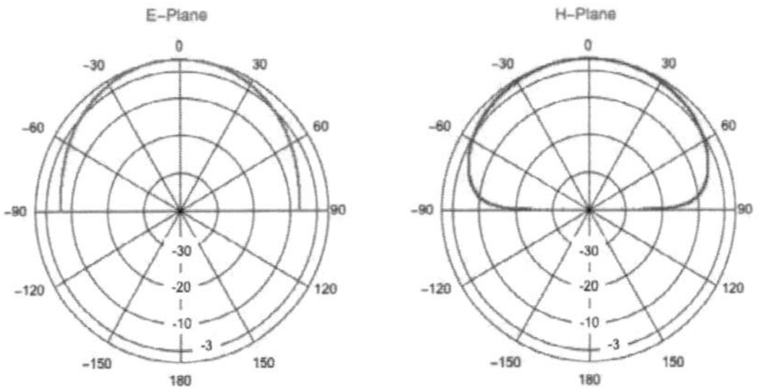

Fig. 3. E- and H-planes, equations (1) and (2), $\boldsymbol{\varepsilon_r = 2.2}$.

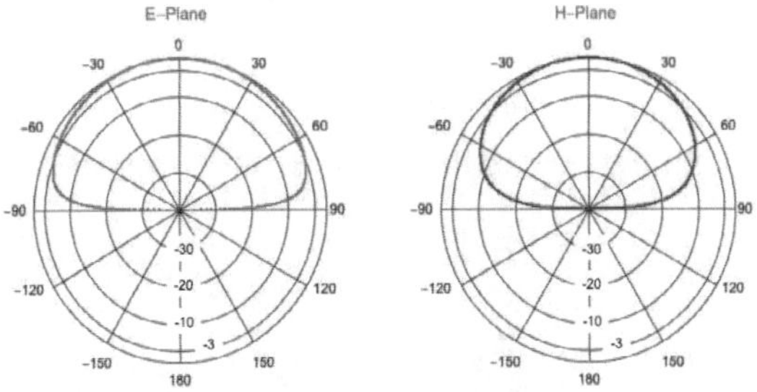

Fig. 4. E- and H-planes, equations (3) and (4), $\boldsymbol{\varepsilon_r = 2.2}$.

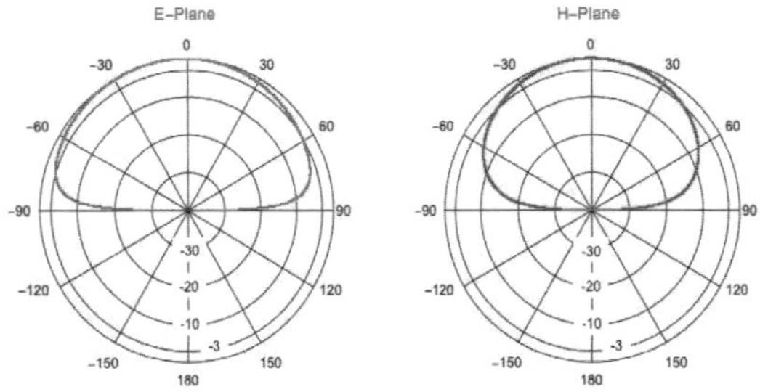

Fig. 5. E- and H-planes, FEKO simulation, $\varepsilon_r = 2.2$.

Equations 1 and 2 are most deficient when plotting the E-plane and fail to take into account the air-dielctric boundary as well as the ground plane. The plots using equations 3 and 4 include the geometry in the formulation of the equations and are more accurate. The FEKO simulations give the most accurate results and take the probe's influence on the pattern measurements. The resonant frequencies are 9.8 GHz and 6.65 GHz for the dielectric constants of 2.2 and 5.0 respectively. The various *(-3 dB)* beamwidths for the three different methods of estimating the performance are given in Table 1.

Table 1. Beamwidth Values.

	Beamwidth for the E- and H-planes (Degrees)		
	Method of Calculation	***E-plane***	***H-plane***
$\boldsymbol{\varepsilon_r = 2.2}$	Equations (1) and (2)	***88.8***	***82.0***
$\boldsymbol{\varepsilon_r = 2.2}$	Equations (3) and (4)	***90.1***	***85.1***
$\boldsymbol{\varepsilon_r = 2.2}$	FEKO	***90.0***	***75.2***
$\boldsymbol{\varepsilon_r = 5.0}$	Equations (1) and (2)	-	***86.2***
$\boldsymbol{\varepsilon_r = 5.0}$	Equations (3) and (4)	***134.7***	***87.7***
$\boldsymbol{\varepsilon_r = 5.0}$	FEKO	***133.5***	***83.8***

As seen in Table 1, the E- and H-plane beamwidth estimates are fairly close for low values of the dielectric constant. As this value gets higher, the results from equations (1) and (2) are not reliable and the more rigorous equations (i.e., equations (3) and (4)) must be used. In particular, the E-plane for Equation (1) using a dielectric constant of 5.0 is never reduced by 3 dB over the entire span of theta. Such a result is clearly incorrect. Similar results can be found when increasing the value of the relative permeability.

References

[1] C. Balanis, Antenna Theory Analysis and Design. Wiley, 4th ed. 2016.

[2] S. Weiss, notes for Antenna Systems class, Johns Hopkins University.

Single Layer Vivaldi Antenna Feed Analysis

William Coburn
US Army Research Laboratory
Adelphi, USA
william.o.coburn.civ@mail.mil

***Abstract*—For many applications tapered slot antennas are attractive with broad bandwidth, medium gain and good pattern stability. Many designs can be found in the literature but the exponentially tapered slot (i.e., Vivaldi aerial) has good performance. The frequencies of interest are 8 to 10 GHz where planar antenna designs are considered for ease of fabrication and integration. A single layer planar Vivaldi tapered slot-type antenna is simulated and fabricated to investigate the simplest way to feed such antennas without limiting performance. The results show that a SMA connector from the rear and soldered on the front can be used but requires an air gap so the SMA does not touch the substrate. This paper summarizes a numerical investigation using FEKO to provide feed alternatives. The results serve to guide the selection of antenna elements and unbalanced feed arrangements for RF system developers.**

Keywords*—*planar antennas, tapered slot antenna, ultra-wideband, Vivaldi antenna.

I. INTRODUCTION

This paper presents a numerical analysis of a single layer Vivaldi tapered slot antenna with FEKO (https://altairhyperworks.com/product/FEKO) software using the Method of Moments. The Vivaldi or notch antenna [1] is designed with different feed configurations for comparing performance such as peak gain, endfire pattern stability, fractional impedance bandwidth (IBW), etc. The reflection coefficient vs. frequency is primarily used to evaluate unbalanced feed alternatives. Although there are many variations of the Vivaldi design a single layer approach directly fed across the slot is considered here. Many designs have more complex balanced feed arrangements to maximize bandwidth [2], but the single layer design sacrifices bandwidth for ease of fabrication. The single layer planar Vivaldi fed through the substrate is an endfire alternative to planar slot or monopole antennas [3] and is well suited for conformal applications.

The objective is to evaluate through simulation and measurements various unbalanced feeds for this type antenna. After model validation, the simulated radiation patterns demonstrate the performance impact of the connector but cannot predict the influence of unbalanced currents on the feed cable. The measured radiation pattern of the most promising feed method will indicate the influence of unbalanced currents. The results provide alternatives to RF system developers to conduct trade studies on size, weight, and power plus cost (SWAP-C) vs. performance. Simulation results for various antenna feed models and measured results will be compared using this approach.

The planar Vivaldi antenna is on Rogers low-loss substrate R4350 having $\varepsilon_r = 3.5$ and $\tan\delta = .0037$ with thickness 0.51 mm (20-mils). Here the objective is to demonstrate good IBW and gain vs. frequency in the most compact size possible without impacting the pattern stability. The antenna is 118 mm L x 56 mm W with minimum slot width 0.5 mm. Scaling this antenna to a smaller size but increasing the minimum slot width to 0.75 mm serves to lower the resonant frequency and limit the peak gain and IBW. If that was acceptable for a given application the antenna can be miniaturized up to a factor of five smaller. The results show that an unbalanced feed for this type antenna is suitable for many applications with an acceptable pattern in the endfire direction.

II. ANTENNA FEED ALTERNATIVES

A planar Vivaldi antenna can be obtained by careful design of the tapered slot commonly fabricated in a multilayer or antipodal design [4]. Single layer designs can be found in the literature [5] typically using an edge connector. For instance in [6] a conformal concept is described but the edge connector defeats the purpose. To be truly conformal the connector should not be in the plane of the antenna. Our single layer approach with unbalanced feed is shown in Fig. 1 indicating the feed point across the slot. The antenna feed variations were simulated with FEKO using different feed models over the desired frequency range where VSWR = 3 is used for the maximum IBW and VSWR = 1.9 for the minimum IBW. The realized gain and endfire pattern stability vs. frequency are also summarized.

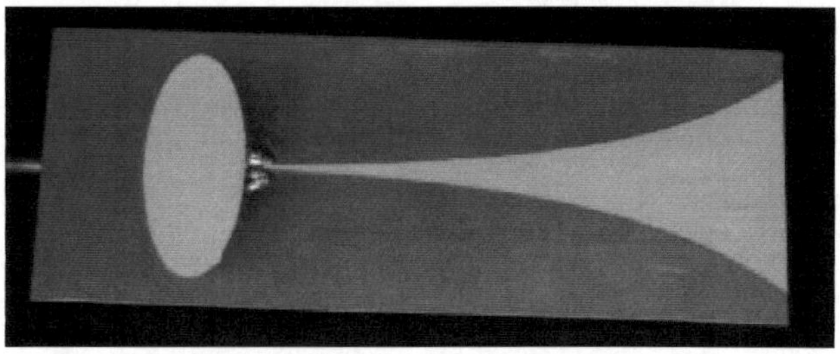

Fig. 1. Single layer Vivaldi antennas: X-Band element (left) and scaled (right).

The numerical results have similar frequency dependence as the measured VSWR. In this investigation prototypes for a pigtailed coaxial cable (Fig. 2 top), a tapered microstrip impedance transformer (Fig. 2 bottom) and a SMA connector are fabricated for comparison. The SMA connector protrudes through the substrate, with or without a gap between the SMA flange and substrate, with soldered connections on top. An analysis of feed alternatives is done primarily by simulation with RF system developers down selecting and modifying the feed arrangement as needed based on mechanical considerations.

Fig. 2. Vivaldi antenna rear view: (top) pigtailed coax and (bottom) transformer.

III. RESULTS

The comparison for the pigtailed cable fed Vivaldi is shown in Fig. 3 indicating good agreement for this idealized feed model with ~67% minimum IBW. The linear tapered microstrip feed does not perform as well with only ~25% IBW.

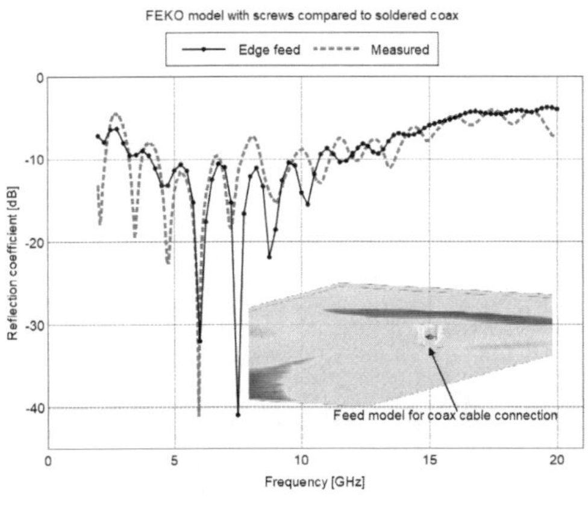

Fig. 3. Vivaldi reflection coefficient with screws and pigtailed coaxial cable.

The comparison for the SMA connector fed Vivaldi is shown in Fig. 4 where an SMA jack model with wave port represents the connector. In the model, if the connector flange touches the substrate the result is in poor agreement with measurements. This indicates that in practice there will be some gap so a 0.5 mm gap is used in simulation with fair agreement to the prototype with no visible gap. Subsequently the SMA was connected with a 1 – 1.3 mm gap that showed better performance. An example is shown in Fig. 5 for this idealized SMA jack model with ~86% minimum IBW. The results indicate that the slot-type antenna with unbalanced feed can be matched with good IBW. Although the simulation results indicate good endfire pattern stability it remains to be seen how unbalanced currents on the feed cable will perturb the radiation pattern. Additional results for this type planar antenna with the available measured data will be included in the presentation.

IV. CONCLUSION

The single layer planar Vivaldi fed with a SMA connector from the rear has been shown to be matched over a broad bandwidth. The realized gain on boresight increases from 7 to 9 dBi over the band. The simulation results indicate good performance for this easily fabricated antenna and soldered SMA connector. However, the simulation cannot predict the effects of unbalanced currents with such an idealized model. So the impact of the feed cable on the radiation pattern vs. frequency has to be measured.

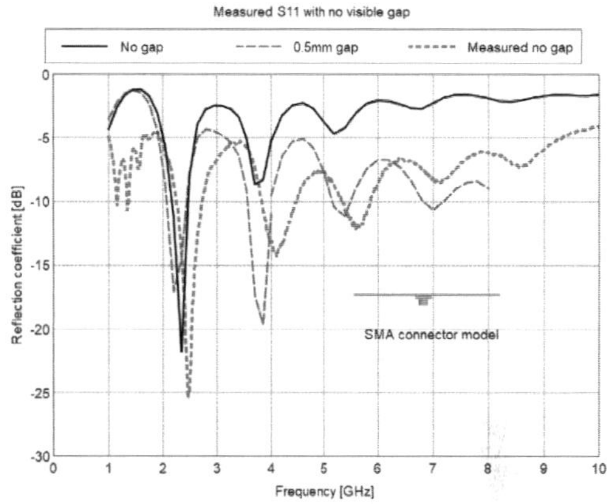

Fig. 4. Vivaldi with SMA connector without a gap between substrate.

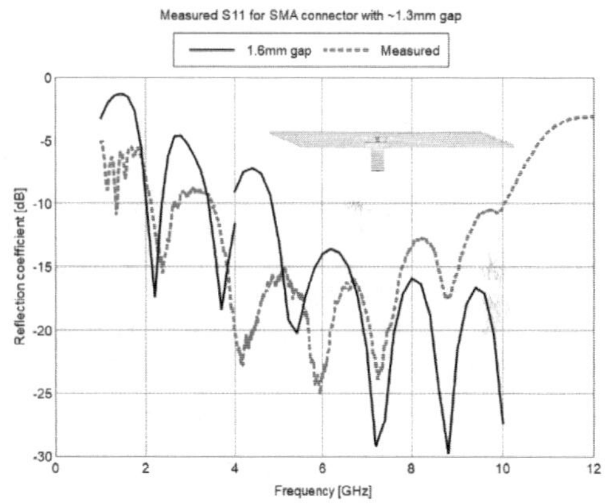

Fig. 5. Vivaldi with connector having a gap between substrate and flange.

REFERENCES

[1] P. J. Gibson, "The Vivaldi aerial," in Proc. 9th Eur. Microwave Conf., Brighton, U.K, pp. 101-105, September 1979.

[2] D. H. Schaubert , S. Kasturi , A.O. Boryssenkol, and W.M. Elsallal, "Vivaldi antenna arrays for wide bandwidth and electronic scanning," IEEE Ant and Propag, EuCAP, Edinburgh, UK, pp. 1-6, Nov. 2007.

[3] W. Coburn, "An ultra-wideband absorber backed planar slot antenna," App. Comp. Electro. Express Journal, vol. 1, no. 1, January 2016.

[4] W. Coburn and S. McCormick, "Ultra-Wideband antenna performance comparison," Proc. Int. App. Comp. Electro.Symposium, April 2018.

[5] M. Ostadrahimi, et. al., "Comparing performance of double layer stripline fed and single layer Y2Y fed Vavaldi antennas," Proc. Int. Sym. Ant. Tech. and App. EM, 2010.

[6] L. Tao, et. al., "Novel conformal Vivaldi antenna fed by CPW," Proc. Micro. And Milli. Wave Tech., vol. 2, pp. 725-727, 2016.

Miniaturized Omnidirectional UHF RFID Antennas

Joseph E. Diener
Electrical Engineering Department
Colorado School of Mines
Golden, CO
jdiener@mines.edu

Atef Z. Elsherbeni
Electrical Engineering Department
Colorado School of Mines
Golden, CO
aelsherb@mines.edu

***Abstract*— UHF RFID reader antennas are often patches operating in the fundamental mode, with broadside radiation patterns. For some applications, it is convenient to have planar antennas with omni-directional patterns, which can have greater angular coverage than conventional reader antennas. A circular-patch antenna operating in a monopole mode is presented. Using both shorting pins and slots, the antenna is highly miniaturized. The effect of different antenna tuning parameters are presented, and their trade-offs are considered. An optimized design is presented and its properties are discussed.**

Keywords—Antenna, Miniaturization, Reader, RFID, Omni-directional, UHF.

I. INTRODUCTION

UHF RFID reader patch antennas traditionally operate in the fundamental mode, with broadside radiation patterns. However, these suffer from radiation nulls at the horizon, and generally low-gain at low-elevation angles. An omni-directional RFID reader antenna overcomes this by operating in a monopole mode, having a moderate gain radiation pattern that covers very low elevation angles, with a null at broadside. This allows for much greater angular coverage than is possible with antennas in the fundamental mode, and consequently, greater probability that the RFID reader will be able to read a tag. Object tracking applications could use a single reader to cover an entire room. A few omni-directional RFID-tag antennas have been proposed in the literature [5-6], attempting to increase tag usability by making the tag-antenna pattern more isotropic. Here, we focus on making the reading antenna coverage broader.

Since UHF antennas are naturally physically large owing to the frequency of operation, integration of UHF RFID into products can be difficult without resorting to large antennas. Printed-patch antennas operating in monopole modes are effective for wide-coverage, small footprint antennas, with relative ease of manufacturing. In [1], authors introduced a patch antenna with a monopole mode. In [2], a patch antenna with monopole radiation using shorting pins to ground was presented. Authors in [3] give good theoretical analysis on broadband implementations of the monopole patch antennas, making use of the TM01 and TM02 modes.

Here, we aim to expand on this previous work by focusing on the addition of slots to the patch antenna, as well as incorporating a coaxial sleeve, such as that in [4], to allow for additional impedance tuning and miniaturization. These features give substantial flexibility over the bandwidth and electrical size of the antenna. We aim to present as miniaturized an antenna as possible, in order to allow for more seamless integration into existing products and preserve space. The presented antenna is $\sim 0.126\lambda_0, 0.126\lambda_0, 0.078\lambda_0$ in the x, y, and z dimensions respectively, with λ_0 the free-space wavelength at the antenna center frequency of 915MHz. The antenna and its relevant features are shown in Fig. 1. All simulations and analysis are performed using CST Microwave Studio.

II. ANTENNA TUNING

The proposed antenna is shown in Fig. 1. Shorting pins, slots, and a coaxial sleeve serve to match and miniaturize the antenna. For simplicity, the number of shorting pins and slots are taken as one parameter, 'slot-via' pairs, with the shorting pins located along the middle of the slot. The substrate is assumed to be 1" thick, representing a compromise between an ordinary monopole height and size considerations. The other main impedance matching features are the patch size, shorting-pin radial distance, and coaxial-sleeve radial distance and vertical height. The antenna is designed on FR4 type materials, as these materials are easily available in thick pieces. The substrate is assumed to have $\epsilon_r = 4.3$, and loss tangent $\delta_d = 0.014$ with a finite ground plane of diameter $0.49\lambda_0$ (160mm).

A. Effect of Coaxial Sleeve

The coaxial sleeve as discussed in [4] is a useful method for matching the printed monopole introduced in [1-2], as seen in [3], since the sleeve helps maintain the 50-Ohm impedance throughout the thick-substrate. Here, we create the sleeve using several wires soldered to the circular ground plane, protruding partially up into the substrate. This allows for integration of the sleeve into the thick substrate with relative ease. Both the radial distance of the sleeve from the central feed via, as well as the height of the sleeve, affect the antenna impedance. Fig. 2. Shows the effect of moving the sleeve radially outward. As the sleeve radial distance increases, the resonant frequency of the antenna decreases. Thus, adjusting the sleeve radial offset is an effective means of matching the antenna, as well as miniaturizing it.

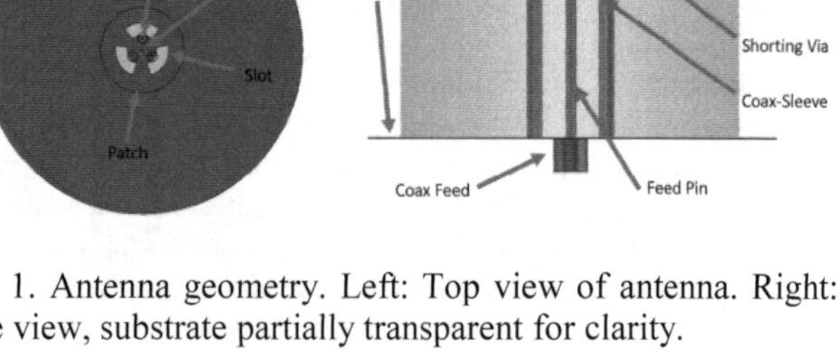

Fig. 1. Antenna geometry. Left: Top view of antenna. Right: Side view, substrate partially transparent for clarity.

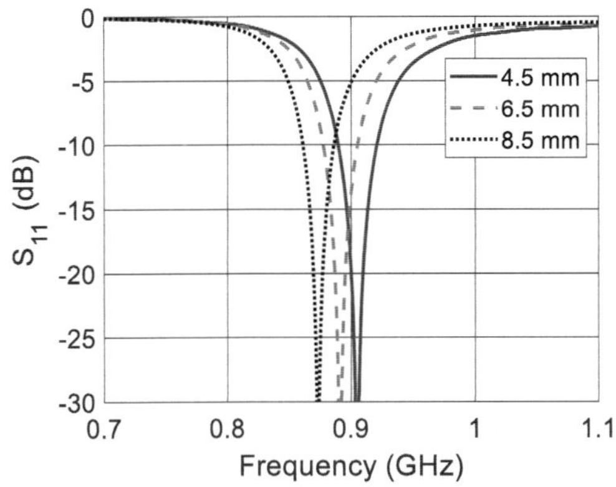

Fig. 2. Effect of changing the coax sleeve distance from the feed.

B. Effect of the Number of Slot-via pairs

The other dominant factor in the antenna matching is the number of slot-via pairs that are used. Results for changing the number of slot-via pairs are shown in Fig. 3. The slot-angle is adjusted so that the total amount of copper removed is kept constant. Fewer slot-via pairs miniaturize the patch more than a larger number does. Three pairs are optimal for US UHF RFID operation for the antenna sizing.

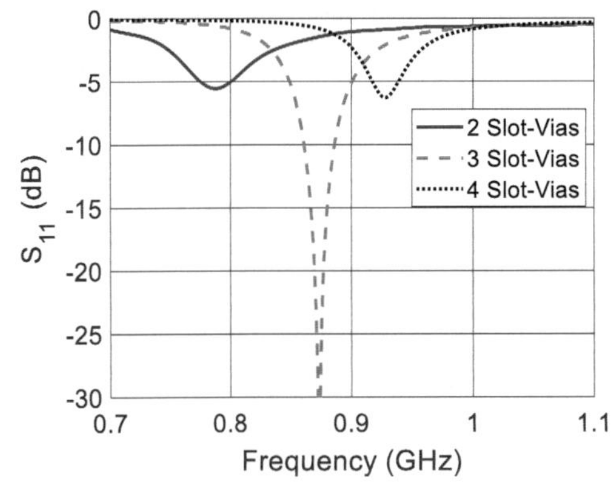

Fig. 3. Effect of changing number of slot-via pairs on impedance match.

III. Impedance Match and Radiation Pattern of Antenna

We present a miniaturized antenna for proof of concept. Three slot-via pairs are used. The slots are 7mm from the patch center, are 6 mm long, and each slot is 80° wide. The patch radius is 20.6 mm, and the shorting pins 5.5mm from the patch center. Each pin is 1mm in size. The coax sleeve is 4.5 mm radially off, and 6.5 mm from the top of the substrate. The antennas simulated match and realized gain are shown in Fig. 4. For an 160mm ground plane, the antenna has realized gains of up to 0.65dB and directivity of 1.26dB, with a maximum efficiency of 86%. The omnidirectional pattern for this ground plane size is seen in Fig. 5. For an 400mm ground plane, the antenna gain is increased substantially, with gains up to 3.4dB – but the pattern is no longer omnidirectional in the XY plane, but instead peaks at $\theta = 40°$, and the antenna becomes less well-matched compared to the smaller ground plane without retuning.

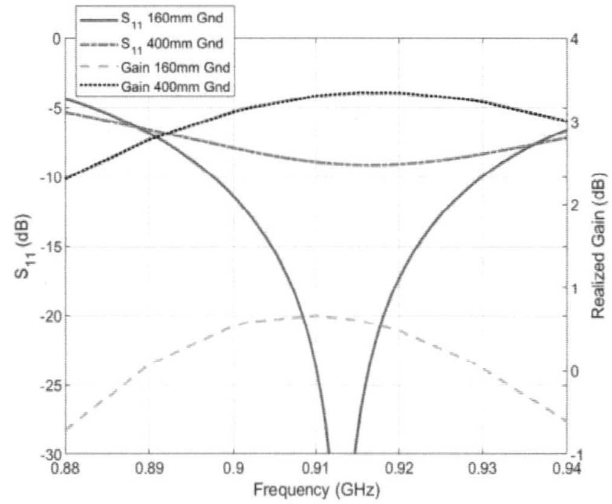

Fig. 4. Antenna match and realized gain for 160mm ground plane and 400mm ground plane.

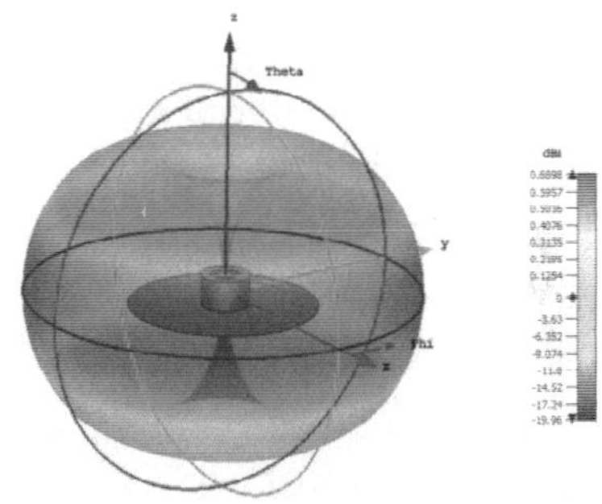

Fig. 5. Antenna pattern at 915MHz for 160mm ground plane.

IV. Conclusion

A miniaturized omni-directional patch antenna is presented. The antenna is matched across the entire U.S. UHF RFID band with realized gains of up to 0.65dB. Future work will be focused on fabrication of the antenna, and comparing measured and simulation results.

References

[1] L. Economou and R. J. Langley, “Patch antenna equivalent to simple monopole,” Electron. Lett., vol. 33, no. 9, pp. 727–728, Apr. 1997.

[2] C. Delaveaud, P. Leveque, and B. Jecko, "New kind of microstrip antenna: The monopolar wire-patch antenna," in Electronics Letters, vol. 30, no. 1, pp. 1-2, 6 Jan. 1994.

[3] J. Liu, Q. Xue, H. Wong, H. W. Lai, and Y. Long, "Design and analysis of a low-profile and broadband microstrip monopolar patch antenna," in IEEE Transactions on Antennas and Propagation, vol. 61, no. 1, pp. 11-18, Jan. 2013.

[4] Z. Y. Zhang, G. Fu, S. X. Gong, S. L. Zuo, and Q. Y. Lu, "Sleeve monopole antenna for DVB-H applications," in Electronics Letters, vol. 46, no. 13, pp. 879-880, 24 June 2010.

[5] K. T. Kaiwen, X. Qing, C. K. Goh, and L. Zhu, "A UHF Omni-directional RFID Antenna," 2010 IEEE Antennas and Propagation Society International Symposium, Toronto, ON, 2010, pp. 1-4.

[6] C. Cho, H. Choo, and I. Park, "Broadband RFID tag antenna with quasi-isotropic radiation pattern," in Electronics Letters, vol. 41, no. 20, pp. 1091-1092, 29 Sept. 2005.

Gain Enhancement of a 94GHz LTCC Integrated Horn Antenna Using High Impedance Periphery

Maxence Carvalho*, Abe Akhiyat, Elias A. Alwan, and John L. Volakis
Electrical & Computer Engineering Dept., Florida International University
Miami, FL USA, mcarvalh@fiu.edu

***Abstract*—There is a growing interest to implement antenna-in-package (AiP) systems for a variety of applications such as imaging, beamforming, integrated transceivers, and radars. Substrate integrated pyramidal antennas are valuable AiP candidates owing to their small form factor, integration ease, and high gain. However, height reduction, dielectric losses and integration of the latter can drastically degrade their gain pattern and limit their applications. This degradation is mainly due to undesired excitations on the surface of the dielectric. For the first time in this paper, we present a Grounded Co-Planar Waveguide-fed (GCPW) 94GHz low temperature cofired ceramic (LTCC) pyramidal horn antenna. To prevent parasitic TE excitations, a mushroom type High Impedance Surface (HIS) periphery is implemented. The combined antenna with HIS surrounding leads to approximately 2.3dB improvement in gain. Concurrently, the 3dB beamwidth is reduced by 26° in both E-Plane and H-Plane.**

***Index Terms*—94GHz, Antenna in Package,High Impedance Surface (HIS), Low Temperature Co-fired Ceramic (LTCC),**

I. Introduction

Low temperature co-fired ceramic (LTCC) is a low cost and high density integration packaging technology. LTCC also enables multilayer antenna fabrication and offers better control on the number of layers as compared to classical printed circuit boards (PCB) [1]. Nevertheless, LTCC fabrication suffers from a number of drawbacks. For instance, a commonly used substrate, the DuPont 9K7 Tape ($\epsilon_r = 7.1$), imposes stringent limitations on the fabrication which can drastically impact the performance of horns and leads to parasitic excitations. Also, the layer-by-layer implementation is done using laser etched via walls technology to create the integrated structure. These imperfect walls cause leakage that can potentially excite parasitic fields on the dielectric and lead to back radiation and directivity loss.

In this paper, we present the fabrication process analysis of a novel substrate integrated pyramidal horn antenna operating at 94GHz. To reduce the parasitic excitations on the surface of the dielectric, we place a high impedance surface ring around the aperture periphery using mushroom structures [2]. The latter were chosen for their design simplicity.

II. Design and Fabrication Process Consideration

A. *Integrated Horn Antenna*

Fig. 1 presents the rendering an integrated pyramidal horn antenna operating at 94GHz. The walls of the metallic horn were discretized according to the *fired* thickness of the LTCC layers. That is, the integrated horn is a stepped version of the smooth surface horn. Few gaps of material are kept on the center of every frame for fabrication purpose. These gaps are carefully chosen to minimize leakage and the current flow inside and outside the antenna. This leakage can excite undesired diffracted fields that may lead to directivity loss and deformation of the radiation pattern.

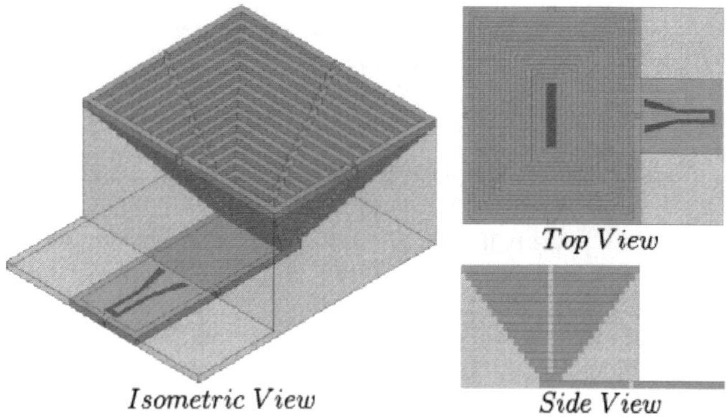

Fig. 1. Substrate Integrated Horn Antenna on LTCC.

As depicted on Fig. 1, the antenna is fed by a grounded co-planar waveguide designed to match a 50Ω W-Band probe. Fig. 2 depicts a side view of the horn antenna showing the etched walls at every layer with respect to two slopes P_x and P_y along the x and y axis, respectively :

$$P_x = \frac{2Nh}{A-a} \text{ and } P_y = \frac{2Nh}{B-b} \quad (1)$$

In the above, A and B refer to the horn's aperture size along the x and y direction respectively, h is the height of one ceramic layer and N is the number of layers comprising the horn. In our case, we use $N = 15$.

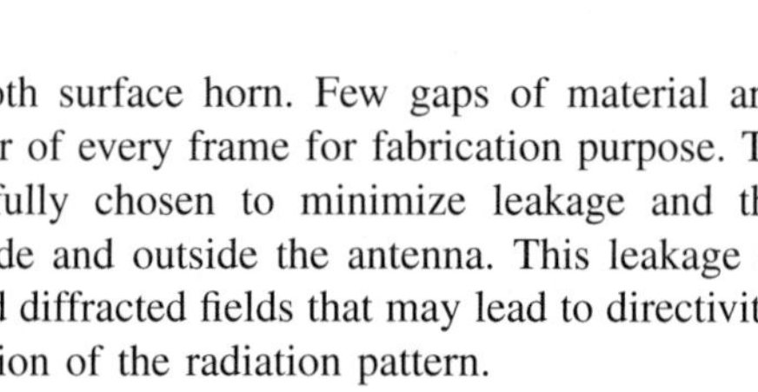

Fig. 2. Integrated horn using rectangular walls to create the inner surface.

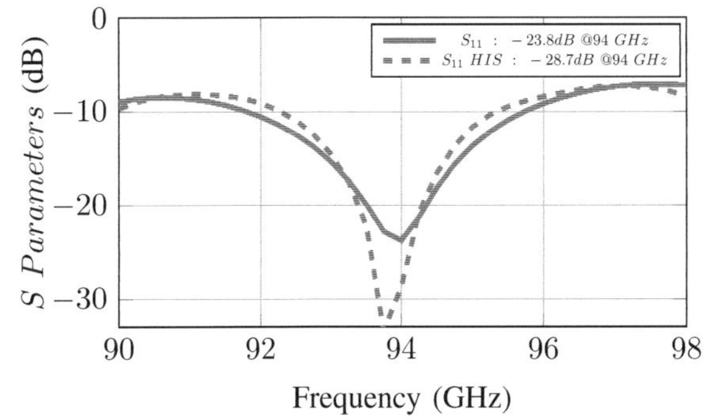

Fig. 3. Reflection coefficient of the GCPW-fed horn, with and without its HIS periphery.

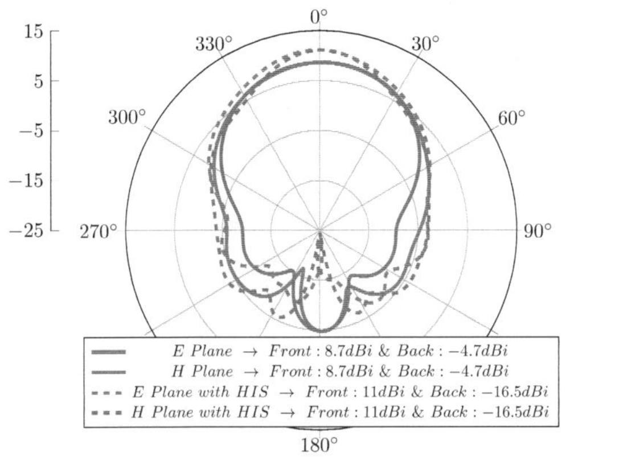

Fig. 4. GCPW-fed pyramidal horn realized gain at 94GHz, with and without its HIS periphery

The radiation pattern, presented in Fig. 4, shows a considerable back radiation with a main back lobe located at $\theta = 180°$. Notably, the front-to-back ratio is slightly higher than 13dB and the 3dB beamwidth in both planes is approximately 62°. An attractive solution to improve the performance of the antenna is using HIS periphery to suppress surface currents and prevent edge diffraction along the aperture's periphery. This is discussed below.

B. High Impedance Surface (HIS)

HIS structures are periodic and frequency selective structures. One of the earliest periodic surfaces is that of the mushroom structure [3], as depicted in Fig. 5. This structure is equivalent to a LC circuit. Notably, it was designed to have a resonance frequency and a maximum impedance at 94GHz. The subject resonance frequency of the HIS is given by:

$$f_r = \frac{1}{2\pi\sqrt{LC}}, \tag{2}$$

where L and C are the equivalent inductance and capacitance, respectively. Here :

$$L = \mu_0 h_e \text{ and } C = \epsilon_0 \frac{1+\epsilon_r}{\pi}.W_e.cosh^{-1}(\frac{W_e}{g_e}+1) \tag{3}$$

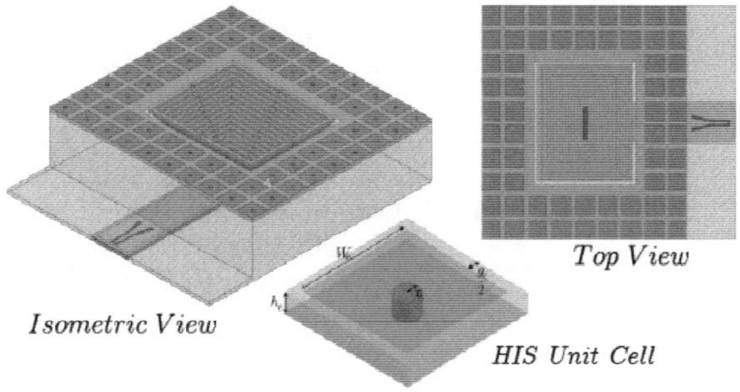

Fig. 5. Integrated Horn Antenna with its HIS Periphery

where μ_0 is the free space permeability, h_e the height of the substrate, W_e the width of the patch forming the mushroom and g_e is the gap between two successive HIS cells.

III. Simulated Performances

The HIS structure is then integrated around the horn antenna. We use two rows of unit cells to ensure efficiency in the suppression of undesired TE excitations from the horn aperture's periphery. As depicted in Figs. 5 the HIS cells are located at the top of the 15 layer structure horn antenna.

The radiation pattern of the horn with the HIS periphery is depicted in Fig. 4. As seen, back radiation is significantly reduced by 11.8dB in both E and H-Planes. The 3dB beamwidth is also reduced and is around 36° for both E and H-planes. This is a reduction of the beamwidth of about 26° as compared to the case without the HIS ribbons around the aperture. The resulting gain improvement is about 1.8dB.

IV. Conclusion and Remark

We presented a 94GHz LTCC approach to fabricate an integrated pyramidal horn antenna with integrated HIS ribbons around its aperture to suppress undesired diffraction. The HIS ribbons around the LTCC pyramidal horn led to significant reduction of the backward radiations lobes. As a result, the realized gain increased by 2.3dB at 94GHz. During the meeting, we will present fabrication details and challenges.

References

[1] N. Ghassemi and K. Wu, "Millimeter-Wave Integrated Pyramidal Horn Antenna Made of Multilayer Printed Circuit Board (PCB) Process," IEEE Transactions on Antennas and Propagation, vol. 60, no. 9, pp. 4432–4435, October 2012.

[2] W. E. McKinzie, D. M. Nair, B. A. Thrasher, M. A. Smith, E. D. Hughes, and J. M. Parisi, "60 GHz Patch Antenna in LTCC with an Integrated EBG Structure for Antenna Pattern Improvements," IEEE Antennas and Propagation Society International Symposium, pp. 1766–1767, July 2014.

[3] D. F. Sievenpiper, "High-impedance electromagnetic surfaces", Ph.D. Diss., Dept. of Electrical Engineering, University of California, Los Angeles, 1999.

Suppressing E-Plane Scan Resonance for UWB Millimeter-Wave Differential Phased Array

Alexander D. Johnson, Satheesh Bojja Venkatakrishnan, Elias A. Alwan, and John L.Volakis
RFCOM Laboratory, College of Engineering and Computing
Florida International University, Miami, Florida, 33174

***Abstract*—Recent advancements in differential Radio Frequency (RF) front-ends at millimeter-waves (mm-wave) create a need for high gain differentially fed arrays for 5G applications. In this paper, we present an ultra-wideband (UWB) mm-wave dual polarized Tightly Coupled Dipole Array (TCDA) with a novel differential feeding network. Notably, we introduce a new H-Wall structure used to eliminate common-mode coupling that causes E-Plane scan resonances with high radiation efficiency and 45° scanning in both planes. This differential TCDA (D-TCDA) is developed for operation across K-Ka and 5G bands (*viz.* 22-80 GHz) in a low profile of 1.38 mm.**

Keywords—5G mobile communication, Antenna arrays, Millimeter-wave communication, Feeds, Ultra-wideband technology.

I. Introduction

With rapidly increasing demand for high data rates, personal electronic devices like cell phones, cars, and watches need multi-functional radios at millimeter-wave (mm-wave) frequencies. To accommodate multiple communication platforms, antennas must be low cost, ultra-wideband (UWB), and integrated with the transceivers. Further, the high path-losses at these frequencies require high gain arrays. Recent UWB arrays have addressed the expensive fabrication problem with flip-chip printed circuit board (PCB) antenna fabrication in mind [1]. However, these arrays lack the differential feeding necessary for 5G applications [2].

Notably, recent advancements in differential RF front-end components, such as commercial push-pull amplifiers provide significant increases in the operational bandwidths of balanced 5G transceivers. These feeds lower the noise in the transceiver chain and allow high dynamic range and linearity. Further, differential signals provide inherent lower distortion in response to noise and interference from power supplies. An unbalanced signal, with unknown signal return path can be distorted by noise while a balanced/differential signal is resistant to noise [3]. Even more, distortions due to even-order harmonics from nonlinear devices can be suppressed by differential feeds [4].

However, differentially fed antenna are plagued by common-mode resonances when scanning in the E-plane nearing angles down to low angles. For instance, the UWB differential feeds in [5-8] were affected by common-mode resonances when scanning in the E-plane nearing angles down to 45°. Hence, the major challenge in the design of full differential radios is the reduction of these common-mode currents present at the aperture when scanning. If not addressed properly, these issues greatly diminished the impedance bandwidth of the balanced antenna structure [9]. These common-modes arise for particular scan angles and frequencies in the differential feed lines due to destructive mutual coupling between elements in presence of a third conductor (i.e. ground plane). These common-modes radiate in a manner that significantly reduces total efficiency. The most prevalent way to suppress these scan-dependent common-modes is to employ a balanced-to-unbalanced feed (i.e. balun), thereby avoiding differential feeding altogether [10]. One method for single polarized arrays is to remove these resonances is by employing conductive E-Plane walls to disrupt the fields between neighboring linear arrays [5-6]. Another approach has been developed to use resistive terminations to attenuate the common-modes, at the cost of acceptable losses [7-8].

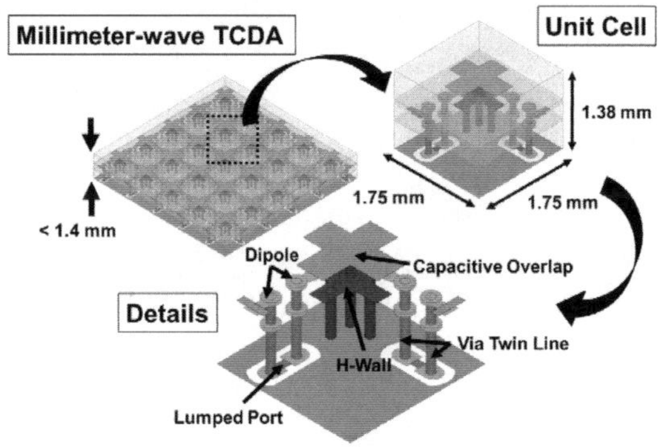

Fig. 1. Pictorial representation of a Dual polarized Differntial TCDA array with Unit Cell of the design.

In this paper, we present an UWB differentially fed mm-wave array with full polarization diversity, developed for operation across K-Ka and 5G bands (*viz.* 22-80 GHz). Our array belongs the family of tightly coupled dipole arrays (TCDA). These arrays have demonstrated large impedance bandwidths and scanning performance in a low profile of $\lambda_{High}/2$. The UWB nature of the TCDA is a product of the continuous current distribution that is achieved across the array, by introducing capacitive coupling between antenna elements to counter the effect of ground plane inductance [11].

II. Tightly Coupled Dipole Element Design

Past TCDA employed balanced feeds to remove the scan-dependent common-mode currents. TCDA with this feed concept have been employed as single polarized arrays up to 70 GHz [10] with standard PCB processes. This design improves on the differential K-band TCDA [3] and the 3:1 single polarized mm-wave TCDA [10] with its dual-polarized differential implementation, providing polarization diversity across a large bandwidth.

In this paper, the tightly coupled dipoles are excited by the differential twin line feed in Fig. 1, where symmetry between the feed lines is maintained for balanced transmission of opposite phase signals from the feed to the aperture over a wide bandwidth. This symmetry adds to the performance of the differential array in creating low cross-polarized gain levels. The design uses coplanar dipoles with a single cross shaped overlapping element to introduce capacitive coupling.

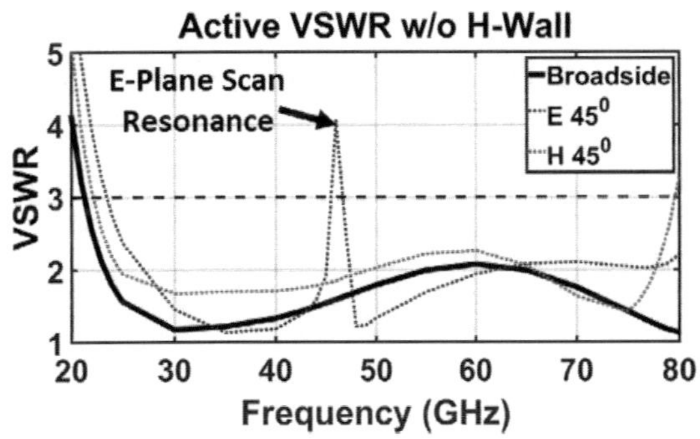

Fig. 2. VSWR in the principle planes (E/H) of D-TCDA using infinite array simulation.

A dielectric superstrate aids in matching the UWB array to scan angles down to 45°. However, as shown in Fig. 2, the issue of common-mode resonances arises at 46 GHz when scanning to 45° from broadside.

III. Removal of E-Plane Scan Resonance

It can be seen in Fig. 3 (left) that a resonance occurs when scanning in the E-plane. The feed lines radiate as monopoles due to the common-modes introduced by the high field intensity between neighboring unit cells in the E-Plane. To remove that resonance, the multi-layer dual-polarized H-wall depicted in Fig. 1 was designed to disrupt and reduce the scan-dependent common-modes, similar to [5-6]. Fig. 3 (right) shows how the fields in the substrate of the dipoles are of much lower intensity and confined between the feed lines for efficient radiation at a steering angle of 45° off broadside. Full wave simulations of the optimized array in an infinite array setup show that the D-TCDA with H-wall has continuous bandwidth with VSWR < 3 across 22-80 GHz, with scanning down to 45°, as depicted in Fig. 4. Broadside gain predictions are given in Fig. 5, showing that a near theoretical realized gain is achieved over each of the K-Ka and 5G bands with polarization purity greater than 40 dB across the operating band.

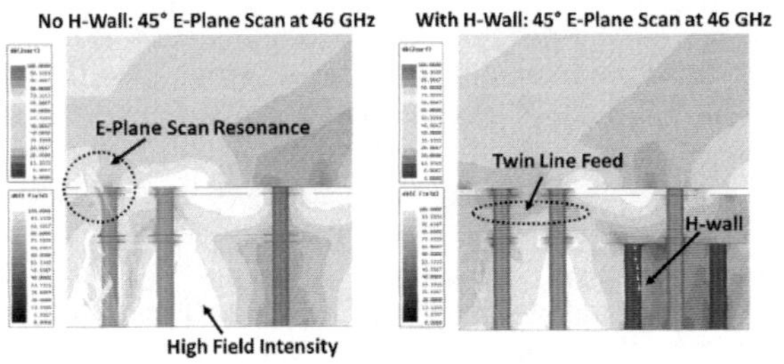

Fig. 3. Magnitude Electric Field E distribtuion and Electric Current J vectors along the E-Plane showing radiation of differntial feed lines (left) and removal of common-mode resonance with H-Wall Structure (right).

IV. Conclusion

We presented a dual-polarized differential array operating across the K to 5G bands (viz. 22-80 GHz). Full-wave simulations show that the array achieved VSWR < 3 for both polarizations in an infinite array setup. The novel H-Wall structure reduces the common-mode coupling that causes E-Plane scan resonances, while allowing for full polarization diversity, without the introduction of resistive losses.

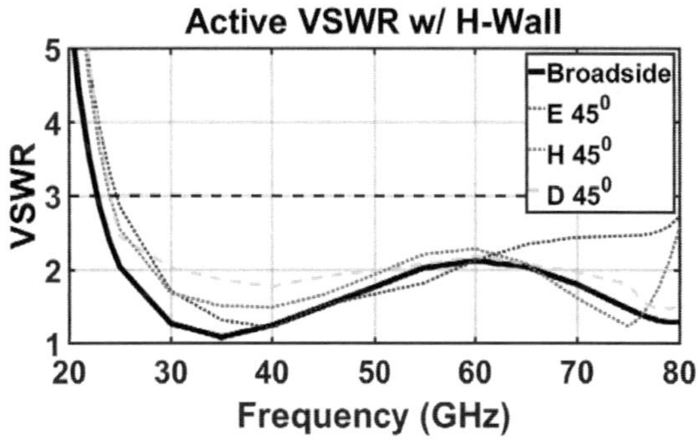

Fig. 4. VSWR in the principle (E/H) and diagonal planes of D-TCDA using infinite array simulation.

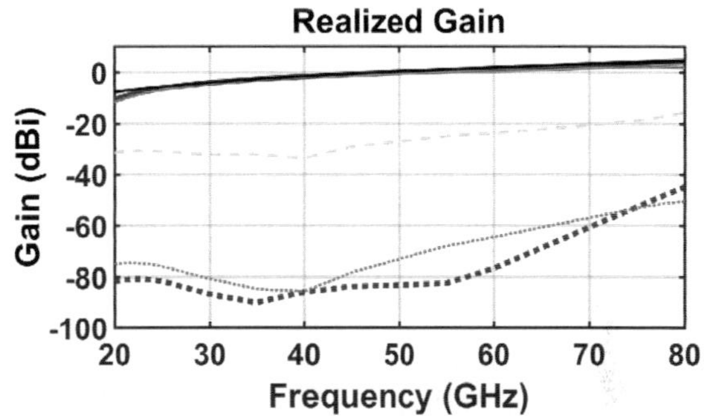

Fig. 5. Realized gain of D-TCDA unit cell with infinite array simulation.

References

[1] Z. N. Chen, X. Qing, M. Sun, K. Gong, and W. Hong, "60-ghz antennas on pcb," in The 8th European Conference on Antennas and Propagation (EuCAP 2014), Apr. 2014, pp. 533–536.

[2] A. Silvian, Toward 5G software defined radio receiver front-ends. Springer International Publishing, 2016.

[3] A. Johnson, J. Zhong, E. A. Alwan, and J. L. Volakis, "Tightly coupled dipole array with wideband differential feeding network," in 2018 IEEE International Symposium on Antennas and Propagation (APSURSI), 2018.

[4] D. M. Pozar, "Microwave engineering education: From field theory to circuit theory," in 2012 IEEE/MTT-S International Microwave Symposium Digest, Jun. 2012, pp. 1–3.

[5] J. R. Bayard, D. H. Schaubert, and M. E. Cooley, "E-plane scan performance of infinite arrays of dipoles printed on protruding dielectric substrates: Coplanar feed line and E-plane metallic wall effects," IEEE Trans. Antennas Propag., vol. 41, no. 6, pp. 837–841, Jun. 1993.

[6] S. Edelberg and A. Oliner, "Mutual coupling effects in large antenna arrays II: Compensation effects," IRE Transactions on Antennas and Propagation, vol. 8, no. 4, pp. 360–367, Jul. 1960, ISSN : 0096-1973.

[7] J. J. Lee, S. Livingston, and R. Koenig, "Performance of a wideband (3-14GHz) dual-pol array," IEEE Antennas and Propagation Society Int. Symp., vol. 1, pp. 551–554, Jun. 2004.

[8] E. de Lera Acedo, E. Garcia, V. Gonzalez-Posadas, J. L. Vazquez-Roy, R. Maaskant, and D. Segovia, "Study and design of a differentially-fed tapered slot antenna array," IEEE Trans. Antennas Propag., vol. 58, no. 1, pp. 68–78, Jan. 2010.

[9] S. G. Hay and J. D. O'Sullivan, "Analysis of Common-mode Effects in a Dual Polarized Planar Connected-Array Antenna," Radio Science RS6S04, vol. 43, Dec. 2008.

[10] M. H. Novak, F. A. Miranda, and J. L. Volakis, "Ultrawideband phased array for millimeter-wave ism and 5g bands, realized in pcb," IEEE Transactions on Antennas and Propagation, pp. 1–1, 2018.

[11] J. Volakis, Ultra-Wideband Phased Arrays. Antenna Engineering Handbook, Mcgraw-Hill Education, 2018.

Large Waveguide Slotted Array With Shaped Patterns

Wang Hongjian[1,2]
[1]CAS Key Laboratory of Microwave Remote Sensing, National Space Science Center, Chinese Academy of Sciences, Beijing, China,100190
[2]University of Chinese Academy of Sciences, Beijing, China,100049
wanghongjian@mirslab.cn

***Abstract*—Genetic Algorithms(GAs) is employed to synthesis the large fan beam shaped pattern waveguide slotted array. Waveguide phase shifters are used to compensate the definite phases for each waveguide. The whole array is divided into eight partitions to broaden the bandwidth. Full wave simulations confirm the design of the shaped pattern antenna that will be used in the altimeter payload.**

***Index Terms*—Genetic Algorithms, shaped pattern, waveguide slotted array**

I. Introduction

Waveguide slot array antennas have been widely due to the advantage of compact structure, light weight, high aperture efficiency, the easy control of aperture distribution [1-6]. Waveguide-fed slot arrays are increasingly used in numerous radar, remote sensing and communications applications. In practice, there is some need that for the antenna patterns with strongly shaped fan beam patterns. One of the key points in the design of a slotted waveguide array with strongly shaped beams is to find an aperture distribution which is realizable. Several methods have been used for the synthesis the shaped patterns [7-8], this paper present a new more flexible GAs method for the optimization. Different from the symmetrical patterns,the shaped one has special and sensitive demand on the phases of the feeding waveguides in addition to the amplitudes. The phase shifting network for each feeding waveguide are used to compensate the phase of each tilt slot. Elliott's design procedure for planar arrays is employed to synthesis this array.

II. GAs Optimization of Shaped Beam Pattern

Longitudinal slots are used as radiating elements of waveguide slot array antenna with broadside radiation. If appropriate aperture field distribution given, the desired patterns will be acquired. We use the Genetic algorithm to optimize array antenna array elements amplitude and phase. The amplitudes and phases are coded in binary. The antenna array works at Ku band,with the 22 rows and 152 columns elements. The pattern in the narrow beamwidth (152 elements) is symmetrical while that in the wide beamwidth (22 elements) has shaped demand. Heredity, mutation, crossover used to optimized the shaped beam patterns. However, due to the limited dimension for space antenna radar use, the most important goal factors are shaped patterns and gain, therefore the goal function can be expressed as antenna patterns (dB) at different angles. The crossover rate is 0.5, the mutation rate is 0.02, population is 50.

Different groups of the radiation slots amplitude and phase after the decoding of the binary can be found after GAs. In order to have high aperture efficiency of the antenna array, the maximum/minimum amplitude ratio among the radiation slots should not be too big; also, the max/min phase difference should be as small as possible to reduce the difficulty of phase compensation needed for the feeding network. The final group of amplitude and phase of the 22 elements is chosen for this antenna is tabulated in Table 1.

TABLE I. Amplitude and Phase of the Elements

Elements		1	2	3	4	5	6	7	8	9	10
Amp		0.20	0.20	0.20	0.25	0.2	0.27	0.2	0.2	0.2	0.42
Phase(°)		225	216	229	205	166	134	86	0	300	300
11	12	13	14	15	16	17	18	19	20	21	22
0.48	0.69	0.82	0.91	0.97	1	1	0.93	0.81	0.69	0.55	0.45
300	287	269	252	236	220	205	191	176	160	142	129

III. Shaped Beam Pattern Slotted Array Antenna

The antenna pattern using the amplitudes and phases of Table 1 is shown in Fig. 1, it is clear that the antenna has strong shaped curve due to the aperture distribution. In order to have relatively wider bandwidth, the waveguide slotted array radiation has 8 subarrays. The phase compensation network lie in the second layer (Fig. 2). The four coupling waveguide lie in the middle of the different subarrays on the third layer. The bottom layer is the feeding waveguide. The half height waveguide dimensions are chosen as 14.87mm*4mm for all the radiation, coupling, feeding and phase compensation networks. The baffle thickness is 0.84mm for the radiation waveguides, while the layer thickness is 0.8mm. All slots widths are 1.6mm, and the slots are ended by half circle with radius of 0.8mm. Elliott's design procedure for planar arrays is employed to synthesis this array.

The phase compensation network utilize the different width waveguide to meet the phase shift needed. Detailed structure of the phase compensation waveguide is shown in Fig. 3. The half height waveguides have been known to have no significant higher-order mode coupling in the junction regions near the tilted coupling slots. With this choice of waveguides, the design based on Elliott's approach generally needs no further iteration to account for higher-order mode coupling effect computed from a full-wave model. Full wave method FDTD is employed to find the normalized admittance and resonant length variation with frequency of an isolated slot (Fig. 4).Elliott's theory is utilized to seek out the radiating slots offsets and lengths. The coupling coefficient of each coupling slot can be obtained by Elliott's equations, then the FDTD is also used to find the coupling slots resistance and length variation with tilt angles (Fig. 5).

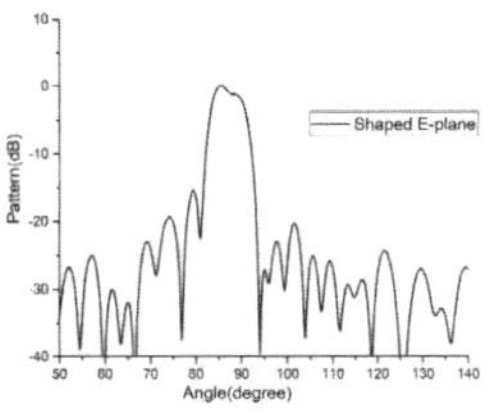

Fig. 1. Diagram of the shaping pattern.

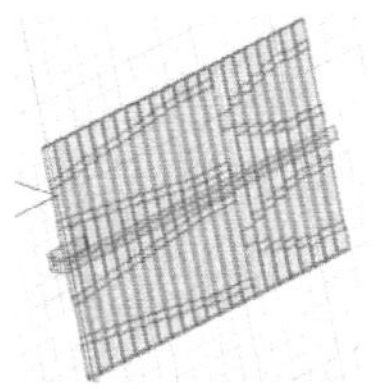

Fig. 2. Diagram of the antenna phase compensation structure.

Elliott's design technique reported gets simplified considerably for the infinite array coupling problem. The active conductance of each radiating slot is obtained by simple formula. Some expert suggests a value of total normalized active conductance of 2 for each radiating waveguide and a value between 2 and 3 for the total resistance in each feed waveguide. The total normalized active conductance is chosen as 2.

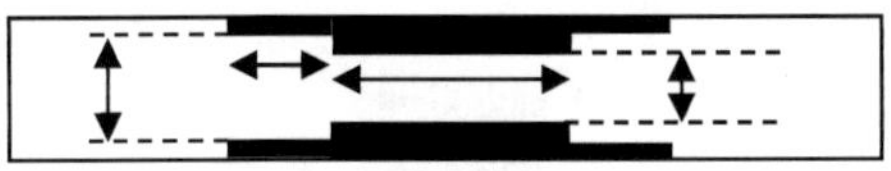

Fig. 3. Structure of the phase compensation waveguide.

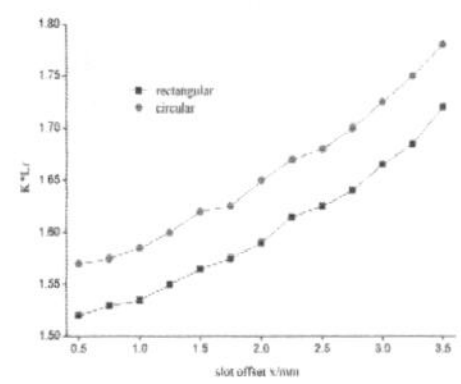

Fig. 4. The resonance length vs offset of the straight slots.

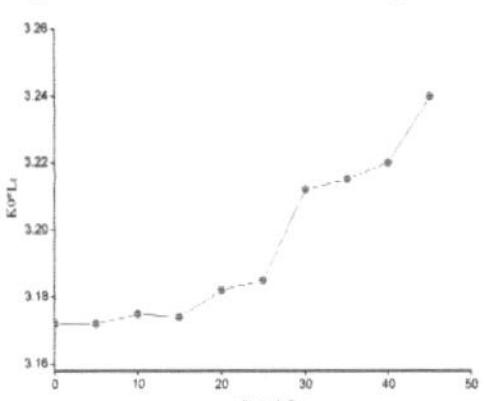

Fig. 5. The resonance length vs offset of the tilt slots.

Due to the fact that the radiating waveguide No.8 has the least phase value, therefore that phase is chosen as the base line. The final phase compensation waveguides can be seen in Fig. 2. The feeding network uses the 8 tilt slots coupling with the coupling waveguides. Finally, the whole array is fed by H-T feeding network.

IV. Simulation Results of the Antenna

The shaped beam pattern waveguide slotted array simulation is finished based on the HFSS full wave simulation. The antenna patterns are shown in Fig. 6. It can be seen that the shaped pattern has -18dB sidelobe level (SLL), while the SLL in the symmetrical plane pattern is about -25dB, in addition, the antenna has aperture efficiency of about 60%. All these results meet the specification for the altimeter demand.

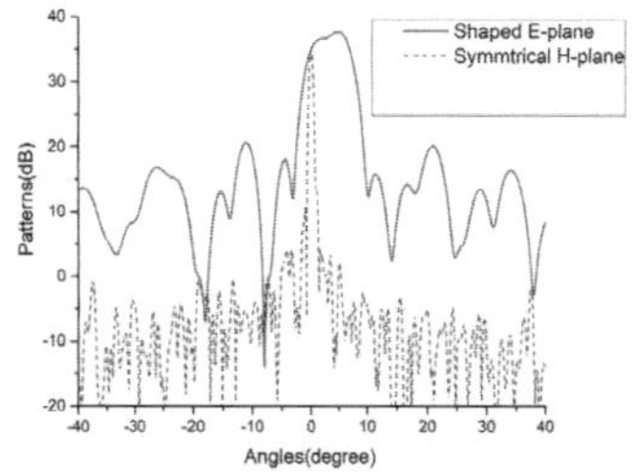

Fig. 6. Shaped patterns in main plane by simulation.

V. Conclusions

22*152 elements shaped beam pattern slotted array antenna is optimized and designed by GAs method. Full consideration and a rigorous analysis is given to the slots end shape and the thickness effect of waveguide. The array mutual coupling effects also influence the radiation, the H-T coupling network is used to realize the wideband characteristics. The full wave simulation showed that the side lobe levels of two principal planes are -18dB and -25dB respectively. The proposed antenna is very suitable for space-borne application.

Reference

[1] R. S. Elliott, Antenna Theory and Design. [M]. Englewood Cliffs, NJ: Prentice-Hall, 1981, pp. 408-411.

[2] H. Jasik, Antenna Engineering Handbook. [M]. 2nd ed., New York: McGraw-Hill, 1989.

[3] L. G. Josefsson, "Analysis of longitudinal slots in rectangular waveguides," [J]. IEEE Transactions on Antennas and Propagation, vol. 35, no. 12, pp. 1351-1357, 1987.

[4] Hamadallah, "Frequency limitations on broad-band performance of shunt slot arrays," IEEE Trans. AP, vol. 37, no. 7, pp. 817-823, July 1989.

[5] M. Ludovico, et al., "Multipaction analysis and power handling evaluation in waveguide components for satellite antenna applications," IEEE AP-S International Symposium (Digest), vol. 2, pp. 266-269, 2001.

[6] S. R. Rengarajan, "Bandwidth enhancement of large planar slot arrays," Antennas & Propagation Society International Symposium, pp. 4405-4408, 2007.

[7] R. S. Elliott, "A new technique for shaped beam synthesis of equispaced arrays," [J]. IEEE Trans. on AP-32, no. 10, pp. 1129-1133, 1984.

[8] H. J. Orchard, "Optimising the synthesis of shaped beam antenna patterns," IEE Proceedings, vol. 132, pt. H, no. 1, pp. 63-68, February 1985.

A Multi-Transmitter Configuration for High-Safety Wireless Power Transfer Applications

Danilo Brizi
Dipartimento di Ingegneria dell'Informazione
University of Pisa, Italy
danilo.brizi@ing.unipi.it

Nunzia Fontana
DESTEC
University of Pisa, Italy

Sami Barmada
DESTEC
University of Pisa, Italy

Agostino Monorchio
Dipartimento di Ingegneria dell'Informazione
University of Pisa, Italy

***Abstract*— A multi-transmitter configuration made by an array of passive resonant elements placed in the proximity of the driver coil for inductive Wireless Power Transfer applications is presented. The array is able to significantly decrease the electric field level produced by the fed loop at the operative frequency of 6 MHz, thus reducing the potentially dangerous radiation over biological tissues (i.e., the Specific Absorption Rate, SAR). Nonetheless, the proposed arrangement preserves the same efficiency level of the simple driver-receiver system and it does not affect the useful working distance. Electromagnetic simulations have been performed to evaluate the SAR reduction and the efficiency levels achieved by the multi-transmitter configuration in comparison with the driver-receiver system. The proposed solution can be extremely useful in all the WPT applications in which the SAR exposure is a concern, such as automotive applications, biomedical implants and rechargeable devices.**

Keywords*— *Array, resonant coils, safety, Specific Absorption Rate, Wireless Power Transfer component, formatting, style, styling, insert

I. INTRODUCTION

Inductive resonant Wireless Power Transfer is nowadays raising a lot of interest in the scientific community. Indeed, a number of different technological areas use a WPT system to deliver energy to a device, such as in automotive applications, biomedical, and rechargeable devices. Due to its capillary diffusion, exposure levels to the electromagnetic field are becoming an important source of concern, especially in all the situations in which the WPT device is operating in close proximity with a human user. Not only biomedical implants, but also commercial solutions, for instance rechargeable stations, fall in such category [1]-[3]. Therefore, it would be strongly desirable to realize WPT systems able to increase the safety of similar applications. This can be translated into the requirement of lower levels of the Specific Absorption Rate (SAR, (W/kg)) in the biological tissues with respect to classically adopted WPT solutions. To the best of our knowledge, in literature the main concern deals with the reduction of magnetic field leakage in WPT systems, by using metamaterial slabs [4]. For this reason, in this paper we propose the insertion of an array of resonant passive elements in between the driver and the receiver coils of a standard 2-coils WPT system principally influencing the electric near field. The array is positioned as close as possible to the driver loop, thus not affecting the useful working distance. Through numerical simulations, we study the possibility to preserve the efficiency level of a typical WPT system, achieving at the same time significantly lower levels of SAR in biological media. The main goal of the paper is to introduce a technical solution thanks to which safer and efficient WPT devices can be developed.

II. NUMERICAL DESIGN

The design process and the numerical simulations were carried out with an electromagnetic solver based on the Methods of Moments (Feko suite, Altair, Troy, MI, USA).

A. *Two-Coils System*

The first step involved the design of a classical 2-coils system, one of the most simple and common configurations used in WPT applications. We selected an operative frequency of 6 MHz, within the typical range for WPT devices. For simplicity, driver and receiver coils were designed equal each other. They consisted in a resonant 4-turns planar spiral, with an average diameter of 20 cm; they are realized with a lossy copper wire with a diameter of 4 mm and placed 20 cm distant each other (i.e., working distance equal to 1 diameter), in a coaxial fashion (Fig. 1). We added, for both the coils, a capacitive load of 108 pF in order to obtain the resonance at the desired frequency; moreover, we added a 5.1 Ω resistor in series with the driver in order to simulate the output impedance of a typical power amplifier. Finally, we equipped the receiver with a useful series resistive load of 50 Ω.

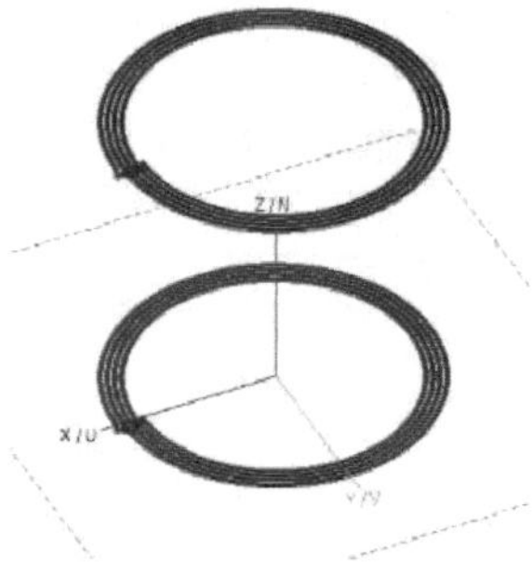

Fig. 1. CAD model of the driver-receiver system: the two coaxial coils are identical and separated by 20 cm.

B. *Multi-Transmitter Array*

After that, we designed the multi-transmitter array to be interposed between the driver and receiver coils, depicted in Fig. 1. The array was composed by a 5×5 matrix of 8-turns passive resonant planar spirals. The average diameter of each element was 4 cm whereas the lossy copper wire had a 1.4 mm diameter (Fig. 2). We equipped each spiral with a 460 pF capacitor in order to obtain the desired resonant frequency. Finally, we placed the array as close as possible to the driver coil (1 mm away), in order to preserve the useful working distance (i.e. the available space between the array and the receiver coil).

Fig. 2. CAD model representing the multi-transmitter array placed in close proximity to the driver coil. The working distance is preserved with respect to the simple driver-receiver system (i.e., 20 cm).

III. Results

Before starting the comparison in terms of exposure levels between the two systems described in Fig. 1 and Fig. 2, we analyzed the efficiency level in both the cases. In particular, for the same working distance (20 cm) and loading configuration (50 Ω), we obtained the same efficiency (i.e., η = 26.2 %). This means that the two systems share equal performance and the comparison in terms of exposure can be fairly performed.

A. Specific Absorption Rate (SAR) comparison

The biological exposure is typically measured in terms of Specific Absorption Rate (SAR (W/kg)), which is defined as:

$$SAR(\vec{r}) = \frac{\sigma(\vec{r})\left|\vec{E}(\vec{r})\right|^2}{2\rho(\vec{r})}, \tag{1}$$

where $\sigma(\vec{r})$ is the punctual conductivity of the tissue (S/m), $\rho(\vec{r})$ is the density (kg/m^3) and $\vec{E}(\vec{r})$ is the electric field value (V/m). In order to compare the exposure level of the driver-receiver system with respect to the case in which we inserted the multi-transmitter array, we placed a simple biological sample (muscle, $\rho = 1040\,kg/m^3$, $\sigma = 0.59\,S/m$, $\varepsilon_r = 60$) in the available space (between the transmitter and the receiver side, Fig. 3). In particular, the distance between the sample and the driver was equal to the distance between the sample and the multi-transmitter array (i.e., 1 mm). From the evaluation of the E-field maps inside the biological load and close to the transmitter side (Fig. 4), it was observed that the multi-transmitter configuration is able to drastically reduce the field peak level (225 V/m vs. 55 V/m, respectively). Moreover, we numerically estimated both the 1-g and the 10-g peak SAR levels, which are the two quantities that the international guidelines [4] take into main consideration. We observed a significant decrease both in the 1-g SAR (1.02 W/kg vs. 0.15 W/kg) and in the 10-g SAR (0.19 W/kg vs. 0.017 W/kg), demonstrating the effectiveness of the proposed solution to significantly reduce the exposure levels.

IV. Conclusions

In this paper we presented a WPT configuration (i.e., the multi-transmitter array) able to reduce the electromagnetic exposure of the biological tissues with respect to a classical driver-receiver system, while maintaining the same efficiency level. The array was made by a 5×5 matrix of passive resonant loops and it was placed as close as possible to the driver coil. Numerical simulations demonstrated that reducing the SAR levels of an order of magnitude between the two cases was possible. Therefore, these results suggest that the multi-transmitter configuration is effective to achieve high safety standards for WPT devices. Such property can be extremely useful in all the WPT applications requiring a close interaction with a human user, as biomedical implants, automotive applications and rechargeable devices. Moreover, in the case in which the SAR exposure is within the limit for a given 2-coils system, through the multi-transmitter array it can be possible to increase the delivered power, thus increasing the current available to the receiver, until that the SAR level becomes comparable with the original system. Future developments can be directed in order to increase the efficiency of the multi-transmitter array, for instance through an increase of the unit-cell Q-factor, achievable with the use of Litz wires.

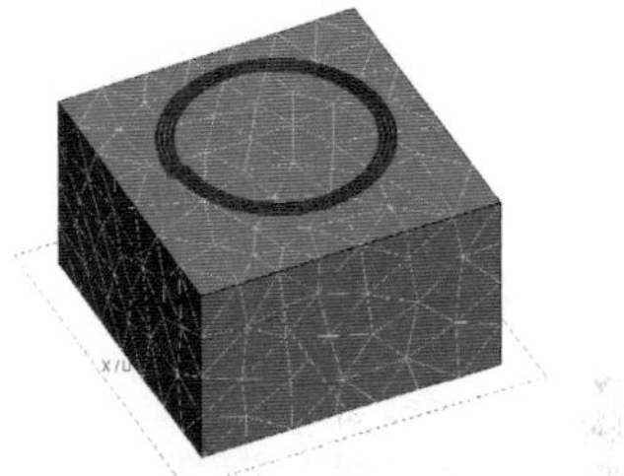

Fig. 3. CAD representation of the WPT system in presence of the biological load (a simple cuboid of muscle).

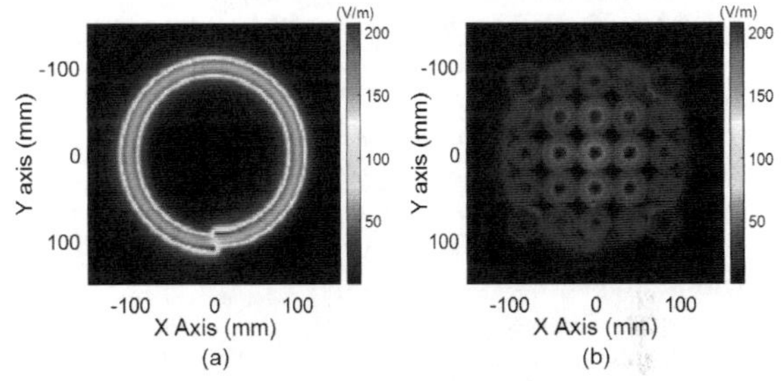

Fig. 4. Electric field maps inside the biological load in close proximity with the driver coil (a) and with the multi-transmitter array (b). As can be seen, the E-field level is significantly lower in the array case.

References

[1] T. Sunohara, A. Hirata, I. Laakso and T. Onishi, "Analysis of in situ electric field and specific absorption rate in human models for wireless power transfer system with induction coupling," Phys. Med. Biol., vol. 59, pp. 3721–3735, 2014.

[2] R. Pinto, V. Lopresto and A. Genovese, "Human exposure to wireless power transfer systems: a numerical dosimetric study," 11th European Conference on Antennas and Propagation (EUCAP), 2017.

[3] T. Campi et al., "Induced effects in a pacemaker equipped with a wireless power transfer charging system," IEEE Transactions On Magnetics, vol. 53, no. 6, june 2017.

[4] Y. Cho et al., "Thin hybrid metamaterial slab with negative and zero permeability for high efficiency and low electromagnetic field in wireless power transfer systems," IEEE Transactions On Electromagnetic Compatibility, vol. 60, no. 4, August 2018.

[5] A. Ahlbom et al., "Guidelines for limiting exposure to time-varying electric, magnetic, and electromagnetic fields (up to 300 GHz)," Health Phys., vol. 74, no. 4, pp. 494–521, 1998.

[6] X. Shi, C. Qi, M. Qu, S. Ye and G. Wang, "Effects of Coil Locations on Wireless Power Transfer via Magnetic Resonance Coupling," ACES Journal Paper, Year: 2016, Vol. 31, N. 3.

Modeling and Simulation of Multilayer Rectangular Coils for Wireless Power Transfer Applications

Huseyin U. Aydogmus* and Hakan P. Partal*†+
* Dept. of Electronics & Communications Eng.
Yildiz Technical University, Istanbul, Turkey.
†Radarcomm, LLC, Istanbul, Turkey.
+ Dept. of Elec. Eng. & Comp. Sci.
Syracuse University, Syracuse, NY, USA
huaydogmus@gmail.com, hpartal@radarcomm.com

***Abstract*—In this paper, miniaturized multilayer rectangular printed circuit board (PCB) coils are investigated and, a method for calculating the total self-inductance, mutual inductance, and power transfer efficiency between two miniature (6.6mm x 6.6mm) coils for wireless power transfer applications is presented. First, in order to reduce the complexity, coil trace turns are modeled as rectangular loops. A formula based on integral solution starting from Biot - Savart's law gives the analytical results of the mutual inductances between each rectangular trace in same and different layers. Then 4-layer rectangular PCB coil based wireless power transfer system is modeled, analyzed and simulated. Mutual inductance and power transfer efficiency parameters according to the distance between coils and trace width of the coils are calculated with analytical methods. Achieved inductance and power transfer efficiency results from the analytical model and simulation results in Ansys – Maxwell and Simplorer environment is compared for verification. The analytical approach proposed in this paper is provide a fast mutual inductance and power transfer efficiency calculation for multilayer rectangular printed circuit board inductors compared to the simulation.**

Keywords—Wireless Power Transfer, Multilayer coil, Printed Circuit Board Coil.

I. Introduction

Wireless power transfer technology provides a great potential for many applications such as consumer electronics, implantable biomedical devices or electric vehicles etc. A typical resonant inductive wireless power transfer system includes two or more coils which uses near field electromagnetic fields in the range of frequencies between 10 kHz and low MHz ranges. Resonant inductive wireless power transfer methods are uses non-radiative near field, so that it has almost no harm to human. With this advantage, this method is suitable for and implantable biomedical systems. However, there are a few limitations and challenges such as compact coil size, high power transfer efficiency, high coupling coefficient between coils etc. To overcome these challenges, coil design parameters can be selected based on the application such as number of turn, trace gaps and track lengths coil shape and material. For biomedical applications, coil sizes must be more compact and self-inductance of the coils must be higher to provide a strong coupling between coils. A lot of works are reported in the literature which analyses inductance, mutual inductance of the different coils and power transfer efficiency between coils. However, number of works focused on calculation methods of the inductance and mutual inductance of the multilayer printed circuit board rectangular coils [1-3] are limited compared to the circular coils designs [4-5]. In this work, analytical calculation of the inductance, mutual inductance and power transfer efficiency parameters for different distance and trace width analysed and compared with the simulation.

A. Inductance Calculation for Single layer Rectangular Coil

The inductance calculation algorithm [1] is used to calculate the magnetic flux density *B* at point (x,y) arising from a current in a straight trace (1) where m is the half length of the wire, x and y are the distance from the centre point of the trace as shown in the Fig. 1(a). A multi-turn rectangular coil in Fig. 1(b) can be simplified as concentric square loops as shown in the Fig. 1(c).

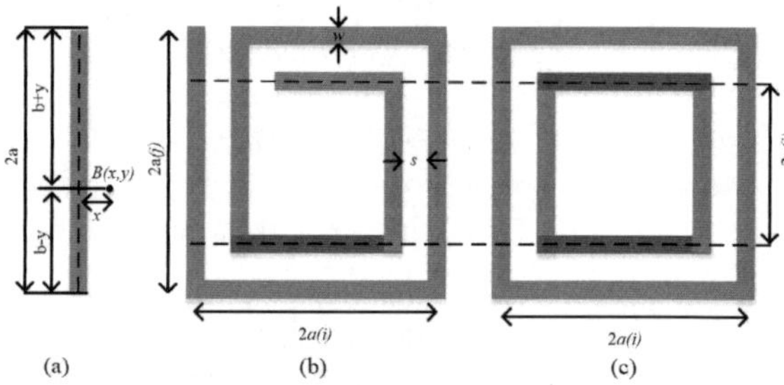

Fig. 1. (a) Straight line - *B* at point *(x,y)*. (b) Multi turn rectangular coil. (c) Single turn concentric rectangular loops.

$$B(x,y) = \frac{\mu I}{4\pi x}\left(\frac{a+y}{\sqrt{(a+y)^2+x^2}} + \frac{a-y}{\sqrt{(a-y)^2+x^2}}\right) \quad (1)$$

Self inductance of each square loop and mutual inductance between square loops can be calculated as in (2) and (3) below by adjusting the integral boundaries. Total inductance is equal to sum of the self and mutual inductances and given in (4):

$$L_s = 4\left(\frac{\mu}{4\pi}\int_{-a(i)}^{a(i)}\int_{w/4}^{2a(i)} B(x,y)dxdy\right) \quad (2)$$

$$M_{a(i)\to a(j)} = 4\left(\frac{\mu}{4\pi}\int_{-a(j)}^{a(j)}\int_{a(i)-a(j)}^{a(i)+a(j)} B(x,y)dxdy\right) \quad (3)$$

$$L_T = \sum_{n=1}^{n<turn} L_m + 2\sum_{m=1}^{m<turn}\sum_{n=m+1}^{n<turn} M_{m\to n} \quad (4)$$

B. Inductance Calculation of 4-Layer Rectangular Coil

In multilayer coils, each layer traces magnetically interacts with the other traces in other layers. Because of the changed geometry of the coils, mutual inductance between two traces on top of each other is calculated by modifying the Biot-Savart formula with adding layer to layer trace distance, *h* (5). The mutual inductance between traces which are not on neighboring layers is calculated by the modified boundary conditions which is given in (6). Total inductance is equal to the sum of self and mutual inductances as given in (4), with the number of turns replaced by the layer index.

$$M_{a(i),h} = 4\left(\frac{\mu}{4\pi}\int_{-a(i)}^{a(i)}\int_{\frac{w}{4}}^{2a(i)} B(x,y,h)dxdy\right) \quad (5)$$

$$M_{a(i),a(j),h} = 4\left(\frac{\mu}{4\pi}\int_{-a(j)}^{a(j)}\int_{a(i)-a(j)}^{a(i)+a(j)} B(x,y,h)dxdy\right) \quad (6)$$

II. WPT LINK PARAMETERS

Equivalent circuit of a 2-coil wireless power transfer system is as shown in the Fig. 2. Mutual inductance is one of the key parameters to calculate the power transfer efficiency between the coils. For a 4-layer rectangular PCB coils, mutual inductance can be written as (7). Power transfer efficiency of the system can be expressed as (8) and (9).

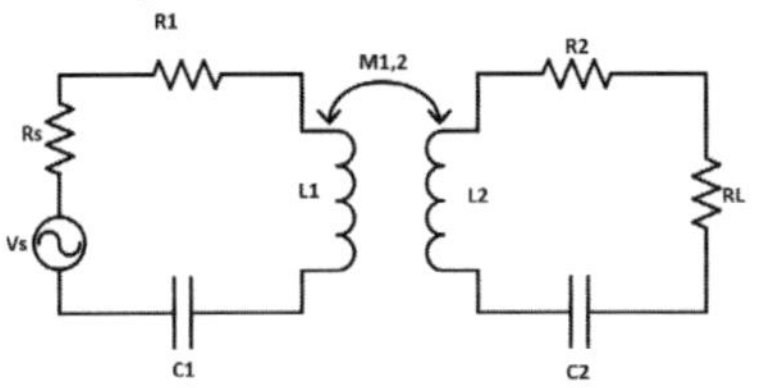

Fig. 2. Equivalent circuit of 2-coil WPT.

$$M_T = \sum_{m=1}^{m=4}\sum_{n=1}^{n=4} L_{m\rightarrow n} \quad (7)$$

$$\begin{bmatrix} V_S \\ 0 \end{bmatrix} = \begin{bmatrix} R_S + R_1 + j\omega L_1 + \frac{1}{j\omega C_1} & j\omega M \\ j\omega M & R_2 + R_L + j\omega L_2 + \frac{1}{j\omega C_2} \end{bmatrix} \begin{bmatrix} I_1 \\ I_2 \end{bmatrix} \quad (8)$$

$$PTE = \frac{P_{out}}{P_{in}} = \frac{(\omega M)^2 R_L}{(R_2+R_L)[(\omega M)^2 + R_1(R_2+R_L)]} \quad (9)$$

III. VERIFICATION OF THE METHOD WITH SIMULATION

To verify the calculation method of the mutual inductance and power transfer efficiency of the coil to coil wireless power transfer system in Fig. 3, two identical 4-layer parallel coils are modeled and mutual inductance of the coils by varying distance from 1mm to 5mm is simulated in Ansys - Maxwell. Maxwell model is used to design a circuit model and simulate the power transfer efficiency at 13.56 MHz in Ansys - Simplorer.

Fig. 3. Maxwell model of the 2-coil wireless power transfer system.

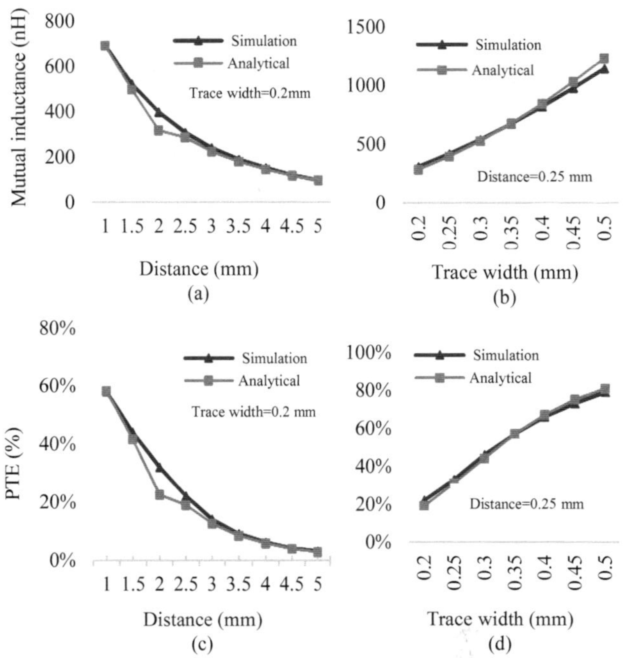

Fig. 4. (a), (b) Coil to coil distance and trace width vs. mutual inductance. (c), (d) Distance and trace width vs. PTE.

CONCLUSION

Analytical calculations of self-inductance, mutual inductance for a 4-layer rectangular compact PCB coil *(6.6 mm x 6.6mm)* and power transfer efficiency of the WPT system with different distances and trace widths are presented. According to the results in Fig. 4, proposed analytical solution shows a good agreement with the simulation. The average relative error is 4.3% for different trace widths and 9% for various distances. This method is simpler and less time consuming than simulations and it can be used for fast calculations of the self and mutual inductance parameters for wireless power transfer systems which utilize multilayer PCB coils.

REFERENCES

[1] Peters, Christian, and Yiannos Manoli. "Inductance Calculation Of Planar Multi-Layer And Multi-Wire Coils: An Analytical Approach". Sensors and Actuators A: Physical 145-146.

[2] Y. Cheng, Y. Shu, "A new analytical calculation of the mutual inductance of the coaxial spiral rectangular coils", *Magnetics IEEE Transactions on*, vol. 50, no. 4, pp. 1-6, April 2014.

[3] A. Islam, S. Islam and F. Tulip, "Design and Optimization of Printed Circuit Board Inductors for Wireless Power Transfer System", *Circuits and Systems*, vol. 04, no. 02, pp. 237-244, 2013R. Nicole, "Title of paper with only first word capitalized," J. Name Stand. Abbrev., in press.

[4] W. Hurley, M. Duffy, J. Zhang, I. Lope, B. Kunz and W. Wolfle, "A Unified Approach to the Calculation of Self- and Mutual-Inductance for Coaxial Coils in Air", *IEEE Transactions on Power Electronics*, vol. 30, no. 11, pp. 6155-6162, 2015.

[5] David M. Beams and Sravan G. Annam. "Calculation of mutual inductance from magnetic vector potential for wireless power transfer applications." IEEE Southeastern Symposium on System Theory (SSST-2012), March 11-13, 2012, pp. 209-213.

Design Guidelines for Magnetically Coupled Resonant Coils with Data Transfer Capability

Sami Barmada, Nunzia Fontana and Mauro Tucci
DESTEC
University of Pisa
Pisa, Italy
sami.barmada@unipi.it

Abstract—**In this contribution the authors investigate the possibility of improving the performances of a coupled Wireless Power Transfer (WPT) - Power Line Communications (PLC) system in case the WPT system is characterised by a four coils structure. The main idea is to use the so-called transmitting and receiving coil (the two "inner" coils) as access point for the PLC modems and use the drive and load loops (the two "outer" coils) as usual access point for power. The simulations results show that a higher wider band for communication is achieved with respect the previously proposed system.**

I. Introduction

Wireless Power Transfer (WPT) technology has lately gained a lot of attention as an alternative way to transmit power with respect to a cabled connection, see for instance [1], [2]. PLC technology uses power cables (where power is typically delivered at $50/60Hz$) to transmit high speed data; PLC communication is now considered one of the main possibility to transmit data in a smart grid environment (when, for instance, long distances do not allow wireless data transmission); see for instance [3] in which the main contribution is the integration of PLC into an electric vehicle. As a matter of fact, the increasing popularity of WPT "cuts the chord" for applications in which PLC can be of potential use. In [4] it is shown that a full integration between WPT and PLC could be a solution allowing the use of WPT without the need of changes to the pre-existing PLC system. In [5] the full system (with coils and filters) have been designed and built showing the actual feasibility of the proposal; in this specific publication, the implemented system is a two coils WPT system, while in [6] the authors investigate the possibility of using different access points for data and power in multiple coils WPT systems. Starting from the results in [6], the authors give the guidelines for the implementation of such system.

II. Background

The usual four coils WPT system is equipped the drive and load loops (where the source and the load are connected) and the transmitting and receiving coils, that are used in order to increase the transmission distance (reducing k_{23}) retaining maximum power transfer. The coils have no access point and are often mounted on the same equipment as the relative loop. Fig. 1 shows the system in which the coils are used for data transmission: this leads in some cases to an increase of the bandwidth, i.e. an increase of the channel transfer capacity with respect of the case in which the drive loop are used both for power and data transmission, represented in Fig. 2.

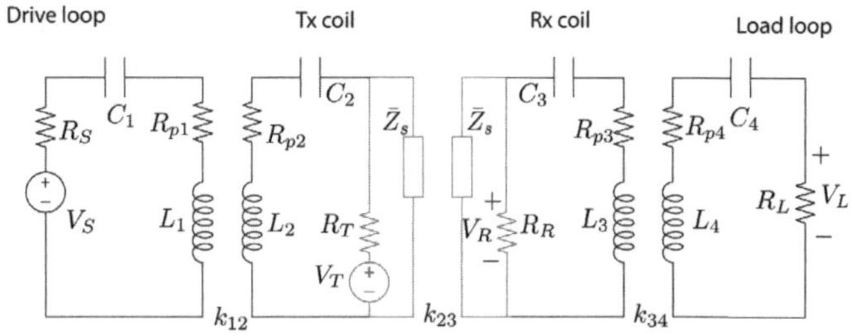

Fig. 1. Four coils equivalent circuit with different power/data access point.

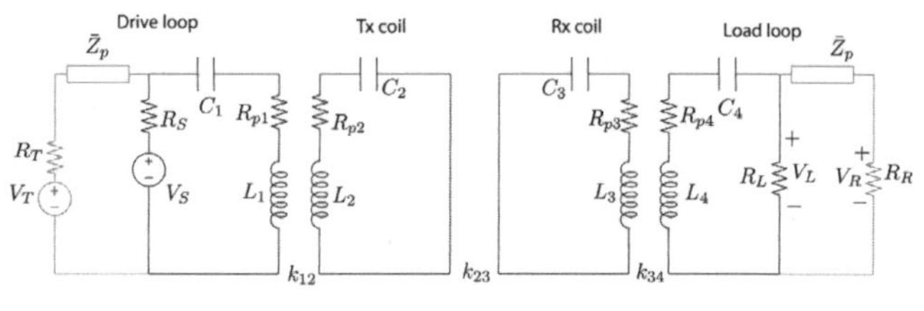

Fig. 2. Four coils equivalent circuit sharing the same power/data access point.

III. Experimental Setup

The design of the WPT system has been performed taking into account the working frequencies and coils dimensions allowing a simple experimental setup. In four coils WPT systems, the loop (power access point) and the short circuited coil are a unique system in which their mutual distance is kept as constant; in most cases two twin loop-coil system are used to create a four coils WPT system. Table I shows the dimension of the loop and the transmission coils supports as designed to be able to allow easy measurement in a laboratory and resonance (with the proper capacitors) in a selected frequency range.

The coils have been realized as single layer coils, whose value of self inductance has been calculated according to [7]

This research is partly founded by the project PRA 2018-2019 of the University of Pisa.

TABLE I
DIMENSIONS OF THE COILS SUPPORT.

	Diameter	Length
Loop	$D_1 = 18cm$	$l_1 = 2cm$
Coil	$D_2 = 12cm$	$l_2 = 8cm$

and the self capacitance according to [8]. These values are reported in Table II.

TABLE II
ELECTRICAL PARAMETERS OF THE INDUCTORS.

	Turns	Self inductance	Self capacitance
Loop	$N_1 = 5$	$L_1 = 8.68\mu H$	$C_1 = 21.57pF$
Coil	$N_2 = 19$	$L_2 = 40.93\mu H$	$C_2 = 30.20pF$

The pairs of loop-coils are winded on supports printed by a 3D printer; in addition also a structure capable of keeping the loop-coil pair coaxial and at the same mutual distance has been created. The coupling coefficient (hence the mutual inductance) according to [9] for such configuration has been consequently calculated, resulting in the following values: $M_{12} = 6.70\mu H$, $k_{12} = 0.3711$.

In order to reduce the resistance due to skin and proximity effect, a Litz wire has been used: the chosen wire is characterized by 600 strands, each of them having a diameter of $0.1mm$; considering that skin depth at the frequency $f = 1MHz$ is about $65\mu m$ we can say that the chosen wire works well for power frequencies not exceeding $1MHz$.

The four coils system is composed by two loop-coil pairs facing each other; the coupling coefficient k_{23} between the two coils have been calculated for distances varying in the range between $3cm$ and $23cm$ according to [9]. In such cases, the optimal frequency (for power transfer) are $f_0 = 1MHz$ for a distance of $3cm$, $f_0 = 55kHz$ for a distance of $23cm$ and $f_0 = 260kH$ for a distance of $10cm$.

Fig. 3. Experimental setup of loop - coil pair.

Figure 3 shows half of the system (a loop and a coil) as realised by the authors, while Figure 4 shows a comparison between the scattering parameters S_{21} calculated by the use of the equivalent circuit and by measurements in a frequency range of interest.

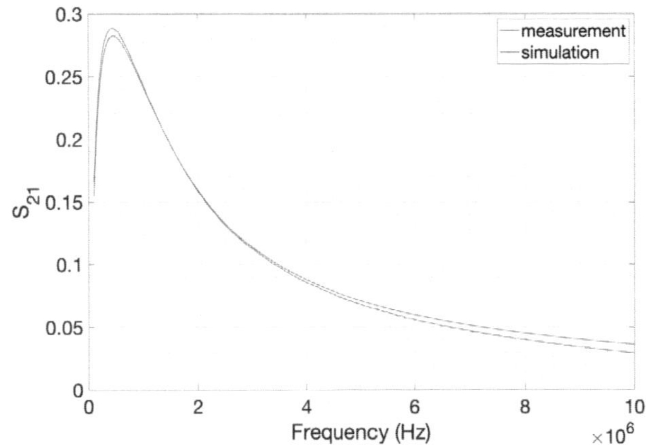

Fig. 4. Comparison between measurements and analytical calculation.

IV. CONCLUSION

This contribution is based on previous work by the authors, relative to multiple access points for combined Wireless Power Transfer - Powerline Communications systems. In this work such 4 coil systems, and its performance have been analysed, in order to give guidelines for future realisation of similar systems of different power.

REFERENCES

[1] A. Kurs, A. Karalis, R. Moffatt, J. Joannopoulos, P. Fisher, and M. Soljacic,: "Wireless power transfer via strongly coupled magnetic resonances", Science, vol. 317, no. 5834, pp. 83-86, Jul. 2007.

[2] X. Shi, C. Qi, M. Qu, S. Ye, G. Wang, : "Effects of Coil Locations on Wireless Power Transfer via Magnetic Resonance Coupling,", Applied Computational Electromagnetics Society Journal, 2016, vol. 31, no. 3, pp. 270 - 278.

[3] S. Barmada, M. Tucci, M. Raugi, Y. Maryanka, and O. Amrani,: "PLC Systems for Electric Vehicles and Smart Grid Applications", Proceedings of IEEE International Symposium of Powerline Communications and its Applications (ISPLC), Johannesburg, South Africa, 2013, pp. 23 - 28.

[4] S. Barmada, M. Raugi, M. Tucci,: "Power line communication integrated in a Wireless Power Transfer system: A feasibility study", Proceedings of IEEE International Symposium of Powerline Communications and its Applications (ISPLC), Glasgow, UK, 2014, pp. 116 - 120.

[5] S. Barmada, M. Dionigi, P. Mezzanotte, M. Tucci,: "Design and Experimental Characterization of a Combined WPT - PLC System", Wireless Power Transfer, Cambridge, Vol. 4, No. 2, pp. 160 - 170, 2017.

[6] S. Barmada, M. Tucci,: "Theoretical Study of Different Access Points in coupled Wireless Power Transfer -Powerline Communication Systems", The Appliced Computational Electromagnetics Society Journal, in press.

[7] H. A. Wheeler: "Simple inductance formulas for radio coils", Proceedings of the institute of Radio Engineers, 1928, Vol. 16, no. 10, 1398 -1400, pp. 1928.

[8] G. Grandi, M. K. Kazimierczuk, A. Massarini, U. Reggiani,: "Stray Capacitances of Single - Layer Solenoid Air - Core Inductors." IEEE Transactions on Industry Applications, 1999, Vol. 35, no. 5, pp. 1162 -1168, 1999.

[9] F. W. Grover,: "Inductance Calculation: Working Formulas and Tables"; Dover Publications, Inc.: New York, USA, 1946.

MULTI BAND ANTENNA SYSTEM for ENERGY HARVESTERs

F. A. Rivera-Abreu [(1)], M. Merghani [(2)] and A. Eroglu[(2)]

[(1)] Department of Electrical and Computer Engineering, Purdue University Fort Wayne, US

[(2)] Department of Electrical and Computer Engineering, North Carolina A&T State University, US

Abstract— **Design, and simulation of dual band planar antenna system for energy harvesting applications is given. The dual band antenna system is based on the modeling and design of microstrip octagonal patch antenna. The proposed dual band antenna has good bandwidth, gain and radiation characteristics at the frequency of interests. It has also lower profile in comparison to conventional microstrip patch antennas. The dual band antenna system is also interfaced with dual band rectifier system in the energy harvester. The performance of the antenna investigated when integrated with dc-RF rectifier and matching network. The simulation and measurement results for dual band antenna system are presented and critical antenna performance parameters when integrated with dual band energy harvesting system is discussed.**

Keywords—Dual band, antenna, energy harvesting, radio frequency, rectanna, rectifier, matching network.

I. INTRODUCTION

Energy harvesting is a key method to overcome the challenges associated with a limited battery life time. However, energy harvester systems consist of several components including antennas, filters, rectifiers, and matching networks. Hence, it is important to design and interface sub components effectively to have an efficient system.

Antennas in the harvesting system capture radio frequency energy exists in the ambient before it is rectified and boosted. Microstrip antennas are among the most commonly used antenna type for several applications including mobile radio communication systems, satellite navigation receivers, satellite communications, direct broadcast radio and television, etc. due to their cost effectiveness, low profile. That is why they are preferred for energy harvesting systems too.

In this paper, a dual band octagonal microstrip patch antenna design is given using a practical method as shown in Fig. 1. The antenna is designed and simulated with HFSS for verification. The antenna that is designed is then interfaced with the rectifier system. Overall system is also measured and it is found that analytical and simulation results are in close agreement.

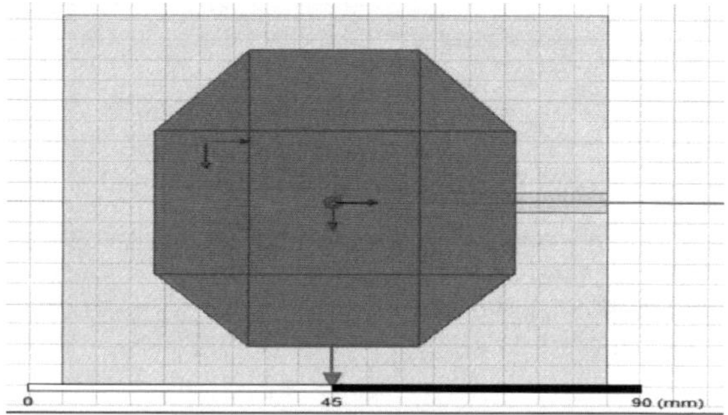

Fig. 1 - Block Diagram of RFEH

II. FORMULATION

The dimensions of geometry of octagonal microstrip patch antenna shown in Fig. 1 are calculated using the equations in [1].

The physical dimensions of the antenna for dual frequency operation are calculated and tabulated in Table I at 900MHz and 1.8GHz, respectively. In Table I, W is the width of the patch, L is the length of the patch, del_l is the additional length on each end due to the fringing field along the widths, ε_r is the relative dielectric constant of the substrate, ε_{eff} is the effective dielectric constant, c is the speed of light in a vacuum, f is target frequency and h is the thickness of the substrate, l_{eff} is the effective length, g_1 is the conductance, g_{12} is the mutual conductance, r_{in} input impedance, inset is the inset feed point distance, Lgmin is the minimum ground plane length, Wgmin is the minimum ground plane width, w_{id} is the transmission line width, g_{is} the gap between path and transmission line, respectively.

The antenna is optimized using optimization tool in HFSS. The optimized values are for the structure show in Fig. 2 are illustrated in Table 2.

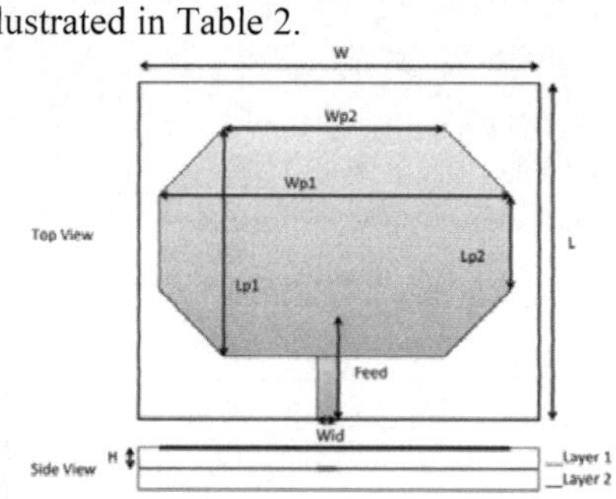

Fig. 2 - Layout of the octagonal patch antenna

TABLE I. CALCULATED PARAMETERS

Param.	Frequency	
	900 MHz	*1.8 GHz*
W	71.7219 mm	35.8610 mm
ε_{eff}	9.3079	8.9509
del_l	0.6916 mm	0.6853 mm
l_{eff}	54.6289 mm	27.8538 mm
L	53.2457 mm	26.4832 mm
la	333.3333	166.6667
k	0.0188	0.0377
x	1.3519	
tl	0.5912	
g_1	0.1397 siemens	
a_1	0.4774	0.4785
$g1_2$	4.0307e-4	4.0403e-4
r_{in}	554.1945 ohm	553.6109 ohm
$inset$	21.4522 mm	10.6684 mm
Lg_{min}	62.8457 mm	36.0832 mm
Wg_{min}	81.3219 mm	45.4610 mm
B	3.7834	
m_1	6.5667	
m	1.8820	
n_1	2.7834	
n	1.0237	
wid	1.3974 mm	
g	0.3592 mm	0.1832 mm

TABLE II. ANTENNA OPTIMIZATION PARAMETERS

Param.	Frequency	
	1.8 GHz	*2.4 GHz*
Lp_1	53 mm	53 mm
Lp_2	35 mm	29 mm
Wp_1	73 mm	73 mm
Wp_2	55 mm	49 mm

III. SIMULATION RESULTS

The simulation results are obtained using ANSYS HFSS and shown in Fig. 3 and Fig. 4. The simulation results show the maximum return of -21.5574dB and -20.3761dB at the resonant frequencies of 900 MHz and 1.76 GHz, respectively.

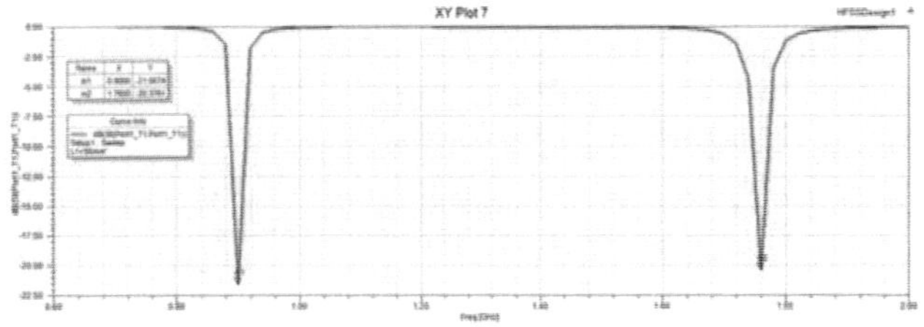

Fig. 3 - Return loss of the optimized octagonal antenna for 900 MHz & 1.8 GHz.

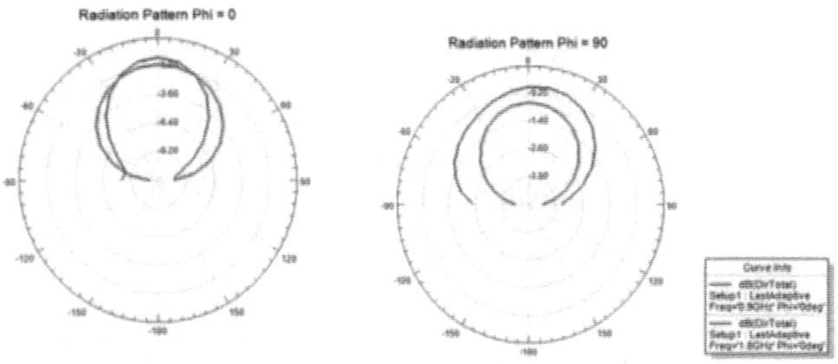

Fig. 4 - Simulated directivity of the optimized antenna for 900 MHz & 1.8 GHz on XY and XZ planes.

IV. CONCLUSION

In this paper, design, and simulation of dual band planar antenna system for energy harvesting applications is given. The proposed dual band antenna has good bandwidth, gain and radiation characteristics at the frequency of interests. It has also lower profile in comparison to conventional microstrip patch antennas. The dual band antenna system is also interfaced with dual band rectifier system in the energy harvester. The performance of the antenna investigated when integrated with dc-RF rectifier and matching network. The simulation and measurement results for dual band antenna system and critical antenna performance parameters when integrated with dual band energy harvesting system are investigated.

REFERENCES

[1] C. A. Balanis, "Microstrip antennas," in *Antenna Theory Analysis and Design*, 3rd ed. Hoboken, NJ, USA: Wiley, 2005.

Wireless Power Transfer Using Magneto-Electric Dipoles

Abdul-Sattar Kaddour
Department of Electrical and Computer Engineering
Florida International University
Miami, USA
https://orcid.org/0000-0001-9929-769X

Stavros Georgakopoulos
Department of Electrical and Computer Engineering
Florida International University
Miami, USA
georgako@fiu.edu

***Abstract*— —In this paper, a wideband Wireless Power Transfer (WPT) system using Magneto-Electric Dipoles (MEDs) is proposed. These elements are based on the concept of the Huygens source and considered as complementary antennas combining electric and magnetic dipoles. This wireless power transfer system is able to achieve 0.58 GHz bandwidth from 1.83 to 2.41 GHz (27%), while maintaining a power transfer efficiency above 80% for a distance equal to 0.2λ_0 (λ_0 is the wavelength at the central operating frequency). A maximum power transfer efficiency of 97% is obtained at 1.93 GHz and 2.2 GHz.**

Keywords—Wireless power transfer, Magneto-electric dipole, Power transfer efficiency.

I. Introduction

Wireless Power Transfer (WPT) was first introduced by Nikola Tesla in the early 1990s. Since that date, WPT has attracted considerable attention and has been used in many different applications. Near-field WPT using inductive coupling, have been applied to Unmanned Aerial Vehicles (UAVs) [1], Implanted Medical Devices (IMDs) [2], and Wearable Devices (WDs) [3]. Although inductive coupling is popular, suffers from short transmission range and low power transfer efficiency. To overcome these problems, many WPT topologies were proposed. A Strongly Coupled Magnetic Resonant (SCMR) method was proposed in [4]. This system consists of transmitting and receiving elements made from coils or loops which deliver higher efficiency and longer ranges compared to classical near-field WPT methods. However, this paper proposes the use of new design topologies for WPT in order to achieve wideband power transfer efficiency. Magneto-Electric Dipoles (MED) [5] are promising solutions with excellent characteristics and can achieve wide impedance matching. These elements are based on the concept of the Huygens source and demonstrated in [6] using spherical wave expansion analysis; the antenna presents the same behavior as a generalized Huygens source with identical contribution of Transverse Electric (TE) and Transverse Magnetic (TM) modes over a wide bandwidth. Here, a wideband MED highly efficient WPT system is proposed. This paper is organized as follows, the magneto-electric dipole is presented in Section II. The WPT system is presented is Section III and finally conclusions are discussed in Section IV.

II. Magneto-Electric Dipole Description

The MED used in this paper is presented in Fig. 1. It combines an electric dipole with a magnetic dipole. The electric dipole is made from two planar rectangular metal sheets, while the magnetic dipole is made from a wideband short-circuited patch. The short-circuited patch is placed vertically and is connected to the planar electric dipole. To excite the antenna, a Γ-shaped probe feed is employed between the two vertical metal sheets. This feed consists of three portions and it is made by folding a straight metallic strip of rectangular cross-section into a Γ-shape. The first portion is considered as a CPW line that transmits the energy from the excitation to the second portion of the probe. The second portion couples the energy to the electric and magnetic dipoles simultaneously. Finally, the third portion is added to create a localized capacitive loading to compensate the inductance produced by the first two portions. A capacitor (C= 2 pF) is added between the vertical walls on each side, as shown in Fig. 1 (a), to tune the MED to the frequency where the structure exhibits maximum Q-factor. The design dimensions are presented in Table I. In this design, the feeding probe is considered as the source/load and the electric and magnetic dipole are the TX/RX resonators.

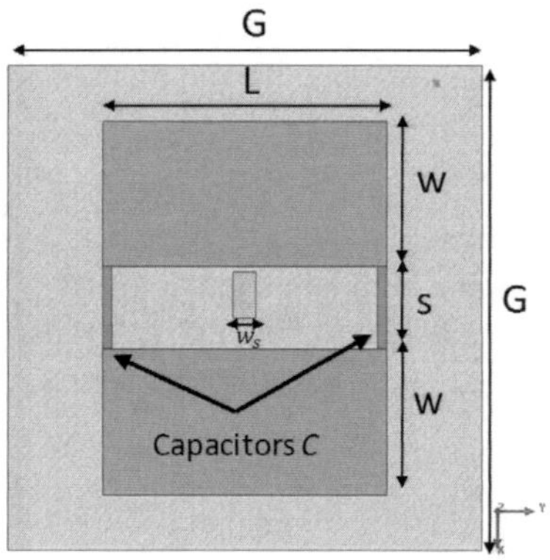

(a)

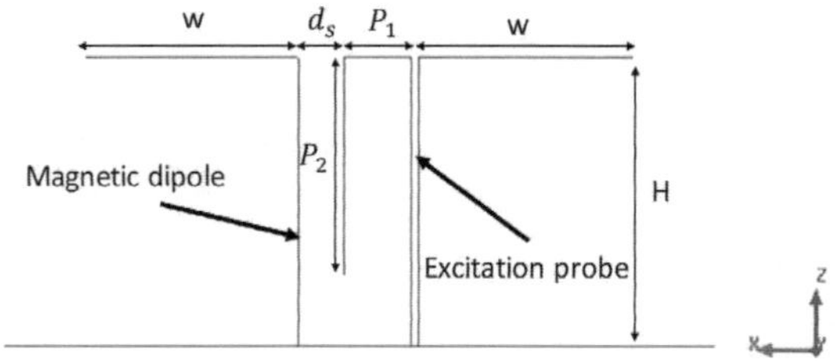

(b)

Fig. 1. MED geometry: (a) Top view and (b) Side view.

TABLE I. Magneto-Electric Dipole Dimensions

Parameter	G	L	W	H	S
Value (mm)	100	60	40	31	17
Parameter	P_1	P_2	Ws	ds	
Value (mm)	8.5	20	4	7	

III. WIRELESS POWER TRANSFER SYSTEM

Two MED's are placed in front of each other and spaced by a distance d=10 mm as shown in Fig. 2. The power transfer efficiency of the MED's system is calculated as follow:

$$\eta = |S_{21}|^2, \tag{1}$$

where η is the power transfer efficiency, including reflection losses. The power transfer efficiency versus frequency is presented in Fig. 3. It can be seen that MED's are able to achieve 0.58 GHz bandwidth from 1.83 to 2.41 GHz (27%), while maintaining a power transfer efficiency above 80%. Also, a maximum efficiency of 97% is obtained at 1.93 and 2.22 GHz.

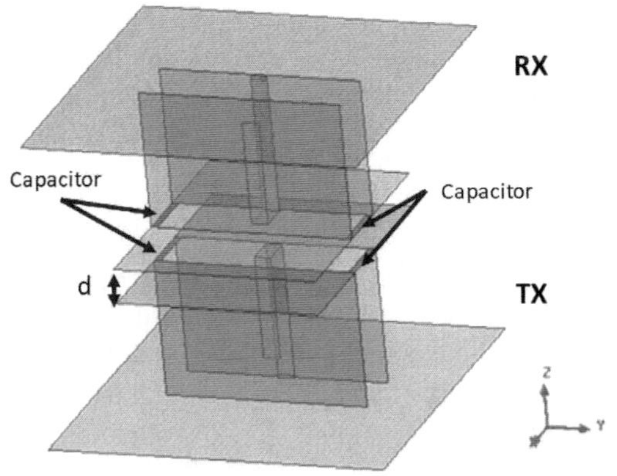

Fig. 2. Geometry of the WPT system using TX and RX MED elements.

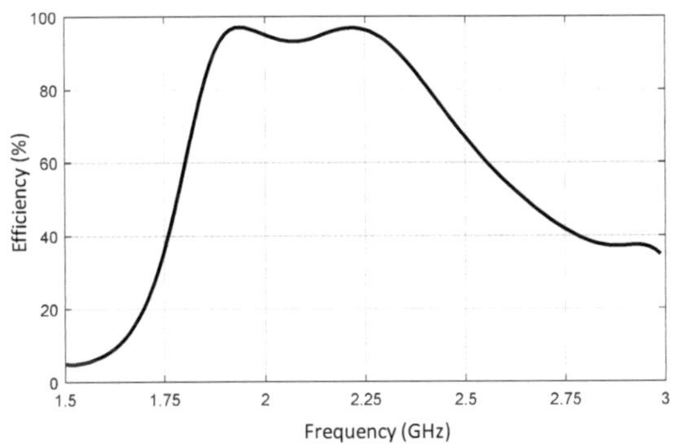

Fig. 3. Power transfer effciency versus frequency.

The power transfer efficiency versus frequency for a distance, d, varying from 10 to 50 mm is presented in Fig. 4. The efficiency is decreased when the distance, d, between the two MEDs is increased. However, the MED-based WPT system achieves an efficiency higher than 60% for a range up to 30 mm (0.2λ) at 1.96 GHz.

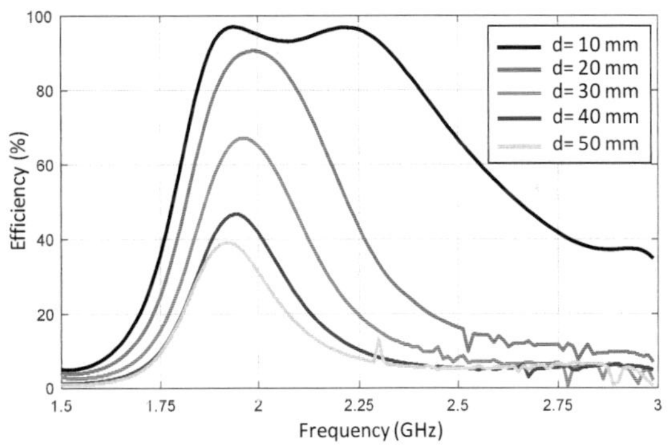

Fig. 4. Power transfer efficiency versus frequency for a distance d varying from 10 to 50 mm.

IV. CONCLUSION

In this paper we presented a new concept for wireless power transfer using magneto-electric dipoles. The obtained results show an excellent power transfer efficiency about 97%. This wireless power transfer system is able to achieve 0.58 GHz bandwidth from 1.83 to 2.41 GHz (27%), while maintaining a power transfer efficiency above 80%.

ACKNOWLEDGMENT

This research was supported by the Air Force Office of Scientific Research under grant FA9550-16-1-0145.

REFERENCES

[1] A. Bin Junaid, Y. Lee and Y. Kim, "Design and implementation of autonomous wireless charging station for rotary-wing UAVs," Aerosp. Sci. Technol., vol. 54 (2016), pp. 253-266, Jul. 2016.

[2] G. Wang, W. Liu, M. Sivaprakasam, M. Zhou, J. D. Weiland, and M. S. Humayun, "A Dual Band Wireless Power and Data Telemetry for Retinal Prosthesis," 28th EMBS Annual International Conference, New York, Aug. 2006.

[3] S. Xu, et al., "Soft microfluidic assemblies of sensors, circuits, and radios for the skin," Science, pp. 70-74, Apr. 4, 2014.

[4] A. Kurs, A. Karalis, R. Moffatt, J. D. Joannopoulos, P. Fisher, and M. Soljacic, "Wireless energy transfer via strongly coupled magnetic resonances," Science, vol. 317, pp. 83-85, 2007.

[5] K. M. Luk and H. Wong, "A new wideband unidirectional antenna element," Int. J. Microw. Opt. Technol., vol. 1, no. 1, pp. 35–44, Jun. 2006.

[6] A. S. Kaddour, S. Bories, A. Clemente, A. Bellion, and C. Delaveaud, "Radiation modes investigation of Huygens source type antenna using spherical wave expansion," in Proc. IEEE Int. Symp. Antennas Propag. (ISAP), Okinawa, Japan, Oct. 2016, pp. 664-665.

Recent Advances in Wireless Systems for Simultaneous Power and Data Transfer

Mahmoud Sharafi Masouleh
Department of Electrical and Computer Engineering, Florida International University
Miami, USA
mshar052@fiu.edu

Abdul-Sattar Kaddour
Department of Electrical and Computer Engineering, Florida International University
Miami, USA
https://orcid.org/0000-0001-9929-769X

Stavros Georgakopoulos
Department of Electrical and Computer Engineering, Florida International University
Miami, USA
georgako@fiu.edu

***Abstract*— Wireless systems that can simultaneously transmit power and data enable the development of battery-less and wire-free sensing for many important applications. In this work, recent advances on simultaneous Wireless Power Transfer (WPT) and wireless data communication are investigated. Moreover, a comparison of WPT methods based on inductive coupling, resonant inductive coupling, Strongly Coupled Magnetic Resonance (SCMR), and Conformal SCMR (CSCMR) is presented.**

Keywords*— *WPT, SCMR, CSCMR, Communication, Wireless power transfer.

I. INTRODUCTION

Wireless Power Transfer (WPT) in its general definition is the propagation of energy from a power source to a load without the use of interconnecting wires. Wireless transmission is useful in highly constraint environments, where interconnecting wires are difficult or not possible to install and/or harmful, Nicola Tesla demonstrated the potential of WPT using the 'Tesla coil', which was a resonant transformer for which he filed a patent in 1902. In his design, the secondary side of the transformer was excited by resonant inductive coupling. After this invention, many researchers demonstrated the use of WPT for various applications including wearable sensors, biomedical devices and infrastructure monitoring [1].

II. WIRELESS POWER TRANSFER METHODS

WPT can be categorized into two types of methods: near-field and far-field. In general, near-field power transfer methods have higher efficiency (η) in comparison to the far-field ones and that is why most of the WPT applications are using the near-field coupling. Also, most biomedical near-field WPT methods use operating frequencies within the range of 100 kHz to 50 MHz. For other applications, operating frequencies must be selected from available ISM bands [2].

There are three major ways to accomplish near-field WPT: (1) capacitive coupling based on electric fields, (2) inductive coupling based on magnetic fields, and (3) magnetic resonant inductive coupling. WPT by inductive coupling and resonant coupling is the main alternative to power implantable devices [3]. The first reported use of inductive power transfer (IPT) was in the 1960s [4]. In the late 1970s, IPT was used to transfer high levels of power. In the mid-1990s, IPT was successfully commercialized in many applications [5].

Inductive coupling, despite its popularity, suffers from short transmission range and low efficiency. These two factors introduce major limitations to real-life applications. A solution to these limitations is given by the Strongly Coupled Magnetic Resonance (SCMR) method, which provides larger efficiency at longer ranges compared to traditional near-field WPT methods. SCMR achieves high efficiency under the condition that the transmitting (TX) and receiving (RX) elements (typically loops or coils) are designed so that they resonate at the frequency where the elements naturally exhibit maximum Q-factor [6]. A disadvantage of conventional SCMR systems is that they are highly sensitive to the alignment between transmitter and receiver. The Conformal SCMR (CSCMR) method, which has a source/load loop that is concentric and coplanar with the TX/RX resonator, was studied in [7]. Therefore, CSCMR systems are easier to implement for small devices as they occupy a very small volume. Even though this system is a very good candidate for wireless power transfer when it comes to data transmission it suffers by its narrow operational bandwidth. To address this issue, Georgakopoulos *et al.*, proposed in [8] a broadband CSCMR. Therefore, broadband CSCMR systems are suitable for applications that require wide bandwidth for transmitting high data rate together with power.

III. SIMULTANEOUS WIRELESS POWER AND DATA TRANSMISSION

The simultaneous transfer of data along with power is an attractive feature to cable-free and battery-less systems, as it allows for diagnostics and sensing capabilities. This is a common practice in wearable or biosensing applications as it is desirable for sensors to be battery-less and cable-free and simultaneously transmit and receive essential data for further processing [9]. Various wireless systems have been proposed that combine power and data. Such systems can be classified into two main groups:

1) Systems that transmit power and data through separate channels. Such systems have to use separate TX/RX circuits for transmitting power and data. at significantly different frequencies, e.g., 2.4 GHz [10] or to introduce an independent second inductive coil system at a different (higher) frequency, e.g., 100 MHz in [9]. Operating at a different frequency or at higher frequency might enable transmitting high-speed data through a larger band, but they have increased complexity [11].

2) Systems that transmit power and data through the same wireless link [11]. Such systems have simpler TX/RX circuits than the first group and utilize LSK (i.e., backscattering modulation) to combine power and data transmission [12].

However, achieving high-speed data transfer on WPT links has proven to be challenging, especially in maintaining high WPT efficiency. So in order to obtain a system which is able to satisfy both mentioned requirements, broadband and highly efficient resonators are needed. The challenge for high-speed data rates comes from the fact that transmission bandwidth is inversely proportional to the quality factor Q of

This work was supported by the Air Force Office of Scientific Research under grant FA9550-16-1-0145.

the power transfer system, which needs to be high in order to maintain high power efficiency.

The selection of the appropriate system depends on the requirements of each application in terms or power, data rate, complexity, and range.

Different modulation schemes such as amplitude, frequency and phase modulation can be used in systems that provide simultaneous wireless transmission of power and data. Amplitude Shift Keying (ASK) or Amplitude Modulation (AM) schemes are the most common and they are based on modulating the amplitude of the carrier signal. Load shift keying (LSK) or load modulation (LM) schemes as a type of (AM) have advantages in terms of power consumption and hardware complexity. However, these schemes cannot support high data rates [13]. FSK and Frequency Modulation (FM) schemes modulate the frequency of the carrier signal. In addition, Phase Shift Key (PSK) or phase modulation schemes modulate the phase of the carrier signal [14].

A strategy for combining wireless power and data communication was suggested in [15], where an analog signal was converted to a series of pulses with varying inter-pulse intervals using a sigma-delta (Σ-Δ) converter. In [16], a system that transmits both power and data through the same link was proposed. This system operated at 13.56 MHz and was capable of supporting a data rate of 3.39 Mbps using QAM modulation with an efficiency reduction of only less than 2 present of overall efficiency. In addition, [17] presented useful information (i.e., relationships between TX/RX distance, data rate, and crosstalk) about PM systems using a near-field magnetic coupling. A system that transmitted power and data transmission via a single inductive link was proposed in [18], which used Passive Phase Shift Keying (PPSK). Cyclic On-Off Keying (COOK) as a means of modulation was suggested in [19], which proposed a platform that can simultaneously support highly-efficient power transfer and high-rate communication with a small loss. The COOK, LSK and PPSK schemes provide similar performance. However, the COOK scheme closes the switch only during a single cycle when the voltage of the secondary coil is zero and the current is at its peak to synchronize the received signal. This synchronized on/off keying does not have a negative effect on resonance. Unlike the multi-carrier schemes, single-carrier schemes experience additional power loss and disruption of the resonance of the WPT elements, which are both caused by the discontinuous power transfer. Also, systems that transmit both power and data face trade-offs between power efficiency and data-rate [20].

IV. Conclusion

In this paper, a review of recent advances in systems that simultaneously transmit power and data is presented. In addition, important challenges are identified and discussed.

References

[1] T. Perera, et al., "Simultaneous Wireless Information and Power Transfer (SWIPT): Recent Advances and Future Challenges", IEEE Commun. Surveys Tuts., vol. 20, no. 1, pp. 264-302, 2018.

[2] H.-J. Kim, et al., "Review of near-field wireless power and communication for biomedical applications," IEEE Access, vol. 5, pp. 21264–21285, 2017.

[3] L. Baby and S. S. Banu, "A survey on wire-free power transmission in biomedical implants, " International Journal of Advanced Research in Electrical Electronics and Instrumentation Engineering, vol. 5, no. 5, pp. 3543–3546, 2016.

[4] J. C. Schuder, "Powering an artificial heart: the birth of the inductively coupled-radio frequency system in 1960," Artificial Organs, vol. 26, no. 11, pp. 909–915, 2002.

[5] J. Dai and D. C. Ludois, "A survey of wireless power transfer and a critical comparison of inductive and capacitive coupling for small gap applications," IEEE Transactions on Power Electronics, vol. 30, no. 11, pp. 6017–6029, 2015.

[6] X. Wei, Z. Wang, and H. Dai, "A critical review of wireless power transfer via strongly coupled magnetic resonances," Energies, vol. 7, no. 7, pp. 4316–4341, Jul. 2014.

[7] O. Jonah, S. V. Georgakopoulos, and M. M. Tentzeris, "Strongly coupled wireless power transfer with conformal structures," in Proc. 29th Annu. Rev. Progress Appl. Comput. Electromagn., Monterey, CA, USA, Mar. 24–28, 2013.

[8] H. Hu and S. V. Georgakopoulos, "Multiband and broadband wireless power transfer systems using the conformal strongly coupled magnetic resonance method," IEEE Trans. Ind. Electron., vol. 64, no. 5, pp, 3595-3607, May 2017.

[9] A. Rush and P. Troyk, "A power and data link for a wireless-implanted neural recording system," IEEE Trans. Biomed. Eng., vol. 59, no. 11, pp. 3255–3262, Nov. 2012.

[10] A. P. Sample, B. H. Waters, S. T. Wisdom, and J. R. Smith, "Enabling seamless wireless power delivery in dynamic environments," Proc. IEEE, vol. 101, no. 6, pp. 1343–1358, Jun. 2013.

[11] G. Yilmaz and C. Dehollain, "Wireless Power Transfer and Data Communication for Neural Implants," Springer, 2017, pp. 14–22.

[12] B. Lee and M. Ghovanloo, "An Overview of Data Telemetry in Inductively Powered Implantable Biomedical Devices," IEEE Communications Mag., vol. 57, iss. 2, Feb. 2019.

[13] Q. Ytrehus, "Communication on inductively coupled channels: Overview and challenges," in Coding Theory and Applications (Lecture Notes in Computer Science), vol. 5228, Á. Barbero, Ed., Berlin, Germany: Springer, 2008.

[14] A. Trigui, S. Hached, A. C. Ammari, Y. Savaria, and M. Sawan, "Maximizing Data Transmission Rate for Implantable Devices Over a Single Inductive Link: Methodological Review," IEEE Review in Biomedical Engineering, vol. 12, pp. 72-87, 2019.

[15] S. Mao, H. Wang, C. Zhu, Z.-H. Mao, and M. Sun, "Simultaneous wireless power transfer and data communication using synchronous pulse-controlled load modulation Measurement," 109 (2017), pp. 316-325.

[16] J. Besnoff, M. Abbasi, and D. S. Ricketts, "Ultrahigh-data-rate communication and efficient wireless power transfer at 13.56 MHz," IEEE Antennas Wireless Propag. Lett., vol. 16, pp. 2634–2637, 2017.

[17] D. Cirmirakis, D. Jiang, A. Demosthenous, N. Donaldson, and T. Perkins, "A fast passive phase shift keying modulator for inductively coupled implanted medical devices," in Proc. Eur. Solid-State Circuits Conf., Sep. 2012, pp. 301–304.

[18] S. Ha, C. Kim, J. Park, S. Joshi, and G. Cauwenberghs, "Energy recycling telemetry IC with simultaneous 11.5 mW power and 6.78 Mb/s backward data delivery over a single 13.56 MHz inductive link," IEEE J. Solid-State Circuits, vol. 51, no. 11, pp. 2664–2678, Nov. 2016.

[19] C.-C. Cheng, M. Di Renzo, F. Graziosi, and A. Zappone, "On Simultaneous Wireless Information and Power Transfer for Receive Spatial Modulation," Access IEEE, vol. 5, pp. 23204-23211, 2017.

[20] J. Besnoff, M. Abbasi, and D. Ricketts, "High data-rate communication in near-field RFID and wireless power using higher order modulation," IEEE Trans. Microw. Theory Techn., vol. 64, no. 2, pp. 401–413, Feb. 2016.

Properties of the Conformal CSCMR System

Stavros V. Georgakopoulos and Constantinos L. Zekios
Department of Electrical and Computer Engineering
Florida International University
Miami, US
georgako@fiu.edu

***Abstract*—In this paper, the evolution of Conformal Strongly Coupled Magnetic Resonance (CSCMR) systems is presented. Such systems are highly efficient and misalignment insensitive. The design and miniaturization of these systems is presented here. The performance of CSCMR systems is validated using simulations and measurements.**

***Keywords*—wireless power transfer system, WPT, misalignment insensitive, broadband**

I. Introduction

Various WPT techniques have been developed based either on far-field, [1], or near field coupling [2]. The far field methods are primarily used for RFID applications where the transmitted power is on the order of $10-30\ \mu W$, [3]. For the case of near field coupling there are two methods that are extensively used: i) the inductive coupling, which has been applied to electric vehicles [4], implanted medical devices [5], and mobile devices [6] and ii) the Strongly Coupled Magnetic Resonance (SCMR) method, which has been used in a variety of applications, such as structural health monitoring sensors embedded in concrete [7]. Even though inductive coupling is the most popular, it suffers from short transmission range and low efficiency, two factors that introduce major limitations in real-life applications. On the contrary, the SCMR method provides larger efficiency at longer ranges, compared to the traditional near-field WPT methods, [8]-[10]. In this paper the authors present the evolution of the conventional SCMR to the Conformal SCMR (CSCMR) systems. The CSCMR systems are highly efficient, compact and misalignment insensitive.

II. Conformal SCMR

The conventional SCMR system is formed by four elements, such as, a source loop, a load loop, and two resonators (one at TX and one RX), each consisting of a single loop and a lumped capacitor. A certain distance is required between the source and the TX resonator as well as between the load and the RX resonator. Depending on the dimension of each element, the distance can be relatively large (around half of the largest dimension of the resonators). Therefore, the traditional three-dimensional structures of SCMR systems occupy significant volume and they cannot be easily printed on substrates and incorporated in modern communications systems and implantable medical devices. In [11], the conformal SCMR (CSCMR) system was proposed, where both the source and the TX resonator (likewise the load and the RX resonator), are placed on the same plane. With this approach the design significantly reduces its size as shown in Fig. 1.

This research was supported by the Air Force Office of Scientific Research under grant FA9550-16-1-0145.

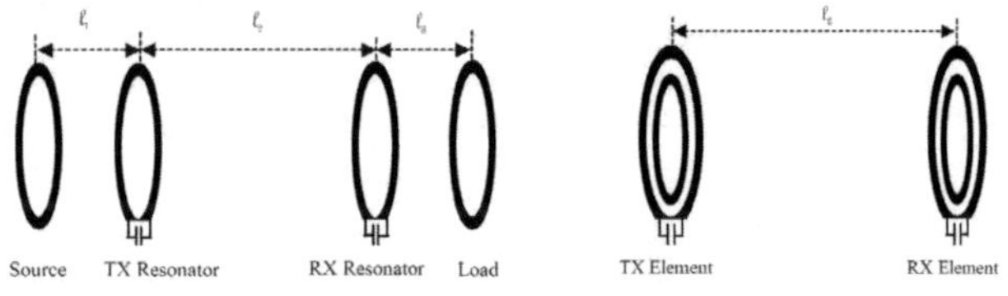

Fig. 1. Schematic of (a) traditional SCMR and (b) CSCMR system.

For the resonator elements a series capacitor is included, as shown in Fig. 1 and its value is appropriately calculated as:

$$C = \frac{1}{4\pi^2 f_r^2 L} \tag{1}$$

where the inductance, L, corresponds to the equivalent self-inductance of the resonator loops. The resonant frequency of the SCMR system is calculated as:

$$f_r = \frac{1}{2\pi\sqrt{LC}} \tag{2}$$

In order to achieve high power transfer efficiency, the TX and RX resonators should be designed at the frequency where the resonators exhibit maximum Q-factor. Choosing an operational frequency for demonstration purposes of $160\ MHz$ using (1) a proper capacitor of $15\ pF$ is chosen. Using a one-sided copper FR-4 substrate ($\epsilon_r = 4$) with copper thickness of $0.035\ mm$ and thickness of $1.5\ mm$ a 50% measured efficiency is reported as shown in Fig. 2, [17].

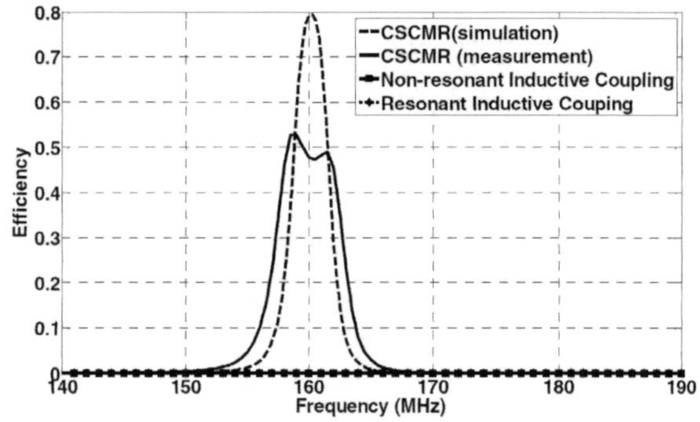

Fig. 2. Measured and simulated results of a CSCMR system, [17].

The disagreement between the measured and simulated results for the CSCMR case is due to the finite Q-factor of the lumped capacitor and the connector losses, which were not considered in the simulation, as they were both modeled as lossless.

III. Misalignment Performance of CSCMR

An important consideration for practical WPT systems is the misalignment between TX and RX. Here, azimuthal angular misalignment is considered for both standard SCMR systems and CSCMR systems. For this misalignment, the RX system (RX resonator and load element) rotates from 0° to 90°, while the TX system (TX resonator and source element) is fixed [13]-[15]. Fig. 3 shows a standard SCMR and a CSCMR system at three different cases of azimuth angular misalignment. The measured efficiency of the SCMR system rapidly decreases as the azimuthal angular misalignment angle increases. On the other hand the measured efficiency of the CSCMR system, for different angles of azimuthal misalignment, remains high and approximately constant up to 70° of azimuthal angular misalignment [14]-[15].

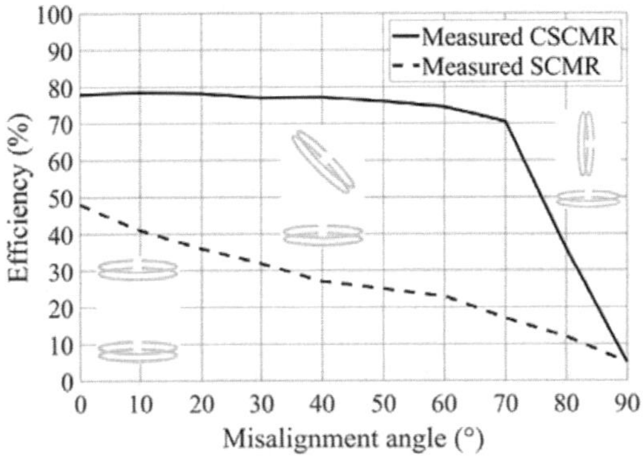

Fig. 3. Measured and simulated results of a CSCMR system.

IV. Miniaturized CSCMR Systems

Low frequency (i.e., 10-100 MHz) CSCMR systems are needed for numerous applications, such as, charging and wireless powering of mobile or medical devices. The traditional method of decreasing the operational frequency of CSCMR systems is to increase their size. However, when the size of CSMR systems increases this makes their implementation in practical systems (e.g., portable, wearable or implantable devices) very difficult and sometimes impractical. A new method of decreasing the frequency of operation of CSCMR systems, while maintaining the same footprint area and only slightly increasing their volume was recently proposed from the authors, [16], where multilayer resonators TX and RX elements are used. This method is equivalent to a miniaturization method for CSCMR systems, since as the frequency of operation decreases, the wavelength increases thereby making the electrical size of the TX and RX significantly smaller. Fig. 4 shows the geometry of a multilayer CSCMR TX or RX element. This geometry is developed by adding multiple identical resonators at multiple layers below the top layer of standard CSCMR TX or RX elements. These multilayer TX and RX elements can be manufactured using multilayer PCBs. All the resonator loops at the different layers are connected in parallel using two vias, as shown in Fig. 4, while a lumped capacitor is connected to the resonator on layer 1. The source loop in the TX element (as well as load loop in the RX element) is located in layer 1. Simulation and measurement results for these miniaturized designs will be presented at the conference.

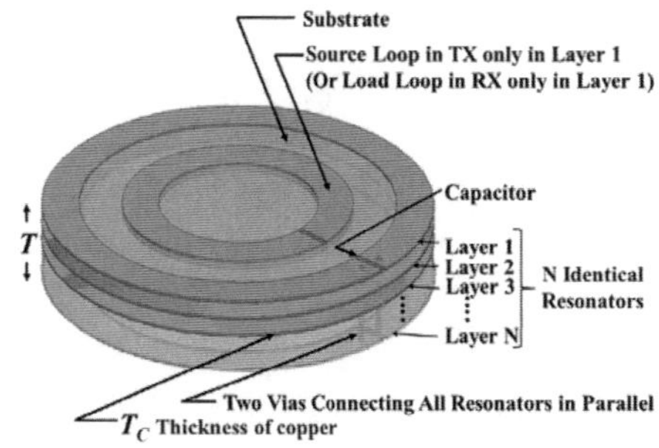

Fig. 4. Geometry of the TX and RX elements of multilayer CSCMR systems

References

[1] W. Brown, "The history of power transmission by radio waves," *IEEE Trans. Microw. Theory Tech.*, vol. MTT-32, no. 9, pp. 1230–1242, Sept. 1984.

[2] Y. Jang and M. M. Jovanovic, "A contactless electrical energy transmission system for portable-telephone battery chargers," *IEEE Trans. Ind. Electron.*, vol. 50, no. 3, pp. 520–527, Jun. 2003

[3] Alien Technology, "HiggsTM – 3 SOT," Higgs 3 datasheet, 2017

[4] J. Lee and B. Han, "A bidirectional wireless power transfer EV charger using self-resonant PWM", IEEE Trans. Power Electron., vol. 30, no.4, pp. 1784-1787, Apr. 2015

[5] D. Ahn and S. Hong, "Wireless power transmission with the self-regulated output voltage for the biomedical implant", IEEE Trans. Ind. Electron., vol. 61, no. 5, pp. 2225-2235, May 2014.

[6] K. Chang-Gyun, S. Dong-Hyun, Y. Jung-Sik, P. Jong-Hu, and B. H. Cho, "Design of a contactless battery charger for the cellular phone", IEEE Trans. Ind. Electron., vol. 48, no. 6, pp. 1238–1247, Dec. 2001

[7] O. Jonah and S. V. Georgakopoulos, "Wireless Power Transfer in Concrete via Strongly Coupled Magnetic Resonance", IEEE Trans. Antennas Propag., vol. 61, no. 3, pp. 1378-1384, March 2013

[8] A. Kurs, A. Karalis, R. Moffatt, J. D. Joannopoulos, P. Fisher, and M. Soljacic, "Wireless energy transfer via strongly coupled magnetic resonances", Science, vol. 317, pp. 83-85, 2007

[9] A. Karalis, J. D. Joannopoulos, and M. Soljacic, "Efficient wireless non-radiative mid-range energy transfer", Annals of Physics, vol. 323, pp. 34–48, Jan. 2008

[10] B. L. Cannon, J. F. Hoburg, D. D. Stancil, and S. C. Goldstein, "Magnetic resonant coupling as a potential means for wireless power transfer to multiple small receivers", IEEE Trans. Power Electron., vol. 24, no.7, pp. 1819-1825, Jul. 2009

[11] F. Hadley, "MIT demos wireless power transmission". Techtalk Serving the MIT Community, vol.51, no. 30, June. 2007

[12] H. Hu, K. Bao, J. Gibson, and S. V. Georgakopoulos, "Printable and Conformal Strongly Coupled Magnetic Resonant systems for wireless powering," Conference: 2014 IEEE 15th Annual IEEE Wireless and Microwave Technology Conference (WAMICON).

[13] O. Jonah, S. V. Georgakopoulos, D. Daerhan and S. Yao, "Misalignment-insensitive wireless power transfer via strongly coupled magnetic resonance principles," in 2014 IEEE Antennas and Propagation Society International Symposium (APSURSI), Memphis, TN, USA, July 2014.

[14] D. Liu, H. Hu and S. V. Georgakopoulos, "Misalignment Sensitivity of Strongly Coupled Wireless Power Transfer Systems," IEEE Transactions on Power Electronics, vol. 32, no. 7, pp. 5509-5519, 2017.

[15] D. Liu and S. V. Georgakopoulos, "Cylindrical Misalignment Insensitive Wireless Power Transfer Systems," IEEE Transactions on Power Electronics, vol. 33, no. 11, pp. 9331-9343, 2018

[16] H. Hu, K. Bao and S. V. Georgakopoulos, "Miniaturized wireless power transfer systems using 3-D strongly coupled magnetic resonance," 2017 IEEE International Symposium on Antennas and Propagation & USNC/URSI National Radio Science Meeting, San Diego, CA, 2017, pp. 1299-1300.

Inverse Design of Three-Dimensional Nanoantennas for Metasurface Applications

Danny Z. Zhu
Department of Electrical Engineering and Computer Science
United States Military Academy at West Point
West Point, NY 10996, USA
danny.zhu@usma.edu

Eric B. Whiting, Sawyer D. Campbell, Pingjuan L. Werner, and Douglas H. Werner
Department of Electrical Engineering
The Pennsylvania State University
University Park, PA 16802, USA
ebw15@psu.edu, sdc22@psu.edu, plw7@psu.edu, dhw@psu.edu

***Abstract*—Recent advances in manufacturing techniques have been made to match the demand for high performance optical devices. To this end, tremendous research activity has been focused on optical metasurfaces as they offer a unique potential to achieve disruptive designs when paired with innovative fabrication techniques and inverse design tools. However, most metasurface designs have revolved around canonical geometries. While these elements are relatively easy to fabricate, they represent only a small portion of the design space, and rarely offer peak performance in transmission, phase range or field of view. In this work, a Lazy Ant Colony Optimization (LACO) technique is applied in conjunction with a full-wave solver using the Periodic Finite Element Boundary Integral (PFEBI) method to reveal high performing three-dimensional nanoantenna designs with potential applications for a variety of optical devices.**

Keywords—three-dimensional nanoantenna, lazy ant colony optimization, metasurface

I. INTRODUCTION

Phase-gradient metasurfaces are desirable for their low profile and ability to abruptly and anomalously refract light [1]. These metasurfaces typically consist of periodic arrays of sub-wavelength unit cells, which leverage the generalized Snell's law to introduce a spatial variation in phase distribution to shape the desired optical wavefront. So far, a large portion of work in this area has revolved around canonical unit cell geometries (*i.e.* patches, strips, split-ring resonators or angled and loaded dipoles) manufactured using conventional fabrication techniques [1]. Although these unit cell geometries are relatively simple to simulate, analyze and fabricate, they represent only a small portion of the design space. As the demand for high performance optics is matched by advances in manufacturing, access to new unexplored three-dimensional design spaces can be exploited. Instead of relying on canonical structures, stochastic combinatorial optimization techniques such as the Multi-Objective Lazy Ant Colony Optimization (MOLACO) algorithm [2] have previously been introduced as an effective method to discover high performance periodic structures in the microwave regime. Unlike the traditional Genetic Algorithm (GA), MOLACO inherently enforces contiguity in its components, making the approach more amenable for three-dimensional fabrication techniques. This approach was first used to optimize multi-band three-dimensional frequency selective structures (which are closely related to metasurfaces) with polarization independent performance over extreme fields of view (up to 80° with respect to the optical axis). A proof of concept was fabricated via additive manufacturing and silver plating, then characterized with a broadband focused beam measurement system [3]. Although dispersion and plasmonic behaviors are negligible at these frequencies, a similar approach can also be applied to discover high performance optical designs [4] for advanced three-dimensional nanofabrication techniques [5].

II. LAZY ANT COLONY OPTIMIZATION

The original Ant System (AS) [6] is a stochastic combinatorial optimization technique which relies on an indirect communication mechanism between ants known as stigmergy. As ants forage for food, they modify their local environment by depositing pheromones along their traveled path. These pheromones influence future ants' decisions on which path to choose, and each path can be interpreted as geometry of a unit cell design. This behavior can be mathematically modeled with some probability that is proportional to the pheromone concentrations. Thus, the probability that an ant would select a path j that is locally accessible in the ith ant's neighborhood N_i at iteration k is dependent on the pheromone concentration associated with that particular direction, τ_j, and is given by:

$$p_{ij} = \frac{\tau_j(k)}{\sum_{j \in N_i} \tau_j(k)} \qquad (1)$$

Pheromones are directly proportional to the quality or fitness of the solution and over time, gradually evaporate at a user-defined rate to balance exploration and exploitation. To further balance this, the Max-Min Ant System (MMAS) introduced in [7] limits the pheromone concentration associated with each path,

Financial support for this work was provided by the DARPA Extreme Optics and Imaging (EXTREME) program under contract HR00111720032.

guaranteeing a non-zero chance of exploring new paths. However, despite the vast number of improvements to the original AS, one underlying assumption remained consistent throughout its many derivatives—that ants travel *indefinitely* throughout the pre-defined design space. Although this is useful for space-filling designs, it offers little value to inverse design of nanoantennas in three-dimensional space. Unlike its predecessors, LACO includes a probability of termination, modeled as an imaginary pheromone concentration which acts like a fatigue factor—the greater the fatigue, the less likely the ant continues traveling:

$$\tau_{imag} = \left({}^{l}/_{L} \right)^{EF} e^{v} \tag{2}$$

where l represents the current number of segments traveled out of L total segments possible, while EF and v are parameters chosen to manipulate the rate of fatigue, and therefore the termination behavior of the ant. As a result, a wide variety of unique and unintuitive design geometries can be discovered, and their performance evaluated.

III. Nanoantenna Optimization

In this study, the inverse design of three-dimensional nanoantennas was performed across four high power computing nodes. Each computer represents a colony with 768 ants operating in parallel across 24 cores over 100 iterations for a total of 161 hours. Nanoantenna designs are optimized based on maximum co-polarized transmission and minimal phase deviation of s-polarized light for various incidence angles at a wavelength of $\lambda_0 = 5.5$ µm, using the following fitness function:

$$T_{fit} = \frac{\min(T_{SS})}{1+\Delta T_{SS}} - \Psi_{correct} \tag{3}$$

where angle independence is assumed, while ΔT_{ss} and $\Psi_{correct}$ represent the maximum deviations of the transmission magnitude and phase angle respectively. Each unit cell is evaluated using a custom full-wave solver that applies the PFEBI method to solve for complex transmission of s-polarized light. By optimizing transmission while simultaneously accounting for phase information to sort results, it is possible to canvas a wide range of designs with high transmission, a variety of phase options and enhanced fields of view in a single procedure. Individual elements can then be manually selected for a particular metasurface application, based on the specific transmission magnitude or phase contribution required. Similarly, reflective metasurface applications can also be discovered by evaluating reflection in place of transmission.

IV. Conclusion

Although canonical structures are fundamental in developing a physical understanding of the behavior of metasurface elements, the increasing demand for high performance optics cannot be met alone with canonical structures and traditional fabrication techniques. Alternatively, advanced manufacturing techniques that leverage three-dimensional design spaces can be employed to discover new, unintuitive nanoantenna structures. In particular, this work applies a LACO algorithm with a full-wave PFEBI solver to discover high performing three-dimensional nanoantennas for advanced optical applications.

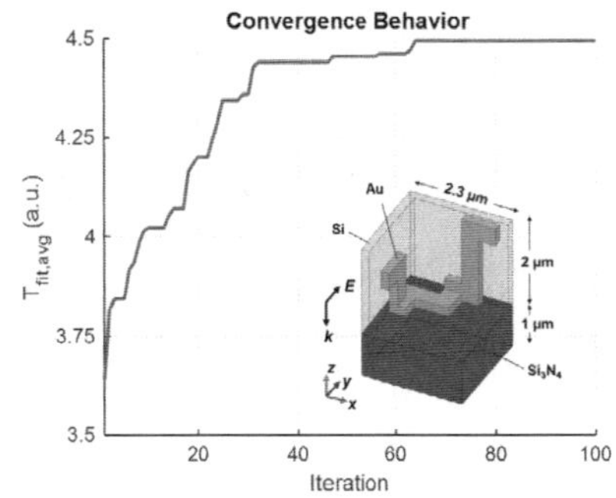

Fig. 1. Convergence behavior of MOLACO with an example unit cell (inset), where an individual ant represents the enclosed gold (Au) trace.

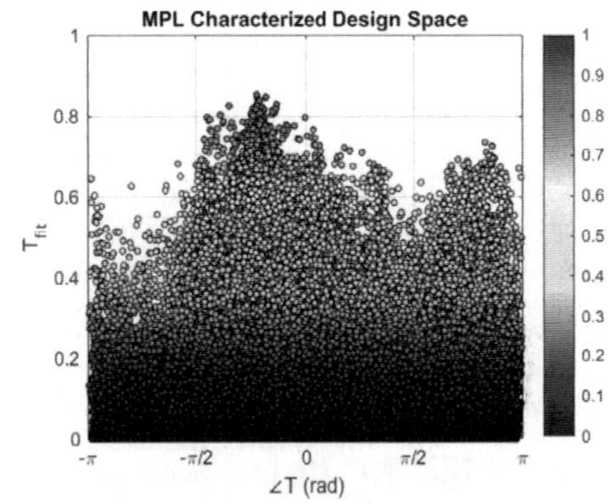

Fig. 2. Archive of designs discovered using LACO.

Acknowledgment

The opinions in this work are solely of the authors and do not necessarily reflect those of the U.S. Military Academy, the U.S. Army, or the Department of Defense.

References

[1] N. Yu, and F. Capasso, "Flat optics with designer metasurfaces," Nature Mater., vol. 13, pp. 139-150, Jan. 2014.

[2] D. Z. Zhu, P. L. Werner, and D. H. Werner, "Design and optimization of 3-D frequency selective surfaces based on a multiobjective lazy ant colony optimization algorithm," IEEE Trans. Antennas Propag., vol. 65, no. 12, pp. 7137-7149, Dec. 2017.

[3] D. Z. Zhu, M. D. Gregory, P. L. Werner, and D. H. Werner, "Fabrication and characterization of multiband polarization independent 3-D-printed frequency selective structures with ultra wide fields of view," IEEE Trans. Antennas Propag., vol. 66, no. 11, pp. 6096-6105, Nov. 2018.

[4] S. D. Campbell, D. Z. Zhu, J. Nagar, R. P. Jenkins, J. A. Easum, D. H. Werner, and P. L. Werner, "Inverse design of engineered materials for extreme optical devices," in Proc. 2019 ACES.

[5] C. M. Soukoulis, and M. Wegener, "Past achievements and future challenges in the development of three-dimensional photonic metamaterials," Nature Photonics, vol. 5, pp. 523-530, Jul. 2011.

[6] M. Dorigo, V. Maniezzo, and A. Colorni, "Ant system: Optimization by a colony of cooperating agents," IEEE Trans. Syst., Man, Cybern., vol. 26, no. 1, pp. 29-41, Feb. 1996.

[7] T. Stützle, and H. H. Hoos, "MAX-MIN ant system," Future Generation Computer Sytems, vol. 16, pp. 889-914, Jun. 2000.

High-performance metasurfaces synthesized via multi-objective optimization

Sawyer D. Campbell, Eric B. Whiting, Douglas H. Werner, and Pingjuan L. Werner
Department of Electrical Engineering
The Pennsylvania State University
University Park, PA 16802, USA
sdc22@psu.edu, ebw15@psu.edu, dhw@psu.edu, plw7@psu.edu

***Abstract*—Metasurfaces show extreme promise for realizing disruptive optical devices due to their ability to tailor reflection and transmission properties at a surface by exploiting the generalized form of Snell's law. Moreover, polarization-, angular- and frequency-dependent performances can also be engineered to achieve dispersive behaviors desired for a particular application. However, how one designs a metasurface that achieves high performances in several of these areas simultaneously is generally not clear. Therefore, synthesizing high-performance metasurfaces requires employing powerful optimization techniques in the inverse design process. To this end, state-of-the-art multi-objective optimization algorithms offer the potential to realize metasurfaces that meet multiple design goals while also presenting the tradeoffs between competing objectives.**

Keywords—nanoantennas; optimization; inverse-design; metasurfaces; metamaterials.

I. Introduction

Synthesizing high-performance optical devices is a challenging problem when there are many design constraints and multiple performance goals. The formal inverse design process for finding a device that satisfies a set of performance requirements given a set of design constrains is known as "system-by-design" (SBD) [1]. Optimization algorithms are commonly employed in SBD to efficiently find designs that minimize a COST function that mathematically describes the performance surface of the problem. Interestingly, the type of problem under consideration often dictates the proper optimization algorithm that should be used. For example, lens design software packages ubiquitously employ the Damped Least Squares (DLS) algorithm [2] due to ease of generating gradient information via ray tracing. Meanwhile, metamaterial and metadevice designers often employ global optimization techniques [3]–[5] which can robustly find a problem's true global minimum and optimize without gradient information. Traditionally, these designs are optimized with single-objective algorithms where multiple design goals are combined as a weighted sum into a single cost function. However, the proper choice of weights requires the designer to possess *a priori* knowledge about the problem's solution space which is typically not available, especially when parameter space is hyper-dimensional. On the other hand, multi-objective optimizers [6] enable the simultaneous optimization of multiple design goals with no required *a priori* knowledge. This is crucially important in realizing high-performance engineered materials [7] which can be used as building blocks to design optical metasurfaces. This paper presents a brief introduction to multi-objective optimization and its potential for synthesizing high-performance metasurfaces.

II. Multi-Objective Metasurface Optimization

One important way that multi-objective optimizers (MOO) differ from single-objective optimizers is that they generate a set of solutions called the Pareto Set (see Fig. 1) which can be examined to visualize the tradeoffs that exist between design objectives. These solutions exist on the Pareto Front, *i.e.*, the surface that contains the solutions for which improvements in a single objective must be accompanied by reductions in all others.

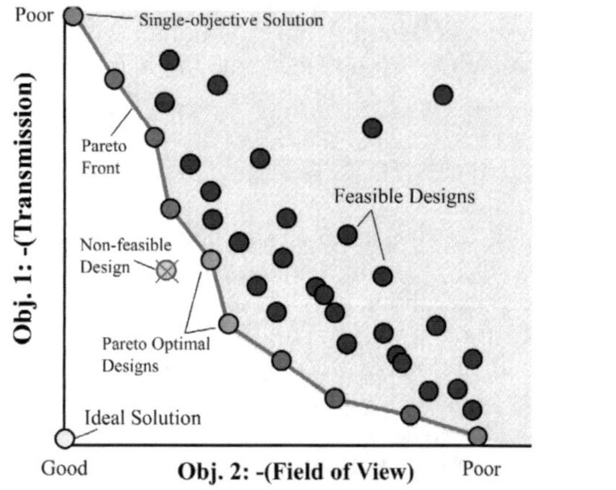

Fig. 1. Visualization of a hypothetical multi-objective optimization problem.

In Fig. 1, all designs to the right of the Pareto Front are considered to be dominated. Designs are dominated when there exist other designs that achieve better performance in all objectives simultaneously. Conversely, there exists no designs to the left of the Pareto Front since those would represent unfeasible designs. Finally, finding a design that achieves the absolute minimum cost in all objectives simultaneously is often impossible and the Pareto Set allows engineers to choose a solution based on the actual tradeoffs present in the system.

Multi-objective optimization is well suited for optical metasurface synthesis. Metasurfaces show extreme promise for realizing disruptive optical devices [8] due to their ability to tailor reflection and transmission behaviors at a surface by

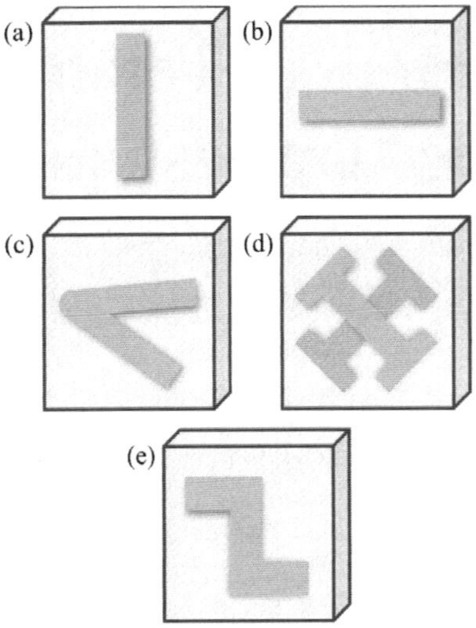

Fig. 2. Example nanoantenna configurations: (a) vertical dipole, (b) horizontal dipole, (c) "v" antenna, (d) crossed end-loaded dipole, (e) "z" antenna.

exploiting the generalized form of Snell's law [9]. Optical metasurfaces are usually constructed with aperiodic arrangements of nanoantennas that have been designed to achieve a desired performance. Nanoantenna performance goals may include frequency bandwidth, field-of-view, co- and/or cross-polarization transmission or reflection phase and magnitude. Consider the nanoantenna geometries shown in Fig. 2. While each geometry is described by a few simple parameters that can be tuned to tailor their reflection and transmission phase and magnitude behaviors, each possesses differing levels of performance in one or more of the goals discussed above. Furthermore, some configurations can be varied enough to cover a full 2π phase range which can be used to synthesize a phase-gradient metasurface for beam-steering applications (see Fig. 3). However, designs that meet the requisite phase options are often found with varying levels of transmission magnitude (see Fig. 3) which can lead to performance degradations when paired together to form a metadevice. To this end, multi-objective optimization is perfectly-suited to synthesize metasurfaces that achieve high performance in all design goals.

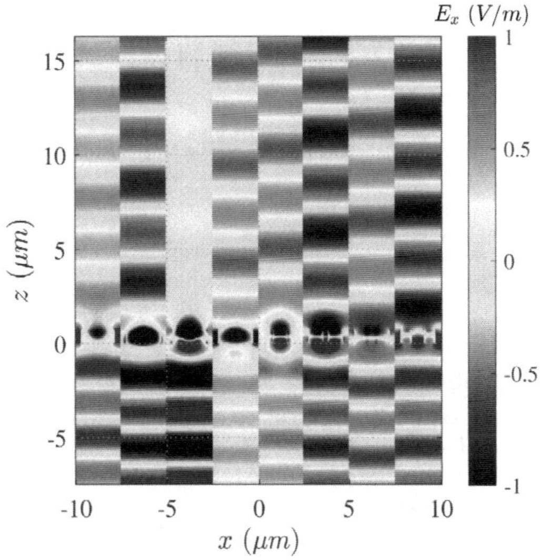

Fig. 3. Side view of the electric field behavior in the vicinity of eight nanoantennas each of which are simulated in doubly-infinitely periodic configurations. The field plots are stitched together to show how staggering the phase across the nanoantennas can lead to beam steering. Note that while the phase options are optimal and uniformly space, the transmission magnitudes are unequal.

III. Futrue Work

There exists a number of multi-objective optimization algorithms with which to design high-performance metasurfaces. The Multi-Objective Optimization with TOLerance (MOTOL) algorithm can optimize designs with robustness as an explicit objective [11] while the Multi-Objective Lazy Ant Colony (MOLACO) algorithm [12] can synthesize contiguous three-dimensional structures which can be paired with state-of-the-art additive manufacturing techniques. Finally, MOO algorithms can be employed to design multi-functional and reconfigurable metasurfaces which are of interest to the optical and RF communities.

Acknowledgments

The authors acknowledge the financial support provided by the DARPA Extreme Optics and Imaging (EXTREME) program under contract number HR00111720032.

References

[1] A. Massa, G. Oliveri, P. Rocca, and F. Viani, "System-by-design: A new paradigm for handling design complexity," in *The 8th European Conference on Antennas and Propagation (EuCAP 2014)*, The Hague, Netherlands, 2014, pp. 1180–1183.

[2] D. W. Marquardt, "An Algorithm for least-squares estimation of nonlinear parameters," *Journal of the Society for Industrial and Applied Mathematics*, vol. 11, no. 2, pp. 431–441, Jun. 1963.

[3] J. H. Holland, "Genetic algorithms," *Scientific American*, vol. 267, no. 1, pp. 66–72, Jul. 1992.

[4] J. Kennedy and R. Eberhart, "Particle swarm optimization," in *Proceedings of ICNN'95 - International Conference on Neural Networks*, Perth, WA, Australia, 1995, vol. 4, pp. 1942–1948.

[5] N. Hansen, S. D. Müller, and P. Koumoutsakos, "Reducing the time complexity of the derandomized evolution strategy with covariance matrix adaptation (CMA-ES)," *Evolutionary Computation*, vol. 11, no. 1, pp. 1–18, Mar. 2003.

[6] K. Deb, "Multi-objective optimization," in *Search Methodologies*, Springer US, 2014, pp. 403–449.

[7] S. D. Campbell *et al.*, "Inverse design of engineered materials for extreme optical devices," in *2018 International Applied Computational Electromagnetics Society Symposium (ACES)*, Denver, CO, 2018, pp. 1–2.

[8] J. Nagar, S. D. Campbell, and D. H. Werner, "Apochromatic singlets enabled by metasurface-augmented GRIN lenses," *Optica*, vol. 5, no. 2, pp. 99–102, Feb. 2018.

[9] N. Yu *et al.*, "Light propagation with phase discontinuities: Generalized laws of reflection and refraction," *Science, New Series*, vol. 334, no. 6054, pp. 333–337, 2011.

[10] J. A. Easum, J. Nagar, P. L. Werner, and D. H. Werner, "Efficient multi-objective antenna optimization with tolerance analysis through the use of surrogate models," *IEEE Transactions on Antennas and Propagation*, Dec. 2018.

[11] D. Z. Zhu, P. L. Werner, and D. H. Werner, "Design and optimization of 3-D frequency-selective surfaces based on a multiobjective lazy ant colony optimization algorithm," *IEEE Transactions on Antennas and Propagation*, vol. 65, no. 12, pp. 7137–7149, Dec. 2017.

Multicsale Multiphysics Modeling of Terahertz Emissions from Field Effect Transistors

Shubhendu Bhardwaj
Electrical and Computer Engineering
Florida International University
10555, W. Flagler Street, Miami, USA
sbhardwa@fiu.edu

***Abstract*—In this work, we show that indeed terahertz emissions are possible from a field effect transistors (FETs) under an influence of strong DC bias under cryogenic conditions and asymmetrical boundary conditions. Such emissions have been hypothesized by researchers in the community, by using analytical models and have been subject of much controversy in terahertz electronics field. Here by using finite-difference-time domain (FDTD) and hydrodynamic modeling, we show that such emissions are indeed possible in the high electron mobility transistors (HEMTs). Specifically, multiphysics modeling tools are developed, and simulations are conducted to demonstrate the terahertz emission phenomenology and effect of device parameters.**

Keywords—FDTD, 2D Electron Gas, HEMT, Hydrodynamic, Plasmonic Modeling, Terahertz.

I. INTRODUCTION

As the search for terahertz sources continues, 2D electron-based terahertz devices have been investigated for their potential for terahertz radiation. The channel dimensions and electron carrier concentrations in these devices allow these oscillations to be in the far-infrared/terahertz frequency range. As a result, field effect transistors and high electron mobility transistors (HEMTs) are capable of terahertz detection and emission, as experimentally shown in various reported results [1]–[6]. A mechanism for creating plasma instability, namely the Dyakonov–Shur (DS) instability, achieved by asymmetric boundary conditions at the source and drain terminals (Fig. 1(a)) was proposed in [8]. This configuration has the potential to provide a range of terahertz devices, including mixers, detectors, and sources [9]. The concept itself is analyzed using linearized hydrodynamic model in [8, 9]. Several numerical studies have also been conducted to study this phenomenon, either using hydrodynamic simulations or using more rigorous Monte Carlo simulations. However, these studies omit the electromagnetic (EM) wave propagation in their modeling.

In this work, we develop multiphysics computational full-wave models by combining the finite difference time domain method for the EM wave propagation with a hydrodynamic modeling of the electron transport. Such integration is intended to produce modeling tools that are apt for modeling semiconductor devices that operate at sub-mm-wave and terahertz frequencies. We then apply it simulating the terahertz emissions from HEMT device in question. In the paper, we first present equations governing device operation and then present the results of the simulations, power calculations and comparison with prior analytical models.

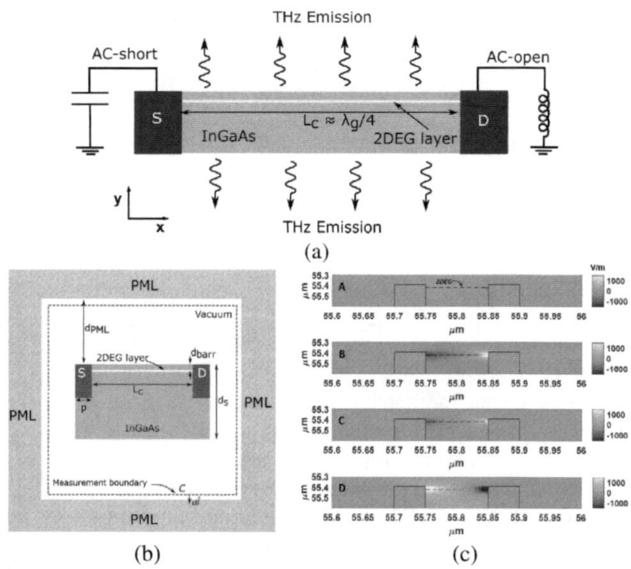

Fig. 1. InGaAs-based HEMT under investigation for terahertz emissions. (a) Asymmetric boundary conditions for generation of current oscillations, (b) simulation domain (c) Electric-field profile at four phase points in an oscillation cycle.

II. GOVERNING EQUATIONS FOR MULTIPHYSICS MODELING

Solution requires modeling of electrodynamic fields via

$$\nabla \times \vec{H} = \frac{\partial \vec{D}}{\partial t} + \vec{J} + \sigma\vec{E}, \quad \text{and} \tag{1}$$

$$\nabla \times \vec{E} = -\frac{\partial \vec{B}}{\partial t} - \sigma^* \vec{H}. \tag{2}$$

For 2D TE_Z solution, electric field $\vec{E} = \hat{x}E_x + \hat{y}E_y$ is used. Electrical and magnetic conductivity parameters, i.e. σ and σ^*, are used for the modeling of anisotropic, perfectly matched layer surrounding the domain. Electron transport in the channel is modelled via hydrodynamic equations, given by,

$$\frac{\partial n_{sh}}{\partial t} + \frac{\partial j}{\partial x} = 0, \quad \text{and} \tag{3}$$

$$\frac{\partial j}{\partial t} + v\frac{\partial j}{\partial x} + \frac{j\partial v}{\partial x} = -\frac{qnE_x}{m_e} - \frac{j}{\tau} - \frac{KT}{m_e}. \tag{4}$$

Here n_{sh} is the sheet carrier density, j ($= n_{sh}v$) is the sheet current and v is the electron velocity within the 2DEG channel. τ refers to the momentum relaxation time and m_e is the effective electron mass, q = 1.6×10−19 C is the charge-magnitude of a single electron, T is the electron temperature in the channel and K is the Boltzmann constant.

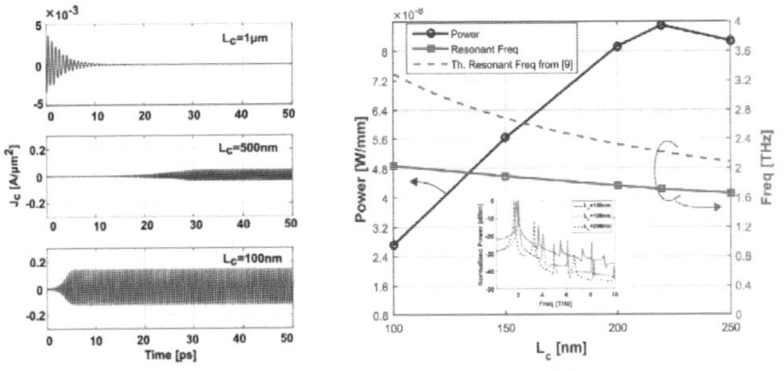

(a) (b)

Fig. 2 (a) Current oscillations recorded at the drain terminal of the HEMT. As shown for small channel length such oscillations are sustained leading to emissions (Chosen n_{sh} = 10^{12} cm^{-2} and v_o = 1 × 10^5 m/s.). (b) Frequency and power dependence on channel length, L_c and its comparison with theoretical estimates taken from [8, 9] (Chosen n_{sh} = 10^{12} cm^{-2} and v_o = 2 × 10^5 m/s).

III. Modeling of THz Emissions

Equations (1) through (4) are numerically solved using FDTD algorithms using details outlined [7]. Using these, the device shown in the Fig. 1(b) is modeled. The domain of the model is shown in Fig. 1(b). For our model, we use drift velocity in the channel as v_o = 10^5 m/s, channel sheet-electron density as n_{sh}=10^{12} cm^{-2}, and varying channel lengths L_c = 1 µm, 500 nm, and 100 nm. As specified in Fig. 1(a), InGaAs substrate with dielectric constant (ϵ_r = 13.9) is used for our purposes. The channel is excited using a square 0.1-ps-long voltage pulse with the amplitude of 1 µV at the drain terminal, D. In practice, this excitation can come from the ambient noise itself (like any other oscillator). Fig. 2(a) shows the effect of channel length of the oscillations occurring in the channel with varying L_c.

For large L_c (=1 µm, 500 nm), the power loss due to the channel scattering and radiation is greater than the gain due to asymmetrical source termination, causing decaying current oscillations. In contrast, for the L_c = 100 nm case, the scattering losses are reduced, due to shorter propagation distance. This causes a net gain in each round trip of the wave, leading to instability. The electric-field profile corresponding to this case is shown in Fig. 1(c). Note that, in such a case, the oscillations do not amplify infinitely, rather saturate at a certain amplitude. This is due to the nonlinearity of the channel hydrodynamics, which balances the current growth with increased propagation losses as the current amplitude increases.

We further mote that the excited oscillations lead to emissions from the channel, which can be recorded by calculating the integral of the Poynting vector along the measurement boundary as shown in Fig. 1(b). This is done using the formula

$$P_{rad} = \int_c \frac{1}{2} \Re(\vec{E} \times \vec{H}^*) \cdot d\hat{l}. \quad (5)$$

The emitted power is shown in Fig. 2(b). Next, the frequency of oscillation is calculated by calculating Fourier Transform of the drain current, which represents the normalized power spectrum (Fig. 2(b) inset).

The results clearly demonstrate instability within the channel leading to oscillations and emissions. Frequency of oscillation shows a decreasing trend with increasing channel length, and oscillations do not survive for larger channel lengths. The power of the emission is found to first increase with increasing channel and then decrease. Thus, multiphysics simulations allow physical simulation of devices leading to evaluation of power emissions which has not be done so far.

IV. Conclusions

The presented work demonstrates the utility of full-wave and hydrodynamic multiphysics computational tools for terahertz semiconductor devices. In our specific example, the tool was used to simulate terahertz emissions from HEMTs, a problem which has been studied by researchers in last several decades. Specifically, power calculations were made revealing that few tens of nm of power per mm width of the device may be expected from HEMT based terahertz oscillators. Furthermore, device operational phenomenology is revealed by instantaneous field profile along the channel. These observations ultimately allow us to learn the utility of such transistors for terahertz source applications.

References

[1] W. Knap, Y. Deng, S. Rumyantsev, and M. S. Shur, "Resonant detection of subterahertz and terahertz radiation by plasma waves in submicron field-effect transistors," Appl. Phys. Lett., vol. 81, no. 24, p. 4637, 2002.

[2] El Fatimy et al., "Resonant and voltage-tunable terahertz detection in InGaAs/InP nanometer transistors," Appl. Phys. Lett., vol. 89, no. 13, pp. 131926-1–131926-3, Sep. 2006.

[3] X. G. Peralta et al., "Terahertz photoconductivity and plasmon modes in double-quantum-well field-effect transistors," Appl. Phys. Lett., vol. 81, no. 9, p. 1627, 2002.

[4] W. Knap et al., "Terahertz emission by plasma waves in 60 nm gate high electron mobility transistors," Appl. Phys. Lett., vol. 84, no. 13, pp. 2331–2333, Mar. 2004

[5] J. Lusakowski et al., "Voltage tuneable terahertz emission from a ballistic nanometer InGaAs/InAlAs transistor," J. Appl. Phys., vol. 97, no. 6, p. 064307, 2005.

[6] Vosseburger et al., "Emission of THz radiation from optically excited coherent plasmons in a two-dimensional electron gas," presented at the Quantum Electron. Laser Sci. Conf. (QELS), Jun. 1996, pp. 206–207.

[7] S. Bhardwaj, F. L. Teixeira and J. L. Volakis, "Fast Modeling of Terahertz Plasma-Wave Devices Using Unconditionally Stable FDTD Methods," in IEEE Journal on Multiscale and Multiphysics Computational Techniques, vol. 3, pp. 29-36, 2018.

[8] M. Dyakonov and M. Shur, "Current instability and plasma waves generation in ungated two-dimensional electron layers," Appl. phys. Lett., vol. 87, no. 11, pp. 111501-1–111501-3, Sep. 2005.

[9] M. Dyakonov and M. Shur, "Detection, mixing, and frequency multiplication of terahertz radiation by two-dimensional electronic fluid," IEEE Trans. Electron Devices, vol. 43, no. 3, pp. 380–387, Mar. 1996.

Modeling of All-Dielectric Metasurfaces Using Deep Neural Networks

Sensong An[1], Clayton Fowler[1], Mikhail Y. Shalaginov[2], Yifei Zhang[2], Peter Su[2], Myungkoo Kang[3], Bowen Zheng[1], Hong Tang[1], Hang Li[1], Anuradha Murthy Agarwal[2], Clara Rivero-Baleine[4], Kathleen A. Richardson[3], Tian Gu[2], Juejun Hu[2], and Hualiang Zhang[1]

[1]ECE Dept., University of Massachusetts Lowell, Lowell, Massachusetts, USA
[2]MSE Dept., Massachusetts Institute of Technology, Cambridge, Massachusetts, USA
[3]CREOL, University of Central Florida, Orlando, Florida, USA
[4]Lockheed Martin Corporation, Orlando, Florida, USA
hualiang_zhang@uml.edu

Abstract—**This paper presents a novel approach using deep neural networks to model all-dielectric meta-atoms over a wide spectrum. A deep neural network is constructed and fully trained in a supervised way to predict the performance of dielectric meta-atoms. The proposed approach has been validated by comparing the obtained results with full-wave simulation results.**

Keywords—deep neural network; all-dielectric; metasurface; predicting neural network.

I. INTRODUCTION

All-dielectric metasurface [1] has drawn a lot of attentions since it offers the capacity of achieving multiple functionalities with low absorption/reflection loss and fabrication complexity. As a crucial part of the all-dielectric metasurface design process, reliable and efficient modeling tools are highly desired. However, such tools can hardly be achieved by exploiting conventional analytical/empirical methods due to the complex physical mechanisms that dominate the light-matter interactions within the all-dielectric nano-structures. In this paper, a data-driven method based on deep neural networks has been proposed to predict all-dielectric meta-atoms' full-spectrum responses.

II. PROPOSED METHOD

As shown in Fig. 1, the metasurface cell we modeled in this work is based on dielectric nanorods placed on a calcium fluoride (CaF_2) substrate while the proposed approach can be widely adopted for other types of meta-atoms and materials systems. Specifically, cylinder-shaped dielectric meta-atoms are explored since they are widely applied to construct meta-optics components due to their robust performance and low fabrication complexity [2-4]. The meta-atoms are arranged in rectangular-shaped lattices. During the modeling, their material properties (i.e. complex refractive indexes), radius, height and lattice size are considered as input variables. The spectrum range under modeling is set in the mid-infrared region (from 30 to 60 THz, i.e. 5um to 10um in wavelength).

One major challenge in applying the data-driven method and forming the spectra predicting neural network (PNN) is the huge dimension mismatch between input and output data [5, 6]. One approach to solve this problem is to introduce binary input design parameters and shrink the size of the output tensors [6]. In addition to the dimension mismatch issue, it becomes even more challenging to model the phase responses of all-dielectric meta-atoms due to the complex multi-order resonant modes involved. To address these two issues and realize the spectra predicting functionality, the neural network as shown in Fig. 2 is proposed. It adopts a bilinear tensor layer to increase the interactions among input variables [7]. The bilinear tensor layer is followed by three fully connected hidden layers containing 500, 500 and 200 neurons, respectively. The output layer contains 31 units, referring to the 31 frequency points that are uniformly distributed within the whole spectrum (30-60 THz).

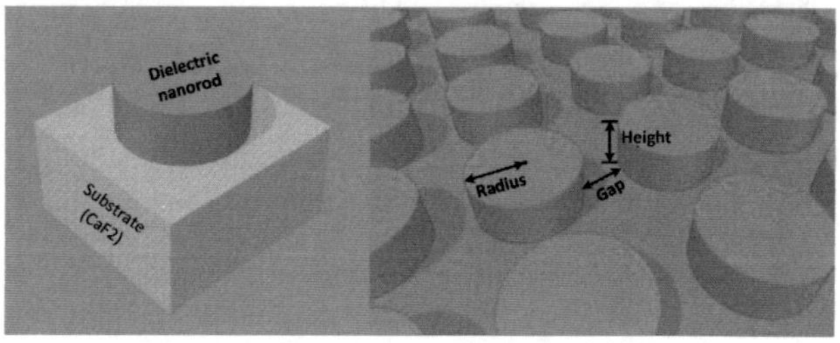

Figure1: General schematic of all-dielectric meta-atoms under consideration.

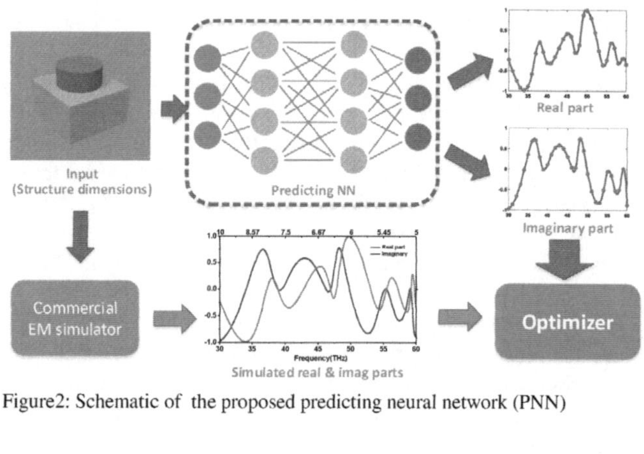

Figure2: Schematic of the proposed predicting neural network (PNN)

III. Results and Discussion

During the modeling process, the constructed neural network is trained in a supervised way. Over 50000 groups of randomly generated 1×4 input vectors are fed into the bilinear tensor layer. 70% of the input vectors are designated as training set, while the rest of them are used as the test set. We then calculate the predicted real & imaginary parts of spectral responses, and compare the results with the full-wave simulation results to derive the prediction error. The typical meta-atom responses obtained by the proposed PNN and full-wave simulations are plotted in Fig. 3. It is found that the proposed PNN is able to achieve high modeling accuracy. Overall, the prediction error is 0.05% for real part, 0.04% for imaginary part and 0.5% for both transmission and phase responses.

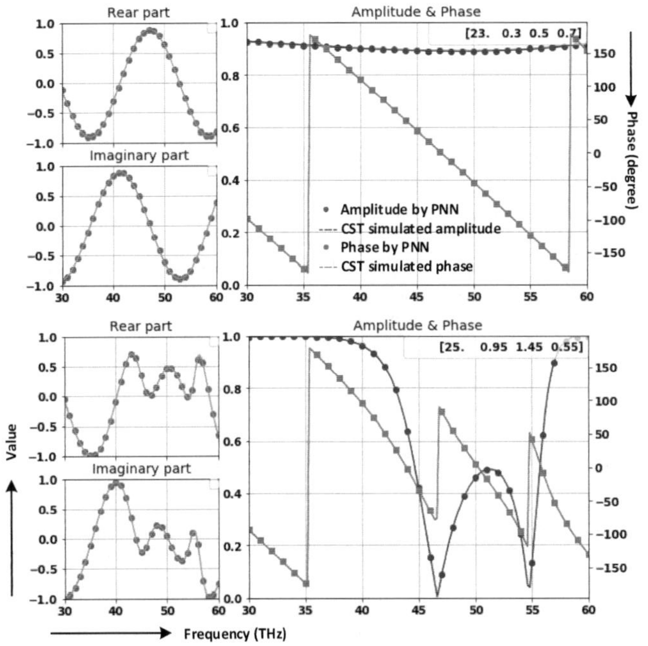

Figure 3: Meta-atom responses modeled by the proposed PNN (dot) and full-wave simulations (solid line).

IV. Conclusion

A deep neural network-based approach is applied to model all-dielectric metasurfaces. Very good consistency between the proposed approach and full-wave simulation has been achieved within the entire spectrum under consideration. It is expected that the proposed approach will pave the way towards the design of multifunctional metasurfaces and meta-optics using deep neural networks.

References

[1] Zhang L, Ding J, Zheng H, et al. Ultra-thin high-efficiency mid-infrared transmissive Huygens meta-optics. Nature Communications, 2018, 9: 1481.

[2] Decker M, Staude I, Falkner M, et al. High-efficiency dielectric Huygens' surfaces. Advanced Optical Materials, 2015, 3(6): 813-820.

[3] Kamali S M, Arbabi A, Arbabi E, et al. Decoupling optical function and geometrical form using conformal flexible dielectric metasurfaces. Nature Communications, 2016, 7: 11618.

[4] Yu Y F, Zhu A Y, Paniagua - Domínguez R, et al. High-transmission dielectric metasurface with 2 π phase control at visible wavelengths. Laser & Photonics Reviews, 2015, 9(4): 412-418.

[5] Ma W, Cheng F, Liu Y. Deep-Learning Enabled On-Demand Design of Chiral Metamaterials. ACS Nano, 2018.

[6] Malkiel I, Nagler A, Mrejen M, et al. Deep learning for design and retrieval of nano-photonic structures. arXiv preprint arXiv: 1702.07949, 2017.

[7] Socher R, Chen D, Manning C D, et al. Reasoning with neural tensor networks for knowledge base completion. Advances in Neural Information Processing Systems. 2013: 926-934.

Metasurface Design using Level-Set and Gradient Descent Optimization Techniques

Mahdad Mansouree
Department of Electrical and Computer Engineering
University of Massachusetts Amherst
Amherst, USA
mmansouree@umass.edu

Amir Arbabi
Department of Electrical and Computer Engineering
University of Massachusetts Amherst
Amherst, USA
arbabi@umass.edu

***Abstract*—Optical dielectric metasurfaces are typically composed of meta-atoms in the form of simple parametrized geometrical shapes. Meta-atoms with more complex cross-sectional geometries may enable better performance and multiple functionalities. Here we present a metasurface design technique based on a combination of the level-set method and the adjoint optimization technique that efficiently explores the available degrees of freedom of meta-atoms. As a proof of concept, we design a 75° metasurface beam deflector with 80% deflection efficiency.**

Keywords*— *Adjoint sensitivity technique, level-set method, optical metasurface, optimization.

I. Introduction

Optical metasurfaces are rationally designed 2D arrays of subwavelength scatterers that control phase, amplitude, and polarization of light, and may replace conventional optical components. They are thin, flat, and can be batch fabricated with high precision using conventional microfabrication techniques, and their transmission efficiency has recently become comparable with conventional components [1]. In contrast to conventional components, metasurfaces can provide multiple functionalities based on different degrees of freedom of light (i.e. polarization, wavelength, incident angle). However, they still suffer from chromatic aberrations, their multi-functionality comes at the cost of lower efficiency. Metasurfaces are typically designed by forming a meta-atom library and creating a lookup table that maps them to desired local optical transformations (e.g. phase shift or polarization conversion). The meta-atoms are heuristically selected as basic parametrized shapes such as circular and rectangular cylinders. As a result, the degrees of freedom potentially available in meta-atom design are not efficiently utilized. To address this issue, several techniques have been recently proposed [2]. Here we present an optimization-based technique to systematically explore the large number of degrees of freedom in meta-atom design. The proposed work is based on a combination of two techniques: the level-set method [3] and the adjoint sensitivity technique. The level-set method allows for the representation of arbitrarily shaped meta-atoms that satisfy fabrication constraints. The adjoint sensitivity technique uses only two simulations (direct and adjoint) and optimally provides the sensitivity of the metasurface scattering response to small variations in the meta-atom shape. As a proof of concept, we present the design of an efficient metasurface beam deflector using the proposed approach.

II. Meta-atom Design using Level-set and Adjoint Optimization Techniques

The conventional design procedure for metasurfaces starts by selecting a set of parametrized meta-atoms in the form of simple geometric shapes and finding their scattering response at the design wavelengths using numerical simulations. After finding the scattering response (e.g. transmission/reflection) of the meta-atoms, a reverse map is generated that serves as a lookup table which maps the desired scattering property (e.g. transmission phase, polarization conversion, etc.) to optimal meta-atoms in the library. The meta-atom library and the corresponding lookup table allows one to design metasurfaces with desired scattering profiles (e.g. phase, polarization conversion, amplitude). This procedure is effective provided the simulated meta-atoms offer the entire range of required scattering responses. This typically can be achieved by scanning meta-atom geometrical parameters. However, the complexity of the meta-atom library formation rapidly increases with the number of target requirements. Furthermore, the number of different fabricatable meta-atom shapes is so large that the direct simulation of all possible meta-atoms is not feasible. For example, for a 500 nm×500 nm unit cell and with a minimum isolated feature size of 50 nm, the number of different fabricatable meta-atom is $2^{100} \approx 10^{30}$. Although the minimum isolated feature size is 50 nm, the size of the features can be typically controlled with less than 5 nm resolution, further increasing the number of fabricatable meta-atoms.

The proposed meta-atom design approach can efficiently explore the large available design domain. We assume that the desired spectral and angular responses of a meta-atom are given, and the goal is finding a meta-atom design that satisfies fabrication constraints and has the closest spectral and angular responses to the desired ones. This is an inverse scattering problem and its solution is generally obtained through an iterative approach, where the object's shape is updated in each iteration. To represent the meta-atom cross-section, we use the level-set method. In this method, a 2D shape is defined by the zero contour of a real-valued auxiliary function $\Phi(x,y)$ which is referred to as the level-set function. We assume that the areas of the unit cell where $\Phi>0$ represents the cross-section of the high refractive index meta-atom. The idea is illustrated in Fig. 1.

The level-set technique can be used to solve the inverse scattering problem and find optimal meta-atom geometries. To this end, we start by defining an objective function (f) that can

This work was funded by the DARPA Extreme Optics and Imaging program.

be the sum of squares of differences between the desired spectral and angular responses and those of the meta-atom.

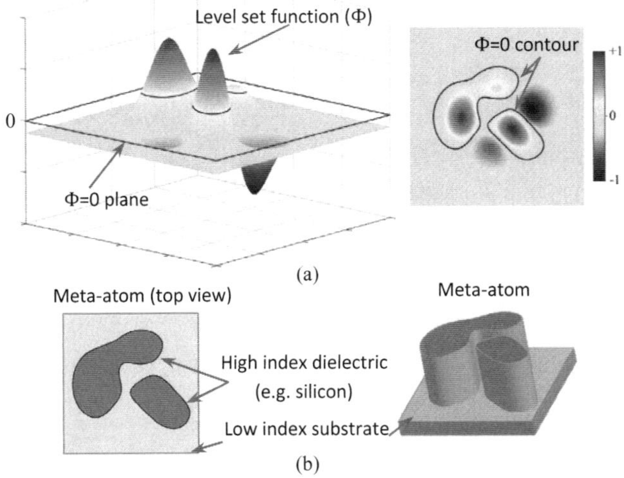

Fig. 1. (a) A level-set function $\Phi(x,y)$ defined over the unit cell of a metasurface. The $\Phi=0$ plane and its crossings with the level-set-function are shown. The color-coded plot of the same level set function and its zero contours are shown on the right. (b) The regions in the unit-cell plane where the level set function is positive (i.e. the areas enclosed in the zero contour) specify the cross section of the meta-atom.

Therefore, solving the inverse problem becomes equivalent to minimizing f which can be performed using the gradient descent method. For example, for designing a periodic metasurface beam deflector with a high efficacy, we can define $f = 1 - |a_1|^2$, where a_1 is the power amplitude of the +1 diffraction order and $|a_1|^2$ represents the diffraction efficiency of this diffraction order. The minimization procedure is iterative, and Φ is updated at the nth iteration step according to the discretized version of the level-set equation [3]

$$\Phi_{n+1} = \Phi_n + \alpha V_n |\nabla \Phi_n|, \quad (1)$$

where V_n represents the velocity of the movement of the constant Φ contours and α is a constant that determines the magnitude of change in each step. If we choose $V(x,y)$ to be the functional derivative of f with respect to meta-atom boundary shift at point (x,y), then updating Φ according to (1) is equivalent to the gradient descent optimization of f [3]. In general, the functional derivative of f can be found using the adjoint sensitivity technique. For the example of metasurface beam deflector, $V = 2\text{Re}\{U a_1^*\}$ and

$$U = j\omega\epsilon_0(\epsilon_r - 1) \int \boldsymbol{E}_{\|\text{d}} \cdot \boldsymbol{E}_{\|\text{adj}} + \frac{1}{\epsilon_r \epsilon_0^2} D_{\perp\text{d}} D_{\perp\text{adj}}\, \text{d}z, \quad (2)$$

where ϵ_r is the relative permittivity of the meta-atom, $\boldsymbol{E}_{\|\text{d}}$ and $D_{\perp\text{d}}$ are the components of the electric field and electric displacement vectors of the direct simulations that are parallel with and normal to the meta-atom side boundaries, respectively. $\boldsymbol{E}_{\|\text{adj}}$ and $D_{\perp\text{adj}}$ are the same quantities but for the adjoint simulation where the beam deflector is illuminated with a plane wave incident from the deflection beam's direction.

III. Results

As a proof of concept, we designed a metasurface beam deflector using the proposed approach. A schematic of the beam deflector is shown in Fig. 2a. The beam deflector is a periodic metasurface with the unit cell dimensions of 700 nm×1600 nm, and deflects a TE-polarized normally-incident wave with the wavelength of 1550 nm by ~75°. We assumed the meta-atoms are 800 nm tall, made of silicon with the refractive index of 3.6, and placed on a glass substrate with the refractive index of 1.44.

To design a metasurface with high deflection efficiency, we used the approach and the objective function described in the previous section ($f = 1 - |a_1|^2$). The design started from an arbitrary initial level-set function that defined three disconnected meta-atoms with smooth boundaries in each unit cell. The direct and adjoint simulations were performed using the finite difference time domain method. At each iteration, the level-set function was updated using (1) and the updated meta-atom geometry was obtained from its zero contour. The deflection (diffraction) efficiency of the metasurface at different iteration steps is presented in Fig. 2b. The inset in Fig. 2b shows the top view of the meta-atom in one unit cell at a few different steps during the design process and illustrates that both the meta-atom shape and topology varies during the design. At the final step, the metasurface reaches a deflection efficiency of 80%, and the meta-atoms have smooth boundaries.

The design technique introduced here is not limited to designating beam deflectors. The technique is highly versatile and can be used to design high-performance metasurfaces with prescribed spectral and angular responses or structural sensitivities.

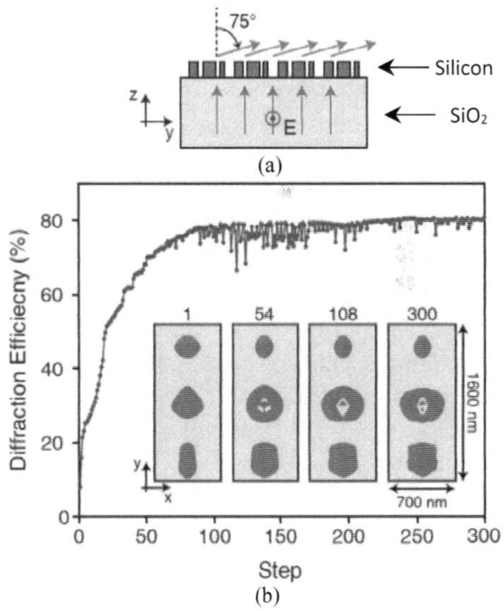

Fig. 2. (a) Schematic of a metasurface beam deflector. (b) Diffraction efficiency of the deflector at different steps during the design process. The inset shows the top views of the meta-atom at steps 1, 54, 108 and 300.

References

[1] S. M. Kamali, E. Arbabi, A. Arbabi, and A. Faraon, "A review of dielectric optical metasurfaces for wavefront control," Nanophotonics, vol. 7, no. 6, pp. 1041–1068, Jun. 2018.

[2] D. Sell, J. Yang, E. W. Wang, T. Phan, S. Doshay, and J. A. Fan, "Ultra-High-Efficiency Anomalous Refraction with Dielectric Metasurfaces," ACS Photonics, vol. 5, no. 6, pp. 2402–2407, Jun. 2018.

[3] F. Santosa, "A level-set approach for inverse problems involving obstacles," ESAIM Control. Optim. Calc. Var., vol. 1, no. January, pp. 17–33, 1996.

A Method-of-Lines Time Domain Method Solver for Dispersive Bianisotropic Maxwell's Equations

Jeffrey W. Banks
Depart. of Mathematical Sciences
Rensselaer Polytechnic Institute
Troy, New York USA
banksj3@rpi.edu

William D. Henshaw
Mathematical Sciences
Rensselaer Polytechnic Institute
Troy, New York USA
henshw@rpi.edu

Alexander V. Kildishev
Electrical and Computer Engineering
Purdue University
West Lafayette, IN 47907, USA
kildishev@purdue.edu

Gregor Kovačič
Mathematical Sciences
Rensselaer Polytechnic Institute
Troy, New York USA
kovacg@rpi.edu

Ludmila J. Prokopeva
Electrical and Computer Engineering
Purdue University
West Lafayette, IN 47907, USA
lprokop@purdue.edu

Derek Olson
Mathematical Sciences
Rensselaer Polytechnic Institute
Troy, New York USA
olsond2@rpi.edu

***Abstract*—Motivated by the emergence of dispersive, bianisotropic materials occurring as an effective medium model of metamaterials, we develop a time-domain algorithm capable of simulating general dispersive, bianisotropic media. This method utilizes auxiliary differential equations for the polarization and magnetization, which are solved in conjunction with Maxwell's equations using a method-of-lines approach with high-order finite-differences in space and integrated using the fourth order Runga-Kutta method.**

***Index Terms*—FDTD, dispersive Maxwell's equations, bianisotropic Maxwell's equations**

I. Introduction

Many homogenization (or effective medium) approximations of metamaterials lead to bianisotropic material parameters whereby the macroscopic polarization and magnetization of the homogenized medium are functions of both the electric and magnetic fields [1]–[3]. In the typical case, frequency domain data (e.g. reflection and transmission) are used to retrieve homogenized permittivity, permeability, and cross-magnetoelectric tensors, whose components are each then fit with Padé approximants. As there may be little *a priori* knowledge of the precise form of the dispersion model generated in such a process, a general Maxwell solver capable of modeling a wide array of dispersion models in *all* of the permittivity, permeability, and cross-magnetoelectric tensors is required.

To that end, we focus on the generalized dispersion model of [4], which is a general framework based on Padé approximants for modeling susceptibility functions which also covers classical models such as Drude, Lorentz, or critical point models. In order to carry out broadband simulations and include the future possibility of incorporating nonlinear effects we develop a time-domain formalism in which the dispersion relationships are Laplace transformed to obtain a set of auxiliary differential equations in conjunction with Maxwell's equations.

This work was partially supported through the NSF RTG Progam, Award 1344962, and the DARPA Defense Sciences Office.

These equations are converted to a system of first order equations which are subsequently discretized in space using centered finite-differences and integrated in time using fourth-order Runga-Kutta. Additionally, artificial dissipation is added in order to stabilize the method in the presence of discontinuous material parameters, as could happen for example when modeling multiple homogenized metamaterial cells.

This method is quite general and can be applied to dispersion in any of the material tensors with an arbitrary number of poles in the dispersion relationship while existing methods time-domain methods for simulating bianisotropic materials typically include some restriction on the material properties. Indeed, the BI-FDTD method [5] has been developed for (dispersive) bi-isotropic materials, the FDTD methods [6], [7] were applied to chiral media, and a Yee-based method was developed for nondisperive bianisotropic materials in [8].

II. Generalized Dispersive Bianisotropic Model

We assume that the materials of interest (perhaps after some homogenization procedure) are described by a generalized dispersive model (GDM) in each of the material tensors. Thus, we consider solving Maxwell's equations

$$\nabla \times \begin{pmatrix} \boldsymbol{H} \\ -\boldsymbol{E} \end{pmatrix} = \frac{\partial}{\partial t} \begin{pmatrix} \boldsymbol{E}+\boldsymbol{P} \\ \boldsymbol{H}+\boldsymbol{M} \end{pmatrix}, \tag{1}$$

where the polarization and magnetization are known in the frequency domain

$$\begin{aligned} \hat{\boldsymbol{P}}(\omega) &= (\epsilon_\infty + \hat{\chi_e}(\omega))\hat{\boldsymbol{E}}(\omega) + (\xi_\infty + \hat{\chi_{eh}}(\omega))\hat{\boldsymbol{H}}(\omega), \\ \hat{\boldsymbol{M}}(\omega) &= (\zeta_\infty + \hat{\chi_{he}}(\omega))\hat{\boldsymbol{E}}(\omega) + (\mu_\infty + \hat{\chi_h}(\omega))\hat{\boldsymbol{H}}(\omega). \end{aligned} \tag{2}$$

Each $\epsilon_\infty, \xi_\infty, \zeta_\infty, \mu_\infty, \chi$ is a *tensor*. For the GDM model, we assume each component, $[\hat{\chi}]_{ij}$, has the form

$$[\hat{\chi}]_{ij} := \sum_{m=1}^{N} \hat{\chi}_{ij}^m(\omega), \quad \hat{\chi}_{ij}^m(\omega) := \frac{\alpha_{ij}^{0,m} - i\omega\alpha_{ij}^{1,m}}{\alpha_{ij}^{2,m} - i\omega\alpha_{ij}^{3,m} - \omega^2}. \tag{3}$$

We next observe that with e_i being the ith standard basis vector,

$$\hat{\chi}\boldsymbol{E} = \sum_{i,j,m} \hat{\chi}_{ij}^m \boldsymbol{E}_j \boldsymbol{e}_i, \quad \hat{\chi}\boldsymbol{H} = \sum_{i,j,m} \hat{\chi}_{ij}^m \boldsymbol{H}_j \boldsymbol{e}_i, \tag{4}$$

so we introduce new, auxiliary variables (no summation)

$$\begin{aligned} \hat{\Xi}_{e,ij}^m &:= \hat{\Xi}_{e,ij}^m \boldsymbol{E}_j, \quad \hat{\Xi}_{eh,ij}^m := \hat{\Xi}_{eh,ij}^m \boldsymbol{H}_j \\ \hat{\Xi}_{he,ij}^m &:= \hat{\Xi}_{he,ij}^m \boldsymbol{E}_j, \quad \hat{\Xi}_{h,ij}^m := \hat{\Xi}_{h,ij}^m, \boldsymbol{H}_j. \end{aligned} \tag{5}$$

Transforming (2), (3), and (5) to the time domain and inserting into (1) yields the dispersive bianisotropic equations

$$\nabla \times \begin{pmatrix} \boldsymbol{H} \\ -\boldsymbol{E} \end{pmatrix} = \begin{pmatrix} \epsilon & \xi \\ \zeta & \mu \end{pmatrix} \frac{\partial}{\partial t} \begin{pmatrix} \boldsymbol{E} \\ \boldsymbol{H} \end{pmatrix} + \frac{\partial}{\partial t} \begin{pmatrix} \sum_{i,j=1}^3 \sum_{m=1}^N \Xi_{e,ij}^m \boldsymbol{e}_i + \sum_{i,j=1}^3 \sum_{m=1}^N \Xi_{eh,ij}^m \boldsymbol{e}_i \\ \sum_{i,j=1}^3 \sum_{m=1}^N \Xi_{he,ij}^m \boldsymbol{e}_i + \sum_{i,j=1}^3 \sum_{m=1}^N \Xi_{h,ij}^m \boldsymbol{e}_i \end{pmatrix}. \tag{6}$$

Furthermore, when we transform (3) to the time domain, we get a collection of second order auxiliary differential equations for the variables $\Xi_{s,ij}^m$ for $i = 1,2,3, j = 1,2,3, m = 1,2,\ldots,N$ and $s = e, eh, he, h$ which are coupled to (6) and take the form:

$$\alpha_{s,ij}^{2,m}\Xi_{s,ij}^m + \alpha_{s,ij}^{3,m}\frac{\partial}{\partial t}\Xi_{s,ij}^m + \frac{\partial^2}{\partial t^2}\Xi_{s,ij}^m = \alpha_{s,ij}^{0,m}\boldsymbol{E}_j + \alpha_{s,ij}^{1,m}\frac{\partial}{\partial t}\boldsymbol{E}_j. \tag{7}$$

III. Numerical Method

The coupled equations (6) and (7) are converted to a first-order system of equations, which are solved using a method-of-lines approach. But first, to combat numerical instabilities caused by discontinuities in the material parameters, a sixth-order artificial dissipation, $(\sigma_1 h^3 + \sigma_2 h^2)\Delta^3 \begin{pmatrix} \boldsymbol{E} \\ \boldsymbol{H} \end{pmatrix}$ is added to (6) for dissipation coefficients σ_1, σ_2. Given a uniform mesh with spacing h, the spatial derivatives are approximated by fourth-order centered finite-differences, and the dissipation is further discretized using centered finite-differences. This produces a semi-discrete system of equations that may formally be written as $\boldsymbol{V}_t = A\boldsymbol{V}$. Time integration is then carried out using fourth-order Runga-Kutta. In practice, forming the coefficient matrix, A, is less than desirable as one can instead directly obtain the update equations for $\boldsymbol{E}, \boldsymbol{H}, \Xi_{ij}^m$ from (6) and (7).

IV. Numerical Results

As a test problem, we apply the method to two one-dimensional examples. The first is the simulation of a standing wave in a homogeneous, dispersive, bianisotropic material with periodic boundary conditions. In this case, we choose our material parameters so that the dispersion relationship is exactly solvable, and we thus have an analytic solution to compare our computed solution to. The results shown in Table I clearly show fourth order convergence.

TABLE I
Error and Convergence Rates in Homogeneous Material.

h	L^2	L^2 Rate	L^∞	L^∞ Rate
1/10	5.627366e-04		1.865827e-04	
1/20	3.391860e-05	4.0523	1.177438e-05	3.9861
1/40	2.073479e-06	4.0320	7.387854e-07	3.9944
1/80	1.283537e-07	4.0139	4.634836e-08	3.9946

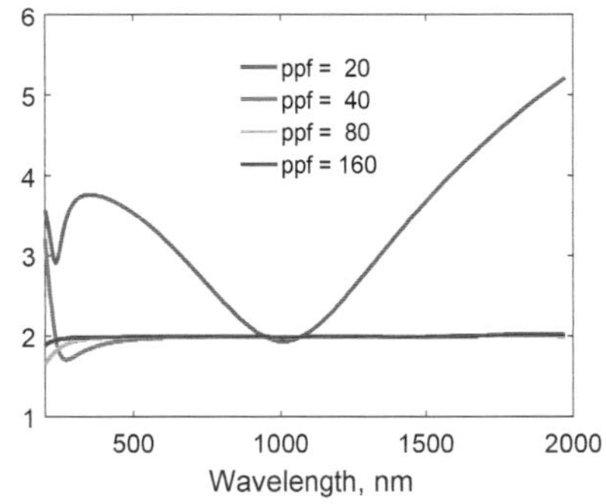

Fig. 1. Convergence of transmission for a BA slab. The material parameters of the slab were obtained from homogenization of the C-shaped in [1].

As a second example, we use our time-domain method to compute the transmission coefficients of a slab of dispersive, bianisotropic material (via a discrete Fourier transform). The exact solution is known in the frequency domain, and we have plotted the convergence rates across a broad range of frequencies in Fig. 1. Here, the presence of discontinuous material parameters causes a decrease in the convergence rate to two.

References

[1] C. . Kriegler, M. S. Rill, S. Linden, and M. Wegener, "Bianisotropic photonic metamaterials," IEEE Journal of Selected Topics in Quantum Electronics, vol. 16, no. 2, pp. 367–375, March 2010.

[2] R. Marqués, F. Medina, and R. Rafii-El-Idrissi, "Role of bianisotropy in negative permeability and left-handed metamaterials," Physical Review B, vol. 65, no. 14, p. 144440, 2002.

[3] A. V. Kildishev, J. D. Borneman, X. Ni, V. M. Shalaev, and V. P. Drachev, "Bianisotropic effective parameters of optical metamagnetics and negative-index materials," Proceedings of the IEEE, vol. 99, no. 10, pp. 1691–1700, 2011.

[4] L. J. Prokopeva, J. D. Borneman, and A. V. Kildishev, "Optical dispersion models for time-domain modeling of metal-dielectric nanostructures," IEEE Transactions on Magnetics, vol. 47, no. 5, pp. 1150–1153, 2011.

[5] A. Akyurtlu and D. H. Werner, "Bi-fdtd: a novel finite-difference time-domain formulation for modeling wave propagation in bi-isotropic media," IEEE Transactions on Antennas and Propagation, vol. 52, no. 2, pp. 416–425, Feb 2004.

[6] V. Demir, A. Z. Elsherbeni, and E. Arvas, "Fdtd formulation for dispersive chiral media using the z transform method," IEEE Transactions on Antennas and Propagation, vol. 53, no. 10, pp. 3374–3384, 2005.

[7] J. A. Pereda, A. Grande, O. Gonzales, and A. Vegas, "Fdtd modeling of chiral media by using the mobius transformation technique," IEEE Antennas and Wireless Propagation Letters, vol. 5, pp. 327–330, 2006.

[8] X. L. Bao, W. X. Zhang, and L. W. Li, "Fdtd formulation for bianisotropic medium," IEEE Antennas and Propagation Society International Symposium. 2001 Digest., vol. 1, pp. 52–55, July 2001.

High-Efficiency Emitter for Thermophotovoltaics: Topology Optimization

Zhaxylyk A. Kudyshev
School of Electrical and Computer Engineering and Birck Nanotechnology Center
Purdue University
West Lafayette, USA
zkudyshev@purdue.edu

Alexander V. Kildishev
School of Electrical and Computer Engineering and Birck Nanotechnology Center
Purdue University
West Lafayette, USA
kildishev@purdue.edu

Vladimir M. Shalaev
School of Electrical and Computer Engineering and Birck Nanotechnology Center
Purdue University
West Lafayette, USA
shalaev@purdue.edu

Alexandra Boltasseva
School of Electrical and Computer Engineering and Birck Nanotechnology Center
Purdue University
West Lafayette, USA
aeb@purdue.edu

***Abstract*— A metasurface-based thermophotovoltaics system directly converts thermal radiation to electricity through the photovoltaic effect. The efficiency of such a system significantly depends on the thermal stability and efficiency of the spectral reshaping of the metasurface. We couple the generative adversarial network technique with the topology optimization to design a new class of high-efficiency metasurface thermal emitters. Numerical simulations confirm that due to non-trivial metasurface topologies the proposed method generates the close-to-ultimate high-efficiency emitters. Comparison with a conventional global optimization technique shows that our topology-optimized designs demonstrate superior spectral control of thermal blackbody radiation than the regular-shape emitters optimized with conventional optimization.**

Keywords— metamaterials, metasurfaces, topology optimization, thermophotovoltaics (TPV)

I. INTRODUCTION

Advanced nanophotonic concepts, such as photonic crystals, metamaterials, and metasurfaces, have enabled unique functionalities including, negative refraction, hyperbolic dispersion, optical magnetism, control of quantum emitters, epsilon near-zero phenomena, and enhanced light-matter interactions to name just a few. With the recent development of new plasmonic/photonic materials and nanofabrication techniques, nanophotonic devices are now capable of providing novel solutions to global challenges including world energy consumption, rapid and accurate chemical/biological detection, quantum computing/security, telecom information densities, and space exploration. In recent years, there has been significant research interest in engineering the optical and spectral properties of materials through the use of photonic metasurfaces for efficient energy conversion, such as solar/thermophotovoltaics (S/TPV) applications. A TPV system directly converts thermal radiation to electricity through the photovoltaic (PV) effect. A typical TPV system consists of a PV cell array and a selective emitter with the emissivity matching absorption band of a PV cell to increase electron-hole pair generation and reduce parasitic out-of-band radiation to suppress heating of the cell. Figure 1a shows a schematic of a TPV system.

It has been predicted that by judiciously tailoring the spectral properties of the absorbers/emitters components using metasurfaces, the efficiency for direct energy conversion from solar/thermal energy to electricity could potentially reach an unprecedented value of about 85% [1] in contrast to the current physical limitation of around 30% imposed by the Shockley-Queisser limit in single silicon p-n junction PV cells [2]. The overall efficiency of the TPV-based energy conversion process significantly depends on the thermal stability and efficiency of the spectral reshaping of a metasurface device. Thus the development of a highly efficient TPV generator is an inherently complex problem due to its multi-disciplinary nature, requiring a manifold of stringent materials and structural constraints in conjunction with the required optical performance. Optimization techniques offer powerful tools to address these multi-faceted challenges. Recently, topology optimization has emerged as a successful approach for the systematic design of photonic structures [3]. Also, it has been demonstrated that inverse design problems applied to metasurface and photonic crystal reconstruction can be efficiently solved using topology optimization techniques to obtain significantly improved performance in comparison with those obtained with direct optimization [4].

II. TOPOLOGY OPTIMIZATION

Here, we applied a topology optimization method to enhance the performance of a thermally stable emitter for a TPV system utilizing GaSb PV cell. We considered a three-layer structure, which consists of 300-nm-thick TiN back reflector, 40-nm-thick SiN dielectric spacer, and 100-nm-thick TiN top layer. Using a topology optimization technique, we optimized the top layer TiN/air binary mixer distribution to achieve the target emissivity spectrum, which in the ideal case is a step function matching the working band of GaSb PV (wavelength range from 400 nm to 1800 nm). Optical properties of plasmonic TiN, as well as SiN were retrieved from temperature-dependent variable angle spectroscopic ellipsometry reported previously [5].

Our topology optimization addressed several critical constraints from the fabrication standpoint. Thus, we limited the minimal feature size of the final design to be no less than 50 nm while ensuring the robustness of the optimized design to the perturbations caused by nanofabrication. This was achieved by: (i) eliminating sub-precision features by averaging the permittivity of the design over neighboring regions and pushing the design to binary structures with evolution of the optimization; (ii) averaging the figure of merit of the device over

Supported by DARPA/DSO Extreme Optics and Imaging (EXTREME) Program (HR00111720032), Air Force Office of Scientific Research MURI Grant (FA9550-14-1-0389), and Air Force Office of Scientific Research grant FA9550-18-1-0002

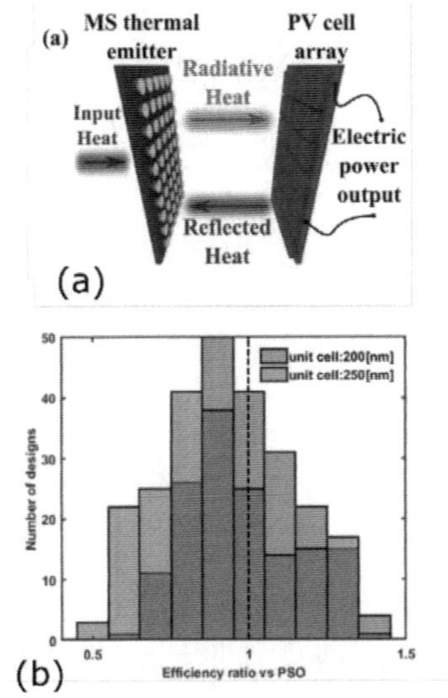

Fig.1. (a) Schematics of a thermophotovoltaics system; (b) Statistics of 200 topology-optimized designs for two different unit cells: efficiency axis is normalized to the performance of the optimal cylindrical emitter (vertical dashed line).

eroded and dilated geometries, thus reducing the impact of geometric variability on the device efficiency. Figure 1b shows the statistics of 200 topology-optimized designs efficiencies obtained from simulation.

For the sake of comparison, we normalize the efficiency scale to the efficiency of a TiN cylindrical gap plasmon emitter optimized with a particle swarm optimization (PSO) technique [6]. The topology-optimized design can be up to 45% more efficient in comparison with the optimized cylindrical emitter. Figure 2a depicts some of the top 10% of the most efficient emitters.

III. Deep-Learning-Based Optimization

Since we used a gradient descent based topology optimization technique, which is a local optimization method, it would have been challenging to find the most efficient design as given by the global extremum of the figure of merit in a given parametric space. To overcome this problem, we coupled the topology optimization with a deep learning algorithm - generative adversarial network (GAN) [7]. GAN forms a class of artificial intelligence algorithms. These algorithms are implemented by a system of two coupled neural networks and are used in unsupervised machine learning. Trained GAN could be employed for generating new patterns from noise, which are unique but have critical features of a training set. Within this work, we trained GAN on the set of topology-optimized designs to generate a new set of high-efficiency thermal emitters. We showed that: (i) GAN-assisted optimization could generate 1000 of new high-efficiency designs within 1 min, while the direct topology optimization takes more than 48 hours to degenerate 200 designs; (ii) training of the GAN could be efficiently coupled with the direct topology optimization to form a self-training loop for a more efficient optimization search in the global parametric space. Figure 2b shows the statistics of the

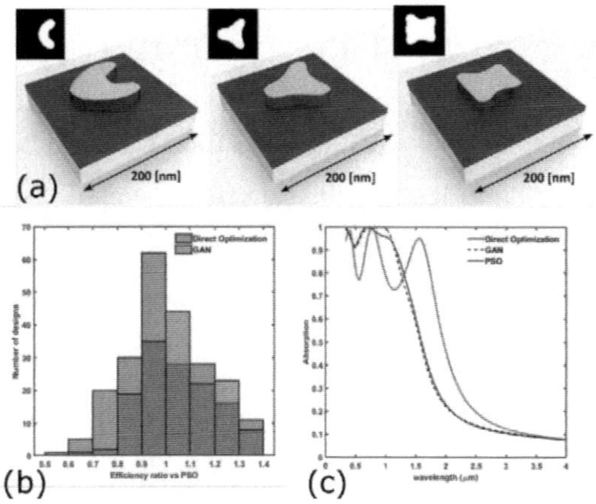

Fig.2. (a) Some of the top 10% most efficient topology optimized unit cell configurations. (b) Comparison of the emissivity/absorption of the most efficient design obtained by direct topology optimization (blue curve), generative adversarial network assisted optimization (dashed black curve) as well as optimized cylinder emitter (red curve); (c) Statistics of obtained GAN based optimization designs efficiencies in comparison with the direct topology optimization: normalization is done in the same way as in (Fig.1b).

simulated design efficiencies compared to the direct topology optimization. Figure 2c shows the comparison of the emissivity/absorption of the most efficient designs obtained from the direct topology optimization and GAN assisted optimization. The trained GAN provided extremely high optimization speed and generated designs with higher efficiencies.

IV. Conclusion

Within this work, we coupled the deep-learning-based technique GAN with the topology optimization of thermal emitters for TPV applications. We have showcased the following advantages of the proposed method: a) generation of high-efficiency metasurface emitters with non-trivial topologies the with the near-to-ultimate spectral reshaping of black-body radiation; and b) significant reduction of the design search time due to the GAN technique that could be used as a "black box" optimization tool.

References

[1] S. Fan, An alternative 'Sun' for solar cells, Nat. Nanotechnol., 9, 92-93 (2014).
[2] W. Shockley et al., Detailed Balance Limit of Efficiency of p-n Junction Solar Cells, J. Appl. Phys. 32, 510 (1961).
[3] F. Wang et al., Robust topology optimization of photonic crystal waveguides with tailored dispersion properties, JOSA B Vol. 28, 3 (2011).
[4] D.Sell et al., Large-Angle, Multifunctional Metagratings Based on Freeform Multimode Geometries, Nano Lett., 17(6) (2017).
[5] H. Reddy et al., Temperature-Dependent Optical Properties of Plasmonic Titanium Nitride Thin Films, ACS Photon., 4 (6) (2017).
[6] A. K. Azad et al., Metasurface Broadband Solar Absorber, Scientific Reports Vol. 6, 20347 (2016).
[7] Z. Liu et al., Generative Model for the Inverse Design of Metasurfaces, Nano Lett. 18(10) (2018).

Phonon-Polariton Resonances in Hexagonal Boron Nitride Transdimensional Lattices

Viktoriia E. Babicheva
College of Optical Sciences
University of Arizona
Tucson, US
vbab.dtu@gmail.com

***Abstract*—We analyze optical antennas made of hexagonal boron nitride which is a natural material with hyperbolic dispersion in mid-infrared range. The antennas in the periodic array support phonon-polariton resonances including electric and magnetic dipoles and higher multipoles. The resonances are controlled by the size and shape of the antenna as well as period of the array. We regard these arrays as transdimensional lattices because of their 2D/3D translational nature. The antenna resonances allow for efficient control of light scattering, reflection, and propagation and can be utilized in metasurfaces and flat optical components.**

Keywords—hexagonal boron nitride, hyperbolic dispersion, optical antenna, transdimensional lattice.

I. INTRODUCTION

Photonic structures that support excitation of phonon-polaritons have recently attracted a lot of attention [1]. One of the reasons is that such phonon-polaritons in strongly-anisotropic van der Waals materials result in the effective hyperbolic dispersion of propagating waves and rich optical phenomena because of it [2].

Antennas made of materials or metamaterials with hyperbolic dispersion is a promising alternative to plasmonic and all-dielectric materials for realizing optical antennas and scattering elements in metasurfaces [3]-[5]. Here we study a metasurface that consists of a periodic array of hexagonal boron nitride (hBN) antennas (Fig. 1) and analyze multipole resonances in the structure. Antenna size and shape play a crucial role in defining the resonances, and an additional degree of control is brought by periodic arrangement of the antennas and their coupling.

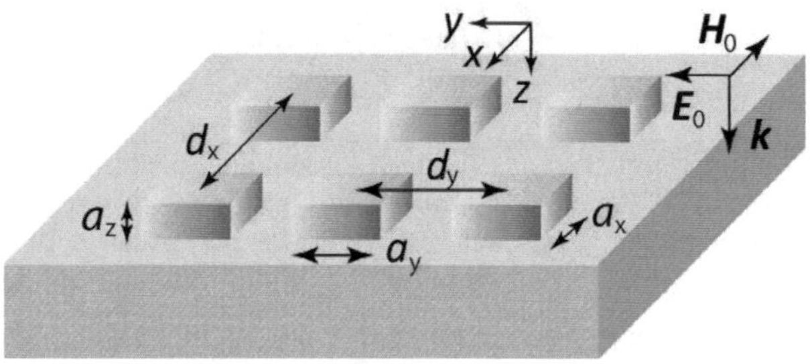

Fig. 1. Periodic array of hBN antennas and illumination conditions. The transdimensional lattice incorporates 3D design of the antenna, including size and shape, and 2D periodic arrangement of the antennas.

II. RESULTS

In the hyperbolic medium, the propagation wavenumber (k_x, k_y, k_z) satisfies the dispersion equation

$$\frac{k_x^2 + k_y^2}{\varepsilon_z} + \frac{k_z^2}{\varepsilon_x} = k_0^2, \tag{1}$$

where ε_x , ε_y, and ε_z are permittivity component of the antenna material, $k_0 = 2\pi/\lambda_0$, and λ_0 is the free-space wavelength. Here we show that in the cuboid particle with dimensions a_x, a_y, and a_z, resonances occur when

$$k_i a_i = \pi n_i, \tag{2}$$

where i = x, y, or z, and n_i are the integers. In the resonance, the following condition is satisfied:

$$\frac{1}{\varepsilon_z}\left(\frac{n_x}{2a_x}\right)^2 + \frac{1}{\varepsilon_z}\left(\frac{n_y}{2a_y}\right)^2 + \frac{1}{\varepsilon_x}\left(\frac{n_z}{2a_z}\right)^2 = \frac{1}{\lambda_0^2}. \tag{3}$$

Fig. 2 shows the results of the calculations of n_z with (3) for hBN in the spectral region where hBN has hyperbolic dispersion of type II. Because of the hBN strong dispersion in the proximity to phonon-polariton resonance, the antenna resonances with $n_z > 10$ are excited at $\lambda \approx 7.3$ μm.

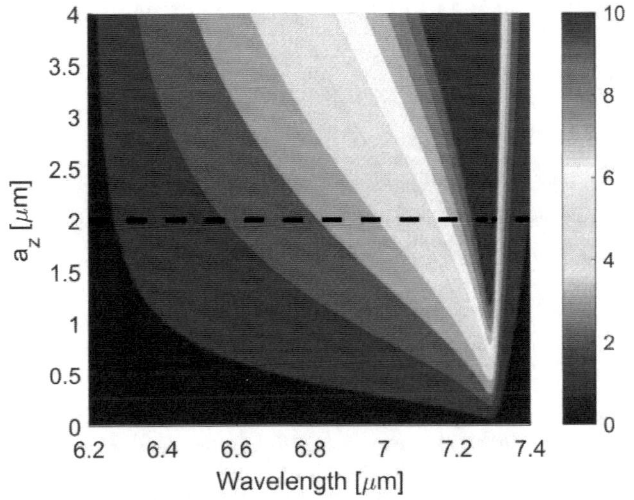

Fig. 2. Resonances supported in the hBN antenna defined through quantum number n_z (see (3)). Antennas parameters are $a_y = 0.5$ μm, $a_x = 0.9$ μm, $n_y = 0$, and $n_x = 1$, and the dashed black line correspond to $a_z = 2$ μm.

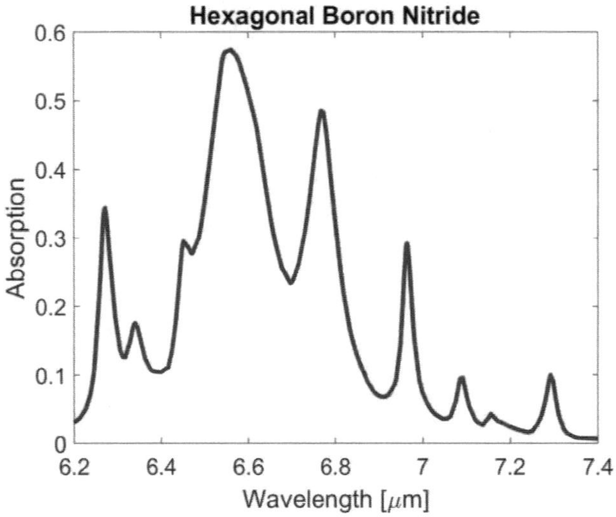

Fig. 3. Absorption in the array of hBN antennas. Structure parameters are $d_x = d_y = 2.5$ μm, $a_x = 0.9$ μm, $a_y = 0.5$ μm, and $a_z = 2$ μm.

To identify hBN antenna resonances in numerical modeling, we perform calculations of hBN antenna periodic array and analyze its absorption spectrum (Fig. 3). Simulation results show that the strongest resonances are excited at $\lambda \approx 6.5 - 6.8$ μm which correspond to small n_z. In turn, at a longer wavelength, resonances are relatively weak. We note that resonances at $\lambda \approx 6.2 - 6.3$ μm are not explained by (3) and all have $n_z = 1$ and different mode properties [5].

III. Conclusion

We have studied cuboid antennas made of hBN arranged in the periodic array. At the wavelength of phonon-polariton resonances, the hBN possesses properties of natural hyperbolic material of type II. This allows for efficient excitation of multipole resonances in the hBN antennas and results in multiple peaks in the absorption spectrum.

Acknowledgment

This material is based upon work supported by the Air Force Office of Scientific Research under Grant No. FA9550-19-1-0032.

References

[1] F. Manene, E. C. Kinzel, B. A. Lail, "Finite element eigenmode analysis of hybrid surface phonon polariton infrared waveguides," ACES Conference Paper - Computational Methods in Nanoelectromagnetics, 2014.

[2] A. M. Shaltout, V. M. Shalaev, A. V. Kildishev, "Waveguides with hyperbolic metasurface claddings," ACES Conference Paper - Computational Methods in Nanoelectromagnetics, 2014.

[3] V. E. Babicheva, "Directional scattering by the hyperbolic-medium antennas and silicon particles," MRS Advances 3, 1913, 2018.

[4] V. E. Babicheva, "Lattice Kerker effect in the array of hexagonal boron nitride antennas," MRS Advances 3, 2783-2788, 2018.

[5] V. E. Babicheva, "Multipole resonances and directional scattering by hyperbolic-media antennas," 2017. arxiv.org/abs/1706.07259

Plasmonic Colors and Memory with Al Metafilms (invited)

Maowen Song
Birck Nanotechnology Center
Purdue University
West Lafayette, USA
Key Lab of Optoelectronic Technology and Systems of Education Ministry of China,
Chongqing University,Chongqing, China smw@cqu.edu.cn

Di Wang
Birck Nanotechnology Center, School of Electrical & Computer Engineering
Purdue University
West Lafayette, USA
wang1292@purdue.edu

Zhaxylyk Kudyshev
Birck Nanotechnology Center, School of Electrical & Computer Engineering
Purdue University
West Lafayette, USA
z.kudyshev@gmail.com

Yi Xuan
Birck Nanotechnology Center, School of Electrical & Computer Engineering
Purdue University
West Lafayette, USA
yxuan@purdue.edu

Honglin Yu
Key Lab of Optoelectronic Technology and Systems of Education Ministry of China,
Chongqing University
Chongqing, China
hlyu@cqu.edu.cn

Alexandra Boltasseva
Birck Nanotechnology Center, School of Electrical & Computer Engineering
Purdue University
West Lafayette, USA
aeb@purdue.edu

Vladimir M. Shalaev
Birck Nanotechnology Center, School of Electrical & Computer Engineering
Purdue University
West Lafayette, USA
shalaev@purdue.edu

Alexander V. Kildishev
Birck Nanotechnology Center, School of Electrical & Computer Engineering
Purdue University
West Lafayette, USA
kildishev@purdue.edu

***Abstract*—We proposed an all-aluminum metasurface for dynamic optical displays and high-density data storage. The metasurface is composed of aluminum nanoantennae attached on aluminum back-reflector. When illuminated with broadband light, such metasurface reflects a broad palette of colors with a rotating polarizer and analyzer. Based on this feature, customized color sequences are created to enable high-density data storage. Also, another metasurface consisting of aluminum gap-plasmon-type centrosymmetric "i-shaped" dimmers is proposed. Full-color generation is theoretically achieved by adjusting the resonator dimensions and polarizer angle.**

Keywords — metasurface, plasmonic colors, polarization multiplexing, surface plasmon resonance.

I. Introduction

Metallic nanostructures are largely used recently to reflect/transmit light of different colors [1], [2]. Such plasmonic color filters gained popularity because of their improved spatial resolution, environmentally-friendliness, and mechanical/chemical robustness in comparison to conventional organic dyes or pigments. Numerous investigations have been carried out to enhance their color tunability by using chemical reactions and heat-induced deformation [3], [4]. Unfortunately, the relatively slow response time and the irreversibility of the tuning process hinder the use of these techniques in real-life applications. Interestingly, the design of asymmetric resonators opens up an avenue for polarization-dependent color metasurface which doubles the information states per nanopixel [5]. However, the rapid development in the area of data storage and encryption calls for extra tuning parameters to increase the number of information states [6]. This need motivates the current study of an anisotropic all-aluminum (Al) metasurface. With respect to color generation performance, a broad palette of colors can be generated and dynamically tuned. Due to the dispersive optical-rotation effect, the generated colors are dependent on both incident and reflected polarizations, which could be highly beneficial for allowing multiple colors to be encoded in a single nanopixel and revealed by unique polarization keys. Hence, judiciously designed Al metasurfaces are suited for dynamic color generation and high-density data storage. The Al gap-plasmon resonators based metasurface achieves nearly perfect absorption, which enhances the color saturation. Full-color generation is theoretically realized when a pair of centrosymmetric "i-shaped" dimmers is introduced to adjust absorption bands.

II. Results

A. Dynamic Color Generation

In our study, we design two types of metasurfaces. One is a surface-relief Al film as shown in Fig. 1(a) (type I), and the other consists of Al gap-plasmon resonators as shown in Fig. 1 (c) (type II). Both metasurfaces are illuminated with broadband visible light, and various colors are generated in the reflection mode. For type I metasurface, the output colors can be tuned by rotating the polarizer (polarizing the incident light) and analyzer (polarizing the reflected light). Such a feature is enabled by the dispersive optical-rotation effect near the localized surface plasmon resonance (LSPR) band of the Al nanoantennae. The elementary structure of type II metasurface is a pair of centrosymmetric "i-shaped" dimers, which tailor the reflection spectrum by polarization-dependent gap-plasmon resonances. Figs. 1 (b) and 1 (d) show the calculated polarization-dependent reflection spectra of type I and II metasurfaces at normal incidence.

Supported DARPA/DSO Extreme Optics and Imaging (EXTREME) Program, Award HR00111720032, Air Force Office of Scientific Research MURI Grant, CSC and National Natural Science Foundation of China

B. High-density Data Storage

Owing to the great diversity in color generation, the type I metasurface can be used to augment current data storage technology. We design a checkerboard-patterned metasurface which contains four differently oriented (0°, 45°, 90°, and 135°, all with respect to the x-direction) nanoantennae to represent four distinct information states. As depicted in Fig. 2 (a), each cell containing identical nanoantennae acts as one storage unit. When the polarizer angle is fixed at 45° and the analyzer angle is set at 0°, 45°, 90°, and 135°, four distinct color images are photographed from the checkerboard pattern and agree well with the calculated images. Four color sequences are created from the calculated results for each nanoantenna orientation at the four analyzer angles. Interestingly, the data storage density in such a metasurface can be further increased by introducing 16 differently oriented nanoantennae from 0° to 168.75° with a step of 11.5°. As shown in Fig. 2 (b). Sixteen distinct color sequences are created, which indicates that 4-bit information can be stored by one nanoantenna orientation. Also, the movable stage and the setup shown in Fig. 2 (a) realize rapid parallel information read-out, surpassing the conventional techniques which read the data stored in one single pit in a point-by-point manner.

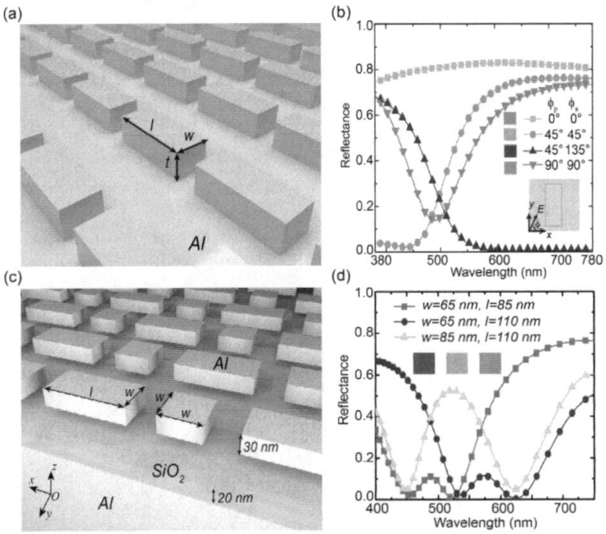

Fig. 1. Two types of Al metasurfaces and their corresponding reflectance. (a) Schematic diagram of type I metasurface, the period of the array is 250 nm and the optimized dimensions of the nanoantenna are: l = 200 nm, w = 80 nm and t = 70 nm. (b) Simulated reflectance under different polarizer and analyzer angles. (c) Schematic diagram of type II metasurface. The period of the array is 400 nm. (d) Simulated reflectance corresponding to varying nanoantenna dimensions. The insets in (b) and (d) depict calculated colors of the corresponding spectra.

III. Conclusion

Diverse colors can be generated from Type I metasurface by tuning the polarization state of the incident and reflected light. Benefiting from the LSPR and carefully chosen dimensions of nanoantennae, the metasurface exhibits great information capacity. By creating customized color sequences, high-density optical data storage is experimentally realized. Type II metasurface uses a pair of centrosymmetric "i-shaped" dimers to adjust gap-plasmon resonance bands, thus enabling full-color generation.

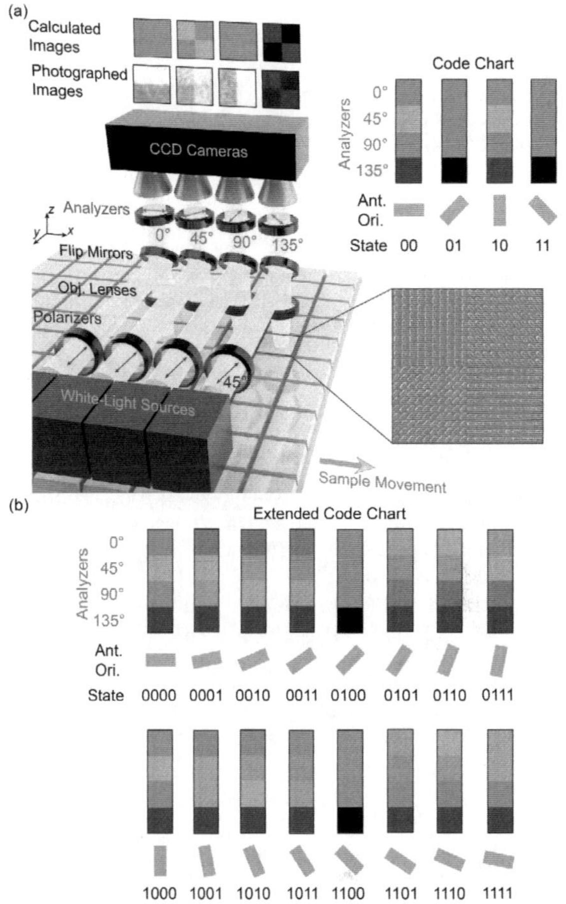

Fig. 2. Type I metasurface as a data storage device. (a) The checkerboard pattern consists of nanoantennae in four orientations arranged in nanopixels each containing 10 × 10 nanoantennae, as shown in the SEM. The schematic depicts a proposed system consisting of 4 white-light sources and a CCD camera with fixed polarizers and analyzers for fast information readout. (b) Calculated color sequences record 4-bit information.

References

[1] J. S. Clausen et al., "Plasmonic Metasurfaces for Coloration of Plastic Consumer Products," Nano Lett., vol. 14, no. 8, pp. 4499–4504, 2014.

[2] A. S. Roberts, A. Pors, O. Albrektsen, and S. I. Bozhevolnyi, "Subwavelength Plasmonic Color Printing Protected for Ambient Use," Nano Lett., vol. 14, no. 2, pp. 783–787, 2014.

[3] X. Duan, S. Kamin, and N. Liu, "Dynamic plasmonic color display," Nat. Commun., vol. 8, p. 14606, 2017.

[4] X. Zhu, C. Vannahme, E. Højlund-Nielsen, N. A. Mortensen, and A. Kristensen, "Plasmonic color laser printing," Nat. Nanotechnol., vol. 11, no. 4, pp. 325–329, 2016.

[5] T. Ellenbogen, K. Seo, and K. B. Crozier, "Chromatic Plasmonic Polarizers for Active Visible Color Filtering and Polarimetry," Nano Lett., vol. 12, no. 2, pp. 1026–1031, 2012.

[6] M. Song et al., "Color display and encryption with a plasmonic polarizing metamirror," Nanophotonics, vol. 7, no. 1, pp. 323–331, 2018.

Digital Metasurfaces Controlled by Light

Wei Xiang Jiang and Xin Ge Zhang
State Key Lab of Millimeter Waves,
Southeast University,
Nanjing 210096, China.
wxjiang81@seu.edu.cn

***Abstract*—In this paper, we will introduce a kind of remote-mode digital metasurfaces that are controlled by the illuminating light. By tuning the intensity of LED light, the digital coding metasurfaces enable dynamically reconfigurable radiation beams or tunable near-field distributions. Experimental demonstrations were carried out at microwave frequencies. The presented dynamical remote-tuning metasurfaces can be tuned in a non-contact remote fashion.**

Keywords*—coding metasurface, electromagnetic wave controlling, light-controllable, microwave.

I. Introduction

Recently, a new class of two-dimensional (2D) ultrathin metamaterials, termed as metasurfaces, has been proposed and developed with versatile functions of manipulating the wavefronts of electromagnetic (EM) waves [1]. Especially, active metasurfaces allow dynamical tuning of EM response. Compared to metamaterials, metasurfaces can reduce the material loss dramatically and overcome the fabrication issue due to the thin thickness. More recently, digital metasurfaces that are described by digital "bits" have been proposed [2], and the concept of using binary codes to quantify phase responses of metasurface unit cells has been verified experimentally.

In this paper, we first introduce a kind of light-controllable digital coding metasurfaces in reflective type [3]. We will present the light-tunable reflective digital element. By controlling the intensity of the illumination light, the reflection phase of the presented digital element can be dynamically tuned as desired. Then, we also present a type of tunable digital coding metasurface for dynamic controlling transmission state of EM waves by tuning the state of external light source or frequency independently [4]. Through tuning the intensity of the illumination light or shifting the frequency remotely, the digital metasurface can realize free switches of EM-wave transmission amplitude. We also fabricated and measured such light-dependent reflective and transmission-type digital metasurfaces.

II. Reflective Light-controlled Metasurface

The presented light-controlled metasurface is composed of an array of tunable digital unit particles that are arranged in a plane, together with an array of photodiodes which provides light-controllable DC bias for the varactor diodes embedded in the digital particles, which is shown in Fig. 1. We first predesign the coding sequence and send the signal by light source array, then the photodiode array receive the coding sequence and transmit it to the metasurface, and finally the incident waves will be dynamically scattered by the digital coding metasurface. Hence, the scattered or radiated waves are controlled by the "coded" light emitted by the source array.

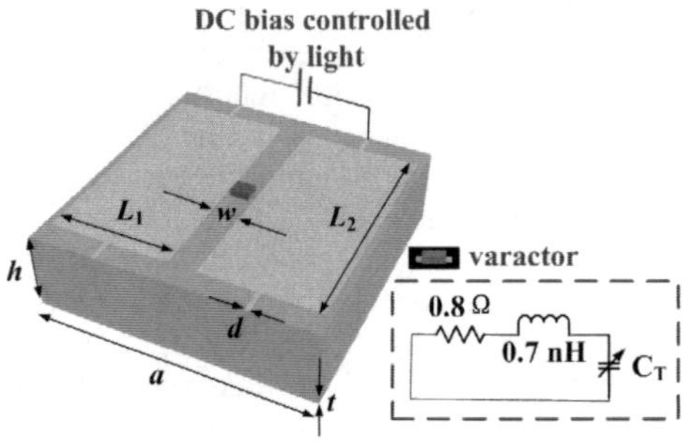

Fig. 1. Unit cell of the light-controllable digital metasurface. The DC bias of the varactor is provided by the photodiodes which are controlled by LED array. The inset shows equivalent lumped elements model of the varactor.

To verify the presented digital coding metasurface controlled by remote illuminating light experimentally, we fabricated the LED-based light source, the photodiode array, and the metasurface. For the fabricated digital metasurface, two 2.0-mm-wide bias lines connects to the positive and negative electrodes of the photodiode array, which is located by the side of metasurface. The illumination source is an array of 50 low-power white LEDs as a tunable handcrafted light source. In experiments, we measured the far-field radiation beams of the digital coding metasurface in the microwave chamber and one of the results is illustrated in Fig. 2.

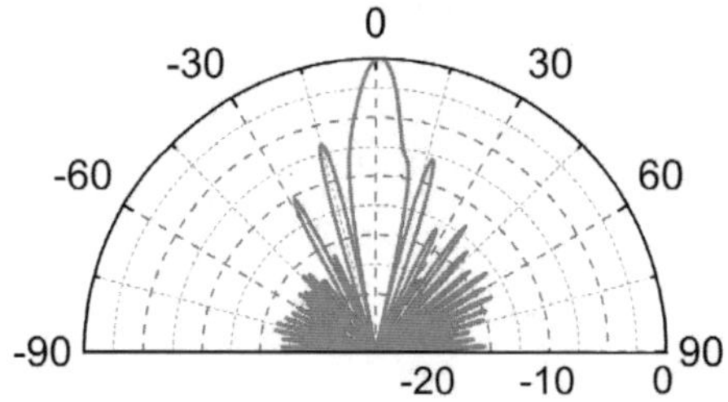

Fig. 2. When light source turns off, the measured reflection beams of the light-controlled digital metasurface with coding "000000" at 3.75 GHz.

III. Transmission-type Coding Metasurface

Next, we discuss the transmission-type digital coding metasurface that can be tuned by light intensity and EM-wave frequency independently. The presented digital particle is illustrated in Fig. 3. On the top square metallic patch, a circular ring gap is excavated outwards along the radius *r*, and a varactor diode is loaded in the gap to connect the circular metallic patch and remaining metallic patch outside the gap. In the center of the circular metallic patch, there is a metallic via connecting to a metallic ground line.

To realize dynamical control of the EM-wave transmission state with external illumination light, we use silicon PIN photodiode series array to provide direct-current

(DC) reverse voltage for tuning the capacitance (CT) of the embedded varactor, as shown in Fig. 3.

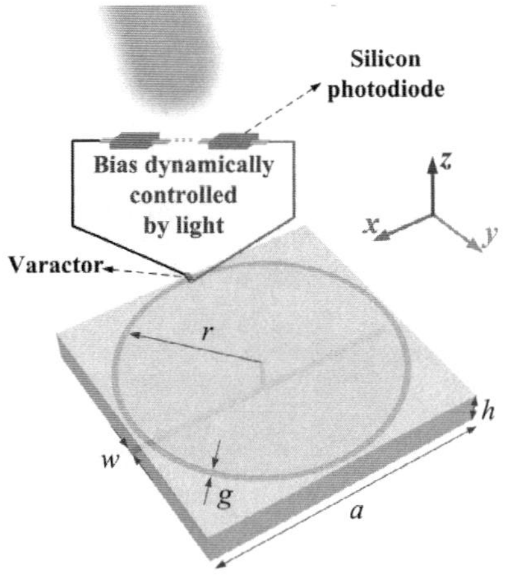

Fig. 3. The proposed transmissive digital coding particle which is controlled by the illumination light and frequency independently.

More importantly, the designed digital particle has two resonance frequencies, corresponding to two different resonant modes, respectively. So, when the illuminating state of the light source is unchanged, the transmission state of EM waves can be also switched by changing the working frequencies.

To verify the coding state of designed metasurface, we make the numerical simulations. The simulated induced surface-current distributions of the digital coding metasurface with different coding patterns are shown in Fig. 4. We also fabricated and measured the digital metasurface, which consists of a 15×15 array of the designed digital particles, and a 70-photodiodes array.

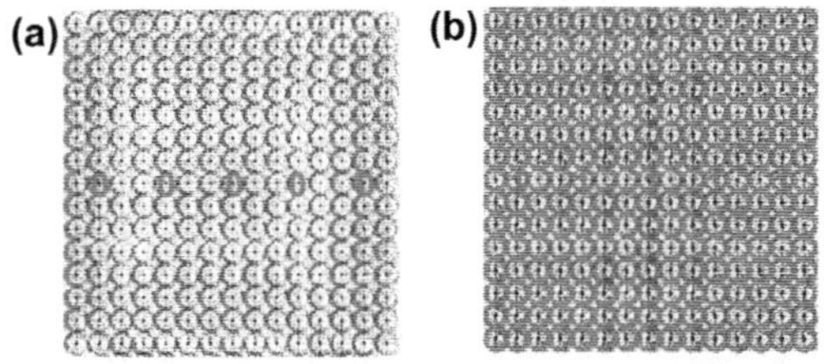

Fig. 4. Simulated induced surface-current distributions of the digital coding metasurface with different coding patterns. (a) 00000; (b) 11111.

IV. SUMMARY

In this work, we have discussed a type of light-controlled digital coding metasurface, including a reflective one and a transmission-type one. Such metasurfaces can be considered as a bridge linking the optics and the microwave.

ACKNOWLEDGMENT

This work was supported by the National Key Research and Development Program of China (2017YFA0700201, 2017YFA0700202, 2017YFA0700203), the National Natural Science Foundation of China (61522106, 61571117, 61501112, 61401089, 61501117 and 61631007), the Foundation of National Excellent Doctoral Dissertation of China (201444), and the 111 Project (111-2-05).

REFERENCES

[1] N. F. Yu, P. Genevet, M. A. Kats, F. Aieta, J. P. Tetienne, F. Capasso, Z. Gaburro, "Light propagation with phase discontinuities: generalized laws of reflection and refraction," Science, vol. 334, pp. 333, 2011.

[2] T. J. Cui, M. Q. Qi, X. Wan, J. Zhao, Q. Cheng, "Coding metamaterials, digital metamaterials and programmable metamaterials," Light: Sci. Appl., vol. 3, pp. e218, 2014.

[3] X. G. Zhang, W. X. Tang, W. X. Jiang, G. D. Bai, J. Tang, L. Bai, C.-W. Qiu, and T. J. Cui, "Light-controllable digital coding metasurfaces," Adv. Sci., DOI: 10.1002/advs.201801028, 2018.

[4] X. G. Zhang, W. X. Jiang, and T. J. Cui, "Frequency-dependent transmission-type digital coding metasurface controlled by light intensity," Appl. Phys. Lett., vol. 113, no. 091601, 2018.

Dual-Band Slot Dipole with AMC using Textiles

[1]Fatin Nabilah Giman, [1,4]*Ping Jack Soh, and[1]Azremi Abdullah Al-Hadi
[1]Sch. of Computer and Comm. Eng, Universiti Malaysia Perlis, 02600 Arau, Perlis, Malaysia.
{pjsoh, azremi}@unimap.edu.my

[2]Mohd Faizal Jamlos
[2]Faculty of Mechanical Eng, Universiti Malaysia Pahang 26600 Pekan, Pahang, Malaysia
faizaljamlos@ump.edu.my

[3]Herwansyah Lago,
[3]Faculty of Engineering Universiti Malaysia Sabah 88400 Kota Kinabalu, Sabah, Malaysia
herwansyahlago@gmail.com

[4]Dominique Schreurs
[4]ESAT-TELEMIC Research Division KU Leuven, Kasteelpark Arenberg 10 3001 Leuven, Belgium
dominique.schreurs@kuleuven.be

[5]Sharul Kamal Abdul Rahim
[5]Wireless Communication Center Universiti Teknologi Malaysia, 81310 UTM Skudai, Johor, Malaysia
sharulkamal@fke.utm.my

[6]Adalbert Beyer
[6]Dept. of Electrical Eng. & Informatics Duisburg-Essen University, Campus Duisburg, 47057 Duisburg, Germany
a.beyer@ieee.org

***Abstract*— A dual band slot dipole antenna integrated with an AMC plane is proposed to reduce SAR when operated on body for WBAN applications. The AMC plane is formed using a 3 x 3 array of unit cells, each consisting of a square patch integrated with diamond-shaped slot. Results indicate that the antenna provides wide upper bandwidth up to 600 MHz (in flat condition) and up to 570 MHz when bent. Besides that, its front-to-back ratio (FBR) is also improved.**

Keywords—antennas, artificial magnetic conductor, metamaterial, multiband antennas, wearable antennas

I. Introduction

Wireless body area networks (WBAN) and Wireless Local Area Networks (WLAN) are two of the most widely researched applications globally. Accordance with this development, wearable antennas made from flexible materials are also widely investigated due to their attractive features: low profile, flexible, inexpensive, lightweight, and most importantly, safe to be worn. However, when placed on body, an antenna with high back radiation or omnidirectional pattern such as dipole antenna [1] tends to increase the electromagnetic absorption in the human body due to its proximity during operation. This almost certainly results in high Specific Absorption Rate (SAR) value which potentially affects human body tissues. The American National Standards Institute (ANSI) and International Commission on Non-Ionizing radiation Protection (ICNIRP) regulated that the exposure for human tissues is limited to 1.6 W/kg averaged per 1g of tissue and 2 W/kg per 10 g of tissue, respectively.

One of the solutions to control the level of the back-radiation is either by selecting an antenna topology with a rear ground plane or to introduce a metallic plane to function as a reflector. However, the conventional reflecting structure interferes with the antenna operation, and is typically placed at an extended distance from the radiator. Such setup, in turn, increases the height of the antenna structure and reduces its suitability to be worn on body due to increased thickness. Moreover, the optimal gap of such structure is frequency-dependent, which requires it to be determined based on the lower frequency in the case of a multi-resonant or wideband antenna, which again increases the thickness. To overcome this, metasurfaces such as Electromagnetic Bandgap (EBG) or Artificial Magnetic Conductor (AMC) with dual-band behaviour can be an ideal solution to balance between thickness and radiation characteristics modification [2]-[7].

II. Design of Dual Band Slot Dipole Antenna

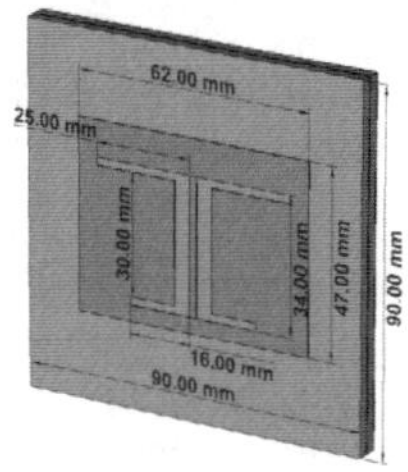

(a)

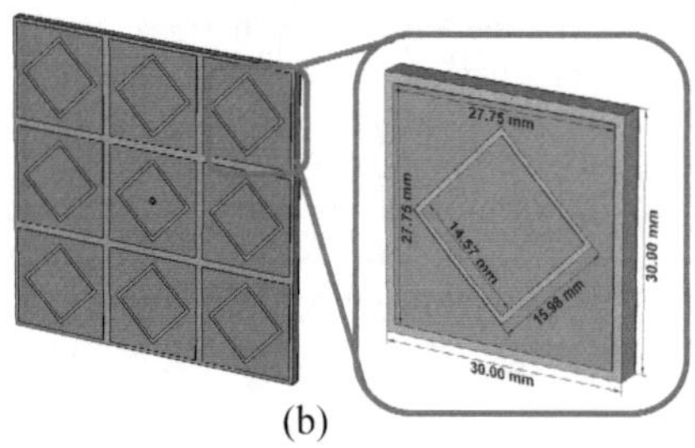

(b)

Fig. 1. Topology of the proposed (a) antenna and (b) AMC unit cell.

The textile antenna is one of the best options for WBAN applications due to flexibility of the material. The proposed antenna structure is illustrated in Fig. 1 (a). It consists of five layers as follows: a ground layer on the bottom-most layer, followed by two layers of substrate, and a layer consisting of the AMC plane in between them. Finally, a radiating layer is placed on the top. Felt, each layer with a thickness of 3 mm is used as its substrate, while ShieldIt Super conductive textile with a thickness of 0.17 mm is used to form the patch, ground and the AMC. The relative permittivity and loss tangent of the felt substrate is 1.44 and 0.044, respectively, whereas the conductivity of the ShieldIt Super is 1.18×10^5 S/m.

Fig. 1 (b) illustrates the proposed AMC plane and unit cell structure. The simulation results indicate that the AMC is capable to achieve zero reflection phase at two operating frequencies, which are 2.45 GHz for the lower band and 5.8 GHz for the upper band. For the upper band, a shorter current path is created in the AMC compared to the lower band. This resulted in a wider reflection phase bandwidth of 15.8% or 891 MHz (from 5.189 to 6.08 GHz) for the upper band, while the achieved phase reflection bandwidth for the lower band is about 7.76% or 187 MHz (from 2.32 to 2.5 GHz).

Both AMC unit cell and proposed antenna have been designed and simulated by using CST MWS software.

III. Results and Discussion

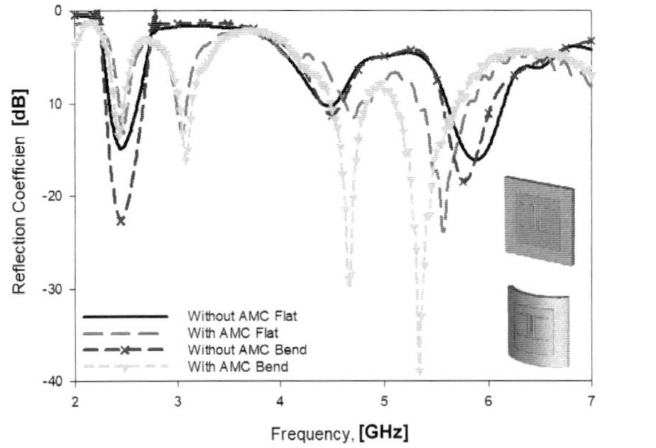

Fig. 2. Reflection coefficient results for the proposed antenna with and without AMC in flat and bending condition.

TABLE I. Performance summary of proposed antenna in planar condition

Parameters	Frequency [GHz]	Antenna	
		Without AMC	*With AMC*
Gain [dB]	2.45	-2.47	5.9
	5.8	7.17	7.2
FBR [dB]	2.45	14.39	20.77
	5.8	13.25	28.61

Fig. 2 shows that the measured reflection coefficient ($|S_{11}|$) in free space planar and bent condition for both antennas is below -10 dB in the lower frequency band (2.45 GHz). However, the proposed antenna with AMC is slightly shifted compared to the antenna without AMC. This is due to the AMC's fabrication inaccuracy. The radiation pattern of both antennas in free space and planar condition is directional in the azimuth plane with a maximum gain of -2.47 dB (without AMC) and 5.9 dB (with AMC) in the lower band. On the other hand, a maximum gain of 7.17 dB (without AMC) and 7.2 dB (with AMC) is observed in the upper band. Table I shows that the realized gain in free space of the flat case of the proposed antenna without AMC produces a negative realized gain. Meanwhile, with presence of AMC, it produces a positive realized gain. This indicates that the dissimilar slot length in the radiator and the integration of the optimized AMC plane contribute in the improved gain in the lower band from -2.47 dB to 5.9 dB, corresponding to a significant increase of about 7 dB. Meanwhile, the realized gain in the upper band for the antenna with AMC is higher than the antenna without AMC. Moreover, the simulated front-to-back ratio (FBR) of antenna with AMC in the flat condition is higher in both bands compared to antenna without AMC.

As wearable antennas are designed to be worn on-body, there is always risks of the radiated energy being absorbed by human body. For that reason, the SAR values for the proposed antenna with AMC are calculated using CST MWS by placing the antennas in proximity of a truncated human voxel model (on the chest). The antenna is placed 10 mm away from these models. The SAR value is calculated based on the IEEE C95.1 standard averaged over 10 g of tissue volume (ICNIRP) and is regulated to be safe when lower than 2 W/kg. A summary of the SAR values is provided in Table I. The SAR distribution at 2.45 GHz and 5.8 GHz did not exceed 0.1 W/kg. Furthermore, with the presence of the AMC plane, the effect of human body towards the antenna's S_{11} result has been reduced, whereas the antenna is capable to operate with the same performance as in free space. It can be observed that the proposed antenna with AMC is capable to balance the performance of S_{11} and gain, besides its reasonably low SAR when operated on body.

IV. Conclusions

A dual band slotted dipole antenna with AMC is proposed for operation in the 2.45 GHz and 5.8 GHz bands for WBAN applications. To ensure a flexible, wearable and low profile structure, felt is used as its substrate and ShieldIt Super as its conductors. It is observed that the integration of the proposed antenna with the AMC produced wider bandwidths up to 600 MHz in the upper band. In the lower band, both antennas produced slightly similar narrow bandwidths of about 100 MHz. Despite this, the present of the AMC improved the realized gain and reduced backward radiation. Maximum gains of 5.9 dB and 7.2 dB are observed in the lower and upper band, respectively, when assessed in a planar free space condition. Finally, calculated SAR values using a detailed human body model for both antennas are below 0.1 W/kg, indicating their safe operation in proximity of the human body (chest) in the planar condition.

Acknowledgment

This work is supported in part by the Fundamental Research Grant Scheme (FRGS) (grant no 9003-00527), and the MyBrain Scholarship, both from the Malaysian Ministry of Higher Education (MOHE), and the Collaborative Research in Engineering, Science and Technology (CREST) (grant no 9002-00035).

References

[1] A Afridi, S Ullah, S Khan, A Ahmed, AH Khalil, and MA Tarar, "Design of dual band wearable antenna using metamaterials," Journal of Microwave Power and Electromagnetic Energy, vol. 47(2), pp.126-37, 2013.

[2] S Yan, PJ Soh, and GAE Vandenbosch, "Low-profile dual-band textile antenna with artificial magnetic conductor plane," IEEE Trans. on Antennas and Propag., vol. 62(12), pp.6487-90, 2014.

[3] ZH Jiang, DE Brocker, PE Sieber, and DH Werner, "A compact, low-profile metasurface-enabled antenna for wearable medical body-area network devices," IEEE Trans. on Antennas and Propag., vol. 62(8), pp.4021-30, 2014.

[4] YH Di, XY Liu, and MM Tentzeris, "A conformable dual-band antenna equipped with AMC for WBAN applications," In: 3rd IEEE Asia-Pacific Conference on Antennas and Propagation (APCAP), pp. 388-391, 2014.

[5] S Yan, PJ Soh, and GAE Vandenbosch, "Wearable dual-band magneto-electric dipole antenna for WBAN/WLAN applications," IEEE Trans. on Antennas and Propag., vol. 63(9), pp. 4165-9, 2015.

[6] A. Alemaryeen, S. Noghanian, "AMC Integrated Textile Monopole Antenna for Wearable Applications," ACES Journal, Volume: 31, Number: 6, 2016.

[7] H. R. Khaleel, H. M. Al-Rizzo, D. G. Rucker, "An AMC Based Antenna for Telemedicine Applications," ACES Journal, Volume: 27, Number: 1, 2012.

Discontinuous Galerkin Time Domain Method for Periodic Dispersive Structure Analysis at Oblique Incidence

Huaguang Bao, Sawyer D. Campbell, Pingjuan L. Werner and Douglas H. Werner
Department of Electrical Engineering
The Pennsylvania State University, University Park, PA, 16802 USA
hub93@psu.edu, sdc22@psu.edu, plw7@psu.edu, dhw@psu.edu

***Abstract*—An efficient discontinuous Galerkin time domain (DGTD) method is presented to analyze the electromagnetic scattering from periodic structures with dispersive components. The time domain periodic boundary conditions are implemented in the DGTD method by introducing transformed field variables. The method is applied to the Drude dispersive media model using an auxiliary differential equation (ADE) approach. Numerical analysis of a dual-band infrared absorber is shown to validate the proposed method.**

Keywords—discontinuous Galerkin time domain method, dispersive material, periodic boundary conditions.

I. Introduction

There has been a recent and growing interest in the modeling, design and application of metamaterials and metasurfaces [1], [2]. Many metamaterials are derived from periodic structures that tailor electromagnetic scattering and radiation behaviors in a desired fashion. When periodic structures are illuminated by a normally incident plane wave, assigning periodic boundaries as pairs of perfect electric conducting (PEC) and perfect magnetic conducting (PMC) boundary conditions is a convenient way to mimic unit cells [4]. However, a more generic boundary condition is required to analyze the scattering from periodic structures at oblique incidence [5]. Furthermore, metamaterials are often comprised from combinations of metallic and dielectric materials arranged in an intelligent way so as to achieve a desired behavior. However, while metals are often modeled as PEC in the RF regime, the dispersive properties of metals should be carefully taken into consideration at terahertz, infrared and optical frequencies. Therefore, an accurate and computationally efficient numerical method for the analysis of periodic structures with dispersive components is of great importance in metamaterial modeling. To this end, the discontinuous Galerkin time domain (DGTD) method has seen rapid development in application to electromagnetic simulations, primarily because of its advantages in dealing with non-conformal meshes and parallel computing [3]. Dispersive materials described by common Debye, Drude and Lorentz models have been incorporated into the DGTD method using the auxiliary differential equation (ADE) approach [6], [7]. In this work, an efficient DGTD method with periodic boundary conditions and the Drude dispersive model is proposed for the analysis of periodic dispersive structures at oblique incidence. A transformed field variable technique is employed to implement the Floquet periodic boundary conditions. The DGTD formulations for a Drude dispersive medium based on transforming Maxwell's equations are derived by using an ADE approach. This work builds the basis for future research on the multiscale design and optimization of highly-complex metasurfaces.

This work was supported in part by the DARPA/DSO Extreme Optics and Imaging (EXTREME) Program, Award # HR00111720032.

II. Formulations

A. Transforming Maxwell's Equations

When a time harmonic plane wave is obliquely incident on a doubly periodic structure with a specific incident angle (θ_i, φ_i), the fields satisfy the Floquet boundary conditions. For time domain solvers, a time shift will be translated from the phase shift introduced by this Floquet periodicity in the frequency domain, which makes its implementation not very straightforward. In order to embed this time shift, transformed field variables [8] are introduced here. Based on this derivation, the time domain transformed Maxwell's equations and their periodic boundary conditions can be described as

$$\varepsilon\frac{\partial \vec{P}_e}{\partial t} = \nabla\times\vec{P}_h - \frac{1}{c}\vec{k}_t\times\frac{\partial \vec{P}_h}{\partial t} \quad (1)$$

$$\mu\frac{\partial \vec{P}_h}{\partial t} = -\nabla\times\vec{P}_e + \frac{1}{c}\vec{k}_t\times\frac{\partial \vec{P}_e}{\partial t} \quad (2)$$

$$\vec{P}_{e,h}(x,y,z,t) = \begin{cases}\vec{P}_{e,h}(x+x_p, y, z, t)\\ \vec{P}_{e,h}(x, y+y_p, z, t)\end{cases}, \quad (3)$$

where x_p and y_p are the period lengths in the x- and y-directions, $\vec{k}_t = (\sin\theta_i\cos\varphi_i, \sin\theta_i\sin\varphi_i, 0)$ is the transverse component of the unit vector of the incident vector wavenumber and c is the velocity of light in the free space.

B. Drude Despersive Media Model

The permittivity of a linear, isotropic, and dispersive material described by a Drude model can be expressed as

$$\varepsilon(\omega) = \varepsilon_0\left(\varepsilon_\infty + \frac{\omega_p^2}{j\omega(v_c + j\omega)}\right) \quad (4)$$

where ε_0 is the free-space permittivity, ε_∞ is the infinite-frequency permittivity, ω_p is the plasma frequency and v_c is the collision frequency. Using a time-frequency transformation and combining (1) and (4), the time domain transformed Maxwell's equations along with the ADE for dispersive materials with a Drude model can be expressed as

$$\varepsilon_0\varepsilon_\infty \frac{\partial \vec{P_e}}{\partial t} = \nabla \times \vec{P_h} - \frac{1}{c}\vec{k_t} \times \frac{\partial \vec{P_h}}{\partial t} - \vec{J_P} \quad (5)$$

$$\mu \frac{\partial \vec{P_h}}{\partial t} = -\nabla \times \vec{P_e} + \frac{1}{c}\vec{k_t} \times \frac{\partial \vec{P_e}}{\partial t} \quad (6)$$

$$\frac{\partial \vec{J_P}}{\partial t} + v_c\vec{J_P} = \varepsilon_0\omega_p^2\vec{P_e} \quad (7)$$

where $\vec{J_P}$ is the auxiliary electric-polarization vector.

C. Discontinuous Galerkin Discretization

In order to obtain the DGTD discrete system, the adjacent elements are coupled with the following upwind flux

$$\vec{n} \times \vec{P_e} = \vec{n} \times \frac{\left(Y\vec{P_e} - \vec{n} \times \vec{P_h}\right) + \left(Y^+\vec{P_e}^+ - \vec{n} \times \vec{P_h}^+\right)}{Y + Y^+} \quad (8)$$

$$\vec{n} \times \vec{P_h} = \vec{n} \times \frac{\left(Z\vec{P_h} - \vec{n} \times \vec{P_e}\right) + \left(Z^+\vec{P_h}^+ - \vec{n} \times \vec{P_e}^+\right)}{Z + Z^+} \quad (9)$$

where $Z = 1/Y$ is the intrinsic impedance and the superscript $+$ implies the variables from adjacent elements. Within the dispersive media, the intrinsic impedance can be described as $Z = Z_0/\sqrt{\varepsilon_\infty}$. Here, a Runge-Kuttta (RK) time stepping scheme was employed for the time discretization.

III. Numerical Results

In order to validate the proposed method, the properties of a dual-band infrared absorber were numerically investigated. The structure of the infrared absorber has been introduced in [4] and it is comprised of a gold elliptical nanodisk array on top of a thin dielectric spacer and an optically thick gold mirror. Figure 1 (a) depicts the unit cell configuration. A Drude model with $\varepsilon_\infty = 1$, $\omega_p = 1.37 \times 10^{16}$ rad/s and $v_c = 1.2 \times 10^{14}$ Hz was employed to describe the gold material. The incident field is taken to be a modulated Gaussian pulse to obtain a wide-band response. Both normal incidence $(\theta_i, \varphi_i) = (0°, 90°)$ and oblique incidence with $(\theta_i, \varphi_i) = (30°, 90°)$ are considered here. Fig. 1 (b) and (c) illustrate the results for the reflectivity of the absorber under normal and oblique incidence, respectively. The results from [4], in which the DGTD method with pairs of PEC and PMC boundaries was employed, are taken as the benchmarks for the normal incident illumination case. To validate the proposed method at oblique incidence, a simulation of this configuration is executed with the CST software package, in which a frequency domain finite element solver was utilized. As shown in Fig. 1 (b) and (c), good agreement is demonstrated, confirming the effectiveness of the proposed method for periodic dispersive structure analysis.

IV. Conclusion

In this paper, a DGTD method with periodic boundary conditions and a Drude dispersive media model has been proposed for the electromagnetic analysis of doubly periodic structures with dispersive materials. The corresponding DGTD formulation, which is based on a transformed version of Maxwell's equations, was derived using an ADE approach. Simulations of periodic dispersive structures illuminated by both normally and obliquely incidence waves have been implemented to validate the proposed computational framework.

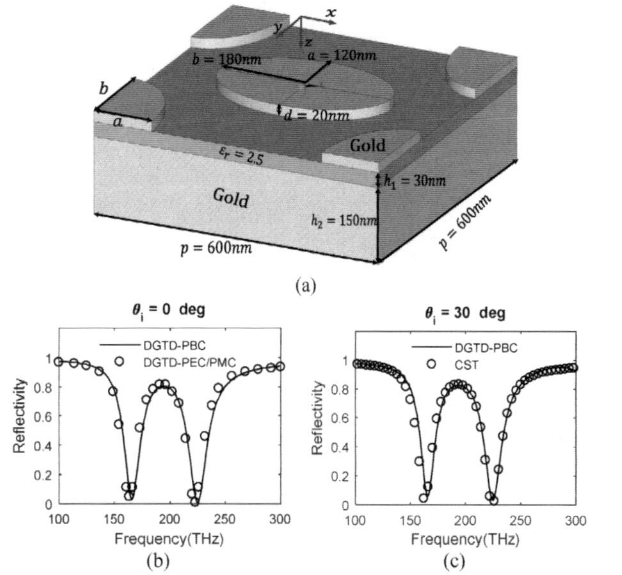

Fig. 1. Geometry and reflectivity of the dual-band infrared absorber. (a) Unit cell geometry. (b) Reflectivity calculated from the proposed method and reference [4] under normal incidence. (c) Reflectivity calculated from the proposed method and CST software package under oblique incidence.

References

[1] H. T. Chen, A. J. Taylor, and N. Yu, "A review of metasurfaces: Physics and applications," Rep. Prog. Phys., vol. 79, no. 7, pp. 076401, Jun. 2016.

[2] Z. H. Jiang, D. E. Brocker, P. E. Sieber, and D. H. Werner, "A compact, low-profile metasurface-enabled antenna for wearable medical bodyarea network devices," IEEE Trans. Antennas Propag., vol. 62, no. 8, pp. 4021–4030, Aug. 2014.

[3] S. Dosopoulos, B. Zhao, and J.F. Lee, "Non-conformal and parallel discontinuous Galerkin time domain method for Maxwell's equations: EM analysis of IC packages," Journal of Computational Physics, vol. 238, pp. 48–70, 2013.

[4] Q. Ren, Y. Bian, L. Kang, P. L. Werner, and D. H. Werner, "Leap-frog continuous–discontinuous Galerkin time domain method for nanoarchitectures with the Drude model," J. Light. Technol., vol. 35, no. 22, pp. 4888–4896, Nov. 2017.

[5] L. E. R. Petersson and J. M. Jin, "A three-dimensional time-domain finite-element formulation for periodic structures," IEEE Trans. Antennas Propag., vol. 54, no. 1, pp. 12–19, Jan. 2006.

[6] S. D. Gedney, J. A. R. J. C. Young, and T. C. Kramer, "A discontinuous Galerkin finite element time-domain method modeling of dispersive media," IEEE Trans. Antennas Propag., vol. 60, pp. 1969–1977, Apr. 2012.

[7] Q. Ren, H. Bao, S. D. Campbell, L. J. Prokopeva, A. V. Kildishev, and D. H. Werner, "Continuous-discontinuous Galerkin time domain (CDGTD) method with generalized dispersive material (GDM) model for computational photonics," Opt. Express, vol. 26, no. 22, pp. 29005–29016, Oct. 2018.

[8] N. C. Miller, A. D. Baczewski, J. D. Albrecht, and B. Shanker, "A discontinuous Galerkin time domain framework for periodic structures subject to oblique excitation," IEEE Trans. Antennas Propag., vol. 62, no. 8, pp. 4386–4391, Aug. 2014.

An Integrated, Broadband Circularly-polarized Millimeter-wave Metasurface-based Transmit-array

Zhi Hao Jiang and Xiao-Wei Zhu
State Key Laboratory of Millimeter-Waves
School of Information Science and Engineering
Southeast, University
Nanjing, Jiangsu, 210096 China

***Abstract*-In this paper, we present the design of an integrated circularly-polarized high-gain antenna with a broad bandwidth at the millimeter-wave Ka-band. The proposed compact antenna is enabled by the integration of a metasurfaces-based transmit-array and a broadband circularly-polarized feed radiator. The feed radiator is a substrate integrated waveguide fed patch with a finite-sized metasurfaces superstrate, while the transmit-array utilizes the rotation phase for collimating the waves emitted from the feeding source. The full-wave simulation results show that the integrated transmit-array antenna achieves an overall bandwidth of about 18.3% within which the S_{11} is below -10 dB, the axial ratio is smaller than 3 dB, and the gain variation is less than 3 dB with a peak gain of 23.5 dBi.**

Keywords—antenna, circularly-polarized, transmit-array

I. INTRODUCTION

The millimeter-wave regime has garnered a great amount of research interest for diverse applications, such as 5G mobile communications, satellite communications, and automotive radars, due to their vast available spectrum resources [1]. At millimeter-wave frequencies, the path loss of electromagnetic waves is much more significant than that at a lower frequency. Hence, high gain directional beams are often required for millimeter-wave wireless systems in order to maintain a high enough signal-to-noise-and-interference ratio. In addition, in order to exploit the wide absolute bandwidth for high speed data transfer or high-precision radar detection, broadband performance is typically preferable.

In the past, many techniques have been employed to achieve broadband directive antennas at millimeter-waves, including planar arrays [2], Fabry-Perot cavity antennas [3], reflect-arrays [4], transmit-arrays [5], and so on. The planar array antennas, which have a low profile, can be designed to achieve a high directivity using cooperate feeding networks. However, as the size of the array expands, the additional gain obtained from adding the number of radiating elements will be consumed by the increased loss caused by a larger feeding circuit. The Fabry-Perot cavity antennas can generate beams with a high degree of collimation, but are usually suffered from a narrow bandwidth. Quasi-optical approaches, such as reflect-arrays and transmit-arrays, are free from loss caused by complicated feeding networks, thus have been often used in cases where a super-high gain is required. When comparing between the two, the transmit-arrays show several advantages over the reflect-arrays in the aspects that they are free from feed blockage and are less sensitive to surface variation induced phase distortion. As a result, more and more transmit-arrays have been developed in recent years for millimeter-wave applications.

So far, the majority of the reported transmit-arrays are using horn antennas as the feeds [6, 7], which results in a large overall volume for the antenna sub-system. Several works have been carried out using planar feeds to reduce the profile [8-10]. However, most of them are suffered from either a narrow bandwidth or only support linear polarization. Here, we present an integrated broadband circularly-polarized (CP) transmit-array antenna at Ka-band which has an overall bandwidth of about 18.3% and a profile of $3\lambda_0$.

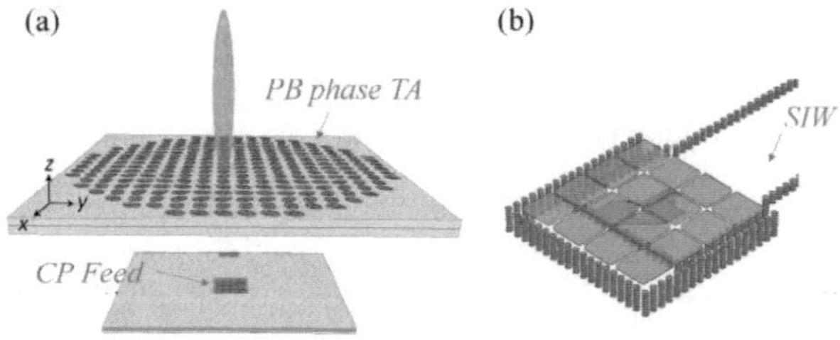

Fig. 1. Configurations of the (a) integrated antenna and (b) feed radiator.

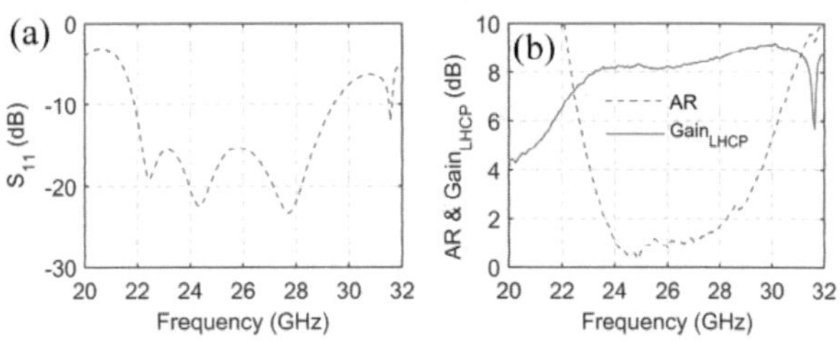

Fig. 2. Simulated (a) S_{11} and (b) AR and gain of the feed radiator.

II. ANTENNA DESIGN AND NUMERICAL RESULTS

The configuration of the integrated antenna is shown in Fig. 1 (a), where a feed source is placed at the bottom fed by a substrate integrated waveguide. Located above the feed at a distance of 30 mm, *i.e.* about $3\lambda_0$, the transmit-array has a diameter of about $9\lambda_0$.

As displayed in Fig. 1 (b), the feed radiator is composed by a patch with a pair of truncated corners and a top metasurface containing 4 by 4 capacitively coupled patches. The patch and the metasurface superstrate jointly provide two axial ratio dips, thus yielding a wide axial ratio (AR) bandwidth. As presented in Fig. 2, the feed radiator has a simulated joint S_{11} < -10 dB and AR < 3 dB band from 23.3 to 29.2 GHz. Within this band, the gain for the radiated left-handed CP waves is about 8 ~ 9 dBi, which are suitable for illuminating a transmit-array.

The metasurfaces transmit-array has unit cells with identical geometries and dimensions but different rotation angles within the plane of the transmit-array. It consists of three metallic layers separated by two dielectric spacers (inset of Fig. 3 (a)), with a total thickness of less than $\lambda_0/3$. Basically, the transmit-array unit cell behaves like a half-wave plate that transforms a left-handed circularly-polarized incident wave into a right-handed circularly-polarized transmitted wave with an imparted transmission phase proportional to twice of the cell rotation angle φ_r. Such a transmission phase delay is independent of the operational frequency, thus is dispersionless [11]. It can be seen that, within the frequency range from 24.5 to 29.0 GHz, the co-polarized transmitted CP wave (T_{LL}) is much weaker than the cross-polarized CP wave (T_{RL}) with T_{RL} > -2.5 dB. As the unit cell rotates around the surface normal by an angle of φ_r, the transmission phase for the cross-polarized CP wave can be controlled, which is linearly proportional to φ_r (Fig. 3 (b)).

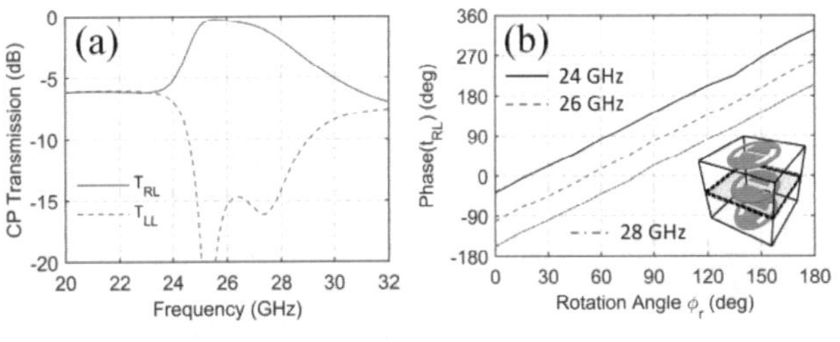

Fig. 3. Simulated CP transmission (a) magnitude and (b) phase of the unit cell.

By designing the cell rotation angle distribution for the metasurfaces-based transmit-array with the actual distribution of fields emitted from the feed radiator taken into account, a high-gain CP beam can be obtained within a wide bandwidth. As shown in Fig. 4 (a), for the integrated antenna, its simulated S_{11} is below -10 dB from 24.1 to 29.6 GHz. The simulated AR < 3 dB spans from 24.3 to 29.8 GHz (Fig. 4 (b)).

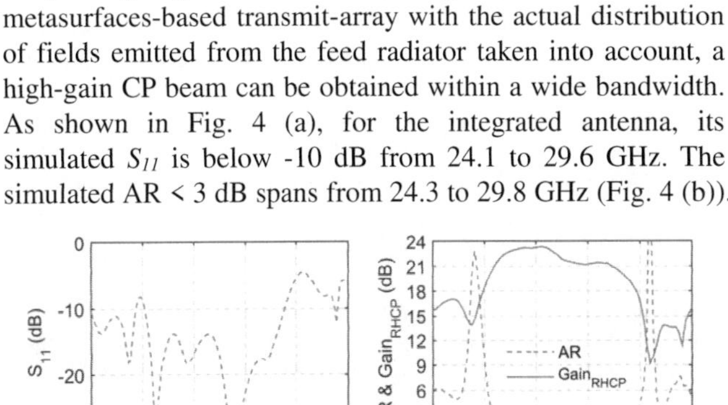

Fig. 4. Simulated (a) S_{11} and (b) AR and gain of the integrated antenna.

Within this band, the peak gain reaches 23.5 dBi. The 3 dB gain bandwidth is 5.1 GHz between 24.2 and 29.2 GHz. Hence, the overall operational band, where S_{11} < -10 dB, AR < 3 dB, and gain variation < 3 dB, is 5 GHz, ranging from 24.3 to 29.2 GHz, indicating a percentage bandwidth of 18.3%. From the simulated radiation patterns in both the *x-z* and *y-z* planes, it can be observed that a directive reft-handed CP beam is pointing at broadside with a low sidelobe level (not shown here).

III. Conclusion

In conclusion, we have presented the design of an integrated broadband CP antenna with a high gain in the Ka-band. The metasurfaces-based feed radiator and transmit-array enable a wide bandwidth of about 18.3%, which makes it a great candidate for wideband millimeter-wave wireless systems. Meanwhile, a prototype is under fabrication for experimental characterization.

Acknowledgment

This work was supported by the Natural Science Foundation of China (NSFC) under Grant 61801109 and Natural Science Foundation of Jiangsu Province under Grant BK20170687.

References

[1] W. Hong et al., "Multibeam antenna technologies for 5G wireless communications," IEEE Trans. Antennas Propagat., vol. 65, no. 12, pp. 6231-6249, Dec. 2017.
[2] X.-P. Chen, K. Wu, L. Han, and F. He, "Low-cost high gain planar antenna array for 60-GHz band applications," IEEE Trans. Antennas Propagat., vol. 58, no. 6, pp. 2126-2129, Jun. 2010.
[3] R. Sauleau, P. Coquet, T. Matsui, and J.-P. Daniel, "A new concept of focusing antennas using plane-parallel Fabry-Perot cavities with nonuniform mirrors," IEEE Trans. Antennas Propagat., vol. 51, no. 11, pp. 3171-3175, Jan. 2003.
[4] J. Huang and J. A. Encinar, Reflectarray Antennas. New York, NY, USA: Wiley, 2008.
[5] L. Di Plama et al., "Circularly-polarized reconfigurable transmitarray in Ka-band with beam scanning and polarization switching capabilities," IEEE Trans. Antennas Propag., vol. 65, no. 2, pp. 529-540, Feb. 2017.
[6] X. Zhao et al., "All-metal beam steering lens antenna for high power microwave applications," IEEE Trans. Antennas Propag., vol. 65, no. 12, pp. 7340-7344, Dec. 2017.
[7] H. Kaouach et al., "Wideband low-loss linear and circular polarization transmit-arrays in V-band," IEEE Trans. Antennas Propag., vol. 59, no. 7, pp. 2513-2523, Jul. 2011.
[8] S. B. Yeap, X. Qing, and Z. N. Chen, "77-GHz dual-layer transmit-array for automotive radar applications," IEEE Trans. Antennas Propag., vol. 63, no. 6, pp. 2833-2837, Jun. 2015.
[9] M. Jiang et al., "Metamaterial-based thin planar lens antenna for spatial beamforming and multibeam massive MIMO," IEEE Trans. Antennas Propag., vol. 65, no. 2, pp. 464-472, Feb. 2017.
[10] A. Clemente et al., "Focal distance reduction of transmit-array antennas using multiple feeds," IEEE Antennas Wireless Propag. Lett., vol. 11, pp. 1311-1314, Nov. 2012.
[11] Z. H. Jiang et al., "Highly efficient broadband multiplexed millimeter-wave vortices from metasurface-enabled transmit-arrays of subwavelength thickness," Phys. Rev. Appl., vol. 9, no. 6, pp. 064009, Jun. 2018.

Reconfigurable Origami Antennas

Stavros V. Georgakopoulos
Department of Electrical and Computer Engineering
Florida International University
Miami, US
georgako@fiu.edu

***Abstract*—Reconfigurable, tunable, multifunctional, deployable, and UWB high-performance antenna systems are expected to play a significant role in next generation communication, reconnaissance, sensing and energy harvesting airborne and spaceborne systems. Towards this goal, in recent years, significant advances have been made in: 1) antenna miniaturization, 2) ultra-wideband (UWB) antennas with as much as 10:1 bandwidth or larger, 3) antenna reconfiguration using MEMS and phase-change material (PCM) switches, 4) conductive textiles for flexible antennas, 5) conductive inks and flexible materials, and 7) smart materials for actuation and sensing. However, to date, adaptable, foldable and deployable electromagnetic structures that can physically self-morph to modify antenna and RF circuit performance for multifunctionality, have yet to be explored in a reliable manner. Recently, origami folding techniques have been used to develop new types of reconfigurable antennas, thereby creating a new class of EM structures The scope of this paper is to give a brief review analysis on the field of origami inspired EM radiating structures, by presenting the past the present and the future of this newly born field.**

Keywords—reconfigurable, tunable, multifunctional, deployable, UWB, origami, antenna, array, FSS

I. INTRODUCTION

Origami structures have the unique ability to morph (i.e., transform) 2-D manifolds (not necessarily flat) into a continuous range of 2-D or 3-D shapes with temporal control via deterministic mechanisms of rigid foldability. Fig. 1 shows an envisioned application of origami in satellites. Correspondingly, flexible materials, thin films and textiles provide the means for realizing novel origami designs. It has already been demonstrated that origami enables the development of new electromagnetic (EM) systems with unprecedented and transformational capabilities. Among them: i) 2-D and 3-D antennas that can morph their geometrical shape to control performance parameters as a function of time and achieve multifunctionality, ii)2-D and 3-D antenna arrays that can change their footprint, shape, and/or element separation to achieve optimal beamforming, beamsteering, and scanning range, and iii) Reconfigurable frequency selective surfaces for tunable and multifunctional antennas and arrays.

Indeed, origami designs have the potential to transform EM structures by enabling RF front-ends that can function across a 10:1 bandwidth while concurrently delivering optimal performance subject to pre-specified physical constraints and performance requirements. Such structures can also be packed and folded. structures, (b) lack of design algorithms for simultaneous electromagnetic physics and origami math analysis, and (c) lack of materials and mechanisms for robust and repeatable actuation.

This work was supported by the Air Force Office of Scientific Research under grant FA9550-18-1-0191 and the National Science Foundation under Grant EFRI 1332348.

Fig. 1. Expandable origami satellite

However, the development of origami EM structures is still hindered by several challenges. Among them: (a) lack of approaches for reconfigurable and multi-functional origami EM. In this paper, the inception of origami antennas is discussed first. Then, current research and future work on origami antennas are presented.

II. ORIGAMI ANTENNAS THE PAST

The design of physically reconfigurable and deployable multifunctional antennas using origami requires combining origami math, mechanics and electromagnetics. The complexity of origami structures is such that in the beginning the first designs followed the conventional origami approach, by assuming zero thickness or very thin substrates such as, paper and/or flexible substrates [1]-[3]. These designs show a performance equally good with the performance of the typical antennas in terms of input impedance matching and radiation efficiency while also offering reconfigurable performance in terms of frequency, polarization and radiation pattern. However, the first origami antennas lacked mechanical robustness. Specifically, after a relatively small number of folding/unfolding cycles (50-150 cycles depending on the thickness of the material) the substrates of these antennas experienced cracks along the creases and around the points of high stress, as shown in Fig. 3(a). Similar results are observed when these designs are exposed to harsh environments with extreme conditions, such as rain, wind and abrupt temperature changes. To address the above problems the following are needed: i) materials that can sustain multiple cycles of folding/unfolding, and ii) design techniques of origami antennas where thick and rigid substrates can be used. In the next section, state-of-the-art origami designs are presented, where we attempt to tackle the aforementioned problems.

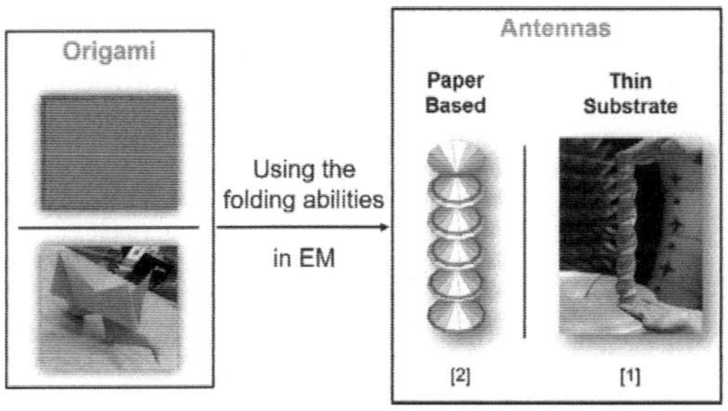

Fig. 2. Using the folding abilities of the origami to design reconfigurable antennas.

III. ORIGAMI ANTENNAS THE PRESENT

Origami antenna designs aim to develop foldable, deployable, reconfigurable, and multifunctional antennas for various applications [4]-[5]. Such applications include reconnaissance, airborne and spaceborne systems, where the deployability as well as the electromagnetic and mechanical robustness of the designs are of high importance. Recently in [6] a new fabrication approach for origami antennas is introduced, that provides robust operation and reduces the stresses at the creases and the corners, as shown in Fig. 3(b).

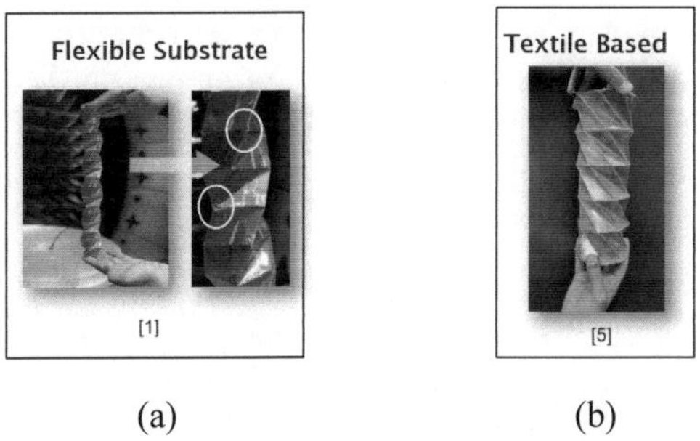

Fig. 3. Origami antenna on various materials. a) The flexible substrate (polyimide) of an origami helical antenna experiences fatigue after 50-100 cycles of folding/unfolding. b) The textile based helical antenna is free of cracks and fatigue at the creases and corners after a large number of cycles.

Even though the design proposed in [6] significantly reduces the stresses of the structure, it cannot be used in harsh environments due to its material properties. For this case, origami antennas are demanded on thick substrates. In [7], Yao et al. proposed the first thick origami antenna, where a dipole antenna is transformed into a conical spiral, using the flasher model. Recently in [8], Muhammad et al. proposed a thick origami array with a hinge that enables the elements of the array to fully fold for any material thickness. A thick array was also recently published in [9]. In this design, however, the authors scored the material using a laser machine, which makes the performance of this design questionable after a small number of folding/unfolding cycles.

IV. ORIGAMI ANTENNAS THE FUTURE

Within the last 5 years of research, significant progress has been achieved in the design of origami antennas. Starting from the design of antennas on paper and moving to designs with both flexible and rigid materials, it can be concluded that that the foundation for the design of origami antennas and EM structures has been established. Fig. 4 shows the progression of origami designs.

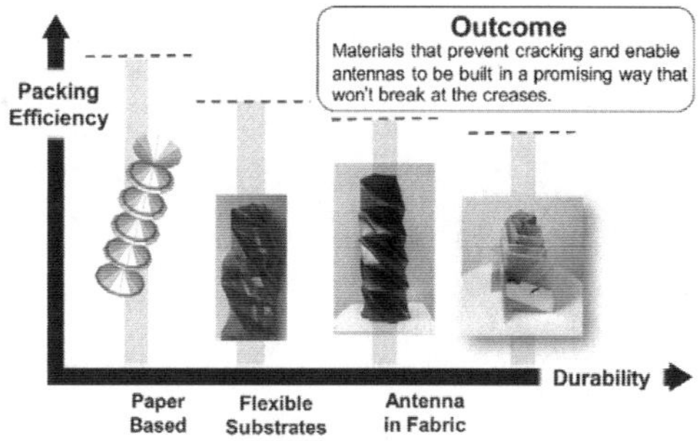

Fig. 4. Origami antenna implementations

The area of origami antennas and EM designs is expected to significantly grow in the following years. Specifically, we expect that game-changing physically reconfigurable foldable and deployable multifunctional antennas will be developed. These antennas will maintain robustness as they dynamically actuate, fold/unfold, morph and/or reshape to enable tunable and reconfigurable EM operation, including RF matching, frequency reconfiguration, beamforming and controllable reflectivity. New mechanisms will also be designed that will enhance the capabilities of origami EM structures. Finally, to appropriately study the mathematical, mechanical and electromagnetic complexity of origami EM designs, unified computational design/optimization tools with multi-physics, origami math, and multi-scale modeling algorithms will be developed.

REFERENCES

[1] X. Liu, S. Yao, B. S. Cook, M. M. Tentzeris, and S. V. Georgakopoulos, "An Origami Reconfigurable Axial-Mode Bifilar Helical Antenna," *IEEE Transactions on Antennas and Propagation*, vol. 63, no. 12, pp. 5897-5903, Sept. 2015.

[2] S. Yao, X. Liu, J. Gibson, and S. V. Georgakopoulos, "Deployable Origami Yagi Loop Antenna," *IEEE Antennas Propagat. Society Internat. Symp.*, pp. 2215-2216, Vancouver, BC, Canada, Jul. 19-24, 2015.

[3] X. Liu, S. V. Georgakopoulos and S. Rao, "A Design of an Origami Reconfigurable QHA with a Foldable Reflector," *in IEEE Antennas and Propagation Magazine*, vol. 59, no. 4, pp. 78-105, Aug. 2017

[4] X. Liu, C. L. Zekios, and S. V. Georgakopoulos, "Analysis of a Packable and Tunable Origami Multi-Radii Helical Antenna," *IEEE Access,* 7, 13003-13014, Jan. 2019.

[5] D. Sessions, K. Fuchi, S. Pallampati, D. Grayson, S. Seiler, G. Bazzan, G. Reich, P. Buskohl, and G. H. Huff, "Investigation of Fold-Dependent Behavior in an Origami-Inspired FSS Under Normal Incidence," Progress In Electromagnetics Research M, Vol. 63, 131-139, 2018.

[6] C. L. Zekios, X. Liu, M. Moshtaghzadeh, E. Izadpanahi, H. R. Radnezhad, P. Mardanpour, and S. V. Georgakopoulos, "Electromagnetic and mechanical analysis of an origami helical antenna encapsulated by fabric," submitted for publication in IDETC-2019.

[7] S. Yao, Y. Bonan, Y. Shafiq, and S. V. Georgakopoulos, "Rigid Origami based Reconfigurable Conical Spiral Antenna," *2018 IEEE International Symposium on Antennas and Propagation & USNC/URSI National Radio Science Meeting* conference, Boston, Massachusetts.

[8] H. Muhammad, C. L. Zekios, S. V. Georgakopoulos, "Thick Origami Based Foldable Patch Antenna Array," *iWAT*, March 3-6, 2019.

[9] S. R. Seiler, et al., "An Origami Inspired Circularly-Polarized Folding Patch Antenna Array," *2018 IEEE International Symposium on Antennas and Propagation & USNC/URSI National Radio Science Meeting*, pp. 181-182, 2018.

Coupled Structural-Electromagnetic Analysis of Origami-Inspired Adaptive Structures

Deanna Sessions and Gregory Huff
Department of Electrical Engineering and Computer Science
Pennsylvania State University
State College, PA, USA
{deanna.sessions}{guh234}@psu.edu

Joshua Ruff
Department of Electrical & Computer Engineering
Texas A&M Univerisity
College Station, TX, USA
joshruff@tamu.edu

Kazuko Fuchi
University of Dayton Research Inst.
Dayton, OH, USA

Alexander Cook
NextFlex Inc.
San Jose, CA, USA

Andrew Gillman
UES Inc.
Dayton, OH, USA

Alexander Pankonien and Philip Buskohl
Air Force Research Laboratory
Wright-Patterson AFB, OH, USA

***Abstract*—This article proposes a method to conduct coupled structural-electromagntic analysis of embedded electromagnetic devices on origami-inspired structures that are deployable and reconfigurable. The method uses a script-based multidisciplinary design and computational anaylsis tool to connect an in-house MATLAB code for nonlinear mechanics analysis and a Python-HFSS library for electromagnetic analysis.**

***Index Terms*—embedded electromagnetic devices, origami, structural-electromagnetic analysis.**

I. Introduction

In recent years, complex electromagnetic (EM) structures have been in the forefront of research topics. These include embedded vascular structures [1], three-dimensional random antenna arrays [2], and origami-inspired frequency selective surfaces [3] and antenna arrays [4]. This reconfigurable design space presents challenges in simulating the structures both in structural and EM solvers.

In this paper, we propose a new method combining structural and EM analysis for origami-inspired EM structures. The structural and EM modes of operation require information to be passed between multiple numerical and computational solvers. This proposed method uses a framework designed to hold structural and material information within a database that can be accessed by multiple solvers.

To demonstrate this concept, a previously designed origami-inspired, linearly polarized stop-band spatial filter [5] acting as a frequency selective surface (FSS) is examined using structural-EM analysis. The filter is comprised of horizontal and vertical dipole components arranged in a square lattice atop a substrate utilizing the Miura-ori origami fold pattern. This fold pattern acts as a mode of configuration for the dipole lattice and allow for multiple filtering frequencies to be achieved depending on the spacing of the components imposed by folded substrate configurations. The proposed analysis method is tested on this filter design as it is deformed in an asymmetric arrangement through structural loading.

This effort was supported in part by the Air Force Office of Scientific Research grant #LRIR 16RXCOR319.

II. Methods

Computational Aircraft Prototype Synthesis (CAPS), a multidisciplinary design and computational analysis framework [6], is used to facilitate the interpretation of the design concept to construct models necessary to conduct structural and EM analyses. The workflow of the analysis of an origami-inspired adaptive structure is summarized in Fig. 1.

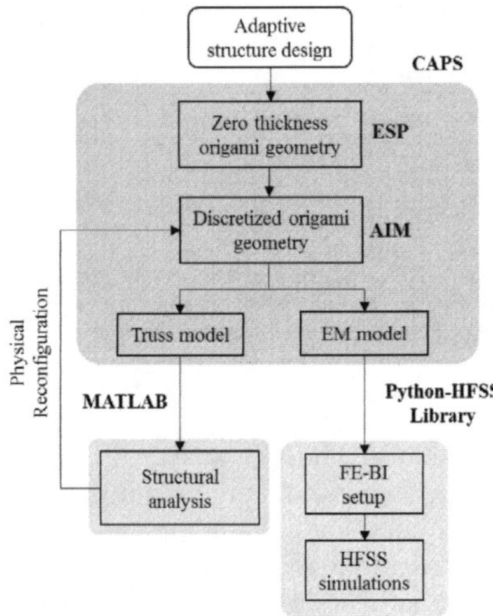

Fig. 1. Flowchart of the coupled structure-electromagnetic analysis method.

The process starts with a mathematical description of the origami surface geometry, prepared in a script-based geometry tool: Engineering Sketch Pad (ESP). The Analysis Interface Module (AIM) is then used to create a data structure that contains relevant information. This information includes locations of vertices in triangulated origami surface geometry fold line connectivity information, and surface attributes to specify conductive prints. The structurally-relevant vertex locations and fold line connectivity information are inputted into a MATLAB code for nonlinear structural analysis using a method based on a modified truss model, first introduced in

[7] and extended for nonlinear analysis in [8] to handle large deformations of the initial configuration through folding.

After the nonlinear structural analysis is conducted, updated vertex locations and the surfaces attributes are passed to a Python script to prepare a finite-element boundary-integral (FE-BI) hybrid model for ANSYS HFSS simulations using a Python-HFSS library [9]. This library accesses individual drawing functions in HFSS to interface with a database of nodal coordinates for the structures. Using these draw functions, we can gnerate complex origami structures with a large variety of structural defromations for electromagentic analysis, simply by providing input files with different nodal coordinate values.

The HFSS simulation space utilizes hybrid FE-BI regions [10] to optimize solving time by solving for fields directly at the surface. For these spatial filtering FSS simulations, shown in Fig. 2, we have employed two waveports represented by waveguides at the top and bottom of the FSS under test. Each of the waveguides and the FSS are surrounded by their own conformal Hybrid-FEBI region. In this case, the baseline filtering structure is comprised of a lattice of dipoles as outlined in [5] and the structure underwent three modes of structural deformation.

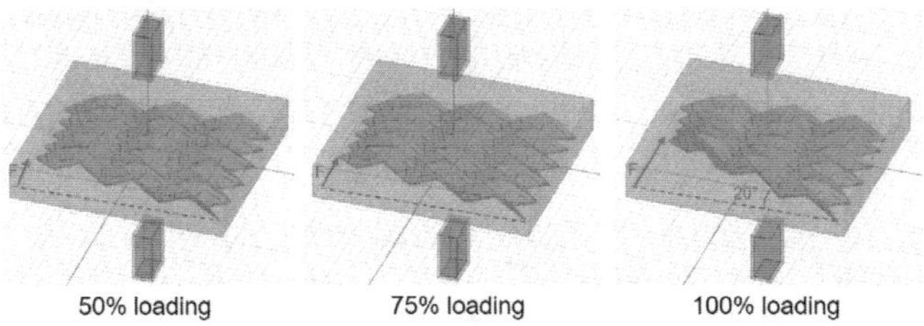

Fig. 2. Miura-ori deformed in Ansys HFSS FE-BI simulation setup with three loading configurations.

III. Results

These deformed Miura-ori substrates provided simulation results presented in Fig. 3. This demonstrates that the asymmetrically deformed origami filter exhibits a stop-band at 3.2 GHz under 50% loading, and the filtered frequency shifts upward as the structure is deformed further. These simulations are in line with the expectation from measured and simulated results of the same structure in a standard folding regime demonstrated in [5].

IV. Conclusion

By linking the structural and electromagnetic analysis through scripting, we can examine more complex geometries and configurations of origami-inspired structures. These structures can undergo deformations in structural analysis and then be analyzed for their electromagnetic response through a simple passing of nodal coordinates. These together can be used to determine the effectiveness of both the structural and electromagnetic designs throughout physical reconfiguration. The ongoing development of this toolset aims to facilitate the design and analysis of complex structures exhibiting deformations that can be used for a multitude of applications such as satellite deployment or deforming aircraft components with embedded antennas.

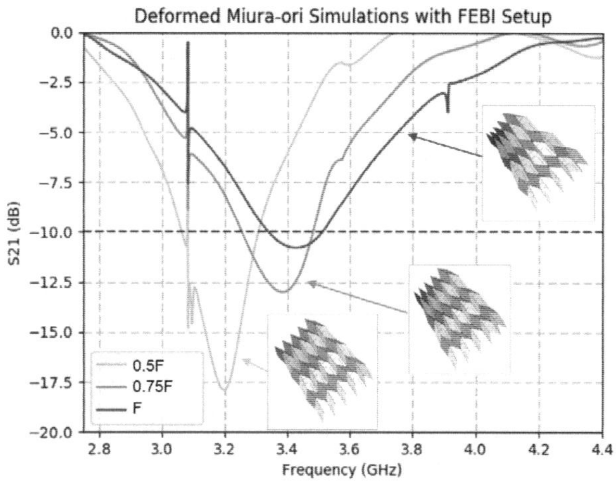

Fig. 3. S21 frequency response of Miura-ori dipole lattice FSS in three modes of deformation.

References

[1] G. H. Huff, H. Pan, D. Hartl, G. J. Frank, R. Bradford, and J. W. Baur, "A physically reconfigurable structurally embedded vascular antenna (SEVA)," IEEE Transactions on Antennas and Propagation, pp. 1-1. 10.1109/TAP, 2017.

[2] K. R. Buchanan and G. H. Huff, "A stochastic mathematical framework for the analysis of spherically-bound random arrays," IEEE Transactions on Antennas and Propagation, vol. 62. iss. 6, pp. 3002-3011, 2014.

[3] K. Fuchi, P. Buskohl, G. Bazzan, M. F. Durstock, J. J. Joo, G. W. Reich, and R. A. Vaia, "Spatial tuning of a RF frequency selective surface through origami," in Proceedings of the Defense and Security, International Society for Optics and Photonics, Baltimore, MD, 2016.

[4] S. R. Seiler, G. Bazzan, K. Fuchi, E. J. Alanyak, A. S. Gillman, G. W. Reich, P. R. Buskohl, S. Pallampati, D. Sessions, D. Grayson, and G. H. Huff, "Physical reconfiguration of an origami-inspired deployable microstrip patch antenna array," in 2017 IEEE International Symposium on Antennas and Propagation & USNC/URSI National Radio Science Meeting, San Diego, CA, 2017.

[5] D. Sessions, K. Fuchi, S. Pallampati, D. Grayson, S. Seiler, G. Bazzan, G. Reich, P. Buskohl, and G. H. Huff, "Investigation of fold-dependent behavior in an origami-inspired FSS under normal incidence," Progress In Electromagnetics Research M, vol. 63, 131-139, 2018.

[6] E. Alyanak, R. Durscher, R. Haimes, J. Dannenhoffer, N. D. Bhagat, and D. L. Allison, "Multi-fidelity Geometry-centric Multi-disciplinary Analysis for Design," in AIAA Modeling and Simulation Technologies Conference, Washington, D.C., 2016.

[7] M. Schenk and S. D. Guest, "Origami folding: A structural engineering approach," in Origami5, Boca Raton, FL, CRC Press, 2011, pp. 291-304.

[8] A. Gillman, K. Fuchi, and P. Buskohl, "Truss-based nonlinear mechanical analysis for origami structures exhibiting bifurcations and limit point instabilities," International Journal of Solids and Structures, vol. 147, no. 15, pp. 80-93, 2018.

[9] J. Ruff, "HFSS Python," Github Repository, 2017. [Online]. Available: https://github.com/ghuff/HRG/tree/master/HFSS_Python

[10] J. Silvestro, "Hybrid Finite Element Boundary Integral Method," ANSYS, Inc., [Online]. Available: https://support.ansys.com/staticassets/ANSYS/staticassets/resourcelibrary/whitepaper/wp-HFSS-Hybrid-Finite-Element-Integral-Equation-Method.pdf

Automated CAD and Modeling of Origami Structures for Reconfigurable Antenna Applications

Md Rayhan Khan, Constantinos L. Zekios, Stavros V. Georgakopoulos and Shubhendu Bhardwaj
Electrical and Computer Engineering
Florida International University
10555 W. Flagler Street, Miami, Florida, USA
Email: mkhan118@fiu.edu, kzekios@fiu.edu, georgako@fiu.edu, sbhardwa@fiu.edu

***Abstract*—Electromagnetic (EM) simulation of origami-inspired antenna structures has been a challenge due to its complex and sometimes counter-intuitive 3-D designs. In this work, we show the development of a unified automated tool that constructs the CAD models for origami type structures for conducting full-wave simulations. In the proposed toolset, we have used the well known Mathematica Notebook called 'Tessellatica', for obtaining origami geometries and subsequently generated CAD models for full-wave simulations in ANSYS High Frequency Structure Simulator (HFSS). The developed toolset can be used to build HFSS 3-D models and conduct full-wave simulations for an arbitrary origami type structure.**

***Index Terms*—Antennas, HFSS, Origami, Tessellatica.**

I. Introduction

Automation of CAD models using scripted design method is a common design approach among Radio Frequency (RF) engineers. Increasing design complexity of antenna structures and the need for automated parametric sweeps with minimal human effort requires the use of such automated tools. Furthermore, counter-intuitive 3-D designs are often used for enhanced RF performances and the modeling could be automated for faster design.

Another crucial feature in modern RF systems is the application of reconfigurable antenna structures [1], [2]. A method for achieving such physical reconfiguration among EM structures is via origami, the ancient art of folding and unfolding. The use of origami structures has led to a new class of antennas known as the origami antennas, where deployability and/or reconfiguration is achieved by transformation of flat substrates and conductors into 3-D antenna shapes [3], [4]. These are typical use-cases for the proposed automated design processes because most origami models are geometrically rigorous and require mathematical algorithms for their modeling. Some tools have recently been developed to perform mathematical modeling and 3-D visualization of origami structures [5]–[8], and can be accordingly employed to create a framework by integrating them with antenna simulation tools for faster modeling.

This work was supported by the Air Force Office of Scientific Research under grant FA9550-18-1-0191.

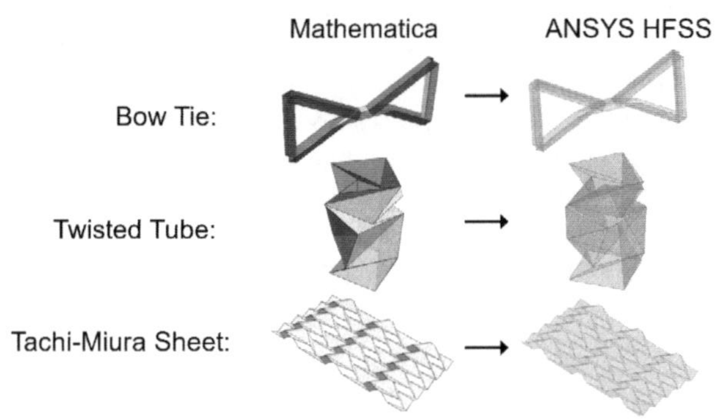

Fig. 1. Examples of Origami models generated using the proposed toolset.

We present a method that uses the available 'Tessellatica' [5] notebook in combination with MATLAB scripting and ANSYS HFSS software for CAD modeling and simulation of origami antennas. In our design approach, origami geometries are generated in Mathematica [9] using the Tessellatica notebook, which makes such structures by employing algorithms for origami folding. Information set related to an origami geometry is then passed onto MATLAB, which after necessary processing generates ANSYS HFSS 3-D models. After specifying the required design parameters, the entire process is completed using a unified interface.

II. Automated Origami-Toolset

Components used in developing integrated design tool are as following.

1) Tessellatica: Tessellatica is a Mathematica package containing functions for generating origami structures. Using the input parameters such as origami type, fold angles, and by using mathematical calculations, Tessellatica checks for design feasibility of origami structures by validating the crease patterns and fold angles using mathematical calculations and provides visualization of the intended geometry.

2) MATLAB: MATLAB was used as an intermediate tool for collecting the origami data from Mathematica and for generating HFSS CAD model. This intermediate MATLAB code performs two tasks. First, generated 3-D vertices, edges, and faces for an origami model are converted into polyline and polygon. Secondly, we used functions to generate VBScript for different operations (e.g., drawing a polyline, uniting HFSS objects, adding a solution setup).

3) MATLink: Matlink, an open source Mathematica application for two-way communication between MATLAB and Mathematica, was used to create automated communication between MATLAB and Mathematica software packages.

4) ANSYS HFSS: As described before, MATLAB was used to generate CAD models and run full-wave simulations in ANSYS HFSS. Specifically, visual basic scripting feature was used in HFSS for automation in the design process.

Available university licensing for Mathematica and MATLAB was used, which did not add any cost over HFSS licensing for this tool-development.

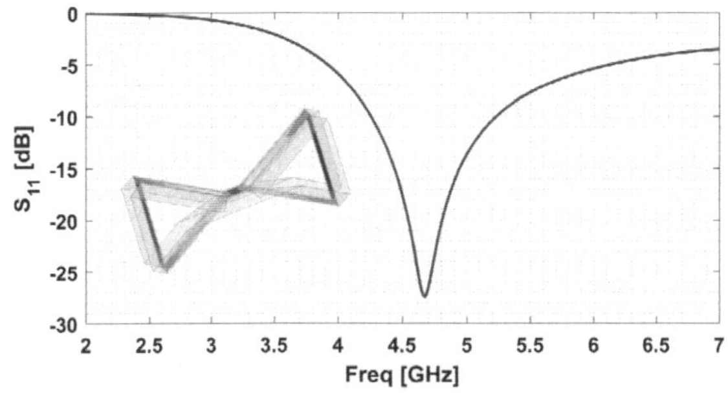

Fig. 2. Simulated S_{11} of an origami bow tie antenna generated using the toolset.

III. Tool Operation and Results

The process starts with initializing Tessellatica notebook along with establishing a connection between MATLAB and Mathematica. Then, Mathematica interface is used for automated generation of an arbitrary origami geometry in HFSS and running the simulations as specified in the intermediate MATLAB code. We tested this generalized toolset for a number of different origami shapes. The toolset successfully demonstrated the ability to model any origami shape in HFSS for the corresponding modeling. Three such origami shapes, namely Bow Tie, Twisted Tube and Tachi-Miura sheet are shown as examples presented in Fig. 1. For illustration purposes, we also generated and conducted full-wave simulations of an origami-substrate based bow tie antenna using the toolset. Here, the bow tie antenna is supported by an origami substrate which allows folding and unfolding of the antenna. That is, the antenna may also transform into a center-fed half wavelength dipole (of length 61.4 mm) in substrate's unfolded form. The bow tie shape has caused a reduction in the effective length of the dipole, thereby shifting the theoretical resonant frequency from 2.3 GHz to 4.67 GHz as shown in Fig. 2.

IV. Conclusion

We presented a generalized toolset which is capable of creating and analyzing origami antennas in ANSYS HFSS. We utilized a Mathematica package named Tessellatica to create the initial origami model and used VBScript to create the model in HFSS and to run the EM simulation. We found that our developed toolset is capable of generating any 3-D origami model in HFSS so that it can be used as a substrate to create an origami antenna by further adding metallic components to it. This work ultimately indicates the utility of the toolset for reducing the human effort in modeling and simulation of origami antennas.

References

[1] C. G. Christodoulou, Y. Tawk, S. A. Lane, and S. R. Erwin, "Reconfigurable antennas for wireless and space applications," Proceedings of the IEEE, vol. 100, no. 7, pp. 2250–2261, 2012.

[2] J. Costantine, Y. Tawk, S. E. Barbin, and C. G. Christodoulou, "Reconfigurable antennas: Design and applications," Proceedings of the IEEE, vol. 103, no. 3, pp. 424–437, 2015.

[3] S. Yao, X. Liu, S. V. Georgakopoulos, and M. M. Tentzeris, "A novel reconfigurable origami spring antenna," in Antennas and Propagation Society International Symposium (APSURSI), 2014 IEEE. IEEE, 2014, pp. 374–375.

[4] X. Liu, S. Yao, B. S. Cook, M. M. Tentzeris, and S. V. Georgakopoulos, "An origami reconfigurable axial-mode bifilar helical antenna," IEEE Transactions on Antennas and Propagation, vol. 63, no. 12, pp. 5897–5903, 2015.

[5] R. J. Lang, "TESSELLATICA," [Accessed: 18-Jan-2019]. [Online]. Available: https://langorigami.com/article/tessellatica/

[6] R. J. Lang, "TREEMAKER," [Accessed: 18-Jan-2019]. [Online]. Available: https://langorigami.com/article/treemaker/

[7] J. Mitani, "ORIPA: Origami Pattern Editor," [Accessed: 18-Jan-2019]. [Online]. Available: http://mitani.cs.tsukuba.ac.jp/oripa/

[8] A. Ghassaei, E. D. Demaine, and N. Gershenfeld, "Fast, Interactive Origami Simulation using GPU Computation," 7th International Meeting on Origami in Science, Mathematics and Education, 2018.

[9] W. R. Inc., "Mathematica, Version 11.3," Champaign, IL, 2018.

Origami-Tunable Frequency Selective Surfaces: A Design Optimization Approach

Kazuko Fuchi
University of Dayton Research Institute
University of Dayton
Dayton, OH
kfuchi1@udayton.edu

Andrew Gillman
Alexander Cook
UES, Inc.
Beavercreek, OH
andrew.gillman.1.ctr@us.af.mil
alexander.cook.1.ctr@us.af.mil

Alexander Pankonien
Aerospace Systems Directorate
Air Force Research Laboratory
Wrigth-Patterson AFB, OH
alexander.pankonien.1@us.af.mil

Philip Buskohl
Materials and Manufacturing Directorate
Air Force Research Laboratory
Wrigth-Patterson AFB, OH
philip.buskohl.1@us.af.mil

***Abstract*—An origami design optimization framework is developed to predict fold topologies of frequency selective surfaces that are tuned through physical reconfiguration. The design methods combines electromagnetics and mechanics into a single tool for fold-based RF performance.**

Keywords—Topology optimization, RF filters, reconfiguration.

I. INTRODUCTION

Origami, the art of paper folding, presents of novel method of shape change, by transforming complex motions into a series of folding operations. The physical reconfiguration of origami has been applied to morphing structures, actuators, robotics, and is gaining traction for electromagnetic applications, such as folding antennas and frequency selective surfaces (FSSs). FSSs are EM filters that block specific frequencies of EM waves due to local resonances within the conductive elements (i.e. dipoles, spirals, etc) of a periodic array. The conductive element shape, size and periodic spacing all contribute to the specificity of the filtering frequency. By embedding the FSS pattern into an origami substrate, the shape, effective size and spacing can be tuned through folding. Origami FSSs have been demonstrated with cross elements [1] and dipoles on Miura-Ori tessellation [2,3]. (see example Miura-Ori dipole FSS in Figure 1A), both exhibiting an increase in resonance of the blocked frequency with folding. However, the inverse problem of predicting an origami topology for a target FSSs resonance is challenging due to the large design space of folding motions possible within a given fold topology, the sensitivity of EM performance to geometric changes and the need to connect the optimal EM shape with a compatible mechanical properties of the origami structure.

II. RESULTS

As a first step to address these challenges, we developed a topology optimization framework that simultaneously evaluates the mechanics and EM performance of an origami frequency selective surface to minimize the transmission coefficient at a specific frequency. The optimization framework is outlined in Figure 1B. First, a unit cell fold topology and dipole arrangement is selected as a reference topology. The fold topology is modeled as a truss structure, with stretch stiffness associated with truss elongation and fold

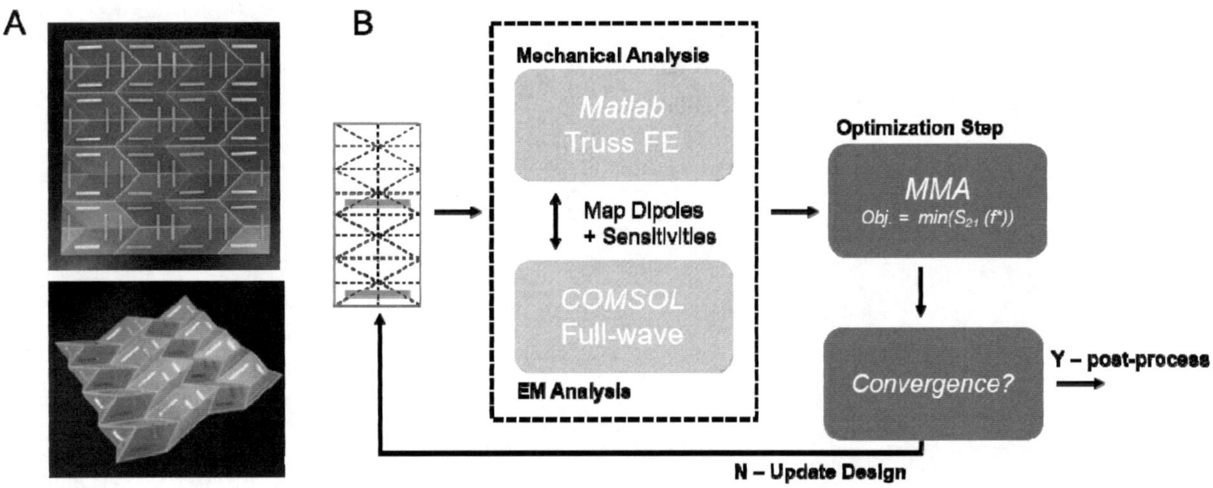

Figure 1 Origami FSS Design Optimization A) Dipole-based Miura-Ori FSS with tunable resonance with folding. B) Optimization framework for origami FSS design with combined electromagnetic and mechanical analysis.

stiffness associated with an angle changed defined by a local triad of truss elements. The optimization routine will down-select which fold lines to use from this reference grid by tuning the fold stiffness parameter of each fold line. Low stiffness values maintain fold-like behavior, while high stiffness values effectively eliminate the local fold. The choice of fold topology determines the spatial reconfiguration of the dipole pair of the unit cell, which includes their lateral spacing, out-of-plane spacing and even shape, as the dipole crosses multiple fold lines. At each iteration, the deformed configuration of the dipoles is ported from the Matlab truss simulation to COMSOL Multiphysics, where the unit cell of the dipoles is modeled with a 2-port setup with perfect matched layers to mitigate artificial reflections at the port boundaries. The transmission coefficient (S_{21}) of the FSS is evaluated at a target frequency, as specified by the objective function. The sensitivities of the transmission coefficient with respect to the deformation and stiffness variables of the origami structure were derived through a series of mappings. They include the mappings between the S_{21} and dipole position, the dipole position to the truss positions and, finally, the truss displacements to the stiffness variables. The sensitivities enable the gradient-based optimization techniques, such as Method of Moving Asymptotes (MMA) to be utilized. After each EM evaluation, the objective function is evaluated and a new stiffness distribution is predicted for the next iteration. The process continues until convergence is reached or the max number of allowed iterations is achieved. The design problems investigated with this framework have focused on shifting the resonance frequency from the flat state of the origami FSS to both higher and lower frequencies. Mechanisms of EM tuning identified through the optimization process include tuning the inductive coupling distance between the parallel dipoles and introducing a phase shift between the dipoles through accessing out-of-plane dipole spacing.

III. CONCLUSIONS

The optimization framework presented here provides an initial toolset to explore mechanisms of FSS tuning mechanisms based on physical reconfigurations that are accessible through origami folding and provides a testbed to further extend to the design methodology to other EM devices.

REFERENCES

[1] Fuchi, K., Tang, J., Crowgey, B., Diaz, A. R., Rothwell, E. J., and Ouedraogo, R. O., 2012. "Origami tunable frequency selective surfaces". Antennas and Wireless Propagation Letters, IEEE, 11, pp. 473–475.

[2] Sessions, D., Fuchi, K., Pallampati, S., Grayson, D., Seiler, S., Bazzan, G., Reich, G., Buskohl, P., and Huff, G., 2018. "Investigation of fold-dependent behavior in an origami-inspired FSS under normal incidence". Progress In Electromagnetics Research,, 63, pp. 131–139.

[3] Nauroze, S. A., Novelino, L., Tentzeris, M. M., and Paulino, G. H., 2017. "Inkjet-printed "4d" tunable spatial filters using on-demand foldable surfaces". In 2017 IEEE MTT-S International Microwave Symposium, pp. 1575–1578

ACKNOWLEDGMENT

This research was supported by the Air Force Office of Scientific Research AFOSR) funding, LRIR 16RXCOR319.

Design of Graded Dielectric Waveguides with Preferential Band-pass Frequencies

Venkatesh Meenakshisundaram
Materials and Manufacturing Directorate
Wright-Patterson AFB
Dayton, OH, USA
venkatesh.meenakshisundaram.ctr@us.af.mil

Daryl Osterloh
Aerospace Systems Directorate
Wright-Patterson AFB
Dayton, OH, USA
daryl.osterloh.ctr@us.af.mil

Andrius Lietuvninkas
Sensors Directorate
Wright-Patterson AFB
Dayton, OH, USA
andrius.lietuvninkas.1@us.af.mil

Jeffrey Massman
Sensors Directorate
Wright-Patterson AFB
Dayton, OH, USA
jeffrey.massman.4.ctr@us.af.mil

Jeremy Tumpak
Aerospace Systems Directorate
Wright-Patterson AFB
Dayton, OH, USA
jeremy.tumpak.ctr@us.af.mil

Joshua Deaton
Aerospace Systems Directorate
Wright-Patterson AFB
Dayton, OH, USA
joshua.deaton@us.af.mil

Philip Buskohl
Materials and Manufacturing Directorate
Wright-Patterson AFB
Dayton, OH, USA
philip.buskohl.1@us.af.mil

***Abstract*—A Neural-Network-biased Genetic Algorithm is employed to design all dielectric waveguide with periodic structures with preferential band-pass frequencies. Preliminary results indicate that an optimum periodic structure design exist for target frequency transmission and highlights the need for robust optimization scheme such as the one described here.**

Keywords—Dielectric waveguides, Genetic Algorithm, Neural Network, Periodic Structures.

I. Introduction

Recent developments in ink formulation for additive manufacturing has enabled design of electromagnetic (EM) dielectric waveguides with robust geometries. Complex geometries were traditionally difficult to develop due to high costs and manufacturing complexity [1]. While these recent advancements have opened doors for novel applications, the behavior of EM waves in complex geometries can be non-intuitive and mathematically challenging. This inverse problem of developing waveguides with target geometries and EM performance cannot be achieved with traditional Edisonian design approach due to high experimental costs. To overcome these limitations, we employ EM finite element modeling (FEM) within a neural-network biased genetic algorithm on a representative waveguide design problem. We introduce and optimize periodic structures [2] within a straight waveguide to transmit a specific frequency (see Fig.1). The study provides an optimization framework to design graded dielectric properties to target EM functionality.

II. Modeling and Design of Dielectric Waveguide

A. EM-FEM Modeling

The waveguide design parameters include the dimensions of periodic structures, the distance between periodic structures, and the permittivity core material and cladding material. The permittivity of periodic structures is same as the cladding material. We optimize these parameters within a neural-network biased genetic algorithm [3] to design a waveguide with transmission at 8.2 GHz waves, while all other frequencies are

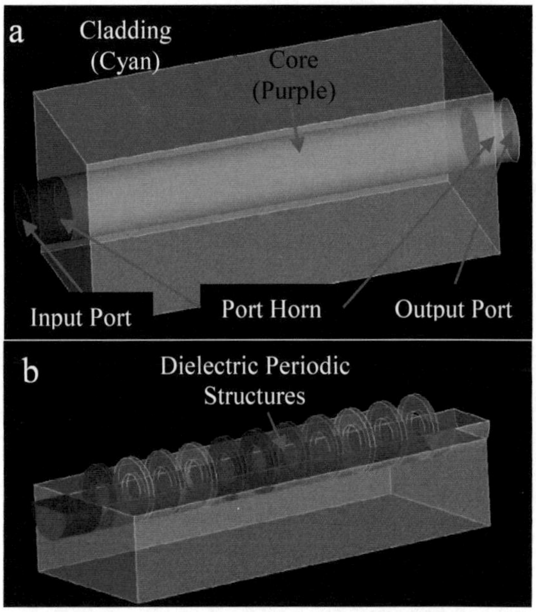

Fig. 1. (a) Waveguide with high dielectric core (purple) and low dielectic cladding (cyan). (b) A cross-section view to highlight periodic structures (disc shaped structures).

filtered. A hybrid finite element – boundary integral (FE-BI) EM solver is utilized for the analysis. The models used in this study are built and meshed with Cubit (Sandia National Laboratories, cubit.sandia.gov) (Fig. 1 (a)). A hexahedral mesh was applied for volume elements and a quadrilateral mesh was applied for surface elements. In order to ensure sufficient integration points for material evaluation, a finer mesh was used with second order elements. This resulted in ~70,000 elements.

B. Neural-Network-Biased Genetic Algorithm

As mentioned earlier, we employ a neural-network-biased genetic algorithm (NBGA) [3] to design all dielectric periodic structures to transmit a target X-band frequency. While standard GAs are effective in optimizing non-convex landscapes, they do suffer from convergence, especially deeper into optimization. NBGA helps overcome this limitation by enlisting an artificial neural network (ANN) in tandem with the FEM-GA. As the FEM-GA generates design candidates each generation, the ANN trains on this data and uses its own GA to test hundreds of thousands of candidates and sends its best candidate as a suggestion to next generation of FEM-GA (see Fig. 2). As more data is generated by FEM-GA, the suggestions from ANN becomes more effective and improves overall convergence. The NBGA has been shown to converge 5X quicker than standard genetic algorithms for open ended material design problems [3].

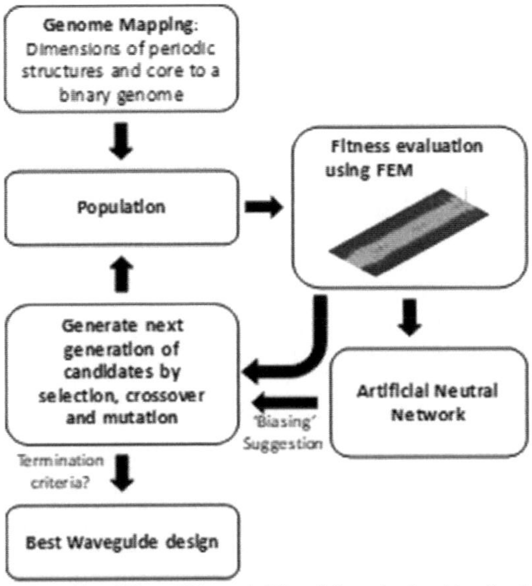

Fig 2. A schematic of Neural-Network-Biased Genetic algorithm for designing all dielectric waveguide.

In this study, inner diameter and thickness of periodic structure, the distance between periodic structures, permittivities of core material and cladding material, were optimized. The properties were encoded to a binary genome with 20 genes with every four genes corresponding to the above mentioned properties. The population size is 50 genomes. The fitness value was defined as the ratio of S_{21} at 8.2 GHz to avg. S_{21} of all higher frequencies in X-band and the NBGA minimized this value. The neural network used here is a feedforward network with five layers (input, output and three hidden layers).

III. Preliminary Results

In order to build intuition on the impact of all dielectric periodic structures, a series of studies were performed on a straight waveguide with periodic structures. The core material had permittivity, $\epsilon = 5$ and the cladding material was set to $\epsilon = 2$ with radiating boundary conditions. In order to avoid impedance mismatch, the horns were set to $\epsilon = 5$ with PEC boundary conditions. The periodic structures were placed at the half and the full period of the guide wavelength of an 8.2 GHz wave and the first periodic structure was placed a full period away from the excited port. The core diameter was 0.028 m. (cutoff diameter for 8.2 GHz) and inner diameter of periodic structure was 0.0093 m. The thickness of the periodic structure was 0.0025 m and a total of 11 periodic structures were used for periodic structures separated by full wavelength of 8.2 GHz and 22 periodic structures were used for periodic structures separated by half wavelength of 8.2 GHz wave. All materials were set to be lossless.

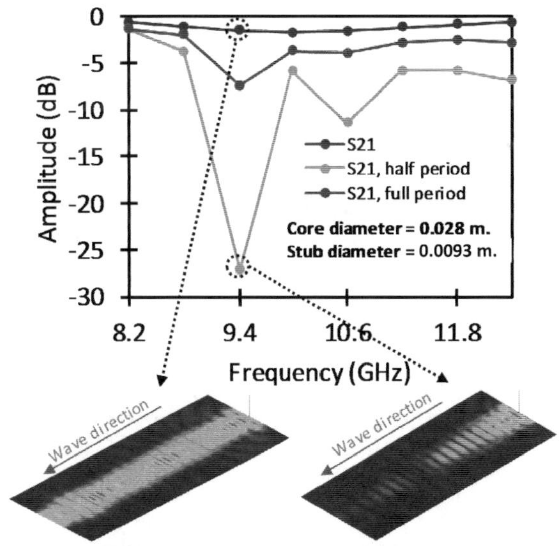

Fig. 3. Transmission coefficient (S_{21}) for a straight waveguide with periodic structures. The inner diameter of the periodic structure (stub) was arbitrarily set to a third of core diameter. S_{21} for waveguide with no periodic structures (Dark blue), periodic structures placed at full period (violet) and periodic structures placed at half period (green). Surface current snapshot at 9.4 GHz for neat system and system with periodic structures is shown.

The transmission coefficients for a straight waveguide with periodic structures are shown in Fig. 3. From the figure, high transmission for entire X-band is observed in neat waveguide (no periodic structures). Introduction of periodic structures at full period of 8.2 GHz moderately reduces transmission of all X-band frequencies except 8.2 GHz compared to neat system. Introduction of periodic structures at half period produces highest transmission at 8.2 GHz while 9.4 GHz is nearly fully reflected. Higher X-band frequencies do transmit but well below -3 dB. It is not intuitive what dimensions of periodic structure will ensure higher X-band frequencies are reflected as well as a 9.4 GHz wave highlighting the need for the NBGA.

IV. Conclusions

The above preliminary results for waveguide with periodic structures with non-optimized dimensions suggest that an optimal waveguide design exists for a frequency-select transmission through the waveguide. Even with this simple waveguide with 5 variables, the design landscape is over 1 million candidates. Introduction of complexity to waveguide geometry such as bending the wave while filtering frequencies highlight the need for a robust optimization scheme.

Acknowledgment

The authors acknowledge DoD High Performance Center for providing computational resources to perform finite element modeling of waveguides.

References

[1] E. MacDonald and R Wicker, "Multiprocess 3D printing for increasing component functionality," Science, 353(6307), p.aaf2093, 2016.

[2] R. E. Collin, Field theory of guided waves, 1960.

[3] T. K. Patra, V. Meenakshisundaram, J. H. Hung, and D. S. Simmons, "Neural-network-biased genetic algorithms for materials design: Evolutionary algorithms that learn," ACS Combinatorial Science, 19(2), pp. 96-107, 2017.

Active Huygens' Box: Arbitrary Synthesis of EM Waves in Metallic Cavities

Kayode A. Oyesina, Omar Zohir Aly, Gabriel G. L. Zhou, and Alex M. H. Wong*
State Key Laboratory of Terahertz and Millimeter Waves
Dept. of Electronic Engineering, City University of Hong Kong
Hong Kong SAR, China
*alex.mh.wong@cityu.edu.hk

***Abstract*— Previously, it was believed that electromagnetic plane waves cannot exist in a closed metallic cavity. However, by applying the electromagnetic equivalence principle, we have demonstrated the formation of an arbitrary waveform in a region enclosed by an active Huygens' metasurface. In this paper, we apply this principle on two cavity shapes — a rectangular and a cylindrical cavity, which we call the Huygens' boxes. We present simulation results to demonstrate the generation of traveling plane waves at 0° and 45° in both Huygens' boxes. We also present measured experimental results that agrees with the simulation results for the Huygens' box. We have thus demonstrated the generation and control of waveforms in a metallic cavity at an unprecedented level. We believe that this novel discovery will find applications in a wide range of applications like imaging, communication, and medical therapy in the nearest future.**

Keywords—antennas, diffraction, metasurface, super-resolution, waveform synthesis.

I. Introduction

Metasurfaces are surfaces artificially engineered to achieve some desirable electromagnetic behavior, even ones that are unusual or difficult to achieve. Recently, researchers have presented works that validate metasurfaces' excellent capabilities for electromagnetic wave manipulation. These surfaces have been applied to a myriad of applications [1]–[3]. In this paper, we report findings on arbitrary waveform generation in metallic cavities enclosed by active Huygens' metasurfaces. We show through theory, simulation and experiment that, with a concept we call the Huygens' box, we can generate and control electromagnetic waveform to unprecedented levels.

II. Concept and Theoretical Formulation

In [4]–[6] we have demonstrated that it is possible to arbitrarily manipulate a waveform if we enclose a region of interest with a Huygens' metasurface. We call this the Huygens' Box. We invoke the electromagnetic equivalence principle developed by Love and Schelkunoff [7], [8] to find the necessary electric and magnetic currents along the boundary that will generate an arbitrary desired electromagnetic waveform within the region of interest. Then we directly generate the required currents using an active Huygens' metasurface. Fig. 1 gives a general outlook of the Huygens' box concept. A set of currents J_s and M_s can generate electromagnetic fields $\{E_a, H_a\}$ within an enclosed area without affecting $\{E_b, H_b\}$, or adjust the electromagnetic field $\{E_b, H_b\}$outside the area without affecting$\{E_a, H_a\}$. We demonstrate this by way of a simple example. The E-field of a plane wave can be written using the equation:

$$\vec{E} = \vec{E}_0 e^{-j(k(\vec{A}_n \cdot \vec{r}))}\,, \qquad (1)$$

where $\vec{A}_n$ is a unit vector in the wave propagation direction, k is the wave number, and η is the wave's intrinsic impedance.

With the provisions of Fig. 1(a) and pre-assuming the fields according to (2);

$$\{E_a, H_a\} = \{E_0 e^{-j(k(A_n \cdot r))}, \frac{1}{\eta}(A_n x E_b)\}$$
$$\{E_b, H_b\} = 0. \qquad (2)$$

We then calculate the required currents using (3).

$$J_s = \hat{n} \times (H_b - H_a)$$
$$M_s = -\hat{n} \times (E_b - E_a). \qquad (3)$$

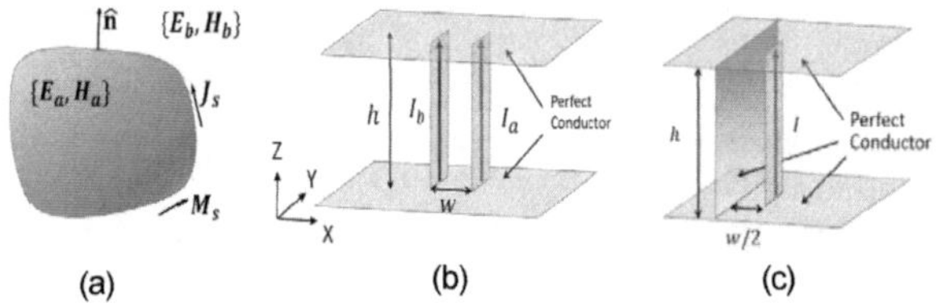

Fig. 1. (a) A diagram showing the equivalence principle where $\hat{n}$ is the outward-pointing normal, $\{E_a, H_a\}$ is the electromagnetic field inside the cavity, $\{E_b, H_b\}$ is the electromagnetic field outside the cavity and J_s and M_s are the electric and magnetic surface currents respectively. (b) A simple active Huygens' metasurface element. (c) The mirrored current filament Huygens' metasurface equivalent [5].

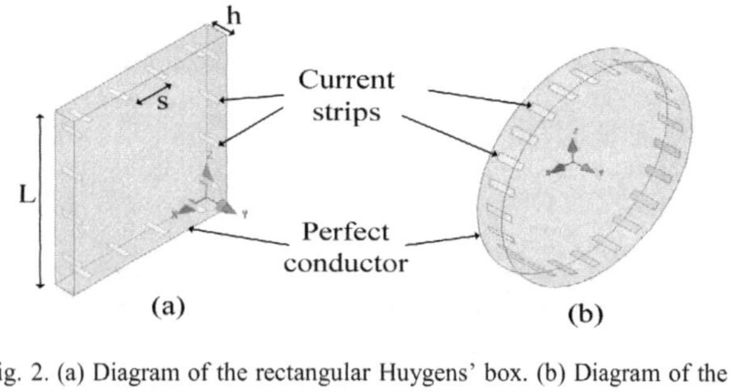

Fig. 2. (a) Diagram of the rectangular Huygens' box. (b) Diagram of the cylindrical Huygens' box

We show the Huygens' boxes in Fig. 2. We implement the Huygens' box using current strips as in Fig. 1(b). Furthermore, we dissect the twin filament of Fig. 1(b) to reduce it to Fig. 1(c) using a perfect electric conductor surface. This serves as an anti-mirror to the single current element, effectively suppressing the electric surface current while doubling the magnetic current. This gives the same effect as the twin current filament setup with fewer current elements [5].

III. RECTANGULAR CAVITY: SIMULATION AND EXPERIMENTAL RESULTS

Fig. 2(a) shows our rectangular cavity simulation model. We performed full-wave simulation using Ansys HFSS at a simulation frequency of 1GHz. We used 16 active Huygens' sources with separation $s = 0.25\lambda$ between any two adjacent sources. We generated a Huygens' box with size $L = \lambda$ in the center of the simulation domain. We present our simulation results in Fig. 3(a-d) showing that upon proper excitation one can excite unconventional waveforms within a rectangular cavity, such as travelling waves, which terminate at the cavity boundaries.

We proceeded to experimentally synthesize and measure the travelling wave (along with several other waveforms) inside the rectangular Huygens' box. Ref. [6] gives a detailed description of our experimental apparatus. We present a comparison between the simulation and the experimental results in Fig. 3(e-h) for a plane wave propagating along the z-axis. The black rectangular frame indicates the movement boundary of the measurement probe used in the experiment. We observe satisfactory agreement in simulation and experiment.

IV. CYLINDRICAL CAVITY: SIMULATION RESULTS

To further demonstrate the concept of the Huygens' box, we also consider plane wave generation in a cylindrical cavity. The curved geometry attracts our attention, as this geometry is amenable to applications in dual (or circular) polarization aperture antennas and medical imaging modalities. We adapt the same methodology as discussed in the previous section.

Fig. 2(b) shows the simulation model. We performed the simulation at a frequency of 1GHz. Again, we used an array of current strips, backed by a perfect conductor, as the metasurface elements. Each of the 24 equidistantly-spaced current strips has a width of λ/10. We present the simulation results in Fig. 4. It shows plane waves generated within the cavity travelling at 0° and 45° from the horizontal axis at different phase intervals.

V. CONCLUSION

In this paper, we have demonstrated the synthesis of plane waves using active Huygens' boxes of two different geometries. Such waveforms would not have been formed in typical metallic cavities. One can synthesize waveforms that are more complicated by simply superimposing the constituent plane waves demonstrated in this paper. Our work hence opens doors to many applications through generating arbitrary

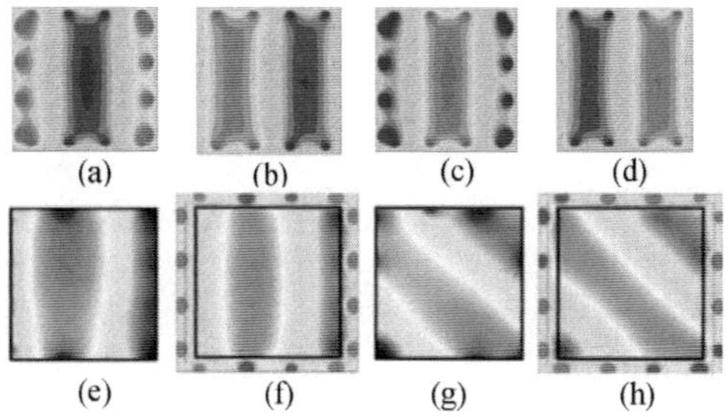

Fig. 3. Generating plane waves inside the Rectangular Huygens' Box. (a-d) Plane wave propagating at 0° from the z-axis at four phase instances. (e) Measured and (f) simulated electric field (real part, at one phase-point) inside the Huygens' box for the 0° plane wave. (g-h) The same for 45° plane wave. The black boxes indicate regions reachable by the probe.

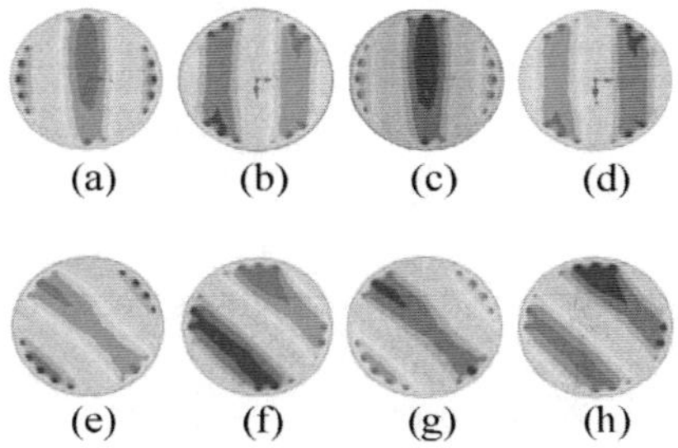

Fig. 4. Generating plane waves inside the Cylindrical Huygens' Cavity. (a-d) Plane wave propagating at 0° (horizontal direction) at four phase instances (e-h) Plane wave propagating at 45° (from the horizontal axis) at four phase instances.

waveforms in closed or partially closed cavities. We expect that this new metasurface device shall find a myriad of applications in imaging, electromagnetic mode management and medical therapy.

REFERENCES

[1] C. L. Holloway E. F. Kuester, J. A. Gordon, J. O'Hara, J. Booth, and D. R. Smith, "An overview of the theory and applications of metasurfaces: the two-dimensional equivalents of metamaterials," IEEE Antennas Propag. Mag., vol. 54, no. 2, pp. 10-35, Apr. 2012.

[2] A. Epstein and G. V. Elettheriades, "Huygens' metasurfaces via the equivalence principle: design and applications," J. Opt. Soc. Am. B, 33 A31-A50 (2016).

[3] N. Yu and F. Capasso, "Light propagation with phase discontinuities: generalized laws of reflection and refraction," Science, vol. 334, pp. 333-337, Oct. 2011.

[4] A. M. H. Wong and G. V. Eleftheriades, "Active Huygens' box: metasurface-enabled arbitrary electromagnetic wave generation inside a cavity," IEEE International Symposium on Antennas and Propagation (AP-S), Boston, USA, Jul. 2018.

[5] A. M. H. Wong and G. V. Eleftheriades, "A simple active Huygens' source for studying waveform synthesis with Huygens' metasurfaces and antenna arrays," IEEE Int. Symp. Antennas Propag., Jul. 2015.

[6] A. M. H. Wong and G. V. Eleftheriades, "Active Huygens' metasurfaces for RF waveform synthesis in a cavity," IEEE Mediterranean Electrotechnical Conf. (MELECON), Apr. 2016.

[7] A. E. H. Love, "The integration of the equations of propagation of electric waves," Phil. Trans. Roy. Soc. London, Ser. A 197, 1-45 (1901).

[8] S. A. Schelkunoff, "Some equivalence theorems of electromagnetics and their application to radiation problems," Bell Syst. Tech. J. 15, 92-112 (1936).

2D Anistropic Media Based Metasurface Absorbing Boundary Conditions

Shraman Gupta*, Abdel Razik Sebak
Department of Electrical and Computer Engineering
Concordia University, Montréal, QC, Canada
*shraman.gupta@concordia.ca

***Abstract*—The metasurface absorbing boundary conditions (MS-ABC) using 2-D finite difference time domain (FDTD) technique for anisotropic media are presented in this paper. These ABC are synthesized using equivalent surface currents based on Generalized Sheet Transition Conditions (GSTCs). The anisotropic media constitutes of variable permittivity and conductivity in the *x-y* computational domain. Therefore, the simulated results are computed on all four metasurface boundary walls with metal cylinders terminated at these walls.**

***Index terms*— Anisotropic media, Generalized Sheet Transition Conditions (GSTCs), Finite difference time domain (FDTD), Metasurfaces.**

I. Introduction

An electromagnetic discontinuity in space consisting of 2D array scattering particles is referred as metasurfaces and offers low loss, compact and controllable transformations properties than polarized selective surfaces [1, 2]. Such surfaces are useful in wave transformations applications such as holograms [3], reflection and transmission [4], and OAM production [5]. Metasurfaces absorbing boundary conditions are governed using Generalized Sheet Transition Conditions (GSTCs) and are implemented using FDTD [6], and FEM technique [7]. The term 'anisotropic' media means the variation in the media material properties in terms of the polarization directions and are controlled through their tensor values. Such media are of great importance and widely used in military and technology fields [8].

In this paper, the metasurface ABC are implemented and analyzed using surface current approach in an anisotropic media where the permittivity and conductivity is varied in *x*-y direction. The metal cylinders are placed at the boundary walls of the metasurface to compute fields for TM_z polarization.

II. Metasurface ABC FDTD Formulation

The electromagnetic field behavior for a metasurface, as illustrated in Fig. 1, is analyzed using GSTCs and are expressed as [6]

$$\hat{n} \times \Delta \vec{H} = j\omega \vec{P}_{||} - \hat{n} \times \nabla_{||} M_{s,n} \quad (1a)$$

$$\Delta \vec{E} \times \hat{n} = j\omega\mu_0 \vec{M}_{||} - \nabla_{||}\left(P_{s,n}\right)/\bar{\bar{\varepsilon}} \times \hat{n} \quad (1b)$$

where $\Delta \vec{H}$ and $\Delta \vec{E}$ represents the magnetic and electric field discontinuity on the two sides of the metasurface. $\vec{P}$ and $\vec{M}$ represents electric and magnetic polarization densities that are expressed in their susceptibility tensors and average fields.

$$\vec{P} = \bar{\bar{\varepsilon}}\, \bar{\bar{\chi}}_{ee} \vec{E}_{av} + \bar{\bar{\chi}}_{em} \sqrt{\bar{\bar{\varepsilon}}\mu_0}\, \vec{H}_{av} \quad (2a)$$

$$\vec{M} = \bar{\bar{\chi}}_{mm} \vec{H}_{av} + \bar{\bar{\chi}}_{me} \sqrt{\bar{\bar{\varepsilon}}/\mu_0}\, \vec{E}_{av} \quad (2b)$$

Assuming $\hat{n} = \hat{y}$, the non-zero field components for TM_z polarization are H_x, H_y and E_z. Therefore, using (1) and (2),

We acknowledge the support of the Natural Sciences and Engineering Research Council of Canada (NSERC). Cette recherche a été financée par le Conseil de recherches en sciences naturelles et en génie du Canada (CRSNG).

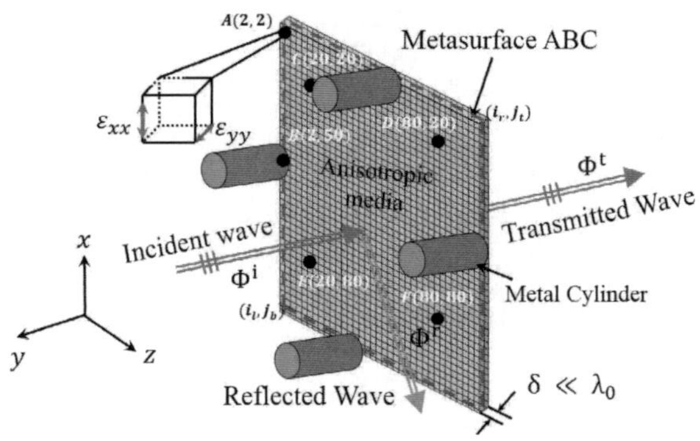

Fig. 1. Metasurface ABC representation with metal cylinders on the boundary walls in an anisotrpic media with evaluating field coordinates.

a set of linear equations for TM_z polarization are expressed as

$$-\Delta H_x = j\omega\bar{\bar{\varepsilon}}\chi_{ee}^{zz} E_{z,av} + j\omega\sqrt{\bar{\bar{\varepsilon}}\mu_0}\,\chi_{em}^{zx} H_{x,av} \quad (3a)$$

$$-\Delta E_z = j\omega\mu_0\chi_{mm}^{xx} H_{x,av} + j\omega\sqrt{\bar{\bar{\varepsilon}}\mu_0}\,\chi_{me}^{xz} E_{z,av} \quad (3b)$$

The metasurface ABC are calculated from surface currents (both electric and magnetic) evaluated from (3) for TM_z polarization using 2-D FDTD technique are presented as

$$J_z^{n-1/2}(i, j_\alpha) = \pm\left[H_x^{n-1/2}(i, j_\alpha + 1) + H_x^{n-1/2}(i, j_\alpha - 1)\right] \quad (4a)$$

$$M_x^{n}(i, j_\alpha) = \pm\left[E_z^{n}(i, j_\alpha + 1) + E_z^{n}(i, j_\alpha - 1)\right] \quad (4b)$$

Here, $\pm$ represents bottom and top walls where α = b, t. Similarly for left and right sides walls where β = l, r.

The E_z field is calculated from conventional 2-D FDTD Maxwell equations in their integral form and using the surface currents from (4) in these equations to update the field equations for top/bottom and left/right walls respectively as

$$E_z^n(i, j_\alpha) = E_z^{n-1}(i, j_\alpha) - \frac{\Delta t}{\bar{\bar{\varepsilon}}}\left[\frac{H_x^{n-1/2}(i, j_\alpha + 1) - H_x^{n-1/2}(i, j_\alpha)}{\Delta y} - \frac{H_y^{n-1/2}(i + 1, j_\alpha) - H_y^{n-1/2}(i, j_\alpha)}{\Delta x} - \frac{J_z^{n-1/2}(i, j_\alpha)}{\Delta y}\right] \quad (5a)$$

$$E_z^n(i_\beta, j) = E_z^n(i_\beta, j) - \frac{\Delta t}{\mu_0}\left[\frac{H_x^{n-1/2}(i_\beta, j + 1) - H_x^{n-1/2}(i_\beta, j)}{\Delta y} - \frac{H_y^{n-1/2}(i_\beta + 1, j) - H_y^{n-1/2}(i_\beta, j)}{\Delta x} - \frac{J_z^{n-1/2}(i_\beta, j)}{\Delta x}\right] \quad (5b)$$

III. FDTD Implementation For Anisotropic Media

The anisotropic media is defined by the change in the material properties tensors. For example, the permittivity and conductivity tensors are responsible for such media in this work. The field equations in the 2-D total field region are governed using Maxwell curl equations followed by their permittivity and conductivity tensors as

$$\nabla \times \vec{E} = -\bar{\bar{\mu}} \cdot \partial \vec{H}/\partial t \quad (6a)$$

$$\nabla \times \vec{H} = \bar{\bar{\varepsilon}} \cdot \partial \vec{E}/\partial t + \bar{\bar{\sigma}} \cdot \vec{E} \quad (6b)$$

where,

$$\bar{\bar{\varepsilon}} = \begin{pmatrix} \varepsilon_{xx} & \varepsilon_{xy} \\ \varepsilon_{yx} & \varepsilon_{yy} \end{pmatrix}, \bar{\bar{\mu}} = \begin{pmatrix} \mu_{xx} & \mu_{xy} \\ \mu_{yx} & \mu_{yy} \end{pmatrix}, \bar{\bar{\sigma}} = \begin{pmatrix} \sigma_{xx} & \sigma_{xy} \\ \sigma_{yx} & \sigma_{yy} \end{pmatrix}$$

The updated field equations for two components of E_z in 2-D FDTD can be written as [8]

$$E_{zx}^{n+1}(i+1, j+1) = \left(\frac{\varepsilon - 0.5\Delta t\sigma_x}{\varepsilon + 0.5\Delta t\sigma_x}\right) E_{zx}^{n}(i+1, j+1) + \frac{\Delta t}{\delta(\varepsilon + 0.5\Delta t\sigma_x)} A$$

$$E_{zy}^{n+1}(i+1, j+1) = \left(\frac{\varepsilon - 0.5\Delta t\sigma_y}{\varepsilon + 0.5\Delta t\sigma_y}\right) E_{zy}^{n}(i+1, j+1) + \frac{\Delta t}{\delta(\varepsilon + 0.5\Delta t\sigma_y)} B$$

where $A = \left(H_x^{n-1/2}(i+1, j) - H_x^{n+1/2}(i+1, j+1)\right)$ and $B = \left(H_y^{n+1/2}(i+1, j+1) - H_y^{n-1/2}(i, j+1)\right)$

IV. Simulated Results and Disscusions

The simulation is done using 2-D FDTD technique where the computational domain (x_{dim}, y_{dim}) is 100 × 100 and each cell size is $\Delta x = \Delta y = 1mm$. The time step is given by$\Delta t = S \times A/c$, where S represents the stability factor i.e. 0.5 is chosen in this work with A as either Δx orΔy. The anisotropic media parameters are taken as

$$\bar{\bar{\varepsilon}} = \begin{pmatrix} 2.2 & 0 \\ 0 & 10.2 \end{pmatrix}, \quad \bar{\bar{\mu}} = \mu_0, \quad \bar{\bar{\sigma}} = \begin{pmatrix} 0.1 & 0 \\ 0 & 0.2 \end{pmatrix}$$

In this work, the excitation source chosen is single Gaussian pulse located at $(x_{dim}/2, y_{dim}/2)$. The metal cylinders are placed at the boundary walls to observe the fields due to unwanted reflections from the metal cylinders. The field analysis is carried out different field observation points i.e. *(A, B)* to illustrate metasurface ABC and *(C, D, E, F)* to show the effect of metal cylinders in an anisotropic media. The electric field distribution at time step 150 and 250 is shown in Fig. 2, where an elliptical field distribution is observed due to anisotropic nature of the media. The unwanted reflections due to metal cylinders are observed.

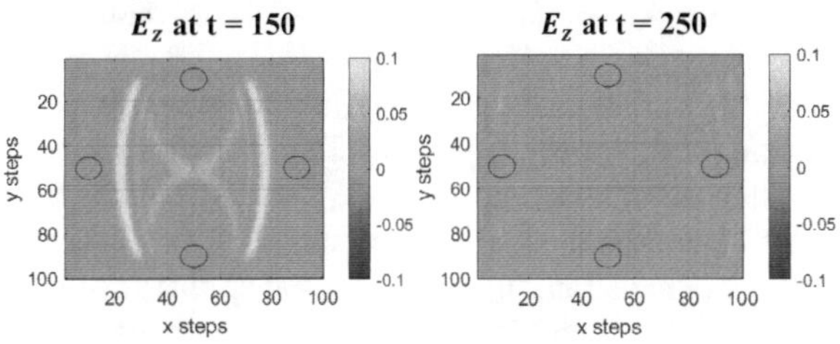

Fig. 2. Electric Field distribution using 2-D FDTD simulation terminated by metasurface absorbing boundary conditions.

The magnitude of electric field at points *A (2, 2)* and *B (2, 50)* is observed in Fig 3 (a), where the electromagnetic waves are truncated to the order of 10^{-4}. The electric field magnitude at point *B* is higher than *A* due to presence of metal cylinder near point *B*. The effect of unwanted reflections from the metal cylinders can be observed at points *C (20, 20), D (20, 80), E (80, 20) and F (80, 80)* in Fig. 3(b), where there are certain reflections between time step 200 and 300. To further illustrate the effect of metal cylinders the field distribution is

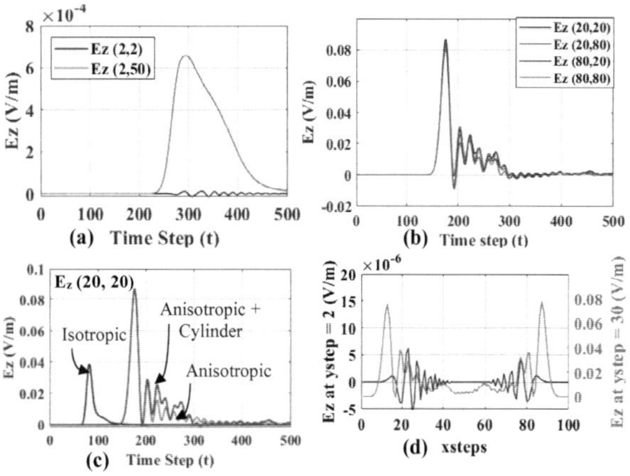

Fig. 3. Electric Field (E_z) simulation (a) at points *(A,B)* (b) at points *(C,D,E,F)* (c) difference between isotropic, and anisotropic media with and without metal cylinders (d) at *ystep =2* and *ystep = 30* over the x-steps.

shown in Fig. 3 (c), where the difference between isotropic, and anisotropic with and without metal cylinders is calculated. It is seen that the unwanted reflections is caused due to the metal cylinders and also there is a time shift in achieving the maximum electric field. Finally, the truncation of EM waves due to metasurface absorbing boundary condition is seen in Fig. 3 (d) at *y-steps* 30 and 2 over the *x-steps* domain from the order of ~ 0.8 to 5 × 10^{-6} V/m respectively.

V. Conclusion

Metasurface absorbing boundary conditions are realized using 2-D FDTD for an anisotropic media in the presence of the metal cylinders at the metasurface boundaries. The updated fields at the boundary is calculated using the surface currents synthesized using GSTCs with an inclusion of effect of variable permittivity and conductivity tensors.

References

[1] E. F. Kuester, M. A. Mohamed, M. Piket-May, and C. L. Holloway, "Averaged transition conditions for electromagnetic fields at a metafilm," *IEEE Transactions on Antennas and Propagation,* vol. 51, no. 10, pp. 2641-2651, Oct. 2003.

[2] C. Pfeiffer and A. Grbic, "Cascaded metasurfaces for complete phase and polarization control," *Appl. Phys. Lett.,* vol. 102, no. 23, p. 231116, 2013.

[3] G. Zheng, H. Mühlenbernd, M. Kenney, G. Li, T. Zentgraf, and S. Zhang, "Metasurface holograms reaching 80% efficiency," *Nature Nanotechnol.* vol. 10, no. 4, pp. 308–312, 2015.

[4] N. Yu and F. Capasso, "Flat optics with designer metasurfaces," *Nature Mater.,* vol. 13, no. 2, pp. 139–150, 2014.

[5] E. Karimi, S. A. Schulz, I. D. Leon, H. Qassim, J. Upham, and R. W. Boyd, "Generating optical orbital angular momentum at visible wavelengths using a plasmonic metasurface," *Light, Sci. Appl.,* vol. 3,no. 5, p. e167, 2014.

[6] K. Achouri, M. A. Salem, and C. Caloz, "General Metasurface Synthesis Based on Susceptibility Tensors," *IEEE Transactions on Antennas and Propagation,* vol. 63, no. 7, pp. 2977-2991, July 2015.

[7] S. Sandeep, J.-M. Jin, and C. Caloz, "Finite-element modeling of metasurfaces with generalized sheet transition conditions," *IEEE Trans. Antennas Propag.,* vol. 65, no. 5, pp. 2413–2420, May 2017.

[8] J. Schneider and S. Hudson, "A finite-difference time-domain method applied to anisotropic material," *IEEE Transactions on Antennas and Propagation,* vol. 41, no. 7, pp. 994-999, July 1993.

Impedance-Matched High-Index Ceramic Microwave Metamaterials at X-band

Quang Nguyen, Max Burnett, and Amir I. Zaghloul
US Army Research Laboratory,
Adelphi, MD, 20783
93nguyen@cua.edu, burnem@seas.upenn.edu
amir.i.zaghloul.civ@mail.mil

Mario J. Mencagli and Nader Engheta
Department of Electrical and Systems Engineering,
University of Pennsylvania,
Philadelphia, PA, 19104
mencagli@seas.upenn.edu, engheta@ee.upenn.edu

***Abstract*—In this paper, we present a design to achieve both impedance matching and high refractive index using dielectric metamaterial resonators in the X-band. This design is based on two cubic dielectric resonators using commercially-available high-κ ceramic. By scaling the size and lattice constant of the individual units, the first magnetic resonance of one cube and the first electric resonance of the other cube can be overlapped in order to achieve the design criteria. The proposed design is then compared with the dielectric Huygens' surfaces inspired by the work of Kivshar, et. al. [1], which is based on a single cylindrical dielectric resonator. For our case, we find that the two-cube resonator design has better performance than the single cylindrical resonator. Thus, it can achieve the reflection-less surface, referred to as a Huygens' surface, and create a high index of refraction at the same time.**

***Index Terms*—Dielectric metamaterial, Huygens' surface microwave materials, electric resonance, high refractive index, impedance matching, magnetic resonance, overlap.**

I. Introduction

CUSTOMIZED magneto-dielectric materials with matching permittivity and permeability have attracted significant attention for their potential to miniaturize the size and to improve the efficiency of antennas and RF devices [1]. Using metallic or dielectric inclusions as the building block, the electric and magnetic properties of the material can be fully customized to achieve the desired scattering *S*-parameters, i.e. minimum reflection or transmission.

Metallic resonators have been developed over the last the two decades. Various practical designs, such as split-ring resonators (SRRs), electric inductive-capacitor (ELC) resonators, and fishnet structures, were introduced in the literature [3]-[5]. Unfortunately, metallic resonators usually suffer from significant Ohmic loss and strong anisotropic properties at the resonance. It is known that dielectric resonators represent a promising alternative solution due to low-loss displacement currents and isotropic designs [6].

In this work, we focus on using high-κ ceramic resonators [7] for developing a fully customized magneto-dielectric material for the microwave frequency around 10 GHz. We present a practical design to minimize the reflection and obtain a high refractive index at the same time. The resonators are assumed to be made of commercial high-κ ceramic, *K-100*, which is developed by National Magnetics Group/TCI Ceramics [8]. The design concept is based on the combination of displacement currents and Mie resonances.

II. Composite Dielectric Cube/Cube Design

In this section, we present the cube/cube resonator design concept. According to Mie theory, a dielectric resonator can exhibit magnetic and electric resonances at different frequencies. In theory, the effective permittivity and permeability of a material comprised of sub-wavelength resonators, can be turned to almost arbitrary values. In practice, due to the loss of the material, only the first or second resonant modes of the Mie series might be considered. The higher-order Mie resonances are weak and often occur at frequencies beyond the long-wavelength limit where the homogenization theory may not be valid. Thus, the design procedure is as follows. First, we design two differently sized dielectric cubes such that the smaller size exhibits the first resonant mode (magnetic) while the larger size exhibits the second resonant mode (electric) at the same frequency. Then, we arrange them into two-dimensional periodic arrays to obtain the matching condition for a plane wave at normal incidence. The proposed design is depicted in Fig. 1a. It is assumed that the unit cell is periodic in the x and y directions. Two cubes have side lengths a_1 and a_2, respectively, with $a_1 < a_2$, surrounded by air as the host material with permittivity ε_0 and μ_0.

III. Single Cylindrical Dielectric Resonator Design

In this section, we present a reference design for Huygens' surface which is based on the seminal work of Kivshar and Decker [1]. A unit cell, shown in Fig. 1b, is comprised of a dielectric cylinder (*K-100)* surrounded by air and Floquet periodic boundary conditions in x and y. By manipulating the dimensions of the cylinder, the magnetic and electric resonance can be made to exist at the same frequency thus creating an overlap. The magnetic resonance of the cylinder (corresponding

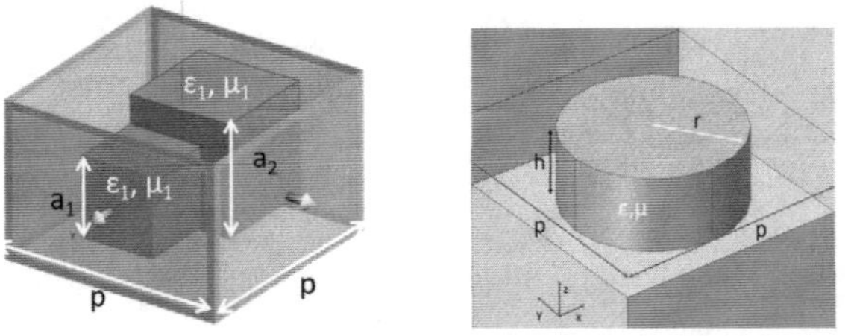

(a) (b)

Fig. 1. Unit cell of a resonator composed of (a) two different size cubes of high-k ceramic and (b) of a single dielectric cylinder of high-k ceramic.

TABLE I. THE PARAMETERS OF CUBE/CUBE RESONATOR

a_1	a_2	p	ε_1	μ_1
2.54mm	3.55mm	7.2mm	100-0.1j	1

to the first Mie resonance) is strongly dependent on the height of the cylinder. The electric resonance (the second Mie resonance), however, is more dependent upon the radius of the cylinder, adjusting these two parameters to obtain an overlap at 9.6GHz yields an aspect ratio (here defined as *h/d*, where *h* is the height and *d* is the diameter) of 0.41.

IV. Numerical Analysis

The S-parameters (amplitude and phase) for the cube/cube resonator arranged in a 2-D array, having parameters indicated in Table I, are computed using FEKO®, assuming a plane wave at normal incidence that propagates along the *z* axis with its electric field directed along the *x* axis.

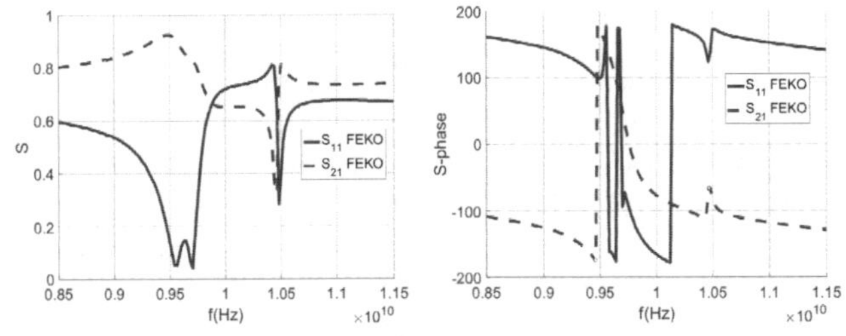

Fig. 2. Magnitude and phase of simulated S-parameters for the cube/cube resonator of high-k ceramic.

As seen in Fig. 2, there is one resonant region (around 9.6GHz), where both the magnetic and electric resonance overlap. This results in relatively high transmission (S_{21} approaching near unity and S_{11} approaching zero, and some absorption). In other words, the input impedance into this structure is similar to that of free space. Furthermore, the phase of S_{11} and S_{21} drops rapidly around 9.6GHz. The effective permittivity and permeability of the metasurface are evaluated numerically, as depicted in Fig. 3, showing high values near the frequency of interest. The second resonant region (around 10.5GHz) is due to higher order mode.

Analysis for the single dielectric cylinder was carried out in COMSOL Multiphysics®, a FEM solver, over the same frequency range, 9-10GHz. The dimensions of the cylinder resulting in an overlap at 9.6GHz are r = *2.3167mm*, h = *1.9mm*, and the width of the unit cell is *6.1334mm*. The material

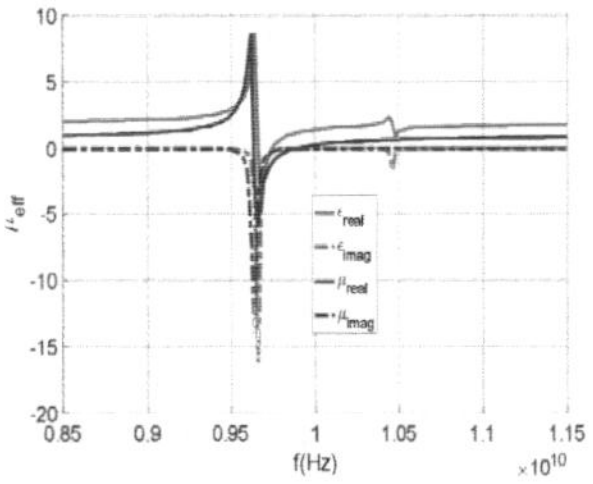

Fig. 3. The effective permittivity and permeability parameters of cube/cube resonator of high-k ceramic

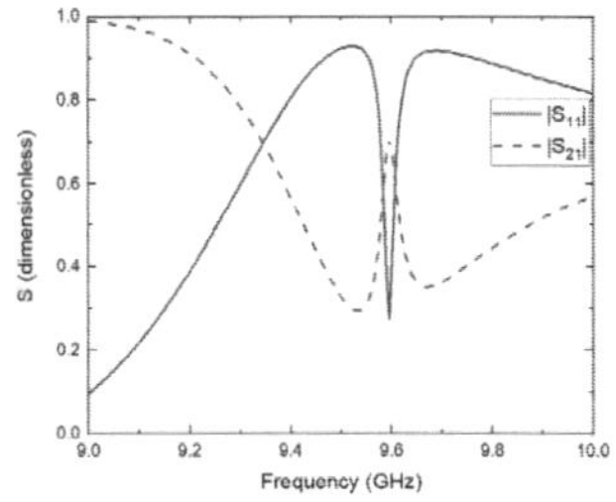

Fig. 4. Magnitude of simulated S-parameters for the single cylinder scenario

was modeled using the same ceramic, *K-100* ($\varepsilon = 100 - 0.1j$), with a unitary electric field polarized along x while propagating along z. As seen in Fig. 4, there is an overlap region resulting in a transmission window where originally a rejection band existed identified by a peak in the transmission and a dip in the reflection.

The presented design (cube/cube resonator) shows the reflection-less surface, referred to as a Huygens' surface, which has a similar performance to the cylinder designed by Kivshar. However, it also shows a high value of effective permittivity and permeability at the resonant frequency. In other words, it can achieve Huygens' surface, and create a high refractive index at the same time.

V. Conclusions

In this work, we presented a cube/cube resonator design that creates a transparent surface, as well as a high refractive index in the X-band. This design may potentially be used as a substrate to miniaturize the antenna size, and to improve its efficiency at the same time.

References

[1] M. Decker, I. Staude, M. Falkner, J. Dominguez, D. N. Neshev, I. Brener, T. Pertsch, Y. S. Kivshar, "High-efficiency dielectric Huygens' surfaces." *Adv. Opt. Mater*, vol. 3, no. 6, pp. 813–820, 2015.

[2] A.O. Karilainen, P.M.T. Ikonen, C.R. Simovski, S.A. Tretyakov, A.N. Lagarkov, S.A. Maklakov, K.N. Rozanov, and S.N. Starostenko. "Experimental studies on antenna miniaturisation using magneto-dielectric and dielectric materials." *IET microwaves, antennas & propagation.*, vol. 5, no. 4, pp. 495-502, 2011.

[3] J. B. Pendry, A. J. Holden, D. J. Robbins, and W. J. Stewart, "Magnetism from conductors and enhanced nonlinear phenomena," *IEEE Trans. Microw. Theory Tech.*, vol. 47, no. 11, pp. 2075–2084, Nov. 1999.

[4] D. Schurig, J. J. Mock, and D. R. Smith, "Electric-field-coupled resonators for negative permittivity metamaterials," *Appl. Phys. Lett.*, vol. 88, no. 4, p. 041109, 2006.

[5] M. Kafesaki, I. Tsiapa, N. Katsarakis, Th Koschny, C. M. Soukoulis, and E. N. Economou. "Left-handed metamaterials: The fishnet structure and its variations." *Physical Review B*, vol. 75, no. 23, pp. 235114, 2007.

[6] A. Ahmadi, and H. Mosallaei, "Physical configuration and performance modeling of all-dielectric metamaterials," *Physical Review B* vol. 77, pp. 045104. 2008.

[7] Q. Zhao, J. Zhou, F. Zhang, and D. Lippens. "Mie resonance-based dielectric metamaterials." *Materials today*, vol. 12, no. 12, pp. 60-69, 2009.

[8] http://www.magneticsgroup.com/

Reconfigurable Metasurfaces for Index Modulation in 5G Wireless Communications

John A. Hodge[1], Kumar Vijay Mishra[2] and Amir I. Zaghloul[1,2]
[1]Virginia Tech, Falls Church, VA 22043 USA
[2]United States Army Research Laboratory, Adelphi, MD 20783 USA
jah70@vt.edu

***Abstract*—Recent research on index modulation (IM) techniques shows great promise in improving the energy and spectral efficiencies of high data-rate 5G wireless communications. In this work, we introduce a reconfigurable software-defined metasurface to implement IM techniques in 5G transceivers. In particular, we define implementation of spatial and subcarrier index modulations using a reconfigurable metasurface antenna, including beam steering and phase modulation capabilities. We present a metasurface aperture that can modulate and multiplex communications signals over the spectral, spatial, and temporal domains using space-time coding of unit elements.**

***Index Terms*—5G, index modulation, OFDM, reconfigurable metasurfaces, spatial modulation.**

I. Introduction

Demands for higher data rates within the limited electromagnetic spectrum have increased multi-fold with the onset of fifth-generation (5G) wireless communications systems. Further, growing global usage of smart phones and internet-of-things (IoT) devices requires 5G networks to support higher spectral and energy efficiencies (SE and EE) [1, 2]. In this context, index modulation (IM) has emerged as a potential 5G waveform because it offers high EE and SE by relying on the indices or permutation of some variable of carrier signals to convey additional bits of information [2]. In this paper, we focus on two particular forms of IM. The first is spatial modulation (SM) which encodes part of the transmit data onto the spatial position of each transmit antenna in the antenna array [3]. The other is the subcarrier index modulation (SIM), also known as orthogonal frequency division multiplexing (OFDM)-IM, wherein the frequency subcarrier-index of the transmitted symbol carries information bits [1–4].

Typically, 5G links employ several multiple-input-multiple-output (MIMO) antenna arrays with many radio-frequency (RF) chains [1], resulting in complex RF systems with prohibitive cost, size, weight, and power (SWaP). These limitations can be offset by employing a variety of techniques. At the modulation level, SM conveys bits of information without additional power through antenna indices and only requires a single RF chain thereby reducing the complexity at both transmitter and receiver, without decreasing the SE or EE of conventional systems [2]. At the RF and antenna stage, recently RF reconfigurable metasurfaces (R-MTSs) have been developed to provide antennas with active beamforming capabilities with significantly lower cost and complexity than the traditional phased arrays [5–9]. In this work, we combine these two ideas to propose MTS-enabled IM to meet the spectral and hardware requirements of next-generation communications systems.

II. Metasurface Control

An MTS antenna is an electrically-large aperture antenna comprising of subwavelength resonant metamaterial elements. By changing the phase coding across the MTS over time, functions such as phase modulation, amplitude attenuation, and frequency-domain multiplexing, are performed all over the MTS surface without RF components such as mixers and phase shifters. Each MTS unit cell is characterized by its transmission or reflection coefficient. This coefficient is tuned to the desired frequency-dependent phase and amplitude by sending a voltage control signal to an active element, e.g. a diode, embedded in the unit cell [10].

In this paper, we assume the active MTS is in a reflectarray configuration [7] and is controlled by a MTS control module, which is an FPGA controller that calculates the necessary phase of each unit cell to perform MTS beam scanning and phase modulation. The MTS control module also sends voltage signals to each unit cell to realize the desired phase states. Let θ_r and θ_i be the reflected and incident wave directions, respectively. If $\frac{d\Phi}{dx}$ is the gradient of phase discontinuity along the MTS, then the MTS beam scanning is modeled using the generalized law of reflection as [11]

$$\sin(\theta_r) - \sin(\theta_i) = \frac{\lambda_0}{2\pi}\frac{d\Phi}{dx}. \tag{1}$$

Assuming $\theta_i = 0$ and taking MTS unit cell parameters into account, the beam scanning equation becomes

$$\theta_r = \sin^{-1}\left(\frac{\lambda_0}{2\pi}\frac{\Delta\phi_e}{Qd}\right), \tag{2}$$

where $\Delta\phi_e$ is the phase tuning range of the unit cell element, Q is the selected period of unit cells, and d is the element spacing of each unit cell. From this relation, we calculate the phase difference between each unit cell necessary to scan the beam in the desired direction. Figure 1 demonstrates a progressive phase shift calculated using (2) that scans the beam to $\theta_r = 30\,\mathrm{deg}$ with a desired phase. The FPGA-based MTS control module computes the values of $\Delta\phi_e$ and Q accordingly for beam scanning and calculates the phase of each unit cell column ($\phi_{steer}(m)$) using

$$\phi_{steer}(m) = \mathrm{mod}(m/Q)(\Delta\phi_e/Q), \tag{3}$$

where $\mathrm{mod}(\cdot)$ denotes the modulo operation. The unit cell grid spacing in each dimension is denoted by d_x and d_y and the wavenumber is $k_c = \frac{2\pi}{\lambda_c}$. The far-field phase of each element due to the array factor of the MTS is

$$\phi_{ff}(m,n) = k_c \sin\theta((m-1)d_x\cos\phi + (n-1)d_y\sin\phi). \tag{4}$$

Let $\phi_{mod}(m,n,t)$ be the time-varying phase modulation term that accounts for the desired phase shift keying (PSK) or quadrature amplitude modulation (QAM) modulation symbols. We denote the reflection amplitude and phase of each MTS unit cell as $a_e(m,n)$ and $\phi_e(m,n)$, respectively [6]. For simplicity, assume $a_e = 1$; in practice, a scan-dependent element pattern may be used. The desired reflection phase of each unit cell is

$$\phi_e(m,n,t) = \phi_{mod}(m,n,t) + \phi_{steer}(m,n) + \phi_{ff}(m,n). \tag{5}$$

From (3)-(5), the far-field radiation pattern of the signal-modulating-MTS is

$$f(\phi,\theta) = \sum_{m=1}^{M}\sum_{n=1}^{N} a_e(m,n)\exp\{j\phi_e(m,n,t)\}. \tag{6}$$

III. MTS-Enabled Index Modulation

We now explain MTS implementation for two 5G IM techniques, i.e., SM and OFDM-IM.

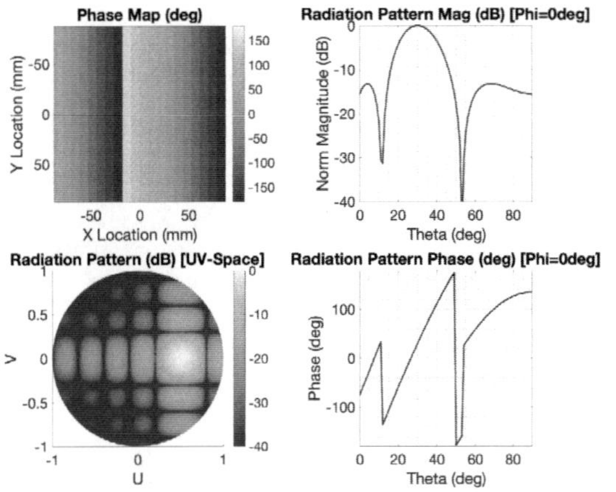

Fig. 1. Phase map of MTS scanning beam to 30° at 6 GHz with far-field radiated phase tuned to +45°. The MTS consisted of 20×20 unit cells with element spacing of 8.3 mm ($\lambda/6$). The radiation pattern is normalized.

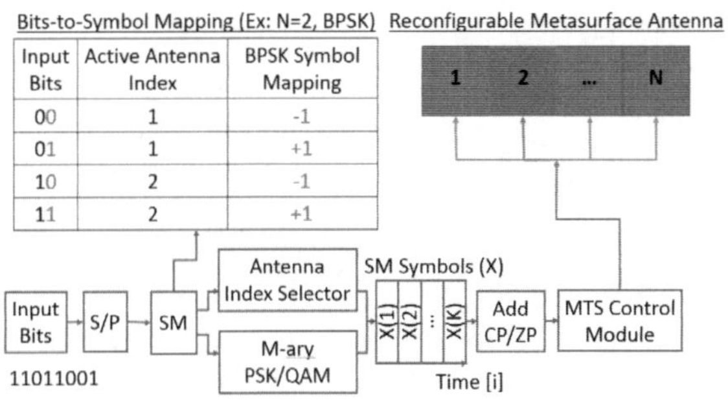

Fig. 2. Simplified system block diagram of an active MTS-based SM transmit chain. The communications signal bit stream input is converted from serial-to-parallel (S/P). The SM splits input into antenna index and M-ary modulation bits; the outputs of the two form SM symbols. Next, zero padding (ZP) or cyclical prefix (CP) add a guard interval. The SM symbols are fed to the MTS Control Module which computes the reflection phase of each unit cell for modulation and outputs voltage signals to control the unit cell at each time step to modulate and transmit the reflected signal from the feed.

In SM, bits are split into index bits and M-ary (PSK/QAM) constellation bits [2]. The R-MTS implements SM by dividing the MTS into sub-apertures with sufficient phase center separation to create a spatial antenna constellation (Figure 2). The SM is particularly well suited for MTS implementation because it employs a single-RF feed. The single-carrier SM MIMO provides the benefits of a low-complexity, low-cost single-RF transmitter while attaining high MIMO multiplexing gain [12]. At the cost of added complexity, generalized spatial modulation (GSM) [2] can be performed using MTSs by illuminating more than one subaperture simultaneously. Additionally, more sophisticated SM modulation schemes, such as space-time block codes (STBCs) (as in, e.g. Vertical-Bell Laboratories Layered Space-Time or VBLAST) [12], can also be implemented using MTSs with most of the added complexity handled digitally inside of the FPGA that controls the MTS.

Many modern wireless communication systems utilize OFDM to multiplex PSK or QAM signals on orthogonal frequency subcarriers to increase data rates. The IM has been extended to OFDM to create SIM (or OFDM-IM) for greater SE and EE. Through space-time coding of an R-MTS, frequency harmonics [13] or subcarriers are generated for SIM. For MTS implementation of OFDM and OFDM-IM, signal amplitude and phase control can each be controlled

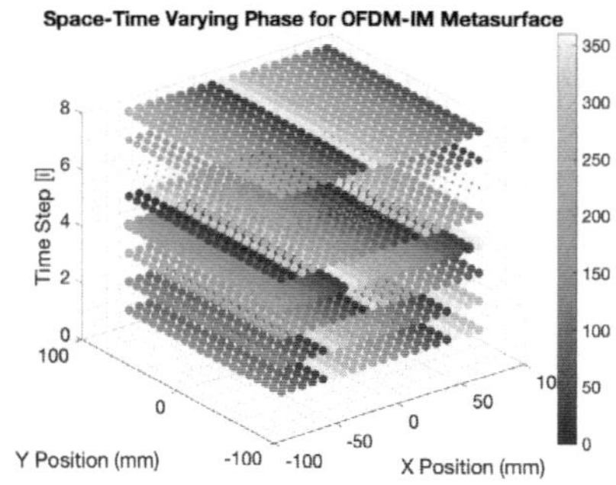

Fig. 3. Illustration of space-time varying phases of an MTS-based OFDM-IM for a random bit signal sequence. The colored dots represent phase in degrees.

either in the RF feed circuitry or directly through switching in the active MTS. Figure 3 shows space-time MTS varying phases that implement OFDM-IM for random bit signal sequence.

ACKNOWLEDGEMENTS

K. V. M. acknowledges support from the National Academies of Sciences, Engineering, and Medicine via Army Research Laboratory Harry Diamond Distinguished Postdoctoral Fellowship.

REFERENCES

[1] X. Cheng, M. Zhang, M. Wen, and L. Yang, "Index modulation for 5G: Striving to do more with less," IEEE Wireless Communications, vol. 25, no. 2, pp. 126–132, 2018.

[2] E. Basar, M. Wen, R. Mesleh, M. Di Renzo, Y. Xiao, and H. Haas, "Index modulation techniques for next-generation wireless networks," IEEE Access, vol. 5, pp. 16 693–16 746, 2017.

[3] R. Mesleh, H. Haas, S. Sinanovic, C. W. Ahn, and S. Yun, "Spatial modulation," IEEE Transactions on Vehicular Techology, vol. 57, no. 4, pp. 2228–2241, 2008.

[4] R. Abu-Alhiga and H. Haas, "Subcarrier-index modulation OFDM," in IEEE International Symposium on Personal, Indoor and Mobile Radio Communications, 2009, pp. 177–181.

[5] D. R. Smith, O. Yurduseven, L. P. Mancera, P. Bowen, and N. B. Kundtz, "Analysis of a waveguide-fed metasurface antenna," Physical Review Applied, vol. 8, no. 5, p. 054048, 2017.

[6] X. Wan, M. Q. Qi, T. Y. Chen, and T. J. Cui, "Field-programmable beam reconfiguring based on digitally-controlled coding metasurface," Scientific Reports, vol. 6, p. 20663, 2016.

[7] K. V. Mishra, J. A. Hodge, and A. I. Zaghloul, "Reconfigurable metasurfaces for radar and communications systems," in URSI Asia-Pacific Radio Science Conference, 2019, in press.

[8] K. Chen, Y. Feng, F. Monticone, J. Zhao, B. Zhu, T. Jiang, L. Zhang, Y. Kim, X. Ding, S. Zhang et al., "A reconfigurable active huygens' metalens," Advanced Materials, vol. 29, no. 17, 2017.

[9] D. Cabric, D. Markovic, and R. W. Brodersen, "On MIMO signal processing for adaptive W-CDMA and OFDM wireless transceivers," in IEEE/ACES International Conference on Wireless Communications and Applied Computational Electromagnetics, 2005, pp. 58–61.

[10] J. A. Hodge, T. K. Anthony, and A. I. Zaghloul, "Utilizing active circuit elements for dynamic tuning and electronic scanning of CLL-loaded dipole antenna structure," in URSI Radio Science Meeting, 2015, p. 16.

[11] N. Yu, P. Genevet, M. A. Kats, F. Aieta, J.-P. Tetienne, F. Capasso, and Z. Gaburro, "Light propagation with phase discontinuities: Generalized laws of reflection and refraction," Science, p. 1210713, 2011.

[12] P. Yang, Y. Xiao, Y. L. Guan, K. V. S. Hari, A. Chockalingam, S. Sugiura, H. Haas, M. D. Renzo, C. Masouros, Z. Liu, L. Xiao, S. Li, and L. Hanzo, "Single-carrier SM-MIMO: A promising design for broadband large-scale antenna systems," IEEE Communications Surveys & Tutorials, vol. 18, no. 3, pp. 1687–1716, 2016.

[13] L. Zhang, X. Q. Chen, S. Liu, Q. Zhang, J. Zhao, J. Y. Dai, G. D. Bai, X. Wan, Q. Cheng, G. Castaldi, V. Galdi, and T. J. Cui, "Space-time-coding digital metasurfaces," Nature Communications, vol. 9, no. 1, p. 4334, 2018.

Generation and Manipulation of OAM Beams in 2D Planar Arrays and Reflectarrays

Shubhendu Bhardwaj
Electrical and Computer Engineering
Florida International University
10555, W. Flagler Street, Miami, USA
sbhardwa@fiu.edu

***Abstract*— In this paper, we develop methods of manipulating OAM beams by using distribution of excitation coefficients in a 2D aperture. The excitation coefficients applied are useful for 2D arrays, reflectarray and reflector antennas. Specifically, we study the effect of spiral phase across the aperture, radial phase gradient in the aperture and gaussian amplitude distribution in the aperture. It is noted that spiral phasing controls the OAM index, radial-phasing controls the beam position and Gaussian amplitude distribution reduces the ripples in the beam-ridge along azimuthal direction.**

Keywords—Orbital Angular Modulation, Gaussian beam, 2D arrays, Beam-forming.

I. Introduction

Orbital angular momentum (OAM) modes represent a class of beams that are known to have spiral phase across the transverse plane of the propagating beam. It has been shown that several modes, with varying rates of spiral phase variations, can coexist in the same region of space, at same frequency and simultaneously, yet they can carry signals distinguishable from one another using appropriate antenna structure [1], [2]. Primarily used for multiplexing modes in lasers and fiber communication [3], more recently the concept has been modified for applications in RF communication as well.

An interesting problem for RF communication is generation of OAM mode using antenna arrays. Prior work in this direction has shown use of uniform circular arrays, use of phase-plates [4] and reflectarray to create such beams [5]. Following these works, in current paper, we study excitation coefficients on large aperture-surfaces to generate OAM beams. Specifically, we investigate methods to control the beam-width and beam-directions to make realistic designs.

II. OAM Modes Formulations

There are two classes of Gaussian beams which are known to carry OAM modes, namely Bessel-Gaussian beams and Bessel-Laguerre beams. Both are indeed solution of Helmholtz equation solved in cylindrical coordinates and under paraxial approximation which states that the changes in phase in the direction of beam-propagation are much stronger than phase changes in the transverse plane of the wave. Here, we first write the mathematical form of cross-sectional fields in Bessel-Gaussian beam

$$|\vec{E}| = A_o J_m(k_t\rho)\exp\left(\frac{-\rho^2}{w_{BG}^2}\right)\exp(-jm\phi), \tag{1}$$

where ρ, ϕ coordinate variables for cylindrical coordinate system, $J_m(\cdot)$ is the Bessel function of first kind with k_t as the transverse component of the wave-vector. w_{BG} is referred to as the waist of the Bessel-Gauss beam. Note that z-variations, i.e., variations in the direction of propagation, are omitted for the sake of simplicity.

Interesting observation is the variation of phase-terms in the expression, which suggests a ϕ variation of phase. By changing the orbital momentum index m (to $\pm 1, \pm 2$ etc), different orthogonal modes may be generated. Furthermore, the distribution of field follows Bessel multiplied by gaussian function from center to edge of the beam. Having understood the basic nature of these waves, we will consider how OAM modes may be generated using a 2D array of elements.

III. Array Coefficients and Corresponding Beams

We consider an array of isotropic elements arranged in 2D fashion over an area of $a \times a$ with interelemental distance chosen to be $d = \lambda/2$. We consider several cases, which ultimately help us understand the effect of array-size, spiral-phase distribution, radial phase distribution and radial amplitude distribution on the beam-direction and beam-width. Before proceeding, we write the general expression of excitation coefficient of (i, j) element located at polar coordinates $(\rho_{i,j}, \phi_{i,j})$ in the aperture as:

$$A_{i,j} = C_{i,j}\, e^{jm\phi_{i,j}}\, e^{j\rho_{i,j} k_o \sin\theta_b}, \tag{2}$$

where $C_{i,j}$ is a real, $k_o = 2\pi/\lambda$ is the free space wave number and θ_B is the intended beam direction [5].

A. *Effect of Rate of Spiral Phase Variation at the Aperture*

To mimic the azimuthal phase-term of the Gaussian OAM beam ($e^{-jm\phi}$), we excite the 2D array with phase coefficients in spiral fashion by using non-zero m. We consider $C_{i,j} = 1$, $\theta_B = \pi/6$, m is varied as -1 and -2 in cases shown in Figs. 1 and 2. Non-zero θ_B leads to radial phase gradient as shown in the figures. The resulting phase distribution over aperture, 3D far-field distribution, and phase/amplitude distribution over the far-field ridge (at $\theta = \pi/6$) is shown in these figures.

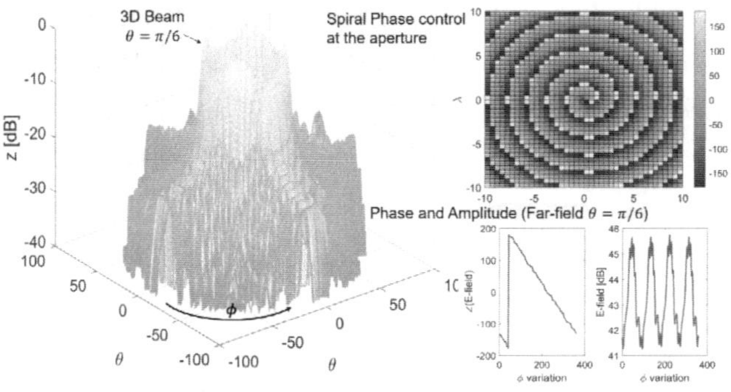

Fig. 1. 3D far-field and beam's phase and amplitude ($\theta = \pi/6$), generated from spiral and radially varying phased array with uniform excitation ($C_{i,j} = 1, \theta_B = \pi/6$, m=-1)

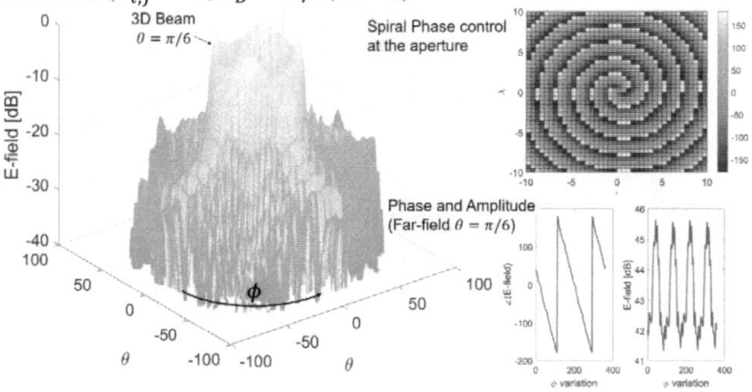

Fig. 2. 3D far-field and beam's phase and amplitude ($\theta = \pi/6$), generated from spiral and radially varying phased array with uniform excitation (a=10λ, $C_{i,j} = 1, \theta_B = \pi/6$, m=-2).

B. *Effect of Gaussian Amplitude Gradation in Aperture*

As noted in previous results (Figs. 1 and 2), the amplitude of the beam at $\theta = \pi/6$ has variations up to 4 dB in amplitude. To correct this, we use a gaussian type gradation of the amplitude across the aperture, as shown in Fig. 3. To realize this, we use, $C_{i,j} = e^{-\rho_{i,j}^2/a^2}$ in (2). As shown in Fig. 3, the ripples in the beam amplitude are minimized to 1.7 dB, by using Gaussian distribution.

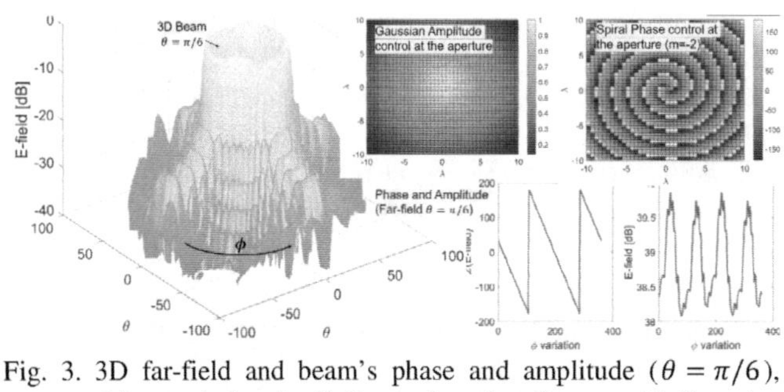

Fig. 3. 3D far-field and beam's phase and amplitude ($\theta = \pi/6$), generated from spiral and radially varying phased array with Gaussian amplitude excitation (a=10λ, $C_{i,j} = 1, \theta_B = \pi/6$, m=-2).

C. *Effect of Phase-Gradation Along Radial Direction*

Next, we investigate the effect of varying $e^{j\rho_{i,j}\, k_o \sin\theta_b}$ term by changing the θ_B in (2). The effect of radial-phase distribution is variation in the beam position (while keeping the m constant). As shown in Fig. 4 (a). As noted, the beam position may be changed to $\theta = 30^o, 45^o$ and 60° by changing the radial phase distribution.

D. *Effect of Increasing Array Size*

Finally, Fig. 4 (b) shows the effect of changing the array size. Results are shown for array sizes $10\lambda \times 10\lambda$ and $20\lambda \times 20\lambda$. Similar to expected effect in phased arrays with uniform phase (non-spiral phase) excitation, the beam-width may be decreased, while maintaining same beam position and phase variations across the beam-ridge.

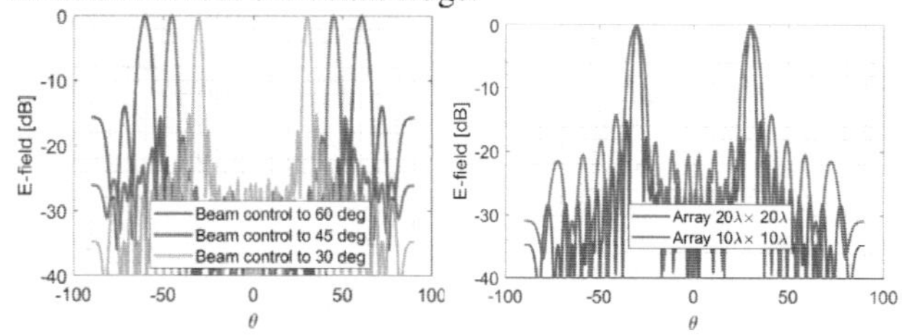

(a) (b)

Fig. 4. (a) Effect of changing the radial phase distribution is changing beam position (θ_B). (b) Controlling beam-width, while maintaining same beam-position, by varying aperture size with same spiral and radial phase gradation.

IV. Conclusion

We consider several cases of 2D arrays featuring spiral (azimuthal) and radial-phase variation as well as Gaussian amplitude variation to manipulate the OAM beams for multiplexed RF communication. We conclude that in order to achieve uniform amplitude of the OAM beam for all ϕ angles, Gaussian amplitude distribution at the aperture should be applied. Secondly, radial phase distribution at aperture allows controlling beam to a certain θ angle, while changing rate of spiral fold controls the orbital angular momentum index m. Finally, beam-width may be controlled by using varying sizes of arrays.

References

[1] G. Xie, et al., "High-capacity millimetre-wave communications with orbital angular momentum multiplexing," Nat. Commun., vol. 5, no. 1, pp. 1–9, 2014.

[2] Y. Yan, et al., "32-Gbit/s 60-GHz millimeter-wave wireless communication using orbital angular momentum and polarization multiplexing," 2016 IEEE Int. Conf. Commun. ICC 2016, pp. 0–5, 2016.

[3] C. Brunet, et al., "Space-division multiplexing in optical fibres," Nat. Phot., vol. 7, pp. 521–531, 2013.

[4] X. Wei, et al., "Generation of arbitrary order Bessel beams via 3D printed axicons at the terahertz frequency range," 2015.

[5] M. Veysi, C. Guclu, F. Capolino, and Y. Rahmat-Samii, "Revisiting orbital angular momentum beams: Fundamentals, reflectarray generation, and novel antenna applications," *IEEE Antennas Propag. Mag.*, vol. 60, no. 2, pp. 68–81, 2018.

An Origami Based Capacity Resilient and Reconfigurable MIMO System

Nicholas E. Russo*, Constantinos L. Zekios, and Stavros V. Georgakopoulos
Department of Electrical and Computer Engineering
Florida International University
Miami, US
nruss006@fiu.edu

***Abstract*—In this work, the ability of a physically reconfigurable, linear uniform, MIMO antenna with variable interelement spacing to achieve maximum capacity is demonstrated for a variety of propagation scenarios. Propagation scenarios are differentiated based upon the angle of incidence. An example situation with two transmit and two receive antennas is analyzed. It is shown that the maximum capacity is achieved by appropriately selecting the inter-element spacing for different propagation scenarios. Demonstrating the resilience of this reconfigurable antenna, high throughput communications are allowed to be reliably achieved.**

***Index Terms*—Multiple-Input-Multiple-Output, MIMO, reconfigurable, Origami structure**

I. Introduction

The next generation communication system (5G) will provide a 10-fold increase in data rate when compared to its predecessor generation [1]. The push into the next generation requires modern antenna designs are made to support large data rates and cover large bandwidths [2]. To achieve this increase in throughput, the degrees of freedom (d.o.f.) of the communication system must be increased. The d.o.f. of a MIMO system consisting of N transmit and M receive antennas are bounded by $min(N, M)$ in a rich scattering environment [3]. In other words, a MIMO system with channel matrix $\mathbf{H}$ is equivalent to $n = rank(\mathbf{H}) = d.o.f.$ orthogonal, parallel single-input-single-output (SISO) channels, each with channel gain λ_i [3]. The channel gains λ_i are a function of the propagation scenario and can be used to evaluate the capacity and the throughput of the MIMO system. For instance, for a given propagation scenario, if the inter-element spacing of the MIMO array is varied, then the channel gains will be altered, resulting in an increase or decrease in achievable data-rate. This is exactly the idea used in the current work. Utilizing an origami mechanism, it is shown how an antenna, by varying the inter-element distance, is able to provide high capacity exploring the relationship between the propagation scenario, channel gains, and capacity.

II. MIMO Capacity Analysis

Orthogonal dipole elements operating in the first mode are mounted on an accordion origami structure as shown in Fig. 1. The accordion structure is selected as it is simply actuated using a modified scissor lift mechanism which inherently provides a variable uniform inter-element distance Δ_r. The channel capacity of this MIMO system [4] is:

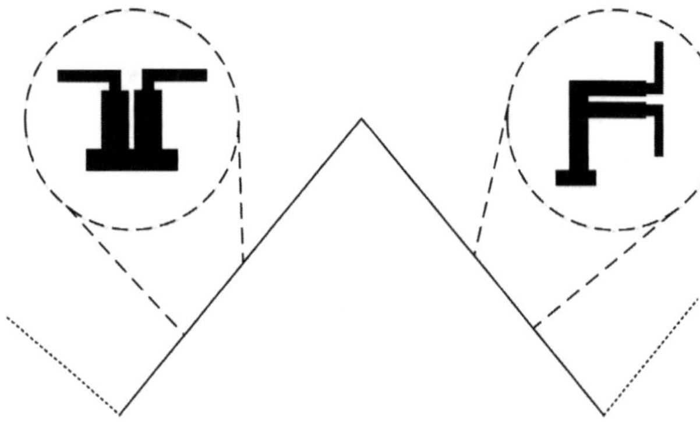

Fig. 1. Orthogonal elements mounted on accordion origami structure.

$$C = \sum_{i=1}^{n} log_2\Big(1 + \frac{P_i \lambda_i^2}{N_0}\Big) \tag{1}$$

where P_i is the power in the ith channel subject to the constraint $\sum_i P_i = P$ and N_0 is the power spectral density of the noise. In a high SNR scenario the capacity is maximized by maximizing the channel gains. Otherwise, all the power is placed in the strongest channel.

Consider a MIMO system consisting of two linear, uniformly spaced arrays. The k element transmit array produces plane waves which strike the r element receive array at angles ϕ_{rk}. The projection of incident plane wave along the axis of the receive array is:

$$\Omega_{ri} = cos(\phi_{ri}) \tag{2}$$

Without loss of generality, let $k = r = 2$ and define $\Omega_r = \Omega_{r2} - \Omega_{r1}$. To obtain the channel gains λ_i, the channel matrix $\mathbf{H}$ must first be defined. The elements of $\mathbf{H}$ are of the form:

$$\mathbf{h}_k = a_k \sqrt{r}\, e^{\frac{-j2\pi d_{1k}}{\lambda_c}} \mathbf{e_r}(\Omega_{rk}) \tag{3}$$

This work was supported by the Air Force Office of Scientific Research under grant FA9550-18-1-0191.

where d_{1k} is the distance between the kth transmit antenna and the first receive antenna, a_k is a constant, and $\mathbf{e_r}(\Omega)$ is given as:

$$\mathbf{e_r}(\Omega) = \frac{1}{\sqrt{r}} \begin{bmatrix} 1 \\ e^{(-j2\pi\Delta_r\Omega)} \\ e^{(-j2\pi 2\Delta_r\Omega)} \\ \vdots \\ e^{(-j2\pi(n_r-1)\Delta_r\Omega)} \end{bmatrix} \quad (4)$$

where Δ_r represents the inter-element spacing of the receive array. Therefore, the channel matrix for this situation reads:

$$\mathbf{H} = [\mathbf{h}_1 \; \mathbf{h}_2] \quad (5)$$

In a high SNR environment, the capacity is maximized by maximizing $\frac{\lambda_2}{\lambda_1}$ for a given Ω_r. The dependence of this ratio upon the propagation scenario, Ω_r, is shown in Fig. 2 for various inter-element spacings. The corresponding effect on channel capacity (assuming $P_i = 1$ and $N_0 = 1$) is shown in Fig. 3.

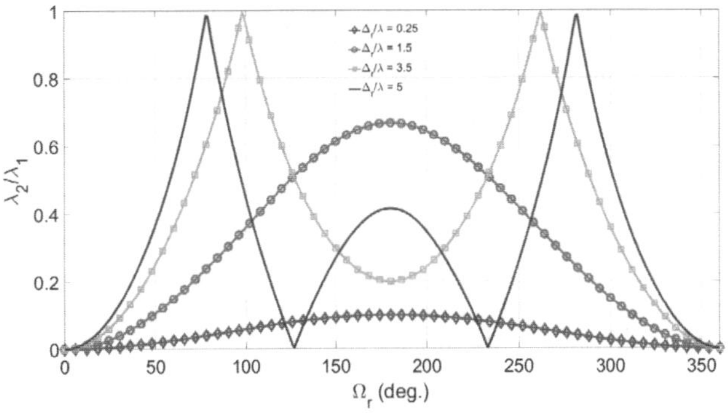

Fig. 2. Channel gain variation for different propagation scenarios.

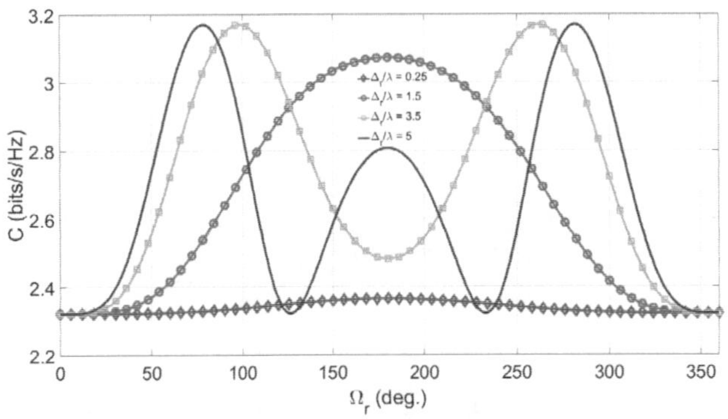

Fig. 3. Capacity dependence on different propagation scenarios.

As expected, there is symmetry about $\Omega_r = 180^o$ in both figures. Moreover, the dependence of capacity on the channel gains as indicated by (1) is observed by comparison of Figs. 2 and 3. When the propagation scenario is such that $\Omega_r = 180^o$, a small inter-element spacing achieves maximum capacity. This is observed by the $\Delta_r/\lambda = 0.25$ and $\Delta_r/\lambda = 1.5$ curves in Fig. 3. However, note that neither of these curves reach the maximum capacity indicating that when the inter-element spacing is too small, maximum capacity will not be achieved regardless of the propagation scenario.

When the propagation scenario is such that $\Omega_r \approx 80^o$ or $\Omega_r \approx 280^o$ by symmetry, an inter-element spacing of $\Delta_r/\lambda = 3.5$ is the best candidate. Similarly, when $\Omega_r \approx 100^o$ or $\Omega_r \approx 260^0$, the inter-element spacing should be set to $\Delta_r/\lambda = 5$ for maximum capacity. Thus, for propagation scenarios where $80^o \leq \Omega_r \leq 180^o$, the maximum capacity is achieved by appropriately selecting the inter-element spacing in the range of $1.5 \leq \Delta_r/\lambda \leq 5$. It is important to note that when the propagation scenario is such that $\Omega_r < 80^o$, the inter-element spacings should be $\Delta_r/\lambda > 5$.

III. Conclusion

The work presented in this paper has demonstrated the ability of a variable length uniform MIMO array to achieve maximum capacity for various propagation scenarios. This capability is shown in an example situation where $k = r = 2$ where it is found that appropriate selection of the inter-element spacing maximizes the channel capacity for a given propagation scenario, Ω_r. This result holds significance as it may be applied to practical antennas designs such as the one presented in Fig. 1.

References

[1] Yinan Qi, M. Hunukumbure, M. Nekovee, J. Lorca and V. Sgardoni, "Quantifying data rate and bandwidth requirements for immersive 5G experience," in *IEEE International Conference on Communications Workshops (ICC)*, Kuala Lumpur, pp. 455-461, 2016.

[2] Yingsong Li, Wenxing Li, and Wenhua Yu, "A Multi-Band/UWB MIMO/Diversity Antenna with an Enhanced Isolation Using Radial Stub Loaded Resonator," in *ACES Journal*, pp. 8-20, vol. 28, 2013.

[3] I. Emre Telatar, "Capacity of Multi-antenna Gaussian Channels," in *European Transactions on Telecommunications*, pp. 585-595, vol. 10, 1999.

[4] D. Tse and P. Viswanath, *Fundamentals of Wireless Communication*. Cambridge UP: Cambridge, 2013.

A Wideband Circularly Polarized GNSS Antenna for Satellite Platforms

Orcun Kiris
Microwave and Antenna Systems Group
TUBITAK Space Technologies Research Institute
Ankara, Turkey
orcun.kiris@tubitak.gov.tr

Kagan Topalli
Microwave and Antenna Systems Group
TUBITAK Space Technologies Research Institute
Ankara, Turkey
kagan.topalli@tubitak.gov.tr

Lokman Kuzu
Microwave and Antenna Systems Group
TUBITAK Space Technologies Research Institute
Ankara, Turkey
lokman.kuzu@tubitak.gov.tr

***Abstract*—This paper presents a wideband circularly polarized antenna for GNSS applications. The antenna consists of four triangular patches excited with 90° phase differences in between to generate right-hand circular polarization. The antenna operating frequency cover the whole GNSS band 1.164-1.610 GHz. The antenna is also modified to incorporate a cavity for LNA placement. The axial ratio and gain measurements indicate a good agreement with the simulations. The antenna presents a compact yet effective GNSS antenna solution for satellite platforms.**

Keywords*—*circular polarization, GNSS, satellites, wideband.

I. Introduction

Wideband antennas operating at different frequencies of the global navigation satellite systems (GNSSs), which are global positioning system (GPS), GLObal NAvigation Satellite System (GLONASS), Galileo, and Compass, have been an interest recently [1]. GNSS antennas operate in circular polarization in order to reduce the polarization mismatch and to alleviate the ionespheric effects. There are two major challenges in the design and implementation of these antennas: the enlarged bandwidth requirement and the constraints by the satellite platform. Antenna size constraint and widened band are conflicting requirements, which is related the fundamental limitation of the gain bandwidth of an antenna to its electrical size. In order to satisfy the requirements of such systems, the antennas should be compact in size and should have wideband, broad beamwidth, a flat gain, and low cross-polarization in the band. Quadrafilar helical antenna is a common solution satisfying the performance requirements [2, 3]. However, these type of antennas have inherently narrow bandwidth and large size. Patch antennas offer planar and easy-to-fabricate structures for such applications [4, 5]. However, the patch antenna is a resonant antenna with a limited bandwidth. There has been an effort to add more bands to such antennas by using stacked patch approach [6] One particular solution is the four-element ring array [7]. The array is composed of four radiating elements fed with a four-way hybrid or beam-former of 0°–90°–180°–270° to generate RHCP. Each radiating element can be a slot, a conducting patch of some shape such as a triangle, a Vivaldi element, an H-slot antenna, or an F or inverted-F antenna [8].

This paper presents a single-feed wideband circularly polarized crossed bowtie dipole antenna operating in 1164-1610 MHz covering the whole GNSS band. First, the simplified version of the antenna is designed without the radome and structural support imposed by the satellite mission constraints. Then an improved model to enhance the robustness is designed and manufactured. The impedance and axial-ratio bandwidths are optimized in the presence of the structural modifications and radome. The simulation and measurement results indicate that the proposed structure is a viable GNSS antenna for satellite platforms. The following part of this work summarize the design approach and simulation results compared with the measurements.

This work was supported in part by TUBITAK Space Technologies Research Institute (TUBITAK UZAY).

II. Antenna Design

The antenna design consists of four triangular patches fed by 0°–90°–180°–270° to generate right hand circular polarization [7]. The signal and ground lines of the 50 Ω coaxial line excite two of the triangular patches providing 180° phase shift in between them. Other triangular patches are connected to the corresponding patches with ring-shaped delay lines to give additional 90° phase shift. The antenna does not need an additional hybrid coupler which reduces reliability of such a structure in space environment. In order to electrically isolate and structurally support four triangular patches, a double-sided PCB has been employed where two of the four triangle are printed on each surface. The PCB material is a 1.575 mm-thick RT/Duroid 5880 ($\varepsilon_r = 2.2$, tanδ = 0.0004) substrate. The PCB that holds four triangular patches is mounted on a ground plane via a metallic hollow cylindrical mast. The coaxial line is extended along the cylindrical mast. Fig. 1 (a) shows the overall view of the simplified antenna structure.

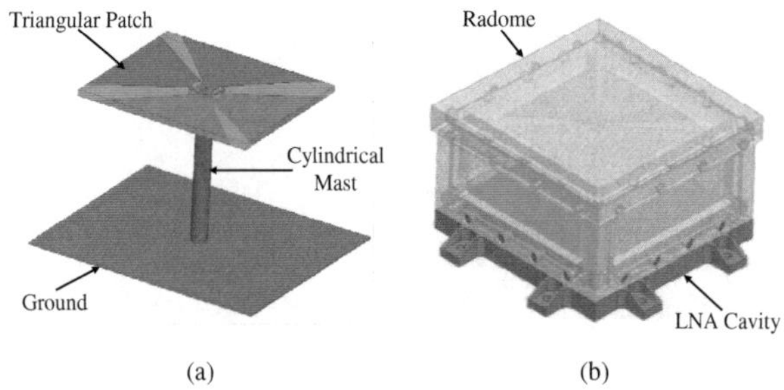

(a) (b)

Fig. 1. The antenna geometry: (a) simplified model and (b) modified antenna with the integrated LNA cavity.

Since the GNSS antenna needs to detect extremely low GNSS signals, the use of LNA close to antenna is highly desirable. Because of the high-performance and low cost, use of LNA as part of GNSS antenna is common today. The simplified antenna design is modified to include a cavity

(a) (b)

Fig. 2. Modified antenna structure: (a) closer viewer of the manufactured antenna, and (b) the measurements setup used for radiation pattern measurements.

for LNA placement at the bottom. A radome for PCB protection and a structural support for robustness are also added. Fig. 1 (b) shows the modified antenna model which includes the details such as mounting apparatus in order to simulate the antenna as close as possible to the manufactured antenna. The antenna models are characterized by the ANSYS-Ansoft High Frequency Structure Simulator (HFSS). Fig. 2 illustrates the manufactured antenna in the measurement setup. The volume of the antenna is 78 mm × 167 mm × 167 mm.

SATIMO StarLab is used for radiation measurements. Figs. 3 (a), (b), and (c) present the simulation results in comparison with measurements for the reflection coefficient, axial-ratio, and gain versus frequency, respectively. The reflection coefficient results show that the antenna is matched for the whole GNSS band. The antenna exhibits a gain of over 6 dBi for the whole band with a cross-polarization level, i.e., left-hand circular polarization, lower than −11 dB. The axial ratio is better than 5 dB, which is sufficient since an LNA is employed for reception. It should be noted that the simplified antenna shown in Fig. 1 (a) has a lower axial ratio. The ground plane of the modified antenna has a limitation due to size constraint of the satellite platform. The size limitation of the ground plane degrades the antenna performance in terms of axial ratio. Although the antenna performance is sufficient for a satellite mission, the optimization process is on-going. The final result of the optimized one will be presented in the conference.

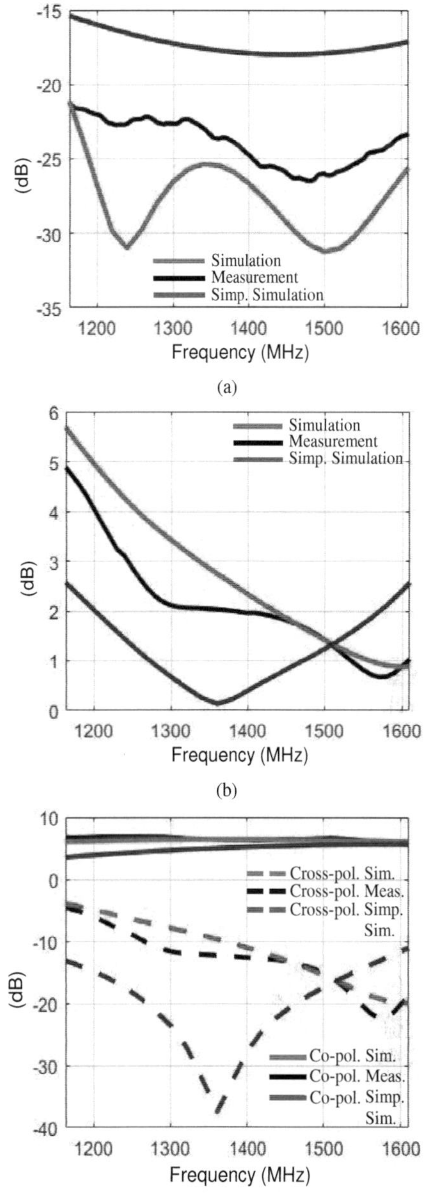

Fig. 3. Simulation and measurements results: (a) reflection coefficient, (b) axial ratio, and (c) gain versus frequency.

ACKNOWLEDGMENT

The authors would like to thank to Dr. Ali Ozdemir for his help in the structural design and manufacturing of the antenna structure.

REFERENCES

[1] P. Misra and P. Enge, Global Position System: Signals, Measurements, and Performance, 2nd ed., Lincoln, MA: Ganga-Jamuna, 2006.

[2] C. Kilgus, "Resonant quadrafilar helix," IEEE Trans. Antennas Propagat., vol. 17, no. 3, pp. 349-351, 1969.

[3] M. Amin and R. Cahill, "Compact quadrifilar helix antenna," Electron Letter, vol. 41, pp. 672-674, 2005.

[4] C. M. Su and K. L. Wong, "A dual-band GPS microstrip antenna," Microwave Opt. Technol. Lett., vol. 33, no. 4, pp. 238-240, May 2002.

[5] Y. X. Guo, L. Bian, and X. Q. Shi, "Broadband circularly polarized annular-ring microstrip antenna," IEEE Trans. Antennas Propagat., vol. 57, no. 8, pp. 2474-2477, 2009.

[6] A. Alphones, K. Agarwal, and Nasimuddin, "Triple-band compact circularly polarised stacked microstrip antenna over reactive impedance meta-surface for GPS applications," IET Microwaves, Antennas Propag., vol. 8, no. 13, pp. 1057–1065, 2014.

[7] H. H. Tran, S. X. Ta., and I. Park, "Single-feed, wideband, circularly polarized, cross bowtie dipole antenna for global navigation satellite systems," J. Electromagn. Eng. Sci., vol. 14, no. 3, pp. 299–305, Sep. 2014.

[8] J. J. H. Wang, "Antennas for Global Navigation Satellite System (GNSS)," Proc. IEEE, vol. 100, no. 7, pp. 2349–2355, Jul. 2012.

Fully Inkjet-printed Tunable Flexible Microfluidic Chipless RFID Sensor

Yepu Cui, Wenjing Su, and Manos M. Tentzeris
School of Electrical and Computer Engineering
Georgia Institute of Technology
Atlanta, GA, USA
yepu.cui@gatech.edu

***Abstract*—In this paper, a tunable flexible microfluidic-based sensor is proposed. The sensor is fabricated using fast, cost-effective, and environment friendly multilayer inkjet printing techniques. Three spiral resonators with microfluidic channels are designed in three different frequencies, each resonator can be tuned individually to encode 3bits information by changing the liquid in the microfluidic channels. The proposed flexible microfluidic RFID sensor can be used for applications such as liquid analysis, healthcare monitoring and wireless sensing.**

***Keywords*— flexible electronics, inkjet printing, microfluidics, resonator, RFID.**

I. INTRODUCTION

Nowadays, the desire for chipless Radio Frequency Identification (RFID) have continuously growing due to it's low cost, reduced complexity, and fully passive features [1]. However, a main disadvantage of traditional multi-resonator RFID tags usually have fixed resonate frequencies that cannot be modified or individually tuned. Microfluidics is an emerging technology that has wide range of applications in biological analysis and chemical synthesis [2]. Introducing microfluidic channels into multi-resonator chipless RFID sensors enables unprecedented capabilities for individual frequency tunability that makes the sensor reconfigurable or "encodable". Usually microfluidic channels are fabricated with photolithography and associated technologies. However, these techniques are primarily subtractive and expensive. Inkjet printing is an additive manufacturing technique featuring no material waste, fast prototyping and low equipment cost. So it becomes a promising alternative to fabricate chipless RFID and microfluidics.

This paper builds on the previous research of [3] by introducing a compact design and improved fabrication process. This new RFID sensor has better repeatability, more accuracy and easier to fabricate. The presented RFID sensor has three slot spiral resonators resonate at frequency 3.4 GHz, 4.5 GHz and 5.9 GHz. Each resonator has an embedded microfluidic channel. By filling or removing the liquid in each channel, three resonate frequency can be tuned independently which enables 3bit encode capability.

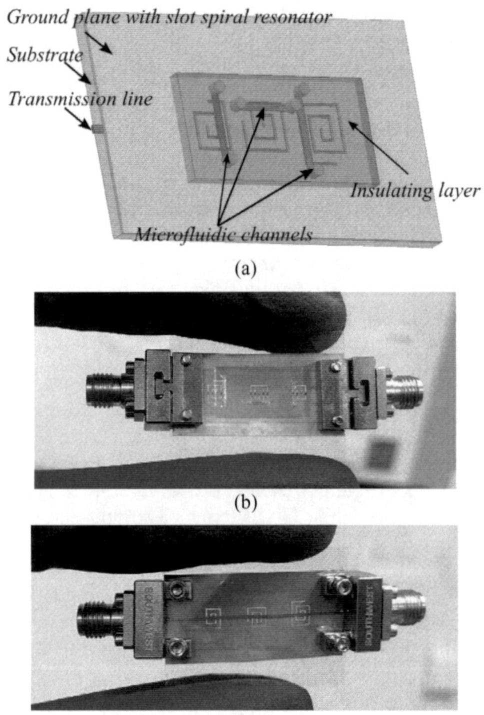

Fig. 1. (a) Design of the microfluidic RFID sensor, (b) Fabricated sample (front), and (c) Fabricated sample (back).

II. DESIGN AND EXPERIMENT

A. Theory of Operation

The design of the microfluidic RFID sensor is shown in Fig. 1(a). A fabricated prototype is shown in Fig. 1(b) and Fig. 1(c). Three slot spiral resonator has different size, so they resonate at different frequency. Microfluidic channels are placed in the spiral's gap between adjacent turns, and they are filled with air in idle status. When a liquid such as water is added to a channel, the change of dielectric constant from 1 (air) to 80 (water) [4] on top of the resonator will cause a frequency decreasement due to capacitance variation. Three idle resonate frequencies represent code '000'. Each frequency shift caused by filling liquid will change the bit from 0 to 1 respectively.

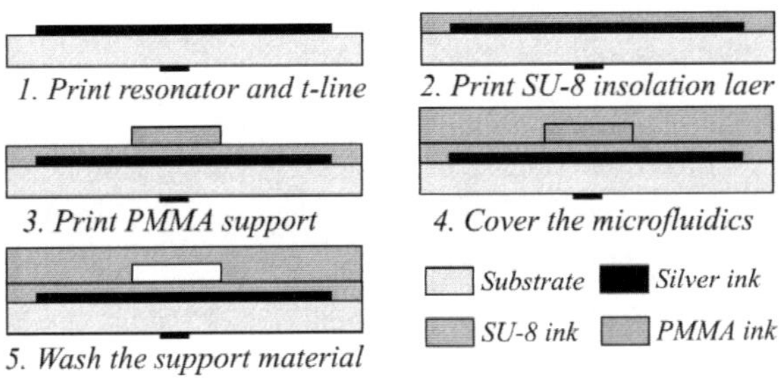

Fig. 2. Fabrication process for the microfluidic RFID sensor.

B. Fabrication Process

The fabrication process is shown in Fig. 2. The sample was printed on a MELINEX ST505 PET substrate using Dimatix DMP-2800 inkjet printer. First, the ground plane with slot spiral resonator was printed on top, the transmission line was printed on the bottom with SunChemical EMD5730 silver nanoparticle ink, and sintering at 150°C for 1 hour. Then 3 layers of SU-8 was deposited to insulate silver traces from the test fluids. After cross-linking the SU-8 with UV light and heat, a 65-um-high 500-um-wide PMMA traces are printed as microfluidic support material. After drying the PMMA at 120°C for 1 hour, another 3 layers of SU-8 was printed on top to cover the PMMA traces. Finally the sample was immersed in anisole solution for 2 hours to remove the PMMA traces.

Compare to the fabrication process in [3], the substrate only sintered once in the new process, this reduces the substrate shrinkage caused by high temperature, so the chance of damage the microfluidic channel during sintering is dramatically reduced. Meanwhile, reduced number of layers will increase fabrication accuracy because less alignment was performed during the printing. Also, the transmission line is placed on the back side away from the microfluidic channels, this eliminates the error caused by accidently spread liquid onto transmission line when filling the microfluidic channel.

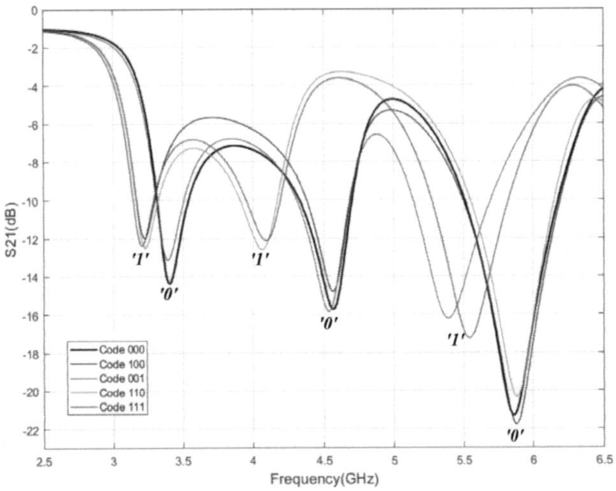

Fig. 3. Simulated insertion loss vs frequency.

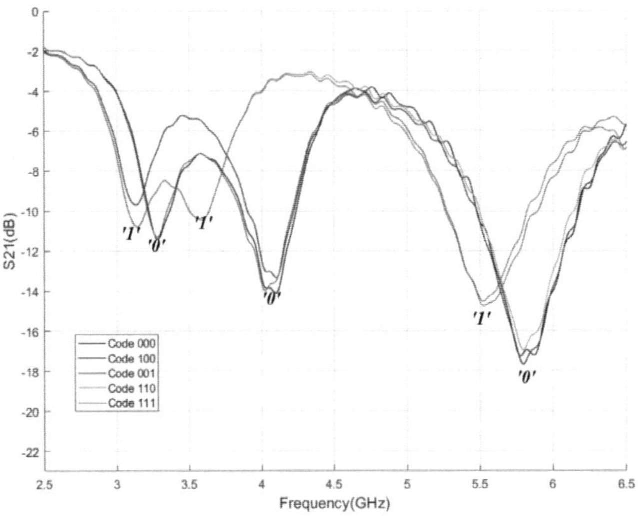

Fig. 4. Measured insertion loss vs frequency.

C. Simulation and Measurement Results

The design was simulated in Ansys HFSS. An Anritsu 37369A vector network analyzer was utilized to measure the insertion loss. As shown in Fig. 3, Fig. 4, the measurements verify the simulation results. The code of the RFID sensor can be tuned by selectively add or remove liquid from microfluidic channel. The channel can be adjusted individually, in pair as well as in triplet.

III. Conclusion

This work propose a novel fully inkjet-printed tunable flexible microfluidic chipless RFID sensor with encode capability. The improved design and process decrease the chance of failure while speed up fabrication cycle. This RFID sensor can find applications in liquid analysis, healthcare monitoring and wireless sensing, etc.

Acknowledgment

The authors would like to thank National Science Foundation for supporting this work.

References

[1] S. Preradovic, I. Balbin, N. C. Karmakar and G. F. Swiegers, "Multiresonator-Based Chipless RFID System for Low-Cost Item Tracking," in IEEE Transactions on Microwave Theory and Techniques, vol. 57, no. 5, pp. 1411-1419, May 2009.

[2] G. M. Whitesides, "The origins and the future of microfluidics," Nature, vol. 442, no. 7101, pp. 368–373, 2006.

[3] W. Su, Qi Liu, B. Cook, and M. Tentzeris, "All-inkjet-printed microfluidics-based encodable flexible chipless RFID sensors," 2016 IEEE MTT-S International Microwave Symposium (IMS), San Francisco, CA, 2016, pp. 1-4.

[4] S. Druart, D. Flandre, and L. A. Francis, "A self-oscillating system tomeasure the conductivity and the permittivity of liquids within a single triangular signal," Journal of Sensors, vol. 2014, 2014.